A Student's Guide to Auditing Practice

A Student's Guide to Auditing Practice

Lisa Weaver and Steve Collings

OXFORD
UNIVERSITY PRESS

OXFORD
UNIVERSITY PRESS

Great Clarendon Street, Oxford, OX2 6DP,
United Kingdom

Oxford University Press is a department of the University of Oxford.
It furthers the University's objective of excellence in research, scholarship,
and education by publishing worldwide. Oxford is a registered trade mark of
Oxford University Press in the UK and in certain other countries

Published in the United States of America by Oxford University Press
198 Madison Avenue, New York, NY 10016, United States of America

British Library Cataloguing in Publication Data
Data available

Library of Congress Control Number: 2024948814

ISBN 978–0–19–878706–8

Printed in the UK by
Bell & Bain Ltd., Glasgow

Preface

External auditing is important. Without a well-functioning audit profession, it is difficult for investors to make decisions based on financial statements. Other stakeholders also rely on good-quality financial—and increasingly—non-financial information, supported by independent assurance. In the absence of credible financial statements and audit reports, people can make poor decisions, companies can collapse, shareholders and other stakeholders lose money, and society suffers.

The auditing profession is attractive to students. In my career in academia I have seen hundreds of undergraduate and postgraduate students with career aspirations to become an auditor. Becoming a member of a professional accountancy body is an important part of that journey, and many students want to earn that badge of success. However, I am frequently surprised at how little students seem to know about this profession that they are so keen to join—they have heard of the bigger audit firms and know something about the different professional bodies, but rarely understand the problems facing the profession or those that challenge how it operates. We want students to enter the profession, if that is their desired career path, with open eyes, understanding the difficulties of being an auditor, as well as the exciting opportunities this can bring.

This book is aimed at students taking audit modules at university. It may also be useful for students taking professional accountancy examinations, as many of the concepts covered in the book are relevant to both university assessments and professional examinations. However, the primary objective of the book is to assist undergraduate and postgraduate students to develop an understanding of the auditing profession and the process of external auditing.

Students at university sometimes find auditing a challenging subject because they lack practical experience in the workplace. It can be hard to understand how auditors plan and carry out their work, make decisions, and interact with clients. The auditing profession can be hard to understand unless you have worked as part of that profession. While many students undertake internships or placements in audit firms, even this only provides limited exposure to the world of auditing, and the insights gained, while being extremely valuable, may not prepare students for university assessments on auditing.

This book aims to bridge the gap between theory and practice. It is written jointly by a professionally qualified academic with over 25 years' experience teaching auditing and related subjects, and an audit partner who also is a well-established author on technical topics. We have worked together on many projects and this book provides a blend of technical and practical content, underpinned with case studies and examples to help students to see how auditors make decisions in the real world. We also want students to think more broadly—about the value of auditing in society, about how the profession operates, and about current developments, for example, the increased use of technology in auditing.

Lisa Weaver and Steve Collings

The authors would like to acknowledge:
Jodie Lucas, Associate Professor, Warwick Business School
Martin Potts, FCA SFHEA

Guide to Using the Book

You can use this book in a number of ways: as a textbook, to help you prepare for seminars, tutorials, and workshops, or in preparation for exams. It can even help if you are getting ready for an audit-related job interview or assessment centre.

The following features can be found throughout the book to support you in your learning.

Introductions outline the key content of the chapter, explaining its relevance and sign-posting any important concepts, theories, regulations, or principles that we will be exploring.

Learning outcomes show you the main objectives of the chapter; the learning outcomes are mapped to sections of the chapter to help provide a logical structure for your learning.

Activities are short 'thought provoker' questions which allow you to practise what you are learning. Some activities are based on short scenarios and others ask you to use your practical skills to apply what you have learned to an auditing task. Suggested answers are provided at the end of each chapter.

Auditing in practice demonstrates a real-life auditing situation through illustration or discussion on an actual or hypothetical situation.

Auditing scenarios provide illustrative examples to explain how auditing concepts or requirements are applied. In these scenarios, we outline an auditing situation and discuss the auditor's response.

Chapter round-ups summarize the key points we have covered in the chapter—this is your checklist of the most important things to remember.

End of chapter case studies provide an opportunity to practise what you have learned; these case studies map to several learning outcomes and are a good way to prepare for classes or assessments.

Outline Contents

Detailed Contents

Scope of the Book

While the overall process of an audit and the general context in which the profession operates is similar in many countries, there are differences in regulations, requirements, and accepted practice depending on where in the world an audit is taking place.

For this book we focus on audit practice in the UK, and as such the regulations we consider are those issued by the Financial Reporting Council, the relevant requirements of the Companies Act (2006), and other UK-specific sources of guidance. In terms of audit regulations, we focus on International Auditing Standards (UK) and International Standards on Quality Management (UK). You can see the word 'international' in the titles of these regulations, so you can rest assured that auditors in other countries are also following these regulations, they just may have been slightly amended to allow for local legal and other requirements and regulations. So, the book is UK focused but the principles are generally applicable across the world.

We focus on the audit of companies. Obviously, other entities such as charities, government bodies, and public sector organizations are subject to audit, but the rules are different, and to avoid any confusion over which rules apply to which type of entity we focus our attention on company audit.

In terms of accounting regulations, we use International Financial Reporting Standards (IFRS), as issued by the International Accounting Standards Board, as the basis for our discussions. Most university financial reporting modules are based on IFRS, and while UK-specific financial reporting exist and are applied by many companies, university students are not likely to be familiar with them. Professional accountancy syllabi are also based on IFRS, and we wish to align the content of the book with the rules that most students will recognize. In the chapters which include financial reporting content (mostly Chapters 14–17) we have provided a summary of the main IFRS requirements relevant to the discussion. We are mindful that university degrees position their audit module(s) differently within the degree programme—sometimes alongside IFRS-based modules, sometimes after these have been completed and sometimes even before. Therefore, you are advised to consider your knowledge of IFRS while reading these chapters, and supplement your knowledge, if necessary, using a financial reporting textbook.

About the Authors

Professor Lisa Weaver BA, FCA, SFHEA, CMBE
Lisa Weaver is a Fellow of the Institute of Chartered Accountants in England and Wales and Professor of Accounting at Warwick Business School. She has published a practitioner's guide on IFRS implementation, authored a large number of online education courses for qualified accountants, and has strong links with the accountancy professional bodies.

For over 20 years, Lisa has specialized in accounting education, from basic financial literacy to advanced courses on specialist topics in auditing, corporate governance, and financial reporting. Lisa is committed to excellence in teaching practice and to building the development of professional skills and competencies into academic teaching. Lisa has won several awards for her teaching.

Lisa is part of a team that has developed an educational business simulation incorporating aspects of financial reporting and sustainability which has been shortlisted for the prestigious Finance for the Future Awards.

Although Lisa is UK based, she has worked in accounting education in many countries in the EU and further afield in Asia and in the Caribbean.

Steve Collings FCCA
Steve Collings is a Director of Leavitt Walmsley Associates, a firm of Chartered Certified Accountants based in Warrington and Sale, where Steve trained and qualified. Steve specializes in UK and Ireland financial reporting, auditing, and Solicitors Accounts Rules.

Steve is the author of several books on UK and Ireland accounting standards, IFRS, and auditing. He also has strong links with accountancy professional bodies and has written authoritative material for ACCA members and several articles for various magazine publishers.

Steve has served as a member of the UK and Ireland GAAP Technical Advisory Group at the Financial Reporting Council and currently represents the North-West of England on the ACCA Practitioners Panel. In addition, Steve is a nationwide lecturer in the UK on financial reporting and auditing topics and has lectured further afield in Barbados and Singapore.

Steve's work has been recognized by his receiving 'Outstanding Contribution to the Accountancy Profession' by the Association of International Accountants and 'Accounting Technician of the Year' at the British Accountancy Awards. Steve has also been highly commended by AAT for his work in the accountancy profession.

Common Abbreviations

ACCA	Association of Chartered Certified Accountants
EFRAG	European Financial Reporting Advisory Group
FRC	Financial Reporting Council
EU	European Union
FTSE	Financial Times Stock Exchange
GAAP	Generally Accepted Accounting Practice
IAASB	International Auditing and Assurance Standards Board
IAS (UK)	International Standard on Auditing (UK)
IASB	International Accounting Standards Board
ICAEW	Institute of Chartered Accountants in England and Wales
ICAS	Institute of Chartered Accountants in Scotland
IESBA	International Ethics Standards Board for Accountants
IFAC	International Federation of Accountants
IFRS	International Financial Reporting Standard
Ltd	limited [company]
plc	public limited company
PIE	public interest entity

1 Introduction to Auditing

Introduction

In this chapter, we will look at some of the basic concepts underpinning the external audit. We will consider the need for audit, the benefits to company stakeholders, and look at how the auditing profession operates. We will also look, in overview, at the process of an individual audit and develop an understanding of the structure of an audit team and how the audit team interacts with the audit client.

Learning outcomes

- Discuss the need for auditing, including the concept of agency theory, and discuss its relevance to audit.
- Describe, and distinguish between 'assurance' and 'audit' engagements.
- Describe the structure of a typical audit team, the process of an audit, and the main features of the auditing profession.

By the end of this chapter, you will be able to:

- Discuss the benefits of audit and assurance to a range of stakeholders.

1.1 Why is there a need for audit?

1.1.1 Separation of ownership and control

To appreciate the need for audit, we need to understand the relationships between a company, its shareholders, and its directors. The key concept here is known as 'separation of ownership and control' and it is based on the fact that a company is a legal entity in its own right and that the shareholders may not be the same people as those running the company.

When a company is first incorporated, often it is 'owner-managed', which just means that the shareholders, who own the company, are also running the company, setting the strategy, and making operational decisions. Some companies retain this structure, but usually, when a company grows, a different structure emerges, whereby the shareholders do not play an active role in running the company. The shareholders appoint company directors, who take on the governance of the company, and who are responsible for the financial performance of the company. This is where the phrase 'separation of ownership and control' comes in—the shareholders own the company, but the directors control it, and they are different sets of people. The directors are accountable to the shareholders who have appointed them, and the shareholders need information so that they can evaluate how well the company is doing, and assess the effectiveness of the directors.

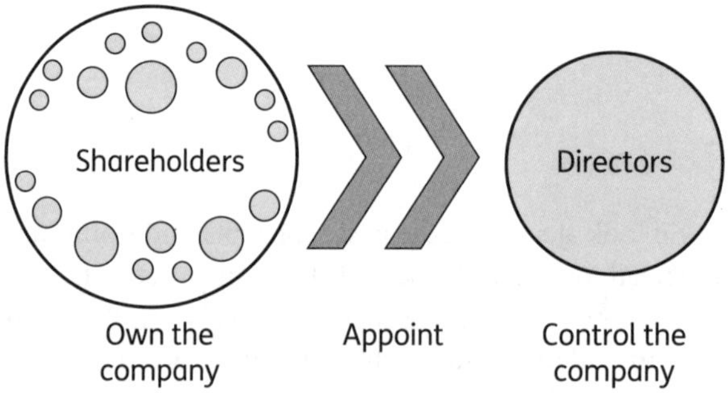

Figure 1.1 Separation of ownership and control

This is why company directors are required to produce financial statements, and other information such as a director's report (and strategic and governance reports for larger companies). The shareholders use this set of information, referred to as an annual report, to perform their evaluation. It is crucial that the shareholders can trust the information produced by the company directors because they have no other way of finding out how the company is performing. The fact that the company directors have access to information which shareholders do not have access to is known as 'information asymmetry'—a term we will look at again later in this section.

So, this is where auditors enter the picture. The shareholders appoint independent auditors to verify the financial statements. We will look much more closely at what this actually means in later chapters—for now, we will just consider that the auditor confirms for the shareholders that they can trust the information that is provided to them by the directors. It is very important that shareholders can trust the auditor's opinion on the financial statements, it must be an objective opinion, and we will see in later chapters how regulations and ethical codes provide a framework for ensuring that auditors are independent of the company they are auditing.

Of course, the directors may have motivations to present misleading information to the company shareholders.

Activity 1.1 Misleading information

What reasons do you think company directors may have for presenting misleading or inaccurate information in the financial statements?

There are many famous cases of company directors presenting false financial information—you have probably heard of cases like Enron, Tyco, or WorldCom, which were huge scandals involving multimillion-dollar frauds. In the UK, Carillion, Patisserie Valerie, and Tesco are all fairly recent examples of company directors attempting to 'fudge' the accounts. As we will see in later chapters, the auditor is almost always investigated when such a scandal takes place because the regulators need to understand why the audit process did not uncover the problem (i.e. why the shareholders thought they could trust the financial statements which turned out to be misleading).

Auditing in practice 1.1 PwC's audit of Kier

In June 2022, the UK Financial Reporting Council (FRC) imposed a financial sanction of £3.35 million on PwC in respect of an investigation into the audit of Kier Group. The key issue in the case is that PwC were found not to have obtained sufficient and appropriate audit evidence in their audit of the Group's long-term contracts, and the investigation found that the Group's 2017 financial statements were misstated.

The FRC's comment on the case included the following statement:

> Rigorous auditing of long-term contract accounting is particularly important in the audit of construction companies, where many contracts are spread over a number of years. Auditors must not only ensure that they obtain sufficient appropriate audit evidence to support the accounting of the contracts, but also apply sufficient professional scepticism. This is vital so that investors can have confidence in the financial statements. The Respondents have accepted that there were deficiencies in the work performed on long-term contracts in this Audit.[1]

The point to appreciate here is that the FRC specifically point out that auditing is, in the words of the FRC, vital to investors, so that they can trust the financial statements. If shareholders cannot trust the auditor's opinion on the financial statements, there is little point in having an audit.

So, what do auditors actually do? We will obviously answer this question in a lot of detail as we work through the chapters of this book! To put it simply, by way of introduction, there are two overall objectives of the auditor according to audit regulations:

- to obtain evidence, about whether the financial statements are free from 'material misstatement'; and
- to report their findings to shareholders.

These objectives are given in auditing standards, known as International Standards on Auditing (ISAs), and basically it means that auditors need to plan an audit so that they

[1] FRC, 'Sanctions against PricewaterhouseCoopers LLP and audit partner (in relation to PwC's audit of Kier)', 2022 <https://www.frc.org.uk/news-and-events/news/2022/06/sanctions-against-pricewaterhousecoopers-llp-and-audit-partner-in-relation-to-pwcs-audit-of-kier/> (accessed 12 January 2024).

identify where things might go wrong in the financial statements (this is known as 'material misstatement'), obtain evidence to evaluate the accuracy of the financial statements, and then report to shareholders as to whether the financial statements can be trusted.

1.1.2 **Agency theory**

Agency theory is an academic concept which was first discussed in the 1970s. Agency theory applies to business relationships, and is often applied in economics and finance. In our context, we apply it to the relationships that exist between shareholders and directors, which we discussed in the previous section, and we are now simply formalizing our understanding.

Figure 1.2 shows the two parties involved.

- Principal: the individual or entity that delegates tasks or decision-making authority to the agent. Principals aim to achieve certain objectives or goals through the actions of the agent. In applying this to the context of auditing, the shareholders are the principals in the relationship.
- Agent: the individual or entity appointed by the principal to carry out tasks or make decisions on their behalf. Agents are expected to act in the best interests of the principal but may also have their own interests. In our case, the directors are the agents.

A further concept within agency theory is that of 'moral hazard', which means that the agent may act in their own self-interest and not in the best interests of the principal. We considered

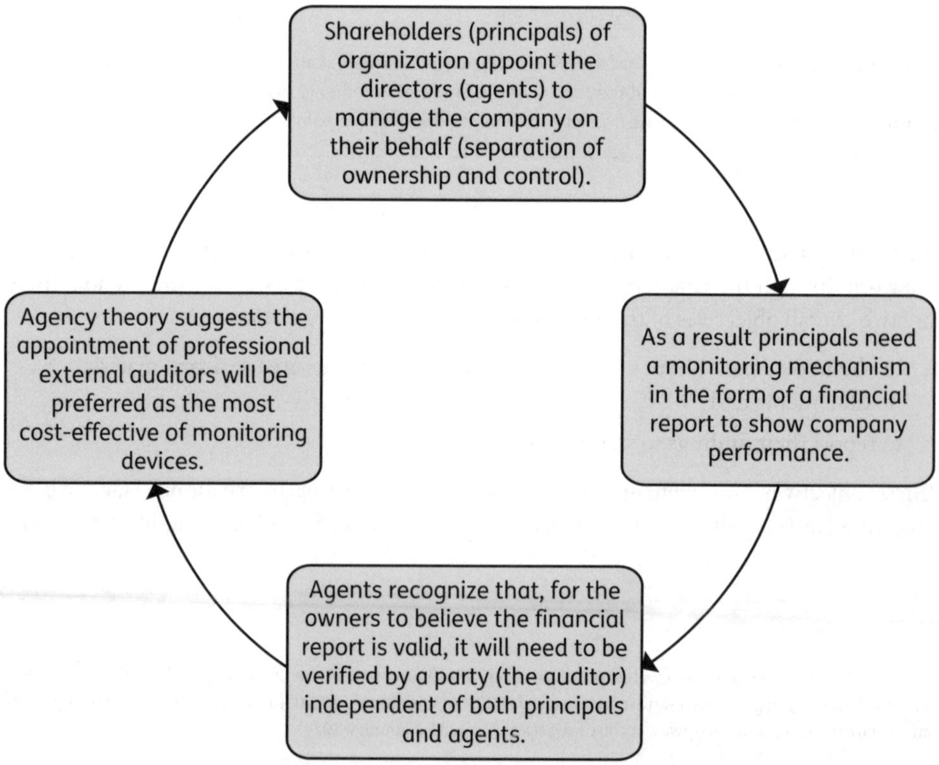

Figure 1.2 Agency theory relationships

some reasons for this in Activity 1.1, for example, the directors might inflate the company's profit as shown in the financial statements in order to receive a financial bonus. This is why the audit is needed—it is a form of monitoring which should ensure that attempts by the directors to present misleading information to the shareholders are prevented or detected. This is linked to the problem of 'information asymmetry', which is when the agents are in possession of information which the principals do not have, making it easy for the agents to prepare misleading financial information.

The implications of agency theory, and the importance of the audit as a monitoring mechanism for shareholders, are that the work of auditors and in particular the output of the audit (i.e. the auditor's report on financial statements) needs to be trusted. To enhance the credibility of the auditor's report, auditing happens within a framework, which should work to ensure the quality of the auditor's work:

- Legislation and other regulations including the Companies Act 2006, and ISAs—we will look at the regulatory framework in Chapter 2.
- An ethical code for auditors—we will look at this in Chapter 4
- Monitoring of the quality of audit work by regulatory and professional bodies—one of the issues we consider in Chapter 5.

As we will see, these mechanisms do not mean that audits are always good quality, and sometimes auditors get it wrong, which can have significant implications for the company, the shareholders, and other stakeholders.

1.1.3 **The wider benefits of audit**

So far, we have seen that audit benefits shareholders because it monitors the activities of directors and should help to ensure that the financial statements are credible.

However, shareholders are not the only beneficiaries of the audit. Companies have a wide range of stakeholders who can benefit from an audit of financial statements taking place. Let's use suppliers as an example. Imagine you have been approached by a company to supply it with a service, say an IT support service. Before agreeing to provide the service, you would want to check that the company will be able to pay you, and to do this you can obtain the company's financial statements and analyse them, to see how profitable it is, and how much cash it generates. You can do this because the company's financial statements and audit report will be on public record—in the UK they can be accessed from the Companies House website. Of course, you could also obtain assurance over the creditworthiness of the company by obtaining a credit rating and by asking for references, but you can see that being able to trust the financial statements is one way to make sure you are happy to enter into an agreement with the company. There is also a benefit to the company—having audited financial statements can help to build good relationships with suppliers.

Activity 1.2 Benefits of audit

Note down as many benefits of audit as you can, thinking from the point of view of a range of stakeholders (i.e. users of financial statements) and the company itself.

Despite all of the benefits of audit, there are some downsides, one of which is the cost to the company being audited. The cost can be very significant, with some UK audits costing over £50 million—though such high audit fees are only seen in the audits of large, listed companies, usually operating in highly regulated sectors such as banking and oil and gas extraction. Audits of smaller and less complex organizations will obviously cost a lot less. A typical listed company audit might cost in the region of £3 to £6 million (e.g. Sainsbury's 2021 audit cost £3.4 million).

Of course, given the number of shareholders that a listed company can have, it would be impractical for every individual shareholder to verify the figures and disclosures in the financial statements, so even with very high audit fees it is valuable to shareholders to have an independent audit of the information prepared by the company directors.

Activity 1.3 Disadvantages of audit

Do you think there are any disadvantages to audit? Note down as many examples as you can think of.

One of the key problems for smaller businesses is that the cost of an audit is likely to outweigh the benefits provided. This is especially the case for owner-managed companies, where the shareholders and directors are the same people, so there is no agency theory issue. In this case, the audit is just a compliance exercise which costs money with little tangible benefit. This is why, in many countries, including the UK, small companies are exempt from audit, an issue we will explore in Chapter 2.

1.2 Audit and assurance

1.2.1 What is assurance?

You have probably heard of 'assurance' as well as 'audit' and you might be wondering what the difference is, or whether they are the same thing. The answer is that they are not the same thing: in fact, audit is just a type of assurance.

An assurance engagement is defined as:

> An engagement in which a practitioner aims to obtain sufficient appropriate evidence in order to express a conclusion designed to enhance the degree of confidence of the intended users other than the responsible party about the subject matter information (that is, the outcome of the measurement or evaluation of an underlying subject matter against criteria).[2]

You can see that there are several important terms within this definition:

- Responsible party—this is the party responsible for the subject matter of the engagement (e.g. a financial controller in a company who has prepared a cash flow forecast).

[2] International Auditing and Assurance Standards Board, *Handbook of international quality control, auditing, review, other assurance, and related services pronouncements* (New York, 2021), 11.

- Subject matter—this is the subject of the assurance engagement, often financial information (e.g. a cash flow forecast), but it could be non-financial (e.g. sustainability performance indicators).
- Criteria—these are the benchmarks used to measure or evaluate the underlying subject matter (e.g. assumptions underpinning a cash flow forecast).
- Intended users—this is the party (or parties) who will be using the assurance report (e.g. a potential provider of finance who will be using the assurance report on a cash flow forecast to help decide about lending).
- Practitioner—this is the provider of the assurance report.
- Sufficient appropriate evidence—this is the evidence obtained by the practitioner to support the conclusion on the subject matter.
- Conclusion—this is the output of the assurance engagement.

There are two types of assurance engagement:

- Reasonable assurance engagements, which result in a positive expression of opinion and where the level of assurance given is deemed to be high—an example of this type of assurance engagement is an audit of historical financial information. The auditor's opinion is phrased in a positive way (e.g. 'in our opinion, the financial statements show a true and fair view').
- Limited assurance engagements, which result in negative assurance and where the level of assurance given is deemed to be moderate—an example here is a review engagement, performed on prospective financial information (e.g. a cash flow forecast). Here, no opinion is expressed. Instead, the practitioner reaches a conclusion, which is phrased using wording like 'nothing has come to our attention to indicate errors in the production of this cash flow statement'. This is sometimes known as 'negative assurance' because of the wording 'nothing has to come to our attention'.

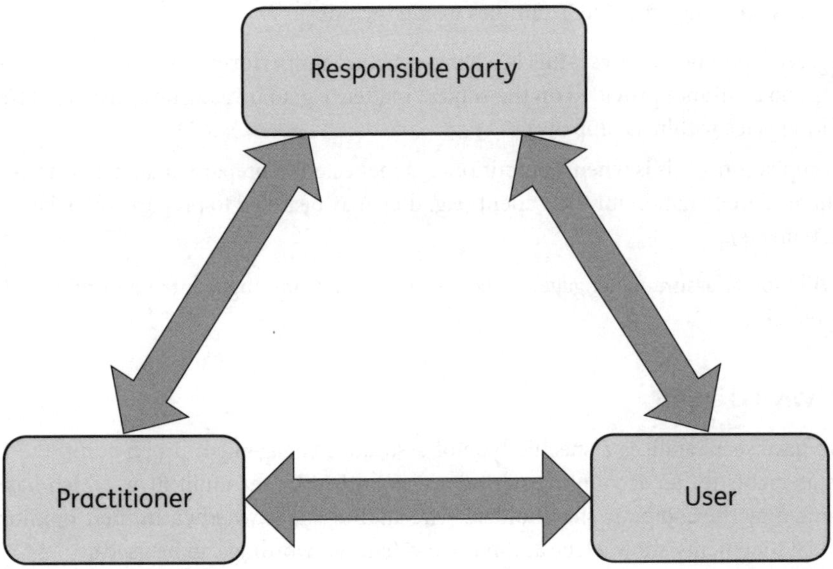

Figure 1.3 Relationships in an assurance engagement

Auditing scenario 1.1 Limited assurance review

Beales Associates is a firm of accountants and auditors, which has been approached by Deans Ltd to perform an assurance engagement on its sustainability report.

Deans Ltd has used a recognized sustainability reporting framework to prepare its report, which includes narrative commentary on the company's strategy towards sustainability, as well as a number of key performance indicators covering issues such as greenhouse gas emissions, water consumption and the impact of the company's operations on biodiversity.

The sustainability report will be published on the company's website, as well as being used internally by the company.

In this situation, the seven elements of the assurance engagement are:

- responsible party—the management of Deans Ltd;
- subject matter—the sustainability report, or just certain elements of the report. It is quite common for assurance to be provided on certain elements (e.g. the key performance indicators, but not on the management commentary);
- criteria—the recognized sustainability framework;
- intended users—the management team of Deans Ltd and readers of the sustainability report;
- practitioner—Beales Associates;
- sufficient appropriate evidence—this is the evidence which will be obtained by Beales Associates to support their conclusion on the subject matter; and
- conclusion—this is the output of the assurance engagement, which will be a limited assurance review.

Before we move on to consider audit, which you should remember is just a type of assurance engagement, we should mention that practitioners are often asked to perform engagements which are not assurance engagements. This type of engagement does not result in an opinion or conclusion being provided. Examples would include:

- Agreed-upon procedures—this is when a practitioner performs a specific piece of work, with no assurance provided on the subject matter (e.g. to investigate a suspected fraud taking place within a company).
- Compilation—this is when a practitioner is requested to prepare financial or non-financial information for their client (e.g. they may be asked to prepare financial statements).

We will look at assurance engagements and non-assurance engagements in more detail in Chapter 23.

1.2.2 **What is audit?**

As we have seen, audit is a specific type of assurance engagement. In an audit, the financial statements for an accounting period are examined by the audit firm, which has been appointed by the company shareholders. The auditor states whether, in their opinion, the financial statements 'show a true and fair view' (similar wording can be used).

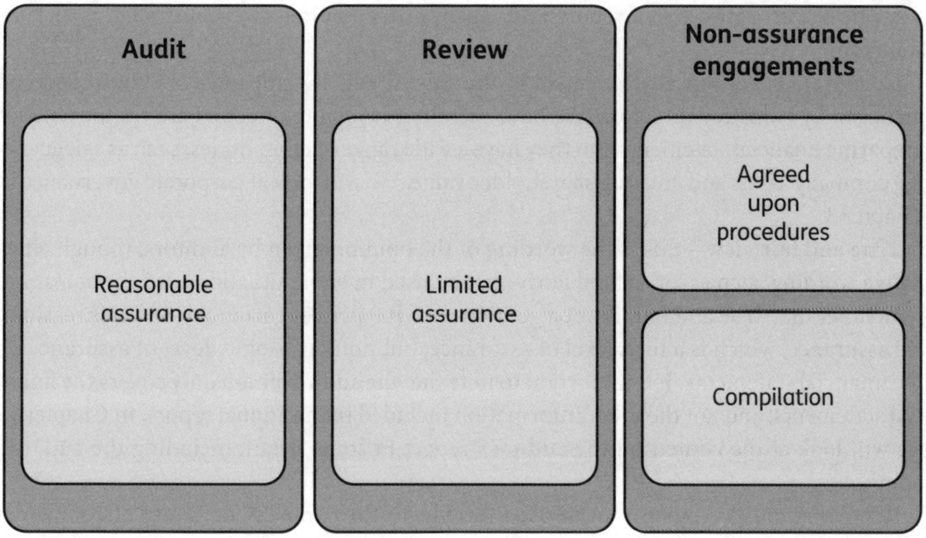

Figure 1.4 Types of engagement and levels of assurance

Activity 1.4 Audit within the assurance framework

We have seen that there are seven elements to an assurance engagement. Can you apply these elements to an audit engagement?

As part of our introduction to auditing, there are some important terms that you need to know, which we will refer to throughout the book and explore in more detail later on. For now, you just need an awareness of a few key concepts.

Financial statements—these are the accounts prepared by company directors. They will include:

- a statement of financial position (sometimes known as the 'balance sheet');
- a statement of profit or loss;
- a statement of cash flows;
- a statement of changes in equity; and
- notes to the financial statements.

In the UK, the general rule is that listed entities use International Financial Reporting Standards (IFRS) while non-listed use UK-specific financial reporting standards. For the purpose of our book, we will use IFRS as the 'applicable financial reporting framework'. These days there is not very much difference between IFRS and UK accounting rules, except for small companies which have a less detailed financial reporting framework. It is not within the scope of our discussions to consider these accounting rules and variations.

Annual report—the annual report contains the financial statements but will also include other information as required by regulations. For larger companies, this will include a strategic report, a governance report, and usually other required disclosures such as sustainability metrics.

Corporate governance—this refers to the way in which companies are controlled and managed by company directors. We have seen that company directors are responsible for preparing financial statements, but they have a wide range of other duties, such as safeguarding company assets and creating shareholder value. We will look at corporate governance in Chapter 3.

True and fair view—this is the wording of the opinion given by auditors, though alternative wording such as 'presented fairly' can be used in some situations. It is important to remember that 'true and fair' is not a guarantee of 100 per cent accuracy, and it is reasonable assurance, which is a high level of assurance, but not an absolute level of assurance on the financial statements. It is important to note that the audit opinion only covers the financial statements, and not the other information included in the annual report. In Chapter 19 we will look at the content of the auditor's report in some detail, including the auditor's opinion.

Reporting entity—this is a term used to refer to the company or group of companies which has prepared the financial statements subject to audit. It might not be a business—a reporting entity could be a charity, a local government authority, or a firm of solicitors. In our book, we will focus on companies, and we use the terms company and entity interchangeably.

Misstatement—this is a term used to refer to something being wrong in the financial statements. It could be due to an error (e.g. some missing information due to an oversight by management), or it could be something more deliberate (e.g. an attempt to overstate profit by recognizing revenue too early). A misstatement can be in any part of the financial statements including the notes.

Materiality—this is a technical term, referring to a level of significance within the financial statements. When auditors give their true and fair opinion, they are saying that the financial statements are free from 'material misstatement'. In simple terms, 'material' means of significance to shareholders. So, when the auditors say the financial statements are free from material misstatement, they are signalling that in their opinion, there is nothing significantly wrong in the accounts. Chapter 10 examines materiality in some detail.

ISAs (UK)—these are the regulations issued by the International Auditing and Assurance Standards Board (IAASB) and adopted for use in the UK by the FRC. All audits should be performed in accordance with the ISAs (UK) requirements. We will look at sources of regulations, including ISAs (UK) and UK-specific legislation in Chapter 2.

Professional judgement—it is important to remember that accounting and financial reporting is at least partly based on the use of judgement. When preparing the financial statements, management will have to use judgement (e.g. when determining the useful lives of assets for depreciation calculations), or for estimating whether any bad debts need to be written off. This means that auditors are often not evaluating whether a figure is 'right or wrong'—instead, they will be evaluating the appropriateness of management's use of judgement in financial reporting.

Professional scepticism—this is an attitude which should be used in auditing, especially when auditing areas of judgement. It means having a questioning mind, challenging management when appropriate, and being alert for contradictory evidence. We will look at how auditors apply professional scepticism in Chapter 4.

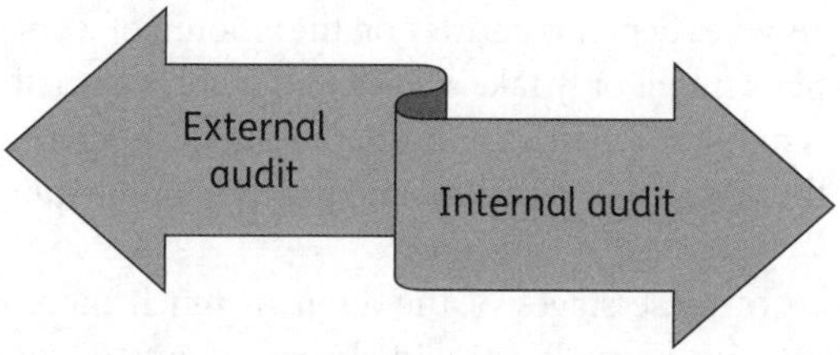

Figure 1.5 External and internal audit

Internal audit—we also need to understand the difference between external and internal audit. This book focuses on external audit, which is when an independent auditor performs an audit of financial statements—this is what we have been discussing so far. Internal audit is different—this is when employees of the company perform assurance work and report internally. We will look at internal audit at various places in the book—in particular in Chapter 3 when we consider corporate governance and in Chapter 12 when we look at the interaction between internal and external auditors.

1.3 How is an audit performed?

1.3.1 The process of an audit

An audit involves a number of stages (see Figure 1.6), beginning with accepting the client and the audit engagement, and ending by issuing the audit report to shareholders. Depending on the size and complexity of the reporting entity and its financial statements, the process will be different, but generally speaking there is a planning stage, evidence gathering (often known as the 'fieldwork stage'), completion, and reporting.

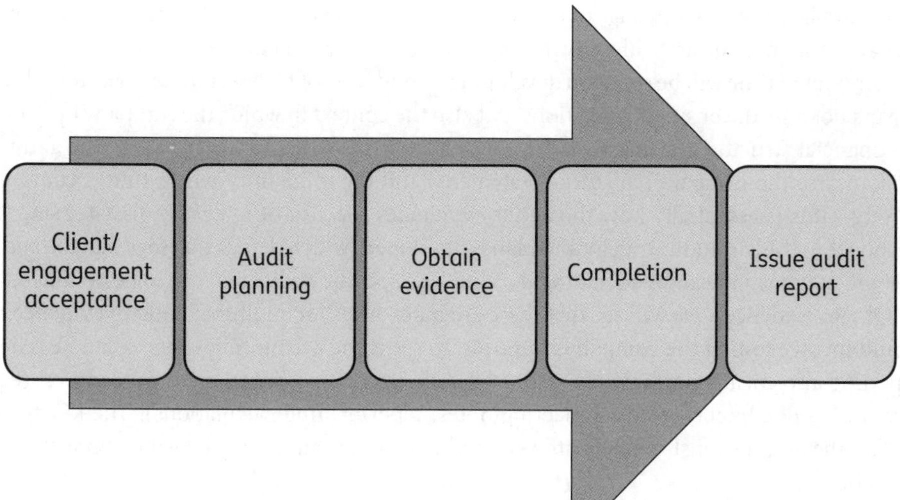

Figure 1.6 Stages of an audit

How long this process takes depends entirely on the amount of work involved. An audit of a relatively small company might only take a week and involve a small audit team. An audit of a large group with complex activities and operations in different countries could take several months, or if there is a tight deadline, the process can be quicker but with a much larger audit team.

We will look at each of these stages of the audit in much more detail later, for now, let's provide an overview. We have also provided some points of comparison between an audit and the provision of a limited assurance review, to contrast the scope of the engagements and the type of evidence obtained.

Client engagement/acceptance—before agreeing to do an audit, the audit firm needs to consider whether they can take on the client, as well as whether they can perform the work required. Many things need to be considered, including whether taking on the client might cause a conflict of interest with other clients and if there are other ethical reasons why the audit firm should not be involved with the client, perhaps because one of the audit partners has a financial interest in the potential client, which is a breach of independence. There are some regulatory requirements as well, such as performing anti-money laundering checks on the potential client, and contacting the existing audit provider to the company, assuming this is not the first time the company has appointed an auditor.

One point of difference here between an audit and a limited assurance review is that for an audit, the scope of the engagement is largely determined by regulations including legislation and auditing standards. The responsibilities and duties of an audit provider are quite fixed, though there is some scope for agreeing additional work with clients. For limited assurance reviews, the scope of the work is more flexible, and is agreed between the client and the assurance provider.

The audit firm should also consider if it has the time and the resources to perform a high-quality audit, and commercial factors will also be considered—will the audit make a profit? Will the client be able to pay the audit fee? Is the client a good strategic fit for the audit firm?

Audit planning—at this stage of the audit the focus is on understanding the client's activities and systems in order to identify the key areas of focus. For a new audit client, a considerable amount of time will be spent on developing a good level of business understanding which covers not only the business operations, but also the context in which the company operates, its financial structure, business model, internal controls—the list is very long. The auditor will analyse the company's financial statements and try to identify where things could go wrong—this is essentially how the auditor evaluates the risk of material misstatement. In response to this, an audit strategy and plan is developed, which details the ways that the auditor will approach the audit, including the details of specific audit evidence to be obtained.

Obtain evidence—we will see that there are many ways for auditors to obtain evidence. It could involve testing the company's controls, to see if the accounting systems can be relied upon. It also means performing 'tests of detail', also called 'substantive procedures' (e.g. examining documents, reading meeting notes, reperforming calculations). The key thing is that the auditor must obtain 'sufficient and appropriate' audit evidence to support their opinion.

This is different from a limited assurance review, when evidence is obtained primarily by analytical review of the financial statements and enquiry with management. The limited range of procedures performed, leading to less robust evidence, is why a lower level of assurance is provided in such an engagement.

Completion—this is where the audit work is finalized, and reviews take place to ensure that a high-quality audit has been performed, and that no issues are outstanding. If the senior auditors think that more evidence needs to be obtained, then additional audit work is performed. At this stage of the audit, specific matters are considered (e.g. events that have taken place since the year end and whether these have been appropriately reflected in the financial statements).

Reporting—the auditor issues their report to shareholders, which is the conclusion of the audit process. As we have seen, the auditor expresses an opinion as to whether the financial statements show a 'true and fair view'. The auditor also reports to the management and those charged with governance of the client on matters which they came across during the audit which are of note to those running the business.

1.3.2 **Timings and audit team personnel**

A related aspect to consider is when the audit takes place. Again, this is largely dependent on the size and complexity of the engagement. Obviously, the audit is based on the financial statements for a financial year end, so the bulk of the audit work will take place after that financial year end, based on draft financial statements prepared by the client. For small audits, the entire process can take place after the financial year end. However, it is quite common for the audit planning to take place before the financial year end, based on projected financial statements. This makes it easier for the audit fieldwork to be completed in good time, which is important for listed companies which need to publish their results to a tight deadline after the year end. When audit work takes place before the year end, this is known as the 'interim audit', and the work after the year end is known as the 'final audit'.

We also need to understand who performs the audit work (i.e. who is involved in the audit team). A typical audit team will involve an audit partner, who signs the audit report and is 'in charge' of the audit process. In Chapter 2 we will look in more detail at the responsibilities of the audit partner, and the regulations around who is allowed to take on this responsibility. The audit team is also likely to include an audit manager and one or more audit assistants—who are often known as 'audit junior' or 'audit senior' depending on their level of experience. Different audit firms use different names for these job titles. Audit juniors are usually trainees progressing through their training contract and professional exams—not yet qualified—however, they will be performing client work, and it is common for audit juniors to interact with clients from a very early stage with the firm.

Other people who might be involved with an audit team could be:

- IT specialists (e.g. to perform data analytics or to obtain evidence on the effectiveness of the client's IT systems).
- Technical specialists (e.g. for a client in a highly regulated sector, a person who has specific expertise on the financial reporting requirements would often be involved).
- Tax specialists, to deal with complex tax arrangements.
- Audit coordinator (e.g. to manage the administrative aspects of the audit, including scheduling, resource allocation, and communication with the client).

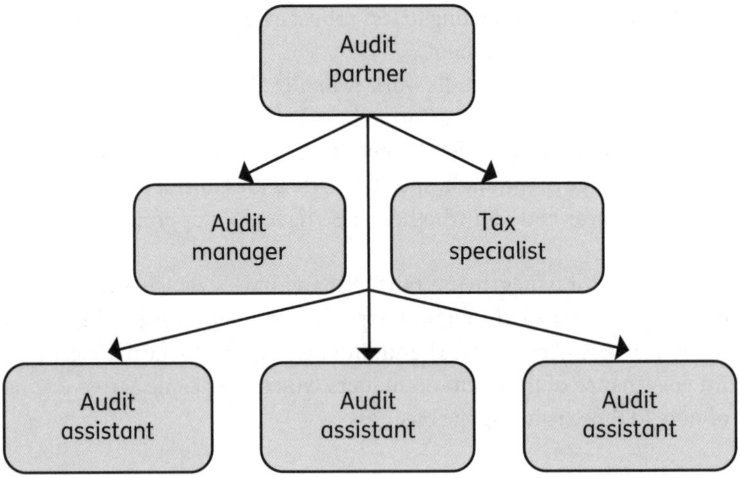

Figure 1.7 Typical audit team personnel

Audit team members may be from outside the audit firm—it is quite common to hire in expertise in specialist areas, or for audit firms to delegate some, often routine and low-risk, audit work to other auditors.

1.3.3 **Audit firms and the auditing profession**

Finally, we bring our attention to how audit firms operate, and the profession in which they operate.

You have probably heard of the big four audit firms—KPMG, Deloitte, Ernst & Young (EY), and PwC. However, there are many audit providers, the largest of which provide audits to public interest entities and which the FRC groups into 'tiers'. Table 1.1 shows the firms in tiers 1, 2, and 3 for 2022/2023.[3]

These firms offer much more to their clients than accounting and audit.

Activity 1.5 Services offered by audit firms

Think of examples of services that are offered by big firms to their clients, other than audit.

It is interesting to note the fees generated by the big four firms for audit and for non-audit services. According to FRC research, in 2020 only 30.2 per cent of fee income was derived from audit fees, of the total services provided by the firms. This had increased from only 28.3 per cent in 2019.[4] This serves to indicate how important the non-audit services are to

[3] FRC, *Tier 1 firms—overview—Audit quality inspection and supervision report* (2023), 41 <https://media.frc.org.uk/documents/Tier_1_Firms__Overview_2023.pdf> (accessed 12 January 2024).

[4] FRC, *Developments in audit 2021* (London, 2021) <https://media.frc.org.uk/documents/Developments_in_Audit_2021.pdf> (accessed 12 January 2024).

the firms, and we should remember that auditing is only one part of the portfolio of services offered to clients.

The audit firms are not providing audit and non-audit services to the same client. Recent regulatory changes mean that for listed companies, auditors can only provide the audit service. It has long been debated in the profession whether it is appropriate for firms to provide an audit client with other services such as tax planning or corporate finance. The issue relates to objectivity and independence—the more services a firm provides to a client, the higher the risk of fee dependency and over-familiarity, which mean that the auditor's opinion on the financial statements may no longer be independent. We will revisit this issue in Chapter 4.

If you remind yourself of the statistic that only 30.2 per cent of big four firm fee income is from providing audit services, this means that the big four firms derive most of their fee income from the provision of non-audit services to non-audit clients.

As we saw in Table 1.1, there are not just four audit firms. The big four are called the big four because they dominate the audit profession. In the UK, almost all audits of FTSE 350 companies are performed by the big four. The FRC monitors audit market share among audit providers, and in 2020 they reported that the big four were the statutory auditors of 93.7 per cent of FTSE 350 companies.[5]

Table 1.1 Tier 1, 2, and 3 audit firms

Tier 1	Tier 2	Tier 3
BDO LLP	Crowe UK LLP	Anstey Bond LLP
Deloitte LLP	Grant Thornton LLP	Beever and Struthers
Ernst & Young LLP	Johnston Carmichael LLP	Begbies
KPMG LLP	MacIntyre Hudson LLP	Bennet Brooks & Co Ltd
Mazars LLP	PKF Littlejohn LLP	Bright Grahame Murray
PricewaterhouseCoopers LLP	RSM (UK) Audit LLP	BSG Valentine (UK) LLP
		CBW Audit Ltd
		Deloitte (NI) Ltd
		Gerald Elderman LLP
		Grant Thornton (NI) LLP
		Hayesmacintyre LLP
		Hazelwoods LLP
		Johnsons Financial Management Ltd
		Kreston Reeves LLP
		LB Group Ltd
		Moore Kingston Smith LLP
		Pointon Young Limited
		Price Bailey LLP
		Royce Peeling Green Limited
		RPG Crouch Chapman LLP
		Shipleys LLP

[5] Ibid.

The FRC commented that, in 2020:

> The non-Big Four firms that audited FTSE 350 companies in 2020 were BDO LLP (15 audits), Grant Thornton LLP (4 audits), MHA Macintyre Hudson LLP (2 audits) and RSM LLP (1 audit), with BDO's LLP market share increasing significantly in the past year as they grew their FTSE 350 audits from 5 to 15.[6]

The issue is whether this dominance of the big four is healthy for the audit market. In 2006, Austin Mitchell MP called for the monopoly of the big four to be broken, to allow a wider range of audit providers to enter the market. He argued that the monopoly and long tenure of the audit firms with their clients had a significant and detrimental impact on audit quality and had implications for auditor objectivity. Many years later, largely due to the collapse of Carillion in 2018, which resulted in questions being asked about the role of all big four audit firms in providing audit and non-audit services to the company, the UK government ordered an investigation into the state of the audit market and the quality of work performed by the largest firms. In December 2018, the Competition and Markets Authority (CMA) published a report which recommended that the audit function is more clearly separated from other lines of service provided by the big four to their clients. It did not rule out more drastic options including a break-up of the big four, capping the number of listed clients they can audit or requiring listed companies to appoint two auditors so that a 'joint audit' is performed (e.g. by one of the big four along with a smaller audit firm). All of these measures, the report argued, would enhance competition, and break the dominance of the big four.

There is also an issue that the big audit firms can charge more for their services because the market operates like a monopoly, pushing up fees but not enhancing audit quality. The big firms are very powerful and can lobby government and the regulatory bodies quite successfully. The lack of choice of audit provider is therefore a problem.

Activity 1.6 Barriers to entry

What do you think prevents firms other than the big four from auditing large, listed companies? Why is it so hard for smaller firms to take on these audits?

The EU brought in regulations which require rotation of audit firms for listed companies after ten years. In the UK, this principle has been adopted, but amended so that after ten years the audit must be put out to tender, and after twenty years, the audit rotated. This has led to changes of auditor (e.g. HSBC moved from KPMG to PwC), but it is just movement between the big four rather than to other audit providers.

[6] Ibid.

Auditing in Practice 1.2 The audit market

Speaking at the Institute of Chartered Accountants in England and Wales in 2018, Rachel Reeves MP, who was at the time the Chair of the Business, Energy and Industrial Strategy Committee, said:

> Misleading audits have been at the heart of corporate failures over recent decades. Recent accounting scandals at BHS, Carillion, and at Patisserie Valerie have shown accounts bearing closer resemblance to works of fiction than an accurate reflection of the true financial performance of the business. Repeated accounting failures have contributed to the collapse of major businesses and undermined public and investor confidence.
>
> The audit market is broken. The Big Four's overwhelming market domination has failed to deliver audits which are fit-for-purpose. The lack of meaningful competition has bred conflicts of interest at every turn. The dice are loaded in the Big Four's favour, as they snap up audit contracts while pocketing huge fees for consultancy work and providing advice on recovering failing businesses. A host of solutions are now proposed to boost competition and improve audit quality. It's important that all options are on the table, including measures to break the stranglehold of the Big 4.[7]

Since this speech was made, there have been several significant reports into the future of the auditing profession in the UK. Progress into implementing measures to reform the profession has been slow, largely due to the Covid-19 pandemic which obviously put different priorities on government. However, in July 2023, draft regulations were laid before Parliament, based on the White Paper 'Restoring Trust in Audit and Corporate Governance'.

In 2022, the FRC issued a policy paper entitled 'Competition in the Audit Market'[8] which outlines the regulator's approach to competition in the audit market. Ultimately, the FRC wants an audit market which supports high-quality auditing and will promote competition if that leads to better-quality auditing and resilience in the audit market. The FRC supports the government's proposals with regard to developing the audit market.

A further FRC report published in 2023 'Audit Market and Competition Developments—A Snapshot',[9] which shows that there is some movement in the audit market. The report shows that 'Since 2019, the number of FTSE 350 audit engagements undertaken by the challenger firms has grown from 13 to 36, and a few FTSE 100 companies are now audited by challenger firms.' The barriers to entry discussed above seem to be working to prevent the challenger firms from breaking into the audit market for the largest listed companies, but the FRC acknowledges that it will take time to promote and achieve effective competition.

The planned changes to the audit profession, and also to some responsibilities of company directors, mean that auditing and company reporting are in a state of change. It is an exciting time to be learning about the role of auditors, the responsibilities of directors, and the value of both high-quality auditing and strong corporate governance to society.

[7] House of Commons, *The future of audit* (London, 2019) <https://publications.parliament.uk/pa/cm201719/cmselect/cmbeis/1718/1718.pdf> (accessed 12 January 2024).

[8] FRC, *Competition in the audit market* (2022) https://media.frc.org.uk/documents/Competition_in_the_audit_market.pdf (accessed 12 January 2024).

[9] FRC, *Audit market and competition developments* (2023) <https://media.frc.org.uk/documents/Audit_market_and_competition_developments_-_a_snapshot.pdf> (accessed 12 January 2024).

Chapter round-up

- Assurance means providing an opinion or a conclusion on a subject matter.
- Auditing is a type of assurance engagement, where the subject matter is financial statements prepared by the management of a company.
- Audit provides a high, but not absolute, level of assurance to shareholders.
- Agency theory is a way of explaining the relationships between the shareholders and the company directors, and the reason for appointing auditors as a mechanism for monitoring the activities of directors.
- Benefits of audit include reducing risk of non-compliance with regulations, recommendations to improve business processes, and reducing the risk of fraud.
- Downsides of audit include the cost and the bureaucracy (e.g. appointment of the auditor).
- Audits are performed in stages, including planning, obtaining evidence, and reporting the opinion to shareholders.
- Audit work is focused on areas of risk, known as the 'risk of material misstatement'.
- Audit teams include staff of different levels of seniority and must include an audit partner, who signs the audit report.
- The audit profession is dominated by the big four firms, but this causes problems for competition and audit quality leading to calls for audit reform.
- Audit firms offer a range of services to clients, and the big four generate most of their income from providing non-audit services to non-audit clients.

Activity solutions

Activity 1.1–Misleading information

What reasons do you think company directors may have for presenting misleading or inaccurate information in the financial statements?

Suggested answer points:

- If the company is not performing well, the directors might inflate revenue or profit to make the company's financial performance look better than it actually is, to keep the shareholders happy and to maintain share price.
- They might also make the company's performance look better than reality for their own job security–shareholders might remove directors from office if the company is not performing well.
- They might want to understate profit, so that the company pays less tax.
- Directors might be paid a bonus based on financial targets (e.g. increase in revenue or maintaining profit at a certain level), leading them to manipulate the financial statements.
- Misleading financial statements might be used to attract investors or lenders by making the company appear more attractive or financially stable than it actually is.
- There may be financial targets attached to debt covenants (e.g. need to maintain a gearing ratio or interest cover), leading to manipulation of figures to ensure the targets are met.

- Directors may try to protect the company's reputation by hiding negative financial information that could damage the brand or lead to a loss of consumer trust or damage other relationships (e.g. with suppliers).

Activity 1.2—Benefits of audit

Note down as many benefits of audit as you can, thinking from the point of view of a range of stakeholders (i.e. users of financial statements) and the company itself.

Suggested answer points:

Benefits to the company:

- Audit has beneficial by-products (e.g. advice on accounting systems and strength of internal controls).
- Linked to this, an audited company may have more efficient operations, improved management decision-making processes, better planning, and budgeting etc.
- Audit can act as a deterrent against error and fraud and other financial irregularities (e.g. money laundering).
- Reduces risk of non-compliance with law and regulations (e.g. payroll tax, VAT, listing rules).
- Having audited accounts makes it easier to raise finance. It can also be cheaper to raise finance as the risk to the provider of finance is reduced.

Benefits to other stakeholders:

- Tax authorities use the information to determine tax due, accurate financial information means that tax is calculated properly.
- For banks, the audited financial statements are critical to lending decisions.
- For employees, they can use audited financial statements to evaluate the company's financial position and performance, which can be relevant for job security.
- Trustworthy financial statements can provide information on wider social issues (e.g. charitable donations made by the company, investment in new technology, of interest to a wide range of stakeholders).

Activity 1.3—Disadvantages of audit

Do you think there are any disadvantages to audit? Note down as many examples as you can think of.

Suggested answer points:

- Cost—an audit can be very expensive, and the directors and shareholders might not see as value for money, especially for smaller, owner-managed businesses where there is no separation of ownership and control.
- Audits can't find every error/fraud because auditors cannot verify every transaction.
- Disruption to business during the audit process.
- Banks use their own lending criteria to make decisions about providing finance to a company, and an audit may not be necessary for this purpose.
- Companies might be reluctant to discuss matters with the auditor or make certain information available to them (e.g. payroll information or commercially sensitive information).

Activity 1.4—Audit within the assurance framework

We have seen that there are seven elements to an assurance engagement. Can you apply these elements to an audit engagement?

Suggested answer points:

- Responsible party—the directors of the company.
- Subject matter—the financial statements of the company.
- Criteria—the financial reporting framework (e.g. IFRS or UK financial reporting standards) and relevant company law.
- Intended users—the shareholders of the company.
- Practitioner—the audit firm.
- Sufficient appropriate evidence—the evidence obtained to support the audit opinion.
- Conclusion—this will be an opinion of reasonable assurance.

Activity 1.5—Services offered by the big firms

Think of examples of services that are offered by big firms to their clients, other than audit.

Suggested answer points:

- Assurance (other than audit) (e.g. limited assurance reviews of forecasts or sustainability information).
- Tax services (e.g. tax planning, compliance, and specialist areas like international tax).
- Consulting services (e.g. management consulting, technology consulting, risk management).
- Mergers and acquisitions (e.g. due diligence engagements and helping clients to value potential acquisitions and to plan successful business integration post-acquisition).
- Corporate finance and financial advisory (e.g. assisting clients in financial planning, raising capital, restructuring).
- Forensic services (e.g. helping clients with fraud detection, investigation, and prevention).
- Legal services (e.g. corporate law, intellectual property, regulatory compliance, litigation support, and dispute resolution).
- Insolvency (e.g. assisting in a company liquidation or administration).
- Sustainability and environmental services (e.g. sustainability reporting, compliance with relevant regulations).
- Technology and data analytics (e.g. using data analytics to provide insights and solutions related to financial management, risk assessment, and business operations).

Activity 1.6—Barriers to entry

What do you think prevents firms other than the big four from auditing large, listed companies? Why is it so hard for smaller firms to take on these audits?

Suggested answer points:

- Resources—it would be hard for a smaller audit firm to allocate sufficient resources to a big audit which might need a large number of audit team members.
- Experience—many larger, listed companies have complex operations which may be highly regulated and international, so smaller audit firms may not be experienced in such areas.
- Reputation—possibly the companies value the 'image' of being audited by a big four firm and the reputational benefits this may bring.

2 The Regulatory Framework

Introduction

Auditors provide a valuable service to company shareholders, to the wider group of organizational stakeholders, and to society. We looked at some of the concepts and theories which underpin this principle in Chapter 1. For the work of auditors to be trusted—in other words, for the service they provide to be truly valuable—there needs to be regulation of the auditing profession. Regulation must work to safeguard the competence and independence of auditors and therefore to maximize the credibility of the auditing profession and the company reports on which they are providing assurance.

In this chapter, we will look at the main elements of the regulatory framework in which auditors operate. It is important to understand the role of the regulatory bodies in setting relevant standards and legislation, and the rationale for the rules and principles which are in place. Regulation of auditors is needed to ensure that high-quality audit work is performed, and the audit profession sets standards which individuals must achieve before they are allowed to sign audit reports.

Regulation exists in various forms. Increased globalization, the rise of e-commerce and cross-border trading, as well as the international harmonization of financial reporting standards, has meant an increased desire for international regulations for the auditing profession. At the international level, there are several regulatory bodies of particular relevance to auditors, namely the International Federation of Accountants (IFAC), and the two independent standard-setting bodies, the International Auditing and Assurance Standards Board (IAASB), and the International Ethics Standards Board for Accountants (IESBA). These bodies issue standards which form the foundation of regulation for auditors in an international context.

At the national level, a country will establish jurisdiction-specific legislation and other regulations relevant to auditors. This book focuses on UK-specific requirements. In the UK, the Companies Act 2006 contains the relevant laws which govern certain aspects of audit practice. In addition to legislation, the UK's Financial Reporting Council (FRC) which is, at the time of writing, set to be replaced by the Audit, Reporting and Governance Authority (ARGA), issues standards and other pronouncements which, while not being law, are mandatory for auditors. The UK has adopted the International Standards on Auditing (ISAs) issued by the IAASB and adapted them where necessary to better fit the UK's legal, economic, and commercial environment. These are referred to as ISAs (UK) or 'ISA pluses'. While the legal framework can differ significantly between jurisdictions, the auditing regulations are often similar, because many countries adopt the ISAs, or make adaptations to them, as is the case in the UK.

Auditors also fall under the scope of other regulations, not aimed exclusively at the auditing profession, but which auditors need to comply with. We will not consider every piece of relevant legislation, but we will look at one very significant issue, that of the Anti-Money Laundering Regulations (AMLR), which auditors are required to follow.

Finally, the professional bodies to which auditors belong, for example the Institute of Chartered Accountants in England and Wales (ICAEW), the Institute of Chartered Accountants in Scotland (ICAS), and the Association of Chartered Certified Accountants (ACCA) have their own regulations with which their members must comply. These professional bodies are a crucial part of the regulatory framework but as this book is not aimed at students or members of any particular professional body, we shall not consider their specific regulations. However, it is worth being aware that they add a further layer to the regulation of auditors.

Learning outcomes

- Discuss the form of regulation which provides the audit framework for auditors in the international context.
- Explain the UK regulatory framework for auditing and discuss relevant current issues.
- Discuss UK-specific audit regulations including the requirements in relation to the appointment and removal of auditors and the rights and duties of auditors.
- Define 'money laundering', describe the main features of AMLR, and explain how accountants meet their obligations to help prevent and detect money laundering.

2.1 The international regulatory framework of auditing

2.1.1 The IFAC

IFAC is the global organization for the accountancy profession. It aims to serve the public interest by strengthening the accountancy profession and contributing to economic development. Its mission covers four aspects:

- supporting the development of high-quality international standards;
- promoting the adoption and implementation of these standards;
- building the capacity of professional accountancy organizations; and
- speaking out on public interest issues.

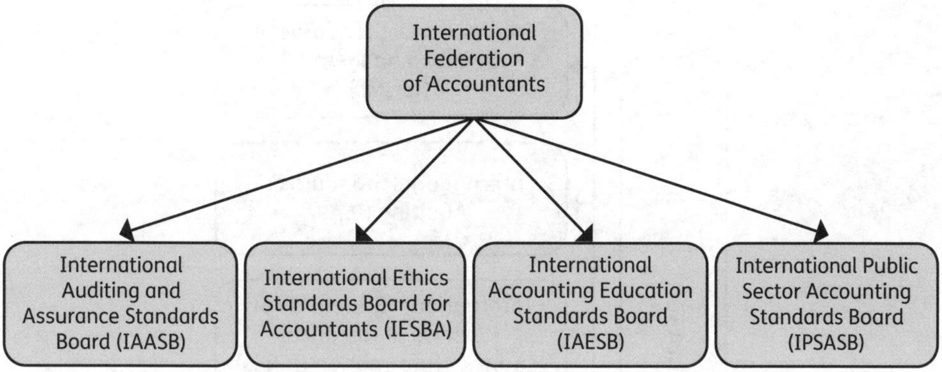

Figure 2.1 IFAC's standard-setting boards

IFAC has over 175 member bodies and associates from countries all over the world, including for example UK representation by ACCA and ICAEW, and it is through cooperation with these member bodies and associates that IFAC initiates, coordinates, and guides efforts to achieve international pronouncements for the accountancy profession.

Four independent standard-setting boards exist within the structure of IFAC (see Figure 2.1).

The IAASB and IESBA are the most relevant to auditors. In this chapter, we will consider the role of the IAASB in setting auditing standards, and in Chapter 4 we will focus on ethics.

In addition to these four standard-setting boards, the Public Interest Oversight Board (PIOB) was established to oversee the boards. The PIOB aims to bring greater transparency and integrity to the audit profession, thereby enhancing credibility and public confidence in the profession and in financial reporting. The PIOB oversees the process of standard setting, which will be described below, to help ensure that standards development is responsive to stakeholder needs and that the process is transparent.

Activity 2.1 International regulation

What do you think are the advantages of having international regulations governing the auditing profession?

2.1.2 **The IAASB**

The IAASB's objective is to serve the public interest by setting high-quality international standards for auditing, assurance, and other related areas, and by facilitating their adoption and implementation. In doing so, the IAASB enhances the quality and consistency of practice throughout the world and strengthens public confidence in the global auditing and assurance profession.

The IAASB issues several types of standard, as shown in Figure 2.2.

Figure 2.2 IAASB standards

2.1.2.1 **ISQMs**

The IAASB has issued two standards dealing with quality management:

- ISQM 1 *Quality Management for Firms that Perform Audits and Reviews of Financial Statements, Or Other Assurance and Related Services Engagements*
- ISQM 2 *Engagement Quality Reviews*

The ISQMs apply not only to audit engagements, but also to the other types of engagements often performed by auditors, for instance, reviews of interim financial information. ISQM 1 is intended to be applied at a firm-wide level, and there is a specific ISA which deals with quality control at the level of the audit engagement. We will look at audit quality management in some detail in Chapter 5.

2.1.2.2 **ISAs**

ISAs are the main source of regulation and guidance for auditors. They are intended to be applied in the audit of historical financial statements. ISAs are numbered according to a codification system which groups ISAs by subject matter as follows:

200–299 general principles and responsibilities
300–499 risk assessment and response to assessed risks

500–599 audit evidence
600–699 using the work of others
700–799 audit conclusions and reporting
800–899 specialized areas
900–999
1000–1100 international auditing practice notes

Over 113 jurisdictions are using or are in the process of adopting or incorporating the ISAs into their national auditing standards or using them as a basis for preparing national auditing standards. In this way, it can be argued that audit practice is becoming more internationally harmonized, as more and more countries implement ISAs, or a close approximation of them, into their national audit regulations. ISAs are not intended to override local laws or other regulations.

Each ISA contains:

- introduction including scope and the effective date of the ISA;
- one or more objectives;
- relevant definitions;
- requirements; and
- application and other explanatory material (including appendices).

The ISA requirements include the phrase 'the auditor shall . . .'. This indicates that a requirement is mandatory. If an auditor considers it necessary to depart from following an ISA requirement, the departure must be justified and fully documented. However, ISA requirements need only be applied to matters which are material to the financial statements. Failure to comply with an ISA requirement can lead to disciplinary action against the auditor, and can be viewed as negligent behaviour, which can have legal implications for the auditor.

ISAs also contain application and explanatory material which provides supplementary guidance on how to apply the ISA requirements and a discussion of the rationale behind the requirements. This material is not mandatory but should be fully read and understood by the auditor.

The IAASB website hosts a list of the current ISAs.

2.1.2.3 **ISREs**

These standards deal with situations when historical financial information is not being audited, and instead is subject to review, which provides a lower level of assurance than an audit. For example, ISRE 2400 *Engagements to Review Historical Financial Information* would be applied when a practitioner is reviewing the financial statements of a company which is below the audit exemption threshold (which will be explained in section 2.3.4) and is therefore not required to have the financial statements audited, but the company wishes an independent review to take place and a conclusion of limited assurance provided. In addition, there is one subject-specific standard, ISRE 2410 *Review of Interim Financial Information Performed by the Independent Auditor of the Entity.*

2.1.2.4 ISAEs

There is a general standard, ISAE 3000 *Assurance Engagements other than Audits or Reviews of Historical Financial Information*, and several subject-specific standards which deal with particular types of assurance engagement, for example ISAE 3400 *The Examination of Prospective Financial Information*.

Auditing in practice 2.1 Assurance on sustainability reporting

Organizations are increasingly required or expected to provide information about sustainability. In the past few years, it has become mandatory in many countries, including the UK, for large listed companies to disclose metrics and narrative information about their environmental and societal impacts. One of the most well-known environmental disclosures is required by the Task Force on Climate-Related Financial Disclosures (TCFD) but there are many different frameworks which are used by organizations, such as Integrated Reporting and the United Nations Sustainable Development Goals.

The issue of whether assurance should be obtained by organizations to support this type of reporting has been a topic of much debate, and the IAASB is supportive of sustainability assurance. ISAE 3000 can be applied to assurance engagements on sustainability engagements and ISAE 3410 *Assurance Engagements on Greenhouse Gas Statements* is also relevant.

In April 2021, the IAASB issued non-authoritative guidance entitled *Applying ISAE 3000 to Sustainability and Other Extended External Reporting Assurance Engagements.* Application of this guidance enhances the credibility of the sustainability report and the assurance report that has been issued on that report. When this guidance was issued, the IAASB commented:

> Non-financial information has become an important topic in reporting circles. As reporting evolves, auditors are increasingly asked to provide assurance on sustainability or Environmental Social and Governance reporting. Where this type of reporting, and assurance thereon, have often been undertaken on a voluntary basis by entities, there is an increasing (and nowadays, urgent) focus on this being mandated by law or regulation. We at the IAASB have taken the view that we must rise to the challenge and assist, particularly as users of corporate reports are demanding a broader base of information to inform capital allocation decisions.[1]

The IAASB is developing a new standard for assurance on sustainability reporting, which will be applicable across all sustainability topics, and reporting frameworks and implementable by all assurance practitioners, including accountants and non-accountants. Explaining the IAASB's objectives with regard to developing this new assurance standard, the Chair of the IAASB commented:

> We at the International Audit Assurance and Standards Board (IAASB) hear the need for a global assurance standards solution. The IAASB already has well-established principles-based and subject-specific standards and guidance that are being effectively applied. But we know there is further work to be done in bringing the existing standards and guidance together and supplementing them to address assurance of sustainability reporting specifically.

[1] Seidenstein, Tom, 'Assurance standards keeping pace on non-financial reporting', 2021 <https://www.iaasb.org/news-events/2021-03/assurance-standards-keeping-pace-non-financial-reporting> (accessed 12 January 2024).

The IAASB is committed to leading this effort to create new 'sustainability bespoke' assurance standards. We are now in the process of identifying the specific approach to building these standards that will have the greatest impact on establishing high-quality assurance to support reliable sustainability reporting. We have determined that the new sustainability assurance standards will need to be framework-agnostic and principles-based—they will need to work with all sustainability/ESG reporting frameworks.[2]

2.1.2.5 ISRSs

ISRSs deal with engagements which are performed as agreed-upon procedures, with no assurance provided. For example, ISRS 4410 *Compilation Engagements* deals with situations where a practitioner is preparing financial information for a client, for example, a profit and cash flow forecast. The practitioner compiles the required information but does not express an opinion on it.

2.1.3 Standard development

IAASB standards are developed following a due process which works to ensure appropriate consultation with relevant stakeholders and these standards are issued in a transparent way (see Figure 2.3). The stages are applicable to the development of all IAASB standards, not just ISAs.

At the end of this process, there will be an approval of the final standard, made by the affirmative vote of at least two-thirds of the IAASB members.

The IAASB has a very open and transparent development process for new and revised standards. It believes that consulting on proposals is a good way to build engagement with the business community, as well as with the audit professionals who will be using the standards. All relevant documents are made available on the IAASB website, including the minutes of meetings where the new or revised standard is discussed, project summaries, and the comments that have been provided in response to consultation documents. It is interesting to note that the vast majority of respondents to IAASB consultations are professional bodies or larger firms of accountants, though on occasion an enthusiastic individual provides a response. The exposure draft, final standard, and the basis for conclusions are all made available, so that the process of developing the regulations is transparent. In addition, the IAASB has started to issue 'At a Glance' documents, which provide a brief summary of the new pronouncement and the rationale for its development.

2.1.4 International Forum of Independent Audit Regulators

Before we move on to look at the audit regulations that are specific to the UK, we should mention the International Forum of Independent Audit Regulators (IFIAR), which was established in 2006 as a way to provide independent audit regulators from different countries

[2] Seidenstein, Tom, 'Balancing urgency and effectiveness in international sustainability assurance standards', 2022 <https://www.iaasb.org/news-events/2022-06/balancing-urgency-and-effectiveness-international-sustainability-assurance-standards#:~:> (accessed 12 January 2024).

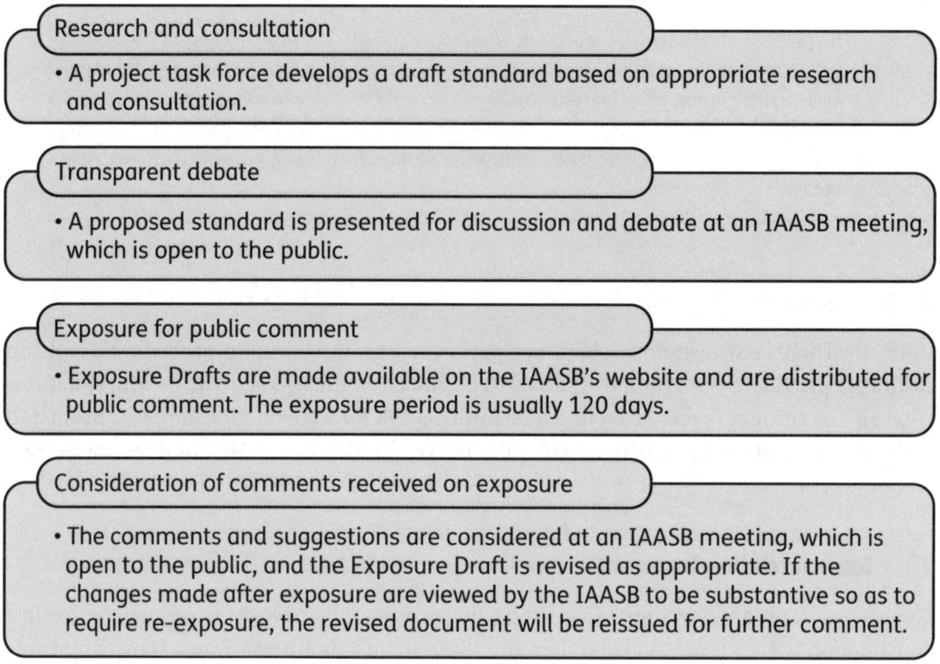

Figure 2.3 Standard development process

an environment in which to share information, promote good practice in audit inspections and monitoring activities, and to share results of members' work. IFIAR comprises fifty independent audit regulators from jurisdictions in Africa, the Americas, Asia, Europe, the Middle East, and Oceania.

The objectives of IFIAR are to:

- improve audit quality globally;
- strengthen IFIAR's role as the international leader on audit matters through strategic thought leadership;
- advance IFIAR's governance structure and operations; and
- facilitate learning and cooperation among IFIAR members.

IFIAR's activities are particularly focused on audit quality, and it carries out an annual inspection findings survey which is made available to the public and is intended to supplement the work of individual countries' audit regulators, who also perform audit quality inspections, which we shall examine in more detail in Chapter 5.

2.2 UK regulation—the FRC

The FRC is the UK's competent authority for audit. The FRC is responsible for issuing, amending, and withdrawing accounting and auditing standards in the UK.

It is expected that in the next few years, the FRC will transition to the ARGA. This transition would follow recommendations by Sir Donald Brydon CBE who carried out an independent review of the auditing profession which was heavily critical of how the FRC operates.[3] A separate review, headed by Sir John Kingman, was specifically tasked with evaluating the current state of the FRC, following the collapse of Carillion and other corporate scandals, which led to a loss of credibility of the FRC.[4] One of those recommendations was that the FRC be renamed and that ARGA is given more powers to sanction directors who commit unorthodox practices. We will explore the reasons for the changes taking place in UK regulation of auditing later in section 2.2.4.

The FRC is responsible for issuing and maintaining ISA in the UK as well as other regulations including Practice Notes (PNs) and Bulletins. In addition to issuing audit regulations, the FRC issues the Ethical Standard to be followed by auditors in the UK. We will look at the Ethical Standard in detail in Chapter 4.

In relation to audit, the FRC also:

- Reports on audit quality inspections of the larger audit firms operating in the UK.
- Exercises professional oversight of the UK professional bodies.
- Issues guidance specific to the audit of Public Interest Entities (PIEs).
- Influences and monitors international standards and policy developments which may affect UK auditors.
- Undertakes research on matters that are of relevance to audit in the UK.

2.2.1 **ISAs (UK)**

ISAs (UK) are based on the ISAs issued by the IAASB and are then tailored to be compliant with the requirements of UK legislation; these UK standards are often referred to as 'ISA pluses'. It is clear where the ISAs (UK) have been tailored to be compliant with UK legislation because any text which is UK specific is in grey shading within the standard.

Table 2.1 presents a list of the ISAs (UK) in issue at the time of writing.

We saw earlier in the chapter that the IAASB has issued a range of standards dealing with non-audit engagements. Several of these have been adopted for use in the UK.

The current list of standards can be found on the FRC's website.

[3] Report of the Independent Review into the Quality and Effectiveness of Audit, *Assess, assure, and inform: Improving audit quality and effectiveness*. Sir Donald Brydon CBE, London, 2019 (the 'Brydon Review') <https://www.gov.uk/government/publications/the-quality-and-effectiveness-of-audit-independent-review> (accessed 15 December 2023).

[4] *Kingman Review, Independent Review of the Financial Reporting Council*, John Kingman, London, December 2018<https://assets.publishing.service.gov.uk/media/5c1bbe68ed915d7327b92162/frc-independent-review-final-report.pdf> (accessed 15 December 2023).

Table 2.1 List of ISAs (UK)

ISA (UK) 200	Overall Objectives of the Independent Auditor and the Conduct of an Audit in Accordance with ISAs (UK) (Revised June 2016 and updated May 2022)
ISA (UK) 210	Agreeing the Terms of Audit Engagements (Revised June 2016 and updated May 2022)
ISA (UK) 220	Quality Management for an Audit of Financial Statements (Updated May 2022)
ISA (UK) 230	Audit Documentation (Revised June 2016 and updated May 2022)
ISA (UK) 240	The Auditor's Responsibilities Relating to Fraud in an Audit of Financial Statements (Revised June 2016 and updated May 2022)
ISA (UK) 250, Section A	Consideration of Laws and Regulations in an Audit of Financial Statements (Revised November 2019 and updated May 2022)
ISA (UK) 250, Section B	The Auditor's Statutory Right and Duty to Report to Regulators of Public Interest Entities and Regulators of Other Entities in the Financial Sector (Revised November 2019 and updated May 2022)
ISA (UK) 260	Communication with Those Charged with Governance (Revised June 2016 and updated May 2022)
ISA (UK) 265	Communicating Deficiencies in Internal Control to Those Charged with Governance and Management (Updated May 2022)
ISA (UK) 300	Planning an Audit of Financial Statements (Revised June 2016 and updated May 2022)
ISA (UK) 315	Identifying and Assessing the Risks of Material Misstatement (Revised June 2020)
ISA (UK) 320	Materiality in Planning and Performing an Audit (Revised June 2016 and updated May 2022)
ISA (UK) 330	The Auditor's Responses to Assessed Risks (Revised July 2017 and updated May 2022)
ISA (UK) 402	Audit Considerations Relating to an Entity Using a Service Organisation (updated May 2022)
ISA (UK) 450	Evaluation of Misstatements Identified During the Audit (Revised June 2016 and updated May 2022)
ISA (UK) 500	Audit Evidence (Updated May 2022)
ISA (UK) 501	Audit Evidence—Specific Considerations for Selected Items (Updated May 2022)
ISA (UK) 505	External Confirmations (Updated May 2022)
ISA (UK) 510	Initial Audit Engagements—Opening Balances (Revised June 2016)
ISA (UK) 520	Analytical Procedures (Updated May 2022)
ISA (UK) 530	Audit Sampling (Updated May 2022)
ISA (UK) 540	Auditing Accounting Estimates and Related Disclosures (Revised May 2022)
ISA (UK) 550	Related Parties (Updated May 2022)
ISA (UK) 560	Subsequent Events
ISA (UK) 570	Going Concern (Revised September 2019 and updated May 2022)
ISA (UK) 580	Written Representations (Updated May 2022)
ISA (UK) 600	Special Considerations—Audits of Group Financial Statements (Including the Work of Component Auditors) (Revised November 2019 and updated May 2022)
ISA (UK) 610	Using the Work of Internal Auditors (Revised June 2013 and updated May 2022)
ISA (UK) 620	Using the Work of an Auditor's Expert (Revised November 2019 and updated May 2022)
ISA (UK) 700	Forming an Opinion and Reporting on Financial Statements (Revised November 2019 and updated May 2022)
ISA (UK) 701	Communicating Key Audit Matters in the Independent Auditors Report (Revised November 2019 and updated May 2022)

Table 2.1 (Continued)

ISA (UK) 705	Modifications to the Opinion in the Independent Auditor's Report (Revised June 2016)
ISA (UK) 706	Emphasis of Matter Paragraphs and Other Matter Paragraphs in the Independent Auditor's Report (Revised June 2016)
ISA (UK) 710	Comparative Information—Corresponding Figures and Comparative Financial Statements
ISA (UK) 720	The Auditor's Responsibilities Relating to Other Information (Revised November 2019 and updated May 2022)
ISA (UK) 800	Special Considerations--Audits of Financial Statements Prepared in Accordance with Special Purpose Frameworks
ISA (UK) 805	Special Considerations—Audits of Single Financial Statements and Specific Elements, Accounts or Items of a Financial Statement

Auditing in practice 2.2 EU Audit Directive

The Statutory Auditors and Third Country Auditors Regulations 2016 introduced several changes for UK auditors and audited entities, including UK implementation of:

- parts of the Competition Commission/Competition and Markets Authority Order relating to the supply of statutory audit services to large companies in the UK; and
- a new EU Audit Directive and Audit Regulation.

The EU Audit Directive and Audit Regulation came into force on 16 June 2014 and all EU member states had two years from that date to transpose the requirements into law. The Directive applies to statutory audits of annual and consolidated financial statements, whereas the Regulation applies only to statutory audits of PIEs. PIEs are entities with securities admitted to trading on a regulated market, banks, building societies, and insurers.

To comply with the EU Audit Directive and Audit Regulation, the FRC made changes not only to ISAs (UK), but also to the UK Corporate Governance Code and the Ethical Standard.

Key areas where changes arose from the implementation of the EU Audit Directive and Regulation include:

- audit regulation, including the single competent authority (which is the FRC in the UK);
- length of audit engagements;
- standards and standard setting;
- removal of auditors;
- cooperation, transferring information, and confidentiality; and
- restrictive clauses in contracts with third parties.

When the UK voted to leave the EU, there was some debate about whether the EU-based regulations would continue to apply in the UK. For example, on leaving the EU, the UK would be free to determine its own audit exemption thresholds and audit firm rotation periods. However, when the UK departed from the EU on 31 January 2020, the EU Audit Regulation continued to apply, albeit with some changes including the definition of a PIE and a change to audit exemption applied to subsidiaries within a group of companies with an immediate parent company in the European Economic Area (EEA). The details of these changes are outside the scope of this book, but it is worth being aware that now that the UK is outside the EU, in the future there may be further divergence in audit regulation in the UK compared with its European neighbours.

2.2.2 **Practice Notes (PNs) and Bulletins**

As well as issuing ISAs (UK), the FRC also issues PNs and Bulletins. PNs are intended to assist auditors in applying auditing standards of general application to particular circumstances and industries. Bulletins are issued to provide auditors with timely guidance on new or emerging issues. PNs and Bulletins are persuasive rather than prescriptive. However, they are indicative of good practice, even though they may be developed without the full process of consultation and exposure used for standards. We have included a list of the current PNs and Bulletins for completeness, and to illustrate the type of circumstances and situations in which they may apply, but any further discussion of these documents is outside the scope of our book.

PNs currently in issue are listed in Table 2.2.

Bulletins currently in issue are listed in Table 2.3.

2.2.3 **Other UK-specific documents**

As well as issuing ISAs (UK), Practice Notes, and Bulletins, the UK regulator has issued the following documents which specifically relate to auditors:

- Glossary of Terms (auditing and ethics)—this defines terms used in the ISAs (UK), the ISQM (UK), and the Ethical Standard. It is based on the IAASB glossary of terms.
- Scope and Authority of Audit and Assurance pronouncements—this outlines the nature of the standards and guidance issued by the UK regulator and their status.
- ISQM (UK) 1 and ISQM (UK) 2—these are the standards on quality management for engagements (audit and non-audit engagements) performed by auditors.
- Staff Guidance Notes—these are intended to support practitioners when they make judgements on the application of standards. The Staff Guidance Notes are prepared

Table 2.2 List of FRC PNs

PN 10	The Audit of Public Sector Financial Statements is now issued by the Public Audit Forum, which has been designated by the FRC to issue a Statement of Recommended Practice (Revised 2020)
PN 11 (Revised)	The Audit of Charities in the United Kingdom (November 2017)
PN 14	The audit of housing associations in the United Kingdom (Revised March 2021)
PN 15 (Revised)	The Audit of Occupational Pension Schemes in the United Kingdom (July 2019)
PN 19 (Revised)	Special Considerations in Auditing Financial Instruments (July 2013)
PN 20 (Revised)	The Audit of Insurers in the United Kingdom (January 2017)
PN 23	Special Considerations in Auditing Financial Instruments

Table 2.3 List of FRC Bulletins

2021	Illustrative Auditor's Reports on United Kingdom Private Sector Financial Statements
2020	Illustrative Auditor's Reports on United Kingdom Private Sector Financial Statements
2020	Miscellaneous Reports by Auditors Required by the United Kingdom Companies Act 2006
2020	Auditor's Reports on Revised Accounts and Reports in the United Kingdom
2017	The Auditor's Association with Preliminary Announcements Made in Accordance with UK Listing Rules
2009/4	Developments in Corporate Governance Affecting the Responsibilities of Auditors of UK Companies
2006/5	The Combined Code on Corporate Governance: Requirements of Auditors under the Listing Rules of the Financial Services Authority and the Irish Stock Exchange

following discussion of the relevant issues at the regulator's Audit Technical Advisory Group, which comprises representatives from audit firms and professional bodies, investors, and audit committee chairs.

- Discussion papers and consultation documents—the regulator is continually considering improvements that can be made to standards and guidance issued, and every so often it issues a consultation on a particular issue.

2.2.4 The reform of the FRC and introduction of ARGA

In December 2018, following an independent review of the FRC, it was recommended that the FRC should be replaced with an independent statutory regulator called the ARGA. This new regulator would be accountable to Parliament, with a new mandate, new clarity of mission, new leadership, and new powers.

The independent review into the FRC was led by Sir John Kingman, and in 2019, the UK government confirmed that it supported the recommendations of his review.

The review was intended to be a 'root and branch' review, evaluating the current state of the regulator and aiming to provide recommendations to ensure that the regulator is highly regarded and can function in an appropriate way. The scope of the Kingman Review included:

- consideration of the governance of the FRC;
- whether the FRC is sufficiently independent from those whom it regulates;
- whether there are appropriate safeguards against conflict of interest;
- the powers of the FRC and whether they should be extended; and
- the resources and capacity of the FRC.

The Kingman Review was initiated following several high-profile company collapses and other accounting and audit scandals in the UK, including Carillion, BHS, and Patisserie Valerie. These scandals had served to highlight several problems in auditing and financial reporting—both of which are regulated by the FRC. The government's dissatisfaction with the FRC was strongly voiced in its investigation into the collapse of Carillion, in relation to which the FRC was called timid and reluctant to use the powers that it does have.

The investigation stated that:

> At present, the role of the FRC is confused. It is the professional regulator for accountants but also responsible for the voluntary codes that guide the behaviour of directors and investors. It has an apparently little-known role in investigating complaints raised relating to its remit by whistle-blowers. The quality of audits, as we have seen, is not of a consistently high standard. The FRC reports that 81 per cent of FTSE 350 audits in 2016 required only limited improvement, meaning that 19 per cent were significantly below standard: not a ringing endorsement of a high quality and competitive audit market. Where standards fall below what is expected, the FRC is far too passive in demanding improvements and monitoring subsequent performance. It therefore offers no effective deterrent to sloppy auditing and accounting, and does nothing to dispel views that it is too sympathetic or close to the accountants and auditors it regulates. The FRC does not appear to acknowledge a link, in terms of its responsibility, between adequate financial reporting, good corporate behaviour and the survival of companies.[5]

[5] Business, Energy and Industrial Strategy and Work and Pensions Committees, *Carillon* (London, 2018), 77–78 <https://publications.parliament.uk/pa/cm201719/cmselect/cmworpen/769/769.pdf> (accessed 12 January 2024).

In simple terms, it was felt that the FRC was not acting to remedy the problem of poor-quality auditing, partly because the regulator is 'too close' to the audit firms it is regulating. Conflicts of interest arise and the FRC fails to address the fact that the large audit firms continually fail to audit to a high enough standard. The lack of independence of the FRC from the audit firms it regulates is an example of 'regulatory capture'—a phenomenon which arises when a regulatory body serves the interests of those it is meant to be regulating, rather than the public interest. This is largely caused by staffing—many senior FRC employees used to work at the large audit firms, creating a familiarity threat to their independence and objectivity when dealing with those firms.

The Kingman Review concludes with eighty-three recommendations, the range and detail of which are not within the scope of our discussion, but we encourage interested students to explore the recommendations, as they are set to have a long-term impact not just on the UK's regulatory framework for auditing, but for the audit profession as a whole.

In April 2022, the FRC set out a three-year plan to form ARGA. Many commentators are disappointed in how long it is taking for the new regulator to be established. The Covid-19 pandemic obviously caused some delay in the implementation of Kingman's recommendations, but by 2027 ARGA should be in place.

The FRC continues to monitor audit quality in the UK to ensure that trust in audit continues to be restored. The FRC and ultimately ARGA will also continue to ensure that UK auditing standards result in a high-quality audit being carried out and will also publish reports on their reviews of audit quality among firms auditing large companies. We will consider the role of the FRC/ARGA in monitoring audit quality in more detail in Chapter 5.

2.3 Requirements of the Companies Act 2006

The Companies Act 2006 has been described as the largest piece of legislation passed by the UK Parliament. We will only be looking at the provisions that apply to a company's financial statements and the audit requirements because the other areas of the legislation are considered less relevant to students of auditing.

2.3.1 Requirement for audited accounts

Only companies and groups that are medium-sized and large are obliged in law to have an audit, although some other types of entity may be required to have an audit, such as an academy school. Micro-entities and small companies generally do not have to have an audit; although some smaller entities choose to have an audit because audited financial statements are more credible than unaudited financial statements. In addition, some smaller companies might have an audit because their financiers or bank may require it to have one even though they may qualify for audit exemption under the law. Sometimes an audit is required by the company's legal documents called the Articles of Association which are drawn up when the company is formed. In addition, if a shareholder holds more than 10 per cent of the share capital, that shareholder can request that the company has an audit (see Table 2.4).

Table 2.4 UK company and group size limits

Size of company	Turnover	Balance sheet total	Employee headcount
Micro-entity	Not more than £632,000 (rising to £1 million for financial years commencing on or after 6 April 2025)	Not more than £316,000 (rising to £500,000 for financial years commencing on or after 6 April 2025)	Not more than 10
Small company	Not more than £10.2 million (rising to £15 million for financial years commencing on or after 6 April 2025)	Not more than £5.1 million (rising to £7.5 million for financial years commencing on or after 6 April 2025)	Not more than 50
Small group	Not more than £10.2 million net; or Not more than £12.2 million gross (rising to £15 million net or £18 million gross for financial years commencing on or after 6 April 2025)	Not more than £5.1 million net (rising to £7.5 million net for financial years commencing on or after 6 April 2025); or Not more than £6.1 million gross (rising to £9 million gross for financial years commencing on or after 6 April 2025)	Not more than 50
Medium-sized company	Not more than £36 million (rising to £54 million for financial years commencing on or after 6 April 2025)	Not more than £18 million (rising to £27 million for financial years commencing on or after 6 April 2025)	Not more than 250
Medium-sized group	Not more than £36 million net; or Not more than £43.2 million gross (rising to £54 million net or £64 million gross for financial years commencing on or after 6 April 2025)	Not more than £18 million net; or Not more than £21.6 million gross (rising to £27 million net or £32 million gross for financial years commencing on or after 6 April 2025)	Not more than 250
Large company	More than £36 million (rising to more than £54 million for financial years commencing on or after 6 April 2025)	More than £18 million (rising to £27 million for financial years commencing on or after 6 April 2025)	250 or more
Large group	More than £36 million net; or More than £43.2 million gross (rising to more than £54 million net or £64 million gross for financial years commencing on or after 6 April 2025)	More than £18 million net; or More than £21.6 million gross (rising to £27 million net or £32 million gross for financial years commencing on or after 6 April 2025)	250 or more

The Companies Act 2006 distinguishes micro-entities, small companies/groups, medium-sized companies/groups, and large companies/groups by specifying thresholds that determines the size of the company or group as follows:

Balance sheet total—The term 'balance sheet total' means gross assets (i.e. non-current (fixed) assets plus current assets). It is *not* the net assets figure because this figure is arrived at after the deduction of liabilities, which is not the same as the balance sheet total.

Employee headcount—When determining the headcount numbers, the Companies Act requires the *average* number of employees to be used and not actual headcount numbers at the balance sheet date. Section 382(6) of the Companies Act 2006 provides the calculation to arrive at the average number of employees as follows:

1. Find for each month in the financial year the number of persons employed under contracts of service by the company in that month (whether throughout the month or not);
2. Add together the monthly totals; and
3. Divide by the number of months in the financial year.

Auditing scenario 2.1 Calculating the average number of employees

Arlo Ltd has an accounting reference date of 31 December each year. The company has a relatively high turnover of staff due to the nature of its production. The Human Resources department has extracted information from the payroll files in respect of the number of employees during the year, as shown in Table 2.5.

The average number of persons employed by the company during the year is fifty-five. This is calculated as the sum of the monthly numbers of staff divided by twelve months and rounded up.

Table 2.5 Employees at Arlo Ltd

Month	Number of employees
January	56
February	52
March	58
April	49
May	52
June	52
July	58
August	57
September	56
October	56
November	55
December	58

The 'two out of three' rule—A company can only qualify as a small company if it meets two out of the above three criteria for two consecutive years. Therefore, if the company was small in the previous year, but in the current year turnover is more than £10.2 million (increasing to £15 million per the above) and gross assets are more than £5.1 million (increasing to £7.5 million per the above), the company will still be small in the current year. If, next year, turnover is again more than £10.2 million (increasing to £15 million per the above) and gross assets are more than £5.1 million (increasing to £7.5 million per the above), then the company will be classed as medium-sized and will not be able to claim audit exemption.

The audit exemption thresholds track the small company thresholds and therefore a company must have an audit if it fails to qualify as a small company (again, the two out of three rule applies). As noted above, the company and group size thresholds will increase in the UK for financial years commencing on or after 6 April 2025. The audit exemption thresholds will automatically increase in line with the small company thresholds.

Auditing in practice 2.3 Determining the size of a company

Sunnie Ltd has been trading for several years and extracts from the financial statements and accounting records are shown in Table 2.6.

Assuming in previous years the company was medium-sized, in 20X1 the company is still medium-sized because the company has turnover of more than £10.2 million (£11.5 million) and gross assets of more than £5.1 million (£6.7 million). The average number of employees is higher than 50 (63). The company is required to have an audit in 20X1.

In 20X2 turnover reduces to £9.8 million which is below the £10.2 million threshold. In addition, gross assets also fall below £5.1 million while the average number of employees remains over 50. Two out of the three criteria for small company classification have been met because turnover and gross asset are both below the small company thresholds. However, as the company was classified as medium-sized in the previous year, it is still classified as such in 20X2.

In 20X3, turnover again falls below the £10.2 million threshold, but gross assets go over the £5.1 million limit. However, the average number of employees falls below 50 and so the company now meets two out of the three criteria for small company classification for two consecutive years and therefore is regarded as small in 20X3. The company can now apply the small companies' regime in the preparation of their accounts and hence claim audit exemption, if the directors so wish.

In 20X4 turnover goes over the £10.2 million threshold, but both gross assets and the average number of employees are below the threshold hence the company is still small.

Please note the size thresholds in this example will increase per the table above for accounting years commencing on or after 6 April 2025.

Table 2.6 Sunnie Ltd

	20X1	20X2	20X3	20X4
	£'000	£'000	£'000	£'000
Turnover	11,500	9,800	10,000	10,900
Gross assets	6,700	5,000	5,350	4,980
Average no. of employees	63	58	48	47

2.3.2 **Recognized Supervisory Bodies**

In the UK, the term 'accountant' is not legally protected and hence anyone can call themselves an accountant, although to be a Chartered Accountant or a Chartered Certified Accountant, a person must be a qualified member of either the ICAEW, ICAS, or a member of the ACCA. Therefore, while anyone can call themselves an accountant, not everyone can call themselves a Chartered or a Chartered Certified Accountant.

An auditor's report can only be signed by a statutory auditor, who must be a member of a Recognized Supervisory Body (RSB) and is recognized as a statutory auditor under the rules of the RSB (see Figure 2.4). In the UK, there are currently four RSBs for the purpose of statutory audit.

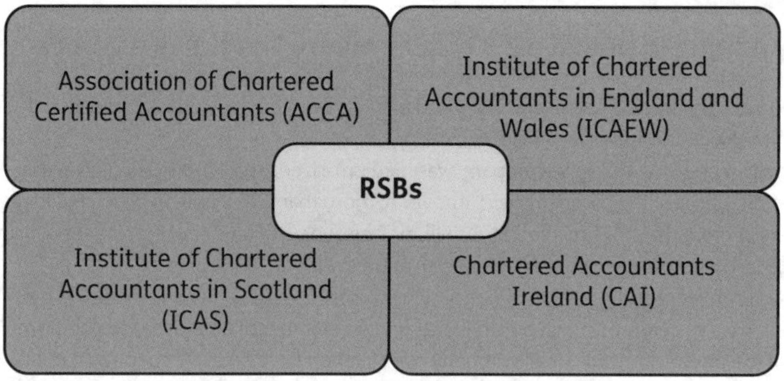

Figure 2.4 Recognized Supervisory Bodies

The RSBs, often referred to as 'professional bodies' have a crucial role to play in the regulation of auditors because it is the RSBs which determine who becomes a qualified accountant and ultimately who can be given the responsibility of being able to sign auditors' reports.

RSBs are subject to supervision by the FRC/ARGA and must demonstrate compliance with various requirements of the Companies Act. The detail of these requirements is outside the scope of our discussion, but, for example, an RSB must have adequate rules and practices designed to ensure that its members who are appointed as statutory auditors:

- hold an appropriate qualification;
- have completed a course of theoretical instruction in the prescribed subjects;
- have undertaken a sufficient period of professional experience;
- continue to maintain an appropriate level of competence in the conduct of statutory audits; and
- adhere to the relevant ethical standards in their work.

The Companies Act also refers to Recognized Qualifying Bodies (RQBs)—an RQB is a body which issues a recognized accountancy qualification. The four professional bodies shown in Figure 2.4 are all RQBs as well as being RSBs. The Association of International Accountants (AIA) is an example of a professional body which is an RQB, because it issues a qualification, but it is not an RSB because it does not supervise its members for the purpose of conducting statutory audits.

The Companies Act 2006 prohibits certain people from acting as a statutory auditor and these include:

- a company's officers (i.e. directors) and employees;
- partners of employees of such people or a partnership of which such a person is a partner;
- anyone who has a connection with the company, or in circumstances where the company has a connection with an associate of any description specified in regulations made by the Secretary of State; and
- anyone who is ineligible to act as auditor of a particular company is also ineligible to act as an auditor of a parent, subsidiary, or fellow-subsidiary of that company.

At this point it is worth highlighting that being a qualified accountant does not give one the right to sign an auditor's report. Normally, after qualification, a member of an RSB would work for several years in audit, building up their experience, before applying for a practising certificate, which is needed in order to perform work in certain situations, for example, becoming a partner in an audit firm or when setting up an independent accountancy service. Holding a practising certificate still does not enable a person to sign auditor's reports—to do this, they need to be a 'responsible individual', a status which can only be awarded after checks on the legal and financial integrity and reliability of the individual have been performed by the RSB.

Activity 2.2 Prohibition from acting as auditor

Looking at the Companies Act requirements, why do you think that certain persons are not allowed to be appointed as auditor of a company?

2.3.3 Compliance with professional body rules and regulatory requirements

Upon successful completion of a professional body's examinations and, where applicable, professional experience requirements, the individual will be assigned designatory letters (such as ACA or ACCA) and be able to call themselves a Chartered Accountant or a Chartered Certified Accountant depending on which professional body the individual has qualified with.

This does not mean, however, that the individual can practise as a qualified accountant (i.e. set up their own firm and sell accountancy and audit-related services) because professional bodies often have additional processes that must be gone through in order for an individual to hold a *practising certificate*. Many people have fallen foul of this prohibition in the past and students need to understand the importance of complying with the professional body's rules because they can, and do, sanction individuals that practise without a practising certificate. In some cases, members have had to resign from professional bodies because they have failed to meet the professional body's requirements for a practising certificate.

When a professional body issues a practising certificate to one of its members, it requires that individual or firm to have professional indemnity insurance (PII) in place. This is a mandatory requirement and, again, some individuals and firms have been sanctioned by their professional body in the past for failing to have PII in place. PII exists to indemnify clients from loss if the firm makes a mistake or acts negligently so that the client is no worse off.

Professional bodies also make it a mandatory requirement for members to remain up to date. This rule applies to all members regardless of whether or not they hold a practising certificate. The purpose of continuing professional development (CPD) is so that the member remains up to speed with changes in their areas of specialism. For example, tax legislation changes frequently and therefore a member of a professional body that works in tax will need to be up to date with changes in tax legislation so that they can advise clients or their company's directors appropriately. Therefore, upon qualification with a professional body, the training requirements do not stop upon admission of a member; professional bodies usually require a minimum number of hours to be devoted to CPD each year and that training will be checked by the professional body during a routine monitoring visit. It is important that the member clearly understands their professional body's requirement for CPD so that they can discharge their obligations satisfactorily.

Professional firms that undertake audit work are also subject to scrutiny by their professional body. In addition, the larger firms are also subject to scrutiny of their audit work by the FRC/ARGA. The objective of these 'monitoring visits' is to ensure that the firm is applying the highest standards possible in audit work and that they also have policies and procedures in place which are appropriate to the size of the practice and the nature of the work they carry out. Where firms are found to be falling short of the standards expected, they will be sanctioned by the professional body. The range of sanctions can vary from having to have their audit work scrutinized by an independent organization (such as a training organization) on a regular basis until the professional body is satisfied that the audit work is of a suitable standard to withdrawal of the firm's auditing practising certificate and heavy fines (both on the firm and on the individual(s) concerned). We will look at some more examples of auditors being monitored when we consider audit quality in detail in Chapter 5.

Unfortunately, not everyone in the auditing profession complies with the rules and therefore professional bodies have codes of conduct and disciplinary proceedings in place which are aimed at ensuring all professional body members undertake work which is of a high standard and sanctioning those members who do not comply with the rules.

Auditing in practice 2.4 Sanctions against Deloitte and an audit engagement partner

In December 2022, the FRC imposed sanctions against Deloitte in respect of an investigation into the audit of SIG plc for the financial years ended 31 December 2015 and 31 December 2016. Sanctions were also imposed on the individual audit engagement partner responsible for the audits.

The investigation found that the audit failed to obtain sufficient appropriate evidence regarding supplier rebates and the auditors involved did not exercise sufficient professional scepticism by failing to investigate indications that supplier rebate receivables balances may have been overstated. In addition, the audit of cash was deficient. The auditors failed to obtain sufficient appropriate audit evidence in respect of cheque payments made around the year end, and failed to exercise sufficient professional scepticism by failing to investigate the cut-off of cash transactions around the year end.

The FRC imposed the following sanctions:

Against Deloitte:

- a financial sanction of £1,250,000 (discounted for admissions and early disposal to £906,250);
- a published statement in the form of a Severe Reprimand;
- a declaration that the 2015 and 2016 audit reports signed on behalf of the firm did not satisfy the Relevant Requirements; and
- an order requiring the firm to take specified action to mitigate the effect or prevent the occurrence of the contravention.

Against the audit engagement partner:

- a financial sanction of £50,000 (discounted for admissions and early disposal to £36,250); and
- a published statement in the form of a Severe Reprimand.

The FRC's Deputy Executive Counsel commented on the case:

> These breaches concerned two discrete areas of the audit of a particular subsidiary of SIG plc. They involved contraventions of requirements which are fundamental to the role of the independent auditor,

and were associated with material misstatements in SIG plc's accounts which had to be corrected. The breaches in respect of supplier rebates were made all the more serious by the fact that the FRC had highlighted these complex supplier arrangements as requiring particular attention from auditors.[6]

You can see that the regulator takes non-compliance with auditing standards and resultant poor audit quality seriously and that the sanctions are imposed on the audit firm and also on the individual partner responsible for the audit.

Over the years, many individuals have been sanctioned for signing auditors' reports when they are not authorized to do so, breaching independence requirements, and failing to comply with the ISAs (UK). Disciplinary proceedings are not confined to a poor standard of work or not having a practising certificate; they also require a member to behave with integrity from a personal standing as well. For example, it is not unheard of for a professional body to bring sanctions against qualified accountants who behave unprofessionally on social media as this is deemed to be a breach of ethical rules. In addition, if a member of a professional body has a criminal conviction that will also result in disciplinary proceedings being instigated by the individual's professional body. Again, the range of sanctions can vary from fines and reprimands to exclusion from membership.

2.3.4 **Appointment of auditors**

Auditors are generally appointed by shareholders by ordinary resolution, meaning that a majority of shareholders vote in favour of the appointment. The exception to this is that a company's first auditors are usually appointed by the directors, and this is then ratified by the shareholders at the company's first annual general meeting (AGM).

2.3.4.1 **Appointing an auditor for a private company**

In general terms, the auditors of a private company must be appointed before the end of a twenty-eight-day period which begins from:

- nine months from the year end, which is the date on which the accounts are sent to the shareholders; or
- if earlier, the date on which the accounts are filed at Companies House.

The auditor's term of office for a private company effectively ends at the end of the equivalent period for the following year.

A private company is not required to have an AGM. The Companies Act allows a private company's auditor to be automatically reappointed and many private companies simply deem its auditors to be automatically reappointed each year. The exception to this rule would be where a private company has provisions in its Articles of Association which stipulate that the auditors must be re-elected by vote at a meeting.

[6] FRC, 'Sanctions against Deloitte LLP and Simon Manning', 2022 <https://www.frc.org.uk/news-and-events/news/2022/12/sanctions-against-deloitte-llp-and-simon-manning/> (accessed 12 January 2024).

In addition, a shareholder that holds more than 5 per cent of the shares may also object to automatic re-election of the auditors and hence an annual appointment will be necessary. In practice, it is quite rare for a shareholder owning more than 5 per cent of the shares to object to automatic reappointment, unless there have been some problems with the auditors in a previous audit(s).

2.3.4.2 **Public companies**

Public companies are required to hold an AGM. At each AGM, at which the financial statements are presented, the company's auditors are appointed. Either the existing auditors are reappointed, or a new auditor is appointed. The incoming auditors must cease to hold office at the end of the next general meeting where the accounts are discussed, unless they are reappointed.

Auditing scenario 2.2 Appointment of an auditor for a public company

Publico plc's previous auditors resigned on 28 August 20X8. The company's financial statements for the year ended 30 September 20X8 are being discussed in a general meeting which is held on 25 October 20X8 and during that meeting the new auditors, Smith & Co LLP, were appointed.

Smith & Co will hold office from 25 October 20X8 until the end of the following general meeting where the 30 September 20X8 year-end accounts are discussed. This period is known as 'the term of office of auditors' (sometimes referred to as the 'tenure of office'). The auditors hold office until the conclusion of the next accounts meeting because they will report on the financial statements for the year ended 30 September 20X8 that are presented at that general meeting, which is within their term of office.

Regardless of whether the company is a public or private company, if it fails to appoint an auditor within the timescales required, the company must inform the Secretary of State, who then has the power to appoint an auditor to fill the vacancy. If a company fails to notify the Secretary of State, both the company and every director who is in default will be committing a criminal offence.

2.3.4.3 **Appointment of auditors for a new company or a company having its first audit**

When a new public company starts in business, the directors can appoint the company's auditors at any time before the first AGM is held that discusses the financial statements (see Figure 2.5). This also applies to a company that was exempt from audit and hence did not have an auditor.

2.3.5 **Small and micro-company audit requirements**

2.3.5.1 **Small companies**

Small companies, defined as we saw earlier, are not required to appoint auditors. In order to be able to claim audit exemption, a company must be a small company and must be able to meet at least two out of the above three criteria for two consecutive years.

When the criteria have been met, the company's directors can claim audit exemption which will relieve the company from the obligation of having its financial statements audited.

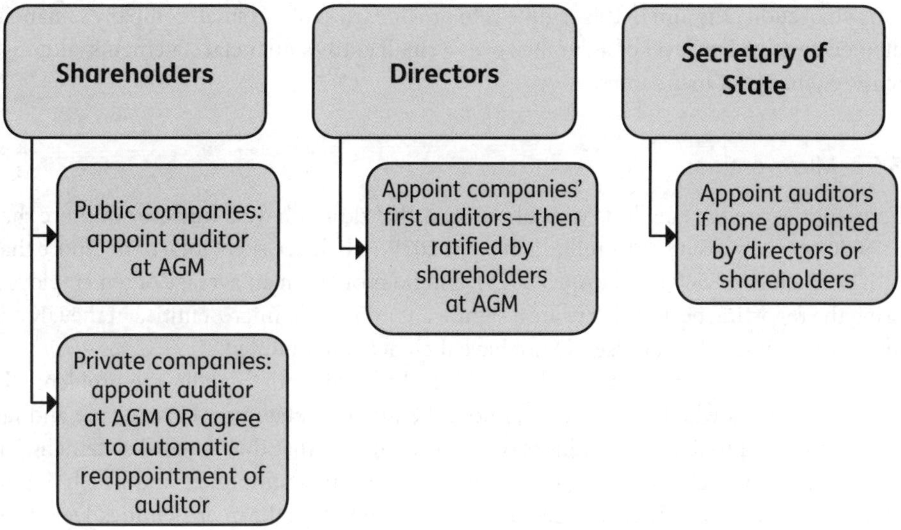

Figure 2.5 Appointment of auditors

Where audit exemption is claimed, the directors must make a statement to this effect on the company's balance sheet (statement of financial position). Audit exemption for a small company is not mandatory. A small company can choose to have an audit if it so wishes and small companies may see a benefit in having an audit, as audited financial statements are effectively viewed as more credible than unaudited ones.

A shareholder that holds not less than 10 per cent of the share capital can also require the company to have an audit. Where the company is reliant on bank finance, the bank or other financier (such as an invoice factoring company) may require the company to have its financial statements audited so that the bank/financier gets comfort that the accounts are credible. Finally, the company's Articles of Association may also require the company to have an audit, even though it would otherwise be eligible to claim audit exemption.

Activity 2.3 Small company audit exemption

Why do you think that small companies, as defined by the Companies Act, are exempt from the requirement for financial statement audit? What are the benefits?

Any increase in the audit exemption thresholds will result in more companies being eligible to claim audit exemption and hence not subjecting their accounts to any external scrutiny. This may lead to undetected errors and omissions within the financial statements and could, to some extent, lead to problems with authorities such as HM Revenue & Customs (HMRC) or other tax authorities who may uncover unorthodox accounting practices or errors as part of their routine examinations of company accounts leading to additional tax and/or penalties.

Some small companies do choose to have their accounts audited because of the discipline that this forces and professional bodies do encourage companies that would be eligible to claim audit exemption to voluntarily obtain assurance. Some professional bodies have introduced an 'assurance "plus"' regime which acts as a sort of 'mini audit' but is not as rigorous as an actual audit. The aim of this regime is to provide users of the small company's financial statements with a low level of assurance over a small entity's financial statements, although such a regime is not mandatory.

2.3.5.2 **Micro-entities**

Micro-entities are the smallest types of business that do not have a turnover of more than £632,000 per year (rising to £1 million in April 2025); a balance sheet total of not more than £316,000 (rising to £500,000 in April 2025); and no more than an average of ten employees during the reporting period. There are a significant number of micro-entities in the UK and most of these types of businesses do not have their accounts audited.

In the event that a micro-entity does subject their accounts to audit, the problems the auditor will face is whether, in their opinion, the financial statements give a true and fair view. One of the problems for auditors of micro-entities is that the financial statements are prepared using special accounting rules which are extremely simplified, and which require very limited disclosures. There are 'deeming' provisions within the micro-entities' legislation which state that if the micro-entity's financial statements have been prepared in accordance with the legal requirements, the financial statements are *presumed* to give a true and fair view. To that end, the directors of a micro-entity do not have to consider any additional disclosure requirements that may be needed for a true and fair view to be achieved.

Consider a micro-entity that has an audit of its financial statements and there are material uncertainties surrounding going concern. Outside of the micro-entities' financial reporting regime, accounting standards would require disclosure of such uncertainties, but a micro-entity need not make any such disclosure and yet their financial statements would still be presumed to give a true and fair view under law. The auditors may take the view that the absence of such going concern disclosures would be misleading (which would invariably be the case) and hence they would more than likely have to resign.

2.3.6 **Auditor resignation or removal from office**

Auditors can cease to act for an audit client either by resigning, or by active removal by the client. An auditor can resign from office at any time, simply by notifying the company. Until recently, the Companies Act required an auditor to notify Companies House of their resignation. However, recent changes to the law means that the auditor's resignation letter may not need to be lodged with Companies House and filed on the public record, provided the reasons for resignation are 'exempt reasons', which are:

- The auditor is ceasing to carry out statutory audit work.
- The company intends to take advantage of audit exemption.
- The company is a subsidiary of a UK company that prepares consolidated financial statements, and the audit is to be carried out by the group auditor (provided that the group auditor is to take over the audit of all UK subsidiaries where an audit is required).
- The company is being wound up under the Insolvency Act or a petition for winding up has been presented and not withdrawn.

Auditors can only be removed from office by the members (i.e. the shareholders of a company). They must give the company twenty-eight days' notice of their intention to put a resolution to remove the auditor, or to appoint somebody else, to a general meeting. A copy of the notice of the intended resolution must be sent to the auditor, who then has the right to make a written response and require that it be sent to the company's shareholders. The shareholders must vote by simple majority (this is known as an ordinary resolution) to remove the auditor.

The law is clear that only a company's shareholders can vote to remove the auditor. This is an important principle because it means that the auditors, in theory, have some protection in that the directors of a company cannot pick and choose who acts as the company's auditor, and cannot force the auditor out of office without the approval of the shareholders. This should lessen the likelihood of intimidation threats made by the directors against the auditors.

However, in reality, the shareholders often simply follow the guidance of the company directors when it comes to voting at the AGM. Not all shareholders are sufficiently informed to make their own decision, so if the directors recommend that the existing auditor is to be replaced by another firm, shareholders are quite likely to follow the recommendation without much discussion or debate.

Companies which have a good corporate governance structure and an effective audit committee offer more protection for the audit firm, as the audit committee is involved with the appointment and removal of the external audit firm, providing independent supervision. However, the auditors of companies without an effective audit committee can find themselves in a difficult situation if the company directors are influencing the body of shareholders to vote on a removal from office.

When an auditor resigns from office, they have the right to call a shareholders' meeting to explain their reasons for resigning. However, this does not apply where the auditor's statement of reasons confirms that there are no matters that need to be brought to the attention of shareholders or creditors.

The Companies Act requires the auditor of a public interest company to send the company a statement of reasons when the auditor ceases to hold office prior to the end of their term of office, and to lodge a copy of that statement at Companies House. This statement must always be sent, regardless of the timing, or reasons, for ceasing to hold office.

When a statement of reasons is required, it should contain the following information:

- the auditor's name, address, and registered number;
- the company's name and registered number; and
- details of any related matters connected with the auditor ceasing to hold office that the auditor believes should be brought to the attention of the company's members or creditors (or a statement that there are no matters to be brought to their attention).

The statement of reasons (formerly known as the statement of circumstances) is an important mechanism for the auditor to explain to shareholders the reasons why they are no longer acting as auditor for a particular client. There is perhaps a distinction to be made between situations where there are 'innocent' reasons for ceasing to act as auditor, and situations where something more sinister might be going on.

? **Activity 2.4** Reasons for resignation or removal of the auditor

List as many reasons as you can think of for an auditor resigning, or being removed from office.

Where there is a more ominous reason for the auditor leaving office, for example, if they have found a fraud or other illegal activity, the auditor must be very careful when preparing the statement of reasons. The auditor should include the relevant facts in their statement of reasons, to bring the issue to the attention of the shareholders who can then take appropriate action. However, the auditor should take legal advice before making any allegations against their client, as explaining these reasons could be construed as slanderous, resulting in potential legal action from the client. In addition, the auditor must be careful not to breach any of the AMLR and inadvertently 'tip off' the client in the statement of reasons.

2.3.7 **Rights of an auditor**

Under the Companies Act 2006, the auditor has certain rights, which are summarized in Figure 2.6.

The auditor has a right of access at all times to the company's 'books, accounts and vouchers'. This means that the auditor has access to the company's accounting records regardless of the format they are in (i.e. in electronic or manual form). These clearly very powerful rights enable the auditor to obtain information including hard and soft versions of documentation, and to discuss matters with company officials. These rights also extend to overseas subsidiaries.

In addition, the auditor can request information and explanations from a range of persons to assist with the performance of the audit including all directors and employees, including those that no longer work at the audit client.

> **Auditing scenario 2.3** Company outsources its payroll function
>
> North Limited is a company specializing in the development of IT programs for the pharmaceutical sector. On 30 September 20X9, the company outsourced its payroll function to a payroll bureau which specializes in payroll preparation. This decision was taken by the directors due to the number of staff it currently employs and hence it was concluded to be more cost-effective to outsource this function.
>
> The two payroll clerks that dealt with the payroll were redeployed elsewhere in the company in administrative roles but since the payroll was outsourced, they have no further responsibility for any payroll-related matters.
>
> In such a situation, the newly appointed payroll bureau must disclose any information the auditors require in respect of the payroll.

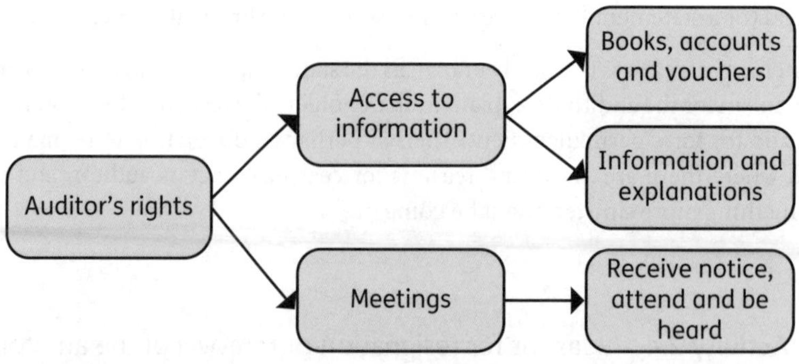

Figure 2.6 Auditor's rights under the Companies Act 2006

Providing misleading, or withholding, information from the auditors is also a criminal offence. A person found guilty of misleading, or withholding information from a company's auditors can receive:

- on conviction of indictment, a prison sentence not exceeding two years or a fine, or both;
- on summary conviction:
  - in England and Wales, a prison sentence not exceeding twelve months or a fine not exceeding the statutory maximum (or both); and
  - in Scotland or Northern Ireland, a prison sentence not exceeding six months or a fine not exceeding the statutory maximum (or both).

In terms of meetings, the Companies Act 2006 gives the auditor the right to:

- to receive all notices of, and other communications relating to, any general meeting which a member of the company is entitled to receive;
- to attend any general meeting of the company; and
- to be heard at any general meeting which they attend on any part of the business of the meeting which concerns them as auditor.

The rights in relation to meetings are important because they allow the auditor to communicate with company members. In particular the combination of the auditor's right to attend any general meeting of the client company, and to speak at any such meeting on matters relating to the audit, protect the auditor's right of access to the company shareholders, and to engage in dialogue with them.

2.3.8 **Duties of an auditor**

The duties of an auditor are set out in the Companies Act 2006. This act refers to the auditors as 'him', but this is intended to cover all genders.

The duties largely relate to the auditor's report—the auditor must form a conclusion on a range of matters and then report to the members on the conclusions reached. However, these sections of the Companies Act do not cover the overall auditor's opinion on the financial statements. Rather, they deal with a number of matters to do with the accounting records that have been maintained by the company directors, the information and explanations received by the auditors, and the sufficiency of disclosure on a number of issues.

The Companies Act requires that the auditor must form an opinion as to:

- whether adequate accounting records have been kept by the company and returns adequate for their audit have been received from branches not visited by them, and
- whether the company's individual accounts are in agreement with the accounting records and returns, and
- in the case of a quoted company, whether the auditable part of the company's directors' remuneration report is in agreement with the accounting records and returns.

These matters are sometimes known as the matters 'reported by exception', a term which is now a little out of date but refers to a time when these matters were only reported by the auditor to the company members if there was a problem which needed to be raised for the attention of the members.

In addition, if the auditor fails to obtain all the information and explanations which are necessary for the purposes of their audit, this must be reported by exception to the shareholders in the auditor's report. This could occur, for example, if the directors refuse to provide the auditors with details of their remuneration or if any accounting records have been lost and the auditors have not been able to verify certain amounts and disclosures in the company's accounts.

The overall duties of the auditor are wide-reaching and the powers the auditor possesses under the Companies Act 2006 should enable their duties to be discharged accordingly. Company directors must make a statement in their directors' report under section 418 of the Companies Act 2006 that each of the directors who held office during the period covered by the accounts have made available all relevant audit information to the auditors and they have taken steps to make themselves aware of any relevant audit information, and ensured that the auditors are made aware of that information.

2.4 Anti-Money Laundering Regulations (AMLR)

So far in this chapter we have looked at the regulatory framework specific to auditors. There is one very important set of regulations which, while not being specifically aimed at the auditing profession, has a significant impact on the activities of auditors—AMLR.

Global money laundering transactions are estimated at 2 to 5 per cent of global GDP, or roughly US$1–2 trillion annually. Yet according to the United Nations Office on Drugs and Crime (UNODC), less than 1 per cent of global illicit financial flows are currently seized by authorities (PwC Global Economic Crime Survey, 2016). For our purposes, we need to understand the principles of money laundering and consider how auditors fulfil their responsibilities in relation to the regulations.

The Financial Action Task Force on Money Laundering (FATF) is an intergovernmental body which sets standards and develops and promotes policies to combat money laundering and terrorist financing. In 1990, FATF drew up a set of recommendations intended primarily to prevent financial systems being used to launder money relating to drug trafficking. The recommendations have since been endorsed by more than 130 countries, including the UK.

2.4.1 What is 'money laundering'?

Money laundering is the process by which criminals attempt to conceal the true origin and ownership of the proceeds of their criminal activity, allowing them to maintain control over the proceeds and, ultimately, providing a legitimate cover for their sources of income. The term is widely defined to include possessing, in any way dealing with, or concealing, the proceeds of any crime, also known as 'criminal property'.

'Criminal property' includes:

- proceeds of tax evasion;
- a benefit obtained through bribery or corruption;

- benefits obtained, or income received, through the operation of a criminal cartel;
- benefits (i.e. saved costs) arising from a failure to comply with a regulatory requirement that is a criminal offence.

Money laundering is a process which often involves three stages, known as placement, layering, and integration. Criminals organize the process to obscure the true nature of what is taking place, so that it is often very difficult to identify that money laundering is happening (see Figure 2.7).

Let's look at a simple example to see how a money laundering scheme can be established. Imagine a drug dealer making a lot of cash through their criminal activity. In order to launder the money and make it 'clean', the drug dealer invests in a cash-based, legitimate business, for example a fast-food restaurant. Customers often pay in cash, and the drug dealer introduces the 'dirty' cash into the business through fictitious sales (placement). The business then invests its cash, perhaps in property or possibly in overseas investments (layering). Ultimately these investments are sold, releasing the funds which are now legitimized (integration) and can be used 'normally' by the criminals.

Professionals, including lawyers and accountants, must be careful not to become inadvertently involved with such a money laundering scheme, for example by providing accounting services to the restaurant, advising on the type of investment to be made, or providing a legal service on the purchase and sale of investments.

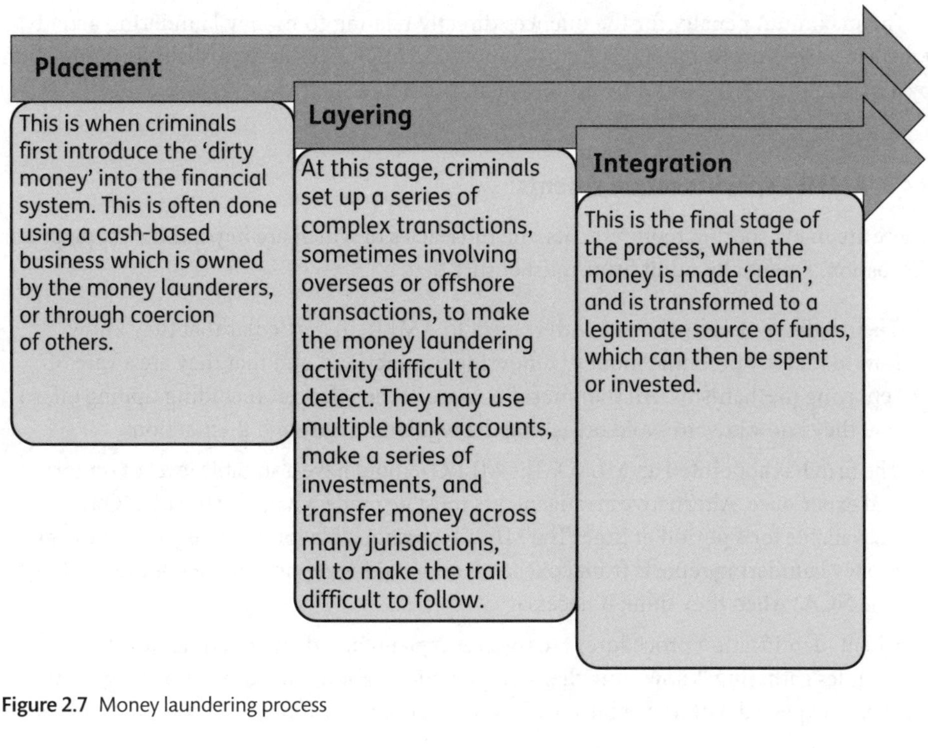

Figure 2.7 Money laundering process

2.4.2 **Money laundering offences**

The Proceeds of Crime Act 2002 created three categories of criminal offence which could impact on auditors:

1. Offences directly relating to money laundering activity—it is an offence to conceal, disguise, convert, transfer, or remove criminal property from England, Wales, Scotland, or Northern Ireland. Concealing or disguising criminal property includes concealing or disguising its nature, source, location, disposition, movement or ownership, or any rights connected with it.
2. Failure to report—individuals operating in the 'regulated sector', which includes auditors, may be guilty of an offence of failing to disclose knowledge or suspicion of money laundering where they know or suspect, or have reasonable grounds for knowing or suspecting, that another person is engaged in laundering the proceeds of crime. Disclosure should be to a Money Laundering Reporting Officer (MLRO) within their organization, or directly to the National Crime Agency (NCA), as soon as is practicable. The report submitted to the NCA is called a 'Suspicious Activity Report.'
3. Tipping off—the criminal offence of tipping off occurs when the professional accountant makes a disclosure which is likely to prejudice an investigation into money laundering activity. If there are indications that money laundering may be occurring, the auditor must exercise caution so that their actions do not tip off the client or prejudice any subsequent investigation.

The maximum penalty for the offences directly relating to money laundering activity is fourteen years' imprisonment. Failure to report and tipping off are punishable on conviction by a maximum of five years' imprisonment and/or a fine.

2.4.3 **AMLR - specific requirements**

There are many specific requirements, the intricacies of which are beyond the scope of our discussion. Essentially, audit firms must ensure that:

- Their staff are all fully trained with respect to AMLR, in particular that they know how to identify potential money laundering transactions, and that they are aware of reporting mechanisms. All staff must be aware of the offences, including tipping off, so that they know how to avoid breaching the regulations through their actions.
- The firm has appointed an MLRO. The MLRO should have a suitable level of seniority and experience. Alternative arrangements must be made whenever the MLRO is unavailable for a period of time. The MLRO is responsible for receiving and assessing money laundering reports from colleagues and making reports to the relevant authority (the NCA) when they think it necessary.
- Client identification procedures are rigorously maintained and documented, this includes gathering 'know your client' (KYC) information, including knowledge of the client's expected patterns of business, its source of funds, and the identity of its owners.

This is known as 'customer due diligence' (CDD). Typical identification procedures would involve:

  - For an individual—obtaining official documents, with a photograph, which establish the client's full name and permanent address (e.g. a driving licence or passport supported by a recent utility bill).
  - For a company or other organization—obtaining from the certificate of incorporation, the registered address and a list of shareholders and directors.
  - Electronic checks can also be carried out on an entity and the individuals connected to the entity.

- All client identification records, together with a full audit trail of all transactions, must be maintained. Records of transactions must be kept in a readily retrievable form for a period of at least five years, with controls to ensure that they are not inadvertently destroyed. Client verification records must be retained throughout the period of the relationship and for five years after termination of the relationship.
- If the audit firm handles money on behalf of their clients, there are internal controls in place to ensure that the firm does not inadvertently become a party to money laundering.

Auditors commit an offence under AMLR if they fail to implement the procedures outlined above. This is why audit firms need to keep meticulous records of their policies and procedures in relation to their compliance with the various requirements. There are other offences which can be committed by the auditor, including:

- Attempting, conspiring with, or inciting another person to commit an offence.
- Aiding or abetting an offence.

Professional bodies are keen to ensure that member firms are complying with their obligations under AMLR and hence carry out routine monitoring visits to ensure compliance. Firms can be sanctioned if they repeatedly fail to make attempts to comply with their obligations. In a recent case, a member of ACCA was expelled from membership of the Association as they repeatedly failed to comply with instructions from ACCA on compliance with AMLR.

2.4.4 **Suspicion–recognition and reporting**

Auditors are legally required to report knowledge or suspicions of money laundering and it is a criminal offence not to do so. There are no *de minimis* concessions, meaning that there is no monetary threshold below which suspicions should not be reported. The obligation to report is irrespective of the amount involved or the seriousness of the offence.

This is an important point—it means that the requirement to report is not just related to matters that could be considered material to the financial statements; auditors must report knowledge or suspicions of money laundering activity that potentially have no material financial statement impact.

Activity 2.5 Suspicious transactions or events

Can you think of some examples of suspicious transactions or events, which might alert you to the fact that money laundering is taking place?

Auditors are normally bound by the ethical principle of confidentiality which means that usually they must not divulge information about a client to a third party without the consent of the client. However, an auditor will not be in breach of any professional duty of confidence if they report money laundering knowledge or suspicions to NCA. It is important to note that disclosure without reasonable grounds will increase the risk of the auditor being sued for breach of confidentiality. Therefore, before making any disclosure, the audit firm must obtain information to back up their suspicions. This can sometimes be difficult, given that the audit firm must not tip off the client or make them aware that the auditor is going to make a disclosure.

Suspicion is not defined by the regulations, and it is up to an auditor's judgement to determine whether a suspicion has strong enough grounds to warrant further action. When faced with suspicious circumstances, the auditor should try to obtain more knowledge about the situation, while remaining alert to the possibility of tipping off the suspect, which as we saw earlier is an offence in itself.

The FRC has included an Appendix in ISA (UK) 250, Section A *Consideration of Laws and Regulations in an Audit of Financial Statements* which deals specifically with money laundering, terrorist financing, and proceeds of crime legislation in the UK. The Appendix to ISA (UK) 250 acknowledges that for auditors, fulfilling the AMLR requirements is onerous, stating that 'the anti-money laundering legislation is complex'. In addition, the Appendix to ISA (UK) 250 confirms that 'in order to obtain a full understanding of the legal requirements auditors will need to refer to the relevant provisions of the legislation and, if necessary, obtain legal advice'.

2.4.5 **AMLR 2017**

On 26 June 2017, new AMLR came into force due to the transposition of the Fourth Anti-Money Laundering Directive into UK company law. The regulations essentially build on the previous framework, although there are some significant changes noted as follows.

2.4.5.1 **Whole-firm risk assessment**

The AMLR 2017 set out a more prescriptive approach to a firm-wide risk assessment, which must be in writing. The risk assessment will depend on the size and nature of the audit firm but the most important point is that auditors properly identify and assess the risk of money laundering or terrorist financing to which the audit firm is exposed and document that assessment.

2.4.5.2 **Internal controls—officer responsible for compliance**

A Money Laundering Compliance Principal (MLCP) must be appointed and that person must be on the board of directors (or equivalent management body) of the audit firm, or a member of senior management. Where a sole practitioner owns an accountancy practitioner, they will be exempt from this requirement.

2.4.5.3 Internal controls–screening of relevant employees

Firms must assess the skills, knowledge, conduct, and integrity of those employees involved in identifying, mitigating, preventing, or detecting money laundering and terrorist financing. Staff must be regularly trained in how to recognize and deal with transactions and other activities which may be related to money laundering or terrorist financing.

2.4.5.4 Internal controls–independent audit function

There should be an independent audit function to assess the adequacy and effectiveness of the firm's AMLR policies, controls, and procedures. Sole practitioners with no employees are exempt from this requirement.

2.4.5.5 Policies, controls, and procedures

Policies, controls, and procedures to prevent activities relating to money laundering and terrorist financing, including data protection requirements, are required which must be in writing. Senior management must also evidence their approval of these policies, controls, and procedures.

2.4.5.6 Enhanced due diligence

Enhanced due diligence (EDD) is required in certain situations as follows:

- there is a high risk of money laundering or terrorist financing;
- where the client or customer operates in a high-risk country;
- the client is a politically exposed person (PEP), or a family member or known close associate of a PEP;
- the client has provided false or stolen identification documentation or information on establishing a relationship; or
- the auditor identifies that the client has entered into complex and unusually large transactions, or there is an unusual pattern of transactions with no apparent legal or economic purpose.

2.4.5.7 PEPs

Procedures must be put in place which will identify whether a client, or the beneficial owner of a client, is a PEP or a family member (spouse, civil partner, children, parent) or known close associate of a PEP.

Auditing in practice 2.5 Banks' lack of AMLR policies and procedures

Standard Chartered

In 2012, Standard Chartered, a London-headquartered bank, was accused by the US authorities of keeping false records, having ineffective anti-money laundering controls in place, and involvement in money laundering for the Iranian government worth US$250 billion.

As a result of the investigation, the bank paid a penalty of US$340 million and agreed to improve its internal controls and undergo external monitoring of its anti-money laundering processes for two years. Unfortunately, in 2014, the bank had to pay a further US$300 million in penalties in 2014 relating to continuing deficiencies in its anti-money laundering processes.

Standard Chartered's problems continued, with it being investigated in Singapore for serious breaches of its anti-money laundering arrangements, resulting in a fine of US$3.65 million.

HSBC

In a high-profile case which was well documented in the media, HSBC was accused of laundering money for Mexican drug cartels.[7] On investigation, HSBC acknowledged that it failed to maintain effective controls against money laundering, including treating millions of dollars of transactions in Mexico as low risk, despite the known connection with drug trafficking, and that it had failed to conduct client identification procedures on many account holders.

As a result of being investigated in 2012 by the US authorities, HSBC paid a fine of US$1.92 million. HSBC forfeited £1.2 billion for having inadequate money laundering controls. A report published by the US Senate suggested that HSBC had, in addition to laundering money relating to drug trafficking, supplied banking services to banks in Saudi Arabia in spite of their connections to terrorist financing and breached international sanctions on trading with Iran and North Korea.[8]

HSBC escaped criminal proceedings after intervention by the British government. The Chancellor of the Exchequer at the time of the investigations, George Osborne, stepped in to warn of the dangers of prosecuting one of the world's largest banks and the financial instability such a prosecution could trigger. If HSBC had been charged and found guilty the US government would have reviewed and possibly revoked the bank's charter to do business in the US.

Chapter round-up

- Auditing is a highly regulated profession, with regulations existing in various forms—legislation, professional body regulations, and international pronouncements.
- In the UK, the FRC (which will eventually become the ARGA) is responsible for issuing, amending, and withdrawing ISA (UK) and other relevant regulations.
- A company is classed as micro, small, medium-sized, or large depending on its level of turnover, balance sheet total, and employee headcount, and this determines the audit requirement.

[7] Blackhurst, Chris, 'Too big to jail: The story of HSBC and the Mexican drug cartel', 2022 <https://www.independent.co.uk/independentpremium/long-reads/hsbc-laundering-mexican-cartel-blackhurst-b2097490.html> (accessed 17 January 2024). Blackhurst, Chris, 'How HSBC laundered millions for Mexican drug lords', 2022 <https://www.newstatesman.com/business/2022/06/hsbc-became-worlds-biggest-money-launderer> (accessed 2 January 2024).

[8] US Department of Justice, 'HSBC Holdings Plc and HSBC Bank USA N.A. admit to anti-money laundering and sanctions violations, forfeit $1.256 billion in deferred prosecution agreement', 2012 <https://www.justice.gov/opa/pr/hsbc-holdings-plc-and-hsbc-bank-usa-na-admit-anti-money-laundering-and-sanctions-violations> (accessed 17 January 2024).

- Auditors are required to abide by the rules of their professional body and keep up to date by means of CPD.
- The Companies Act 2006 prescribes the procedures necessary on the appointment, removal, and resignation of auditors, with more relaxed regulations for private companies.
- The auditor has certain rights and duties which are specified by law—in the UK this is governed by the Companies Act 2006.
- AMLR apply to auditors and the penalties for non-compliance are severe.
- Auditors must be alert to money laundering activities and report their suspicions to the NCA.
- Audit firms must establish firm-wide procedures relating to client identification, maintain records of transactions with clients and training for staff in relation to money laundering.
- Audit firms must appoint an MLRO who makes the necessary disclosures.

End of chapter case study

Introduction

Auditors must work within a regulatory framework which comprises UK-specific legislation, ISAs (UK) which are based on standards issued by the IAASB, AMLR, among others. Auditing is therefore recognized to be a highly regulated activity, and auditors must be able to apply the regulations in a wide variety of client scenarios.

This case study provides three situations which are not untypical of the kind that may arise in any audit practice and requires application of some of the regulations which we have looked at in this chapter.

This activity links to the following learning outcomes:

- Discuss UK-specific audit regulations including the requirements in relation to the appointment and removal of auditors and the rights and duties of auditors.
- Define 'money laundering', describe the main features of AMLR and explain how accountants meet their obligations to help prevent and detect money laundering.

Scenario

You are an auditor working in a medium-sized audit practice in the Midlands. You have been asked by a colleague to review several situations which have arisen recently in relation to two audit clients—Star Ltd and Planet Ltd. Information about each of these clients is given below, along with the questions which have been raised by your colleague.

Star Ltd

Star Ltd manufactures steel components which are used in the automotive industry and has five factories—four located in the Midlands and one in Scotland. The company's draft financial statements recognize revenue of £14.5 million (prior year: £13.3 million), and total assets of £6.7 million (prior year: £4.5 million).

The audit planning relating to the current year's financial statements began last week. The audit manager, Kirsty, who is preparing the audit strategy and audit plan requested information relating to the year-end inventory counts so that they can arrange for audit team members to attend the count at each factory. Star's finance director, George Balmain, has provided the necessary information including the date and time of the inventory count to be held at each factory but has requested that the audit team do not attend the count at the factory in Scotland. The reason given by George is that there is only a small amount of inventory at the Scottish location, and therefore it is not necessary for the audit team to incur travel expenses just to observe the count of a few items of inventory.

George has also asked that the auditor does not attend Star's AGM, though George has invited the audit partner to join the next meeting of the board of directors. George thinks that it will be more worthwhile for the audit partner to come to the board meeting because the partner will be able to provide some advice to the directors about a business acquisition which the company is considering. George says that the AGM is a 'waste of time' and only lasts for an hour.

Required

Discuss the issues raised by the finance director's requests for the audit firm not to attend Star's inventory count in Scotland, and not to attend the company's AGM.

You should also comment on the request from the finance director for the audit partner to attend the next meeting of the board of directors and provide advice to the directors.

Planet Ltd

John is the audit manager responsible for the audit of Planet Ltd, a company which operates funfairs at seaside resorts. Almost all the company's sales are paid for in cash, with customers paying a cash entrance fee to the funfairs which allows them four activities within the funfair. If customers want extra activities, such as additional rides, they pay as they go. Planet Ltd is required to have a statutory audit due to its size.

Planet Ltd is owned and managed by Barry Taylor, who deals with all aspects of the company's operations including its finances. He maintains the company accounts and files the necessary tax returns and other paperwork.

While conducting the company audit for the year ending 31 December 20X7, John discovered several bank transfers to a bank account in the Cayman Islands. On asking Barry about this, Barry explains that they are transferring money to the Caribbean with the aim of buying a house on one of the islands. There have also been a large number of smaller bank transfers to a bank account in South Africa, which Barry said was a 'good investment given the exchange rate'. Barry has provided John with the company's accounting records in respect of these transactions, but has asked John not to contact the overseas banks because they will charge a fee for dealing with requests from the company's auditor.

Required

Identify and explain the matters which may lead the audit manager to suspect that Barry could be involved with money laundering, and describe the actions which the audit manager should take in respect of their suspicions.

Answer

Star Ltd

The Companies Act gives the auditor various rights, including that the company's auditor is entitled to receive all notices of any general meeting which a member of the company is entitled to receive, to attend any general meeting of the company, and to be heard at any general meeting on matters which concerns the auditor. The finance director is therefore denying the auditor the opportunity to attend and speak at the AGM, which is a legal entitlement of the auditor.

The right to attend and speak at a company's AGM is important because it allows the auditor and shareholders to have a face-to-face dialogue regarding the audit, giving the shareholders opportunity to ask relevant questions. Equally, the auditor may have important issues to discuss and raise with the shareholders.

The finance director is also suggesting that the audit team does not attend one of the company's inventory counts. The Companies Act gives the auditor a right of access at all times to the company's books and records and the right to request the information and explanations that are necessary to the audit process. Therefore, the finance director cannot deny the auditor the right to attend to inventory count in Scotland; it is a criminal offence to withhold information from the auditor, which would include information obtained at the inventory count.

It is up to the auditor to decide whether the inventory count is necessary, including assessment of whether the inventory held in Scotland is sufficiently material to the financial statements to warrant inventory account attendance. The fact that the finance director does not want the auditor to attend the inventory count could mean that they have something to hide, and the auditor may wish to approach the audit of inventory as high risk, especially given the significant increase in the company's total assets for the year.

The suggestion that the audit partner should attend the board meeting would seem inappropriate. Auditors cannot be seen to be acting in a management capacity, and should not provide business advice as this gives rise to a threat to objectivity. The audit partner should politely decline the invitation to attend the board meeting, explaining that it is a breach of ethical principles relating to auditor independence.

Planet Ltd

First, the funfair is a cash-based business. It would be very easy for Barry to introduce 'dirty' cash into the business without raising much suspicion—this is known as placement. An increase in the company's cash could simply be explained away by an increase in customers.

The transfers to overseas bank accounts raise a suspicion. There is no real business rationale for a funfair to make such investments, and Barry's claim about buying a house in the Caribbean may not be true. The fact that a large number of small transfers have been made to the South African bank could indicate that Barry is hoping that these, being of a low monetary value, will not be picked up during the audit.

The fact that Barry does not want the auditor to contact either of the overseas banks is suspicious, indicating that they may have something to hide.

Finally, given that Barry deals with all aspects of the company's finances himself, Barry can more easily hide illegal activities. It is unusual for a company of this size not to employ an accountant to deal with this aspect of the business.

The audit manager should attempt to obtain more information, especially in relation to the overseas bank transfers. However, care must be taken not to commit a tipping-off offence. It might be difficult to contact the banks in the Caribbean and in South Africa without the consent of Barry, and asking for consent could be considered as tipping off.

Facts surrounding the bank transfers can be found by normal audit procedures, presumably from the company's accounting records. The audit manager should confirm how many transfers were made and their monetary value. They should also try to find out if any other transfers have been made into different bank accounts, and also whether any money has been moved back into the UK from these overseas locations.

The audit manager should report their suspicions to the audit firm's MLRO. It is up to the MLRO to consider the facts and the suspicions and then to report to the relevant authority—the NCA in the UK. Any failure to report, either by the audit manager to the MLRO, or by the MLRO to the NCA is itself an offence under the Money Laundering Regulations.

Activity answer points

Activity 2.1—International regulation

What do you think are the advantages of having international regulations governing the auditing profession?

Quality—standards developed by international regulators are developed using a robust process involving extensive consultations which should ensure that the resulting standards are of high quality. This in turn means that high-quality auditing should be performed, enhancing the credibility of auditing on a global scale.

Ease of adoption—the existence of international regulations makes it easier for individual countries or groups such as the EU to decide to adopt the standards, promoting high-quality auditing in these jurisdictions. This is particularly important for emerging economies who may not have existing auditing regulations, so they can simply adopt the international regulations as their own.

Consistency—using international standards helps to promote consistency in how audits are performed across the world. Audit evidence should be of a consistent high quality and audit reports should be comparable. This in turn could support cross-border investment and the functioning of the global economy.

Practicalities—for audit firms or networks of audit firms that operate on a global scale, using international auditing regulations make it easy for them to standardize work processes, making audits more efficient.

According to the PIOB website:

> Independent oversight is necessary for financial markets: investors want to know that the financial information on which they base their capital allocation decisions is credible and reliable. By overseeing the establishment and adherence to high-quality professional standards, the PIOB seeks to further the international adoption and implementation of such standards and improve the comparability of financial statements across the globe.

Activity 2.2—Prohibition from acting as auditor

Looking at the Companies Act requirements, why do you think that certain persons are not allowed to be appointed as auditor of a company?

The primary purpose of the Companies Act requirements is to protect the independence of auditors. Auditors must be, and be seen to be, conducting their role in an independent and objective manner. Any circumstances which threaten the integrity or objectivity of an auditor will also threaten the independence. So, a person with a close connection with a company or its directors cannot be sufficiently independent to give an objective opinion on the financial statements.

Activity 2.3—Small company audit exemption

Why do you think that small companies, as defined by the Companies Act, are exempt from the requirement for financial statement audit?

The cost of an annual audit can be relatively high for small companies and many people think that this creates an unnecessary financial pressure on small companies. There is also an administrative burden in terms of time and disruption to the business when the audit is taking place, which is not seen as a fair burden to place on smaller companies.

In addition, there is sometimes little benefit to having an audit conducted for an owner-managed company. This is because one of the objectives of audit—to report to the shareholders with regard to how the directors have prepared the financial statements—is unnecessary given that the shareholders and directors are the same people.

Activity 2.4—Reasons for resignation or removal of the auditor

List as many reasons as you can think of for an auditor to resign, or to be removed from office.

There are many reasons why an auditor may resign (or be removed) from office, which the auditor may choose to declare to the shareholders. For example:

- The client has outgrown the audit firm, which can no longer provide the support needed to the client or perform the necessary audit work due to a lack of resources.
- The client put the audit out to tender, and awarded the audit to a different audit firm.
- The audit is not profitable for the audit firm.
- The client is bought by another company, who wishes to replace the incumbent auditor with their own auditor.
- The auditor retires, or sells their audit practice to another firm.
- There are ethical reasons, for example, the auditor has acted for the client for a long period, and a familiarity threat to objectivity has arisen.

There could be more ominous reason for the auditor leaving office, for example:

- The auditor has suspicions that the client is conducting illegal activities.
- The client has a poor reputation or bad publicity, and the auditor no longer wishes to be associated with them.
- The auditor is threatened by the company directors, creating an intimidation threat to objectivity.

Activity 2.5—Suspicious transactions or events

Can you think of some examples of suspicious transactions or events, which might alert you to the fact that money laundering is taking place?

Examples of potentially suspicious transactions or events can include:

- unusually large cash deposits;
- frequent exchange of cash into other currencies;
- transactions or other activities inconsistent with normal business activity;
- unusual investment activity;
- transactions with little or no supporting documentation;
- offshore business arrangements with no clear business rationale.

3 Corporate Governance

Introduction

Corporate governance refers to the way that companies are directed and managed. It considers how senior decision-makers act, how they set strategic goals, and their responsibilities and behaviours. It also regulates how company directors are paid for their work and how they should be held accountable for their actions and decisions.

Corporate governance has grown in importance in the last few decades with corporate scandals bringing the actions of company directors to public attention. Infamous scandals like Enron and WorldCom, and more recently in the UK, Carillion, demonstrate poor corporate governance. In response to such scandals and to try to prevent reoccurrence, improved governance codes and tighter regulations for company directors have been introduced. The UK's own globally influential set of corporate governance principles was first developed in the 1990s, including principles on the composition and selection of the board, and the responsibility of both executive and non-executive directors (NEDs).

So why is corporate governance relevant to auditors? We have already considered the concept of agency theory in Chapter 1, in which we saw that external audit acts as a mechanism for monitoring the activities of company directors. As we will see in this chapter, corporate governance regulations set specific requirements for company directors in respect of internal controls, financial reporting, and audit. So, the auditor needs to understand these requirements because they impact how the auditor engages with the client—in other words, which committee or individual company directors the auditor will have most contact with. The auditor also needs to form a view as to how well the company's senior management have applied the relevant corporate governance requirements, as this forms part of the auditor's understanding of the business and will impact the auditor's assessment of audit risk, which we will look at in Chapter 9. For certain companies, the auditor is required to review the extent of compliance with corporate governance requirements and to pass on this report to the shareholders.

Learning outcomes

- Discuss the underpinning principles of corporate governance including agency theory and explain the relevance and importance of corporate governance to external auditors.
- Explain best practice in corporate governance relating to directors' responsibilities.
- Explain best practice in corporate governance relating to board structure and directors' remuneration.
- Discuss the role of audit committees, describe their benefits and limitations, and explain the relationship between the audit committee and the external auditor.

By the end of the whole chapter, you should be able to:

- Evaluate whether a company has implemented best practice in corporate governance, identify any deficiencies, and recommend necessary changes.

3.1 Corporate governance approaches

3.1.1 Agency theory

As we saw in Chapter 1, a traditional way to consider corporate governance from a conceptual perspective is to use agency theory. In this theory, there are two key players—principals and agents. As a brief reminder, the principals are the owners or shareholders of a company. The agents are the managers or directors, who are put in place to run the company on behalf of the shareholders. Agency theory suggests that the agents are inherently likely to act in their own interests, rather than in the best interests of the principals. So, left to their own devices, the agents may pay themselves excessively, use company assets for their personal use, or make strategic decisions which benefit themselves personally (e.g. to maximize their bonuses). Corporate governance principles therefore aim to regulate the activities of agents to ensure they act in the best interests of other parties (mainly shareholders and other stakeholders), rather than themselves, and to make the agents more accountable for their actions.

Auditing in practice 3.1 The Maxwell scandal

This is an old scandal, but one that illustrates well the concept of agency theory, and how company directors can operate in their own best interest, rather than that of company shareholders and other stakeholders—in this case, members of the company pension scheme. Despite this being an old example, it is worth considering, as the Maxwell scandal was one of the catalysts for the development of corporate governance principles in the UK.

Robert Maxwell's two companies Mirror Group Newspapers and Maxwell Communication were both listed on the London Stock Exchange. As far back as 1971, Maxwell had been investigated by the Department of Trade, who found him 'unfit' to run a listed company.

Maxwell established a board of directors which failed to challenge his actions. The board was made up of close family members and other hand-picked individuals who were afraid to criticize him. He acted as both chair of the board and chief executive and the concentration of power in the hands of one intimidating individual meant that his unethical and fraudulent activity went unchecked.

After his death in 1991, his sons Ian and Kevin were the subject of investigation as they had both served on the board in senior executive positions. The Maxwell business empire collapsed, and the two sons were made personally bankrupt.

The audit firm at the time, Coopers & Lybrand, was also criticized for not speaking out about Maxwell's management style, and for not highlighting the financial distress of the companies being audited. The auditors (now part of the merged audit firm PwC) were eventually fined £3.2 million. The auditors were accused of poor audit quality and in particular of failing to address the going concern problems facing the company as part of their audit procedures.

The Maxwell scandal was one of a number of corporate scandals (others include BCCI and Polly Peck) which occurred in the late 1980s and early 1990s. These scandals prompted the UK's regulatory authorities to instigate an inquiry into how investors could be better protected. Sir Adrian Cadbury was charged with this task, which culminated with the publication of the Cadbury Code in 1992,[1] a voluntary code of conduct with which directors of listed companies were expected to comply. This was the first iteration of today's UK Corporate Governance Code.

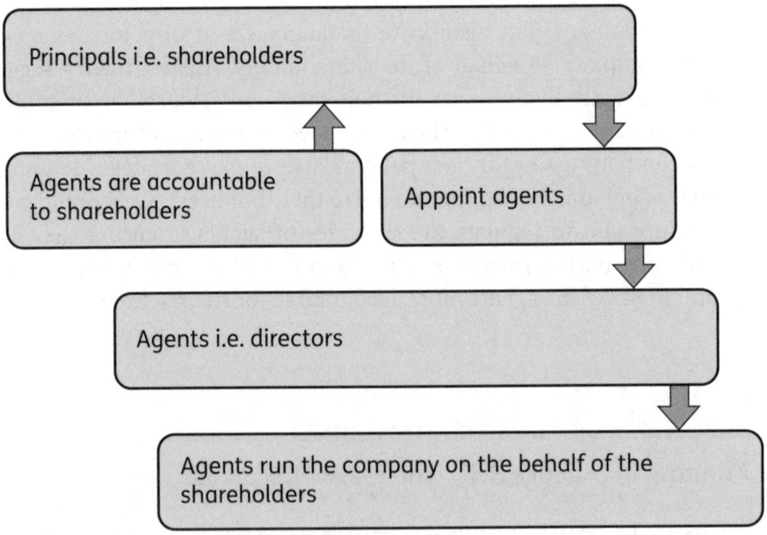

Figure 3.1 Agency relationships

[1] Cadbury, A., *Report of the Committee on the Financial Aspects of Corporate Governance.* (London, 1992).

3.1.2 **Approaches to corporate governance**

There are two basic approaches to corporate governance—an approach based on a code of best practice—often referred to as the 'comply or explain' approach, and an approach based on legislation. Comply or explain is the underpinning principle of corporate governance codes in many countries including the UK's Corporate Governance Code ('the Code'). The key issue is that the comply or explain framework is not a rigid set of rules. There is some flexibility which allows company directors to consider the best way to apply the principles in their own situation without having to go through a 'tick-box' exercise. Companies can declare non-compliance with certain elements of governance principles and then explain why the non-compliance is appropriate to the company's circumstances.

The UK Corporate Governance Code states:

> The Code does not set out a rigid set of rules; instead it offers flexibility through the application of Principles and through 'comply or explain' Provisions and supporting guidance. It is the responsibility of boards to use this flexibility wisely and of investors and their advisors to assess differing company approaches thoughtfully.[2]

Listed companies are expected to follow the Code. As mentioned previously, if there is a good reason to deviate from it, this can be explained in the annual report, leaving it to the shareholders to form a view as to whether the departure from the Code's principles is justified. For example, smaller listed and newly listed companies may feel that some of the aspects of the Code are too costly or onerous to apply or are not very relevant to their operations.

Non-compliance with the Code is not a breach of the Code, but failure to fully disclose the non-compliance in a transparent manner is. Of course, disclosing a non-compliance is likely to attract negative publicity and a higher level of scrutiny from the various interested stakeholders of the company, which the directors may wish to avoid.

Auditing in practice 3.2 Comply or explain

In 2008 Marks & Spencer (M&S) made the headlines in the financial press following the announcement of a non-compliance with the UK Corporate Governance Code (or Combined Code, as it was then known). Shareholders were left unhappy with the board's disregard for one of the key principles of corporate governance–that the roles of chairman and chief executive should be separate.

Stuart Rose had been appointed M&S's chief executive in 2004, and had proved a strong corporate leader, implementing strategies which led to a steady improvement in the company's financial performance and share price. In 2008 the company's chairman, Terence Burns, was due to retire. The board decided that instead of appointing an external person as chairman, Stuart Rose would fulfil both roles of chairman and chief executive. This was a clear breach of one of the fundamental principles of the UK Corporate Governance Code–that no one person should act as both chief executive and chair of the board.

[2] FRC, 'The UK Corporate Governance Code', 2018.

The rationale for this decision was that the board considered that Stuart Rose had unique skills to lead the company, and it confirmed that the combined role provided an appropriate leadership structure for the company.

This decision caused anger among shareholders, in particular the institutional investor Legal & General which owned about 5 per cent of M&S shares and was quick to challenge the board's decision and to voice concerns over the non-compliance with a key principle of the Corporate Governance Code, even if it had been disclosed and, to some extent, explained. Other commentators argued that with M&S's clear disregard for the Code's principles, it was setting a poor example for other listed companies.

The M&S board did not change their decision, and Stuart Rose performed the roles of chair and chief executive until his departure from the company in 2010.

In February 2021, the FRC issued specific guidance on helping companies to achieve transparency in their reporting related to the comply or explain principle. This guidance states that, 'The FRC encourages companies to embrace the flexibility offered by the Code, consider their circumstances carefully and choose what is best for them, while clearly explaining any departures from the Code. Companies and shareholders should not favour strict compliance over effective governance and transparency.'[3]

Every year the rate of compliance with the UK Corporate Governance Code is monitored by the FRC. Their report issued in November 2022 found that only twenty-seven companies from one hundred sampled reported full compliance with the Code.[4] You might be surprised at the low level of full compliance, and assume that the FRC would not be happy to see this. However, in this report, the FRC states that they are 'pleased to see that more companies are using the comply or explain nature of the Code' and that, 'Such an increase in non-compliance demonstrates the benefits of a code-based approach to governance, which allows companies to choose bespoke governance arrangements most suitable to their particular circumstances in both the short and long-term. We have seen instances where it is clear how non-compliance benefits the company and its strategy.'[5]

You can see that many companies do not fully comply with the Code. The most common reasons for non-compliance tend to be due to lack of independence of the chair of the board and the chair remaining in post for longer than the nine-year recommended period for chair tenure. Sometimes a non-compliance is unavoidable, for example if a director resigns at short notice, meaning that there is not an appropriate balance of independent directors for a period of time until a replacement can be recruited.

Some commentators argue against comply or explain because of the high incidence of non-compliance in some countries. They suggest that it is not an effective 'enforcement mechanism' and favour a more prescriptive approach where non-compliance is punished.

[3] FRC, 'Improving the quality of "comply or explain" reporting', 2021 <https://media.frc.org.uk/documents/Improving_the_Quality_of_Comply_or_Explain_Reporting.pdf> (accessed 17 January 2024).

[4] FRC, 'Review of corporate governance reporting', 2022. <https://media.frc.org.uk/documents/Review_of_Corporate_Governance_Reporting_2022.pdf> (accessed 17 January 2024).

[5] FRC, 'The UK Corporate Governance Code', 2024 <https://media.frc.org.uk/documents/UK_Corporate_Governance_Code_2024_a2hmQmY.pdf> (accessed 17 January 2024).

In contrast to the comply or explain approach, in the United States, following the various corporate scandals of the early 2000s, the notorious Sarbanes–Oxley Act (SOX) was introduced as a legislative mechanism aimed at improving corporate governance. The rules are exactly that—rules—and if broken could result in severe penalties, including prison sentences and large fines for directors found guilty of acting in breach of those rules. The requirements of SOX were considered so onerous that some companies delisted their shares from the US stock exchange to end the need to comply with it.

SOX was issued in 2002 largely in response to the Enron/Andersen corporate scandal in the US. Effective in 2004, it requires companies with a listing on the US stock exchange to submit an annual assessment of the effectiveness of their internal financial controls to the Securities and Exchange Commission (SEC).

SOX aims to enhance corporate governance and strengthen corporate accountability by formalizing and strengthening internal controls and monitoring those controls and increasing the level of transparency regarding disclosures of control deficiencies. Following the rules of SOX should ensure that not only are the company's financial statements complete and accurate, but the company has confidence in them because adequate controls are in place to safeguard financial information. In addition, the company's external auditors are required to audit and report on the internal control effectiveness in a process known as 'attestation'.

Non-compliance carries heavy penalties, which vary depending on which section of the legislation has not been complied with. Penalties range from the company losing its SEC listing and a chief executive officer (CEO) or chief finance officer (CFO) who submits an accurate certification can be fined up to $1 million and imprisoned for up to ten years, even if this is done as a result of a genuine mistake. If an inaccurate certification was submitted purposefully, the fine can be increased up to $5 million and the prison term can be increased up to twenty years.

Activity 3.1 Approaches to corporate governance

There are two very different approaches to corporate governance—'comply or explain' and legislative.

What do you think are the advantages of the comply or explain approach?

3.2 The UK Corporate Governance Code

In the UK, companies with a premium listing of equity shares are required under the Listing Rules to apply the Principles and Provisions of the Code and to report to shareholders regarding governance arrangements. Until 2018, the Code did not apply to companies listed on the Alternative Investment Market (AIM). However, from 28 September 2018 AIM companies were required to report on their application of a recognized corporate governance code. An AIM listed company may choose to apply the UK Code, or an alternative such as the Quoted Companies Alliance Code.

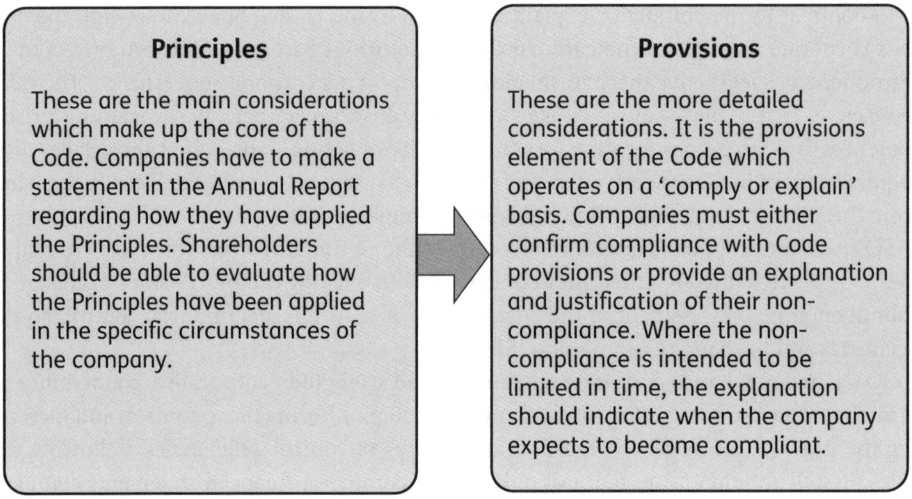

Figure 3.2 Code Principles and Provisions

3.2.1 **What are the Principles of the Code?**

The Code contains two key components: Principles and Provisions.

The Code comprises five sections, each containing a number of Principles. Remember that listed companies have to make a statement about how they have applied the Principles so that shareholders can evaluate the situation. The statement should include actions and outcomes in order to be meaningful.

While it is important for auditors to understand the corporate governance principles and how they have been applied by an audit client, students do not need such a deep understanding. For this reason, a detailed exploration of all the issues outlined in Table 3.1 is not

Table 3.1 Code sections and main requirements

Code section	Principles[6]
Board Leadership and Company Purpose Every company should be headed by an effective board which is collectively responsible for the long-term success of the company and should lead and control the company's operations. The board should establish the company's strategy and values, encourage dialogue with a range of stakeholders including shareholders and employees.	• A successful company is led by an effective and entrepreneurial board, whose role is to promote the long-term sustainable success of the company, generating value for shareholders and contributing to wider society. • The board should establish the company's purpose, values and strategy, and satisfy itself that these and its culture are aligned. All directors must act with integrity, lead by example and promote the desired culture. • The board should ensure that the necessary resources are in place for the company to meet its objectives and measure performance against them. The board should also establish a framework of prudent and effective controls, which enable risk to be assessed and managed. • In order for the company to meet its responsibilities to shareholders and stakeholders, the board should ensure effective engagement with, and encourage participation from, these parties. • The board should ensure that workforce policies and practices are consistent with the company's values and support its long-term sustainable success. The workforce should be able to raise any matters of concern.

[6] FRC, 'The UK Corporate Governance Code', 2024 <https://media.frc.org.uk/documents/UK_Corporate_Governance_Code_2024_a2hmQmY.pdf> (accessed 17 January 2024).

Code section	Principles[6]
Division of Responsibilities There should be a clear division of responsibilities at the head of the company between the running of the board and the executive responsibility for the running of the company's business. This should ensure a balance of power and authority, such that no one individual has unfettered powers of decision. The chair is responsible for leadership of the board and ensuring its effectiveness on all aspects of its role. The board should include a balance of executive and non-executive directors (including independent non-executives) such that no individual or small group of individuals can dominate the board's decision taking. Non-executive directors should constructively challenge and help develop proposals on strategy.	• The chair leads the board and is responsible for its overall effectiveness in directing the company. They should demonstrate objective judgement throughout their tenure and promote a culture of openness and debate. In addition, the chair facilitates constructive board relations and the effective contribution of all non-executive directors, and ensures that directors receive accurate, timely and clear information. • The board should include an appropriate combination of executive and non-executive (and, in particular, independent non-executive) directors, such that no one individual or small group of individuals dominates the board's decision-making. There should be a clear division of responsibilities between the leadership of the board and the executive leadership of the company's business. • Non-executive directors should have sufficient time to meet their board responsibilities. They should provide constructive challenge, strategic guidance, offer specialist advice and hold management to account. • The board, supported by the company secretary, should ensure that it has the policies, processes, information, time and resources it needs in order to function effectively and efficiently.
Composition, Succession and Evaluation The board should comprise a combination of skills, experience and knowledge. Appointments to the board should be made using a formal and transparent procedure, with a promotion of diversity relating to gender, ethnicity and social backgrounds. Board members should be evaluated regularly to ensure objectives are being met.	• Appointments to the board should be subject to a formal, rigorous and transparent procedure, and an effective succession plan should be maintained for board and senior management. Both appointments and succession plans should be based on merit and objective criteria and, within this context, should promote diversity of gender, social and ethnic backgrounds, cognitive and personal strengths. • The board and its committees should have a combination of skills, experience and knowledge. Consideration should be given to the length of service of the board as a whole and membership regularly refreshed. • Annual evaluation of the board should consider its composition, diversity and how effectively members work together to achieve objectives. Individual evaluation should demonstrate whether each director continues to contribute effectively.
Audit, Risk and Internal Control The board should present a balanced and understandable assessment of the company's position and prospects. The board is responsible for determining the nature and extent of the significant risks it is willing to take in achieving its strategic objectives. The board should maintain sound risk management and internal control systems. The board should establish formal and transparent arrangements for considering how they should apply the corporate reporting and risk management and internal control principles and for maintaining an appropriate relationship with the company's auditor.	• The board should establish formal and transparent policies and procedures to ensure the independence and effectiveness of internal and external audit functions and satisfy itself on the integrity of financial and narrative statements. • The board should present a fair, balanced and understandable assessment of the company's position and prospects. • The board should establish procedures to manage risk, oversee the internal control framework, and determine the nature and extent of the principal risks the company is willing to take in order to achieve its long-term strategic objectives.

Continued

Table 3.1 Continued

Code section	Principles[6]
Remuneration Levels of remuneration should be sufficient to attract, retain and motivate directors of the quality required to run the company successfully, but a company should avoid paying more than is necessary for this purpose. A significant proportion of executive directors' remuneration should be structured so as to link rewards to corporate and individual performance. There should be a formal and transparent procedure for developing policy on executive remuneration and for fixing the remuneration packages of individual directors. No director should be involved in deciding his or her own remuneration.	• Remuneration policies and practices should be designed to support strategy and promote long-term sustainable success. Executive remuneration should be aligned to company purpose and values and be clearly linked to the successful delivery of the company's long-term strategy. • A formal and transparent procedure for developing policy on executive remuneration and determining director and senior management remuneration should be established. No director should be involved in deciding their own remuneration outcome. • Directors should exercise independent judgement and discretion when authorising remuneration outcomes, taking account of company and individual performance, and wider circumstances.

within the scope of our book. We will look at some of the key principles in the next section of this chapter and concentrate on issues relating to the structure of the board and audit and internal controls, which are most relevant to the external auditor.

3.2.2 **Board committees**

A board will form a number of committees, some of which are required by the Code, such as the audit committee, but the board is free to create other committees which it considers to be appropriate to the circumstances of the company.

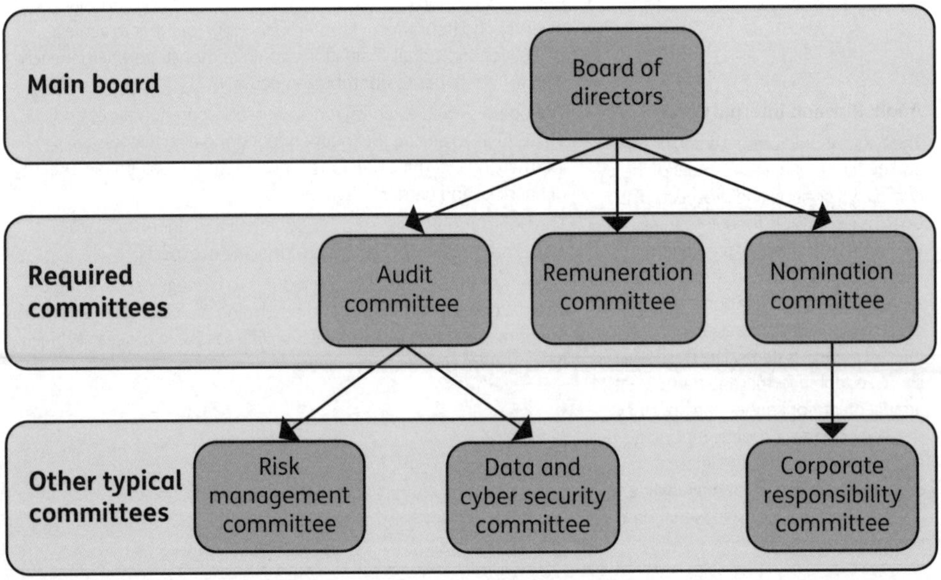

Figure 3.3 Board committees

Auditing in practice 3.3 Board committees

To provide an example of how a listed company structures its board, we can look at the example of Sainsbury's plc. Its annual report discloses that it has the following board committees, each with a range of responsibilities:

> The Board Committees support the Board in specific areas of its responsibilities, as outlined below. The Chairs summarise Committee meetings and provide updates to the Board.
>
> **Audit Committee**
>
> - Reviews integrity of financial information prior to publication
> - Oversees systems of internal control and risk management
> - Approves the internal and external audit process
> - Maintains relationship with auditors
> - Carries out in-depth reviews of specific risks, including information security and data governance
>
> **Corporate Responsibility and Sustainability (CR&S) Committee**
>
> - Reviews the sustainability strategy, Net Zero by 2040 plan, and broader environmental and social matters
> - Monitors engagement of the business with colleagues, customers, suppliers, the community, shareholders and government on sustainability and corporate responsibility matters
>
> **Nomination Committee**
>
> - Reviews the balance of skills, knowledge, experience, independence and diversity of the Board
> - Proposes new Board appointments
> - Plans succession at Board and senior management levels
>
> **Remuneration Committee**
>
> - Recommends and reviews the Remuneration Policy, ensuring it is aligned to the long-term success of the business
> - Approves the remuneration and benefits of Executive Directors and the Operating Board
> - Approves the remuneration principles throughout the business[7]

You can see that there are four committees. Three of these—the audit committee, nomination committee, and remuneration committee, are required by the UK Corporate Governance Code. The CR&S committee is something that the company has decided to establish in order to ensure that sustainability and corporate responsibility issues are given appropriate status within the organization and discussed at board level.

Like many other listed companies, Sainsbury's plc also has an Operating Board, which concentrates on the day-to-day management of the company, and which ensures that decisions made by the board are implemented in the business.

[7] J Sainsbury plc 'Annual report and financial statements 2021', 2021 <https://www.about.sainsburys.co.uk/~/media/Files/S/Sainsburys/documents/reports-and-presentations/annual-reports/sainsburys-ar2021.pdf> (accessed 17 January 2024).

3.2.3 **Governance Report and statement of compliance**

Listed companies should present a Governance Report within their annual report. The specific requirements of what needs to be disclosed come from a variety of regulations—the Code, the Listing Rules, and the Companies Act 2006. We do not need to look at the details of all these requirements, but it is important to understand broadly the type of content and disclosure within a typical Governance Report.

The company must make a statement on how it has applied the Principles set out in the Code, to enable shareholders to evaluate whether the corporate governance arrangements are appropriate. Remember that if there is any non-compliance with the Code, there should be a full disclosure on what has not been complied with, and why.

Auditing in practice 3.4 Statement of compliance

Looking again at Sainsbury's plc, in 2021 the company explained a non-compliance with a provision of the UK Corporate Governance Code relating to pension contribution rates for directors. The following is an extract of the disclosure contained in the Governance Report.

> The UK Corporate Governance Code 2018 (Code) is the key governance measure to which we referred during the financial year to 6 March 2021. The Company makes every effort to comply with the Code in full. Provision 38 of the Code requires that pensions contribution rates, or payments in lieu, for executive directors are aligned with those available to the workforce. Kevin O'Byrne's contractual cash pension supplement is not yet aligned with the pension contribution rates available to the workforce. This has been addressed by a clear incremental reduction plan, as set out in full in our Directors' Remuneration Report within the 2020 Annual Report and Accounts, which shareholders approved by 98.87 per cent. Full compliance will be achieved by the end of the 2022 calendar year. Further detail is outlined in the Directors' Remuneration Report on page 71. The Board considers that the Company has complied with the Principles and Provisions of the Code in all other respects.[8]

You can see that the company makes a full disclosure about the specific details of the non-compliance, and outlines the time period by which the non-compliance will be resolved. This is considered to be sufficient information for shareholders to evaluate the situation.

A Governance Report is likely to contain the following disclosures:

- Information about each of the executive and NEDs, often presented as a short biography including the directors' experience and skills.
- A summary of the structure of the board into various committees and subcommittees.

[8] Ibid.

- Each committee of the board (audit, remuneration, nomination, etc.) will prepare a report to be included in the Governance Report. Each committee outlines its purpose, key activities during the year, outputs, and recommendations.
- There should also be a statement on the appropriateness of the going concern basis of accounting in the financial statements, and an assessment by the directors of the future prospects of the company. This is known as the 'Viability Statement'.
- A lot of information is usually provided on directors' remuneration, which is a statutory requirement. For example, in Sainsbury's plc 2021 Governance Statement, information on directors' remuneration is over sixteen pages in length.
- Additional statutory information is provided on a range of matters including information relating to major shareholders, sustainability and environmental matters, and employment policies.

Activity 3.2 Governance disclosures

You can see that companies are required to provide a lot of detailed information about their governance, and that this information is included in the Governance Report.

What are the benefits to shareholders of being provided with this information? Can you think of any disadvantages of the disclosure?

3.2.4 Auditor's responsibilities

For listed companies, the external auditor does have a responsibility to report to shareholders in respect of the corporate governance report or statement that has been included in the annual report. In particular, the auditor is required to review the parts of the corporate governance disclosures relating to going concern and longer-term viability as well as other areas of relevance to the audit and financial statements, including the directors' disclosures relating to risk management and internal control, the audit committee, and directors' remuneration.

Typically, and assuming there are no problems identified by the auditor, a statement can be made that confirms that the company's corporate governance statement is consistent with the financial statements and with the knowledge obtained during the audit. Further details would be provided in the auditor's report if the auditor identified any errors or inconsistencies in the corporate governance disclosures made by the directors.

3.2.5 Private companies

Until recently there were no specific requirements for private companies in relation to corporate governance. However, large, non-listed companies can come under pressure from shareholders and possibly other stakeholders such as external providers of finance, to comply with all or some of the provisions of the Code. For example, they may decide that in the interests of effective decision-making at board level, they should install one or two NEDs to the board.

The important thing is that smaller or non-listed companies should follow the principles that generate the most benefit to the business, and as such a lot of the Code's principles are based on good business sense. It would seem beneficial for most companies to follow as many of the principles as possible, bearing in mind the associated cost of compliance.

In June 2018 the Companies (Miscellaneous Reporting) Regulations were issued by the UK government.[9] The new legislation requires all companies of a significant size to disclose their corporate governance arrangements. They are not required to follow the UK Corporate Governance Code.

The criteria for 'significant size' are:

- more than 2,000 employees; or
- turnover of more than £200 million and a balance sheet total (i.e. total assets, not net assets) of more than £2 billion.

A company meeting *either one* of the criteria must disclose as part of the Directors' Report a statement of corporate governance arrangements stating which corporate governance code, if any, it has applied and how it has been applied. The comply or explain principle applies—any instances of non-compliance must be reported along with the reasons. If the company has not applied any corporate governance code, the statement must explain the reasons for this and explain what arrangements for corporate governance were applied. The requirement is applicable for accounting periods commencing on or after 1 January 2019.

The Coalition Group was asked to prepare some principles to assist first-time adopters of this legislation. This resulted in the publication of the 'Wates Principles' which provide a set of six high-level, flexible, and voluntary principles. The idea is that by following these principles, a company should be able to effectively explain their governance arrangements.

The six principles are:

- purpose and leadership;
- board composition;
- directors' responsibilities;
- opportunity and risk;
- remuneration; and
- stakeholder relationships and engagement.

[9] Companies (Miscellaneous Reporting) Regulations 2018 (SI 2018/860) <https://www.legislation.gov.uk/uksi/2018/860/contents/made> (accessed 17 January 2024).

There are also requirements of company law that directors must consider. Section 172 of the Companies Act 2006 requires that the directors of a large, private company must include in the company's annual report an explanation of how they considered the interests of shareholders and a number of other matters. The detail of this disclosure is beyond the scope of our discussion.

3.3 The structure of the board and executive pay

In this section we will look at two of the principles of good governance—how the board of directors is structured, and how directors' pay should be determined. The auditor should understand these issues, for the reporting required in the auditor's report for listed companies, and because knowledge of these aspects of the company's governance arrangements can assist the auditor in understanding the attitude of the directors towards governance and control and also helps them to form a view on the integrity of the directors.

3.3.1 The roles of chair and chief executive

It is a cornerstone of good corporate governance that the chair of the board and chief executive have separate and clearly defined roles. Though it is up to the board as a whole to determine the exact nature of each of the roles, generally the chair of the board is responsible for running the board, determining its priorities, and setting the timetable and agenda for board meetings. The Code specifically states: 'The chair leads the board and is responsible for its overall effectiveness in directing the company'. The chair of the board should encourage debate at board meetings, and ensure that there is sufficient time spent on discussing operational and strategic matters. The chief executive's responsibility lies with managing the company.

Activity 3.3 Roles of chair and chief executive

What do you think are the reasons for separating the roles of the chair of the board and the chief executive?

The chair of the board should not have operational management responsibilities, and the chief executive should not influence the management of the board. The chief executive is accountable to the company's shareholders in terms of company performance, and having one person in this position of ultimate accountability allows them to focus on delivering good results to shareholders. The chair of the board, who is independent of operational management, is then in a position to watch over and monitor the actions of the chief executive and the company's performance on behalf of the shareholders.

The key issue is that combining the roles of chair and chief executive creates a conflict of interest. When the roles are combined, the chair/chief executive is both running the board and running the company, which means that the board's monitoring of company performance becomes a self-review process. The Code further provides that the chair should not remain in post for longer than nine years. This is partly to ensure that bad practices do not accumulate over a long period of time, and to allow a fresh perspective to come into the board when a new chair is appointed.

A matter to be determined by the board is the amount of time that the chair of the board needs to devote to their role. Often, the chair's position is not full-time, with many spending two or three days per week on their responsibilities. The fact that the chair of the board is not at the company on a day-to-day basis means they are less likely to become involved with operational issues.

3.3.2 The role of NEDs in good governance

The Code provides that at least half of the board, excluding the chairman, should comprise NEDs determined to be independent. The role of NEDs is not defined in law. NEDs should be able to bring an external perspective to the board.

Activity 3.4 NEDs

Why do you think it is important to have external people appointed as NEDs to a company's board?

The key characteristic of NEDs is that they are independent of executive responsibility, which means that they fulfil several important functions. NEDs should constructively challenge and help develop proposals on strategy. They should also review the performance of the board.

As we saw earlier, the Code requires that remuneration and nomination committees should be established, with the majority of members of the nomination committee, and at least three members of the remuneration committee, being independent NEDs. The aim of the remuneration committee is to ensure that executives receive appropriate remuneration, and that any targets relating to remuneration are reasonable. The nominations committee ensures that the board contains a balance of skills, experience, independence, and knowledge appropriate for its size and the needs of the business.

NEDs should take the lead where potential conflicts of interest arise. An important aspect of effective corporate governance is the recognition that the interests of the executive directors and the wider interests of the company and its shareholders may at times diverge, for example when dealing with boardroom succession or directors' pay. Independent NEDs, whose interests are less directly affected, are well placed to help to resolve such situations.

NEDs can bring a wealth of experience to the board, especially in smaller companies, where they may contribute valuable knowledge and expertise not otherwise available to management. In this capacity, NEDs can act as a sounding board for the executive directors when discussing, for example, strategic matters. One of the independent NEDs should be appointed as the senior independent director to discuss matters with the chair, and to act as a communication channel between shareholders and the board.

A particular role of NEDs is to form an audit committee—which we will look at in more detail shortly.

Auditing in practice 3.5 The role of NEDs in the financial crisis

It is widely recognized that poor corporate governance, and in particular ineffective NEDs, contributed to the financial crisis of 2008 by failing to challenge the senior management of financial institutions.

In 2009, David Walker was commissioned to investigate and report on corporate governance in UK banks and other financial institutions. In his report,[10] Walker suggested that the comply or explain approach to corporate governance remains valid, but argued more should be done to strengthen the contribution of NEDs to board decisions.

Walker found that strategic decisions were not properly debated in the board room, and that NEDs were often side-lined because the financial issues being debated were too complex or specialist for them to make a meaningful contribution. Many NEDs found it difficult to challenge the banks' investment strategies proposed in the board room by more dominant and 'knowledgeable' board members, because they lacked financial industry experience. This led Walker to recommend that to ensure that NEDs have the knowledge and understanding of the business to enable them to contribute effectively to the board, each NED should be provided with a substantive personalized approach to induction, training, and development to be reviewed annually with the chair of the board.

Walker also discussed the behavioural aspects of board room discussions, recognizing that there is sometimes a culture that does not promote discussion of strategic matters, and that there may be pressure to conform and not to challenge other board members for fear of being seen to be disruptive or disloyal. It is the responsibility of the chair to encourage an atmosphere in which debate and challenge is encouraged.

The time commitment of NEDs in relation to the board to which they are appointed is also an important issue. NEDs who do not commit an appropriate amount of time are unlike to have the necessary knowledge and insight into the company's operations to make an effective contribution to board meetings.

3.3.3 **Executive remuneration**

Executive remuneration is a very controversial topic. Many corporate scandals involve scrutiny of directors' pay, and shareholders will become angry if they perceive that executives are being paid excessively, especially when the company is in financial difficulties or when a company collapses. This type of situation is known as the 'fat cat' controversy.

Auditing in practice 3.6 Carillion

Carillion plc was a listed UK company which worked on large contracts including construction, catering, and cleaning. It was the country's second-largest construction company, with many of its contracts being carried out for the government. Carillion went bankrupt in January 2018, resulting in thousands of employees being made redundant, and, at the time of its bankruptcy, the company owed more than £1.5 billion to various creditors. The collapse of Carillion also caused the insolvency of many hundreds of subcontractor businesses as well as distress for thousands of members of its pension scheme. It is estimated that the company collapse has cost UK taxpayers over £148 million.

[10] Walker, David, 'A review of corporate governance in UK banks and other financial institution entities—Final recommendations', 2009 <https://www.ecgi.global/sites/default/files/codes/documents/walker_review_261109.pdf> (accessed 17 January 2024).

One of the most high-profile themes emerging from the scandal is that of executive remuneration. The company's chief executive earned a £750,000 salary and a total of £4 million was paid in bonuses to the company's directors in the year leading up to the company's insolvency. Controversially, the company had changed its remuneration policy in 2016 to avoid any of these bonuses having to be paid back by the directors in the event of the company collapsing.

Ultimately, the government took legal action in the public interest against the company's former directors to disqualify them from acting in an executive capacity in the future. Rachel Reeves, chair of the investigating committee, said:

> What we found in Carillion was a board focused on short-term fixes and growing pay outs, with no plan for what would happen when the illusion was shattered. Looking at the poor treatment of suppliers when the company was solvent and the trail of destruction the management of the company has caused, I cannot see how Carillion's directors can make any claim that they had anything other than their own personal interests at heart. Let me be clear: the directors of Carillion are culpable for the company's collapse. They should be ashamed of their performance, and they should not be allowed to take the helm of a company ever again.[11]

To promote fairness and transparency, a remuneration committee should be established to decide on executive remuneration. The remuneration committee should comprise NEDs who should scrutinize all aspects of remuneration—salaries and bonuses, pension contribution, and share options. The chair of the board may be a member of the remuneration committee but should not chair the committee.

The Code makes it clear that remuneration should be linked to performance, and performance-related elements of remuneration packages should be designed to promote the long-term success of the company, and targets should be used to monitor performance. The ultimate aim is to avoid paying excessively for poor performance. On the other hand, it can be dangerous to pay too little. Remuneration packages offered should be in line with market rates, otherwise low-calibre executives will be the only ones attracted to the company.

3.4 Audit committees and the external audit

The relationship between a company's audit committee and its external auditor is very important. The audit committee, which, as a reminder, is made up of NEDs, have a significant role to play in deciding who should be a company's auditor, how much they will be paid, and the scope of the work which they will perform.

3.4.1 Audit committee responsibilities

The audit committee is such an important part of corporate governance that it is the subject of its own guidance document, the FRC's 'Guidance on Audit Committees'. This document states that 'While all directors have a duty to act in the interests of the company the audit committee has a particular role, acting independently from the executive, to ensure that

[11] UK Parliament, debate in the Commons, 12 July 2018 https://hansard.parliament.uk/Commons/2018-07-12/debates/2D8B6F0E-B8C0-47C6-B9D0-D274EC5D72DD/Carillion, accessed 20 January 2024.

the interests of shareholders are properly protected in relation to financial reporting and internal control.'[12]

The audit committee should be made up of at least three independent NEDs, one of whom should have recent and relevant financial experience. All members of the audit committee should receive appropriate training so that they understand key principles in corporate reporting and regulation.

The audit committee should monitor the integrity of the company's financial statements and announcements. This means that committee members should scrutinize all published financial information, and question and be ready to challenge the executive directors on any contentious matters arising. The audit committee's review of financial information should consider the appropriateness of accounting policies, estimates, judgements, and disclosures.

If the audit committee is not satisfied with the quality of financial reporting, their concerns should be raised with the board of directors. The audit committee should also review the other information presented with the financial statements including the strategic report and governance statements.

In addition, the audit committee members have a responsibility to review the company's internal financial controls and systems (and risk management systems, unless there is a separate risk committee). The purpose of controls is to manage risk, and many large companies have a separate risk management committee as part of the board. Controls, if properly designed and operating effectively, should contribute to the smooth running of the business, help to ensure that company's objectives are met, and reduce the risk of fraud. Therefore, it

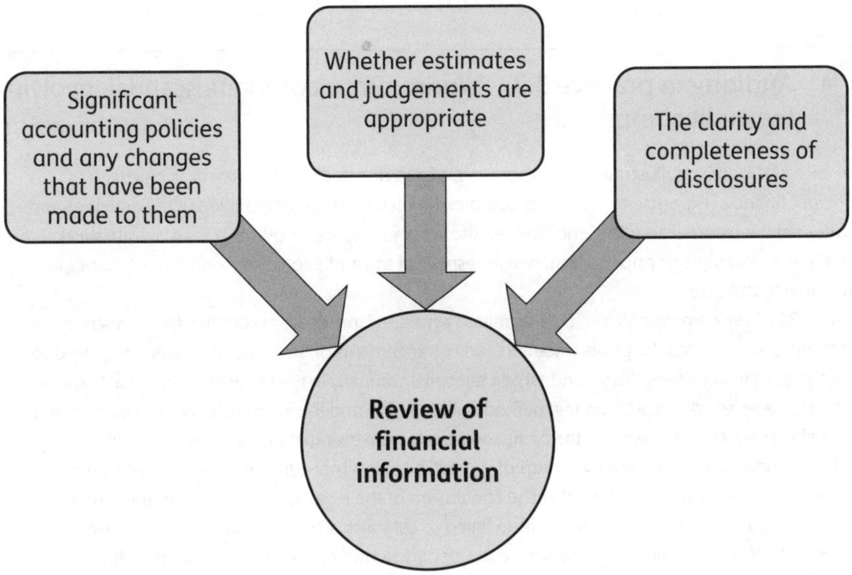

Figure 3.4 Audit committee review

[12] FRC, 'Guidance on audit committees', 2016 <https://media.frc.org.uk/documents/Guidance_on_Audit_Committees_April_2016.pdf> (accessed 17 January 2024).

is in the interests of all stakeholders that controls are adequately monitored, so that shareholder value is maintained, and company assets protected.

Most large companies have an internal audit function, in which case the audit committee has specific responsibilities. We will look at internal audit in more detail later, when we consider internal controls more specifically. For now, we just need to understand that an internal audit function exists to provide independent assurance on risk and internal controls within an organization. Such a function plays a crucial part in the whole governance structure of the company, as the internal auditors aim to provide assurance that all aspects of the company's controls and risk management systems are operating effectively at all times. The results of the internal auditors' testing will provide the basis for the directors' disclosure in the annual report regarding the review of the effectiveness of internal controls. To avoid a threat to objectivity in reporting, it is best practice for the internal audit function to report to the audit committee.

When an internal audit function has been established, the audit committee should:

- Review and approve the role and mandate of the internal audit function.
- Approve the annual internal audit plan, ensuring that it is aligned with the key risks of the business.
- Review the effectiveness of internal audit and ensure that internal audit has unrestricted scope in its activities and sufficient resources to perform high-quality work.

Finally, the audit committee plays a part in fraud prevention and detection in that whistleblowing arrangements should be made so that staff of the company may raise concerns about possible improprieties in respect of financial reporting matters.

Auditing in practice 3.7 WorldCom: a corporate scandal involving the audit committee

The case of WorldCom illustrates the importance of a strong audit committee which possesses sufficient financial expertise to scrutinize complex financial statements, challenge the activities and conduct of the external auditors, and oversee the work of internal auditors. It is an old situation, but a famous example of poor governance in respect of the audit committee, so it is worth being familiar with the case.

In 2002 US telecoms giant WorldCom admitted a multi-billion-dollar accounting fraud which prompted questions into the governance and audit arrangements of the company. WorldCom was once a highly respected business, the second-largest telecoms company in the US, with exceptional levels of profit. However, fraudulent accounting methods were used to under-report costs and overstate revenue to the effect that it is estimated that the company's assets were eventually inflated by $9 billion.

The scandal was uncovered by a team of WorldCom's internal auditors, who worked in secret to uncover the fraud. The report issued at the conclusion of the legal investigation into the directors' actions concluded that the audit committee failed to establish a strong reporting mechanism between itself and the company's internal audit department. As a result, the internal auditors fell under the control of the executive directors and spent most of their time performing operational functions. This meant that the internal audit procedures did not identify the risk of fraud nor identify the fraudulent financial reporting which was taking place. While this in isolation did not cause the company's failure, the poor governance arrangements allowed this and other financial irregularities to continue, undetected, for a long period of time.

WorldCom is an old case, but there are plenty of other more recent examples of poor corporate governance and company financial scandals which involve the audit committee. In fact, you could argue that in any situation where a company's accounting and internal controls are significantly deficient, there is some blame to be taken by the audit committee, because as we have seen, the responsibilities of the audit committee include scrutiny of the company's accounting policies and practices. Institutional investors have suggested that they will target the chairs of audit committees that are associated with poor accounting, and could encourage their removal from the board. In addition, one of the potential powers of the new regulator ARGA, is to investigate the actions of company directors, including audit committee members. So, it is more likely that future audit committees will be held to account for financial irregularities that happen under their governance.

3.4.2 **Audit committee and the external auditor**

The audit committee has specific responsibilities in respect of the external auditors.

The audit committee should approve the terms of the engagement and the remuneration to be paid to the external auditors. The committee should also review and agree the engagement letter issued by the external auditor at the start of each audit, ensuring that it has been updated to reflect changes in circumstances arising since the previous year. The audit fee should be appropriate, and an effective audit must be feasible for that fee.

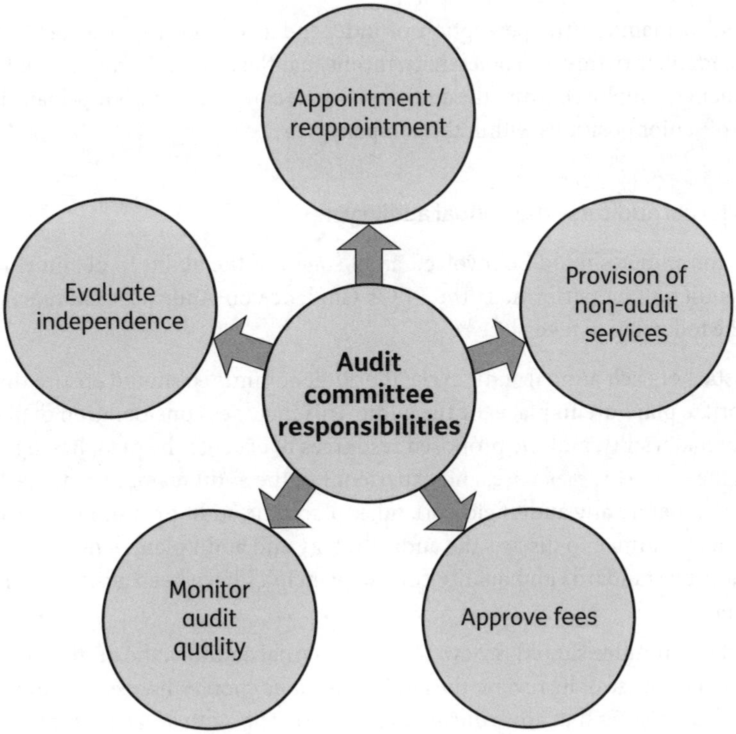

Figure 3.5 Audit committee responsibilities regarding external auditor

If the external auditor resigns, the audit committee should investigate the issues giving rise to such resignation and consider whether any action is required.

The audit committee should assess annually the qualification, expertise, resources, and independence of the external auditors and the effectiveness of the audit process. The audit committee section of the annual report should explain to shareholders how it reached its recommendation to the board on the appointment, reappointment, or removal of the external auditors, which should help to ensure transparency and full disclosure on these important matters.

One of the most important roles of the audit committee is in relation to overseeing the independence of the external auditor. The audit committee should obtain assurance that the audit firm itself has established procedures for monitoring its own objectivity, and that relevant ethical codes standards for auditors have been complied with.

A particular area that the audit committee should consider is the provision of any non-audit services by the external auditor. The provision of such services, which can sometimes provide more fee income than the audit itself, can severely impair the auditor's objectivity for many reasons, including that the auditor may be seen to be dependent on fees obtained from the client. Therefore, any non-audit services should be subject to preapproval by the audit committee who should consider not only the level of fees to be paid, but also whether the skills and experience of the audit firm make it the most suitable supplier of the non-audit service. The nature and effectiveness of any safeguards put in place to protect auditor's objectivity should also be considered, and such matters should also be explained in the company's annual report, in the interests of transparency.

The need to maintain the perception of independence, and in particular to safeguard against the familiarity threat to objectivity, means that the audit committee should monitor the movement of employees from the audit firm to the company. This is especially important in respect of senior positions within the company.

3.4.2.1 **External auditors—the annual audit cycle**

The audit committee should be involved at all stages of the audit, to obtain comfort that a quality audit will be performed. The FRC's Guidance on Audit Committees specifically requires the following to take place:

- At the start of each annual audit cycle, the audit committee should ensure that appropriate plans are in place for the audit. This includes consideration of planned levels of materiality, and the proposed resources to execute the plan, having regard also to the seniority, expertise, and experience of the audit team. In practice this means that before any audit fieldwork takes place, the audit firm should meet with the audit committee to discuss the audit strategy and audit plan, demonstrating that auditing standards and quality control principles have been adhered to in their development.
- The audit committee should review, with the external auditors, the findings of their work. In the course of its review, the audit committee should discuss with the external auditor major issues that arose during the course of the audit and have subsequently been resolved and those issues that have been left unresolved; review key accounting

and audit judgements; and review levels of errors identified during the audit, obtaining explanations from management and, where necessary, the external auditors as to why certain errors might remain unadjusted. The audit committee should review and monitor management's responsiveness to the external auditor's findings and recommendations. Thus, all key audit findings should be shared with the audit committee and discussed with them as the audit progresses.

At the end of the annual audit cycle, the audit committee should assess the effectiveness of the audit process, by:

- reviewing whether the auditor has met the agreed audit plan and understands the reasons for any changes, including changes in perceived audit risks and the work undertaken by the external auditors to address those risks;
- considering the robustness and perceptiveness of the auditors in their handling of the key accounting and audit judgements identified and in responding to questions from the audit committee;
- obtaining feedback about the conduct of the audit from key people involved, for example the finance director and the head of internal audit;
- reviewing and monitoring the content of the external auditor's management letter (report to those charged with governance), in order to assess whether it is based on a good understanding of the company's business and establish whether recommendations have been acted upon and, if not, the reasons why they have not been acted upon; and
- reporting to the board on the effectiveness of the external audit process.

In summary, the audit committee carefully monitors the conduct of the audit and plays an important part in ensuring the quality and rigour of the external audit of the financial statements.

Auditing in practice 3.8 Audit committees and audit quality—an international perspective

The International Forum of Independent Audit Regulators (IFIAR) has published a thought paper focusing on the relationship between audit committees and audit quality.[13] The paper recognizes that audit committees contribute to audit quality where certain requirements are in place, for example, that the audit committee is independent, that it communicates effectively with the auditor and it plays an active role in auditor selection and fee determination.

These requirements are not present in all jurisdictions, being dependent on local corporate governance requirements and relevant legislation, which vary from country to country or may even be absent. The thought paper provides a good resource for organizations and their audit committees operating without the robust corporate governance framework that exists in the UK, and it should serve to enhance audit quality by strengthening the role of the audit committee.

[13] IFIAR, 'Audit committees and audit quality: Trends and possible areas for further consideration', 2017 <https://www.ifiar.org/?wpdmdl=6632> (accessed 17 January 2024).

Chapter round-up

- Corporate governance is about promoting best practice by company directors, to ensure that they act in the best interests of shareholders.
- In the UK, corporate governance is regulated by a 'comply or explain' approach, with principles laid out in the UK Corporate Governance Code.
- If a company does not follow the principles, under the 'comply or explain' approach, they should disclose within their annual report the circumstances of the non-compliance including a time frame for eliminating the non-compliance, if relevant.
- Listed companies are required to include information about their corporate governance arrangements in their annual report, and the external auditor is required to review this disclosure and report to shareholders on whether the information is consistent with their understanding.
- The UK Corporate Governance Code contains principles in relation to a number of broad areas including board leadership, division of responsibilities, directors' remuneration, board composition, succession, and evaluation.
- Important principles of good governance include having a balance of executive and NEDs, separating the roles of chair of the board and chief executive, and forming remuneration and nomination committees.
- The part of the UK Corporate Governance Code of most direct relevance to external auditors deals with audit, risk, and internal control.
- An audit committee should be established to perform a range of responsibilities including having oversight of the company's financial reporting practice, the internal audit function, and liaising with the external auditor.
- The audit committee has specific duties with respect to external audit, including setting the audit fee, oversight of the external audit process including audit effectiveness, and preapproving the services to be provided by the external auditor.

End of chapter case study

Introduction

We have looked at some of the important aspects of corporate governance in this chapter and developed an understanding of best practice in relation to company directors and their relationship with the external auditor. One of the key issues for auditors is that they should evaluate whether an audit client adopts good governance practices because it has an impact on planning and performing the annual audit, as well as the specific reporting responsibilities which need to be fulfilled.

This case study links to the following learning outcomes:

- Explain best practice in corporate governance relating to board structure and directors' remuneration.
- Evaluate whether a company has implemented best practice in corporate governance, identify any deficiencies, and recommend necessary changes.

Scenario

You are a member of the audit department at Hound & Co, working on the audit of Bertie's Bathrooms plc, a listed company with a financial year ended 31 December 20X8.

You have only recently joined the audit team, and you have some information about the company, which the audit partner has asked you to read through to build up your knowledge of the client. You should read the information below and use it to answer the requirements at the end of the case study.

Bertie's Bathrooms plc—notes taken at an audit planning meeting with the finance director, George Marley

Bertie's Bathrooms plc (BB) is based in the West Midlands and has been trading for forty years. The company became listed in 20X2 and has recently undergone a significant restructuring. The company's main activity is the design and manufacture of bathroom fixtures, which it sells to high street stores.

BB does not have a dedicated internal audit department, and this function is outsourced to an audit firm called Fountain Associates. Because BB does not have an established audit committee, Fountain Associates sends its internal audit reports and recommendations to the main board for consideration. Many of the recommendations of Fountain Associates have not been implemented because the board consider them to be too expensive and not providing the company with value for money.

The company's IT system is a bespoke system introduced in September 20X8 and was developed by a small local company IT-Pathways Ltd. Any operational problems with the system are resolved by IT-Pathways Ltd. All the accounting and finance staff had training in the new system when it was introduced. There was some resistance to the new software and documentation as many of the accounting and finance team thought it was over-complicated and difficult to understand compared to the previous system. There is still some reliance on manual records that were used in the old system.

The finance director, George Marley, was recruited from a Big Four firm in January 20X8. The previous finance director left following a disagreement with the other company directors.

George produces a set of management accounts each month which is emailed to the directors. George is responsible for performing analytical review on the management accounts and for explaining variances on actual versus budgeted figures to the Board. Other than this analytical review, no formal analysis is produced by George, but he answers any questions raised about the management accounts at board meetings, which are held every quarter.

The board of directors is chaired by Bert Hobson, whose father founded the company. Bert is also the CEO of the company. Bert's brother Dickie acts as sales director. Bert and Dickie have both worked at BB since they left school, and they own 20 per cent of the company between them. The directors decide their own salary and pay rises are approved at board meetings every three months.

The company is dominated by Bert, who has extensive influence on all aspects of company operations. Bert is known to have a short temper and, in the past, has threatened employees in the accounting and finance department with no pay rise if they failed to help him achieve company goals.

Currently there are six executive directors and two NEDs. One of the NEDs is Bert's wife, and the other is Dickie's son. Bert's wife has relevant business experience, including an accounting background, prior senior management and board positions, and senior regulatory posts. Dickie's son is young with no relevant business or financial experience. The board is trying to recruit two more NEDs but is finding it difficult to find people with experience in the industry or financial reporting familiarity. This is largely because Bert and Dickie will only pay a nominal fee to NEDs, as they don't see the point of having them at all. There is currently no formal audit or other specialized committee, a fact which is disclosed in the company's annual report.

The audit is due to commence shortly, and the directors have requested that the audit be completed in four weeks. Due to the restructuring during the year, there is considerable media attention expected on the 20X8 results and the Annual General Meeting (AGM). It is planned that George Marley will present the operating and financial results at the AGM, as Bert and Dickie are worried about being asked about internal controls, which they don't fully understand.

As well as providing the audit service, Hound & Co have been asked to provide corporation tax planning advice to BB, and to advise on the selection and implementation of a new management information system to be used in the company.

Required

Discuss whether the governance structure and internal control of BB is appropriate for a listed company.

Make recommendations for improving BB's governance arrangements.

Answer

Board composition

There is no separation in the role of chair of the board and CEO because Bert performs both of these roles. This means that power is concentrated in the hands of one person who seems to be a domineering character. This means that Bert's decisions may go unchallenged, and he may make decisions in the best interests of himself, rather than in the best interests of the company and the shareholders. For example, the company has recently undergone a significant restructuring, and this strategic decision may not have been appropriately debated by the board. The board of directors should be restructured to separate the roles of chair and the CEO.

The ineffective composition of the board may have contributed to the previous finance director resigning. The finance director had a disagreement with the other directors which has not been explained but could be due to difficult working relationships and the domineering characters involved.

There are not enough NEDs. There should be a balance of executive and NEDs so that decisions are not totally in the hands of the executive directors. However, only two of the eight board members are NEDs. Also, the NEDs are family members of the chair and CEO, so they are not independent and are not likely to challenge the chairman/CEO on decisions that are being made. One of the NEDs has limited experience and knowledge so cannot bring the necessary skills to the board. The company must make more effort to attract more NEDs with relevant experience and not family members so that they can offer independent challenge to board discussion and decisions. It may be necessary to pay a higher fee to attract good NEDs.

The directors also need to understand the role of NEDs because currently they seem not to realize the importance of having good NEDs who can bring valuable experience and skills to the board, acting as a sounding board when important decisions are being made.

There are no formal committees—there should be an audit committee and a remuneration committee with NEDs being the members of these committees. Some important roles are going unperformed. The audit committee has many roles including liaising with the external audit firm and should oversee the internal audit function.

A remuneration committee should be formed to discuss and approve pay rises, bonus payments, and other compensation paid to the directors. They should not be able to make the decision about their remuneration. The board restructuring should include the appointment of more NEDs and the creation of an audit committee and a remuneration committee.

Internal audit and internal controls

The board seem to lack knowledge and understanding about internal controls. Bert and Dickie do not want to answer questions about internal controls at the AGM indicating that they do not want to take accountability.

In addition, they don't take on board the recommendations of the internal auditors, and they don't seem to pay much attention to the IT function which is also outsourced. Directors are responsible for maintaining a sound control environment and it seems here that controls are not taken very seriously. The board may have valid reasons not to implement the recommendations of Fountain Associates, but there should not be a general attitude of considering the recommendations a waste of money. The directors should have some training on these matters so that they understand the importance of controls and good systems.

There is nothing wrong with outsourcing the internal audit function—this is common practice and can strengthen the independence of the internal auditors. However, the internal audit function at BB does not have appropriate organizational status as their recommendations are ignored and perhaps the function is only present as a 'box-ticking' exercise, so that the company at least complies with the requirement to have an internal audit function.

The internal audit team should be tasked with evaluating the controls relating to the new bespoke IT system that has been introduced. It is worrying that staff have not been trained and that the system does not appear to be used properly due to manual records still being maintained. This means that operational and financial reporting systems are likely to have poor internal controls and there is a high risk of error and operational problems. If BB had an effective audit committee, they would direct the work of internal audit to focus on this area of the business.

There does not seem to be any detailed evaluation of the company's performance at board level, other than a superficial analysis prepared by the finance director. It is hard to see how the company's board can properly monitor performance and make strategic decisions based on a simple variance analysis prepared for the board meetings.

This is made worse by the fact that there are only four board meetings each year. This is not enough for the company to maintain control over its operations. It will not be able to react quickly if business conditions change. Board meetings should be more regular, usually once a month for a listed company.

All of the above points indicate that BB is unlikely to have a good 'tone at the top' (i.e. a weak control environment, characterized by inappropriate attitude and behaviours of the directors).

Note: Remember that under the UK Governance Code there is a 'comply or explain' approach which means that the Code contains best principles that plc companies should comply with. However, the Code is not legislation, so it is not illegal if a company does not comply. Any non-compliance should be disclosed and explained in the company's annual report. In BB's case, for example, the lack of an audit committee should be disclosed with the reason explained, and if this is adequately disclosed there is no breach of the Governance Code. However, non-compliance is frowned upon and will lead to negative media attention and could make it difficult for the company to raise finance.

Non-audit services

BB has asked Hound & Co to provide several non-audit services. An audit committee should be involved in requesting additional, non-audit services from the external auditor. The problem is that should Hound & Co provide these services, they may not be objective and independent in performing the external audit. For example, if the audit firm provides advice on tax and management systems, as requested, the auditor ends up auditing their own work. In addition, if the audit firm provides a tax service, the tax figure that is in the financial statements has been calculated by the audit firm, and the figure is then audited. The auditor is basically auditing their own work which cannot be independent—this is called a self-review threat. Other threats to independence may arise, which we will look at in more detail later on. In the UK generally, non-audit services can be provided for non-listed companies if there are safeguards in place to reduce the threat to independence, for example the audit firm can use a separate team to do the audit and to provide the non-audit services. However, for listed companies generally non-audit services cannot be provided, and the suggestion in the case of BB and Hound & Co is therefore not appropriate.

Activity solutions

Activity 3.1—Approaches to corporate governance

There are two very different approaches to corporate governance—'comply or explain' and legislative.

What do you think are the advantages of the comply or explain approach?

- It is flexible and can be tailored to individual company circumstances—some companies and their shareholders may not benefit from full compliance, as some parts of the regulations may be irrelevant to them.
- It is likely to be cheaper and much less time-consuming for companies to implement the relevant portions of a code than to implement full compliance with detailed legal requirements.
- It attracts people to serve on the boards of companies—under the legislative approach it can be hard to recruit board members as they are fearful of the consequences of any non-compliance, even if not deliberate.
- It is easy to amend and can react quickly when necessary (e.g. at the time of the global financial crisis)—it is less time-consuming to change a code of best practice than a piece of legislation, which would have to go through a potentially lengthy parliamentary process for any changes to be made.
- It should encourage boards to make sound business decisions based on proper risk assessment and encourage competitive behaviour, whereas a strict rules-based approach can hamper entrepreneurial spirit.

Activity 3.2—Governance disclosures

You can see that companies are required to provide a lot of detailed information about their governance, and that this information is included in the Governance Report.

What are the benefits to shareholders of being provided with this information? Can you think of any disadvantages of the disclosure?

- The information is useful to shareholders because it helps them to understand how the directors are organized (e.g. what committees have been established, and this provides insight into decision-making processes).
- The statement of compliance with the Code provides some comfort that best practice in governance is being followed, and if any instances of non-compliance are disclosed, the shareholders can evaluate and take action if necessary.
- The disclosures about remuneration can help shareholders to understand whether directors' pay appears to be fair, and again, they can act if they are not happy with the level or type of remuneration.
- However, there is a lot of information, and there could be 'information overload'—it is not likely that many shareholders will read all of the Governance Report and some of the content, for example, the detail of individual directors' remuneration, may not be very relevant.

Activity 3.3—Roles of chair and chief executive

What do you think are the reasons for separating the roles of the chair of the board and the chief executive?

- reduces potential for conflict of interest;
- makes chief executive more accountable to shareholders;
- encourages effective debate at board meetings; and
- allows appropriate monitoring of operational activities.

Activity 3.4—NEDs

Why do you think it is important to have external people appointed as NEDs to a company's board?

- provide independent viewpoint for all boardroom discussions;
- can bring additional skills and experience to the board;
- allow effective monitoring of directors' performance; and
- may defuse conflicts of interest and allow proper debate on strategic matters.

4 The Ethical Framework

Introduction

Ethics is at the forefront of the duties of an auditor. All auditors are required to act in the public interest and uphold fundamental principles and integrity.

Any threats to integrity, objectivity, and independence must be reduced to an acceptably low level. If this is not possible, the auditor must resign from or decline the engagement.

The Financial Reporting Council (FRC)[1] in the UK has issued the Ethical Standard which is also used as a framework by the UK professional bodies when developing their Codes.

Generally, all professional bodies in the UK have their own form of a *code of ethics* which must be adhered to by members of that body (including students). For example, the Institute of Chartered Accountants in England and Wales (ICAEW) has issued a Code of Ethics and ACCA has a Code of Ethics and Conduct, both of which are based on the IESBA Code of Ethics.

All of these ethical codes and the Ethical Standard tend to apply a principles-based regime. This means that, rather than adopt a rules-based approach, the Codes rely on the assurance provider's professional judgement. However, the UK Ethical Standard does contain some rules based on legislation which are prescriptive rather than principle-based in nature. Any breaches of the ethical codes can carry serious sanctions that can be imposed by professional bodies including fines and expulsion from membership. It is therefore particularly important that all professional accountants are aware of their relevant *code of ethics* and comply as far as possible with it. Breaches of the UK Ethical Code must be notified to the relevant appropriate authority, such as the professional body or the FRC.

There are often specific rules to be applied in the audit of public interest entities (PIEs), which are broadly defined as listed entities and entities that are of public interest due to their size or type of business.

Many of the ethical rules relate to independence, which is a key characteristic of sound ethical behaviour, but other aspects of ethics are important, including integrity and confidentiality. While we will focus on audit engagements, you should be aware that the ethical codes also apply to other types of engagements performed for clients.

[1] The FRC will eventually transition to the Audit, Reporting and Governance Authority.

Learning outcomes

- Explain the fundamental principles of professional ethics: integrity, objectivity, professional competence and due care, confidentiality, and professional behaviour.
- Define and explain the various threats to ethical behaviour and recommend potential safeguards to minimize threats to integrity, objectivity, and independence to an acceptable level.
- Discuss specific threats relating to long association, provision of non-audit services, fees, and smaller audit firms.
- Explain how the auditor may handle conflicts of interest and confidentiality issues.

4.1 The fundamental principles

There are five fundamental principles which must be applied at all times by auditors, as illustrated in Figure 4.1.

4.1.1 **Integrity**

This means being straightforward and honest in all professional and business relationships.

4.1.2 **Objectivity**

This requires the auditor to exercise professional or business judgement without being compromised by:

- bias;
- conflict of interest; or
- undue influence of, or undue reliance on, individuals, organizations, technology, or other factors.

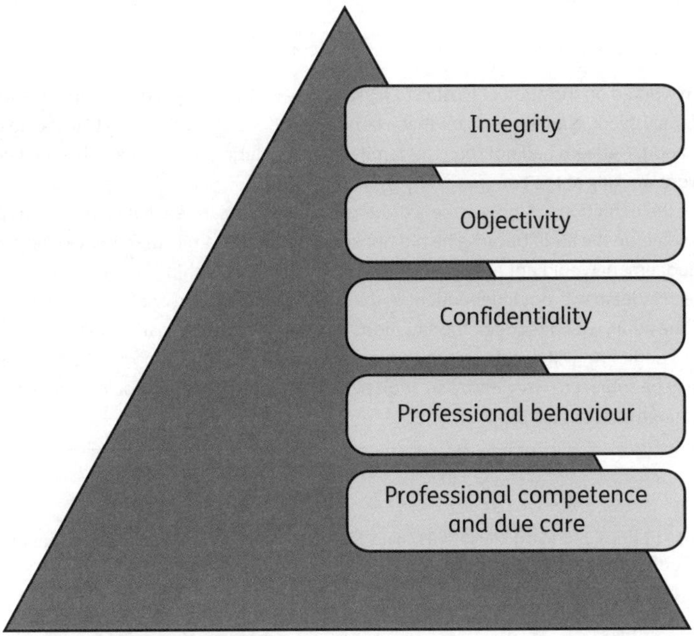

Figure 4.1 Five fundamental ethical principles

The words 'objectivity' and 'independence' might appear to mean the same thing but there is a difference. The FRC Ethical Standard defines the two terms as follows:

> *Objectivity*—acting and making decisions and judgments impartially, fairly and on merit (having regard to all considerations relevant to the task in hand but no other), without discrimination, bias, or compromise because of commercial or personal self-interest, conflicts of interest or the undue influence of others, and having given due consideration to the best available evidence.
>
> *Independence*—freedom from conditions and relationships which, in the context of an engagement, would compromise the integrity or objectivity of the firm or covered persons.[2]

One way to differentiate between the terms is to think that objectivity is about a state of mind and overall behaviour, whereas independence is more about whether the auditor complies with the relevant regulations. You should also note that perceptions are important. Actual threats to the fundamental principles need to be considered, and so do situations that might be perceived as threats by a reasonable and informed observer even if they are not actual threats.

Auditing scenario 4.1 Objectivity vs independence

Nadeem is an audit manager, recently assigned to the audit of Hosta Ltd. Prior to being assigned to the audit, Nadeem completed his audit firm's independence checklist to confirm that there were no barriers to being assigned to the audit. The firm's checklist includes questions such as:

- Do you own any shares in the company?
- Do you have any other financial interest in the company?
- Do you have personal, family, or business relationships with any directors or employees of the company?
- Have you ever worked at the company?
- Have you ever received gifts or hospitality from the company?

Nadeem worked on the audit of Hosta Ltd for four weeks. A few days after completing this work, when at a family event, Nadeem realizes that a family member started to work at Hosta Ltd during the time of the audit. Nadeem had not seen this family member during the audit and had no knowledge that they were working at the company.

Applying the definitions of independence and objectivity, we can see that Nadeem was objective when he worked on the audit because he did not know about the family member working at the client. Nadeem's judgement would not have been impaired by the relationship.

However, Nadeem was not independent of the client because a personal relationship did exist at the time of the audit, which is one of the situations dealt with by the Ethical Standard.

Nadeem's audit firm will decide on appropriate action, for example, the work he performed on the audit may be subject to a review by an audit partner and the situation should be reported to the partner in charge of ethics for the firm.

[2] FRC, 'Revised Ethical Standard 2024', 2024, para I23 <https://media.frc.org.uk/documents/Revised_Ethical_Standard_2024.pdf> (accessed 17 January 2024).

4.1.3 **Confidentiality**

An auditor must respect the confidentiality of information acquired as a result of professional and business relationships. They must not disclose any such information to a third party. However, the exception to this would be where there is a legal or professional right or duty to disclose. Section 4.3 examines confidentiality in more detail including the situations where the duty of confidentiality is overridden. Under no circumstances must confidential information be used for the personal advantage of the auditor.

4.1.4 **Professional behaviour**

This principle requires the auditor to comply with relevant laws and regulations and avoid any action which may discredit the profession. This is not necessarily just about professional behaviour in the workplace. Nowadays, this can extend to the auditor's behaviour on platforms such as social media as there have been some disciplinary cases where auditors have been sanctioned by professional bodies for behaving in an inappropriate manner on social media platforms.

Auditors must also consider the impact of their behaviour outside of the profession. For example, criminal acts or civil acts of misconduct are likely to result in the auditor being sanctioned or even expelled from membership in more serious cases.

4.1.5 **Professional competence and due care**

Auditors must maintain professional knowledge and skill at a level that is required to ensure a client or employer receives competent professional services based on current developments in practice and legislation. They must also act diligently in accordance with all applicable technical and professional standards.

Failing to keep up to date with developments in areas such as accounting standards and international standards on auditing is more likely to result in a poor level of service being provided and a failure to act in accordance with technical standards, which can also result in disciplinary action being taken by the professional body.

Auditing in practice 4.1 PwC fined for lack of competence and due care

In 2019, PwC was fined £6.5 million and given a severe reprimand over poor-quality auditing in respect of their client Redcentric plc. Two partners at the firm also received sanctions and were both fined £140,000.

In issuing the penalties, the FRC commented that 'the breaches of relevant requirements were numerous and in certain cases were of a basic and/or fundamental nature, evidencing a serious lack of competence in conducting the statutory audit work'.[3]

[3] FRC, 'Sanctions against PwC and partners in relation to Redcentric plc', 2019 <https://www.frc.org.uk/news-and-events/news/2019/06/sanctions-against-pwc-and-partners-in-relation-to-redcentric-plc/> (accessed 17 January 2024).

In response, PwC commented:

> We are sorry that our work fell below the professional standards expected of us. Since the work in question was completed, we have taken numerous steps to strengthen processes. In addition, this month we announced an additional £30m investment annually as part of a new wide-ranging action plan to provide greater focus on the quality and public interest responsibilities of PwC's statutory audit services.[4]

Table 4.1 provides some examples of how the fundamental principles can be breached.

Table 4.1 Examples of fundamental ethical principles

Scenario	Fundamental principle breached
An auditor carried out an audit of a client in which they owned shares which means that they have a financial interest in the audit client. The auditor may therefore fail to be objective when performing the audit.	Objectivity and independence
An auditor signed an unmodified auditor's report without conducting an appropriate amount of audit work.	Integrity and professional competence and due care
An auditor lost the audit working papers file for a client which contained sensitive client information.	Confidentiality
An auditor carried out a poor-quality audit on a pension fund because they were unaware of changes in the guidance on auditing such a fund.	Professional competence and due care
An auditor was found guilty of misconduct because they had posted several allegations on social media about another audit firm.	Professional behaviour

Breaches of a code of ethics can result in the following sanctions being imposed by the relevant professional body:

- suspension of membership;
- exclusion from the professional body;
- fines;
- payment of costs incurred during the investigation into the situation; and
- publication of the disciplinary proceedings on the professional body's website, including the name of the auditor and/or firm they are associated with.

Auditing in practice 4.2 EY and KPMG misconduct cases

In 2022, the US arm of EY was given a record fine of $100 million by the SEC. Employees at the audit firm had been found guilty of cheating in exams which form part of the CPA qualification. The worst part is that the cheating related to ethics exams.

[4] Sweet, Pat, 'FRC fines PwC £6.5m over Redcentric audit failures', 2019 <https://www.accountancydaily.co/frc-fines-pwc-ps65m-over-redcentric-audit-failures> (accessed 17 January 2024).

On issuing the fine, the SEC commented that 'It's simply outrageous that the very professionals responsible for catching cheating by clients cheated on ethics exams'.[5] The fine levied against EY was the highest ever imposed on an audit firm, indicating how seriously this situation was viewed by the regulators. EY was informed about possible cheating several years before by a whistle-blower, but rather than reporting the suspicions to the regulator, they conducted their own investigation, which failed to adequately address the problem. The firm also failed to inform the regulator, providing a misleading response when asked about possible misconduct at the firm.

In a similar case, in 2019, the US branch of KPMG was fined $50 million as a result of an SEC investigation into misconduct at the firm. The SEC found that KPMG staff were cheating in training exams. Members of staff, including senior partners, were guilty of sending the exam answers to other partners as well as to their subordinates in the audit firm. In addition, the SEC found that KPMG employees manipulated an internal server hosting the firm's training exams to lower the score required for passing. As a result, audit professionals achieved passing scores while answering less than 25 per cent of the questions correctly.

As part of the same investigation, the SEC looked into allegations that senior staff at KPMG had altered audit working papers which they knew would be inspected by the Public Company Accounting Oversight Board (the auditing regulatory body in the US). It is clearly wrong to revise audit working papers for fear of them being found to be of poor quality, but what made the situation even worse was that the information regarding which audits would be subject to inspection was confidential and had been obtained using 'unethical practices', including offering jobs to PCAOB employees in exchange for the information. Senior personnel at KPMG set up the programme of altering audit documentation because the firm was under intense pressure to improve its audit quality from the regulators and changing the documentation reduced the likelihood of further deficiencies being found.

When the SEC report was published, the SEC Chair said, 'KPMG's ethical failures are simply unacceptable' and the director of the SEC Enforcement Division said, 'The breadth and seriousness of the misconduct at issue here is, frankly, astonishing. This settlement reflects the need to severely punish this sort of wrongdoing while putting in place measures designed to prevent its recurrence.'[6]

As well as imposing the $50 million fine, the SEC required KPMG to evaluate its quality controls relating to ethics and integrity and to identify the audit professionals that violated ethics and integrity requirements in connection with training examinations.

4.2 Identifying and responding to threats to integrity, objectivity, and independence

4.2.1 Identifying ethical threats

Threats to integrity, objectivity, and independence are common in practice but they must be carefully managed with appropriate safeguards. The relevant safeguard(s) to be applied will all depend on professional judgement, and, in some more contentious cases, it is likely that the auditor will have to seek third-party advice or resign from or decline the engagement.

[5] US Securities & Exchange Commission, 'Ernst & Young to pay $100 million penalty for employees cheating on CPA ethics exams and misleading investigation', 2022 <https://www.sec.gov/news/press-release/2022-114> (accessed 17 January 2024).

[6] US Securities & Exchange Commission, 'KPMG paying $50 million penalty for illicit use of PCAOB data and cheating on training exams', 2019 <https://www.sec.gov/news/press-release/2019-95> (accessed 17 January 2024).

Auditors must exercise extreme care when it comes to handling threats to integrity, objectivity, and independence. Remember, these three traits are crucial in auditing and so any threats to them must be minimized to an acceptably low level.

There are six threats to the objectivity of an auditor identified in the FRC Ethical Standard.

- Self-interest threat—this is when an auditor has financial or other interests in a client which may impact the auditor's work. For example, if the auditor owns shares in an audit client, they would be reluctant to issue an audit opinion other than 'true and fair' because of the adverse impact this would have on the company's share price and therefore on the auditor's investment in the company.
- Self-review threat—this arises when the audit firm has provided a non-audit service to the audit client, for example, performed a valuation of an asset, and the subject matter of the non-audit service falls under the scope of the audit engagement. This means that the audit team would need to re-evaluate the asset valuation as part of the audit. They may over-rely on the fact that a colleague from the audit firm performed the valuation, thereby failing to obtain sufficient appropriate evidence and failing to apply professional scepticism. This leads to poor-quality audit work and a lack of integrity.
- Familiarity threat—this is also known as the trust threat. It arises when the auditor fails to challenge the audit client, over-relying on representations made by them. This could happen when a member of the audit team has a family member or personal friend working at the audit client. The familiarity threat is linked to a lack of professional scepticism.
- Intimidation threat—this can arise when the auditor's actions are impacted by threats or fear. Thankfully this does not mean physical intimidation! An example is when an audit

Figure 4.2 Threats to integrity, objectivity, and independence

client threatens the audit firm with being removed from their position as auditor. This would mean the audit firm tries to 'keep the client happy' for fear of losing the audit.

- Advocacy threat—this happens when the audit firm takes a position which is seen to be supporting or promoting management of the client, in effect, advocating for them, for example, if supporting management in a legal situation. This results in the auditor's position being so closely aligned with that of management that it is difficult to act in an impartial manner.
- Management threat—auditors should not be involved in management's decision-making. For example, if an audit firm provides a non-audit service such as tax planning, the ultimate decisions should be taken by management, not by the auditor.

Activity 4.1 Examples of threats to independence and objectivity

For each of the six threats to the fundamental principles, note down at least two other examples of situations which may give rise to the threat.

Some situations can give rise to several threats. For example, if an audit firm provides non-audit services to a client, the fees generated from providing the services create a self-interest threat, and depending on the nature of the services there may also be a self-review and a management threat.

Auditing scenario 4.2 Identifying threats

Baddie & Co provides the external audit service to Milo Ltd, a training provider. The management of Milo Ltd has approached the audit partner to see if Baddie & Co will invest £50,000 in a business arrangement with the company. The funds would be used to set up and advertise an accounting training course, with the speakers provided by the audit firm. The profits made by the business arrangement would be split equally between Baddie & Co and Milo Ltd.

Several threats to the fundamental principles would arise if Baddie & Co invests in the business arrangement. A financial self-interest threat arises because of the financial investment which would be provided to the audit client and because of the profit-sharing arrangement. Baddie & Co would be working with the client in this business venture, and presumably making decisions with them, creating a management threat. A familiarity threat may also arise if the audit firm starts to work closely with Milo Ltd's employees over a period of time, especially if the audit firm provides speakers for Milo Ltd's events. In addition, the audit firm could be seen as advocating for the client, supporting and promoting their business.

So, you can see from this simple example, that one situation can result in a range of threats arising. Of course, Baddie & Co should not be involved with this business arrangement and should decline to make the £50,000 investment or to provide speakers for the events.

4.2.2 **Responding to threats to ethical principles**

In practice, many firms will face threats to integrity, objectivity, and independence. It is how the firm manages these threats and reduces them to an acceptably low level which is crucial. Safeguards are actions which the audit firm puts in place to either eradicate the threat in its entirety or to minimize the threat to an acceptably

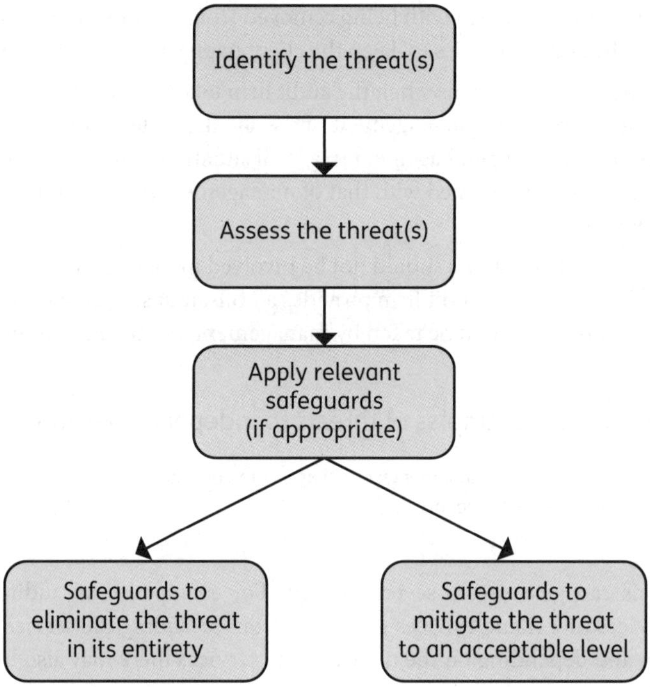

Figure 4.3 Responding to ethical threats

low level. Where the threat cannot be minimized to an acceptable level, the audit firm must resign or decline the engagement.

Where a threat is clearly insignificant, no safeguards are needed.

An audit firm will generally apply the process outlined in Figure 4.3.

Safeguards which a firm can apply come from two sources:

- Safeguards created by the profession as a whole, for example: mandatory Continuing Professional Development, review and monitoring, good corporate governance, application of professional standards.
- Safeguards created by the audit firm, for example: rotation and removal of audit team members, external file reviews ('hot' or 'cold' reviews), use of separate teams.

Table 4.2 provides details of some threats to independence, objectivity, and integrity, together with the relevant safeguard(s) which may be applied by the firm. It should be emphasized that the safeguard(s) are merely suggestions, and, in practice, other relevant safeguard(s) may be used as an alternative to resignation.

Remember, whenever a threat to independence, objectivity, or integrity presents itself, the auditor must always apply safeguards to reduce the threat to an acceptable level. This will always require professional judgement, and, in some cases, the auditor may determine it necessary to seek third-party advice on how to handle the threat. It is important that the auditor has contemporaneous documentation on file which explains:

- the type of threat that has presented itself;
- the safeguards that the auditor deems applicable in the situation; and
- how those safeguards reduce the threat to an acceptable level.

Table 4.2 Examples of ethical threats and relevant safeguards

Self-interest threat	Safeguard(s)
The audit engagement partner has a non-controlling interest in the shares of the client Owning a beneficial interest in an audit client creates a self-interest threat as the audit engagement partner would want to maximize his/her return on the investment and hence may overlook adjustments which could potentially affect the value of that investment	• Immediate disposal of the interest by the engagement partner • Remove the audit engagement partner from the engagement team
An audit client has not paid their audit fee from the previous year and the current year's audit is about to commence Overdue fees could be akin to a loan, or, for the fees are not paid, it could be perceived as performing the audit for free, both of which are strictly prohibited	• Request that the client pays the prior year's audit fee immediately before commencing any work on the current year
The audit client has suggested that the whole audit team accompany him on a weekend away to a luxury villa which he owns The value of this hospitality is unlikely to be trivial. The audit team may feel indebted to the client if they accompany the client on this weekend away.	• Gifts such as this cannot be accepted by the audit team. Only gifts and/or hospitality which are trivial should ever be accepted and, even then, the firm must have protocol in place such as documenting the gifts and hospitality and them being authorized by the engagement partner
Self-review and management threats	**Safeguard(s)**
The audit client has requested the audit firm to carry out the year-end tax calculation and complete the company's tax return Performing this service for an audit client would give rise to a self-review threat. The audit team would tend to over-rely on the work performed by their colleagues, not obtain sufficient audit evidence and be reluctant to point out mistakes. In addition, there may be some judgements to make in preparing the tax calculations, which means the audit firm is taking on management responsibility.	• Separate teams must be used to carry out the tax service. The team used must not be involved in any aspect of the audit to preserve independence • Managerial decisions must not be made by the audit firm. Source data, underlying assumptions and any subsequent adjustments must be actioned by the audit client. • If the audit client is listed, the audit firm would not be able to carry out this work, which we will explain in section 4.3.2
The audit client has requested the audit firm carry out a valuation of its portfolio of investments. The investments are significantly material to the financial statements. Valuations inherently involve making significant estimates and judgements and this could also give rise to the audit firm making managerial decisions. The investments would also be subject to audit, and hence a self-review threat arises, as seen with the tax example.	• Valuations of matters which are material to the financial statements and involve a significant degree of subjectivity should not be provided • The audit firm should politely decline the work and suggest another independent third-party expert carry out the valuation • If the client is a listed entity, valuation services which are material to the financial statements (irrespective of subjectivity) cannot be provided, which we will see in section 4.3.2
Familiarity threat	**Safeguard(s)**
Three senior members of the engagement team (including the audit engagement partner) have been involved in the audit of an unlisted entity for eleven years Long association with an audit client increases the risk that the audit team become too trusting and familiar with the audit client hence less sceptical and may fail to challenge certain assumptions or estimates	• Rotate personnel where long association has been (or will be) reached • Ensure independent engagement quality reviews are conducted on a cyclical basis by either a pre-issuance (hot) review or a post-issuance (cold review) • Where the personnel are retained on the audit, ensure documentation is in place explaining *how* the familiarity threat has been reduced to an acceptably low level

Continued

Table 4.2 Continued

Self-interest threat	Safeguard(s)
The finance director of the audit client is married to the audit manager There is overlap in this relationship between a familiarity threat, a self-interest threat, and an intimidation threat. This is because the finance director is in a position to exert significant influence over the financial statements. In addition, such a threat may also arise when a partner or employee of the audit firm has a family or personal relationship with someone at the client who is in a position to exert significant influence over the financial statements (or subject matter) even if the individual is not a member of the engagement team.	• Remove the individual from the engagement team • Ensure that the composition of the engagement team is such that the individual concerned does not deal with any matters which are the responsibility of the relation
Intimidation threat	**Safeguard(s)**
The audit client has informed the audit engagement partner that they must have an unmodified opinion this year as they are approaching the bank for additional finance and the bank wish to see the financial statements before making any decision The request for an unmodified opinion is pressure from the client to express a specific opinion. There is an added risk that the financial statements could be manipulated to ensure the best possible financial performance and position if the bank wish to see the financial statements.	• Inform the audit client that the opinion is based on the audit evidence obtained during the course of the audit and if any material misstatements (either in isolation or in the aggregate) are discovered, they must be corrected if an unmodified opinion is to be expressed • If the audit client continues to exercise undue influence over the audit, it may be necessary for the auditor to resign
Advocacy threat	**Safeguard(s)**
An audit client has received notice of a tax enquiry from the tax authority in respect of the prior year's company tax return. The finance director has requested the audit engagement partner is involved in representing the company as they have audited the tax calculation. Representing the client in a tax enquiry or in a court of law would mean that the audit firm is 'taking sides' with the client.	• The firm must politely decline the request to represent the client in front of the tax authority and may advise them to seek representation from another third party (such as a tax specialist)
The audit client has asked the audit engagement partner to attend a meeting with the bank to negotiate a new ten-year loan to assist with the company's expansion plans. Again, such negotiations would give rise to the audit firm 'taking sides' with the client which would mean the audit firm is not being independent.	• The audit engagement partner must decline the request to meet with the bank

Under the FRC Ethical Standard, the audit firm must appoint an ethics partner, who is responsible for ensuring that the firm complies with the relevant ethical regulations. The ethics partner's responsibilities include ensuring that the audit firm has adequate policies and procedures and that these are effectively communicated within the firm. The ethics partner should provide guidance to staff of the audit firm should an ethical situation arise, and breaches of the ethical regulations should be reported to the ethics partner. Breaches may also need to be reported to the audit client—usually to the audit committee (AC), and to the FRC.

Activity 4.2 Responding to a client request to provide training

Several audit clients have requested that your audit firm provide technical training on financial reporting and tax issues. This is not a service that your firm wishes to provide, and it has referred its audit clients to a training firm, which will be paying a referral fee of 20 per cent of the cost of the training to your audit firm.

Consider the ethical threats present, and how the audit firm should respond.

Activity 4.3 Responding to a client request relating to the audit team

The finance director of Magpie Ltd has requested that a certain audit senior, Rita Scott, be assigned to the audit team. Rita has not previously been assigned to the audit of Magpie Ltd. On further investigation, it transpired that Rita Scott is the sister of Magpie Ltd's financial controller.

Consider the ethical threats present, and how the audit firm should respond.

4.3 Prohibitions and specific regulations

In some situations, the ethical codes simply prohibit a course of action, because it is considered that the threats to integrity, objectivity, and independence are so significant that they cannot be reduced to an acceptable level by the use of any safeguards.

Specific rules and prohibitions vary between the ethical codes and standards, and it is not within the scope of our discussion to list out every single rule. Instead, we will look at some of the more significant prohibitions in the IESBA Code and the FRC Ethical Standard, to illustrate why these specific regulations are in place.

4.3.1 Long association with clients

When an audit firm has a long association with a client, several threats to independence can arise, in particular self-interest, self-review, and familiarity threats. It is argued that acting for a client for a long period means that auditors' professional scepticism becomes impaired (i.e. they become overly trusting of the client, with potential significant impacts on audit quality).

4.3.1.1 **Long association of audit partners**

The FRC Ethical Standard requires audit firms to monitor the length of time and extent of involvement that partners and other senior staff have with an audit client. Safeguards can be used to reduce the threats including:

- rotating the members of staff after a certain number of years;
- involving an additional partner to review work performed on the audit; and
- performing an engagement quality review on the audit (e.g. a pre-issuance (hot) review or a post-issuance (cold) review).

The FRC Ethical Standard requires that for PIEs, the key audit partner must be removed after five years of involvement with the client, and they cannot be involved with the audit for a further five years. Some flexibility is allowed in the Ethical Standard, for instance, the engagement partner can act for a total of seven years if this is necessary to safeguard the quality of the audit. This would need to be disclosed to the audit client's shareholders.

For non-PIEs, the rules on partner rotation are not as strict. Where an audit engagement partner has acted for an audit client for more than ten years then the firm should ideally rotate the partner off and replace them with a new audit engagement partner. If this is not possible then the audit work should be reviewed for audit quality management purposes (i.e. a 'pre-issuance/hot' review or a 'post-issuance/cold' review). In addition, the audit firm must also document the safeguards that have been put in place where long association is concerned together with the reasons why the audit engagement partner can still act for the client. The audit client must also be informed of the long-association threat.

As part of the revisions of the Ethical Standard, a table is included setting out the rotation rules for various partners on an audit engagement. In addition, further guidance has been included setting out circumstances such as maternity/paternity leave and sickness absence which may be relevant to those rotation rules.

Auditing scenario 4.3 Long association with an audit client

Frances has been the audit engagement partner for Almeria Ltd for eleven years. Almeria is an owner-managed business which is not a public interest or listed entity. Frances is one of three audit engagement partners in the audit firm.

For non-PIEs, according to the FRC Ethical Standard, anything beyond ten years is considered to be a long association with an audit client. This creates a familiarity threat as the auditor is unlikely to apply the same level of professional scepticism as they would had it been a relatively new audit client.

The situation should be reported to the ethics partner within the audit firm, who should evaluate the situation and decide on an appropriate course of action.

Rotation of the audit engagement partner is one option that the firm can apply, particularly as Frances is one of three engagement partners. However, if this is impracticable for whatever reason, the firm could have each audit engagement reviewed either before the auditor's report is signed (a 'pre-issuance' or 'hot' review) or immediately after the auditor's report is signed (a 'post-issuance' or 'cold' review). These reviews will ensure that the audit has been conducted in accordance with the ISAs and other regulation and legislation as well as ensuring that appropriate levels of professional scepticism have been maintained throughout the audit.

If Frances is to remain as audit engagement partner, despite the long association, then the firm must ensure it documents the reasons how independence, objectivity, and integrity are maintained in light of the long association. The reasons should also link back to the safeguards which the firm has put in place. For example, ensuring that pre- or post-issuance reviews of the work are carried out each year (on a cyclical basis, if necessary).

In addition, the firm must also ensure that they adequately communicate the long association threat to management and/or those charged with governance as it may be the case that the client requests a new audit engagement partner be assigned to the audit.

The IESBA Code is less strict than the FRC Ethical Standard. For PIEs, a key partner cannot be in place for more than seven years, but this can be extended by one year to maintain audit quality. There are no specific requirements relating to the audit of non-public entities.

4.3.1.2 **Long association of audit firms**

In addition to considering the length of time that individual partners have been involved with an audit, the length of tenure of the audit firm is another important matter. Tenure means how long the audit firm has acted as auditor for a particular client. Until recently there were no rules governing audit firm tenure, and some auditor–client relationships were very long and well established. It can be argued that when the auditor works with the client for a long period, close relationships develop, causing the auditor to lose their professional scepticism and 'side with management' rather than acting in the best interest of the company shareholders.

Auditing in practice 4.3 Auditor tenure

Prior to mandatory audit firm rotation rules being implemented in the UK, many audit firms had acted for their clients for a very long time. You may be surprised to learn how long!

Research performed by Audit Analytics[7] revealed that in 2017, around the time that the new requirements for audit rotation were introduced, an average tenure, by which we mean how long the auditor has acted for the client, was between sixteen and twenty-three years.

However, some audit tenures were much longer. For example, Lloyds Banking Group plc had been audited by PwC for 127 years, Proctor & Gamble were audited by Deloitte for 126 years, and BP plc by Ernst & Young for 107 years.

A case which has become infamous is the audit of Carillion plc by KPMG. Carillion plc went bankrupt in 2018, having been audited by KPMG for the entire existence of the company, leading to allegations that the auditor could not be objective in their audit due to their over-familiarity with the company and its directors.

[7] Erickson, Mercedes, 'A century of opinions: Companies with auditor tenure over 100 years', *Audit Analytics*, 2017 <https://blog.auditanalytics.com/paper/the-changing-landscape-of-auditor-liability/page/76/> (accessed 17 January 2024).

4.3.1.3 Mandatory firm rotation

In some jurisdictions, regulators believe that mandatory firm rotation (MFR) is a solution to the problems caused by long association of an audit firm with their audit clients. MFR basically means enacting law or introducing other regulations to force companies to change their auditor after a certain number of years. In the EU, legislation requires that for PIEs, there is a ten-year mandatory audit firm rotation. However, member states were allowed some flexibility in implementing this rule. In the UK, a maximum tenure of twenty years was introduced, as long as a public tendering process is conducted after ten years. Some countries decided on a shorter period of maximum tenure: in Italy, it was decided that nine years would be the maximum tenure.

Mandatory rotation is not really a 'current issue' because it has been debated in the profession for many years. When company scandals occur, the issue tends to re-emerge, with the main arguments in favour of mandatory rotation being the strengthening of auditor independence and the advantages created by the new auditor having a 'fresh pair of eyes'. The main argument against being increased costs for the client and possible impairment of audit quality as the new auditor lacks knowledge and experience with the client's business.

There is a further possible benefit from mandatory rotation, relating to competition in the audit market. The argument is that when companies have to change auditor regularly, the audit firms compete with each other for the clients, meaning that they need to improve their audit service to differentiate themselves from the competition. However, when an audit market is dominated by a small number of large firms, as in the UK, audit clients are often left with little choice when they need to appoint a new auditor.

Auditing in practice 4.4 Choice of audit providers

The UK's Competition and Markets Authority published a review of the audit market in 2019, which noted the lack of choice in the audit market.

The report comments that: 'There are only four firms auditing the biggest companies—100% of the FTSE100; 97% of FTSE350 companies, 99% of fees [. . .] Worse than that, choice for any given company can be as few as two or even one of these four.'[8]

The reason why a large company might only have two options when looking to appoint a new audit firm is that, assuming they wish to appoint one of the big four, one firm is being replaced, so cannot tender, and the other firms are likely to be providing the company with other services, such as tax planning or corporate finance work. A firm that is already providing a company with services might not be allowed to tender for the audit, or they might not want to, given that providing the non-audit services can be very lucrative.

For this reason, the argument that mandatory audit firm rotation will introduce more competition to the audit market and choice for companies is not strictly true.

In the UK, for the audit of a listed entity, after ten years has elapsed, a tendering process must be arranged, and it will usually be the audit committee (AC) that has overall responsibility for the selection process.

[8] Competition & Markets Authority, 'Statutory audit services market study: Final summary report', 2019 <https://assets.publishing.service.gov.uk/media/5cb74577e5274a7416b64f01/final_summary_report.pdf> (accessed 17 January 2024).

For non-listed companies, there is no such mandatory requirement. However, long association must be considered where the audit engagement partner has acted in that capacity for more than ten years.

4.3.2 **Non-audit/additional services**

Another controversial issue is whether audit firms should provide their audit clients with other services. It may seem sensible that the audit provider should also perform other work for the audit client, as they have knowledge and experience of the client's business and already have a working relationship with key members of staff. The client often prefers just to deal with one firm rather than have to liaise with different firms who are all providing different services to the company. There can be benefits in terms of consistency when one firm provides a range of services to a client.

Because of these benefits, until a few years ago it was quite common for an audit provider to also perform other engagements for their audit clients. For example, in 2016, a survey found that PwC charged their client GlaxoSmithKline £15.6 million for their audit, £4 million for 'audit-related' services, and £13.6 million in non-audit fees.[9] In the same year, Ernst & Young charged £300,000 for the audit of Greene King, but earned a lot more for the non-audit services, with £1.3 million being charged for services relating to a significant acquisition made by the company.

Activity 4.4 Threats caused by provision of non-audit services

For each of the types of threat to independence, explain how the threat can arise, should an audit provider also perform non-audit services for their audit client.

In 2019, the FRC issued a revised Ethical Standard which extended the prohibition on the provision of non-audit services to public interest and other audit clients. Prior to the revision, audit firms were allowed to perform a limited range of non-audit engagements for PIEs as long as they were not on a list of prohibited services. The revised Ethical Standard prohibits the provision of any non-audit service, other than a small number of audit-related services and those required by specific regulations.

In addition to extending the range of banned services, the revised Ethical Standard also extends the scope of the prohibitions. The new rules apply not only to PIEs, but also to 'other entities of public interest' which includes large private sector companies.

A separate rule, which was introduced as a result of a new EU Audit Directive in 2016, limits the proportion of non-audit fees that can be earned in a year to 70 per cent of the audit fee. This rule applies to PIEs. Given the prohibition discussed previously following the revision of the FRC Ethical Standard, it is unlikely that audit firms will be close to breaching this imposed fee limit in the future.

[9] Financial Director, 'Audit Fees Survey', 2016.

4.3.3 **Fees**

Performing an audit is expensive and there is a risk that the audit could become loss-making for the audit firm. Audit firms are under increasing amounts of pressure to ensure audit quality is as high as possible which means spending more time and incurring more costs. However, it is a fact of life that a lot of companies view the cost of the audit as a 'distressed cost'—in other words, some companies view the audit as being a cost of compliance with the requirements of law with little benefit. To that end, a lot of companies look unfavourably at increases in the annual audit fee.

Of course, the cost of an audit must be recovered by an audit firm as far as possible, and firms must ensure that they charge a fee which is representative of the level of skill and expertise required and enables a high-quality audit to be carried out which complies with the ISAs and other regulatory or legislative requirements.

There is also an issue with contingent fees, which is when the fee for an audit engagement is calculated on a predetermined basis relating to the outcome or result of a transaction, or other event, or the result of the work performed. The FRC Ethical Standard states that audits must not be performed on a continent fee basis because the self-interest threat created cannot be reduced to an acceptable level by the use of safeguards.

Auditing scenario 4.4 Contingent fee

Stefan is the audit engagement partner for Berlin Industries Ltd and has recently held a planning meeting with the finance director to discuss the forthcoming audit of the company's financial statements for the year ending 31 March 20X9.

During that discussion, the finance director suggested that the audit firm calculate their audit fee at 5 per cent of Berlin Industries' profit before the tax figure. The finance director feels that this would be a mutually beneficial means of calculating the audit fee as the higher the profit before tax, the higher the audit fee.

Stefan cannot agree to this method of calculating the audit fee because it would be classed as a contingent fee. In other words, the audit fee would depend on the level of profit before tax. If this were allowed, the audit team would be inclined to overlook any audit adjustments that would reduce the company's profit before tax and therefore the audit fee.

Fees based on a particular outcome, such as levels of profits or total assets are not permitted for assurance services. They must be based on the level of skill, seniority, and time spent by audit staff on the audit engagement.

Consequently, Stefan must politely decline the offer to calculate fees on a contingent basis and inform the finance director that fees will be calculated based on staff charge-out rates and the time spent on the audit.

4.3.3.1 **Fee dependence**

A self-interest threat can arise when the audit firm is dependent, or is perceived to be dependent, on a particular audit client for their fees. The point is that when an audit firm depends on the income from a particular client, their behaviour will be impacted, for example, the audit firm is less likely to challenge the judgements used by management in preparing the financial statements and ultimately will be reluctant to issue a modified opinion, for fear of losing the client and the income from performing the audit engagement.

This situation also gives rise to an intimidation threat, because the client could threaten the audit firm with being removed from office, knowing that the audit firm is reliant on performing the audit for income.

For this reason, the ethical codes have limits on the amount of income generated by one client. In the UK, where it is expected that the total fees for services receivable from a PIE will regularly exceed 10 per cent of the annual fee income of the firm, the firm must not act for the client. For non-PIEs, this benchmark is increased to 15 per cent.

For PIEs, where the fees generated from one client are 5 to 10 per cent of the audit firm's annual income, the situation needs to be monitored closely, disclosed to the ethics partner and to those charged with governance, and safeguards such as enhanced audit quality reviews implemented. Where the recurring fees received from a non-public interest entity are 10 to 15 per cent of the firm's annual income, a similar response is necessary.

Auditing scenario 4.5 Fee limits

Dahlia LLP is appointed as auditor to Hibiscus plc, a listed entity, and to Salvia Ltd, a large private company. Dahlia regularly receives 11 per cent of its practice income from Hibiscus plc, and 14 per cent from Salvia Ltd.

To comply with the FRC Ethical Standard, Dahlia LLP must resign as auditor to Hibiscus plc as the recurring fee income is more than 10 per cent.

Safeguards, such as performing an audit quality review, must be implemented in respect of the audit of Salvia Ltd as the recurring audit fee is between 10 per cent and 15 per cent.

The IESBA Code is less strict. It requires that for PIEs, where the total fees from the client exceed 15 per cent, there is no requirement to step down from performing the audit. Instead, safeguards must be used to monitor the quality of the audit performed, including performing an engagement quality review and a post-issuance review on the audit, and the situation must be disclosed to those charged with governance of the client.

It is important that the firm regularly reviews its audit fee income to ensure that it does not breach these thresholds. Any such breaches may result in the firm being sanctioned by its relevant professional body or by a regulator, such as the FRC. During the course of any routine monitoring inspection by a professional body, they are likely to ask for a list of current audit clients and will also ask for details of the last fee charged to ensure that there are no breaches of ethical standards in this respect.

Activity 4.5 Fee dependence

While monitoring levels of fees generated by its clients, an audit manager realizes that one client, a non-listed company, is likely to generate 16 per cent of the audit firm's income this year. The audit firm provides a range of services to this client.

What steps could the audit firm take to reduce the fee dependence on this client?

Auditing in practice 4.5 Fee dependence

As part of good governance arrangements, PIEs usually develop a policy regarding fees paid to their audit provider for any non-audit service provided. This is to ensure that the fees paid do not breach any of the ethical regulations, as well as providing a mechanism for fees to be approved at an appropriate level in the organization.

Here is an example of a policy of this type, taken from the Corporate Governance policy of Barratt Developments plc:[10]

- In any one financial year, the Chief Financial Officer has the authority to approve projects, which in aggregate do not exceed £50k in anticipated or approved fees.
- Where, in aggregate, anticipated and approved non-audit fees, in any one financial year, exceed £50k but are less than £150k, the projects must be approved by the Chief Financial Officer following consultation with the Chairman of the AC.
- Where, in aggregate, the anticipated and approved fees, in any financial year, exceed £150k, the projects must be approved, in advance of any formal commission, by the AC.
- The AC will review, at each of its meetings, the cumulative year to date and annual estimated audit and non-audit fee expenditure to ensure that the 70 per cent regulatory limit on non-audit service fees is not breached.

4.3.3.2 **Lowballing**

It is not only high fees which can create ethical problems. Charging too low an audit fee is also an ethical issue. Offering to perform the audit for a discounted fee is known as 'lowballing'. While this is not specifically prohibited, it does create a risk that the audit firm will not be able to perform a high-quality audit for the fee they are charging.

The audit team might be tempted to cut corners in order to minimize any loss that might be made on the audit, for example, skipping audit procedures, reducing sample sizes, over-relying on the client's internal controls. This is a threat to the fundamental ethical principle of professional competence and due care.

To ensure that the audit firm does not 'cut corners', the FRC Ethical Standard requires that 'The engagement partner shall be satisfied and able to demonstrate that the engagement has assigned to it sufficient partners and staff with appropriate time and skill to perform the engagement in accordance with all applicable Engagement and Ethical Standards, irrespective of the engagement fee to be charged.'[11]

Auditing scenario 4.6 Lowballing

Field Associates is preparing a tender document for the external audit of Hedgerow Ltd, a non-listed company. The tender document proposes a fee for the external audit which is approximately 30 per cent less than the market rate for this type of engagement. The audit fee discount is being

[10] Barratt Developments plc, 'Corporate governance', 2023 <https://www.barrattdevelopments.co.uk/investors/corporate-governance/policy-on-auditor-independence-and-non-audit-fees> (accessed 17 January 2024).

[11] FRC, 'Revised Ethical Standard', 2024, para 4.1 <https://media.frc.org.uk/documents/Revised_Ethical_Standard_2024.pdf> (accessed 17 January 2024).

offered to undercut competitors. Hedgerow Ltd operates in a sector in which Field Associates does not currently have any clients, so winning the client would be a great strategic move for the firm.

Charging a fee for the audit which is below the market rate is not prohibited, but it means that unless Field Associates is willing to accept making a loss on performing the audit, the firm will be tempted to cut back resources and 'under-audit', in order to minimize the loss or make a small profit. This will have an impact on audit quality.

The risk is elevated by the fact that Field Associates does not have existing clients in this sector, so they may lack knowledge and experience of this type of client. The audit firm should not prioritize its commercial ambitions i.e. to secure a client in a new sector, over audit quality. To do so would mean a lack of integrity of the audit firm.

The FRC Ethical Standard requires that the engagement partner must be able to demonstrate that the audit has assigned to it sufficient partners and staff with appropriate time and skill to perform the audit to a high standard, irrespective of the engagement fee to be charged.

4.3.4 Applying ethical standards in smaller firms

Smaller audit firms are also subject to compliance with ethical standards in the same way that larger firms are. For example, there is still a requirement to handle threats to independence, objectivity, and integrity in the same way that a larger firm would handle them; and there is still a requirement for auditors in smaller firms to act with integrity, demonstrate technical competence and due care and preserve confidentiality.

Depending on the jurisdiction, there may be certain provisions which can be applied for small entity audits which allow a relaxation of the more stringent rules which apply to larger audit clients. For example, in the UK, the Ethical Standard makes certain provisions available to small entities in section 6 Provisions Available for Audits of Small Entities which provides alternative provisions for auditors of small entities which are not PIEs. As we saw in Chapter 2, a 'small' entity is one which meets two out of the following three thresholds for two consecutive years:

- turnover not more than £10.2m (increasing to £15 million for accounting years commencing on or after 6 April 2025);
- total assets not more than £5.1m (increasing to £7.5m for accounting years commencing on or after 6 April 2025); or
- not more than an average of fifty employees.

The provisions which are available allow auditors of small entities to apply alternative provisions to threats which arise from the provision of tax or accounting services. However, the auditor is required to disclose in the auditor's report the fact that the firm has applied the FRC's ES—Provisions Available for Audits of Small Entities.

The Provisions Available for Audits of Small Entities provide the following alternative provisions.

- Economic dependence

  Where there is a risk of fee dependence, the audit engagement partner must disclose the expectation that fees will amount to between 10 per cent and 15 per cent of the firm's annual fee income to the ethics partner and to those charged with governance of the entity.

- Non-audit services

  The firm need not apply safeguards to address a self-review threat *but only on the basis that* the small entity has 'informed management'; and the audit firm performs appropriate reviews of audit work performed in line with requirements for audit quality management. 'Informed management' is defined as a 'Member of management (or senior employee) of the entity relevant to the engagement who has the authority and capability to make independent management judgments and decisions in relation to non-audit/additional services on the basis of information provided by the firm'. Management of the client must accept responsibility for any decisions taken.

4.4 Confidentiality and conflicts of interest

One of the fundamental principles in the IESBA's *Code of Ethics* is confidentiality. It goes without saying that an auditor must respect the confidential nature of a client's information. Clients must be able to trust auditors, in much the same way that a patient must trust their doctor; or a client must trust a lawyer. To that end, members of an assurance team cannot disclose any information to anyone outside of the engagement team, regardless of the fact that they may work for the same firm.

In addition, an auditor must not use confidential information acquired for their own advantage, for example, make an investment because of confidential information obtained during an audit.

Information can only be disclosed to a third party with specific authority from the client, or if there is a legal or professional right or duty to disclose.

Activity 4.6 Confidential information

What type of confidential information do you think an auditor is likely to come across while conducting an audit? Note down your ideas.

Auditing scenario 4.7 Liaising with a predecessor auditor

Currie Ltd has appointed a new firm of auditors, Mata'utia & Co to audit the financial statements for the year ending 31 July 20X9. Currie Ltd is based in the UK where auditors have a right to inspect the predecessor firm's audit files in order to obtain sufficient appropriate audit evidence concerning opening balances.

Mata'utia & Co is required to write to the predecessor audit firm as a matter of courtesy to ask if there are any reasons (professional or otherwise) why they should not accept appointment as auditor. However, before they can do this, Currie Ltd will need to give permission to the outgoing firm to liaise with Mata'utia & Co. This is because the outgoing firm is still subject to client confidentiality and will not be able to enter into any discussion with Mata'utia & Co if this permission is not obtained.

Once permission by Currie Ltd has been granted, Mata'utia & Co can liaise with the outgoing audit firm to request professional handover information (sometimes referred to as 'professional clearance') and then make arrangements to attend the outgoing firm's office to review the audit files to obtain sufficient appropriate audit evidence over opening balances.

4.4.1 Circumstances when disclosing client information is appropriate

There are some situations when auditors may be, or are required, to disclose confidential client information.

When disclosure is permitted by law and is authorized by the client, it is important that the auditors obtain written permission from the client.

In some situations, disclosure is required by law, and client permission is not needed. This could arise as a result of legal proceedings which require the production of documents or other forms of evidence; or disclosure needs to be made to the appropriate authority because a law has been breached.

Sometimes there is a professional duty or right to disclose, where this is not prohibited by law, such as:

- to comply with audit monitoring requirements by a professional body;
- to respond to an inquiry or investigation by a professional body in respect of a complaint;
- to protect the professional interests of an auditor during legal proceedings; or
- to comply with technical standards and ethical requirements.

There may also be situations that the auditor comes across during their work which may give rise to the need to disclose confidential client information, without informing the client of this disclosure. For example, in the UK, anti-money laundering regulations (AMLRs) are in place that aim to combat money laundering and other such offences. If the auditor suspects that the client is committing such offences against the public good, then disclosure to the relevant authority (e.g. the National Crime Agency (NCA)) will be required.

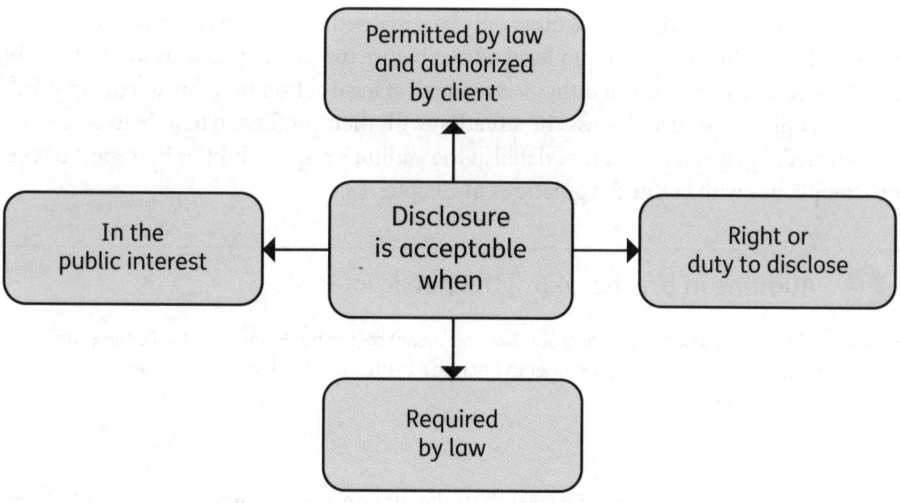

Figure 4.4 Circumstances when disclosure of client information is permitted

Auditing scenario 4.8 Act of fraud

During the audit of Jardins Enterprises Ltd, the audit senior noticed a number of invoices from a supplier which appeared to be fictitious. The values on these invoices are significant and value added tax (VAT) has been reclaimed on these invoices resulting in large refunds of VAT being repayable from the tax authority. The audit senior has concluded that they need to report this matter in accordance with AMLRs.

AMLRs would require the audit senior to report the matter to the firm's money laundering reporting officer (MLRO). The MLRO would then decide whether, or not, the allegations warrant a Suspicious Activity Report being made to the NCA. If a Suspicious Activity Report is to be made by the MLRO, the client must not be informed because this would constitute 'tipping off' the client and hence the auditor would then be committing a criminal offence.

In this scenario, the duty of confidentiality is overridden by the requirement to comply with law. The impact on the auditor's opinion where this alleged fraudulent activity is concerned would be determined by the audit engagement partner.

Disclosure to relevant authorities can also be required when it is in the public interest. This is because maintaining client confidentiality would be considered unethical if, for example, the auditor came across dangerous or unethical business practices or significant environmental pollution being conducted by the client.

ISA 250 Consideration of Laws and Regulations in an Audit of Financial Statements contains some UK-specific guidance about reporting in the public interest. ISA 250 makes it clear that reporting in the public interest requires very careful consideration and should only be done if the auditor has discussed a serious matter with the company's directors which they refuse to disclose.

ISA 250 provides examples of 'rare circumstances' for which, 'according to common law, disclosure might be justified in the public interest (e.g. where the public is being misled or their financial interests are being damaged); where a miscarriage of justice has occurred; where the health and safety of members of the public or the environment is being endangered'.[12]

Matters of a confidential nature must only be disclosed to appropriate regulatory authorities and the auditor should obtain legal advice before making any disclosure in the public interest to ensure they protected themselves against legal action for a breach of confidentiality. The auditor may also discuss the situation with their professional body to ensure they are protected. We will look in more detail at the auditor's responsibilities in respect of client non-compliance with law and regulations in Chapter 13.

Auditing in practice 4.6 The public interest

There has been considerable debate around what is meant by 'the public interest'. While there are definitions to help auditors assess whether to disclose a matter in the public interest, it remains a matter of judgement.

[12] FRC, 'ISA 250 (UK)', 2019, para A33-4 (18a) <https://media.frc.org.uk/documents/ISA_UK_250A_Revised_November_2019_Updated_May_2022.pdf> (accessed 17 January 2024).

IFAC defines the public interest as 'the net benefits derived for, and procedural rigour employed on behalf of, all society in relation to any action, decision or policy'.[13]

This definition basically means that auditors need to consider the wider impact on society when dealing with a problematic situation discovered while performing an audit.

To help auditors to determine whether disclosure should be made in the public interest, ISA 250 contains guidance where there has been a non-compliance with law and regulations.[14]

'Public interest' is a concept that is not capable of general definition. Each situation must be considered individually. In the UK, legal precedent indicates that matters to be taken into account when considering whether disclosure is justified in the public interest may include:

- The extent to which the issue is likely to affect members of the public.
- Whether those charged with governance have rectified the matter or are taking, or are likely to take, effective corrective action.
- The extent to which non-disclosure is likely to enable the situation to continue without remedy.
- The gravity of the matter.
- The weight of evidence.

It is very rare for an auditor to have to make a disclosure in the public interest because those charged with governance would almost always rather disclose the information themselves in order to protect their reputation.

4.4.2 **Conflicts of interest**

It is implicit in the professional business relationship that an auditor must act in the best interests of their client. However, situations can present themselves which may cause conflicts of interest. For example, a firm may act for a competing client; in such a situation, the firm should ensure they have procedures in place which avoid the interest of one party being adversely affected by another party as well as preventing any breaches of confidentiality.

To deal with this threat properly, the firm must notify all affected clients when a conflict of interest is noted. The firm must also obtain the client's consent to act.

Auditing scenario 4.9 Managing a conflict of interest

Starling & Co is a firm of auditors. It has acted for Bury Enterprises Ltd for a number of years and has just been invited to accept appointment as auditor for Ethan Environmental Ltd. Ethan Environmental is a direct competitor of Bury Enterprises and Starling & Co have been granted permission by Bury Enterprises to act for Ethan Environmental provided that the firm ensures strict confidentiality is maintained at all times.

[13] International Federation of Accountants, 'A definition of the public interest: IFAC policy position 5', 2012 <https://www.ifac.org/_flysystem/azure-private/publications/files/PPP5-Definition-of-Public-Interest-At-a-Glance.pdf> (accessed 17 January 2024).

[14] FRC, 'ISA 250 (UK)', 2019, para A33-5 <https://media.frc.org.uk/documents/ISA_UK_250A_Revised_November_2019_Updated_May_2022.pdf> (accessed 17 January 2024).

To comply with Bury Enterprises' instructions, Starling & Co must adopt safeguards to maintain confidentiality and to deal with the conflict of interest effectively. Such safeguards could include the following:

- The use of separate engagement teams with different audit engagement partners and team members.
- The use of 'barriers to information' which would prevent access to information across the firm such as confidential and secure data filing and/or the use of separate teams from different offices.
- Confidentiality agreements signed by all the relevant staff members and audit engagement partners concerned.
- Regular review of the safeguards utilized by the firm by an external reviewer with appropriate levels of skill and expertise.
- Advising the client to seek independent advice.

Should Starling & Co be unable to apply adequate safeguards to handle the conflict of interest, they should decline the invitation to accept appointment by Ethan Enterprises or resign as auditors of Bury Enterprises.

Auditing in practice 4.7 KPMG, Silentnight, and HIG Capital

In 2021, the FRC completed their investigation of KPMG in respect of their client Silentnight, a UK manufacturing company, finding that a significant conflict of interest impaired the objectivity and integrity of KPMG and one of its partners. The conflict of interest arose in 2011, when KPMG acted as adviser to Silentnight, as well as advising the private equity firm, HIG Capital, which was seeking to acquire Silentnight.

The FRC argued that the partner involved had helped HIG Capital to devise a strategy to acquire Silentnight's profitable business but without the company's significant pension liability, ultimately pushing Silentnight to the brink of insolvency.

KPMG earned £1.6 million from its work with Silentnight but has received more than £8 million in fees from HIG since 2011.

The tribunal found that the partner and KPMG had failed to consider threats to objectivity and integrity arising from their involvement with both HIG Capital and Silentnight, or whether a conflict of interest arose. The tribunal also found that KPMG had the desire to 'keep HIG onside'—indicating that the firm's actions were motivated by keeping HIG happy—a clear self-interest threat to objectivity. The tribunal concluded that concluded that the lack of objectivity went to the core of the relationship between Silentnight and KPMG, and that in addition to a lack of objectivity, the partner had acted dishonestly.

Following their investigations, the FRC imposed significant sanctions against KPMG including a £13 million fine, a severe reprimand, and ordered KPMG to conduct an internal review to establish why threats to fundamental ethical principles were not identified and safeguarded.

The partner involved was fined £500,000, severely reprimanded, excluded from membership of the ICAEW for thirteen years, and precluded from holding an insolvency licence for the same period.

The FRC commented on the case as follows:

> In determining the sanctions, the Tribunal considered the Misconduct was very serious, noting that to a professional accountant the conflicts of interest should have been obvious and that the Misconduct

risked the loss of significant sums of money. It put at risk Silentnight's ability to survive and tens of millions of pounds of creditors' claims, potentially exceeding £100 million as the liability to the Pension Scheme would crystallize. The Misconduct potentially adversely affected a significant number of people. The majority of the membership of the Pension Scheme comprised factory workers, many of whom had worked for Silentnight and contributed to the pension scheme for much of their working life. The standards of integrity and objectivity are of fundamental importance. They express the most basic requirements that society expects of professional accountants. Members of the profession have a privileged and trusted role in society. In return, they are required to live up to their own professional standards. Society expects high standards from professional persons; and the professions expect high standards from their own members.[15]

4.5 Professional scepticism

4.5.1 What is 'professional scepticism'?

ISA (UK) 200 defines 'professional scepticism' as:

> An attitude that includes a questioning mind, being alert to conditions which may indicate possible misstatement due to error or fraud, and a critical assessment of audit evidence.[16]

Professional scepticism is something that cannot be taught. However, professional bodies and regulators frequently criticize audit firms for failing to evidence that they have exercised professional scepticism during the audit.

Adopting an approach of professional scepticism will involve a critical assessment of audit evidence and being alert for audit evidence that may contradict other audit evidence, or may call into question the reliability of the information gathered from management and those charged with governance. We often link being sceptical to challenging something—usually information. It's about not taking things as face value and asking for more evidence. It's about having an analytical approach, using critical evaluation skills and being willing to hold meaningful conversations around the subject matter. It can also mean being assertive, being brave at times, because sometimes being sceptical means asking questions that people do not want to answer, or asking for information that they don't want to provide. Being sceptical means auditors will sometimes be outside of their comfort zone.

Professional scepticism is linked to the auditor's use of judgement, which is defined as follows:

> The application of relevant training, knowledge and experience, within the context provided by auditing, accounting and ethical standards, in making informed decisions about the courses of action that are appropriate in the circumstances of the audit engagement.[17]

[15] FRC, 'Sanctions against KPMG and former partner in relation to Silentnight', 2021 <https://www.frc.org.uk/news-and-events/news/2021/08/sanctions-against-kpmg-and-former-partner-in-relation-to-silentnight/> (accessed 17 January 2024).

[16] FRC, 'ISA (UK) 200', 2016, para 13(l) <https://media.frc.org.uk/documents/ISA_UK_200_Updated_May_2022.pdf> (accessed 17 January 2024).

[17] 'ISA (UK) 200' Overall Objectives of the Independent Auditor and the Conduct of an Audit in Accordance with International Standards on Auditing, para 13(k) <https://media.frc.org.uk/documents/ISA_UK_200_Updated_May_2022_V8vTA3V.pdf> Date of document: 2022 Accessed 17 January 2024.

Activity 4.7 Professional judgement

Can you think of any examples where auditors need to use judgement when performing their work?

Auditing in practice 4.8 Regulator's views on professional scepticism

In recent years audit firms have been criticized by regulators where they have not demonstrated clearly enough that they have approached audits with an appropriate level of professional scepticism. In particular, after the global financial crisis of 2008–2009, when financial statements were particularly affected by significant areas of judgement, the auditing profession came under scrutiny for not challenging certain accounting treatments. At this time, impairment of assets and fair value measurements had material impacts on the financial statements, and it seems that in some cases the audit firms were too accepting of management's accounting treatment of these matters.

In 2012, Professor Arnold Schilder, Chairman of the IAASB, stated in a conference speech that:

> today's financial reporting involves more complexity, more areas of judgment, and more qualitative disclosures; and users have higher expectations than ever before ... Perhaps most importantly, the global financial crisis has triggered questions concerning the quality of audits, their effectiveness, and the role of professional judgment and scepticism—which have given way to fundamental questions to the profession about relevance and trust.[18]

Thus, applying professional scepticism is seen by the regulatory bodies as a cornerstone in maintaining audit quality and safeguarding the credibility of the auditing profession.

This situation led the regulatory bodies to focus on audit quality in their work programmes, with professional scepticism being a key component of audit quality. In 2012 the IAASB issued *Professional Scepticism in an Audit of Financial Statements*, a question-and-answer publication that re-emphasized to auditors the importance of an attitude of professional scepticism when performing their role.

The FRC is also concerned with auditors obtaining the skills to practise professional scepticism and has issued several documents on the matter, many of which are linked to audit quality.

The issues that arise in FRC audit inspections indicating poor-quality audit practice linked to a lack of professional scepticism include:

- Being over-reliant on management representations, especially management assumptions in a matter of accounting judgement.
- Not obtaining corroboratory evidence in relation to management assertions.
- Assuming that management's calculations are correct and not performing additional work to come to an independent conclusion on a monetary value.
- Placing too much reliance on the work of internal auditors.
- Not performing proper audit risk assessment; assuming that risks have not changed since the prior year audit.

Audit firms need to ensure that their staff apply professional scepticism, and that this is adequately documented in the audit files.

[18] Schilder, Arnold, 'The evolving role of auditors and auditor reporting', International Auditing and Assurance Standards Board, 2013 <https://www.iaasb.org/news-events/2013-08/evolving-role-auditors-and-auditor-reporting> (accessed 17 January 2024).

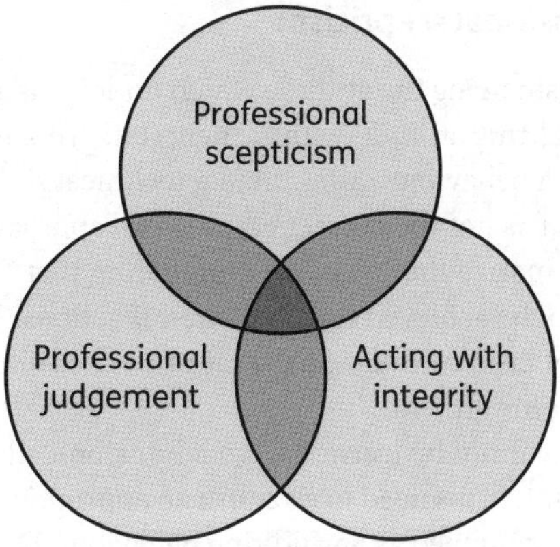

Figure 4.5 Professional behaviours

4.5.2 **Professional scepticism and ethics**

Auditors must appreciate that professional scepticism is an integral part of their work and is closely interrelated to the fundamental concepts of independence, integrity, and objectivity. While the use of professional scepticism is a requirement of auditing standards, it is not just relevant to auditors. All professional accountants should comply with the code of ethics issued by their professional body. These codes highlight the importance of principles such as acting with integrity and objectivity, which include requirements that accountants should not allow bias or undue influence of others to impact on their professional or business judgement. Professional scepticism is a mindset which we all should adopt, flexing the degree of scepticism to the situation we find ourselves in.

Auditing scenario 4.10 Ethics and professional scepticism

Mary is an audit manager at Cross Associates, a firm of Chartered Accountants. Mary is the manager responsible for the audit of Bingley Ltd, an important manufacturing client of the audit firm. Caitlin is an audit partner within the firm. The finance director of Bingley Ltd has just retired, and Caitlin is leaving Cross Associates having been offered the finance directorship by the management of Bingley Ltd.

An ethical issue arises in that Cross Associates is no longer independent of Bingley Ltd. There is a familiarity threat to independence due to the relationship between the audit firm and the finance director of the client company. There is a perception that the audit opinion could be biased due to this relationship.

There is also an issue with professional scepticism. When Mary is planning and conducting the next audit of Bingley Ltd she is likely to be too trusting of Caitlin's work. She may not feel the need to challenge the accounts prepared by Caitlin having worked with her at Cross Associates. She will be less inclined to approach the audit as high risk and may not identify risks of misstatement due to relying on the statements made by Caitlin to be true and accurate.

For both of these reasons, it is unlikely that Cross Associates could continue to provide the audit service to Bingley Ltd.

Audit firms must therefore ensure that when evaluating threats to independence they bear in mind any potential compromise to their professional scepticism. Safeguards can sometimes be used to reduce threats to independence to an acceptable level, and these same safeguards should also protect the auditor's ability to employ professional scepticism during the audit.

4.5.3 **Enhancing professional scepticism**

With professional scepticism being the attitude which underpins a quality audit, it is imperative that audit firms instil this attitude within their staff. This is not easy to do however because being sceptical is a behaviour rather than a technical skill, so training and passing an exam in 'being sceptical' is not the correct educational approach. A wider perspective is needed. The ICAEW summarize the issue by commenting that 'The proper application of scepticism in audits cannot be achieved through one-off actions. The key driver in improving the application of scepticism by individual auditors is the culture within their firm. This will require an on-going commitment.'[19]

Professional scepticism cannot be learned from a book and education needs to focus on practical development. Audit firms need to establish an appropriate 'tone at the top' whereby scepticism is valued and encouraged as an auditing behaviour. Developing the culture of an audit firm in this way could involve establishing mentoring schemes for junior members of staff so that they feel supported by senior colleagues, giving them confidence to develop sceptical behaviours when performing client work.

Staff should receive training, though this should be practical in nature. Audit firms can develop a training programme involving case studies to enable staff to develop their skills. Real-life client scenarios could be used to illustrate where professional scepticism needs to be employed.

Recruitment of appropriate personnel is also important. Good auditors with the ability to approach matters sceptically will be technically competent but also have the right attributes to use their technical ability. Audit staff should be confident enough to challenge clients and to question what they are told when obtaining audit evidence.

Audit staff need to have good communication skills and the confidence to enter into dialogue with members of clients' senior management. Training on effective communication, listening and interviewing skills, assertiveness, and report writing (for documenting discussions) will all help. Audit firms are sometimes reluctant to devote much resource to this kind of 'soft skills' training, but it is crucially important and goes hand in hand with technical ability. It is no good having all of the technical knowledge if you don't have the confidence or ability to discuss issues with your client.

Audit firms should encourage sceptical behaviours by including professional scepticism as part of performance appraisal and linking it to promotion and possibly remuneration packages.

At the level of an individual audit engagement, there are ways to safeguard the application of professional scepticism. Some such examples include:

- Encouraging the audit team to act in a sceptical way, for example the audit engagement partner can discuss this at the audit planning meeting, highlighting any areas of risk where the need to be sceptical is heightened, such as fraud risks.
- Identifying whether there are any points brought forward from the previous year's audit which indicate a need to apply professional scepticism to a certain part of the audit process.

[19] ICAEW, 'Professional scepticism and other key audit issues', 2015.

- Allowing enough time for the audit to be properly planned and conducted. Regulatory bodies note that time pressure is an impediment to audit quality generally and professional scepticism in particular as it causes auditors to look for 'easy' evidence and discourages debate with the client.
- As part of the review of audit work that takes place during the audit more senior members of the audit team should be ready to challenge the conclusions reached by less-experienced team members and request more evidence to be obtained where necessary.
- Ensuring proper direction and supervision of staff, in particular junior members of the audit team. It is important that audit juniors feel comfortable to ask questions of the more senior members of the team especially on areas of judgement, where they have identified risks and where evidence seems contradictory. Proper direction and supervision should encourage confidence in the audit team to challenge management assertions.
- Creating an audit team using the principles of good team building, encouraging an atmosphere where questions are encouraged, team members invited to give their opinion on a matter. The two behaviours that are most important in developing good relationships in a team are openness and supportiveness.

4.5.4 Demonstrating the application of professional scepticism

The problem that many auditors have with the concept of professional scepticism is that there is no single way of demonstrating its application. Notwithstanding this problem, professional scepticism is a mindset, and a sceptical mindset will enable the auditor to question aspects of the entity and its financial statements rather than merely accepting information at face value.

Professional scepticism is an attitude, and it can therefore be very hard to document how it has been applied. An auditor can have performed an audit with an appropriately sceptical mindset but if there is no documentation to support this the perception of quality of the audit is under threat. ISA 230 Audit Documentation states that 'there may be no single way in which the auditor's professional scepticism is documented. But the audit documentation may nevertheless provide evidence of the auditor's exercise of professional scepticism in accordance with the ISAs.' The regulatory bodies agree that it is difficult to prove that an auditor has been sceptical but criticize audit firms who fail to properly document matters relating to professional scepticism.

Some regulatory bodies suggest that specific documentation relating to professional scepticism is prepared. An example is provided by the Institute of Chartered Accountants Australia and the Chartered Professional Accountants of Canada who have released a joint publication *Practical Guide to Exercising Professional Scepticism in Auditing* which recommends the use of a checklist to record how scepticism was applied during an audit.

Professional scepticism is important when auditing management judgements, and there should be documentation on:

- How management has reached a judgement.
- What has been discussed with management, including the auditor's challenges of management's assumptions.

- The evidence obtained in support of management's assumptions.
- An evaluation of other relevant evidence and consideration of whether it corroborates, or is contradictory, to management's judgement.

Applying scepticism often involves a discussion with the client and it is crucial that discussions are fully documented. It is best to write up the notes from a meeting as soon as possible to ensure the completeness and accuracy of what is recorded in the audit working papers.

Auditors should document the application of professional scepticism at all relevant stages of the audit.

Auditing scenario 4.11 Demonstrating professional scepticism

During the audit of Murphy Ltd, management have made an assertion regarding the outcome of a court case against the company, concluding that the court case will not result in a cash outflow.

A key element of the audit evidence will be a discussion with management regarding their assertion, the auditor should ask questions to understand management's rationale for this assertion, and consider the validity of the reasoning behind it. The auditor is likely to ask many questions about the matter, and should reach an independent view on the situation. The audit working papers should contain a full account of the discussion with management including:

- Who was present at the meeting.
- The questions asked by the auditor, specifically whether any management assumptions were challenged.
- The discussion and answers from management.
- Whether management could provide any corroboratory evidence to substantiate their assertion.
- The tone of the discussion (for example was management aggressive or defensive).
- The time taken for the discussion (this can indicate whether a discussion was too superficial or appropriately detailed).
- The auditor's conclusion.
- Any further actions (for example need to obtain more evidence, matter to be discussed with AC).

4.5.4.1 **Audit planning meeting**

Notes from the audit planning meeting should include points relating to professional scepticism, for example any areas of the audit considered to be high risk and where it is especially important to be sceptical of management assertions. This is evidence that the audit team as a whole has been reminded of the need to be sceptical.

4.5.4.2 **Audit working papers**

- Notes of discussions with client including questions and answers and detailing how the auditor's questions constitute a challenge of facts presented by management (see example on court case, Auditing scenario 4.11).
- Where there is conflicting audit evidence, a written explanation of how the contradictory evidence has been assessed by the auditor and a conclusion on the overall reliability and sufficiency of the evidence.

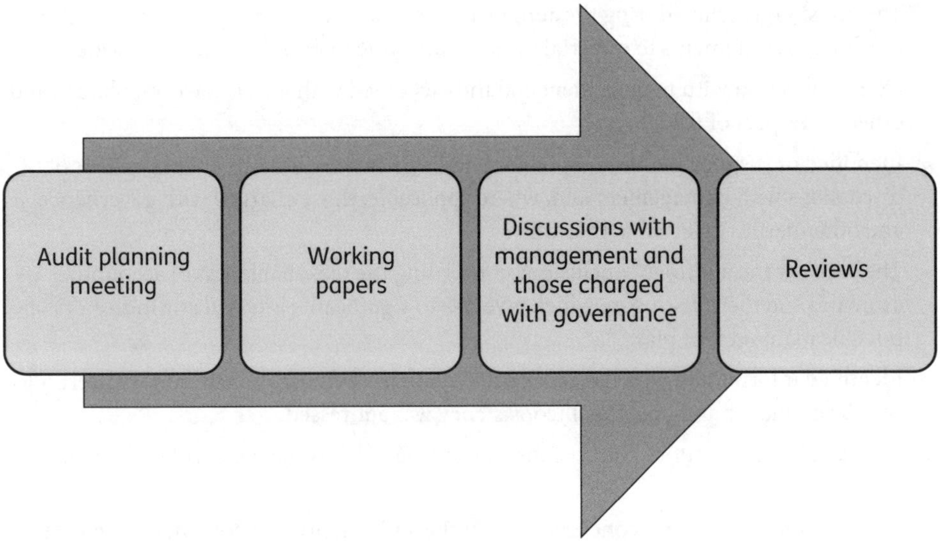

Figure 4.6 Documentation of professional scepticism

- Where additional audit evidence has been obtained to corroborate facts, opinions, or other evidence, a written evaluation of whether the additional evidence does actually corroborate or whether it fails to do so, in which case the further actions to be taken by the auditor should be explained in the working papers.
- Audit conclusions should be very clearly explained—not just a statement of the conclusion that has been reached but an explanation of the thought process leading to the conclusion. It is especially important to detail any matters of judgement.
- If the client has changed their assumptions following a challenge by the auditor this also should be documented.

4.5.4.3 **Notes of meetings with management, ACs, or those charged with governance**

Notes should be comprehensive and include a full account of discussions held on contentious matters and the conclusions reached.

4.5.4.4 **Engagement Quality Review and other reviews**

One of the objectives of an EQR (or other audit file review such as concurring partner review) is that the reviewer should be considering the rigour of the audit. The EQCR itself should challenge the judgement of the audit team as well as evaluating whether the audit has been conducted with an appropriate attitude of professional scepticism. The review documentation should include this as a specific matter and should also conclude as to whether there is sufficient documentation relating to professional scepticism on the audit file.

The following is a non-comprehensive list of examples where appropriate audit documentation should be on file and where the matters and judgements are significant:

- The decisions reached during the audit team discussion concerning the susceptibility of the financial statements to material misstatement due to fraud.

- The decisions reached during the audit team discussion concerning the susceptibility of the financial statements to material misstatement due to fraud with related parties.
- Communication with management and those charged with governance, regulators, and others in respect of fraud.
- Identified or suspected non-compliance with laws and regulations and the results of discussions with management and, where applicable, those charged with governance and other parties external to the entity.
- The basis for the auditor's conclusions concerning the reasonableness of accounting estimates and their disclosure which give rise to significant risks and any indicators of possible management bias.
- Identified information which is inconsistent with the auditor's conclusions concerning a significant matter and how that inconsistency was addressed.
- The basis for the auditor's conclusions concerning the reasonableness of subjective judgements.
- The basis for the auditor's conclusion about the authenticity of a document when the procedures applied by the auditor caused them to believe that the document may not be authentic.

4.5.5 **Professional scepticism and judgement in financial reporting**

It is also particularly important to apply professional scepticism when addressing areas of the financial statements that are complex, significant or contain a high degree of judgement on the part of the client and challenge management's assumptions, for example:

- Accounting estimates, including fair value accounting estimates and related disclosure—particularly:
  - evaluating the reasonableness of the significant assumptions used by management for accounting estimates that give rise to significant risks;
  - determining whether changes in accounting estimates or in the method for making them from the prior period are appropriate in the circumstances; and
  - reviewing the judgements and decisions made by management in the making of accounting estimates to identify whether there are indicators of possible management bias.
- Related party transactions and relationships and remaining alert during the audit for information which may indicate previously unidentified or undisclosed related party relationships or transactions.
- Significant transactions outside the ordinary course of business and evaluating whether the business rationale (or lack thereof) of the transactions suggests that they may have been entered into so as to engage in fraudulent financial reporting or to conceal misappropriation of assets or the reliability of external confirmation requests.
- Consideration of laws and regulations and remaining alert when performing the audit for instances of (suspected) non-compliance which may have a material effect on the financial statements, or that could have a fundamental effect on the operations of the

client causing the business to cease trading or bring into question the entity's ability to continue as a going concern.

- Considering whether the going concern presumption is appropriate in the company's circumstances, such as evaluating management's plans for future actions, and whether the outcome of these plans is likely to improve the situation and whether such plans are feasible.
- If the auditor is auditing significantly unusual or highly complex transactions, they must apply professional scepticism because the nature of such transactions may give rise to a material misstatement of the financial statements and hence will merit heightened attention by the auditor.

Chapter round-up

- Ethics is at the forefront of an auditor's role and the relevant ethical codes must be complied with at all times.
- The fundamental principles relate to integrity, objectivity, confidentiality, professional behaviour, professional competence, and due care.
- There are several threats to the objectivity of an auditor: self-interest threat, self-review threat, familiarity threat, intimidation threat, management, and advocacy threats.
- Where there are threats to independence, objectivity, or integrity, these must be reduced to an acceptable level through the use of appropriate safeguards.
- Safeguards are those which are created by the profession as a whole (e.g. review and monitoring) and those created by the audit firm (e.g. use of separate teams).
- Certain jurisdictions require audit firms to be rotated on a mandatory basis.
- Professional accountants owe a duty of confidentiality to all clients but there are certain situations where this duty of confidentiality is overridden.
- Audit firms must have procedures in place which handle conflicts of interest effectively.
- Auditors of smaller clients may be entitled to some reliefs from complying with some areas of ethical standards.
- Professional scepticism is an attitude required of auditors, meaning to challenge the client when appropriate.
- It can be difficult to document that an audit has been performed with an appropriate level of professional scepticism.

End of chapter case study

In this chapter, we have looked at the fundamental ethical principles which should be applied by auditors in their work. We have seen that auditors are expected to act with integrity at all times, applying their skills and knowledge in a diligent manner, maintaining client confidentiality, and avoiding conflicts of interest. We have considered the specific threats to auditor independence, and seen many examples of how these threats arise and how they can be safeguarded against. We also saw illustrations of real-life situations where even the biggest audit firms have been found to be lacking in their ethical approach, often letting the desire for commercial success override the key principles of auditor integrity and objectivity.

This case study links to the following learning outcomes:

- Define and explain the various threats to ethical behaviour and recommend potential safeguards to minimize threats to integrity, objectivity, and independence to an acceptable level.
- Explain how the auditor may handle conflicts of interest and confidentiality issues.

Scenario

You are an audit manager at Zachary and Partners LLP (ZAC), a large firm of accountants and auditors which offers a range of services to its clients. You are assisting Louisa Griffin, the partner responsible for ethics in ZAC, and several situations have recently been brought to your attention. The partner has asked you to assess each situation in line with the FRC Ethical Standard and other relevant regulations, making recommendations for Louisa to review.

Information with respect to three existing audit clients is given below.

Elijah Ltd

This client operates in the food processing sector, the audit for which is currently taking place. During the audit, Joanne, an audit assistant, found that 5,000 units of a particular food product, which were sent out to shops just after the company's year end, had been given the incorrect 'best before' date on their packaging. The audit assistant mentioned this to the company's operations director, who told Joanne that 'it didn't matter because the products are not dangerous'. However, Joanne made further enquiries and discovered that the food contains ingredients which can become dangerous if the food is not consumed by the best-before date. The audit partner has discussed this with the company's directors, but they are reluctant to make any announcement about the best-before date error, saying that it will destroy the company's reputation. The directors are urging ZAC not to disclose anything about the situation, and have hinted that if any disclosure is made, they will be looking for a new audit provider.

Lily Ltd

Lily Ltd operates in the agriculture sector, growing fruit which is sold to retailers. The directors plan to expand the company's operations by tendering for lucrative contracts to supply major supermarkets. ZAC is also the auditor of Saveaway plc, a national supermarket chain, and the directors of Lily Ltd have asked ZAC to review their tender document prior to it being submitted to Saveaway plc. The directors of Lily Ltd have hinted that should the tender be successful, they will pay a bonus of 5 per cent of the audit fee to ZAC.

Goose Ltd

Goose Ltd is an expanding company, looking to achieve a listing on the London Stock Exchange in two years' time. The company is changing its financial reporting framework from UK accounting standards to International Financial Reporting Standards (IFRS) in preparation for the listing. The company's finance director has requested ZAC to provide training on IFRS to the accounting department at Goose Ltd. The finance director has also requested the audit partner to assist them in developing new accounting policies which are IFRS-compliant.

Required

In respect of the matters outlined above, discuss the ethical and any other professional issues arising, and recommend relevant actions to be taken by ZAC.

Answer

Elijah Ltd

Elijah Ltd has manufactured goods which potentially could cause illness to a consumer, should they consume food which is past its best-before date. The directors have decided not to recall any products, or even make an announcement, which indicates a serious lack of integrity.

Even though the risk of any customers becoming ill has been assessed by the directors as low, it would still be ethically appropriate to announce the problem, allowing customers to return or destroy potentially dangerous goods which are past the best-before date. The directors' claim that the risk to human health is 'low' should be treated with scepticism.

The audit firm should encourage the directors of Elijah to make the error with the best-before date public. The auditors explain the reasons why they should disclose, and hopefully convince the directors that this would be the ethically correct way to proceed.

If the directors still refuse to make a disclosure, ZAC should consider their duty of confidentiality. Ethical codes recognize that information discovered while performing a professional engagement must not be disclosed without proper and specific authority to do so, or unless there is a legal or professional right or duty to disclose. ZAC should consider whether to disclose in order to protect consumers from potential harm, but the firm must be very careful to consider whether it has a right or duty to disclose.

ISA 250 Consideration of Laws and Regulations in an Audit of Financial Statements provides relevant guidance in this situation. Selling food which is potentially dangerous to consume is likely to be a non-compliance with food safety law and regulations, the auditor may have a statutory right or duty to report the situation to the appropriate authority.

ZAC should also consider if there is a necessary disclosure in the public interest. In deciding whether to disclose in the public interest, the auditors should consider the seriousness of the matter (i.e. the likelihood of harm being caused), and the relevant laws and regulations. ZAC may also take legal advice, and ensure that they have knowledge of the facts and circumstances of the situation.

Lily Ltd

This situation creates a conflict of interest for ZAC, which provides the audit to both Lily Ltd and Saveaway plc. A conflict of interest arises because the interests of one client conflicts with acting in the interests of another client. In this case, ZAC may be tempted to help Lily to obtain the contract at a high price, but this is not in the interest of Saveaway, who would prefer to pay a lower price for the goods.

In addition, confidentiality could be a problem. ZAC will have information about Saveaway that could be used to prepare Lily's tender for the supply of goods, which may give Lily an unfair advantage over other companies submitting a tender.

There could also be a threat to objectivity and independence, because ZAC could be perceived as acting in the role of management of Lily, depending on how involved they become with the tender process. There could also be a perception of advocacy, if ZAC is perceived to be promoting the interests of Lily to Saveaway.

In responding to this situation, ZAC should make full disclosure to both Lily and Saveaway, and should only provide advice if both parties acknowledge the situation and give permission for ZAC to proceed. In the event that this disclosure is made and permission received, ZAC should ensure that there is a separation between staff who have worked on either audit and those who provide advice on the tender.

Finally, the 5 per cent audit fee bonus is not allowed. This is a contingent fee, dependent on a favourable outcome of the tender process, and as such is prohibited. Should ZAC provide this service to Lily, it must be a separate engagement, not related to the audit, and with its own fee payable by the client.

Goose Ltd

Providing training to staff at an audit client could create a number of threats to objectivity and independence. One issue that that a self-review threat can arise, especially because the client has also requested the audit firm the assist in developing accounting policies. This is a significant issue, because the audit team will be auditing the policies that have been developed, to some extent, with assistance from the audit firm. A management threat also arises, because determining accounting policies is the responsibility of management, and should not be performed by the auditor.

It would not be possible to reduce this threat to an acceptable level, so the audit firm must not help management to decide on accounting policies. The training could be provided, if it were provided by people who are not involved with the audit of Goose Ltd. However, ZAC may prefer to be cautious in this situation, and not provide the training or the assistance with accounting policies.

Activity solutions

Activity 4.1—Examples of threats to independence and objectivity

For each of the six threats to the fundamental principles, note down at least two other examples of situations which may give rise to the threat.

Table 4.3 Types of threat

Type of threat	Example of a situation which can create the threat
Self-interest	• An investment in the client (e.g. shares or other investments) • Overdue fees - the auditor's objectivity is threatened by wanting to 'keep the client happy' to recover the fees • Contingent fees - which is when an auditor receives an enhanced fee, dependent on the outcome of the engagement e.g. an unmodified audit opinion • The auditor provides a loan to the client • The auditor guarantees a loan to the client • An audit team member is planning on taking up employment with the client • The client provides gifts and/or hospitality to the audit firm
Self-review	• The audit firm is involved in the accounts preparation and taxation work as well as the audit • Other services are provided by the audit firm in addition to the audit, such as a share valuation exercise • Internal audit services are provided by the external auditor • A member of the client's staff joins the audit firm
Familiarity	• There is long association with the audit client • There is a personal relationship between senior officials at the client and staff at the audit firm • The client provides gift and/or hospitality to the audit firm • Sharing staff between the client and the audit firm
Intimidation	• The audit firm is dependent on the fees from the client • An audit engagement partner leaves the firm to join the client • The audit firm becomes involved in litigation involving the client

Type of threat	Example of a situation which can create the threat
Advocacy	• The audit firm represents the client • The audit firm promotes the client • The audit firm enters into negotiations on behalf of the client
Management	• The audit firm performs non audit engagements for the client which involve making decisions which should be made by the client (e.g. tax planning, asset valuation) • The audit firm loans staff to the client, especially senior roles • The audit firm enters into a business arrangement with the client

Activity 4.2—Responding to a client request to provide training

Several audit clients have requested that your audit firm provide technical training on financial reporting and tax issues. This is not a service that your firm wishes to provide, and it has referred its audit clients to a training firm, which will be paying a referral fee of 20 per cent of the cost of the training to your audit firm.

Consider the ethical threats present, and how the audit firm should respond.

A self-interest threat can arise when referral fees are received, as the audit firm gains a financial benefit for each audit client which receives training from the training firm. Without knowing the number of audit clients who take up the training and how much the training costs, it is difficult to evaluate the significance of the threat.

Assuming that the self-interest threat is not significant, the referrals and payments can continue, provided that safeguards are put in place. Safeguards could include:

- Disclosing to the audit clients that a referral fee arrangement exists, and the details of the arrangement.
- Receiving confirmation from the audit clients that they are aware of the referral arrangement.

Activity 4.3—Responding to a client request regarding the audit team

The finance director of Magpie Ltd has requested that a certain audit senior, Rita Scott, be assigned to the audit team. Rita has not previously been assigned to the audit of Magpie Ltd. On further investigation, it transpired that Rita Scott is the sister of Magpie Ltd's financial controller.

Consider the ethical threats present, and how the audit firm should respond.

Rita is a relative of the financial controller of the audit client. A family or personal relationship between a member of the audit team, and a director or employee of the audit client can create a number of threats to objectivity and independence:

- Familiarity—Rita may fail to approach the audit with professional scepticism and be willing to overlook any errors in the accounts which had been caused by the financial controller.
- Intimidation—the financial controller may be able to exert influence on Rita because of their relationship.

The degree of threat depends on the level of seniority of the close family member. In this case, Rita is related to the financial controller, who is clearly in an influential position.

The most appropriate course of action is for Rita not to take part in the audit of Magpie Ltd.

Allocation of staff to an audit team should be the decision of the audit firm, and should not be influenced by the wishes of the client.

Activity 4.4—Threats caused by provision of non-audit services

For each of the types of threat to independence, explain how the threat can arise, should an audit provider also perform non-audit services for their audit client.

Self-interest threat—the fees charged for performing non-audit services can be very high and create a fee dependence on the client. This is particularly the case for specialist work for which a high fee can be charged (e.g. mergers and acquisitions and corporate finance advisory services).

Self-review threat—depending on the type of non-audit engagement, the audit work might involve obtaining evidence about the subject matter of the engagement. This may impact the quality of evidence obtained in relation to the subject matter and impair the auditor's professional scepticism. For example, if the audit firm was engaged to value assets such as financial instruments, when these are subject to audit, the audit team may over-rely on the figures, fail to challenge how the financial instruments were valued and fail to obtain sufficient and appropriate audit evidence.

Familiarity threat—it can be argued that the more work an audit firm performs for a client, the closer the relationship that develops between the audit firm and the staff at the client. This can impair the quality of the audit, as the auditor may become 'too trusting' of the client and fail to exercise appropriate professional scepticism.

Intimidation threat—the behaviour of the auditor can be influenced by the provision of non-audit services. For example, if the client threatens to take lucrative non-audit work away from the auditor and appoint a different firm unless the auditor acts in a certain way, e.g. overlooks errors or agrees with management judgements.

Advocacy threat—some non-audit services will lead to the audit firm taking a position of advocacy in respect of the client, for example, if performing litigation work and arguing in support of the client in a legal case.

Management—providing some non-audit services will lead to the auditor making management decisions (e.g. if performing tax planning work). The more non-audit services that are provided, the more the line is blurred between the auditor and the management of the company.

Activity 4.5—Fee dependence

While monitoring levels of fees generated by its clients, an audit manager realizes that one client, a non-listed company, is likely to generate 16 per cent of the audit firm's income this year. The audit firm provides a range of services to this client.

What steps could the audit firm take to reduce the fee dependence on this client?

- The audit firm could resign from some of the services provided to this client, to reduce the proportion of the audit firm's income which it receives from the client.
- Alternatively, the audit firm could increase its client base to reduce dependence on this one client.
- The firm can implement safeguards which could reduce the threat to an acceptable level, including performing external quality reviews on the audit and other services provided.

Activity 4.6—Confidential information

What type of confidential information do you think an auditor is likely to come across while conducting an audit?

- payroll and directors' remuneration;
- details of legal claims involving the client company;
- commercially sensitive information about new products in development, market research, etc.;
- business reorganizations (e.g. selling off part of the business), which may impact on the share price;
- takeover bids planned by the client company;
- results of regulatory inspections or monitoring visits.

5 Quality Management and Auditor Liability

Introduction

Quality management is at the heart of any audit firm and has become even more important over recent years due to the attempts by regulators to restore confidence in the auditing profession. Recent high-profile corporate scandals, such as Carillion and Patisserie Valerie, have rocked the auditing profession and many stakeholders have been questioning the value of audit.

Carrying out a high-quality audit is important. Not only does it ensure that the financial statements can be relied upon, but it also ensures that the firm complies with professional standards and legal and regulatory requirements. Auditing is a regulated profession, and professional bodies and regulators are keen to ensure that standards are maintained. To that end, audit firms are subject to scrutiny by professional bodies and the Financial Reporting Council (FRC) to ensure that audits are carried out in accordance with ISAs and other regulatory and legislative requirements. Where it is found that the firm is falling short of the standards, the firm can expect to receive sanctions which can involve follow-up visits to ensure any deficiencies noted in the inspection have been addressed to more serious sanctions such as withdrawal of auditing practising certificates and expulsion from membership of a professional body.

There are three specific standards which address quality management, although there is overlap with other ISAs:

- ISQM 1 *Quality Management for Firms that Perform Audits or Reviews of Financial Statements, or Other Assurance or Related Services Engagements*;
- ISQM 2 *Engagement Quality Reviews*; and
- ISA 220 *Quality Management for an Audit of Financial Statements*

The three standards above deal with quality management in slightly different ways.

Remember, all firms which issue assurance reports to clients (whether they are auditor's reports or other assurance reports) are exposed to some form of risk. Audit itself has

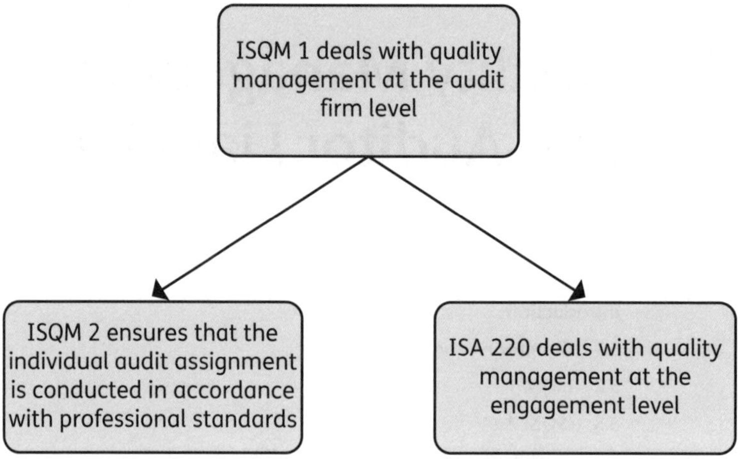

Figure 5.1 Audit quality standards

inherent limitations (e.g. reliance on internal controls, management representations and the use of sampling) which may result in the expression of an incorrect opinion. Even where an audit has been carried out in accordance with the ISAs and other requirements, there will always be an element of audit risk present because of the inherent limitations. The firm must mitigate these risks through a comprehensive programme of quality management and compliance with ISQMs 1 and 2 and ISA 220 should enable that.

Despite audit firms' efforts to enhance audit quality, it is perhaps inevitable that things will go wrong in some audits. There have been many cases of audit firms being investigated by the professional and regulatory bodies and sometimes legal action is taken against firms, the aim of which is to determine whether a financial loss has been suffered as a result of auditor negligence. Audit firms can face significant financial penalties and reputational damage as a result of investigations or court cases. In this chapter, we will consider how audit firms can seek to manage their risk exposure and protect themselves by reducing potential liabilities which could arise as a result of poor-quality auditing.

Learning outcomes

- Explain the importance of quality in the context of auditing and discuss the factors which may cause poor-quality auditing.
- Discuss and apply the requirements for a system of quality management which should be in place at audit firm level.
- Explain the importance of engagement quality reviews and evaluate whether appropriate reviews have taken place.
- Evaluate quality management deficiencies and provide recommendations to allow compliance with quality management standards.
- Describe the auditor's liability in both criminal and civil law and explain how the auditor's liability may be limited.

5.1 Monitoring audit quality

Auditing is a regulated profession in most jurisdictions and the work of auditors is subject to scrutiny by regulators. In the UK, for example, the FRC monitors the work of audit firms which act for public interest entities. Professional bodies such as the Institute of Chartered Accountants in England and Wales and Association of Chartered Certified Accountants (ACCA) monitor the work of audit firms which act for non-public interest entities.

Activity 5.1 Audit quality

Why should audit firms be concerned about the quality of the audits they perform?

In recent years, there have been several high-profile corporate collapses which have triggered investigations into the audit work which took place prior to the scandal. These investigations will often look back over more than one audit to ascertain whether audit work identified issues leading up to the collapse, or whether the audit was deficient. Unfortunately, nowadays it is not unusual to hear about a firm being on the receiving end of a substantial fine for carrying out deficient audit work. Sanctions do not just stop at fines either; the individual audit engagement partners can, in more serious situations, be expelled from the profession by regulators or face personal financial penalties. It is not just audit partners who face sanctions when audit quality is not good enough—even junior members of an audit team can come under investigation and can be financially punished or reprimanded.

Auditing in practice 5.1 Annual Enforcement Review

Every year the FRC's Enforcement Division investigates cases which may have arisen from complaints made to the FRC, referrals from other FRC teams, audit firms, professional bodies, or from information obtained from whistle-blowers. Outcomes of the investigations can include constructive engagement, which is when the FRC attempts to work with the audit firm to improve their practice. Alternatively, the FRC can impose penalties including unlimited fines, reprimands, and exclusion of individuals from membership of a professional body.

From 2021 to 2022, twenty-four cases were resolved through constructive engagement. Cases which result in constructive engagement tend to be those where issues involved have not had a significant impact on stakeholders. Constructive engagement can mean requiring an audit firm to provide further training for staff, updating its audit methodology, or introducing more reviews on high-risk audits.

From 2021 to 2022, thirteen investigations resulted in sanctions being imposed on audit firms and individuals. As an example, in the investigation into the audit of Patisserie Valerie by Grant Thornton (GT), it was found that the audits for three consecutive years were deficient in relation to four areas–revenue, cash, journals, and non-current assets. According to the FRC's report on this investigation, there were serious lapses in professional judgement, a failure to exercise professional scepticism, failure to obtain sufficient appropriate audit evidence, and/or to prepare sufficient audit documentation. The sanctions imposed on GT were as follows:

- £4 million fine (reduced to £2.34 million for admissions and early settlement);
- severe reprimand;
- GT to perform root-cause analysis and to report findings to the FRC;

- a review of the audit firm's culture;
- additional monitoring of audit work; and
- The audit partner received a fine of £150,000 (reduced to £87,750 for admissions and early settlement) and a three-year prohibition on performing statutory audit work.[1]

The FRC's Annual Enforcement report for the year to March 2022 showed a record level of financial penalties imposed by the FRC, a total of £46.5 million.[2] In Chapter 2, when we considered the regulatory framework of auditing, we discussed the fact that the FRC has, in the past, been called a 'toothless regulator' and been accused of not being aggressive enough in its actions against audit firms who have got it wrong. The record level of penalties seen in 2022 can be seen as a response to these accusations. In other words, the FRC is acting more aggressively when an audit firm's quality of work is not good enough.

Monitoring audit quality is important because it helps to identify deficiencies in audit work which may need to be remedied. Professional bodies and regulators publish reports on their monitoring activities which can be used by other firms as a means of identifying deficiencies within their own firms that may need remedial action taken. It is hoped that making the results of the FRC's audit quality inspections public makes the audit firms more accountable for their actions. However, despite many years of less than favourable results, there is still room for improvement in audit quality.

In 2022, the FRC Chief Executive Sir Jon Thompson said:

> While it is encouraging to see some improvement in audit quality at the largest audit firms, consistent, long-term improvement is still required across the market. We will monitor closely the potentially negative impact on the public interest that the de-risking by firms of challenging audits may have on audit quality. The FRC will continue to build on our assertive supervisory approach to ensure firms are consistently delivering high quality audit which will drive increased choice and resilience in the market over time.[3]

Auditing in practice 5.2 *Annual Audit Quality Inspection Results for 2020/21*

On 23 July 2022, the FRC issued their *Annual Audit Quality Inspection Results for 2020/21*. The FRC reviewed 103 audits. Out of these, 29 per cent (2019/20: 33 per cent) required improvement or significant improvement and 71 per cent (2019/20: 67 per cent) were assessed to be of a good standard or requiring only limited improvement.[4]

The FRC inspected seven firms as follows.

BDO

The individual findings of the audits performed by BDO include the following:

- Urgently improve the quality of the firm's audit of revenue.

[1] https://www.frc.org.uk/news-and-events/news/2021/09/sanctions-against-grant-thornton-uk-llp-and-david-newstead/ (accessed 2 January 2024).

[2] https://www.frc.org.uk/news-and-events/news/2022/07/frc-reports-record-cases-resolved-and-record-financial-sanctions-of-465m/ (accessed 2 January 2024).

[3] FRC, 'FRC publishes latest audit quality review results', 2022 <https://www.frc.org.uk/news-and-events/news/2022/07/frc-publishes-latest-audit-quality-review-results/> (accessed 2 January 2024).

[4] https://www.frc.org.uk/news-and-events/news/2021/07/frc-annual-audit-quality-inspection-results-202021/ (accessed 2 January 2024).

- Improve audit teams' understanding and assessment of significant and presumed fraud risks, together with required audit response.
- Improve, as a matter of urgency, the challenge and testing of estimates and assumptions in key areas of judgement.
- Strengthen the audit work performed over the existence and valuation of assets within defined benefit pension balances.
- Implement enhancements to improve audit quality in response to other issues driving lower audit quality assessments.

Deloitte

- Improve the evaluation and challenge of management's key assumptions of impairment assessments of goodwill and other assets.
- Enhance the consistency of group audit team's oversight of component audit teams.
- Strengthen the effectiveness and consistency of the testing of revenue.

EY

- Enhance the valuation or challenge of aspects of management's impairment and going concern assessments.
- Strengthen the testing or evidence over aspects of the assessment of the expected credit loss allowance.
- Enhance the evidence and justification for the recoverability of deferred tax assets.

Grant Thornton

- Improve the challenge and corroboration of key judgements and estimates.

KPMG

- Urgently and comprehensively address the continuing deficiencies in the quality of audit work on banks and similar entities.
- Improve the quality of the firm's audit work on certain areas of revenue.
- Enhance the evaluation and challenge of management's impairment assessment for tangible and intangible non-current assets.
- Implement enhancements to improve audit quality in response to other issues driving lower audit quality assessments.

Mazars

- Improve the challenge of management's impairment assessments in relation to goodwill and other assets.
- Strengthen the quality and effectiveness of audit work on revenue.
- Enhance the oversight of component audit teams by the group auditor.
- Take further steps to strengthen the quality of audit work on areas of judgement, including the expected credit loss model.

PwC

- Improve the evaluation of aspects of management's impairment and going concern assessments.
- Enhance the testing for the valuation of certain pension assets.
- Improve the audit procedures for the residual journal population in response to the risk of management override.

5.2 **ISQM 1**

ISQM 1 became effective on 15 December 2022 and replaced ISQC 1 Quality Control for Firms that Perform Audits and Reviews of Financial Statements, and Other Assurance and Related Services Engagements.

5.2.1 **Fundamental principles**

The fundamental principle is that ISQM 1 focuses on quality **management**; whereas previous ISQC 1 focused on quality **control**. ISQM 1 deals with an audit firm's responsibility for having a system of quality management (SOQM). The SOQM creates an environment that enables and supports engagement teams in performing consistently high-quality engagements.

ISQM 1 brought changes to the way in which audit firms ensure a sound system of quality management as follows:

- A more proactive and tailored approach to managing quality which is focused on achieving quality objectives by identifying risks to those objectives and developing responses to those risks.
- Requirements to address the firm's governance and leadership, including increased leadership responsibilities.
- Requirements which modernize the standard and reflect factors that affect the firm's environment, including requirements to address technology, networks, and the use of external service providers.
- Requirements which address information and communication, including communication with external parties.
- Requirements for monitoring and remediation to promote more proactive monitoring of the system of quality management as a whole and effective and timely remediation of deficiencies.

Auditing in practice 5.3 Development of the ISQMs

Three new auditing standards relating to quality of audit work became effective in December 2022. The IAASB announced back in 2014 that it intended to focus on enhancing audit quality as a main strategic objective. At this time, the IAASB issued 'A Framework for Audit Quality: Key Elements that Create an Environment for Audit Quality', which outlined a holistic approach to support audit quality. The Framework encouraged audit firms to enter into an active dialogue with other stakeholders in the audit process including the preparers of the financial statements and audit committees to discuss mechanisms of improving audit quality.

In 2016, the IAASB began its project to develop the ISQMs. The main objective of the project was to enhance audit quality through improvements in quality management at the audit firm and audit engagement level. The project also focused on group audit quality, in particular in strengthening and clarifying the audit procedures and communications necessary when working with other audit firms.

After completing a series of consultations and issuing a proposed ISQM for comment, the IAASB, issued the new audit quality standards in 2020. At the time, the Chair of the IAASB, Tom Seidenstein made the following comments:

> The passage of our three Quality Management standards is the culmination of our response to the changing environment, the challenges of the effectiveness of our pre-existing quality control standards, and growing market participant needs. The resulting suite of standards are aimed at a more robust System of Quality Management for firms using the IAASB's standards, and marks an evolution from a traditional, more linear approach to quality control.
>
> The new and revised standards facilitate an integrated and iterative process to manage the quality for the firm's engagements where the quality standards are applicable. The standards are aimed at comprehensively and actively managing risks to quality, through greater accountability, improved focus on leadership and culture, and continuous improvement through a required monitoring and remediation feedback loop. Moving from binary, compliance-based processes to a much more proactive, dynamic, risk-based quality management approach is crucial to the audit profession staying a step ahead.[5]

The ISQMs have been developed to improve audit quality, which in turn should enhance the credibility of audit reports and the financial reporting process. For audit firms, adherence to some of the requirements can be challenging, but the IAASB has produced detailed implementation resources to support firms.

5.2.2 **Establishing quality objectives**

According to ISQM 1:

> The objective of the firm is to design, implement and operate a system of quality management for audits or reviews of financial statements, or other assurance or related services engagements performed by the firm, that provides the firm with reasonable assurance that:
>
> (a) The firm and its personnel fulfil their responsibilities in accordance with professional standards and applicable legal and regulatory requirements, and conduct engagements with such standards and requirements; and
>
> (b) Engagement reports issued by the firm or engagement partners are appropriate in the circumstances.[6]

It might be helpful to visualize the objectives.

These objectives are high-level and, consequently, ISQM 1 contains specific quality objectives for eight specified components of the firm's system of quality management so that it is clear what outcomes need to be achieved by the firm to have an effective system of quality management.

[5] IFAC, 'With new standards in place, proactive quality management will underpin the next era of audit transformation', 2020 <https://www.ifac.org/knowledge-gateway/supporting-international-standards/discussion/new-standards-place-proactive-quality-management-will-underpin-next-era-audit-transformation#:~:text=Theper cent20newper cent20requirementsper cent20reinforceper cent20firm,swiftper cent20remediationper cent20of> (accessed 2 January 2024).

[6] International Auditing and Assurance Standards Board, 'ISQM 1', 2020, para 14 <https://www.ifac.org/_flysystem/azure-private/publications/files/IAASB-Quality-Management-ISQM-1-Quality-Management-for-Firms.pdf> (accessed 17 January 2024).

Objective of the firm

To design, implement, and operate a SOQM

→

Objective of the SOQM

To provide the firm with reasonable assurance that:

1. The firm and its personnel fulfill their responsibilities in accordance with professional standards and applicable legal and regulatory requirements, and conduct engagements in accordance with such standards and requirements.

2. Engagement reports issued by the firm or engagement partners are appropriate in the circumstances.

Figure 5.2 Objectives of ISQM 1

The quality objectives in each component help the firm in properly identifying and assessing quality risks, because the quality objectives focus the firm on specifically what needs to be achieved and what could go wrong in achieving those quality objectives.

Audit firms must establish the quality objectives specific to each component. However, ISQM 1 recognizes situations when a quality objective, or an aspect thereof, may not be relevant to the firm because of the nature and circumstances of the firm or its engagements. It is important to bear in mind that there is no 'one-size-fits-all' approach to establishing quality objectives and the way this is achieved will vary from firm to firm. Essentially, it is established by the nature and circumstances of the firm, including how the firm is structured and organized. Scalability is an important feature of ISQM 1, with recognition that the SOQM will be very different in a smaller audit practice compared with a large, global audit firm.

ISQM 1 requires the audit firm to:

The key point is that the approach to audit quality management is based on a risk assessment process. So, the audit firm needs to establish a process which tailors the SOQM to the audit firm's individual circumstances. This risk assessment process will be very different in a smaller audit firm with no listed company clients compared to a large audit firm with a more high-profile client base.

Auditing scenario 5.1 A sole practitioner with two audit clients

Sandeep is a sole practitioner and has two audit clients which are private companies. Sandeep has been considering how the introduction of ISQM 1 is going to affect their practice and is concerned about the following requirement in ISQM 1, para 31(b):

> The firm shall establish the following quality objectives that address the performance of quality engagements:

(b) The nature, timing and extent of direction and supervision of engagement teams and review of the work performed is appropriate based on the nature and circumstances of the engagements and the resources assigned or made available to the engagement teams, and the work performed by less experienced team members is directed, supervised and reviewed by more experienced engagement team members.

Sandeep is concerned that because they are a sole practitioner, they will not be able to fully comply with this requirement.

ISQM 1 takes a risk-based approach and hence there may be situations when a quality objective, or part thereof, is not relevant to an audit firm due to the nature and circumstances of the firm and/or the engagement. In this example, ISQM, para 31(b) which addresses direction and supervision is likely to be irrelevant to a sole practitioner. Review can be performed by engaging an external party to perform reviews when this is considered necessary.

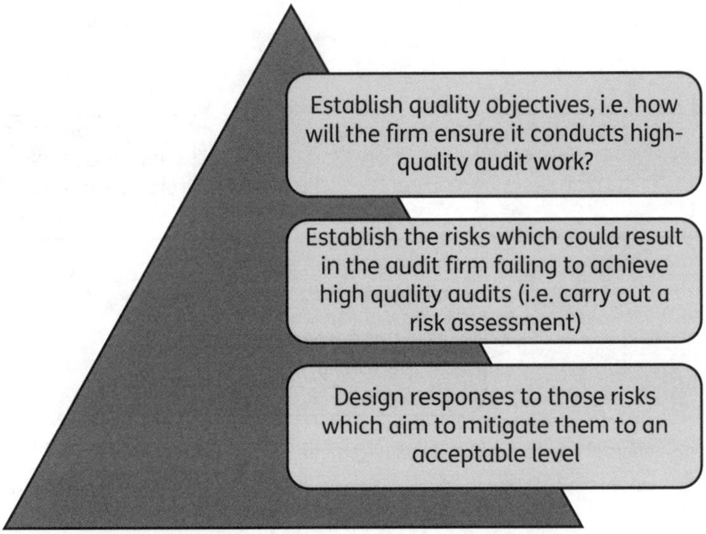

Figure 5.3 Overall requirements of ISQM 1

5.2.3 **Components of a system of quality management**

ISQM 1 requires quality objectives to be set, and the SOQM is effective when those objectives have been met. ISQM 1 provides a framework containing eight components, quality objectives must be set for each component.

5.2.3.1 **The firm's risk assessment process**

The firm must follow a risk-based approach in applying ISQM 1 which focuses on the risks that may arise to quality management given the nature and circumstances of the firm and the engagements it performs. There is no prescribed method of carrying out a risk assessment, and the way in which a firm identifies and assesses quality risks will vary from firm to

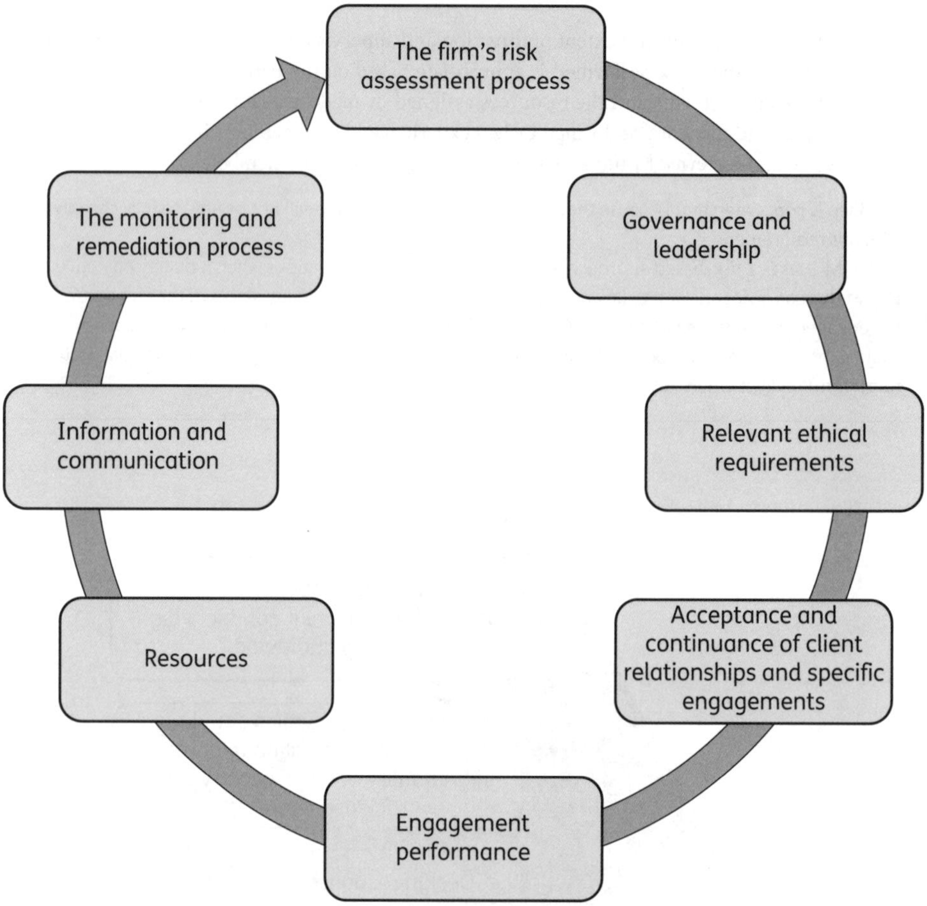

Figure 5.4 Components of a system of quality management

firm. Matters that may be considered in determining the risks specific to an individual audit firm could include the nature of technology involved in the firm's audit methodology, the firm's use of external providers, and the nature of the client portfolio. Larger audit firms will carry out a more rigorous risk assessment on a regular basis, whereas a smaller firm may be able to carry out annual risk assessments.

5.2.3.2 **Governance and leadership**

Governance and leadership establish the environment in which the SOQM operates. Governance and leadership are seen as being of paramount importance to quality management. It is about the culture of the audit firm and its leadership, which should set the 'tone from the top' and hence is the way in which the firm embeds an appropriate culture, approach to ethics and self-regulation. Essentially, governance and leadership are the foundation for the framework under which the firm makes decisions. The chief executive or managing partner is ultimately responsible for the audit firm's SOQM, and they must demonstrate commitment to quality and ethics, an attitude which should permeate through the audit firm.

5.2.3.3 **Relevant ethical requirements**

All auditors must adhere to the requirements and principles of the relevant ethical code, as we saw in Chapter 4. This element of SOQM is about ensuring that personnel understand the regulatory ethical requirements and also any specific or additional requirements set by the audit firm, and how to fulfil their responsibilities in respect of ethics.

> **Auditing scenario 5.2** SOQM and ethical requirements
>
> Windsor Associates, an audit firm, has a firm-wide policy which prohibits the acceptance of gifts and hospitality from clients. This policy is more specific than the requirement of the FRC Ethical Standard, which allows the acceptance of goods and hospitality that are 'trivial' in value. Windsor Associates has communicated its policy to all staff, and the policy is included in a training programme which all staff complete on an annual basis. The firm monitors the staff training as a way to ensure that the requirements are understood.

The audit firm is only responsible for the relevant ethical requirements which apply to others in the context of the firm and the firm's engagements. Other professionals (for example, valuation agents and lawyers) are subject to other ethical requirements which do not apply to the firm.

An example of relevant ethical requirements would be in respect of an expert carrying out a valuation of complex financial instruments for an audit client. The audit firm is not responsible for the expert's fulfilment of the ethical requirements of their own professional body. This is the responsibility of the expert themselves. The audit firm is, however, responsible for ensuring that the auditor's expert understands the confidentiality provisions in the relevant code of ethics, for example, the expert must treat the client's information as confidential.

5.2.3.4 **Acceptance and continuance of client relationships and specific engagements**

This section of ISQM 1 includes principles-based requirements to establish quality objectives that address the acceptance and continuance of client relationships and specific engagements. The overarching focus is on the firm's judgements in determining whether, or not, to accept or continue the client relationship of specific engagement. The SOQM should ensure that the audit firm's commercial considerations do not lead to inappropriate decisions regarding the acceptance or continuance of a client engagement.

5.2.3.5 **Engagement performance**

There are principles-based requirements in ISQM 1 which require the audit firm to establish quality objectives that address engagement performance. These include consultation and addressing the assembly, maintenance, and retention of engagement documentation.

There should also be quality objectives in respect of the exercising of appropriate professional judgement and professional scepticism, and how differences of opinion are resolved.

Engagement teams must understand their responsibilities for ensuring a quality audit. Less experienced engagement team members should be appropriately supervised and reviewed. In addition, the audit engagement partner is responsible for achieving quality on an engagement and ISQM 1 specifically states that one quality objective must relate to the audit partner being sufficiently and appropriately involved throughout the engagement.

5.2.3.6 **Resources**

The firm must establish quality objectives which address the need for technological and intellectual resources (for example the firm's audit methodology or other policies and procedures) to enable the operation of the system of quality management and performance of engagements.

There must be competent and capable staff involved in ensuring the efficient operation of the firm's SOQM and the firm must ensure only competent and capable staff are involved in performing activities within the system of quality management. Competence is described as:

> the ability of the individual to perform a role and goes beyond knowledge of principles, standards, concepts, facts, and procedures; it is the integration and application of technical competence, professional skills, and professional ethics, values and attitudes. Competence can be developed through a variety of methods, including professional education, continuing professional development, training, work experience or coaching of less experienced engagement team members by more experienced engagement team members.[7]

It is imperative that an audit firm hires, develops, and retains personnel with the right level of competence, in order to support the performance of high-quality audits.

Activity 5.2 Developing capabilities and competence

How can audit firms ensure that they hire, develop, and retain personnel with the right level of competence and capabilities?

A key point is that 'engagement team members are assigned to each engagement, including an engagement partner, who have appropriate competence and capabilities, including being given sufficient time, to consistently perform quality engagements'.[8] This means that not only must the audit firm employ high calibre personnel—they must be appropriately assigned to audit teams.

There is a requirement that addresses service providers. ISQM 1 requires that resources from service providers are appropriate for use in the system of quality management and performance of engagements.

[7] Ibid., para A88. [8] Ibid., para 32(d).

5.2.3.7 **Information and communication**

This was a new component introduced into ISQM 1. There are requirements for obtaining, generating, or using information and communication information to enable the design, implementation, and operation of the firm's system of quality management. For example, information and communication could relate to the firm's policy on ethics, keeping a register of training undertaken by individuals, communication between an audit team and an external expert or component auditor.

5.2.3.8 **The monitoring and remediation process**

ISQM 1 requires that 'the firm shall design and perform monitoring activities to provide a basis for the identification of deficiencies'.[9]

The monitoring and remediation process must be designed in such a way that it allows the firm to take appropriate actions to respond to identified deficiencies, such that those deficiencies are rectified in a timely manner and do not reoccur. It should be emphasized that identifying and remediating deficiencies is constructive and is an essential component of an effective system of quality management. Monitoring and remediation should be a continual cycle, resulting in improvements to audit quality.

Auditing scenario 5.3 Monitoring within the SOQM

Westminster LLP is an audit firm which has identified that due to time pressure on senior staff, there is a quality risk in relation to how much time audit partners spend on audit engagements. To mitigate this risk, and to provide monitoring of the risk, Westminster LLP has established a tool within the software used by the firm which tracks how much time each partner logs in respect of working on each client. The tool also raises alerts at particular points, for example, if an audit partner has not logged any time to a client during the weeks designated for audit completion and file review. Westminster LLP can monitor the output of the tool including the alerts which have been raised, to follow up with the audit partners concerned.

ISQM 1 requires that the inspection of completed engagements is part of the firm's monitoring activities. The inspections should be designed to evaluate whether policies or procedures or other aspects of the SOQM are designed, implemented, and operating in the manner intended. Not all audits need to be inspected, and the selection of engagements for inspection should be based on the risks associated with the engagements. However, ISQM 1 does require that an engagement quality review is performed on:

- Audits of financial statements of listed entities;
- Audits or other engagements for which an engagement quality review is required by law or regulation; and
- Audits or other engagements for which the firm determines that an engagement quality review is an appropriate response to address one or more quality risk(s).[10]

[9] Ibid., para 36. [10] Ibid., para 34(f).

Activity 5.3 Engagement inspections

What factors do you think should be considered in determining which completed audit engagements should be inspected?

ISQM 1 does not specify who is required to perform the monitoring activities. However, it is required that the audit firm needs to have policies or procedures dealing with the competence and capabilities (including sufficient time) of the individuals performing the activities, and the objectivity of the individuals. It further specifies that for inspections of engagements, the individual cannot be an engagement team member or the engagement quality reviewer of the engagement.

When monitoring activities, including inspections of completed engagements identifies deficiencies, the firm is required to evaluate the severity and pervasiveness of the deficiencies. This evaluation should include a root cause analysis (RCA) and an evaluation of the impact of the deficiencies on the SOQM. Prior to it becoming a requirement of ISQM 1, RCA was becoming more prevalent in the auditing profession as a response to poor-quality auditing identified in regulatory and professional body reviews. RCA means employing techniques to identify the cause of an issue, in this case, deficiencies in audit quality. Identifying the cause of a problem, and resolving the fundamental problem, is more effective than just dealing with the symptoms.

Auditing in practice 5.4 RCA

In 2016, the FRC published a review entitled 'Audit Quality Thematic Review—Root Cause Analysis', which included the findings of an FRC review of how the big audit firms carry out RCA. The thematic review defines RCA as, 'a process for identifying the causes of problems or events in order to prevent them from recurring. It is based on the idea that effective management requires more than putting out fires for problems that develop, but finding a way to prevent them. RCA can also be a means of identifying good practice as part of continuous improvement'.[11]

Prior to the FRC's report, global bodies including the International Forum of Independent Auditors (IFIAR) and the European Audit Inspection Group (EAIG) had also commented on the benefits of RCA for audit firms looking to identify and respond to issues with audit quality.

In their review of how audit firms carry out RCA, the FRC observed that practices varied greatly between the audit firms, but that in all firms one feature of the RCA process was interviews with audit partners and sometimes audit managers. The FRC comments that interviews are a good source of information about audit quality, because the audit team members will be able to provide insight into what went wrong during an audit, and suggest the reasons. The FRC recommends that interviews should involve not just audit partners and managers; more junior members of the team should also be able to express their opinions.

In addition, most firms use Audit Quality Measures (AQMs) to measure audit performance, for example an AQM to measure the time spent by audit partners or managers on an audit.

[11] FRC, 'Audit quality thematic review—Root cause analysis', 2016 <https://media.frc.org.uk/documents/Audit_Quality_Thematic_Review_Root_Cause_Analysis.pdf> (accessed 17 January 2024).

The FRC found that most of the root causes for deficiencies in audit quality relate to:

- audit team members' lack of knowledge or skill (e.g. not understanding the client's business);
- inappropriate behaviours of audit team members (e.g. lack of professional scepticism);
- lack of care in audit work performed (e.g. not preparing sufficiently detailed audit conclusions);
- lack of direction by senior members of the audit team (e.g. lack of review of working papers);
- problems with resourcing or managing the audit (e.g. time pressure, too few staff);
- lack of clarity in guidance (e.g. relating to the firm's audit methodology).

In response to these root causes identified, the firms provided more training to staff and issued better guidance and communications on audit methodology. Other responses included improving project (i.e. audit) management, enhancing audit methodology, review of resourcing and providing better support to new members of the audit firm.

5.2.4 **Evaluating and documenting the SOQM**

ISQM1 requires that the SOQM must be evaluated at least annually, by the individual(s) who are ultimately responsible for it. This evaluation must conclude on the following:

- The system of quality management provides the firm with reasonable assurance that the objectives of the system of quality management are being achieved.
- Except for matters related to identified deficiencies that have a severe but not pervasive effect on the design, implementation, and operation of the system of quality management, the system of quality management provides the firm with reasonable assurance that the objectives of the system of quality management are being achieved; or
- The system of quality management does not provide the firm with reasonable assurance that the objectives of the system of quality management are being achieved.[12]

If the conclusion is that there is reasonable assurance that the objectives of the SOQM are not being achieved, the firm must take prompt and appropriate action and ensure that appropriate communication is made within the firm and to relevant external parties.

Auditing scenario 5.4 Evaluation of deficiencies in the SOQM

Melody LLP is a large audit firm with twelve offices across the UK. The partner responsible for the firm's SOQM identifies that in the office located in Birmingham there have been many instances of non-compliance with the firm's audit methodology. The partner performs RCA and identifies that the culture in this office is not appropriate because commercial considerations are prioritized over audit quality; the partners tolerate and even encourage non-compliance if it improves the profitability of the engagements performed. The Birmingham office performs the audit of several of Melody LLP's largest and high-risk clients, including a listed group of companies, which involves one other audit firm which performs the audit on a subsidiary of the group.

[12] International Auditing and Assurance Standards Board, 'ISQM 1', 2020, para 54.

In accordance with ISQM 1, the partner needs to determine whether this is a severe and pervasive deficiency. This is, of course, a matter of judgement. In this case, let's assume that the partner concludes that it is a severe deficiency because it stems from the attitude and behaviour of senior partners in the firm, and it is pervasive because this office works on the firm's largest and highest risk audits.

The partner responsible for SOQM must now take prompt action which should include remedial actions to resolve the deficiencies identified, for example, training staff on the importance of prioritizing audit quality over commercial considerations. There should also be appropriate communications within the firm, for example, to highlight the audit quality deficiencies identified, and communications may potentially be necessary with the other audit firm that is involved in the group audit performed by the Birmingham office.

ISQM 1 requires specific documentation of the SOQM including documentation relating to the firm's quality objectives and quality risks, evidence of monitoring activities, evaluation of findings, remedial actions, and communications.

According to the implementation guide which supports ISQM 1, documentation of the SOQM is important because:

- It helps personnel understand the SOQM and what is expected of them, so that they are able to perform engagements, and fulfil their roles and responsibilities with respect to the firm's SOQM.
- It enables the responses to be implemented and operated in the manner that the firm intended.
- It helps the firm retain organizational knowledge and the basis for why decisions related to the SOQM were made.
- It helps the firm monitor the SOQM, and provides information so that leadership is able to evaluate and conclude on the SOQM.
- It establishes accountability for the firm by evidencing that the firm has designed, implemented and operated a SOQM in accordance with ISQM 1 and applicable legal and regulatory requirements.
- It helps external oversight authorities in fulfilling their duties in inspecting the firm's SOQM, which is an important element to the financial reporting ecosystem. The firm's SOQM may change and evolve over time.[13]

Auditing in practice 5.5 Audit Firm Governance Code

The FRC published the Audit Firm Governance Code (AFGC) in 2016 and updated it in 2022. The Code is intended to be used by the larger audit firms, which audit Public Interest Entities. It works in a similar way to the UK Corporate Governance Code, which we looked at in Chapter 3, in that it operates on a 'comply or explain' basis. Audit firms should comply with the AFGC, or explain why they have not done so.

[13] International Auditing and Assurance Standards Board, 'ISQM 1: First time implementation guide', 2021.

The reason for introducing the AFGC is because one of its stated principal objectives is to promote audit quality. The provisions of the AFGC relate to leadership of the audit firm, people, values, behaviour, operations, and resilience. It also requires independent non-executives to be appointed, who should observe, challenge and influence decision-making in the audit firm.

When an audit firm implements the AFGC, they are supporting audit quality in a number of ways. For example, as part of an appropriate culture, the AFGC's principle states that the audit firm should encourage people to consult, challenge, contribute ideas and share problems, knowledge, and experience. This should lead to a higher level of knowledge and skill within the audit firm, and a better demonstration of professional scepticism. Following the AFGC means that the audit firm should have an appropriate 'tone at the top', which means that the leadership of the audit firm (i.e. the senior partners should lead by example and set a high level of integrity to be followed by members of the audit firm).

You should be able to see some overlap with the requirements of ISQM1, because applying the AFGC should certainly help in the development of a System of Quality Management within the firm.

5.3 ISQM 2

ISQM 2 *Engagement Quality Reviews* became effective for audits and reviews of financial statements for periods commencing on or after 15 December 2022, and other assurance and related services engagements commencing on or after 15 December 2022.

An 'engagement quality review' is an objective evaluation of the significant judgements made by the engagement team and the conclusions reached thereon, performed by the engagement quality reviewer and completed on or before the date of the report.

As with ISQM 1, ISQM 2 focuses on quality management at the **firm** level and was a new standard introduced by the International Auditing and Assurance Standards Board which aims to achieve effective quality management systems.

It has always been the case that audit firms must ensure that audit work is properly reviewed to ensure that:

(a) the firm's system of quality control has been complied with; and
(b) that the audit has been performed in accordance with the ISAs, other guidance, and legislative requirements.

Reviews of audit work are often performed prior to issuing the auditor's report (known as a 'pre-issuance' or 'hot' review) or after the auditor's report has been issued (known as a 'post-issuance' or 'cold' review). These reviews can take place within the audit firm provided they are carried out by someone who has not been involved in the detailed audit fieldwork. However, in practice, a lot of audit firms tend to outsource this review to an external third-party because this enables a 'fresh pair of eyes' to review the audit work and make suggestions for improvements.

ISQM 2 promotes a system which is tailored to the nature and circumstances of the firm and its audits. It also deals with the appointment and eligibility of the engagement quality reviewer.

The overarching objective of ISQM 2 is for the firm to appoint an eligible engagement quality reviewer who will perform an objective evaluation of the significant judgements

Figure 5.5 Pre- and post-issuance reviews

made by the engagement team and the conclusions reached thereon. The engagement quality reviewer for the purposes of ISQM 2 is a partner, other individual in the firm, or an external individual appointed by the firm to perform the review.

5.3.1 Eligibility of an individual to be appointed as engagement quality reviewer

ISQM 2 requires the audit firm to establish policies or procedures which set forth the criteria for eligibility to be appointed as an engagement quality reviewer. There are strict eligibility requirements for those carrying out the engagement quality review to ensure there is sufficient independence, competence, time, and seniority for all reviews.

Those policies and procedures must require that the engagement quality reviewer is **not** a member of the audit team. This is crucial, to ensure that the review is conducted in an objective and independent manner and to allow the reviewer to 'stand back' from the work performed and consider whether the audit team has applied appropriate professional scepticism.

ISQM 2 includes a specific requirement that the firm's policies or procedures must specify a cooling-off period of two years, or a longer period if required by relevant ethical requirements, before the engagement partner can assume the role of the reviewer.

In addition, the reviewer must have the competence and capabilities, including sufficient time, and the appropriate authority, to perform the engagement quality review. Competence and capabilities impact the ability of the reviewer to exercise appropriate professional judgement in performing the review. For example, a reviewer who lacks relevant industry experience may not have the ability or confidence to evaluate and, where appropriate, challenge significant judgements made, and the exercise of professional scepticism, by the engagement team on a complex, industry-specific accounting or auditing matter.

Activity 5.4 Competence and capabilities of the reviewer

What matters do you think an audit firm should consider in determining whether an individual has the necessary competence and capabilities to perform an engagement quality review?

The engagement quality reviewer must also have appropriate authority and will usually be a senior partner in the firm. This is to ensure that the reviewer can confidently challenge the audit engagement partner, for example on matters of judgement. Authority also means that the reviewer's evaluation and conclusions are taken seriously.

The reviewer must also comply with the relevant ethical requirements, including in relation to threats to objectivity and independence of the reviewer, for example, there should not be intimidation of the reviewer by the audit engagement partner. The reviewer must also comply with the provisions of law or regulation, if any, that are relevant to the eligibility of the reviewer, for example, for the review of entities operating in regulated industries the reviewer may need to hold specific qualifications.

Where the entity is a public interest entity, the audit firm must also ensure that the review is performed by an engagement quality reviewer who is eligible for appointment as a statutory auditor and is not involved in the performance of the audit to which the engagement review relates.

Some audit firms appoint external people to perform engagement quality reviews and they must think very carefully about who they will appoint. There are many training organizations that carry out reviews for firms who are highly experienced and competent professionals that provide a comprehensive review service and provide the firm with a report after the review which details their findings. Some firms also ask for specific details to ascertain the eligibility of the reviewer, such as requesting a CV of the person carrying out the review, to ensure they have the relevant knowledge and experience. This can provide comfort to the audit firm who may need an engagement quality review for a specialist audit, such as a pension scheme.

ISQM 2 forms part of the firm's system of quality management. It builds on the requirements of ISQM 1 by including specific requirements for the appointment and eligibility of the review, the performance of the engagement quality review and the documentation of the review.

5.3.2 **What is *not* an engagement quality review?**

As we discussed above, an engagement quality review is an objective evaluation of the significant judgements made by the audit engagement team and the conclusions reached thereon. The reviewer's evaluation of significant judgements is performed in the context of professional standards and applicable legal and regulatory requirements.

An engagement quality review is not intended to be an evaluation of whether the entire engagement complies with professional standards and applicable legal and regulatory requirements, or with the firm's policies or procedures.

As we mentioned earlier, the reviewer cannot be a member of the audit engagement team. In addition, the performance of an engagement quality review does not change the responsibilities of the engagement partner for managing and achieving quality on the engagement, or for the direction and supervision of the members of the engagement team and the review of their work. The review is not required to obtain audit evidence to support the opinion or conclusion on the engagement, but the engagement team may obtain further evidence in responding to matters raised during the engagement quality review (for example, it may be the case that audit evidence is found to be insufficient in a specific area once a review has been completed).

5.3.3 **Requirements of the engagement quality review**

The review should focus on significant judgements and other significant matters which arose during the audit. The reviewer is required to discuss these with the audit engagement partner and other relevant members of the audit team, as well as review the audit documentation. In addition, the reviewer should evaluate how ethics requirements have been fulfilled. This requirement demonstrates the close link between ethics, in particular auditor objectivity, and audit quality.

ISQM 2 requires the engagement quality reviewer to:

(a) Read and obtain an understanding of information communicated by the engagement team regarding the nature and circumstances of the engagement and the entity as well as the firm and its monitoring and remediation process (in particular, identified deficiencies which may relate to, or affect, the areas involving significant judgements made by the engagement team).

(b) Discuss with the engagement partner and, if applicable, other members of the engagement team, significant matters and significant judgements made in planning, performing, and reporting on the engagement.

(c) Review selected engagement documentation relating to the significant judgements made by the engagement team and evaluate the basis for making those judgements, including, where applicable, to the type of engagement, the exercise of professional scepticism by the engagement team, and whether the engagement documentation supports the conclusions reached as well as whether those conclusions are appropriate.

(d) Evaluate the basis for the engagement partner's determination that relevant ethical requirements relating to independence have been fulfilled.

(e) Evaluate whether appropriate consultation has taken place on difficult or contentious matters or matters involving differences of opinion and the conclusions arising from those consultations.

(f) Evaluate the basis for the engagement partner's determination that the engagement partner's involvement has been sufficient and appropriate throughout the audit engagement such that the engagement partner has the basis for determining that the significant judgements made, and the conclusions reached, are appropriate given the nature and circumstances of the engagement.

(g) Review the financial statements and the auditor's report including, if applicable, a description of the Key Audit Matters.

(h) For review engagements, review the financial statements or financial information and the engagement report thereon.

(i) For other assurance engagements and related services engagements, review the engagement report and, when applicable, the subject matter information.[14]

Auditing in practice 5.6 Audit quality and professional scepticism

One of the core features of an engagement quality review is that the reviewer must evaluate the exercise of professional scepticism by the audit team in making significant judgements and reaching conclusions.

When auditors fail to exercise professional scepticism there can be an impact on audit quality. Regulators frequently comment on the lack of demonstration of professional scepticism found during their reviews of audit work, and in specific investigations of poor-quality auditing. For example, the FRC's Developments in Audit report 2021 states that one of the most significant thematic weaknesses identified in the 2020/21 inspection cycle related to the lack of professional scepticism including the failure to adopt an attitude to sufficiently challenge management's assumptions.

[14] International Auditing and Assurance Standards Board, 'ISQM 2', 2020, para 25 <https://www.iaasb.org/_flysystem/azure-private/publications/files/IAASB-Quality-Management-ISQM-2-Engagement-Quality-Reviews.pdf> (accessed 17 January 2024).

In July 2022, the FRC published guidance for auditors on professional judgement and in issuing this guidance, the FRC reiterated that professional scepticism is a key part of an appropriate auditor mindset, supporting the quality of judgements during an audit engagement and enhancing the overall effectiveness of auditing.

The link between professional scepticism and judgement and audit quality is clear, and this is why the requirement for an engagement quality review to carefully evaluate the use of professional judgement and professional scepticism is so important.

If the reviewer has concerns over significant judgements or other issues arising from their review, these should be brought to the attention of the audit engagement partner. If the issues are not resolved, they should be escalated to other relevant personnel, likely to be the individual responsible for the firm's SOQM.

In the UK, the FRC has amended ISQM 2 to include some additional requirements for the engagement quality review when an audit client is a public interest entity, including consideration of the independence of the firm from the entity, the significant risks which are relevant to the audit, and the measures taken to adequately manage those risks, the reasoning of the audit partner, in particular with regard to the level of materiality and the significant risks referred to earlier. In addition, there must be consideration of the subjects discussed with the audit committee and management and/or supervisory bodies of the entity.

5.3.4 **Documentation**

In terms of documentation, the audit firm must establish policies and procedures that require the engagement quality reviewer to take responsibility for documentation of the engagement quality review. That documentation must be included within the engagement documentation.

In addition, the reviewer must ensure that the review includes:

(a) The name(s) of the reviewer(s) and individuals who assisted with the engagement quality review.
(b) An identification of the engagement documentation that has been reviewed.
(c) The basis for the reviewers determination in respect of completion of the engagement quality review.
(d) The notifications required.
(e) The date of completion of the engagement quality review.[15]

In the UK, where the engagement quality review is for a public interest entity, there are additional documentation requirements in relation to the oral and written information provided by the key audit partner to support the significant judgements as well as the main findings of the audit procedures carried out and the conclusions drawn from those findings, and the opinions of the key audit partner, as expressed in the draft of the reports required by ISA 260 *Communication with Those Charged with Governance and ISA 700 Forming an Opinion and Reporting on Financial Statements.*

The reviewer must also keep a record of the results of the review, together with the considerations underlying those results within the audit documentation.

[15] Ibid.

5.4 Quality management at the engagement level

So far, we have looked at quality management at the firm level by examining some of the issues in ISQMs 1 and 2. Quality management at the engagement level is dealt with in ISA 220 *Quality Management for an Audit of Financial Statements*.

In order to ensure a high-quality audit is carried out, the firm's system of quality management must be such that it ensures the firm complies with professional standards and that reports are appropriate in the circumstances.

ISA 220 contains a clear description of the audit engagement partner's responsibilities as well as how the engagement team, as a whole, manages and achieves audit quality. The overall objective of ISA 220 is to ensure that the audit engagement team has fulfilled their responsibilities and has conducted the audit in accordance with ISAs as well as other regulatory requirements. Remember, everyone on the engagement team is responsible for ensuring high-quality work is carried out; but ultimately the audit engagement partner is responsible for ensuring this is done correctly.

5.4.1 Leadership responsibilities and ethical requirements

Among other things, ISA 220 requires the audit engagement partner to take responsibility for creating an environment for the engagement which emphasizes the firm's culture and expected behaviour of engagement team members. It requires the engagement partner to be sufficiently and appropriately involved in the audit, such that the engagement partner has the basis for determining whether the significant judgements made, and the conclusions reached, are appropriate in the engagement's circumstances. If the audit engagement partner does not have sufficient involvement in the audit work, they will be unable to ensure the work is being done in accordance with the ISAs and the firm's system of quality management.

To that end, ISA 220 requires the audit engagement partner to ensure that:

- all engagement team members to take responsibility for contributing to the management and achievement of quality at the engagement level;
- the importance of professional ethics, values and attitudes are communicated to the audit engagement team;
- there is open and robust communication within the engagement team as well as supporting the ability of the team to raise concerns without fear of reprisal; and
- the importance of professional scepticism being applied throughout the audit engagement is emphasised.[16]

ISA 220 requires the engagement partner to understand all relevant ethical requirements and to:

- take responsibility in ensuring other members of the engagement team have been made aware of the relevant ethical requirements applicable given the nature and circumstances of the audit engagement, including the firm's related policies or procedures;

[16] FRC, 'ISA (UK) 220', 2021 <https://media.frc.org.uk/documents/ISA_UK_220.pdf> (accessed 17 January 2024).

- remain alert throughout the audit assignment, through observation and enquiry as necessary, for breaches of relevant ethical requirements or the firm's related policies or procedures by members of the engagement team;
- take appropriate action where matters come to the engagement partner's attention via the system of quality management (or other sources) which indicate that relevant ethical requirements applicable to the nature and circumstances of the audit engagement have not been fulfilled; and
- prior to signing the auditor's report, the engagement partner must take responsibility for determining whether ethical requirements, including those related to independence, have been fulfilled.[17]

5.4.2 Acceptance and continuance of client relationships and audit engagements and engagement resources

ISA 220 requires the audit engagement partner to consider information obtained in the acceptance and continuance process in planning and performing the audit engagement. In practice, this will involve considering:

- the integrity of management;
- the competence of the engagement team;
- compliance with ethical requirements; and
- any significant matters that have arisen during the current or previous audit and their implications for continuing the relationship.

We will look at client acceptance in detail in Chapter 6.

In terms of resources, the audit engagement partner is responsible for ensuring that the engagement team have been provided with sufficient and appropriate resources to perform the engagement in a timely manner. This includes ensuring that any external experts and internal audit who are not part of the engagement team have the appropriate competence and capabilities, including sufficient time, to perform the engagement.

If the engagement partner determines that the resources are insufficient or inappropriate, they must take appropriate action.

5.4.3 Engagement performance, consultation, and review

The audit engagement partner is responsible for ensuring that the nature, timing, and extent of direction, supervision, and review is responsive to the nature and circumstances of the audit engagement and the resources assigned or made available to the engagement team. Part of this is to consider matters such as providing coaching and on-the-job training to help engagement team members develop skills or competencies. A good supervisory environment is one where engagement team members raise questions and concerns without fear of reprisals.

[17] FRC, 'ISA (UK) 200', 2016, paras 17–21 <https://media.frc.org.uk/documents/ISA_UK_200_Updated_May_2022.pdf> (accessed 17 January 2024).

Activity 5.5 Direction and supervision

What do you think direction and supervision mean in the context of an audit engagement?

The audit engagement partner must also review audit documentation at appropriate times during the audit, including documentation relating to:

(a) Significant matters

(b) Significant judgements, including those relating to difficult or contentious matters and the conclusions reached

(c) Other matters that, in the partner's professional judgement, are relevant to the partner's responsibilities.[18]

The audit engagement partner must also carry out a review of the financial statements (including a description of the Key Audit Matters, if applicable) and related documentation to determine that the report to be issued is appropriate in the circumstances. This review must take place *before* the auditor's report is signed and dated. In addition, the audit engagement partner must also review formal written communications to management, those charged with governance and/or regulatory authorities prior to their issuance to ensure they are also appropriate in the circumstances.

Auditing in practice 5.7 Audit failure at BHS

British Home Stores (BHS), collapsed in 2016, leading to more than 11,000 redundancies, and leaving a pension deficit of over £570 million. PwC, the firm that had audited the company, and the audit partner, admitted instances of misconduct during the audit.

PwC commented that there were 'serious shortcomings' in the quality of the audit performed and stated that 'at its core this is not a failure in our audit methodology, the methodology simply was not followed'.[19]

One of the significant findings of the investigation was how the audit work was allocated amongst the audit team. The FRC report states that the audit engagement partner recorded only two hours of work on the BHS audit during the completion stage, and delegated almost all of his audit review to a more junior colleague, who had only one year of post-qualification experience. In addition, audit working papers relating to several high-risk areas, including revenue recognition and impairment, had been reviewed by the partner.

As a result of his misconduct, the audit partner was fined £350,000 and banned from performing audits for fifteen years.

If PwC had an effective SOQM in place, and applied good quality management on the BHS audit, it is likely that the firm's audit methodology would have been followed, the partner would have spent an appropriate amount of time on this audit, and the misconduct would not have taken place.

[18] FRC, 'ISA (UK) 220', 2021, para 31.

[19] *BBC News*, 'PwC partner banned over BHS audit' (2018) <https://www.bbc.co.uk/news/business-44462835> (accessed 2 January 2024).

The audit engagement partner must take responsibility for the engagement team undertaking consultation on difficult or contentious matters. ISA 220 requires those difficult or contentious matters to be those which the firm's policies or procedures require consultation on as well as other matters which, in the audit engagement partner's professional judgement, require consultation.

This could be on, for example, the valuation of complex financial instruments or taxation issues.

The engagement quality review has been discussed in detail earlier in the chapter. ISA 220 requires the audit engagement partner to cooperate with the EQR and inform other members of the engagement team of their responsibility to do so. Sometimes, however, there may be a difference of opinion between the audit engagement partner or team and the EQR, and it is important that the firm has procedures in place to handle these differences of opinion.

Where differences of opinion arise, the audit engagement partner has additional responsibilities and must:

(a) Take responsibility for the differences of opinion being addressed and resolved in accordance with the firm's policies or procedures.
(b) Determine that the conclusions reached are documented and implemented.
(c) Not date the auditor's report until any differences of opinion are resolved.[20]

The audit engagement partner must take responsibility for obtaining an understanding of the firm's monitoring and remediation process. In practice, monitoring and remediation is directly linked with the engagement quality review so ISQM 2 will be particularly relevant where this is concerned.

Where deficiencies are noted, these must be discussed with the audit engagement partner and remedial action taken to prevent the deficiencies from reoccurring. This may involve additional staff training, improvements to the system of quality management, arranging additional quality reviews, or taking disciplinary action against those who are found not to be complying with the firm's system of quality management.

5.4.4 **Responsibility for managing and achieving audit quality and documentation**

Prior to dating the auditor's report, the audit engagement partner must assess whether their involvement in the engagement has been sufficient and appropriate such that the partner has the basis for determining the significant judgements made and the conclusions reached thereon are appropriate given the nature and circumstances of the engagement.

It is the audit engagement partner who is ultimately responsible for managing and achieving audit quality. In practice, the audit engagement team also have responsibilities to ensure their work is carried out to a high standard to ensure a high-quality audit. It is important that there is always adequate supervision and that there are review processes in place during the audit (especially where junior team members are concerned). Where there are effective supervision and reviews processes in place, this will ensure that the audit is not only

[20] FRC, 'ISA (UK) 220', 2021, para 38.

conducted to a high quality, but it will also ensure that it is conducted in a timely manner as well.

The audit documentation must contain:

(a) Matters identified, relevant discussions with personnel and conclusions reached with regards to:
    (i) fulfilment of responsibilities relating to relevant ethical requirements, including those related to independence; and
    (ii) the acceptance and continuance of the client relationship and audit engagement.
(b) The nature and scope of, and conclusions resulting from, consultations undertaken during the audit engagement and how such conclusions were implemented.
(c) If the audit engagement is subject to an engagement quality review, that the engagement quality review has been completed on or before the date of the auditor's report.[21]

The auditor must include all significant threats to the firm's independence together with safeguards that have been applied to mitigate those threats to an acceptable level.

5.5 Auditor liability

Auditor liability is an important topic, both in terms of its relationship with audit quality and the reputation of the profession but also in terms of the cost to the individual audit firms should they face a legal claim. Auditors are potentially liable for both criminal and civil offences. A criminal offence takes place when an auditor breaks the law, for example, being found in breach of the Companies Act 2006. Civil offences include breach of contract and the law of tort, under which an auditor can be sued for negligence.

5.5.1 Criminal liability

Auditors are required to comply with relevant legislation. Different countries will, of course, have different types of law to comply with. For example, in the UK, section 507 of Companies Act 2006 states that an auditor will be committing a criminal offence if they knowingly or recklessly cause a report to include any matter which is misleading, false, or deceptive in a material aspect of the financial statements. Specifically, an offence is committed if the auditor knowingly or recklessly causes a report to omit a statement in respect of:

(a) a statement that the entity's financial statements do not agree with accounting records and returns;
(b) a statement that necessary information and explanations have not been obtained; or
(c) a statement that the directors wrongly took advantage of the exemption from preparing consolidated financial statements (group accounts).

This means that auditors could be prosecuted in a criminal court for either knowingly or recklessly issuing an inappropriate audit opinion. The term 'knowingly or recklessly' gave rise to some contention when it was first introduced into the UK's Companies Act 2006. The concern was that some auditors may be deemed to be committing a criminal offence for

[21] FRC, ISA 220 (2021) para 41.

negligence or honest mistakes as there was no definition of the term 'recklessly'. However, the government considers 'recklessness' to be a very high hurdle, and it must be demonstrated that the auditor knew that they were taking unreasonable risks in their actions. One of the MPs involved in drafting the legislation said, 'a person who is merely negligent will not be guilty of this offence, even if the negligence is gross'.

5.5.2 Civil liability

There are two types of civil law which are relevant to the audit profession: contract law and the law of tort. These establish the principles for auditor liability to clients and to third parties, respectively.

The concept of contract law is straightforward. The auditor enters into a contractual agreement with their client. If there is a breach of this contract, the client can take legal action against the audit firm. The contract between the auditor and the client is in the form of the letter of engagement. This letter of engagement sets out the respective responsibilities of both management (of the audited entity) and the auditor. Consequently, as there is a contract between the client and the auditor, the auditor can be sued for breach of contract if they provide a negligent auditor's report which results in loss to the client.

The law of tort is more complicated. Under this law, auditors can face civil liability and be sued for negligence. In order to successfully claim negligence, the plaintiff (the party bringing the legal claim against the auditor) must prove a number of things.

The key points are around duty of care—who does the auditor owe a duty of care to? How is a duty of care breached?

The auditor owes an automatic duty of care to the parties to which they report, i.e. the company shareholders. However, the law is unclear about the extent of the auditor's duty of care beyond the shareholders, and this is where case precedent is important. A number of significant cases have shaped this duty of care, and we will shortly look at the details of some of these cases.

The second issue is about the breach of duty of care. Auditors must exercise reasonable care and skill when carrying out their work. International Standards on Auditing, company law, and other guidance that auditors may apply do not define 'reasonable care and skill' and the level of reasonable care and skill the auditor adopts will be driven by the nature, size, and complexity of the audit client.

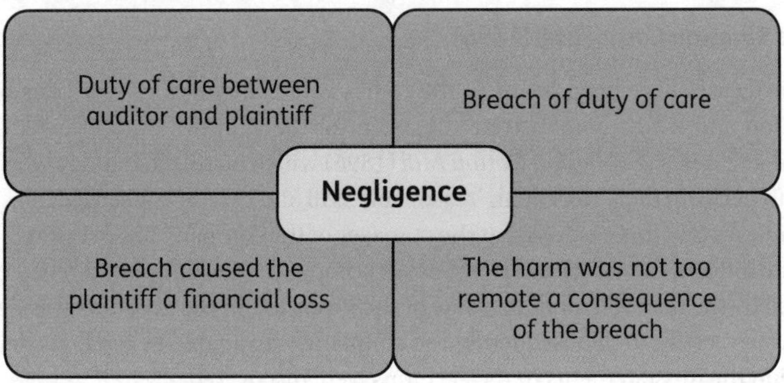

Figure 5.6 Components of a claim of negligence

Activity 5.6 Reasonable care and skill

What do you think it means for an auditor to act with 'reasonable care and skill'?

One of the ways in which an auditor can minimize the risk of negligent auditing is to ensure that they carry out their audit work in accordance with the ISAs and other professional standards and legislation. Remember, though, that even when an audit has been properly planned and executed, this does not guarantee that the auditor has 'found' everything; even a material misstatement can go undetected, especially if it as a result of fraud, which has been hidden from the auditor.

If an auditor fails to apply reasonable care and skill in carrying out their work, it is inevitable that:

- fraud or material error(s) may go undetected;
- the auditor may express an opinion that the financial statements give a true and fair view when they don't;
- a third party relying on the financial statements and the auditor's report thereon may lose money.

As we mentioned previously, the law of tort works on the basis of case precedence. This means that a series of legal cases shape how the law is applied. We will look at some of these cases now, to develop understanding of how the judges in certain cases have interpreted the law, and the impact on auditor's liability under tort.

5.5.3 **Relevant legal cases**

There are two important cases which deal with the issue of 'duty of care' and which illustrate that there are limits to how much an auditor is expected to do in exercising their duty of care: *Kingston Cotton Mill* and *Thomas Gerrard & Son*. You will see that *Kingston Cotton Mill* is a very old case, but is very important, because it introduces that the auditor is a 'watchdog and not a bloodhound' (i.e. the fact that the auditor cannot be expected to investigate everything they come across in an audit).

5.5.3.1 ***Re Kingston Cotton Mill* (1896)**

A number of cases have been heard in the courts where an auditor's work has been called into question and which demonstrate the extent of the auditor's duty of care. One of the more familiar cases is in *Kingston Cotton Mill* (1896) which is still cited today where an auditor's duty to perform their work with 'reasonable skill and care' is concerned.

The simple facts of this case are that the manager of the company has overstated inventory and thereby inflated the assets and profit of the company. The auditor had relied on a certificate signed by the manager, and the value of the inventory in the accounts was described as 'per manager's certificate'. Subsequently the company was unable to repay its debts and on investigation the misstatements in the accounts were discovered.

In considering the issue of 'duty of care', Mr Justice Lopes said:

> It is the duty of an auditor to bring to bear on the work he has to perform that skill, care, and caution which a reasonably competent, careful, and cautious auditor would use. What is reasonable care, skill and caution must depend on the particular circumstances of each case.
>
> An auditor is bound to be a detective, or, as was said, to approach his work with suspicion, or with a foregone conclusion that there is something wrong. He is a watchdog, but not a bloodhound.
>
> Auditors must not be made liable for not tracking out ingenious and carefully laid schemes of fraud, when there is nothing to arouse their suspicion . . . So, to hold would make the position of an auditor intolerable.

In summary, this case laid out that auditor's duty of care must be assessed based on the facts of a particular audit. In addition, the case shows that the auditor cannot be expected to discover a fraud if there is nothing to indicate that a fraud is going on, because it has been concealed.

The auditing profession has held this judgement close since it was first issued in 1896. However, in today's modern auditing profession it is less likely to carry as much weight as it did back then. At the time of the case there were no auditing regulations, it was not common practice for auditors to inspect inventory, and it was common to rely on 'certificates' from management. These days, ISA 240 *The Auditor's Responsibilities Relating to Fraud in an Audit of Financial Statements* has placed more responsibility on the part of the auditor to recognize that the possibility of fraud may exist and to set aside their previous dealings and past experiences of the directors in terms of their honesty and integrity to one side. Since the issuance of ISA 240, auditors must apply professional scepticism in their approach to audit work and have to recognize that there could well be sophisticated schemes of fraud in existence, which will be concealed by management and that any representations made by management may not be truthful.

5.5.3.2 ***Re Thomas Gerrard & Son* (1968)**

The *Thomas Gerrard & Son* (1968) case demonstrates the importance of professional scepticism. The managing director of the company falsified the closing inventory valuation in order to manipulate profits and allow the payment of dividends to the shareholders. This was done by including non-existent inventory in the final valuation as well as creating fictitious invoices. These acts were discovered by the auditor, but nothing was done about them.

The auditor's defence was that they were not responsible for counting the year-end inventory; their responsibility was to verify the figure in the financial statements and rely on assurances provided by a responsible individual at the company and nothing else.

In the previous case we looked at, *Kingston Cotton Mill* (1896), Mr Justice Lopes stated that the auditor:

> is justified in believing tried servants of the company in whom confidence is placed by the company.

Reliance on 'believing tried servants of the company' did not work in the Thomas Gerrard case because the auditors had already discovered what was going on, hence they should have investigated the matter further. Had this been done, the fraud would have been revealed and so the outcome of this case was that the auditors were found guilty of negligent auditing (i.e. there had been a breach of duty of care). The case of Thomas Gerrard & Son emphasizes the importance of corroborating assertions by management and challenging management's assumptions.

The judge in the Thomas Gerrard case also noted that 'the standards of reasonable care and skill are, upon the expert evidence, more exacting than those which prevailed in 1896'. This comment indicates that developments in the profession do impact on the evaluation of duty of care, and that more is expected of auditors now than in 1896.

The next two legal cases deal with to whom the duty of care is owed. Remember that to be found guilty of negligence, it has to be proven that there was a breach of duty of care, and that the duty of care is owed to the plaintiff. The connection between the audit firm and the plaintiff is the crucial issue: this is sometimes called 'proximity'.

5.5.3.3 ***Caparo Industries v Dickman*** **(1990)**

Caparo Industries alleged that it had based decisions to carry out a successful takeover of Fidelity plc based on the strength of Fidelity's 1984 financial statements which had been audited by Touche Ross. Dickman in this case was the audit engagement partner at Touche Ross (and Touche Ross is the audit firm which eventually became Deloitte). Prior to the takeover bid, Caparo Industries were a minority shareholder in Fidelity, and they built up their shareholding in a series of share acquisitions based on the 1984 financial statements.

Caparo argued that the financial statements on which they had relied were misleading because they recognized a profit of £1.3 million which should have been a loss of £400,000. Hence, subsequent to the takeover being completed, Caparo sued the auditor for negligence, arguing that a duty of care was owed to them, as investors and potential investors, by Touche Ross. The Court of Appeal originally found in favour of Caparo; however, on appeal to the House of Lords, the decision was overturned on the grounds that in the circumstances, the auditor did not owe a duty of care to *potential* investors. Instead, the House of Lords held that the duty of care was owed to the shareholders as a body and not to individual shareholders for purposes of them making investment decisions. The House of Lords decision also included consideration of the fact, that in their view, there is no special relationship created between the auditor and potential investors just because a takeover bid may take place.

Lord Bridge stated that for a duty of care to arise in respect of advice or information provided, the person who it is alleged owes the duty of care must be fully aware of the following:

- the identity of the third party who purports to rely on the adviser's advice;
- the nature of the transaction contemplated by the third party;
- that the advice or information provided will be passed to a third party, either directly or indirectly; and
- that it would be very likely that the third party intends to rely on that advice or information when deciding whether, or not, to engage in the transaction.

In summary, the *Caparo* case narrowed the auditor's potential liability to third parties and implies that parties other than the shareholders as a body are unlikely to have sufficient 'proximity' to the audit firm for a duty of care to be created.

5.5.3.4 *ADT Ltd v BDO Binder Hamlyn* (1996)

This case changed the view of 'proximity' and was an important development in case law. BDO Binder Hamlyn were the auditors of the Britannia Security Group ('Britannia') which was acquired by ADT in 1990 for £105 million. However, subsequently, it was found that the company was worth only £40 million and that the financial statements were misleading. ADT sued BDO for damages, claiming a breach of duty of care.

However, in this case, in contrast to the ruling in the *Caparo* case, the decision went in favour of the plaintiff, not the audit firm. This was because the judge ruled that 'proximity' had been created by the BDO partner saying that he 'stood by' the financial statements in a meeting with ADT prior to the takeover. BDO Binder Hamlyn were aware that ADT were looking to acquire Britannia and hence the assurances provided to ADT created a relationship between ADT and BDO Binder Hamlyn.

Unfortunately for the audit firm, there was insufficient insurance to pay the damages and costs, and the partners of the firm were personally liable for £34 million. As a result of this case, the BDO Binder Hamlyn partnership was broken up, some offices merged with other audit firms and staff of other offices were either made redundant or offered positions in other audit firms.

5.5.4 **Risk management**

It is sensible for audit firms to attempt to minimize the risk associated with their liability and there are various ways that risk can be managed. Of course, having a sound SOQM, as discussed earlier in the chapter, should reduce the risk of poor-quality or negligent auditing. However, other mechanisms are in place to reduce the risk exposure of audit firms.

All audit firms are required to have professional indemnity insurance (PII) in place. This is a mandatory requirement and firms which do not have PII in place, or have inadequate PII in place, face disciplinary action from their professional body. PII is there to protect partners from loss, but all audit firms recognize that any claims can have significant reputational damage, especially when findings are published.

Other ways of minimizing the risk of negligence claims include:

- Ensuring the audit is planned and performed correctly and risks are sufficiently addressed.
- Ensuring that audit work is conducted in accordance with the ISAs.
- Ensuring an up-to-date letter of engagement is in place, including carefully documenting the respective responsibilities of management and the auditor. The engagement letter should also explain that the report of the auditors should be used for the purposes for which it has been prepared and that the client cannot use the report for any other purpose.
- Describing the work undertaken in the auditor's report, including the fact that audit work has inherent limitations.
- Using a *Bannerman* paragraph in the auditor's report (see below).
- Having a 'limitation of liability' agreement in place with the client which has a limit on the amount of damages that can be claimed in a negligence claim (see below).

5.5.4.1 *Bannerman* paragraphs

The use of *Bannerman* paragraphs in auditors' reports was borne out of the Scottish case of *Royal Bank of Scotland v Bannerman Johnstone Maclay & Others* (2005). Following *Caparo Industries v Dickman* (see above), auditors have been liable for negligence to third parties (i.e. those parties other than the client and its shareholders as a whole) if:

- the third party was known to the auditor at the time of signing the auditor's report to be placing reliance on that report; and
- the reason for that reliance was known to the auditor.

In the case of *Bannerman*, the court held that the company's bankers, who had extended the company's lending arrangements, may not have done so if they had known that the financial statements contained misstatements due to fraud which had not been detected by the auditor. The court held in favour of the bank on the grounds that the auditors knew the identity of the third party, the use to which the information would be put and that the bank intended to rely on it for the known purpose. The courts dismissed the auditor's arguments that, for a duty of care to arise, there must be an express assumption of responsibility to the third party by the auditor.

In this case, the judge commented that, having become aware of the details of the lending arrangements, the auditors could have disclaimed responsibility to the bank. This led to the inclusion of *Bannerman* paragraphs in auditors' reports.

The three chartered bodies (Institute of Chartered Accountants in England and Wales, Scotland, and Ireland) recommend that an extra paragraph be included to form a disclaimer that auditors may wish to use to manage the risk of liability to third parties. The ACCA do not recommend the use of *Bannerman* paragraphs as ACCA take the view that audit work carried out in accordance with ISAs and other regulatory requirements would be enough to minimize the risk of negligence claims arising.

The recommended wording of a *Bannerman* paragraph is as follows:

> This report is made solely to the company's members, as a body, in accordance with Sections 495 and 496 of the Companies Act 2006. Our audit work has been undertaken so that we might state to the company's members those matters we are required to state to them in an auditor's report and for no other purpose. To the fullest extent permitted by law, we do not accept or assume responsibility to anyone other than the company and the company's members as a body, for our audit work, for this report, or for the opinions we have formed.

The *Bannerman* paragraph limits the audit firm's duty of care to third parties and is very common in auditors' reports as well as other reports issued by professional firms.

5.5.4.2 *Barclays Bank plc v Grant Thornton*

The use of a *Bannerman* paragraph was highlighted in the case of *Barclays Bank plc v Grant Thornton*. In this case, Grant Thornton prepared non-statutory auditor's reports on Von Essen Hotels Limited Group (VEH) and expressed unqualified opinions for both 2006 and 2007. Barclays Bank alleged that the financial statements had been manipulated to show that VEH was capable of meeting bank covenants on its loan facility when, in fact, it could not. Consequently, Barclays Bank suffered losses of some £45m when VEH went into administration in April 2011. The bank also stated that it relied on the unqualified opinions when making the loans to VEH.

Barclays Bank claimed Grant Thornton owed a duty of care to them and that this duty of care was breached because the auditors had failed to uncover the alleged fraud. Barclays Bank also said that Grant Thornton would have been aware that they would be placing reliance on the auditor's report. Grant Thornton's auditor's report contained a *Bannerman* paragraph which set out that they did not accept or assume responsibility in respect of the reports to anyone other than the company and its directors.

The judge accepted Grant Thornton's argument and struck out the claim. The judge stated that Barclays Bank should have been aware of the *Bannerman* paragraph contained in the auditor's report—particularly as it was included in the first two paragraphs and, therefore, if Barclays Bank had not read it, then they should have.

5.5.5 **Limiting the auditor's liability**

As we discussed earlier in this chapter, auditors must have PII in place, and this is a mandatory requirement. However, it cannot be the *only* protection against losses arising from negligence claims. PII is merely a defence from the audit firm being at risk of collapse due to claims.

Many audit firms now structure themselves as limited liability partnerships (LLPs), which provides some protection to the audit partners should there be a legal claim brought against the audit firm. In a LLP, the partnership is a distinct corporate body with a legal existence separate from the partners, who are called 'members' of the LLP.

The key point is that under UK legislation, the LLP is responsible for its own debts, in the same way that a company is responsible to its creditors. The individual members (partners) are only liable up to the extent of their investment into the LLP. There is no concept of 'joint and several' liability, which is seen in a non-LLP partnership structure, and which means that partners are individually and collectively responsible for the liabilities of the partnership. The members of an LLP have limited liability, similar to shareholders in a company.

The downside of LLP status is that the audit firm's financial information is available on public record—like companies, LLPs have to prepare and publish financial statements, which may need to be subject to audit.

Over the years it has become more common for audit firms to enter into a liability limitation agreement (LLA) with an audit client. In the UK, such agreements are governed in company by sections 534–538 of Companies Act 2006. Such agreements enable the auditor and the client to agree to limit the liability of the auditor in respect of any negligence, breach of duty, default of breach of trust arising during an audit. The LLA is between the shareholders of both public and private companies and the auditor and will be arranged by way of an ordinary resolution in general meeting.

There are, however, some conditions in the legislation, including that:

- The LLA cannot reduce the auditor's liability to less than what is considered to be 'fair and reasonable' in the circumstances, taking into consideration the auditor's responsibilities, their contractual obligations and the professional standards that are expected of them.

- Shareholder approval can be obtained either before, or after, the company enters into an LLA. The shareholders have the right, by way of an ordinary resolution, to terminate the LLA and the LLA must be renewed on an annual basis—one agreement cannot cover all subsequent audits.
- Any LLA made with the auditors must be disclosed in the directors' report or in the notes to the financial statements.
- The limit on the auditor's liability need not be a monetary amount or a multiple of the audit fee. It could be, for example, a percentage of any loss suffered by the company taking into consideration the auditor's responsibility for such a loss.

Chapter round-up

- ISQM 1 and ISQM 2 both deal with quality management at the audit firm level. ISA 220 deals with quality management at the engagement level.
- The EQR cannot be a member of the audit engagement team. A firm may appoint an EQR in-house, or they may be external to the audit firm.
- Audit quality has moved up the ranks of importance over recent years and is monitored closely by both regulators and professional bodies around the world to ensure audits are being conducted in accordance with professional standards and legislation. Sanctions can (and often are) brought against audit firms for negligent audit work.
- Auditors can be prosecuted for negligent audit work where clients suffer a loss as a result of reliance on the auditor's report.
- Over the years case law has evolved meaning auditors can be held to account for negligent audit work where this can be proven.
- Auditors can protect themselves against negligence claims by including a *Bannerman* paragraph in their auditor's report, but this can only go so far. If a negligent audit has been carried out, the firm can be liable to a fine.
- Audit firms often use a limited liability partnership as a corporate structure which provides a degree of protection against excessive monetary fines.
- Auditors and their clients can enter into liability limitation agreements provided certain protocol has been followed. There are, however, restrictions on what these agreements can limit.

End of chapter case study

In this chapter we have considered the important issue of audit quality. We have seen that in recent years, the regulatory and professional bodies have focused on audit quality and that several new ISQMs have been issued to try to address problems with audit quality. It is important to understand that without good quality auditing there will be little trust in auditor's reports or financial reporting. We have also seen that auditors can face significant financial repercussions if they do not perform to a high standard, either due to fines and penalties being imposed by the professional and regulatory bodies, or because they are sued for negligence.

In this case study we will ask you to comment on deficiencies in audit quality.

This case study links to the following learning outcomes:

- Discuss and apply the requirements for a system of quality management which should be in place at audit firm level.
- Evaluate quality management deficiencies and provide recommendations to allow compliance with quality management standards.

Scenario

Mulligan & Co is the audit provider to the Bryn Group plc, which is based largely in the UK and has a financial year ended 28 February 20X9. The Group, which is listed, has diverse operations including construction, infrastructure support services, and supply chain management. The Group financial statements for the year to 28 February 20X9 recognize profit before tax of £23 million, and total assets of £190 million, and the audit of these financial statements is in the completion stage.

Mulligan & Co was appointed as auditor to the Group in September 20X8, and has previously performed a non-audit service to the Group, when the firm performed a due diligence engagement in 20X7.

Based on a review of the audit working papers and also a discussion with the audit engagement partner and several other audit team members, there are concerns over the quality of the audit work which has been performed, which are described below:

Client acceptance

Mulligan & Co performed appropriate client identity checks and all other relevant Anti-Money Laundering procedures prior to accepting the client. However, there was no communication with the Group's previous audit provider, Connemara Associates, until October 20X8. You are aware, from a conversation with the audit engagement partner, that the Group audit was a 'significant win' for Mulligan & Co, and that the partners of the audit firm decided to delay communicating with Connemara Associates in case there were any 'skeletons in the closet'. One of the partners also commented that due to performing a due diligence engagement in 20X7, client acceptance procedures were not relevant.

Tax

One of the audit team members helped the Group finance director to prepare the calculation of the Group's deferred tax position. The audit manager said that this was acceptable because the audit team member had not been involved with the audit of tax, and it would save time as we would not have to audit the deferred tax.

Audit partner review

The audit engagement partner reviewed the audit working papers towards the completion of the audit fieldwork. One of the audit assistants said that 'The audit partner asked me if there had been any problems on the sections of the audit which I had worked on, and when I said that there were no issues for him to be aware of, he signed off the working papers after a quick look through them.'

Engagement quality review

An engagement quality review was carried out by Sarah Hill, a partner who was not involved with the Group audit, but was involved with the due diligence engagement performed for the Group in 20X7.

Required

Evaluate the quality management issues that have arisen in respect of the audit of the Bryn Group and recommend further actions to be taken in respect of the issues identified.

Answer

Client acceptance

ISQM 1 requires that there should be a System of Quality Management (SOQM) place to deal with the acceptance and continuance of client relationships. In this case, it appears that the partners of the audit firm were more concerned with winning the client than communicating with the Group's previous audit provider. The SOQM should work to ensure that commercial considerations are not given priority over other factors, such as whether the audit firm has the resource and capability to perform the audit. There is a risk that the Group has been taken on as a client without proper consideration of whether a quality audit can be performed.

It is not relevant that Mulligan & Co had previously performed a due diligence assignment– client and engagement procedures must still be followed. If the partners do not understand this then they should be trained in the relevant requirements for client and engagement acceptance.

Mulligan & Co may not have a SOQM in place with respect to client acceptance decisions, which is a breach of ISQM 1 and must be remedied urgently.

It concerning that the partners did not want to find out about 'skeletons in the closet', implying that the decision not to carry out proper client acceptance procedures was deliberate. This is evidenced by the fact that the communication with the previous auditor of the Group took place after Mulligan & Co had been appointed as auditor. If the audit firm has a SOQM in place with respect to client acceptance decisions, but the partners chose to ignore it, this indicates that the partners are not acting with integrity, and it is questionable whether good audit firm governance is in place at Mulligan & Co. The audit firm should investigate whether this is the case, and, if so, they should stress to the partners the importance of compliance with ISQM 1 and the firm's SOQM.

Tax

According to ISQM 1, the SOQM should ensure that all audit personnel understand the relevant ethical requirements, whether these are regulatory requirements, or the rules relating to ethics that have been set by the audit firm.

In this case, there has been a breach of ethical requirements. An audit team member has assisted the Group finance director with determining the Group's deferred tax, a figure which will be included in the financial statements. This creates threats to objectivity and independence, including a self-review threat and a potential lack of professional scepticism. The deferred tax will not have been subject to robust audit procedures, because of over-reliance on the involvement of the audit team member in determining the figure. In fact, the audit manager has said that there is no need to audit the deferred tax at all. There could also be a management threat because the auditor may have been involved in making management decisions about the deferred tax position.

The audit quality issue is that the audit manager was fully aware of the situation and allowed it to take place. The audit manager either does not understand the ethical threat raised, or does understand it and chose to ignore it. In addition, the member of the audit team should also know that helping the client to prepare elements of the financial statements is likely to give rise to an ethical threat.

At the firm-wide level, Mulligan & Co should review the SOQM in relation to relevant ethical requirements, and ensure that all staff members are fully trained in how to identify and respond to ethical threats to their objectivity and independence.

At the level of the individual engagement, the deferred tax should be subject to audit, and the work performed should be reviewed by someone independent from the audit team.

Audit partner review

ISA 220 requires the audit engagement partner to review the audit documentation at appropriate times. This review should be thorough, especially in respect of any significant matters that arose during the audit and significant judgements that were made. In this case it appears that the partner has not performed a detailed review, having signed off the working papers after asking the audit assistant if there had been any problems. This means that there may not be sufficient and appropriate audit evidence to support the audit opinion and there is a risk that material misstatements have not been detected by audit procedures.

A detailed partner review must now take place, before the audit report is issued, to reduce the risk that the audit firm gives the wrong opinion on the financial statements.

Engagement quality review

ISQM 2 requires that the EQR is not a member of the audit team. This requirement has been adhered to, because Sarah Hill was not on the Group audit. However, they were involved with the due diligence engagement which took place in 20X7. This does not necessarily prohibit Sarah from performing the engagement quality review, as long as the review is conducted in an objective manner.

The Group is a listed company, and to comply with ISQM 2, Sarah must be eligible for appointment as a statutory auditor in order to carry out the review. This needs to be confirmed and documented.

Activity solutions

Activity 5.1–Audit quality

Why should audit firms be concerned about the quality of the audits they perform?

- The audit client is likely to look for a different audit provider if the audit is found to be of poor quality, meaning a loss of income for the firm.
- There could be reputational damage to the audit firm if it becomes well known that the firm's audits are not of a high standard.
- If the audit firm performs poor-quality audit work and is investigated, they could have to pay a significant fine if they are found to have breached regulatory requirements.
- There could be legal action against the audit firm, if there is a suspicion of negligence.
- Poor-quality audits damage the reputation of the whole profession and impact on the credibility of auditing and financial reporting.

Activity 5.2–Developing capabilities and competence

How can audit firms ensure that they hire, develop, and retain personnel with the right level of competence and capabilities?

Suggested answer points:

- Ensuring that an appropriate recruitment policy is in place (e.g. only employing staff with a good educational record or appropriate qualifications).
- Having a promotion system which rewards further training and demonstration of competence whilst performing audit work.
- Setting up a mentoring scheme, so that more senior staff can pass on the benefits of their knowledge and experience.
- Providing in-house CPD for qualified staff, or paying for staff to attend CPD events.

Activity 5.3—Engagement inspections

What factors do you think should be considered in determining which completed audit engagements should be inspected?

Suggested answer points:

Engagements which are likely to be selected for inspection include:

- audits of listed companies;
- audits involving a high level of complexity or judgements;
- audits of companies which operate in highly regulated environments (e.g. financial services);
- engagements with a high level of public interest (e.g. audit of charities);
- where the audit client is new;
- audits with a history of risk (e.g. past instances of fraud or material misstatements);
- if there have been complaints made, or allegations that the audit was not of a good quality, from members of the audit team; and
- if a new partner has been assigned to an audit.

Activity 5.4—Competence and capabilities of the reviewer

What matters do you think an audit firm should consider in determining whether an individual has the necessary competence and capabilities to perform an EQR?

Answer points are provided below.

Matters that the firm would consider include:

- Does the individual understand the relevant professional standards including legal and regulatory requirements—this may be particularly important for an audit involving a specialized industry or a high-risk engagement.
- Do they understand the firm's policies and procedures relevant to the engagement? (For example, how the firm's audit methodology should be applied)
- Do they have knowledge of the entity's industry, to provide context to the review?
- Have they been involved with or reviewed engagements of a similar nature and complexity?
- Do they understand the responsibilities of the EQR in performing and documenting the engagement quality review?

Activity 5.5—Direction and supervision

What do you think direction and supervision mean in the context of an audit engagement?

Suggested answer points:

Direction is about making sure that the audit team members have been informed about their responsibilities, including:

- ensuring that the audit team understand the objectives of the audit work that they are performing;
- informing the audit team about detailed instructions as laid out in the audit strategy and audit plan;
- ensuring that the audit team understands how to fulfil relevant ethical requirements;
- reminding the audit team about the need to exercise professional scepticism; and
- making sure that budgetary issues or resource constraints do not impact on the quality of the audit work.

Supervision is about keeping the audit on track and should be an ongoing monitoring of the audit as it progresses. This could include:

- Providing feedback to the audit team about whether work is being carried out in accordance with the planned approach.
- Addressing significant issues arising and modifying the plan (e.g. if the level of materiality needs to be changed).
- Identifying matters for consultation or consideration by more experienced personnel.

Activity 5.6—Reasonable care and skill

What do you think it means for an auditor to act with 'reasonable care and skill'?

Suggested answer points:

Auditors practise reasonable care and skill by:

- following the requirements of ISAs, relevant law, and other regulations;
- exercising appropriate professional judgement and professional scepticism;
- adhering to relevant ethical codes and principles;
- maintaining their level of knowledge and expertise (e.g. through annual continuing professional development and training); and
- applying their knowledge and expertise appropriately in the context of a specific engagement.

6 Client and Engagement Acceptance

Introduction

Audit clients will come and go in practice, although some audit clients may stay with the firm for a number of years, subject to ethical considerations such as long association. To that end, it is important that the firm has adequate procedures in place to deal with accepting new work and continuing with existing audit engagements. In this chapter, we will see that there are some specific regulations which must be adhered to when a firm is considering taking on a new client, including those relating to audit quality.

As well as following the relevant regulations, audit firms have practical and commercial considerations when evaluating whether to take on a new client, including the level of resources required, the fee that can be charged, and whether the engagement will make a profit. We must remember that audit firms are businesses, so these are important issues. A new audit engagement may not generate a huge profit, but the new client might be an important strategic win for the firm, allowing them to break into a new market, so these commercial issues can be very important.

Once a client has been accepted onto the firm's portfolio, the audit engagement partner is responsible for ensuring that they can continue to act for the client in each subsequent year. This is important because there may be ethical threats that have arisen in the current year which might mean the firm can no longer act for the client; or it may simply be that the client has grown so large that the audit firm no longer has the resources to staff the audit. Continuance of client relationships is therefore something that needs to be carefully considered each year.

Learning outcomes

- Explain the process by which the audit firm obtains audit engagements.
- Explain and evaluate the matters to be considered before accepting a new client or engagement.
- Explain and discuss the issues relating to agreeing the terms of an audit engagement that an audit firm must consider such as resources, fees, and the purpose and content of an audit engagement letter.

6.1 Obtaining professional appointments

6.1.1 Advertising and tendering for work

There are several methods by which an audit firm will obtain new audit clients.

Figure 6.1 Obtaining professional appointments

6.1.1.1 Direct approach

The 'direct approach' means that the prospective audit client has directly approached the audit firm and has requested that they provide a quotation for services. This is usually because the audit firm has been recommended to the prospective client by a third party or the audit firm has a good reputation in the area.

6.1.1.2 Advertising

Advertising is another way in which a firm can generate audit clients, although care must be taken with advertising to ensure that it does not breach any of the rules of the professional body of which the audit firm is a member. For example, some professional bodies prohibit firms from making unflattering reference to, or comparisons with, the services of others. Advertisements must not be misleading. Any promotional material which the firm uses must contain factual statements of truth which they can justify to avoid potential clients being misled.

Auditing scenario 6.1 Advertising for work

Pippa Associates is a small audit firm with three audit partners and twenty staff. The partners are trying to obtain more audit clients and have prepared an advertisement which they plan to use in a social media campaign. The advertisement is shown below.

Pippa Associates—the most professional firm in the city!

We offer a friendly, professional service to businesses of all sizes. Appointing us to audit your business will:

- ✓ Allow you access to the best audit and tax experts in the area
- ✓ Guarantee business improvements if you follow our strategic advice
- ✓ Ensure that you pay less tax

Call us now for more information—we guarantee a better service than your current audit provider!

The advertisement is not appropriate for the following reasons.

Pippa Associates cannot claim to be 'the most professional firm'—it implies that other firms are not acting in a professional way, and it is not possible to 'prove' which firm is the most professional. The comment is misleading. Similarly, it is not appropriate to claim that Pippa Associates has 'the best experts' in audit and tax.

The audit firm cannot guarantee that clients will see business improvements—this implies that one of the objectives of the audit is to provide strategic advice, which is not true, and providing strategic advice could impair the objectivity of the audit firm.

Pippa Associates should not claim that they can save all clients tax, as they do not know the specific tax situations of all potential clients. It may not be possible to pay less tax, and this could be seen as helping clients to evade tax, which is at least unethical and at worst illegal.

Finally, they cannot claim to offer a better service than their competitors: this is unflattering to other audit firms operating in the same area and is misleading. A small firm with only three partners and twenty staff may not be able to offer a good service, for example, to audit a large company or one that operates in a highly regulated or specialist sector.

The advertisement should be rewritten before it is promoted on social media or other advertising platforms.

6.1.1.3 **Tendering**

Tendering is another means by which audit clients are obtained and has become increasingly common nowadays as audit work becomes more competitive. Most large audits will be awarded as a result of a tendering process. A tender can be prepared in response to an open invitation to tender, issued by a company, or the audit firm could be approached by a potential client.

The audit firm will put together a tender document, sometimes called an 'audit proposal', which provides details of the services it can offer, the proposed audit fee, and any other relevant points outlined in the tender document such as timescale for the audit. The firm then meets with company management to 'pitch' for the engagement. The pitch usually involves a presentation to management, and for larger companies with an established audit committee, the tendering process must involve the committee.

At the end of the process, the client will decide on the audit firm they feel is most appropriate for their circumstances.

Activity 6.1 Audit tenders

Imagine that you are an audit partner, and your firm has been invited to tender for the audit of a prestigious company. You are keen to obtain the engagement and there are no ethical reasons why you should not accept the client.

List the matters that you think the audit firm should include in the tender document.

6.1.2 **The involvement of the audit committee**

For companies applying the UK Corporate Governance Code, and with an established audit committee, the audit committee should be involved with client appointment. The overall objective of the audit tendering process is to ensure that the audit firm which is appointed will be able to provide a high-quality, efficient audit.

The FRC's Guidance on Audit Committee recommends the following:

- The audit committee should have primary responsibility for the appointment of the auditor. This includes negotiating the fee and scope of the audit, initiating a tender process, influencing the appointment of an engagement partner and making formal recommendations to the board on the appointment, reappointment, and removal of the external auditors.
- The audit committee should be responsible for the selection procedure for the appointment of audit firms. When considering the selection of possible new appointees as external auditors, it should oversee the selection process, and ensure that all tendering firms have such access as is necessary to information and individuals during the duration of the tendering process.[1]

You can see that the role of the audit committee is very important in respect of auditor appointment. As we saw in Chapter 3, the audit committee members are non-executive directors, and their objectivity should ensure that the auditor appointment process is fair and transparent. In simple terms, the involvement of the audit committee means that the executive directors do not have the power to recommend the appointment of whichever firm they want to the shareholders.

Further specific regulations are contained in the 2016 Statutory Audit Regulation and Directive, which applies to UK public interest entities (PIEs), and which requires that:

- Audit Committees must submit two possible audit firm options for the engagement to the Board, together with a justified preference for one of them.
- The tender process cannot preclude the participation of non-big four firms.
- The tender process provides information to the participating firms that allows them to understand the audited entity's business.
- The tender process uses transparent and non-discriminatory selection criteria to evaluate the proposals and that a report on the conclusions of the selection procedure is prepared and validated by the Audit Committee.
- The Audit Committee should consider the findings and conclusions of the public reports on the UK audit firms published by the competent authority (in the UK this is the FRC).[2]

The final point is important—it is saying that the audit committee should review reports issued by the FRC on the audit quality of specific firms. As we saw in Chapter 5, the FRC publishes annual reports which evaluate the quality of audits performed by audit firms involved with PIE audits, and these reports can provide valuable information to the audit committee about the overall quality of audits.

[1] FRC, 'Guidance on audit committees', 2016 paras 58–59 <https://media.frc.org.uk/documents/Guidance_on_Audit_Committees_April_2016.pdf> (accessed 17 January 2024).

[2] FRC, 'Audit tenders: Notes on best practice', 2017 <https://media.frc.org.uk/documents/Audit_Tenders_-_Notes_on_best_practice.pdf> (accessed 18 January 2024).

Auditing in practice 6.1 The costs of an audit tender

In 2018, the audit firm Grant Thornton decided that it would no longer tender for providing the audit service to UK listed companies. The audit firm reported that the cost of involvement in an audit tender process can be as much as £300,000 and that due to the dominance of the big four audit firms, Grant Thornton rarely wins a tender for listed entities. The cost clearly outweighs the benefit. The head of audit at Grant Thornton UK, Sue Almond, stated that, 'Despite the firm's experience and track record of delivering quality audits, we have been unable to impact the dominance of the big four firms.'[3] Grant Thornton often came second place in the tendering process, and the firm believed that listed companies did not want to 'take the risk' of appointing a non-big four firm as their audit provider.

6.2 Client and engagement acceptance

6.2.1 Acceptance considerations

Whichever method is used to market the audit firm's services and attempt to obtain work, an audit firm can only accept clients within an acceptable level of risk. Neither ISAs (UK) nor law prescribes a specific level of risk—it is very much firm-specific. Audit firms will consider various attributes when assessing their acceptable levels of risk and must only take on clients that they are competent to act for and have staff who possess the appropriate levels of skill and technical ability required to carry out the audit in accordance with ISAs (UK) and other legal and regulatory requirements.

Firms have a duty to ensure they only accept clients for whom they can provide a high level of service. To that end, the firm must not accept clients that are beyond their specialisms; nor must they accept clients for which they do not have the appropriate resources at their disposal to service the client adequately.

Auditing scenario 6.2 Acceptance of an inappropriate audit client

Sunnie Ltd has approached Dexter & Co LLP to act as auditors for the forthcoming financial year ending 31 July 20X1. Sunnie Ltd is an entity that specializes in investment management for entities such as pension schemes and hedge funds. Dexter & Co LLP currently has no other client that operates in this sector and has not acted for such clients in the past.

Sunnie Ltd is a specialized entity which will have complex accounting policies and transactions. Therefore, such a client must have a team assigned to it that has the specialist knowledge and experience required to carry out the audit in accordance with ISAs (UK) and other regulatory requirements.

[3] Shoaib, Alia, 'Grant Thornton to exit FTSE 350 audit market, citing big four dominance', 2018 <https://www.accountancyage.com/2018/04/03/grant-thornton-exit-ftse-350-audit-market-citing-big-four-dominance/> (accessed 2 January 2024).

The audit engagement partner has downloaded some information from the internet about investment management entities and has circulated this to the audit staff claiming this will be sufficient to gain an adequate background to the client. In addition, the engagement partner has enrolled three of the team on a three-hour training course on how to audit investment management companies which is specifically aimed at partner level.

In this scenario, Dexter & Co LLP does not have the resources available to carry out this audit. The firm has not acted for an investment management entity before and simply downloading information from the internet (which may be out of date and/or technically inaccurate) is not sufficient. The training course the engagement partner has enrolled the audit staff on is inappropriate as well, as it is aimed at partners and hence will be a high-level course, therefore will not cover crucial basic elements that need to be considered when auditing such a specialized entity.

The audit engagement partner must decline the offer to act as auditor to Sunnie Ltd because they do not have the ability to service the client. They do not have specialist knowledge of investment management and hence will not be able to properly understand the client's transactions, accounting policies, and levels of risk. To act for this client would be reckless and audit risk (the risk that the auditor expresses an incorrect audit opinion on the financial statements) would be very high.

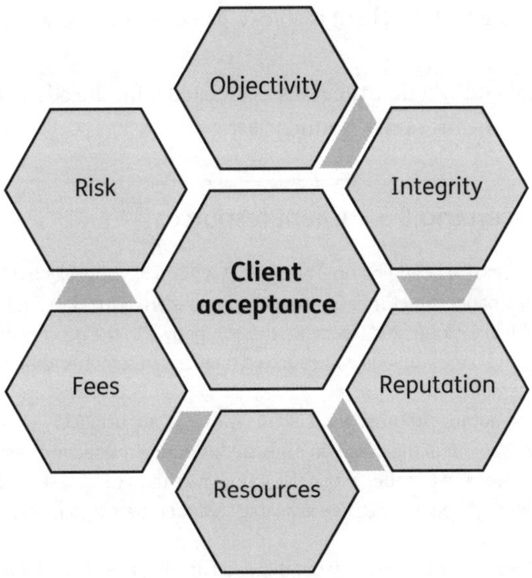

Figure 6.2 Matters relevant to client acceptance

It is not just levels of competence and skill that the audit firm must consider, although, of course, these are two attributes which are vitally important.

Figure 6.2 highlights client acceptance issues that a firm must consider.

- Whether the firm can demonstrate it is *independent and objective* and that this independence and objectivity can be maintained throughout the course of the audit.
- Whether there is sufficient *management integrity* in place. It would not be appropriate to act for a client whose management have a reputation for acting recklessly or have

a record of running the business without integrity. Frequent changes of auditor could indicate management integrity is in doubt.

- The *reputation* of the client—if the client has a bad reputation or has received a large amount of adverse publicity, this may be a reason not to act for the client as the audit firm would not want to be associated with this type of client.
- Whether the firm has *adequate resources* to service the client. We discussed this issue briefly above, but ensuring the firm has adequate resources available not only includes consideration as to whether there is a sufficient level of suitable staff to carry out the audit work; but also, whether those staff will be available at the time the audit is scheduled to be carried out. Audit firms often have busy periods where audit staff availability is limited. In considering the resources needed to perform the audit, the firm should also think about whether experts may be needed (e.g. if there are particularly complex issues to deal with) and if specific technological resources are in place.
- The fee level must be proportionate to the levels of skill and time needed to carry out the audit in accordance with the firm's quality assurance standards, ISAs (UK), and other legislative and regulatory requirements. In addition, the firm may also wish to refer to a credit check to ensure that the client is able to pay the audit fee within specified credit periods.
- The firm's risk level and whether the risks associated with the client are acceptable to the firm and are within the firm's risk boundaries.

Auditing scenario 6.3 Client resources

Osbourne Ltd has a financial year ending on 31 August 20X1 and has approached Maisie & Co to act as the auditors. The finance director of Osbourne Ltd has advised that the audit must take place during the second week of October 20X1 because the company is in the process of buying out another company and the bank would like the audited financial statements to be made available before the start of December.

Maisie & Co act for a number of other audit clients with a 31 August 20X1 year end. Thirteen of its twenty audit staff will be out of the office on other audits during the second week of October. In addition, the second week of October is also the school half-term week so a further four staff members will be on holiday. This leaves three available staff members to carry out the audit of a new audit client.

The resources currently available to carry out this audit are likely to be inadequate as things currently stand. Unless the firm can release further resources to carry out this new audit, then it may be the case that Maisie & Co will have to decline the engagement. However, it may also be the case that three members of staff may be sufficient enough to carry out the audit in accordance with the ISAs (UK) and other regulatory requirements, depending on the size and complexity of Osbourne Ltd. This will be a decision for the audit engagement partner to make having considered all other risks associated with accepting this client.

The acceptance considerations discussed above are formalized as audit quality management issues under the requirements of ISQM (UK) 1 *Quality Management for Firms that Perform Audits or Reviews of Financial Statements, and Other Assurance or Related Services Engagements*, which requires the following:

The firm shall establish the following quality objectives that address the acceptance and continuance of client relationships and specific engagements:

(a) Judgments by the firm about whether to accept or continue a client relationship or specific engagement are appropriate based on:

(i) Information obtained about the nature and circumstances of the engagement and the integrity and ethical values of the client (including management, and, when appropriate, those charged with governance) that is sufficient to support such judgments; and

(ii) The firm's ability to perform the engagement in accordance with professional standards and applicable legal and regulatory requirements.

(b) The financial and operational priorities of the firm do not lead to inappropriate judgments about whether to accept or continue a client relationship or specific engagement.[4]

The first part of the requirement focuses on integrity and ethical values, meaning that the auditor must obtain information in respect of these matters and evaluate them to reach a conclusion. To obtain the relevant information, the audit firm may discuss the potential new client with other professional services providers, bankers, and lawyers. In addition, the incoming auditor will always contact the outgoing auditor in a handover process, which we will look at later in the chapter. Background information can also be found by using an internet search about the business and using relevant databases.

The second part of the ISQM (UK) 1 requirement states that the audit firm should not prioritize income and profit over the other client acceptance considerations. Of course, the audit firm will want to make a profit, and an appropriate fee should be determined, which we will look at next, but the overriding consideration should be whether the audit firm can provide a high-quality audit.

Activity 6.2 Integrity and ethical values

Imagine that you are evaluating whether to take on a new audit client. What are examples of matters or issues you could find out about the potential client which could lead you to believe there is a lack of integrity and ethical values? List as many as you can.

As well as considering the ethical values of the client, the audit firm must also consider whether there are other ethical threats which mean that the engagement should not be accepted, in particular whether there are any threats to auditor objectivity. Potential threats could arise for example, if members of the audit firm hold shares in the client or there are family relationships. If threats are discovered, it may not mean that the client must be turned down, as safeguards could potentially reduce the threats to an acceptable level.

There may be other ethical matters to evaluate in relation to a potential new engagement, for example, whether any conflict of interest or confidentiality issues could arise, and, if so, whether appropriate safeguards can be put in place. Also, the firm's competence

[5] FRC, ISQM (UK) 1, 2021 para 30.

to perform the potential work should be evaluated from an ethical perspective, especially if the potential client operates in a specialized industry, or if the client has a complex structure. A self-interest threat to professional competence and due care is created if the engagement team does not possess, or cannot acquire, the competencies necessary to properly carry out the engagement.

6.2.2 **Fees**

In practice, one of the sticking points in onboarding a new audit client is the level of fee to be charged. A lot of audit clients view the audit as a 'necessary evil' which provides the company with little benefit—some audit clients view the audit process as a disruptive 'compliance exercise'. To that end, many prospective audit clients will be driven by the lowest fee they can obtain, rather than looking at the overall benefits that an audit brings, such as a level of comfort that the financial statements are credible and a 'fresh pair of eyes' observing the company's system of internal control.

Fee levels for an audit must reflect the level of work to be carried out and the level of skill and competence of the personnel that are needed to carry out the engagement.

The act of 'lowballing' has unfortunately become more prevalent in recent years as fee pressure for audit firms increases. Lowballing is where an audit firm will deliberately set a low fee in an attempt to secure the audit. The problem with this approach is that it results in a poor-quality audit because not enough time will be devoted to carrying out all of the necessary audit procedures. This is because the fee level will invariably dictate the amount of time that can be spent on the audit before the audit becomes loss-making (i.e. where time spent on the audit by the audit team exceeds the fee that is charged). There is a higher risk that the audit procedures which have been carried are incomplete or sample sizes are too small to keep the time spent on the audit within the fee level.

Poor audit quality results in higher audit risk—that is the risk that the auditor expresses the incorrect opinion on the financial statements. Therefore, the audit fee proposed must be conducive to the work involved which also must comply with the ISAs (UK) and other regulatory requirements.

There are generally two main methods for determining the audit fee—charge-out rates and fixed fees.

- Charge-out rates are used when the audit firm determines the audit fee using an hourly rate for the audit staff multiplied by the estimated time to perform the audit work. This way of determining the audit fee is easy for the client to understand but it can be difficult to predict how much time the audit will take, especially for a new audit client, leading to changes in the fee, which may not please the client.
- Using fixed fees for quotes can be simpler and it may be preferable for the audit client as they know exactly how much the audit will cost. However, there is a risk for the audit firm in that if the audit takes longer than expected, the engagement becomes less profitable and can even become loss-making.

It is important that the audit firm is very clear in providing information to the client about the basis of the fee and the work that will be performed for that fee. This is included in the engagement letter (which we look at in section 6.3.3).

Auditing scenario 6.4 Determining the audit fee

The audit engagement partner of Wolves & Co has been approached by the board of Warrington Ltd to provide external audit services.

Warrington Ltd has approached four audit firms to provide a tender and quotation for audit services, including Wolves & Co, and the company has requested a fixed fee so they know exactly how much the audit will cost them.

A meeting took place last week between the finance director and the audit engagement partner to enable the audit partner to obtain a basic understanding of the business, its structure, and controls, and to obtain a copy of the prior year's financial statements. Given the size and nature of Warrington Ltd, the audit engagement partner has suggested that a manager, senior, semi-senior, and junior will be needed to carry out the audit to be able to meet the deadline for the board to approve the financial statements.

The charge-out rates of staff at Wolves & Co who will potentially be deployed on the audit are as follows:

- audit engagement partner £500 per hour
- audit manager £400 per hour
- audit senior £310 per hour
- audit semi-senior £250 per hour
- audit junior £200 per hour

The audit engagement partner has estimated that the audit fee in the first year of the audit will be approximately £87,720 which is made up as follows (note a standard working day at Wolves & Co consists of seven hours):

Table 6. 1

Activity	Performed by	Estimated number of hours required	Total (£)
Obtaining information required for the permanent audit file and planning section, where applicable	Manager	7	2,800
Obtaining an understanding of the entity and the environment in which it operates	Manager	7	2,800
	Partner	7	3,500
	Senior	7	2,170
	Semi-senior	7	1,750
	Junior	7	1,400
Undertaking the audit planning and documenting the client's system of internal control	Manager	14	5,600
	Partner	7	3,500
Obtaining audit evidence (substantive procedures and tests of controls)	Manager	35	14,000
	Senior	35	10,850
	Semi-senior	35	8,750
	Junior	35	7,000
Review of audit evidence	Partner	7	3,500
Dealing with difficult/contentious matters by expert	Expert	Estimate	2,500
Audit completion	Manager	14	5,600
	Partner	10	5,000
Finalization	Partner	14	7,000
Estimated fee			87,720

Wolves & Co may expect to make a loss in the first year of auditing Warrington Ltd due to the additional work involved in the first year of any audit. This includes obtaining an understanding of the client, its accounting policies, transactions, and balances, and putting together the permanent audit file. However, the audit engagement partner will usually 'build in' an element of additional time for staff to be given sufficient time to obtain a detailed understanding of the client and obtain additional information to mitigate any such losses. This can often be done by over estimating the time needed at each stage of the audit.

Activity 6.3 Setting an audit fee

Imagine that your audit firm has tendered for the audit of a new client, Ghost Ltd, a small company which chooses to have an audit performed on its financial statements. The audit partner has proposed an audit fee which is 25 per cent below the market rate for this type of engagement. The partner is hoping to win the audit and then be able to provide Ghost Ltd with tax and other non-audit services, on which a high profit will be made.

What are the ethical problems caused by the audit partner's proposed audit fee?

6.2.3 **Client handover**

Once the firm has determined that it is acceptable to take on a new audit client and is satisfied that the risks are within acceptable levels to act for the client, the next step is to arrange for the handover process to be implemented.

The handover process is often referred to in practice as 'professional enquiry' or 'professional clearance' although this term is somewhat a misnomer nowadays as the incoming audit firm does not need 'clearance' to act for the client and the process is usually referred to in practice as a 'change in professional appointment'. The incoming auditor must make their own decisions, based on the information they receive from the outgoing auditor, as to whether, or not, to act for the client.

The handover process is usually straightforward. In the UK, all audit firms are regulated by a professional body so compliance with that professional body's *Code of Ethics and Conduct* will be mandatory and hence the outgoing audit firm will usually cooperate with the incoming audit firm. Only in very rare situations will an incoming audit firm conclude that a complaint to the outgoing firm's professional body is necessary due to the outgoing auditor being uncooperative.

The steps that are usually involved in the client handover process are as follows:

Step 1 The incoming audit firm will ask the client to provide permission for the outgoing auditor to liaise with the incoming auditor. This is necessary due to client confidentiality rules. The outgoing firm cannot discuss any aspect of the client with a third party without the express permission of the client. If the client refuses this permission, the incoming auditor must refuse the engagement. In the majority of cases, this permission is granted.

Step 2 When permission is granted, the incoming auditor contacts the outgoing auditor and asks for all relevant information that should be considered by the incoming auditor when deciding whether, or not, to accept the engagement. Relevant information may include fee disputes or breaches of laws and regulations (although the outgoing auditor will be subject to anti-money laundering regulations so may not be able to discuss anything in respect of money laundering that could constitute 'tipping off').

If the incoming auditor does not receive a written reply from the outgoing firm, the incoming auditor must attempt to receive a response by other means such as by telephone. If a response is still not received, the incoming auditor should seek advice from their professional body as to the way forward. It may be that the professional body advises the firm to accept the appointment, but to proceed with caution. In most cases, the firm will send notification that if a response is not received within, say, seven days from the date of the final communication, it will be assumed that the outgoing firm has no objection.

However, if handover information relating to the previous year's accounts is not received due to a non-response by the outgoing audit firm, this will create a problem for the incoming auditor as they may not have enough information to audit the opening balances. This could give rise to the incoming auditor expressing a modified audit opinion on the grounds of insufficient audit evidence.

Step 3 Where a response is received, consider the outgoing auditor's response and assess if there are any ethical or professional reasons as to why the incoming auditor should not accept the appointment.

Step 4 For UK-based companies, the incoming auditor can ask to be given access to the outgoing auditor's prior year's audit file to collate certain audit evidence they will need for their audit—such as audit evidence over opening balances. The outgoing auditor is compelled to allow this under company law but does not have to do so for certain clients, such as pension schemes.

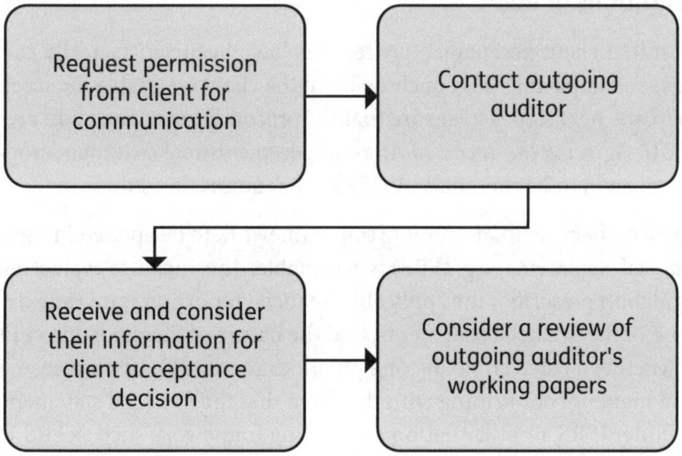

Figure 6.3 Stages in the change in professional appointment process

6.2.4 **Client due diligence**

Another important exercise which must be carried out by the audit firm during the client acceptance process is client due diligence. As we saw in Chapter 2, anti-money laundering regulations must be complied with by all professional firms. As a brief reminder, as this is highly relevant to client acceptance, this involves carrying out client due diligence to ascertain whether there is a risk that the client may be engaged in money laundering. Generally, the audit firm will:

- Carry out searches on the audit client, such as searches at Companies House, or equivalent public register, to identify who the beneficial owners are.
- Obtain identification of the company, such as the certificate of incorporation and other evidence to prove that the company exists for genuine reasons.

- Obtain identification of the company's beneficial owners, such as the directors and shareholders (especially for those that own more than 25 per cent of the business). This identification will include photographic identification, such as a passport or driving licence and proof of residential address of the owner(s) by obtaining a copy of a recent utility bill such as a council tax bill.
- Carry out electronic searches on the client, such as credit checks.

The firm may also carry out other ad hoc due diligence checks as it sees fit depending on the levels of risk associated with the client. This is known as 'enhanced due diligence' and is usually carried out on clients that are considered to be higher risk.

At this point, you may wish to revisit Chapter 2 to refresh your knowledge of the Anti-Money Laundering Regulations, especially in respect of 'know your client' procedures.

6.3 Agreeing the terms of an audit

6.3.1 Preconditions of audit

Once all the initial client acceptance procedures have been satisfactorily carried out and the audit engagement partner has concluded that the client is suitable for acceptance on the firm's portfolio, the next step is to ensure that the preconditions of an audit are present.

ISA (UK) 210 *Agreeing the Terms of Audit Engagements* makes it mandatory for the preconditions of an audit to be present. ISA (UK) 210 requires the auditor to:

- Determine whether the financial reporting framework to be applied in the preparation of the financial statements (e.g. IFRS) is acceptable. This includes evaluating whether law or regulation prescribes the applicable financial reporting framework, considering the purpose of the financial statements, and the nature of the reporting entity (for example, whether a listed company or a public sector entity). In most cases this will simply be a matter of confirming with the client that the financial statements will be prepared under IFRS, or other national reporting framework such as FRS 102 *The Financial Reporting Standard applicable in the UK and Republic of Ireland.*
- Obtain the agreement of management that it acknowledges and understands its responsibilities for the following:
  - preparing the financial statements in accordance with the applicable financial reporting framework;
  - internal control necessary for the preparation of the financial statements to be free from material misstatement; and
  - providing the auditor with access to information relevant for the audit and access to staff within the entity to obtain audit evidence.[5]

If the auditor cannot confirm that the preconditions for an audit are present, the auditor must discuss the situation with management. The auditor must not accept the engagement unless the preconditions for an audit are present, unless required to do so by law or regulation.

[5] FRC, 'ISA (UK) 210', 2016, para 6 <https://media.frc.org.uk/documents/ISA_UK_210_-_Revised_June_2016_Updated_May_2022.pdf> (accessed 18 January 2024).

Auditing scenario 6.5 Preconditions for an audit are *not* present

Zico Ltd is a new audit client of Morley & Co which manufactures chemicals for use in domestic cleaning products. The audit manager has held a meeting with the company's finance director and has supplied a copy of the notes of that meeting to the audit engagement partner. An extract of the notes from the conversation with the finance director is as follows:

> I understand that you will need access to certain other staff members within the company to obtain your audit evidence. However, I am reluctant for this to happen because the company is currently very busy and having our staff deal with the auditors will not be productive. I therefore am not willing to provide you with unrestricted access to other personnel within the company. You must deal only with myself when requiring audit evidence.

The audit engagement partner decided to contact the finance director straightaway once they had reviewed the content of these notes. The partner informed the finance director that it is a requirement of ISA (UK) 210 that unrestricted access to other staff members be granted so the audit team could obtain audit evidence. The finance director has continued to express their unwillingness for this to happen.

It is strange why the finance director is reluctant to provide unrestricted access to staff members for the audit team. There will be some aspects of the company's business which would be better dealt with by other staff of Zico, when responding to requests for information from the auditors. For example, it would be unusual for the finance director to have a deep understanding of production processes which may need to be reviewed by the audit firm when carrying out tests of control over the various cycles of the business. Such processes would best be looked at with the production director.

In this situation, if the finance director remains unwilling to provide the auditor with unrestricted access to other individuals within the company from which to obtain audit evidence the audit engagement partner has no alternative but to either not accept the audit engagement or resign from it. The exception to this would be where the audit firm is required to continue with the engagement because they are required to do so by law or regulation.

The preconditions for an audit are outlined in the auditor's letter of engagement which we will look at shortly.

6.3.2 **The terms of the engagement**

ISA (UK) 210 outlines the auditor's responsibilities in agreeing the terms of the audit engagement with management and, where appropriate, those charged with governance. It is critical that the terms of the audit engagement are set out clearly and that both parties have a clear understanding of their responsibilities.

The objective of the auditor is to accept or continue an engagement only when the basis upon which it is to be performed has been agreed. This agreement is twofold:

- The auditor must be satisfied that the preconditions for an audit are present.
- The auditor must confirm that there is common understanding between the auditor and management and, where appropriate, those charged with governance, of the terms of the audit appointment.

As mentioned above, agreeing the terms of the engagement includes ensuring that the responsibilities of the auditor and of management are clear and that management accepts various responsibilities, including preparing the financial statements in accordance with financial reporting standards and providing the auditor with the information required to perform the audit.

Auditing scenario 6.6 Agreement of terms cannot be obtained

The finance director of Tennyson Ltd has approached the audit engagement partner of Churchill & Co to act as auditor for the forthcoming year end 31 October 20X1. Preliminary investigation carried out by the audit engagement partner has revealed that the previous audit firm resigned because they expressed a disclaimer of opinion on the financial statements for the year ended 31 October 20X0 due to an inability to obtain written representations from the directors.

The audit engagement partner has discussed the situation with the finance director who said:

> Oh yes, we did have a problem with that. The problem is that we don't view the supply of written representations as being important. They only confirm information that is already in the financial statements so that should be sufficient enough. Our chief executive officer is also clear on the issue—there is no requirement for us to provide written representations in law and so we won't be willing to provide them to any other audit firm.

Written representations are an important source of audit evidence as they complement existing forms of audit evidence over which the representations relate. On their own, they are insufficient forms of audit evidence, but ISA (UK) 580 *Written Representations* requires the auditor to obtain them for certain areas of the financial statements.

The finance director has expressed the entity's unwillingness to supply the audit firm with written representations. This would result in a further disclaimer of opinion in the financial statements for the year ending 31 October 20X1.

ISA (UK) 210 states that if management, or those charged with governance, impose a limitation on the scope of the auditor's work in terms of a proposed audit engagement, such that the auditor believes the limitation will result in the auditor disclaiming an opinion on the financial statements, the auditor must not accept such a limited engagement as an audit engagement, unless required by law or regulation to do so.

In this situation, the auditor must refuse the engagement as there is a management-imposed scope limitation that will result in a disclaimer of opinion if it cannot be resolved. The preconditions for audit have not been met because management fails to understand its responsibilities with regard to providing the auditor with appropriate written representations.

6.3.3 **The audit engagement letter**

As we have already seen, ISA (UK) 210 requires the auditor to agree the terms of the audit engagement with management or those charged with governance, as appropriate. This agreement will be in the form of an engagement letter. The engagement letter is essentially a contract between the audit firm and the audit client.

Audit engagement letters are very important because they set out, in writing, the responsibilities of management and, where appropriate, those charged with governance and the auditor. If an audit engagement letter is not issued there can be very serious problems at a later date. Also, where an audit engagement letter is not issued, the professional body to

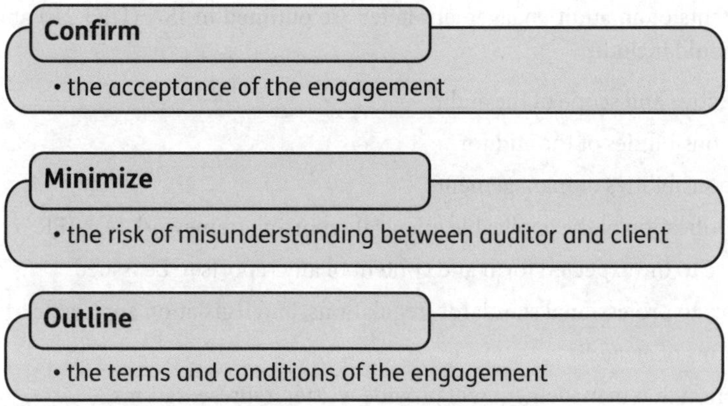

Figure 6.4 The purposes of an engagement letter

which the auditor belongs will impose sanctions on the firm for failing to comply with the ISAs (UK). These sanctions can include a requirement to improve their processes and a 'follow-up' visit to ensure procedures have been improved or disciplinary action where there are multiple deficiencies in the firm's audit work as well as the absence of an engagement letter (or an up-to-date engagement letter).

The purpose of an engagement letter is to confirm the acceptance of the engagement, minimize the risk of misunderstanding between the auditor and the client and outline the terms and conditions of the engagement (Figure 6.4). It also outlines the scope of the audit (i.e. what are the boundaries of the work that is being agreed, for example, is the audit of a single company, or a group of companies), and is the work solely the audit, or are other related services being provided to the client?

In all cases, the audit engagement letter must be in place (i.e. signed by both parties) before the audit commences.

Once the audit engagement letter is in place it needs to be reviewed every year to make sure its terms and conditions are appropriate. The letter itself does not need to be reissued every year, but a review does need to be carried out every year to make sure it remains appropriate. If there have been any changes to the terms and conditions or scope of the audit engagement, a new letter must be issued. In addition, ISA (UK) 210 requires the auditor to consider reminding the client of the existing terms and conditions of the audit engagement for continuing engagements.

A revised engagement letter may need to be sent to the audit client where there has been a change to the statutory duties of an auditor—for example, due to new legislation. New or revised ISAs (UK) may be introduced that change the auditor's professional duties which will also give rise to the audit engagement letter being reissued. In addition, the audit client may also request other services from the auditor which would warrant a revised engagement letter to be issued. However, for non-audit services which may be requested, and for which the audit firm is permitted to carry out without breaching any ethical rules, a separate letter of engagement will usually be provided which deals with those non-audit services.

The contents of an audit engagement letter are outlined in ISA (UK) 210 and the main contents should include:

- The objective and scope of the audit.
- The responsibilities of the auditor.
- The responsibilities of management.
- The identification of the applicable financial reporting framework (e.g. IFRS or FRS 102).
- Reference to the expected form and content of any reports to be issued.
- Reference to professional standards, regulations, and legislation applicable to the audit.
- Limitations of an audit.
- Expectation that management will provide written representations.
- Basis on which the fees are calculated.
- Agreement of management to notify the auditor of subsequent events (subsequent events are events arising between the reporting date and the date of the auditor's report).
- Agreement of management to provide the draft financial statements in time to allow the audit to be completed before any agreed or imposed deadline.
- Form and timing of any other communications during the audit.

The audit engagement letter may also refer to limitation of an auditor's liability to third parties as well as the (planned) use of the entity's internal audit function.

The Appendix to this chapter contains an illustrative letter of engagement for reference.

6.3.4 **Recurring engagements**

As we noted earlier in the chapter, it is unusual for an audit client to change auditors on a frequent basis. Some clients stay with the audit firm for many years, although you should remember that there are ethical issues that must be considered by the auditor in these circumstances, such as long association, which will need adequate safeguards.

When the first audit is complete, the auditor must then revisit the acceptance procedures and review the documentation to ensure that it is appropriate to continue with the engagement for the following year. This is necessary because some issues may have been identified during the course of the audit that could mean the audit firm no longer wishes to continue acting for the client. For example, the auditor may have discovered some aspects of the business which call into question the integrity of the management; or the auditor could have been asked to agree to some course of action that would be unethical and inappropriate. In these situations, it is likely that the auditor will consider resigning.

In practice, for the most part, auditors will continue acting for the client.

Each year the audit firm must revisit certain aspects of the engagement to ensure they discharge their obligations correctly, such as:

- updating customer due diligence procedures;
- obtaining additional identifications for money laundering purposes, where necessary;
- revisiting the audit letter of engagement to ensure it is up to date or whether it needs reissuing;

- considering whether it is necessary to remind the client about the terms and conditions of the engagement; and
- reviewing the prior year's audit file to check what issues arose last year that may impact on this year's decision to continue acting as auditors to the client.

These steps are necessary to ensure that it is appropriate to continue acting for the client in light of the firm's levels of acceptable risk.

Chapter round-up

- New audit clients can be acquired through direct requests from the client, advertising the services of the firm or by submitting a tender for the audit assignment.
- There are several steps that must be carried out prior to commencing work for the new audit client such as client due diligence, ascertaining whether the preconditions for an audit are present, obtaining anti-money laundering identification, and liaising with the outgoing audit firm.
- There are preconditions that must be present for an audit: determining the applicable financial reporting framework; and obtaining acknowledgement from management that it acknowledges and understands certain responsibilities.
- Various risks must be considered by the audit firm to ensure the risk profile of the new audit client fits into the firm's accepted levels of risk.
- Once it has been agreed the firm can act for the client, the handover process is commenced which involves liaising with the outgoing auditors, considering the response of the outgoing auditor and reviewing their audit files for evidence (e.g. for opening balances), where applicable.
- Audit fees should be based on chargeable time, though fixed fees are sometimes used. Audit fees should be sufficient to allow for a quality audit to be performed.
- Both the auditor and the client must agree to the terms of the engagement which is usually set out in a letter of engagement that is signed by both parties and is reviewed each year to ensure it remains appropriate. The engagement letter must contain certain clauses to comply with ISAs (UK) 210.

End of chapter case study

Introduction

This chapter has covered a range of matters that relate to how audit firms obtain clients. We have seen that auditors have to follow regulations regarding client acceptance including evaluating client integrity and ethical values as well as more practical points about competence to take on the work and the level of resources that are needed. Auditors also need to confirm, in an engagement letter, that management acknowledges its responsibilities in respect to the financial statements and internal controls.

This case study links to the following learning outcomes:

- Explain and evaluate the matters to be considered before accepting a new client or engagement.
- Explain and discuss the issues relating to agreeing the terms of an audit engagement that an audit firm must consider such as resources, fees and the purpose and content of an audit engagement letter.

Scenario

You work in the audit department of Thomson & Co, a large audit firm. You have been asked to evaluate whether Thomson & Co should take on a new audit client, Jones Ltd, and to respond to the company's managing director's questions in relation to the audit engagement letter.

Jones Ltd was established five years ago. The company is a food processor, producing a range of organic frozen foods and ready meals. The company's founders, two sisters called Lena and Suzanna Connor, provided start-up investment of £5 million and they have recently introduced a further £4 million as an equity investment to help fund further expansion of the business.

Due to the company's small size, the financial statements have not previously been subject to independent audit or review. However, Lena and Suzanna are hoping to raise a further £3 million bank finance to build a new factory. As a basis for this lending decision, the bank has requested to see the company's financial statements accompanied by an independent auditor's report. The bank also wants to see a cash flow and profit forecast for the next two years, and Lena and Suzanna have asked Thomson & Co to prepare these forecasts and to provide an opinion on them as well as on the financial statements.

For the last year, the company's accounts have been maintained by Lena, who studied management and accountancy at university and went on to work in risk management at a large manufacturing company before setting up Jones Ltd. Prior to Lena maintaining the accounts, the company engaged a firm of accountants called Khalil Associates to provide the accounting function, including the preparation of annual financial statements. Khalil Associates also submitted tax returns and ran the monthly payroll. Jones Ltd decided not to renew their contract with Khalil Associates two years ago, when Lena and Suzanna disagreed with some of the accounting policies being used by Khalil Associates which they believe resulted in too much corporation tax being paid. You have searched for the company's most recent financial statements filed at Companies House and note that they were submitted two months late.

Since the relationship with Khalil Associates was terminated, the company's payroll function has been outsourced to a service organization, which is responsible for payroll preparation and the submission of payroll-related tax returns to HM Revenue & Customs.

To develop your understanding of Jones Ltd, you carried out an internet search, and an interesting point came to light. Recently, it has been reported in the news that not all of the company's suppliers use organic farming practices. Jones Ltd has denied these allegations, but one dairy farmer, who has a contract to supply the company with milk and cheese, claims that Jones Ltd is happy to pay a lower price for his non-organic products.

Finally, Lena and Suzanna have sent you the following email:

To: Audit Manager
From: Lena and Suzanna Jones
Subject: Audit appointment

Hello
Further to our conversations about appointing your firm to audit Jones Ltd, we have some further information and a couple of questions:

First, we want to let you know that we have just started to discuss expanding the business by acquiring one of our competitors–Deli Ltd. We know the company's directors well and we believe that they are keen to sell their majority shareholding to us. We believe that you know this company too, as the directors told us that you have been the company's auditor for the last few years. Hopefully, you can help us plan the acquisition and value the company. We think we will need to raise £30 million to buy Deli Ltd and we will probably approach our bank for this.

Second, we would like you to explain the audit engagement letter to us –what it is for? We are not experts in accounting, so we are not confident in signing the letter without understanding what is included.

Thank you
Lena and Suzanna

Required

- Evaluate the matters which should be considered by Thomson & Co in deciding whether to accept Jones Ltd as an audit client.
- Briefly respond to the question raised by Lena and Suzanna in their email, in relation to the audit engagement letter.

Answer

Acceptance issues

There are a number of matters which are relevant to the acceptance decision. One issue is that the financial statements have not been audited before, due to the company's small size. This increases the risk of material misstatement and means that there is a high risk of error in the financial statements. This risk is elevated by the fact that for the last year, the accounts have been maintained by Lena, who is not an expert in accounting. She studied accounting at university, but her knowledge could be out of date, so the accounts may not be technically accurate. This means that should Thomson & Co take on the audit, they will need to ensure sufficient resources are available to perform sufficient audit procedures and reduce the audit risk to an acceptable level.

A related matter is that there was a disagreement with Khalil Associates about accounting treatments, leading to a discontinuance of the professional relationship. This implies a lack of management integrity, particularly because the nature of the disagreement seems to imply that Lena and Suzanna are keen to avoid or evade paying tax, which could be a serious and possibly criminal activity.

Thomson & Co should consider whether it is appropriate to take on a client with a history of removing previous professional advisors. Management could be difficult to work with, make unreasonable demands, possibly acting with intimidation.

Submitting the financial statements two months late is not necessarily a 'deal-breaker' but it could indicate that the company's management have a lax attitude to company administration and that the general control environment could be quite weak. There could be a disregard for compliance with relevant law and regulations.

The fact that payroll is outsourced to an external provider should not impact significantly on the acceptance decision, as long as Thomson & Co can arrange access to information held by the service provider and can ascertain the strength of internal controls applied to payroll.

In terms of client integrity and business ethics, in addition to the potential tax avoidance/evasion noted above, there is also an issue relating to the company's supply chain. Jones Ltd sells organic goods but one of its suppliers claims that he is supplying non-organic products to the company. This indicates that management is making unethical business decisions in order to save costs. Thomson & Co should carefully consider whether they wish to have a business relationship with such a company and its management. Any damage to the reputation of Jones Ltd, should the unethical business practice become widely publicized, could impact on the reputation of Thomson & Co.

In terms of anti-money laundering regulations, Thomson & Co will need to perform the necessary procedures for example confirming the identity of key shareholders and all directors of the company and understanding the company's business model. One issue they should look into is the sources of funding of the business, in particular the £9 million that has been introduced by the company's two founders.

There is nothing in the scenario to suggest that Thomson & Co lacks the necessary competence and resources to perform a good-quality audit. In fact, the firm already provides the audit to Deli Ltd, which operates in food processing, indicating that the audit firm has some experience in this sector. The firm should bear in mind that if Jones Ltd acquires Deli Ltd, the enlarged group will have a much bigger size, and the scope of the audit will increase which will impact the resources required.

The company is looking to obtain a significant amount of bank finance—£3 million to build a new factory and a further £30 million should the acquisition of Deli Ltd go ahead. In respect of the £3 million finance, Thomson & Co has been asked by Lena and Suzanna to be involved with preparing forecasts and to provide an opinion on the forecasts. This gives rise to several ethical threats to objectivity. A self-review threat arises because the forecasts will be reviewed as part of the audit and therefore the audit team will be reviewing work performed by themselves or by colleagues from Thomson & Co, so they are less likely to challenge the forecasts and the assumptions on which they are based. There is also a potential advocacy threat because Thomson & Co would be supporting their client and promoting their interests to the bank by being involved with securing the finance. In addition, a management threat arises, particularly given the small size of Jones Ltd and lack of expertise in accounting and finance matters of the company's management.

Therefore, should Thomson & Co accept the audit, they can only perform the non-audit service in respect of preparing the forecasts if safeguards can be used to reduce these threats to an acceptable level, for example, using separate personnel who are not involved with the audit and having both engagements subject to independent review.

Thomson & Co would not be in a position to provide an opinion on the forecasts if they have prepared them, and this should be explained to the company's management.

Further ethical threats exist in relation to the potential acquisition of Deli Ltd. It appears that Deli Ltd is an existing client of Thomson & Co leading to a conflict of interest. This arises when an audit firm provides a service in relation to two or more clients whose interests in respect of the matter are in conflict. In this case, the interests of Jones Ltd and Deli Ltd will be conflicting; Jones Ltd will want to purchase the shares for the lowest possible amount and the owners of Deli Ltd will want to sell them for the highest possible amount. This creates, therefore, a significant threat to the objectivity of the audit firm, who may be seen to be acting in the interest of one party at the expense of the other.

In all cases of conflict of interest, the audit firm should make full disclosure to both parties and ask them both to confirm that they are happy for the service to be provided. In reality, it is likely that one of the parties will refuse permission in which case the service should not be provided.

Finally performing a valuation service would also create a self-review threat because the audit firm would have a significant influence over the valuation of Deli Ltd, which would consequently be used to consolidate their accounts into the new, enlarged group which the audit firm would be responsible for auditing in the future.

Audit engagement letter

Engagement letters are mandatory and must be issued as soon as an engagement is accepted and evaluated every year to ensure it is up to date and whether the entity needs to be reminded of the terms of the audit engagement. Engagement letters are reissued whenever there is a change in law or regulation or when changes to the terms of the audit engagement are agreed. The engagement letter forms the basis of a contractual relationship between the audit firm and the client company.

The engagement letter must outline the scope of the audit engagement (i.e. work that is to be performed). It should also document the basis on which the fees will be charged. The engagement letter must detail management's responsibilities and the preconditions of the audit, to ensure that management acknowledges responsibility for certain things (e.g. for adhering to the applicable financial reporting framework and establishing appropriate internal controls).

One of the reasons for having an engagement letter is to agree the terms of the engagement and to document them. This limits misunderstandings between auditor and client about the audit process and the amount that will be paid for the audit. If a dispute were to arise, for example in relation to the responsibilities of auditor or management, a signed engagement letter offers protection to both the audit firm and the client company.

Activity solutions

Activity 6.1—Audit tenders

Imagine that you are an audit partner, and your firm has been invited to tender for the audit of a prestigious company. You are keen to obtain the engagement and there are no ethical reasons why you should not accept the client.

List the matters that you think the audit firm should include in the tender document.

Suggested answer points:

- An outline of the audit firm including key specialisms relevant to the client.
- An introduction to the personnel likely to be involved with the audit (e.g. the audit engagement partner).
- An evaluation of the client's expectations e.g. the scope and nature of the work required, any important deadlines.
- An explanation of how the firm will meet these expectations—this could include a summary of audit methodology.
- The proposed audit fee, and how it has been determined.
- Confirmation that there are no ethical barriers to accepting the appointment.

Activity 6.2—Integrity and ethical values

Imagine that you are evaluating whether to take on a new audit client. What are examples of matters or issues you could find out about the potential client which could lead you to believe there is a lack of integrity and ethical values? List as many as you can.

Suggested answer points:

- The client appears to be involved in unethical business practices (e.g. poor track record in respect of how employees are treated).
- Instances of non-compliance with relevant law and regulations (e.g. lack of regard for health and safety requirements).
- Connections with other people or companies which appear to lack integrity (e.g. using suppliers with a poor reputation).
- Frequent investigations by relevant regulatory bodies (e.g. tax investigations).
- Resignation or removal of previous audit provider or other professional services providers over matters relating to integrity and ethics (e.g. disagreements over accounting issues).
- Unrealistic expectations regarding the audit fee i.e. management intends to pay as little as possible for the audit.

Activity 6.3—Setting an audit fee

Imagine that your audit firm has tendered for the audit of a new client, Ghost Ltd a small company which chooses to have an audit performed on its financial statements. The audit partner has proposed an audit fee which is 25 per cent below the market rate for this type of engagement. The partner is hoping to win the audit and then be able to provide Ghost Ltd with tax and other non-audit services, on which a high profit will be made.

What are the professional and ethical problems caused by the audit partner's proposed audit fee?

Suggested answer points:

The audit partner's proposal is effectively lowballing. This means deliberately providing the audit for a low fee, which will probably mean that the audit engagement is loss-making. There is a risk that the audit team will not carry out enough audit procedures in order to save time and costs. There is a high detection risk, and the audit firm is at risk of not obtaining sufficient appropriate evidence. From an ethical point of view, the audit firm will not be acting with due professional care.

If the audit firm provides non-audit services to Ghost Ltd, threats to auditor objectivity will arise including a self-review threat because the audit team may over-rely on work performed by their colleagues in respect of tax and other areas relevant to the financial statements. There may also be a self-interest depending on the level of fee charged for the non-audit services, if this creates any fee dependency on Ghost Ltd. Given that Ghost Ltd is a small company, there is unlikely to be 'informed management' and therefore the audit firm may become involved in making management decisions, a further threat to objectivity.

Appendix—Illustrative audit engagement letter

Auditor & Co LLP
123 High Street
Anytown
County
AB1 2CD

14 April 20X1
Board of dircctors
Harper Limited
456 Low Street
Downtown
EF1 3GH

Dear Directors

This letter, together with the attached terms of business dated 14 April 20X1, set out the basis on which we are to act as auditors to your company. This letter also sets out both your and our responsibilities.

You have requested that we carry out an audit of the financial statements for the year ended 31 March 20X1. The financial statements comprise the statement of financial position as at 31 March, the statement of comprehensive income, the statement of changes in equity, the statement of cash flows for the year then ended, and a summary of significant accounting policies and other explanatory information.

We are pleased to confirm our acceptance and our understanding of this audit engagement by means of this letter. Our audit will be conducted with the objective of our expressing an opinion on the financial statements.

1. Responsibilities of management

Our audit will be conducted on the basis that management acknowledge and understand that they are responsible for:

(a) The preparation and fair presentation of the financial statements in accordance with International Financial Reporting Standards.

(b) Such internal control as management determines is necessary to enable the preparation of financial statements that are free from material misstatement, whether due to fraud or error.

(c) Providing the auditor with:
   (i) access to all information of which management is aware that is relevant to the preparation of the financial statements, such as accounting records, documentation, and other matters;
   (ii) additional information that we may request from management for the purposes of the audit; and
   (iii) unrestricted access to persons within the entity from whom we determine it necessary to obtain audit evidence.

As part of our audit procedures, we will request written confirmation from management in the form of representations made to us in connection with the audit.

2. Responsibilities of the auditor

We will conduct our audit in accordance with International Standards on Auditing (UK) (ISAs (UK)). Those standards require that we comply with ethical requirements issued by the FRC (Audit, Reporting and Governance Authority) and our professional body and plan and perform the audit to obtain reasonable assurance about whether the financial statements are free from material misstatement. An audit involves performing procedures to obtain audit evidence about the amounts and disclosures in the financial statements. The procedures selected depend on the auditor's judgement, including the assessment of the risks of material misstatement of the financial statements, whether due to fraud or error. An audit also includes evaluation the appropriateness of accounting policies selected, and the reasonableness of accounting estimates made by management, as well as evaluating the overall presentation of the financial statements.

Due to the inherent limitations of an audit, together with the inherent limitations of internal control, there is an unavoidable risk that some material misstatements may not be detected, even though the audit is properly planned and performed in accordance with the ISAs (UK).

In making our risk assessments, we consider internal control relevant to Harper Limited's preparation of the financial statements in order to design audit procedures that are appropriate in the circumstances, but not for the purpose of expressing an opinion on the effectiveness of Harper's system of internal control. We will communicate to you, in writing, about any significant deficiencies in internal control relevant to the audit of the financial statements that we have identified during the course of the audit.

3. Form of our report

We will report to the shareholders of Harper Ltd as a body whether, in our opinion, the financial statements present fairly, in all material respects, the financial position of Harper Ltd as 31 March, and its financial performance and cash flows for the year then ended in accordance with International Financial Reporting Standards. The form and content of our report may need to be amended in light of our audit findings.

4. **Fees**

Our fees will be based on the time required by the individuals assigned to the engagement, plus VAT and out-of-pocket expenses. Individual hourly charge-out rates vary depending on the degree of responsibility involved and the skill and experience required.

5. Limitation of liability

To the fullest extent permitted by law, we will not be responsible for any losses, where you or others supply incorrect or incomplete information, or fail to supply any appropriate information or where you fail to act on our advice or respond promptly to communications from us.

Our work is not, unless there is a legal or regulatory requirement, to be made available to third parties without our written consent and we will accept no responsibility to third parties for any aspect of our professional services or work that is made available to them.

6. Confirmation of the terms and conditions of the audit engagement

We would be grateful if you could please sign and return the attached copy of this engagement letter to indicate your acknowledgement of, and agreement with, the arrangements for our audit of the financial statements including our respective responsibilities.

If this letter and the attached terms of business are not in accordance with your understanding of our terms of appointment, please contact the audit engagement partner immediately.

Yours sincerely
Auditor & Co LLP

We understand and agree to the terms and conditions of this letter of engagement and agree to be bound by them.

....

For and on behalf of the board of directors of Harper Ltd
Date

The above engagement letter contains some specific elements that are worthy of explanation.

Table 6.2

Element in the engagement letter	Why it is important
It is addressed to the directors of Harper Ltd	The auditor's report will be addressed to the shareholders (members) of Harper Ltd, but the directors will sign the engagement letter on behalf of the shareholders
Responsibilities of management and responsibilities of the auditor	These paragraphs set out the expectations of each party to reduce the expectations gap. In addition, the auditor's responsibilities will include the scope of the audit which is the basis on which the auditor will form their opinion
The responsibilities of the auditor confirm they will obtain reasonable assurance about whether the financial statements are free from material misstatement, whether caused by fraud or error	This is one of the limitations of an audit. The auditor does not strive for maximum assurance as this is not practicable due to time constraints and audit evidence is persuasive rather than conclusive. The auditor will provide reasonable assurance in the auditor's report which is a high level of assurance, but is not a 100 per cent guarantee that the financial statements are completely accurate
The auditor will report to the shareholders of Harper Ltd as a body	This defines who the intended users of the auditor's report are and therefore who can place reliance on it
Confirmation of agreement to the terms	Both the client and the auditor must sign and retain a copy of the engagement letter to confirm their understanding and agreement to the terms of the audit engagement letter which is essentially a contract between the parties

7 Audit Planning—The Objectives of Audit Planning and Understanding the Entity

Introduction

The planning stage is crucial to the success of the audit and planning must be detailed and thorough to ensure that the overall objectives of the audit are met.

In general terms, the planning stage of the audit involves developing an understanding of the audit client, identifying risk factors that may indicate a risk of material misstatement in the financial statements, performing analytical review, determining financial statement and performance materiality levels, and developing an audit strategy and audit plan. Planning is a dynamic process that may evolve during the audit and must always respond to changes in the circumstances of the audited entity.

Adherence to the requirements of the relevant International Standards on Auditing (ISAs) should result in a well-focused audit, staffed by appropriate personnel, performing relevant and appropriate audit procedures. Proper planning should reduce audit risk (the risk that the auditor forms an incorrect opinion on the financial statements), and the auditor must document their planning carefully, to ensure that the audit is performed in the way it was intended. Any deviations from the audit plan can increase audit risk.

In this chapter, we begin our exploration of audit planning by considering the requirements of ISA (UK) 300 *Planning an Audit of Financial Statements*, which provides the overall objectives of audit planning and therefore is the starting point in developing an understanding of this stage of the audit. We will think about how audit planning should be documented, in particular the form and content of an audit strategy and an audit plan. We will also start to consider a long and detailed standard—ISA (UK) 315 *Identifying and Assessing the Risks of Material Misstatement*, which we will continue to explore in Chapters 8 and 9.

We will also look at something quite practical—how does the auditor obtain understanding of the audit client and the environment in which it operates? This is especially important when auditing a new client, when the auditor will have to build up knowledge and understanding from scratch.

When does audit planning take place, and what does it include?

Naturally, it is reasonable to assume that planning occurs towards the start of an audit engagement. However, planning should not be seen as a discrete and separate part of the overall audit. When auditors refer to the 'planning stage' of an audit, this can include:

- Obtaining information in the form of an update from clients about business development or significant events that have taken place during the year.
- Documenting and evaluating changes to systems that have taken place.
- Obtaining and reviewing recent financial information, for example, the latest management accounts.
- Performing risk assessment and determining financial statements and performance materiality levels.
- Deciding on how to approach the audit—which areas should be prioritized, what type of audit evidence should be obtained?
- Preparing the audit strategy and audit plan.
- Planning the practical things—who will form the audit team? When will be audit fieldwork take place? What is the deadline for issuing the auditor's report?

Planning does not follow a set sequence: the elements overlap with each other—for example, evaluating systems informs the risk assessment process and the audit plan. Audit planning should be revisited during the audit and revised if necessary, for example, if new information comes to light which impacts risk assessment.

For a large and complex audit, for example when the client is a listed, multinational organization, planning often begins shortly after, or in connection with, the completion of the previous audit, for example, with a review of issues that were discussed with management, such as control deficiencies or unadjusted errors. Such matters are relevant to the next year's audit and need to be considered when planning.

Learning outcomes

- Describe the objectives of planning and explain the benefits of a well-planned audit and preliminary planning activities.
- Explain the components of an audit strategy and an audit plan, and distinguish between the two.
- Explain what is meant by obtaining understanding of the audit client and discuss the methods by which this understanding is obtained.
- Explain the difference between an interim audit and a final audit and the type of work performed at each stage.

7.1 Planning an audit of financial statements—benefits and preliminary activities

Effective planning should focus the auditor's attention on key areas of the audit and ensure that sufficient resources are allocated to the engagement team. Planning should result in an audit which is well directed and supervised, and which is cost-efficient. All of the auditor's duties as outlined in the engagement letter, as discussed in Chapter 6, will be performed, and the quality of the engagement should be assured.

ISA (UK) 300 *Planning an Audit of Financial Statements* deals with audit planning in overview. The overall objective of ISA (UK) 300 is that the auditor must plan the audit so that it will be performed in an effective manner. An efficient and effective audit will only take place if adequate audit planning is performed, leading to the development of the overall audit strategy and audit plan.

We will explore the nature and purpose of the audit strategy and audit plan later in the chapter. Before doing this, we need to understand the reason for audit planning; in other words, what are the benefits of a well-planned audit?

7.1.1 **Benefits of adequate planning**

Planning should ensure that transactions, balances, and disclosures that are at risk of material misstatement are identified early in the audit process. This enables adequate resources to be allocated to the audit of these high-risk areas, thereby reducing the overall level of audit risk. The auditor can plan to audit less significant areas with fewer resources or a different type of resource, for example, using junior members of the audit team. In this way, attention is focused on the key areas of the audit right from the start.

One of the benefits of audit planning is that it helps the auditor to identify and respond to problems. Significant problems should be identified early in the planning process, so that the auditor can plan to address them effectively. For example, if, during planning, the auditor discovers that an expected source of evidence is not available, alternative means of obtaining evidence can be devised.

In addition, planning ensures that the audit is conducted in a reasonable timeframe, and procedures and activities can be planned to coincide with key dates such as the financial year end and anticipated date of approval of the financial statements. A poorly planned audit may not meet its deadline, causing problems for the client, for example, delaying the release of the financial statements to shareholders or regulatory bodies.

Activity 7.1 Benefits of audit planning

In addition to the benefits previously outlined, what do you think are the other benefits of audit planning?

7.1.2 **Audit planning activities**

According to ISA (UK) 300, two types of planning activities must take place—preliminary engagement activities and developing the audit strategy and audit plan.

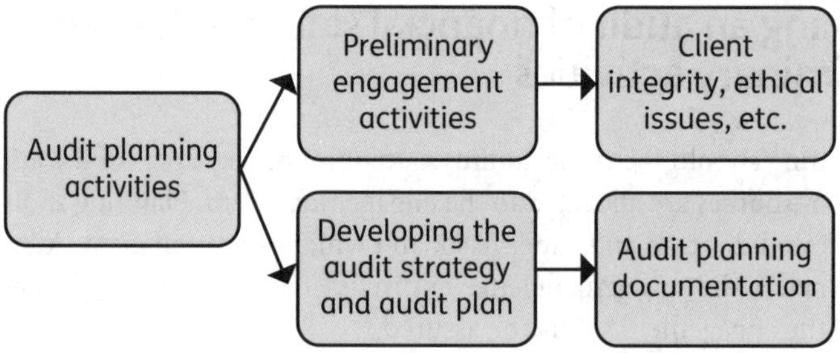

Figure 7.1 Audit planning activities

7.1.2.1 **Preliminary engagement activities**

ISA (UK) 300 requires that the auditor undertake the following preliminary engagement activities at the beginning of the current audit engagement.

- Performing procedures regarding the continuance of the client relationship and the specific audit engagement;
- Evaluating compliance with relevant ethical requirements, including independence; and
- Establishing an understanding of the terms of the engagement.[1]

The purpose of these activities is to ensure that the auditor has identified potential problems which might impair the quality of the audit, for example, issues relating to auditor independence or client integrity. ISA (UK) 300 reiterates the importance of preliminary engagement activities as they may influence the auditor's response to assessed risks. For example, the terms of the engagement may require the auditor to perform a specific task, which then needs to be reflected in the audit plan.

Undertaking the above procedures also allows the auditor to ensure that there is no misunderstanding with the audit client as to the terms of the engagement.

It is important to understand that consideration of client continuance and relevant ethical requirements should continue throughout the audit engagement. Auditors must ensure that they remain alert to changes in circumstances or specific events which might impact matters such as independence or client integrity, in which case the auditor must consider an appropriate response, for example changing planned audit procedures.

The points above included in ISA (UK) 300 are themselves requirements of other ISAs: ISA (UK) 210 *Agreeing the Terms of Audit Engagements* and ISA (UK) 220 *Quality Management for an Audit of Financial Statements*. They will not be considered again in detail in this chapter because we have explored the relevant issues in previous chapters (Chapter 5 on audit quality management and Chapter 6 on agreeing the terms of audit engagements), but it is important to note the interrelated nature of the planning ISAs, which need to be considered holistically by the auditor.

[1] FRC, 'ISA (UK) 300', 2016, para 6 <https://media.frc.org.uk/documents/ISA_UK_300_Updated_May_2022.pdf> (accessed 18 January 2024).

Before we move on to focus on the development of the audit strategy and audit plan, we should point out that ISA (UK) 300 requires that the engagement partner and other key members of the engagement team be involved in planning the audit, including planning and participating in the discussion among engagement team members. This will ensure that people with seniority and experience are involved in the planning process, which should work to improve the efficiency of the audit and the quality of the audit work performed.

7.2 The audit strategy and audit plan

Audit planning activities must include establishing an overall audit strategy for the engagement and developing an audit plan.

The audit strategy sets out in general terms how the audit is to be conducted and sets the scope, timing, and direction of the audit. This should then be used to develop the audit plan, which contains the detailed responses to the auditor's risk assessment. The audit plan contains specific planned audit procedures which will be carried out to implement the strategy and obtain sufficient appropriate audit evidence to support the audit opinion.

7.2.1 Developing the audit strategy

ISA (UK) 300 states that, 'the auditor shall establish an overall audit strategy that sets the scope, timing and direction of the audit, and that guides the development of the audit plan.'[2]

Developing an appropriate audit strategy should mean that sufficient and appropriate resources are deployed. This is a key consideration and does not just mean the number of auditors assigned to an audit team. It also involves matters such as:

- How will the audit team be managed? How many audit managers and partners are needed?
- The timing of resource allocation—when will the interim and final audits be performed? Is there sufficient time allotted for file reviews by senior members of the audit team?
- When will specialists be engaged, and when will their work be required for evaluation?
- Will resources be required in remote locations, or at specific times, for example, to attend inventory counts?

Essentially this is all part of good project management—it is helpful to think of the audit as a significant project to be managed, and developing a good audit strategy is similar to producing a project scope, budget, and Gantt chart to ensure the project is properly planned.

There are a number of matters to be considered when establishing the audit strategy.

[2] Ibid., para 7.

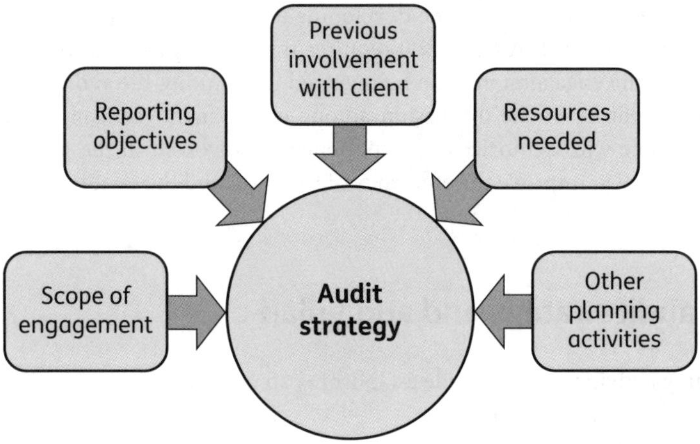

Figure 7.2 Matters impacting audit strategy

7.2.1.1 **The scope of engagement**

Essentially, the scope of an audit means 'what needs to be audited'—it could be just the financial statements or include other information such as additional published reports. The financial statements could be simple (a small single company) or complex (a large multinational group). Therefore, some audit engagements have specific characteristics that mean the audit has a wider scope than the audit of other entities. Other circumstances which would widen the scope of the audit include the status of the reporting entity (listed or non-listed), whether there are overseas operations, or whether there are industry-specific or other regulatory reporting requirements. In some circumstances, the client may need to prepare specific information which falls under the scope of the audit. For example, in the public sector, organizations are often required to report specific performance measures, which while not necessarily part of the financial statements, are subject to external audit under the relevant regulations. All these circumstances would indicate a wider scope of engagement, and that specific or additional resources are likely to be needed.

The auditor must also consider the financial reporting framework of the financial statements, including whether reconciliations may be required to other frameworks, and whether currency retranslations will be needed, both of which again increase the scope of the audit. This is common in multinational organizations where several financial reporting frameworks are applied (e.g. IFRS and US GAAP).

Auditing in practice 7.1 Audit engagements with additional scope

The following are examples of regulatory bodies in the UK which may require organizations operating under their remit to submit specific reports in addition to financial statements. Depending on the terms of their engagement, the auditor of a regulated company or other type of reporting entity may face an increased scope in their work due to additional reporting requirements.

- Charity Commission for England and Wales
- Environment Agency

- Financial Conduct Authority
- Pensions Regulator
- Solicitors Regulation Authority
- Civil Aviation Authority
- Ofgem (Office of the Gas and Electricity Markets)
- Ofwat (Water Services Regulation Authority)

7.2.1.2 **Reporting objectives**

The auditor will need to determine the date by which the audit needs to be completed, bearing in mind the client's scheduled date for release of the financial statements. In addition, other communications to the client should be considered, for example, reports to those charged with governance, and the expected timings of these. The auditor should also consider how to communicate within the audit engagement team, including the need for, and the timings of, team meetings. Communication with other auditors in a group audit engagement always needs careful planning to ensure that messages are communicated effectively and on a timely basis. In addition, certain regulatory bodies require financial statements to be fully audited by specific dates—for example, an academy school regulated by the Department for Education in the UK must have their financial statements for the year ended 31 August audited and submitted to the Education and Skills Funding Agency by 31 December each year.

7.2.1.3 **Previous involvement with the client**

The results of previous years' audits can be very significant in determining the audit strategy. For example, if significant problems were encountered in performing the audit in the previous year, the reasons for those problems should be considered, and if possible, the audit strategy should be developed so that the same problems are not encountered again in the subsequent year.

Activity 7.2 Impact of previous involvement with the client

Can you think of two examples of how the auditor's previous involvement with a client may impact planning the audit?

7.2.1.4 **Resources**

The key issue here is to ensure that the audit strategy will result in the formation of an audit team with sufficient skills and resources to perform a high-quality audit, and that tasks are allocated appropriately within the team. High-risk and complex areas should be audited by more senior members of the audit team. Budgeting for resources should include an element of contingency, in case some areas take longer than anticipated to audit.

Timing is also a key feature of the audit strategy in terms of resources. If the audit is time pressured due to a tight deadline, then more resources will need to be allocated to ensure that all necessary audit work is completed and can be reviewed in time to meet the deadline. Different resources may be needed at the interim audit, at the final audit, and at particular points in time, for instance when the organization plans to hold an inventory count, which could be very labour intensive for the audit team.

The audit strategy should also consider how the resources are managed, directed, and supervised, such as when team briefing and debriefing meetings are expected to be held, how and when engagement partner and manager reviews are expected to take place, and whether engagement quality control reviews are required.

7.2.1.5 **Other planning activities**

The auditor should bear in mind the results of other planning activities that have been performed, such as the determination of materiality, the results of risk assessment, and preliminary analytical procedures. The assessment of the client's internal control environment is particularly significant, as this will determine the overall audit strategy that is adopted—this is discussed in more detail in Chapter 8.

Auditing in practice 7.2 Extract from an audit strategy document

The audit is to be carried out in accordance with ISAs (UK). The sampling methodology is to be based on the prior year audit approach and will aim for a 95 per cent assurance level.

Overview of the audit

The audit will concentrate on:

- Testing assets and expenses for overstatement and liabilities and income for understatement.
- Documenting and evaluating the client's internal control environment.
- Obtaining audit evidence to support the relevant assertions (e.g. rights and obligations for non-current assets).
- Carrying out risk assessment procedures.
- Forming a conclusion on the material areas of the financial statements and minimizing audit risk to the maximum extent possible.

Key dates

The following milestones are relevant:

• Audit fieldwork to commence:	20 April 20X7
• Issue of draft report for management comments:	14 May 20X7
• Final report to be issued for management comments:	21 May 20X7
• Present audit findings to management:	26 May 20X7
• Approval of the financial statements:	27 May 20X7

Review of audit work will be performed by the audit senior and audit manager on a daily basis as each task is completed.

Internal control

Management have asserted to us that they are committed to the design, implementation, and maintenance of sound internal controls which will prevent and detect and correct, on a timely basis, misstatements. Internal control reviews are carried out internally quarterly, and throughout the reporting period, all controls have been subject to some internal review for operating effectiveness.

Inventory count

The client's inventory count will be taking place on 31 March 20X7. Inventory is located in three warehouses which are local to the audit firm. Each warehouse will be counted by members of staff from the finance department. Four auditors will be required to attend the inventory count to ensure management's instructions are being carried out and the inventory count reduces the risk of material misstatement of the final inventory valuation to an acceptable level.

Financial reporting framework

The financial reporting framework to be used is International Financial Reporting Standards (IFRS).

Materiality levels (based on forecast financial statements)

Financial statement materiality:	£85,000
Performance materiality:	£25,000

Fraud

Management and those charged with governance have responsibility for the design and implementation of internal controls which prevent or detect fraud and/or error and to ensure regulatory compliance. The audit team is to be informed by management of any fraud or material misstatements.

Management representations

ISA (UK) 580 *Written Representations* requires us to obtain representations from management and/or those charged with governance on material areas of the financial statements. We will require these written representations be provided to us before we can sign the auditor's report.

Results of the prior year audit

The prior year auditor's report was unmodified with an emphasis of matter paragraph included in respect of the entity's restructuring exercise which was deemed to be a material subsequent event.

7.2.2 The audit plan

The audit plan is a detailed programme giving instructions as to how each area of the audit will be conducted. In other words, the audit plan details the specific procedures to be carried out to implement the strategy and complete the audit. The audit plan should also contain details such as whether the use of experts is required. Throughout, the auditor must ensure that the audit plan is developed with its prime objective in mind which is to reduce audit risk to an acceptably low level.

The establishment of the overall audit strategy and the detailed audit plan are not necessarily discrete or sequential processes but are closely interrelated since changes in one may result in consequential changes to the other. Therefore, it is not necessarily the case that the audit strategy is prepared and completed before the audit plan is devised, and in practice it is typical for the two to be developed together.

ISA (UK) 300 provides guidance on what should be included in the audit plan, stating that the audit plan should describe:

- the nature, timing, and extent of planned risk assessment procedures
- the nature, timing, and extent of planned further audit procedures at the assertion level
- other planned audit procedures that are required to be carried out so that the engagement complies with ISAs.[3]

Typically an audit plan will include sections dealing with business understanding, internal controls, risk assessment procedures, materiality, results of analytical procedures, and planned audit procedures (i.e. the responses to the risks identified and other mandatory audit procedures).

To give you an idea of the typical sections of an audit plan, an outline of the main headings is provided.

Procedures to obtain business understanding, for example:

- review of entity's governance and management structure;
- confirmation of applicable financial reporting framework;
- documentation of systems and controls; and
- preliminary analytical review on latest available management accounts.

Risk assessment procedures, for example:

- inquiries with management regarding financial and operating issues;
- discussion with internal audit personnel with respect to their recent activities;
- analytical procedures on financial and non-financial information; and
- review of information obtained in prior years (e.g. identification of past misstatements).

Planned audit procedures in response to identified risks at the assertion level, for example:

- circularization of trade receivables;
- attendance at year-end inventory count;
- physical verification of a sample of additions to non-current assets; and
- substantive analytical procedures on expenses included in operating profit.

Other mandatory procedures include:

- final analytical procedures;
- going concern review;
- subsequent events procedures; and
- obtaining written representations from those charged with governance.

The plan in respect of:

- the direction and supervision of engagement team members; and
- the review of their work.

[3] Ibid., para 9.

ISA (UK) 300 also requires the auditor to plan the nature, timing, and extent of direction and supervision of engagement team members and the review of their work. This is to ensure that the requirements of ISA (UK) 220 in relation to quality control are fulfilled. It is crucial that the audit plan includes the detail as to how supervision and review should be conducted during the audit, in order to perform a high-quality audit. Inadequate supervision and review can lead to the audit team making errors, for example, selecting inappropriate items for sampling, or failing to properly conclude on audit procedures.

The amount of detail included in the audit plan in relation to supervision and review will depend on factors such as the size and complexity of the entity being audited, the assessed risk of material misstatement, and the capabilities and competence of the audit team members. It is wise to build some contingency time into the audit plan, so that in the case of delays or other disruption to the audit team's work, there is still ample time for proper review to take place.

While it is not a requirement of ISA (UK) 300 that the auditor should discuss the audit strategy and plan with management of the audit client, in practice there is usually communication of certain aspects of the auditor's approach. This should help with the smooth running of the audit, for instance, so that management know when information will be required or that they will need to allow the auditor access to the accounting systems. When discussing audit planning matters with management, the auditor must take care not to reveal information which may impair the quality and effectiveness of the audit. For example, details about materiality levels or the nature of planned audit procedures should not be made available, as this could allow the client to hide facts or information from the auditor or obscure their work in other ways.

7.2.2.1 **Planning the audit of disclosures**

The auditor must consider the audit of disclosures in the notes to the financial statements at the planning stage. It is perhaps easy to focus on the audit of the balances and transactions that are contained in the statement of financial position and the statement of profit or loss, as the draft or projected versions of these will often be the key information on which the audit is planned. However, ISA (UK) 300 emphasizes the importance of disclosures within the financial statements, to ensure that sufficient resources are allocated to their audit and that there is enough time for review of the audit work performed. The timing of auditing disclosures can be problematic, as the notes are often not drafted until late in the process of the audit, leaving little time for proper attention by the audit team.

This issue is particularly important for companies required to produce significant and complex disclosures, for example those relating to financial instruments, segmental reporting, and pension plans.

Auditors will need to consider whether new or revised disclosures are necessary, for example, due to change in business circumstances or new IFRS requirements. Many audit firms use disclosure checklists to verify the adequacy of the disclosures. It is important that these are up to date, reflecting any changes made to accounting standards, to ensure that the disclosures are technically correct. If the checklist is out of date, this increases audit risk as a material disclosure may be inadequate.

7.2.3 **Documentation and changes to the audit strategy and audit plan**

The audit strategy and audit plan are not fixed once the planning stage of the audit is complete. It is important that both are updated and changed as necessary as the audit progresses. For example, as a result of unexpected events, or changes in conditions, the auditor may need to modify the overall audit strategy and audit plan and thereby the resulting planned nature, timing, and extent of further audit procedures, based on the revised consideration of assessed risks.

This may be the case when information comes to the auditor's attention that differs significantly from the information available when the auditor planned the audit procedures, for example, an event may take place after audit planning has been initially completed which creates doubt over going concern. Or, as a result of performing planned audit procedures additional information may come to light which may lead the auditor to amend initial risk assessment, or level of performance materiality, for all, or part, of the audit.

Documentation is crucial, because key decisions about how the audit will be performed are contained in the audit strategy and audit plan. Documentation should contain a record of the key matters evaluated during the development of the strategy.

Any significant changes made to the audit strategy during the audit process must also be documented accordingly, along with the rationale for the changes made. The documentation must therefore include the response made by the auditor to any significant changes that occur during the audit.

The audit strategy and audit plan do not need to be documented in a particular way. Some audit firms use memoranda, others use standard checklists. Some use standardized documentation while others tailor the specific form of the documentation to each audit engagement. The form of the documentation does not matter as long as it provides a clear record of how the audit was planned. Standard audit documentation often includes checklists to demonstrate that a full range of appropriate matters have been considered, and this can evidence compliance with the requirements of ISA (UK) 315 *Identifying and Assessing the Risks of Material Misstatement*. When standard audit documentation is used, it should be tailored to the client's circumstances and requirements as far as possible. Otherwise, the development of the audit strategy becomes generic, loses client-specific focus, and ends up as a 'tick-box' exercise rather than a proper consideration of issues specifically relevant to the client.

7.3 **Obtaining and documenting an understanding of the entity and its environment**

7.3.1 **Overview of ISA (UK) 315**

At this point we begin to look at one the of key standards relevant to the audit process, ISA (UK) 315 *Identifying and Assessing the Risks of Material Misstatement*. ISA 315 (UK) lays down the principles which must be followed when planning an audit. Planning an audit is based on risk assessment, which in turn is based on a thorough understanding of the audit client.

Before we start thinking about obtaining this understanding, it will be helpful to see how the overall audit planning approach required by ISA 315 works.

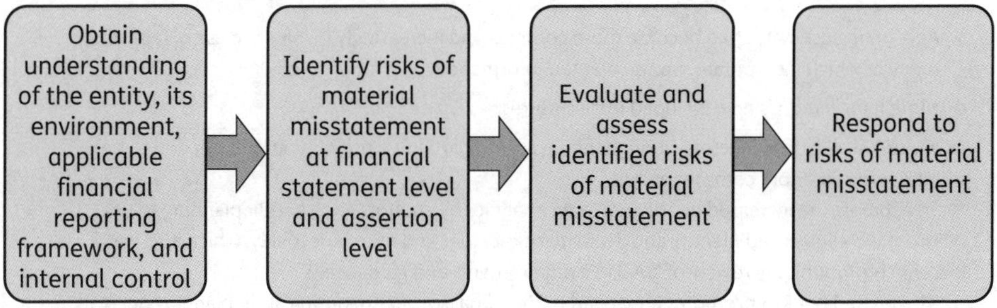

Figure 7.3 ISA (UK) 315 Approach to audit planning

ISA (UK) 315 is a long and detailed standard and we are going to look at it over a number of chapters. In this chapter, we begin with considering the requirements in relation to obtaining an understanding of the audit client and its environment. Perhaps it sounds obvious, but without an in-depth understanding of the audited entity, it is impossible to properly plan the audit. Obtaining a sound understanding of the client is therefore fundamental to audit planning. In Chapter 8 we will look specifically at internal controls and in Chapter 9 move on to think about risks of material misstatement.

We should also at this point mention that there are other relevant planning procedures which must take place, in particular the determination of materiality, and performing analytical procedures, which we cover in Chapter 10.

The key elements of the business understanding obtained must be documented. However, the ISA (UK) does not stipulate a method or level of detail required for this documentation, leaving it to the auditor's judgement to determine the extent of documentation needed. In the audit of smaller entities, which often have a small range of products or services, operate from a limited number of locations, and have a simple ownership structure, the documentation may be simple in form and relatively brief. Documentation may be prepared by using narrative notes or by completing a structured form. The notes may be maintained separately or incorporated into the documentation of the overall audit strategy.

Auditing in practice 7.3 Revision of ISA 315

In 2019, the International Audit and Assurance Standards Board (IAASB) approved major changes to ISA 315. The key aims of the changes related to better quality and more consistent risk assessments being performed as part of audit planning, enhancing the assessment of IT risks, as well as promoting the exercise of professional scepticism.

The IAASB recognized the need to review and update ISA 315 for the following reasons:

- The financial reporting frameworks under which their financial statements are prepared had evolved further and become more complex.
- Processes and systems including financial reporting systems were using technology to a much greater extent.
- Ownership and governance structures had become more complex, with an increased focus on enterprise risk management.

- Accounting estimates had become more complex and increasingly involve the use of fair values, many of which incorporate future-oriented information.
- More information is now included in disclosures.

As a result of all of these factors, audit planning and, in particular, risk assessments needed to be more rigorous or more comprehensive.

In addition, the increased use of audit data analytics by auditors allows audit planning to use different techniques and identify and evaluate risks earlier and more effectively, which also was a factor in promoting the review of ISA 315's requirements and guidance.

The revised ISA 315 promotes enhanced professional scepticism during audit planning and this is particularly relevant to obtaining understanding of the client. According to the IAASB, 'it becomes more difficult for auditors to apply appropriate professional skepticism if they do not have a sufficient understanding of the entity and its environment'.[4]

The Financial Reporting Council (FRC) issued ISA 315 (UK) in July 2020, based on the revised IAASB ISA 315. The effects of the revisions to ISA 315 were significant, and while students do not need to know the differences between the old and new versions of the standard, it is worth being aware that the requirements changed a few years ago.

7.3.2 **Obtaining an understanding of the business**

The phrase 'obtaining an understanding of the entity' has a very wide remit. ISA (UK) 315 requires the auditor to not just understand the entity, but also to obtain an understanding of the applicable financial reporting framework and the entity's system of internal control.

The audit team's understanding of the entity needs to emphasize the relevant aspects of the client's business model and includes an understanding of how the client measures its performance. This requirement intends for the audit team to understand how the entity operates and measures its performance from management's point of view, as that may better help the auditor understand where risks of a material misstatement could arise.

Activity 7.3 Enquiring about the client's business

What questions might an auditor ask a new client, to obtain preliminary understanding of the client's business?

To help the auditor focus on matters that are potentially relevant to the audit of financial statements, ISA (UK) 315 contains an appendix which provides specific examples of the information about the entity and its environment that the audit team should consider and document, where relevant, such as:

- The scope of the entity's activities and why it does them.
- The entity's structure and scale of its operations.
- How the entity's business model integrates the use of IT in its interactions with customers, suppliers, lenders and other stakeholders through IT interfaces and other technologies.[5]

[4] International Auditing and Assurance Standards Board, 'Revision of ISA315 (Revised)—IAASB Project Proposal', 2016 <https://www.iaasb.org/_flysystem/azure-private/meetings/files/ISA-315-Revised-Project-Proposal_Final-September-2016.pdf> (accessed 18 January 2024).

[5] FRC, 'ISA (UK) 315', 2020, para 3 <https://media.frc.org.uk/documents/ISA_UK_315_Jul_2020.pdf> (accessed 18 January 2024).

Activity 7.4 Understanding the business model

List examples of useful information that the auditor can enquire about and obtain, to develop their understanding of the client in respect of their:

- business model;
- business operations; and
- financing activities.

The auditor needs to build up an understanding of the environment in which the audit client operates. It may be helpful to think of this as a series of questions and in practice auditors use models such as PESTLE (Political, Economic, Social, Technological, Legal, Environmental) which is a model that helps the auditor to understand the external factors that may impact the client's business decisions. Porter's Five Forces is another model which considers the threat of new entrants to the market, the bargaining power of suppliers and of buyers, the threat of substitute products or services and the extent of competition between rivals. Both of these models can be used to help the auditor to understand external factors that influence a business. The auditor may use a checklist of questions, which would typically cover the following matters:

- What are the entity's lines of business? What are its key products or services?
- Who are the main suppliers?
- Who are the key customers?
- Is the market competitive?
- Is business seasonal?

7.3.2.1 Strategies, objectives, and financial performance

As part of obtaining business understanding the auditor will obtain information about the entity's objectives and strategies. 'Objectives' are the overall plans for the entity, determined by management. 'Strategies' are the approaches by which management intends to achieve its objectives.

An organization's objectives and strategies may change over time, so every year the auditor must discuss with management to identify any important changes which may have a bearing on the audit. Examples of matters which the auditor may consider include:

- the introduction of new products and services;
- starting significant research and development activities;
- introducing new technology to a production process or management information systems;
- expansion of the business into new geographical areas.

Auditing in practice 7.4 Sources of information for business understanding

When obtaining an understanding of the entity and its environment, the auditor needs to use a wide variety of information sources. Here are some examples of information sources, categorized as to whether they are publicly available or derived from the audit client.

Publicly available information

- Client's website—background about the company, its products, areas of operation, etc. If the company is listed, it is likely to have an investor relations section on its website which will contain a lot of very relevant information, such as published reports, investor presentations, operating/financial reviews.
- Trade press and industry websites—to provide general information about the industry and may also contain articles specific to the company (e.g. on recent developments or news stories affecting the client).
- Companies House—holds details of company directors, registered address, as well as financial statements filed.

Client information

- management accounts, forecast financial information, and related business plans;
- minutes of board meetings;
- organizational structure;
- internal audit reports and other relevant information (e.g. systems documentation); and
- correspondence with tax authorities.

Other ways to obtain information

- visit to client's premises to observe its operations;
- correspond with previous auditor and other professional advisers.

The auditor should also form an understanding of how the entity measures and reviews its financial performance. Organizations should have some system of measuring, monitoring, and reviewing their financial performance. Many organizations implement key performance indicators (KPIs) such as earnings per share, earnings before interest, tax, depreciation, and amortization (EBITDA), like-for-like sales, which are monitored internally but also published as part of the annual report.

The auditor needs to understand the measures which are seen as crucial to management because the existence of such measures creates a pressure for management bias. There is incentive for these measures to be shown in a positive light, especially when there is pressure from stakeholders and/or the measures are linked to performance targets and financial incentives. There is therefore potentially a high risk of misstatement and fraud in relation to published measures of financial performance.

To obtain understanding about performance measures used by management, the auditor can consider internal information such as budgets, forecasts, management accounts, and other internal reports. For listed entities, the auditor must also consider the type of KPIs that are disclosed in the annual report, mentioned in press releases, and other publicly available information, for example, investors presentations, and information on the company website. All of these published performance measures are sources of pressure for management to manipulate results. Auditors can also review external documentation such as reports from credit rating agencies, or bank correspondence. This type of documentation can offer a lot of information to auditors to help them understand the entity and in particular the pressures which may be present to maintain certain targets or metrics. For example, a bank agreement may contain a particular covenant relating to interest cover or gearing, which management will be under pressure to adhere to.

Auditing in practice 7.5 Tesco's accounting scandal

In 2014, the UK supermarket company Tesco was accused of applying incorrect accounting techniques for the recognition of income received from suppliers in the form of rebates, sometimes known as commercial income. It is common in retail, and especially in the supermarket sector, for the retailer and supplier to enter into an agreement whereby the supplier pays the retailer a 'rebate' based on sales volumes. For example, if the supermarket has entered into such an agreement with a cosmetics supplier, the supermarket will promote the supplier's brands, placing them in prominent positions on the grocery shelves, in order to boost sales of the brand. The supplier then pays the supermarket an amount which is linked to the sales volume.

There is nothing illegal about this practice. However, the issue for Tesco was that it overestimated the value of these 'rebates', recognizing too much revenue and boosting profit. The overstatement in Tesco's 2014 financial statements was found to be £263 million, around 8.5 per cent of the company's profit for the year.

Why this is relevant to our discussion is that Tesco had been under pressure from other supermarkets, in particular the cut-price discount stores which were taking Tesco's customers and reducing market share. Tesco's profit was declining, and management was under pressure to stop the deterioration in performance. The company's auditors should have identified this situation as a business risk, impacting the measurement of financial performance, which then led to aggressive accounting treatments.

Indeed, the company's auditors, PwC, did discuss the issue of commercial income in their auditor's report, highlighting that the accounting treatment for this type of transaction is highly judgemental, and required particular attention during the audit.

7.3.2.2 The regulatory environment

As discussed earlier in the chapter, the more highly regulated a client, the wider the potential scope of the audit. Therefore, the auditor must understand the regulatory environment, including the legal and political context in which the client operates, in order to determine the scope of the engagement and associated risks.

The auditor may consider the following to obtain understanding of the regulatory environment:

- Does the client operate within a regulated sector? (e.g. a charity, a financial institution).
- Is there any specifically relevant legislation? (e.g. environmental law, minimum wage legislation).
- What is the tax regime the client operates under?
- Are there relevant political issues which affect the client? (e.g. government monetary policy, tariffs, foreign exchange controls).

If an audit client has to adhere to specific legislation, the auditor is not expected to be a legal expert and obtain understanding of the minute detail of the law. However, the auditor has to be aware of relevant legislation to understand any potential impact on the financial statements. For example, if a client operates in a legal environment which includes environmental legislation, the auditor has to be aware of the possibility that laws have been breached, which in turn means that provisions may be necessary for fines and penalties within the financial statements.

7.3.3 Understanding the financial reporting framework

The requirement to understand the applicable financial reporting framework means identifying not only the relevant financial reporting standards (IFRS or national standards) but also whether there are any relevant industry-specific reporting regulations.

How an audit client determines and applies its accounting policies is clearly of vital importance to the financial statements. Accounting policies must be based on the applicable financial reporting framework including its conceptual framework. Auditing is not just a check of compliance with the relevant financial reporting requirements (e.g. whether the financial statements adhere to IFRS requirements); the auditor must also consider the appropriateness of accounting policies that have been developed for new types of balances and transactions for which there may be little guidance within the financial reporting framework. This part of obtaining business understanding also includes consideration of any changes in accounting policy, whether these are voluntary or through the introduction of new financial reporting requirements. It is reasonably common for companies to change accounting policies and auditors must evaluate any changes in accounting policies to ensure they have been correctly accounted for, disclosed correctly in the notes to the financial statements, and that they present a more relevant and reliable view of the company's financial position and performance.

It is important to remember that financial reporting is dynamic. Accounting standard-setters are continually revising existing financial reporting requirements or bringing out new accounting rules. For example, in the last few years, organizations reporting under IFRS requirements have had to implement major new IFRSs in relation to revenue recognition, leases, and financial instruments.

For the auditor, any significant change in the financial reporting framework brings a heightened audit risk. The auditor will need to consider:

- how new accounting policies were developed;
- whether the policies are in compliance with the new requirements;
- whether transitional rules have been appropriately dealt with;
- how comparative financial information has been restated, where relevant; and
- the adequacy of disclosure in the notes to the financial statements.

Auditing in practice 7.6 Accounting for cryptocurrency

In recent years, cryptocurrencies such as bitcoin have become increasingly common. The IASB considers that cryptocurrencies have the following characteristics:

a. A cryptocurrency is a digital or virtual currency that is recorded on a distributed ledger and uses cryptography for security.

b. A cryptocurrency is not issued by a jurisdictional authority or other party.
c. A holding of a cryptocurrency does not give rise to a contract between the holder and another party.[6]

Organizations including Subway and Expedia, charities such as Save the Children, and even PwC accept bitcoin to settle transactions.

There is no IFRS dealing specifically with cryptocurrency, and so organizations have to develop an appropriate accounting policy to deal with transactions involving cryptocurrency, and holdings of them at the year end. It is even difficult to decide what type of balance a cryptocurrency is—while intuition might lead you to think that it is cash, because it is not backed by government, it does not fall under the definition of cash. Perhaps treating it as some kind of financial instrument, inventory or intangible asset is more appropriate. The management of an organization using a cryptocurrency needs to consider this carefully, and will probably ask for external guidance to develop an appropriate accounting treatment.

For the auditor, how this new accounting policy is developed is important, as there is a high risk of misstatement in the absence of any specific financial reporting framework.

7.4 Interim and final audit

Now that we understand some of the elements of planning at audit, we can consider the timing of this work more carefully. Typically, the detailed audit fieldwork is done at two stages, which are known as the interim audit and the final audit.

The interim audit usually takes place a few months before the client's financial year end. This is when much of the audit planning will take place, and audit work is likely to include:

- obtaining understanding of business developments and significant events in the year;
- documenting systems, including changes to systems;
- performing tests of control and evaluating the systems; and
- some substantive audit procedures (e.g. some tests of detail on significant balances).

As a result of the work performed on the interim audit, the audit strategy and plan will be developed. The strategy and plan will be revised later during the audit process if necessary. There is no requirement to perform an interim audit. In deciding whether to perform one the auditor will consider matters such as the size and complexity of the company along with the effectiveness of internal controls.

The benefit of performing work at the interim stage is that it allows early identification of issues, which can then be resolved at the final audit. If a potential problem area is identified at the interim audit, there is time for the auditor to devise a solution. For instance, if the interim audit reveals a significant risk of material misstatement in relation to a property valuation, the auditor can plan to involve a property expert to provide objective evidence on that matter. If the issue had not been picked up until the final audit, there may be a delay in obtaining evidence, or there is a risk that the auditor would accept less reliable evidence for the sake of meeting the audit deadline.

[6] International Financial Reporting Standards Foundation, 'Tentative agenda decision and comment letters—Holdings of cryptocurrencies' <https://www.ifrs.org/projects/completed-projects/2019/holdings-of-cryptocurrencies/tad-holdings-of-cryptocurrencies/> (accessed 18 January 2024).

Some audit firms use a strategy which involves performing a great deal of substantive procedures at the interim stage. This means that less work is required at final audit. Essentially, if the results of the interim testing are wide-ranging and do not highlight risk of material misstatement, it is possible that at the final audit, the auditor only needs to audit the period of time between the interim and final audit. This can be a useful strategy if the deadline for issuing the audit opinion is very tight.

Auditing in practice 7.7 Continuous auditing

Continuous auditing means exactly what it says—obtaining audit evidence on a continual basis during the financial year. It is something that is becoming more prevalent due to advances in technology such as cloud accounting, as companies and their auditors can use data analytics techniques to provide information on a continual basis which can be monitored throughout the year. It is most commonly used by internal audit teams, but external audit firms are also starting to explore its possibilities. The benefits of continual auditing include the following:

- It provides an early warning of fraud and other financial irregularities.
- Advice can be given to the client during the year rather than after the year end, thus resolving potential problems sooner.
- Earlier completion of final audit and issuance of auditor's report quickly after the financial year end.

Chapter round-up

- Adequate audit planning ensures an efficient and high-quality audit being performed.
- Audit planning includes preliminary activities such as reviewing client acceptance and evaluating ethical compliance.
- Planning must involve the audit engagement partner and other key members of the audit engagement team.
- The audit strategy establishes and documents the scope, timing, and direction of the audit and informs the development of the audit plan.
- The audit strategy must include the nature, timing, and extent of direction and supervision of engagement team members and the review of their work.
- The audit plan is a detailed document which sets out the nature, timing, and extent of planned risk assessment and audit procedures.
- The audit strategy and audit plan must be reviewed as the audit progresses and revised if necessary as a result of new facts and information.
- The auditor is required to obtain detailed information about the audit client to obtain an understanding of the business.
- Obtaining business understanding is a crucial aspect of audit planning, especially in respect of new audit clients.
- The interim audit is performed before the financial year end and usually involves work on systems and controls, as well as updating business understanding.
- The final audit is usually when the majority of audit fieldwork is performed.

End of chapter case study

Introduction

This chapter has shown the importance of the auditor obtaining full understanding of the client in order to effectively plan the audit. If an audit is performed in the absence of thorough business understanding, then the auditor may not identify risks of material misstatement. The audit would be low quality and there is a danger that an inappropriate audit opinion is issued. This is particularly an issue when an auditor takes on a new audit client, therefore having limited knowledge of the client and understanding of the environment in which it operates.

This case study links to the following learning outcomes:

- Explain what is meant by obtaining understanding of the audit client and discuss the methods by which this understanding is obtained.
- Explain the difference between an interim audit and a final audit and the type of work performed at each stage.

Scenario

Sparrow Ltd is a new audit client of Kyla Associates, a firm of accountants and auditors. Sparrow appointed Kyla Associates to replace their previous audit firm as the company has grown rapidly in the last few years and the previous audit firm no longer had the necessary resources to perform the audit.

Sparrow, a retail organization, operates in several countries. Sparrow specializes in clothing retail, having around 300 stores across Europe. Its stores are mostly in large towns and cities, and it has recently opened several stores at airports and train stations, which are proving successful. Like many other retailers, online sales now generate a significant proportion of income for Sparrow, and the company has invested in new IT to ensure that online orders are quickly fulfilled, and to monitor inventory levels.

The company produces monthly management accounts which are discussed at board meetings. Sparrow has an internal audit department, but as it is not a listed company, it has not set up an audit committee.

Required

(a) Identify and explain the sources of information that could be used by Kyla Associates to develop understanding of Sparrow Ltd.

(b) Provide examples of audit work that could be performed at the interim stage of the audit.

Answer

Sources of business understanding

- Prior year financial statements—provides the key accounting policies and disclosure notes as well as the financial statements which can be used for analytical review.
- Current year management accounts—helps with analytical review and understanding any significant changes in the year to date (e.g. the impact of opening the new stores at airports and train stations, has this led to a significant increase in revenue?). The management accounts may also break down information by geographical area, so that the auditor can understand the relative scale of operations and the sales per country.
- Accounting manual—information on the company's accounting policies, estimation techniques, and procedures used in the accounting system.

- Internal auditor reports—provides information on the effectiveness of controls and how well the systems operate—this may be particularly useful in respect of the new IT which has been put in place for online sales and inventory management.
- Minutes of board meetings and other meetings of senior management—information in relation to any important issues which have arisen and been discussed by management, along with their responses.
- Sparrow's website—this can provide information about its product ranges, areas of operation, number of stores, and their location. The website may also contain news/press releases from the company (e.g. in relation to new stores being opened).
- A general internet search—the auditor can search Sparrow to find a wealth of information such as customer reviews, news stories about the company, and its management.
- Financial statements of competitors—this will provide information about Sparrow's competitors, to enable a comparison of their financial results.
- Information from Know Your Client procedures—assuming that Kyla Associates has performed appropriate client screening, the audit firm should have information already on file in respect of a range of matters including the ownership of Sparrow, its key management, the nature of its business and source of funds.
- Correspondence with the previous audit firm—this is essential information, to understand if there were any issues raised by the previous audit firm. Kyla Associates could also ask to view the working papers (e.g. review the previous year's auditor's report to management to understand the nature of adjustments made as a result of their audit and information on any deficiencies found with internal controls).
- Visit stores—the audit firm can simply visit a number of stores to develop an understanding of product ranges, the business model (e.g. high-end retail or mass market).

Interim audit work

- documenting all accounting systems;
- performing tests of control and evaluating the strength of internal controls;
- discussing business developments and significant events with management;
- performing analytical review on forecast or year-to-date financial statements;
- performing some substantive audit procedures (e.g. attend inventory counts).

Activity solutions

Activity 7.1—Benefits of audit planning

In addition to the benefits previously outlined, what do you think are the other benefits of audit planning?

Suggested answer points:

Audit team selection—without proper planning, it will not be possible to select an audit team with skills and experience commensurate with the requirements of the audit. Also, without a detailed audit strategy and plan it will not be possible to effectively delegate audit work among the audit team.

Some audit engagements, for example, audits of public interest entities, or those in highly regulated industries, require specialist knowledge, and it is essential to plan this input as early as possible as specialist resources may be limited within the audit firm.

Scheduling audit reviews—Thorough planning should involve consideration of quality control requirements such as direction, supervision, and review. In particular, sufficient time must be planned to facilitate review procedures as required by ISA (UK) 220 *Quality Management for an Audit of Financial Statements*.

Identifying whether experts may need to be engaged—When planning an audit, it may become apparent that the auditor may need to, or choose to, rely on the work of others. For example, specialist inventory valuers may be required for elements of inventory in certain types of business. Without thorough planning, this may be overlooked. In group audits, it is essential that the work of component auditors is coordinated carefully to ensure that no areas of the consolidated financial statements go un-audited.

Activity 7.2—Impact of previous involvement with the client

Can you think of examples of how the auditor's previous involvement with a client may impact planning the audit?

Suggested answer points:

In previous years' audits, the audit team may have evaluated the client's internal controls and found them to be robust. While it is not possible to simply rely on the controls again, the previous evaluation will have some bearing on the amount of work on controls that is needed in the current year's audit.

The audit firm may have performed other services for the client that may be relevant in determining the audit strategy, for example, reviews of business plans or cash flow forecasts. This can provide useful information about the client's business and the environment in which it operates.

Activity 7.3—Enquiring about the client's business

What questions might an auditor ask a new client, to obtain preliminary understanding of the client's business?

Suggested answer points:

The auditor should consider the following:

- Does the client have a simple or a complex structure—in particular, is it a group of companies?
- Does it have a range of investments?
- Who owns the client? It is owner-managed, owned by numerous shareholders, or controlled by another company?
- Who are the related parties (i.e. connected people or other organizations) of the client?
- What is the business model? What are its main inputs and outputs?
- What are the main sources of revenue?
- Where does the client operate? How widely dispersed are its operations?
- What type of finance does the client have? It is financed mainly by debt or by equity?
- What is the organizational structure? Who are the key management personnel?
- Are there any significant changes in business operations in the year?

Answering these questions will allow the auditor to gauge the level of complexity and scale of the organization.

Activity 7.4—Developing business understanding

List examples of useful information that the auditor can enquire about and obtain, to develop their understanding of the client in respect of their business model, business operations and financing activities.

Suggested answer points:

Useful information about the business model may include:

- The markets or geographical or demographic spheres, parts of the value chain in which it operates, how it engages with those markets or spheres (main products, customer segments, and distribution methods), and the basis on which it competes.
- The entity's business or operating processes (e.g. investment, financing, and operating processes) are employed in performing its activities, focusing on those parts of the business processes that are important in creating, preserving, or capturing value.
- The resources (e.g. financial, human, intellectual, environmental, technological) and other inputs and relationships (e.g. customers, competitors, suppliers, employees) that are necessary or important to its success.

Information about business operations can include:

- Nature of revenue sources, products or services, and markets, including involvement in electronic commerce such as internet sales and marketing activities.
- Conduct of operations (e.g. stages and methods of production, or activities exposed to environmental risks).
- Alliances, joint ventures, and outsourcing activities.
- Geographic dispersion and industry segmentation.
- Location of production facilities, warehouses, offices, and location/quantities of inventories.
- Key customers and important suppliers of goods and services, employment arrangements (including the existence of union contracts, pension, and other post-employment benefits, stock option or incentive bonus arrangements, and government regulation related to employment matters).
- Research and development activities and expenditures.
- Transactions with related parties.

Information about financing and financing activities includes:

- Ownership structure of major subsidiaries and associated entities, including consolidated and non-consolidated structures.
- Debt structure and related terms, including off-balance-sheet financing arrangements and leasing arrangements.
- Beneficial owners (e.g. local, foreign, business reputation, experience) and related parties.
- Use of derivative financial instruments.[7]

[7] FRC, 'ISA (UK) 315', 2020, Appendix 1, para 5.

8 Internal Control

Introduction

All organizations should employ robust internal controls which operate across the organization to ensure its smooth running. For auditors, internal controls over financial reporting have a particular significance, because stronger controls should mean less risk of error or deliberate misstatement in the financial statements. In other words, good internal controls work to reduce audit risk. Remember that audit risk is the risk that the auditor expresses an incorrect opinion on the financial statements.

However, internal controls apply not only to accounting systems and other elements of the financial reporting process. Internal controls operate over every aspect of a well-run organization, covering all functions, including human resources (HR), procurement, legal, treasury management, to name a few. Internal control is a broad concept. As we will see, it also includes matters such as the attitude of management, the cultural norms of an organization, and monitoring activities.

In this chapter, we will consider which elements of internal control are most significant for the auditor, and examine the requirements of ISA (UK) 315 *Identifying and Assessing the Risk of Material Misstatement* relating to documenting and understanding controls. ISA (UK) 315 requires the auditor to obtain an understanding of the internal control relevant to the audit. Systems and controls need to be thoroughly documented by the auditor. This can be done in a variety of ways, including the use of questionnaires, flowcharts, diagrams, and narrative notes.

Information systems and the related control activities are key to audit planning. The auditor must understand the systems that generate the figures in the financial statements and how well those systems operate. Robust internal controls should mean that the business is well run, and from the auditor's perspective, if accounting systems are well controlled then the financial statements are less likely to contain material misstatement.

The auditor must gain an understanding of internal controls in order to design the nature, extent, and timing of planned audit procedures. Generally, the auditor would prefer an audit strategy which allows reliance to be placed on a client's internal controls. This is because, once the controls have been tested and confirmed as sufficiently robust for the auditor to place reliance on them, the amount of detailed audit testing can be reduced. This typically is an efficient way to audit, reducing the time and resources that need to be allocated to the audit. It is important to note that the auditor must obtain sufficient, appropriate evidence to conclude on the strength of controls, and this is often done by performing tests of control at both the interim and final stages of the audit.

Learning outcomes

- Describe and explain the components of a system of internal control.
- Discuss the limitations of internal controls and explain the matters specific to small organizations.
- Explain the design, operation, and evaluation of internal controls in computerized environments.
- Explain how auditors document internal controls.
- Describe the main accounting systems used in organizations and identify the controls that should be in place.

By the end of this chapter, you should be able to:

- Identify and discuss deficiencies in internal control and recommend relevant remedies to deficiencies in internal control.
- Analyse information in respect of internal controls to identify audit planning issues.

8.1 The system of internal control

8.1.1 **What are controls?**

ISA 315 defines controls as:

> Policies or procedures that an entity establishes to achieve the control objectives of management or those charged with governance. In this context:
> (i) Policies are statements of what should, or should not, be done within the entity to effect control. Such statements may be documented, explicitly stated in communications, or implied through actions and decisions.
> (ii) Procedures are actions to implement policies.[1]

The purpose of internal control is to identify and mitigate the business risks that may threaten the achievement of any of the organization's objectives concerning three matters:

- the reliability of financial reporting;
- the effectiveness and efficiency of operations; and
- compliance with applicable laws and regulations.

[1] FRC, 'ISA (UK) 315', 2020, para 12 (c) <https://media.frc.org.uk/documents/ISA_UK_315_Jul_2020.pdf> (accessed 18 January 2024).

It might be reasonable to assume at first glance that it is only the first of these three objectives which will concern the auditor. However, the other two objectives, and the controls which relate to them, are important because they can impact the financial statements and are therefore relevant to the audit. For example, if a company has poor controls over credit control and therefore is inefficient in managing its liquidity, this can impact the collectability of trade receivables and their valuation. The associated audit risk is that receivables could be overstated in value in the statement of financial position. Therefore, the auditor must approach internal control with a broad mindset, and not ignore controls that on the face of it appear irrelevant to the audit of financial statements.

It is a matter of the auditor's professional judgement whether a control, individually or in combination with others, is relevant to the audit. The auditor should carefully document their rationale in respect of the application of this judgement. Particularly when concluding that a control is not relevant to the audit, the auditor should be able to demonstrate why this is the case. For example, a control operating in relation to a matter which is clearly immaterial to the financial statements can be considered not relevant to the audit.

'Internal control' is a big topic, so we will start with a high-level overview of the components of a system of internal control, then look at each component in turn. Remember that internal control is something that the auditor must obtain an understanding of, as part of audit planning. Ultimately, the auditor will evaluate the strength of the audit client's internal controls, because this has a significant bearing on the audit strategy and audit plan.

Internal control has five components, each of which must be understood, documented, and evaluated, when relevant to the audit:

- the control environment;
- the entity's risk assessment process;
- the entity's process to monitor the system of internal control;
- the information system and communication, and control activities; and
- control activities.

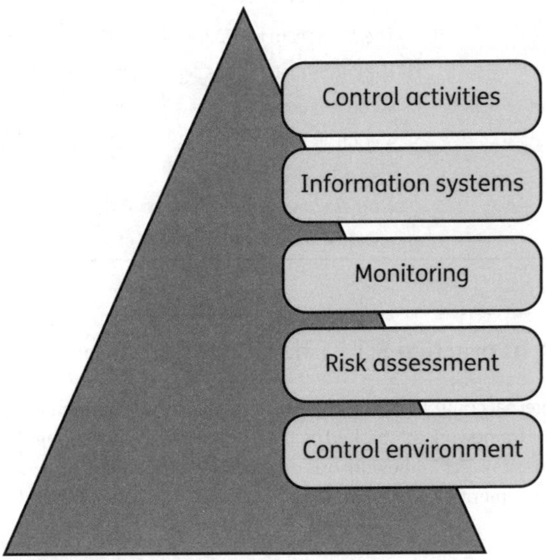

Figure 8.1 The system of internal control

You can think of the elements of internal control as a pyramid Figure 8.1, with the control environment at the bottom, indicating the foundation of the system of internal control. If a strong control environment foundation is not present, it is unlikely that the rest of the elements of internal control built on top will be effective.

ISA (UK) 315 contains Appendix 3 which provides guidance to the auditor on understanding the audit client's system of internal control and each relevant component.

Audit teams need to understand several key aspects of an audit client's system of internal control. Table 8.1 outlines the elements of an internal control system:

Table 8.1 Elements of a system of internal control

Element	What it means
Control environment	The culture and top-down commitment to integrity, ethics, and nurturing competent and accountable staff
The entity's risk assessment process	How the entity internally identifies, assesses, and responds to business risks
The entity's process to monitor the system of internal control	How the entity monitors its control system (e.g. by using internal audit (IA) or other compliance checks)
The information system and communication	How transactions are initiated, and the relevant details captured and processed, along with the accounting records, financial reporting processes, and IT resources How accounting matters are communicated, including to those charged with governance (if they are separate from management)
Control activities	The specific controls over significant risks, journal entries, along with any other controls that the auditor plans to test for operating effectiveness and any related IT applications. Control activities include: • authorizations and approvals • reconciliations • verifications • physical or logical controls • segregation of duties The audit team is required to identify and design procedures on: • controls that address significant risks • controls over journals • controls for which the auditor plans to test the operating effectiveness of controls • other controls the auditor considers appropriate based on the auditor's professional judgement

Auditing in practice 8.1 The COSO framework

The framework of internal control that was used in developing the requirements of ISA (UK) 315 is based on the controls framework established by the Committee of Sponsoring Organizations (COSO) of the Treadway Commission. The framework was originally developed in 1992, and it provides guidance on the design and implementation of internal controls, and on assessing their effectiveness. COSO's stated aim is to provide thought leadership on matters relating to enterprise risk management (ERM), internal control, and fraud deterrence.

In 2013 a revised COSO framework on internal controls was issued. The revised version reflects changes in business and operating environments and more clearly articulates the supporting principles of the COSO framework. It also includes illustrative examples and case studies to help organizations establish and implement appropriate internal controls.

The COSO framework indicates that an internal control system should be developed for the three objectives of internal control—business operations, compliance, and reporting. and that the controls should function at all levels and across all activities of an organization's operations.

8.1.2 **The control environment**

The control environment relates to the attitudes, awareness, and actions of those charged with governance and management in respect of the organization's internal control. The control environment sets the tone of an organization; this is often referred to as the 'tone at the top'. Essentially, an appropriate control environment means that senior people within the organization take internal control seriously, support actions to improve internal control, and that this ethos filters down throughout the organization.

Companies with good corporate governance mechanisms will strive to maintain a strong control environment. This means that honesty and integrity are valued among management and employees, whereas dishonesty and acting without integrity are not tolerated. Management should design and implement policies and procedures with the objective of deterring employees from engaging in dishonest, illegal, or unethical acts. This has relevance to the auditor because controls are less likely to be circumvented where the control environment is strong, allowing the auditor to place more reliance on the operating effectiveness of procedural controls that are in place, and reducing the risk of material misstatement. However, a strong control environment can only deter, and never prevent fraud or other abuse of controls.

In evaluating the control environment, the auditor may consider these matters, and obtain an understanding by asking relevant questions (see Table 8.2).

Activity 8.1 Control environment

The management of Giles Ltd has recently discovered a fraud operating, whereby an employee stole £5,000 of goods from the warehouse. What actions should management take to strengthen the control environment?

8.1.3 **Risk assessment**

It is fundamental to audit planning that the auditor must evaluate the audit client's business risk. The requirements of ISA (UK) 315 in relation to risk assessment are broad, with the objective of ensuring that the auditor understands how the audit client identifies and manages business risk.

Table 8.2 Evaluation of control environment

Matter relating to control environment	Questions/evidence
Communication and enforcement of integrity and ethical values The organization should demonstrate its commitment to high moral values	• Does the organization have an ethical code of conduct? • Do anti-corruption and anti-bribery policies exist? • Is there a whistle-blowing policy? • Are these codes and policies communicated to employees?
Commitment to competence If the organization employs staff who are not fully competent, then it is not likely that business objectives will be met, increasing business risk	• Does management recruit staff with appropriate skills and competencies? • Are employee performance reviews regularly conducted? • Is there an appropriate budget for staff training? • Has a mentoring scheme been established?
Participation by those charged with governance The experience and knowledge of those charged with governance should be utilized in an appropriate way, including proper scrutiny of the organization's activities and results	• Do the actions of those charged with governance comply with relevant codes (e.g. the UK Corporate Governance Code)? • How do those charged with governance interact with management, the external auditors, and other advisers? • Is the board of directors independent from management? • What matters are discussed at board meetings, and what actions are taken based on decisions made?
Management's philosophy and operating style The approach to taking and managing business risks, attitudes, and actions towards financial reporting and towards information processing and accounting functions and personnel can heavily influence the control environment	• What is management's attitude to taking risk? • How are risks debated in the board room? • Is there an appropriate mechanism for the challenge of management's decisions? • Is debate/consultation encouraged, especially in relation to significant business decisions?
Organizational structure The structure of the organization should include clear reporting lines, appropriate authorities, and responsibilities	• Is there a clear organizational chart for each segment/business function? • Are changes in the organizational structure properly debated and approved?
Assignment of authority and responsibility Internal control is weaker where reporting lines are complex and responsibilities are unclear, meaning that duties can go unfulfilled	• Are job specifications clear, including reporting lines, specific responsibilities, and limits to delegation?
HR policies and practices HR policies and procedures should reinforce the organization's commitment to integrity, ethical behaviour, and competence	• Do appropriate HR policies exist in relation to recruitment and induction to the organization? • Are promotion pathways clear? • Are disciplinary procedures transparent and fair? • How are pay levels determined?

Robust processes to manage an organization's risk exposure strengthen internal control, whereas an absence of risk management process, or failure of established risk management processes indicates that a significant deficiency in internal control may exist. Therefore, the auditor must evaluate the client's risk management processes as this forms part of the auditor's overall evaluation of internal control. The auditor should form a view as to the processes by which business risks are evaluated by those charged with governance and by management, how their potential significance for the business is determined, and the way in which responses are decided upon and carried out.

8.1.3.1 Business risk

It is worth exploring what is actually meant by the term 'business risk'. The definition from ISA (UK) 315 states that a business risk is, 'A risk resulting from significant conditions, events, circumstances, actions or inactions that could adversely affect an entity's ability to achieve its objectives and execute its strategies, or from the setting of inappropriate objectives and strategies.'[2] In other words, a business risk is something which causes problems for an organization, having a negative impact on operations, finance, or even the long-term survival of the organization. The key thing is to understand that a business risk is anything which might prevent or delay the objectives of the business being met.

Business risks are often categorized as to whether they relate to operations, finance, or compliance:

- Operational risk—these are risks relating to a failure in the organization's operations (i.e. the core of its business model). These risks will obviously be quite specific to the type of business and its strategy, but could include for example, loss of key members of staff, running out of raw materials, loss of a key customer, decline in market share, or IT failure.
- Financial risk—these risks relate to financial problems, for example, failing to collect cash quickly enough from trade receivables, inability to raise long-term finance, increase in interest rates or adverse movements in exchange rates.
- Compliance risk—is the organization complying with all the necessary laws and regulations that apply to the business? For example, employment law, health and safety regulations, tax legislation, environmental regulations, and data protection regulations.

You might be thinking that understanding a business's risk management process is 'background' information, but in actuality, this understanding is often the first step in identifying risks of material misstatement in the financial statements. For example, for a company operating in a high-tech industry, technological developments might make a particular product obsolete, thereby causing inventory to be more susceptible to overstatement.

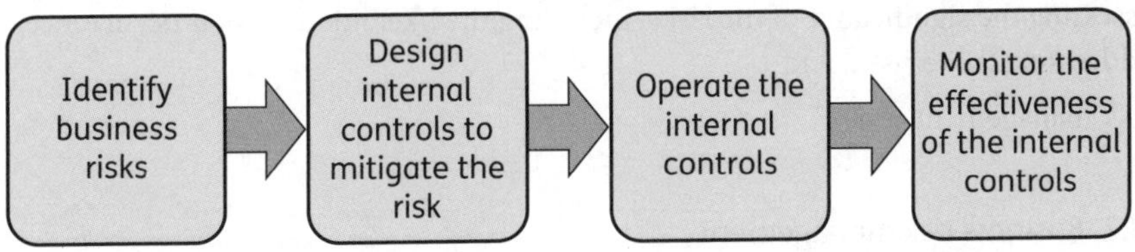

Figure 8.2 Management's risk management process

[2] Ibid., para 12(b).

If an auditor fails to adequately consider business risk, the quality of the whole audit is placed in jeopardy.

It is also important that the audit team are fully briefed on business risks. Throughout the audit process, as a result of performing planned audit procedures, audit team members may come across information which impacts business risk evaluation. The evaluation of business risk and its impact on risk of material misstatement therefore may change as the audit progresses.

Auditing scenario 8.1 Business objectives and business risk

Pulp Products Ltd is a company based in the Midlands which manufactures packaging from recycled paper and cardboard. The company's auditor, Brandon Associates, has obtained the following list of business objectives and business risks which have been discussed at a recent meeting of the company directors.

The audit team can now consider whether any of these business objectives and risks translate into issues relevant to the audit. For example, if the company fails to comply with the relevant health and safety legislation, it may incur fines and penalties which require accounting for and/or disclosure in the financial statements. Other business risks may have less of a direct impact on the audit in terms of specific risks of material misstatement but developing understanding of these matters is important because they assist the auditor in other ways, for example in performing analytical review on the financial statements.

Table 8.3

Business objective	Business risk
Maximizing profit	Increase in costs of production due to inflation
Maintaining liquidity	Failure to collect amounts owed from trade receivables
Innovate product lines	Lack of investment in research and development
Retain key members of staff	Failure to keep pay rates commensurate with market rates
Compliance with relevant legislation	Lack of capital expenditure on health and safety equipment
Maintain reputation of the company	Adverse publicity based on company's actions

For the auditor, in relation to risk assessment, the exact requirements of ISA (UK) 315 are that the auditor obtain an understanding of whether the entity has a process for:

- identifying business risks relevant to financial reporting objectives;
- assessing the significance of the risks, including the likelihood of their occurrence, and addressing those risks; and
- risk management.[3]

8.1.3.2 Business risk management

The auditor's work may indicate that the client has established such a risk assessment process, in which case the auditor is required to obtain an understanding of the process. In many organizations, especially larger ones, there should be a well-established risk management process.

[3] Ibid., para 22.

In smaller organizations, the risk assessment process may exist but be less well defined, which, in itself, is not a weakness as smaller organizations tend to have less formal risk assessment processes in place, but which are still equally effective given the size of the entity.

During the audit, the auditor may identify risks that management failed to identify. In this case, the auditor should evaluate whether there was a failure in the risk assessment process established by management and why that process failed to identify it. The failure of the risk assessment process could indicate that there is a significant deficiency in internal control, which has implications for audit risk.

Auditing in practice 8.2 Risk management

Business risk should not be viewed as a 'bad thing'. Organizations seeking to maximize wealth need to accept risk in order to grow and achieve strategic objectives. However, risk needs to be carefully managed to ensure that risk-taking is not excessive, which can lead to erosion of wealth. Most larger organizations utilize Enterprise Risk Management (ERM) techniques to try to identify, assess, and respond to risks. The objective of ERM is to assess identified risks and to gauge their potential significance to the organization. Risks should be prioritized and managed to ensure that management's attention is focused on the key risks and to help in the determination of an appropriate response. Some risks can be tolerated, and part of ERM is to establish the organization's risk appetite, which refers to the scale and nature of risk that an organization is willing to accept in order to meet its objectives.

In the UK, the Financial Reporting Council (FRC) issues guidance on risk management and internal controls. In the document *Guidance on Risk Management, Internal Control and Related Financial and Business Reporting* (2014), the FRC makes it clear that the board has responsibility for an organization's overall approach to risk management and internal control, and lists the board's responsibilities as follows:

- To ensure that appropriate risk management and internal control systems are designed and implemented to enable identification and assessment of the risks facing the company.
- To determine the nature and extent of the principal risks faced and to determine the risk appetite of the company.
- To ensure that appropriate culture and reward systems have been embedded.
- To agree on how the principal risks should be managed or mitigated to reduce the likelihood of their incidence or their impact.
- To monitor and review the risk management and internal control systems, to evaluate that they function effectively.
- To ensure sound internal and external information and communication processes.

ISA (UK) 315 notes that there is unlikely to be an established risk assessment process in a small entity. In such cases, it is likely that management will identify risks through direct personal involvement in the business. Irrespective of the circumstances, however, inquiry about identified risks and how they are addressed by management is still necessary. In smaller organizations, risk assessment will be performed in an ad hoc manner by the company's owners and/or managers. In this case, it is required that the auditor discuss with management whether business risks relevant to financial reporting have been identified and addressed, and should then consider whether this represents a significant deficiency in internal control.

Activity 8.2 Business risks

Oriole Ltd manufactures circuit boards and most of the components of the manufacturing process are imported from one supplier, located in South America.

Can you identify three business risks facing Oriole Ltd?

We will return to the topic of business risk in Chapter 9, when we consider the auditor's evaluation of business risk as a way to identify risks of material misstatement.

8.1.4 **The process to monitor the system of internal control**

Management should continually monitor internal control to ensure its continual effectiveness. Like any other part of the business, if it is not monitored it is likely to deteriorate in its usefulness to the organization. Put simply, if an organization's internal control becomes weaker, there is more risk of material misstatement, and increased audit risk. Therefore, the auditor should form an understanding of the monitoring procedures put in place by management, and the type of remedial actions that may be needed.

ISA (UK) 315 requires that the auditor obtain an understanding of the entity's process for monitoring the system of internal control relevant to the preparation of the financial statements.[4]

The procedures to be performed in this respect include obtaining understanding of how the audit client monitors the effectiveness of controls and how deficiencies in controls are identified and resolved.

Matters that may be considered include:

- the design of the monitoring activities (e.g. whether it is periodic or ongoing monitoring);
- the performance and frequency of the monitoring activities;
- the evaluation of the results of the monitoring activities, on a timely basis, to determine whether the controls have been effective;
- how identified deficiencies have been addressed through appropriate remedial actions, including timely communication of such deficiencies to those responsible for taking remedial action.[5]

Activity 8.3 Enquiries regarding monitoring of internal control

Can you create a list of examples of questions which the auditor may ask in order to obtain understanding of monitoring activities?

[4] FRC, 'ISA (UK) 315', 2020, para 24. [5] Ibid., para A116.

8.1.4.1 **Internal Audit (IA)**

As we saw in Chapter 3, IA is a cornerstone of good corporate governance. The establishment of an IA function is likely to form a key part of an organization's monitoring activities; therefore, the auditor must obtain a thorough understanding of the work of IA in order to properly appraise the monitoring component of internal control. Additional guidance in this area is contained in ISA (UK) 315, Appendix 4. The auditor may consider it necessary to read reports issued by IA that have been prepared for management or those charged with governance in describing the findings of the IA function's work.

IA is a significant component of an entity's system of internal control as it carries out important work during the year on assessing whether internal controls are operating effectively. IAs ultimately advise management of any weaknesses in controls (or absent controls) and provide recommendations on how these weaknesses can be strengthened or which controls need to be in place. Remember, IAs do not implement controls—they only assess the effectiveness of the controls.

The external auditor may make inquiries of the appropriate individuals within IA to obtain information that may be helpful in understanding the entity and its environment, the applicable financial reporting framework; and the entity's system of internal control.

This understanding will then serve to help the auditor in identifying and assessing the risks of material misstatement at the financial statement and assertion levels.

Understanding the entity's control environment

The auditor may consider how management has responded to the findings and recommendations of IA regarding identified control deficiencies relevant to the preparation of the financial statements. This will include an assessment of whether (and how) such responses have been implemented and whether they have been subsequently evaluated by the IA function.

If management have a disregard for the recommendations by IA, the auditor is likely to place less reliance on the relevant control(s) because doing so will effectively waste audit time. Instead, the auditor is likely to devise more substantive procedures to address the risk of material misstatement.

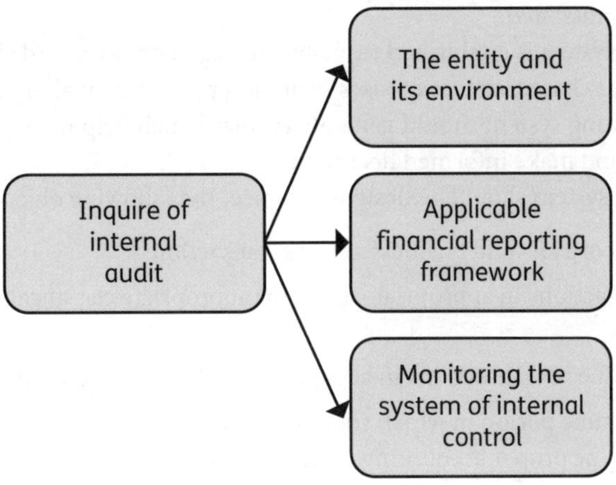

Figure 8.3 Inquiries of IA

Applicable financial reporting framework

IA can assist the auditor in understanding the company's interpretation of the financial reporting framework including its accounting policies and how management exercises judgement in financial reporting, in particular in respect of estimates.

Monitoring the system of internal control

When the IA's responsibilities are related to the entity's financial reporting, the auditor may be able to use the work of IA. In some countries (e.g. the UK), the IA function *cannot* provide direct assistance to the external auditor; however, the auditor may be able to use the work of the IA function if they consider this appropriate. The advantage this usually has is that the detailed work carried out by the external auditor may be reduced (e.g. sample sizes can be reduced; or less substantive testing may be carried out due to reliance on sound internal controls). There is overlap with ISA (UK) 240 *The Auditor's Responsibilities Relating to Fraud in an Audit of Financial Statements* as well. The auditor may obtain information from IA concerning any actual, suspected, or alleged fraud. The auditor must take this information into consideration when carrying their identification of risk of material misstatement due to fraud.

8.1.5 **The information system and communication**

Obtaining an understanding of the information system is critical to the success of the audit. The information system generates the figures that are included in the financial statements, so any deficiencies in the system itself or the controls over it, could lead to a high risk of material misstatement. The auditor needs to determine which elements of the information system are relevant to financial reporting (also described as an accounting system)—there is no requirement for the auditor to obtain understanding of other management information systems. While the auditor is interested in ensuring there is no material misstatement in the 'final' figure stated in the financial statements, they are equally interested in *how* this figure has been arrived at (i.e. its 'route' into the financial statements). This 'route' is the process which generates the figure and whether this process is robust enough to prevent the final figure from being misstated.

An accounting system is established to enable management to record all types of transactions, including purchases, sales, expenses including payroll, capital expenditure, and cash flows. The accounting system should generate reports which help management to monitor financial activity and make informed decisions.

The accounting system should be designed to meet the following objectives:

- Identify and record all valid business-related transactions.
- Detail the transactions in appropriate detail for appropriate classification of transactions.
- Measure the value of transactions in accordance with stated accounting policy.
- Determine the time period in which transactions occurred to permit recording of transactions in the proper accounting period.
- Accurately present the transactions and related disclosures in the financial statements.

Components of an accounting system could include:

Accounting software packages—a typical accounting software package would include as a minimum functionality relating to accounts payable, accounts receivable, cash book, payroll, general ledger, and trial balance. Examples of off-the-shelf software include those available from SAGE, SAP, and Oracle. Some organizations make use of bespoke accounting software, though this can be expensive and is becoming less popular. Smaller organizations use simple software such as QuickBooks or XERO. Larger and more complex organizations may use an enterprise resource planning (ERP) software package which integrates many business systems together (e.g. integrates accounting software with HR and supply chain management software).

Hard copy documents—though there is a trend towards paperless offices, almost all organizations will keep hard copies of certain documents.

Cloud accounting—this is accounting—including input and processing of transactions, and reporting accounting information—over the internet. Accounting software is hosted on a remote server, data is input into the cloud in real time, where it is processed and returned to the user. An example of a common cloud accounting software is XERO, which is becoming more popular as businesses in the UK prepare for Making Tax Digital (MTD) which requires a business to use an MTD-compliant software system which will report financial information to HM Revenue & Customs on a quarterly basis.

People—accounting systems are not just about data. People input data, manage controls, operate processes, and perform activities within an accounting system.

Auditing in practice 8.3 Cloud accounting

Cloud accounting is growing rapidly in popularity and is used by many organizations. Ease of access is a significant advantage of cloud accounting. Financial data held on the cloud can be accessed anywhere, at any time, allowing flexibility in working. You are no longer tied to the office to perform accounting tasks, which can be performed anywhere, at any time, as long as there is internet connection, and you have a smartphone or tablet. You can easily share information with other people.

Other benefits of cloud accounting include:

- Price—cloud accounting can be cheap in comparison with desktop accounting software and paying monthly by subscription allows the cost to be spread.
- Security—all accounting data is backed up and held securely as long as a reputable provider is used.
- Real-time information—financial information is up to date, allowing fast response from business owners.

Disadvantages of cloud accounting include:

- Cost— the monthly subscription costs build up over time and depending on the software used, this could work out to be more expensive over time than the one-off cost of buying a software package.
- Reliability—the provider could be located anywhere, and you need to trust them to keep your data safe from hackers.
- Outages—any provider can be affected by outages which impact your access to data.

To comply with the requirements of ISA (UK) 315, the auditor must obtain an understanding of the accounting system, regardless of whether the system is hosted on the cloud, maintained within the organization's software, or simply held on a spreadsheet. The matters over which understanding should be obtained include the following:

- The significant classes of transactions—this could include purchases, sales, payroll, capital expenditure.
- The procedures by which those transactions are input to the system, processed, recorded in the general (nominal) ledger, and reported in the financial statements. These procedures could be manual or driven by software.
- The related accounting records, which may be in hard or soft copy.
- How necessary corrections are identified and processed.
- How events and conditions other than transactions are identified and recorded, if they are significant to the financial statements.
- The process used to produce the financial statements, including how significant accounting estimates are determined and disclosures are prepared.
- In relation to journal entries, including those used to record non-recurring, unusual transactions or adjustments, controls over how journals are initiated and the mechanisms by which they are processed.

The auditor should also obtain an understanding in relation to information that impacts the financial statements that is obtained from outside of the accounting system. Examples of such information may include:

- tax records and submitted tax returns;
- legal correspondence;
- lease agreements; and
- the value of investments, and information may be held by a treasury management function in a large organization.

8.1.6 **Control activities**

ISA (UK) 315 requires the auditor to obtain understanding of the control activities that are relevant to the audit. We will start by considering first, what do we mean by the term 'control activities'?

Control activities are policies and procedures which aim to ensure that management's directives are being carried out. Control activities should work to mitigate risks identified by management. For example, management may design procedures which have the objective of keeping the organization's assets safe—something as simple as implementing swipe card access to an inventory store to prevent unauthorized access is an example of a control activity.

The requirement to understand internal control can seem onerous, and indeed for large and complex organizations, the documentation of internal control can be laborious. However, it is important to remember that it is only required that the auditor understand and document those elements of internal control which are relevant to the audit. In determining whether a control is relevant to the audit, matters such as the significance of the related risk, materiality, and the complexity of operations should be considered.

Control activities may be preventive or detective in nature and include a wide range of manual and automated activities such as authorizations and approvals, reconciliations, and performance reviews.

Auditors are only required to understand and document internal controls that are relevant to financial reporting. A business will have controls relating to business objectives that are not relevant to an audit and therefore need not be considered. For example, a delivery company may design and implement extensive controls to provide an efficient and effective delivery service to its customers (e.g. vehicle tracking), but these controls ordinarily would not be relevant to the audit. The auditor need not develop an understanding of these controls as they do not relate to financial reporting.

Control activities will have certain objectives:

- Completeness—ensuring that there are no missing transactions in an account balance (e.g. using sequentially numbered documents and performing sequence checks to identify missing items).
- Accuracy—ensuring the recording of transactions is correct (e.g. by performing control account reconciliations).
- Validity—ensuring that balances and transactions when recorded properly represent commercial reality and economic substance (e.g. by having appropriate authorization procedures for the entry of one-off, unusual journals). Validity also means ensuring that only genuine business transactions are recorded (e.g. that only assets meeting the definition of an asset are recorded, that only genuine employees are paid for work done, that invoices raised relate to genuine sales made by the company).
- Existence—ensuring that all balances and transactions relate to items which exist and belong to the organization (e.g. by performing inventory counts).
- Restricted access—to ensure that financial information can only be accessed by the appropriate personnel (e.g. to make sure that employees cannot amend their payroll details, that warehouse staff cannot change inventory levels inappropriately, or only authorized individuals in the finance department can access the online banking system).

Note that some control activities will meet more than one objective.

Due to the increased use of IT, automated controls are now much more common than manual. Automated controls are of two types—general controls and application controls. These will be considered in more detail later in the chapter when we focus specifically on controls in a computerized environment (see section 8.3).

It is helpful to think of control activities as being preventative, detective, or corrective in nature. This means that some controls exist to prevent errors or fraud, while other controls will find them if they take place, and ensure that an appropriate corrective action is taken.

ISA (UK) 315 gives some examples of control activities—these are explained below, and see Figure 8.4.

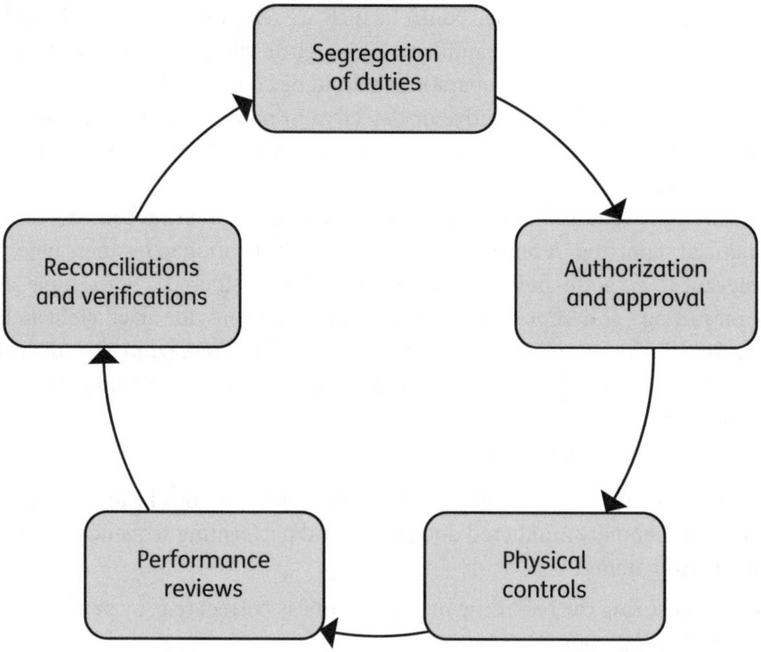

Figure 8.4 Examples of control activities

8.1.6.1 **Segregation of duties**

This is often thought of as the most important type of control activity. Segregation of duties means not allowing one person to have control of a complete transaction, or to separate roles so that one person cannot access both the organization's accounting records and the organization's assets.

Imagine what could happen if one employee had complete control of purchasing an asset such as a computer. That person could raise the order with the supplier, receive the computer when it is delivered, arrange for payment to be made from the organization's bank account, and ultimately take the computer home without anyone else realizing what had happened.

Segregation of duties simply means having more than one person involved, so going back to the example above, in a well-controlled organization, there would be different people to raise the order, take delivery of the asset, and to arrange payment. The example illustrates the principle that most transactions can be broken down into three separate duties: the authorization or initiation of the transaction, the handling of the asset that is the subject of the transaction, and finally recording the transaction in the accounting system.

Establishing segregation of duties across the organization means there is much less risk of fraud. It also should reduce the likelihood of error or deliberate manipulation of the accounting system and financial records by having several people involved with the transaction or event that is being recorded. However, people may collude together to deliberately bypass the control.

Auditing scenario 8.2 Segregation of duties in a purchasing system

Holly Ltd is a software developer, and its audit provider, Berry & Co, has identified that there is a lack of segregation of duties over the purchase ledger function because it is primarily operated by one individual, Carolyn Byrne. To improve the internal control over the system, recently other various functions of the purchase ledger function are now dealt with by other individuals. For example:

1. Carolyn Byrne runs the due payments report.
2. The finance director reviews the report authorizing which payables are to be paid.
3. A member of the finance department prepares the payments and provides backing documentation the payments (purchase invoices).
4. Two signatures (e.g. the finance director and managing director) sign the payment.

The introduction of these measures means that Carolyn is no longer solely responsible for the purchase ledger, so errors are prevented and detected, and fraud is much less likely to occur.

8.1.6.2 **Authorization and approval**

This control is quite easy to understand—it simply means ensuring that everything is subject to authorization or approval before being initiated, recorded, or changed.

Activity 8.4 Authorization and approval

Can you list some examples when authorization and approval can be used within an accounting system?

There should be clear limits to authorization, and approval should work in a hierarchy, so that significant transactions, changes, or events should be approved by senior managers or board members.

8.1.6.3 **Reconciliations and verifications**

These controls operate to ensure the accuracy and completeness of information, and can also check that authorization has taken place. They can be manual or automated. A good example of a manual control is a physical inventory count performed by an organization's staff. Other examples include performing reconciliations and maintaining control accounts, and arithmetic checks, such as checking that an invoice received from a supplier is accurate.

8.1.6.4 **Physical controls**

The objective of these controls is usually quite obvious—they should work to restrict access to assets or to the accounting system. Physical controls can include the use of passwords, swipe cards, biometric access devices, installing CCTV cameras and use of a safe for valuable assets and documents.

8.1.6.5 **Performance reviews**

Performance reviews are any reviews that are conducted on an organization's performance. This could include comparing:

- actual financial data to budgeted data or prior period data;
- non-financial data to financial data;
- data across business segments within the organization, or with an industry average.

The point of the performance review as an internal control is to identify variances and to investigate their cause. For example, if a performance review indicates that operating margins have fallen unexpectedly, this could indicate accounting errors in how the operating profit has been determined.

8.2 Limitations of internal control and considerations for smaller organizations

Now that we understand the elements of a system of internal control, we can think about why no system of control is perfect—they all have inherent limitations which means the auditor must always exercise professional scepticism and challenge the strength of internal controls.

8.2.1 **Limitations of internal control**

Even the most well-designed internal controls can be manipulated or overridden by employees or management. Or, a control system may not be operating effectively for less sinister reasons, perhaps due to staff shortages meaning that appropriate segregation of duties or authorization and approval has not taken place. These reasons mean that auditors should be alert to the fact that internal controls may not be effective and that control objectives have not been met even if appears that a company has well-designed controls.

There are some common limitations which could be present in any system of internal controls:

- Human error: the employees or members of management who are operating controls might not understand the purpose of the control or how it is meant to operate. Or they might just make mistakes. The risk of human error will increase when controls are changed, or new technology is introduced.
- Management override: members of management may be able to override prescribed controls. This could be a deliberate action, for example, in order to achieve some kind of personal gain, or it could be for other reasons, for example, time pressure leading to a control being ignored.
- Collusion: this is when several employees or members of management work together to circumvent internal controls. This is usually linked to fraud, and is very difficult to identify, as the fraudsters will conceal their activity.

8.2.2 Internal controls in small organizations

Small organizations are unlikely to have the same breadth and depth of internal controls compared to a large organization. Smaller entities may simply not have the resources to devote to internal controls, for example they are not likely to have an IA department, so the monitoring element will be reduced. Looking at specific control activities, some are less able to work well in smaller organizations. In particular, segregation of duties is going to be difficult if there is a small number of staff. There may also be limited scope for authorization and review elements of control activities.

Even where controls are in place, they are less likely to be formally documented compared to in a larger organization. For example, an owner-manager of a small business may review the monthly management accounts but is perhaps unlikely to prepare formal documentation of the review such as noting formal review points or documenting unexpected trends in the figures and how these were investigated. It is not likely that the owner-manager would even sign and date the management accounts to indicate that they had been subject to review.

This does not mean that controls are completely absent in small organizations. Indeed, in owner-managed businesses, the person in charge might be very 'hands-on', involved in the business on a day-to-day basis, and performing supervisory control over business activities, as well as more specific control activities such as authorization controls. In this situation the owner-manager may well instil a strong culture of trust in the business, leading to a strong control environment where fraud and deliberate misstatements are unlikely. For instance, if one person has sole authority for granting credit to customers and approving significant purchases, this can provide strong control over important account balances and transactions, reducing the need for more detailed control activities.

However, in many cases, the owner-manager will be more focused on business operations and growing the business than on internal controls. They will simply see business development as more important than internal controls, which then become a much lower priority than, for instance, building customer relations and driving growth. In addition, the owner-manager may not have the knowledge and skills to develop robust systems and internal controls.

All of the points above mean that the auditor is likely to take a particular approach when planning the audit of a smaller organization. The auditor will still need to understand and document the systems, which are likely to be quite simple, so this should not take too much time and effort. There will be some controls in place, for example, the owner-manager is likely to sign off the monthly payroll and payments to suppliers. However, because the existence of a wide range of robust internal controls is not likely, the auditor will not test the controls as a key part of their audit strategy. There is little point in testing controls which either do not exist or are not likely to be operating effectively—this is a waste of the auditor's time and resources. Instead, the auditor will take a substantive approach to the audit, obtaining evidence from performing detailed testing, rather than from placing reliance on internal controls.

Auditing scenario 8.3 Internal controls in a small company

Boris Ltd operates a small construction company. The company was established two years ago, and despite rapid growth since it started to trade, recently sales have reduced, and the company is struggling to manage its working capital.

Boris Ltd has not computerized all of its financial reporting function and some of its operations are manual, including the raising of sales invoices to its customers. Boris Ltd's managing director is Lee Richards, and he is assisted in running the business by Rowena Smith, who is his sister. Lee and Rowena spend most of their time visiting potential customers and at meetings with the subcontractors who they use on their construction contracts. They employ a part-time bookkeeper who maintains accounts using an off-the-shelf software package on the office laptop computer.

Supplier payments are made when the suppliers issue reminders because the bookkeeper often deals with other daily tasks such as the allocation of cash and the authorizing of credit notes due to mistakes made on sales invoices raised. Unfortunately, these mistakes are quite common and have resulted in the loss of customers.

The credit control function is relatively poor as Lee and Rowena are often out of the office. This also contributes to the poor administration of supplier payments because Lee and Rowena are the only signatories on the bank account.

You can see that in this small company there are practically no controls in place to prevent, detect, and correct misstatements in a timely manner. Indeed, this is accentuated by the fact that those charged with governance (i.e. Lee and Rowena), are hardly ever present in the office where the bookkeeper is attempting to maintain the accounting records.

There is no scope for segregation of duties or for proper authorization of transactions. This is leading to mistakes being made in raising sales invoices. Boris Ltd has already seen a downturn in sales which could partly be due to its lack of internal controls.

The lack of resources means that suppliers' payments are being delayed, and there is little emphasis on collecting cash as quickly as possible from customers. These factors are undoubtedly contributing to the working capital problems experienced by the company.

If Boris Ltd engages an auditor, management's failure to commit sufficient resources to internal controls will have an effect on that auditor's strategy. This is because the auditor would not test the controls in place as they are clearly weak. Instead the auditor would undertake a mainly substantive audit which could result in extra costs and time. There is a high risk of material misstatement, and the auditor will need to be sure to obtain sufficient and appropriate audit evidence from the testing performed.

8.3 Controls in a computerized environment

Even the smallest and simplest of businesses will have some form of computerized element in their accounting system. Straightforward sets of accounts can be maintained using software packages on computers. Larger organizations will have almost fully computerized systems, with only small manual elements. As mentioned earlier in the chapter, many companies also make use of cloud accounting, and the use of this is increasing rapidly—especially in the UK in the light of MTD, which requires software through which the business will report quarterly figures to HM Revenue & Customs.

Activity 8.5 Benefits of IT

Can you list the reasons why IT can benefit a system of internal controls?

Auditors need to understand and document systems and controls regardless of the extent to which the environment is computerized. In addition to considering the types of controls discussed earlier—authorization and physical controls for example—in a computerized environment, the auditor must also consider the existence of controls which work to maintain the integrity and security of data.

Auditing in practice 8.4 Cybersecurity

Cybersecurity is the term given to the measures put in place to protect systems, networks, and data in cyberspace. Cyberattacks can arise from deployment of viruses and malware, with the objective of fraud or perhaps deliberate sabotage in an act of malicious damage.

According to a UK government report published in 2023, across all UK businesses in the twelve months surveyed there were approximately 2.39 million instances of cybercrime and approximately 49,000 instances of fraud as a result of cybercrime; 32 per cent of businesses and 24 per cent of charities reported a cybersecurity breach or attack, with the cost estimated at £15,300 per victim.[6]

When developing understanding of an audit client's IT, it is important to consider the IT security controls that have been put in place to combat cybercrime. Simple practical measures such as password control and physically restricted access to vulnerable areas (e.g. location of servers) are very important. A log should be maintained for unauthorized attempts to access an IT system. Staff should be trained so that they are alert to instances of cybercrime and there should be recovery procedures so that the intended consequences of cyberattacks are minimized.

8.3.1 **Considerations for understanding the use of IT**

ISA (UK) 315 places a lot of emphasis on IT controls, the IT environment, and IT risks. For our purposes, we just need to develop an awareness of the key issues which impact audit planning.

As a starting point, the auditor must obtain an understanding of the following aspects of IT in order to understand the information system:

- The IT environment relevant to the information system.
- The entity's use of IT (i.e. IT applications relevant to the flows of transactions and processing of information in the information system).

[6] Department for Science, Innovation & Technology, 'Cyber security breaches survey 2023', 2023 <https://www.gov.uk/government/statistics/cyber-security-breaches-survey-2023/cyber-security-breaches-survey-2023> (accessed 18 January 2024).

ISA (UK) 315 requires the auditor to gain an understanding of information processing activities. Auditors must then identify the IT applications and other aspects of the entity's IT environment (e.g. the database or network) that are subject to risks arising from the use of IT:

- Databases will store the data used by IT applications and may consist of many interrelated data tables. There may also be database management systems that pull together information directly from databases into accounting packages or other linked software (e.g. payroll).
- The operating system is responsible for managing communications between hardware, IT applications, and other software used in the network.
- A network is used in the IT infrastructure to transmit data and to share information, resources, and services through a common communications link. The network typically establishes a layer of logical security (through the operating system) for access to the underlying resources.

This is an area which has historically been poorly documented or understood by audit teams, with resulting over-reliance on software systems as a base for audit testing without fully exploring the risks and reliability aspects of it. Keep in mind that if the client uses a very complex accounting system, the risk of material misstatement may become higher because of the system's complexity as those in the finance department may struggle to use it.

The auditor must assess what controls the client has over the IT system, for example, who can access certain areas of the accounting system, as well as how reliable the IT is and whether certain procedures, such as backup procedures, are adequate.

Considerations for understanding IT are outlined in ISA (UK) 315, Appendix 5, and considerations for understanding general IT controls are outlined in Appendix 6. These two appendices are long and detailed and are designed to guide audit teams in a practical way through the requirements of the standard, including detailing various characteristics of commercial software applications relevant to financial reporting, indicating how these are found in non-complex IT environments and in large or complex applications.

8.3.1.1 Non-complex IT environment

Where the entity has a non-complex IT system (e.g. where the audit client is a smaller audit with a relatively simple system of internal control), the auditor will have to test a few more IT controls (such as access level controls, backup processes, software updates, antivirus, and malware software) to ensure that the IT system is stable. Remember, the auditor is primarily concerned with how the IT system processes information that eventually ends up in the financial statements or helps that information 'on its journey' into the financial statements together with the relevant IT controls over that information.

To that end, the auditor must document the IT system, the controls over the IT system, and devise appropriate audit procedures to test the operating effectiveness of the system. Where the auditor considers that controls over the IT system are lacking or are weak, a more substantive approach to the audit will be needed.

8.3.1.2 **Complex IT environment**

Similar requirements for a non-complex IT environment as above will generally apply. However, the key difference is that the audit team may not be able to complete the assessment of the reliability of the IT systems without specialist input.

Where an audit client has applications that support finance, purchasing, stock, sales, and HR/payroll, these may be part of an ERP system, which is generally considered to be complex. Such clients may have a separate IT department/staff or use the software provided (and supported) by a parent company or another part of the group.

The issue with these systems is that, generally, the client has a lot of flexibility with the system and control over it, such as by having an administrator account or 'super user' who can manage access and tailor or design bespoke reports and manage upgrades and changes to the source code. Many of these sorts of changes (and the evidence that no untoward changes have been made) can only be adequately assessed and checked by someone with specific experience of that ERP system or similar experience that can be applied. Many external auditors are unlikely to have this experience.

Where specialist input is deemed necessary, ISA (UK) 620 *Using the Work of an Auditor's Expert* will apply. In practice, when a client has an extensive and/or a complicated IT infrastructure, the auditor may consider using IT specialists to obtain an understanding of the systems and controls, and to obtain evidence to allow the systems and controls to be evaluated. Larger audit firms have specialist departments who can perform this work.

8.3.2 **General IT controls**

General IT controls support the continued effective functioning of information processing controls, upon which the entity and the auditor may be able to place some reliance.

ISA (UK) 315 contains the following definition of general IT controls:

> Controls over the entity's IT processes that support the continued proper operation of the IT environment, including the continued effective functioning of information processing controls and the integrity of information (i.e., the completeness, accuracy and validity of information) in the entity's information system.[7]

The auditor is required to evaluate the design of each general IT control and carry out testing to establish whether or not it has been implemented.

As we have already seen, controls are put in place to mitigate risks—remember that one way to think about risk is to ask, 'what could go wrong?' Here we are considering what could go wrong in the IT environment.

Appendix 5 to ISA (UK) 315 offers a range of examples of relevant risks, including:

- Unauthorised access to data that may result in destruction of data or improper changes to data, including the recording of unauthorised or non-existent transactions, or inaccurate recording of transactions.

[7] FRC, 'ISA (UK) 315', 2020, para 12(d).

- Unauthorised changes to data in master files.
- Inappropriate manual intervention.
- The possibility of IT personnel gaining access privileges beyond those necessary to perform their assigned duties thereby breaking down segregation of duties.
- Potential loss of data or inability to access data as required.
- Unauthorised changes to IT applications or other aspects of the IT environment.[8]

The organization should put controls in place to mitigate these risks. Controls can be simple, such as using password protection and ensuring regular backups of data.

Auditing scenario 8.4 Passwords

The accounting system of Ratchford Industries Ltd is accessible to all fifteen employees in the finance department. No access level rights are implemented meaning that all members of staff have full access to the system. The password to access the accounting system is 'password'.

The principal risks in this situation are that the accounting system can be accessed by anyone in the finance department. Users may be able to make inappropriate changes to data and audit trails would likely lack sufficient information.

To remedy this situation, all staff should be provided with access level rights meaning they can only access the areas of the accounting system that they need to perform their role. In addition, each member of the finance department must be given a unique password which they must not divulge to other staff members. These passwords must be automatically changed on a regular basis (e.g. monthly).

General IT controls are typically grouped into controls over three processes (see Figure 8.5).

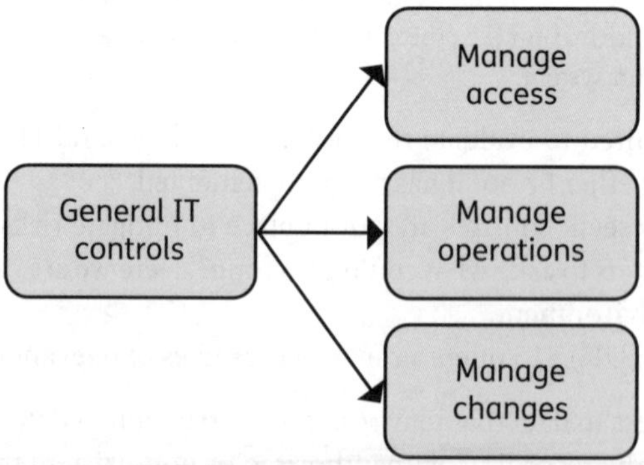

Figure 8.5 General IT controls

[8] Ibid., Appendix 5, para 18.

Processes to manage access—those that ensure a user accessing the system is appropriately authorized to do so, has been given an appropriate level of access which is regularly reviewed and revoked when the individual no longer needs such access to perform their role within the organization.

Processes to manage IT operations—those that control access to schedule and initiate jobs or programs that may affect financial reporting, job monitoring to check successful execution of jobs, backup and recovery, and intrusion detections. IT operations may well be outsourced to third-party IT providers.

Process to manage program or other changes to the IT environment—those that implement a change management process to ensure that changes to the design and implementation of the system are suitably tested, appropriately authorized, and that data is correctly converted.

Examples of general IT controls include:

- Access to certain areas of the IT system is restricted to authorized personnel who each have their own credentials and whose access is limited to that which is required for their specific role within the business. The list of users and their access rights is reviewed by management each month.
- Passwords must meet minimum standards with regard to complexity. These include being more than twelve characters long, including both upper and lowercase characters, and at least one 'special' character (e.g. # or !).
- Changes to programs are tested and approved prior to being moved into a production environment.
- The system will not permit the same person to set up and approve a supplier payment.

Auditing scenario 8.5 Software updates

You are working on the audit of Connor Ltd, which allows most of its staff to work from home, and all staff have a company-owned and -maintained laptop for this purpose. From a discussion with the company's IA team, you know that staff have not been regularly updating their software, including antivirus software on their laptops, during the year.

If the antivirus software is not updated regularly, the employees' laptops are vulnerable to cyberattacks. This could be in the form of malware (i.e. malicious programs being introduced into the systems for deliberate sabotage or an attempt to steal data, which can result in the loss, theft, or misuse of data). In relation to this, there is a risk of a breach of data protection legislation, depending on what can be accessed and how it is used.

There is the associated business risk that outdated software impacts the performance of the laptops, because software updates enhance efficiency so failing to run software updates means that systems are slower and may not be compatible with other software.

Connor Ltd needs to understand why it is that employees are not running regular software updates and ensure that controls are implemented to improve the situation and reduce the risks created. This could be through staff training, so that employees are aware of the risks created, and setting up alerts so that laptops that have not been updated recently are flagged and the employee contacted to ensure that an update is performed.

8.3.3 Information processing controls

Information processing controls are the controls that are implemented in relation to a specific computer application (e.g. over the payroll system or the inventory management system). Information processing controls can be manual or automated procedures, and they should help to ensure that transactions that have occurred are authorized and completely and accurately recorded. Information processing controls relate to procedures used to initiate, record, process, and report transactions or other financial data.

Information processing controls should exist over input, the processing itself, and the output (see Figure 8.6).

Controls over input are important as they should work to ensure that data input into the system is complete and accurate. Examples include:

- Checking the numerical sequence of transactions to ensure no duplications or missing items.
- Using check data to confirm the accuracy of data inputted into the system—for example, using digit verification to ensure that reference numbers (e.g. an invoice number) are valid, or using an existence check to ensure that data is valid (e.g. a customer reference).
- Applying range checks to ensure that transactions fall within an accepted, predetermined range (e.g. to check that overtime payments are no more than £1,000 per employee).
- Comparison of manual total to input total (e.g. to check the total number of invoices and also their monetary value posted in a day). This can be done by simple comparison of a manually derived total, and the total showing in the system after the data has been input.
- Checks to ensure that data input has been appropriately authorized.

Information processing controls tend to be inbuilt with the software, and include controls over master files and standing data, which should work to ensure that no unauthorized changes are made. Controls over processing are often dealt with by a specialist due to the complex nature of the work involved.

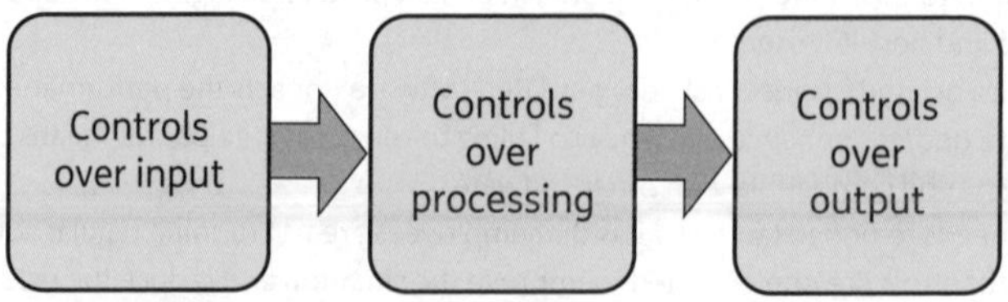

Figure 8.6 Information processing controls

Output controls should ensure that output is distributed in a timely manner, only to prescribed authorized users. Typical output controls could include:

- Formal written instructions notifying data processing personnel of prescribed distribution procedures.
- Ongoing monitoring by a responsible official of the distribution of output to ensure it is distributed in accordance with authorized policy.

8.4 Documenting accounting systems and internal control

The understanding and documentation of accounting systems and associated systems of internal control should be commensurate with the nature, size, and complexity of the entity. The extent of documentation should also be appropriate to the experience and capabilities of the audit engagement team, as less experienced members of the audit team may require more detailed documentation to assist them to obtain appropriate understanding of the entity and its controls.

In a smaller entity, the audit documentation on internal control is likely to be relatively simple, focusing on how sales and purchasing cycles operate and highlighting the risks of material misstatement that arise from the controls (or lack of) that are in place. It is tempting to think that in a simple system operating in a small company, there is little risk of material misstatement, but of course there are specific risks associated with this type of company, especially the risks posed by opportunities for management override, and the limited scope for segregation of duties and authorization controls. In a smaller company, the extent and nature of management's involvement in internal control is likely to be a key aspect in the documentation of internal control.

The auditor will have to include IT system controls within their understanding. For a complex system, this may take significant time and effort, whereas for a more basic system, it will be more straightforward.

There are three main methods used by auditors to document systems and controls, which we will examine shortly, explaining each method and considering the advantages and disadvantages of each:

- narrative notes;
- flowcharts; and
- questionnaires.

A walk-through test is performed by auditors to test their understanding of the systems. It means selecting transactions and tracing their path through the various stages of the financial reporting system. The purpose of walk-through testing is not to evaluate the effectiveness of internal controls. It is to check that the auditor has correctly documented the system and understands the processes involved.

Typically, the auditor will select a number of transactions for each transaction cycle, making sure to include transactions at various points in time during the year (e.g. on a quarterly basis). This ensures that any changes in how transactions are processed will be picked up.

8.4.1 Narrative notes

Narrative notes simply explain how the systems and controls operate in words. The notes record what occurs in the system at each stage and include the detail of any controls which operate at each stage. Narrative notes can work well when systems are simple and are often used for smaller clients where there are only a small number of transactions cycles (e.g. sales, purchases, payroll), and when the transaction cycles have a limited number of stages.

8.4.1.1 Advantages

- Narrative notes are easy to prepare, an audit team member simply needs to write down their understanding of the system.
- The notes should be easy to understand by all audit team members, as they are simply a description of how the system works.
- Assuming that the notes are maintained on a word processor, they are easy to update each year when changes are made to the systems and controls.
- This method is quite flexible and therefore the format of the notes and the level of detail required can be tailored to each client's circumstances.
- The notes can be augmented to include other relevant information, for example, the auditor's evaluation of the controls present.

8.4.1.2 Disadvantages

- Notes can be cumbersome, and if systems are even slightly complex, it can be hard to describe in words how the system operates compared with a diagrammatical representation in a flowchart.
- If the notes are made manually, it is difficult to update them.
- It may be easy to miss out elements of the system or to omit controls if there is no standard template for the narrative notes which forces the auditor to consider all possible ways in which the system operates, or if the notes are prepared by a less experienced auditor who does not realize that elements are missing.

Auditing scenario 8.6 Problem with recording systems and controls using narrative notes

Jia Huang is a junior auditor who has been assigned to the audit of Fin Ltd, a small manufacturing company which produces wooden furniture. Jia has been given the task of documenting the sales system using narrative notes. As an existing client, there is already a document which describes and explains how the system works, but there have been some changes in the year which Jia needs to ask the client about.

The system changes have arisen due to Fin Ltd starting to sell its products online, using a sales portal built into its website. Due to Jia's inexperience, they do not know the detailed questions to ask the client about how this new part of the system operates. Jia lets the client explain about its operation, and diligently records the conversation, so the audit team does have a record of how the sales made on the company's website are recorded. However, the client fails to tell Jia that a small number of sales are being made overseas, or about how management is monitoring the success of this new sales method. Therefore, the auditor has no record about the overseas transactions, how the transactions are recorded and controlled, and there is no record of management monitoring, which is an important aspect of internal control.

8.4.2 **Flowcharts**

Flowcharts are diagrammatical representations of how a system operates, including relevant internal controls. Lines usually demonstrate the sequence of events and standard symbols are used to indicate the existence of documents and internal controls.

Figure 8.7 shows some examples of symbols that are used in constructing a systems flowchart.

Symbol	Meaning
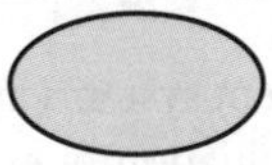	The start or end of a process
	Link between stages of the process
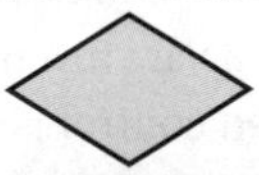	Decision
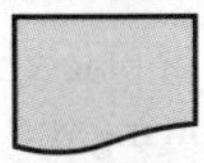	Document
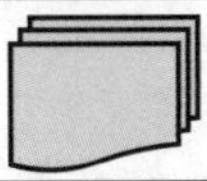	Multiple linked documents
	Database
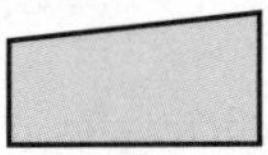	Manual input
	Sequential data

Figure 8.7 Flowchart symbols

8.4.2.1 **Advantages**

- Using off-the-shelf software (e.g. Microsoft Visio), it is quick and easy to create flowcharts. Even auditors with relatively little experience can produce accurate flowcharts from information provided by the client.
- When flowcharts incorporate standard templates and symbols it is quite easy to understand and interpret the system represented by the flowchart. For example, it is easy to spot missing controls over part of a transaction cycle.
- They are quick to review, especially compared with narrative notes—a picture speaks a thousand words.

8.4.2.2 **Disadvantages**

- As they are usually based on software templates, it can be difficult to depict unusual systems using flowcharts.
- They can sometimes be difficult to amend, as any amendments may require the whole flowchart to be redrawn, though the use of software makes updating easier.
- Narrative notes are often used as supplementary information supporting flowcharts, which could be viewed as a duplication of effort.

8.4.3 **Questionnaires**

Auditors use two types of questionnaire in order to document systems and controls—internal control questionnaires (ICQ) and internal control evaluation questionnaires (ICEQ). Both contain a list of questions but with slightly different purposes.

ICQs are designed to evaluate whether expected controls are in place, with questions usually worded to elicit a 'yes or no' response. For example, the ICQ could ask 'are purchase requisitions authorized prior to a purchase order being raised?', or 'are inventory counts held on a monthly basis?'—answering yes indicates that the expected control is in place, answering no indicates that the expected control is absent.

ICEQs are used to evaluate not only whether controls are in place, but also the effectiveness of the controls. ICEQs therefore go a step further in allowing the auditor to assess and conclude on the strength of the internal controls.

8.4.3.1 **Advantages**

- Questionnaires are quick to prepare, usually based on a standard list of questions, which means they are an efficient method for recording the system.
- They are easy to understand and review.
- Using questionnaires means that missing controls or deficiencies are clearly highlighted.

8.4.3.2 **Disadvantages**

- Using a standard list of questions may miss out more unusual controls which may have been specifically designed for a particular purpose.
- If not tailored, the questionnaires may include a lot of information about less relevant controls.
- They may create the impression that all controls are of equal importance—for example, segregation of duties is seen as a key control which, if lacking, is a serious deficiency, regardless of the extent of other controls that are in place.

Auditing scenario 8.7 ICQ and ICEQ

Bobbi is auditing Fields Ltd, an events management company which specializes in organizing music festivals. Bobbi has been tasked with documenting the company's internal controls over purchases, for which Bobbi has prepared an ICQ. Bobbi also documented the good inwards process, using an ICEQ. Extracts from each document are shown in Tables 8.4 and 8.5.

Table 8.4 ICQ

	Yes	No	Comment
Do all purchases made by the company derive from written orders?	X		
Are all purchase orders sequentially numbered?	X		
Are manual sequence checks performed on purchase orders on a regular basis?		X	The system is computerized
Do orders have to be authorized by a manager?	X		
Does the company have approved suppliers?	X		
Does the purchase order contain details of:	X		
Quantities?			
Prices?			
Terms of payment?			
Person who authorized the order?			
Date of order?			
Are individuals given a limit as to the value of orders they can place with a supplier?	X		Purchasing director has to authorize orders over £5,000
Are copies of the purchase order sent to the purchase ledger department?	X		
Are purchase orders matched to invoices?	X		
Does the purchasing department retain a copy of all orders?	X		

Table 8.5 ICEQ

	Yes	No	Comment
Can goods inwards be accepted without being inspected for quality/damage		X	
Are goods inwards signed for on receipt?	X		
Are the individuals dealing with goods inward the same as those who deal with the recording of the goods in inventory?	X		Warehouse staff deal with goods inwards
Are the individuals dealing with goods inward the same as those who deal with the purchasing of the goods?		X	A separate purchase ordering department deals with purchasing the goods
Is it possible for goods to be paid for without them having been received?		X	Invoices are not paid for unless there is a goods received note (GRN) attached to the invoice
Can goods be accepted without being ordered?		X	A copy of the order is emailed to the warehouse department on authorization of the order
Are damaged goods stored in the same part of the warehouse as goods held for resale?		X	A separate area is maintained which stores damaged goods

8.4.5 **Evaluating control activities**

ISA (UK) 315, para 26 states:

> The auditor shall obtain an understanding of the control activities component, through performing risk assessment procedures, by:
>
> (a) Identifying controls that address risks of material misstatement at the assertion level in the control activities component as follows:
>
> (i) Controls that address a risk that is determined to be a significant risk;
>
> (ii) Controls over journal entries, including non-standard journal entries used to record non-recurring, unusual transactions or adjustments;
>
> (iii) Controls for which the auditor plans to test operating effectiveness in determining the nature, timing and extent of substantive testing, which shall include controls that address risks for which substantive procedures alone do not provide sufficient appropriate audit evidence; and
>
> (iv) Other controls that the auditor considers are appropriate to enable the auditor to meet the objectives of paragraph 13 with respect to risks at the assertion level, based on the auditor's professional judgment;
>
> (b) Based on controls identified in (a), identifying the IT applications and the other aspects of the entity's IT environment that are subject to risks arising from the use of IT;
>
> (c) For such IT applications and other aspects of the IT environment identified in (b), identifying:
>
> (i) The related risks arising from the use of IT; and
>
> (ii) The entity's general IT controls that address such risks; and

(d) For each control identified in (a) or (c)(ii):

(i) Evaluating whether the control is designed effectively to address the risk of material misstatement at the assertion level, or effectively designed to support the operation of other controls; and

(ii) Determining whether the control has been implemented by performing procedures in addition to inquiry of the entity's personnel.[9]

To summarize these lengthy requirements, the auditor should not just document how a system and relevant controls works, but also needs to evaluate whether controls have been properly designed, including whether they have appropriate objectives, and also whether they are operating in the manner intended. In other words, understanding the design and implementation of controls is necessary regardless of whether or not the auditor intends to place any reliance on internal controls. More work is needed for controls that address 'significant risks'—we will consider how the auditor determines whether a risk is significant in Chapter 9.

When evaluating the design of a control, the auditor should consider whether the control, individually or in combination with other controls, is capable of effectively preventing, or detecting, and correcting, material misstatements. The design of a control should be considered before its implementation. An improperly designed control may represent a significant deficiency in internal control.

Evaluating the implementation of a control means considering whether the control exists and whether it is being used within the organization. If a control has been designed but there is no evidence of it actually operating, then clearly it is ineffective.

If the auditor intends to place reliance on internal controls, tests of control must be performed, to obtain audit evidence which demonstrates that internal controls are sufficiently robust. ISA (UK) 330 *The Auditor's Responses to Assessed Risks* defines 'tests of controls' as:

> An audit procedure designed to evaluate the operating effectiveness of controls in preventing, or detecting and correcting, material misstatements at the assertion level.[10]

To summarize, there is theoretically a three-step process to be used by auditors (Figure 8.8).

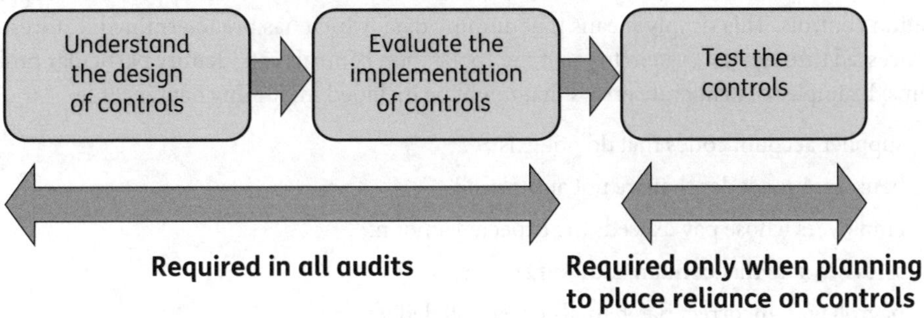

Figure 8.8 Understanding, evaluating, and testing control activities

[9] Ibid., para 26.

[10] FRC, 'ISA (UK) 330', 2017, para 4(b) <https://media.frc.org.uk/documents/ISA_UK_330_-_Revised_July_2017_Updated_May_2022.pdf> (accessed 18 January 2024).

The problem for auditors is that in order to evaluate the implementation of controls, some form of testing will need to take place. It is difficult to understand whether a control has been implemented without testing it in some way. In other words, the process does not really work in a linear fashion. Auditors therefore often perform some tests of control as a way of evaluating implementation and then perform further tests of controls (i.e. obtain audit evidence with regard to the controls if they chose to rely on the controls). Tests of control are often performed at the interim audit stage. We will look at tests of control, focusing on using them as a means of obtaining audit evidence in Chapter 11.

8.4.5.1 **Journal entries**

You can see that IAS (UK) 315 places a specific requirement for the auditor to identify controls over journal entries. This is because journal entries can be used to carry out a fraud, for example, if a company wishes to improve the appearance of their financial statements, a journal could be made to create fictitious sale invoices or to remove accrued expenses, thus inflating the profit for the year. At a more specific level, a fraudster can use journal entries to hide their activity and make it difficult to spot. Fraudulent journal entries are linked to deficiencies in internal controls because they are often the result of management override (i.e. when senior employees are able to circumvent internal controls in order to post the journal, or happen due to controls not operating properly, e.g. if journals can be posted without the necessary approval).

? **Activity 8.6** Fraudulent journal entries

What do you think could indicate that a journal entry is a fraudulent transaction? What might indicate that it is unusual?

8.4.6 **Test data**

Various techniques are used to help the auditor evaluate controls in a computerized accounting system. For example, test data can be input into the system to test the operation of application controls. This simply means that dummy data, which has predetermined features, is processed through the system to see if the application controls can identify particular problems. Examples of deliberate errors that might be included in dummy data include:

- supplier account codes that do not exist;
- bank account codes that are not authorized;
- employees whose pay exceeds the expected amount;
- sales invoices that contain addition errors;
- payroll with incorrect batch totals or payroll deductions.

If the client's systems and controls do not detect these deliberate errors, this indicates problems with the system and that controls are not sufficiently robust.

As well as using data with deliberate errors, the dummy data should also include valid data which can demonstrate that correct data is properly processed by the system and produces the correct output.

Activity 8.7 Problems in using test data

Why do you think the audit client may be reluctant for the auditor to use test data?

8.5 Control objectives and activities in main transaction cycles

Any business will have transaction cycles, by which we mean the process of recording business activity for a particular area of the business, for instance the sales cycle and the purchasing cycle. In this final section of the chapter, we explore the typical elements of both of these transaction cycles, to consider the control objectives and the type of control activities that would be expected to be in place.

The illustrations are simply meant to indicate examples of transaction cycles. It is important to understand that these should be specifically tailored to an organization's specific circumstances, however, many very similar controls will be in place in most organizations.

Note that some objectives are more related to operational matters than specifically related to financial reporting. While the auditor is only required to understand and document controls relating to financial reporting, it is very difficult to understand and document a system without considering the operational objectives and control activities as well as the financial reporting objectives and activities, so these have been included for the sake of completeness.

When the auditor discovers deficiencies in internal controls, they are reported to management in accordance with ISA 265 *Communicating Deficiencies in Internal Control to Those Charged with Governance and Management*. We will look at the details of this reporting in Chapter 22. For now, we just need to focus on understanding the control objectives and the relevant controls, so that we can evaluate the strength of internal control.

8.5.1 Sales cycle

The sales (or revenue) cycle applies to how a business records its transactions with customers. Some sales may be cash but of course most sales transactions are now digital in nature. There will be different control objectives and activities for different types of sales. See Table 8.6 which outlines an example sales cycle for a manufacturing business, selling physical items to its customers.

8.5.2 Purchasing cycle

This cycle could be applied to the purchase of inventory (raw materials, components to be used in manufacturing, etc.), or items such as stationery and laptops for use in the business. See Table 8.7.

8.5.3 Other transactions cycles–payroll and capital expenditure

Organizations will of course have transactions other than described above in respect of the sales and purchasing cycles. It is not within the scope of this textbook to describe in detail every possible transaction cycle, but we will provide some discussion on payroll and capital

Table 8.6 Controls in a sales cycle

Stage in the cycle/ documentation	Objectives	Controls that should be in place
Customer places an order and an order form is raised	Sales only accepted from creditworthy customers	Credit check on the customer—for new customers, a reference may be required or a credit rating record obtained
		For existing customers, a check should be made on their credit limit and payment history
		Approval of new customers by sales manager
		Limit placed on the amount the customer can order
	Achieve the best sales price possible	Discounts subject to manager's approval
		Monthly review of level of discounts offered as a % of total sales
		Monthly review of gross profit margins and levels of sales—to monitor the completeness of sales and whether too many discounts are being offered
	All orders can be fulfilled and can promptly despatched	Inventory levels are checked before the order is accepted
		Standard order forms are used (so that 'rogue' items cannot be ordered and that sufficient information is on the form for the order to be processed)
		Customer contacted if goods are unavailable
	All orders are dealt with (i.e. none go missing)	Use sequentially numbered order forms
		All order forms are clearly labelled when they have been fulfilled
Order form is passed for packing and delivery. A delivery note (goods despatched note or GDN) is raised.	All orders are quickly sent out to customers	Regular review of order forms which have not been labelled as fulfilled
		IT control to produce an exception report of orders not fulfilled after a certain period
	Inventory levels will be replenished	All items taken out of inventory are entered into inventory records
		Regular reports of inventory levels to be reviewed
		IT control to flag when inventory lines reach a certain reorder level, to prompt reordering
	Goods only delivered to valid customers	All delivery notes are matched to approved customer orders
		Delivery is authorized by a responsible official
	The correct goods are packed and despatched and are in saleable condition	Goods should be checked back to order and the quality of the goods is inspected
		Bar codes can be used to accurately monitor the date, quantity, details of the items and delivery address

Stage in the cycle/ documentation	Objectives	Controls that should be in place
Goods delivered to customer. Delivery note is raised	Goods are confirmed as received by the customer	Customer signs a copy of the delivery note, or receipt is confirmed by electronic means
		Receipt confirmations are retained in case of disputes
	All goods are delivered to valid customers	Company checks all delivery notes signed by customer back to original order form
		Use a reputable courier if delivery is not an internal function
		Delivery notes should be sequentially numbered—a check should be made to ensure none are missing
Invoice raised and sent to the customer	The correct amount is invoiced for the goods	Invoices raised are checked back to GDN and original order for quantities of goods ordered
		The price charged is agreed to order, and to price list
		Any discounts offered are approved at this stage, if not already approved at ordering stage.
		IT controls to ensure totals are correct and VAT added at correct rate
	All goods despatched are subsequently invoiced	Sequence check on GDN and invoices to look for gaps in the sequence
		IT controls to ensure that all recorded despatches prompt production of an invoice
	All invoices are entered into the accounting records	Use sequentially numbered invoices and perform input/sequence checks to identify any missing numbers in the sequence
		Sales ledger control account reconciliations—to ensure the accuracy and completeness of receivables
	All invoiced amounts are subsequently collected	Credit control function to monitor customer balances and to chase slow-paying customers
		Monthly review of ageing of debtors' balances—to check the level of slow-paying debtors
		Any disputed invoices are quickly resolved
Payment received from customer	Money is promptly and securely banked	Encourage use of electronic payment by customers
		For cash receipts, daily banking by responsible personnel
		Use two people to deal with cash (a supervisory control to deter theft)
		Segregation of duties between those who: • Raise invoices • Deal with cash receipts (to prevent fraud known as teeming and lading)

Table 8.7 Controls in a purchasing cycle

Stage in the cycle/ documentation	Objectives	Controls that should be in place
Employee requires goods to be purchased. A purchase requisition is raised	Goods should only be requested where these is a valid business purpose	All purchase requisitions to be approved by a manager—usually the higher the value of item being requested, the more senior the level of approval is needed For non-routine items a business case/justification document may be needed and approved For inventory items the requisition should only be approved after inventory levels have been checked to ensure the goods are actually needed Segregation of duty to avoid people both ordering items and approving the requisition
	All items requested can actually be delivered	Use an approved suppliers list—only reputable suppliers can be used Authorization by a responsible official needed for new suppliers
	Value for money is achieved	For standard items, review supplier price lists and identify the best price For non-standard items/high value orders a tender process may be used, or quotations obtained and reviewed Discounts negotiated and written confirmation obtained from the supplier Monthly review of gross profit margins and levels of purchases—to monitor whether all discounts are being taken up
	All items requested are actually ordered	Requisition forms should be sequentially numbered, and sequence checks performed to ensure all forms have been actioned.
Order is raised	Orders only placed where there is a valid business purpose	All orders placed to be matched back to approved requisition document A standard order form should be used —this will highlight any unusual items being ordered
	All orders end up being placed	Order forms should be sequentially numbered and regularly checked for gaps in the sequence
	All orders will be delivered promptly	Obtain written confirmation from the supplier regarding the likely delivery timescale, and match this to the order form and requisition
Receipt of goods, a Goods Received Note (GRN) is raised	Goods are only accepted where they have been ordered	GRN is a standard form showing the quantity of goods received and the supplier/delivery details which should be matched back to order and requisition. Goods not matching the order and requisition should not be accepted
	Goods are only accepted in acceptable condition	GRN should only be raised when the goods have been checked for quality Unacceptable goods should not be signed for on the suppliers delivery note

Stage in the cycle/ documentation	Objectives	Controls that should be in place
	Inventory levels updated	IT control so that raising a GRN automatically updates inventory levels In a manual system a regular sequence review of GRN for any not yet entered into the accounting records
	Inventory is secure and risk of theft is minimized	Physical controls over inventory Regular check on the physical quantity of inventory HR controls over recruitment of staff for the warehouse and delivery function (to deter theft)
	All orders are fulfilled	Unmatched order forms to be regularly reviewed and suppliers contacted IT control to produce a weekly report of unfilled orders
	The person who requested the goods is promptly notified	A copy of the GRN to be passed to the relevant department
Supplier sends invoice	Liability only accepted where goods have been ordered and received	All invoices received to be matched to GRN, order, and requisition
	Invoices received charge the correct amount	Arithmetic check on invoice totals, VAT, and other items included (e.g. delivery charges) Level of discount agreed to suppliers file or order agreed with the supplier Agree invoice amounts to supplier statements received
	Invoices are recorded completely and accurately	Invoices received should be given an internal reference/ sequence number and gaps in the sequence should be flagged by the IT system Daily posting of invoices received to nominal ledger Batch total checks to ensure the total value of invoices posted agrees from manual record to computer record Purchase ledger control account and supplier statement reconciliations—to ensure the accuracy and completeness of creditors
Payment made to suppliers	Payments only made to meet valid liabilities	Cheques signed/electronic transfers approved by responsible officials Approval of payment only after agreeing amounts to verified invoice received Segregation of duty to ensure one person cannot order goods, check them in, and arrange payment of supplier
	Invoices only paid once	Invoices stamped as 'PAID' Supplier accounts promptly updated after payment
	Suppliers are paid on time and no late payment fees are incurred	Monthly review of ageing of creditors balances

Table 8.8 Controls in a payroll cycle

Payroll—internal control objectives	Example control activities
Payment is made only to valid employees of the company for work performed	Personnel files to be maintained for all employees
	Robust authorization procedures to avoid unapproved amendments to payroll information (e.g. in relation to starters and leavers)
	Use of exception reports and 'before and after' reports to show changes to master payroll files
	Overtime is subject to approval by a responsible official
	Payroll is approved by a responsible official (e.g. finance director, having checked names/payroll numbers of personnel to whom payment is being made)
	Segregation of duty between HR and payroll functions
	Swipe cards, clock cards, or other methods of monitoring hours worked by employees, and/or use of time and attendance software
Payroll costs are accurately determined, including payroll deductions such as tax and pension contributions	Payroll software uses application controls such as range checks to detect payments of an unusual size
	Review of total payroll and payroll deductions to detect unusual trends in monthly payments
	Double checking a sample of tax calculations and agreeing the elements of the calculation to current tax rates
	Reconciliations of payroll records and employee costs as recognized in the general ledger
	Regular comparison of payroll with budgets for wages and salaries to identify unusual trends

expenditure cycles as these are common to most audit clients. We will approach these cycles by selecting illustrative internal control objectives and providing some examples of typical control activities for each. See Tables 8.8 and 8.9.

Auditing scenario 8.7 Deficient controls over payroll leading to fraud

Patrick is working on the audit of Bryn Ltd, a small company which processes soft fruit for use in the food industry. When auditing payroll, Patrick found that six new employees had been added to the company's payroll during the year, with combined payments of £75,000 being made to them. These additions to payroll had not been authorized and Patrick could not find any personnel files in the HR database relating to these people. When Patrick questioned the payroll supervisor who had made the amendments, she commented that authorization was not needed because the new employees are only working for the company on a temporary basis.

On further investigation, Patrick found that the payroll supervisor had been filling in time sheets for the six people and submitting them along with the other time sheets collected from employees. The wages of the six fictitious employees were being paid into one bank account, which the payroll supervisor had set up.

The amendment of payroll and falsification of time sheets indicates that a fraud, known as a ghost employee fraud, is being carried out by the payroll supervisor. This type of fraud is quite common, and for it to be successful the perpetrator will ensure that having created the fictitious employees on the payroll and falsified the record of work carried out, they are also able to arrange payment to be made into their own, or an accomplice's, bank account.

The controls that should be in place to prevent this fraud include segregation of duty and authorization of amendments to payroll information and of time sheets.

In this example, additional procedures should be conducted to determine whether the supervisor has made any other amendments to payroll to determine the possible scope of any fraud. Verification should be sought as to the existence of the new employees, in case they are valid employees of Bryn Ltd. The bank accounts into which their salaries are being paid should also be examined, to see if the payments are being made into the same account.

Table 8.9 Controls in a capital expenditure cycle

Capital expenditure–internal control objectives	Example control activities
Assets are only acquired for valid business purposes	All asset acquisitions to be approved by a responsible official—with significant expenditure requiring board-level approval
	For non-routine items, a business case/justification document may be needed and approved
	Segregation of duty to avoid people both ordering items and approving the requisition
The non-current asset register is a complete and accurate record of the company's assets	Regular asset counts with reconciliation of totals to the non-current asset register
	Additions to the non-current asset register are supported by documentation i.e. purchase requisition/approved order/suppliers' invoice
	Asset disposal is authorized by a responsible official
	Restricted access to non-current asset master files using password protection
	Use of exception reports to show changes to master file data
	Regular comparison of additions to the non-current asset file with capital expenditure budgets

Chapter round-up

- There are five elements of a system of internal control—control environment, the entity's risk assessment process, the entity's process to monitor the system of internal control, the information system and communication, and control activities.
- The auditor is required to understand and document the elements of the client's system of internal control that relates to financial reporting.
- Different methods can be used for documenting systems and controls, including narrative notes, flowcharts, and questionnaires.
- The auditor evaluates the strength of internal control in order to devise an appropriate audit strategy and to help evaluate the overall risk of material misstatement.
- Internal controls have limitations and in particular they can be overridden by management or circumvented by collusion. Therefore, the auditor can never rely wholly on a client's systems and controls.
- In a computerized environment, specific IT-related controls should be present. The auditor may wish to rely on a specialist in evaluating the strength of such systems.
- Control activities should be devised by management to meet particular control objectives, such as accuracy of recording transactions and restricted access to records.

End of chapter case study

Introduction

In this chapter, we have considered the wide range of matters which auditors should consider when they obtain understanding of a client's system of internal control. Especially when dealing with a new audit client, the auditor needs to ensure that sufficient time and resources are available to enable a proper breadth and depth of understanding in relation to internal controls to be developed. Without a good level of understanding there is a risk that an inappropriate audit strategy is developed, leading to an inefficient audit and possibly an increased audit risk.

This case study links to the following learning outcomes:

- Describe and explain the components of a system of internal control.
- Identify and discuss deficiencies in internal control and recommend relevant remedies to deficiencies in internal control.
- Analyse information in respect of internal controls to identify audit planning issues.

Scenario

Windsor Ltd retails luxury fashion accessories, mainly bags, scarves, and jewellery. Its operations are international, with over 120 stores in fifteen countries worldwide. Its products are aimed at female customers with a high level of disposable income, as the items are expensive. The company has a high-profile brand 'Miss Windsor', on which a great deal of marketing budget is spent every year to support the worldwide presence of the brand name.

The company is a new audit client of your audit firm, and you are planning the audit. The audit engagement partner has asked you to develop business understanding in order to effectively plan the audit. You need to prepare a section of the audit file which contains a summary of the matters you have investigated in developing your business understanding.

You are aware that Windsor Ltd has set up an internal audit (IA) department, but this function appears to be quite small in relation to the size of the organization. When asked about this, the finance director, to whom the IA department report, said that the board does not want to spend much money on IA, as they do see the value in it. The IA department is staffed by three members of staff who used to be part of the marketing team, who were offered a choice of leaving the company, or moving into IA, when the marketing team was rationalized last year.

Following a discussion with the finance director, you have been documenting the purchasing system in order to evaluate the controls that operate within that system. Given the company's operations, purchasing is a significant class of transaction, and the trade payables figure recognized in the statement of financial position represents 20 per cent of the total assets. You have discussed the system with Windsor Ltd's financial controller, and the notes that you have made are shown below.

Ordering process

Inventory ordering is managed by a purchasing manager. The purchasing manager determines how much inventory each store needs by reviewing current inventory levels and comparing them to next month's sales forecast. On the basis of this, the purchasing manager raises a purchase order for each individual store. A member of the purchasing department collates all the purchase orders each month and checks the information on these manual forms. Individual orders below £1,500 in value do not have to be approved. Individual orders above £1,500 in value are passed to one of the company directors for authorization. Any one of the company directors has the authority to sign the purchase order.

The purchase orders are not sequentially numbered and often not all of the sections of the form are completed. The purchasing manager says that they are too busy to complete the form in total, and as many of the details are the same on every order, it doesn't matter if some sections are blank. The purchasing manager also says that as long as the product code and quantity are filled in, that is all that matters.

Goods received

The company does not have a central warehousing facility—all goods are delivered directly from the suppliers to the stores. On receipt of goods, the quantities received are checked by the store manager against the supplier's delivery note, relevant details are input into the inventory management system, and a Goods Received Note (GRN) is printed off. At the end of each week, the GRNs are sent to the finance department at head office to be matched against purchase orders.

Inventory counts are held every three months at each store. The inventory count is supervised by the store manager and sales assistants perform the count. The store manager agrees the results of the inventory count to the inventory management system by comparing the total number of goods from the manual count sheets to the total on the system. Any discrepancies are sent to head office for the finance team to investigate.

Invoicing and payment

When purchase invoices are received from suppliers, they are matched to GRNs and original orders. Any discrepancies are investigated promptly. Any invoices with a noted discrepancy (e.g. showing the incorrect quantity of goods delivered, are not entered into the accounting system).

You also have the extract of a report prepared by the company's IA department:

Internal Audit Report: Fraud

During the year, one of the store managers was found to be carrying out a fraud. The manager was selling some items in the store for cash, but not registering the sale or the cash receipt. He then kept the cash and noted on the inventory management system that the goods were faulty and had been thrown away. When senior management were told about the fraud, they were shocked, as this manager had previously been thought to be conscientious and had been given rewards in the past for having such high sales at his store. In light of his previous record, management decided not to punish the store manager, and instead he was moved to another, larger store, where his management responsibilities would be shared with another manager.

Required

1. Discuss the factors which indicate problems with the control environment at Windsor Ltd.
2. In respect of the purchasing system prepare a summary for management which:

   (a) identifies and explains the deficiencies in the system; and

   (b) explains the possible implication of each deficiency.

Answer

Problems with the control environment

The IA department seems to be too small for the size of the organization and is probably lacking in expertise as it is staffed by people from the marketing department rather than people with skills in accounting, audit, and IT. The attitude of management indicates a problem with the control environment, as management should try to instil an attitude in the company which emphasizes the importance of internal controls generally, and therefore management should support the development of a skilled IA department with sufficient resources to provide an adequate monitoring function.

In addition, the IA department should not report to the finance director. This is not good practice, as the internal auditors should be independent of the finance team. Any problems highlighted by the internal auditors, or recommendations made by them, could just be ignored by the finance director. There should be an effective audit committee to whom the internal auditors report, and which supervises and directs their work.

The attitude of management in relation to the fraud also indicates problems with the control environment. Fraud should not be tolerated, and while the store manager has been moved to another location, this is hardly punishment, and indicates that management were willing to ignore the actions of the store manager because of his sales record. This does not send a good message, and management could be seen to be too tolerant of fraud. There should be an appropriate 'tone at the top', which seems to be deficient in this situation.

Control deficiencies

Deficiency	Implication
Individual orders below £1,500 do not have to be authorized	The purchasing manager could place orders which do not have a valid business purpose
Any of the company's directors can sign individual orders	The authorization appears to be a 'box-ticking' exercise rather than a proper check by a knowledgeable official. The directors could be authorizing fraudulent transactions without realizing it
Orders are not sequentially numbered	It is very likely that orders go missing, as there is no way to check the completeness of the total orders being processed at any time
Orders are not always fully completed	Some important information could be missing (e.g. special requirements for a particular order). This could lead to the wrong goods being delivered or delays in receipt of goods
The store managers confirm the correct quantities but not quality of good received	If a delivery is subsequently disputed there may be little recourse for the company to the supplier
Goods are being accepted without any checks being made against purchase orders	This could result in Windsor receiving and subsequently paying for goods it did not order
Inventory counts are only held every three months	Discrepancies between actual inventory levels and those recorded in the inventory management system will not be investigated quickly
The store manager supervises the inventory count as well as inputting data into the inventory management system	There is little segregation of duties. The store managers control too much of the inventory management system. This has contributed to the fraud carried out by one of the store managers
Invoices received from suppliers are not input into the system if they contain a discrepancy	The recording of purchases and trade payables will be incomplete. All invoices should be recorded, and discrepancies followed up once they are on the system

Activity solutions

Activity 8.1–Control environment

The management of Giles Ltd has recently discovered a fraud operating, whereby an employee stole £5,000 of goods from the warehouse. What actions should management take to strengthen the control environment?

Suggested answer points:

- Take appropriate disciplinary action against the employee to demonstrate that theft will not be tolerated.
- Openly address the issue to indicate that problems are not being 'swept under the carpet'.
- Ensure that the company has appropriate procedures in place for recruitment (e.g. taking up references for all employees).
- Investigate how the theft took place, was there a breakdown in internal controls? If so, ensure the control deficiency is rectified and that the relevant controls are regularly monitored.

Activity 8.2–Business risks

Oriole Ltd manufactures circuit boards and most of the components of the manufacturing process are imported from one supplier, located in South America.

Can you identify three business risks facing Oriole Ltd?

Suggested answer points:

- Imported goods–this exposes the company to exchange rate volatility and consequentially cash flow fluctuations.
- Transportation issues–heavy reliance on imports means that transportation costs will be high and need to be carefully managed.
- Reliance on single supplier–disruption to the supplier's operations (e.g. due to financial difficulties or political interference) could result in the supply of components being cut off, which could disrupt the company's manufacturing process.

Activity 8.3–Enquiries regarding monitoring of internal control

Can you create a list of examples of questions which the auditor may ask in order to obtain understanding of monitoring activities?

Suggested answer points:

- Have monitoring roles been assigned to people with appropriate capabilities, objectivity, and authority?
- Has there been any external monitoring of controls in the year? (e.g. by industry regulators to assess compliance with industry standards).
- What activities has the IA function focused on during the year?
- What has been the output of IA in terms of reports or other communications to those charged with governance?
- What actions have been taken in response to reports by the IA function?
- What quality assurance reviews have taken place on the work of IA?

Activity 8.4—Authorization and approval

Can you list some examples of when authorization and approval can be used within an accounting system?

Suggested answer points:

- approving overtime payments to staff;
- authorizing the acquisition of new assets;
- approving a new contract (e.g. a bank agreement or rental agreement);
- approving the purchase of goods or services from a new supplier;
- approving a discount to a customer; and
- authorizing a new credit limit to a customer.

Activity 8.5—Benefits of IT

Can you list the reasons why IT can benefit a system of internal controls?

Suggested answer points:

These are the benefits suggested by ISA (UK) 315:

- Consistently apply predefined business rules and perform complex calculations in processing large volumes of transactions or data;
- Enhance the timeliness, availability and accuracy of information;
- Facilitate the additional analysis of information;
- Enhance the ability to monitor the performance of the entity's activities and its policies and procedures;
- Reduce the risk that controls will be circumvented; and
- Enhance the ability to achieve effective segregation of duties by implementing security controls in IT applications, databases and operating systems.[11]

Activity 8.6—Fraudulent journal entries

What do you think could indicate that a journal entry is a fraudulent transaction? What might indicate that it is unusual?

- The journal is accounted for at an unusual time or on a day when people are not usually working—at the weekend or in the middle of the night.
- The journal is made in an unusual account or a new account has been created for it.
- It is made by someone who does not usually enter journal entries.
- There is no evidence of it having been approved or authorized.
- It is a round sum figure.

Activity 8.7—Problems in using test data

Why do you think the audit client may be reluctant for the auditor to use test data?

Suggested answer points:

Clients may not want to allow access to the auditor, or their appointed expert, to run the test data through the system. They may be concerned that the test data cannot be extracted from the system, or what if the data corrupts the client's systems? One way around this problem is to use test data on the system but outside of normal processing, using copies that have been made of the master files. This avoids running the test data during 'live' processing, so there is less chance of corruption or that the test data becomes integrated with real transactions.

[11] FRC, 'ISA (UK) 315', 2020, Appendix 5, para 1.

9 Evaluating the Risk of Material Misstatement

Introduction

The planning stage of the audit is a crucial aspect in the audit process. If the auditor fails to carry out sufficient planning, audit risk is increased as the auditor will not fully understand the risk factors, which may mean that the financial statements are prone to contain significant errors or deliberate misstatements.

In Chapters 7 and 8 we looked at some of the requirements of ISA (UK) 315 in relation to obtaining understanding of the audit client and the need to understand and document the client's internal controls. In this chapter, we will concentrate on the requirements of ISA (UK) 315 which relate to identifying and assessing audit risk as a key part of the audit planning process. We will explore audit risk and its components, and business risk, and how the two interact. We also look at how a client's systems and controls are evaluated.

It is important to remember that audit planning does not follow a set sequence, instead, audit planning should be seen as an iterative process, with the various elements of audit planning informing each other. Auditors may perform parts of planning at different points in time (e.g. obtain business understanding), then perform analytical procedures, then determine materiality, and after that assess the risk of material misstatement. But this is not a rigid step-by-step approach, and the auditor should be flexible in their approach (e.g. having performed analytical procedures the auditor may then decide that they need to obtain further business understanding).

Therefore, as you are working through this chapter, keep in mind that the planning exercise does not stop at a certain point in time—the ISAs (UK) themselves refer to the audit planning as a 'continuous and iterative process'. During the course of the audit fieldwork, matters may come to the auditor's attention which they were unaware of at the planning stage. This could result in changes to the original risk assessment, audit strategy, audit plan, and materiality levels. Significant changes to the audit plan during the course of the audit must be documented by the auditor.

Learning outcomes

1. Explain the audit risk model and identify and explain audit risks.
2. Discuss the concept of business risk and its relationship to audit risk.
3. Describe the use of tests of control as a way to evaluate and respond to control risk.

By the end of the chapter, you will be able to:

- Discuss and apply the use of the risk-based approach to audit planning.
- Comment on the use of professional judgement in planning an audit of financial statements.

9.1 The audit risk model

9.1.1 Audit risk

Before considering what is meant by the risk of material misstatement, we should consider what is meant by audit risk. According to the International Auditing and Assurance Standards Board's 'Glossary of Terms', 'audit risk' is defined as:

> The risk that the auditor expresses an inappropriate audit opinion when the financial statements are materially misstated. Audit risk is a function of material misstatement and detection risk.[1]

In simple terms, audit risk is the risk that the auditor forms an incorrect opinion on the financial statements (i.e. expresses an unmodified opinion when, in reality, the opinion should be modified). Another way of thinking of this is that the auditor fails to spot a significant error or deliberate misstatement, and says that the financial statements are 'true and fair' when really, they are not.

The auditor will want to minimize the risk of giving an incorrect opinion. To do this, a risk-based approach is used when planning the audit. The auditor takes a risk-based approach to auditing because auditors are unable to check every transaction that makes up the financial statements. In a perfect world perhaps the auditor would be able to check every single transaction and how it has been accounted for, however, this is not possible and so the auditor has to manage the risk that they fail to identify misstatements. A risk-based approach should minimize the chance of expressing an inappropriate audit opinion.

Auditors must focus their attention on those areas of the financial statements which are at higher risk of misstatement and those areas of the financial statements where it is more likely that errors in transactions and balances will lead to a material misstatement in the financial statements.

There is a traditional audit risk model which dates back to before ISA (UK) 315 was issued but it continues to remain appropriate to the audit process. It works as follows:

$$Audit\ risk = Inherent\ risk \times Control\ risk \times Detection\ risk$$

[1] International Auditing and Assurance Standards Board, 'Glossary of terms', 2000 <www.iaasb.org/_flysystem/azure-private/publications/files/A006%202012%20IAASB%20Handbook%20Glossary.pdf> (accessed 18 January 2024).

We will look at each component of the audit risk model in more detail below, but we should understand the model in simple terms at this point by defining the components:

- Audit risk—the risk that the auditor gives an inappropriate audit opinion.
- Inherent risk—the risk that that financial statements contain material misstatements due to the nature and circumstances of the business, before considering internal controls.
- Control risk—the risk that the client's controls fail to prevent or detect material misstatement.
- Detection risk—the risk that the auditor fails to detect material misstatement.

9.1.2 **Risk of material misstatement**

At this point, it is also worth clarifying that ISA (UK) 315 focuses on the 'risk of material misstatement', which is the combination of inherent risk and control risk, see Figure 9.9. In fact, the overall objective as given in ISA (UK) 315 is as follows:

> The objective of the auditor is to identify and assess the risks of material misstatement, whether due to fraud or error, at the financial statement and assertion levels thereby providing a basis for designing and implementing responses to the assessed risks of material misstatement.[2]

The key point to remember is that by requiring the auditor to focus on the risk of material misstatement, and designing appropriate audit responses to the risks identified, audit risk should be minimized.

If something is 'material' it means that it could (or would) influence the decisions of those assessing the financial performance, financial position, and cash flows of the business.

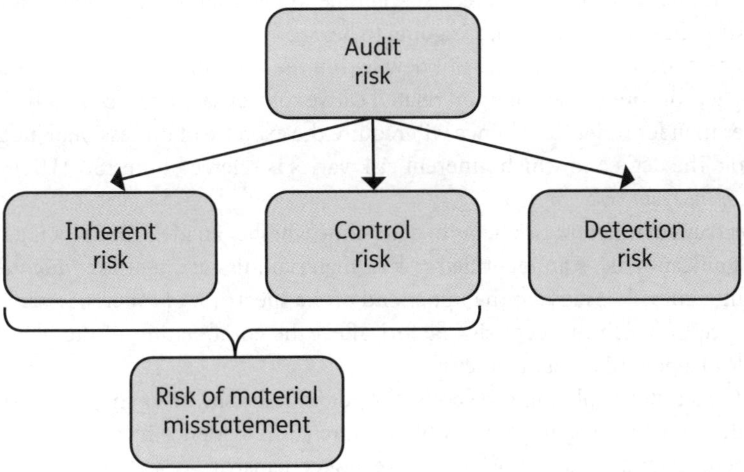

Figure 9.1 The audit risk model

[2] FRC, 'ISA (UK) 315', 2020, para 11 <https://media.frc.org.uk/documents/ISA_UK_315_Jul_2020.pdf> (accessed 18 January 2024).

We will explore the technical meaning of materiality in Chapter 10. For now, we will use a simple example to illustrate the concept. Consider a potential investor who is reviewing a set of financial statements for a company which shows a healthy profit and a strong financial position. However, if those financial statements contain a material misstatement, for example, if sales are overstated by a significant amount, then profit will reduce and so will receivables in the statement of financial position. When the misstatements are corrected, the financial statements will not look as healthy and the potential investor may change their opinion and decide not to invest. The auditor therefore has to think about risk from the point of view of the 'third person' (i.e. 'what would a third person think if this was missed or that was not disclosed or this contained a material misstatement?').

ISA (UK) 315 also introduces the term 'significant risk' which is defined as:

> An identified and assessed risk of material misstatement:
>
> (i) For which the assessment of inherent risk is close to the upper end of the spectrum of inherent risk due to the degree to which inherent risk factors affect the combination of the likelihood of a misstatement occurring and the magnitude of the potential misstatement should that misstatement occur; or
>
> (ii) That is to be treated as a significant risk in accordance with the requirements of other ISAs (UK).[3]

Where significant risks are identified, ISA (UK) 315 requires that the auditor obtain an understanding of the entity's system of internal control, including control activities, relevant to that risk. As we saw in Chapter 8, internal controls need to be documented and procedures such as walk-throughs are performed to ensure that the auditor understands how systems operate.

It is a matter of judgement for an auditor to decide whether a risk is 'significant'. ISA (UK) 315 introduces the concept of a risk spectrum, which involves evaluating risks on a continuum, ranging from lower to higher risks. The greater the degree to which a class of transactions, account balance, or disclosure is susceptible to material misstatement, the higher on the spectrum the assessment of risk is going to be.

The concept of a risk spectrum is not new within the ISAs and audit methodologies. Risk will be higher for some assertions and related classes of transactions, account balances, and disclosures than for others and hence will require the exercise of professional judgement by the auditor. The degree to which inherent risk varies is referred to in ISA (UK) 315 as the *spectrum of inherent risk*.

The spectrum of inherent risk helps to determine whether an identified risk is a significant risk. A 'significant risk' is an identified risk of material misstatement for which the assessment of inherent risk is close to the upper end of the spectrum of inherent risk. This is due to the degree to which inherent risk factors affect the combination of the likelihood and magnitude of a potential misstatement.

When the auditor is planning responses to identified risks, risks may need to be prioritized as the auditor needs to plan to obtain more audit evidence in relation to significant risks (remember, audit evidence is persuasive, not conclusive).

[3] Ibid., para 12(l).

9.1.3 **Risk assessment procedures**

Before looking at the audit risk model in detail, we should clarify the procedures which the auditor should perform in order to identify risks. ISA (UK) 315 defines 'risk assessment procedures' as:

> The audit procedures designed and performed to identify and assess the risks of material misstatement, whether due to fraud or error, at the financial statement and assertion levels.[4]

Further, ISA (UK) 315 identifies the three types of risk assessment procedures as inquiries, analytical procedures and observation and inspection (Figure 9.2).

9.1.3.1 **Making inquiries of management and other appropriate individuals within the entity**

Auditors must have discussions with the client's management about its objectives and expectations, and its plans for achieving those goals. In addition to discussing matters with management, the auditor may wish to make inquiries from others, for example:

- Internal auditors could be asked about the client's systems and controls and about the results of their testing during the year.
- Members of the sales team could provide information about new products, key customers, and marketing strategies.
- IT personnel could be asked about changes to operating systems and to provide information about systems failures during the year.
- The client's legal team could be asked about litigation that the client is facing.[5]

This list is not meant to be exhaustive—clearly the people who can provide useful information relating to risk assessment will vary for each client.

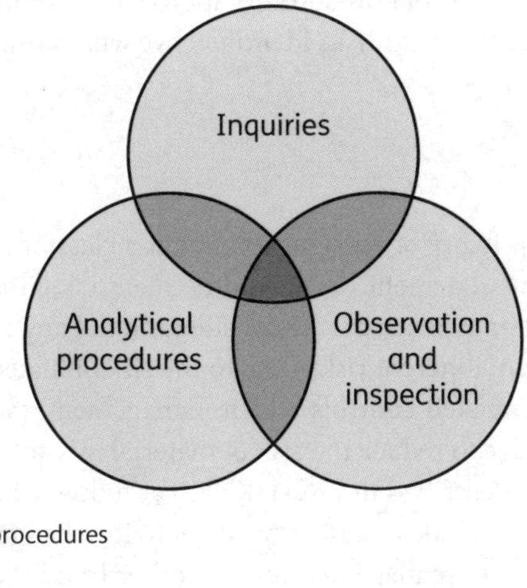

Figure 9.2 Risk assessment procedures

[4] Ibid., para 12(j). [5] Ibid., para 14.

9.1.3.2 **Analytical procedures**

Analytical procedures performed as risk assessment procedures should help the auditor in identifying unusual transactions or positions. They may identify aspects of the entity of which the auditor was unaware, and may assist in assessing the risks of material misstatement in order to provide a basis for designing and implementing responses to the assessed risks. We will consider analytical procedures in Chapter 10.

9.1.3.3 **Observation and inspection**

Observation and inspection may also provide information about the entity and its environment. Examples of such audit procedures can potentially cover a very broad area, including observation or inspection of the entity's operations, documents, and reports prepared by management, and also of the entity's premises and plant facilities.

ISA (UK) 315 requires that risk assessment procedures should, at a minimum, comprise a combination of the above three procedures, and the standard also requires that the engagement partner and other key engagement team members should discuss the susceptibility of the entity's financial statements to material misstatement. Key risks can be identified at any stage of the audit process, and ISA (UK) 315 requires that the engagement partner should also determine which matters are to be communicated to those engagement team members not involved in the discussion.

Note that we have discussed risk assessment procedures at this point as they are crucial to the application of the audit risk model. They are essentially the same procedures that would be used by the auditor to obtain an understanding of the business, as discussed in Chapter 7. This is a good illustration of why audit planning is an iterative process—obtaining business understanding and risk assessment are not separate stages of audit planning, they are all part of the process by which the auditor identifies and evaluates audit risk.

To develop our understanding of how auditors approach the evaluation of risk of material misstatement, and their responses to risks identified, we will examine each individual component of audit risk in turn.

9.1.4 **Inherent risk**

Inherent risk is the susceptibility of an assertion about a class of transaction, account balance, or disclosure to a misstatement that could be material, either individually or when aggregated with other misstatements, before consideration of any related controls.

Note that the definition of inherent risk refers to the risk of material misstatement **before** the auditor considers any related controls which management and/or those charged with governance have put in place to reduce the risk of material misstatement.

Inherent risk factors are described in ISA (UK) 315 as follows, 'Such factors may be qualitative or quantitative, and include complexity, subjectivity, change, uncertainty or susceptibility to misstatement due to management bias or other fraud risk factors insofar as they affect inherent risk.'[6]

[6] Ibid., para 12(f).

One of the reasons why it is so important for auditors to obtain a thorough understanding of the audit client's business and the environment in which it operates is to make it possible for the auditor to appropriately evaluate inherent risk. Remember that to understand business risk, auditors ask, 'what could go wrong in the business?'. One way to think about inherent risk is to ask, 'does the company's business and operations make it likely that something will go wrong in the financial statements?'.

Some examples to illustrate the concept are set out in Table 9.1.

You might notice from the examples in Table 9.1 that the first two business issues lead to quite specific inherent risks (i.e. the risk of misstatement relates to one area of the financial statements). The third and fourth business issues lead to inherent risks that apply to several areas of the financial statements.

This illustrates the difference between what are known as 'assertion level' inherent risks, and 'financial statement level' inherent risks. Assertion level simply means that the risk of misstatement is specific to one issue, or 'assertion'—in Table 9.1 this is the valuation of inventory and the completeness of liabilities. Financial statement level risk just means that the issue could possibly impact on several areas of the financial statements. It is a specific requirement of ISA (UK) 315 that the auditor must identify and assess risks of material misstatement, whether due to fraud or error, at both the financial statement and assertion levels and design audit procedures in response.

You should now be able to understand why the auditor's understanding of the business is so crucial to effective audit risk assessment. Without obtaining an understanding of the business it would be very difficult for the auditor to identify risks of material misstatement, especially financial statement level inherent risk.

Inherent risk is most likely to arise when an entity's transactions are complex or in situations which require a high degree of judgement where financial estimates are concerned. Remember that the definition of inherent risk refers to the risk of material misstatement **before** the auditor considers any related controls which management and/or those charged with governance have put in place to reduce the risk of material misstatement. In other words, it is a 'worst case scenario' risk.

Table 9.1 Business issues and inherent risk

Business issue	Why this leads to inherent risk
A company makes hi-tech products such as mobile phones	The inventory is more likely to be obsolete, leading to complexities in its valuation (i.e. there is a higher risk of misstatement of the inventory balance)
A company operates in a highly regulated environment	There is risk of non-compliance with the regulations, making it more likely that provisions need to be minimizing (i.e. there is a higher risk of misstatements of liabilities)
A company that has established a profit-based bonus scheme for management	There is risk that management deliberately overstate profit, for example by early recognition of revenue, manipulating expenses, not making provisions
A company that has going concern and liquidity issues	There will be pressure on management to present healthy financial statements, for example, by boosting profit, minimizing liabilities (i.e. there is a risk of misstatement across the whole financial statements)

Consider an entity which has a significant amount of complex financial instruments that must be remeasured to fair value at each reporting date, for example, a bank or other financial institution. The inherent risk is that the valuation exercise carried out in relation to the financial instruments is so complex that a material misstatement could easily be made, even by an experienced accountant. This is a risk which the auditor must consider before they consider any controls present within the entity over the valuation exercise.

This type of risk is not confined to specialized businesses or particularly complex situations. For example, in a typical manufacturing situation, if the client operates in an industry where inventory becomes obsolete very quickly, the inherent risk is that the inventory will be overvalued at the reporting date because net realizable value is lower than cost. Keep in mind that IAS 2 *Inventories* requires inventory to be valued at the lower of cost or net realizable value. Inherent risk arises not because the accounting treatment is particularly complex, but because the business situation can change very quickly and there is a chance that the accounting records do not reflect the new conditions.

ISA (UK) 315 provides Appendix 2 *Understanding Inherent Risk Factors* which provides the auditor with further guidance concerning inherent risk factors applicable to the entity. Such factors may be qualitative or quantitative and include:

- complexity;
- subjectivity;
- change;
- uncertainty; and
- susceptibility to misstatement due to management bias or other fraud risk factors.

These five factors are examined further Table 9.2.

Table 9.2 Inherent risk factors

Complexity	This may arise due to the nature of the information or the way that the information is prepared. For example, complex accounting issues or reporting requirements, such as the reporting requirements for a large multinational listed group
Subjectivity	This arises from inherent limitations in the ability to prepare information objectively. For example, where there is a choice of valuation methodology, or basis for accounting estimates
Change	Events or conditions which affect the entity's business, industry, regulatory, or economic environment. For example, customer change or geographical expansion
Uncertainty	This arises when the required information cannot be prepared based on sufficiently precise and comprehensive data. For example, the entity may have a contingent liability, or uncertainty over key issues such as environmental, legal, or financial issues
Susceptibility to misstatement due to management bias or other fraud risk factors	These are conditions which create susceptibility to intentional or unintentional failure by management to maintain neutrality. For example, transactions with related parties, the use of manual adjustments and bonus schemes which are profit dependent

Activity 9.1 Inherent risk factors

ISA (UK) 315 states that there are five inherent risk factors: complexity, subjectivity, change, uncertainty, and susceptibility to misstatement due to management bias or fraud risk factors.

Can you think of examples for each of these risk factors—that is, matters which would lead the auditor to think that there is a high level of inherent risk?

9.1.5 **Control risk**

Control risk is the risk that a misstatement could occur in relation to a transaction, account balance or disclosure, and that the misstatement will not be prevented or detected and corrected, on a timely basis, by the entity's internal control. In other words, the internal controls established will not pick up on the misstatement in good time, leading to material misstatement in the financial statements.

As we saw in Chapter 8, all organizations should have adequate internal controls in place to prevent, detect and correct, on a timely basis, misstatements which may arise whether these misstatements are due to fraud and/or error. If an audit client does not have adequate internal controls, perhaps having been judged by the auditor to be ineffective, or even absent, control risk is increased. Hence, the risk of material misstatement in the financial statements is higher due to control risk where controls are weak or do not exist.

Control risk is influenced by a number of factors, such as:

- The attitude of the directors, management and those charged with governance of an entity towards internal control. If management and those charged with governance have little regard to internal control systems, control risk is higher as the controls in place are likely to be ineffective.
- The overall internal control environment and the capabilities of staff who maintain and operate them.
- The level of supervision within the business.
- The integrity of staff, management, and those charged with governance.

In Chapter 8 we considered internal controls in depth, so there is no need to repeat the detail at this point. The key thing to remember is that the auditor must have a thorough understanding of the audit client's internal controls in order to assess their strengths and identify deficiencies, as a means of evaluating the control risk component of audit risk.

As discussed in the previous section, ISA (UK) 315 requires the auditor to consider risks of material misstatement at the financial statement level and at the assertion level. In addition, ISA (UK) 315 requires the auditor to carry out a **separate** assessment of inherent risk and control risk. Some control issues lead to financial statement level risk of material misstatement, others will be more specific and apply at the assertion level.

For example, if a company has a poor control environment, such that management does not establish an appropriate 'tone at the top', or where an internal audit function has not been established to monitor the effectiveness of controls, this could have an impact on the integrity of the financial statements as a whole, and would be considered a financial statement level risk.

In contrast, a company could have a good control environment, and established effective internal audit, but controls could still be deficient in specific areas, for example if there is an IT failure relating to a component of the financial reporting system, or a particular control activity is not performed due to staff shortages. These would be more likely to give rise to control risks at the assertion level.

9.1.6 Detection risk

Detection risk is the risk that the procedures performed by the auditor to reduce audit risk to an acceptably low level will not detect a misstatement that exists and that could be material, either individually or when aggregated with other misstatements. Detection risk is the residual risk after the auditor considers inherent risk and control risk and the overall risk which the auditor is willing to accept.

Detection risk is the only risk in the audit risk model which is under the control of the auditor. It comprises 'sampling risk' and 'non-sampling risk'.

Sampling risk is the risk that the auditor's conclusion based on a sample is different from the conclusion that would be reached if the whole population were tested (i.e. the sample size may be too small).

Non-sampling risk is the risk that the auditor's conclusion is inappropriate for any other reason, such as the application of inappropriate audit procedures or the misinterpretation of audit evidence.

We will look at sampling in detail in Chapter 11 when we consider its use by the auditor in obtaining audit evidence.

There is an inverse relationship between detection risk and control risk. If inherent risk or control risk increase, the auditor must strengthen their audit procedures (i.e. reduce detection risk in order to keep overall audit risk to an acceptable level).

Auditors must apply relevant audit procedures over the material areas of the financial statements to detect material misstatements whether caused by fraud or error. If the auditor misapplies audit procedures or does not carry out critical audit procedures, detection risk is increased because it is likely that the auditor will fail to detect a material misstatement which may exist in the area being audited. Some detection risk will always be present because of the inherent limitations of an audit (for example because the auditor will not be testing every transaction in the financial statements which makes up an account balance and the fact that audit evidence is persuasive rather than conclusive). However, an auditor can decrease detection risk as far as possible by increasing their sample sizes to obtain more robust audit evidence.

Auditing scenario 9.1 Risks and the audit risk model

Jackson Enterprises Group Plc is a new audit client of ABC Accountancy LLP. The company's year end is 31 December 20X8 and key information from the client's background is as follows:

- The Group was listed on the London Stock Exchange in January 20X8 and is required to comply with the UK Corporate Governance Code. The Group has not yet implemented an internal audit department as the finance team have been extremely busy due to expansion of its operations.

- The Group has a large network of subsidiaries and associates.
- Part of the business operates in the financial services sector which is regulated by the Financial Conduct Authority (FCA) in the UK.

The audit manager has used this information to produce a summary of relevant audit risks to be considered in planning the audit.

Inherent risk

Inherent risk is high because the entity is highly regulated and has a complex structure. As part of the Group is a financial institution there will be many transactions and balances which are complex to account for and require extensive disclosure in the financial statements. In addition, the Group will be required to provide disclosures under the listing rules and to the FCA. This adds a layer of complexity to the reporting process, making it more likely that errors, for example, incomplete disclosures, are made.

As the Group obtained its stock market listing quite recently, the management may be inexperienced in following the relevant regulations, so competence could be questioned. This exacerbates the risk of inappropriate financial reporting through errors being made.

The recent expansion of operations also leads to inherent risk, as the Group may have struggled to keep pace with the volume of transactions being recorded. Finally, the recent stock market listing means that shareholder expectations will be high. Management may feel under pressure to present healthy financial statements in this first year following the Group's flotation. There is a risk that management will 'window-dress' the financial statements, perhaps to boost profit to support a positive view of the Group's financial performance for the year.

Control risk

Control risk is likely to be high because the Group has not established an internal audit department. Internal audit provides an important monitoring mechanism, which is absent for the Group. Establishing internal audit is a requirement of the UK Corporate Governance Code, so the fact that there is no compliance with the Code in this respect is significant.

The Group has a large network of subsidiaries and associates and there is a risk that each Group member's internal control environment is weak, or significant internal controls that should be present do not exist. In an attempt to reduce this risk to an acceptable level, the auditor will gain an understanding of group-wide controls and carry out tests of those controls to establish whether, or not, they are operating effectively.

Detection risk

Detection risk is high because this is the first year ABC Accountancy LLP has audited the client and hence the firm does not have experience of the client nor is it familiar with the client's transactions, accounting policies and disclosure requirements. The audit firm must ensure that they carry out sufficient audit procedures to address this risk and apply further substantive procedures where necessary. In addition, the audit team must be given sufficient time to gain an understanding of the entity and its environment and document the systems and controls in place.

9.1.7 Quantifying the audit risk model

We have seen that the audit risk model contains three components. The auditor evaluates the risk of material misstatement (inherent risk and control risk) and then responds by managing detection risk in order to minimize audit risk. This process of evaluation is very subjective and requires the auditor to exercise a great deal of professional judgement.

The auditor can also determine an acceptable level of audit risk—this also requires the use of significant judgement and would be decided on a client-by-client basis. For instance, for a complex audit client operating in a regulated industry where the financial statements are subject to significant external scrutiny, the auditor will only accept a very low level of audit risk. Conversely, the auditor may be willing to accept a higher level of audit risk for an audit client which has few stakeholders and with simple financial statements.

Theoretically, the audit might assign a percentage to the acceptable level of audit risk. Then, having evaluated inherent risk and control risk will assign a percentage to these also. This leaves detection risk as a 'balancing figure' in the following equation:

$$Detection\ risk = \frac{Audit\ risk}{Inherent\ risk \times Control\ risk}$$

This calculative approach is used in some audit software but it is rarely performed manually by an auditor.

Auditing scenario 9.2 Audit risk model

Ashbrook Co Ltd is operating in a market which is experiencing a fall in demand for its products and several new entrants to the market have been able to instigate a 'price war' which has had a detrimental impact on the company during the year to 31 December 20X8.

The company does not have an internal audit department and the audit engagement partner has deemed control risk to be high because the company has changed accounting systems during the year which resulted in significant problems being encountered and various information having to be recreated in order to compile the financial statements. This was because the old and the new accounting system were not run 'in parallel' and some data was lost in the transfer from old to new system.

The audit engagement partner wishes to keep overall audit risk at a maximum of 10 per cent and the partner has assessed inherent risk and control risk to be both 70 per cent. The partner can quantify **detection risk** using the audit risk model:

$$\textbf{Audit Risk} = \textbf{Inherent Risk} \times \textbf{Control Risk} \times \textbf{Detection Risk}$$

$$10\% = 70\% \times 70\% \times ?$$

If inherent risk and control risk are both 70 per cent, detection risk has to be set at 20.4 per cent in order to prevent overall audit risk from exceeding 10 per cent as follows:

$$0.10 / 0.49 \times 100 = 20.4\%$$

Setting a percentage for detection risk can impact audit strategy and audit procedures. Where detection risk is to be minimized (i.e. set at a very low level), the auditor will for example:

- extend audit procedures (e.g. by increasing sample sizes);
- obtain more auditor-generated evidence rather than relying on management for evidence; and
- include more senior and more experienced staff in the audit team.

These measures will allow more assurance to be provided on the financial statements through the generation of high-quality audit evidence.

It is important to note that ISAs (UK) do not require auditors to use the audit risk model in this precise way to assign specific percentage scores to the components of the model or to assign a percentage to audit risk overall. In practice, auditors are more likely to approach the model in more general terms, without using percentages. This reflects the degree of judgement which is involved with assessing audit risk. Audit firms are likely to evaluate risk factors as 'high, medium, or low' rather than approach audit risk mathematically.

In addition, the auditor will look at the different elements of the financial statements and assess the risks in a component fashion rather than by looking at the audit as a whole. This means that elements of the financial statements will be evaluated as having their own level of inherent risk and control risk and therefore the auditor's detection risk response will be tailored specifically to that element of the financial statements.

Auditing scenario 9.3 Applying the audit risk model

As part of planning the audit of Merlin Ltd, the audit team has assessed the risk of material misstatement for provisions, payroll, and share capital and has produced a schedule summarizing the results in the audit working papers.

Provisions are assessed as high inherent risk, due to the high degree of judgement involved in determining an appropriate accounting treatment. At the same time, control risk is assessed as high, meaning that the client's internal controls are unlikely to prevent or detect errors or deliberate misstatements in relation to provisions. In order to have a high level of confidence that the provisions do not contain a material misstatement, a low level of detection risk is needed, so a lot of detailed audit work will be needed in order to obtain assurance that provisions are not misstated.

For the payroll balance, again there is a high inherent risk, but this time control risk is assessed as low, indicating that the audit client has good controls over payroll. This means that the controls are likely to prevent or detect misstatements. The auditor can now set a moderate level of audit risk and perform a moderate amount of audit work in order to be confident that payroll is free from material misstatement.

With share capital, both inherent risk and control risk are assessed as low. This means that share capital is unlikely to be misstated. The auditor need only perform limited audit procedures to be happy that the share capital figure is not misstated.

The key thing to remember is that all of these assessments are based on the use of the auditor's professional judgement, and that is not possible to precisely quantify these risks or the appropriate auditor's response.

Table 9.3 Applying the audit risk model

Account balance	Inherent risk assessment	Control risk assessment	Planned level of detection risk	Planned amount of audit evidence required
Provisions	High	High	Low	HIGH
Payroll	High	Low	Moderate	MODERATE
Share capital	Low	Low	Moderate	LOW

9.1.8 Documentation and discussion of risk assessment

ISA (UK) 315, requires the following to be documented:

(a) The discussion among the engagement team and the significant decisions reached;

(b) Key elements of the auditor's understanding; the sources of information from which the auditor's understanding was obtained; and the risk assessment procedures performed;

(c) The evaluation of the design of identified controls, and determination whether such controls have been implemented; and

(d) The identified and assessed risks of material misstatement at the financial statement level and at the assertion level, including significant risks and risks for which substantive procedures alone cannot provide sufficient appropriate audit evidence, and the rationale for the significant judgments made.[7]

As noted above, ISA (UK) 315 requires that the auditor document the identified and assessed risks of material misstatement at the financial statement level and at the assertion level. There is no set way for the documentation to be presented, the format of the documentation and the level of detail provided is a matter of professional judgement. In some audits, especially when relating to small and relatively uncomplicated audit clients, the documentation can be simple and is often incorporated in the auditor's documentation of the overall audit strategy and audit plan, or as part of the audit programme where audit procedures in response to the risks identified have been documented.

ISA (UK) 315 also requires discussion among audit team members regarding the risk of material misstatement. The audit engagement partner and other senior members of the audit team must discuss the susceptibility of the audit client's financial statements to material misstatement, as well as discussing the relevant financial reporting framework. It is not necessary for every member of the audit team to be present when these matters are discussed, but the audit engagement partner must decide how to inform the audit team about these important planning issues.

Activity 9.2 Audit team discussion

Why do you think it is important that there is a discussion about risks of material misstatement among the audit team?

9.2 Business risk as part of auditor's risk assessment

9.2.1 Translating business risk into risk of material misstatement

ISA (UK) 315 defines 'business risk' as, 'a risk resulting from significant conditions, events, circumstances, actions or inactions that could adversely affect an entity's ability to achieve

[7] Ibid., para 38.

its objectives and execute its strategies, or from the setting of inappropriate objectives and strategies'.[8]

In Chapter 8 we looked at how organizations should identify and manage their risk. To briefly recap at this point, a business risk is something which causes a problem for a business which, in turn, causes a negative impact on operations, finance, or even the longer-term future for the business. Business risks are often linked to inherent risk which, as we know, is itself a component of the risk of material misstatement. This is why ISA 315 requires auditors to obtain understanding of the business risks facing an audit client, as this can translate into risks of material misstatement as shown in Figure 9.3.

Remember that business risks are often categorized as:

- operational risks;
- financial risks; and
- compliance risks.

As the auditor needs to understand business risk in order to identify and evaluate risks of material misstatement, we will look at how an organization's business risk can impact audit risk.

It is important to understand that business risk is broader than the risk of material misstatement of the financial statements, although it does include the latter. Some business risks have no impact at all on the financial statements and hence they are outside the scope of the audit.

Examples of matters which the auditor may consider when obtaining an understanding of the entity's objectives, strategies, and related business risks which may result in a risk of material misstatement include:

- Industry developments—a potential related business risk may be, for example, that the entity does not have the personnel or expertise to deal with the changes in the industry.
- New products and services—a potential related business risk might be that there is increased product liability.
- Expansion of the business—a potential related business risk might be that the demand has not been accurately estimated.
- New accounting requirements—a potential related business risk might be incomplete or improper implementation, or increased costs.

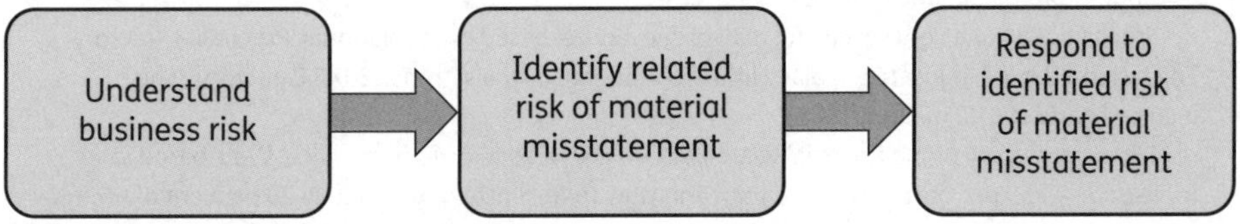

Figure 9.3 Translating business risk into risk of material misstatement

[8] Ibid., para 12(b).

- Regulatory requirements—a potential related business risk might be that there is increased legal exposure.
- Current and prospective financing arrangements—a potential related business risk might be the loss of financing due to the entity's inability to meet requirements.
- Use of IT—a potential related business risk might be that systems and processes are incompatible or cybersecurity risk is increased.
- The effects of implementing a strategy, particularly any effects that will lead to new accounting requirements—a potential related business risk might be incomplete or improper implementation.

The key consideration for the auditor is whether the business risks identified give rise to an associated risk of material misstatement. Sometimes this is obvious—for example, if there is a business risk relating to IT failure, this can clearly have an impact on computerized accounting records leading to risk of material misstatement. For some business risks, it may be harder to identify a specifically related risk of material misstatement, but all business risks identified should be evaluated by the auditor to determine if risk of material misstatement arises.

Auditing scenario 9.4 Business risk and risk of material misstatement

Prochain Ltd is a manufacturer and high street retailer of fashion clothes and home products. It has 200 stores located all over the UK and has recently expanded into France, the Netherlands, and Germany. It is approaching year end 31 August 20X7.

In order to maximize revenue in a rapidly changing market, the company aims to have new fashion lines in the stores every ten weeks. However, it is struggling to recruit good graduates from art school, where most designers are trained.

Prochain Ltd uses an external provider for moving inventory from the factories to and between branches. Deliveries are particularly rapid in the run up to the January and July sales. At these times of the year, the stores recruit a large number of temporary employees.

In the last twelve months, the city centre stores in Birmingham, Manchester, and Liverpool have suffered from declining sales, caused by new out-of-town shopping centres which have attracted customers out of the city centres. Prochain Ltd has flagship stores in these new shopping malls, so overall revenues have not suffered significantly. However, there is now serious discussion about pulling out of city centre locations. The Birmingham and Manchester stores are owned, whereas the Liverpool store is held under an operating lease.

Prochain Ltd has a very successful mail order service, based on its biannual 'Prochain Directory'. The fashion shoot has just taken place in the Caribbean for the summer 20X8 Directory, which incurred costs of £1.2 million.

The success story of the financial year has been the website ordering service. Web-based sales increased by 750 per cent during the year. This now represents approximately 20 per cent of total revenue, and many of the sales are to customers located in foreign countries.

Based on the information above, the audit manager, who is planning the audit of Prochain Ltd, has prepared a working paper summarizing the company's business risks and the related risks of material misstatement to be considered in planning the audit.

Table 9.4 Business risk and risk of material misstatement working paper

Business risk	Risk of material misstatement
Overseas expansion—the company is now having to manage exchange rate fluctuation which may be volatile	Recognition of exchange gains and losses and retranslation of monetary items at year end—there are risks in the recording of transactions, for example, that incorrect exchange rates are used resulting in errors in the monetary value of the amounts recognized
Lack of designers—items quickly out of date, may be unable to react quickly enough to new fashion trends	Inventory valuation—there is a risk that product lines are out of date, unlikely to sell, or only sell with a discount. It is likely that net realizable value will be less than cost, so a risk that inventory is overvalued, and profit overvalued if any necessary write down in value is not recognized
High volume of deliveries around year end—risk in controlling the volume of inventory and possible risk of theft of items	Inventory records likely to be incomplete, items could be in transit at the year end, the risk may be increased because deliveries outsourced to another company, so a risk of incomplete recognition of inventory. Alternatively, inventory could be overstated if items have been stolen and not written off in the accounts
Large number of part-time and temporary employees—risk that tax legislation is not complied with and the right amount of tax is paid	Inappropriate payroll deductions if casual workers are not dealt with appropriately in the payroll system
Loss of revenue in city centre stores—this brings cash flow problems to the company and could have wider going concern implications if the reduction in sales is part of a long-term trend	There are several risks associated with this: Stores likely to be impaired, so non-current assets and profit could be overvalued if any necessary impairment is not recognized In addition, if the reduction in revenue is significant there could be a going concern issue for the company which creates an inherent risk at the financial statement level. There is a risk of management bias if the preparers of the financial statements attempt to window-dress (e.g. to make sales and profit look healthier than they actually are)
Large spend on next year's catalogue immediately prior to year end—cash outflow in advance of sales being received is a drain on cash and could have liquidity implications	There is a risk that the advertising spending has been inappropriately recognized, for example, the company may try to defer the cost or recognize as an intangible asset. Therefore, there is a risk of understated expenses
Web-based sales—while the cash and revenue being generated mitigates the lost revenue from stores the rapid increase in e-commerce brings many business risks including, for example, those related to cybersecurity (can the company keep customers' details safe?), compliance with international regulations (payment of customs duties when selling overseas), the logistical issues of selling and distributing overseas (deliveries may be delayed or items lost in transit)	Timing of revenue recognition Possible unrecorded sales (if website not integrated with nominal ledger) Cut-off problems—with large amounts of inventory in transit at the year end, it may be difficult to determine when sales should be recognized There may also be general control issues, for example, if the systems can't keep pace with the increased volume of transactions, leading to incomplete recording of revenue and inventory movements

Table 9.5 Business risk versus inherent risk

Business risk	Inherent risk
Business risk is concerned with the occurrence of an event which will have a detrimental impact on the business as a whole.	The risk that the financial statements are materially misstated before the auditor considers any related controls and is a function of the audit risk model
Business risk should be reviewed continuously by management	Inherent risk is only assessed at the time of the audit
Business risks are identified by management	Inherent risk is identified by the auditor

9.2.2 **Business risk versus inherent risk**

It is important to understand that both business risk and inherent risk both have an impact on the audit risk model and the nature, timing, and extent of audit procedures which the auditor will apply. Neither risk can be eliminated in totality and neither is under the control of the auditor (only detection risk is under the control of the auditor). However, they are not the same thing.

Table 9.5 summarizes the differences between business risk and inherent risk.

9.2.3 **The 'top-down' audit approach**

The method of evaluating audit risk which we have examined is known as the 'top-down' approach to audit. As we have seen, the auditor is required by ISA (UK) 315 to use their understanding of the audit client's business entity and its environment when making risk assessments. Business risks are used to help the auditor to identify risks of misstatement. In the name of this approach to risk identification and evaluation, the 'top' refers to the starting point of the risk assessment—understanding the operations of the entity and the environment in which it operates, and 'down' refers to the financial statements of the entity. The auditor starts the risk assessment at the entity level and works down to the balances and transactions within the financial statements, and the presentation of those items.

This is in contrast to other possible audit strategies, for example, a 'bottom-up' approach would begin with the financial records and work 'up' to consider the business model.

The 'top-down' approach gained favour after the Enron scandal and other high-profile corporate collapses which led to questions over the effectiveness of audit, as well as concerns over corporate governance. Supporters of the 'top-down' approach consider that it ensures that the auditor develops an understanding of the client's business in its entirety, so that the auditor has a broader view of sources of audit risk. In addition, the auditor is better placed to provide added value to clients, by being in a better position to discuss the business risks facing the client.

The 'top-down' approach is used in other areas of management, for example in internal audit, risk management, and project management.

In their article 'Standards of Innovation in Auditing', academics from the National University of Ireland, Galway, and the University of Manchester discuss the evolution of the business risk approach (BRA) to auditing. They argue that 'The essential premise of BRA was based on the notion that audit failures typically arose from a failure on the part of auditors to identify and address client business risk in the course of their audit rather than from failures in the application of detailed testing procedures.'[9]

Prior to the BRA approach, auditors had traditionally performed risk assessment focusing on the balances and transactions in the financial statements—this was known as 'financial statement risk'. Several reasons prompted the move away from this towards the BRA approach, including that BRA more suited the complexities of modern business and would be more likely to alert auditors to going concern problems facing their clients. It is also argued that the BRA approach is more efficient and delivers a more cost-effective audit. There is also a view that the big audit firms had an interest in developing the BRA approach in their own audit methodology, and for it to be endorsed through the pronouncements of the international regulatory bodies for auditors. This is because BRA aligned with the consultancy services offered by the big audit firms to their clients, and would also be viewed favourably by audit clients as it could allow more 'value' to be added to the audit engagement.

9.3 Evaluating systems and controls

As we saw in Chapter 8, as part of the planning phase of the audit, the auditor must obtain an understanding of systems and controls relevant to financial reporting. The auditor must also carry out an evaluation of the client's systems and controls, which is our focus now to help in identifying and responding to audit risk.

The entity's internal control function plays a vital role in the financial statement preparation process. If controls are weak or non-existent, there is a much higher risk of material misstatement in the financial statements. In such instances, the auditor will place less reliance on the control environment and carry out a more substantive approach to the audit. This does, effectively, increase the time spent on the audit but it serves to reduce audit and detection risk and would be considered necessary where controls are weak or non-existent.

9.3.1 Understanding systems and controls–a reminder

To briefly recap, 'systems' can be thought of as the means by which a process is carried out. Consider the sales, purchases, and payroll cycle of a business—each cycle will involve a system having to be implemented including appropriate internal controls.

For example, in a sales cycle, the system might work as follows:

- an order is received from the customer
- the order is input into the sales ordering system
- the sales order generates a picking list for the warehouse

[9] Curtis, E., Humphrey, C., & Turley, W.S., 2016, 'Standards of innovation in auditing', *Auditing: A journal of practice & theory*, vol. 35, no. 3, pp. 75–98.

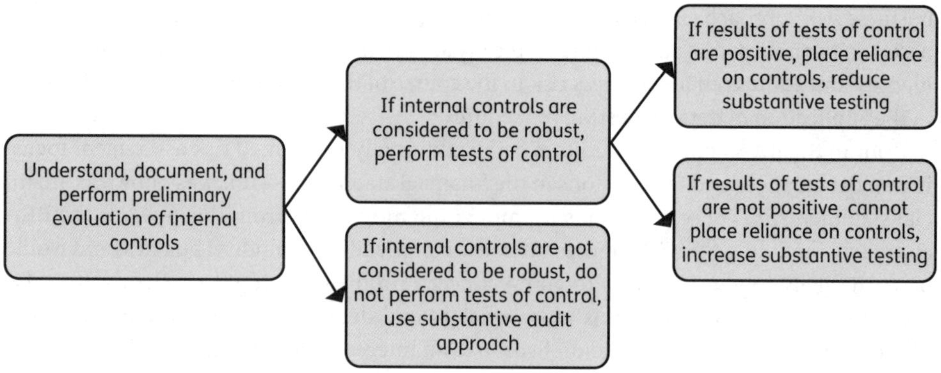

Figure 9.4 Evaluating internal controls

- the goods are picked and prepared for despatch to the customer
- a goods received note (GRN) is prepared
- the goods are despatched
- a copy of the order and GRN are sent to the finance department
- the sales invoice is prepared
- the sales invoice is transferred onto the customer's account in the sales ledger and general ledger

If this system is followed correctly at all times during the year, including effective operation of well-designed internal controls, the auditor can place some reliance on the fact that the revenue figure in the financial statements is not materially misstated (although they will have to perform other types of audit procedure over the revenue figure).

In the vast majority of entities nowadays, systems are automated via a computer system. However, even automated systems can have their faults which could give rise to a misstatement being present in the financial statements.

An evaluation of the systems and internal control involves the auditor considering the effectiveness of an organization's system of internal control. This assists the auditor in determining the extent of other tests which must be performed in order to arrive at a conclusion. A robust system of internal control will reduce the risk of material misstatement in the financial statements, whether caused by fraud or error. When the auditor considers a client's internal control environment to be robust, they can place more reliance on it which will result in less detailed substantive testing being performed. See Figure 9.4.

As we saw in Chapter 8, the auditor needs to make a preliminary evaluation of internal control to form an initial conclusion as to whether controls appear to be sufficiently robust for tests of control to be performed. Remember that if, based on an initial evaluation, controls are not considered to be good, the auditor does not test the controls, but will instead use substantive audit procedures. They will also inform the client's management about control deficiencies and recommend improvements.

Activity 9.3 Evaluating systems and controls

What do you think auditors consider when performing an initial evaluation of systems and controls? This is not performing tests on the controls, just forming an initial view as to whether the systems and controls are good enough for tests of control to be carried out.

9.3.2 Tests of control

The auditor must assess the risk of material misstatement within the financial statements and to do this, the audit risk model will be used. Remember that:

$$Audit\ Risk = Inherent\ Risk \times \mathbf{Control\ Risk} \times Detection\ Risk$$

Internal controls are a vital component of an organization because they are the mechanism designed by the client to prevent, detect, and correct misstatements.

In order to place reliance on the entity's internal controls, the auditor must:

- determine how the system operates;
- document the system in the audit working papers;
- test the operation of the system;
- assess the design and operating effectiveness of the control system; and
- determine the impact on the audit approach for a specific class of transaction, account balance, or disclosure.

The focus of a test of control is not on the monetary amount of a transaction and a test of control does not test the figure in the financial statements (this is the purpose of substantive procedures). A test of control provides evidence of whether a control procedure is operating correctly. A test of control provides *indirect* evidence over the financial statements and the auditor can assume that if the controls are working effectively, there is a lower risk of material misstatement in the financial statements.

If the control is judged to be ineffective, the auditor will not place reliance on it. There would be little to be achieved by relying on weak internal controls. Where internal controls are ineffective or do not exist, the auditor will carry out more substantive procedures which aim to test for material misstatement at the assertion level.

Table 9.6 outlines some examples of the tests of control an auditor may perform when evaluating the control environment of an entity.

The purpose of a test of control is to test whether the control operates effectively and whether it has operated effectively throughout the reporting period.

Table 9.6 Controls and relevant tests of control

Control	Test of control
In relation to payroll, staff who are paid in cash must produce their identification and sign for the pay packets	Attend a cash wages payout and observe the staff members producing their identification and signing for the pay packets
In relation to cash, bank reconciliations are performed on a regular basis and checked by a supervisor	Review the bank reconciliations to confirm they have been performed and to view evidence that they have been checked (i.e. signature of the supervisor and date)
In relation to inventory, where a company holds periodic inventory counts, prior to the inventory count, the counting staff are issued with written instructions by management explaining how the count is to be performed	Review the instructions issued by management and consider if they are sufficiently effective to reduce the risk of material misstatement in the final inventory valuation Attend the inventory count and carry out sample counts to obtain evidence that management's instructions are being complied with
In relation to capital expenditure, all purchases of fixed assets over £20,000 have to be authorized by the capital expenditure committee	For a sample of fixed asset additions over £20,000 during the year, review the purchase order/purchase invoice for evidence of authorization by the capital expenditure committee
In relation to credit control, credit limits for certain customers must not exceed £10,000 so as to avoid the risk of excessive bad debts being incurred	With the client's permission, attempt to input an order for goods which takes a customer over the £10,000 credit limit. The system should reject the order

Auditing scenario 9.5 Controls and tests of control in a payroll system

Larch Ltd is a manufacturing company. Most of the company's employees are paid on an hourly basis and work in the factory. Larch Ltd has established a dedicated human resources (HR) department, which is responsible for recording information on all staff, including new recruits. When a new employee joins Larch Ltd, the HR department completes a 'new joiner' form, including personal information such as bank details and home address for the new employee. This information is input to a master file, stored in the company's computer, and a copy is sent to the payroll team to set up the employee's wages on the system.

All factory workers have a swipe card which they must use when they start and leave work every day. The information from the swipe card, which calculates the hours worked by the employee, is used to determine the worker's pay for each week. Any overtime worked is recorded in a separate document, prepared by the factory manager, and sent to the payroll department for processing at the end of each month.

The audit manager, who is planning the audit of Larch Ltd, has compiled the following working paper, indicating for identified controls, the test(s) that are to be performed.

Table 9.7 Examples of tests of control

Control	Test(s) of control
The new joiner forms should be in a standard format, to avoid details being missed. New joiner forms should be approved by an HR manager before being input into the system and passed to the payroll department, to ensure that only valid additions are made to the HR records	Review a sample of new joiner forms to check that all details are completed and that they have been signed as approved by the HR manager For a sample of new joiners, meet the new employee in person to confirm their existence

Control	Test(s) of control
HR master file information can only be amended by the HR manager to prevent unauthorized amendments. In particular, payroll staff should not be able to access the HR files	Attempt to log in to the HR master file information using a payroll clerk's password. The system should reject the request.
An exception report should be produced which shows changes made to the master file information	View the exception reports which show changes made to the HR master file, confirm that the changes are valid by agreeing to supporting documentation (e.g. if an employee's bank details have changed, has this been confirmed by the employee?)
Factory employees are required to use their swipe cards so that they are only paid for hours worked and this process should be supervised (e.g. by a factory manager, to prevent staff from swiping in cards for workers not actually present)	Audit team members to observe the factory workers clocking in and out of the factory, ensuring that it is supervised With client's permission, attempt to swipe a card containing 'dummy data' to check the data is identified by the system as invalid
Overtime worked reports must be authorized by the factory manager prior to being sent to payroll so that only valid overtime that has been worked is paid to the employee	Review a sample of overtime worked reports for evidence that they have been authorized by the factory supervisor (i.e. they have the factory supervisor's signature on them)

Chapter round-up

- Auditors are required to use a risk-based approach to audit planning, to minimize audit risk (i.e. the risk they give an inappropriate opinion on the financial statements).
- The planning stage of the audit is crucial to maintaining high audit quality as it is at the planning stage that the auditor identifies the risks that the financial statements could be misstated.
- Risk of material misstatement is comprised of inherent risk and control risk.
- Detection risk is the only risk that can be controlled by the auditor.
- Auditors are required to perform risk assessment procedures which include inquiry, analytical procedures, and observation/inspection.
- A business risk approach to identifying risks of material misstatement should ensure that the auditor considers a broad range of risks of material misstatement.
- The auditor evaluates the effectiveness of internal controls using tests of control. If results are positive, the auditor can conclude that control risk is low, and can place reliance on the controls, this reduces the amount of detailed audit procedures that are required.

End of chapter case study

Introduction

This chapter has looked at some important matters which the auditor must consider when planning an audit. It is crucial that the auditor has performed risk assessment procedures to identify risks of material misstatement as a way to reduce audit risk to an acceptable level. We have seen that auditors use a risk-based approach to identify risks of material misstatement. This involves understanding the audit client's business including its business risks and internal controls as a way to identify audit planning implications.

This case study links to the following learning outcomes:

- Explain the audit risk model and identify and explain audit risks.
- Discuss and apply the use of the risk-based approach to audit planning.

Scenario

It is 1 November 20X1. You are a manager in the audit department of Lavender & Co, a firm of Chartered Accountants. You specialize in the audit of companies in the retail sector and you are assigned to the audit of Frankie plc, which has a financial year ending 31 December 20X1. The company, which is listed, operates twenty-five large department stores across the UK.

Lavender & Co has been appointed as auditor to Frankie plc for the last five years, with the audit opinion being unmodified each year.

Background information

Frankie plc's department stores are all located in prime locations in city centres, and they sell a range of goods, including clothing, beauty products, home furnishings, and electrical equipment. One product line is a range of luxury items branded as 'Frankie's Finest' goods. The company owns the buildings in which its stores in London, Manchester, and Leeds operate. The rest of the stores operate from rented premises.

In addition to the department stores, Frankie plc also makes sales through its website and has a distribution division which supports the online sales.

The company implements best practice in respect of corporate governance, with a balance of executive and non-executive directors appointed to the board, and it has an internal audit department which reports to the company's audit committee.

Minutes of meeting

Financial performance

Increased competition following the opening of new stores by a rival retail organization has resulted in lower revenue in most stores in 20X1. However, online sales have increased significantly, and the company is planning to invest a significant amount to strengthen this aspect of its business model. The Chief Finance Officer (CFO) is not planning to test the properties owned by the company for impairment, justifying this on the basis that the company's operating profit is projected to be slightly higher than the operating profit recognized in the previous financial year.

Data loss

In March, a cybersecurity attack meant that the credit card details of some customers who had purchased goods from the company's website were stolen. As a result of this data loss, the company may have to pay a fine equivalent to 3 per cent of revenue. The fine will be payable if an investigation by the regulatory authorities concludes that the data loss was caused by deficiencies in the company's internal controls which allowed hackers to access its systems.

Closure of Birmingham city centre store

Last month, a decision was made to close the department store located in Birmingham city centre. This was one of the company's largest stores, opened six years ago, but competition from new department stores has caused declining customer footfall and reduced revenue, leading to the decision to shut the store. The store will close on 31 January 20X2.

The company will retain approximately half of the employees of the Birmingham store, the rest will be made redundant. The CFO has calculated that a restructuring provision of £21 million should be recognized in the year-end financial statements, comprised of the following elements:

Redundancy payments	£10m
Retraining staff who will transfer to the distribution division	£3m
Transport of inventory to different stores	£3m
Lease cancellation fee	£5m

Extracts from projected financial statements and comparative information

The financial information shown in Table 9.10 is extracted from the management accounts and was presented to the board of directors at their meeting on 30 October 20X1.

The company is projected to have profit before tax of £18 million (20X0: £19 million) at the year end.

Required

Evaluate the significant risks of material misstatement to be considered in planning the audit of the financial statements of Frankie plc for the year ended 31 December 20X1.

Table 9.10 Revenue and operating profit

	Projected to 31.12.20X1		**Actual to 31.12.20X0**	
Revenue and operating profit by store location:	**Revenue £million**	**Operating profit £million**	**Revenue £million**	**Operating profit £million**
London	100	9.2	108	9.8
Manchester	66	5.2	67	5.5
Birmingham	50	4.5	81	7.5
Liverpool	52	5.1	55	5.3
Bristol	31	2.8	30	3.1
Leeds	27	2.5	35	2.9
Glasgow	25	2.5	28	2.9
Edinburgh	34	3.2	31	3.3
Other stores	98	12	95	10
Total revenue and operating profit from stores	483	47	530	50.3
Revenue and operating profit from online sales	42	4.9	33	4.5
Total revenue and operating profit	525	51.9	563	54.8

Table 9.11 Information extracted from the statement of financial position

Statement of financial position	**Notes**	**Projected at 31.12.20X1 £million**	**Actual at 31.12.20X0 £million**
Non-current assets: Property, plant, and equipment	1	360	334
Current assets: Inventory		190	125

Table 9.11 (Continued)

Statement of financial position	Notes	Projected at 31.12.20X1 £million	Actual at 31.12.20X0 £million
Receivables		90	85
Cash		35	38
Total assets		675	582

Note 1
Property, plant, and equipment include £220 million (20X0: £228 million) which relates to the properties owned in London, Manchester, and Leeds.

Answer

The increased competition faced by the business has resulted in declining revenue in Frankie's stores. This creates a pressure on the company's directors to use accounting treatments which may overstate revenue and/or profit. This is an inherent risk at the financial statement level as numerous accounts could be impacted (e.g. expenses could be understated, revenue overstated, in an attempt to improve the company's profitability).

This risk is amplified by the fact that the company is planning to invest heavily to promote its online sales. If it needs to raise finance to do so, there is more pressure to create a healthy set of financial statements to support any application for loans.

The declining revenue at many of the stores should prompt an impairment review of each separate cash-generating unit. The fact that the finance director is trying to justify not performing impairment reviews should be treated with professional scepticism as this could just be a way to avoid charging impairment losses in profit for the year. There is a risk that the properties are overstated in value and that profit is also overstated if any necessary impairment loss is not recognized. This potential misstatement could be material given that three stores (London, Manchester, and Leeds) have a combined carrying value of £220 million, which is 32.6 per cent of total assets, and all of these stores are projected to see a decline in revenue and profit and should be tested for impairment.

The cybersecurity attack indicates that there could be internal control deficiencies which allowed the attack to take place. More information is needed to enable the auditor to evaluate the specific control activities which should have been in place to prevent the attack which seemed to target customer's details. The attack may have impacted on systems used for financial reporting purposes—this should be discussed with Frankie so that the auditor can evaluate the potential control risk and implication, if any, for the evaluation of risk of material misstatement.

The potential fine of 3 per cent of revenue related to cybersecurity attack is material to the financial statements, amounting to £15.75 million, and the auditor needs to consider the recognition of a provision or disclosure of a contingent liability in respect of this. Given management's incentive to portray a healthy profit figure, and to avoid the possible reputational damage, it is likely that they will not wish to recognize this in the financial statements. It is an area of judgement, as it may not be certain by the time the financial statements are finalized as to whether the amount should be accounted for (if it is probable to be paid), or disclosed in a note to the financial statements (if it is possible to be paid) in accordance with IAS 37 *Provisions, Contingent Liabilities and Contingent Assets.* The level of subjectivity elevates the risk of material misstatement regarding this potential fine.

The closure of the Birmingham store creates an assertion level risk of material misstatement in respect of the provision which the finance director wishes to recognize. IAS 37 contains specific requirements around what can and cannot be included in a restructuring provision. The lease cancellation fee and redundancy costs can be included, but staff retraining and transport of inventory to other stores are both associated with the ongoing operations of the business and cannot be included. If the finance director creates a provision as intended, for the full £21 million, the provision and associated expense will be overstated by £6 million, which is 1.1 per cent of projected revenue and 33.3 per cent of projected profit which would be considered material to the financial statements.

Looking at the projected inventory, this shows an increase of 52 per cent in the year. Given the increased competition facing Frankie, there is a business risk that some of this inventory is not going to be sold, or may be sold at a loss should the products needs to be discounted. The inventory should be valued at the lower of cost and net realizable value in accordance with IAS 2 *Inventories* and there is a risk that inventories and profit are overstated if any necessary write down is not recognized.

Activity solutions

Activity 9.1—Inherent risk factors

ISA (UK) 315 states that there are five inherent risk factors: complexity, subjectivity, change, uncertainty, and susceptibility to misstatement due to management bias or fraud risk factors.

Can you think of examples for each of these risk factors—that is, matters which would lead the auditor to think that there is a high level of inherent risk?

Suggested answer points:

Complexity

- Regulatory complexity (e.g. operations that are subject to a high degree of complex regulation such as financial institutions, charities, certain sectors such as oil and gas production).
- Business model complexity (e.g. the existence of large and complex group structures).
- Financial reporting (e.g. complex valuation methods such as impairment or accounting for hedge transactions).

Subjectivity

- Accounting estimates (e.g. depreciation, revenue recognition over time, recognition of provisions and contingencies).

Change

- Changes in economic conditions (e.g. inflation, volatility in interest rates, or exchange rates).
- Changes in market conditions (e.g. increased competition).
- Changes in the business model (e.g. introducing a new product or entering a new geographical area of operations).
- Change in key personnel particularly those with influence over financial reporting.
- Changes in accounting regulations (e.g. a new or significantly changed IFRS standard).
- Changes in regulations (e.g. new environmental legislation).

Uncertainty

- Economic uncertainty (e.g. during an economic recession or when a new government comes into power).
- Litigation against the entity for which the outcome is uncertain.

Bias or fraud

- Significant related party transactions.
- Significant unusual transactions.

Activity 9.2–Audit team discussion

Why do you think it is important that there is a discussion about risks of material misstatement among the audit team?

Suggested answer points:

- It allows more experienced audit team members, especially the partner and key managers involved, to share their experience and knowledge with the rest of the team.
- It enables a discussion about business risks and other planning issues such as fraud risks.
- It promotes better understanding among members of the audit team of how the work assigned to them may impact the audit as a whole, and the work of other audit team members.
- It establishes a communication channel so that audit team members can more easily share their findings and information obtained during the audit.

Activity 9.3–Evaluating systems and controls

What do you think auditors consider when performing an initial evaluation of systems and controls? This is not performing tests on the controls, just forming an initial view as to whether the systems are controls are good enough for tests of control to be carried out.

Suggested answer points:

- whether there is adequate segregation of duties;
- whether regular checks are performed on certain areas of the financial statements (e.g. regular bank reconciliations and regular control account reconciliations);
- the adequacy of the accounting records and how these are safeguarded;
- the training level and competence of employees; and
- the effectiveness of the entity's internal audit function (if one is present).

10 Materiality and Analytical Review

Introduction

As we saw in the previous chapters, the auditor needs to obtain detailed business understanding and identify risks of material misstatement. In this chapter, we will focus on two specific elements of auditing, which are very important at the planning stage of the audit, but which are also relevant to other stages in the audit process. The ISAs we are going to look at are:

- ISA (UK) 320 Materiality in Planning and Performing an Audit
- ISA (UK) 520 Analytical Procedures

Remember that audit planning, including the evaluation of materiality and performing robust analytical procedures, informs the development of the audit strategy and production of the audit plan so both are important aspects of the audit process. In this chapter, you will see how auditors must use their judgement in deciding on the significant elements of the financial statements which need to be prioritized. You might be surprised to see that there are few strict rules on materiality, so audit firms have different approaches, some being more cautious than others.

Analytical procedures are about interrogating information—focusing on the client's financial information but also involving comparisons to competitors, industry averages, and non-financial information. The auditor is looking for clues that might indicate that something is wrong in the financial statements—for instance, an increase in revenue is not matched by an increase in cost of sales, prompting the auditor to enquire with the client about the possible reasons for this. If the client cannot provide a good reason, there is a risk of misstatement. This analysis is made easier these days with the advent of audit data analytics, which can perform extremely detailed analysis in a matter of seconds and present the results in a way that is easy for the auditor to interpret. This powerful technology can reduce audit risk—but only if the auditor is skilled in interpreting the output.

Learning outcomes

- Explain the concept of materiality.
- Determine and justify levels of materiality and performance materiality in an audit.
- Describe and explain the nature, and purpose of, analytical procedures in an audit.
- Perform analytical review including the computation and interpretation of relevant trends and ratios.
- Comment on how audit data analytics tools can be used in performing analytical procedures.

10.1 The concept of materiality

10.1.1 What is 'materiality'?

A simple way to think of materiality is that it is a way for the auditor to decide whether something in the financial statements—a balance, transaction, or disclosure—is important enough for it to have an impact on the users of the financial statements. If the financial statements contain material misstatements, the auditor cannot give the true and fair opinion.

ISA (UK) 320 *Materiality in Planning and Performing an Audit* refers to materiality as follows:

> Misstatements, including omissions, are considered to be material if they, individually or in the aggregate, could reasonably be expected to influence the economic decisions of users taken on the basis of the financial statements.[1]

You can think of materiality as a way for the auditor to prioritize the elements of the financial statements which need more attention. It is a way of managing audit risk—the more material an element of the financial statements, the more audit attention it is likely to require, to ensure that the appropriate audit opinion is given.

Materiality is a matter of professional judgement and can be revised during the course of an audit. It is set at the planning stage of the audit based on the draft financial statements or other sources of financial information. If matters come to light during the audit which the auditor was not previously aware of, the auditor may choose to increase or decrease materiality levels as appropriate.

When considering materiality, there is not a 'set method' for deciding whether something is material or not—the auditor uses their judgement to make this decision, using the framework provided in ISA (UK) 320.

ISA (UK) 320 confirms the importance of professional judgement when determining materiality by stating:

- Judgments about materiality are made in light of surrounding circumstances, and are affected by the size or nature of a misstatement, or a combination of both; and
- Judgments about matters that are material to users of the financial statements are based on a consideration of the common financial information needs of users as a group. The possible effect of misstatements on specific individual users, whose needs may vary widely, is not considered.[2]

[1] FRC, 'ISA (UK) 320', 2022, para 2 <https://media.frc.org.uk/documents/ISA_UK_320_Updated_May_2022.pdf> (accessed 18 January 2024).

[2] Ibid.

Auditing in practice 10.1 Guidance on materiality for financial reporting

Materiality is as much a financial reporting concept as an auditing concept. Financial reporting frameworks such as IFRS have their own definitions and application requirements or guidance on materiality to be used by preparers of financial statements.

In 2017 the IASB issued non-mandatory guidance on materiality in IFRS Practice Statement 2 *Making Materiality Judgements*. The Practice Statement aims to promote a more consistent approach to materiality by preparers of financial statements at the same time as acknowledging that materiality decisions are made specifically in the context of the reporting entity. The Practice Statement also refers to the use of judgement in making materiality decisions, stating:

> When assessing whether information is material, an entity considers its own specific circumstances and the information needs of the primary users of its financial statements. Materiality judgements are reassessed at each reporting date.

The IASB is keen that preparers of financial statements and their auditors use a similar approach when determining materiality.

10.1.2 Material classes of transactions, account balances, and disclosures

ISA (UK) 320 contains the fundamental requirement relating to materiality:

> When establishing the overall audit strategy, the auditor shall determine materiality for the financial statements as a whole. If, in the specific circumstances of the entity, there is one or more particular classes of transactions, account balances or disclosures for which misstatements of lesser amounts than materiality for the financial statements as a whole could reasonably be expected to influence the economic decisions of users taken on the basis of the financial statements, the auditor shall also determine the materiality level or levels to be applied to those particular classes of transactions, account balances or disclosures.[3]

The ISA (UK) 320 requirement refers to 'a class of transaction and account balance'. This means the various categories into which the financial statements are divided. For example, expenditure may be classed as 'cost of sales', 'administration expenses', or 'distribution costs'. A 'class' of account balance will be 'non-current assets' and 'current assets' as well as 'current' and 'non-current' liabilities. See Table 10.1.

The auditor is concerned with material classes of transactions, account balances, and disclosures to ensure there is no material misstatement. Immaterial account balances and disclosures will not be a major concern of the auditor on the grounds of their immateriality, but that is not to say they can be forgotten about entirely during the course of the audit—immaterial transactions, balances, and disclosures may become material if there are any revisions to materiality levels during the course of the audit.

[3] Ibid., para 10.

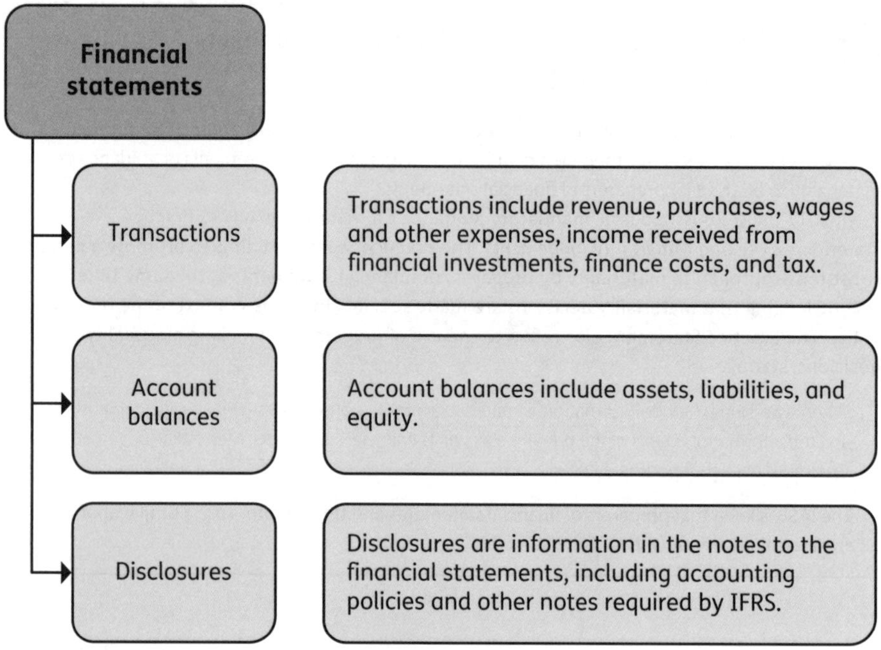

Figure 10.1 Transactions, account balances, and disclosures

An item in the financial statements should be considered from different points of view in order to determine its materiality. An item could be material from one point of view, but immaterial from another point of view. The important thing to remember is that materiality should be judged from the perspective of the users of the financial statements. Let's use a simple example to illustrate the idea.

Imagine that a company has made an investment during the financial year. The monetary amounts involved, in the auditor's judgement, are not material. Therefore, the amount at which the balance is recorded in the financial statements is not considered to be something which would influence the user's view of the financial statements. However, disclosure about the investment in the notes to the financial statements could be material, as this is where the users can discover information which is important to them e.g. the reason why the investment was made. Therefore, a different materiality would be applied to the account balance and the disclosure relating to that investment.

10.2 Applying materiality in an audit

10.2.1 Determining materiality for the financial statements as a whole

As we have seen, the auditor's objective is to obtain sufficient appropriate audit evidence over the figures that appear in the financial statements and the auditor is also concerned with evaluating whether the narrative information relevant to the organization's financial performance, financial position, and cash flows is complete and accurate. The auditor must also consider the overall impact that immaterial misstatements may have on the financial statements when they are combined, for example, could they turn a reported profit into a loss?

There are two important factors to consider where materiality is concerned: whether an item is material by **size** or whether it is material by **nature**—in other words, there are both **qualitative** and **quantitative** factors where materiality is concerned.

ISA (UK) 320 does not prescribe a definitive calculation for materiality because the ISA (UK) recognizes that materiality is down to the auditor's professional judgement. However, percentage 'benchmarks' can be a useful starting point in determining materiality levels, such as:

- 0.5 to 1 per cent of revenue
- 5 per cent to 10 per cent of profit before tax
- 1 per cent to 2 per cent of total assets (non-current assets plus current assets)

These benchmarks are common, but are not definitive. Different audit firms may use different benchmarks or different thresholds for each client. For a profit-oriented entity, a benchmark based on profit before tax is commonly used. However, materiality should be assessed each year and the method may need to change in response to new circumstances. For example, if profit before tax becomes volatile, the auditor may no longer conclude that it is an appropriate benchmark, so could decide to use a different benchmark, such as gross profit, total revenue, or a normalized profit figure.

Auditing scenario 10.1 Calculating materiality using monetary benchmarks

The draft financial statements of a company for the year ended 31 October 20X9 show the following:

	20X9 (draft)
	£'000
Revenue	12,600
Profit before tax	2,500
Total assets	32,000
Current assets	18,000

Financial statement materiality has been determined at 1 per cent of revenue, 5 per cent of profit before tax, and 2 per cent of total assets.

During the audit, the audit senior discovers an error in the accounts: £1.2m has been capitalized as non-current assets, but this should be recognized as revenue expenditure as the expenditure does not meet the recognition criteria for an asset according to IAS 16 *Property, Plant and Equipment*.

The misstatement represents 3.8 per cent (1,200/32,000) of total assets and 48 per cent (1,200/2,500) of profit before tax and hence is a material amount because it goes over the benchmarks of 2 per cent of total asset, and 5 per cent of profit before tax. Management should be requested to correct the misstatement to avoid the auditor modifying the auditor's opinion due to material misstatement from non-compliance with IAS 16.

It is important that the auditor considers misstatements against the correct benchmarks. In this scenario, the auditor compared the incorrectly capitalized expenditure against the benchmarks for total assets and profit before tax which is correct. It would be inappropriate to compare such a misstatement against revenue or current assets because the misstatement does not affect revenue.

'Material by nature' refers to the fact that materiality is not just concerned with the numbers disclosed in the financial statements. Some items may be material by nature because of the impact they have on the financial statements. You can think of these as matters which impact the users of the financial statements regardless of the monetary size of the matter.

Auditing Activity 10.1 Material by nature

Can you think of examples of matters which could be material by their nature?

10.2.2 **Performance materiality**

In a lot of cases, it is unlikely that auditors will be able to design tests which identify individually material misstatements. It is much more common that misstatements are material when combined (i.e. considered in aggregate). For this reason, ISA (UK) 320 includes a concept of 'performance materiality'.

ISA (UK) 320 defines 'performance materiality' as:

> The amount or amounts set by the auditor at less than materiality for the financial statements as a whole to reduce to an appropriately low level the probability that the aggregate of uncorrected and undetected misstatements exceeds materiality for the financial statements as a whole. If applicable, performance materiality also refers to the amount or amounts set by the auditor at less than the materiality levels for particular classes of transactions, account balances or disclosures.[4]

Performance materiality is a level of materiality which is set **lower** than financial statement materiality. This lower level of materiality is used when designing and performing audit procedures. For example, if performance materiality for trade receivables is £40,000 then essentially all individual trade receivables accounts that are over £40,000 are included in the sample.

Auditing scenario 10.2 Performance materiality

During the audit planning of Lowton Enterprises Ltd, a manufacturing company, the auditor determines a materiality level for the financial statements as a whole of £90,000. The assessment of risk of material misstatement indicates that the valuation of the company's work in progress is susceptible to a high risk of accounting error because it relies on significant estimates and judgements. The total work in progress is valued at £1.2 million, so the balance as a whole is material. The £1.2 million comprises many individual items, valued individually between £15,000 to £105,000.

To reduce audit risk, the auditor can apply a specific performance materiality level to the work in progress. How this is determined is very judgemental.

Performance materiality could be determined as a percentage of financial statement materiality, for example, 75 per cent—that is, a performance materiality of £67,500 (£90,000 x 75 per cent). However, the audit team could use a different percentage, or even use a different calculation depending on their professional judgement. Using £67,500 means that all individual balances within the total work in progress that are valued at this amount or over would be included in the

[4] Ibid., para 9.

audit testing, as individually material items. The auditor could then test the items valued at less than £67,500 on a sample basis.

If a misstatement of £80,000 was identified *without* performance materiality, the auditor would conclude that work in progress is not materially misstated. However, the auditor may not have detected further misstatements which, when added to the £80,000 identified would result in a material misstatement. When the auditor uses performance materiality, this reduces the risk that the auditor expresses an incorrect opinion on the financial statements.

10.2.3 **Materiality in practice**

You can see that materiality is quite a complex issue and you probably can understand why some users of financial statements would not understand what materiality is and how it is applied by auditors. The significant use of judgement by auditors when they are determining materiality makes the issue even more hard for lay people to understand. A research paper published in 2011[5] puts forward some views on the use of materiality by auditors and whether it is a concept that is understood. Key findings include that many investors struggle to understand the concept of materiality and that even those charged with governance of an audited entity may not understand how it is determined or used in the context of financial reporting and audit. The authors of the article link this lack of understanding to the audit expectation gap and consider that audit firms could better explain the use of materiality to interested stakeholders. They also conclude that audit committees should have detailed conversations with their audit provider to ensure that they understand how it is applied during the audit process.

Auditing in practice 10.2 FRC Thematic Review on Materiality

In their 2017 Thematic Review on Materiality,[6] the UK Financial Reporting Council found that the most common way to determine a materiality threshold (in their survey of the eight largest audit firms) is based on 5 per cent of profit before tax. The FRC commented that: 'It may be appropriate to use a profit-based measure for some sectors, such as construction, general retailing, and support services; in others, such as mining and equity investment instruments, however, earnings before interest, tax, depreciation and amortisation (EBITDA) and net asset values may be more appropriate.' This highlights the fact that auditors need to use their judgement when determining how to apply materiality—the same approach will not be suitable for all audit clients.

In addition, the review noted that some firms use materiality benchmarks based on a rolling average, which should work to eliminate volatility in profits and therefore in the materiality benchmark applied in audits of clients in industries where profit volatility is prevalent.

One of the significant findings of the review was that there is a considerable difference in how audit firms determine materiality, with some audit firms using considerably lower materiality levels than others on their audits. Perhaps this is not too surprising given the extent of professional judgement that needs to be used when setting a level of materiality for audit clients. In the review,

[5] Houghton, K.A., Jubb, C., & Kend, M. (2011) 'Materiality in the context of audit: The real expectations gap', *Managerial auditing journal*, vol. 26, no. 6, pp. 482–500.

[6] FRC, 'Audit Quality Thematic Review: Materiality', 2017 <https://media.frc.org.uk/documents/Audit_Quality_Thematic_Review_-_Materiality.pdf> (accessed 18 January 2024).

the FRC comments that it is possible that the materiality levels set by some audit firms 'could be around 100% higher than that of the more prudent firms'. These different approaches to materiality could lead to significantly different audits being conducted, impacting on the scope and detail of audit work performed and possibly on the conclusions reached by the audit firm.

The Thematic Review also encourages Audit Committees to engage with their audit provider to discuss and where necessary challenge the auditor's determination of materiality. The review reported that only 17 per cent of Audit Committees have engaged with their auditor regarding materiality which goes against the principle that the Audit Committee should monitor the quality and effectiveness of the external audit.

Audits of UK companies which fall under the scope of extended audit reports (which we will consider in detail in Chapter 19) are now required to provide an explanation of the significant judgements made by the auditor in determining materiality. The disclosure should enable readers of the auditor's report to understand how the auditor applied materiality in planning and performing the audit, and the disclosure should be specifically tailored to the circumstances of the audit. The disclosure should include:

- The rationale for the determination of performance materiality.
- Significant qualitative considerations relating to the auditor's evaluation of materiality.
- Materiality level or levels for those classes of transactions, account balances or disclosures where such materiality levels are lower than materiality for the financial statements as a whole.
- Any significant revisions of materiality thresholds that were made as the audit progressed.
- The threshold used for reporting unadjusted differences to the audit committee.[7]

It is tempting to assume that investors and other users of the annual report would use these disclosures about materiality in their evaluation of financial statements and audit reports. However, there is little evidence that this is the case. Indeed, academic research indicates that disclosures about materiality are not understood by many users of annual reports and that disclosures about materiality do not impact investment decisions.[8]

Auditing in practice 10.3 Materiality disclosures

The 2022 audit report for Tesco, issued by Deloitte, discloses the following in relation to materiality:

> The materiality that we used for the Group financial statements was £100m which was determined on the basis of 4.60% of adjusted profit before tax from continuing operations... In the prior year materiality was determined based on 0.13% of revenue from continuing operations due to the impact of COVID-19 on the profitability of the group as a whole. Our determined materiality in the current year equates to 0.16% of revenue from continuing operations.[9]

[7] FRC, 'ISA (UK) 701', 2022, para A59-2 <https://media.frc.org.uk/documents/ISA_UK_701_Updated_May_2022.pdf> (accessed 18 January 2024).

[8] Christensen, B.E., Eilifsen, A., Glover, S.M., & Messier, W.F. (2020) 'The effect of audit materiality disclosures on investors' decision making', *Accounting, organizations and society*, vol. 87.

[9] Tesco plc, 'Annual report and financial statements 2022', 2022 <https://www.tescoplc.com/investors/reports-results-and-presentations/annual-report-2022/> (accessed 18 January 2024).

In common with many other audits, and in line with the FRC's research on the application of materiality, Deloitte uses a profit-based measure for its retail client.

In the audit of Anglo American, a large mining company with global operations, PwC include the following in relation to their use of materiality:

> Overall Group materiality: \$300 million (2020: \$200 million) based on approximately 3.0% of the Group's three year-average consolidated profit before tax, special items and remeasurements . . . Profit before tax, special items and remeasurements is used as the materiality benchmark. The directors use this measure as they believe that it reflects the underlying performance of the Group. We consider that it is most appropriate to calculate materiality based on a three-year average of profit before tax, special items and remeasurements to respond to longer-term trends in commodity markets and to dampen the impact of short-term price volatility. We used judgement to cap our materiality at \$300 million.[10]

It is interesting to note the use of materiality based on a three-year average of adjusted profit—here the auditor is using their judgement to respond to potential volatility in profit by determining a more stable measure of materiality.

Not all audits use a profit-based materiality benchmark. In the audit of the Crown Estate, conducted by the National Audit Office, materiality is based on gross assets. The Crown Estate manages a significant and diverse portfolio of national assets so it is appropriate that materiality is not focused on profit:

> Materiality: £168 million
> Basis for determining materiality: 1% of gross assets of £16.8 billion
> Rationale for the benchmark applied: I chose gross assets as a benchmark as I consider it to be the principal consideration for users assessing the financial performance of the Group.
> As well as quantitative materiality there are certain matters that, by their very nature, would if not corrected influence the decisions of users, for example, any errors in respect of the Board and Executives' remuneration as reported in the Remuneration Committee report. Assessment of such matters would need to have regard to the nature of the misstatement and the applicable legal and reporting framework, as well as the size of the misstatement.[11]

The extract above also shows an example of how auditors explain qualitative materiality in the context of an audit.

The key point to appreciate from looking at these three short examples is how different the determination of materiality can be, and to understand that materiality must be very specific to the audit being performed.

10.2.4 **Materiality and audit risk**

As we saw in Chapter 9, audit risk is the risk that the auditor expresses an incorrect opinion on the financial statements. Remember that the auditor must try to reduce audit risk to the lowest possible level, although the reality is they cannot remove audit risk completely.

There is an inverse relationship between materiality and the level of audit risk. Hence, the higher the assessed level of audit risk, the lower the level of materiality, and vice versa see Figure 10.2. Another way of thinking of this is that, if the auditor wishes to reduce audit risk,

[10] Anglo American, 'Integrated annual report 2021', 2021 <https://www.angloamerican.com/~/media/Files/A/Anglo-American-Group-v5/PLC/investors/annual-reporting/2022/aa-annual-report-full-2021.pdf> (accessed 18 January 2024).

[11] Crown Estate Annual Report, 2022 <https://www.thecrownestate.co.uk/about-us/annual-report-archive>, (accessed date 30 September 2023).

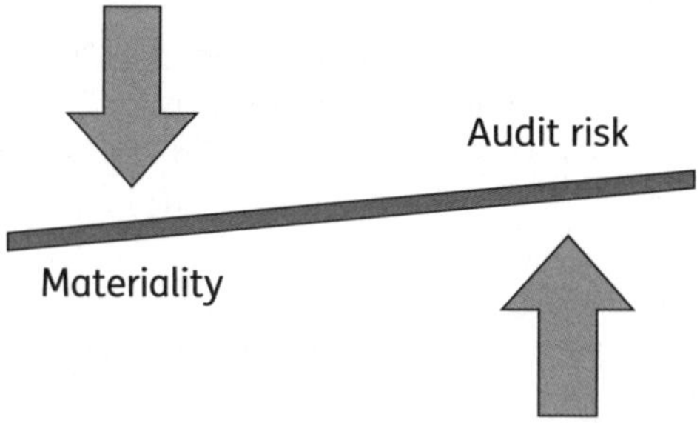

Figure 10.2 Inverse relationship between materiality and audit risk

they should increase the materiality level—this means that more balances, transactions, and disclosures will become material (based on quantitative materiality) and larger sample sizes will used to obtain audit evidence.

Let's illustrate this using a simple example. Imagine that during the audit of a company, the auditor discovers significant weaknesses in the controls over the payroll cycle; the payroll department has weak segregation of duties and a lack of authorization controls in place. During the last four months of the year, there have had to be significant revisions made to the company's payroll due to mistakes made in the payroll processing. In this situation, there is a high audit risk relating to payroll transactions. The auditor reduces audit risk by increasing materiality levels hence there is a higher likelihood that the auditor will detect more misstatements by performing more audit procedures on payroll. You can see that the auditor is using materiality as a way to reduce their risk exposure.

This example also demonstrates that materiality does not remain 'fixed' during the course of an audit. Matters may come to light during the audit which may cause the auditor to revise materiality levels either upwards or downwards depending on the issues identified. Where misstatements, fraud risks, or weaknesses/override of controls are identified, the auditor is likely to increase materiality levels and carry out additional substantive procedures.

In fact, this is a requirement of ISA (UK) 320, which requires the auditor to revise the level of materiality during the audit, 'in the event of becoming aware of information during the audit that would have caused the auditor to have determined a different amount (or amounts) initially'.[12] This can happen, for example, if the initial assessment of materiality is based on projected financial information, and the actual financial results for the period turn out to be quite different to the projections.

Auditing Activity 10.2 Applying materiality

Based on what we have learned about materiality, what do you think are the difficulties faced by auditors in determining and applying materiality?

[12] FRC, 'ISA (UK) 320', 2022, para 12.

10.3 Analytical procedures

10.3.1 Analytical procedures throughout the audit

We have seen that ISA (UK) 315 identifies analytical procedures as a risk assessment procedure to be used at the planning stage of the audit. Analytical procedures are used to identify unusual trends, fluctuations or relationships which might indicate a risk of misstatement.

Analytical procedures are dealt with in ISA (UK) 520 *Analytical Procedures*. In addition to discussing the use of analytical procedures at the planning stage of the audit, ISA (UK) 520 provides guidance on the auditor's use of analytical procedures as substantive procedures (i.e. as a means of obtaining audit evidence). It also deals with the auditor's responsibility to perform analytical procedures towards the end of the audit to assist the auditor in forming an overall conclusion on the financial statements.

The term 'analytical procedures' is defined in ISA (UK) 520 as:

> Evaluations of financial information through analysis of plausible relationships among both financial and non-financial data. Analytical procedures also encompass such investigation as is necessary of identified fluctuations or relationships that are inconsistent with other relevant information or that differ from expected values by a significant amount.[13]

In simple terms, analytical procedures are a way of looking at the relationships that exist, or should exist, in the financial statements, to identify possible misstatements. For example, if a company has taken out a significant loan during the year, you would expect to see an increase in finance costs recognized as an expense. The absence of such an increase in finance costs could indicate that the costs are understated and that there is a risk of material misstatement.

In another example, a company's sales have increased by 10 per cent in the year. The auditor may compare this increase to the projected change in sales from the company's management accounts and find that the projected increase was only 5 per cent. The discrepancy between the recorded increase in sales and the expectation of the increase in sales could indicate that there is a misstatement in how sales have been recognized in the financial statements (i.e. there is an overstatement). The analytical procedure has helped the auditor to identify that revenue could be overstated, and this will impact on the audit strategy for that component of the financial statements.

Analytical procedures are used throughout the audit process and are conducted for three primary purposes (Figure 10.3).

10.3.2 Improving the effectiveness of analytical procedures

There are three key factors which affect the precision of analytical procedures:

10.3.2.1 Disaggregation

The more detailed the level at which analytical procedures are performed, the greater the potential precision of the procedures. When the auditor performs analytical procedures at a high level, this may not reveal detailed enough information. If the auditor disaggregates the data into smaller groupings, such differences are more likely to come to the auditor's attention.

[13] FRC, 'ISA (UK) 520', 2022, para 4 <https://media.frc.org.uk/documents/ISA_UK_520_-_Updated_May_2022.pdf> (accessed 18 January 2024).

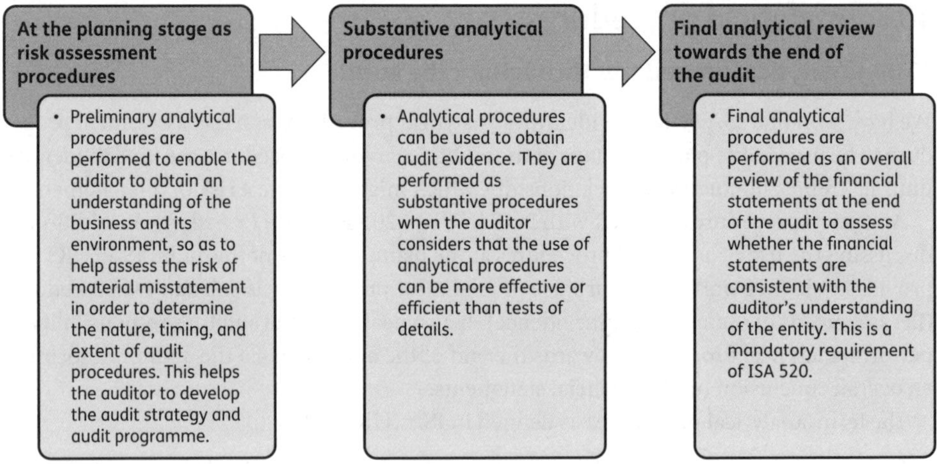

Figure 10.3 Use of analytical procedures throughout the audit

The objective of the audit procedure will determine whether data for an analytical procedure should be disaggregated and the extent to which it should be disaggregated. For example, disaggregating sales data into weekly or monthly sales, by geographic region or by product to understand the various elements.

10.3.2.2 **Data reliability**

If the source data used by the auditor is reliable, then it is likely the expectation will be more precise. The data used could consist of external industry information gathered through research activities. The source of the information will be a particularly important factor for the auditor because information produced by the entity's systems and records which cannot be manipulated by individuals is generally considered to be more reliable. The reliability of the data is also influenced by the comparability of the information available and the relevance of information made available.

10.3.2.3 **Predictability**

The more precise an expectation is for an analytical procedure, the greater the potential reliability of that data will be. For example, the use of non-financial data, such as the number of employees or electricity consumption in developing an expectation may increase the auditor's ability to predict relationships among the accounts.

10.4 **Performing analytical procedures at the planning stage of the audit**

There are a variety of ways in which the auditor carries out analytical procedures Figure 10.4.

10.4.1 **Comparison**

Analytical procedures can be used to compare financial information. For example, the payroll expense in the current year's financial statements can be compared against the prior

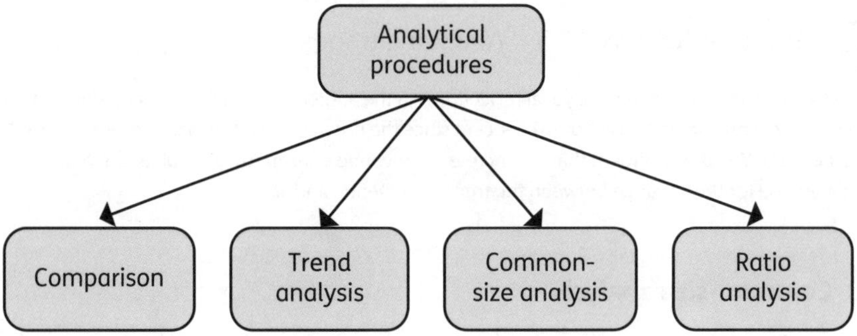

Figure 10.4 Types of analytical procedure

year and the auditor will investigate any significant differences. Similarly, current year gross profit margins can also be compared against the prior year or against another entity in the same industry. Again, the auditor will investigate any significant variations.

Comparison is an effective means of carrying out analytical review. For example, if gross profit margins are considerably higher or lower than the previous year, this will indicate a risk of material misstatement. It could be that cut-offs of sales or purchases are incorrect or there is a misstatement in the year-end inventory valuation. Similarly, if administrative expenses are disproportionately higher or lower than the previous year, this, too, could also indicate a risk of material misstatement. It is not necessarily the case that there is a misstatement in every case where current year figures are higher or lower than prior year figures—there may well be genuine reasons for the variation and the auditor will gather sufficient appropriate audit evidence to corroborate the reasons.

As well as comparisons from year to year, the auditor could also make comparisons of:

- actual results against forecast or budgeted results of the entity; and
- industry information, such as a comparison of information from the entity with its competitors or against industry averages.

Analytical procedures can also include the auditor's evaluation of relationships between financial information and relevant non-financial information, such as for a retail organization, comparing increase in revenue with changes in the number of sales people employed, or number of retail sites.

10.4.2 **Trend analysis**

Trend analysis is just a specific form of comparison—the analysis of changes in an account over time (i.e. the comparison of a current account balance with the same balance from the previous accounting periods). The longer the period used for the trend analysis, the more meaningful the results are likely to be. An auditor may choose to use evaluate if the current year's balance on the account deviates significantly from the trend established in the previous accounting periods for that account. Alternatively, the auditor may calculate a balance expected for that account and then compare it to the actual amount.

Auditing Activity 10.3 Analysing trends

You are an auditor performing analytical procedures in the audit of a manufacturing company. You notice that revenue has increased by 10 per cent since the previous year but wages have increased by 25 per cent. You are confident that the increase in revenue is justified. What plausible reasons could there be for the variance between the trends in revenue and wages?

10.4.3 **Common-size analysis**

Common-size analysis is a tool the auditor can use to analyse financial statements. It evaluates the financial statements by expressing each line item as a percentage of the base amount for that period. The idea of common-size analysis is that it helps the auditor to understand the impact of each item in the financial statements and its contribution to the final figure.

Common-size analysis is calculated using the following formula:

$$Percentage\ of\ base = \frac{Amount\ of\ individual\ item}{Amount\ of\ base\ item} \times 100$$

For example, in the statement of financial position, the common size analysis mostly utilizes the total assets value as the base value. The auditor can use the common-size analysis to see how a client's capital structure may compare to other entities in the same industry.

Common-size analysis is an extremely useful tool for the auditor because it can identify significant changes in a company's financial statements and can also indicate areas of the financial statements which contain misstatements.

Auditing scenario 10.3 Common-size analysis

Fields Ltd is a company that operates a chain of restaurants in the UK. The auditor is planning the company's audit and has prepared a common-size analysis on the statement of profit or loss, using revenue as the base figure. The auditor has obtained figures for a competitor, Pastures Ltd, to compare to those of Field Ltd.

Table 10.5 shows the analysis performed by the auditor.

Table 10.1

	Amount		**Percentage**	
	£'000	**£'000**	**%**	**%**
	Fields	**Pastures**	**Fields**	**Pastures**
Revenue	390.455	286,900	100	100
Cost of sales	(145,655)	(114, 700)	37.3	40
Gross profit	244,800	172,200	62.7	60
Operating expenses	(171,360)	(100,500)	43.9	35
Operating profit	73,440	71,785	18.8	25
Finance cost	(4,000)	(2,450)	1	0.8
Profit before tax	69,440	69,335	17.8	24.2
Tax	(13,890)	(19,455)	3.6	6.8
Profit after tax	55,550	49,880	14.2	17.4

The auditor makes the following observations based on the common-size analysis and comparison to the industry competitor.

Field's cost of sales as a percentage of sales is slightly less than Pastures. It is not a significant variance, and could be explained by a genuine business reason, such as Fields having a more efficient manufacturing process than Pastures. The auditor may choose to investigate further why Field's gross margin is better than Pastures. It could indicate accounting errors (e.g. incorrect valuation of closing inventory).

Field's operating expenses as a percentage of sales is significantly higher than Pastures. This could be caused by one-off expenses being included in Field's operating expenses this year, such as a large irrecoverable debt write-off. It could indicate accounting errors, for example, over-accruing year-end expenses, or, misclassification of expenses between cost of sales and operating expenses.

Field's tax expense as a percentage of sales is much lower than Pastures. Fields may have a valid reason for this—perhaps it is utilizing tax losses which have been carried forward from previous years, or maybe it has been granted some tax relief on certain expenditure. Alternatively, there could be an error in Field's tax calculation.

You should be able to see that common-size analysis is just a method for the auditor to identify possible accounting misstatements. All of the trends could be explained by a valid business reason or by an accounting error or deliberate misstatement—it is up to the auditor to respond to the issues identified to discover the explanation for the variances observed.

10.4.4 **Ratio analysis**

Ratio analysis is one of the most common methods of analytical procedure. It is important to understand that when using ratio analysis, the auditor must have something to compare the current year's ratio against (i.e. a ratio is meaningless on its own). For example, if a company's gross profit margin in 20X8 was 40 per cent this would not tell the auditor very much other than the company is making 40p gross profit for every £1 it sells. However, if the company's gross profit margin in 20X8 was 40 per cent and in 20X7 was 30 per cent this would be useful information as the auditor would want to identify the reasons why the margins have increased significantly in the year when, generally speaking, gross profit margins are expected to remain relatively consistent.

There are many different ratios that can be used in this analysis—there is no 'right or wrong' set of ratios, and there are different ways that each ratio can be calculated. We are not going to look at every possible ratio—instead, we will look at some broad categories of ratio and several examples of ratios that can be used. The Appendix to this chapter has more detail on ratio analysis, and is there for further reading if you would like to see more detail on this topic.

Broadly, four categories of ratio are used in financial analysis (see Figure 10.5).

We will now look at each of these broad categories of ratios and explain their use in the context of audit planning. Remember, we are just showing you some examples with brief explanations—if you want to see more detail then look at the appendix to this chapter.

10.4.4.1 **Profitability ratios**

- Gross profit margin = gross profit / sales revenue x 100
- Net profit margin = net profit / sales revenue x 100
- Return on capital employed (ROCE) = profit before interest and tax / equity + borrowings)

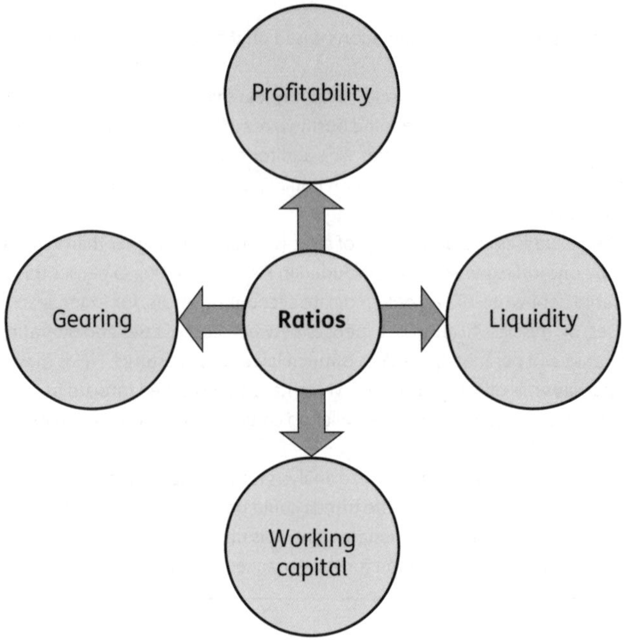

Figure 10.5 Categories of ratio analysis

Auditors generally expect the relationships between costs and revenues to stay relatively consistent. Profitability ratios can be affected by changes in sales prices, bulk purchase discounts, economies of scale, changing energy costs, and payroll increases.

Hence, any unusual fluctuation in the profitability ratio could indicate a risk of material misstatement.

Auditing Activity 10.4 Profit margins

The draft financial statements of an audit client for the year ended 31 December 20X8 show gross profit margins have increased by 6 per cent during the year. Can you suggest some accounting errors which could explain the change in the ratio?

10.4.4.2 **Working capital ratios**

- Receivables days = trade receivables / revenue x 365
- Inventory days = inventory / cost of sales x 365
- Payables days = trade payables / purchases x 365

These ratios show how long, on average, companies take to collect cash from customers and pay suppliers and how long inventory is being held for. A company should try as far as possible to reduce receivables and inventory days and maximize payables days because this assists the company's cash flow. Care should be taken to maximize payables days in accordance with credit terms because if credit terms are breached, supplier goodwill is lost and this could interrupt the supply of goods or withdrawal of credit facilities which would be detrimental to the business.

Any changes in efficiency ratios can indicate significant issues to the auditor, for example:

- worsening credit control, indicated by an increase in receivables days, may give rise to the need for receivables to be written off;
- ageing and possibly obsolete inventory, indicated by increasing inventory days, which could be overvalued; and
- poor cash flow could lead to material uncertainties related to going concern which would require disclosure in the financial statements.

10.4.4.3 **Liquidity ratios**

- Current ratio = current assets/current liabilities
- Quick ratio = (current assets – inventory)/current liabilities

Liquidity ratios indicate how able a company is to meet its short-term debts. Liquidity ratios are particularly important for the auditor when they are assessing the ability of the entity to continue as a going concern.

10.4.4.4 **Gearing ratios**

- Gearing = borrowings/share capital + reserves
- Interest cover = operating profit/finance costs

Gearing is a measure of external debt to internal equity and interest cover shows the ability of the company to pay finance costs from operating profit.

Any change in gearing or interest cover may indicate a change in the financing structure of the entity or changes in overall performance of the business. These ratios are important for identifying potentially material changes to the statement of financial position such as new loans taken out in the year or share issues.

Auditing scenario 10.4 Ratio analysis as a method of performing analytical procedures

Extracts from the draft financial statements of Farsley Ltd for the year ended 31 December 20X8 show the following:

Using the information in Table 10.2, the audit manager has calculated several ratios for both years. The audit manager then provides a review of the ratios, identifying possible risks of material misstatement.

This is typical of how an audit working paper would be presented, for review by the audit engagement partner.

Table 10.2

	20X8 (draft) £'000	20X7 (audited) £'000
Revenue	190,000	180,000
Cost of sales	(105,000)	(75,000)
Gross profit	85,000	105,000
Operating expenses	(62,000)	(68,000)
Operating profit	23,000	37,000
Inventory	25,000	22,000
Receivables	60,000	51,000
Cash	9,000	15,000
Trade payables	26,000	20,000
Bank overdraft	8,000	-

Relevant ratios

Table 10.3

	20X8	20X7
Gross margin	85,000/190,000 = 44.7%	105,000/180,000 = 58.3%
Operating margin	23,000/190,000 = 12.1%	37,000/180,000 = 20.6%
Inventory days	25,000/105,000x365 = 87 days	22,000/75,000x365 = 107 days
Receivable days	60,000/190,000x365 = 115 days	51,000/180,000x365 = 103 days
Current ratio	94,000/34,000 = 2:8	88,000/20,000 = 4:4

Analysis and identification of risks of material misstatement

Gross profit margins are generally expected to remain relatively consistent. In Farsley Ltd's draft financial statements, the gross profit margin has reduced from 58.3 per cent to 44.7 per cent which may indicate a cut-off problem within sales (sales may be understated) or purchases from the next accounting period could be recognized in error or there may be a problem with the valuation of inventory at the year end.

Operating margin has also decreased quite significantly from 20.6 per cent to 12.1 per cent. This could indicate that the company has experienced an increase in overhead expenditure which has had a detrimental impact on profit. If this is expected to continue, the company will eventually start to sustain a loss if it is not addressed by management. There could also be an overstatement of expenses which is reducing the operating margin, for example, there could be errors in calculating this year's depreciation expense, or the amount of accrued expenses recognized. Another explanation is that the operating expenses could contain a significant large one-off item, for example, a large impairment of an asset. The auditor will need to obtain more information about what is included in operating expenses in order to identify any specific risk of material misstatement.

Inventory days have reduced from 107 days to 87 days which suggests that the company is holding inventory for a shorter period of time which is encouraging as there are costs associated with holding inventory for long periods of time. However, if the inventory is undervalued (as may be the case given the reduced gross profit margins), any adjustment to increase inventory will increase the inventory holding days. Inventory could be understated if not all inventory has been recognized in the financial statements (i.e. there is a risk attached to the completeness of inventory, as well as issues with its valuation).

Receivables days has increased which means that the company is taking longer to receive payment from its customers. From a working capital point of view this is not a good sign, and perhaps the company needs to improve its credit control procedures. The increase in trade receivables could also indicate a risk that the balance is overstated—perhaps no adjustments have been made to write off bad debts or to recognize an allowance against slow paying customers' balances.

The current ratio has decreased in the year, indicating liquidity problems for Farsley Co. As discussed above, there could be undervaluation of inventories which helps to explain the reduction in the current ratio.

From this example, you can see that analytical procedures can provide information in two ways. Firstly, the trends can reveal information about the performance of the business in the year (e.g. for Farsley Ltd there appeared to be problems with liquidity as well as a reduction in profit margins in the year). This information, assuming that the source data is reliable, helps the auditor to understand the business and supports the requirements of ISA (UK) 315 in terms of obtaining business understanding.

Secondly, the analytical procedures can indicate possible misstatements (e.g. for Farsley Ltd there may be problems with how inventory is recognized in the financial statements—in particular, the valuation and completeness of inventory). This informs the auditor's risk assessment and can help to shape the audit strategy, as the auditor will want to devote more time to areas of the financial statements where analytical procedures reveal unusual trends or relationships.

To summarize this section on analytical procedures, you should be able to see how important these techniques can be in helping the auditor to identify where there could be misstatements in the financial statements.

The general process involved in performing analytical procedures can be summarized as in Figure 10.6.

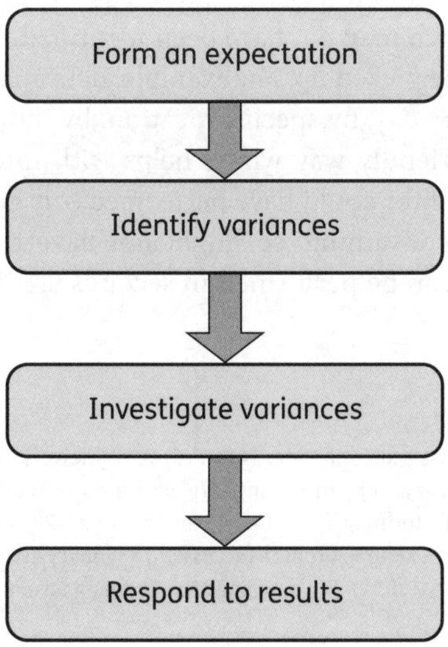

Figure 10.6 The process of performing analytical procedures

10.5 Using audit data analytics

Data analytics tools can be used to great effect when planning the audit, and perhaps the most significant impact is on performing analytical procedures. Auditors can use their client's accounting information, sourced from software such as Xero or SAGE and feed this into the auditor's data analytics software, to perform powerful data analytics and produce useful data visualization. This process is quick—performing analytical procedures manually or using excel can be time consuming, so making use of data analytics makes audit planning efficient.

In fact, audit data analytics can be used for than analytical procedures, a point acknowledged by the regulatory bodies. The IAASB has commented that, 'In a complex and high-volume environment, the use of technology and data analytics offers opportunities for the auditor to obtain a more effective and robust understanding of the entity and its environment, enhancing the quality of the auditor's risk assessment and response.'[14] Academic research also suggests that using data analytics provides a cost effective way for auditors to obtain high-quality audit evidence. For example, in their article 'Big Data Analytics in Financial Statement Audits',[15] the authors argue that audits can be made more efficient and effective by the use of big data analytics tools.

Audit data analytics can be used to perform several aspects of analytical review including performing all calculations—trend and common-size analysis, ratio calculations, industry comparisons, identifying anomalies, and highlighting significant variances for further investigation by the auditor.

The analysis is not confined just to accounting information. The auditor can import data from accounting-related systems such as payroll and inventory management, and even external information like exchange rates, interest rates, and inflation.

Using data analytics to perform analytical procedures is not just efficient—it should also enhance the auditor's ability to detect risks of material misstatement. This is because it allows the auditor to sort and filter large amounts of data quickly and easily, so that variances or anomalies which may not have been identified from performing high-level analytical procedures can be picked up. For example, data analytics can be used to quickly analyse revenue trends by day, by specific location, by individual customer, and present the results in a user-friendly way which helps with interpretation. Prior to using audit data analytics, the auditor could have performed this granular level of analysis but it would have been time consuming, so might not have been worth the effort. Now that this detailed analysis can be performed in seconds, auditors can include it in their audit planning easily.

[14] International Auditing and Assurance Standards Board, 'A framework for audit quality key elements that create an environment for audit quality', 2013 <https://www.iaasb.org/publications/framework-audit-quality-key-elements-create-environment-audit-quality-3#:~:text=Through%20this%20Framework%2C%20the%20IAASB,key%20stakeholders%20on%20the%20topic> (accessed 18 January 2024).

[15] Min C., Roman, C., & Trevor S. (2015) 'Big data analytics in financial statement audits', *Accounting horizons*, vol. 29, no. 2, pp. 423–429.

Another way that audit data analytics can be useful is in comparing actual to forecast results. In their article 'Making Audits More Effective through Data Visualization',[16] the authors suggest that:

> Forecasting provides expectations based on historical values and other factors and reflects previous patterns in recorded amounts. Seeing the results of a forecast visually and comparing them to actual results can help auditors quickly identify unusual changes or unexpected trends, helping auditors with their understanding of the client and supporting risk assessment.

You can see how this is a great help in identifying potential risks of material misstatement. Auditors have always compared actual to forecast figures, but using audit data analytics makes this much more efficient and powerful as a tool in audit planning.

Chapter round-up

- Materiality is a way of identifying account balances, classes of transaction, and disclosures which may influence the users of the financial statements.
- Auditors determine an initial level of materiality, but need to revise this as the audit progresses.
- Benchmarks are typically used to set the overall level of materiality, for example, 5 per cent of profit before tax, but this is a matter of judgement and ISA (UK) 320 does not prescribe percentages to be used.
- Performance materiality is used to ensure that individually immaterial errors do not accumulate into a material misstatement.
- Analytical procedures are used at the planning stage of the audit to identify unusual trends or relationships which may indicate a risk of material misstatement.
- A range of techniques can be used to perform analytical procedures, including ratio analysis and trend analysis, as well as comparisons with competitors and industry averages.

End of chapter case study

Introduction

This chapter has looked at some important matters which the auditor must consider when planning an audit. It is crucial that the auditor has performed risk assessment procedures to identify risks of material misstatement as a way to reduce audit risk to an acceptable level. Risk assessment procedures include analytical procedures, which help to identify unusual trends, relationships, and fluctuations which warrant further attention during the audit.

This case study links to the following learning outcomes:

- Discuss and apply the use of the risk-based approach to audit planning (Chapter 9).
- Perform analytical review including the computation and interpretation of relevant trends and ratios (Chapter 10).
- Explain and apply the concepts of materiality and performance materiality (Chapter 10).

[16] Higginbotham, N., Nash, L., & Demeré, W. (2021) 'Making audits more effective through data visualization', *Journal of accountancy* [online], vol. 231, no. 4, pp. 12–17.

Scenario

The Monique Group operates in distribution and haulage, and is based in the UK with its headquarters in Manchester. The Group has a number of subsidiaries, one of which, Davies Ltd, has been loss-making this year due to a new competitor entering the market and taking several key customer contracts from it.

The Group has twenty warehouses and depots across the country, all located near major motorway junctions, airports, and docks. The Group is not listed on a stock market, but it adheres to many principles of the UK Corporate Governance Code. For instance, there are several non-executive directors on the board, and an audit committee and internal audit function have been established.

You are planning the audit of the Group for the financial year ending 20X9, and the information provided below has been given to you by the audit engagement partner, following a meeting he recently held with the Group finance director and representative of the audit committee.

Internal audit findings

Only last week, the internal audit team discovered as a result of their work, that two members of the finance department had colluded in conducting a fraud. The finance team members, who had access to the Group's payroll records, had entered fictitious employees into the payroll system. The salaries of these fictitious employees were paid into a bank account accessed by the finance team members to withdraw the money. The internal audit team discovered the operation of the fraud, but have not investigated how much money was stolen.

In addition, the internal audit team found that an employee working in the procurement department has downloaded a free trial of an inventory management software. His manager, being impressed with the software, has been using it across all of the Group's subsidiaries for the last month. The free trial expires in two weeks.

Financial statement extracts

Table 10.4

Income statement	Notes	Year to 31 March 20X9 (projected) £'000	Year to 30 March 20X8 (actual) £'000
Revenue		45,000	42,500
Operating expenses		(20,500)	(20,000)
Operating profit		24,500	22,500
Finance costs		(5,000)	(5,000)
Profit before tax		19,500	17,500
Tax expense		(4,000)	(4,300)
Profit after tax		15,500	13,200

Table 10.5

Statement of financial position	Notes	31 March 20X9 (projected) £'000	30 March 20X8 (actual) £'000
Non-current assets:			
Property, plant, and equipment	1	130,000	120,000
Intangible assets	2	15,000	15,000
Financial assets	3	7,000	3,500
		152,000	**138,500**

Statement of financial position	Notes	31 March 20X9 (projected) £'000	30 March 20X8 (actual) £'000
Current assets:			
Inventory		200	170
Trade receivables		3,100	3,900
Cash		5,200	4,500
		8,500	**8,570**
Total assets		**160,500**	**147,070**
Equity:			
Share capital		50,000	50,000
Retained earnings		32,500	21,970
		82,500	**71,970**
Non-current liabilities:			
Loans	4	**71,200**	**67,000**
Current liabilities:			
Trade payables		1,500	3,600
Tax and other liabilities		5,300	4,500
		6,800	**8,100**
Total equity and liabilities		**160,500**	**147,070**

Notes to the financial statements:

1. The Group's properties include its head office and storage facilities. The Group accounting policy is to depreciate property over a forty-year useful life. Property, Plant, Equipment also includes the Group's fleet of lorries and delivery vans, which are depreciated over a fifteen-year useful life. According to the finance director, the depreciation policies are 'standard in the haulage industry'. The net book value of the vehicles is £30,000 (20X8–£33,000).
2. The intangible assets comprise goodwill of £15 million arising on the acquisition of the Group's subsidiaries over the years.
3. The Group invests surplus cash in a portfolio of investments. The portfolio is managed by an external financial adviser who takes all decisions regarding the investments and who maintains all accounting records in relation to the investments bought and sold, and the income received from the portfolio.
4. The Group took out some additional long-term finance of £4.2 million, to help fund capital expenditure.

Required

Identify and explain the risks of material misstatement to be considered in planning the audit of the Monique Group's consolidated financial statements for the year ended 31 March 20X9. Use analytical procedures to assist in the identification of risks. Where possible, comment on the materiality of the issues you explain.

Answer

Fraud

The internal audit team have discovered that a fraud has been taking place. While the amount stolen as a result of the fraud might be immaterial (this will be investigated during the audit), the fact that a fraud was not prevented by the Group's internal controls indicates that the control risk of the audit could be high. A risk of misstatement arises in relation to payroll, which may be incorrectly recorded in the financial statements.

Software

Using software which has been downloaded for free without any approval or testing indicates that the control risk of the audit should be approached as a high risk. Any software used in the company's operations should be evaluated and authorized for use prior to being implemented. As the free software has not been tested, it might not the appropriate for use in the Group's operations, and errors might have arisen in recording the movement of inventory. There is a risk of misstatement in relation to inventory. The fact that the software has been used across the Group increases the risk.

Analytical review

Revenue has increased 5.9 per cent, while operating profit has increased 8.9 per cent. This could indicate that profit is overstated, and possibly there is incomplete recording of operating expenses.

The finance cost has remained constant despite the Group taking out a loan of £4.2 million. This could indicate that finance costs are understated (though if the loan was taken out very close to the financial year end, the finance cost would not be expected to increase).

The tax charge has reduced by 7 per cent despite an increase in profit before tax of 11.4 per cent. Another way of looking at this is that the effective tax rate has fallen from 24.6 per cent to 20.5 per cent (the effective tax rate is calculated as tax expense/profit before tax). There is a risk that tax expense is understated.

The receivables days (calculated as trade receivables/revenue x 365) have fallen from 33 (3,900/42,500 x 365) days in 20X8 to 25 (3,100/45,000 x 365) days in 20X9. This indicates a possible understatement of trade receivables.

Property, plant, and equipment

The depreciation period applied to property appears reasonable at forty years. However, the policy of depreciating the lorries over fifteen years seems quite long. This is an estimate and so not capable of precise determination, however, it might not be the case that most lorries will have a useful life which is that long. The rationale that it is 'industry average' is not appropriate—the depreciation policy should be specific to the company's assets. There is a risk that property, plant, and equipment are overstated and depreciation expense is understated. The net book value of the vehicles amounts to 18.7 per cent of the Group's total assets, which would be considered material to the financial statements.

Goodwill

IFRS 3 *Business Combinations* requires goodwill to be reviewed for impairment every year. The goodwill figure has remained the same over the two-year period, indicating that no impairment of goodwill has been recognized during this time. However, one of the subsidiaries, Davies Ltd, is loss-making, and this is a clear indicator of impairment. We are not given information specifically on the monetary value of the goodwill relating to Davies Ltd, but goodwill as a whole amounts to 9.3 per cent of total assets, so the balance in total is material to the financial statements. It is likely that the goodwill relating to Davies Ltd is impaired, and any necessary impairment loss is not recognized, intangible assets will be overstated, and operating expenses are understated.

Financial assets

The financial assets are managed by an external financial adviser, who also records the transactions relating to these investments. There is a risk that the transactions are not properly accounted for during the year or measured appropriately. Financial assets can be complex and subjective, for example, they may need to be measured at fair value at the year end. It is not clear that the financial adviser has the necessary accounting knowledge to ensure that the requirements of IFRS 9 *Financial Instruments* is followed. The financial assets category accounts for 4.4 per cent of total assets and would be considered material to the financial statements.

Activity solutions

Activity 10.1—Material by nature

Can you think of examples of matters which could be material by their nature?

Suggested answer points:

Examples of such items include:

- Misstatements that, when adjusted, would turn a reported profit into a loss.
- Misstatements that, when adjusted, would turn reported net assets into net liabilities or net current assets to net current liabilities.
- Transactions with directors, such as directors' remuneration and personal use of company assets.
- Material uncertainties related to going concern.
- Disclosures relating to potential future legal claims against the company.

Activity 10.2—Applying materiality

Based on what we have learned about materiality, what do you think are the difficulties faced by auditors in determining and applying materiality?

Suggested answer points:

- Use of professional judgement—materiality is by its nature subjective and in particular, inexperienced auditors may find it difficult to apply materiality.
- Lack of prescriptive guidance—ISA (UK) 320 does not contain rules about how materiality should be determined and applied, so different audit firms can have very different methods for using materiality in their audits.
- Quantitative and qualitative materiality—auditors need to consider both factors and it can be challenging to identify non-monetary items such as related party transactions.
- Perspective of the users of the financial statements—materiality should be judged from the point of view of someone making economic decisions based on the financial statements, which can be difficult for auditors to consider.

Activity 10.3—Analysing trends

You are an auditor performing analytical procedures in the audit of a manufacturing company. You notice that revenue has increased by 10 per cent but wages have increased by 25 per cent. You are confident that the increase in revenue is justified. What plausible reasons could there be for the variance between the trends in revenue and wages?

Suggested answer points:

Reasons for the increase in wages could be:

- Wages are increasing as a result of labour market conditions (e.g. there is a short supply of workers, pushing up the cost of labour).
- The government has imposed a regulatory increase in wages that must be paid, which the company has complied with.
- The manufacturing process has become more complex or more inefficient, so employees are working longer hours and therefore being paid more.
- The company has taken on some highly skilled workers, paying higher wages to attract them.

Alternatively, if management cannot provide justifications for the higher-than-expected wages, such as those above, the increase could be due to error or fraud impacting the wages figure.

Activity 10.4—Profit margins

The draft financial statements of an audit client for the year ended 31 December 20X8 show gross profit margins have increased by 6 per cent during the year. Can you suggest some accounting errors which could explain the change in the ratio?

Suggested answer points:

- Overstated revenue: cut-off may be incorrect or the company could have recognized revenue too early.
- Understated cost of sales: purchases may be incomplete (e.g. if accruals have not been made for purchases made before the year end but for which invoices were not received until after the year end).
- Understated cost of sales: this could be due to overvaluation of closing inventory. This would create an overstatement in both the statement of profit or loss and the statement of financial position (i.e. profit and assets would be both overstated).
- Incorrect analysis of expenses: classifying cost of sales expenses as administration expenses would cause an increase in gross margin.

Appendix—Ratios

This appendix is a more detailed explanation of the ratios that are commonly used in financial analysis, including when auditors perform analytical procedures.

1. Profitability and efficiency ratios

$$Return\ on\ equity\left(ROE\right)=\frac{Profit\ after\ tax}{Equity}\times 100$$

$$Return\ on\ capital\ employed\left(ROCE\right)=\frac{Operating\ profit}{Capital\ Employed}\times 100\%$$

$$Asset\ turnover=\frac{Sales\ revenue}{Capital\ employed}$$

$$Sales\ revenue\ to\ non\text{-}current\ assets=\frac{Sales\ revenue}{Non\text{-}current\ assets}$$

$$Gross\ profit\ margin=\frac{Gross\ profit}{Sales\ revenue}\times 100\%$$

$$Operating\ profit\ margin=\frac{Operating\ profit}{Sales\ revenue}\times 100\%$$

$$Operating\ expenses\ to\ sales=\frac{Operating\ expenses}{Sales\ revenue}\times 100\%$$

Return on Capital Employed (ROCE)/Return on Equity (ROE)

Measures performance (i.e. profitability and efficiency as a whole). Higher ROCE indicates better financial performance and efficiency. It means that the capital is being used to generate as much profit as possible. Some companies are capital intensive and have traditionally low ROCE e.g. manufacturing, whereas less capital-intensive businesses have a much higher ROCE. If new assets are being purchased, watch this figure for fluctuations, it takes time for new assets to reach optimal efficiency.

- ROCE: Considers all sources of long-term finance (i.e. capital employed).
- ROE: considers only the shareholders' equity (i.e. ordinary/equity shares and reserves and not preference shares and long-term liabilities).

Asset turnover (or sales revenue to capital employed)

This is similar to ROCE but measures the efficiency in generating sales revenue rather than profit. A higher ratio indicates a more efficient use of total capital.

Sales revenue to non-current assets

Similar to asset turnover but measuring how efficiently non-current assets are used to generate revenue. This is useful for capital-intensive manufacturing businesses where non-current assets are the main type of asset used within the business model.

Gross margin

A higher margin indicates more profitability and is therefore good. It indicates that costs are being controlled. The margin is also affected by sales price, product mix, and cost of sales, including inventory valuation.

What is considered a good or bad margin will depend upon the nature of the industry. Businesses with a rapid turnover tend to have lower gross profit percentages than those with low turnover of goods.

Operating margin

A higher margin indicates more profitability and is therefore good. Operating margins should be stable to indicate a good control over costs, though in times of rapid growth, this can be difficult to achieve. What is considered a good or bad margin will again depend upon the nature of the industry.

A good or bad margin could arise out of a mixture of things.

- degree of competitiveness in the marketplace;
- the economic situation;
- the ability of the company to make its product stand out;
- the ability of managers to control expenses;
- one-off or exceptional items which distort expense in a particular year.

Operating expenses to sales

A lower operating expenses-to-sales ratio indicates good control of operating expenses (or overheads) and so is good for profitability.

2. Liquidity ratios

$$Current\ ratio = \frac{Current\ assets}{Current\ liabilities}$$

$$Quick\ ratio = \frac{Current\ assets - inventory}{Current\ liabilities}$$

Current ratio

Compares current assets with liabilities due within the same period. It tells us if the company has sufficient short-term assets (inventory, receivables, and cash) to meet current liabilities when they are due for payment.

A current ratio greater than 1 is considered necessary for traditional manufacturing companies. If the ratio = 1, it means that there is just enough current asset to pay off current liabilities.

A high current ratio is not necessarily a good thing—it could indicate that inventories are stockpiling, may be obsolete or not sellable, customers are unable to pay, or just very slow paying. Even having a very high cash balance could indicate poor management, as the cash could be invested for a better return.

Service and retail companies often have a current ratio less than 1.0 and this does not indicate liquidity problems. This can be related to the company's working capital cycle, and so working capital ratios (inventory turnover period, settlement period for trade receivables, and settlement period for trade payables) can help to provide further explanation.

Quick ratio

Same as current ratio but inventory is omitted. The quick ratio is a tighter test of liquidity for manufacturing companies, where it is not always possible to sell inventories quickly to realize cash, especially if a large proportion of the inventory is raw materials or work in progress.

It is also known as the acid test ratio.

3. Working capital management

Inventory days

$$\frac{Inventory \times 365\,days}{Cost\ of\ sales}$$

Receivables days

$$\frac{Trade\ receivables \times 365\ days}{Sales\ revenue}$$

Trade payables days

$$\frac{Trade\ payables \times 365\ days}{Cost\ of\ sales}$$

Inventory days

This measures how long the business takes to sell its inventory, on average.

For many manufacturing companies, an inventory turnover period of thirty to sixty days is considered normal, but if they are operating a just-in-time system this would be expected to be lower. Generally, businesses will try to keep inventory days as short as possible, to ensure sales are made quickly. Holding high levels of inventory can cause problems with short-term cash flow as well as incurring costs relating to storage and insurance.

Retailers usually have lower inventory turnover periods than manufacturers, as they do not hold raw material or work in progress. Many businesses try to implement 'just in time' inventory systems to reduce their inventory holding period as much as possible. In a just-in-time system, deliveries from suppliers arrive 'just in time' for the goods received to enter production or go onto the shelves of a retail organization.

Service companies would be expected to have very limited inventory.

Receivables' collection period

This tells us how long, on average, it takes for the company to collect money from its customers. This will depend on the credit terms offered by the company. Thirty to sixty days are quite common for manufacturers, but retailers are usually paid in cash or by debit or credit card and so have much lower settlement periods on average.

Generally, it should be lower than payables' payments days (see below).

If this ratio is rising, it may raise questions about company ability to collect money (i.e. problem with credit control), and may cause cash flow problems.

Payables' payment period

This tells us how long, on average, it takes for the company to pay its suppliers and other short-term liabilities.

If it is falling or very low, it raises the question as to whether the company is paying its bills too fast. This may be a deliberate action to receive prompt payment discounts from suppliers.

Extending the payables payments period can be considered an essential source of finance by companies, helping them to manage their overall cash flow.

Operating cycle

You can combine together the inventory holding period, receivables settlement, and payables settlement periods to calculate the operating cycle or working capital of the company. This shows how well short-term cash flows are managed and links to the level of cash generated from operating activities. The operating cycle shows the balance between the time it takes to collect cash from customers and the time it takes to pay suppliers. It is usually calculated as inventory days + receivables days – payables days. If the cash is paid on average to the supplier before the cash is received from customers, this can indicate working capital (i.e. short-term cash management) problems.

4. Gearing/long-term financial stability

$$Gearing = \frac{Debt}{Debt + equity} \times 100\%$$

$$Debt\ to\ equity = \frac{Debt}{Equity} \times 100\%$$

$$Interest\ cover = \frac{Operating\ profit}{Finance\ charges}$$

Gearing ratio

Financial gearing measures the level of financial risk a company has taken. A ratio of less than 30 per cent is often considered to indicate a safe level of gearing. Some suggest that a ratio of more than 50 per cent indicates high (risky) levels of financial gearing.

There are several accepted ways to look at gearing—some analysts prefer the debt–equity ratio—but it doesn't really matter which you use as long as you are consistent.

It is very useful to also consider the interest cover ratio to get a clearer understanding of the levels of financial risk.

Interest cover

This measures how easily operating profits cover interest expense. If this is less than 1.0, then the company's operating profit is not sufficient to cover finance charges. This is not likely to be sustainable in the long run. Safer levels are given by an interest cover of over 3 or 4.

Interest cover is affected by both the company's level of debt and its profitability.

11 Audit Assertions and Obtaining Audit Evidence

Introduction

As we saw in Chapter 7, the auditor must carry out a significant amount of work during the planning stage of the audit. We have already seen that during audit planning, the auditor develops a thorough understanding of the client, the environment in which it operates, and the nature of the internal controls in place, and that this understanding drives the development of the audit strategy and the audit plan. The audit plan contains detailed audit procedures which are performed during audit fieldwork. Ultimately, the audit engagement partner will use this audit evidence obtained from performing audit procedures to conclude on whether the financial statements give a true and fair view (or present fairly, in all material respects)—that is, express their opinion on the financial statements.

In this chapter, we will examine the principles which the auditor should follow when designing the audit procedures included in the audit plan. A key consideration when designing audit procedures is the financial statement assertions and the vital part which they play in the financial reporting process. We will also consider the sources of audit evidence and the requirements for the auditor to obtain sufficient and appropriate audit evidence to support the audit opinion. We will then move into the area of audit sampling which is a technique used by the auditor to obtain audit evidence without testing every transaction that makes up a particular figure in the financial statements. We will also consider the increased use of audit data analytics tools and think about the benefits, but also the challenges, of implementing these techniques. We will then round off the chapter by considering the timing of audit fieldwork, focusing on the interim audit, when particular types of work are likely to be performed.

The key ISAs we will be looking at in this chapter are:

- ISA (UK) 330 The Auditor's Responses to Assessed Risks
- ISA (UK) 500 Audit Evidence
- ISA (UK) 530 Audit Sampling

Learning outcomes

- Explain how the auditor responds to assessed risks at the financial statement level and the assertion level.
- Discuss the types of procedure used to obtain audit evidence including tests of controls and substantive procedures.
- Explain how an audit strategy is determined and explain the use of audit programmes.
- Describe the methods used to obtain audit evidence, including inspection, observation, external confirmation, recalculation, reperformance, analytical procedures, inquiry, and recommend relevant sources of audit evidence.
- Discuss and apply the requirements relating to obtaining sufficient and appropriate audit evidence.
- Define audit sampling, explain the need for sampling, and discuss how auditors apply sampling techniques to obtain audit evidence.
- Describe the use of audit data analytics and discuss the associated benefits and challenges.
- Outline the type of work that is typically performed at the interim stage of the audit.

By the end of the chapter, you should be able to:

- Discuss factors impacting the quality and quantity and the relevance and reliability of audit evidence.
- Assess how the nature, timing, and extent of tests of controls and substantive procedures are impacted by audit planning.

11.1 Responding to assessed risks

ISA (UK) 330 *The Auditor's Responses to Assessed Risks* provides guidance on how the auditor should design audit procedures. ISA (UK) 330 states:

> The objective of the auditor is to obtain sufficient appropriate audit evidence regarding the assessed risks of material misstatement, through designing and implementing appropriate responses to those risks.[1]

ISA (UK) 330 requires the auditor to respond to risks identified at two levels: the financial statement level, and the assertion level.

We explored the concept of risk identification at these two levels in Chapter 9. In this section, we will consider how the auditor responds to the risks identified.

[1] FRC, 'ISA (UK) 330', 2017, para 3 <https://media.frc.org.uk/documents/ISA_UK_330_-_Revised_July_2017_Updated_May_2022.pdf> (accessed 18 January 2024).

11.1.1 **Responding to risks at the financial statement level**

Responses to risks at the financial statement level are also known as overall responses. These are responses to risks that potentially pervade the whole financial statement and are not specific to particular transactions or balances. Audit planning, especially risk assessment, may indicate many different factors that create risk at the financial statement level. We saw many examples of this in Chapter 9. As a reminder, financial statement level risks identified by the auditor could include:

Going concern difficulties—this may increase the risk of management bias in financial reporting, as management wish to present healthy financial statements (e.g. by overstating profit or understating liabilities).

Lack of management competence—lack of personnel, especially at senior level within the organization, with appropriate accounting and financial reporting skills means that the entity's financial statements could be incorrectly prepared.

Risk of management override—where controls can be easily overridden (e.g. if there is not an effective supervisory control or segregation of duty).

Non-recurring events such as a significant reorganization—unusual events increase the risk of incorrect accounting treatments or a lack of disclosure.

The common feature of all of the examples above is that they could lead to misstatements in many areas of the financial statements and are not necessarily specific to particular transactions or balances.

There are many ways the auditor could choose to respond to the financial statement level risks identified (Figure 11.1).

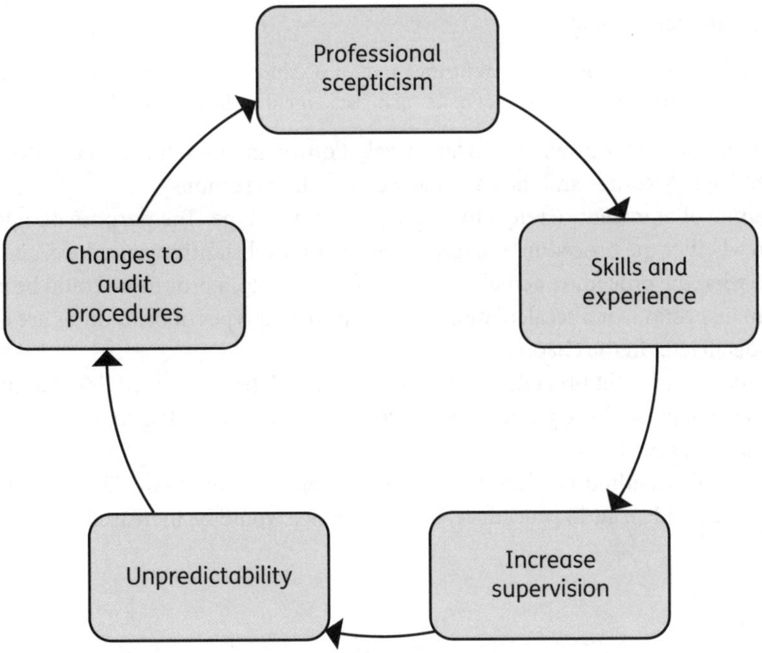

Figure 11.1 Overall responses to risks at the financial statement level

Emphasizing to the audit team the need to maintain professional scepticism

This is particularly important where the auditor identifies a risk in relation to the reliability of representations made by management. Professional scepticism is also crucial where fraud risks have been identified.

Assigning more experienced staff or those with special skills or using experts

The use of experts or experienced audit staff would be a response to risks created by complex or highly subjective accounting issues or disclosure requirements.

Providing more supervision

Supervision is an element of good quality management, so increasing the amount of supervision is an appropriate response in any audit where a relatively high level of risk at the financial statement level has been identified.

Incorporating elements of unpredictability in the selection of further audit procedures to be performed

Unpredictability can be used as an effective response where the auditor has identified risks relating to fraud.

Making general changes to the nature, timing, or extent of audit procedures

This can include performing substantive procedures at the period end instead of at an interim date.

11.1.2 **Responding to risks at the assertion level**

ISA (UK) 330 requires that:

> the auditor shall design and perform further audit procedures whose nature, timing and extent are responsive to the assessed risks of material misstatement at the assertion level.[2]

This is an important requirement, so let's break it down and look first at the 'nature, timing and extent' of procedures and then at what we mean by 'assertions'.

The *nature* of a procedure refers to its purpose and its type. The purpose of a procedure relates to whether the procedure is a test of control or a substantive procedure, and the type relates to what the procedure actually involves, for example, a procedure could be an observation, an inspection, or a recalculation. The purpose and types of procedures are discussed in more detail later in the chapter.

The *timing* of an audit procedure refers to when it will be performed, for example, at the interim stage of the audit (e.g. a receivables circularization), or at the completion stage (e.g. a going concern review).

The *extent* of an audit procedure relates to the amount of work that will be carried out, for example, to extend an audit procedure, the sample size would be increased.

[2] Ibid., para 6.

Financial statement **assertions** are claims made by an entity's management with regard to the financial statements. ISA (UK) 315 *Identifying and Assessing the Risks of Material* defines the term 'assertions' as:

> Representations, explicit or otherwise, with respect to the recognition, measurement, presentation and disclosure of information in the financial statements which are inherent in management representing that the financial statements are prepared in accordance with the applicable financial reporting framework. Assertions are used by the auditor to consider the different types of potential misstatements that may occur when identifying, assessing and responding to the risks of material misstatement.[3]

Auditing scenario 11.1 Management assertion

The financial statements of Morley Industries Ltd for the year ended 31 December 20X9 show that the entity has purchased a freehold building during the year amounting to £1.2 million.

In this example, management have 'asserted' that they have the right to include this building in the financial statements because they have capitalized it on the statement of financial position as freehold property.

The auditor will therefore test this assertion, known as the rights and obligations assertion, by tracing the asset to title deeds to ensure that the company does, in fact, own the building. The title deeds should show the name of Morley Industries Ltd as owner. If it does, the auditor can take comfort in the fact that the company does rightly own the asset and that audit evidence is available to support the rights and obligations assertion.

There are three types of assertions (see Figure 11.2).

11.1.2.1 Assertions about classes of transactions and events, and related disclosures

According to ISA (UK) 315, there are six assertions related to classes of transactions and events, and related disclosures which are set out in Table 11.1.

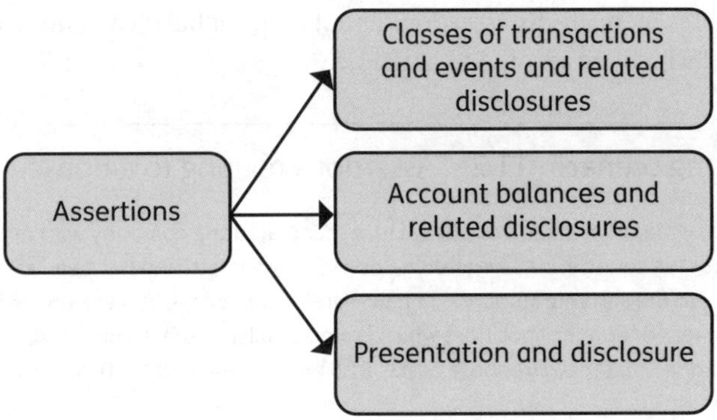

Figure 11.2 Types of assertions

[3] FRC, 'ISA (UK) 315', 2020, para 12(a) <https://media.frc.org.uk/documents/ISA_UK_315_Jul_2020.pdf> (accessed 18 January 2024).

Table 11.1 Assertions relating to transactions and events

Occurrence	Transactions and events that have been recorded or disclosed, have occurred, and such transactions and events pertain to the entity
Completeness	All transactions and events that should have been recorded have been recorded, and all related disclosures that should have been included in the financial statements have been included
Accuracy	Amounts and other data relating to recorded transactions and events have been recorded appropriately, and related disclosures have been appropriately measured and described
Cutoff	Transactions and events have been recorded in the correct accounting period
Classification	Transactions and events have been recorded in the proper accounts
Presentation	Transactions and events are appropriately aggregated or disaggregated, and clearly described, and related disclosures are relevant and understandable in the context of the requirements of the applicable financial reporting framework

Table 11.2 Assertions relating to account balances

Existence	Assets, liabilities, and equity interests exist
Rights and obligations	The entity holds or controls the rights to assets, and liabilities are the obligations of the entity
Completeness	All assets, liabilities, and equity interests that should have been recorded have been recorded, and all related disclosures that should have been included in the financial statements have been included
Accuracy, valuation, and allocation	Assets, liabilities, and equity interests have been included in the financial statements at appropriate amounts and any resulting valuation or allocation adjustments have been appropriately recorded, and related disclosures have been appropriately measured and described
Classification	Assets, liabilities, and equity interests have been recorded in the proper accounts
Presentation	Assets, liabilities, and equity interests are appropriately aggregated or disaggregated and clearly described, and related disclosures are relevant and understandable in the context of the requirements of the applicable financial reporting framework

11.1.2.2 Assertions about account balances, and related disclosures

ISA (UK) 315 states there are six assertions about account balances, and related disclosures at the period end which are set out in Table 11.2.

Auditing scenario 11.2 Assertions relating to a non-current asset

Lizzie has been assigned to the audit of Rocky Ltd, a manufacturing company with many properties around the country. Lizzie is auditing non-current assets, and has been asked to obtain evidence relating to the carrying amount of a new warehouse, recognized at £1.5 million in the company's statement of financial position, which is a material amount. From the accounting records, Lizzie can see that the warehouse cost is £1.6 million, and £100,000 depreciation was charged this year.

In terms of existence, Lizzie should physically verify the warehouse (i.e. go and see it) to make sure that it really exists. This, however, does not provide assurance that Rocky Ltd has the right to include the asset on its statement of financial position. Lizzie should check that the company occupies the building, which again can be done through physical verification, and that the warehouse is being used. This is basically to confirm that the warehouse meets the definition of property, plant, and equipment (PPE) in accordance with IAS 16 *Property, Plant and Equipment*, which relates to the classification assertion.

Lizzie will also obtain evidence in respect of rights and obligations, by obtaining the title deeds to the property, confirming that Rocky Ltd is named as the owner. Lizzie can also review the legal documents relating to the purchase of the warehouse which should state that the company owns the warehouse.

Lizzie needs to confirm the cost of the asset, for example, by agreeing the cash payment to a bank statement. This will provide evidence as to the valuation assertion. Lizzie will also need to examine the appropriateness of the depreciation charge, in particular the estimated useful life of the warehouse, as this is an area of judgement.

In terms of completeness, Lizzie should check that all of the relevant costs associated with the purchase of the warehouse have been capitalized into its cost, again in accordance with IAS 16. This might include legal fees, site preparation, and other costs to get the warehouse ready for use in the manner intended by management.

Presentation relates to how information relating to the warehouse is presented in the financial statements. The warehouse will be categorized within PPE, so Lizzie needs to check the disclosures in the notes to the financial statements are in line with IAS 16.

11.1.2.3 **Assertions about disclosures**

ISA (UK) 315 states that the assertions described in respect of transactions, events, and balances, adapted as appropriate, may also be used by the auditor in considering the different types of potential misstatements that may occur in disclosures not directly related to recorded classes of transactions, events, or account balances.

When testing assertions about disclosures, the auditor will often use a disclosure checklist to ensure the disclosures are complete and conform to accounting standards and the requirements of the company law. It is important that the checklist is up to date for any developments or changes in accounting standards that impact on disclosures.

11.2 **Designing audit procedures**

Audit procedures are the methods used by the audit team to obtain audit evidence. There are two types of audit procedure—tests of control and substantive procedures. Substantive procedures are then subdivided into substantive analytical procedures and tests of detail. See Figure 11.3.

11.2.1 **Tests of control**

Tests of control involve the auditor ascertaining whether the client's internal control environment is operating effectively (i.e. to enable the auditor to evaluate the operating effectiveness of a specific control that either prevents or detects misstatements at the assertion level).

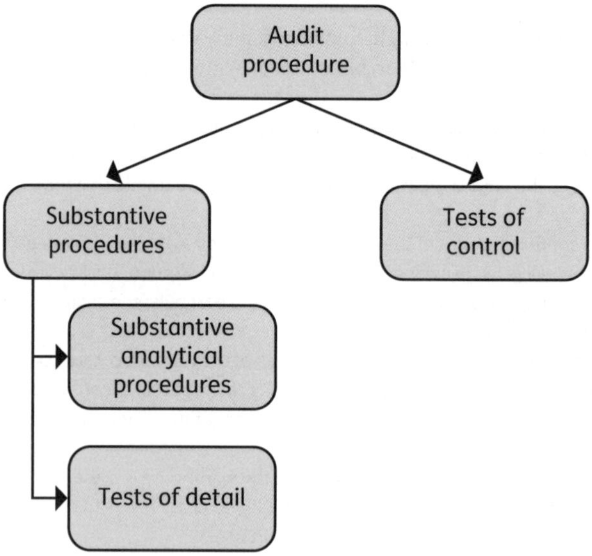

Figure 11.3 Types of audit procedure

Note that tests of control do not focus on any monetary amounts stated in the financial statements—they provide evidence of whether a control procedure has operated effectively.

Placing reliance on internal controls can be an efficient audit strategy, but the auditor cannot simply assume that controls are operating effectively. As we saw in Chapter 8, when the auditor wishes to rely on an internal control, they must test the control to obtain evidence that it is effective, including that the control has operated throughout the year.

Examples of tests of controls could include:

- *Block testing*—this is where one aspect of a control system is tested. For example, a block of 200 suppliers' invoices received could be tested to confirm that they have been signed as approved prior to being entered into the accounting system. Another example is that a block of, say, one hundred credit application forms from customers are inspected by the auditor to ensure that credit limits are authorized by a responsible official. This test provides comfort to the auditor that credit is not granted to customers who may not be able to pay, so indirectly provides evidence of the valuation of trade receivables.
- *Observing staff at work*—this could be important at an inventory count, for the auditor to get an impression as to whether the inventory count procedures are being followed. Another example is that the auditor may observe staff clocking in and out of the factory or warehouse; this type of test provides the auditor with assurance that staff are not paid for hours not worked.
- *Testing of outputs*—the auditor may trace the output of an element of the accounting system back to source documentation, to gain comfort on the audit trail, for example, tracing a payroll run summary back to HR records.

ISA (UK) 330 states:

> The auditor shall design and perform tests of controls to obtain sufficient appropriate audit evidence as to the operating effectiveness of relevant controls if:
>
> (a) The auditor's assessment of risks of material misstatement at the assertion level includes an expectation that the controls are operating effectively (that is, the auditor intends to rely on the operating effectiveness of controls in determining the nature, timing and extent of substantive procedures); or
>
> (b) Substantive procedures alone cannot provide sufficient appropriate audit evidence at the assertion level.[4]

Tests of control should only be performed where the auditor expects that controls are properly designed and are operating well. There is no point in testing controls if the auditor thinks that they are ineffective. In this situation, the auditor will base their audit plan on performing substantive audit procedures, and will discuss the internal control deficiencies with management.

In rare situations, the auditor may have to perform tests of controls because the use of substantive procedures cannot provide sufficient, appropriate audit evidence. ISA (UK) 330 provides an example where this may be the case, describing an entity which conducts its business using IT and no documentation of transactions is produced or maintained, other than through the IT system. In this case, it would not be possible to perform substantive procedures such as inspecting documents, so tests of control on the IT system would be used to provide audit evidence.

11.2.1.1 Tests of controls versus obtaining an understanding of controls

Testing of controls (i.e. testing the operating effectiveness of controls) is different from obtaining an initial understanding of controls and evaluating their design and implementation. It would be logical to obtain an initial understanding, then to evaluate, and then depending on the results decide the extent of tests of controls which should be performed. However, the same types of audit procedures are often used to obtain understanding, evaluate, and test the controls. The auditor may, therefore, decide it is efficient to test the operating effectiveness of controls at the same time as evaluating their design and determining that they have been implemented.

Activity 11.1 Reliance on internal controls

What matters should an auditor consider in deciding whether to place reliance on a client's internal controls?

11.2.1.2 Nature, extent, and timing of tests of controls

The nature of tests of controls refers to the type of procedure that is performed. ISA (UK) 330 states that inquiry alone is not sufficient to obtain audit evidence about the operating

[4] FRC, 'ISA (UK) 330', 2017, para 8.

effectiveness of the controls. Other types of procedure must be performed as well as, or instead of, inquiry. This is so that the auditor's evidence is not solely based on discussion or representations from management regarding the operating effectiveness of controls. Additional procedures could include the inspection of documentation relevant to the particular control being tested.

In terms of the extent of tests of controls, this will be driven by consideration of a number of matters including the extent of planned reliance on controls by the auditor, the expected rate of deviation from a control which has operated, and the consistency of application of controls during the period being audited.

The auditor needs to consider when tests of control should be performed. If planning to rely on a control throughout the whole period which is subject to audit, then it makes sense to test that the control has operated effectively throughout that period. If the auditor only tested the control at the year end, this would not provide evidence that the control has operated effectively during the whole year.

This means that tests of control are often performed during the year, at the interim phase of the audit. We will consider the interim audit in more detail later on in the chapter.

11.2.1.3 **Using audit evidence relating to internal controls obtained in previous audits**

In many situations, the design of the client's internal controls will not change substantially year on year, in which case it might be a waste of audit effort to test the controls in exactly the same way every year. However, just because the design of the internal controls may not have changed, their operating effectiveness could vary year on year.

A simple illustration is that a company might have a control designed over a particular matter (e.g. a member of staff performs a supplier statement reconciliation every month). However, due to staff shortages, the staff member does not have the time to perform the reconciliation each month. The design of the control has not changed, but clearly its operating effectiveness is reduced.

This means that the auditor cannot simply rely on the audit evidence obtained in previous years with regard to internal controls. Some work has to be performed every year. However, ISA (UK) 330 takes a pragmatic approach and does not require full tests of controls to be performed every year. The approach that is required is as follows.

The auditor obtains audit evidence, using inquiry, observation, and inspection, about whether significant changes in those controls have occurred since the previous audit. Then, depending on the outcome of this:

- If there have been changes in internal controls which means that the audit evidence previously obtained is no longer relevant, the auditor performs test of controls in the current audit.
- If there have not been changes in internal controls impacting on the relevance of previously obtained audit evidence, the auditor must test the controls at least once in every third audit, and must also test some controls in each audit.
- However, if the auditor plans to rely on controls over a risk the auditor has determined to be a significant risk, the auditor must test those controls in the current period.

11.2.1.4 Evaluating the results of tests of controls

It is important to remember that when performing tests of control, the auditor is obtaining evidence relating to the effectiveness of a control procedure rather than a specific transaction. If the results of the controls testing indicates that the control is not operating effectively, the auditor should consider the following:

- Is the control failure revealed by the test of control an isolated incident, or is it systematic and indicative of wider control failure?
- What is the reason for the control failure?
- Did the control fail at one particular time, or throughout the period being audited?
- Should the controls testing be extended to include a wider sample?
- Should the sample not be extended, which might not be an efficient response, and instead further substantive procedures be performed?

These considerations are in accordance with ISA (UK) 330 which states that:

> If deviations from controls upon which the auditor intends to rely are detected, the auditor shall make specific inquiries to understand these matters and their potential consequences, and shall determine whether:
>
> a) The tests of controls that have been performed provide an appropriate basis for reliance on the controls;
>
> b) Additional tests of controls are necessary; or
>
> c) The potential risks of misstatement need to be addressed using substantive procedures.[5]

It is quite common to find instances of control failure when performing tests of control. No organization's systems and controls are perfect, no matter how well designed they might be. Instances of non-compliance with prescribed controls are known as deviations, and might be caused by simple issues such as changes in personnel leaving a control unperformed, or human error. ISA (UK) 330 recognizes that deviations are common and suggests that the auditor should compare the detected rate of deviation to an expected rate of deviation to consider whether the control can be relied upon or not.

If the auditor concludes that the control which has been tested now cannot be relied upon, further substantive procedures should be performed.

In addition, the auditor may need to discuss the control failure with management in accordance with ISA (UK) 265 *Communicating Deficiencies in Internal Control to Those Charged with Governance and Management*—we will explore this ISA (UK) in Chapter 18.

Auditing scenario 11.3 Tests of controls

Kate is working on the audit of Barca Ltd, and has just completed tests of controls on the authorization of discounts offered to customers. Discounts have to be approved by the company's sales manager, and the operation of this control is evidenced by the manager's signature on the

[5] Ibid., para 17.

customer order documentation and the sales invoice. Kate found that in four cases out of fifty orders and invoices selected for testing, there was no signature to evidence that the discount had been approved by the sales manager.

In this case, Kate should:

- Discuss the results of the testing with the sales manager, to understand the reason for the control failure in four cases out of fifty.
- Consider extending the sample to determine if the four instances of the control not operating were isolated or not.

If further testing reveals that the control failure was relatively isolated (e.g. only occurred at a certain time), for instance, when the sales manager was on holiday, then the control can be relied upon to some extent, to reduce substantive testing.

If further testing reveals that the control failure is not isolated, further substantive procedures should be planned and the control deficiency notified to management in accordance with ISA (UK) 265.

11.2.2 **Substantive procedures**

Substantive procedures are procedures adopted by the auditor that aim to detect material misstatement at the assertion level and focus on monetary amounts stated in the financial statements. There are two types of substantive procedure:

- *tests of detail* which provide audit evidence relating to individual transactions and balances; and
- *substantive analytical procedures* which involve the evaluation of financial information through the analysis of plausible relationships among both financial and non-financial data.

Tests of detail involve the auditor obtaining evidence in relation to the individual amounts that make up classes of transactions, account balances, or financial statement disclosures. Tests of detail provide assurance over a particular transaction, balance, or disclosure in the financial statements, for example, over individual trade receivables balances which make up the total balance.

Examples of tests of detail could include:

- physical verification of a sample of additions to non-current assets;
- obtaining confirmation from trade receivables of the amounts outstanding at the year end;
- reperforming a selection of supplier statement reconciliations;
- recalculating a complex figure, such as an exchange rate gain or loss; and
- tracing a selection of items recognized in revenue back to supporting documentation (i.e. signed customer order, goods despatched note, invoice raised).

The benefits of performing tests of detail are that they are a reliable source of evidence because they are performed by the auditor. Also, tests of detail provide specific evidence over particular balances, so are effective in providing assurance on high-risk transactions and balances.

Tests of detail are often performed on a sample basis, in which case the reliability and sufficiency of the evidence obtained will be subject to sampling risk, which will be discussed in more detail later in the chapter.

Substantive analytical procedures are performed as a means of obtaining audit evidence by analysing the relationships between financial and non-financial information in order to evaluate the reasonableness of financial information. Substantive analytical procedures provide assurance over classes of transactions or balances, for example, over trade receivables as a whole.

ISA (UK) 330 (para 18) requires that irrespective of the assessed risks of material misstatement, the auditor shall design and perform substantive procedures for each material class of transactions, account balance, and disclosure.

11.2.2.1 Nature and extent of substantive procedures

It is down to the auditor's judgement to decide whether to use just tests of detail or a combination of tests of detail and substantive analytical procedures. In some cases, for example, where there is persuasive evidence from tests of controls, performing only substantive analytical procedures will provide sufficient audit evidence. Conversely, the extent of substantive procedures (both tests of detail and substantive analytical procedures) may need to be increased when the results from tests of controls are unsatisfactory.

The auditor will normally plan to perform substantive analytical procedures before performing tests of detail because the results of substantive analytical procedures can impact the nature and extent of detailed testing. Substantive analytical procedures might direct attention to areas of increased risk and therefore more tests of detail will be needed, and conversely the assurance obtained from effective substantive analytical procedures can reduce the number of tests of detail that need to be conducted.

Substantive analytical procedures are often quick to conduct and provide reliable, auditor-generated evidence. The application of substantive analytical procedures is based on the expectation that relationships among data exist. The presence of these relationships provides audit evidence as to the completeness, accuracy, and occurrence of transactions. Therefore, substantive analytical procedures can respond to risk at the assertion level.

The extent of audit procedures, whether tests on controls or substantive procedures, must always be linked to materiality and audit risk (ISA (UK) 330 para A15). Generally, the lower the level of materiality and the higher the level of audit risk assessed, the more extensive the audit procedures that will need to be performed, including increasing sample sizes.

Keep in mind that tests of controls focus on the client's internal control environment, whereas substantive procedures focus on the amounts and disclosures in the financial statements themselves.

Also, it is common to use substantive analytical procedures in combination with tests of detail on the same assertion—this increases the persuasiveness of the evidence obtained. But it still may not be possible to use substantive analytical procedures alone to provide sufficient evidence.

11.2.2.2 Mandatory use of substantive audit procedures

The auditor must perform substantive procedures related to the financial statement closing process, in relation to:

- Agreeing or reconciling the financial statements with the underlying accounting records, including agreeing or reconciling information in disclosures, whether such information is obtained from within or outside of the general and subsidiary ledgers; and
- Examining material journal entries and other adjustments made during the course of preparing the financial statements.[6]

The nature and extent of substantive procedures performed in relation to the above will depend on the nature and complexity of the financial reporting process and the associated risks of material misstatement. For example, if a client has a newly appointed finance director, the auditor is likely to conclude that there is a relatively high risk of misstatement due to the finance director's lack of experience with the audited entity's financial statement closing procedures and may therefore extend substantive testing in this area.

The auditor is also required to perform substantive procedures to evaluate whether the overall presentation of the financial statements, including related disclosures, is in accordance with the applicable financial reporting framework. This includes an assessment of the classification and description of financial information, the terminology used, and the amount of detail given.

ISA (UK) 330 states that

> If the auditor has determined that an assessed risk of material misstatement at the assertion level is a significant risk, the auditor shall perform substantive procedures that are specifically responsive to that risk. When the approach to a significant risk consists only of substantive procedures, those procedures shall include tests of details.[7]

We have already seen that audit procedures generally should respond to assessed risks. ISA (UK) 330 para 21 extends that principle to require that when a significant risk is identified, the auditor MUST conduct substantive procedures.

To summarize, substantive procedures (either tests of detail or substantive analytical procedures) are performed on:

- all material classes of transactions, balances, and disclosures;
- all assertions that are evaluated to contain a significant risk of material misstatement;
- the financial statement closing process;
- presentation and disclosures in the financial statements.

[6] Ibid., para 20. [7] Ibid., para 21.

11.3 Audit strategy and audit programmes

11.3.1 Determining an appropriate audit strategy

In Chapter 7 we considered the requirements for the auditor to develop an audit strategy and audit plan. As a reminder, the audit strategy sets out in general terms how the audit is to be conducted. It sets the scope, timing, and direction of the audit, which should then guide the development of the audit plan. The audit plan contains the detailed responses to the auditor's risk assessment including the specific planned audit procedures which will be carried out to implement the strategy and obtain sufficient appropriate audit evidence to support the audit opinion.

This is a very important part of the audit, so let's recap what we have seen so far. In some circumstances, the auditor may plan to use an audit strategy that is based on tests of controls. This depends very much on the auditor's initial assessment of the control environment. If the auditor concludes that the internal control environment of an entity is weak or non-existent, the auditor will not place reliance on it. Instead, the auditor will carry out extended substantive procedures in an attempt to generate sufficient and appropriate audit evidence for the relevant assertion being tested.

Tests of control should only be performed on controls that the auditor has determined are suitably designed to prevent, or detect and correct a material misstatement in an assertion. As we have already discussed, there is no point in testing a control that is not considered to be effective. Therefore, generally, if an audited entity is considered at initial assessment to have properly designed controls that have operated effectively through the accounting period, the auditor may choose to test the controls in order to place reliance on them. The auditor is likely to adopt this audit strategy in situations where:

- There have been little deviations from internal control procedures in the past during previous audits.
- Interim audit procedures applied suggest the internal control environment has been operating effectively during the year.

To summarize, depending on the risks of material misstatement, the auditor may decide to place reliance on the entity's internal control environment. This does not mean, however, that auditors do not have to do any detailed substantive testing because they do—auditors cannot just place 100 per cent reliance on the control environment, but they can use reliance on the internal controls to reduce the level of substantive testing they do.

Alternatively, the auditor may choose not to place reliance on the entity's internal control environment and carry out more detailed substantive testing. The auditor may choose a more substantive approach to reduce detection risk. This may be the case when the auditor concludes that the client's internal control environment is weak or has not been operating effectively throughout the accounting period. Figure 11.4 summarises different audit strategies.

A strategy focusing on substantive procedures (which can be tests of detail or substantive analytical procedures) is typically used when the initial assessment is that controls cannot be relied upon. Table 11.3 sets out where this may occur.

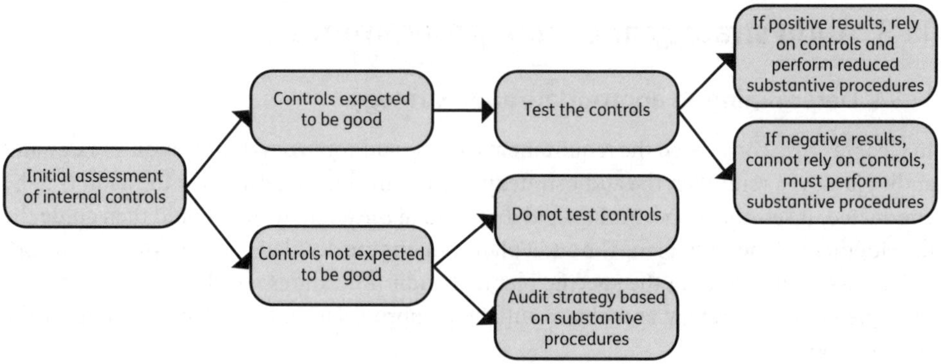

Figure 11.4 Audit strategies

Table 11.3 Matters impacting on audit strategy

Situation	Examples
There is a poor control environment	• where management does not encourage a culture which embraces controls • where an appropriate 'tone at the top' has not been established • there is no established internal audit function • there has been a history of fraud due to manipulation of weaknesses in the internal control environment • management have an aggressive operating style and there is scope for management override of the controls
There is a lack of controls	• in a newly established system where controls have not yet been established • there are few staff meaning that segregation of duty is not possible • there are non-routine transactions and events over which no controls have put in place
Controls are ineffective	• there is management override of controls • there are too few staff to properly operate controls • controls have not been properly designed

A substantive audit strategy would be appropriate where a test of controls would be less efficient. However, the auditor needs to be satisfied that performing only substantive procedures for the relevant assertions would be effective in reducing the risk of material misstatement to an acceptably low level.

Auditing scenario 11.4 Weak internal controls over the payroll cycle

The audit senior has been testing the internal controls over the payroll cycle which have been documented as follows:

- The hours worked report is extracted from the electronic clocking-in system.
- The hours worked are input into the payroll software by Caroline Smith who is the payroll clerk.

- Overtime worked is input into the payroll software by Caroline Smith.
- A first draft of the payroll is produced and is reviewed by Caroline Smith.
- If the figures on the payroll are in line with last month's payroll, the payroll is finalized by Caroline Smith and she prepares the bank transfer form.
- The bank transfer form is signed by the finance director but no checks are carried out by the finance director.
- The employees are paid by bank transfer once the transfer authority has been signed.

In this example, there is no segregation of duties over the payroll. It would therefore be inappropriate for the auditor to rely on the controls over the payroll because the only one that seems to be present is the fact that the bank authority transfer is signed by the finance director, who carries out no independent checks to ensure the accuracy of the payroll. This also gives rise to a fraud risk factor because one person having so much responsibility in a key area of the business is in a position to commit fraud. This is referred to as a 'fraud risk factor' and means the risk of fraud is higher, but it does not necessarily mean that a fraud has taken place.

The auditor must devise extended substantive procedures over the payroll to ensure that the payroll expense in the financial statements together with any related asset or liability in the statement of financial position does not contain material misstatement, such as:

- Recalculating the payroll expense in the statement of profit or loss.
- Reperforming the employment tax control account to prove the year-end asset/liability.
- Disaggregating the payroll expense into months and comparing it to the prior year and investigating any significant differences.
- Developing an expectation of the payroll figure by taking last year's payroll expense and adjusting it for starters/leavers and pay increases, and arriving at an expected expense and investigating any significant differences.
- Comparing this year's payroll expense to the prior year and investigating any significant differences.
- Using data analytics tools to identify any duplicate names on the payroll or duplicated bank account details.
- For a representative sample, agreeing the total net pay per the payroll records to the bank transfer listing and the cash book.
- Agreeing individual wages and salaries per the payroll to human resources records of hours worked or the hours worked report.

In this scenario, the auditor has not relied on the controls over the payroll cycle but has instead carried out additional substantive procedures which aim to detect material misstatement in the area being tested (payroll).

11.3.1.1 Dual-purpose tests

The auditor may also choose to use tests of control where a control is specifically linked to an assertion which is at risk of misstatement. The test of control may be performed at the same time as a substantive procedure. This is known as a dual-purpose test. For example, when auditing purchases, the auditor may agree a recorded purchase invoice back to supporting documentation which is a test of detail, and at the same time confirm that the invoice was approved prior to payment, which is a test of control. This is an efficient method of auditing which generates reliable auditor-generated evidence.

Dual-purpose tests are also often used for risks where highly persuasive evidence is needed, for example, a highly material balance which is at high risk of material misstatement, or where substantive procedures alone cannot provide sufficient appropriate audit evidence. It is likely for this type of risk that substantive procedures alone cannot reduce the risk of misstatement to an acceptable level. For example, where an audited entity conducts its business using IT and maintains minimal documentation of transactions, the auditor must use both tests of control and substantive procedures—one of these alone would not provide adequate evidence.

11.3.2 **Audit programmes**

The audit programmes contain instructions in relation to the procedures that are necessary to obtain sufficient, appropriate audit evidence including detailed information regarding audit fieldwork, including audit objectives, planned audit procedures, sample selection, and sample size. The audit programmes should be sufficiently detailed to allow a less experienced member of the audit team to understand the objective of the audit procedure, and how to conduct and conclude on that audit procedure.

Audit programmes also contain instructions in respect of documentation, to ensure that there is properly documented evidence that audit procedures have been conducted, the results or evidence obtained, and an appropriate conclusion. Completion of all audit programmes during the audit should ensure that all audit risks have been properly responded to, and should ensure the overall quality of the audit by facilitating thorough review of work carried out.

There are two types of audit programme, which we now consider in turn.

11.3.2.1 **Standardized audit programmes**

These are a pre-prepared set of audit instructions that can be used on any audit. They are not tailored to be specifically relevant to the entity being audited. The benefit is that they are quick to prepare and because they are comprehensive there should be reduced risk that audit procedures are omitted.

11.3.2.2 **Tailored audit programmes**

These are specifically tailored to the circumstances of the entity being audited, considering the entity's size, complexity, and specific risk factors. They will contain audit procedures which respond to the specific risks identified, therefore reducing audit risk. They should also prevent over-auditing, as unnecessary procedures will not be included in the audit programme and they will match the exact systems and controls in place at the audited entity, ensuring that an efficient audit is conducted.

Activity 11.2 Audit programmes

What do you think are the pros and cons of using standardized versus tailored audit programmes?

For the rest of this chapter, we will look at how the auditor designs the audit procedures which form the audit programme. This involves consideration of many factors including the assessed risk of material misstatement and results of preliminary analytical review and the materiality of balances, transactions, events, and disclosures, which we covered in previous chapters.

11.4 Sources of audit evidence

As we have seen, the auditor obtains audit evidence from tests of controls and substantive procedures. Substantive procedures are then split into tests of details and analytical procedures. ISA (UK) 500 *Audit Evidence* goes into detail regarding the sources of evidence and the relevance and reliability of information to be used as audit evidence.

11.4.1 Types of audit procedure

ISA 500 identifies seven types of audit procedure which the auditor can apply in order to obtain sufficient appropriate audit evidence (Figure 11.5).

Table 11.4 examines these procedures in further detail.

11.4.2 Analytical procedures as a source of audit evidence

Substantive analytical procedures can be used during the audit fieldwork stage, when they are used to identify trends and understand relationships between sets of data.

Analytical procedures will not detect specific misstatements (this is done by tests of detail), but they will identify possible sources of misstatement. Hence, it is important that the auditor understands that analytical procedures cannot be used on their own to obtain sufficient and appropriate audit evidence; instead, they must be used in conjunction with other forms of audit procedures, such as inquiry of management or reperformance.

Analytical procedures do not simply entail the auditor comparing one figure to another (e.g. revenue in the current year against revenue in the prior year). Various other analytical procedures are used by the auditor including:

- Ratio analysis—such as profitability ratios, liquidity ratios, and return ratios.
- Trend analysis—this is the analysis of changes in an account over time (i.e. the comparison of a current account balance with the previous year's balance). An auditor may choose to examine in more detail if the current year's balance on the account deviates significantly from the trend established in the previous year's balance for that account.
- Proof in total tests—these create an independent expectation of a figure, for example, payroll, by taking the payroll charge in the prior year and increasing this for pay rises, bonuses, and changes in staff numbers.

In order to use substantive analytical procedures effectively, the auditor has to create an expectation.

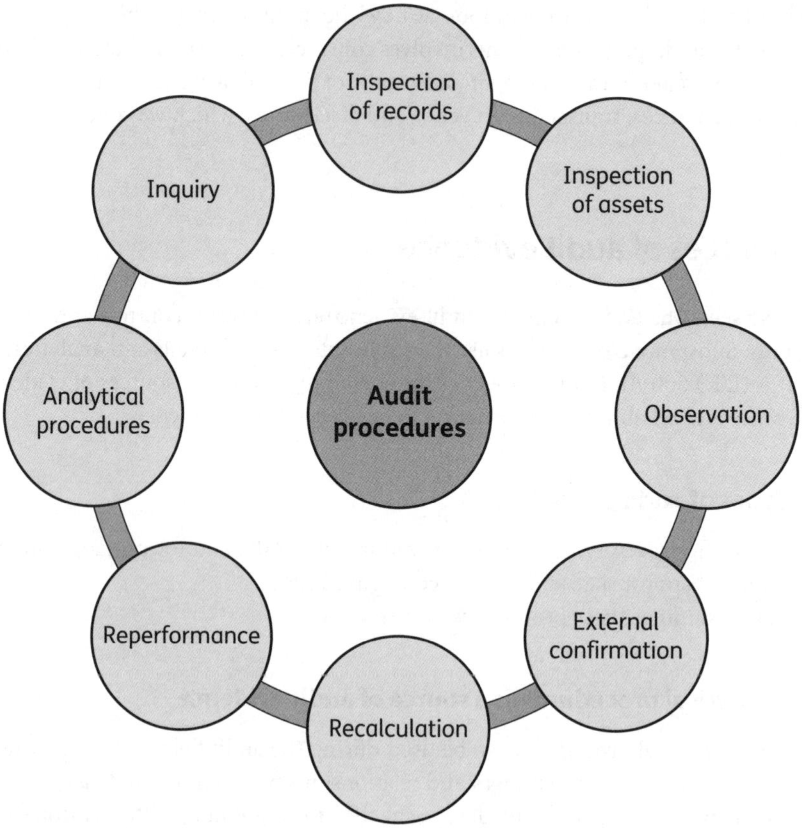

Figure 11.5 Types of audit procedure

Table 11.4 Examples of audit procedures

Type of audit procedure	Examples of evidence obtained
Inspection of records or documents This may involve the inspection of internal or external records or documents in paper or digital format (e.g. inspecting a share certificate, inspecting books and records of the accounting system, inspecting contracts, invoices, minutes of meetings, and correspondence)	• Can provide evidence over rights and obligations (e.g. inspection of title deeds for a property or inspection of an invoice for ownership of an asset) • Can provide evidence that a control is operating effectively (e.g. a timesheet is authorized or an invoice is authorized) • Can provide evidence over cut-offs (e.g. the date on a goods dispatched note and an invoice) • Can confirm the value of a sale or purchase
Inspection of assets Typically, this is the physical verification of non-current assets (e.g. properties, plant, or fixtures). It can also be applied to other assets (e.g. the inspection of inventories).	• Provides evidence that an asset exists (e.g. physically inspecting a machine in the warehouse from the non-current assets register) • Provides evidence over valuation (e.g. inspecting an asset for evidence of any impairment) • Inspecting tangible assets may help to provide evidence for other balances (e.g. inspecting assets used for research and development could provide evidence regarding the recognition of intangible development assets)

Table 11.4 (Continued)

Type of audit procedure	Examples of evidence obtained
Observation—observing a process or procedure being performed by others, often performed as a test of control Observation can be limited in terms of its appropriateness because it only provides evidence that a control is operating properly at the time of the observation. The fact that the auditor is present may have an influence over the operation of the control.	• Can provide evidence that a control is being operated correctly (e.g. segregation of duties) • Can provide evidence that the inventory count is being conducted properly by the auditor attending the count
External confirmation—obtaining a direct response from an external third party (usually in writing) ISA (UK) 505 *External Confirmations* provides specific guidance	• Circularization of trade receivables/trade payables, where customers/suppliers are asked to confirm the year-end balance owed to/from the company • Obtaining a bank confirmation letter • Obtaining confirmation from lawyers concerning litigation at the year end • Confirmation of inventories held by third parties
Recalculation—checking the arithmetical accuracy of documents, records, or the client's calculations	• Recalculating values on a sample of sales invoices • Recalculation of foreign currency translation • Recalculating payroll information • Recalculating depreciation calculations • Recalculating the trial balance and the financial statements themselves
Reperformance—the auditor reperforms a process or control which was originally executed by the company, and is often done as a test of control	• Reperforming the bank reconciliation at the year end • Reperforming the employment tax control account to verify the year-end employment tax accrual • Reperforming the ageing of accounts receivable
Analytical procedures—evaluating financial information through the analysis of plausible relationships among both financial and non-financial data ISA (UK) 520 *Analytical Procedures* provides guidance in this area	• Comparing this year's payroll expense to the prior year and investigating any significant differences • Comparing the current year's gross margin to the prior year • Use of analytical procedures as substantive tests
Inquiry—seeking information from those internal and external to the entity Inquiry can range from formal written inquiries to informal verbal conversations Evaluating responses to an inquiry is an important part of the inquiry process Inquiry is often a limited procedure and is insufficient on its own as audit evidence and it is usually performed in addition to other types of procedure The results of inquiry procedures will need to be corroborated in some other way through other audit procedures	• Making inquiries of the sales director to ascertain the procedure for opening credit accounts • Inquiring of management as to the control environment • Discussing the valuation of receivables with a credit controller • Inquiries made to the company's lawyers regarding a legal claim against the company. • Corroborating the results of analytical procedures

Auditing scenario 11.5 Forming an expectation of revenue

Marcus is auditing a company which operates a chain of cafés for the year ending 31 December 20X5. Marcus knows from prior year financial statements that the total revenue for the previous year end was £5,400,000, and that there were ten cafés in operation during that year.

From initial discussions with directors this year Marcus understands that two new cafés opened on 1 July 20X5 and from obtaining business understanding, Marcus knows that customer demand has been strong this year and there is an expectation that sales will increase 10 per cent for this financial year.

Marcus forms an expectation of revenue for the 31 December 20X5 as follows:

Sales for the previous year were £5,400,000, generated by ten cafés, so an average revenue of £540,000 each.

Assuming that sales per café increase by 10 per cent due to the increase in customer demand, each café will now generate £594,000.

During 20X5 there were ten cafes open for the whole year, and two for six months of the year. So, assuming that all cafes generate the same average revenue, the expected revenue for the year would be £6,354,000.

The suitability of substantive analytical procedures depends on four issues (Figure 11.6).

11.4.2.1 Assertions under scrutiny

The assertions under scrutiny should be suitable for the assertions which are being tested. For example, analytical procedures would not be suitable for testing the existence of work in progress. However, they would be suitable for assessing whether any write-down may be required for slow-moving inventory by using the inventory holding period ratio.

The use of analytical procedures is appropriate for those balances which are likely to be predictable over time because the auditor needs to analyse the relationships between the sets of data. This is why it is important to only use substantive analytical procedures in specific situations as they are not always appropriate. Hence, the use of analytical procedures would

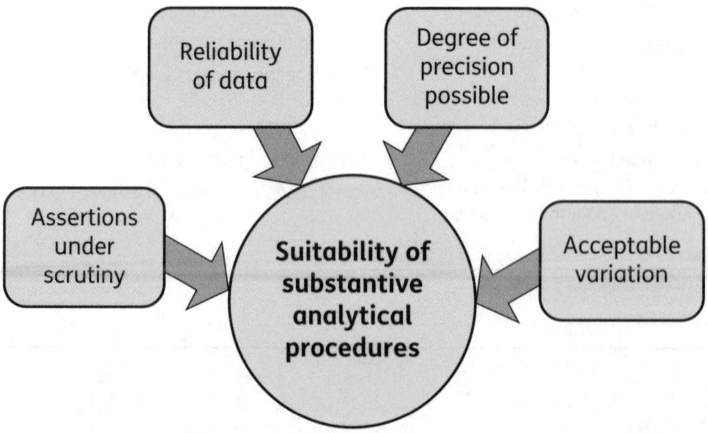

Figure 11.6 Matters impacting substantive analytical procedures

be inappropriate in a business which has experienced a significant restructuring during the year or has diversified into several new areas because the business would be too different in order to conduct a sensible comparison.

11.4.2.2 The reliability of the data

In a business where controls over the financial information are weak, the risk of material misstatement is higher. In this situation, the use of analytical procedures is not a suitable basis for assessment because it may not be possible to rely on the accuracy or completeness of the source data.

11.4.2.3 The degree of precision possible

Analytical procedures are viewed as a high-level approach to test a balance. If the auditor needs to test with a high level of precision, analytical procedures are unlikely to detect misstatements. A degree of precision will be involved if the auditor is to disaggregate the balance being tested. For example, if the auditor were to disaggregate revenue into products/divisions/regions. By disaggregating a balance, the auditor will be applying analytical procedures over a smaller balance and analytical procedures are therefore likely to be more effective.

11.4.2.4 The amount of variation which is acceptable

The auditor needs to create an expectation to compare against the actual amount recorded in the financial statements. If the level of variation from actual is higher than the level of variation which the auditor is willing to accept, the auditor will have to carry out further audit procedures to ensure that the balance in the financial statements is not materially misstated.

11.5 Sufficient and appropriate audit evidence

Audit evidence is made up of information that supports and corroborates management's assertions, and also information that contradicts management's assertions. Both types of information can provide evidence that will help the auditor to form an opinion on the financial statements. Audit evidence is defined as, 'Information used by the auditor in arriving at the conclusions on which the auditor's opinion is based. Audit evidence includes both information contained in the accounting records underlying the financial statements and information obtained from other sources.'[8]

Obtaining evidence is a cumulative process, and the auditor can obtain evidence from many different sources including the following:

- the accounting records (i.e. general ledgers, journal entries, and all supporting documentation);
- minutes of meetings;

[8] FRC, 'ISA (UK) 500', 2022, para 5 <https://media.frc.org.uk/documents/ISA_UK_500_Updated_May_2022.pdf> (accessed 18 January 2024).

- confirmations from third parties;
- analysts' reports;
- comparable information about competitors;
- controls manuals;
- information accumulated from previous years' audits; and
- evidence generated by the auditor through observation, inquiry, and inspection.

A key concept in auditing is that the auditor must obtain **sufficient appropriate audit evidence** to be able to draw reasonable conclusions on which to base the auditor's opinion (Figure 11.7).

11.5.1 Sufficient audit evidence

Sufficient means that there is the right amount (quantity) of evidence. Sufficiency will be determined by factors such as the level of risk associated with the item in question, by the quality of evidence obtained, and it is also linked to materiality. The auditor must use judgement to decide when sufficient evidence has been obtained, and in reaching this decision the type of procedures that have been used to obtain evidence must be considered. For example, it is important to appreciate that inquiry alone does not usually provide sufficient audit evidence on the operating effectiveness of controls.

11.5.2 Appropriate audit evidence

Appropriate means that the evidence is relevant and reliable. Relevance means that evidence should be pertinent to the assertions inherent in the item in question. For example, when gathering evidence about a property, a physical verification will provide evidence of existence, but not of the right to recognize the property on the balance sheet. So further procedures would be necessary to obtain evidence of the right to recognize the asset. Therefore, the auditor should take care to gather evidence for all necessary assertions for a particular balance or transaction.

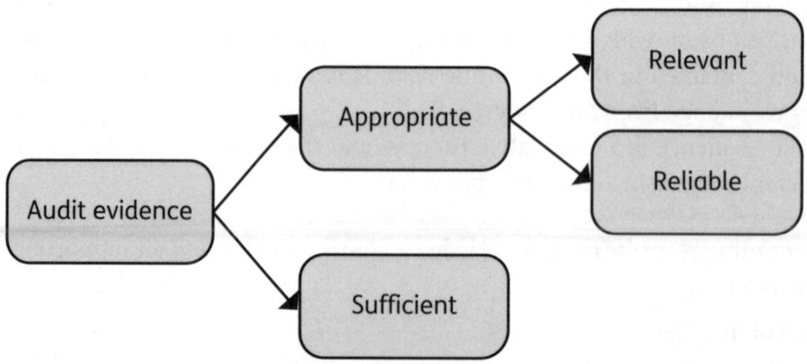

Figure 11.7 Sufficient appropriate audit evidence

Reliability means that the auditor can trust the evidence. If the information used as the basis of an audit procedure is not auditor-generated (i.e. has been provided by the client or by an auditor's expert), the auditor must carefully evaluate the accuracy and completeness of the information and whether it is detailed enough to support the planned audit procedure.

The reliability of evidence is influenced by factors such as:

- The source of the evidence (e.g. whether it is client-generated or auditor-generated).
- The nature of the evidence (e.g. whether it is documentary or based on inquiry).
- The circumstances under which it was obtained (e.g. whether there were effective controls over the preparation of the evidence).

ISA (UK) 500 (para A31) provides a guideline as to the reliability of evidence (Table 11.5).

11.5.3 **Link between sufficient and appropriate evidence**

Sufficiency and appropriateness should not be considered in isolation. For example, the more reliable the source of evidence, the lesser quantity of evidence may need to be gathered.

For example, if an auditor is obtaining evidence in relation to a lease that has been entered into. If the audit client can present the auditor with the original signed copy of the lease, which is a reliable source of evidence, then limited further procedures need to be performed. However, if the client presents the auditor with a photocopy of the lease, or cannot produce the document in any form at all, then extensive further procedures should be carried out.

Table 11.5 Examples of reliable audit evidence

Type of reliable evidence	Examples
Generated by third parties independent of the client	• Confirmation of a trade receivables balance by a customer • A letter from the bank confirming an overdraft limit, rates of interest, etc. • Evidence obtained by auditor's experts, for example, specialist property valuers
Generated by the auditor rather than by the entity	• Financial performance measures such as trends and ratios prepared by audit software • Recalculations of complex computations such as foreign exchange gains or losses
Documented in a written form rather than an oral representation	• Written management representations • Written confirmations of matters discussed with people outside the audited entity such as lawyers, finance providers
Gathered from original documentation rather than photocopies or scanned documents	• Original signed documents such as lease agreements, loan covenants, contracts with suppliers and customers • Original version of board minutes and meetings with shareholders
Produced by the entity when controls are deemed to be effective	• Evidence obtained from a well-organized and well-controlled inventory count • Evidence based on the audited entity's accounting records when controls are effective

11.5.4 **Corroborating evidence**

Where evidence obtained from different sources is consistent it provides corroborating evidence. This improves the reliability of evidence obtained. For example, imagine a company that is facing a legal claim from a customer, which will be settled in the next financial year. Management has provided a written representation that states that the claim is unlikely to lead to a cash outflow. This evidence on its own is not very reliable, as it is client-generated. If the auditor can obtain evidence from an independent source, for example, a legal expert that the claim is unlikely to be successful, then the two sources of evidence are consistent and corroborate each other, and the evidence when combined is reliable.

11.5.5 **Professional judgement**

ISA (UK) 200 *Overall Objectives of the Independent Auditor and the Conduct of an Audit in Accordance with International Standards on Auditing* requires the auditor to conclude whether sufficient appropriate audit evidence has been obtained. It is a matter of professional judgement to decide whether the evidence obtained is sufficient and appropriate as a basis for forming the auditor's opinion.

There is no 'one-size-fits-all' where sufficient and appropriate audit evidence is concerned and it is down to the auditor's professional judgement to decide when enough evidence of the right type has been obtained in order to support the auditor's opinion. This is why reviews of audit working papers should be performed by senior members of the audit team during the completion stage of the audit—to ensure that more work is performed if necessary—and the decision should be based on matters such as the assessed level of risk of material misstatement, the nature of audit procedures performed and the timeliness of financial reporting.

11.5.6 **Risk and evidence**

ISA (UK) 330 indicates a link between the auditor's assessment of risk and the persuasiveness of evidence obtained. The correlation is that the higher the assessment of risk, the more persuasive evidence should be obtained. To obtain more persuasive evidence, the auditor can:

- increase the quantity of evidence obtained;
- obtain evidence that is more relevant;
- obtain evidence that is more reliable.

For example, imagine an auditor is obtaining evidence on the recognition and valuation of trade receivables. A circularization of trade receivables balances has indicated a higher risk than previously identified during audit planning. The auditor could respond in several ways to improve the persuasiveness of evidence, for example:

- extend the sample of trade receivables that was circularized; or
- extend other procedures which are relevant and reliable, such as after-date cash receipts testing.

11.6 Audit sampling

It is usually impracticable for the auditor to test every item in an accounting population because of the costs involved and time constraints. This leads to almost all audits involving the use of sampling as audit evidence is obtained. Remember that the auditor only gives reasonable assurance (not absolute assurance) that the financial statements are free from material misstatement, whether caused by fraud or error. Hence, the auditor is not certifying that the financial statements are 100 per cent accurate as the auditor is not verifying 100 per cent of the transactions that are included in the financial statements. Sampling is therefore an accepted way for auditors to obtain evidence.

Audit sampling is dealt with in ISA (UK) 530 *Audit Sampling*. The definition of 'audit sampling', as described in ISA (UK) 530 is:

> The application of audit procedures to less than 100% of items within a population of audit relevance such that all sampling units have a chance of selection in order to provide the auditor with a reasonable basis on which to draw conclusions about the entire population.[9]

The term 'population' refers to the entire set of data from which a sample is selected and about which the auditor wishes to draw conclusions.

Auditing scenario 11.6 Use of sampling

ABC Industries Ltd operates approximately 600 credit accounts through its receivables ledger and raises approximately 2,500 sales invoices each month.

Sales invoices at 2,500 multiplied by 12 months is equivalent to 30,000 sales invoices each year. It would be impracticable for the auditor to test every single sales invoice during the year as this would prove very expensive and would take a significant amount of time to complete. For this reason, the auditor will extract a sample from the population of sales invoices and test that sample.

If errors are noted within the sample, the auditor will extend the sample to decipher whether, or not, the error(s) is/are isolated or if the error(s) indicate further problems which may need to be discussed with management and/or those charged with governance. Errors in the sample will also give rise to potential adjustments being made to the financial statements if the errors are material both in isolation and when combined with other errors noted by the auditor.

11.6.1 Sampling risk

As discussed in Chapter 9, sampling risk is a component of detection risk. Detection risk is the risk that the auditor will not detect a misstatement which exists in an assertion that could be material, either individually or when aggregated with other misstatements. In the audit risk model, detection risk is the only risk that is under the control of the auditor.

[9] FRC, 'ISA (UK) 530', 2022, para 5(a) <https://media.frc.org.uk/documents/ISA_UK_530_-_Updated_May_2022.pdf> (accessed 18 January 2024).

The term 'sampling risk' is defined in ISA (UK) 530 as:

> The risk that the auditor's conclusion based on a sample may be different from the conclusion if the entire population were subjected to the same audit procedure. Sampling risk can lead to types of erroneous conclusions:
>
> (i) In the case of a test of controls, that controls are more effective than they actually are, or in the case of a test of details, that a material misstatement does not exist when in fact it does. The auditor is primarily concerned with this type of erroneous conclusion because it affects audit effectiveness and is more likely to lead to an inappropriate audit opinion.
>
> (ii) In the case of a test of controls, that controls are less effective than they actually are, or in the case of a test of details, that a material misstatement exists when in fact it does not. This type of erroneous conclusion affects audit efficiency as it would usually lead to additional work to establish that initial conclusions were incorrect.[10]

This means that auditors should aim to reduce sampling risk so that audits are high quality and likely to result in the detection of material misstatement, but also to ensure that audits are performed in an effective and resourceful way, avoiding unnecessary audit work.

The term 'non-sampling risk' is defined as:

> The risk that the auditor reaches an erroneous conclusion for any reason not related to sampling risk.[11]

Auditors are faced with sampling risk in both tests of controls and in substantive procedures. Essentially, sampling risk is the risk that the auditor's sample from a population will not be representative.

11.6.1.1 Sampling risk within tests of control

As we discussed earlier in the chapter, tests of controls are designed to evaluate the operating effectiveness of controls in preventing or detecting and correcting material misstatement. The risk to auditors where test of controls is concerned is that controls are either more or less effective than they actually are because the rate of errors in the sample is not the same as the actual rate of errors in the population.

Sampling risk affects tests of control because the wrong conclusion over the operating effectiveness of controls could lead the auditor to rely too heavily on controls, hence failing to detect a material misstatement and expressing an incorrect audit opinion. Or the auditor could place less reliance on internal controls which results in more substantive procedures having to be applied, which results in audit inefficiencies due to more work having to be performed which increases the cost of the audit.

Auditing scenario 11.7 Attendance at inventory count

During the initial audit planning meeting with Pelway Enterprises Ltd, the audit engagement partner was told by Samina Rai, the finance director, that all staff involved in the year-end inventory count are provided with detailed instructions drawn up by Samina and the company's production

[10] Ibid., para 5(c). [11] Ibid., para 5(d).

director, Joshua Johnson. Samina confirmed that at each warehouse there will be a number of teams counting the inventory in different numbered sections of each warehouse which has been mapped. Each team will comprise two individuals: one will count the inventory and another will record the inventory on the sequentially numbered inventory count sheets.

The audit engagement team will be attending each warehouse on 31 December 20X8 to carry out a sample of test counts in a two-way direction: from inventory count sheets to inventory (testing the existence assertion) and from the physical inventory to the inventory count sheets (testing the completeness assertion). As each section of a warehouse has been counted, it will be crossed out on the map to indicate that counting is complete in that area.

In this example, the sampling risk is the risk that the auditor's sample from the entire inventory count is not representative of the population (the population being the entire inventory). This can arise because the auditor's sample is inadequate (i.e. it is too small). In order to reduce sampling risk, the auditor needs to increase the size of the sample selected.

However, the auditor may consider that increasing the sample size need not be necessary on the grounds that Pelway Enterprises has a number of controls in place over the inventory count as follows:

- Detailed instructions are provided to counting staff by management.
- Each section of the warehouse has been numbered on the warehouse map.
- Teams are comprised of two individuals—one counting and one recording.
- Sequentially numbered inventory count sheets are being used.

Sampling risk can lead the auditor to erroneously conclude that the above controls are more effective than they actually are. This means that the auditor's sample of inventory counts will be lower than would otherwise be the case (as they are placing reliance on the effectiveness of the controls) and is more likely to lead to an inappropriate audit opinion being expressed because those items of inventory which have not been sampled may contain material misstatement due to the incorrect conclusion over the controls over the inventory count.

Conversely, sampling risk can lead the auditor to erroneously conclude that the above controls are less effective than they actually are. This results in the auditor increasing sample sizes than would otherwise have been the case which creates additional work (and costs) and hence reduces audit efficiency.

11.6.1.2 **Sampling risk within substantive procedures**

As we have already seen earlier in the chapter, substantive procedures are aimed at detecting material misstatement at the assertion level. Tests of detail, which are one type of substantive procedure, are often performed on a sample basis.

Remember that sampling risk is the risk that the auditor's sample from a population is not representative. If the sample is too small, the sampling risk is that the auditor fails to detect a material misstatement (detection risk). On the flip side, if the auditor has concluded that a material misstatement exists and hence requires a large sample to be tested, the auditor is carrying out more substantive procedures than is actually necessary which increases time spent on the audit.

Let's use an example to illustrate this point. During the audit of trade receivables, the auditor picked a sample of twenty receivables. The population of receivables (i.e. the number of customers owing money at the year end) was 330.

In this example, the sample may be too low because it only represents 6.1 per cent (20/330 x 100) of total trade receivables balances. There is a risk that those trade receivables balances which remain untested if the sample is not increased will contain material misstatement. This increases detection and audit risk and hence the auditor should increase their sample accordingly so that it is representative of the population.

11.6.2 **Non-sampling risk**

Non-sampling risk is the risk that the auditor's conclusion is inappropriate for any other reasons, such as the application of inappropriate audit procedures or the failure to recognize a misstatement. Non-sampling risk can also arise by the auditor misinterpreting the audit evidence obtained.

Auditing scenario 11.8 Non-sampling risk

Wayne Roberts is the audit supervisor of ABC & Co Accountancy Services who is attending the inventory count of Whitaker Enterprises Ltd with a team of four other audit engagement team members. The inventory count is being carried out as at Whitaker Enterprises' year end of 31 December 20X8.

During December 20X8, a significant problem arose in the company's inventory control system. A junior member of the warehouse team incorrectly inputted the selling prices of goods as opposed to their cost prices into the stock control system. This resulted in overstated inventory valuations for approximately 20 per cent of the company's products. The issue only came to light due to complaints from customers who had been overcharged for goods they had purchased from the company.

Jackson Ludlow, the company's production director, carries out monthly reviews of the prices input into the stock valuation system to ensure they are cost prices so the inventory valuation complies with IAS 2 *Inventories* 'lower of cost and net realizable value' principles. However, in December 20X8, Jackson was absent due to illness and hence could not carry out the checks—nor did any other responsible official.

Wayne Roberts has fully documented the controls over Whitaker Enterprises' inventory cycle, including the checks carried out by Jackson Ludlow, but has not been made aware of this control deviation, nor has he asked Jackson Ludlow or the finance director about any problems arising in the system during the year.

The issue here is that further inputting errors could have been made by the junior member of staff. The failure of the auditor to identify this problem is a non-sampling risk. Hence, Wayne Roberts could conclude that controls over the inventory cycle have been operating effectively enough during the year to reduce the risk of material misstatement, when, in fact, there has been a deviation from the internal control which should result in more substantive procedures being carried out.

11.6.3 **Statistical versus non-statistical sampling**

ISA (UK) 530 defines 'statistical sampling' as:

> An approach to sampling that has the following characteristics:
>
> (i) Random selection of the sample items; and
>
> (ii) The use of probability theory to evaluate sample results, including measurement of sampling risk.

A sampling approach that does not have characteristics (i) and (ii) is considered non-statistical sampling.[12]

While statistical sampling requires the use of mathematical procedures, it still requires the auditor to exercise professional judgement—for example, in determining what constitutes a misstatement or deviation and what the performance materiality level is. In practice, a certain level of mathematical competence is required if valid conclusions are to be drawn from the sample evidence.

The main advantage of statistical sampling is that it should lead to efficiencies in performing the audit because the sample size will not be excessive and it should also enhance audit quality. Most audit firms use software to determine the size of the sample that is necessary—based on variables including the level of risk of the item under audit, its materiality, and the size of the population. So, it can be quick and easy to select the sample. However, it can involve complex mathematical processes which need to be understood by the audit team.

Non-statistical sampling means selecting an appropriate sample size based on the auditor's judgement and without the use of probability theory.

Activity 11.3 Non-statistical sampling

What do you think are the advantages and disadvantages of non-statistical sampling?

11.6.4 Audit sampling techniques

There are a variety of sampling techniques (both statistical and non-statistical) which the auditor can use in devising a sample of a population to perform audit procedures over. The technique used will ultimately be at the discretion of the auditor's professional judgement and there are various factors which need to be carefully considered by the auditor because not every technique will be appropriate in the circumstances.

ISA (UK) 530 recognizes that there are many methods of selecting samples (Figure 11.8).

Random selection—this can be achieved through the use of random number generators or tables.

Systematic selection—where the number of sampling units in the population is divided by the sample size to give a sampling interval. For example, every twentieth sales invoice. While the starting point may be determined on a haphazard basis, the sample is more likely to be truly random if it is determined by the use of a computerized random number generator or by way of random number tables. It is important when auditors use this sampling technique that they ensure that the sampling units within the population are not structured in such a way that the sampling interval corresponds with a particular pattern in the population.

Monetary unit sampling—this is a method of sampling which uses the monetary unit value as opposed to the items as the sampling population. This technique results in a sample which

[12] Ibid., para 5(g).

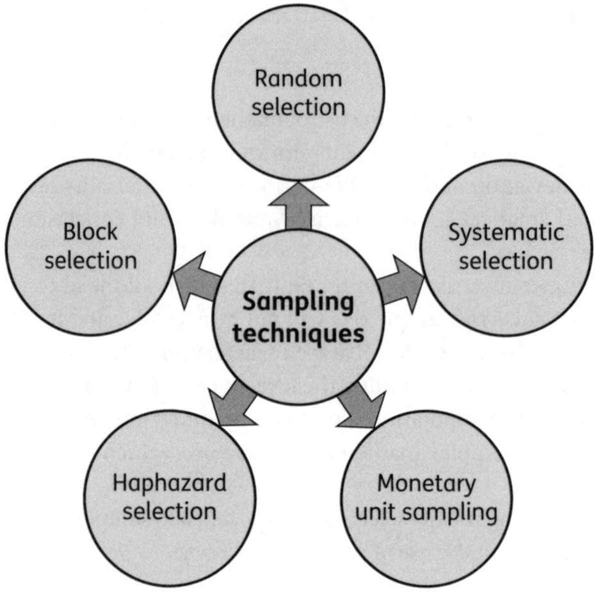

Figure 11.8 Sampling techniques

usually focuses on higher-value items and it should be set up so that all material items in a population are included in the sample.

Monetary unit sampling is generally applied to large variance populations such as receivables or inventories where the individual members are of varying degrees of size.

The sample size will take into account:

- the size of the population;
- the level of tolerable misstatement which is related to performance materiality; and
- the assurance level required.

Auditing scenario 11.9 Monetary unit sampling

The auditor has extracted a list of trade receivables from Howard Enterprises Ltd which shows a total population value of £750,000. The sample size is set to 120. The sampling interval is therefore £6,250 (£750,000/120).

Table 11.6 contains extracts from the receivables ledger.

If the auditor starts at £0:

- The first balance, ABC Co, has within it the first sampling interval of £6,250, so this is selected.
- The next £12,500 (£6,250 + £6,250) arrives in the balance belonging to JKL Co.
- Finally, (in the list above), the sampling interval has reached £18,750 (£6,250 + £6,250 + £6,250) which is in the balance belonging to MNO Co, and so on.

Table 11.6

Customer name	Balance (£)	Cumulative (£)	Selected
ABC Co	10,250	10,250	Yes
DEF Co	600	10,850	No
GHI Co	1,300	12,150	No
JKL Co	4,050	16,200	Yes
MNO Co	2,820	19,020	Yes
And so on. . .			
	750,000	750,000	

The sample is random because the starting point for sampling can be random although the amount which the auditor starts off with does not have to be zero. This will be left to the professional judgement of the auditor.

When the auditor uses monetary unit sampling, the larger balances have a greater chance of being selected and this reduces detection risk.

Haphazard selection—when the auditor adopts a haphazard technique it is not a structured technique. When no structured technique is followed, the auditor would nonetheless avoid any conscious bias or predictability (e.g. avoiding difficult-to-locate items or always avoiding items on the first or last page of the general ledger account). This ensures that all items in the population stand a chance of selection. ISA (UK) 530 acknowledges that haphazard selection is inappropriate when using statistical sampling.

Block selection—this involves selecting a block of contiguous (i.e. next to each other) items from the population and is often used when testing cut-offs. ISA (UK) 530 clarifies that such a technique would rarely be appropriate where the auditor intends to draw valid inferences about the entire population based on the sample.

When non-statistical methods (haphazard and block) are used, the auditor must use professional judgement to select the items to be tested. This increases the risk of auditor bias, but it does support the risk-based approach whereby the auditor focuses on those areas of the financial statements which are more susceptible to material misstatement.

11.6.4.1 **Stratification**

Stratification is the process of breaking down a population into smaller subpopulations. Each subpopulation is a group of sampling units which have similar characteristics.

Auditing scenario 11.10 Stratification

Hoylake Enterprises Limited has a large sales ledger which is made up of customers in the UK, Ireland, Asia, America, and Poland. The auditor has concluded that because the client supplies the majority of its goods to overseas customers, overseas receivables are high risk because they could be translated

Table 11.7

	Number of items in stratum	Value of stratum	Test size
Above £1m	9	£25m	9
£750,000–£1m	28	£21m	20
£250,000–£750,000	40	£40m	30
£50,000–£250,000	95	£80m	60
£10,000–£50,000	120	£60m	60
£0–£10,000	200	£15m	20

at the year end at inappropriate foreign exchange rates. The auditor therefore divides the population (the population being the trade receivables) into strata (layers) as set out in Table 11.7.

The sample chosen is weighted towards the higher-value items because they are most material. If one transaction in excess of £1m contains a misstatement, it may be material to the financial statements whereas an error in a transaction totalling £50,000 may not be.

11.6.5 Factors to consider when selecting a sample

There are various factors which the auditor must consider when selecting a sample to test. These are outlined as follows:

- The purpose of the procedure—what is the overall objective of the test? What contribution does the test make to the overall assessment of the financial statements presenting a true and fair view?
- The combination of procedures that are being performed—are tests of control being carried out and can they contribute as audit evidence? What other audit procedures are being carried out over the area being audited?
- The nature of audit evidence sought—is external, third-party audit evidence available? Can auditor-generated evidence be obtained?
- The possible misstatement conditions—is the area being audited at a higher risk of material misstatement or are controls over the area weak or non-existent?

Auditing scenario 11.11 Factors when selecting a sample

Derano Industries Ltd operates approximately 400 sales ledger accounts and the majority of these sales ledger accounts are expected to owe the company money at the year end 31 December 20X8. The audit engagement partner has decided that a trade receivables circularization will not be carried out this year due to the low response rate received in the previous year's audit and the fact that they are generally viewed as a weak form of audit evidence.

The audit engagement partner has requested extended post-year-end cash receipts testing be performed to support the valuation and existence assertions.

Given the number of sales ledger accounts in existence, it is highly likely that the trade receivables balance at the year end will be material. When designing the sample, the auditor must consider:

- The purpose of the procedure—which is to provide reasonable assurance that the trade receivables amount in the statement of financial position does not contain material misstatement and the valuation of receivables is appropriate.
- The combination of the procedures that are being performed—extended post-year-end cash receipts testing will be in addition to other audit procedures to support the trade receivables amount (such as agreeing the sales ledger control account to the list of balances and selecting a sample of year-end balances and agreeing back to goods dispatched notes and sales order).
- The nature of the audit evidence sought—the extended post year-end cash receipts testing will confirm (or otherwise) that trade receivables exist at the year end and that they are appropriately valued as they will be traced to monies received after the reporting date from the receivable.
- Possible misstatement conditions—the auditor must consider the possibility that some receivables balances may not be recoverable (especially if they cannot be traced to post-year-end cash receipts) and hence an allowance for receivables (or a further allowance for receivables) may be necessary to avoid overstating trade receivables and profit.

11.6.5.1 **Factors that influence the sample size**

As we have seen, there are various sampling techniques and various factors which the auditor must consider and not all techniques and factors will apply to every audit. Sample sizes must be representative of the population because if they are too small there is a greater risk that the auditor will form an incorrect opinion on the financial statements (i.e. audit risk is increased). Conversely, if they are too large there will be a resulting increase in audit inefficiencies (i.e. increased costs).

The most important factor to be considered when determining the sample size is the risk of material misstatement. The higher the auditor's assessment of the risk of material misstatement, the larger the sample size needs to be.

11.6.6 **Evaluating results of audit sampling**

ISA 530 requires the auditor to investigate the nature and cause of any deviations or misstatements identified, and evaluate their possible effect on the purpose of the audit procedure and on other areas of the audit.[13]

[13] Ibid., para 12.

For tests of controls performed on a sample basis, it is important for the auditor to understand whether a deviation represents a breakdown in internal controls. ISA 530 explains that:

> For tests of controls, an unexpectedly high sample deviation rate may lead to an increase in the assessed risk of material misstatement, unless further audit evidence substantiating the initial assessment is obtained.[14]

Auditing scenario 11.12 Analysing a deviation in the results of a test on controls

The auditor of Driscoll Ltd has performed a test of controls operating over employee expense claims, whereby the auditor checked that expense claims had been signed as approved by the employee's line manager. The test was performed on a sample basis, and forty expense claims were selected using systematic selection.

The results of the test indicate that four of the expense claims had not been authorized. This is a deviation rate of 10 per cent for the sample selected.

The auditor should consider whether there is a common feature relevant to the four deviations, for example, they may have occurred during the same month, or in respect of the same employee. The auditor will then extend testing to obtain further evidence. This could reveal, for example, that no expense claims were signed as approved during a particular time period, when a particular line manager was away from work, indicating a deficiency in how the internal control has operated during the year.

When evaluating the results of tests of detail performed on a sample basis an unexpectedly high misstatement amount in the results of test may cause the auditor to believe that there is a material misstatement in the balance or account being tested.

The auditor is required to project misstatements identified as a result of sample testing. ISA 530 explains that:

> The auditor is required to project misstatements for the population to obtain a broad view of the scale of misstatement but this projection may not be sufficient to determine an amount to be recorded.[15]

The projected misstatement is an estimate of the misstatement in the population being tested.

There are different methods for projecting misstatements, ISA (UK) 530 does not prescribe a specific method that must be used. A common way to project misstatements is by using this formula:

$$\begin{aligned} &\textit{projected misstatement} \\ &\quad = \textit{misstatement in population} \\ &\quad \times \textit{number of items in population/number of items in sample} \end{aligned}$$

[14] Ibid., para A21. [15] Ibid., para A18.

Auditing scenario 11.13 Projecting misstatements

Wendy has performed a test of detail on discounts allowed, which are calculated manually and entered into the accounting system on an individual basis. Wendy selected twenty-five invoices containing a discount allowed to test, from a population of 1,500 invoices. The testing revealed that three invoices contained arithmetic errors with a total monetary value of £67.

Wendy should project the misstatement as follows:

$$\text{Projected misstatement} = £67 \times 1{,}500/25$$
$$= £4{,}020$$

The projected error is unlikely to be the same as the actual value of a misstatement, the projection is an estimate. Wendy needs to use judgement to consider whether a material misstatement is likely, and if Wendy concludes that it is likely she must take further action, which could include extending the testing (i.e. increase the sample size of this audit procedure) or perform alternative procedures.

11.7 Data analytics

Over the last couple of years, the use of data analytics has been gathering pace in the audit profession, although it has been around for a long time. In general terms, the use of data analytics in an audit involves the analysis of complete sets of data to identify unusual fluctuations and trends which the auditor may need to investigate (in a similar manner to analytical review). Data analytics can also serve as audit evidence.

'Audit Data Analytics' is defined by the IAASB as follows:

> Data Analytics, when used to obtain audit evidence in a financial statement audit, is the science and art of discovering and analysing patterns, deviations and inconsistencies, and extracting other useful information in the data underlying or related to the subject matter of an audit through analysis, modelling and visualization for the purpose of planning and performing the audit.[16]

11.7.1 Advantages and challenges of audit data analytics

Auditors have used computer-assisted audit techniques (CAATs) for many years and the increasing use of technology in auditing means the auditor can quickly analyse entire populations of data rather than use a sample. Audit tests that used to take hours, or even days to complete can now take a matter of seconds and eliminate sampling risk. Inherently, this provides the auditor with more persuasive audit evidence, particularly when entire populations are examined, and the audit is more efficient.

One of the main advantages of data analytics is the fact that the auditor can use them at a very early stage in the audit to identify problem areas. Analytical review, for example, can be carried out much more efficiently using data analytics because they can uncover unusual

[16] International Auditing and Assurance Standards Board, 'The IAASB's work to explore the growing use of technology in the audit, including data analytics', IAASB, 2016 <https://www.iaasb.org/_flysystem/azure-private/meetings/files/20160621-IAASB-Agenda_Item_8A-Data-Analytics-Working-Group-Publication-final_0.pdf> (accessed 18 January 2024).

trends. Data analytics increase audit efficiencies so the auditor can spend more time focusing on those areas of higher risk. Data analytics can also be used as part of a continuous auditing approach rather than having audit procedures concentrated on year-end balances and transactions.

Another advantage of data analytics is that it can uncover more anomalies within the financial statements or client's internal control environment than traditional audit procedures, the auditor can communicate more issues to those charged with governance which may be of interest to them.

There are also some disadvantages to data analytics. For example, their use can be restricted if the client's data is of poor quality or the data cannot be converted into the same format which is used by the data analytics software.

The use of data analytics will involve training audit staff in their use. This will involve additional costs in bringing audit staff up to the required level to be able to use data analytics correctly. If the audit firm is small, the costs of this training may outweigh the benefits.

Activity 11.4 Audit data analytics

Can you think of other challenges that audit firms face with implementing audit data analytics?

Suggested answer points are provided at the end of the chapter.

Auditing in practice 11.1 FRC thematic review into data analytics

In January 2017, the FRC issued a thematic review into the use of data analytics in the audit of financial statements. In a thematic review, the FRC looks at a sample of firms' policies and procedures in respect of a specific area or aspect of the audit or firm-wide procedures so they can make comparisons to identify good practice and areas of common weakness.

The FRC reviewed the use of data analytics at the six largest UK audit firms.[17] They found that data analytics is most commonly used to:

- Provide an analysis of all transactions within a population, stratify that population, and identify outliers which the auditor must examine further.
- Reperform calculations relevant to the financial statements.
- Match transactions as they are processed through the relevant cycle.
- Assist in the segregation of duties testing.
- Compare entity data to data that has been obtained externally.
- Manipulate data to assess the impact of different assumptions.

As expected, the thematic review identified that data analytics provides positive contributions to audit quality, including:

- deepening the auditor's understanding of the entity;
- facilitating the focus of audit testing to those areas of high risk by stratifying large populations;

[17] FRC, 'Audit quality thematic review: The use of data analytics in the audit of financial statements', 2017 <https://media.frc.org.uk/documents/Audit_Quality_Thematic_Review_The_Use_of_Data_Analytics_in_the_Audit_of_Financial_Statements.pdf> (accessed 18 January 2024).

- strengthening the exercise of professional scepticism;
- improving consistency and central oversight in group audits;
- enabling the auditor to perform tests on large or complex datasets where a manual approach may not be practical;
- general improvements to audit efficiencies;
- identifying instances of fraud; and
- enhancing communications with audit committees.

Typical areas of the financial statements where data analytics are used in practice include:

- testing journal entries;
- general ledger (nominal ledger) analysis;
- revenue analytics;
- process analytics;
- valuation of financial instruments including derivative financial instruments;
- impairment modelling;
- tracing individual revenue transactions to receivables and after-date cash received;
- recalculation of inventory ageing;
- recalculation of receivables ageing;
- tracing supplier income to agreements and cash received; and
- recalculation of fund management fees based on value of assets under management.

The FRC's thematic review clarifies that data analytics are not used in isolation, but they form part of a body of audit evidence. To that end, the FRC recommend that audit firms:

- Consider whether a data analytic is a 'good tool' for the client's specific environment. The thematic review identifies one audit where an analytic was designed on the basis that the entity posts granular journals but the entity, in fact, posts large batch journals. This analytic would therefore produce a number of anomalies in the output and hence significant follow-up work was required.
- Ensure that all the relevant assertions are covered for the balance which is being tested. The FRC identified one audit where the completeness assertion for revenue was not addressed and one audit where the classification assertion was relevant but also not addressed.
- Assess whether audit testing in other areas needs to be 'flexed' to provide the necessary supporting evidence for the use of data analytics. The FRC identified four audit firms that use data analytics in various ways to provide assurance over revenue by tracing sales transactions through to receivables and cash. This technique may then rely on testing of receivables and cash to provide substantive audit evidence for revenue. The FRC observed one such audit where the cash procedures were inappropriately performed on a sample basis and the bank account used for sales receipts was omitted from the sample.

11.7.2 **Application of audit data analytics**

An important feature of the application of audit data analytics is the use of 'dashboards' or other data visualization tools. The process is simple—the auditor imports client's data into their audit analytics software, which then analyses the data and presents the results in a visual form which can be reviewed and interpreted by the auditor. As a result of this process, the auditor will decide how to respond—the data analytics can identify unusual transactions which then need to be investigated, and it can highlight control failures or shown other anomalies in the data.

It is important to understand that audit data analytics is just a way for the auditor to quickly analyse a population—the results still need to be carefully examined and an appropriate response formulated. The audit data analytics does not provide a conclusion—the auditor must use their skills in interpreting the results to reach a conclusion or decide that further work is necessary. This may involve a more detailed analysis of data, but it is also likely to mean the auditor uses more traditional techniques such as physical verification of assets, discussion of issues with management, or transaction testing.

Auditing scenario 11.14 Audit data analytics

Maddie is an auditor, assigned to the audit of Prospero Ltd. Maddie has used her audit firm's audit data analytics software to analyse the average transaction value of journals that have been posted into the sales ledger control account.

The software presents Maddie with a visualization (Figure 11.9).

The visualization shows Maddie that in April and December there are unusually high average values for the journals that have been posted to the client's sales ledger. Maddie will need to investigate further, to find out the reason for this unusual activity. There may be a genuine business reason, for example, in April and December, there may be large, one-off transactions that have been posted, perhaps to write off irrecoverable balances.

Without the audit data analytics software, it would have taken a lot longer for Maddie to determine the trends and possibly the unusual values of journal entries in these two months would not have been identified.

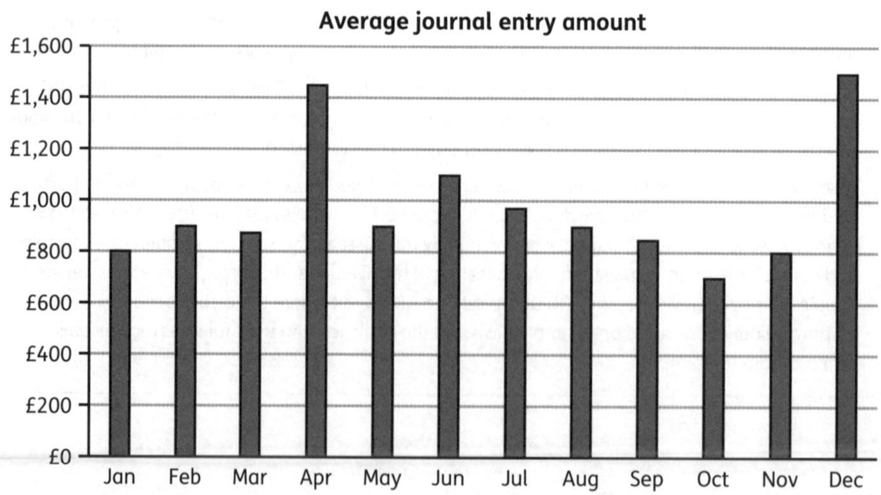

Figure 11.9 Average journal entry amount

11.7.2.1 Data analytics and audit sampling

One of the key impacts of auditors using data analytics techniques is on sampling. As we have discussed, sampling is traditionally used as a way to select and test a representative sample of a population. However, audit data analytics tools now mean that it can be relatively easy and quick for entire populations to be tested. The benefit of this should be obvious—the audit test covers the whole population, thereby reducing, perhaps even eliminating sampling risk. There is therefore a strong argument that using data analytics could improve the quality and the efficiency of audit evidence.

However, the results of data analysis performed will need careful evaluation, and it is likely that this evaluation will take time and require skill. For example, when testing an entire population using data analytics, the results are likely to highlight many more anomalies or exceptions (known as 'outliers') than if the test had been performed on a sample basis, so the skill will be in deciding which of these to investigate further (i.e. how to set a threshold in terms of the number or perhaps the monetary value of exceptions to look at in more detail) and how to carry out the further investigative procedures.

11.8 Procedures during the interim audit

As we saw in Chapter 7, when we briefly introduced the concept of the interim audit, this is when audit procedures are performed during the audited entity's financial year (i.e. prior to the year end). For example, if the financial year end is 30 September, it would be common for the audit firm to conduct some audit work in the last few months of the financial year, starting possibly in June or July.

Interim audits allow the auditor to carry out audit procedures during the year and the evidence from those procedures can be used at the final audit.

Activity 11.5 Benefits of interim audit

What do you think are the benefits of performing an interim audit?

11.8.1 Types of procedures performed at interim audit

Now that we understand more about the different types of audit procedures and sources of evidence, we can consider in more detail the procedures that would typically be performed at the interim audit.

It is common for the auditor to make an initial assessment of controls and possibly to perform tests of controls at the interim period. The advantage of obtaining evidence about controls at this point is that it allows for early planning, especially the early identification of risks of material misstatement.

Substantive procedures may also be performed at the interim audit, which allows at least some detailed testing to be performed ahead of the year end. For example:

- additions to non-current assets acquired prior to the interim audit date can be physically verified to gain assurance on their existence;
- inventory counts which take place during the year can be attended by the auditor; and
- substantive tests of detail can be performed on transactions such as sales, purchases, and payroll for the year to date.

However, it is not always the case that procedures will always be performed at the interim date. Table 11.8 includes factors which should be considered.

When procedures have been performed at the interim stage, consideration needs to be given to how to roll forward the audit procedures to the year-end date.

11.8.2 **Roll-forward–tests of control**

ISA (UK) 330 states:

> If the auditor obtains audit evidence about the operating effectiveness of controls during an interim period, the auditor shall:
>
> (a) Obtain audit evidence about significant changes to those controls subsequent to the interim period; and
>
> (b) Determine the additional audit evidence to be obtained for the remaining period.[18]

Table 11.8 Matters to consider in respect of interim audit procedures

Factor	Matters to consider
Control environment	If the auditor is planning to rely on the controls during the audit, then it is sensible to perform an initial assessment and possibly some tests on the controls as early as possible, in order to confirm if a test on controls strategy is appropriate for the audit
Risk assessment	For specific balances and transactions that are considered high risk, it may be more efficient to leave the detailed audit work until the year end, so that audit procedures are focused on detailed testing of the balance that will appear in the financial statements However, if a significant class of transaction that has operated throughout the accounting period is considered high risk, then some testing can be performed at the interim stage to gain assurance on the transactions that have occurred up to that point in time
Nature of specific risk	There are some risks that can only be audited at or after the year end, for example, risks to do with cut-off, or the stage of completion of work in progress
Logistics	It will usually be preferable for an audit firm to perform work at the interim stage as it allows more flexibility in the allocation of work to members of the audit team. It avoids audit work being too bunched at and just after the financial year end.
Availability of information	Some audited entities may have limited information available at an interim date, for example, smaller entities may not produce management accounts at each month end, which restricts the work that the auditor can conduct prior to the year end

[18] FRC, 'ISA (UK) 330', 2017, para 12.

It is essential that the auditor considers any changes that have occurred in the control systems between the interim stage and final stage of the audit. For example, controls may have deteriorated in that period, in which case the auditor would need to re-evaluate the assessment of the control environment.

The amount of additional audit evidence that may be needed in relation to the controls that were operating during the period between the interim audit and the financial year end includes (but are not limited to) the following:

- The specific controls that were tested at the interim audit, and any significant changes to them
- The length of the interim period
- The extent to which the auditor intends to reduce the use of further substantive procedures based on reliance on controls
- The significance of the assessed level of risk of material misstatement.[19]

To obtain evidence on the operation of controls in the interim period, the auditor can perform additional tests on controls, or can gain assurance from testing and assessing the audited entity's monitoring of controls.

11.8.3 Roll-forward–substantive procedures

ISA (UK) 330 states:

> If substantive procedures are performed at an interim date, the auditor shall cover the remaining period by performing:
>
> (a) substantive procedures, combined with tests of controls for the intervening period; or
>
> (b) if the auditor determines that it is sufficient, further substantive procedures only, that provide a reasonable basis for extending the audit conclusions from the interim date to the period end.[20]

When the auditor has performed substantive analytical procedures and/or tests of detail at the interim stage, the auditor is required to perform further procedures relevant to the period from the interim to the final stage of the audit. There is an obvious risk that a risk of misstatement may arise in the period between the interim and final stages of the audit, and that risk is increased the longer the period of time between the interim and final stages.

ISA (UK) 330 suggests the matters that should be considered in deciding whether further substantive procedures are necessary[21]:

- Whether the period-end balances of the particular classes of transactions or account balances are reasonably predictable—in which case little or no further substantive procedures may be necessary
- Whether the entity's procedures for analysing and adjusting classes of transactions or account balances at interim dates and for establishing proper accounting cut-offs are

[19] Ibid., para A33. [20] Ibid., para 22.

[21] ISA (UK) 330, 'The Auditor's Responses to Assessed Risks', para A57.

appropriate (i.e. the better the general control environment, and specific controls over cut-off, the fewer roll-forward procedures will be necessary)

- Whether the information system relevant to financial reporting will provide information concerning the balances at the period end and the transactions in the remaining period that is sufficient to permit investigation of:
  - Significant unusual transactions or entries (including those at or near the period end);
  - Other causes of significant fluctuations, or expected fluctuations that did not occur; and
  - Changes in the composition of the classes of transactions or account balances.

When conducting substantive procedures at the interim stage, the auditor may detect an unexpected misstatement. In this situation, the auditor will modify the procedures performed, for example, by extending the procedures or repeating them.

Chapter round-up

- The audit strategy can be controls based or substantive in focus, or a mixture.
- The audit plan contains details of the planned audit procedures which respond specifically to risks identified.
- The auditor must plan to obtain sufficient and appropriate audit evidence to support the audit opinion.
- Tests of controls provide evidence on the operating effectiveness of internal controls.
- A strategy based on tests of controls is appropriate where the auditor's expectation is that controls will be operating effectively.
- Substantive procedures are designed to provide evidence on specific balances and transactions.
- A strategy based on substantive procedures is appropriate where there is a weak control environment, a lack of controls, or controls are considered to be ineffective.
- Sampling can be used as an efficient way to obtain audit evidence where there is a large population of items.
- Sampling risk is part of detection risk and sampling involves the use of auditor's judgement when selecting the sample and evaluating the results.
- Audit data analytics is increasingly being used by audit firms to make obtaining audit evidence more efficient and to reduce detection risk through comprehensive testing of client's accounting systems.
- The interim audit is often used to make an initial assessment of the effectiveness of internal controls.

End of chapter case study

Introduction

The auditor must ensure that planned audit procedures respond to specific risks that have been identified during audit planning. The exact nature of audit procedures will depend on the type of risks that have been identified and the materiality of the balances and transactions concerned.

ISA (UK) 500 requires that audit evidence is obtained that is sufficient and appropriate and that forms a basis for the forming of the auditor's opinion. Generally speaking, the higher the risk of material misstatement, the more persuasive the audit evidence that should be obtained.

This activity will test your ability to plan audit procedures in response to specific risks identified at the assertion level. This is a key skill that is crucial to the successful planning of an efficient and effective audit.

This activity links to the following learning outcomes:

- Explain how the auditor responds to assessed risks at the financial statement level and the assertion level.
- Discuss the types of procedure used to obtain audit evidence including tests of controls and substantive procedures and discuss the use of audit programmes.
- Describe the methods used to obtain audit evidence, including inspection, observation, external confirmation, recalculation, reperformance, analytical procedures, inquiry, and recommend relevant sources of audit evidence.

Scenario

Madrid Ltd has a financial year ending 30 September 20X2 and you are working on the audit. Madrid Ltd is a property development company, specializing in the renovation of old warehouses into luxury residential apartment buildings. Extracts from the draft financial statements and comparative information are given below.

Statement of profit or loss	Notes	Year to 30 September 20X2 (draft) £'000	Year to 30 September 20X1 (actual) £'000
Revenue	1	45,000	42,500
Operating expenses	2	(20,500)	(20,000)
Operating profit		24,500	22,500
Finance costs		(5,000)	(5,000)
Profit before tax		19,500	17,500
Tax expense		(4,000)	(4,300)
Profit after tax		15,500	13,200

Figure 11.10

Statement of financial position	Notes	30 September 20X2 (draft) £'000	30 September 20X1 (actual) £'000
Non-current assets:			
PPE	3	30,000	20,000
Financial assets	4	7,000	3,500
		37,000	**23,500**
Current assets:			
Inventory	5	120,000	117,000

Figure 11.10 (Continued)

Statement of financial position	Notes	30 September 20X2 (draft) £'000	30 September 20X1 (actual) £'000
Trade receivables		450	390
Cash		5,000	4,500
		125,450	**121,890**
Total assets		**162,450**	**145,390**
Equity:			
Share capital		50,000	50,000
Revaluation surplus	6	10,000	–
Retained earnings		32,450	20,290
		92,450	**70,290**
Non-current liabilities:			
Loans	7	**61,200**	**67,000**
Current liabilities:			
Trade payables		3,500	3,600
Tax and other liabilities		4,300	4,300
Provisions		1,000	200
		8,800	**8,100**
Total equity and liabilities		**162,450**	**145,390**

Notes to the financial statements:

1. In January 20X2 Madrid Ltd changed its accounting policy on revenue recognition. The new accounting policy is to recognize revenue when the sale of a property has been agreed with the purchaser and a legally binding contract has been signed. The previous accounting policy was to recognize revenue on completion of the contract, when all proceeds relating to the disposal had been received.
2. Operating expenses include an amount of £750,000 regarding a legal claim that has been made against the company. The claim relates to a breach of planning permission which is alleged to have occurred on a major property development.
3. PPE comprises the company's head office, storage facility, and construction equipment. No major additions have been made to PPE during the year.
4. Madrid Ltd invests surplus cash in a portfolio of investments. The portfolio is managed by an external financial adviser who takes all decisions regarding the investments and who maintains all accounting records in relation to the investments bought and sold, and the income received from the portfolio. The adviser uses a specialist to provide valuations for investments in non-listed shares.
5. All properties that are currently being developed or are awaiting sale to a customer are recognized as inventory.
6. Madrid Ltd revalued its head office on 1 April 20X2. The revaluation was performed by a property consultant who is independent of Madrid Ltd.
7. Madrid Ltd paid off some of its long-term finance during the year. The finance was provided by the company's bankers several years ago to fund expansion.

Required

You have been asked you to help with planning the audit of Madrid Ltd. The tasks that you are required to perform are as follows:

1. Identify and explain the risks of material misstatement in the financial statements of Madrid Ltd.
2. Identify the specific assertions impacted by the risks identified.
3. Recommend an audit response (i.e. an audit strategy and at least one planned audit procedure for each risk identified).

Answer

Risk of material misstatement	Specific assertion affected	Planned audit response
The new accounting policy on revenue may not be in compliance with the applicable financial reporting framework Changes in accounting policy require specific adjustments to be made to comparative information and disclosure in notes to the financial statements. There is risk that this has not happened	Revenue—occurrence Revenue—accuracy Revenue—cut-off Completeness of disclosure Accuracy of disclosure Valuation of opening balances of retained earnings	Substantive testing on revenue, focusing on testing to obtain assurance that revenue is not overstated Specific procedures may include: Discussion with management regarding the reason for the change in accounting policy Scrutiny of the new accounting policy to ensure it is compliant with the applicable financial reporting framework Agreement of a sample of revenue items back to legal agreement signed by the customer, focusing on transactions recorded just prior to the year end Review of disclosures made in relation to the change in accounting policy Perform a reconciliation of opening and closing retained earnings to ensure any adjustment necessary in respect of the changed accounting policy has been made
A provision has been recognized in relation to a legal claim. There is a risk that an insufficient amount has been provided In addition, the notes to the financial statements should disclose information about the matter giving rise to the provision. There is a risk that disclosure has not been made	Provisions—valuation Completeness of disclosure Accuracy of disclosure	Discuss the situation with management to form an understanding of the events leading up to the claim being made against the company Obtain the claim documentation to confirm that the amount provided is equal to the amount claimed. Review legal correspondence to gain evidence on the likelihood of the claim against Madrid Ltd being successful Obtain written management representation regarding the outcome of the legal claim Review the disclosures made in the financial statements and ensure the information given is consistent with auditor's understanding of the situation

Risk of material misstatement	Specific assertion affected	Planned audit response
The financial assets have doubled in value during the year. This is a significant increase and indicates potential overvaluation, especially because the assets are held at fair value. The determination of fair value is subjective and therefore risk arises in the valuation of the assets Risk also arises in relation to the recognition of fair value gains or losses—the draft financial statements do not show where these are classified The accounts being maintained by an external party means that the audit team must determine how much reliance can be placed on the accounting systems and controls of the external party. Risk arises if controls are deficient	Valuation of assets Fair value gains and losses—accuracy and classification Financial assets and fair value gains and losses—completeness, measurement, accuracy, cut-off	Select a sample of listed investments held in the portfolio at the year end and agree valuation to external sources, for example, published stock exchange values For non-listed investments discuss the method of valuation with the external party and consider the reasonableness of the valuation method and any assumptions used in the valuation Perform substantive analytical procedures, comparing the return received on investments with market rates of return Recompute a selection of profits/losses made on investment disposals Confirm the accounting policy regarding recognition of gains and losses and agree consistent treatment in previous years' financial statements Plan to audit the accounting records held by the external party in accordance with ISA (UK) 402 *Audit Considerations Relating to an Entity Using a Service Organization*. This should include documentation and evaluation of the external party's systems and controls
The inventory of properties being developed will be at various stages of completion at the year end. Valuation will be complex and needs to be performed on an individual basis for each property	Inventory—valuation	The audit team should physically inspect each property at, or close to, the year end, to form a judgement as to the stage of completeness of each property development The costs incurred to date on each property redevelopment should be obtained, and a sample of costs agreed to supporting documentation such as invoices for materials, payroll sheets for labour costs Consider the use of an auditor's expert in relation to property valuation

Risk of material misstatement	Specific assertion affected	Planned audit response
The head office has been revalued during the year. The revaluation gain represents 6.2% of total assets and is therefore material to the financial statements. Valuations are subjective and give rise to risk of misstatement, especially the risk of overstatement Depreciation should have been recalculated at the date of the revaluation. The risk is that this has not happened so depreciation expenses are not correct	PPE—valuation Depreciation—accuracy	The audit team must consider the independence of the expert who provided the valuation of PPE and confirm there is no threat to objectivity The professional qualifications and experience of the expert should also be determined The methods used by the expert to arrive at the property valuation should be evaluated. Any assumptions should be reviewed for reasonableness and to ensure they are in line with auditor's understanding of the business Management's calculations of depreciation should be reviewed and reperformed to ensure the expense is correctly determined
The company's loan balance is disclosed as a non-current liability. However, an amount has been paid off this year, indicating that part of the amount should be classified as a current liability	Loan liability—classification	The loan documentation should be obtained and repayment terms verified. Any amounts due for repayment within twelve months should be classified as a current liability Cash payments in the post-year-end period can be reviewed for any repayments of the loan balance
Finance costs have remained static at £5 million in both 20X2 and 20X1. It is unusual for the amount to remain the same, especially given the loan repayment that has been made, and that the gains and losses on financial investments should have been netted or added to the finance cost figure	Finance costs—accuracy	Obtain a breakdown of the amounts included in the £5 million finance costs for both years and compare the component parts Form an expectation of the finance costs attached to the loan using the loan documentation's stated interest rate and amount outstanding Agree investment gains and losses included in the £5 million to external party's workings
Tax expense is lower this year despite Madrid Ltd making more profit. The effective tax rate is 20.5% this year compared to 24.6% last year. Also, the tax liability has not changed at this year end. This indicates that the tax accrual for the year may not be properly calculated or accrued for	Tax expense—accuracy	Recompute the estimated tax charge for the year Review correspondence with tax authorities to form an expectation of the expense that should be recognized

Activity solutions

Activity 11.1—Reliance on internal controls

What matters should an auditor consider in deciding whether to place reliance on a client's internal controls?

Suggested answer points:

- Any improvements that have been made to internal controls including the overall environment, systems, and processes during the year.
- Following up on recommendations made by the auditor in the previous year to see if they have been implemented.
- The approach used in previous years and any relevant points brought forward from last year's audit.
- The results of any interim testing that has taken place and any preliminary evaluation of internal controls.

Activity 11.2—Audit programmes

What do you think are the advantages and disadvantages of using standardized compared to tailored audit programmes?

Suggested answer points:

Standardized audit programmes have the advantage of consistency and a reduced risk that audit procedures will be missed out. Standardized programmes can also make the review process more efficient because the reviewer will be familiar with the documentation.

Standardized audit programmes can be efficient, quick to set up and use, and are often sufficient for a smaller audit client with a simple business model and few complex balances and transactions.

Tailored programmes encourage audit teams to respond specifically to the audit risks identified, leading to higher-quality audit evidence being obtained. The audit teams will have a better understanding of the objective of the procedures if they have been designed specifically for the audit in question.

However, tailored programmes can be time-consuming to create and review. In addition, there is increased detection risk if the programme is not properly designed (e.g. objectives of audit testing are not appropriate). Experienced auditors need to be involved with developing tailored programmes, to reduce this risk.

Activity 11.3—Non-statistical sampling

What do you think are the advantages and disadvantages of non-statistical sampling?

Suggested answer points:

Advantages	Disadvantages
It can be an established process which is well understood	It can result in large sample sizes which can increase the costs of the audit; it can also result in sample sizes which are too small which render the test invalid
It brings in auditor's judgement and expertise	The results are not statistically valid
No time is spent on complex mathematical formulae or interpretations	It can result in bias in the sample chosen
No specialist knowledge is required	It can be indefensible if there is a lack of logic in the selection of the sample or its size
Non-statistical sampling has been refined by experience	There is no consistency of results—different auditors can produce different samples

Activity 11.4–Audit data analytics

Can you think of other challenges that audit firms face with implementing audit data analytics?

Suggested answer points:

- If the quality of the underlying data/input to the audit data analytics software is not good, then the results may not be reliable.
- Auditors need training, which can be expensive, if auditors are not properly trained, they will not be able to interpret the results, leading to poor quality work being performed.
- There could be problems with cybersecurity.
- The client may be reluctant to allow the audit firm access to systems if they are worried about confidentiality or loss of data.

Activity 11.5–Benefits of interim audit

What do you think are the benefits of performing an interim audit?

Suggested answer points:

- Fewer substantive tests being performed at the final audit if the controls tested at the interim stage provide evidence that the controls are effective.
- Fewer substantive procedures being performed at the final stage if they have been carried out at the interim stage as only substantive procedures between the interim audit date and the year-end date will need to be carried out.
- A shorter timescale involved in completing the final audit if an interim audit has been carried out.
- The audited financial statements can be available earlier as the auditor's report will be signed closer to the year end.

12 Other Issues Relating to Audit Evidence

Introduction

As we know, the objective of an audit is for the auditor to express an opinion on the financial statements as to whether they are true and fair (or present fairly, in all material respects). The auditor expresses this opinion through the auditor's report and is based on the audit evidence obtained throughout the audit. In the previous chapter, we developed an understanding of the assertions which are relevant to the audit of financial statements, appreciating that it is a matter of judgement for the auditor to determine when they have obtained sufficient appropriate evidence to support the audit opinion. We also looked at the types of audit procedures that the auditor can perform and considered sources of evidence.

In this chapter, we are going to look at some specific ways in which the auditor can obtain evidence and some particular areas over which the auditor needs to obtain audit evidence.

Many entities have an internal audit function which reports to management on the operating effectiveness of the system of internal control and will make recommendations where they detect weaknesses in controls or absent controls. In this respect, the external auditor may decide to use the work of internal audit if they think the work carried out by internal audit is relevant to the external audit and fit for purpose. Sometimes, the audit client may use a service organization to carry out certain functions of its business. Here the auditor will need to gather sufficient appropriate audit evidence to ensure that the use of any service organizations does not increase the risk of material misstatement in the financial statements.

In this chapter, we will look at these and other relevant issues relating to how auditors can obtain sufficient and appropriate audit evidence, including the requirements of the following ISAs:

- ISA (UK) 610 Using the Work of Internal Auditors
- ISA (UK) 620 Using the Work of an Auditor's Expert
- ISA (UK) 580 Written Representations
- ISA (UK) 540 Auditing Accounting Estimates and Related Disclosures
- ISA (UK) 402 Audit Considerations Relating to an Entity Using a Service Organization
- ISA (UK) 510 Initial Audit Engagements—Opening Balances
- ISA (UK) 505 External Confirmations

Learning outcomes

- Describe the role of internal audit and explain its interaction with external audit and discuss the extent to which external auditors are able to rely on the work of internal audit.
- Explain when the use of an auditor's or management's expert will be required and the type of audit evidence that must be obtained.
- Discuss the circumstances where written representations are necessary and the matters on which representations are commonly obtained; describe the content of a written representation letter and discuss its usefulness as audit evidence.
- Discuss the problems associated with the audit and review of accounting estimates; explain the procedures that may be used to obtain evidence in respect of accounting estimates.
- Explain the use of a service organization and the factors that must be considered by the auditor when a client uses a service organization for a specific function of the business.
- Describe the audit procedures to be applied on opening balances.
- Describe the types of external confirmation the auditor may require and how they serve as audit evidence.

By the end of this chapter, you will be able to:

- Recommend an audit approach when faced with a range of issues including the need to obtain external confirmations, representations from management, and obtain evidence in respect of opening balances.
- Discuss and evaluate the impact on the audit when an audit client uses a service organization.

12.1 Internal audit and its role in an external audit

12.1.1 The role of internal audit

We introduced the concept of internal audit in Chapter 3, when we looked at corporate governance, and again in Chapter 8 when we explored internal audit as part of a system of internal control. In this chapter, we will look in more detail at the work performed by internal audit and consider how this relates to the external auditor's work.

As a reminder, an internal audit function is defined as:

> A function of an entity that performs assurance and consulting activities designed to evaluate and improve the effectiveness of the entity's governance, risk management and internal control processes.[1]

[1] FRC, 'ISA (UK) 610', 2022, para 14(a) <https://media.frc.org.uk/documents/ISA_UK_610_Updated_May_2022.pdf> (accessed 18 January 2024).

Remember that many businesses, particularly companies required to comply with corporate governance, and other large organizations, have an internal audit function. The existence of an internal audit function does not change the responsibilities of the external auditor but the external auditor can choose to rely on some of the work performed by internal audit if the work is relevant to the scope of the external audit and of good quality.

As we saw in Chapter 8, one of the main objectives of internal audit that is relevant to the external audit is to provide assurance on the operation of a company's internal controls. When an internal audit function is efficient, it will reduce **control risk**, which is the risk that a material misstatement in the financial statements will not be prevented or detected and corrected on a timely basis by the entity's system of internal control.

It is important to remember that internal auditors should be independent from the operations they evaluate, so that they can provide an unbiased and objective view. The Institute of Internal Auditors says that, 'it is important to think of the internal auditor as the organization's critical friend—someone who can challenge current practice, champion best practice and be a catalyst for improvement, so that the organization as a whole achieves its strategic objectives'.[2] Internal auditors should not be involved in designing or implementing operational activities or internal controls. Their role is evaluation of operations and providing assurance on internal controls.

Activity 12.1 The work of internal audit

Here is a brief scenario for you to consider.

Pearl Ltd operates a number of manufacturing sites across the country. The company has an internal audit team. The finance director has suggested that the internal auditors could perform the following tasks:

- Assist the accounts department, which is very short-staffed, in preparing the financial statements.
- Develop a new credit control procedure, to help combat the company's poor cash flow.
- Perform an evaluation of compliance with health and safety regulations in the company's manufacturing sites.

Briefly comment on whether you think it is appropriate for the internal auditors to perform these tasks.

The external auditor may decide to use the work of internal audit with a view to reducing the level of detailed substantive testing that is to be carried out. This promotes audit efficiency and therefore allows the external auditor to devote more audit resources to higher-risk areas of the financial statements. The work of an internal audit function varies across entities: for larger businesses, the internal audit function will be more complex, whereas for smaller businesses it is likely to be a simple process.

At the outset, it is worth understanding the differences between internal and external audit. The notable differences are set out in Table 12.1.

The type of work that the external auditor would wish to rely on will also vary and will be considered at a very early stage in the planning process. Typically, the external auditor may decide to use the work of internal audit in respect of a number of areas.

[2] Institute of Internal Auditors, 'Internal Auditing: Adding Value Across the Board'.

Table 12.1 Internal audit compared with external audit

External audit	Internal audit
Objective The main objective of the external auditor is to provide an opinion on whether the financial statements give a true and fair view (or present fairly, in all material respects).	The main objective of internal audit is to improve the entity's operations by reviewing the efficiency and effectiveness of the system of internal control.
Reporting External auditors report to the shareholders or members of the company. External auditor's reports are included in the annual report and financial statements and are therefore publicly available.	Internal audit reports are not publicly available and are only intended to be seen by the addressee of the report. The reports are normally provided to the company directors and those charged with governance, such as the audit committee, to whom internal audit reports.
Scope of work The external auditor's work is limited to verifying the truth and fairness of the financial statements.	The internal auditor may have a wide remit. Their work is determined by the requirements of management or those charged with governance. Generally, internal audit will focus their attention on the company's internal control environment, but any other area of the company's operations can also be reviewed.
Relationship External auditors are appointed by the shareholders and hence are independent of the company.	Internal auditors are appointed by management. They are normally internal employees of the company and hence will not be independent. In some cases, an entity's internal control function can be outsourced which can increase independence.

Figure 12.1 Work of internal audit relevant to external audit

Auditing in practice 12.1 Internal audit

Internal auditors have a unique position in a company, having cross-functional insight across the operations of business divisions. This means that the internal audit function can provide a wealth of information to the external auditor. At the planning stage of the audit, the external auditor should consider how best to utilize the knowledge of the internal audit team and whether they wish to rely on their work. Some examples of how the work of internal auditors can be useful to external auditors include:

- Accounting policies—internal auditors will be familiar with the organization's accounting policies, so they can provide information about current policies and any planned changes to accounting policies.
- Financial analysis—internal auditors may perform their own financial analysis (e.g. to compare the performance of different business divisions), and this analysis can be useful to the external auditor for audit planning purposes and to gain further insight into company performance over time.
- Systems and controls—the internal audit function is likely to have extremely good knowledge of the organization's systems and controls, which again will help with audit planning, helping the external auditor to understand the level of control risk. The external auditor may choose to rely on tests of controls performed by internal audit, subject to appropriate evaluation in accordance with ISA (UK) 610 *Using the Work of Internal Auditors*. Even if there is no reliance on tests of controls over the systems, the internal auditor can provide documentation regarding the systems.
- Risk management—internal audit often plays a supporting role in risk management within an organization, so is well placed to provide information to the external auditor about risks facing the business, which can enhance the auditor's understanding of the business and inform the audit risk assessment process.

ISA (UK) 610 *Using the Work of Internal Auditors* provides guidance on the external auditor's responsibilities when using the work of a client's internal audit function. This ISA will only apply where the entity has an internal audit function. ISA (UK) 610 does not apply if the responsibilities and activities of the internal audit function are irrelevant to the external audit; or if the external auditor does not expect to use the work of internal audit when obtaining audit evidence.

Where the entity has an internal audit function, ISA (UK) 610 does not mandate the auditor to use the work of the internal audit function. Whether the work of internal audit will be used by the external auditor is a matter for the external auditor to decide. Prior to using the work of the entity's internal audit function, the external auditor must assess its overall effectiveness.

Where the external auditor does plan to use the work of the internal audit function, the responsibility for the auditor's opinion still rests with the external auditor. ISA (UK) 610 acknowledges that while internal auditors may perform similar audit procedures to those which the external auditor may perform, neither the internal audit function nor the internal auditors are **independent** of the entity as is required of the external auditor by ISA (UK) 200 *Overall Objectives of the Independent Auditor and the Conduct of an Audit in Accordance with International Standards on Auditing (UK).*

ISA (UK) 610 provides specific objectives where the external auditor is planning to use the work of the internal audit function as follows:

(a) To determine whether the work of the internal audit function or direct assistance from internal auditors can be used, and if so, in which areas and to what extent; and having made that determination:

(b) If using the work of the internal audit function, to determine whether that work is adequate for purposes of the audit; and

(c) If using internal auditors to provide direct assistance, to appropriately direct, supervise and review their work.[3]

12.1.2 **Using the work of the internal audit function**

As we have mentioned above, when the external auditor is planning to use the work of the internal audit function, the external auditor must first evaluate the work of internal audit. To that end, the auditor must evaluate three matters as shown in Figure 12.2 the extent to which the internal audit function's organizational status and relevant policies and procedures support the objectivity of the internal auditors, the level of competence of the internal audit function, and whether the internal audit function applies a systematic and disciplined approach, including quality control.[4]

Activity 12.2 Using the work of internal audit

Thinking from a practical point of view, what questions do you think an external auditor might ask, to evaluate the organizational status, objectivity, and competence of internal audit, and whether they operate using a systematic and disciplined approach?

Figure 12.2 Matters to consider in respect of using the work of internal audit

[3] FRC, 'ISA (UK) 610', 2022, para 13. [4] Ibid., para 15.

It is worth making clear at this point that we are discussing the external auditor using the work that is performed by internal audit as they are performing their regular duties within the organization. This is not the same as the internal auditor providing direct assistance to the external auditor, which is when the internal auditor performs work under the direction of the external auditor. We will consider direct assistance later in this chapter.

When the auditor does decide that it is appropriate to use the work of internal audit, care must be taken in determining how much reliance to place on this work, and whether the external auditor should perform their own procedures in addition. ISA (UK) 610 suggests that

> the higher the assessed risks of material misstatement, the more persuasive the audit evidence required by the external auditor will need to be, and, therefore, the external auditor will need to perform more of the work directly.[5]

In addition:

> where the risk of material misstatement is other than low, the use of the work of the internal audit function alone is unlikely to reduce audit risk to an acceptably low level and eliminate the need for the external auditor to perform some tests directly.[6]

In other words, the external auditor will need to obtain their own evidence, and not use the work of internal audit as a sole source of audit evidence for areas of the audit which have a high risk of material misstatement.

When the auditor does decide to use the work of internal audit, the auditor needs to discuss and coordinate with the internal audit function. It is important to remember that the internal audit function is simply performing its usual work, which is being made available for use by the external auditor. The external auditor is not asking the internal auditor to perform specific tasks for the purpose of the external audit or directing and supervising their work. Matters which need to be discussed include the timing of work, the type of work performed, and how it will be documented. It is important that there is good communication between the external and internal auditors, so that any significant issues that arise when the internal auditors are performing their work are notified to the external auditors, who can then consider implications for the audit.

The auditor must set aside adequate time and resources to be able to review the work of internal audit. This is to ensure that the work is of a high quality and has been performed in an objective manner. As well as reviewing documentation, the external auditor may choose to observe procedures being performed by internal audit and discuss matters with members of the internal audit function.

The review process will typically involve:

- Ascertaining if internal audit's work has been properly planned, performed, supervised, reviewed, and documented.
- Determining whether sufficient appropriate evidence has been obtained.
- Considering whether the conclusions reached are appropriate in the circumstances.
- Concluding whether the reports prepared by internal audit are consistent with the work performed.

[5] Ibid., para 20. [6] Ibid., para A21 (extract).

At this stage, the auditor may consider it necessary to reperform some of the procedures which internal audit have carried out to ensure the external auditor reaches the same conclusion.

Auditing scenario 12.1 Internal audit

The Lurcher Group is a large bank, with operations in many countries across the world. It has an internal audit team of 200 individuals, headed up by Max Macha, who reports to the Group audit committee every month.

The internal audit team operates under an 'Internal Audit Charter' which provides principles in relation to how the internal audit team will operate and other relevant matters. Here is an extract from the Internal Audit Charter:

- The Group Head of Internal Audit reports to the Chair of the Group Audit Committee and attends the Group board meetings but does not participate in decision-making.
- The internal audit team has unrestricted access at any time to all the records, personnel, property, and operations of the Group.
- The internal audit team determines the scope of its work and the procedures it will perform including the frequency and timing.
- Members of the internal audit team are required to undertake relevant professional and technical training, to ensure they perform work with a high level of competence.

The Internal Audit Charter provides a robust framework for the activities of the internal auditors. It means that the external auditors are more likely to be able to use the work of internal audit, but the requirements of ISA (UK) 620 *Using the Work of an Auditor's Expert* in respect of evaluating their organizational status, competence, and the quality of their work will still need to be followed.

The key points to bear in mind where an entity has an internal audit function is that this can reduce control risk, provided the internal audit function is efficient, well structured, and systematic in its approach. The auditor must also consider management's attitude to the work of internal audit. For example, if management has a dismissive attitude where internal audit is concerned, it is likely that any recommendations made by internal audit to improve the company's controls have been ignored. In this respect, the external auditor is unlikely to place reliance on the work of internal audit as their recommendations may not have been implemented. Conversely, if management have a history of always implementing recommendations made by internal audit, this can help the auditor in reducing the level of substantive testing they carry out (if the external auditor decides to place reliance on the work of internal audit).

12.1.3 **Direct assistance**

ISA (UK) 610 defines 'direct assistance' as:

> The use of internal auditors to perform audit procedures under the direction, supervision and review of the external auditor.[7]

[7] Ibid., para 14(b).

In the UK, the Financial Reporting Council (FRC) have modified ISA 610 (as issued by the International Auditing and Assurance Standards Board (IAASB)) to prevent the external auditor from using internal audit to provide direct assistance. The prohibition on direct assistance is largely due to the threat to objectivity that is present when internal auditors perform work for the external auditor. In the UK, the regulatory body considers that such threats cannot be reduced to an acceptable level, hence the prohibition.

Activity 12.3 Prohibition on direct assistance

Why do you think that in some jurisdictions, including the UK, there is a prohibition on the internal audit function providing direct assistance to the external auditor?

Where law or regulation does not prohibit the internal audit function providing direct assistance to the external auditor, the following factors must be considered:

- *Objectivity of internal audit*—if there are any threats to the objectivity of internal audit, the significance of them and whether they can be reduced to an acceptably low level must be considered.
- *Competence of internal audit*—direct assistance should only be provided if the internal auditor is competent to perform high-quality work.
- *Type of work to be assigned*—the external auditor cannot assign work to the internal auditor which involves significant judgement, a high risk of material misstatement, or work in which the internal auditor has been involved.
- *Communication*—the planned work must be communicated with those charged with governance in accordance with ISA 260 *Communication with Those Charged with Governance* to ensure that agreement to use internal audit can be obtained and that the use of internal audit is not excessive.

When the internal audit function is used to provide direct assistance to the external auditor (i.e. when national auditing standards do not prohibit the provision of direct assistance), the following must be complied with:

(a) The external auditor must obtain written confirmation from management that the internal auditor can provide direct assistance and that they will not intervene in that work.

(b) The internal auditor must provide written confirmation to the external auditor so that they will keep the external auditor's information confidential.

(c) The external auditor must provide direction, supervision, and review of the internal auditor's work.

(d) At all times, the external auditor must keep in mind the risk that the internal auditor may not be objective or competent.

12.1.4 **Documentation**

When the external auditor uses the work of the internal audit function, ISA (UK) 610 requires certain documentation to be prepared as follows:

(a) The evaluation of:
- (i) Whether the function's organizational status and relevant policies and procedures adequately support the objectivity of the internal auditors;
- (ii) The level of competence of the function; and
- (iii) Whether the function applies a systematic and disciplined approach, including quality control;

(b) The nature and extent of the work used and the basis for that decision; and

(c) The audit procedures that have been performed by the external auditor to evaluate the adequacy of the work used.[8]

Where the external auditor uses internal auditors to provide direct assistance on the audit, the external auditor's audit documentation must include:

(a) The evaluation of the existence and significance of threats to the objectivity of the internal auditors, and the level of competence of the internal auditors used to provide direct assistance;

(b) The basis for the decision concerning the nature and extent of the work performed by the internal auditors;

(c) Who reviewed the work performed and the date and extent of that review;

(d) The written agreements obtained from an authorized representative of the entity and the internal auditors; and

(e) The working papers prepared by the internal auditors who provided direct assistance on the audit engagement.[9]

12.2 Using an auditor's expert

Auditors cannot be experts in every aspect of a client's business. Indeed, audits often need the involvement of specialists to arrive at the amounts recognized in the financial statements, for example, amounts in respect of a defined benefit pension scheme or valuations of complex financial instruments.

The use of experts will generally be needed where complex items are included in the financial statements and ISA (UK) 620 *Using the Work of an Auditor's Expert* provides guidance to auditors when an individual or organization is used to obtain sufficient appropriate audit evidence. Auditors may also choose to rely on the work of others where they conclude that it would be efficient and effective to do so. However, simply engaging an expert is not enough to provide sufficient audit evidence—the auditor does have to do some other work where the expert is concerned to ensure that the work performed is suitable as audit evidence.

[8] Ibid., para 36. [9] Ibid., para 37.

It is important to emphasize that even when an auditor uses the work of an expert, this does not relieve the auditor of any of their responsibilities for the audit opinion. The auditor has sole responsibility for the opinion expressed in the auditor's report and the fact that an expert may have been used in a material area of the financial statements does not reduce this responsibility.

ISA 620 requires that

> If expertise in a field other than accounting or auditing is necessary to obtain sufficient appropriate audit evidence, the auditor shall determine whether to use the work of an auditor's expert.[10]

Activity 12.4 External experts

Suggest areas for which an expert may be brought in to provide audit evidence.

There are two types of expert an auditor may use: an 'auditor's expert' and a 'management's expert'. ISA (UK) 620 defines an 'auditor's expert' as follows:

> An individual or organization possessing expertise in a field other than accounting or auditing, whose work in that field is used by the auditor to assist the auditor in obtaining sufficient appropriate audit evidence. An auditor's expert may be either an auditor's internal expert (who is a partner or staff, including temporary staff, of the auditor's firm or a network firm), or an auditor's external expert.[11]

ISA 620 also defines a 'management's expert' as follows:

> An individual or organization possessing expertise in a field other than accounting or auditing, whose work in that field is used by the entity to assist the entity in preparing the financial statements.[12]

Auditing scenario 12.2 looks at the use of a management's expert.

There are a number of stages involved in using the work of an expert (Figure 12.3).

Auditing scenario 12.2 Use of a management's expert

Sunnie Ltd is an investment management business and has several complex financial instruments which are required to be remeasured to fair value at the reporting date. The company engaged the services of Morley & Co who specialize in valuing complex financial instruments. For the year ended 31 May 20X9, the investments significantly increased in value compared to the prior year.

The audit firm, Esme & Co LLP, has started to plan the audit of Sunnie Ltd's financial statements for the year ended 31 May 20X9. As the increase in the fair value of the financial instruments is material, the auditor must devise specific procedures to obtain sufficient and appropriate audit evidence to corroborate the valuation assertion. Some of these procedures will involve assessing the competence and experience of the valuer.

[10] FRC, 'ISA (UK) 620', 2022, para 7 <https://media.frc.org.uk/documents/ISA_UK_620_Revised_November_2019_Updated_May_2022.pdf> (accessed 18 January 2024).

[11] Ibid., para 6(a). [12] Ibid., para 6(b).

Figure 12.3 Stages involved in using the work of an auditor's expert

Typical procedures the auditor will carry out include:

- make inquiries of the expert, in particular the scope of the work to be performed;
- review the expert's working papers and reports;
- examine reputable reports and other authoritative published data;
- perform analytical procedures and reperform various calculations; and
- review the report of the expert for consistency.

The fact that the client has used the work of an expert does not preclude the auditor from carrying out their own procedures to address the risk of material misstatement within the valuation.

12.2.1 **Nature, timing, and extent of audit procedures**

ISA (UK) 620 confirms that the nature, timing, and extent of audit procedures where the work of an expert is concerned will vary depending on the circumstances. There are certain matters which the auditor must consider as follows:

(a) The nature of the matter to which the expert's work relates;

(b) The risks of material misstatement in the matter to which that expert's work relates;

(c) The significance of the expert's work in the context of the audit;

(d) The auditor's knowledge and experience with any previous work that the expert has performed; and

(e) Whether the expert is subject to the audit firm's quality management policies and procedures.[13]

[13] Ibid., para 8.

The key point to appreciate here is that the external auditor will require different or more extensive procedures to be performed where the expert is being engaged to provide evidence in respect of matters which are highly material to the financial statements, if the matter involves complex judgements or is very subjective in nature.

12.2.2 **Assessing the auditor's expert**

ISA (UK) 620 requires the auditor to assess the competence, capabilities, and objectivity of the expert. Where the expert is an auditor's expert, the evaluation of objectivity must include inquiry concerning any interests and relationships which may create a threat to the expert's objectivity. Remember, independence is vitally important where an external audit is concerned.

'Competence' relates to the nature and level of expertise of the expert and 'capability' relates to the expert's ability to exercise that competence in the performance of specific duties on the audit engagement. Competence and capability are not the same thing. A specialist may be competent to perform a valuation of a work of art for example, but they might not have the capability to value it in accordance with the International Financial Reporting Standard (IFRS).

? **Activity 12.5** Assessing the competence of an expert

How might an external auditor evaluate and conclude on the competence of an expert?

The term 'objectivity' relates to the potential effects of bias, conflict of interest or the influence that others may have on the judgement of the expert. For example, if an expert owns shares in the entity then their opinion is likely to be influenced by the fact they are a shareholder, and hence the auditor is unlikely to place any reliance on the expert's work.

In some jurisdictions (for example, the UK), there is a requirement for the auditor to obtain a confirmation from the expert concerning their independence where the entity is a public interest entity.

12.2.3 **Agreeing the work to be performed**

Prior to carrying out any work, an auditor's expert will need to agree the scope of their work and reporting responsibilities, which is usually in the form of an engagement letter or other formal agreement. This engagement letter essentially forms a contract between the auditor and their expert and will aim to minimize any misunderstanding between the two parties.

Typically, the engagement letter will include:

- The nature, scope, and objectives of the work to be performed by the auditor's expert, including any relevant technical standards or industry requirements.

- The roles and responsibilities of the auditor and the expert—this may refer to whether the expert is required to test any source data they are using in their work. There should also be agreement regarding access to, and retention of, each other's working papers.
- The nature, timing, and extent of communication between the two parties, for example, the form of the expert's report and deadlines for the completion of the work
- The need for the expert to observe confidentiality.[14]

Both parties should sign the engagement letter prior to any work being carried out. A more detailed agreement will be needed in situations where:

- the auditor has not previously used the work of the expert,
- the matter on which the expert is providing evidence is highly complex, or
- the expert will need to have access to confidential information.

12.2.4 **Evaluating the expert's work**

Once the work has been completed, the auditor must then assess it to ensure that it is appropriate for the purposes of the audit. When carrying out this evaluation, the auditor must consider the following issues:

- The relevance and reasonableness of the expert's findings and/or conclusions. The auditor must also assess the consistency of the findings with other audit evidence (to see if there are any contradictions with other audit evidence).
- Where the expert's work involves the use of significant assumptions and methods, evaluate the reasonableness of those assumptions and methods in the client's circumstances.
- If the expert's work involves the use of source data which is significant to the expert's work, consider the relevance, completeness, and accuracy of that source data.[15]

Activity 12.6 Evaluating the work of an auditor's expert

What matters do you think the auditor would consider when evaluating the adequacy of an auditor's expert's work?

There may be circumstances when the auditor determines that the work of the expert is inadequate for the purposes of the audit. There could be many reasons for this, such as the basis of the work carried out by the expert being inconsistent with the financial reporting framework; or the auditor discovering that the expert is not independent of the client.

In such situations, the auditor must agree with the expert the nature and extent of further work (if any) that is to be performed by the expert. Alternatively, the auditor must perform additional audit procedures that are appropriate in the particular circumstances.

[14] Ibid., para 11. [15] Ibid., para 12.

We mentioned earlier in the chapter that in some situations, management of the audit client will appoint their own expert, typically to provide a valuation within the financial statements. When this happens, the auditor must evaluate the work performed by the management's expert in much the same way as they would for an auditor's expert—considering the competence and capability as well as the objectivity of the expert in addition to looking at the adequacy of the actual work performed.

Auditing scenario 12.3 Evaluating the work of management's expert

Freya Enterprises Ltd is a property management company with a year end of 31 May 20X9. The company has thirty-five commercial investment properties all within a radius of 30 miles of each other, which it rents out to third parties. The investment properties are measured at fair value through profit or loss in accordance with IAS 40 *Investment Property*. This year the directors decided to appoint a new firm of surveyors to carry out the valuation of the investment properties and appointed Matautia & Co as a management's expert.

The work to be performed was agreed in a letter of engagement which was signed prior to the valuation being carried out.

The draft valuation report shows that the portfolio of investment properties has increased in value by £1.2m. Press reports in the area suggest that commercial property prices in the area have decreased considerably in the last twelve months due to the declining economic situation.

Majid, the audit senior, has exercised professional scepticism and has questioned the reliability of the valuation. On average, each property in Freya Enterprises' portfolio has increased by £34,286 (£1.2m/35 properties). This is inconsistent with what is happening in the market because press reports suggest the commercial properties should have decreased in fair value.

Upon investigation, it was found that the managing partner of Matautia & Co is married to the finance director of Freya Enterprises.

Clearly in this situation the auditor cannot place reliance on the expert's work because they are not independent of the entity. The fact that other commercial properties in the same area have declined in value to the worsening economic situation is inconsistent with the expert's valuation which shows that each property in the client's portfolio has increased in value by just over £34,000.

The auditor is unlikely to request that Matautia & Co carry out any additional work because they are not independent of the client. It may be appropriate for the auditor to engage the services of an auditor's expert to carry out a valuation of the properties or the auditor may request the client engages another expert to perform the valuation.

If the client refuses to have another valuation carried out, it is likely that the auditor will have to modify their audit opinion on the grounds of insufficient audit evidence.

12.2.5 **Relying on the work of the expert and the auditor's report**

In practice, an auditor will generally rely on the work of an expert provided the expert is independent and objective, technically competent, and possesses the expertise required to carry out the work adequately.

When the auditor relies on the work of the expert and has carried out all the procedures required by ISA (UK) 620, they must not make any reference to the work of the expert in the auditor's report.

Remember, it is the external auditor who is responsible for the audit opinion in the auditor's report. If any reference to an expert is made in the auditor's report, this is likely to devalue the opinion and mislead the user of the report. The only exception to not making any reference to an expert in the auditor's report is if law or regulation requires such reference to be made.

Even if law or regulation require reference to an expert to be made in the auditor's report, the auditor must indicate in the report that the reference does not reduce the auditor's responsibility for the auditor's opinion.

In the event that the auditor refers to the work of an expert in the auditor's report because doing so enables a better understanding of a modification to the auditor's opinion, the auditor must indicate in the auditor's report that such reference does not reduce the auditor's responsibility for that opinion.

12.3 Written representations

ISA (UK) 580 *Written Representations* contains the requirements for obtaining written representations from clients during the course of the audit. ISA (UK) 580 defines a written representation as:

> a written statement by management provided to the auditor to confirm certain matters or to support other audit evidence. Written representations in this context do not include financial statements, the assertions therein, or supporting books and records.[16]

Written representations, on their own, cannot be regarded as sufficient appropriate audit evidence. This is because they are internally generated and hence must serve to complement other forms of audit evidence. In practice, audit firms are often criticized when having an audit file reviewed because of over-reliance on written representations as audit evidence.

There are a few matters on which ISA (UK) 580 requires a written representation to be obtained. In addition, written representations are useful where other forms of evidence may be unavailable, especially in respect of matters requiring management judgement or knowledge which is restricted to management (Figure 12.4).

12.3.1 Written representations about management's responsibilities

The auditor must request that management provide a written representation to confirm that they have fulfilled their responsibilities for the preparation of the financial statements in accordance with an applicable financial reporting framework (e.g. IFRS), including, where relevant, their fair presentation. Management must also confirm that the financial statements are complete and hence they must provide a written representation that:

(a) It has provided the auditor with all relevant information and access as agreed in the terms of the audit engagement; and

(b) All transactions have been recorded and are reflected in the financial statements.[17]

[16] FRC, 'ISA (UK) 580', 2022, para 7 <https://media.frc.org.uk/documents/ISA_UK_580_Updated_May_2022.pdf> (accessed 18 January 2024).

[17] FRC, 'ISA (UK) 580', 2022, paras 10–11. <https://media.frc.org.uk/documents/ISA_UK_580_Updated_May_2022.pdf> (accessed 18 January 2024).

Mandatory written representations

- Confirm financial statements prepared by management in accordance with IFRS
- Auditors provided with all relevant information
- All transactions are recorded in the financial statements

Other written representations

- Where other forms of evidence may not be available, e.g.:
  - Compliance with certain laws or regulations
  - Plans or intentions which may affect the carrying amounts of assets and/or liabilities
  - Title to, or control over, assets
  - Confirmation of values which involve judgement such as provisions for liabilities

Figure 12.4 Written representations from management

12.3.2 **Other written representations**

In practice, the auditor will collate a list of issues during the evidence-gathering stage of the audit for which written representations are required. They will then draft the written representation letter but it must be transcribed onto the client's letterhead. The written representations letter must then be signed by one or more responsible officials of the client, usually the chief executive and/or chief financial officer.

It is also important to emphasize that the date of the written representations letter must be either on the *same date as the date of the auditor's report* or *very close to the date of the auditor's report.* It must not be dated after the date of the auditor's report. This is because the auditor's report must cover all issues up to and including the date of the auditor's report. If the written representations letter is dated after the date of the auditor's report, this implies there are issues which may be relevant to the financial statements that have not been addressed by the auditor.

The content of the written representation should be discussed with those charged with governance, as required by ISA (UK) 260 *Communication with Those Charged with Governance.*

We have provided an example of a written representation in the Appendix to this chapter.

12.3.3 **Reliability of written representations**

Written representations are internally generated by the client and hence may be subject to bias. This is one of the main reasons why written representations can be unreliable forms of audit evidence (even though they must be obtained).

If the auditor has any doubts concerning the client's competence, integrity, ethical values, or diligence, or concerns relating to the enforcement of those values, the auditor must carefully consider the effect those concerns have on the reliability of the written representations received (whether they have been received orally or in writing). This is because the representations received may be inconsistent with other audit evidence obtained by the auditor.

Auditing scenario 12.4 Contradictory evidence

It is 17 November 20X9 and the audit of Revere Ltd for the year ended 31 May 20X9 is nearing completion. The file is due to be passed to the audit engagement partner for their review next week. Written representations have been received by the auditor, one of which confirms that the directors are not aware of any breach of laws or regulations which may require a provision or disclosure of a contingent liability in accordance with IAS 37 *Provisions, Contingent Liabilities and Contingent Assets*.

An article published in a leading newspaper reported that last month the company was found guilty of breaching environmental legislation by dumping toxic chemicals in a nearby river. The company has been fined £300,000 plus costs by the water authority following a court case that was heard two weeks ago. The environmental incident took place in April 20X9.

The fact that management have confirmed in the written representation letter that there has been no breach of law or regulation is inconsistent with the facts of the court case that was heard two weeks ago. This means that the directors' representation is factually incorrect and cannot be relied upon.

As the offence took place prior to the year end a contingent liability disclosure should at least be made in the financial statements for the year ended 31 May 20X9. If a reliable estimate of the amount required to settle the case was able to be made as at the reporting date, then a provision for liabilities should be included instead.

If this situation cannot be resolved (i.e. if the directors refuse to correct the record in the financial statements), the auditor must determine the potential effect on the auditor's opinion which is likely to be modified.

12.3.4 **Management fails to provide written representations**

If management fail to provide one, or more, of the written representations requested by the auditor, the auditor must discuss the situation with them to understand the reasons why they will not provide the representations. Remember, written representations are a form of audit evidence and the auditor will request certain representations for specific areas of the financial statements which are material.

In addition to discussing the reasons for the refusal with management, the auditor must also re-evaluate the integrity of management and consider the effect that this may have on the reliability of representations (whether oral or written) together with the other audit evidence in general.

As written representations are a form of audit evidence for material areas of the financial statements, the auditor must also consider the impact of the refusal on the audit opinion.

Auditing scenario 12.5 Management refusal to provide written representations

The audit of Ratchford Ltd for the year ended 31 May 20X9 is nearing completion and the auditor's report is due to be issued in two weeks. The auditor has requested various written representations from the board and the CEO has sent an email to the audit manager confirming that the board is unwilling to provide the relevant representations on the basis that they do not feel they are necessary.

The audit engagement partner has discussed the necessity of the written representations with the finance director and CEO, but management still refuse to provide them.

In this situation, the auditor is unable to obtain sufficient appropriate audit evidence. Consequently, the potential effects on the financial statements of this inability to obtain written representations are not confined to specific elements, accounts, or items in the financial statements. This gives rise to a pervasive matter and hence the auditor will be required to express a disclaimer of opinion on the financial statements.

12.4 Auditing accounting estimates

One of the inherent limitations of an audit is the fact that all financial statements will contain some degree of accounting estimate. This is a fact of life in accountancy and audit. Even simple sets of accounts will contain some estimates, for example, in relation to allowances for receivables and useful lives of property, plant, and equipment on which depreciation is based. In determining the amounts to be recognized or disclosed in the financial statements—this is known as 'management's point estimate', management will need to exercise some judgement, which creates a risk of management bias.

An accounting estimate is defined as

> a monetary amount for which the measurement, in accordance with the requirements of the applicable financial reporting framework, is subject to estimation uncertainty.[18]

Accounting estimates can also relate to more complex areas of financial reporting, for example, the valuation of financial instruments, which can also involve volatility in the measurement of these items.

The problem with accounting estimates is that they can be tricky to audit because they are subjective. They are not 100 per cent 'correct'; and, in some cases, they may lack supporting documentary evidence. There can also be areas in which the auditor does not have specialist knowledge, particularly in the case of fair value accounting for items like financial instruments.

The objective as stated in ISA (UK) 540 *Auditing Accounting Estimates and Related Disclosures* is that the auditor must obtain sufficient and appropriate audit evidence about whether accounting estimates and related disclosures are reasonable and in line with financial reporting requirements. ISA (UK) 540 requires the auditor to obtain an understanding of how management identifies those transactions, events, or conditions that give rise to the need for an accounting estimate.

Activity 12.7 Accounting estimates

Note down five examples of accounting estimates which are recognized or disclosed in financial statements.

[18] FRC, 'ISA (UK) 540', 2022, para 12(a) <https://media.frc.org.uk/documents/ISA_UK_540_Revised_December_2018_Updated_May_2022.pdf> (accessed 18 January 2024).

Auditing in practice 12.2 ISA 540 (Revised)

In 2016, the IAASB initiated a project to revise the original version of ISA 540. This revised edition of ISA 540 was adopted in other jurisdictions, such as the UK. The IAASB consulted with key stakeholders and the evaluation of the feedback obtained indicated a perceived lack of consistency in the extent to which auditors obtained an understanding of accounting estimates together with evidence of insufficient and inappropriate work effort by auditors in this area. Other regulators, including the FRC in the UK, commented that audit quality in respect of the audit of accounting estimates was not always good and improvements in the regulations were needed.

The consultation process also identified a lack of professional scepticism being exercised by auditors and a need for more specific risk assessment requirements and more granular requirements regarding obtaining audit evidence. It also identified a need to enhance communication between auditors and those charged with governance about accounting estimates.

Another driving force behind the development of ISA 540 is the increased prevalence of fair value accounting in financial reporting and the increasing complexity of business models and the environments in which they operate. In particular, the issuance of IFRS 13 *Fair Value Measurement* and IFRS 9 *Financial Instruments* meant that more companies and their auditors were developing models to determine and to audit complex and subjective accounting estimates.

In relation to complex accounting estimates, a particular problem is that the measurement is likely to be performed infrequently for external reporting purposes only, and outside the normal accounting and management systems. As a non-routine event, the assessment of fair value is likely not to have the same level of monitoring or controls as a day-to-day business transaction and may give rise to high control risk.

ISA 540 was revised in 2017 to address these, and other issues, and to promote high-quality auditing in respect of accounting estimates, including fair values. As noted earlier, this revised edition of ISA 540 was subsequently adopted by other jurisdictions.

12.4.1 **Risk assessment for accounting estimates**

There is an overlap between ISA (UK) 540 and that of ISA (UK) 315 *Identifying and Assessing the Risks of Material Misstatement* because these two ISAs (UK) share the 'spectrum of inherent risk'. This was not a new concept when the latest edition of ISA (UK) 540 was published and most audit methodologies include a spectrum (albeit only on a three-point scale: 'low', 'moderate', or 'high').

A spectrum of risk is important so the auditor can assess risk effectively, and to ensure that the focus of audit procedures is given to the areas with most inherent risk. It is also a key part of ensuring that the ISAs (UK) are scalable, since auditors are expressly permitted to vary the nature, timing, and extent of their work (including elements of risk assessment itself) based on the assessed inherent risk.

According to ISA (UK) 540:

> The process of making accounting estimates involves selecting and applying a method using assumptions and data, which requires judgment by management and can give rise to complexity in measurement. The effects of complexity, subjectivity or other inherent risk factors on the measurement of these monetary amounts affects their susceptibility to misstatement.[19]

[19] Ibid., para 2 (excerpt).

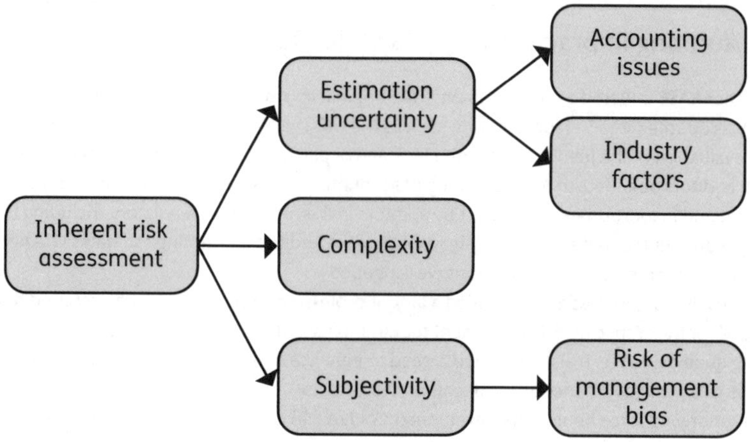

Figure 12.5 Assessing the inherent risk relating to estimates

ISA (UK) 540 recognizes that there can be a high risk of management bias in the preparation of information relating to accounting estimates, and the requirements of the ISA (UK) largely relate to how the auditor should design audit procedures which respond to this risk.

ISA (UK) 540 requires the auditor to separately assess inherent and control risk when evaluating the risk of material misstatement relating to an accounting estimate and includes three specific risk factors to consider when the auditor is assessing inherent risk (Figure 12.5).

12.4.1.1 **Estimation uncertainty**

The degree of uncertainty may be affected by a prescribed method within the financial reporting framework (e.g. IFRS) or by assumptions which are highly uncertain, such as where the forecast period is long or where the underlying data is unobservable. Certain industry sectors may be highly volatile as well, particularly if they are not well established and this can increase uncertainty, as can the inherent unpredictability of certain types of events.

12.4.1.2 **Complexity**

Some estimates may need specialized skills or knowledge and may be calculated by models based on complex algorithms. Other estimates may be the product of several interrelated variables which need to be tracked; whereas other estimates may not be inherently complex.

12.4.1.3 **Subjectivity**

Some estimates are not subject to specific prescribed approaches within a financial reporting framework and management is therefore free to select its own approach. This increases the risk of management bias and hence higher subjectivity. In other cases, external data to support the accounting estimate may not exist and it is subject solely to the professional judgement and experience of management.

ISA (UK) 540 requires the auditor to understand the entity and its environment including matters related to accounting estimates, such as:

- Events and conditions that give rise to the need for estimates (e.g. whether there are any new types of balances and transactions involving estimates or changes in relevant terms and conditions).
- The requirements of the relevant financial reporting framework and the regulatory environment (e.g. Companies Act 2006) and whether there have been any changes in these regulations.
- Management's governance and oversight of the estimation process (e.g. does management have the necessary skills to develop methods and models to make estimates?).
- The role of the entity's IT system including methods, assumptions, and input data.
- The outcome of previous estimates and the implications for the estimation process.
- Whether specialist skills will be required to perform risk assessment and audit procedures (e.g. will a management's expert be required to make estimates?).

12.4.2 Assessment of inherent risk and control risk

ISA (UK) 540 requires the auditor to separately assess inherent risk and control risk when assessing the risks of material misstatement at the assertion level.

The auditor must carry out tests of controls (i.e. test the operating effectiveness of the system of internal control). If the auditor does not do this, it will mean that the auditor will not be able to reduce their risk assessment at the assertion level for the effective operation of those controls. In addition, the auditor will need to carry out tests of controls if substantive procedures alone cannot provide sufficient appropriate audit evidence. This may be the case if an estimate is generated using a complex system with inputs or outputs that cannot be observed directly.

12.4.3 Responses to assessed risks

There are three distinct approaches the auditor can take to respond to assessed risks of material misstatement where accounting estimates are concerned. One or more of these three approaches can be used by the auditor (Figure 12.6).

12.4.3.1 Obtain audit evidence from subsequent events (i.e. those events which occur between the reporting date and the date of the auditor's report)

Obtaining audit evidence from events occurring up to the date of the auditor's report may provide sufficient appropriate audit evidence in respect of an estimate. For example, the sales value of inventory after the year end may provide sufficient appropriate audit evidence relating to the estimate of its net realizable value at the period end.

However, some estimates relate to events or conditions which occur over a longer time scale, in which case it is unlikely that events taking place up to the date of the auditor's report will provide sufficient and appropriate evidence.

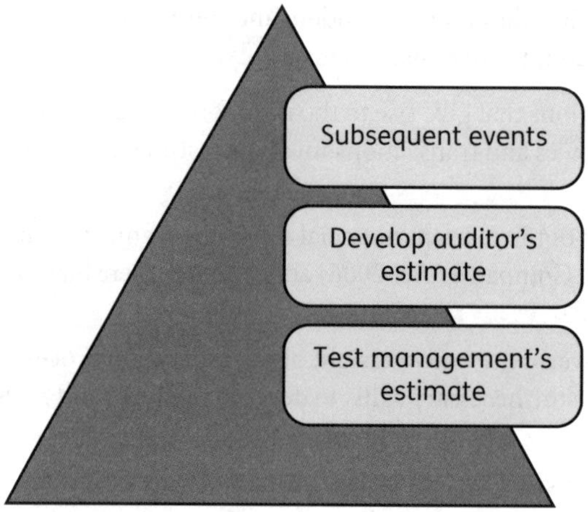

Figure 12.6 Responding to assessed risks in respect of estimates

Auditing scenario 12.6 Evidence from subsequent events

Catalan Ltd manufactures engineering components for medical hardware manufacturers. It sells goods on credit to corporate customers and trade receivables are usually collected within forty-five to sixty days of invoices.

Each year, management estimates the value of irrecoverable receivables for the purpose of preparing the financial statements. Over the last couple of years, there has been an increase in the number of irrecoverable balances suffered due to an overall decline in the market due to cheaper medical hardware being available overseas.

The audit fieldwork is due to commence shortly after Catalan's year end. The audit team decide that the most appropriate way of assessing the estimate made in relation to the valuation of trade receivables is to select a sample of high-value pre-date sales and trace these to after-date cash receipts.

12.4.3.2 **Test how management made the accounting estimate**

This is where the auditor obtains evidence in relation to:

- The selection and application of the methods, significant assumptions and the data used by management in making the accounting estimate; and
- How management selected the point estimate and developed related disclosures about estimation uncertainty.[20]

This approach may be used when:

- prior period evidence suggests that management's method is appropriate;
- the population consists of a large number of individually insignificant items;
- the financial reporting framework suggests how the estimate needs to be derived; and
- the estimate is based on routine data processing.

[20] Ibid., para 22.

The auditor must consider the appropriateness, presence of bias indicators, consistency or accuracy, and whether they were used properly. ISA (UK) 540 requires that audit procedures must address:

- Whether the method selected is appropriate in the context of the applicable financial reporting framework and, if applicable, changes from the method used in prior periods are appropriate;
- Whether judgments made in selecting the method give rise to indicators of possible management bias;
- Whether the calculations are applied in accordance with the method and are mathematically accurate;
- When management's application of the method involves complex modelling, whether judgments have been applied consistently and whether, when applicable:
  - The design of the model meets the measurement objective of the applicable financial reporting framework, is appropriate in the circumstances, and, if applicable, changes from the prior period's model are appropriate in the circumstances; and
  - Adjustments to the output of the model are consistent with the measurement objective of the applicable financial reporting framework and are appropriate in the circumstances; and
- Whether the integrity of the significant assumptions and the data has been maintained in applying the method.[21]

In addition to the above, specific procedures are required when significant assumptions have been used in developing the estimate (e.g. whether the assumptions are consistent with each other and with other business activities).

The auditor is also required to consider whether the data underpinning the estimate is appropriate, relevant, and reliable, and whether it has been appropriately understood or interpreted by management, including with respect to contractual terms. ISA (UK) 540 also refers to the possibility of management bias in the selection of data, and the auditor must consider whether judgements made in respect of data selection and use are appropriate.

Auditing scenario 12.7 Testing how management make an estimate

Potts Ltd sells machine parts under warranty. The terms and conditions of sale have not changed in the last five years and management has developed a simple model based on expected values for estimating how many machine parts will be returned under the warranty. For the current financial year, an estimate of £67,000 has been made.

The auditor knows from past experience that management's model for predicting the rate of return is quite accurate. The auditor has also confirmed that the method for determining the estimate is in line with relevant financial reporting requirements.

[21] Ibid., para 23.

In this situation, the estimate relates to a large number of individually insignificant items and the auditor can test how management has determined the £67,000 estimate by confirming that the method for determining the estimate has not changed from previous years, confirming the reliability of source data, reperforming elements of the calculation and considering whether any assumptions used are reasonable and in line with the auditor's understanding of the business. The auditor will also perform analytical procedures and test the controls over the development of the estimate and how it has been accounted for.

12.4.3.3 **Develop an auditor's point estimate or range**

This approach may be relevant when management's point estimate cannot be relied upon, which could arise when:

- Prior period evidence suggests that management's method is likely to be ineffective.
- Management controls are not well designed or implemented.
- Post-date evidence has either not been properly considered by management or contradicts management's point estimate.
- There are appropriate alternative assumptions or evidence sources which could be applied.
- Management has failed to consider the level of estimation uncertainty.

The auditor is required to evaluate their own methods, assumptions, and data regardless of whether they are basing their estimate on management's approach or designing their own method. The auditor must also consider whether a range is reasonable and carry out procedures to confirm the risk of material misstatement within accompanying disclosures. For complex and/or subjective estimates, it is common that the auditor may engage an expert, as we saw earlier in the chapter, to develop the point estimate or range as illustrated in Auditing scenario 12.8.

Auditing scenario 12.8 Developing an auditor's point estimate

Paris Properties Ltd rents out properties to individuals and families. It has a portfolio of approximately 600 properties in the south of England. Each property is classed as an investment property and is measured at fair value through profit or loss in accordance with IAS 40 *Investment Property*.

The year-end values of the investment properties are estimated by the directors based on a model which incorporates local price indices, rental yields, and occupancy rates. The auditor has concluded that the aggregate fair value of the property portfolio is the most significant item in the financial statements. Post-date evidence is unavailable and the auditor remains unconvinced that the client's model is sufficiently reliable or well designed.

The auditor has decided to engage a chartered surveyor with experience of valuing these types of properties. The scope of work to be performed has been agreed whereby the surveyor will appraise a small sample of the properties to review the fair values for a selection of towns to generate a range.

Once the expert has carried out this valuation work, the auditor can extrapolate from the surveyor's findings to determine an aggregate fair value range to evaluate whether management's estimate is reasonable or otherwise.

12.4.4 **Other audit procedures for accounting estimates**

Other typical audit procedures the auditor will adopt when auditing accounting estimates include the following:

- Inquire of management as to how the accounting estimate was derived and the data on which it is based.
- Determine if subsequent events can provide sufficient appropriate audit evidence regarding the accounting estimate.
- Review management's method of measurement and assess the reasonableness of the assumptions made in arriving at the accounting estimate.
- Test the operating effectiveness of the controls over how management arrived at the accounting estimate.
- Review the judgements and decisions made by management when determining the accounting estimate to identify if there are any indicators of management bias.
- Evaluate whether the accounting estimates in the financial statements are reasonable or whether they indicate a risk of material misstatement at the assertion level.
- Obtain sufficient appropriate audit evidence over the disclosures made in the financial statements concerning the accounting estimate (e.g. considering whether the disclosures in respect of a provision for liability comply with IAS 37).
- Obtain written representations from management and, where appropriate, those charged with governance whether they believe significant assumptions used in making accounting estimates are reasonable.

Auditing in practice 12.3 Shell plc

In the audit report of Shell, the audit firm Ernst & Young LLP discloses as a key audit matter the estimation of oil and gas reserves. This is a material issue within the financial statements, and the audit firm describes why it is identified as a key matter in the audit, and how they responded to the risks of material misstatement.

Below, you can read an extract from the section of the audit report issued on the 2021 financial statements, where this issue is described.

The estimation of oil and gas reserves

Description of the key audit matter

> This is a forecast-based estimate. Oil and gas reserves estimates are used in the calculation of depreciation, depletion and amortisation (DD&A), impairment testing and in the estimation of decommissioning and restoration (D&R) provisions. The risk is the inappropriate recognition of proved reserves that impacts these accounting estimates.
>
> If proved reserves are recognised that are not ultimately produced, depreciation will be understated, and the recoverable amount of assets may be overstated. In-year reserve movements are driven by revisions of previous estimates resulting from reclassifications, changes to recovery assumptions, extensions and discoveries, and purchases and sales of reserves in place. Revisions generally arise from new information, for example additional drilling results, changes in production patterns, and changes to development plans, which are an input to the cash flows used in the measurement of production assets and D&R provisions.

Auditing the estimation of oil and gas reserves is complex, as there is significant estimation uncertainty in assessing the quantities of reserves and resources in place. The estimates are based on the Company's central group of experts' assessments of petroleum initially in place, production curves, and certain other inputs, including forecast production volumes, future capital and operating cost assumptions and life of field assumptions, all of which are inputs used by reservoir engineers to estimate oil and gas reserves. Estimation uncertainty is further elevated given the transition to a low-carbon economy, which could impact life-of-field assumptions and increase the risk of underutilised or stranded oil and gas assets. Also, given the estimation of oil and gas reserves is complex, there is a risk that inappropriate management bias influences the estimate.

Our response to the risk

We obtained an understanding of the controls over Shell's oil and gas reserves' estimation process. We then evaluated the design of these controls and tested their operating effectiveness. For example, we tested management's controls over review of changes to year-on-year estimated oil and gas reserves volumes.

We involved professionals with substantial oil and gas reserves audit experience, including a partner with relevant qualifications in energy economics, to assist us in evaluating the key assumptions and methodologies applied by management.

Our procedures included, amongst others:

- testing that significant additions or reductions in reserves had been made in the period in which the new information became available by understanding the change in circumstance that drove the change;
- verifying that they were in compliance with Shell's reserves and resources guidance;
- evaluating the professional qualifications and objectivity of management's experts (internal reservoir engineers) who performed the detailed preparation of the reserve estimates and those who are primarily responsible for providing independent review and challenge, and ultimately endorsement of, the reserve estimates;
- evaluating management's estimation of the point at which the operating cash flow from a project becomes negative (the economic limit), as this impacts DD&A and impairment. Where relevant, we assessed whether the economic limit test incorporated Shell's estimate of future carbon costs to reflect the potential impact of climate change and the energy transition;
- evaluating the completeness and accuracy of the inputs used by management in estimating the oil and gas reserves by agreeing the inputs to source documentation;
- performing back-testing of historical data to identify indications of estimation bias over time; and
- evaluating management's development plan for compliance with SEC rules that undrilled locations must be scheduled to be drilled within five years, unless specific circumstances justify a longer period. This evaluation was made by assessing the consistency of the development projections with Shell's development plans and capital allocation framework. Also, where reserves are recognised beyond current licence terms, we obtained evidence to support the assumption that the licence would be renewed.[22]

12.4.5 **Evaluation and concluding on accounting estimates**

ISA (UK) 540 requires the auditor to evaluate, based on the evidence obtained, whether accounting estimates are reasonable. When the auditor has developed their own point estimate, this should be compared with the estimate developed by management. If there is a

[22] Shell plc, 'Annual report and accounts', 2021 <https://reports.shell.com/annual-report/2021/_assets/downloads/shell-annual-report-2021.pdf> (accessed 18 January 2024).

difference between the point estimates developed by the auditor and by management, this may be a misstatement which results in modification of the auditor's opinion.

Overall evaluation must also include consideration of whether disclosure is sufficient. Accounting estimates are often subject to a high degree of estimation uncertainty, and IAS 1 *Presentation of Financial Statements* requires disclosure of key sources of estimation uncertainty and judgements that have been used in the preparation of the financial statements. According to ISA (UK) 540:

> when an accounting estimate is subject to a higher degree of estimation uncertainty, the auditor may determine that additional disclosures are necessary to achieve fair presentation. If management does not include such additional disclosures, the auditor may conclude that the financial statements are materially misstated.[23]

Therefore, the auditor must reach a conclusion not only on the amounts recognized in the financial statements in respect of accounting estimates, but also on whether there is sufficient supplementary information given in the notes to the financial statements for a fair presentation to be achieved.

As we saw earlier in this chapter, written representations can be an important source of audit evidence. ISA (UK) 540 specifically requires written representations in respect of accounting estimates:

> The auditor shall request written representations from management and, when appropriate, those charged with governance about whether the methods, significant assumptions, and the data used in making the accounting estimates and the related disclosures are appropriate to achieve recognition, measurement or disclosure that is in accordance with the applicable financial reporting framework. The auditor shall also consider the need to obtain representations about specific accounting estimates, including in relation to the methods, assumptions, or data used.[24]

The auditor should also discuss estimation uncertainty with those charged with governance in accordance with ISA (UK) 260, in particular any risks of material misstatement which arise relating to estimation uncertainty and the effects of complexity and subjectivity in relation to estimates.

Finally, ISA (UK) 540 contains extensive documentation requirements, to ensure that the audit files contain sufficient information on how the auditor has responded to the risks of material misstatement identified. The ISA (UK) makes a point of discussing that the auditor should consider how to document their use of professional scepticism when auditing accounting estimates, for example, in how the auditor has addressed any indicators of possible management bias.

12.5 Service organizations

A lot of businesses outsource various parts of their organization to specialists. In some cases, a company might outsource a specific task, for example, a business may decide to outsource its payroll function to a payroll specialist. In other cases, an entire business function could be outsourced, for example, internal audit may be outsourced to an internal audit specialist.

[23] FRC, 'ISA (UK) 540', 2022, A143 (excerpt).
[24] Ibid., para 37.

Whenever a business outsources a function to a third party, that third party is referred to as a 'service organization'.

Guidance for auditors on the use of a service organization is provided in ISA (UK) 402 *Audit Considerations Relating to an Entity Using a Service Organization.* Not all outsourced services are relevant to the auditor, but in many cases, they are.

There are many reasons why a business would choose to use a service provider and there are advantages and disadvantages of an audit client doing this from the perspective of the external auditor (as set out in Table 12.2).

ISA (UK) 402 states that the objectives of the auditor, when the client uses a service organization are to:

(a) To obtain an understanding of the nature and significance of the services provided by the service organization and their effect on the user entity's system of internal control, sufficient to provide an appropriate basis for the identification and assessment of the risks of material misstatement; and

(b) To design and perform audit procedures responsive to those risks.[25]

12.5.1 **Obtaining an understanding of the services provided**

ISA (UK) 402 requires the auditor to obtain an understanding of how the audited entity (also known as 'the user entity') uses the services of a service organization in the user entity's operations, including the following matters:

- The nature of the services provided by the service organization and the significance of those services to the user entity, including the effect thereof on the user entity's internal control;
- The nature and materiality of the transactions processed or accounts or financial reporting processes affected by the service organization;

Table 12.2 Advantages and disadvantages of outsourcing

Advantage	Disadvantage
As the service organization is independent of the entity, this may increase the reliability of audit evidence obtained	It may prove difficult obtaining information from the service organization, particularly if there are restrictions in law, such as through the General Data Protection Regulation or other local legislation
As a service organization will be a specialist in the service they offer, there is usually increased reliability in the data in which they process	Tests of controls at the service organization may be difficult to perform or the auditor may not be allowed to test such controls due to confidentiality/practicality reasons
Control risk may be reduced and hence the auditor may be able to place reliance on the reports produced by the service organization	Any difficulties in obtaining information from the service provider or testing controls may lead to a lack of sufficient appropriate audit evidence being obtained by the auditor which could result in a modified opinion if alternative sources of audit evidence cannot be obtained

[25] FRC, 'ISA (UK) 402', 2021, para 7 <https://media.frc.org.uk/documents/ISA_UK_402_-_Updated_May_2022.pdf> (accessed 18 January 2024).

- The degree of interaction between the activities of the service organization and those of the user entity; and
- The nature of the relationship between the user entity and the service organization, including the relevant contractual terms for the activities undertaken by the service organization.
- If the service organization maintains all or part of a user entity's accounting records, whether those arrangements impact the work the auditor performs to fulfil reporting responsibilities in relation to accounting records that are established in law or regulation.[26]

The reason for the auditor being required to understand these matters is so that any risk of material misstatement created by the use of the service organization can be identified and an appropriate response planned. When a material area of the client's business is outsourced to a service organization the auditor will need to devote more time in carrying out audit procedures.

Auditing scenario 12.9 Client outsources its payroll function

Dwyer Ltd manufactures textiles and has a year end of 31 May 20X9. During the year, the company decided to outsource its payroll function to a specialist payroll provider in order to free up time in the finance department. Payroll is a material area of the financial statements being one of the highest costs of the business.

The audit manager is responsible for auditing the payroll cycle of the business and has held preliminary inquiries with the finance director who has confirmed that the move to the payroll provider was smooth and no problems have been encountered during the year.

In this case, the service organization is simply providing a payroll service, but the auditor will be required to:

- Determine the materiality of the transactions to the entity.
- Ascertain the level of interaction between the activities of the service organization and Dwyer Ltd.
- Understand the relationship between the service organization and the client including contractual terms. This is important to assess whether the service organization is independent of the entity and the respective responsibilities of both the service organization and the client.

There are different levels of reliance that the audit client may place on the service provider, ranging from the service provider simply processing information, such as payroll information, to a service provider preparing the financial statements (Figure 12.7).

In some situations, the service organization may maintain all, or part, of the client's accounting records. For example, a payroll provider may maintain payroll records including processing and posting the transactions, such as the payment of payroll taxes. In an extreme situation, a company may use an external bookkeeping service to maintain their accounts and prepare the financial statements.

The client will be provided with a copy of the various reports produced by the service organization, and the auditor is required to carefully evaluate the impact of this arrangement

[26] Ibid., para 9.

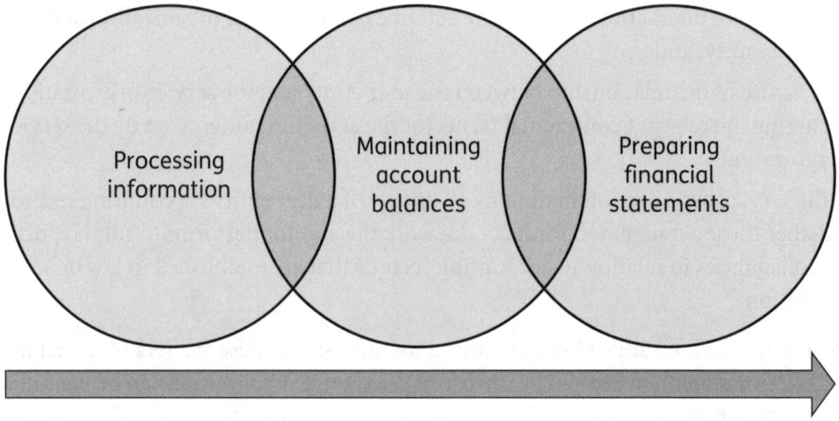

Figure 12.7 Increasing level of reliance on service providers

on the audit. In some countries (such as the UK), company law requires the entity to maintain adequate accounting records which enable the business to assess its financial performance and position with reasonable accuracy. This obligation could be impacted if a service organization maintains all, or part, of the client's accounting records because the auditor may not be able to assess the state of the applicable records.

12.5.2 **Sources of information in obtaining an understanding of the services provided**

In addition to obtaining an understanding of the relevant services provided to the client by the service organization, the auditor must also obtain an understanding of the impact the service organization has on the entity's system of internal control. This is to obtain understanding of the control risk associated with the outsourced function, for example, whether the transactions and information provided by the service organization are monitored and whether checks are performed prior to inclusion in the financial statements. This provides a basis for the identification and assessment of risks of material misstatement. Just because a client may use a service organization, this does not automatically reduce the risk of material misstatement at the assertion level. There could be inherent problems either in the records provided to the service organization or at the service organization itself which may give rise to a risk of material misstatement in the financial statements.

Information should be available from the audited entity to enable this understanding to be obtained, for example, through reports received from the service organization, technical manuals and the contract between the audited entity and the service organization. The auditor may decide that further work is necessary in order to evaluate the risk of material misstatement associated with the outsourcing arrangement's impact on the financial statements.

ISA (UK) 402 provides four sources of information the auditor may use in obtaining an understanding as follows:

(a) Obtaining a type 1 or type 2 report, if available; (see below)

(b) Contacting the service organization, through the user entity, to obtain specific information;

(c) Visiting the service organization and performing procedures that will provide the necessary information about controls at the service organization; or

(d) Using another auditor to perform procedures that will provide the necessary information about the relevant controls at the service organization.[27]

A type 1 report provides a description of the design of the controls at the service organization. It will also include a report by the service organization's auditor which provides an opinion on the description of the system and the suitability of the controls. If the service organization's auditor has modified their report in any way (e.g. due to weaknesses identified in the control environment), the client's auditor is less likely to place reliance on the report.

A type 2 report is a report on the description, design, and operating effectiveness of controls at the service organization. It contains a report prepared by the service organization's management as well as a report by the service organization's auditor that provides an opinion on:

- the description of the system;
- the suitability of the controls;
- the effectiveness of the controls; and
- a description of the tests of controls performed by the auditor.

In practice, a type 1 or type 2 report is often used as this is more practicable, but the auditor may decide that any of the other methods may need to be used as well, particularly if there are concerns about the type 1 or type 2 report received.

12.5.3 **Responses to assessed risks**

During the risk assessment stage, the auditor will consider whether or not to place reliance on the system of internal control of the service organization. If the auditor expects controls to operate effectively, they can carry out one or more of the following procedures:

- Obtaining a type 2 report, if available;
- Performing appropriate tests of controls at the service organization; or
- Using another auditor to perform tests of controls at the service organization on behalf of the user auditor.[28]

All of these methods of evaluating the service organization's controls require permission and can be time-consuming to perform. However, it is important that the auditor obtain evidence in respect of the controls at the service organization in order to place reliance on them.

When using a type 2 report, ISA 402 (UK) requires the auditor to determine whether the service auditor's report provides sufficient appropriate audit evidence concerning the effectiveness of the controls. To that end, the auditor must consider:

- whether the date covered by the report is appropriate for the audit (remember the client's reporting date and the service organization's reporting date may be considerably different. In such cases the auditor may need to obtain a 'bridging' letter/report covering the intervening period);

[27] Ibid., para 12. [28] Ibid., para 16.

- whether the client has any complementary internal controls in place;
- the time that has elapsed since tests of controls were last carried out; and
- whether tests of controls performed by the auditor are relevant to the financial statement assertions.

If the auditor believes that the type 2 report does not provide sufficient appropriate audit evidence, for example, if the report does not contain a description of the service auditor's tests of controls and conclusions, the auditor may perform other work to obtain the necessary evidence regarding the controls. This could include:

- discussion with the service auditor about the scope and results of the service auditor's work; or
- request that the service auditor perform additional procedures.

Alternatively, the auditor may perform additional procedures.

The auditor must inquire of the client whether the service organization has reported any frauds to them, or whether they are aware of any frauds. This is usually a matter that is covered in the written representation letter. These inquiries must also extend to non-compliance with laws and regulations or uncorrected misstatements affecting the financial statements of the client.

These are important procedures to carry out because it will help the auditor to understand how such matters will affect the nature, timing, and extent of further procedures the client's auditor has to carry out as well as the effect on the client auditor's conclusions and auditor's report.

12.5.4 **The use of service organizations and effect on the auditor's report**

If the auditor concludes that they are unable to obtain sufficient appropriate audit evidence regarding the services provided by the service organization and there are no further procedures that the auditor can undertake which will provide sufficient appropriate audit evidence, the auditor must modify their opinion accordingly. This will usually be due to a limitation of scope (or insufficient audit evidence) and the type of modification will depend on whether the potential effects on the financial statements are material (qualified 'except for') or pervasive (adverse or disclaimer of opinion).

The auditor cannot make any reference to the work of a service organization's auditor in the client auditor's report where the audit opinion is unmodified. The exception to this rule would be where law or regulation specifically requires reference to be made to the service organization's auditor. Even if law or regulation requires reference to be made to the service organization's auditor, the auditor's report must indicate that the reference does not diminish the auditor's responsibility for the audit opinion. Remember, the auditor is fully responsible for the opinion expressed in the financial statements; the auditor cannot delegate that responsibility to a third party (this will also apply even if reference to the work of a service organization's auditor is relevant to an understanding of any modification to the audit opinion).

12.6 Initial audit engagements—opening balances

12.6.1 What are opening balances?

Opening balances are those account balances which exist at the start of a new accounting period. They are based on the closing balances of the prior period and reflect the effects of transactions and events of prior periods and accounting policies that the entity applied in the prior period. They also include matters which require disclosure that existed at the start of the period (e.g. commitments and contingencies).

Where the audit engagement is a recurring engagement, the auditor will check that the opening balances from the prior year have been correctly brought forward into the current year. They will also check that the client's accounting policies have been consistently applied to the opening balances.

When an audit firm engages a new audit client and performs their initial audit engagement, they must obtain sufficient appropriate audit evidence to confirm that the opening balances are free from material misstatement. This is because the current year's financial statements are based on the opening statement of financial position at the start of the year. If there are any misstatements in the opening balances, the closing balances will also be misstated. The auditor also needs to consider the appropriateness of the accounting policies applied in the financial statements.

This is particularly important when it is the first time that the client's financial statements have been subject to audit—typically this happens if the company has previously been exempt from audit due to small size, but has grown sufficiently so an audit is now mandatory.

ISA (UK) 510 *Initial Audit Engagements—Opening Balances* provides guidance to the auditor on how to obtain sufficient appropriate audit evidence in connection with the entity's opening balances.

ISA (UK) 510 requires the auditor to:

> read the most recent financial statements, if any, and the predecessor auditor's report thereon, if any, for information relevant to opening balances, including disclosures.[29]

In addition, ISA (UK) 510, requires the auditor to carry out the following:

(a) Determine whether the prior period's closing balances have been correctly brought forward into the current period or, where appropriate, have been restated.

(b) Determine whether the opening balances reflect the application of appropriate accounting policies.

(c) Perform one, or more, of the following:

   (i) if the prior year financial statements were audited, review the predecessor auditor's working papers to obtain evidence regarding the opening balances;

   (ii) evaluate whether audit procedures performed in the current period provide evidence relevant to the opening balances; or

   (iii) perform specific audit procedures to obtain evidence regarding the opening balances.

[29] FRC, 'ISA (UK) 510', 2016, para 5 <https://media.frc.org.uk/documents/ISA_UK_510_Revised_June_2016.pdf> (accessed 18 January 2024).

For some balances recognized in the statement of financial position, it is likely that the current year's audit procedures will provide some evidence relating to the opening balances. For example, audit work on trade receivables will provide some evidence as to the existence, completeness, and valuation of the opening balance of trade receivables. However, it is likely that specific procedures may be necessary on opening balances, for example, in relation to inventory, current-year inventory records can be reconciled to opening balances, and for significant assets and liabilities including loan balances, direct confirmation can be used to confirm the accuracy of the opening balance.

12.6.2 **Predecessor auditor audited the prior year's financial statements**

Often, when a new auditor is appointed, they are replacing a predecessor auditor. However, just because the prior year's financial statements have been audited by a different audit firm, this does not mean that the incoming auditor can just assume that the opening balances are correct. The incoming auditor must be satisfied, through obtaining sufficient appropriate audit evidence, that the opening balances are free from misstatement and have been correctly brought forward into the current year from the prior year.

To obtain sufficient appropriate audit evidence when the auditor had not audited the prior year, they will review the predecessor auditor's working papers file to obtain the audit evidence they need to support the opening balances. This is not an inspection as to the quality of the audit carried out by the predecessor firm; it is merely an exercise to obtain audit evidence to support the opening balances and reduce the likelihood of a modified audit opinion due to insufficient evidence concerning the opening balance sheet position.

Auditing scenario 12.10 Opening balances audited by a predecessor auditor

Zoe & Co was appointed on 1 July 20X2 to audit Scoot Ltd, a manufacturing company with a financial year ending 31 July 20X2. Scoot Ltd had previously been audited by Lois Associates.

When planning the initial audit engagement (i.e. the first audit of Scoot Ltd by Zoe & Co), the audit team at Zoe & Co must perform the procedures outlined in ISA (UK) 510 in respect of the opening balances. The extent of work to be performed on the opening balances will depend on matters including the company's accounting policies and the significance of the opening balances to the current period financial statements. Essentially, Zoe & Co needs to evaluate the risk of material misstatement in the opening balances and respond accordingly.

Because Scoot Ltd was previously audited by Lois Associates, the audit team at Zoe & Co may be able to obtain audit evidence relating to the opening balances by reviewing the working papers prepared by Lois Associates during the previous year's audit. In some countries, including the UK, the predecessor auditor is required by law to provide the auditor with access to all relevant information concerning the entity, including information concerning the most recent audit.

When reviewing the working papers of Lois Associates, the audit team at Zoe & Co should consider the competence and objectivity of Lois Associates, as part of evaluating whether the working papers provide sufficient appropriate audit evidence.

In practice, the successor auditor will write to the predecessor auditor to request access to the predecessor auditor's working papers file in order to obtain such evidence. There is no mandatory requirement for a successor auditor to make this request but the successor auditor must, as part of the planning process, decide if such access is required and the areas to cover as well as the amount of information to request.

Auditing in practice 12.4 Illustrative letter requesting access to predecessor auditor's working papers file

Dear Sir/Madam

Provision of information pursuant to Audit Regulation 3.09 relating to the audit of Greaves Industries Ltd

This firm was duly appointed statutory auditor (as defined by Companies Act 2006, s 1210 ('the Act')) on 10 April 20X9 to Greaves Industries Ltd.

Pursuant to paragraph 9(3) of Sch 10 to Companies Act 2006 and Audit Regulation 3.09, we request for the purposes of our audit work access to the following information:

- The working papers in respect of your auditor's report on the financial statements of Greaves Ltd relating to the year ended 31 May 20X8.

We may also request explanations from you in connection with our consideration of the above information, and on the same basis.

We will meet reasonable costs that you will incur in giving access, provided that a maximum amount is agreed first.

We look forward to receiving your confirmation letter in response to this request, which should be addressed for the attention of Mr B Currie, engagement partner.

Yours faithfully

Auditor & Co LLP

12.6.3 **Misstatements in opening balances**

If the auditor concludes that the opening balances contain misstatements which could be material to the current period's financial statements, the auditor must perform audit procedures which are appropriate in the circumstances to determine the effect on the current period's financial statements. This situation could arise when the predecessor auditor issued a modified opinion on the previous year's financial statements, which impacts the opening balances and has not been corrected by management.

If material misstatements within the opening balances remain uncorrected, the auditor must communicate the misstatements to the appropriate level of management and those charged with governance as required under ISA (UK) 450 *Evaluation of Misstatements Identified during the Audit*. The auditor will also express a modified audit opinion because of the misstated opening balances. The type of modified opinion expressed will depend on whether the misstatements are material (thus giving rise to a qualified 'except for' opinion) or pervasive (potentially resulting in an adverse or disclaimer of opinion).

The auditor must also carry out procedures to ensure that the client's accounting policies have been consistently applied in relation to the opening balances and are compliant with the applicable financial reporting framework.

12.7 External confirmations

12.7.1 What are external confirmations?

External confirmations are a source of audit evidence which the auditor may place reliance upon. ISA (UK) 505 *External Confirmations* provides the guidance which auditors must apply where external confirmations are concerned.

ISA (UK) 505 (Revised) defines an 'external confirmation' as

> audit evidence obtained as a direct written response to the auditor, or by the auditor directly, from a third party (the confirming party), in paper form, or by electronic or other medium. Electronic or other medium could include auditors directly accessing information held by third parties through web portals, software interfaces or other digital means.[30]

Remember that audit evidence is more reliable when it is obtained from independent sources outside the entity, so obtaining an external confirmation can be a very useful source of audit evidence.

Examples of external confirmations include:

- Bank audit letter (or bank certificate/bank confirmation request) sent directly to the auditor from the client's bank confirming bank balances, loan balances, and details of secured debt.
- Trade receivables circularization letter which is a letter from the client trade receivables customers asking them to confirm the balance on their purchase ledger (or otherwise provide a reconciliation of any difference) which the auditor can use as a form of audit evidence (note that circularizations are generally considered to be a weak form of evidence on their own as they do not verify the valuation assertion, i.e. whether the balance will actually be paid, and hence they should complement other forms of evidence).

An important point to emphasize where external confirmations are concerned is that ISA (UK) 505 (Revised) requires the auditor to maintain control over them. To achieve this, the auditor must:

(a) Determine the information that is to be requested as well as the information to be included in the request.

(b) Select the sample of external parties from which to obtain confirmation.

[30] FRC, 'ISA (UK) 505', 2023, para 6(a) <https://media.frc.org.uk/documents/ISA-UK-505-Revised-October-2023.pdf> (accessed 18 January 2024).

(c) Design the confirmation request, including determining that requests are appropriately designed which will provide evidence relevant to the assertions identified. There is overlap here with ISA (UK) 330 *The Auditor's Responses to Assessed Risks* as the auditor must determine the need for a confirmation request based on their risk assessment.

(d) Send the requests to the confirming party, including follow-up requests when applicable.

Auditing in practice 12.5 Trade receivable circularization letter

The following is an illustrative trade receivables circularization letter which will be sent by the auditor on the client's letterheading with a request to the receivable to return the letter back to the audit firm:

4 June 20X9
Manchester Engineering Ltd
123 Street Name
Any County
Any Town
AB1 2BC

Dear Sir/Madam

For audit purposes, would you please confirm to our auditors, ABC Accountancy LLP, of 456 Lane Name, Any County, Any Town AB3 4DE, your indebtedness to us as at 31 May 20X9 which, according to our records amounted to £140,233.

If the above is in agreement with your records, please sign in the space provided below and return this letter direct to our auditors in the enclosed self-addressed envelope.

If the amount is not in agreement with your records, please notify our auditors direct of the amount shown by your records and, if possible, send them full particulars of the difference.

Please note that this is not a request for payment.

We should be grateful if you could give this request your early attention.

Yours faithfully

A Brown

Finance Director

The amount shown above *is/is not in agreement with our records as at 31 May 20X9.

Signed . . . . Date. . . . .

Title or position . . . .

*delete as appropriate

The above illustrates a trade receivables **positive** confirmation letter. A 'positive' confirmation letter is a request that the confirming party responds to indicating whether they agree or disagree with the information in the request, or providing the requested information. A 'negative' circularisation is when the letter sent asks the customer to respond directly to the auditor only if they disagree with the stated balance. Negative confirmation requests are no longer permitted under ISA (UK) 505 (Revised).

An alternative procedure could be for the auditor to omit the balance outstanding in the letter and ask the client's customer to confirm how much is outstanding on their payables ledger and then compare this amount to the amount outstanding on the client's receivables ledger.

The inherent problem with receivables and payables circularization letters is that the response rate may be low because of the extra effort required by the client's customer/supplier in providing such information.

In some instances, external confirmations may be sent out but replies not received. The auditor must follow up non-replies and if they are still not forthcoming, the auditor must adopt additional procedures to obtain sufficient appropriate audit evidence. In respect of trade receivables, the additional audit procedures adopted could be extended after-date cash receipt testing to confirm the valuation of trade receivables. 'After-date cash receipt or payment testing' is where the auditor will look at the cash received after the reporting date to see if the receivable has paid their balance owing to the company; or if the company has paid their balance owing to the supplier. This type of procedure provides evidence over the valuation assertion. The extent to which these are tested will depend on the auditor's assessment of risk and the nature and complexity of the audit client as well as the account balance and assertion in question.

If management refuse to allow the auditor to send an external confirmation request, this essentially gives rise to a limitation on audit scope (insufficient evidence) and the auditor is required to discuss with management the reasons for such refusal. The auditor must also corroborate management's reasons because it may be that management are refusing permission to send an external confirmation request in an attempt to conceal a fraud or error. Where the auditor suspects that the refusal is due to a fraud risk factor, they must revise the risk of material misstatement.

12.7.2 Reliability of external confirmations and evaluating responses

In considering whether the external confirmation request received serves as sufficient appropriate audit evidence, the auditor must consider various risk factors which could affect the reliability of the external confirmation. For example, external confirmation requests are usually required to be sent directly to the auditor. Where such requests are sent direct to the audit client, this could indicate a problem (e.g. the client could 'doctor' the information in the confirmation).

Electronic communications are a popular way of sending correspondence nowadays (and one of the reasons ISA (UK) 505 was updated was to reflect the fact that confirmations can be obtained electronically). However, for audit purposes this can cause a risk. For example, it may be difficult to verify the sender of such correspondence, but the auditor may reduce these risks by having a secure electronic communication environment.

The auditor must evaluate the results of external confirmations in order to determine whether sufficient appropriate audit evidence has been obtained. The auditor achieves this by looking at all surrounding circumstances, such as:

- the rate of non-responses;
- responses that have been received which disagree with information contained in the entity's accounting records;
- unreliable responses.

ISA (UK) 505 requires that where exceptions are noted in the confirmation, the auditor must investigate them to identify if they are indicative of a misstatement. In addition, the auditor must also consider the following factors:

(a) Is the exception indicative of a fraud or suspected fraud?
(b) Is the exception indicative of a deficiency in the entity's system of internal control?
(c) How will additional procedures enable the auditor to obtain sufficient appropriate audit evidence?

The auditor may conclude that the external confirmation does not give rise to sufficient appropriate audit evidence, in which case they must adopt additional audit procedures to satisfy the relevant assertion.

Chapter round-up

- Internal audit is a function of the entity's internal control system and the external auditor may decide to place reliance on the work of internal audit. In some jurisdictions, including the UK, the internal audit function cannot provide direct assistance to the external auditor.
- Auditors may use the work of an auditor's expert or management's expert to obtain sufficient appropriate audit evidence.
- Written representations are a necessary form of audit evidence but, on their own, they are not sufficient appropriate audit evidence and must serve to complement other forms of audit evidence. Written representations must be dated as near to, or on the same date as, the auditor's report, but they cannot be dated after the date of the auditor's report.
- Accounting estimates can prove difficult to audit because they are subjective and are never 100 per cent 'correct'. There are specific procedures which the auditor may carry out to test accounting estimates for material misstatement.
- An audit client may use a service organization for specific functions of the business, such as outsourcing the payroll. The auditor must obtain an understanding of the nature and significance of the services provided and their effect on the client's internal control and design and perform audit procedures to address the identified risks.
- Specific audit procedures must be carried out on an entity's opening balances to ensure they have been brought forward correctly into the current year. For new audit clients, this will involve additional audit procedures, such as reviewing the predecessor auditor's working papers file. In addition, the auditor must also ensure that accounting policies have been correctly applied to the opening balances and remain appropriate.
- External confirmations are a form of audit evidence which the auditor must maintain control over. Examples include bank confirmation letters and trade receivables circularization letters. Where a confirmation is deemed not to be sufficient appropriate audit evidence, the auditor must carry out additional procedures to minimize the risk of material misstatement.

End of chapter case study

Introduction

In this chapter, we have looked at several important issues that auditors should consider when obtaining evidence. Many of these points have been practical in nature and it is important that you can think about how these methods of obtaining audit evidence work in real-life audit situations.

This case study links to the following learning outcomes:

- Explain when the use of an auditor's or management's expert will be required and the type of audit evidence that must be obtained.
- Explain the use of a service organization and the factors that must be considered by the auditor when a client uses a service organization for a specific function of the business
- Describe the audit procedures to be applied on opening balances

Scenario

You are an audit manager in Racket & Co, a firm of accountants and auditors. You are assigned to the audit of Voyage Ltd, a manufacturing company which specializes in producing electrical goods including TVs and game consoles. The company has a financial year ending 31 December 20X5, and your firm has recently been appointed as auditor. The previous audit provider, Hilltop Associates, issued an unmodified opinion on the financial statements for the previous financial year.

It is 20 January 20X6 and you have been given the following information to help you to plan certain parts of the audit. The audit engagement partner has determined that the financial statement materiality level to be applied during the audit is set at £250,000.

Inventory

The company holds an inventory count at the end of each financial year. The company has over one hundred product lines, and the opening balance of inventory is valued at £340,000. You are aware that the company regularly offers discounts to its retail customers, in order to sell obsolete stock and make way for new product lines. The audit partner has asked you to focus on the audit of the opening balance of inventory, as the closing balance will be audited by one of your colleagues who attended the inventory count on 31 December 20X5.

Painting

In November 20X5, one of the company's original founders, Vincent Voyage died and he bequeathed a painting by a well-known artist to the company. This painting, which meets the definition of an asset of the company, is displayed in the company headquarters. Management has appointed an expert to value the paining, and the expert has recommended a value of £1.2 million.

Payroll

Voyage Ltd outsources its payroll function to a service organization, Aloe Processing (AP). Payroll costs are approximately £80,000 each month. AP deals with all aspects of payroll including determining salary payments to individuals and the amounts to be paid to the tax authorities. The payments are authorized by the finance director of Voyage Ltd, based on the monthly reports provided by AP.

Internal audit

Voyage Ltd has a small internal audit team, comprising one qualified accountant, Kelly Smith, and two part-time employees who both used to work in other business divisions of Voyage Ltd. Kelly reports to the finance director of the company and there is no audit committee.

Required

For each of the issues described, explain the impact on planning the audit. You should consider how the auditor should plan to obtain audit evidence. In the case of the inventory, consider how the auditor should obtain evidence in respect of the opening balance, as well as the year-end balance.

Answer

Inventory

The accounting policy that was applied to the opening balance of inventory should be confirmed by reading the previous year financial statements. Given the materiality of the opening balance and its impact on this year's profit, Racket & Co should approach the predecessor audit firm and ask to review their working papers in respect of the work they performed on inventory.

In addition, the following procedures are recommended:

- Inspection of client's records of the inventory count held at the prior period year end, 31 December 20X4, to confirm the quantity of items held in inventory confirms the underlying accounting records.
- Using information obtained at this year's inventory count, reconcile the closing inventory quantities back to opening inventory quantities.
- Perform analytical procedures on gross profit margins per product line, comparing the opening and closing gross profit margins year on year and discussing any unusual fluctuations with management.
- Perform an after-date sales test by obtaining the sales value in the current financial year of items held in inventory at 31 December 20X4, and comparing the sales value with cost. This should provide evidence that inventory is correctly valued at the lower of cost and net realizable value.
- Inspect management accounts for evidence of any inventory items written off in the current financial period—this is particularly important for slow-moving items which are likely to be obsolete.

Painting

The painting is highly material and the auditor must plan to obtain robust evidence in relation to the valuation of the painting because it was gifted to the company and has no cost. Management has appointed an expert to provide a valuation, and the report of this expert must be scrutinized.

Racket & Co must obtain details about the expert appointed by management and assess their expertise through assessment of their professional certification, experience, reputation, and connections with Voyage Ltd. Their objectivity should be approached with professional scepticism, given that they were appointed by the company and there is risk of bias in the valuation they have provided.

The auditor must review the expert's working papers and reports and consider whether the valuation is in accordance with any relevant financial reporting requirements, for example, whether a fair value has been determined in accordance with IFRS 13. Any assumptions used must be evaluated to consider whether they are in line with auditor's understanding (e.g. in respect of the intended use of the painting).

The auditor should also attempt to obtain further information about the painting (e.g. confirm the artist, the age of the painting). Given the materiality of the valuation provided by the expert appointed by management, the audit firm may wish to appoint its own expert to obtain a second opinion on the value.

Payroll

A service organization is being used in respect of a material expense to the business. In accordance with ISA (UK) 402, Racket & Co must obtain a detailed understanding of the relationship between Voyage Ltd and AP, including reviewing the service agreement between the two companies to understand the exact nature and scope of the service provided.

From the information given, it appears that AP fully processes the payroll transactions and provides the company with a report which is used as a basis for authorizing payment and making the relevant accounting entries. The auditor needs to obtain a good understanding of the controls which AP has implemented in order to assess the risk of material misstatement in the payroll figures and to respond to the risk with appropriate audit procedures. With the permission of Voyage Ltd, the auditor should contact AP with the objective of obtaining more information which can be used to assess how the payroll has been processed, and the controls which are in place. Racket & Co should then consider obtaining a type 1 or type 2 report on the internal controls at AP to obtain further information (and assurance if a type 2 report is obtained) on the controls which AP has in place.

The controls which Voyage Ltd uses to verify the information received from AP also need to be understood. The controls in place at Voyage Ltd should be documented and tested. The company's internal audit team may be able to provide information in this regard.

Internal audit

According to ISA (UK) 610 the external auditor may decide to use the work of the audit client's internal audit function to modify the nature or timing, or reduce the extent of audit procedures to be performed directly by the external auditor.

Racket & Co must evaluate the internal audit department to determine whether its work is suitable for use by the external audit team. The evaluation should consider a number of factors including the competence of the internal audit function. The internal audit team is managed by a qualified accountant who is presumably technically competent, though the nature and status of their qualification should be determined. Racket & Co should consider whether the other part-time employees are sufficiently competent and whether overall the internal audit team has sufficient resources to operate effectively.

A further key issue to consider is objectivity—the internal audit department should be unbiased in their work and be able to report their findings without being subject to the influence of others. The fact that the internal audit reports are addressed to the company's finance director could indicate that there is a lack of objectivity. In addition, the two part-time employees previously worked in other business divisions of the company, so there may be familiarity and self-review threats to their objectivity, when auditing the business divisions in which they previously worked.

If there are doubts over either the objectivity or the competence of the internal audit department, then Racket & Co should not rely on their work.

In order to determine whether the internal audit department works in a systematic and disciplined way, Racket & Co should consider matters including the nature of documentation which is produced by the department and whether effective quality control procedures are in place such as direction, supervision, and review of work carried out.

Activity solutions

Activity 12.1—The work of internal audit

Pearl Ltd operates a number of manufacturing sites across the country. The company has an internal audit team. The finance director has suggested that the internal auditors could perform the following tasks:

1. Assist the accounts department, which is very short-staffed, in preparing the financial statements.
2. Develop a new credit control procedure, to help combat the company's poor cash flow.
3. Perform an evaluation of compliance with health and safety regulations in the company's manufacturing sites.

Briefly comment on whether you think it is appropriate for the internal auditors to perform these tasks.

Suggested answer points:

1. It is not appropriate for the internal auditor to assist the accounts department because this impacts the objectivity of the internal audit team (e.g. when evaluating compliance with company accounting policies).
2. It is not appropriate to design credit control procedures because internal auditors need to be independent of the operations they are auditing.
3. It is acceptable to perform this task. Internal auditors can be involved with evaluating compliance and recommending improvements if necessary.

Activity 12.2—Using the work of internal audit

Thinking from a practical point of view, what questions do you think an external auditor might ask, to evaluate the organizational status, objectivity, and competence of internal audit, and whether they operate using a systematic and disciplined approach?

Suggested answer points:

Organizational status

Are there any restrictions on the operations of the internal auditors?
Who directs their activities?
Who does internal audit report to?
Does management take internal audit seriously, and act on their recommendations?
Is the head of Internal Audit on the board of directors or in a senior management position?

Objectivity

Is internal audit a completely separate function with no close ties to any operational function of the business?
Is internal audit free to determine the scope and nature of the work it performs?
Do members of internal audit have to declare any conflicts of interest or other threats to objectivity—for example, family members working at the company?
How are such situations dealt with?
Can the internal auditors communicate with external auditors without restrictions?

Competence

Does the company provide appropriate training?
Are members of internal audit appropriately qualified and members of relevant professional bodies?
Are there sufficient resources for internal audit?

Approach to work

Are there internal audit manuals and standardized documentation?
Is there an effective quality control or quality management process?
Is adequate time spent on reviewing work carried out?

Activity 12.3—Prohibition on direct assistance

Why do you think that in some jurisdictions, including the UK, there is a prohibition on the internal audit function providing direct assistance to the external auditor?

Suggested answer points:

It is largely due to the threat to objectivity. Internal auditors are employees of the organization meaning that there may be significant problems with the internal audit function being truly independent of the business divisions which they are auditing. For example, a familiarity threat can arise, because the internal auditors are auditing the work of their co-employees. Whilst organizations can put safeguards in place to strengthen independence, for example, by ensuring that lines of reporting are appropriate, there may still be a concern over independence.

According to ISA (UK) 610:

> in evaluating the existence and significance of threats to the objectivity of an internal auditor, the following factors may be relevant:
>
> - The extent to which the internal audit function's organizational status and relevant policies and procedures support the objectivity of the internal auditors.
> - Family and personal relationships with an individual working in, or responsible for, the aspect of the entity to which the work relates.
> - Association with the division or department in the entity to which the work relates.
> - Significant financial interests in the entity other than remuneration on terms consistent with those applicable to other employees at a similar level of seniority.[31]

Activity 12.4—External experts

Suggest areas for which an expert may be brought in to provide audit evidence.

Suggested answer points:

Examples of matters on which an expert may be commissioned include:

- property valuations;
- work-in-progress valuations;
- valuation of specialist assets (e.g. works of art, biological assets, minerals);
- provisions for liabilities;
- valuation of financial instruments; and
- actuarial valuations for pension schemes.

This list is not comprehensive, but it aims to illustrate that the auditor may need to rely on the work of an expert when it comes to auditing these areas of the financial statements.

Activity 12.5—Assessing the competence and capability of an expert

How might an external auditor evaluate and conclude on the competence of an expert?

Suggested answer points:

- discussion with other auditors who have used the expert to obtain evidence;
- obtaining references regarding the work of the expert;
- obtaining confirmation that the expert is a member of a relevant professional body, is appropriately qualified, and has a licence to practise;
- reviewing papers or books written by the expert;
- considering whether the expert's work is subject to quality reviews;
- evaluating whether the expert is familiar with relevant aspects of financial reporting (e.g. they may be experts in property valuation but may have limited experience with applying valuation models as prescribed by IFRS requirements).

[31] FRC, 'ISA (UK) 610', 2022, para A32.

Activity 12.6–Evaluating the work of an auditor's expert

What matters do you think the auditor would consider when evaluating the adequacy of an auditor's expert's work?

Suggested answer points:

- confirm by reference to the engagement letter or other agreement, that all work as agreed with the expert has been performed;
- review the expert's working papers and discuss conclusions with the expert;
- evaluate any assumptions used by the expert;
- review any source data used for completeness and consistency;
- reperform calculations where appropriate;
- discuss the report with the client's management;
- consider whether the evidence is in line with the auditor's knowledge of the business and with other evidence obtained;
- ensure that the work covers an appropriate period and that subsequent events have been considered.

Activity 12.7–Accounting estimates

Note down five examples of accounting estimates which are recognized or disclosed in financial statements.

Suggested answer points:

- valuation of inventory–relating to slow-moving inventory and obsolescence;
- estimated useful lives and residual values of tangible and intangible assets–impacting depreciation;
- outcome of legal claims against the company–impacting provisions and contingent liabilities;
- valuation of investment properties;
- valuation of financial instruments;
- measurement of obligations in relation to warranties;
- determination of value of goodwill and assets acquired in a business combination;
- impairment of tangible and intangible assets;
- valuation of defined benefit pension plans.

Appendix–Illustrative written representation letter

Dear Sir/Madam

The following representations are made on the basis of inquiries of management and staff with relevant knowledge and experience such as we consider necessary in connection with your audit of the company's financial statements for the year ended 31 May 20X9. These inquiries have included inspection of supporting documentation, where appropriate, and are sufficient to satisfy ourselves that we can make each of the following representations. All representations are made to the best of our knowledge and belief.

General

1. We have fulfilled our responsibilities as directors, as set out in the terms of your engagement letter dated 17 February 20X9 under the Companies Act 2006, for preparing financial statements in accordance with applicable law and International Financial Reporting Standards, for being satisfied that they present fairly, in all material respects and for making accurate representations to you.
2. All the transactions undertaken by the company have been properly reflected and recorded in the accounting records.
3. All the accounting records have been made available to you for the purpose of your audit. We have provided you with unrestricted access to all appropriate persons within the company, and with all other records and related information requested, including minutes of all management and shareholder meetings.
4. The financial statements are free from material misstatement, including omissions.
5. The effects of uncorrected misstatements are immaterial both individually and in the aggregate.

Internal control and fraud

6. We acknowledge our responsibility for the design, implementation, and maintenance of internal control systems to prevent and detect fraud and error. We have disclosed to you the results of our risk assessment that the financial statements may be misstated as a result of fraud.
7. We have disclosed to you all instances of known or suspected fraud affecting the entity involving management, employees who have a significant role in internal control or others that could have a material effect on the financial statements.
8. We have also disclosed to you all information in relation to allegations of fraud or suspected fraud affecting the entity's financial statements communicated by current or former employees, analysts, regulators, or others.

Assets and liabilities

9. The company has satisfactory title to all assets and there are no liens or encumbrances on the company's assets, except for those that are disclosed in the notes to the financial statements.
10. All actual liabilities, contingent liabilities, and guarantees given to third parties have been recorded or disclosed as appropriate.
11. We have no plans or intentions that may materially alter the carrying value and, where relevant, the fair value measurements or classification of assets and liabilities reflected in the financial statements. We are satisfied that the inventory value of £2,500,000 has been valued at the lower of cost and net realizable value and that all stock on hand as at 31 May 20X9 is complete and exists.

Equity

12. We confirm that the bonus issue of shares carried out during the year has been properly recorded and adequately disclosed in the financial statements. Other than the bonus issue of shares, there have been no further changes to the company's capital structure.

Accounting estimates

13. The methods, data, and significant assumptions used by us in making accounting estimates, and their related disclosures, are appropriate to achieve recognition, measurement and disclosure that is reasonable in the context of the applicable financial reporting framework.

Significant assumptions used by us in making accounting estimates, including those measured at fair value, are reasonable.

Loans and arrangements

14. The company has made advances to directors during the year of £21,074 which have been properly disclosed in the financial statements. The directors acknowledge their indebtedness to the company as follows:

Mr A Smith	£100,000
Mr B Jones	£100,000

The directors confirm they have the means available to repay debts due to the company on demand.

We also confirm that all directors' personal guarantees have been properly disclosed in the financial statements.

Legal claims

15. There are no legal claims or demands which need to be disclosed in the financial statements.

Laws and regulations

16. We have disclosed to you all known instances of non-compliance or suspected non-compliance with laws and regulations whose effects should be considered when preparing the financial statements.

Related parties

17. Related party relationships and transactions have been properly accounted for and disclosed in the financial statements. We have disclosed to you all relevant information concerning such relationships and transactions and are not aware of any other matters which require disclosure in order to comply with the requirements of company law or IFRS.

Subsequent events

18. All subsequent events to the date of the financial statements which require adjustment or disclosure have been properly recorded and disclosed.

Going concern

19. We believe that the company's financial statements should be prepared on a going concern basis on the grounds that current and future sources of funding or support will be more than adequate for the company's needs. We also confirm our plans for future action(s) required to enable the company to continue as a going concern are feasible. We have considered a period of 12 months from the [reporting date]/[date of approval of the financial statements].[32] We believe that no further disclosures relating to the company's ability to continue as a going concern need to be made in the financial statements.

We acknowledge our legal responsibilities regarding disclosure of information to you as auditors and confirm that so far as we are aware, there is no relevant audit information needed by you in connection with preparing your auditor's report of which you are unaware.

Each director has taken all the steps that he ought to have taken as a director in order to make himself aware of any relevant audit information and to establish that you are aware of that information.

Yours faithfully

....

Signed on behalf of the board of directors
30 September 20X9

[32] Some financial reporting frameworks (e.g. IFRS) require going concern to be assessed for a minimum period of twelve months from the reporting date. Others require going concern to be assessed for a minimum period of twelve months from the date of approval of the financial statements (for example, UK and Ireland GAAP).

13 Fraud and Laws and Regulations

Introduction

The responsibility of the external auditor in relation to fraud prevention and detection is often misunderstood. There have been many press reports in recent years about well-known companies where fraud has taken place. For example, in the UK in 2019, Patisserie Valerie was the subject of a fraud which forced the company into administration. The story was widely reported in the press, and the audit firm Grant Thornton came under considerable scrutiny as Patisserie Valerie's external auditor. There are plenty of other famous examples of big companies which have suffered significant frauds—you have probably heard of Wirecom, Toshiba, Tesco, and of course Enron—an old example but possibly the most notorious.

When a well-known company suffers a significant fraud, one of the first questions asked, particularly where fraud is concerned, that appears to have been going on for a long time, is why did the auditors not spot it?

Many people mistakenly think that the auditor's primary duty is to detect fraud, but the International Standards on Auditing (ISAs) (UK) confirm that the prevention and detection of fraud is not the responsibility of the auditor. It is the responsibility of management. There is an 'expectation gap' between what an auditor does and what the general public *thinks* the auditor does when it comes to fraud detection.

Fraud is an extremely significant problem for companies and it appears that it is becoming more prevalent. According to a PwC study,[1] in 2020, 56 per cent of organizations surveyed had experienced some form of fraud, corruption, or economic crime, increased from 50 per cent when the same question was asked in 2018. Accounting fraud, defined in the

[1] *PwC Fraud and economic crime survey—An evolving challenge, 2020 UK findings.*

PwC survey as 'the intentional manipulation of accounting records to misstate a company's true financial position', increased from being reported by 14 per cent of survey respondents in 2014 to 26 per cent of survey respondents in 2020. As shown by these figures, fraud is an extremely serious problem for companies of all sizes.

We need to understand the auditor's responsibility where fraud and compliance with laws and regulations are concerned, as well as management's responsibility. There are high expectations that auditors should find frauds, but in actuality the external auditor only discovers a small proportion of frauds—the same PwC survey suggests that in only 10 per cent of cases of fraud was the external auditor involved in the detection.

In this chapter, we will also examine appropriate responses to suspected or identified fraud and non-compliance with laws and regulations (NOCLAR) by the external auditor because frauds and non-compliance could significantly affect the whole audit process, including the auditor's opinion.

The two ISAs (UK) we will be looking at in this chapter are:

- ISA (UK) 240 *The Auditor's Responsibilities Relating to Fraud in an Audit of Financial Statements*
- ISA (UK) 250 Section A—*Consideration of Laws and Regulations in an Audit of Financial Statements*

Learning outcomes

- Distinguish between 'fraud' and 'error' and identify different types of fraud.
- Explain the auditor's responsibilities in respect of fraud, and distinguish them from the responsibilities of management.
- Discuss the effect of fraud on the audit strategy and audit plan and recommend how the auditor should respond to the discovery of fraud, including reporting responsibilities.
- Discuss the expectation gap in relation to fraud.
- Explain the auditor's responsibilities in respect of law and regulations and recommend responses should a non-compliance with law and regulations take place.

By the end of this chapter, you will be able to:

- Identify and explain the factors which indicate a high risk of fraud and recommend appropriate auditor responses.

13.1 Fraud and error

It is important to understand the difference between a fraud and an error because the two are very different. A misstatement in the financial statements arising from fraud is deliberate, whereas a misstatement arising from error is generally unintentional.

13.1.1 **Errors in accounting and financial reporting**

ISA (UK) 240 does not define the term 'error' but the key issue is that errors are mistakes, often human errors, and errors can arise at any stage in a process, for example:

- posting purchase invoices to incorrect accounts in the general (nominal) ledger;
- misinterpreting or misunderstanding facts or the requirements of accounting standards (particularly complex accounting standards such as IFRS 9 *Financial Instruments*);
- an incorrect manual calculation (e.g. sales taxes on sales invoices);
- duplicating payments to a supplier, employee or other third party unintentionally;
- sending out incorrect quantities of goods to a customer.

This list is by no means exhaustive but provides examples of how errors can arise in everyday business.

Auditing Activity 13.1 Examples of errors

Can you think of any other common errors which might arise in relation to accounting or financial reporting?

As we have seen in previous chapters, during the planning stage of the audit the auditor will assess the client's system of internal control to ascertain whether internal controls are effective at preventing, detecting, and correcting, on a timely basis, errors such as those listed. The auditor will carry out tests of controls to test their operating effectiveness. Remember, tests of control do not focus on any monetary amounts in the financial statements—their focus is on whether the entity's controls have been operating effectively.

How this links to fraud is that during the audit process, when planning the audit in accordance with ISA (UK) 315 *Identifying and Assessing the Risks of Material Misstatement*, the auditor, by evaluating the client's internal controls, is also assessing the risk of error and fraud.

Auditing in practice 13.1 Consideration of errors at the planning stage of the audit

Common reasons for errors occurring, which the auditor may identify at the planning stage, include:

- errors in gathering the relevant data and information from which the financial statements are drawn up;
- errors in applying the requirements of financial reporting standards;
- misinterpretations of facts giving rise to an error in an accounting estimate; or
- incorrect classifications in the financial statements.

For recurring audits, the auditor can draw on their previous experience of the client when considering such issues. For example, if the finance department has a history of making mistakes in processing financial information, then the risk of material misstatement due to error will be deemed higher by the auditor.

For new audit clients, audit risk is higher because the auditor has no previous experience. Therefore, for a new audit client, it would normally be the case that specific audit procedures are designed at the planning stage to address fraud and error. This may include less reliance on tests of control and a more substantive approach.

13.1.2 **Errors and misstatements discovered during the course of the audit**

In practice, in all audits, the auditor will discover errors within the financial statements. While effective internal controls help to prevent and detect errors, no system of controls is perfect and errors in accounting and financial reporting are certainly not unusual. As the auditor progresses throughout the course of the audit, they document all errors and misstatements on a 'Schedule of Audit Adjustments' or 'Uncorrected Error Schedule'. Typical errors discovered may include:

- Some goods and/or services received by the reporting date but not invoiced have not been accrued in the financial statements.
- Depreciation charges have been calculated incorrectly.
- A mis-posting has been discovered in the financial statements (e.g. posting directors' remuneration to staff salaries).
- Transactions in a foreign currency may have been translated at the incorrect exchange rates.
- A disclosure note may contain incorrect information or have been omitted by error.

Once all the audit fieldwork (the evidence-gathering) is complete, the auditor will review the total errors and misstatements discovered during the course of the audit which will help them to form a conclusion as to the adequacy of the accounting records. In addition, the auditor must also assess the errors and misstatements against materiality levels to identify if any further work is required or if the financial statements are materially misstated. The auditor discusses the errors or misstatements with the client and requests that appropriate adjustments be made. In the case of unintentional errors or misstatements, there should be no reason for the client not to make the necessary adjustments. These issues are examined further in Chapter 18.

The errors and misstatements that the auditor discovers during the course of the audit fieldwork may have arisen because of weaknesses in the accounting records or deficiencies in the entity's internal control environment which may need to be notified to management and/or those charged with governance.

13.1.3 **Types of fraud**

Remember that fraud is a deliberate act. ISA (UK) 240 defines fraud as:

> An intentional act by one or more individuals among management, those charged with governance, employees, or third parties, involving the use of deception to obtain an unjust or illegal advantage.[2]

[2] FRC, 'ISA (UK) 240', 2022, para 12(a) <https://media.frc.org.uk/documents/ISA_UK_240_Updated_May_2022.pdf> (accessed 18 January 2024).

Note that the definition is quite broad and refers to management and those charged with governance, acknowledging that fraud can be, and often is, conducted by senior people within the company.

Generally, fraud committed by a member of management or those charged with governance of the entity arises through the overriding of the entity's system of internal control. The senior status of the person within the organization allows the management override to take place. ISA (UK) 240 recognizes that management override of internal controls is a significant fraud risk and therefore the auditor must devise procedures at the planning stage which respond to this risk.

Fraud committed by an employee of the entity usually arises through the manipulation of weaknesses in the internal control environment of the business—for example, through a lack of segregation of duties or a lack of oversight by senior officials. This type of risk is assessed through the auditor's tests of controls. Where a fraud risk factor is present, the auditor will tailor their procedures to address the fraud risk factor.

Auditing in practice 13.2 Who commits fraud?

It is interesting to think about who is most likely to commit fraud within an organization. According to a survey published by the Association of Certified Fraud Examiners (ACFE) in 2020,[3] employees commit 41 per cent of occupational fraud, managers commit 35 per cent, and owners/executives commit 20 per cent.

The financial loss caused by fraud correlates with the seniority of the perpetrator. The average size of the fraud for each category of perpetrator is as follows:

Employee—$60,000

Manager—$150,000

Owner/executive—$600,000

Men are much more likely to carry out fraud, with 72 per cent of frauds having male perpetrators, and only 28 per cent female perpetrators. Men are also more 'successful' fraudsters, with an average fraud size of $150,000, compared to $85,000 for women.

Perhaps not surprisingly, the ACFE survey reveals that the highest risk departments for frauds to take place are operations and accounting. The survey also shows that 51 per cent of frauds were carried out by two or more individuals working in collusion. The more people involved with a fraud, the higher the financial loss caused by the fraud.

The vast majority, 96 per cent, of fraud perpetrators have no prior charges or convictions for fraud.

ISA (UK) 240 explains that there are two types of fraud which the auditor is concerned with: misappropriation of assets and fraudulent financial reporting (Figure 13.1).

[3] Association of Certified Fraud Examiners, 'Report to the nations: 2020 global study on occupational fraud and abuse', 2020 <https://acfepublic.s3-us-west-2.amazonaws.com/2020-Report-to-the-Nations.pdf> (accessed 18 January 2024).

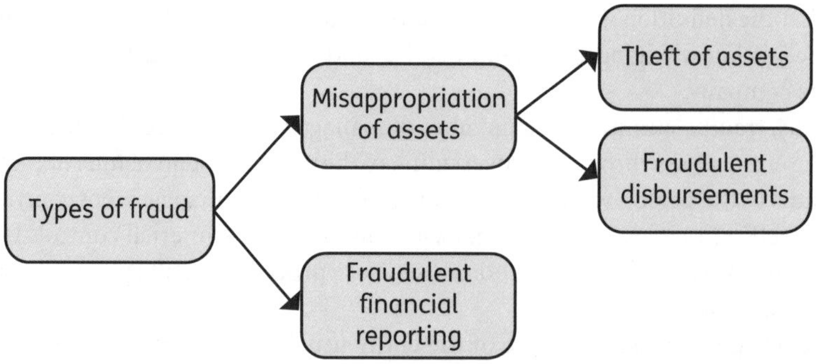

Figure 13.1 Types of fraud

13.1.3.1 **Misappropriation of assets**

This type of fraud involves the theft of cash or other assets from an organization such as theft of high-value inventory and computer equipment. In addition, using an entity's assets for personal use is classed as misappropriation of assets, for example, if an employee uses a company car for personal use when this is against company policy.

Misappropriation of assets can also include fraudulent disbursements—this is when company funds are being used to make fraudulent payments. Common examples include when payments are made to a fictitious supplier with the funds going into the perpetrator's bank account, and payroll schemes such as 'ghost employee' where salary is paid to a fictitious employee.

13.1.3.2 **Fraudulent financial reporting**

This refers to deliberate manipulation of the financial statements so that they reflect a predetermined outcome. It can include deliberate falsification of accounting records; omission of transactions, balances, or disclosures from the financial statements; or the deliberate misapplication of financial reporting standards. This is often carried out with the intention of presenting the financial statements with a particular bias, for example, concealing liabilities in order to improve any analysis of liquidity and gearing, possibly to secure finance or to attract investment into a company. Fraudulent financial reporting is characterized by a deliberate breach of accounting standards.

ISA (UK) 240 states that fraudulent financial reporting may be accomplished by the following:

- Manipulation, falsification (including forgery), or alteration of accounting records or supporting documentation from which the financial statements are prepared.
- Misrepresentation in, or intentional omission from, the financial statements of events, transactions or other significant information.
- Intentional misapplication of accounting principles relating to amounts, classification, manner of presentation, or disclosure.[4]

[4] FRC, 'ISA (UK) 240', 2022, para A3.

It is important to note that fraudulent financial reporting is not the same as creative accounting, which is when the financial statements are prepared in a way that uses the flexibility allowed by financial reporting standards to present a certain picture. Creative accounting is not a breach of financial reporting standards, but it can mean that the financial statements are not 'true and fair' because they are not a faithful representation of the entity's financial position and performance. Creative accounting is often thought of as bending the rules rather than breaking the rules.

Activity 13.2 Examples of creative accounting

Can you think of examples of creative accounting?

13.1.4 **Why does fraud take place?**

ISA (UK) 240 suggests that an incentive or pressure to commit fraudulent financial reporting may exist when management is under pressure to achieve an expected, and perhaps unrealistic, earnings target or financial outcome. For example, shareholders may require a certain level of profit to be achieved in order that they can receive a certain level of dividend.

Auditing scenario 13.1 Tesco

In 2015, the UK-based supermarket chain Tesco revealed that it had overstated its profits by £263 million due to revenue recognition accounting irregularities. Effectively, Tesco had recognized supplier rebates in its financial statements that it had not received, nor was expected to receive, because the rebates were based on targets that the supermarket was never going to reach. The impact of this was that the company's profit and earnings per share figure were higher than they should have been, meaning that shareholders thought the supermarket was doing better than it actually was.

This is an example of fraudulent financial reporting—deliberately misstating the financial statements to reflect fictitious transactions, events, or conditions. An internal whistle-blower told the company's legal department of their concerns, who in turn informed the chairman and CEO. The whistle-blower was a member of the finance department who initially was concerned about the lack of documentation regarding revenue transactions.

The revenue rebates were based on estimates therefore it is not easy to 'prove' that they were right or wrong at the point in time when they are recognized. The external auditor, PwC, had raised the issue as a key audit matter but Tesco's audit committee had said that it was not a problem. However, internal controls over revenue recognition were either not robust enough or were overridden by management. The audit committee had dismissed the issue as a significant risk.

The figure of £263 million is large, but it was not material in individual years or cumulatively when looking at the monetary amounts involved which were less than 10 per cent of the company's profit before tax. However, the misstatement could be considered material by nature (i.e. due to the risk of fraud and the level of subjectivity involved in the accounting).

Tesco was underperforming due to pressure from cut-price supermarkets like Aldi and Lidl. There was a perceived 'need' by management to improve results. Targets were not being met which led to a motive to overstate revenue and profit. Bonuses were based on performance, so senior managers had a personal incentive to maximize revenue and profit. So, there was a lot of motive for overstatement of profit, and senior management have the opportunity to override internal controls, to put in place fraudulent financial reporting.

Other examples of fraudulent financial reporting include:

- Processing fictitious journals very close to, or at, the reporting date to deliberately manipulate the information in the financial statements.
- Advancing or delaying recognition in the financial statements of events or transactions which have taken place during the accounting period.
- Failing to disclose facts which would affect the amounts recorded in the financial statements.
- Failing to disclose contingent liabilities or significant going concern difficulties.
- Inappropriately changing assumptions and judgements used in estimating account balances.
- Engaging in complex transactions which are deliberately engineered to provide a misleading picture in the statement of financial position or statement of profit or loss.

As we saw earlier, high-value fraud is more likely to be carried out by individuals in a senior position in the entity than a mid-tier manager or lower-level ranking staff member. Nowadays, criminal record checks carried out on individuals prior to them commencing work will indicate if the potential employee has been prosecuted for fraud in the past. However, individuals in any position can commit fraud or even collude with others to commit a fraud and it is for this reason that the auditor must maintain professional scepticism. Fraudsters tell lies—a lot—and for this reason the auditor must not just accept an explanation at face value; they must obtain corroborative evidence of any oral explanations or evidence provided to them by someone internal to the audit client.

Auditing in practice 13.3 The 'fraud triangle'

Why do people commit frauds? The 'fraud triangle' is a behavioural model, developed by Donald Cressey,[5] which explains why individuals commit fraud (see Figure 13.2).

Motivation

Most people commit fraud in order to make money. Financial pressure is often the root cause. During economic recessions, it is observed that there is an increase in occupational fraud, particularly asset misappropriation. Many fraudsters begin by embezzling small amounts of cash or stealing other assets from their employer but fraud schemes can quickly escalate. Of course, greed is also a motivation, as is job dissatisfaction.

[5] Cressey, Donald R. (1973) *Other People's Money*, Patterson Smith, Montclair.

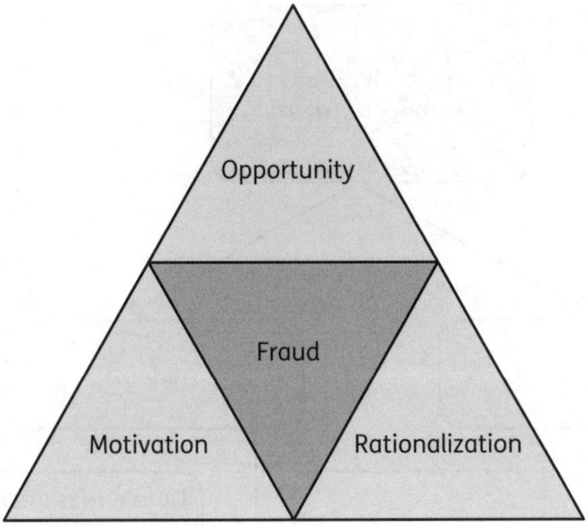

Figure 13.2 The 'fraud triangle'

Opportunity

Opportunity must exist within an organization for a fraudulent activity to occur. This relates to both the means to commit a fraud and the ability to conceal it. This is why many frauds are committed by individuals who have access to the accounting system and the ability to override controls (i.e. relatively senior members of the accounting department are very well-placed to establish a fraud).

Rationalization

It is typical that a fraudster believes that he or she is doing nothing wrong, though as schemes escalate in complexity and value this becomes less the case. Fraudsters often do not believe they are acting illegally or see themselves as criminals. For example, fraudulent financial reporting which hides liabilities or overstates profitability is often rationalized by the perpetrator as an attempt for the company to obtain more finance in times of economic distress, appease investors, and ultimately save a failing company.

13.2 Responsibilities in respect of fraud

Fraud can be very difficult to detect and, in some cases, it can be years before suspicions are roused. When a fraud is discovered, it can lead to significant tensions within the entity and where a fraud has been ongoing for a long time, quite often the auditors are questioned as to why they never spotted it in prior years' audits. Management may often try to blame the auditor. However, ISA (UK) 240 makes it very clear that the auditor does not bear the responsibility for fraud prevention and detection (see Figure 13.3).

13.2.1 Management's responsibilities

ISA (UK) 240 states that the primary responsibility for the prevention and detection of fraud rests with those charged with governance and management of the entity. Hence, it is not the auditor's responsibility to prevent and detect fraud.

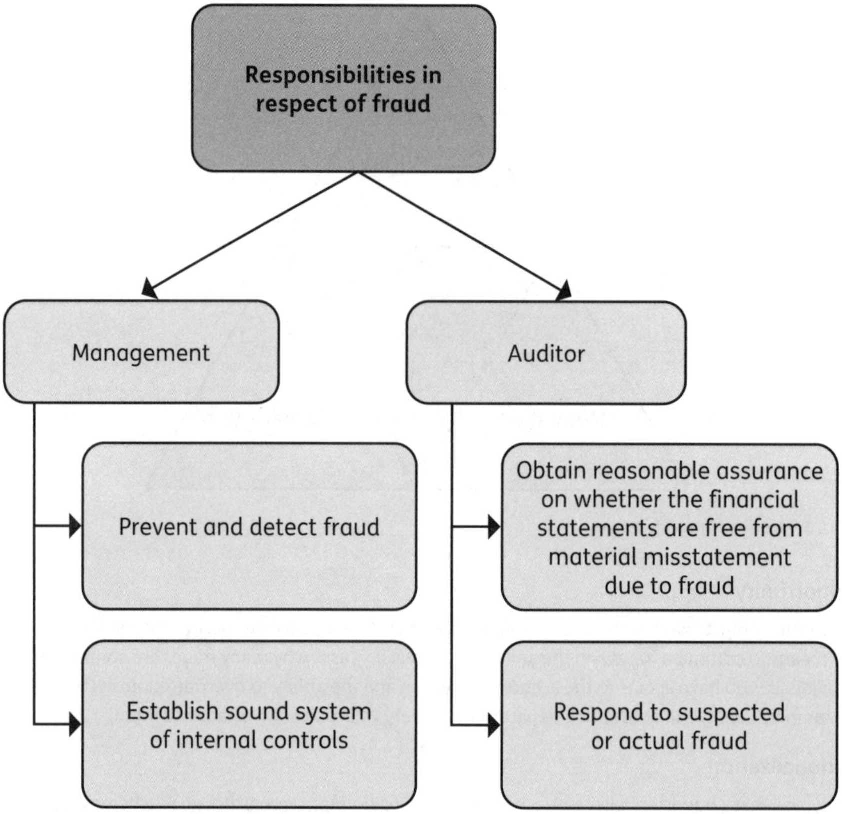

Figure 13.3 Responsibilities in respect of fraud

Establishing a sound system of internal control, which is also the responsibility of management, will help to reduce the risk of fraud and error. An effective system of internal control will reduce opportunities for fraud to take place and it will also increase the likelihood of fraud being discovered if it does take place. In addition, management should also create a culture of honesty, ethical behaviour, and active oversight by those charged with governance.

However, no system of internal control will ever be so robust that it will entirely prevent a fraud or error. This is largely because of the risk of management override of the internal control system.

Auditing scenario 13.2 Internal controls relating to fraud

You are carrying out the audit of the payroll cycle for your client, Montserrat Ltd, for the year ended 31 December 20X9 and are reviewing the internal controls documentation. You have noted the following points:

- Montserrat Ltd has a human resources (HR) function that is responsible for recruiting staff. However, the payroll department is responsible for completing joiner and leaver forms and processing these within the payroll.

- The payroll is completed on a monthly basis and there are no staff paid weekly. The payroll is prepared by the payroll clerk who processes the payroll, finalizes it, and prepares the bank transfer listing that is sent to the finance director.
- The finance director reviews the total amount of the bank transfer listing and compares this to his cash flow forecast to ensure that the amount to be paid to the employees is reasonable.
- The bank transfer listing is then signed by the finance director and sent back to the payroll clerk for processing.

Table 13.1 outlines the weaknesses in the payroll cycle of the business together with suggested improvements to reduce the risk of fraud occurring within the payroll cycle:

Table 13.1 Weak controls and fraud risk

Weakness and fraud risk	Suggested improvement
Montserrat Ltd has an HR department who are responsible for recruiting staff. The payroll department complete the joiner and leaver forms and process these through the payroll. This provides an opportunity for the payroll department to complete a joiner form for a fictitious employee and process them as if they were a real person. This creates a fraud risk factor within the payroll department as it would be easy for a 'ghost employee' fraud to be set up.	The HR department should be responsible for completing all joiner and leaver forms. These should be sent to the payroll department who should review them for completeness and then process the joiner forms in the payroll. They should then be signed as completed and returned to the HR department.
The payroll clerk completes the payroll on a monthly basis, finalizes it, and prepares the bank transfer listing which is sent to the finance director. The payroll clerk has too much responsibility. In addition to completing the joiner forms (noted above), there is no evidence of a review of the payroll by a senior official. This not only creates a fraud risk factor in that ghost employees could be being paid via the payroll, but also friends and family of the payroll clerk could be receiving unauthorized payments via the payroll.	Once the payroll has been completed, it should be reviewed by a payroll supervisor or another payroll clerk. If such a person does not exist, the payroll should be reviewed by a senior member of the finance team. Once reviewed, the senior official should evidence their review by way of signature and inform the payroll clerk of any amendments or to finalize the payroll.
Only the total amount of the bank transfer listing is reviewed by the finance director for cash flow purposes. No other reviews are carried out. Any deliberate changes to individual payments made will not be detected if a detailed review of the amount to be paid is not carried out	The finance director should review the bank transfer listing in conjunction with the payroll reports produced by the payroll system to ensure that the amounts being paid to the employees are accurate and that only bona fide employees are being paid

As you can see from Table 13.1, a weak system of internal control can easily create fraud risk factors. The example does not mention that any fraud has actually taken place, but it does highlight the type of fraud risk factors which auditors may identify when planning the audit.

Management should be aware of fraud risks within their business and this should inform elements of their risk assessment and corporate governance procedures. Where the entity has an audit committee, this committee should review these procedures to ensure that they are in place and are working effectively and this will usually be done in conjunction with the internal audit function, if one is in place.

Management needs to be made aware of any weaknesses in the entity's system of internal control which create fraud risk factors so that they can implement measures to reduce the risk of fraud to an acceptable level. This will involve either implementing controls or strengthening existing controls.

For many companies, the internal audit function is a key element of the battle against fraud. Remember that one of the roles of internal audit is to review systems of internal control. Management can request that internal audit carry out various tasks to reduce the risk of fraud, including:

- testing the effectiveness of the entity's system of internal control that is designed to prevent and detect fraud and provide recommendations for management on their improvement;
- investigate any frauds that have been discovered and identify:
  - how the fraud was committed;
  - the extent of the fraud; and
  - provide recommendations to management on controls that need to be implemented or strengthened to prevent the fraud from happening again; and
- carry out random checks on assets (such as cash counts and checks of the non-current assets register to the physical asset).

The mere presence of an internal audit function can also act as a deterrent to fraud itself as there is more chance of fraud being detected.

13.2.2 **Auditor's responsibilities**

According to ISA (UK) 240, in respect of fraud, the objectives of the auditor are:

a) To obtain reasonable assurance about whether the financial statements as a whole are free from material misstatement due to fraud, including:
   - Identifying and assessing the risks of material misstatement of the financial statements due to fraud;
   - Obtaining sufficient appropriate audit evidence regarding the assessed risks of material misstatement due to fraud, through designing and implementing appropriate responses; and

b) To respond appropriately to fraud or suspected fraud identified during the audit.[6]

There is some interaction with ISA (UK) 700 *Forming an Opinion and Reporting on Financial Statements*. This is very much a UK-specific issue. Under ISA (UK) 700, the auditor's report must include a section within the 'Auditor's responsibilities for the financial statements' section as to how the audit was designed to detect irregularities, including fraud. This could include matters like:

- assessing compliance with laws and regulations;
- assessing compliance with tax legislation;

[6] FRC, 'ISA (UK) 240', 2022, para 11.

- reviewing correspondence (especially from lawyers) to identify any potential NOCLAR;
- discussions with management and those charged with governance concerning any irregularities, including fraud.

The ISA (UK) also acknowledges that due to the inherent limitations of audit, there is an unavoidable risk that some material misstatements of the financial statements may not be detected, even though the audit has been properly planned and performed.

Activity 13.3 Why are frauds difficult to detect?

Think of as many reasons as you can which might explain why it is difficult for the auditor to detect frauds at a client.

Frauds perpetrated by senior management in particular can be very difficult to discover, because it is relatively easy for a senior person, for example the finance director of a company, to manipulate accounting records, override controls, destroy evidence, and even intimidate their junior members of staff to cover up the fraudulent activity.

13.3 Auditor's fraud risk assessment procedures and responses

ISA (UK) 240 requires the auditor to consider fraud risk factors when performing risk assessment at the planning stage of the audit. ISA (UK) 240 defines a 'fraud risk factor' as:

> Events or conditions that indicate an incentive or pressure to commit fraud or provide an opportunity to commit fraud.[7]

13.3.1 Fraud risk indicators

Unfortunately, there is no exhaustive list available to auditors to provide definitive indicators that fraud is present at an audit client. ISA (UK) 240 requires the auditor to maintain professional scepticism throughout the audit. Maintaining an inquiring mind and not relying on the past integrity and honesty of management and, where applicable, those charged with governance will help the auditor to identify indicators of fraud which may include:

- aggressive management or aggressive responses from management and staff to the auditor's requests;
- staff becoming nervous when asked certain questions;
- dismissive attitude towards internal controls and/or evidence of management override of the entity's internal controls;
- inadequate accounting records or lack of explanations for certain transactions;

[7] Ibid., para 12(b).

- tolerance of petty theft and other minor breaches of laws and regulations or company policy;
- staff members not taking holidays (for fear of a fraud being discovered in their absence);
- large numbers of write-offs on control account reconciliations;
- management and staff maintaining an expensive lifestyle when their wages or salaries would not otherwise allow them to do so;
- use of business assets for personal use.

Within an IT system, the following might indicate actual or attempted frauds:

- a higher-than-average number of failed log-in attempts;
- log-ins at unusual times of the day or at weekends or by a person who is on leave;
- system access controls being disabled.

Documentary 'red flags' could include:

- Photocopied rather than original documents—the photocopied version could have been altered (which is difficult to spot on a photocopy).
- Documents not being in an appropriate style (e.g. missing a logo, lines missing on an invoice).
- Incomplete information on documents (e.g. missing VAT number, company registration number).
- Incorrect contact details on a document (e.g. a non-existent email address or website).
- 'Companies' not being registered on public registries (e.g. Companies House).
- Documents being created via a word-processing package and converted to PDF format when the 'properties' section of the PDF indicates that the document has been recently created.

ISA (UK) 240 requires that there is discussion among the audit engagement team focusing on fraud risk indicators. Engagement team members may discuss matters including management incentives to commit fraud, factors relating to the business environment, and how frauds could be perpetrated. This discussion must involve the audit engagement partner and should take place regardless of past history with the client and the level of trust which the auditor has in relation to the integrity of the client. The discussion can be particularly useful for more junior members of the audit team because they can learn from the insights of the more experienced auditors.

The key to the audit team discussion is primarily to discuss *how* fraud *could* occur at the client, even if there has not been any past history of frauds.

As part of the audit risk assessment process, the auditor should specifically assess the risk of material misstatement due to fraud. ISA (UK) 240 requires the auditor to consider how management assesses the risk of fraud taking place within the company and how management responds to the risk of fraud. The auditor should also discuss fraud risks with management and obtain an understanding of how management's views on business practices and ethical behaviour are communicated to employees.

The auditor should also inquire with management and those charged with governance to find out if any actual, suspected, or alleged fraud has taken place.

When planning the audit, normal audit procedures such as analytical review may indicate that fraud is taking place. For example, if a company's operating profit margin unexpectedly reduces due to increased payroll costs, this could be due to a 'ghost employee' fraud.

It is fundamental that the auditor obtains a good level of business understanding when planning the audit. Knowledge of the business environment may lead the auditor to conclude that there are specific circumstances which increase the risk of fraud, for example, if the company is facing financial difficulties, there will be pressure on management to present a good picture of the company's financial performance and position, which creates a motivation for fraudulent financial reporting.

Auditing in practice 13.4 Fraud and Covid-19

During the Covid-19 pandemic, many governments around the world implemented various schemes to help businesses. These included various grants, reliefs, and loans. One of the grants in the UK was the Job Retention Scheme (JRS) grant.

Under the JRS, an employee who was furloughed (the word 'furlough' means a member of staff has been put on temporary leave due to the Coronavirus restrictions) would receive a certain percentage of their salary for hours not worked.

Some employers took advantage of this grant inappropriately. That is, the employer claimed the JRS grant but continued to have the staff member(s) working for them. This is fraud because the employer has claimed a grant that they are not entitled to.

Where an audit client took advantage of the JRS, the auditor needed to be alert to the possibility that the employer may not have furloughed all the staff members for whom the business has received the JRS grant. Specific procedures such as looking at time sheets, clocking-in information, staff holiday requisitions and discussions with various individuals at the entity helped the auditor to identify any fraudulent claims.

Where a fraudulent claim is identified during the course of any audit, care needs to be taken by the auditor to ensure they comply with anti-money laundering regulations. For that reason, auditors must have a sound understanding of their obligations under those regulations and the audit firm's internal procedures in respect of money laundering.

13.3.2 **Fraud risks in revenue recognition**

One part of the financial statements which is singled out by ISA (UK) 240 for special consideration by the auditor in relation to fraud, is revenue. The presumption that there are fraud risks in revenue recognition can be rebutted, but generally ISA (UK) 240 requires that:

> When identifying and assessing the risks of material misstatement due to fraud, the auditor shall, based on a presumption that there are risks of fraud in revenue recognition, evaluate which types of revenue, revenue transactions or assertions give rise to such risks. Paragraph 48 specifies the documentation required where the auditor concludes that the presumption is not applicable in the circumstances of the engagement and, accordingly, has not identified revenue recognition as a risk of material misstatement due to fraud.[8]

[8] Ibid., para 27.

Revenue is at risk of deliberate over or understatement. Overstatement could occur, for example, if revenue is deliberately recognized too early (as in the Tesco example we looked at earlier), perhaps to boost poor performance or to maximize a bonus based on revenue growth. Understatement could be done to reduce profits, perhaps to reduce tax payable. Revenue may be more susceptible to manipulation in cash-based businesses.

13.3.3 **Responding to the assessed risk of material misstatement due to fraud**

Once the auditor has assessed the fraud risk, they must consider the impact on the audit plan. Where there is an elevated risk of material misstatement due to fraud, perhaps due to economic pressures in the business environment and financial distress facing the audit client, the auditor may respond by:

- assigning more senior and experienced personnel to the audit engagement team; or
- using unpredictable audit procedures (e.g. a 'surprise' cash count or a non-routine inspection of physical assets).

As discussed earlier, the auditor will always assess whether a client's system of internal control is effective or not. Part of this assessment relates to management's ability to override internal controls. Management is in a unique position to be able to carry out fraudulent financial reporting—remember one of the elements of the 'fraud triangle' which we looked at earlier is 'opportunity'—and management often have the opportunity to manipulate the financial statements using inappropriate or unauthorized journal entries. These adjustments are often made around the year end and especially when the adjustments are made manually, they are often done outside of the normal accounting processes, so can bypass internal controls over financial reporting.

ISA (UK) 240 requires that because management are able to override controls which otherwise appear to be operating effectively, the auditor must design and perform audit procedures which fulfil three objectives (see Figure 13.4).

ISA 240 (UK) requires that auditors:

a) Test the appropriateness of manual or automated journal entries recorded in the general ledger and other adjustments made in the preparation of the financial statements, including consolidation adjustments in the preparation of group financial statements. In designing and performing audit procedures for such tests, the auditor shall:

    i. Make inquiries of individuals with different levels of responsibility involved in the financial reporting process about inappropriate or unusual activity relating to the processing of journal entries and other adjustments;

    ii. Select journal entries and other adjustments made at the end of the reporting and post-closing entries; and

    iii. Consider the need to test journal entries and other adjustments throughout the reporting period.

b) Review accounting estimates for biases and evaluate whether the circumstances producing the bias, if any, represent a risk of material misstatement due to fraud. In performing this review, the auditor shall:

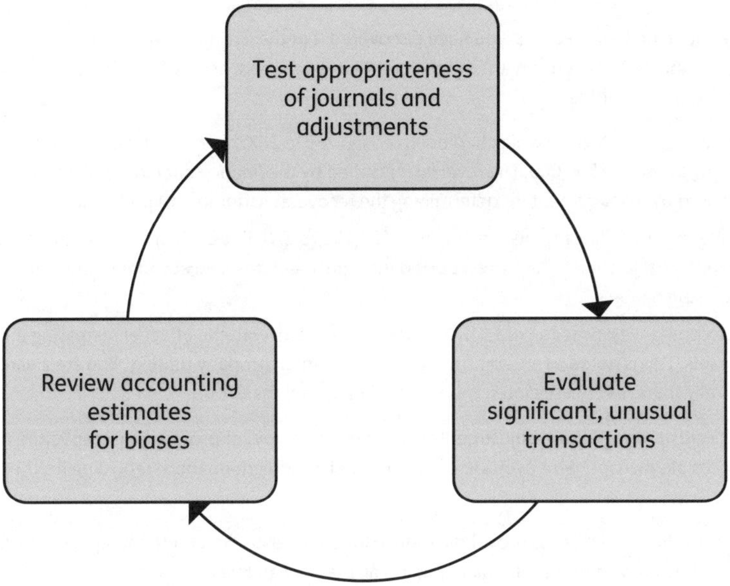

Figure 13.4 Procedures relating to management override of controls

i. Evaluate whether the judgments and decisions made by management in making the accounting estimates included in the financial statements, even if they are individually reasonable, indicate a possible bias on the part of the entity's management that may represent a risk of material misstatement due to fraud. If so, the auditor shall re-evaluate the accounting estimates taken as a whole; and

ii. Perform a retrospective review of management judgments and assumptions related to significant accounting estimates reflected in the financial statements of the prior year.

c) For significant transactions that are outside the normal course of business for the entity, or that otherwise appear to be unusual given the auditor's understanding of the entity and its environment and other information obtained during the audit, the auditor shall evaluate whether the business rationale (or lack thereof) of the transactions suggests that they may have been entered into to engage in fraudulent financial reporting or to conceal misappropriation of assets.[9]

Auditing scenario 13.3 Journal entries

You are auditing the Shaker Group, a business that manufactures glassware for use in the hospitality sector. The Group is facing some financial difficulties and has applied for a significant bank loan. The financial year ended on 31 December 20X4 and you have established the audit materiality level to be £350,000.

[9] Ibid., para 33.

As a result of audit procedures, you have discovered that the Group's finance director has made a number of manual journal entries around the company's year end, none of which were discussed with the Group audit committee:

- An impairment of a factory which had been recognized in 20X2 has been reversed, with the effect of increasing profit by £500,000. The reversal is justified by the finance director on the basis of a new model used by management for determining the recoverable number of properties.
- A number of small adjustments ranging from £24,000 to £78,000, each of which reduces the company's total liabilities, have been posted through a seldom-used account in the nominal ledger, with no explanation.
- An intercompany transaction of £340,000 has been posted, with the effect of increasing the Group's total assets. This is noted as an 'adjustment relating to intercompany trading'. You are aware that historically there is very little intercompany trading within the Group.

You should approach these adjustments with a very high level of professional scepticism, as they indicate possible management override of controls and fraudulent financial reporting for the following reasons:

- The Group's financial distress provides a motive for the finance director to manipulate the financial statements to show better profit, higher assets and fewer liabilities.
- The finance director presumably has the ability to make these adjustments using his or her access to the accounting system and no approval or authorization from the Group audit committee has been sought.
- Reversal of any impairment is unusual, and the impact of the adjustment improves the Group's profit. Using a new model to determine the recoverable amount may not be an appropriate justification.
- Adjusting a seldom-used nominal ledger account is again highly unusual, especially as all of the adjustments work to boost profit and have not been explained.
- The number of individually small adjustments could accumulate into a large impact on profit.
- Intercompany transactions can be used as a mechanism for moving transactions around the Group and it is unusual that an adjustment for intercompany trading would increase assets—usually such as adjustments (e.g. a provision for unrealized profit), would reduce Group assets.
- The intercompany adjustment appears to have no justified business rationale, which also indicates possible manipulation.
- The fact that all of these adjustments are round-sum figures is also unusual and this can indicate deliberate manipulation of the transactions.
- The adjustment relating to an intercompany transaction is just below the auditor's materiality threshold—if the Group finance director is aware of this threshold, the adjustment may have been set up deliberately less than £350,000 to try to avoid it being looked into by the auditor.

You will need to consider how to respond to this evidence of management override of controls and the implications of these fraud risk factors for the audit. The responses should include planning further testing on all of these manual adjustments and considering performing further audit procedures on other areas of the audit where management override of controls could have taken place.

To summarize: before we move on to consider how the auditor should respond if a fraud is discovered or suspected, while the auditor does not have a primary responsibility to prevent and detect fraud, ISA (UK) 240 makes it clear that the auditor has a responsibility to evaluate the client's susceptibility to fraud and to plan the audit accordingly. In order to discharge their responsibilities properly, the auditor must:

- Maintain professional scepticism throughout the entire audit so as to recognize the possibility that a material misstatement due to fraud could occur.
- Set aside previous experience of the client's integrity and honesty.
- Consider any incentives to commit fraud, such as a profit-related bonus or a lavish lifestyle where the individual's income would not normally allow such a lifestyle.
- Discuss the susceptibility of the financial statements to fraud among the engagement team (including fraud in respect of related parties).
- Identify and assess the risks of material misstatement due to fraud.
- Identify through discussion with management how they respond to the risks of fraud.
- Inquire of internal audit and management whether they are aware of any actual or suspected fraudulent activity.

13.3.4 **Responding to suspected or identified fraud**

It is not unusual for an auditor to discover a fraud operating at a client, or at least have strong suspicions that a fraud is taking place. In this situation, there are specific actions which the auditor must take. Essentially, the auditor needs to report their suspicions to an appropriate person—who that is depends on the nature of the fraud that is taking place, including who is perpetrating the fraud (Figure 13.5).

- Communicate the matter on a timely basis to the appropriate level of management. It is important that the client is alerted to an actual or suspected fraud as soon as possible, even if the fraud is not significant from a monetary point of view. The level of management to which the fraud should be reported would normally be at least one level above the individual involved with the fraud.
- When the suspected fraud involves management, the auditor must communicate the matter to those charged with governance. If the auditor has any doubt in their mind about the integrity of those charged with governance (e.g. they may suspect they are also involved in the fraud), then legal advice should be taken by the auditor.
- The auditor also needs to consider whether it is appropriate to report actual or suspected fraud to an appropriate authority outside the client. This may be required by law, regulation, or ethical requirements. However, remember that auditors are bound by confidentiality, so they must only make disclosures outside of the client once confidentiality has been considered. Whether to disclose information about fraudulent activity outside the client is a complex decision for the auditor's judgement, who may wish to consult with a regulator or professional body to help determine an appropriate course of action.

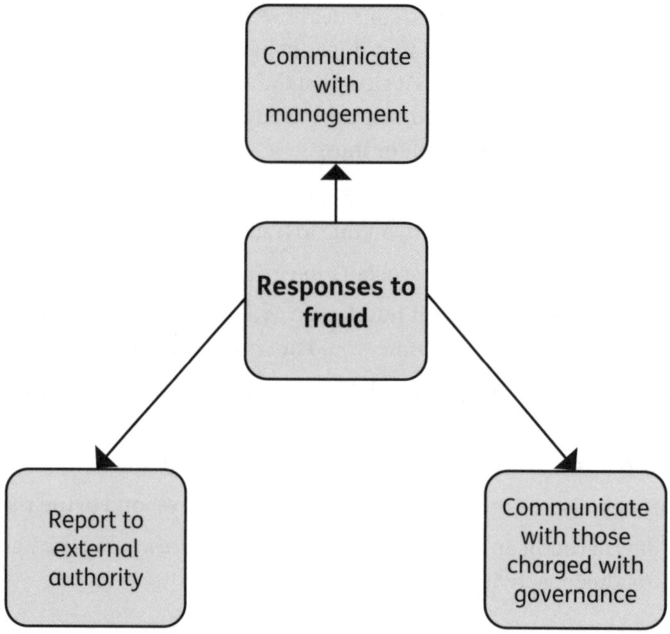

Figure 13.5 Responding to suspected or identified fraud

Extreme care needs to be taken where fraud is concerned because auditors are obliged to comply with anti-money laundering regulations and they need to ensure that they do not commit the act of 'tipping off'. Tipping off arises when the auditor may rouse suspicion in the perpetrator's or management's mind that the auditor has discovered the fraud and that they are going to take further action about it, such as making a money laundering report. Tipping a client off can happen very easily, even when the auditor does not think they have done anything wrong, so caution needs to be exercised to handle this issue carefully. If a member of the audit team has discovered the fraud, they should report it, in the first instance, to the audit engagement partner who will then deal with the issue.

Auditors are bound by the rules about confidentiality in that they cannot divulge information that they acquire during the course of their work.

When it comes to fraud, an auditor may need to seek legal advice from a third party about the course of action they need to take. In addition, the auditor may also need to inform the audit firm's Money Laundering Reporting Officer (MLRO) where the fraud involves acts of money laundering. The MLRO will then evaluate the situation and report externally when appropriate. In such instances, any legal responsibility will override the duty of confidentiality.

In exceptional situations, as a result of actual or suspected fraud, the auditor may consider that it is not possible to continue the audit engagement. This could happen, for example:

- If the client does not take appropriate action following the auditor alerting management to an actual or suspected fraud.
- Where there are doubts over the integrity of management or those charged with governance (e.g. if they have been involved with fraudulent activity).

If the auditor decides to discontinue the audit engagement, they should follow the appropriate regulatory and legal frameworks, and should take legal advice.

Auditing scenario 13.4 Suspected money laundering

You are the audit manager of Churchill Ltd, carrying out the audit for the year ended 31 March 20X1. During the year, Churchill Ltd acquired a government-backed loan for £400,000. You have obtained details of the loan, including the loan application, from the finance director and noted that a number of details in the application are factually incorrect—for example, the turnover declared on the loan application is overstated and bears no resemblance to the actual turnover in the financial statements. You have also noted that as soon as the loan was credited into the company's bank account, some of the proceeds of the loan were immediately transferred into the personal bank account of the chief executive and treated as a director's loan in the financial statements.

The fact that the loan application contains false information is a 'red flag' of fraud and the audit manager should report this issue to the audit engagement partner. The audit engagement partner should then consider whether a report to the firm's MLRO is needed. It is likely, in this situation, that a report will be needed.

The auditor does not have to check what the loan proceeds have been spent on, but the fact that some of the proceeds have been paid into the chief executive's personal account should also be a 'red flag' and the audit manager should also report this to the audit engagement partner.

Under no circumstances should the audit manager or the audit engagement partner notify the client that they have made a suspicious activity report (SAR) to the audit firm's MLRO. SARs are filed with the National Crime Agency by the audit firm's MLRO and if the auditor notifies the client, or even drops any hint, that they have made a SAR, this will constitute tipping off the client, for which the auditor may be prosecuted.

The audit firm should also consider how to withdraw from the audit, given the serious lack of integrity shown by the company's chief executive. This will need to be discussed with a legal adviser as giving the client notice of intending to withdraw from the audit engagement could be seen as 'tipping off', and the situation needs to be handled with extreme caution.

13.4 The expectation gap in relation to fraud

Now that we have seen the requirements as they relate to the external auditor and fraud, we can consider the issue of the expectation gap. Generally speaking, the expectation gap is described as the difference between what auditors actually do, and what people expect auditors to do.

13.4.1 Public perception of auditor's responsibilities for fraud

The issue of the expectation gap has been around for decades, it is not a 'current issue'. However, media attention on high-profile company scandals involving fraud and sometimes the collapse of the organization has caused a recent focus of attention on the expectation gap. As we mentioned in the introduction to this chapter, when a high-profile fraud is discovered, a question which is often asked is 'why didn't the auditors prevent or detect the fraud?'.

Different academic papers and the reports of professional and regulatory bodies over the years have discussed and explained the components of the expectation gap in a variety of ways, usually distinguishing between a lack of knowledge of the users of the audit report—the knowledge gap, and auditors not doing what they are supposed to—the performance gap.

Professional and regulatory bodies in the last few years have raised the issue of the expectation gap again. The resurgence of interest in the expectation gap is linked to a crisis of confidence in the audit profession and in financial reporting, and there is pressure on regulatory bodies to make changes with the aim of restoring trust in the auditor's opinion and report on financial statements.

In 2019, the Association of Chartered Certified Accountants (ACCA) published a paper[10] which discusses the expectation gap as arising from three elements, including a 'new' component called the evolution gap (see Figure 13.6).

- The knowledge gap arises from misunderstandings around the role and responsibilities of auditors, and the ISA (UK) requirements, for example, a mistaken belief held by the public that an objective of audit is to *prevent* and detect fraud.
- The performance gap relates to auditors not following the requirements. This can indicate poor-quality auditing, for example, the auditor not following the requirements of ISA (UK) 240 by not presuming a fraud risk in relation to revenue, or not properly evaluating fraud risk indicators. It could also mean that ISA (UK) requirements are not clear and are open to misinterpretation.

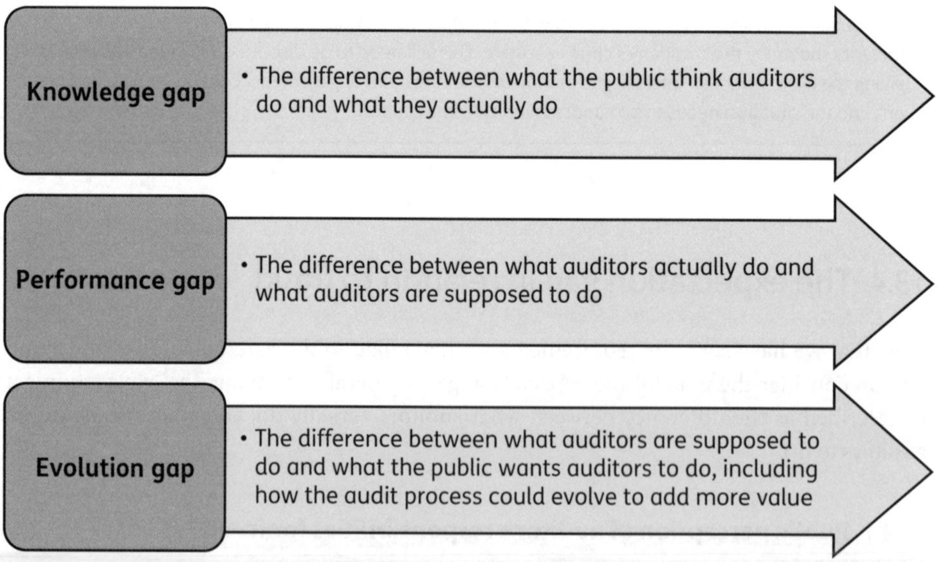

Figure 13.6 The expectation gap including the 'evolution gap'

[10] Association of Chartered Certified Accountants (2019) 'Closing the expectation gap in audit' <https://www.accaglobal.com/content/dam/ACCA_Global/professional-insights/Expectation-gap/pi-closing-expectation-gap-audit.pdf> (accessed 18 January 2024).

- The evolution gap considers where auditing may need to change to take account of the expectations of users of the auditor's report, for example, evolution may be driven by technological advances.

The survey performed by ACCA in preparing their paper supports the view that an expectation gap exists: for example, only 25 per cent of UK survey respondents could correctly identify the overall objective of an external audit, clearly indicating that a knowledge gap exists. Other evidence shows that a performance gap exists, for example, the reports from regulatory bodies such as the UK's Financial Reporting Council (FRC), which every year show that audits performed by the largest audit firms do not meet the standards expected.

The ACCA paper asked a specific question about fraud, focusing on the evolution gap. The question asked respondents to select the statement which best reflects their expectations of the auditor's responsibility for fraud. The survey responses showed that generally speaking, the public want the auditor to have more responsibility, with 35 per cent agreeing that 'I expect auditors to always detect and report any fraud'. We know from looking at the ISA (UK) 240 requirements earlier in the chapter that this is not the case—ISA (UK) 240 requires an auditor to obtain reasonable assurance that the financial statements taken as a whole are free from material misstatement, whether caused by fraud or error.

13.4.2 **The Brydon Report**

Several national reviews have also been conducted recently which include discussion on the issue of the expectation gap in relation to fraud. In the UK, the Brydon Report[11] included several significant recommendations relating to the auditor's role in respect of fraud, all linked to an expectation gap.

The report comments that fraud is the most commonly misunderstood area in relation to auditors' duties and Brydon recommends some extension of auditors' duties in relation to fraud including:

- A revision to ISA (UK) 240 to ensure that an obligation of the auditor is to detect material fraud in all reasonable ways.
- The auditor's report to contain information on work performed in relation to fraud risk assessment and assessment of relevant controls. This is now required by ISA (UK) 700 *Forming an Opinion and Reporting on Financial Statements* as the auditor must describe how the audit was designed to detect irregularities, including fraud. This disclosure is set out in the 'Auditor's responsibilities for the financial statements' section of the auditor's report.
- Training in forensic accounting and fraud awareness for all auditors with these topics to be included in the professional examination syllabi.
- The regulatory body to maintain a publicly available set of case studies on real-life frauds for auditors to use to build their expertise.

[11] *Assess, assure and inform—Improving audit quality and effectiveness.* Report of the Independent Review into the Quality and Effectiveness of Audit (2019) <https://assets.publishing.service.gov.uk/media/5df8edfced915d0938597e1f/brydon-review-final-report.pdf> (accessed 27 June 2023).

In addition, the Brydon Report recommends that directors should also report on the actions they have taken to fulfil their responsibilities in relation to fraud prevention and detection and fraud risk assessment.

It is hoped that extending the auditor's duties may help to reduce the expectation gap, by bringing the auditor's responsibilities closer to those expected by the public. Whether this will work to reduce the expectation gap, or whether further changes are needed, for example, in relation to education of the public or better monitoring and enforcement activities in relation to audit quality, remains to be seen.

Auditing in practice 13.5 Grant Thornton, Patisserie Valerie, and the audit expectation gap

In 2018, accounting irregularities were discovered at Patisserie Valerie, the company which ran a successful chain of over 200 cafés and sandwich shops in the UK. The irregularities came to light when HMRC acted against the company for an unpaid tax bill and it transpired that rather than having over £28 million in the company bank account, there was actually £10 million debt in two secret overdrafts which the company directors did not know about. Further investigations revealed that the company's cash position was overstated by £54 million, liabilities were understated by £17 million, and other assets overvalued by £23 million.

The company had been audited by Grant Thornton, which had issued unmodified audit opinions on its previous years' financial statements. Questions were asked about why the fraud had not been discovered during the external audit and David Dunckley, CEO at Grant Thornton, was called to the parliamentary Business Energy and Industrial Strategy (BEIS) Committee to discuss the audit. The conversation took many interesting turns, with politicians angrily asking why the fraud had not been discovered during the audit, and at one point the expectation gap was discussed.

When asked why his firm had not uncovered the accounting irregularities, David Dunckley said:

> We are not doing what the market thinks. We are not looking for fraud and we are not looking at the future and we are not giving a statement that the accounts are correct. There is a clear expectation gap, and audit fundamentally gives a reasonable opinion on historic information, and doesn't look for fraud. We're saying [the accounts] are reasonable, we are looking in the past and we are not set up to look for fraud.[12]

The members of the committee were not pleased with this answer, clearly thinking that Grant Thornton should have found the fraudulent activity. Rachel Reeves MP and chair of the BEIS committee said:

> In a shop that sells teas and cakes you'd think that sort of thing might be spotted. It's not a multinational complex organisation.

Peter Kyle MP added:

> Of course the audit company isn't committing a crime, in that case, but its fingerprints would be all over the crime scene. If an audit company isn't picking up on this type of behaviour, what is the point of audit in the first place?[13]

[12] Reported in the *Financial Times*, 30 January 2019 <https://www.ft.com/content/f8828dc8-24b0-11e9-8ce6-5db4543da632>.

[13] Kollewe, J. & Butler, S. (2019) 'Ex-Patisserie Valerie auditor says "not his role to uncover fraud"' <https://www.theguardian.com/business/2019/jan/30/ex-patisserie-valerie-auditor-says-not-his-role-to-uncover#:~:text=Heper cent20saidper cent20inper cent20anper cent20ideal,notper cent20aper cent20multinationalper cent20complexper cent20organisation.per centE2per cent80 per cent9D> (accessed 18 January 2024).

In 2021, the FRC published the report of their investigation into the audit of Patisserie Valerie by Grant Thornton for the financial years ended 2015, 2016, and 2017. In the relevant press release, the FRC comments as follows:

> In each of the three years, the audit work included serious breaches of Relevant Requirements across . . . four different audit areas, often repeated year on year, and in relation to several legal entities. The breaches reveal a pattern of serious lapses in professional judgement, failures to exercise professional scepticism, failures to obtain sufficient appropriate audit evidence and / or to prepare sufficient audit documentation.Consequently, each of the FY15, FY16 and FY17 Audits failed in their principal objectives of providing reasonable assurance that the financial statements were free from material misstatement, whether caused by fraud or error.[14]

A financial sanction of £4 million (discounted to £2.34 million) was applied to Grant Thornton, as well as a requirement for the audit firm to report to the FRC annually for three years on the corrective action being taken in light of the audit failure. An individual partner was fined £150,000 (discounted to £87,750) and they were banned from performing statutory audits for three years.

13.5 Laws and regulations

All entities are subject to some form of laws and regulations—some more than others. For example, some entities operate in highly regulated industries such as financial services, agriculture, and chemical processing, all of which have complex regulations. Others are subject to non-industry-specific laws and regulations which relate to the operating aspects of the business, such as employment law. Auditors are required to comply with ISA (UK) 250—Section A *Considerations of Laws and Regulations in an Audit of Financial Statements*. ISA (UK) 250 recognizes that the effect of laws and regulations varies considerably. For example, there are laws and regulations which directly affect the financial statements (e.g. tax legislation) and there are laws and regulations which do not directly affect the financial statements (e.g. health and safety legislation).

The financial reporting implication where laws and regulations are concerned is that any non-compliance with law and regulation (NOCLAR) may result in fines, litigation, or other consequences for the entity which may have a material effect on the financial statements. This is why the auditor needs to consider relevant laws and regulations under which an audited entity operates.

ISA (UK) 250 is one of the standards up for change by the FRC. In October 2023, the FRC issued an Invitation to Comment—Proposed Revisions to ISA (UK) 250 A and B. It is expected that the FRC's revised ISA (UK) 250 will be effective for audits of financial statements for periods commencing on or after 15 December 2024 (i.e. for 31 December 2025 year ends or short periods).

In the proposals, the FRC wish to remove the reference to direct and other laws and regulations and instead apply a more risk-based approach. This risk-based approach will direct the auditor's attention to identifying those laws and regulations where non-compliance may have a material impact on the financial statements. It will also enable the auditor to devise

[14] FRC (2021) 'Sanctions against Grant Thornton UK LLP and David Newstead' <https://www.frc.org.uk/news-and-events/news/2021/09/sanctions-against-grant-thornton-uk-llp-and-david-newstead/> (accessed 3 January 2024).

specific audit procedures to address the risk of material misstatement. In turn, this will also mean there will be a need for more professional judgement by the auditor.

The FRC are also looking at enhancing the risk assessment procedures, so under the proposals, the auditor will be required to:

(a) Understand those laws and regulations that relate to the applicable financial reporting framework, or which arise from regulatory factors.
(b) Understand management's process concerning compliance with laws and regulations and how those charged with governance oversee this process.
(c) Determine whether there are any deficiencies in internal control relevant to non-compliance with laws and regulations.
(d) Make inquiries of management, those charged with governance and other individuals to obtain their views on which laws and regulations could have a material impact on the financial statements.
(e) Inspect documentation for indications of non-compliance with laws and regulations.[15]

It is also expected that there will be explicit requirements for the auditor to identify, assess, and respond to the risks of material misstatement due to fraud or error relating to NOCLAR.

You'll have noticed that we have often referred to a 'stand back' requirement in a lot of the ISAs (UK) and the proposed changes to ISA (UK) 250 Section A are no different. The proposed 'stand back' requirement will require the auditor to assess whether they have obtained sufficient appropriate audit evidence regarding whether there is a material misstatement of the financial statements relating to NOCLAR. This will also include a requirement for the auditor to conclude whether non-compliance (or suspected non-compliance) with laws and regulations has resulted in a material misstatement of the financial statements.

13.5.1 **Management's responsibilities**

You should remember from Chapter 8, when we looked at internal controls, that management should establish risk assessment procedures. One element of risk assessment relates to compliance risk—that is, management should ensure that the organization is complying with all the necessary laws and regulations that apply to the business and manage the risk of non-compliance.

ISA (UK) 250 confirms that management is responsible for compliance with laws and regulations. To that end, management must monitor legal requirements and develop a system of internal control that ensures compliance with the entity's legal and regulatory framework.

13.5.2 **Auditor's responsibilities**

ISA (UK) 250 states that the auditor is not responsible for preventing and detecting NOCLAR.

The overall objective of the auditor is to identify any (potential) NOCLAR (see Figure 13.7). If any such non-compliance is identified, the auditor needs to obtain an understanding of the situation and obtain evidence to enable them to consider the possible impact on the financial

[15] FRC, 'Invitation to comment, proposed International Standard on Auditing (UK) 250 (Revised)', 2023, para 18 <https://media.frc.org.uk/documents/Invitation_to_Comment_Proposed_ISAs_UK_250.pdf> (accessed 18 January 2024).

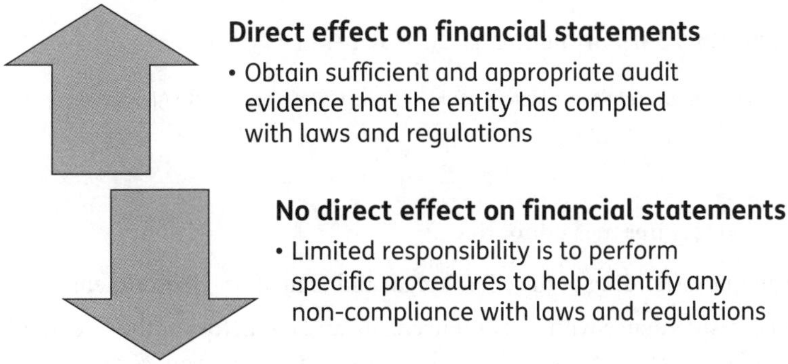

Figure 13.7 Auditors responsibilities regarding NOCLAR

statements, for example, whether any provision for liabilities should be recognized for potential fines and penalties or whether any contingent liability should be disclosed. In more serious cases, fines and penalties for non-compliance may also impact the going concern basis.

Remember, in the proposed amendments to ISA (UK) 250, Section A, the FRC are looking at removing the distinction between laws and regulations which have a direct and an indirect effect on the financial statements. Instead, the proposals will require the auditor to identify those laws and regulations where non-compliance may have a material impact on the financial statements.

The auditor will need to obtain sufficient and appropriate audit evidence that the entity has complied with laws and regulations that have a direct effect on the amounts and disclosures in the financial statements. In respect of laws and regulations which do not have a direct effect on the financial statements, the auditor has a limited responsibility to perform specific procedures to help identify any NOCLAR. Where the auditor discovers any NOCLAR or suspected NOCLAR, they must respond appropriately.

Auditing in practice 13.6 Compliance with laws and regulations

Some laws and regulations do have a direct effect on the entity's financial statements: for example, the Companies Act 2006, and tax legislation. In addition, an entity is required to prepare its financial statements in accordance with the applicable financial reporting framework, such as International Financial Reporting Standards (IFRS), and hence IFRS would be regarded as a regulation that has a direct impact on the amounts and disclosures reported in the financial statements.

The auditor must devise procedures that provide sufficient and appropriate audit evidence to confirm compliance with the entity's applicable laws and regulations which have a direct effect on the financial statements.

Where any NOCLAR is identified, this could give rise to a need for a provision for a liability (i.e. a fine or a penalty for non-compliance). The auditor would need to consider the materiality of the NOCLAR and whether any NOCLAR leading to a fine or a penalty gives rise to the recognition criteria for a provision in IAS 37 *Provisions, Contingent Liabilities and Contingent Assets* being met.

The risk of NOCLAR is considered at a very early stage in the audit and procedures are devised through the audit plan to obtain the necessary audit evidence. The principal audit risk is that where the audit client has not complied with laws and regulations, provisions for liabilities and expenses are understated or disclosures of a contingent liability are incomplete.

Activity 13.4 Indications of NOCLAR

If you were planning an audit, what factors could indicate to you that a NOCLAR was taking place?

ISA (UK) 250 requires the auditor to:

- Obtain an understanding of the client's legal and regulatory environment.
- Review correspondence with relevant licensing and regulatory authorities to identify any potential breaches of laws and regulations (e.g. if the relevant authority is investigating any (potential) non-compliance).
- Inquire of management and those charged with governance as to whether the entity has been compliant with laws and regulations during the period under audit.
- Review documentation such as board meeting minutes and correspondence with regulatory bodies and legal advisers to identify any (potential) NOCLAR.
- Review documentation after the reporting date to identify if any non-compliance has been discovered after the reporting date and, if so, consider whether the entity had an obligation at the reporting date as a result of a past event (i.e. considering whether the recognition criteria for a provision had been met at the reporting date).
- Obtain a written representation from the directors that they have disclosed all known instances and possible NOCLAR to the auditor.

Auditing in practice 13.7 BP's NOCLAR

In April 2010, the Deepwater Horizon explosion in the Gulf of Mexico caused the death of eleven people, and created the world's largest marine oil spill—an unprecedented ecological disaster. The Deepwater Horizon oil rig was operated by BP (British Petroleum) plc. The numerous legal claims against the company in the years following the Deepwater Horizon disaster ultimately resulted in BP paying out $18.7 billion. Of this amount, $5.5 billion resulted from legal action brought against the company by the United States Department of Justice in relation to non-compliance with a specific piece of legislation, the Clean Water Act. The settlement is reported to be the largest amount paid by a single company due to a NOCLAR in history. The impact on the financial statements was the recognition of a significant provision, and the matter is discussed at length within the annual report, noted as an area of significant risk by the auditor Ernst & Young.

ISA (UK) 250 also requires the auditor to discuss suspected or identified instances of non-compliance with management and those charged with governance, where appropriate. This is the case in all situations unless the non-compliance is clearly inconsequential. If management and those charged with governance fail to provide enough information to the auditor, and where the impact on the financial statements could be material, the auditor may consider taking legal advice.

In some cases, the auditor will need to consider reporting the non-compliance to third parties outside the client company. As discussed earlier in relation to fraud, the issue of client confidentiality is important. In some situations, depending on the type of actual or suspected non-compliance and the relevant laws and regulations, the duty of confidentiality may be overridden by legal requirements. We saw this earlier in the chapter when looking at money laundering as an example of fraud.

Auditing in practice 13.8 Disclosure in the public interest

In some countries, for example in the UK, auditors can report specific instances of non-compliance in the public interest if the auditor does not have confidence that management or those charged with governance will make any necessary disclosures to an outside authority. This is a clear indication of a lack of integrity, as it implies that the client is attempting to hide the non-compliance, perhaps to avoid regulatory investigation.

The auditor needs to be extremely careful about making disclosure in the public interest because there is no clear definition of what is meant by 'public interest'. A situation where a non-compliance could endanger life would be an example of when disclosure in the public interest could be justified.

Chapter round-up

- There is a clear distinction between misstatements that arise due to fraud and those which arise due to error. A deliberate misstatement is fraud because it is intentional, whereas an innocent misstatement would be classed as an error.
- Fraud can involve the misappropriation of assets (e.g. stealing cash) or fraudulent financial reporting (e.g. deliberately inflating profit to achieve a predetermined outcome).
- Fraud risk factors do not necessarily mean that a fraud has taken place, but it does indicate a higher risk that a fraud could take place.
- Management is responsible for the prevention and detection of fraud. The auditor is responsible for obtaining sufficient and appropriate audit evidence that the financial statements, taken as a whole, are free from material misstatement whether caused by fraud or error.
- The expectation gap means that there is a difference between what the pubic expects auditors to do in relation to fraud, and what they actually do. At this time there are several regulatory body discussion papers and reviews which are looking at how the expectation gap could be reduced.
- Acts of suspected money laundering must be dealt with carefully and in accordance with the audit firm's anti-money laundering procedures. The auditor must be careful to ensure they do not 'tip off' the client in the event that a SAR is made to the audit firm's MLRO.
- Some laws and regulations pertinent to an entity could have a direct impact on the amounts and disclosures contained in the financial statements, such as tax legislation. Others may not have a direct impact on the financial statements, but any breach may give rise to a material fine.
- Management is responsible for ensuring the entity complies with all its laws and regulations. The auditor is responsible for obtaining sufficient and appropriate audit evidence that the entity has complied with laws and regulations that have an effect on the financial statements.

End of chapter case study

Introduction

This chapter has examined the responsibilities of the auditor in relation to fraud and NOCLAR. We have seen that fraudulent activity is very common but is often difficult to detect, particularly because it will be concealed. Auditors need to know how to identify fraud risks, and how to respond appropriately to both indicators of fraud and instances of NOCLAR. This case study will test your understanding and application skills in these areas.

This case study links to the following learning outcomes:

- Explain the auditor's responsibilities in respect of fraud, and distinguish them from the responsibilities of management.
- Discuss the effect of fraud on the audit strategy and audit plan and recommend how the auditor should respond to the discovery of fraud, including reporting responsibilities.
- Identify and explain the factors which indicate a high risk of fraud and recommend appropriate auditor responses.

Scenario

You are the auditor in charge of the audit of Maypole Ltd, a company which operates a chain of successful fast-food restaurants under a franchise business model. You have just been assigned to the audit of the company's financial statements for the year ended 31 December 20X2 and you have been given some information to help you familiarize yourself with the client's business, as well as some recent findings from the audit fieldwork.

Maypole Ltd background and past audit experience

Maypole Ltd was established twenty years ago and there are now sixty-five restaurants operating under the 'Maypole Burgers' brand name. The fast-food restaurants offer burgers and other meals to diners and have recently expanded their menu to include plant-based meals, which are proving successful.

The company's business model operates on a franchise basis, with each restaurant operated by a franchisee, who is licensed to use the Maypole Burgers brand name, business support, and operating systems in return for a royalty payment based on the revenue of the restaurant under licence. Typically, a franchisee is the sole manager of their restaurant, and the other employees are the kitchen and front-of-house staff, usually young people, and staff turnover is quite high.

Maypole Ltd is owner-managed by Peter Maypole, who owns 75 per cent of the company's shares. There is a small internal audit department but no audit committee. The finance director, Clarissa Columbo, is an old friend of Peter's, and she manages the internal audit team. Clarissa is always present when the audit team meet with the internal auditors.

In previous years, Peter and Clarissa have been quite helpful to the audit team. In fact, Clarissa prepares an 'auditor's file' of information each year, containing copies of all key information required by the audit team. She asks for advance warning from the audit team of any additional information required, so that she can get it ready and save time for them. The audit is therefore quite efficient, though on occasion there are delays caused by last-minute adjustments made to the financial statements by Clarissa, which the audit team have little time to investigate before the audit is signed off by the partner.

Cash payment

An audit assistant was reviewing the company's cash book for large cash payments when she came across an unexplained transfer on 30 October 20X1 of £10,000 to 'BN', which had been authorized by Peter Maypole. On investigation, the audit assistant could not identify a supplier called 'BN' or any other payable with those initials. The amount was not material so was not investigated further at that time.

On reading some correspondence dated 5 November 20X1 relating to a health and safety inspection conducted at a sample of restaurants, you notice that the inspector is called Barry Nightingale. The restaurants were assessed by Barry Nightingale to have passed their inspections on his second visit, which took place on 25 October 20X1. There are no records of his first visit or any correspondence relating to it.

Required

- Using the background information, identify and explain the fraud risk indicators present.
- Discuss how the auditor should respond to the issues identified in relation to the cash payments.

Answer

1. Fraud risk indicators

Franchisee business model—the franchisees have an incentive to understate the revenue being made in their restaurants, as this means a lower value of royalty payments being made to Maypole Ltd. This gives a risk of fraudulent financial reporting by the franchisees, for example, they may misclassify revenue as other income, or move revenue into the next financial reporting period to delay royalty payments. At the company level, revenue is therefore at risk of being fraudulently understated.

Sole management of restaurants—where the franchisee is the sole manager of their restaurant, there is a high risk of management override of controls at this level of the organization. The fact that the restaurant employees are typically young people means that the franchisee can easily intimidate the staff and this is compounded by the high staff turnover.

Owner-managed business—at the company level, Peter Maypole can override controls and there is a risk of collusion with his friend Clarissa who is the company's finance director. If Peter and Clarissa colluded to establish a fraud, it could be difficult to find, given their seniority and the ease with which they could conceal fraudulent activities.

Internal audit—the presence of an internal audit team should reduce the risk of fraud. However, as the internal auditors report to Clarissa, she could cover up or ignore any suspicions of fraud raised by the internal auditors. It is also suspicious that, as she will not allow the internal auditors to meet privately with the external audit team, she may not want them to reveal their findings to the external auditors.

Auditor's file—Clarissa prepares this for the audit team, allegedly to save them time. However, the file could contain photocopies of documents which have been tampered with or have items missing. This could be to conceal fraudulent activity, especially given that she needs 'advance warning' to prepare other documents for the audit team.

Last-minute adjustments—Clarissa could be making adjustments late in the audit process, in the knowledge that the audit team will have little time to obtain sufficient, appropriate evidence. Manual adjustments to year-end figures indicate a fraud risk.

2. Cash payment

The cash payment could be a bribe paid to Barry Nightingale to secure a successful health and safety inspection of the restaurants. Health and safety regulations would be crucial for restaurants to follow and there is a risk that operating licences would be revoked if the regulations are not followed.

It is therefore in the interests of the company that restaurants pass these inspections. The evidence indicates that shortly after the second inspection, a cash payment of £10,000 was made. This could indicate that Barry Nightingale was bribed to ensure that the restaurants passed their inspection. It is suspicious that there is no evidence of his first inspections—the documentation could have been destroyed.

In accordance with ISA (UK) 250, the auditor should attempt to obtain more evidence regarding both the health and safety inspections and the cash transfer. The franchisees whose restaurants were visited may be able to provide information about when the inspections took place, and any conversations they had with Barry Nightingale as he was carrying out the inspection.

Regarding the cash transfer, this is more difficult, as the cash payment was authorized by Peter Maypole, who may be unwilling to discuss it or to provide any further explanation or evidence. The auditor could contact the health and safety regulatory body, though this would raise the issue of client confidentiality, so Peter Maypole would have to give permission for this.

Ultimately, if the auditor considers that a bribe may have been paid, they should take legal advice on how to proceed, as this would be covered by specific legislation, in this case the Bribery Act 2010. After taking this legal advice, the auditor may be compelled to report to an outside agency and consider resigning from the audit.

Activity solutions

Activity 13.1—Examples of errors

Can you think of any other common errors which might arise in relation to accounting or financial reporting?

Suggested answer points:

- Making an inappropriate judgement call regarding an accounting treatment (e.g. incorrect estimation of the useful life of an asset).
- Incorrect calculations related to payroll (e.g. incorrect tax or pension deductions from employees' pay).
- Incorrect quantities of inventory counted at a year-end stock take.
- Allocating a payment made to the wrong supplier.
- Forgetting to remove employees who have left the company from the payroll and/or HR records.
- Applying the wrong discount to a customer's order and sales invoice.
- Incorrect calculation of year-end adjustments such as accruals and prepayments.

Activity 13.2—Examples of creative accounting

Can you think of examples of creative accounting?

Suggested answer points:

- Underestimating the amount to be recognized for a provision, with the objective of minimizing liabilities.
- Overestimating the amount to be recognized for a provision, with the objective of releasing unused provisions in future years.
- Overvaluations of assets held at a revalued amount, to increase the asset base of the company.
- Overestimating the useful life of property, plant, and equipment, to reduce the depreciation expense and therefore increase profits.

Note that all of the above are based on inappropriate judgements being made within the flexibility which is allowed by financial reporting standards.

Activity 13.3—Why are frauds difficult to detect?

Think of as many reasons as you can which might explain why it is difficult for the auditor to detect fraud at a client's.

Suggested answer points:

- Frauds will be hidden, so normal audit procedures might not detect them (e.g. if documentation is falsified or destroyed).
- Fraudsters will lie to cover up their dishonest activity.
- Fraudsters might collude and back each other up when questioned about suspicious activity.
- Fraudsters are clever and junior members of the audit team might be easy to deceive.
- If a fraud is immaterial, it is much less likely to be detected.
- Performing audit procedures on a sample basis means that a fraudulent transaction may not be spotted. It is likely that a fraudulent transaction will not be captured in the auditors' sample, and therefore will go undetected.
- Audit procedures are 'routine' and predictable—so someone wanting to carry out a fraud can plan their activity accordingly as they know what the auditor will be testing (e.g. if the client knows that the auditor will look at transactions over £5,000 in value, then they know that a fraudulent transaction under £5,000 is not likely to be detected by audit procedures).
- Auditors lack the knowledge, training, and experience to recognize various fraud schemes, especially complex schemes.
- Lack of professional scepticism and not being suspicious enough—this can be linked to the familiarity threat and long association with the client.

Activity 13.4—Indications of NOCLAR

If you were planning an audit, what factors could indicate to you that a NOCLAR were taking place?

Suggested answer points:

- Evidence of regulatory investigations (e.g. by the tax authorities or by an industry regulator).
- Stories in the news or on social media which relate to actual or alleged non-compliance.
- The company engaging consultants or legal advisers in respect of regulatory matters.
- Payments of fines or penalties in respect of non-compliance.
- Internal control deficiencies relating to the assessment of compliance risk, and/or an ineffective risk management function.

14 Auditing Assets

Introduction

In previous chapters, we have seen how the auditor plans the audit, so by now you should have a good understanding of the main processes involved in audit planning including risk assessment, determining materiality and how to design the audit strategy and audit plan.

In the next few chapters, we are moving on to look at what is often called the 'fieldwork' stage of the audit (i.e. what happens when the auditor is obtaining their evidence). We are going to think about the different elements of the financial statements and how the various balances and transactions are audited. In this chapter, we begin by looking at how evidence is obtained in relation to assets, which often forms a very substantial part of the audit fieldwork.

As we have a lot of balances, transactions, and disclosures to consider, we are going to look in turn at the audit of assets, liabilities, income, expenses, and equity. While we are considering each of these separately, to help in your understanding of each area of the financial statements being audited, it is important to remember that the auditor does need to 'stand back' and consider the overall impact of the item they are considering on the financial statements. For example, when auditing the recoverability of trade receivables, there is an impact on profit, should any balances need to be written off, and possible additional disclosure, should the write-off be significant.

Auditors need to have a good understanding of the applicable financial reporting framework in order to determine whether balances and transactions are fairly presented in the financial statements. For this reason, we need to remind ourselves of the relevant financial reporting requirements. The chapter therefore includes some information regarding IFRS requirements on the recognition, measurement, and disclosure rules relating to different types of assets.

Each section of the chapter, dealing with different types of assets, contains three parts:

- accounting treatment;
- audit risks;
- audit procedures.

Depending on your level of familiarity with accounting for assets, you may or may not need to read the first part of each section which describes the key features of the financial reporting requirements in relation to assets. The audit risks and audit procedures are essential reading for all students.

Let's begin with a brief reminder of some fundamental accounting relating to assets—this is important for everyone.

The statement of financial position lists the assets, liabilities, and equity all of which are separately defined in the International Accounting Standards Board's (IASB) *Conceptual Framework for Financial Reporting* (Conceptual Framework). The definition of an 'asset' according to the Conceptual Framework is:

> A present economic resource controlled by the entity as a result of past events. An economic resource is a right that has the potential to produce economic benefits.[1]

In the broadest sense of the term, an asset is something which the entity uses in its business. However, the definition does not contain the words 'own' or 'ownership'. Instead, the focus of the definition is on the concept of control. To be classified as an asset, an entity must be able to control the item including who can access the asset and how the asset will be used within the entity as well as control over the timing of its ultimate disposal.

Assets are presented in the statement of financial position as 'non-current' or 'current'. Non-current assets are those assets which an entity controls that are expected to be used within the business for more than one accounting period, hence the term 'non-current'. Non-current assets can be 'tangible' (i.e. they have a physical form such that you can touch them); or they can be 'intangible' (i.e. they do not have a physical form). Examples of tangible non-current assets include the following:

- land and buildings;
- fixtures and fittings;
- plant and machinery;
- motor vehicles;
- computer equipment.

Examples of intangible assets include the following:

- goodwill (in consolidated financial statements);
- patents and licences;
- acquired brand names;
- development costs.

As we will see later in the chapter, auditing intangible assets is inherently more complex than auditing tangible assets because of the subjectivity involved.

[1] IASB Conceptual Framework 'asset'.

Current assets are those which are expected to be 'realized' (i.e. turned into cash) within twelve months from the reporting date. Current assets are usually presented in the statement of financial position in the 'order of liquidity' (i.e. the least liquid (inventory) first and the most liquid (cash and bank balances) last). Examples of current assets, listed in the order of liquidity include the following:

- inventory and work in progress;
- trade receivables;
- other receivables (such as loans made by the entity);
- bank balances;
- cash in hand.

This order follows the order in which inventory and work in progress turn into cash. Inventory is sold to customers on credit, resulting in trade receivables; the receivable will then pay the entity and ultimately the cash is received.

When the auditor is auditing assets, they are primarily concerned with whether assets are overstated in the statement of financial position. Examples of how assets can be overstated include the following:

- inappropriate depreciation policies (i.e. the asset is being depreciated too slowly);
- recognition of repairs and maintenance expenditure as a non-current asset;
- failure to recognize an impairment loss when an asset is impaired;
- not writing inventory down to net realizable value (NRV) when this value is lower than cost;
- not writing off receivables balances which are unlikely to be paid.

Key assertions

The key assertions for assets are:

- Existence—non-current assets exist and meet the relevant definition of an asset.
- Valuation—assets are stated at an appropriate value in accordance with the applicable financial reporting framework.
- Completeness—all assets that meet the recognition criteria are recognized as assets (i.e. there are no assets missing from the financial statements).
- Rights and obligations—the entity is able to exert control over recognized assets and the benefits they generate.

Learning outcomes

- Design and explain audit procedures in respect of tangible non-current assets including depreciation and profits/losses on disposal of assets.
- Design and explain audit procedures in respect of intangible assets including research and development (R & D) costs.

- Design and explain audit procedures in respect of impairment of assets.
- Design and explain audit procedures in respect of inventory including those relating to inventory counting procedures in respect of both year-end and perpetual inventory counts, cut-off testing, valuation, and direct confirmation of inventory held at third parties.
- Design and explain audit procedures in respect of trade receivables including circularization procedures and the completeness and occurrence of revenue.
- Design and explain audit procedures in respect of bank and cash including the use of bank confirmation reports.

By the end of this chapter, you will be able to:

- Discuss the areas of complexity in auditing assets and recommend relevant audit procedures.
- Recognize situations when it is appropriate to use an auditor's expert to obtain evidence in respect of assets.

14.1 Property, plant, and equipment

14.1.1 Accounting treatment

Property, plant, and equipment (PPE) are tangible assets controlled by the entity which will be used within the business for more than one accounting period. IAS 16 *Property, Plant and Equipment* deals with the accounting and disclosure requirements for these types of assets. Figure 14.1 shows different types of PPE. According to IAS 16, an entity must recognize an asset on the statement of financial position if, and only if:

(a) it is probable that future economic benefits associated with the item will flow to the entity; and

(b) the cost of the item can be measured reliably.[2]

'Future economic benefits' essentially means that the asset will generate something, often another asset, for the business. For example, a manufacturing company will have various items of machinery that produce goods that will be sold to the entity's customers. This results in sales from which the cash inflow is an economic benefit.

The 'cost' of an item of PPE does not just include the purchase price but it also includes all other costs involved in bringing the asset to the location and condition intended by management. For example:

- costs of transporting the asset to its location;
- costs of site preparation;
- installation costs;
- related professional fees (e.g. for architects and engineers);
- irrecoverable taxes such as import duties; and
- an initial estimate of costs of dismantling and removing the item and restoring the site on which it is located.

[2] International Financial Reporting Standards Foundation, 'IAS 16 Property, Plant and Equipment', 2023, paras 7(a) and (b) <https://www.ifrs.org/issued-standards/list-of-standards/ias-16-property-plant-and-equipment/#-standard> (accessed 19 January 2024).

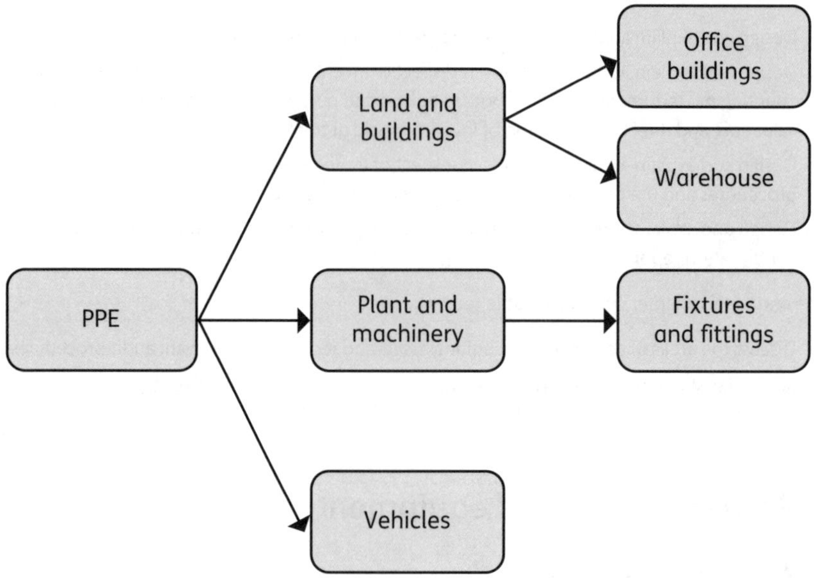

Figure 14.1 Categories of PPE

Such costs are called 'directly attributable' and, generally speaking, they are costs which the entity could have avoided had they not purchased the item of PPE in the first place.

Some costs should not be included in the cost of the asset, and should be recognized as an expense in the statement of profit or loss:

- administration and other general overhead costs;
- start-up and similar pre-production costs;
- staff training costs;
- incidental costs.

The cost of an asset is usually easy to audit, as the purchase costs can be confirmed by underlying documentation (e.g. a purchase invoice). Other issues including depreciation and revaluations can be more challenging.

Other features of IAS 16 which you should be aware of include:

Deprecation—most PPE assets are depreciated over the asset's useful life. The exception is land, which is not depreciated. The residual value and the useful life of an asset should be reviewed at least at each year end and the deprecation charge may need to be adjusted—this is dealt with as a prospective adjustment. Depreciation should be charged as an expense to profit or loss. Different methods of depreciation are possible (e.g. straight line or reducing balance).

Revaluation—IAS 16 allows PPE assets to be carried at a revalued amount, being its fair value at the date of revaluation, provided that fair value can be measured reliably. Under the revaluation model, revaluations should be carried out regularly, so that the carrying amount of an asset does not differ materially from its fair value at the balance sheet date. There are no timescales in IAS 16 as to how frequently management must carry out a revaluation so this will require professional judgement being applied. In addition, if an item is revalued, the entire class of assets to which that asset belongs should be revalued (this is to stop an entity deliberately revaluing assets in a class that have increased in value and ignoring those that have not). Assets which have been revalued are still subject to depreciation.

When auditing revalued properties, the auditor may wish to engage an auditor's expert. As we looked at this in Chapter 12, we will not revisit the issue here. However, remember that when engaging an expert, the auditor must carefully evaluate their work, to ensure that it provides sufficient appropriate audit evidence, in this case in respect of a revalued asset.

Leased assets—it is very common for assets to be used under a lease contract, in which case a lease liability arises. We will look at the audit implications of leasing activity when we look at auditing liabilities, in the next chapter.

Auditing in practice 14.1 How are items of PPE presented in the financial statements?

The financial statements will show the carrying amount (also known as net book value, or carrying value of the assets) as a single line item on the face of the statement of financial position. This figure will be cross-referenced to a note to the financial statements which contains a full breakdown of how the net book value is made up.

Banbury Ltd
Statement of financial position (extract)
As at 31 December 20X9

	Note	31.12.20X9	31.12.20X8
		£	£
Non-current assets			
PPE	7	192,855	130,047

Notes to the financial statements (extract)
For the year ended 31 December 20X9

7. **PPE**

Table 14.1

	Plant and machinery	Fixtures and fittings	Motor vehicles	Totals
	£	£	£	£
Cost				
At 1 January 20X9	998,856	355,751	24,300	1,378,907
Additions	53,956	23,782	25,850	103,588
Disposals	(51,979)	(19,026)	(24,300)	(95,305)
At 31 December 20X9	1,000,833	360,507	25,850	1,387,190
Depreciation				
At 1 January 20X9	887,749	336,811	24,300	1,248,860

	Plant and machinery	Fixtures and fittings	Motor vehicles	Totals
Charge for year	20,498	13,820	6,462	40,780
Eliminated on disposal	(51,979)	(19,026)	(24,300)	(95,305)
At 31 December 20X9	856,268	331,605	6,462	1,194,335
Net book value				
At 31 December 20X9	144,565	28,902	19,388	192,855
At 31 December 20X8	111,107	18,940	–	130,047

The auditor's primary concern is to ensure that the net book value of £192,855 is not materially misstated, and they will carry out both tests of controls and substantive procedures to obtain sufficient and appropriate audit evidence over the items of PPE. This will involve ensuring that the company does, in fact, own, and have the ability to control, the assets and that any additions to PPE during the year have not been incorrectly recognized on the statement of financial position when they should be expensed to the statement of profit or loss.

The auditor will ensure that the company's accounting policies have been correctly applied over items of PPE, such as depreciation rates and will test a sample of calculations to ensure that this is the case.

The auditor will also ensure that those items of PPE that have been disposed of during the year have been correctly removed from the non-current assets register and that any profit and loss on disposal is correctly stated in the financial statements.

14.1.2 **Audit risks**

Auditing PPE involves the auditor applying audit procedures over several areas, including:

- existing items of PPE brought forward from the previous year;
- additions to PPE during the year;
- disposals of PPE;
- ensuring the depreciation charges have been correctly calculated;
- any revalued assets have been accounted for in accordance with IAS 16; and
- ensuring that related disclosures in respect of PPE are in accordance with IAS 16 and relevant legislation.

Activity 14.1 Assertions at risk for PPE

What do you think are the key risks in auditing PPE? Try to link the risks to relevant assertions.

The principal audit risk in respect of PPE is that of overstatement. Overstatement can arise because of under-depreciation (i.e. the depreciation policy is inappropriate). When a company disposes of an item of PPE any significant gains or losses on disposal is an indicator that the depreciation method applied by the entity is inappropriate. For example, it would not be appropriate to depreciate a computer over ten years as this would not be consistent with the useful economic life; such equipment is usually depreciated over three to five years, although there is no 'hard and fast' rule as to how long assets should be depreciated over, the accounting treatment is based on an estimate.

Overstatement can also arise because the entity may have capitalized items as PPE when, in fact, the expenditure should have been recognized in profit or loss as repairs and maintenance expenditure. Overstatement could also arise if the statement of financial position includes assets which do not exist, perhaps because they have been disposed of, but they have not been removed from the accounting records.

The other audit risk is that PPE is understated. This could arise because the entity has recognized items of PPE in expenses when they should have been capitalized. This is usually evident because the relevant expense in the general (nominal) ledger (e.g. repairs and maintenance expenditure or computer costs) may be higher than the prior year and hence performing analytical procedures (comparing current year repairs and maintenance expenditure against the prior year) may indicate this as a risk of material misstatement.

Another principal audit risk relates to assets measured at a revalued amount. There is a risk of management bias, because the fair value of an asset is based on a judgement. This is particularly the case where the entity does not use an independent valuer—for example, where a director of the entity may carry out an internal valuation. There is also a risk that the person carrying out the valuation lacks technical competence and professional expertise in valuing PPE in accordance with financial reporting requirements. In these cases, the auditor may determine it necessary to use their own expert to obtain sufficient and appropriate audit evidence over the valuation exercise.

Another risk arises in relation to the accounting treatment applied to a revaluation. Revaluation gains on items of PPE must be taken to the revaluation reserve within the equity section of the statement of financial position and reported as other comprehensive income. Revaluation losses are taken to the revaluation reserve to the extent of a surplus on the revaluation reserve in respect of that asset; excess losses are then reported in profit or loss. The principal audit risk in this respect is that the revaluation has not been accounted for correctly in accordance with IAS 16 (e.g. recognized the gain in profit or loss when it should be in other comprehensive income) (see Figure 14.2).

14.1.3 **Audit procedures**

Remember that the auditor needs to obtain evidence that is relevant to the assertions. When designing audit procedures, it is important to think about the assertion, which is similar to asking yourself 'what is the objective of the procedure'? We have provided some examples in Table 14.2 where you can see that each procedure is linked to a specific assertion and states the objective of the procedure.

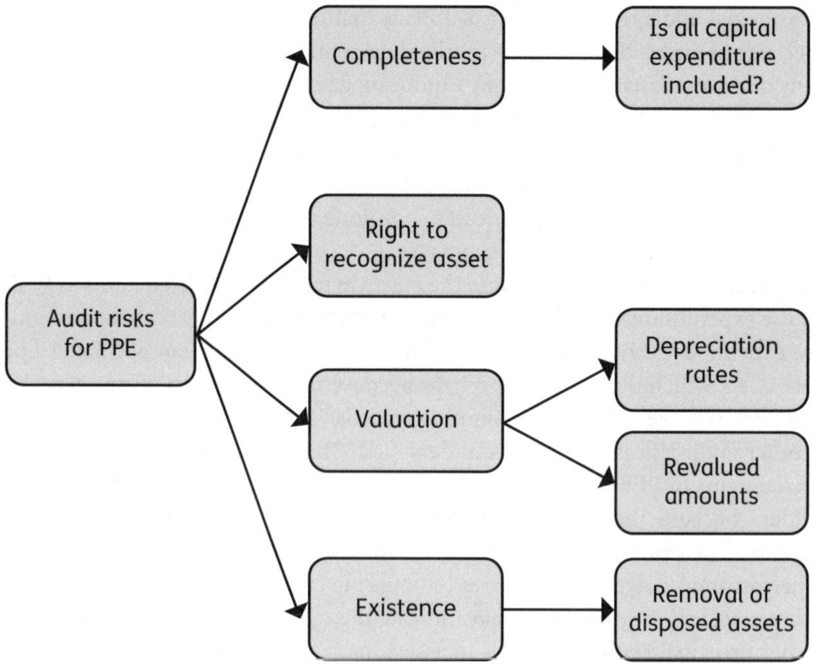

Figure 14.2 Key audit risks for PPE

Table 14.2 Assertions and procedures for PPE

Assertion	Example procedure
Completeness	Select a sample of physical assets (e.g. office fixtures), and confirm that they are included in the non-current asset register
Existence	Select a sample of items (e.g. additions to assets in the year), from the non-current asset register and physically inspect them to confirm that they exist
Valuation	Review the depreciation rates applied to assets and evaluate whether the rates are reasonable and in line with business understanding
Rights and obligations	Select a sample of items (e.g. additions to assets in the year), from the non-current asset register and inspect purchase documentation to confirm ownership of the assets

Substantive procedures that the auditor will carry out over non-current assets include the following:

- Obtain the non-current assets register, cast the register, and agree the totals to the financial statements, and ensure cost and accumulated depreciation have been correctly brought forward from the prior year (verifies *completeness*, *classification*, and *presentation*).
- Select a sample of non-current assets from the non-current assets register and physically inspect them. Ensure they are in working order and are not showing indicators of impairment such as damage (verifies *existence* and *valuation*).
- Select a sample of physical assets and inspect the non-current assets register to ensure they have been included (verifies *completeness*).

- For assets which have been revalued during the reporting period, inspect the valuation report, and agree the revalued amount to the general ledger and the financial statements and ensure that all assets within the same asset class have been revalued as well (verifies *valuation*).
- Select a sample of additions to non-current assets during the reporting period and agree the cost to the supplier invoice or other supporting documentation (verifies *valuation*).
- Select a sample of additions and agree that the supplier's invoice is in the name of the company (verifies *rights and obligations*).
- Obtain a schedule of additions to non-current assets during the period and confirm they are capital in nature rather than repairs and maintenance expenditure (verifies *existence*).
- For assets which have been self-constructed, obtain a schedule of costs that have been incurred, cast the schedule to check arithmetical accuracy, and agree a sample of costs to supporting documentation (e.g. labour costs to payroll records and material costs to supplier invoices) (verifies *valuation*).
- For non-current assets that have been disposed of during the period, agree sales proceeds to supporting documentation such as sundry sales invoices (verifies *accuracy* of profit or loss on disposal).
- For a sample of disposals, recalculate the profit or loss on disposal and agree to the trial balance and financial statements (verifies *accuracy* of profit or loss on disposal).

Tests of controls (which test the operating effectiveness of controls during the period) that the auditor may carry out include the following:

- Review board minutes for evidence of authorization of capital expenditure by the directors (particularly significant items of capital expenditure).
- Inspect purchase orders for capital expenditure for evidence that these have been approved by a responsible individual.
- Inspect the reconciliation of the non-current assets register for evidence of approval that the reconciliation has been reviewed by a responsible individual.
- Inspect insurance policies and compare these with the value of non-current assets to ensure that the value of non-current assets is sufficiently covered.
- Inspect management accounts and revenue expenditure schedules for evidence of review to ensure that capital items are not incorrectly written off to the statement of profit or loss as expenditure.
- For a sample of disposals of non-current assets, review board minutes to ensure that such disposals have been formally approved by the board prior to disposal taking place.

The auditor must also carry out audit procedures over the depreciation charges to ensure that these do not contain material misstatement and that they are compliant with the company's declared accounting policies. Audit procedures include the following:

- For a sample of non-current assets, recalculate the depreciation charge for the period and agree to the non-current assets register (verifies *valuation*).

- Inspect the financial statement disclosures in respect of the accounting policies for depreciation and agree that these have been consistently applied and adequately disclosed (verifies *presentation*).
- For revalued assets during the year, recalculate the depreciation charge based on the revalued amount and agree the charge to the statement of profit or loss (verifies *valuation*).
- Review profit and loss on disposal of assets to assess the reasonableness of the depreciation policies. If depreciation policies are reasonable, there should not be any significant profits or losses on disposal (verifies *valuation*).
- Perform a proof in total calculation for the depreciation charge for each category of non-current asset and discuss any significant variations with management (this is an *analytical procedure* which verifies *completeness* and *valuation*).
- Inspect budgets for the next few years to assess the appropriateness of the useful economic lives in comparison to the company's asset replacement cycle (verifies *valuation*).

Auditing scenario 14.1 Creating an expectation of the depreciation charge

The audit junior has obtained a copy of the non-current assets register for Bury Enterprises Ltd for the year ended 31 December 20X9 and is auditing the depreciation charge for plant and machinery. The charge for the year has been recorded in the financial statements at £81,500 and the company's depreciation policy is to depreciate plant and machinery over their useful economic lives of five years on a straight-line basis. The total cost of the plant and machinery is £410,000 and the materiality level is 2 per cent of total assets. There have been no disposals or additions to plant and machinery during the year.

You have asked the audit junior to create an expectation of the total depreciation charge for plant and machinery for the year ended 31 December 20X9.

The total cost of the plant and machinery is £410,000 and the depreciation policy is to depreciate such items of PPE on a straight-line basis over five years. Hence, the expected depreciation charge is £82,000 (£410,000/5). The actual depreciation charge is £81,500 which is understated by £500. This difference represents 0.6 per cent (£500/£82,000) less than our expectation and therefore we can conclude that the depreciation charge for plant and machinery is not materially misstated.

14.2 **Intangible assets**

14.2.1 **Accounting treatment**

An intangible asset is a non-current asset held by the entity which does not possess a physical form (i.e. it cannot be touched). Intangible assets are accounted for under IAS 38 *Intangible Assets* and this standard contains strict criteria which must be met before an intangible asset can be recognized on the statement of financial position.

IAS 38 states that an intangible asset shall be recognized if, and only if:

(a) it is probable that the expected future economic benefits that are attributable to the asset will flow to the entity; and

(b) the cost of the asset can be measured reliably.[3]

[3] International Financial Reporting Standards Foundation, 'IAS 38 Intangible Assets', 2023, paras 21(a) and (b) <https://www.ifrs.org/issued-standards/list-of-standards/ias-38-intangible-assets.html/content/dam/ifrs/publications/html-standards/english/2023/issued/ias38/> (accessed 19 January 2024).

In addition, the asset must be:

- controlled by the entity as a result of events in the past, and
- something from which the entity expects future economic benefits to flow.

Examples of intangible assets that can be recognized include:

- licences;
- copyrights and patents;
- trade marks;
- acquired brands;
- acquired goodwill;
- development costs.

There are certain types of intangible asset which can never be recognized on the statement of financial position such as internally generated goodwill, brands, and customer lists because these do not meet the recognition criteria.

Activity 14.2 Audit of intangible assets

Why do you think intangible assets can be difficult to audit?

14.2.1.1 R & D

An entity may be actively involved in R & D—for example, a pharmaceutical company will incur high levels of expenditure on R & D in the search for new drugs to treat illnesses or the enhancement of existing drugs. IAS 38 also deals with R & D expenditure and requires research expenditure (both pure and applied) to be immediately expensed to the statement of profit or loss. Development expenditure is capitalized when it meets the recognition criteria in IAS 38, which states that development expenditure is recognized as an intangible asset if, and only if, an entity can demonstrate that a number of criteria have been met (Figure 14.3).

The key issue is that the auditor must obtain evidence that all of these criteria have been met. In particular, the issue regarding technical feasibility of completing the development is important, because if development is not likely to be successful, then future economic benefits are in doubt and the definition of an asset is therefore not met. The auditor will want to see demonstration of the existence of a market for the output of the intangible asset or the intangible asset itself or, if it is to be used internally, the usefulness of the intangible asset.

14.2.1.2 Determining the useful life

Intangible assets need to be categorized as to whether they have a finite or indefinite life. Those with a finite life, which means that the asset provides economic benefit for a limited period (e.g. a patent with a ten-year life), are amortized over that period. Amortization is essentially the same as depreciation applied to PPE assets. The amortization method should reflect the pattern of benefits generated by the asset; if the pattern cannot be determined reliably, amortization is by the straight-line method.

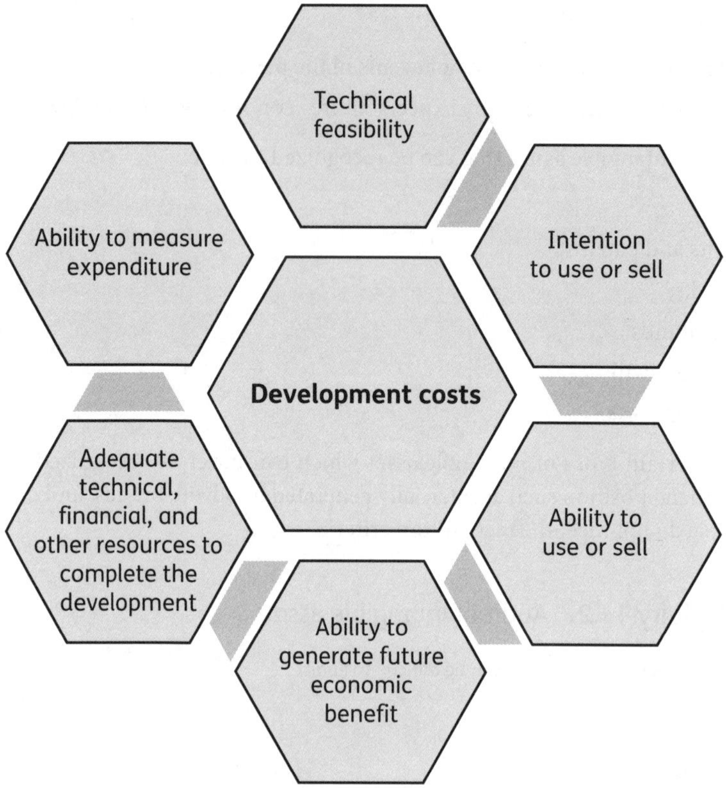

Figure 14.3 Criteria for capitalization of development costs

Some intangible assets have an indefinite life. This means that there is no foreseeable limit to the period over which the asset is expected to generate net cash inflows (e.g. an acquired brand name with very little competition, which is heavily supported by marketing). These assets are not amortized, but they must be tested for impairment (see section 14.3) each year.

14.2.2 **Audit risks**

The principal audit risk where intangible assets are concerned is that some items may have been recognized on the statement of financial position (capitalized) in contravention of IAS 38. This audit risk gives rise to intangible assets being overstated.

Auditing in practice 14.2 Recognition of internally generated goodwill

During the year to 31 December 20X9, Mulberry Ltd included an amount of £200,000 worth of goodwill on the statement of financial position. The audit senior held a discussion with the finance director who stated the following:

> The board decided that it would be appropriate for the company to recognize the value of its brand as goodwill on the statement of financial position. The company has been established for over 70 years

and we consider that the amount of £200,000 reflects the potential sale value of the business if it were to be marketed for sale.

In this scenario, the goodwill recognized is internally generated and has been recognized in contravention of IAS 38 which states that internally generated goodwill must not be recognized as an asset. The reason IAS 38 prohibits the recognition of internally generated goodwill as an intangible asset is because there is no 'active market' from which a fair value can be obtained. An 'active market' is one in which the intangible asset is frequently traded and as there is no active market for internally generated goodwill, IAS 38 prohibits the recognition of it on the grounds that a reliable measure of cost cannot be obtained.

In order to avoid the auditor expressing a modified audit opinion, the internally generated goodwill must be removed from the statement of financial position.

Another principal audit risk is that research expenditure in an R & D project has been incorrectly capitalized as an intangible asset. As noted above, only development expenditure is recognized as an intangible asset when the recognition criteria are met.

Auditing scenario 14.2 Distinguishing between the R & D phase of an internal project

Chatsworth Ltd is in the process of rapid expansion and is considering the development of a new accounts production software system for accountancy firms in countries where there is a lack of such resources available.

The project team involved have structured the project as follows:

(1) Identify the need for a new accounts production software.

(2) Commission research for any existing equivalent accounts production systems in that part of the world.

(3) Commission research for any existing equivalent accounts production systems that may have the features which Chatsworth believe are currently only unique to themselves.

(4) Undertake research for any other competitors that may be involved in producing equivalent accounts production systems in the timescale that the project team have devised.

(5) Commission the design of the new accounts production system.

(6) Prepare a shortlist from step (5).

(7) Obtain a budget from the finance department for the new system and then compare this budget to the shortlist prepared in step (6).

(8) Prepare a further shortlist of two possible alternatives based on feedback from the project management team.

(9) Send the shortlist to the board of directors for their approval.

(10) Develop the new accounts production system based on the directors' approval.

(11) Undertake testing.

(12) Roll out the new system.

The recognition criteria at each stage must be considered in order to establish when capitalization of development costs can commence and hence when the recognition criteria in IAS 38 have been met. At stage (5) of the project, the technical feasibility of completing the project has been confirmed. At the end of stage (7), it has been established how the project will generate future economic benefits. At the beginning of stage (10), all of the recognition criteria have been met and the board of directors have approved the project which, in turn, provides evidence of the company's intention to complete the project. The budgeted information will also provide evidence of the entity's ability to measure the expenditure.

Therefore, the costs from stage (10) onwards should be capitalized as an intangible asset. All costs incurred up to this point must be recognized as an expense. The audit risk is that Chatsworth Ltd has not appropriately determined the point at which capitalization should commence, leading to a risk of misstatement regarding the valuation of the intangible asset and the expenses charged to profit. The auditor would need to perform robust procedures around the capitalization of costs, to ensure that the company has only capitalized costs from stage (10) onwards.

The key point to note here is how late in the development the recognition criteria are met. There is a significant audit risk that development costs are capitalized too early, overstating assets and overstating profit.

A further audit risk where intangible assets are concerned is that they may be overstated due to inappropriate amortization policies. If an intangible asset is being amortized over an excessively long period of time, there is a risk that the asset is materially overstated in the statement of financial position and hence the associated amortization expense is also understated.

14.2.3 **Audit procedures**

For intangible assets, other than development costs, the auditor should carry out the following procedures:

- Inspect purchase documentation for purchased intangible assets and agree amounts recognized on the statement of financial position are appropriate (verifies *existence*, *rights*, *obligations*, and *valuation*).
- Confirm, through a review of board minutes, that significant acquisitions have been approved (supporting evidence of *existence*).
- Inspect any specialist valuer's report and agree the amount on the report to the amount included in the general ledger, trial balance, and financial statements (verifies *valuation*).
- Agree the opening balances of intangible assets (both cost and amortization) to the prior year's audit file and ensure they have been correctly brought forward into the current financial year (verifies *valuation* and *completeness*).
- Carry out an assessment of the intangible assets to identify if any intangible assets are showing indicators of impairment (e.g. review sales returns and statistics to verify the reasonableness of income derived from patents, trademarks, licences (verifies *valuation*)).

Audit procedures which would be applied to amortization are the same as those of depreciation.

Audit procedures in respect of development costs would include the following:

- Obtain a schedule of development costs capitalized during the period, cast the schedule, and agree the amount to the financial statements (verifies *valuation*).
- Discuss details of the project with management and evaluate compliance with IAS 38 to ensure that only development costs are capitalized and research costs have been recognized as expenditure in the statement of profit or loss (verifies *existence*).
- Inspect documentation to assess compliance with IAS 38 criteria regarding measurement of expenditure (e.g. confirm that the project is clearly defined and costs separately identified by having a separate cost ledger or general (nominal) ledger codes (verifies *existence*)).
- Inspect the company's budgets including cash flow forecasts to confirm the project is financially viable (verifies *existence*).
- To confirm technical feasibility, review project documentation (e.g. results of scientific testing, reports of experts, existence of working prototypes).
- To confirm future profit, review market research reports, feasibility studies, inquire as to existence of customer orders.
- Inspect board minutes for discussions relating to the intended sale or use of the asset (verifies *existence*).
- For a sample of costs, agree them to purchase invoices or labour costs to payroll records (verifies *valuation*).
- Agree the opening balances of development costs (cost and amortization) to the prior year's audit file and ensure they have been correctly brought forward into the current year (verifies *valuation* and *completeness*).
- For amortization, confirm that it begins when commercial production starts by agreeing the date to production schedules and that it is charged on a systematic basis.

Auditing in practice 14.3 Verifying the cost of intangible assets

The audit senior is auditing the intangible assets of Hanbury Ltd for the year ended 31 December 20X9 and is being assisted by an audit junior. The company produces tyres used for motor vehicles and the financial statements recognize a material number of licences which have been recognized as intangible assets during the year so that the company can produce a certain type of wet-weather tyre for three years, the design of which is protected by copyright. The audit junior is unsure as to why such licences have been recognized as an intangible asset and has also asked what audit procedures should be carried out to ensure there is no material misstatement of the intangible assets.

A licence is an example of an intangible asset. For Hanbury Ltd, the company is able to produce a certain type of wet-weather tyre which is protected by copyright which it can then sell onto its customers which will create economic benefits for the entity in the form of sales revenue. IAS 38 only allows an intangible asset to be recognized on the statement of financial position if future economic benefits associated with the intangible asset will flow to the entity. In this case, it will because the company has obtained a licence to produce the tyres that it can then sell to customers. IAS 38 also requires that the intangible asset has a cost or value that can be reliably measured. This can be obtained from the purchase invoice or relevant agreement or where a class of intangible assets comprises several items, the auditor can select a representative sample of licences and trace these back to supporting documentation (i.e. the licence documentation).

The licence should be amortized over its useful economic life of three years and the company would usually amortize the whole licence fee over a three-year period on a straight-line basis.

Principal audit procedures would include the following:

- Obtain a copy of the licence and agree that the licence has been correctly capitalized as an intangible asset.
- Review the terms of the licence and agree that three years is the correct length of time.
- Agree the amount capitalized on the statement of financial position to the licence agreement.
- Recalculate the amortization charge for the year based on three-years straight-line and discuss any significant variations with management. Agree the amortization charge for the year to the statement of profit or loss.

14.3 Impairment

14.3.1 Accounting treatment

Impairment is when an asset has fallen in value below the amount at which it is recognized in the financial statements. The financial reporting requirements are contained in IAS 36 *Impairment of Assets*, which prescribes the procedures that should be followed to ensure that assets are not held at more than their recoverable amount. IAS 36 provides the requirements to write down assets for impairment and the circumstances when an impairment can and should be reversed.

IAS 36 contains some important definitions:

- An *impairment loss* is the amount by which the carrying value of an asset exceeds its recoverable amount.
- *Recoverable amount* is the higher of an asset's fair value less costs to sell (also known as net selling price) and value in use.
- *Value in use* is the present value (PV) of estimated future cash flows expected to arise from the continuing use of an asset and from its disposal at the end of its useful life. The calculation of value in use is based on assumptions about the future use of the asset and must reflect the following:
  - an estimate of the future cash flows the entity expects to derive from the asset;
  - expectations about possible variations in the amount and timing of future cash flows;
  - the time value of money; and
  - other factors that would be reflected in pricing future cash flows from the asset.

Assets should be reviewed for possible impairment where there are indications that the asset could be impaired. These indications would include both internal and external factors to the business (e.g. damage of asset, new competitors).

Activity 14.3 Causes of impairment

Note down five indicators that an asset could be impaired, which an auditor might identify when planning the audit.

Key features of the accounting rules are as follows:

- Goodwill and intangibles with indefinite lives should be tested annually for impairment.
- Where possible the review should be carried out on individual assets, but if this is impractical a group of assets should be considered. The group of assets should be the smallest group on which cash flows can be identified and is called a cash-generating unit (CGU).
- If an asset has impaired in value, the asset should be written down to its recoverable amount. If a CGU is impaired, it should be written down to recoverable amount but charging the impairment in the order:
  - goodwill allocated to the CGU; and
  - other assets pro-rated according to their carrying value (or on some more reasonable basis).
- The impairment losses should be charged to the statement of profit or loss unless the asset had previously been revalued upwards in which case the impairment losses can be charged against the revaluation reserve to reduce the asset to depreciated historical cost, with any additional losses going to the statement of profit or loss.
- Reversals of impairment losses can be recognized in the statement of profit or loss to the extent that the original impairment was charged there with the exception of impairments of goodwill. It is not pernitted to reverse an impairment of goodwill.

14.3.2 **Audit risks**

In relation to impairment, the primary objective of the auditor is to obtain sufficient appropriate audit evidence that assets are not stated in the statement of financial position in excess of recoverable amount.

Auditing scenario 14.3 Impairment of a business unit

In 20X2, the management team of Boheme Co, a retail organization, identified that one of its stores should be subject to an impairment review due to a new competitor opening a rival store in the same street. The store is recognized at a net book value of £9 million in the financial statements and its fair value less cost to sell is £8.5 million. In order to determine the value in use of the store, management has prepared an eight-year cash flow forecast as set out in Table 14.3.

In determining the present value, the following assumptions have been made:

- There will be no significant growth in sales until 20X5 at which time growth is expected, based on the assumption that Boheme Co will have launched new product ranges and carried out advertising which will lead to an increase in customers to the store.
- The patterns of growth 20X3–20X7 are consistent with the company's five-year business plan.

Table 14.3

Year	Growth rate	Cash flow	PV factor at 8% interest rate	PV
	%	£,000		£,000
20X3	0	1,500	0.9259	1,389
20X4	0	1,520	0.8573	1,303
20X5	1	1,580	0.7938	1,254
20X6	1.5	1,600	0.7350	1,176
20X7	2	1,630	0.6806	1,109
20X8	2	1,680	0.6302	1,059
20X9	2	1,700	0.5835	992
20Y0	3	1,750	0.5403	946
Total present value				**9,228**

- An interest rate of 8 per cent is used as the basis for the discounted cash flow, this is consistent with the company's cost of capital.

The assumptions, in particular regarding the patterns of growth, are based on management judgement. For the auditor of Boheme Co, this is an area of considerable audit risk. They will need to obtain evidence regarding the rationale for, and application of the assumptions and obtain robust corroboratory evidence. This is particularly the case given that the value in use (based on the present value of cash flows) is greater than the net book value of the store, meaning that no impairment loss needs to be recognized. Management could have manipulated the assumptions to achieve a value in use higher than new book value, thereby avoiding having to recognize an impairment loss in relation to the store.

14.3.3 **Audit procedures**

The auditor will carry out these procedures in relation to impairment:

- Discuss with management whether any indicators of impairment (or reversals of previously recognized impairments) have arisen during the reporting period (*existence* and *valuation*).
- Review board minutes for discussions relating to evidence of any assets which have indicators of impairment (*existence* and *valuation*).
- Where an impairment review has been performed (*valuation*):
  - Obtain management's calculations of recoverable amount, and review to ensure the calculation uses reasonable assumptions and the method is compliant with IAS 36, paying particular attention to estimates and judgements used in the calculations.
  - Reperform all parts of the determination of recoverable amount, to check accuracy.
  - For the value in use element of the impairment review:
    - o compare the cash flow projections to recent budgets and projections approved by the board to ensure that they are realistic;
    - o confirm that the growth rates assumed in the calculation of value in use are in line with auditor's understanding of the business and information published by the company;
    - o confirm that the income from disposal of the asset at the end of its life has been included in the calculation;

    - confirm that cash flows from financing activities and income tax have been excluded; and
    - compare discount rate used to published market rates to ensure that it correctly reflects the return expected by the market.
  - For fair value less cost to sell:
    - review any specialist valuer's report which indicates the market value of assets; and
    - compare the value of the asset to similar assets (e.g. in competitor companies).
- Where impairment has been recognized in the year, review the accounting treatment to confirm the expense has been recognized within profit.
- For reversals of impairments in prior periods, discuss the rationale for the reversal with management, in particular to obtain understanding as to why the reasons for the original impairment loss no longer apply and corroborate this explanation with further evidence.

Auditing in practice 14.4 Difficulties in auditing impairment

Impairment is a notoriously difficult area to audit, largely because of the degree of judgement which is inherent in the calculations. As we have seen, management has to use a number of assumptions and judgements, particularly in calculating value in use. Often, audit firms need to approach impairment as a high-risk area of the audit and exercise an appropriate degree of professional scepticism.

The audit of impairment is sometimes criticized. In their inspection of firms' audit quality, regulators mention impairment as an area where firms need to improve their procedures and obtain more audit evidence.

For example, in the FRC's 2019 audit inspection report on KPMG, the audit of goodwill impairment was cited as a problem area, with the report stating that the firm should:

> Improve the consideration and challenge of cash flow forecast assumptions in relation to the impairment of goodwill.[4]

The report goes on to state that:

> We reviewed the audit of impairment on almost all audits that we inspected where this was identified as a significant risk. While the audit work in this area was often performed to an acceptable standard, on two of these audits there was insufficient consideration and challenge of management's short-term cash flow forecasts used in the impairment models, including:

- On one of these audits, there was insufficient corroboration and challenge of management adjustments to increase the estimated cash flow forecasts, partly due to an expectation that recently declining profitability would return to historical levels and growth rates.
- On another audit, there was insufficient evidence that the growth assumptions used in the impairment assessments were consistent with those modelled for individual businesses and contracts. There was also insufficient evidence to support certain other assumptions (not covered by these models) such as the achievability of estimated cost savings.

KPMG responds that the audit procedures around obtaining corroboratory evidence to support management assumptions in relation to impairment are being enhanced and that training is being provided to staff on complex areas of audit.

[4] Financial Reporting Council, 'KPMG LLP Audit Quality Inspection', 2019 <https://media.frc.org.uk/documents/KPMG%20Audit%20Quality%20Inspection%202018/19.pdf> (accessed 19 January 2024).

14.4 Inventory

14.4.1 Accounting treatment

Inventory can be a particularly sensitive area of the financial statements not only due to the inherent estimates that are contained within certain types of inventory (especially work in progress) but also the fact that a misstatement of inventory can have a direct impact on both the statement of financial position and the statement of profit or loss. Any significant variance in a company's gross profit margin between the current and prior year can indicate a risk of material misstatement within the final inventory valuation.

Inventories are assets:

- held for sale in the ordinary course of business; or
- in the process of production for such sale; or
- in the form of materials or supplies to be consumed in the production process or in the rendering of services.

The key accounting principle contained in IAS 2 *Inventories* is that inventories should be valued at the lower of cost and net realisable value (NRV) of separate items of inventory, or of groups of similar items (see Figure 14.4).

Inventories can be valued using the first-in first-out (FIFO) or weighted average method. Last-in first-out (LIFO) is not an acceptable method for determining the cost of inventories under IAS 2.

Inventories should be disclosed in the notes to the financial statements into main categories (e.g. raw materials, work in progress, and finished goods).

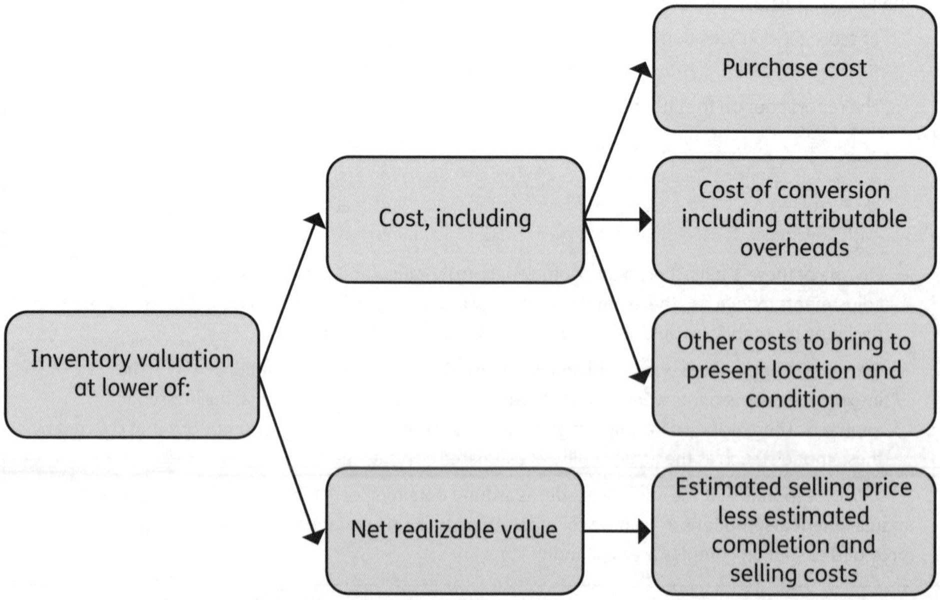

Figure 14.4 Inventory valuation rules

14.4.2 **Audit risks**

The principal risk of material misstatement is that inventory is overvalued which results in overstated current assets and overstated gross profit.

Activity 14.4 Inventory valuation risks

List five factors which could lead to incorrect valuation of inventory at the year end.

It may help to think that inventory valuation is comprised of the quantity of inventory as well as the valuation per item of inventory. So, there can be errors or deliberate manipulation of either element of the valuation. For example, if the management of a company wanted to inflate inventory, they could invent additional, non-existent inventory which might be hard to audit, such as items in transit at the year end.

While auditors are primarily concerned with overstated inventory, they will also test for understatement as well. This could arise, for example, if the year-end inventory count was incomplete or if items of inventory have not been included in the count, perhaps if there are items held at numerous locations at the year end. Such instances would also be indicative of control weaknesses which the auditor may need to communicate to management and/or those charged with governance of the entity.

The audit work performed on inventory will include cut-off testing. This involves checking that all transactions including sales and purchases are recorded in the correct accounting period. For example, if goods are delivered from the company to a customer prior to year-end, the goods are excluded from inventory and are included in the cost of goods sold. When looking at purchases, goods received before the year end should be recorded in inventory and as a purchase, whereas any goods arriving after the year end should not be recognized in the financial statements. If a company has a large volume of transactions, it is particularly important that they have good controls over cut-off to avoid inaccurate recording of transactions around the year end. This might seem obvious, but when dealing with receipt of goods from suppliers, sometimes the invoice might be sent before the goods arrive, perhaps because of delays with deliveries, which means that establishing cut-off is not always easy.

Auditing scenario 14.4 Cut-off testing

Cheddar Co is a producer of crisps and snacks. It receives deliveries from suppliers on a regular basis and on the receipt of each item into the warehouse a goods received note (GRN) is raised and attached to the goods and a copy is printed to be attached to the supplier's invoice when it arrives.

The audit team attended the inventory count on the company's financial year end at 30 June 20X9. The last GRN prior to the year end was GRN number 9091.

The table below shows details of the invoices received from suppliers around the year end, and the relevant GRN.

Table 14.4

Supplier	Invoice date	Invoice amount	Invoice received	GRN
		£		
Pickle Co	27 June	675	29 June	9090
Chilli Co	28 June	890	30 June	9092
Chive Co	21 June	390	4 July	9088
Onion Co	29 June	215	30 June	9091
Salt Co	1 July	975	2 July	9089
Olive Co	1 July	650	3 July	9093

Purchases should be recognized for all goods delivered up to and including GRN 9091, therefore the deliveries received from Pickle Co, Chive Co, Onion Co, and Salt Co. For all of these, the inventory was received before the year end, so should be included within current assets and a purchase recognized within cost of sales. For the goods delivered after the year end, which are GRNs 9092 and 9093, the goods were received after the year end, so should be excluded from inventory and from purchases.

14.4.3 **Attendance at inventory count**

ISA (UK) 501 *Audit Evidence—Specific Considerations for Selected Items* requires the auditor to attend the physical inventory count (unless this is impracticable) when the client's inventory balance is material to the financial statements. The auditor attends the inventory count to obtain evidence relating to the existence of inventory, but evidence is also obtained in relation to the completeness and valuation of inventory, the inventory 'cut-off', and the design and implementation of the entity's internal control systems.

The important point to emphasize is that the auditor does not carry out the inventory count; their responsibility is to attend during the inventory count to ensure that management's instructions are being adhered to and those instructions will reduce the risk of material misstatement in the final inventory valuation. In addition, the auditor will also carry out tests over the inventory records to determine whether they accurately reflect the count results. Effectively, when the auditor attends the inventory count process, they are carrying out a test of control.

The primary objectives of the auditor where the inventory count is concerned are to:

- evaluate management's instructions and procedures for the inventory count;
- observe the client's staff performing the inventory count;
- inspect the condition of the inventory; and
- perform test counts in a two-way direction (from shelf to sheets and from sheets to shelf).

14.4.3.1 **Prior to the inventory count**

Before attending the inventory count, the auditor must:

- Obtain a copy of the instructions issued by management to the staff to understand how the count will be undertaken and assess the effectiveness of the counting process.

- Obtain the prior year's working papers file and review the counting process and audit evidence acquired during last year's count process to identify any issues which may need to be taken into account this year—for example, any control weaknesses that were noted last year.
- Establish the location(s) of the inventory and whether any third parties are holding inventory on behalf of the client. If third parties are holding inventory which is material, consider how sufficient and appropriate audit evidence will be gathered over such inventory.
- Consider circularizing (writing to) third-party warehouses requesting confirmation of inventory balances held at the reporting date together with quantities and conditions of inventory.
- Consider the need to utilize the services of any experts who may need to assist in valuing the inventory being counted.

14.4.3.2 **During the inventory count**

As we noted earlier, the auditor attends the inventory count while the count is being conducted because one of the primary objectives of attendance at inventory count is to ensure that management's instructions are being carried out. If the auditor attends **after** the inventory count, this objective will not be achieved. The auditor will carry out tests of controls and substantive procedures during the inventory counting process to gather sufficient appropriate audit evidence that the inventory counting process will reduce the risk of material misstatement within the final inventory valuation.

Tests of controls which the auditor will usually carry out during the inventory count include the following:

- Ensure that staff who are normally employed in the warehouse are not involved in the inventory counting process. This is to ensure there is adequate segregation of duties in place because if the warehouse staff were to be involved in the counting process not only would they not be independent, but if there was any fraud being committed, they would be in a position to conceal the discrepancies.
- Ensure that once a section of inventory has been counted it is flagged as counted to avoid double-counting or not counting at all.
- Ensure there are no movements of inventory during the counting process.
- Where movements of inventory cannot stop (e.g. because the client operates twenty-four hours a day, seven days a week), ensure items requiring despatch are moved to a different location than the other inventory. Also ensure that any deliveries of goods are made to a different location while the count is taking place. A separate count can then be performed on these segregated items which can be added to the warehouse count.
- Ensure that count sheets which record the inventory and quantities run in numerical sequence (gaps in the sequence indicate missing count sheets).
- Ensure that there are at least two people in each counting team performing the count (one counting and the other recording the quantities on the count sheets).

- Ensure that damaged and/or obsolete items of inventory are segregated from other inventory to enable them to be valued appropriately.
- Ensure the count sheets do not show expected quantities of goods (i.e. to stop staff from deliberately not counting the inventory).
- Ensure there is adequate review of the counting process once each area of the warehouse has been counted to ensure full and complete coverage.

Substantive procedures which the auditor would normally carry out during the inventory counting process include the following:

- Select a sample of inventory from the inventory counting sheets to the physical inventory in the warehouse and highlight these once counted for subsequent checking to the final inventory valuation (verifies *existence*).
- Select a sample of inventory from the physical inventory in the warehouse to the inventory counting sheets and highlight these once counted for subsequent checking to the final inventory valuation (verifies *completeness*).
- For goods held on behalf of third parties, discuss with management the process for ensuring these are not included in inventory and ensure they are not included in the inventory count (verifies *rights and obligations*).
- Obtain details of the last deliveries into the warehouse immediately prior to, or at, the reporting date and retain a record of these deliveries so that during the final audit procedures the auditor can ensure that no further adjustments have been made which may misstate the final inventory valuation (verifies *completeness* and *existence*).
- Attend the inventory count at third-party warehouses where inventory balances are material or where the level of exceptions are expected to be high and carry out test counts and inspect the condition of the inventory (verifies *completeness* and *existence*).
- Inspect inventory being counted for evidence of any damage or obsolescence which may indicate the need to write down the inventory to its NRV (verifies *valuation*).

Auditing in practice 14.5 Attendance at the inventory count

Harper Ltd is a chemical manufacturer and operates twenty-four hours a day, seven days a week. Production staff work day and night shifts to ensure continued production. The directors have confirmed that production cannot stop during the inventory count as this will have a detrimental impact on the company and customer orders may not be fulfilled on time.

The audit junior is attending the inventory count with an audit supervisor and this is going to be carried out at the year-end date of 31 March 20X9. The audit junior is unsure as to how the inventory count will be possible if production is not stopped, commenting that inventory values will constantly change and that there may inevitably be a material misstatement in the final inventory valuation.

The audit junior has asked you to explain how a company that produces goods twenty-four hours a day, seven days a week can ensure that the final inventory valuation does not contain a material misstatement due to the ongoing production.

Ideally during the inventory count movements will stop. However, there are some industries, such as manufacturing, where this is impracticable because of the level of disruption that stopping production will cause.

Management must ensure that they move the items requiring despatch to a different location to that being counted prior to the count being carried out. Any deliveries of goods must be made to a different location while the count is being undertaken. A separate count can then be carried out on those items delivered or produced during the count which can then be added to the warehouse items counted.

Where the auditor ensures that such controls are in place, the completeness and existence assertions can be verified and the auditor can also check that cut-offs for purchases and sales have also been correctly applied.

14.4.4 **Perpetual inventory counts**

A perpetual inventory count (often referred to as 'continuous counting systems') is a system whereby all lines of inventory are counted on a regular basis, such as monthly throughout the accounting period so that by the reporting date all lines of inventory have been counted.

There are advantages and disadvantages of a perpetual inventory counting system as follows.

14.4.4.1 **Advantages**

- Perpetual inventory counting enables the auditor to attend counts relating to lines of inventory which stand a higher chance of material misstatement and can also reduce the time spent by the auditor on the overall inventory count.
- Slow-moving and damaged inventory is identified on a continuous basis with relevant adjustments being made to the inventory valuation so that by the reporting date the inventory valuation should be more accurate.

14.4.4.2 **Disadvantages**

- The auditor must obtain sufficient and appropriate audit evidence that the perpetual inventory counting system is operating effectively at all times rather than at the reporting date.
- Additional audit procedures will need to be applied by the auditor to ensure that the final inventory balance is appropriate in terms of the cut-off assertion and allowances to reduce certain inventory to NRV (e.g. damaged and/or obsolete inventory) which is the valuation assertion.

Where the audit client uses a perpetual inventory counting system, the auditor must:

- Attend at least one inventory count to ensure there are adequate internal controls in place during the counting process.
- Confirm that all of the inventory lines have been counted or are due to be counted at least once a year by reviewing the schedules of counts that have taken place.
- Inspect the number of exceptions that have arisen as a result of the count. Where significant variations arise, this may indicate that the inventory valuation at the reporting date is unreliable and hence a full inventory count at the year end may be necessary.

- Carry out additional tests to verify cut-off, valuation and rights and obligations, even where the perpetual inventory counting process is deemed to be reliable.
- Inspect GRNs and goods despatched notes immediately pre- and post-year end to verify the entity has applied correct cut-offs.
- Carry out an NRV test to ensure that goods are being sold in excess of cost (if NRV is lower than cost this would indicate inventory impairment).
- Calculate the inventory holding period and compare with the prior year to identify if there is any slow-moving inventory which may need an allowance to bring its valuation down to NRV.

14.4.5 **Consignment inventory**

Consignment inventory is inventory which is legally owned by one party (the principal) but is being held by another party (the agent). Generally, this means that the risks and rewards of ownership of the goods remain with the principal, but the agent is responsible for distribution or retail of the inventory.

An auditor usually considers consignment inventory as high risk because it can be a complex accounting issue. The auditor is primarily concerned with the rights and obligations assertion.

Any consignment stock must be segregated from other inventory owned by the client. The auditor must inquire of management as to the process involved in ensuring that such consignment inventory is excluded from the inventory valuation.

If the auditor is auditing the principal's financial statements, the agent must tell the principal how many of the agent's goods are in its possession. The principal will then calculate the cost value of those goods and include that value in its own inventory. If the value of the consignment inventory belonging to the principal is material the auditor may consider attending the inventory count of the agent to verify the existence, completeness, and condition of the consignment inventory.

14.4.6 **Audit procedures over the final inventory valuation**

During the audit fieldwork (the evidence-gathering stage), the auditor must carry out audit procedures over the final inventory valuation. These procedures include the following:

- Trace items counted during the inventory count and check against the final inventory valuation and check to confirm that any errors identified during the inventory count have been corrected (verifies *completeness* and *presentation*).
- Obtain a schedule of inventory disaggregated into raw materials, finished goods and work in progress. Cast the list to ensure it is mathematically correct and agree the final total to the financial statements (verifies *completeness* and *classification*).
- For a sample of inventory items, agree cost prices to purchase invoices (verifies *valuation*).
- For a sample of inventory items, inspect post-year-end sales invoices to establish if NRV is determinable. Compare NRV to cost to determine if inventory is held at the lower of cost and NRV to comply with IAS 2 (verifies *valuation*).

- Use audit data analytics techniques to age the inventory items in order to identify any slow-moving inventory which may need an allowance and discuss these with management (verifies *valuation*).
- Trace goods received immediately prior to the reporting date and agree these to year-end payables balances and inventory records (verifies *completeness* and *existence*).
- Trace goods despatched immediately prior to the reporting date to ensure these goods are not in inventory at the reporting date (they should be included in revenue and receivables) (verifies *completeness* and *existence*).
- Agree the valuation of raw materials to invoices and price lists (verifies *valuation*).
    - Agree labour costs to payroll records (verifies *valuation*).
    - Review standard labour costs in the light of actual costs and production (verifies *valuation*).
    - Reconcile labour hours to time records (verifies *valuation* and *completeness*).
    - Compare actual manufacturing overhead costs with budgeted or standard manufacturing overhead costs (verifies *valuation* and *completeness*).
- For inventory in transit, review transfer documentation to ensure that inventory quantities are adequately reflected in the inventory valuation (verifies *completeness*).
- Review GRNs after the reporting date to ensure that the goods were genuinely in transit (verifies *completeness* and *existence*).

IAS 2 allows an entity to use standard costs which take into account normal levels of materials, labour, efficiency, and capacity utilization. Where an entity uses standard costs, it must ensure that the standard costs are updated on a regular basis and revised in light of current conditions. If the entity uses standard costs, the auditor must carry out the following procedures to verify the valuation assertion:

- Obtain a breakdown of the standard cost calculation and agree a sample of costs to purchase invoices.
- Discuss with management the basis for the standard costs and how often they are updated to reflect current costs.
- Inspect a variance report and assess the level of variances for reasonableness. For any significant variances arising, discuss these with management to establish the reasons why.

Analytical procedures which the auditor can perform over the final inventory valuation are as follows:

- Calculate inventory holding days or inventory turnover ratio and compare this to the prior year to determine if the company is holding inventory longer than the prior year which may indicate the need for an allowance to write the inventory down to NRV (verifies *valuation*).
- Calculate the gross profit margin (gross profit/turnover x 100) and compare this to the prior year and investigate any significant fluctuations which may highlight an error in the closing inventory valuation (verifies *valuation*).

14.4.6.1 **Audit procedures for inventory held at third parties**

For inventory which is held by third parties, the auditor should carry out the following procedures:

- Obtain external confirmation from the third party concerning the quantity and condition of the goods (verifies *rights and obligations*).
- Consider obtaining a report from the third party's auditors over the internal controls over inventory at the third party and consider whether these have been operating effectively.

14.5 Receivables and prepayments

14.5.1 **Accounting treatment**

Trade receivables can be very simple to account for. For most small businesses with simple income streams, trade receivables are not complex to account for and audit risk tends to be limited to the recoverability of the balances.

The problem arises because under IFRS, trade receivables meet the definition of a financial asset and therefore should be accounted for under IFRS 9 *Financial Instruments.* IFRS 9 is a notoriously complex accounting standard, which unfortunately means that accounting for trade receivables is therefore sometimes difficult.

The good news is that, for the purpose of this chapter, we are going to keep it quite simple. We are just going to consider the key accounting issue involved with recording trade receivables, which relates to their collectability. Remember that assets can only be recognized if they provide a future economic benefit. This means that companies must continually review their list of trade receivables to assess whether there are any slow paying customers or balances which they think may not be received. If balances are considered to be irrecoverable, they must be written off (i.e. treated as a bad debt), with an expense recognized within profit or loss.

14.5.2 **Audit risks**

The principal audit risk where receivables and prepayments are concerned is overstatement. If receivables are overstated, then this would mean that revenue is also overstated. By performing procedures to ensure that receivables are not overstated, the auditor is also indirectly testing whether profit is also overstated (Figure 14.5).

Receivables and prepayments are usually presented as current assets in the statement of financial position and the key assertions which the auditor is concerned with where receivables and prepayments are concerned are valuation and existence.

Incorrect cut-offs may mean that sales that should be recorded in the next accounting period are recorded in the current accounting period which would overstate revenue and receivables and present a misleading picture in the financial statements. On the flip side, management may want to suppress the levels of sales reported in the financial statements in order to manipulate the profit figure (e.g. to pay less tax). This would mean that revenue recognition has been delayed, resulting in understated revenue and understated receivables.

Receivables could be overstated due to bad debts not being recognized, as discussed previously, or due to incorrect cut-offs being applied.

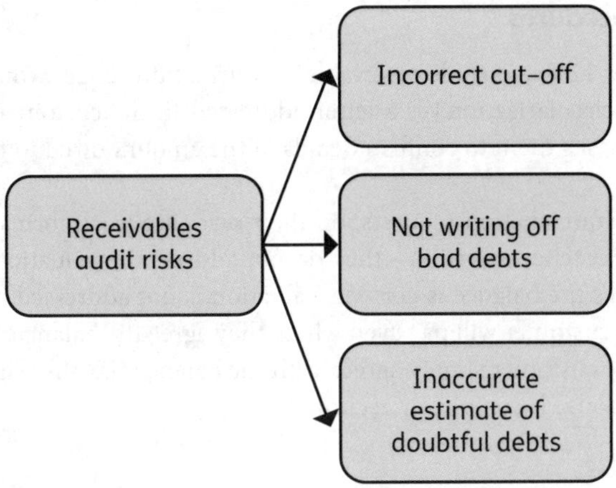

Figure 14.5 Key audit risks for receivables

Overstated receivables can also arise if a customer is unable to settle its debts due to cash flow difficulties. In these situations, the entity should recognize an allowance against that receivable (sometimes called a 'bad debt provision'). Existing allowances for receivables might also need to be increased to reflect additional credit risks.

General bad debt provisions will need to be made under IFRS 9 because this standard requires an entity to account for 'expected credit losses' rather than recognize a loss when it is actually incurred. However, there are some frameworks, such as UK and Ireland GAAP, which do not allow general bad debt provisions, so only *specific* bad debts are allowed. The auditor must therefore consider the requirements of the relevant financial reporting framework and tailor procedures accordingly.

Auditing in practice 14.6 Irrecoverable receivable

The draft financial statements of Harper Ltd for the year ended 31 December 20X9 recognize profit before tax of £4.3 million and total assets of £15 million.

During the audit of trade receivables, it was noted that a balance of £685,000 was significantly overdue from a customer. The credit control clerk has informed you that it is unlikely this amount will be received because the customer is experiencing significant cash flow difficulties and is likely to cease trading in the next few weeks. The finance director has refused to make an allowance for this receivable as he insists that this should only happen when the customer officially ceases to trade, and argues that the amount in question is immaterial to the financial statements.

According to the information provided by the credit controller, it is unlikely that the balance of £685,000 will be received. If an allowance for the receivable is not made in the financial statements trade receivables, then profit will be overstated and hence will be misleading.

The receivable represents 15.9 per cent (£685,000/£4.3m) of pre-tax profit and 4.6 per cent (£685,000/£15m) of total assets and hence is material to the financial statements. The finance director's argument that an allowance should not be made until the customer officially ceases to trade is irrelevant and the financial statements should recognize an allowance with a corresponding increase in bad debt expense recorded in the statement of profit or loss.

If the finance director refuses to make an allowance for the receivable, there is a material misstatement, and receivables and profit are overstated.

14.5.3 **Audit procedures**

We saw in Chapter 12 that a trade receivables confirmation request (often referred to as a 'trade receivables circularization') is a letter addressed to the customer directly from the audit client which asks them to confirm details of the amount owed to the company at the reporting date.

As a reminder, confirmation requests, on their own, are weak forms of evidence. They only address the existence assertion—they do not address the valuation assertion, even if the customer agrees the balance is correct. Valuation is not addressed because there is no guarantee that the customer will pay even where they agree the balance. In addition, it may be the case that the customer simply agrees with the balance (i.e. there is no guarantee that the customer's response is completely accurate).

Activity 14.5 External confirmations

Here is a short scenario to remind you of the audit issues relating to external confirmations.

You are working on the audit of Quizzer Ltd, a company which produces and retails board games. You are helping a junior member of the audit team who has been given the task of preparing the trade receivables circularization. She has asked for your advice, as she is unsure about the different types of circularizations and how to select trade receivables balances for inclusion in the sample.

She has asked you, 'I don't understand the difference between positive and negative circularizations, and I am not sure which balances to include—is it just the biggest ones?'

Note down your answers to the audit junior's questions—what is the difference between positive and negative circularizations, and which balances should be included in the sample?

Audit procedures which the auditor should carry out over the entity's receivables, other than an external confirmation, are as follows:

- Obtain an aged receivables listing, cast the list, and agree the total to the financial statements (verifies *valuation* and *presentation*).
- Agree the receivables ledger control account in the general (nominal) ledger to the list of trade receivables at the year end and investigate any reconciling items (verifies *completeness* and *existence*).
- Inspect post-year-end cash receipts and follow through to pre-year-end trade receivables balances (verifies *valuation*, *rights and obligations*, and *existence*).
- Select a sample of year-end trade receivable balances and agree back to supporting documentation such as goods despatched notes and sales orders (verifies *existence*).
- Select a sample of goods despatched notes immediately pre- and post-year end and follow through to the sales invoice to ensure that the sale has been recorded in the correct accounting period (verifies *completeness*, *existence*, and *cut-off* of revenue).
- Perform a trade receivables circularization by selecting a representative sample of trade receivables and sending a confirmation letter on the client's letterhead asking the customer for confirmation of the balance on their purchase ledger at the year end (verifies *rights and obligations* and *existence*).

- Review the valuation of trade receivables to ensure that an appropriate allowance has been made in accordance with the relevant financial reporting framework.
- Discuss the aged receivables with the credit control manager to assess whether any further allowance is required (verifies *valuation*).
- Inspect any customer correspondence to identify if there are any material disputed items that may require a balance to be written off (verifies *existence*, *valuation*, *rights*, and *obligations*).
- Inspect the list of trade receivables for any credit balances to assess whether these need to be reallocated to payables (verifies *existence* and *completeness* (of payables) and *presentation*).

The auditor may also carry out analytical procedures such as calculating trade receivables days (sometimes referred to as the 'receivables collection period'); comparing the current year's calculation to the prior year's and investigating any significant differences (verifies *completeness* and *valuation*).

Auditing in practice 14.7 Trade receivables

You are the audit senior of Orange & Co LLP and are carrying out the audit of the trade receivables of Lineham Ltd for the year ended 31 December 20X9. Lineham Ltd sells high-value precious metals to a small number of retailers. Credit terms are granted to these retailers of between thirty and sixty days. The finance director of Lineham Ltd has provided you with the following trade receivables listing as at 31 December 20X9 (Table 14.5).

During the audit, you will be primarily concerned with the valuation assertion of these receivables. For example, the company's standard credit terms are between thirty and sixty days. However, there are two balances amounting to £122,000 that have gone past these terms.

Table 14.5

Lineham Ltd
Aged receivables listing as at
31 December 20X9

	0–30 days	30–60 days	60–90 days	120 days +	Total
	£	£	£	£	£
Apple Ltd	71,250				71,250
Banana Ltd	12,000	1,000	500		13,500
Berry Ltd	89,000	120,000	76,000	55,000	340,000
Cherry Ltd	125,000	17,000		67,000	209,000
Nectarine Ltd	800	100			900
Pomegranate Ltd	19,600	15,120	700		35,420
Tomato Ltd	91,200	14,660			105,860
Total	408,850	167,880	77,200	122,000	775,930

The auditor must therefore obtain sufficient appropriate audit evidence that these balances are actually recoverable. If they are not recoverable, the auditor must request that they are written off as a bad debt because otherwise trade receivables will be overstated in the statement of financial position (as will profit before tax). If the finance director refuses to write off the balances and they are material to the financial statements, the auditor will have to modify their auditor's report (see Chapter 20).

The auditor cannot just focus their attention on older balances—they must also focus their attention on balances which are within credit terms and ensure the assertions of valuation, existence and completeness are also covered. In Lineham Ltd, the auditor would be able to satisfy these assertions by carrying out the audit procedures above, for example:

- Carrying out a trade receivables circularization (remember this only covers the existence assertion—it does not cover valuation).
- Selecting a sample of year-end trade receivables and agreeing these balances back to supporting documentation (goods despatched notes and sales orders).
- Inspecting post-year-end cash receipts to identify when the balances were cleared.
- Discussing whether any balances are irrecoverable and hence may need writing off in the financial statements for the year ended 31 December 20X9.
- Inspecting customer correspondence to identify any disputes.

At all times, the auditor must bear in mind that when it comes to assets in the statement of financial position, they are primarily testing for overstatement.

14.5.4 **Prepayments**

Prepayments are goods or services which the organization has paid for in advance of receiving them. Procedures to test prepayments include the following:

- Inspect the cash book and bank statements to ensure that the payment has been made (verifies *existence*).
- Inspect invoices to ensure that the payment relates to a good or service that has not yet been delivered or rendered (verifies *existence*).
- Inspect the trade payables listing to identify any debit balances and assess whether these debit balances relate to on-account payments (prepayments) (verifies *classification* and *existence* (of prepayments)).
- Recalculate the amount prepaid to confirm mathematical accuracy (verifies *valuation*).

The auditor can also apply analytical procedures over the prepayments by comparing the level of current-year prepayments against the prior year and investigating any significant differences. For example, there may be some items that have not been prepaid in the current year, but which were prepaid in the prior year, and vice versa, hence the auditor will investigate the reasons for such variations (verifies *existence*, *valuation*, and *completeness*).

14.6 Bank and cash

The key assertions which the auditor is concerned with over bank and cash are existence and valuation. The auditor will also look to two important sources of audit evidence:

- the bank confirmation letter (sometimes called the 'bank certificate' or 'bank audit letter'); and
- the year-end bank reconciliation.

14.6.1 Audit risks

The principal audit risk for bank balances is that of understatement due to 'window-dressing'. Window-dressing is a term used in auditing referring to when an audit client treats a payment (or multiple payments, such as a BACS run to pay suppliers) as being made at, or immediately before, the reporting date. For example, a client with a 31 December reporting date treating a BACS run carried out on 2 January as being made on 31 December. This understates positive bank balances and understates payables—the purpose of doing this is to make the company's liabilities appear to be smaller in value than the reality.

Where window-dressing is apparent, the auditor will request that the client adds the payment back into payables and removes it from the bank reconciliation.

Auditing scenario 14.5 Window-dressing

You are the audit senior of Tennyson Ltd carrying out the audit of the bank and cash balances as at 31 December 20X9. The financial controller has provided you with the year-end bank reconciliation for the current account which is shown in Table 14.6.

Upon investigation, you note that the bank transfer of £19,825 was carried out on 3 January 20X0 and not on 31 December 20X9. The finance director has informed you that he wishes for this to remain on the year-end bank reconciliation because it relates to payments to six suppliers whose invoices were due to be paid by 31 December 20X9 but due to the online banking system being unavailable on this date it had to be delayed until 3 January 20X0.

Regardless of whether the finance director 'intended' for the payment to be made to the suppliers on 31 December 20X9 or not, the fact is that the payment was made on 3 January 20X0 which is after the reporting date. As a consequence, this is evidence of window-dressing. The current asset of £120,055 which will be shown in the statement of financial position in the year-end financial statements will be understated by £19,825 and there will also be a corresponding understatement of trade payables by the same amount. This will present a misleading picture in the financial statements.

If the finance director refuses to make the amendment and write the payment back into the year-end payables balance, the auditor will modify their opinion if the transaction is material.

Table 14.6

Churchill Ltd
Bank reconciliation
For the year ended 31 December 20X9

				£
Balance per bank statement at 31 December 20X9				151,224
Less outstanding payments:	Date cleared	Cheque no.	£	
	05.01.X0	122020	15,621	
	05.01.X0	122021	9,651	
	06.01.X0	122022	1,000	
	03.01.X0	Bank transfer	19,825	
				(46,097)
				105,127
Plus outstanding lodgements:	Date cleared	Pay-in ref	£	
	04.01.X0	235665	150	
	05.01.X0	235666	14,778	
				14,928
Balance per cash book at 31 December 20X9				120,055

Activity 14.6 Audit risks for bank and cash

Can you think of any situations where the audit of bank and cash could be complex, increasing the audit risk?

14.6.2 **Bank confirmation requests**

A key source of audit evidence for the auditor over the entity's bank balances at the reporting date is the bank confirmation request. This is a letter sent directly by the auditor to the client's bank (after permission has been obtained from the client to the bank to liaise directly with the auditor in this respect). This letter provides details of balances on each account at the reporting date together with details of any security pledged by the company in respect of borrowings.

Prior to the reporting date, the auditor will send a confirmation request to the client's bank asking for certain information. The bank will usually need a few weeks to collate the information (ordinarily it takes about six weeks at present) so the auditor will need to send the letter in good time to receive it by the time they are carrying out the detailed audit fieldwork.

The standard content of a confirmation request to the bank includes the following:

- company name;
- details of current, deposit, loan, and other accounts;
- account number and sort code;
- currency;
- audit confirmation date (i.e. the reporting date);
- contact name (usually the audit engagement partner); and
- contact details of audit firm.

Auditing in practice 14.8 Bank confirmation request

Harper Grace Accountants and Statutory Auditors
123 Street Name
County
AB1 2CD
30 November 20X9

The Manager
Client Bank PLC
456 Street Name
County
BC1 2DE

Dear Sir/Madam
Churchill Ltd
In accordance with the agreed practice for the provision of information to auditors, please would you provide the following information for our client as at 31 December 20X9. This request, and your response, does not create any contractual or other duty with us.

Client name:	Churchill Ltd
Account numbers:	12345678
	87654321
Sort code:	11-22-33
Audit confirmation date:	31 December 20X9
Information required:	Terms of finance
	Custodian arrangements
	Security
Audit contact name:	Stefan Ratchford

The authority to disclose information has previously been signed by our mutual client and is held by you. This authority is dated 31 July 20X9.

Yours faithfully
Harper Grace Accountants and Statutory Auditors

Bank confirmation requests are a reliable source of evidence because they are external and are always sent directly to the auditor. They also provide evidence of security that has been pledged by the client for borrowings which will need to be disclosed in the financial statements.

In practice, however, there can be errors or omissions on the bank confirmation letter and so it is important that the auditor does not rely wholly on the content. For example, they will wish to verify the balances on the bank confirmation letter to the year-end bank balances on an original bank statement and to the year-end bank reconciliation. They will also wish to verify the completeness of security disclosures by carrying out checks on public registries such as records on file at Companies House which can provide details of mortgage charges and other security pledged for borrowings.

14.6.3 **Attendance at cash counts**

Where cash on hand is material to the financial statements, e.g. when auditing a bank or a retailer, the auditor will usually attend the physical cash count that will take place at the close of business on the reporting date. The objective of this procedure is to ensure that the cash on hand at the reporting date is accurately stated in the statement of financial position.

If the audit client has a large cash balance, the auditor will need to ensure the reasons for such large cash balances on hand together with checking the company is adequately insured. Cash is susceptible to theft and if it is not kept secure there is a high risk that it could be stolen. If the company is not adequately insured and cash is stolen this means the company could suffer a loss. Levels of insurance must also be considered by the auditor because cash-on-hand balances might exceed the limits in the insurance policy and hence any excess cash over the insurance limit will usually be uninsured.

The auditor will count the petty cash on hand at the reporting date and agree this total to the balance included in the financial statements. This verifies **accuracy**, **valuation**, and **existence**.

The auditor will consider the controls in place over the cash to assess whether these are effective. For example, if cash is not kept in a secure place, there is a higher risk of material misstatement due to fraud. If the auditor concludes that controls over cash are weak, they will rely less on those controls and carry out additional substantive procedures.

14.6.4 **Audit procedures**

Substantive procedures (test of detail) which the auditor may perform over the bank and cash balances of the entity include the following:

- Obtain the bank reconciliations for all accounts, cast the reconciliation to ensure mathematical accuracy and agree the balance per the cash book to the trial balance, general ledger, and financial statements (verifies *accuracy* and *valuation*).
- Obtain a bank confirmation letter from the bank and agree the balance on the bank confirmation to the year-end bank reconciliation (verifies *accuracy* and *valuation*).
- Agree the balance per the cash book to the year-end bank reconciliation (verifies *accuracy* and *valuation*).
- Agree the balance per the bank statement on the bank reconciliation to an original bank statement and to the bank confirmation letter (verifies *accuracy* and *valuation*).
- Trace all outstanding payments on the bank reconciliation to the post-year-end bank statements and note the date the payment clears the bank (verifies *accuracy*, *valuation*, and *completeness*).

- Trace all outstanding lodgements (cash in transit) to the pre-year-end cash book and post-year-end bank statements (verifies *accuracy*, *valuation*, and *existence*).
- Examine old unpresented payments to determine whether these should be written back into the payables ledger (purchase ledger) if they are no longer valid to be presented (verifies *accuracy*, *valuation*, and *completeness*).
- Inspect the bank confirmation letter for details of security pledged by the company or any legal right of set-off of overdrafts against positive bank balances which may require disclosure in the financial statements (verifies *presentation*, *rights*, and *obligations*).
- Review the cash book for any large or unusual items, particularly around the reporting date, as this may indicate window-dressing (verifies *completeness* and *existence*).
- If cash on hand at the year end is material, attend the year-end cash count to ascertain the closing balance on hand at the year end is accurate (verifies *completeness* and *valuation*).

The auditor will also carry out tests of controls over the bank and cash cycle which may include the following:

- Review a sample of bank reconciliations prepared during the period for evidence of review by a responsible official (e.g. the finance director).
- Inquire of management as to who has access to the online banking system and attempt to log into the banking system using an unauthorized staff member's details. The system should reject access.
- Inspect petty cash requisitions to ensure they have been authorized by a responsible official.
- Review the payments cycle to assess whether supporting documentation is presented before payment is authorized (such as an invoice).
- If cash on hand is material at the reporting date, attend the cash count to ascertain the closing balance on hand at the year end and whether this is accurate.
- Observe whether the entity's staff are following instructions of the cash count as this will help to ensure that the cash count is complete and accurate.
- Perform test counts to ensure procedures and internal controls are operating effectively.

Chapter round-up

- The auditor is primarily concerned with the overstatement of assets; although they will also have to obtain sufficient appropriate audit evidence that they are not understated as well.
- Non-current assets are often highly material to the statement of financial position and a wide range of audit evidence needs to be obtained in relation to their existence, valuation, completeness.
- Significant judgements are involved in accounting for tangible and intangible assets, particularly around their valuation. Auditors must obtain robust audit evidence relating to the valuation assertion.
- The auditor must attend the year-end inventory count where inventory is material to the financial statements. This is an observation test which aims to ensure that the controls over the inventory count will serve to reduce the risk of material misstatement in the final inventory valuation.

- A trade receivables circularization can either be a positive or negative request. A negative request should only be carried out where the auditor determines the risk of material misstatement to be low.
- Trade receivables circularizations should not be used as sole audit evidence as they are weak forms of evidence and do not address the valuation assertion.
- Bank confirmation requests can provide external audit evidence to the auditor although they should be verified for accuracy.
- The auditor will carry out tests to ensure that no window-dressing has taken place at the reporting date which may understate liabilities and assets.

End of chapter case study

Introduction

The ability to design appropriate audit procedures is a key skill which auditors must possess. While some 'standard' audit procedures which can be applied to any audit client are useful, it is usually necessary to tailor audit procedures to fit the particular circumstances of the audit client. This is the best way to ensure that sufficient, appropriate evidence is obtained for all of the relevant assertions for a specific balance or transaction.

This activity will test your ability to design audit procedures for use in obtaining sufficient, appropriate evidence in relation to several types of assets.

This activity links to the following learning outcomes:

- Design and explain audit procedures in respect of tangible non-current assets including depreciation and profits/losses on disposal of assets.
- Design and explain audit procedures in respect of intangible assets including R & D costs.
- Design and explain audit procedures in respect of impairment of assets.

Scenario

You are working on the audit of Fettler Co, a pharmaceutical company which develops a wide range of medicines which are sold to health authorities for use in hospitals. The company also produces vitamins and other health supplements which are sold to pharmacies and supermarkets for retail to the general public.

The company acquires patents for all of its newly developed products. The typical lifespan of a patent is ten years.

Your audit manager has provided you with some information about some of the non-current assets recognized in the company's draft financial statements. She wants you to design the audit procedures to be performed. In each case, the matter described is material to the company's financial statements for the year ended 31 December 20X9, which recognize total assets of £280 million and profit before tax of £45 million.

R & D

Fettler Co spends a significant amount of cash every year on R & D; in this current financial year, the cash outflow on R & D amounted to £32 million. The company follows IAS 38 *Intangible Assets*, it expenses all research costs and development costs are only capitalized when the IAS 38 recognition criteria are met. All of the medicines used in hospitals are subject to a government licence, without which the products cannot be sold.

At this time, the company has two new products in the pipeline:

- Nutgo—this is a tablet being developed to relieve headaches. The development of the drug is at an early stage, but the company directors are confident that the drug will be a success. It is planned that Nutgo will be on general sale to the public through pharmacies and supermarkets. An intangible asset of £2.5 million is recognized in relation to Nutgo.
- Maxleve—this is a medicine which will be used in hospitals to relieve pain after patients have had surgery. The development project is almost finished with clinical trials successfully completed in the last month. An intangible asset of £8 million is recognized in relation to Maxleve.

Once commercial production of a new product is started, the company begins to amortize the development costs over a systematic period, in accordance with IAS 38. Ventamore is a new product which began commercial production this year. It is being amortized over a twelve-year useful life, twelve years being the period over which management believe they will generate sales from this product.

New research laboratory

In June 20X5, Fettler Co began construction of a new research laboratory which will replace its existing laboratory when construction is complete in 20X6. By 31 December 20X5, £14 million had been spent on the construction, including the cost of acquiring the site on which the laboratory is being built, which cost £3 million. This includes all directly attributable costs, and borrowing costs capitalized relating to loans taken out to finance the acquisition of the site and construction of the laboratory.

Trade receivable

In December 20X5, a major pharmacy chain called Greymart announced its insolvency and procedures to shut down the company began shortly after the year end. Greymart was a major customer with whom Fettler Co had several significant contracts.

The professional advisers dealing with the closure of Greymart have suggested that the company may be able to pay approximately 25 per cent of the amounts owed to its trade payables. A trade receivable of £8 million is recognized on Fettler Co's statement of financial position in respect of Greymart.

Required

For each of the matters described above, explain any relevant risks of material misstatement.

You should recommend the audit procedures to be performed including a brief explanation of the purpose of the procedure.

Answer

R & D

Development costs should only be capitalized as an intangible asset if the recognition criteria of IAS 38 *Intangible Assets* have been demonstrated in full:

- intention to complete the intangible asset and use or sell it;
- technical feasibility and ability to use or sell;
- ability to generate future economic benefit;
- availability of technical, financial, and other resources to complete; and
- ability to measure the expenditure attributable to the intangible asset.

Research costs must be expensed, as should development costs which do not comply with the above criteria. From the information provided, the company has an acceptable accounting policy because it expenses all research costs and only capitalized development costs where the criteria are met.

However, there is a risk that the stated accounting policy is not properly applied. The auditors must consider how Fettler Co differentiates between R & D costs.

There is risk that not all of the criteria have been demonstrated, for example:

- Pharmaceutical development is highly regulated. If the government does not license the product, then the product cannot be sold, and economic benefits will therefore not be received. For example, the Nutgo product is in an early stage of development and government licence may not yet have been given, indicating that there is not yet the ability to use or sell the development.
- Market research should justify the commercial viability of the product. The launch of any rival products would mean that the products will not generate an overall economic benefit if future sales will not recover the R & D costs already suffered, and yet to be suffered, prior to launch.
- Fettler Co may struggle to maintain the cash flow which is devoted to developing new products. This year, £32 million was spent. If the company cannot maintain good liquidity, then there is no ability to complete the project and therefore generate future economic benefit.

Overall, because of these issues, there is a risk that development costs are overstated, and expenses understated.

Audit procedures:

- Review the results of scientific tests and clinical trials performed on the products, for example, the results of animal or human testing of the products. The development should also be discussed with the project leaders, who should provide their view on the likely outcome of the development. This will provide evidence on the technical feasibility of the products.
- Inquire whether any licences necessary for continued development and/or commercial production have been granted by the government, particularly in relation to Nutgo, which is at an early stage of development.
- Using management accounts, compare expected to actual development costs incurred per product being developed. This will help the auditor to form a view on the ability to separately identify costs relating to each project, and whether there is any cost over-run which may mean that the project will not generate a future economic benefit.
- Review board minutes for relevant discussion of the product development taking place during the year. This will help the auditor to understand management intention in relation to the projects, in particular intentions to complete the projects and sell the products.
- Inquire if any orders have yet been placed for Nutgo or Maxleve—this is more likely for Maxleve which is nearing the end of its development phase. This will assist in demonstrating the future economic benefit to be derived and the commercial viability of the products.
- By reference to the company's cash position and available finance, evaluate whether Fettler Co has sufficient funds to complete the development projects.
- Obtain a breakdown of the amounts capitalized and for a sample of items:
    - Agree the amount spent to date to invoices, payroll records and other relevant source documentation and to the company's cash records.
    - Confirm that the expenditure specifically relates to the development project and is not a general cost of the business.

For the Ventamore product, which began commercial production this year, there is a risk that the amortization period of twelve years is not appropriate. Patents relating the company's products typically last for ten years, so the auditor needs to understand why twelve years seems to be the expected product lifespan for Ventamore. The amortization should correspond with the pattern of economic benefits generated from the sale of the product. The audit risk is that the amortization period has not been appropriately assessed.

The auditor must obtain evidence regarding actual sales of the product since its launch, to confirm that orders are being placed and that income is being generated.

Audit procedures to determine the validity of the amortization rate of twelve years being applied could include the following:

- Obtain market research carried out on Ventamore and review to ascertain that the market research supports a product lifespan of twelve years.
- Review actual sales patterns since the launch of Ventamore and compare to the predicted sales as indicated by the market research.
- Review the assumptions underpinning the market research sales projections, and consider whether these assumptions agree with the auditors' understanding of the business.
- Discuss sales trends with the sales/marketing directors and ascertain whether sales are in line with management's expectations.
- Read correspondence with retail outlets and obtain customer orders to ensure there is continued demand for Ventamore.
- Obtain marketing/advertising budgets and ascertain enough expenditure is continuing on Ventamore to support continued sales.
- Obtain the patent relating to Ventamore and confirm the period covered by the patent. If the period is less than twelve years, inquire with management regarding why they have determined that twelve years is an appropriate lifespan for the product.

New research laboratory

The main issue for the auditor is to confirm that the costs which have been capitalized are all directly related to the construction of the new research laboratory. IAS 16 *Property, Plant and Equipment* requires all costs which are directly attributable to be capitalized into the cost of the asset, so items such as the site itself, labour and material costs should be capitalized. Revenue items should not be capitalized.

In addition, IAS 23 *Borrowing Costs* requires directly attributable finance costs to be capitalized during the period of construction. In this case, finance costs should be included in the cost of the asset from June 20X5.

Audit procedures:

- Obtain a breakdown of the £14 million capitalized and agree the total to the general ledger and non-current asset register.
- Agree the site acquisition cost of £3 million to legal documentation, purchase invoice(s) and bank statement.
- Agree a sample of other costs for supporting documentation (e.g. labour costs to approved payroll records and time sheets), materials (such as cement, bricks), and fixtures and fittings to suppliers' invoices.
- Compare the amounts capitalized with an approved capital expenditure budget and discuss significant variances with an appropriate employee, for example, the project manager.
- Review any relevant signed contracts (e.g. from building contractors, electricians, architects), and discuss any significant deviations from the amounts stated in the contract and the amount capitalized.
- Review the list of amounts capitalized to ensure that revenue items have not been capitalized by mistake (e.g. staff training costs, consumable items which are operating expenses which should not be capitalized).

- For the capitalized finance cost:
  - Recalculate the amount, agreeing that the finance cost has only been capitalized during the period of the construction (i.e. from June 20X5).
  - Agree the rate of interest to the terms of finance.
  - Read the terms of finance to see that the finance was taken out specifically in relation to the construction of the laboratory.

Trade receivable

Trade receivables are recognized at fair value, which is the PV of estimated cash inflows. According to the information provided by Greymart's administrators, it is possible that 25 per cent of the amount outstanding will be paid. Therefore, it seems that 75 per cent of the £8 million trade receivable is irrecoverable, and this should be recognized as a bad debt expense in the statement of profit or loss. The receivables balance should be written down by at least £6 million within current assets and the expense charged against profit for the year. It could be that all of the amount is irrecoverable in which case the total should be written off.

The audit risk is that the company does not account for the bad debt, which would mean that current assets and profit for the year are overstated. Given that the bad debt expense represents 13.3 per cent (£6m/£45m) of profit before tax, management of the company has an incentive not to recognize it, a risk of management bias therefore exists.

Audit procedures:

- Obtain the correspondence from the professional advisers dealing with the closure of Greymart confirming that the company is insolvent and that only 25 per cent of amounts outstanding may be paid to creditors of the company.
- Obtain written confirmation from the professional advisers stating the amount that is likely to be paid, and an anticipated payment date.
- Agree the amount owed by Greymart to the receivables ledger, and to confirmation from the professional advisers.
- As a post-year-end procedure, review the cash book for any amounts received from Greymart.
- Discuss the accounting treatment with the management of Fettler Co, to understand their intention regarding writing off the debt.
- Perform recalculations of the amounts involved, confirm accounting entries relating to the bad debt agree to the nominal ledger.

Activity solutions

Activity 14.1—Assertions at risk for PPE

What do you think are the key risks in auditing PPE? Try to link the risks to relevant assertions.

Suggested answer points:

A key risk is overvaluation (i.e. either through error or deliberate manipulation), the assets are stated at a value greater than their 'true' value according to IAS 16. This could happen, for example, if depreciation is charged at too low a rate or if the carrying amount of assets includes costs that are not capital expenditure (e.g. if repair costs have been capitalized).

PPE could be overvalued if the value includes assets which the company does not have the **right** to include, for example, assets being used under short-term rental agreements which should not be recognized as assets in the company's financial statements.

There is also a risk relating to **existence** (i.e. the carrying amount of assets is overstated because non-existent assets are included). This could happen if assets that have been disposed of have not been correctly removed from the financial statements.

Completeness is also a risk—if assets are 'missing' from the financial statements. This could happen if capital expenditure is expensed rather than capitalized.

Activity 14.2—Auditing intangible assets

Why do you think intangible assets can be difficult to audit?

Suggested answer points:

Intangible assets create a specific issue for auditors because they are invisible—they have no physical substance. Therefore, it is not possible for the auditor to physically count or inspect, so it is difficult to 'prove' that they exist. The auditor will need to use other procedures to obtain evidence regarding the existence of the asset.

In addition, there can be a lot of judgement in determining whether an asset will give rise to future economic benefit and the length of the useful life of intangible assets, creating inherent risk. For example, if a company buys a brand name, the cost is certain and not an audit risk, but the period of time over which the brand name will generate sales is likely to be uncertain.

Activity 14.3—Causes of impairment

Note down five indicators that an asset could be impaired, which an auditor might identify when planning the audit.

Suggested answer points:

External sources of information regarding possible impairment:

- A decline in the market value of an asset.
- Adverse changes in technology, markets, economy, or legal environment.
- Increases in market interest rates that are likely to affect the discount rate using to calculate value in use.

Internal sources of information regarding possible impairment:

- obsolescence or physical damage to an asset;
- significant changes with an adverse effect on use (e.g. asset will become idle or is part of a business restructuring);
- worse economic performance of the asset than was expected.

Activity 14.4—Inventory valuation risks

List five factors which could lead to incorrect valuation of inventory at the year end.

Suggested answer points:

- Determining the cost of goods incorrectly (e.g. including inappropriate costs such as non-production related overheads or abnormal costs).
- Using out-of-date standard cost cards (e.g. not factoring in cost increases of raw materials).
- Inappropriate % completion applied to items of work in progress at the year end.
- Incorrect cut-offs.
- Slow-moving or obsolete inventory that has not been written down to NRV.
- Calculative errors or deliberate manipulation.

Activity 14.5—External confirmations

You are working on the audit of Quizzer Ltd, a company which produces and retails board games. You are helping a junior member of the audit team who has been given the task of preparing the trade receivables circularization. She has asked for your advice, as she is unsure about the different types of circularizations and how to select trade receivables balances for inclusion in the sample.

She has asked you 'I don't understand the difference between positive and negative circularizations, and I am not sure which balances to include—is it just the biggest ones?'

Note down your answers to the audit junior's questions—what is the difference between positive and negative circularizations, and what balances should be included in the sample?

Suggested answer points:

A positive circularization is when the customers relating to the trade receivables balance which are included in the auditor's sample, are asked to confirm the accuracy (or otherwise) of the balance as shown in the trade receivables ledger. If they do not agree with the amount, they are asked to state the amount which they believe to be correct.

A negative circularization is when the customers relating to the trade receivables balance which has been included in the auditor's sample are asked to respond only if they disagree with the balance as shown in the trade receivables letter.

The following balances would normally be included in the circularization:

- material balances;
- negative (credit) balances;
- nil balances;
- balances with little activity or dormant accounts;
- balances where there is evidence of disputes;
- balances which are long overdue;
- balances on which there have been contras with trade payables account balances;
- any balances containing unusual transactions (e.g. with employees of the company);
- balances where there is evidence of window-dressing (e.g. credit notes or journal entries issued around the year end).

Activity 14.6—Audit risks for bank and cash

Can you think of any situations where the audit of bank and cash could be complex, increasing the audit risk?

Suggested answer points:

- Where a company has numerous bank accounts with different organizations (e.g. there could be different interest rates for different bank accounts which adds some complexity).
- If there are both positive and negative (overdrawn) bank accounts.
- Where some bank accounts are held in a foreign currency, which needs to be retranslated to £ at the year-end exchange rate.
- Where there is a high risk of theft of cash (e.g. in a cash-based business).

15

Auditing Liabilities and Equity

Introduction

In this chapter, we examine how the auditor gathers sufficient, appropriate audit evidence over an entity's liabilities and components of equity presented in the statement of financial position. Liabilities can create audit risks, largely because management may wish to minimize the liabilities included in the accounts, to present a healthier picture of liquidity and solvency.

In addition, the measurement and recognition of some liabilities is quite judgemental, for example in the case of provisions.

We will follow a similar structure to that used in Chapter 14, when we considered how to audit assets—for each area we will have a summary of the key financial reporting requirements, consider the key audit risks, and look at relevant audit procedures.

Let's begin with a reminder of some basic definitions. The definition of a 'liability' according to the International Accounting Standard Board's (IASB) *Conceptual Framework for Financial Reporting* (Conceptual Framework) is as follows:

> A liability is a present obligation of the entity to transfer an economic resource as a result of past events.[1]

In order for the entity to have a present obligation, an 'obligating event' has to have taken place. For example, if the directors of an entity decide to take out a bank loan to provide additional finance, this, in itself, does not create a present obligation because a mere 'intention' to do something does not give rise to an obligating event. For a liability to crystallize in respect of the bank loan, the entity has to become a party to the contractual terms and conditions of the loan; hence the obligating event in this respect is the signing of the bank loan's term and conditions. At this point, the entity has a legal obligation to the bank to make repayments of the loan.

[1] International Financial Reporting Standards Foundation, *Conceptual Framework for Financial Reporting*, 2023, para 4.26 <https://www.ifrs.org/issued-standards/list-of-standards/conceptual-framework/#standard> (accessed 19 January 2023).

So, in the simplest of terms, a liability is something a business owes to a third party and to settle that liability they will have to pay cash or transfer another financial asset in settlement.

Some of the most common forms of liability a business may have include the following:

- trade creditors;
- tax liabilities;
- bank loans;
- accrued expenses.

In this chapter, we also look at the various different components of equity within the statement of financial position. According to the IASB's Conceptual Framework, the definition of 'equity' is as follows:

> Equity is the residual interest in the assets of the entity after deducting all its liabilities.[2]

Equity is also known as 'shareholders' funds' and represents the net assets of a business—that is, the amounts that belong to the shareholders and usually consists of the following:

- equity share capital (also known as ordinary share capital);
- share premium;
- revaluation reserve;
- retained earnings.

We will look at how the auditor gathers sufficient and appropriate audit evidence over the equity composition of the client's statement of financial position. There are some principal audit risks that need to be addressed where both liabilities and equity are concerned because there are some transactions which an entity may enter into that could give rise to an entity recognizing *both* a liability and equity and which can be complex to account for, giving rise to inherent risk of misstatement due to error.

Key assertions

The key assertions for liabilities and equity are:

- Existence—liabilities and equity balances exist and meet the relevant definition of a liability or equity.
- Valuation—liabilities and equity balances are stated at an appropriate value in accordance with the applicable financial reporting framework.
- Completeness—all liabilities and equity balances that meet the recognition criteria are recognized in the financial statements (i.e. there are no liabilities or equity balances missing from the financial statements).
- Rights and obligations—the entity bears the obligation in respect of liabilities recognized.

[2] Ibid., para 4.63.

Learning outcomes

- Design and explain the audit procedures relevant to trade payables, accruals, and tax payables.
- Design and explain the audit procedures relevant to provisions and contingent liabilities.
- Design and explain the audit procedures relevant to loans and debt (financial liabilities) including lease arrangements.
- Design and explain the audit procedures relevant to elements of equity, including share capital, revaluation reserve, dividends, and other items recognized in equity.

By the end of this chapter, you will be able to:

- Discuss the areas of complexity in auditing liabilities and equity and recommend relevant audit procedures.
- Recognize situations when it is appropriate to use an auditor's expert to obtain evidence in respect of liabilities.

15.1 Trade and tax payables and accruals

15.1.1 Accounting treatment

Trade payables are the most common form of liability. A trade payable arises when a company enters into an agreement with a supplier to pay for goods and/or services within a certain number of days. For example, a business may agree to pay a supplier within thirty days from the date of the invoice and this agreement is set out in the 'terms of credit' agreed with the supplier.

Trade payables are recorded in a payables ledger (often referred to as the 'purchase ledger'). At the end of the reporting period, a list of trade payables is extracted from the payables ledger which should agree to the value of trade payables presented in the financial statements of the business at the year end. Any discrepancies between the list of payables and the amount stated in the financial statements must be investigated as it could be an error or deliberate manipulation such as 'window-dressing' (i.e. an attempt to improve the appearance of the financial statements by reducing liabilities).

Where payables (and accruals) are concerned, the key assertion that the auditor is concerned about is completeness (i.e. all payables that should have been recorded have been recorded and there are no missing liabilities). The auditor will therefore be concerned with ensuring that payables and accruals are not understated. When the auditor *directly* tests payables and accruals for understatement, they are also *indirectly* testing cost of sales and overhead expenditure for understatement. If a trade payable is understated, this means that cost of sales or an overhead expense is understated as well, meaning profit is overstated. A trade payable could also be overstated (e.g. if a transposition error has taken place when posting a purchase invoice), meaning cost of sales and overheads are overstated and profit is understated.

Activity 15.1 Assertions for trade payables

Explain how the following assertions relate to the audit of trade payables: completeness, existence, valuation, rights, and obligations.

15.1.2 **Audit risks**

As we mentioned previously, the principal audit risk where trade payables and accruals are concerned is that of understatement.

Understated trade payables and accruals can arise because of cut-off errors (i.e. the payables ledger has been closed down too early or the schedule of accruals at the year end is incomplete). If the payables ledger is closed down too early, then the accounting system may not have captured all the invoices that may still be in transit that relate to the accounting period in question. Some companies close their purchase ledger on the first day of every month, so the business must have adequate controls in place to ensure that any late purchase invoices received after the month end are adequately accrued for in the financial statements. An accrual represents amounts owed by the entity for goods and/or services received up to and including the reporting date that has not yet been invoiced. In some cases, management may need to use a 'best estimate' for accruals and the auditor must devise procedures to ensure that such estimates are not inaccurate as estimates are a key area where misstatements are likely due to their subjectivity.

Accruals are expenses which have been incurred but not yet paid for. Imagine a company has used electricity in the final month of the accounting period, but they pay their electricity bills in arrears, at the end of each quarter. The company will have to 'accrue' for the final month's electricity expense by estimating the amount and making this journal:

DR Electricity expense
CR Accruals (current liability)

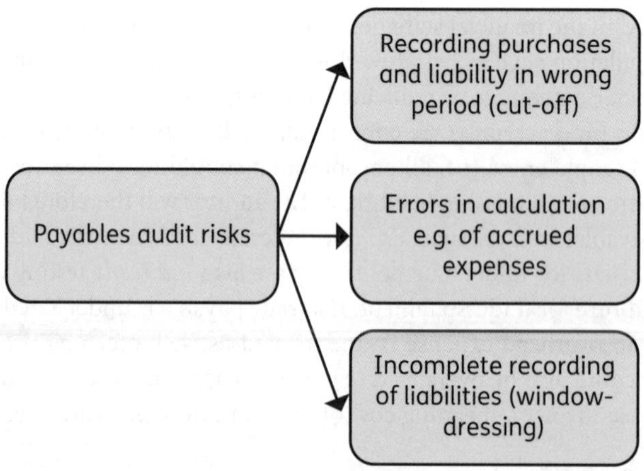

Figure 15.1 Audit risks relating to payables

There is a risk that accruals are not accurate, either through error, or a deliberate attempt to minimize them, to understate liabilities.

Activity 15.2 Indicators of incomplete payables and accruals

Imagine you are auditing a company's payables and accruals. From a review of the company's accounting records, what might indicate to you that there are unrecorded payables and accruals?

15.1.3 **Audit procedures**

For trade payables and accruals, the auditor should carry out the following procedures:

- Obtain a list of trade payables from the payables ledger, cast the list to ensure mathematical accuracy and agree the total of the payables ledger listing to the general (nominal) ledger, trial balance, and financial statements (verifies *completeness*, *classification*, and *presentation*).
- Reconcile the total of the payables ledger listing with the payables ledger control account. In practice, this should agree automatically if the accounting system is computerized but differences can arise if journals have been incorrectly posted into the payables ledger control account (verifies *completeness*).
- Inspect payments made by the company post-year end and where they relate to the current year, agree them to invoices on the payables ledger or schedule of accruals (verifies *completeness*).
- Inquire of management as to any unrecorded liabilities (verifies *completeness*).
- Select a sample of trade payable balances and perform a trade payables circularization—we will discuss this specific procedure in more detail later. Follow up any non-responses and any reconciling items between balances confirmed and the trade payables balance per the payables ledger (verifies *completeness* and *existence*).
- Obtain supplier statement reconciliations and agree these to the balance on the payables ledger at the year end and investigate any reconciling items (verifies *completeness*, *rights*, *obligations*, and *valuation*).
- Review invoices received post-year end and if any relate to the current year agree them to the schedule of accruals (verifies *completeness*).
- Select a sample of goods received notes immediately pre- and post-year end and ensure those received pre-year end are included in the trade payables balance and those received post-year end are excluded (verifies *completeness* (of payables) and *cut-off* (of purchases)).
- Inspect the payables ledger listing for any debit balances and for material amounts, discuss with management how they have arisen, and consider whether reclassification as a receivable is appropriate (verifies *classification* and *completeness* (of receivables)).

- Obtain a schedule of accruals, cast the schedule to ensure mathematical accuracy and agree the total to the general ledger, trial balance and financial statements (verifies *completeness* and *classification*).
- Inspect invoices received post-year end and compare to the list of accruals to ensure the accrual at the year end is reasonable (verifies *valuation*).

Analytical procedures over payables and accruals which the auditor should carry out include the following:

- Compare total payables and accruals to the prior year and investigate any significant variations (verifies *completeness* and *valuation*).
- Calculate trade payables days (trade payables/cost of sales x 365), compare to the prior year and investigate any significant differences (verifies *completeness* and *valuation*).

15.1.4 **Supplier statement reconciliations**

A key audit procedure to verify the completeness of trade payables is to obtain supplier statement reconciliations. A supplier statement is sent by the supplier to the client and is therefore considered to be a strong form of audit evidence because it is external to the entity. Supplier statement reconciliations reconcile the balance on the supplier's receivables ledger (sales ledger) to the balance on the client's payables ledger at the reporting date. Such reconciliations can highlight errors or discrepancies which may need further investigation or discussion with management.

Auditing in practice 15.1 Supplier statement reconciliation

McSorley Ltd is one of the major suppliers of Cahill Ltd, a retailer of home furnishings. The supplier statement issued by McSorley as at 31 December 20X9 shows a balance of £1.2 million owing by Cahill. Cahill's payables ledger shows an amount of £975,200 owing. The difference is reconciled as set out in Table 15.1.

Table 15.1

	£	£
Balance per McSorley's supplier statement		1,200,000
Less:		
Cash in transit not recorded by McSorley		(730,000)
		470,000
Plus:		
Invoice 2240 dated 30/12/X9 not on purchase ledger	250,000	
Invoice 2250 dated 31/12/X9 not on purchase ledger	243,500	
Transposition error on invoice 2232	11,700	
		505,200
Balance per Cahill payables ledger		975,200

The auditor should carry out the following procedures:

Cash in transit

- Review the date of the payment sent to McSorley Ltd for £730,000–it could form one of several payments made immediately pre- or post-year end. If it was made after the reporting date, then it must be added back into the payables ledger.
- If payment was made pre-year end, agree the date of clearance. If the payment has cleared shortly after the reporting date, it would seem that the cash had not been processed by McSorley before the reporting date and the reconciling item is valid. It should also be shown as an unpresented item on the year end bank reconciliation if the payment has not cleared the banking system by the reporting date.

Invoices not on the payables ledger

- Discuss with the warehouse manager as to whether these goods had been delivered prior to the year end, or inspect goods received notes to assess whether the goods had been received by the reporting date.
- Inspect correspondence with McSorley Ltd to establish whether these invoices are in dispute.
- If a purchase invoice has been received prior to the reporting date, inquire of management as to why it has not been included in the payables ledger as this may indicate a cut-off problem or there could be a dispute.
- If the goods relating to these invoices are in Cahill's inventory, or have been sold, the invoices should be included in the accruals schedule so verify the invoices to the schedule of accruals. If they are not on the accruals list, then include them on the schedule of uncorrected adjustments.
- If the goods have not been received by the reporting date, then no adjustment is necessary.

Transposition error

- Review the original copy of invoice 2232 from McSorley Ltd and agree that there has been a transposition error in the posting of the invoice onto the payables ledger.
- No adjustment to the payables ledger will be necessary if the invoice has been posted at the correct value and the error relates to the sales invoice posting in McSorley's accounting records.

15.1.5 **Trade payables circularization**

We looked at trade receivables circularizations in Chapter 14, whereby the auditor will select a sample of receivables and arrange to contact them in writing to confirm the balance on their payables ledger (a 'positive' circularization) or reply only if there is a disagreement with the balance (a 'negative' circularization). Similar principles apply to a trade payables circularization and the auditor may determine it necessary to carry out such a confirmation request. In practice, payables circularizations are less common than receivables because the auditor can use other external sources to verify the balances owing by the audit client, such as supplier statements as we saw previously. However, they can be used when the supplier has not sent a statement at the year end.

In a trade payables circularization, the auditor will select a sample of balances from the payables listing extracted from the payables ledger at the reporting date and ask the client to write to the suppliers asking for positive confirmation that the balance owing per the payables ledger agrees to their receivables ledger. A negative confirmation request will ask the supplier to respond if the balance on the confirmation request differs from the balance on their receivables ledger. The response from the supplier will be sent directly to the auditor and not directly to the audit client so as to prevent any unauthorized tampering of the payables confirmation.

A trade payables circularization verifies the assertions of completeness and existence. However, as with a trade receivables circularization, it does not cover valuation. Therefore, additional procedures will be necessary to cover the valuation assertion.

The auditor's focus is primarily on large supplier balances when they conclude that the internal control environment is strong, and the auditors believe that all liabilities have been recorded. However, where the auditors suspect that there may be unrecorded balances, they will include regular suppliers with small or zero balances in their sample.

The auditor will follow up on any non-responses, usually through a further letter or, with the client's permission, a telephone call. Alternatively, the auditor can obtain sufficient appropriate audit evidence through extended post-year-end cash testing (extended post-year-end cash testing also covers the assertion of valuation).

An important point to emphasize where a trade payables confirmation letter is concerned is that it must not be used as sole audit evidence because it is insufficient audit evidence on its own. The supplier could just say that the balance agrees when, in fact, it does not. Hence, supplier confirmation letters must complement other forms of audit evidence covering the completeness and existence of trade payables.

The auditor will consider whether supplier statements are available for major suppliers and also those suppliers with a nil balance at the reporting date. If a supplier has a nil balance in the current year but had a large balance in the prior year, this may be indicative of an understatement in the current year and the auditor may consider requesting a confirmation of a nil balance at the reporting date. Major suppliers may also be requested to confirm their balance in the absence of a supplier statement so the auditor can investigate any significant differences.

Auditing in practice 15.2 Difficulties in performing a trade payables circularization

Performing a trade payables circularization is a good way to obtain evidence regarding the existence of trade payables, but the response rate is not always good, and there may be other difficulties in performing the circularization. This means that the results of the procedure may not be robust, and the effort of performing the procedure may not be worth it in terms of sufficiency of evidence obtained.

A key issue is that the trade payable to whom the circularization has been sent is under no obligation to reply. There is no benefit to the trade payable in doing so, for this reason, the request is often simply ignored. Responses could also be inaccurate (e.g. the balance is just confirmed without the trade payable really checking), or they agree an amount which is wrong but is in their favour.

There is little that the auditor can do to solve the problem of inaccurate replies. However, a better response rate could be encouraged by:

- Sending out the circularization letters as soon as possible after the year end, or even before the year end as an interim audit procedure.
- Easing administrative burden by providing a prepaid and addressed envelope for the reply.
- Making sure that the balance to be confirmed (or not) is clearly stated.

15.1.6 **Current tax payable**

Related to the audit of trade payables, we will now look at tax payable. We all know that companies have to pay tax on their profits. For the purpose of our discussion, we don't need to know anything about the actual tax calculation—that is beyond the scope of this book. But we do need to understand how the auditor should obtain evidence relating to the tax that is owed to the tax authorities, so a bit of background about the tax regulations is useful. There are a variety of taxes applicable to a company (Figure 15.2).

Taxes can either be payable to HMRC or receivable from HMRC. For example, a company may receive refunds from HMRC in respect of VAT because their purchase taxes (input VAT) exceed VAT on sales (output VAT). This just means that the company is owed some VAT from HMRC. Similarly, a company might receive a refund of corporation tax because they have made a loss in the year that has been 'carried back' to profits generated in the previous year.

The auditor's focus is on the completeness and valuation of taxes whether they are receivable or payable.

If the company has failed to pay its taxes on time or has not completed any returns within specific deadlines, the auditor will also need to assess whether there are any penalties and interest

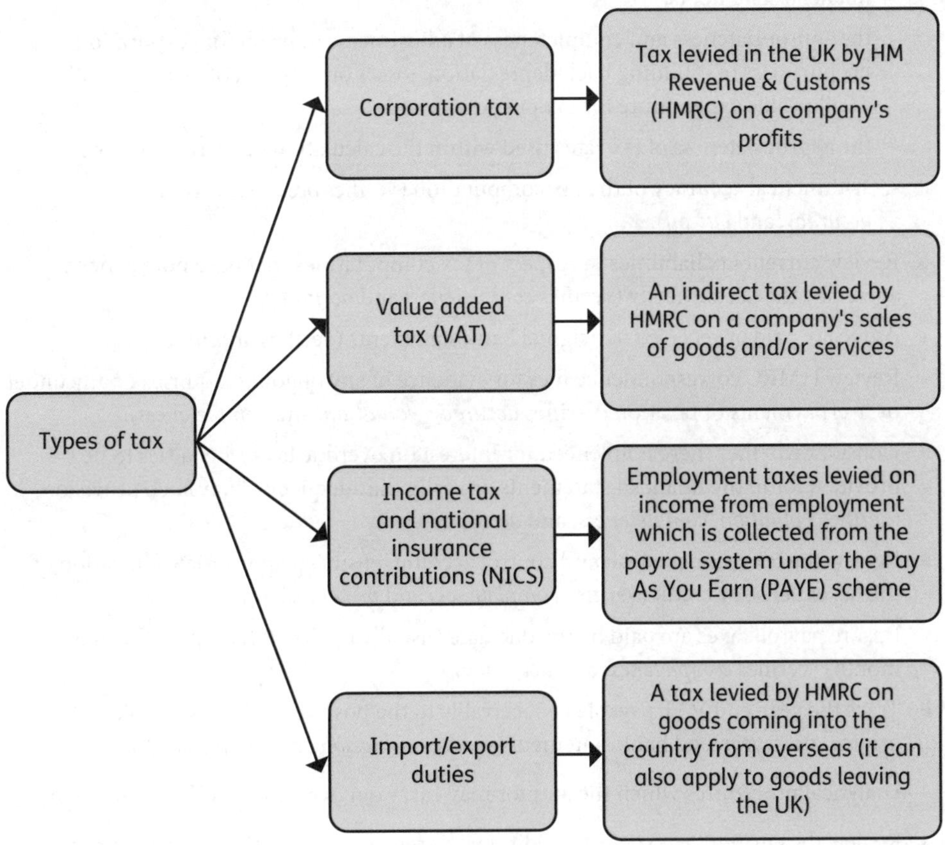

Figure 15.2 Types of tax

that may be levied, and which may need to be provided for (accrued) in the financial statements. In addition, the client may have undergone a tax inquiry that could have yielded additional taxes payable that may need to be provided for in the financial statements if the liability relates to the current or previous year (i.e. there is a present obligation as a result of a past event).

Claiming incorrect amounts of taxes may also be indicative of a weakness in the entity's controls or it may call into question the integrity of management—for example if they have deliberately claimed for things that they should not have or have deliberately overstated amounts in tax returns that have triggered a refund of tax. In such cases the auditor must maintain professional scepticism and determine whether non-compliance with tax legislation is indicative of a fraud risk factor as this may need to be reported to the audit firm's anti-money laundering officer under the UK's Anti-Money Laundering Regulations.

15.1.6.1 **Audit procedures–taxation**

Typical audit procedures which the auditor may perform over taxation include the following:

- Review the corporation tax computation to ensure:
  - consistency of amounts within the computation to underlying amounts in the financial statements;
  - the appropriateness and completeness of adjustments to profit for corporation tax purposes (e.g. adding back depreciation, losses on disposal of assets and other disallowable expenditure for tax purposes); and
  - the appropriateness of tax rates used within the calculation of current tax; and
  - arithmetical accuracy of the tax computation (verifies *occurrence*, *completeness*, *accuracy*, and *cut-off*).
- Review current tax liabilities in respect of tax computations that have not yet been agreed by the tax authority (verifies *completeness* and *accuracy*).
- Agree tax paid or received to original bank statements (verifies *accuracy*).
- Review HMRC correspondence files for evidence of any ongoing inquiries or any under or overpayments of taxation (verifies *accuracy*, *valuation*, and *completeness*).
- Consider whether there is any need for interest on overdue tax or penalties to be provided for in the financial statements or verify the adequacy of any such provision (verifies *valuation*, *completeness*, and *accuracy*).
- Review the tax reconciliation and control account, ensuring appropriate allocation of the tax expense or credit (verifies *completeness* and *presentation*).
- Ensure payroll taxes are paid by the due date (usually by the 19th of the following month) (verifies *completeness* and *accuracy*).
- Trace the year-end VAT payable or receivable to the post-year-end cash book and the original post-year-end bank statement (verifies *valuation* and *completeness*).

Analytical procedures which the auditor may carry out over tax include the following:

- Review the current tax expense (credit) by reference to expectations, such as previous periods (verifies *occurrence*, *completeness*, *accuracy*, and *cut-off*).

- Review the computation adjustments by reference to expectations, such as previous periods (verifies *occurrence*, *completeness*, *accuracy*, and *cut-off*).
- Review the proof of tax for large or unusual items (verifies *occurrence*, *completeness*, *accuracy*, and *cut-off*).
- Review the current tax asset or liability by reference to expectations, such as taxable profit/applicable rates of tax and payments on account (verifies *occurrence*, *completeness*, *accuracy*, and *cut-off*).

15.2 Provisions and contingent liabilities

15.2.1 Accounting treatment

Provisions and contingent liabilities are dealt with in IAS 37 *Provisions, Contingent Liabilities and Contingent Assets* and this is an area which can cause problems for auditors due to the subjectivity involved in provisions and contingencies.

IAS 37 defines a provision as 'a liability of uncertain timing or amount'.[3]

A provision differs from other types of liabilities because the amount and timing of settlement are both uncertain. Ordinary payables will have specific payment dates and amounts which is what distinguishes payables from provisions.

An entity can only recognize a provision when three criteria have been met by the reporting date. If these conditions are not met, a provision should not be recognized (Figure 15.3).

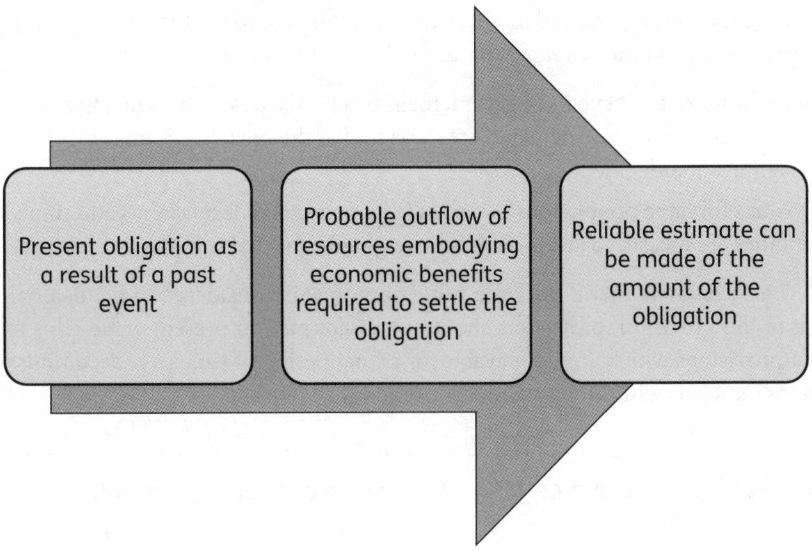

Figure 15.3 Criteria for recognizing a provision

[3] International Financial Reporting Standards Foundation, *IAS 37 Provisions, Contingent Liabilities and Contingent Assets*, 2023, para 10 <https://www.ifrs.org/issued-standards/list-of-standards/ias-37-provisions-contingent-liabilities-and-contingent-assets.html/content/dam/ifrs/publications/html-standards/english/2023/issued/ias37/> (accessed 19 January 2024).

If payment is only *possible* rather than probable (probable being defined as 'more likely than not'), the entity will have a contingent liability. A contingent liability is disclosed in the notes to the financial statements where material—it is not recognized in the statement of financial position. This is explored in more detail later on.

It is crucial that the auditor can conclude whether these criteria have been met because provisioning is an area which lends itself to manipulation. For example, if profits are higher than what management would like, they could recognize a provision to bring profit down to a more 'acceptable' level. This could happen if management want a lower accounting profit to avoid paying tax. It is for this reason that there are accounting standards which provide strict rules on when a provision can be made to stop deliberate manipulation of the profit (or loss) figure. As noted above, where the phrase 'probable' is concerned, it should be taken to mean 'more likely than not', which of course is a matter of significant judgement.

Activity 15.3 Provision for a legal claim

Imagine a simple situation involving a provision–an audit client is involved with a legal claim, as a result of which the company may have to pay damages of £500,000.

How might you obtain evidence in respect of this, to help you decide if a provision should be recognized?

In terms of measurement, the amount recognized as a provision should be the best estimate of the expenditure required to settle the present obligation at the year end. This means that there are different measurement bases for different types of provisions:

- Provisions for one-off events (e.g. settlement of a legal claim, restructuring costs, costs relating to environmental damage) are measured at the most likely amount, which can be a significant judgement.
- Provisions for large populations of events (e.g. many small legal claims and some warranties are measured at a probability-weighted expected value).

IAS 37 also requires that if the time value of money is considered to be material to the amount of the provision, provisions should be discounted to present value. This tends to arise for provisions which are not payable for a long period of time (e.g. decommissioning provisions for assets with a long estimated useful life).

Auditing in practice 15.3 BP's provisions relating to Gulf of Mexico oil spill

British Petroleum (BP) recorded extremely large provisions in relation to the Gulf of Mexico oil spill which happened in 2010. The recognition of the provisions had a highly material impact on the financial statements. Numerous provisions were recognized–in relation to litigation and claims against the company, environmental restoration, and the costs of responding to the oil spill from an operational point of view. Penalties were also imposed under the relevant legal framework including the Clean Water Act.

In its 2010 financial statements, BP recognized a provision of $16,335 million relating to the disaster and there is extensive disclosure relating to the provision and associated contingent liabilities.

The auditor's report contained an emphasis of matter paragraph relating to the significant uncertainty over the provisions and contingencies related to the oil spill:

> In forming our opinion we have considered the adequacy of the disclosures made in Notes 2, 37 and 44 to the financial statements concerning the provisions, future expenditures for which reliable estimates cannot be made and other contingencies related to the Gulf of Mexico oil spill significant event. The total amounts that will ultimately be paid by BP in relation to all obligations relating to the incident are subject to significant uncertainty and the ultimate exposure and cost to BP will be dependent on many factors. Actual costs could ultimately be significantly higher or lower than those recorded as the claims and settlement process progresses. Our opinion is not qualified in respect of these matters.[4]

Note that the auditor has commented on the significant uncertainty involved with the provisions and that the costs could end up being quite different from those reflected in the financial statements.

In 2010, auditors had no further reporting responsibilities regarding what we would now call key audit matters—the emphasis of matter paragraph was used to highlight that a significant issue is present in the financial statements and that the auditor is highlighting this issue for the readers of the report.

15.2.1.1 **Restructuring provisions**

Under IAS 37, a restructuring provision is recognized only when both of the following conditions are met:

- there is a detailed formal plan for the restructuring; and
- a company has raised a valid expectation in those affected that the plan will be implemented (i.e. either by starting to implement the plan or announcing its main features to those affected).

For example, a company might decide to shut down one of its manufacturing facilities. If the company announces its plan, specifying the facility to be closed, the estimated timing of the closure and the approximate number of employees it plans to make redundant, then it recognizes a restructuring provision. The approval of the restructuring plan by the company's board is not by itself sufficient to recognize a restructuring provision.

Restructuring provisions should only include the direct costs arising from the restructuring (e.g. employee redundancy payments and contract termination costs). Costs associated with ongoing activities are not included in restructuring provisions (e.g. the costs of retaining or relocating employees).

[4] BP, 'Annual report and Form 20-F 2010', 2010 <https://www.bp.com/content/dam/bp/business-sites/en/global/corporate/pdfs/investors/bp-annual-report-and-form-20f-2010.pdf> (accessed 19 January 2024).

15.2.1.2 Contingent liabilities and contingent assets

A *contingent liability* is a possible obligation that arises from past events whose outcome is based on uncertain future events or, an obligation that is not recognized because it is not probable or cannot be measured reliably.

Contingent liabilities should not be recognized in the statement of financial position however disclosure should be made unless the possibility of the transfer of economic benefits is remote.

A *contingent asset* is a possible asset that arises from past events and whose existence will only be confirmed by uncertain future events not wholly within the control of the enterprise.

Contingent assets should not be recognized as an asset within the statement of financial position. They should be disclosed in the notes to the financial statements where an inflow of economic benefits is probable. An asset is only recognized when the receipt of income is virtually certain, in which case the balance is not contingent and its recognition is appropriate.

15.2.2 Audit risks

The principal audit risk where provisions are concerned is that they are understated or incomplete. Understated provisions will also mean understated expenses because of the double entry used to record most provisions when they are established:

DR Expenses
CR Provisions

Conversely, a provision may have been included in the financial statements that does not meet the three recognition criteria above. This would mean that liabilities and expenses are both overstated. In addition, there could also be tax implications if the company has claimed tax relief on the provision. If the provision does not meet the recognition criteria, the tax relief cannot be claimed and hence the tax expense (or credit) may also be misstated.

As we have seen, contingent liabilities are disclosed in the notes to the financial statements unless the possibility of settlement is remote. The principal audit risk here is that disclosures may be inadequate or even incomplete. This could arise, for example, if the directors do not want to disclose a contingent liability because doing so would present them in an unfavourable light with shareholders, potential investors, financiers, and suppliers. Only material contingent liabilities require disclosure, and so professional judgement will be required to determine whether the event giving rise to the contingent liability is material or whether any amounts that may need to be paid if the liability crystallizes are material.

Activity 15.4 Auditing contingent liabilities

It can be difficult to obtain audit evidence on contingent liabilities because they relate to uncertain future events or outcomes.

Can you suggest some ways that auditors can obtain relevant evidence?

It may be the case that disclosing information relating to a contingent liability or provision for liability could seriously prejudice the position of an entity which is involved in a dispute with other parties on the matter giving rise to the contingency/provision. IAS 37 makes an exception to disclosing the information required by the standard, but the entity must still provide particulars of the general nature of the dispute, together with the fact that, and reason why, the information has not been disclosed. This exception should only be used by reporting entities in extremely rare circumstances. It must also be noted that the prejudicial exemptions from disclosure under accounting standards only relate to the disclosure of them—a provision must still be recorded in the financial statements if the recognition criteria are met. The audit risk here is that management have misinterpreted the prejudicial disclosure exemptions, thus not recognizing a provision where one is needed, or have applied them incorrectly resulting in inadequate disclosure.

To summarize: the key problem with provisions and contingencies is that they are, by definition, uncertain. This means that management will have to use judgement when deciding on the appropriate accounting treatment. There is a very high risk of management bias, and auditors will need to apply professional scepticism when obtaining evidence regarding provisions and contingencies.

Auditing scenario 15.1 Provisions and application of professional scepticism

You are the audit senior planning the audit of your client, McLaughlin Ltd, for the year ended 31 December 20X9, which prepares its financial statements under IFRS. The audit engagement partner has had a meeting with the finance director and has flagged up an issue arising from that meeting as follows.

On 20 December 20X9, McLaughlin Ltd received a letter from a former employee claiming unfair dismissal. The directors have refuted the claim stating that employment legislation was followed, and the claim is currently being actively defended by the company. The case is due to be heard by an employment tribunal in May 20X0, by which time the year-end financial statements will have already been issued.

The directors have not included a provision in the year-end financial statements; nor have they made any disclosures in respect of a contingent liability. The finance director has informed the audit engagement partner that under no circumstances will the company make any disclosures that may present them in an unfavourable light because doing so could damage their reputation. The directors have stated that, in their view, the legal claim will not succeed against the company because the former employee has no evidence to support their claim of unfair dismissal.

The principal audit risk in this situation is that the company has a present obligation as a result of a past event and payment to the former employee is, in fact, probable. In such a situation, the company would be required to recognize a provision if the amount of the payment could be reliably measured. If payment is only possible, rather than probable, the company must disclose a contingent liability.

The auditor should apply professional scepticism to the comment made by the directors regarding the claim not being likely to succeed. This statement should be challenged, and the directors should provide some corroboratory evidence to back up their comment (e.g. correspondence with a legal adviser). For the auditor, it is important that independent evidence is obtained so that they can assess whether it is probable that payment will be made by the entity, and then discuss the situation further with the directors.

15.2.3 Audit procedures

Audit procedures which the auditor should carry out over provisions for liabilities and contingent liabilities include the following:

- Obtain a breakdown of provisions, cast the schedule, and agree the total to the general ledger, trial balance, and financial statements (verifies *valuation*).
- Discuss the schedule of provisions with the directors and/or inspect relevant supporting documentation to confirm that the entity has a present obligation as a result of a past event at the reporting date (verifies *rights and obligations*).
- Inquire of the directors, or inspect relevant board minutes, to ascertain if payment is probable (verifies *existence*).
- Where necessary, recalculate the components of the provision and agree the calculation to supporting documentation (verifies *valuation* and *completeness*).
- Obtain the post-year-end cash book, review the cash book for any payments made in respect of the provision in the next accounting period, and agree such payments to an original bank statement and compare the payments made to the provision to assess its reasonableness (verifies *valuation*).
- With the client's permission, obtain confirmation from the lawyer as to the likely outcome of the case and how probable it is payment will be made. Alternatively, inspect correspondence from lawyers regarding the issue to confirm whether a provision should be recognized and if the amount provided for is reasonable (verifies *existence*, *rights and obligations*, and *completeness*).
- Review the financial statement disclosures in respect of the provision or contingent liability and confirm they are in compliance with the requirements of IAS 37.
- Perform a review of legal expenses in the general (nominal) ledger to identify any items which may indicate the need for a provision at the year end (verifies *existence* and *completeness*).
- Obtain a written representation from management that they believe the provision is appropriately valued and is complete (verifies *valuation* and *completeness*).

Auditing in practice 15.4 PwC audit of Stora Enso Oyj

Stora Enso Oyj is a company based in Finland and is a manufacturer of pulp, paper, and other forest products. The company's financial statements for the year ended 31 December 2019 include significant provisions in relation to environmental restoration costs and restructuring.

The company's audit firm, PwC includes a key audit matter disclosure in the auditor's report which describes the risk of material misstatement relating to provisions and contingencies and how the audit approach dealt with these risks. This is an extract from the key audit matter disclosure:

> Key audit matter in the audit of the group
>
> As of 31 December 2019, the Group had environmental, restructuring, and other provisions totalling EUR 165 million. In addition, the Group has disclosed significant open legal cases and other

contingent liabilities in Note 29. The assessment of the existence of the present legal or constructive obligation, the analysis of the probability of the outflow of future economic benefits, and the analysis of a reliable estimate, require management's judgement to ensure appropriate accounting or disclosures. Due to the level of judgement relating to recognition, valuation and presentation of provisions and contingent liabilities, this is considered to be a key audit matter.

How our audit addressed the key audit matter

We obtained an understanding of management's process to identify new obligations and changes in existing obligations. We analysed significant changes in material provisions from prior periods and obtained a detailed understanding of these changes and assumptions applied. Our audit procedures related to material provisions recognized included:

- Assessment of the recognition criteria for the liability;
- Evaluation of the methodology adopted by management for the measurement of the liability;
- Testing of the mathematical accuracy of the measurement calculation;
- Assessment of the discount rates applied in the measurement; and
- Assessment of the other key measurement assumptions and inputs.

We obtained legal letters on the main outstanding legal cases. We reviewed minutes of the board meetings including sub committees. We assessed the appropriateness of the presentation of the most significant contingent liabilities in the consolidated financial statements.[5]

15.2.4 Litigation and claims

ISA (UK) 501 *Audit Evidence—Specific Considerations for Selected Items* contains specific requirements for situations when the audit is the subject of litigation and claims, as follows:

- The auditor shall design and perform audit procedures in order to identify litigation and claims involving the entity which may give rise to a risk of material misstatement, including:
- Inquiry of management and, where applicable, others within the entity, including in-house legal counsel;
- Reviewing minutes of meetings of those charged with governance and correspondence between the entity and its external legal counsel; and
- Reviewing legal expense accounts.[6]

In addition to these procedures, where a risk of material misstatement arises in relation to litigation and claims, the auditor should seek to communicate directly with the company's external legal counsel regarding the matter. Written representations should also be obtained from management to state that all actual or possible litigation and claims which are relevant to the financial statements have been disclosed to the auditor and accounted for in accordance with the relevant financial reporting requirements.

[5] PwC, 'Auditor's report (translation of Finnish original): To the annual general meeting of Stora Enso Oyj', 2019 <https://www.storaenso.com/-/media/documents/download-center/documents/annual-general-meetings/2020/storaenso_auditors_report_2019_eng.pdf> (accessed 19 January 2024).

[6] FRC, 'ISA (UK) 501', 2022, para 9 <https://media.frc.org.uk/documents/ISA_UK_501_-_Updated_May_2022.pdf> (accessed 19 January 2024).

Auditing scenario 15.2 Litigation and claims

Parklife Co runs a number of hotels in Europe and the Caribbean. Parklife Co's management team has received notification from an environmental protection agency, SafeBeaches, that they intend to take legal action against the company. SafeBeaches is claiming that the hotel guests are causing environmental damage to the beaches on which the Parklife hotels are situated. If the legal action against the company is successful, fines of £50,000 are potentially payable. This would be material to the financial statements.

In planning the audit, the auditor should consider the requirements of IAS 37, which requires that a provision should be recognized if there is a present obligation as a result of a past event, and that there is a probable outflow of future economic benefits for which a reliable estimate can be made.

The auditor must plan to obtain sufficient, appropriate evidence as to whether it is probable that the company will be held liable for the damage to the beaches and whether the £50,000 is likely to be payable. If it is less than probable that the fine will be paid, then it will be appropriate for Parklife Co to disclose a contingent liability in the notes to the financial statements.

Relevant audit procedures would include the following:

- Obtain correspondence received from SafeBeaches and/or their legal advisers and review to understand the basis of the claim, for example, to confirm if it refers to a specific incident when damage was caused to beaches.
- Discuss the issue with Parklife Co's legal adviser, to understand whether, in their opinion, the company could be liable for the fine.
- Discuss with the company's legal adviser to obtain understanding of the relevant legislation.
- Obtain confirmation from SafeBeaches' legal adviser regarding the claim, to confirm its basis, the evidence which underpins the claim, and the amount of the fine.
- Discuss the situation with management, and read minutes of relevant meetings, to confirm management's understanding of the situation and their views on the likelihood of the claim against the company being successful.
- Obtain a written representation from management, as required by ISA (UK) 501, that all known litigation and claims have been disclosed to the auditor.
- Read the other information published with the financial statements, including the chairman's statement and directors' report, to assess whether any disclosure relating to the issue has been made, and, if so, whether it is consistent with the financial statements.

There is also an issue arising in relation to ISA (UK) 250—Section A *Consideration of Laws and Regulations in an Audit of Financial Statements*, which requires that if the auditor becomes aware of information concerning an instance of non-compliance or suspected non-compliance with laws and regulations, the auditor must obtain an understanding of the act and the circumstances in which it has occurred, and further information to evaluate the possible effect on the financial statements. Therefore, the audit plan must contain planned audit procedures which are sufficient for the audit team to conclude on the accounting treatment and on whether the auditor has any reporting responsibilities outside the company, for example, to communicate a breach of legislation to the appropriate authorities.

15.3 Loans and debt (financial liabilities) and lease liabilities

15.3.1 Accounting treatment

Loans and debt are also known as financial liabilities, a type of financial instrument. Some companies have very complex debt arrangements, but even very simple businesses may have the most common type of debt, which is a bank loan.

A financial liability arises when the client becomes a party to the contractual terms and conditions of the financial instrument. The *issuer* (i.e. the borrower) has to make payments to the *holder* (i.e. the lender) in the form of interest and principal; hence there is a contractual obligation to transfer cash or other financial assets in settlement of the liability. As we discussed earlier, the obligating event that creates a legal obligation, thus a liability, for the entity, is the signing of the loan agreement.

Loans payable are presented in the statement of financial position as current (i.e. the portion falling due within one year from the reporting date) and non-current (i.e. the portion falling due after more than one year from the reporting date). This is to comply with the requirements of IAS 1 *Presentation of Financial Statements* and company law.

In terms of measurement, IFRS 9 *Financial Instruments* requires loans to be measured at amortized cost using the effective interest method.

The primary concern of the auditor is to ensure that financial liabilities are complete and are presented appropriately in the statement of financial position (i.e. as current and non-current). In addition, certain financial liabilities will be secured over the assets of the company and in this respect the auditor is concerned with ensuring the entity has adequately disclosed the nature of security pledged by the business for its borrowings.

15.3.2 Audit risks

The principal audit risk where financial liabilities are concerned is that of understatement. Companies may want to keep liabilities out of their financial statements to present a healthier picture of their financial position, in particular, they may want their debt to look lower which improves gearing. This can be a significant risk where the company has quite high levels of debt and where there are debt covenants which include a metric relating to gearing. A loan covenant may stipulate that the entity must maintain a certain level of assets, or make a certain level of profit or keep gearing within a particular target, which aims to protect the lender against default. Any breach of loan covenants will mean the loan becomes repayable on demand and this could place considerable strain on a company's cash flow and call into question the going concern ability of the entity. This creates a pressure for management bias (i.e. management may deliberately use accounting techniques which may result in off-balance sheet finance to keep within the gearing criteria of the covenant).

15.3.2.1 Complex financial liabilities

Financial liabilities can be difficult transactions to account for and IFRS 9 and IAS 32 are particularly complex standards which automatically gives rise to an **inherent risk**. We saw

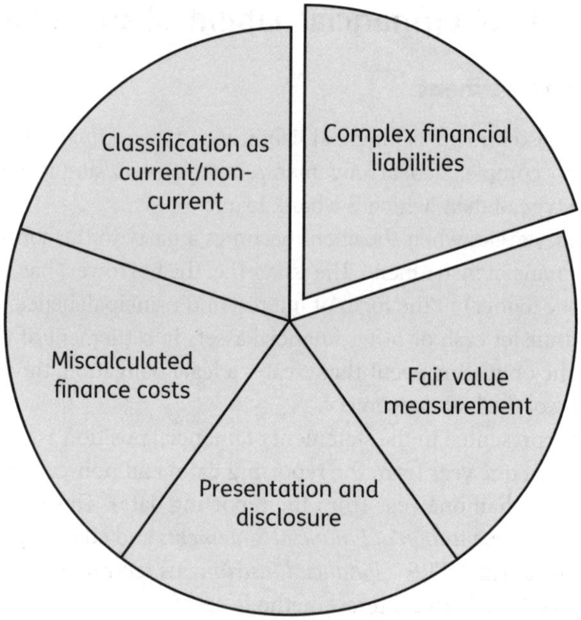

Figure 15.4 Audit risks in respect of complex financial liabilities

in Chapter 9 that an inherent risk is the risk of material misstatement before the auditor considers any related controls that may be present in the entity that aim to reduce the risk of material misstatement.

A specific audit risk relating to measurement is that a loan has not been accounted for under the amortized cost method using the effective interest rate. This could also give rise to a misstated liability and finance cost in the financial statements if, for example, the incorrect interest rate has been used or the effective interest rate has been calculated incorrectly.

Risk of misstatement in presentation is also a principal audit risk where financial liabilities are concerned. Liabilities have to be presented in the financial statements as current and non-current. If this allocation is not done correctly, then current and non-current liabilities will both be misstated. A company may try to deliberately understate current liabilities to present a higher net current assets figure, therefore showing a misleading picture in the statement of financial position. In some situations, the monetary value of any correction to the current and non-current liability apportionment may be immaterial, but if it turns net current assets into net current liabilities, then it will be material regardless of the amount. Remember that materiality has both qualitative and quantitative traits.

Certain financial liabilities can be measured at fair value through profit or loss. We won't spend much time looking at these more complex financial liabilities, but a brief overview is useful. These financial liabilities tend to be more difficult to account for than, say, a basic bank loan. Fair value fluctuations for loans measured at fair value are generally taken to profit or loss and the audit risk here is that the fair value is incorrect or the gain or loss at the reporting date has been misposted in the financial statements (e.g. the fair value gain or loss has been presented in other comprehensive income rather than profit or loss). There can also be a risk that the fair value is incorrectly determined, and, again, this is linked to the complexity of the financial liability.

While the detail is outside the scope of our discussion, it is worth mentioning that there is a specific IFRS standard which deals with the disclosure requirements for financial instruments—IFRS 7 *Financial Instruments: Disclosure*. This is a very detailed standard which contains extensive disclosure requirements relating to information about the significance of financial instruments to an entity, and the nature and extent of risks arising from those financial instruments, both in qualitative and quantitative terms. Auditors need to plan procedures to confirm the completeness and accuracy of these disclosures. Due to some financial liabilities being very complex to account for, the audit firm may use in-house specialists to plan and perform the audit procedures in this area.

Auditing in practice 15.5 Lehman Brothers, EY, and off-balance sheet finance

EY audited the US company Lehman Brothers from 2001 until its bankruptcy in 2008. The Lehman Brothers scandal involves many issues—poor corporate governance, bad decision-making, acceptance of high risk, and corruption at the highest level of the organization. The collapse of Lehman Brothers was the biggest corporate failure in history and it had a huge impact on the global financial markets. The US government had to bail out the banking sector by $700bn. The effects were also felt in the UK where the government had to step in to rescue the Royal Bank of Scotland. Central banks all over the world needed to support the banking sector to avoid a global collapse.

The accounting fraud set up by the Lehman Brothers management team, and which played a significant role in the company's bankruptcy, used a now infamous mechanism known as 'Repo 105', which was a form of off-balance sheet finance involving complex financial liabilities. The Repo 105 scheme resulted in tens of billions of dollars of debt being removed from the financial statements. Using Repo 105, 'toxic assets' (i.e. risky loans) were sold just before the date of the reporting period and repurchased just after. The temporary absence of the bad debt gave the impression of a much healthier balance sheet. Essentially, this is just 'window-dressing' and Repos were a common type of transaction, but in Lehman Brothers' case it was on a massive scale, with $50bn taken out of the accounts in the second quarter of 2007.

In 2010 the New York attorney general sued EY for its part in what was alleged as 'a massive accounting fraud' involving hidden liabilities which made Lehman Brothers' financial position appear healthier and less debt-heavy than it actually was. The attorney general said:

> Ernst & Young approved Lehman's accounting for the Repo 105 transactions and issued unqualified opinions certifying Lehman's financial statements, in spite of knowing that Lehman was not disclosing the existence or impact of the Repo 105s in its annual and quarterly consolidated financial statements, all of which Ernst & Young audited or reviewed.

As part of the investigation, the bankruptcy examiner looked into how EY audited the Repo 105 transactions and was scathing of the approach taken by the firm. The examiner's report stated:

> EY's review . . . applied only to the accounting basis for these transactions, not to their volume or purpose. Specifically, EY's review and analysis of Lehman's Repo 105 program did not account for the volumes of Repo 105 transactions Lehman undertook at quarter-end.[7]

7 Report of Anton R. Valukas, Examiner, United States Bankruptcy Court, Southern District of New York, 2010.

The report goes on to state that:

> EY's audit did not require EY to consider or review the volume or timing of Repo 105 transactions. Accordingly, as part of its year-end 2007 audit, EY did not ask Lehman about any directional trends, such as whether its Repo 105 activity was increasing during fiscal year 2007. Notably, as part of its quarterly review process, EY did not audit any of Lehman's Repo 105 transactions.

Despite these accusations, ultimately, EY was not found guilty of any negligence in their audit of Lehman Brothers, but did agree to pay $99 million to settle a lawsuit brought against them by Lehman Brothers' investors and a further $10 million to New York state.

In a statement regarding the closure of the legal action against the firm, EY stated:

> Lehman's audited financial statements clearly portrayed Lehman as what it was—a highly leveraged entity operating in a risky and volatile industry; and Lehman's bankruptcy was not caused by any accounting issues. After many years of costly litigation we are pleased to put this matter behind us, with no findings of wrongdoing by EY or any of its professionals.[8]

15.3.2.2 **Preference shares**

A particular audit risk relates to preference shares. Reference to 'shares' may, at first glance, suggest that preference shares are treated as equity. In some cases, they can be treated as equity if they are non-redeemable (i.e. the company doesn't have to buy the preference shares back from the holder at a future date, or it can at its own discretion) and dividends on the preference shares can be paid at the discretion of the entity rather than as a mandatory requirement.

However, preference shares often mandate the company to pay 'dividends' on them—for example, a 5 per cent coupon rate per annum. Where a preference share mandates the company to pay cash to the holder—either in the form of 'dividends' or there is a requirement to redeem the preference shares at a future date—they are treated as a financial liability. The dividends paid to the preference shareholders are presented as finance costs in the statement of profit or loss—they are not treated as equity dividends paid in the same way as dividends paid to ordinary shareholders. This is because the preference share is accounted for as a financial liability and not equity.

The audit risk where preference shares are concerned is that they have been incorrectly treated as equity when they should be treated as a financial liability (or vice versa). This would give rise to a corresponding risk of misstatement in respect of the dividends paid on these preference shares which should be treated as finance costs if the preference shares are financial liabilities. The auditor must pay careful attention to the terms of any preference share issuances to ensure the client has correctly accounted for them as debt or equity, as appropriate.

15.3.2.3 **Convertible debt**

Convertible debt can be tricky to account for because it is classed as a compound financial instrument, which is a financial instrument that contains both liability and equity

[8] Brown, N. (2013) 'Ernst & Young to pay $99 mln to end Lehman investor lawsuit' <https://www.reuters.com/article/idUSDEE99H0EE/> (accessed 3 January 2024).

features. Compound financial instruments are dealt with in IAS 32 *Financial Instruments: Presentation.*

Convertible debt is where the lender has the option at the maturity date to convert some, or all, of the principal amount outstanding at the redemption date to equity shares of the business. This might prove an attractive option for the lender because the company could be generating a high level of profits on which they would receive a return if they are a shareholder (in the form of dividends). The return received by way of dividends may prove to be more lucrative than just receiving the principal amount in cash at the date of maturity.

'Split accounting' is used to deal with compound financial instruments, including convertible debt where the liability portion is calculated first and the balance is treated as equity. The balance treated as equity represents the lender's option to convert the principal outstanding at the redemption date to equity shares.

Auditing scenario 15.3 Calculation of liability and equity portion of a convertible loan

The draft financial statements of Hall Ltd for the year ended 31 December 20X9 recognize a convertible loan taken out in the year. It was issued on 2 January 20X9 at a nominal value of £600,000 and is redeemable in four years' time or it may be converted into equity shares at the discretion of the bondholder. Coupon rates of interest are paid to the bondholder at 8 per cent and an equivalent loan note without the conversion option would have carried interest at 10 per cent.

The audit manager has expressed concern that the finance director has accounted for this convertible debt incorrectly and has asked you to reperform the calculation of the initial recognition of the loan to verify the value of the liability in the statement of financial position, and to test the finance cost charged to the statement of profit or loss.

You have obtained the present value rates as set out in Table 15.2.

Table 15.2

End of year	8%	10%
1	0.926	0.909
2	0.857	0.826
3	0.794	0.751
4	0.735	0.683

The audit procedure involves calculating the amount that has to be recognized as a liability in the entity's financial statements, with the balance being recognized in equity. To calculate this, the cash flows are discounted using the discount rate that would apply to a similar loan without the conversion option as this is a requirement of IAS 32. In this example, that rate is 10 per cent and the calculation reperformed by the auditor is as set out in Table 15.3.

Table 15.3

Year	8% interest (£600k x 8%)	10% factor	Present value
	£		£
1	48,000	0.909	43,632
2	48,000	0.826	39,648
3	48,000	0.751	36,048
4	648,000	0.683	442,584
Liability portion			561,912
Proceeds			(600,000)
Equity portion			38,088

Table 15.4

	£
Dr Cash at bank	600,000
Cr Financial liability (loan payable)	(561,912)
Cr Equity	(38,088)
Being initial recognition of convertible debt	

The journals to record the above transaction in year 1 are as set out in Table 15.4.

The auditor can compare this working to the journal posted in Hall Ltd's financial statements, to verify that the liability is valued correctly at initial recognition.

15.3.3 **Audit procedures**

Audit procedures which the auditor should apply over the entity's financial liabilities include the following:

- Where a loan is material, obtain a confirmation from the borrower as to the amount outstanding at the reporting date (verifies *existence*, *rights*, and *obligations*).
- Recalculate the interest accrual on each loan and agree to the general ledger, trial balance and financial statements (verifies *accuracy*, *valuation*, and *completeness*).
- Examine loan documentation and ensure that the loan terms are being complied with (verifies *valuation*).
- Review any loan covenants in place to ensure these have not been breached. Where they have been breached the loan may need to be presented as wholly current (verifies *presentation*).
- If a loan is secured, examine the security and consider its value and whether the security is sufficient—for example if it has to be sold quickly to cover outstanding balances (verifies *valuation*).
- For loans taken out in the period, review loan documentation, agree the loan proceeds to the cash book and an original bank statement and recalculate the interest charge.

Agree the closing balance to external confirmations (verifies *valuation*, *completeness*, *existence*, *rights*, and *obligations*).

- Agree opening balances of existing loans to the prior year audit working papers file and ensure the opening balances have been correctly brought forward into the current year (verifies *valuation* and *completeness*).
- Agree closing loan liabilities to the external confirmations, general ledger, trial balance, and financial statements (verifies *accuracy*, *valuation*, *completeness*, *rights*, and *obligations*).
- For preference shares, agree they have been treated as a financial liability if there is a requirement to pay cash to the preference shareholders or they are redeemable at a specific point in time in the future (verifies *accuracy*, *completeness* (of liabilities) and *presentation*).
- For compound financial instruments, ensure the discount rates used in the calculation of the liability and equity portion are correct and they reflect the rate of interest which would be paid on an equivalent loan without an option to convert the principal outstanding to equity at the redemption date (verifies *accuracy*, *completeness*, and *presentation*).

15.3.4 **Lease arrangements**

Leasing is a common form of finance for businesses and lease arrangements are very common in many types of organization. Over the years there have been considerable changes to the way in which leases are accounted for in the financial statements through IFRS 16 *Leases*. We will not look at the detail of the accounting requirements, which can be complex. Instead, we will look at the key elements of a lease, from the point of view of the 'lessee' (i.e. the party to the lease contract that is paying for the right to use an asset under a lease contract).

IFRS 16 requires an entity to recognize a 'right-of-use' asset and a corresponding lease liability at the commencement of a lease. The right-of-use asset is calculated as set out in Table 15.5.

Table 15.5

	£
Value of lease liability at initial measurement (see below)	X
Plus lease payments made at, or before, inception of the lease	X
Less lease incentive received	(X)
Plus initial direct costs	X
Plus an estimate of any dismantling costs	X
Right-of-use asset per statement of financial position	**X**

The lease liability is recognized at the commencement of the lease at the present value of the lease payments which are not paid at the date of initial recognition. The present value of the lease liability is measured using the interest rate implicit in the lease. Hence, the lease liability is calculated as set out in Table 15.6.

Table 15.6

	£
Fixed payments less lease incentives receivable	X
Plus variable lease payments	X
Plus amounts payable under residual value guarantees	X
Plus the exercise price of a purchase option (if expected to exercise)	X
Penalties for early termination (if applicable)	X
Lease liability per statement of financial position	**X**

15.3.4.1 Common audit risks

The principal audit risk is whether an arrangement constitutes a lease under IFRS 16. IFRS 16 defines a lease in terms of the right to control the use of the asset for a period of time in exchange for consideration. Where an arrangement does constitute a lease, the financial statements must include a right-of-use asset and a lease liability.

Leases are likely to be material. The auditor is primarily concerned with ensuring that the right-of-use asset has been recognized at an appropriate value in line with IFRS 16 requirements. The risk is that the calculation of fixed/variable payments is incorrect, resulting in a misstated right-of-use asset, or that additional amounts have been included in the right-of-use asset which are either incorrect or will not arise, hence overstating the value of the asset.

In addition, a lease liability may be correctly recognized on initial recognition, but there is a risk that incorrect accounting entries have been made during the year and that the closing lease liability is misstated. The auditor will therefore be concerned with ensuring that interest added to the lease liability during the year has been correctly calculated using the interest rate implicit in the lease, because any misstatement can also have an effect on the statement of profit or loss.

Another audit risk relates to the depreciation charged on the right-of-use asset. This could be misstated if the entity is unaware of the requirements of IFRS 16 and IAS 16 *Property, Plant and Equipment*.

IFRS 16 also requires extensive disclosures to be made in the financial statements concerning leasing transactions. There is a risk that the disclosures are inadequate or do not comply with the requirements of the standard. In particular, the lease liability must be presented as an analysis to show the present value of the minimum lease payments in time bands which are appropriate.

15.3.4.2 Audit procedures

Typical audit procedures the auditor may carry out on leasing transactions include the following:

- Agree prior year finance lease liabilities with the prior year's working papers file and agree that they have been correctly brought forward into the current year (this verifies *completeness*).

- Obtain a schedule of finance leases in existence at the reporting date, cast the schedule, and agree with the total in the general ledger and the financial statements (this verifies *completeness* and *valuation*).
- For leases entered into during the year, obtain a copy of the leasing agreement, recalculate the right-of-use asset and lease liability, and agree these totals with the general ledger (this verifies *completeness* and *valuation*).
- Agree the depreciation charge for the right-of-use asset is in accordance with the company's declared accounting policy and IAS 16, and agree the charge with the statement of profit or loss (this verifies *valuation*).
- Ensure the interest rate implicit in the lease is the rate which causes the present value of:
  - the lease payments; and
  - the unguaranteed residual value to equal the sum of:
  - the fair value of the underlying asset; and
  - the initial direct costs of the lessor

  (this verifies *valuation*).
- Reperform the calculation of the closing lease liability for a sample of leases taking the opening balance, deducting the payments made and recalculating the interest using the interest rate implicit in the lease and agree with the client's calculations (this verifies *completeness* and *valuation*).
- Review the financial statement disclosures for compliance with IFRS 16 and IFRS 7 (this verifies *presentation* and *disclosure*).

15.4 Equity

15.4.1 Accounting treatment

As we mentioned earlier in the chapter, 'equity' is the residual in the assets of a company after all its liabilities have been deducted. Equity is also commonly referred to as 'shareholders' funds' (see Figure 15.5).

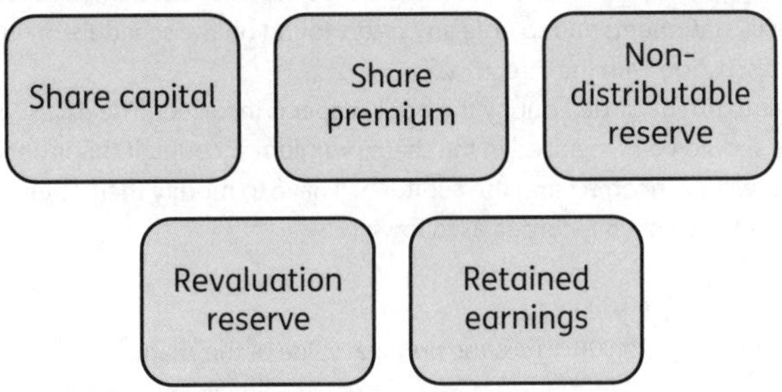

Figure 15.5 Common categories of equity

Share capital represents the amount invested by the shareholders of the entity and their shares may attract *dividends* which are paid at the company's discretion (usually on ordinary shares). Share capital may also be issued by the company at a higher price than its face value, which is known as a 'premium' and the equity section of the statement of financial position will include a 'share premium' account which is where the excess of face value over proceeds is taken to comply with company law.

Where a company revalues an item of property, plant, and equipment as permitted in IAS 16 *Property, Plant and Equipment*, revaluation gains are taken to the revaluation reserve. Revaluation losses are also taken to the revaluation reserve to the extent that there is a surplus on the revaluation reserve in respect of that asset.

'Reserves' comprise the retained profits which the company has reinvested back into the business (hence the term 'retained earnings'). These retained profits are the profits that are left after tax and dividends have been accounted for.

Finally, a non-distributable reserve can be used by a business to ring-fence those reserves which are non-distributable ('non-distributable' means they cannot be paid to the shareholders in the form of a dividend or other form of distributable). Such reserves can be classified in this way to prevent them from being unlawfully distributed.

15.4.2 **Audit risks**

The audit of equity is mainly concerned with ensuring the company's compliance with legal and regulatory requirements.

Common risks of misstatement include share capital being issued at a premium and the premium element not being treated correctly. As we mentioned earlier, a company issuing shares at a premium is required to present the face value of the shares within share capital and the excess of face value over proceeds received is shown in share premium.

Auditing scenario 15.4 Shares issued at a premium incorrectly accounted for

On 1 January 20X9, Whitaker Ltd issued 20,000 shares with a nominal value of £1 for £2 each. The bookkeeper has credited the entire £40,000 (20,000 shares x £2) to ordinary share capital. The audit manager has asked you to ensure that this share issue has been accounted for correctly in the year-end financial statements and to note any errors found on the schedule of uncorrected misstatements for discussion with the directors.

The accounting treatment carried out by the bookkeeper is incorrect. The excess of proceeds over nominal value should be recognized in the share premium account. If this is not corrected, the financial statements will be incorrect and the auditor will have to modify their opinion accordingly. The share issue should have been recorded as follows:

Dr Cash at bank	£40,000
Cr Ordinary share capital	£20,000 (this is the nominal value of the shares)
Cr Share premium	£20,000 (this is the excess of par value over proceeds)

An audit error of £20,000 which debits ordinary share capital and credits share premium will need to be recorded on the schedule of uncorrected misstatements.

Another common risk of misstatement includes errors in accounting for revalued assets within the revaluation reserve. If the entity has revalued an item of property, plant, and equipment as permitted under IAS 16, which requires revaluation gains to be recognized within equity, there is a risk that the entity may have taken the gain (or loss) to profit or loss rather than the revaluation reserve, thereby overstating profit. However, under IAS 40, when accounting for investment properties, a different accounting treatment is required. For investment properties, the fair value gain (or loss) should be recognized in profit and not within equity.

Auditing scenario 15.5 Investment property increases in value

The financial statements of Heaton Ltd recognize an investment property on the statement of financial position that is accounted for at fair value under IAS 40 *Investment Property*.

You are auditing the company's non-current assets and have been asked by the audit manager to ensure that the finance director has included the fair value adjustment in respect of the investment property correctly because the audit manager is concerned that the finance director lacks knowledge of the requirements under IAS 40.

At the year end 31 December 20X9 the fair value of the property had increased by £50,000 and the finance director recorded the transaction as follows:

Dr Investment property	£50,000
Cr Revaluation reserve	£50,000

Being increase in fair value of investment property at year end.

In this example, the finance director had incorrectly credited the fair value gain on investment property to the revaluation reserve. The finance director's accounting treatment is incorrect and understates profit. The auditor should request that the £50,000 be removed from equity and reported in profit or loss. If the error is not corrected and is material, the auditor would have to express a modified audit opinion.

You can see from this example that there are a few ways in which revalued assets can cause problems for the auditor and it is important, therefore, that the auditor clearly understands the requirements of the applicable financial reporting framework to ensure the audit client has accounted for fair value/revaluation gains and losses correctly.

Another audit risk concerns dividends paid to ordinary shareholders. If a dividend has not been declared by the reporting date, the entity has no legal obligation at that date to pay a dividend and therefore no liability is recognized—even if the company has paid dividends in previous years as normal practice. Only when a dividend has been properly declared is it legally binding on the entity. The audit risk is that a dividend may have been recognized in the financial statements that has not been properly declared resulting in overstated liabilities and understated equity. Conversely, a dividend that has been properly declared by the reporting date but not paid until after the reporting date may not have been recognized as a liability despite the entity having a legal obligation at the reporting date. This would mean that liabilities are understated and equity is overstated.

15.4.3 **Audit procedures**

In respect of the entity's share capital, the auditor should carry out the following procedures:

- Agree share capital and nominal value of share capital to underlying shareholder agreements/statutory records, such as share certificates (verifies *existence* and *completeness*).
- Agree prior year amounts of share capital have been properly brought forward (verifies *completeness*).
- For share issues during the year, agree the proceeds from the share issue to the cash book and bank statements (verifies *existence* and *completeness*).
- For share issues at a premium, agree the split of the issue between par value and premium and ensure they have been correctly allocated into ordinary share capital and share premium (verifies *presentation*).
- For shares called up but not yet paid, agree that these have been correctly presented as 'Called-up share capital not paid' (verifies *presentation*).
- Inspect board minutes to verify the issue of share capital during the year (verifies *existence*).

In respect of the entity's retained earnings, the auditor should carry out the following procedures:

- Agree prior year reserves have been correctly brought forward into the current year and reconcile all movements (verifies *completeness*).
- Agree movements in reserves to supporting documentation—for example, agree movements on the revaluation reserve to the valuation report (verifies *accuracy* and *completeness*).
- For non-distributable reserves, where presented, ensure these have been correctly segregated and reconcile the movements on the non-distributable reserve (verifies *accuracy* and *presentation*).

In respect of dividends declared and paid by the entity, the auditor should carry out the following procedures:

- Inspect board minutes for evidence that the dividend has been declared at, or prior to, the reporting date (verifies *rights and obligations*).
- Recalculate the dividend based on the announced dividend per share and agree the amount to the general ledger, trial balance and financial statements (verifies *accuracy* and *completeness* (of liabilities)).
- Agree the dividend to the post-year-end cash book and bank statement (verifies *completeness*).
- Ensure the dividend has been included as a movement on equity and not as an expense in profit or loss (verifies *presentation*).
- Review the financial statement disclosures in respect of the dividend and ensure compliance with the applicable financial reporting framework and company law (verifies *presentation*).

Chapter round-up

- The auditor is primarily concerned with the completeness of liabilities and, in particular, whether liabilities have been understated.
- Payables may need to be accrued for depending on the date on which the payables ledger is closed. Accruals represent goods and/or services received up to the reporting date that have not yet been invoiced. The auditor needs to carefully consider cut-offs when auditing payables and accruals.
- Reconciling items on the payables ledger control account should be carefully examined by the auditor because these may represent errors (the control account should agree to the list of payables outstanding at the reporting date).
- Tax liabilities include amounts of current tax (e.g. corporation tax) payable on the company's profits at the reporting date.
- Provisions are liabilities of uncertain timing or amount and are recognized in the financial statements when three criteria are met. The auditor must ensure that contingent liabilities are adequately disclosed where material.
- Provisions and contingencies are often difficult to audit because of the level of subjectivity involved.
- Financial liabilities can be complicated transactions to account for which gives rise to an automatic inherent risk of material misstatement.
- There is a risk of management manipulation of debt balances, as there may be pressure to 'window-dress' the financial statements using off-balance-sheet finance arrangements.
- Equity can comprise several items and the auditor should verify that all movements in each component of equity is correctly stated.
- Revaluation gains arising on property revaluations need careful consideration as the gains and losses are recognized differently for items of property, plant, and equipment compared to investment property.
- Dividends must only be recognized as a liability when the entity has declared them at, or prior to, the reporting date.

End of chapter case study

Introduction

The ability to design appropriate audit procedures is a key skill which auditors must possess. While some 'standard' audit procedures which can be applied to any audit client are useful, it is usually necessary to tailor audit procedures to fit the particular circumstances of the audit client. This is the best way to ensure that sufficient, appropriate evidence is obtained for all of the relevant assertions for a specific balance or transaction.

This activity will test your ability to design audit procedures for use in obtaining sufficient, appropriate evidence in relation to several types of liabilities.

This activity links to the following learning outcomes:

- Design and explain the audit procedures relevant to provisions and contingent liabilities.
- Design and explain the audit procedures relevant to loans and debt (financial liabilities).

Scenario

You are auditing Lavender Ltd, a company which manufactures household electrical items such as washing machines, cookers, and dishwashers. The company's financial year ended on 31 December 20X8. You have been assigned to the audit of provisions and you also have information relating to a debt instrument which the company issued during the year. Information about two provisions and the debt instrument, all of which are material to the financial statements, is given below.

Warranty

Lavender Ltd's products are all sold with a two-year warranty, under the terms of which products can be returned and either repaired by Lavender Ltd or replaced with a new product if they cannot be repaired. Your firm's technical advisory department have confirmed that the warranty provision should be determined in accordance with IAS 37.

The finance director has estimated that a warranty provision of £1.4 million should be recognized this year end. This estimate is an expected value, based on past experience of the proportion of warranty claims made applied to this year's sales. In the previous year, a warranty provision of £1.6 million was recognized.

Restructuring

On 1 November 20X8, the board of directors of Lavender Ltd agreed a restructuring plan which will make the company more cost-effective and competitive. On 1 December 20X8, Lavender Ltd announced the closure of its largest factory because production is moving overseas. This is a significant restructuring, which will take place over the next nine months. As a result of the factory closure, 600 staff will be made redundant, and 150 will be retrained to work in a different factory. A provision of £4 million has been recognized in respect of the restructuring which is made up as follows:

Redundancy costs	£2 million
Retraining costs	£1.5 million
Factory disposal costs	£0.5 million

Convertible debt

On 1 January 20X8, Lavender Ltd issued a £6 million debenture at par. The debenture carries interest at 2 per cent, payable in arrears on 31 December. The debt is redeemable after five years, at which point the holder of the debenture has the option to convert their holding into debenture into ten million £1 ordinary shares in Lavender Ltd. In the draft financial statements, the debt is recognized within non-current liabilities at a value of £6 million.

Required

For each of the matters described above, explain any relevant risks of material misstatement.

You should recommend the audit procedures to be performed including a brief explanation of the purpose of the procedure.

Answer

Warranty provision

A provision should be recognized if there is a probable outflow of economic benefit as a result of an obligation which can be reliably estimated. The sale of products under a warranty gives rise to a legal obligation and it is appropriate for the finance director to estimate the value of the provision.

IAS 37 requires a best estimate to be used to measure provisions, and for a large population of items, an expected value should be used.

The provision has reduced in value by £200,000, which is a reduction of 12.5 per cent. This could indicate an under-provision, unless significant improvements had been made to the quality of Lavender Ltd's products meaning that fewer claims are likely to be made under the warranty.

Audit procedures should include:

- Obtain a copy of the terms of sale offered to customers to confirm the length of the warranty period and the terms of the warranty.
- Discuss the basis of the expected value calculation with the finance director to confirm the basis of measuring the provision (e.g. the rate of return of different product lines).
- Reperform the expected value calculation to check for arithmetical accuracy.
- Analytically review the provision in comparison to previous years, disaggregated as far as possible (e.g. across different product lines). Discuss significant variances with the finance director to try to obtain explanations for the variances.
- Inquire for reasons why the provision is 12.5 per cent less than the previous year (e.g. have some items with a high return rate in the past now been withdrawn from sale? Have significant improvements been made to product quality? Have the terms of the warranty changed to make it more difficult for goods to be returned?).
- Analyse the level of returns received after the year end, and confirm that the provision appears adequate.
- Review correspondence with customers during the year end to gain an understanding of the level of claims and adequacy of the provision.
- Review board minutes for discussion of ongoing warranty claims, and approval of the amount provided.
- Use management accounts to ascertain normal level of warranty rectification costs during the year.
- Compare the prior year provision with actual expenditure on warranty claims in the accounting period to assess the adequacy of the prior year provision.

Restructuring

IAS 37 requires that in order for a restructuring provision to be recognized, there must be a present obligation as a result of a past event. For a restructuring, an obligation only exists when a detailed formal plan is in place and the entity has started to implement the plan, or announced its main features to those affected. It is therefore appropriate to recognize the provision at the 31 December year end because the announcement to employees was made on 1 December.

However, the retraining costs should not be included in the provision. This is because IAS 37 requires that costs associated with the ongoing activities of the business should not be provided. Currently, the provision is overstated by £1.5 million, and operating expenses are also overstated. The auditor should discuss this with management who should correct the error, resulting in a provision of £2.5 million being recognized.

Audit procedures should include:

- Read minutes of board meetings where the restructuring plan was discussed and approved, in order to gain an understanding of the business rationale.
- Confirm the date on which the plan was publicly announced, using supporting documentation such as press releases, notifications to employees, internal meetings held with employees, and trade union representatives.

- Obtain a copy of the announcement and review for details (e.g. to confirm the factory closure and the number of employees to be made redundant).
- Agree the £2 million redundancy cost to supporting documentation (e.g. a schedule indicating the number and grade of staff to be made redundant).
- For a sample of those to be made redundant, confirm the redundancy payment to payroll and employment contract details.
- Obtain a breakdown of the factory closure costs and arithmetically check to ensure accuracy.
- Scrutinize the list of factory closure costs to ensure they are all eligible to be included in the provision (i.e. they are direct costs of the restructuring and not related to ongoing business activities).
- Agree a sample of the factory closure costs to supporting documentation (e.g. quotes for dismantling plant and equipment.
- Using the results of the discussion with management, assess the planned restructuring in the context of the auditor's knowledge of the business, considering whether any further costs are likely to be incurred.
- Review the post-year-end cash book to identify whether any redundancy payments have been made, compare actual payments to the amounts provided to evaluate the completeness of the provision.
- Obtain a written representation from management to confirm the completeness of the provision.
- Review the disclosure of the provision to ensure compliance with IAS 37.

Convertible debt

The convertible debt should be split into its equity and liability components. It is not correct to recognize the full £6 million within liabilities.

The liability element should be calculated as the present value of the future cash flows of the debenture, discounted using the discount rate that would apply to a similar loan without the conversion option. The remainder of the £6 million proceeds represents the fair value of the right to convert, and this element of the proceeds received should be classified as equity. If no correction is made, equity is understated and liabilities overstated. The issue should be discussed with management, who should determine the liability–equity split, and adjust the financial statements accordingly.

Audit procedures would include:

- Obtain a copy of the debt agreement to confirm the terms of the loan including the maturity date, terms of conversion, and the date and amount of the annual interest payments.
- Recalculate the equity element of the proceeds received, using interest rates quoted for similar debt without conversion rights.
- Agree the £6m cash receipt on 1 January 20X8 and the interest payment of £120,000 made on 31 December 20X4 to bank statement and cash book.
- Review the board minutes to confirm the approval of the convertible debt being issued.
- Reperform the calculation of the split of the proceeds between debt and equity, and request that management amend the amounts recognized in the financial statements accordingly.

Activity solutions

Activity 15.1—Assertions for trade payables

Explain how the following assertions relate to the audit of trade payables: Completeness, existence, valuation, rights, and obligations.

Suggested answer points:

- Completeness: are all trade payables balances recorded in the accounts and recognized as liabilities in the financial statements?
- Existence: do all trade payables relate to valid purchases and do all the associated liabilities exists at the year end?
- Valuation: are trade payables balances accurately valued—for example, having accounted for VAT and discounts received from suppliers?
- Rights and obligations: are the trade payables balances actually obligations of the company—for example, they relate to goods received or services incurred by the year end?

Activity 15.2—Indicators of incomplete payables and accruals

Imagine you are auditing a company's payables and accruals. From a review of the company's accounting records, what might indicate to you that there are unrecorded payables and accruals?

Suggested answer points:

- The payables ledger appears to be missing balances relating to major suppliers
- Suppliers with significant balances outstanding at the previous year end are not in the payables ledger.
- Balances that are usually accrued for (e.g. electricity, rent) are not on the list of accruals.
- The current ratio shows an unexplained improvement (current ratio measures current assets: current liabilities, so an improvement means either (or both) an increase in current assets and a decrease in current liabilities)

Activity 15.3—Provision for a legal claim

Imagine a simple situation involving a provision—an audit client is involved with a legal claim, as a result of which the company may have to pay damages of £500,000.

How might you obtain evidence in respect of this, to help you decide if a provision should be recognized?

Suggested answer points:

- Discuss the facts of the legal claim with the client's management to verify whether an obligation exists, ask them to confirm the situation that has led to the legal claim against the company, and when it occurred.
- Obtain confirmation from the client's legal advisers or in-house legal team as to the possible outcome and probability of having to make a payment.
- Obtain and review correspondence between the company and the claimant/their legal representatives.
- Review subsequent events—by the time the final audit is taking place the legal claim may have been resolved.
- Obtain a letter of representation from the client as the matter is one of judgement and uncertainty.

Activity 15.4—Auditing contingent liabilities

It can be difficult to obtain audit evidence on contingent liabilities because they relate to uncertain future events or outcomes.

Can you suggest some ways that auditors can obtain relevant evidence?

Suggested answer points:

- Review board minutes for evidence of discussion of significant events which could give rise to contingent liabilities (e.g. court cases, breaches of law and regulations).
- Review relevant business websites or journals for new or other indications of industry-wide situations which could create contingent liabilities (e.g. possible fines to be imposed).
- Discuss with management their approach to identifying possible contingent liabilities—this should be part of the entity's risk management process.
- Obtain correspondence files relating to the entity's legal advisers and review contents for any relevant information.

16 Auditing Income and Expenses

Introduction

In Chapters 14 and 15 we looked at the audit of the statement of financial position (balance sheet) including assets, liabilities, and equity. In this chapter we look at how the auditor gathers sufficient and appropriate audit evidence over an entity's income and expenditure which are included in the statement of profit or loss.

Unlike the statement of financial position which presents the assets, liabilities, and equity of the business as at the close of business on the last day of the reporting period (i.e. a 'snapshot' of the company's financial position at the year end); the statement of profit or loss shows the performance of the business from the first day of the reporting period to the last. The statement of profit or loss is used to show how profitable a company is as well as the different types of income streams it has to generate a profit. It is sometimes referred to as a 'performance statement' as it presents the company's financial performance during the year.

As well as shareholders, banks, financiers, and potential investors will all be interested in the statement of profit or loss to determine whether the company's profits will generate an adequate return in the form of interest or dividends. The higher the profit, the more comfortable a potential investor will be in making an investment or a bank in providing a loan.

A risk for the auditor when examining income and expense is the issue of earnings management, which occurs when companies deliberately manipulate their revenues and/or expenses in order to inflate (or deflate) figures relating to profits and earnings per share. In other words, it is when companies use 'creative accounting' to construct reported figures that show the position and performance that management want to show. Preparers of financial information are often under pressure from other members of the senior management team to present a certain level of profitability. This is especially the case when going concern is a problem, when a company's revenue may have reduced significantly, or if profit is being eroded by significant expenses arising from asset impairments or other exceptional losses.

Before we explore how an auditor gathers sufficient and appropriate audit evidence over income and expenditure, it is worthwhile looking at how certain items in the statement of profit or loss are distinguished according to the IASB's *Conceptual Framework for Financial Reporting* (Conceptual Framework).

The Conceptual Framework recognizes that income encompasses both revenue and gains and it is important to understand the distinction between the two. Revenue arises in the ordinary activities of the entity. Revenue is often referred to as 'sales' or 'turnover' and is derived from the entity's day-to-day activities. For example, a manufacturer of chemicals will generate revenue from selling those chemical products to its customers; and a retailer of clothing will generate revenue from selling its clothing products to members of the public. The Conceptual Framework also recognizes that revenue can be called different things, for example fees or royalties.

Gains, on the other hand, are not revenue. The Conceptual Framework recognizes that gains represent other items which meet the definition of income and may, or may not, arise in the ordinary activities of the entity. Gains which are recognized as part of profit may arise from:

- A profit on disposal of an item of non-current assets;
- Fair value gains on the revaluation of investment property; or
- A gain on an investment measured at fair value.

As we saw in Chapter 14, some gains might be recognized outside of profit or loss—for example, where the entity has a revaluation gain on an item of property, plant, and equipment in which case the credit (the gain) is taken to a revaluation surplus and reported in the financial statements as other comprehensive income rather than as income in the statement of profit or loss.

Expenses are costs which the entity incurs in carrying out its principal activity and will usually include items such as:

- Cost of sales
- Payroll costs
- Depreciation
- Overheads such as rent and rates, electricity and insurance.

In addition, expenses can also encompass losses. Losses may, or may not, arise in the ordinary course of activities of the entity. The Conceptual Framework recognizes that losses represent decreases in economic benefits so they are not really any different in nature from other expenses. Examples of losses incurred by a business include:

- A loss on disposal of an item of non-current assets;
- A fair value loss on the revaluation of an investment property;
- A decline in fair value of an investment measured at fair value; and
- An impairment loss on an item of property, plant, and equipment.

Losses are recognized as a debit in the trial balance and contribute to a reduction in profit or an increase in a loss.

Learning outcomes

- Design and explain audit procedures to obtain sufficient and appropriate audit evidence over an entity's revenue and gains.
- Design and explain audit procedures to obtain sufficient and appropriate audit evidence over different expense cycles of the business including cost of sales, administrative expenses, and other expenses.
- Design and explain audit procedures to obtain sufficient and appropriate audit evidence over directors' remuneration and payroll costs.

16.1 Revenue

16.1.1 Accounting treatment

In many audits, revenue is not complex or subjective because revenue recognition is as simple as raising an invoice for goods or services sold to a customer. There are still audit risks to be considered, but the accounting treatment is straightforward and there is a relatively low level of risk of material misstatement.

16.1.1.1 Key assertions

The key assertions which the auditor is concerned with in respect of revenue are:

- Cut-off: sales are recognized in the correct accounting period
- Accuracy: sales are recognized in the financial statements at correct amounts and related disclosures have been appropriately measured and described
- Completeness: all sales that should have been recorded have been recorded, and all related disclosures that should have been included have been included
- Occurrence: sales recorded and disclosed have occurred and relate to the entity

However, in some audits, revenue can give rise to a high level of audit risk. The application of IFRS 15 *Revenue from Contracts with Customers* can add a layer of complexity and judgement which auditors will need to carefully consider. This is because some revenue - generating activities are complex and judgement may be needed in determining the timing of revenue recognition and the measurement of revenue.

It is also the one figure that is singled out by the International Standards on Auditing (ISAs) as containing a risk of material misstatement due to fraud, so the auditor needs to tread very carefully where revenue is concerned.

We won't be going through the detailed accounting for revenue because we are primarily concerned with how revenue is to be audited. However, we do think it is important that we give a general overview of the accounting requirements in IFRS 15 purely because it is such an important topic.

There are five criteria in IFRS 15, all of which must be met, before the entity can recognize revenue (Figure 16.1). The idea behind these steps is that the entity recognizes the correct amount of revenue at the correct point in time. For some entities this will be fairly straightforward, however, for others, especially those that are involved in more complex activities, such as construction companies, revenue recognition can be a difficult issue to account for.

The five-step model approach to revenue recognition incorporated within IFRS 15 is as follows:

So, from an accounting perspective, it is crucial that the entity has a sound system in place that enables its revenue recognition controls to comply with IFRS 15. The auditor will need to gather sufficient appropriate audit evidence that provides reasonable assurance that the entity has recognized the right amount of revenue at an appropriate time. Remember, revenue is a particularly sensitive area of the financial statements because it can easily be manipulated to achieve a desired outcome. For example, management may want to inflate the revenue figure to achieve a higher profit, particularly where profit- or sales-related bonuses are concerned. On the flip side, management may want to suppress revenue to reduce profits to achieve a lower tax liability.

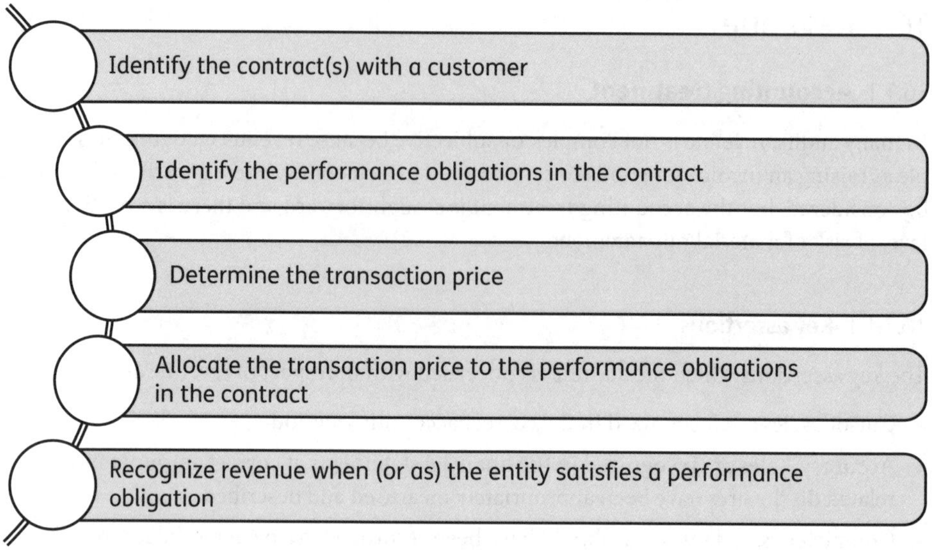

Figure 16.1 Five step model for revenue recognition

16.1.2 **Audit risks**

The most significant audit risk is that revenue could be materially overstated. There are several ways that revenue can be overstated, either by error, or intentionally (Figure 16.2).

Overstated revenue distorts the financial statements by falsely improving the financial performance of the business for the year and could lead a potential investor/financier into believing the entity is more successful than it is. Deliberate overstatement of revenue also affects the statement of financial position because the trade receivables figure in current assets will also be inflated by the value of the overstatement.

Activity 16.1 Audit risks relating to revenue

Here is a short scenario to explore audit risks relating to revenue.

Trinity Ltd sells garden furniture and the audit team is working on the audit of revenue for the current accounting period. The draft financial statements include revenue of £3.5 million.

Audit procedures have revealed that on the last day of the accounting period, sales invoices totalling £90,000 were posted, but the inventory to which these invoices relate was still in Trinity's warehouse until three days after the year end.

The audit team is aware that Trinity Ltd has in place a bonus scheme for management based on the company meeting certain targets, one of which is based on revenue growth.

What are the audit risks indicated in this scenario?

Deliberately manipulating the financial statements to show a desired financial performance or financial position is a criminal offence and auditors can also be questioned where it is proved that an entity has committed such an act. This is why auditors must always demonstrate **professional scepticism** which allows them to maintain a questioning mind and challenge management's assertions within the financial statements.

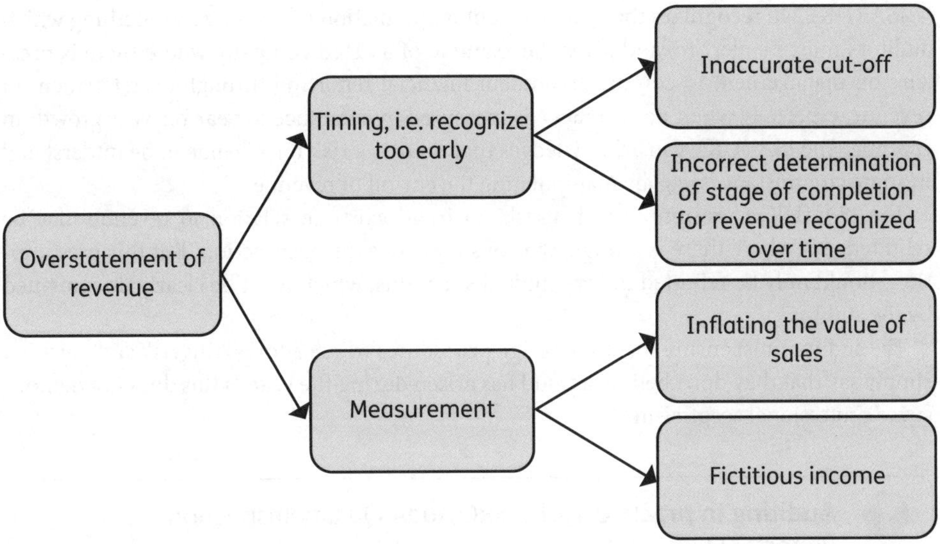

Figure 16.2 Methods of overstatement of revenue

Auditors are particularly interested in ensuring that the company's revenue is recognized at an appropriate time and at an appropriate amount, i.e. measured appropriately.

Timing, i.e. when revenue is recognized, can be a significant risk. This could happen because the entity has recognized sales in the current year's financial statements that should be recognized in the next period and could be due to incorrect cut-offs—this can be due to errors in the accounting system or deliberate manipulation. In more complex situations, where revenue is being recognized over time, e.g. when an entity is providing a service which spans several accounting periods, judgement is needed in determining the stage of completion of the service being provided. If this judgement is not appropriate, revenue can be recognized too early (or too late).

In terms of measurement of revenue, there could be problems in how the entity has applied the requirements of IFRS 15, resulting in inflated revenue. This could happen for example when revenue is measured at fair value, and management has used inappropriate assumptions to determine the fair value. The entity could also deliberately overstate its revenue figure by recognizing fictitious revenue, i.e. sales that are not genuine and have not actually occurred (see the occurrence assertion above).

16.1.3 **Fraud risks**

We looked at ISA (UK) 240 *The Auditor's Responsibilities Relating to Fraud in an Audit of Financial Statements* in Chapter 13. It's worth reminding ourselves at this point that ISA 240 contains a specific requirement in relation to the audit of revenue:

> When identifying and assessing the risks of material misstatement due to fraud, the auditor shall, based on a presumption that there are risks of fraud in revenue recognition, evaluate which types of revenue, revenue transactions or assertions give rise to such risks.[1]

[1] Financial Reporting Council, 'ISA (UK) 240', 2022, para 27 <https://media.frc.org.uk/documents/ISA_UK_240_Updated_May_2022.pdf> (accessed 18 January 2024).

ISA (UK) 240 recognizes that management manipulation of revenue is something which auditors must be alert to, and gives the example of a listed company where there is pressure on management to commit fraudulent financial reporting through overstatement of revenue, especially when performance is measured by reference to year-on-year growth in revenue. The ISA (UK) also acknowledges that there is a risk for revenue to be understated in some circumstances, e.g. by manipulating the cut-off of revenue.

The ISA (UK's) presumption that risks of fraud exists in relation to revenue may be rebutted, e.g. where there is a single type of simple revenue transaction. But this presumption should only be rebutted in very limited situations, which must be clearly documented by the auditor.

The auditor must ensure that they design procedures which address this risk and must not simply say that they don't believe a fraud has arisen during the year as this does not demonstrate professional scepticism.

Auditing in practice 16.1 FRC Audit Quality Inspection Report 2022

The FRC's Audit Quality Inspection Report in 2022 highlighted that the audit of revenue needs to be improved at many of the large audit firms. The report states that the inspection teams found numerous examples of where the audit teams did not obtain sufficient audit evidence over the revenue recognized in respect of:

- Long-term contracts, including inadequate challenge of significant judgements and accounting treatment.
- Sample testing, including where some of the revenue had not been subject to sample testing.
- Substantive analytical procedures, including not corroborating material differences identified or not adequately setting the expectation for the level of revenue.[2]

The FRC also found instances of poor sampling techniques being applied, for example, not testing revenue from across the year, not testing the completeness of revenue, and not obtaining sufficient appropriate evidence in relation to journals made to revenue figures. In addition, there was sometimes a lack of challenge to management where assumptions were important in determining the recognition of revenue.

These findings show that even the biggest audit firms sometimes need to improve the quality of their audit work in respect of revenue. This is particularly concerning given that there is a presumption of fraud risk in respect of revenue.

16.1.4 **Audit procedures**

For revenue, the auditor should carry out the following **substantive procedures**:

- Inspect a sample of goods dispatched notes (GDNs) before and after the year end and ensure they have been recorded in the correct accounting period (verifies *cut-off*).
- Recalculate any sales discounts and sales tax applied for a representative sample of sales invoices (verifies *accuracy*).

[2] Financial Reporting Council, 'Tier 1 Firms – Overview, Audit Quality Inspection and Supervision Report', FRC, 2022 <https://media.frc.org.uk/documents/FRC_Audit_Quality_Inspection_and_Supervision_Public_Report_2022_-_Tier_1_Firms_Overview.pdf> (accessed 19 January 2024).

- Select a sample of GDNs and agree these to sales invoices and follow through to inclusion in the sales day book (verifies *completeness*).
- Inspect post-year-end credit notes, trace to the GDN and sales invoice and if the credit note relates to a pre-year-end sale, ensure the sale has been reversed (verifies *occurrence*).
- Recalculate amounts of deferred income at the year end and agree this amount to the statement of financial position (verifies *completeness* (of revenue and liabilities) and *accuracy*).
- For a sample of service revenue invoices, agree service revenue has been recognized when the contractual obligations to the customer have been fulfilled and any remaining obligations are recognized as deferred income (verifies *occurrence* and *completeness*).

Tests of control over revenue which the auditor should carry out are as follows:

- Ensure the sales system only accepts orders which can be fulfilled (goods not dispatched promptly can result in a loss of customer goodwill). Attempt to enter an order for goods which are out of stock and the system should reject the order.
- Inspect GDNs for evidence of being matched to invoices to ensure the invoice is raised from the GDN and not the original order.
- Inspect a sample of sales invoices for evidence of approval by a responsible official prior to it being sent to the customer.
- Obtain a copy of the entity's price list which is currently in use and for a sample of sales invoices ensure that correct prices have been used.
- Enquire of management who has the authority to amend standing data in the sales system (such as amending customer discounts). Try to input a change of standing data using the ID of an employee not authorized to make such a change and ensure the system does not allow the change to be made.
- With the client's permission, attempt to process an invoice with a sales discount without authorization from a responsible official. The system should reject the discount and the invoice.
- For sales orders where discounts are given, review the order for evidence of a signature approving the discount by a responsible official.
- For a sample of customers who are entitled to discounts, review the credit agreement for evidence that the discount has been approved by a responsible official.

Analytical procedures which the auditor should carry out over the entity's revenue are as follows:

- Compare the revenue figure in the current year to the prior year and investigate any significant fluctuations.
- Compare revenue with the entity's budgets/forecasts and investigate any significant fluctuations.
- Where budgets/forecasts are prepared on a monthly or quarterly basis, disaggregate the revenue for the current year and compare each month/quarter against budget and investigate any significant differences.

- Compare revenue against industry averages or benchmarks and investigate any significant fluctuations.
- Calculate the gross profit margin (gross profit/sales x 100) and compare to the prior year and investigate any significant fluctuations.

Activity 16.2 Audit procedures over revenue

Here is a short scenario to practice designing audit procedures over revenue:

Stour Ltd manufactures four types of engine which are used in large vehicles. Sales are made to commercial customers through the company's team of business development managers. Each business development manager can allow a discount of up to 5% on list price, with all discounts needing approval of the company's sales director. Customer orders are taken by the business development managers, who then inform the warehouse. At the point at which an engine is despatched, a Goods Despatch Note is raised and a sales invoice generated, based on the customer order details.

Can you recommend four audit procedures relevant to the audit of Stour Ltd's revenue?

16.1.5 **Revenue recognized over time**

So far, we have only considered the audit of a simple revenue transaction. However, many organizations have more complex arrangements relating to their revenue, which create specific risks which the auditor needs to evaluate and address. We don't have scope in our discussion to cover many of these more complex issues, but we will address some of the most common:

- When a company is constructing an asset for a customer, and
- When a company is providing several goods or services to its customers at the same time.

Construction contracts are often long-term contracts under which the company agrees to create an asset for a customer such as a building or infrastructure, e.g. road or railway. IFRS 15 allows revenue and profit to be recognized over time, and the company needs to determine the stage of completion of the contract at the year end, as a basis for estimating how much of the revenue and profit it is appropriate to recognize. Simply put, if a contract which commenced during the year is say 40 per cent complete at the year end, the accounting treatment would be to recognize 40 per cent of the revenue and profit this year.

The risk for the auditor in this case is that the estimate of percentage completion can be a matter of judgement. Various methods are allowed for the basis of this estimate, e.g. by reference to cost incurred to date compared to the total estimated contract cost, or by reference to sales value. Robust audit procedures need to be performed to obtain evidence surrounding the percentage completion which has been determined.

Auditing scenario 16.1 Construction contract audit issues

Bluebottle Ltd, which has a financial year ended 31 March 20X5, is working on a major contract relating to the construction of a road for its customer Dragonfly Ltd. Work on the contract started in July 20X4, and it is estimated that the contract will be completed in September 20X5. The contract price is £10 million, and it is estimated that a profit of £2 million will be made on completion of the contract.

Bluebottle Ltd's management team has estimated that the contract is 70% complete by the year end. This estimate is based on a comparison of the total costs which were incurred on the contract up to 31 March 20X5, which amounted to £5.6 million. Total estimated contract costs are £8 million.

On this basis, revenue of £7 million (£10 million contract price x 70%) and costs of £5.6 million will be recognized in the financial statements to 31 March 20X5, resulting in profit recognized of £1.4 million (£2 million estimated profit x 70%).

The auditors of Bluebottle Ltd should clarify that the company's accounting policy is to measure revenue and profit by reference to costs. Evidence should be obtained to determine the stage of completion of this contract at the reporting date, including:

- The contract terms should be scrutinized to agree the fixed price of £10 million and to evaluate terms and conditions e.g. terms relating to completion of stages of the contract which may trigger the recognition of contract revenue at a specific point in time.
- Surveys of work performed by 31 March 20X5 should be reviewed to estimate the stage of completion at the reporting date.
- Discuss the contract with the project manager or other appropriate personnel to assess if the percentage completion appears reasonable, if any cost overruns are expected and if the timeframe for completion of the contract is feasible.
- A sample of costs should be agreed back to supporting documentation such as suppliers' invoices and labour costs.
- The road should be physically seen by the audit team, to ensure its existence and to obtain understanding of the completeness of the road.
- Correspondence with Dragonfly should be read to confirm that the contract is progressing in a satisfactory way.

Another common issue with revenue, which increases audit risk, is when a combination of goods and services are provided as a 'bundle' to the customer. This means that the customer is paying for two distinct goods or services as part of one contract. Here are a few examples to illustrate when this might happen:

- A telecommunications company provides a free iPhone to each customer who signs up for access to their mobile phone network. The iPhone is a distinct good, separate from the provision of access to the mobile phone network.
- A car manufacturer sells cars to its customers with an agreement within the sales contract to provide free service and maintenance for the car for a period of two years. The service and maintenance is a distinct service, separate from the sale of the car.

You can see from these examples how common the provision of multiple goods or services can be. IFRS 15 requires a specific accounting treatment here, based on the fact that the products or services are distinct. Without going into all of the detail, the company selling the 'bundle' of goods and services is required to split the revenue between the two elements and recognize revenue when the separate performance obligations are met. So, using the car example to illustrate, the car manufacturer would recognize the revenue allocated to the sale of the car immediately, once the customer has taken delivery of the car, and part of the revenue relating to the service and maintenance would be deferred and recognized over a two-year period.

Audit risk arises due to the complexity of the accounting treatment. In particular, how the revenue is allocated between the distinct goods and services can be tricky to determine, and as with anything complex or subjective, an inherent risk of error exists.

Auditing in practice 16.2 Vodafone Key Audit Matters

Revenue is a high-risk audit area in the telecoms industry, and it is common to see auditor's reports on their telecoms clients to refer to revenue recognition as a Key Audit Matter. To illustrate, here is an extract from the annual report of Vodafone Group plc for the year ended 31 March 2020, where the auditor, EY LLP, describes the Key Audit Matter relating to revenue recognition as follows:

> Risk
>
> Under IFRS 15, management must determine if there are separate performance obligations for the services and goods it provides to customers and assign values thereto, based on the selling prices of goods or services in separate transactions under similar conditions to similar customers (the 'stand-alone selling price'). Determining the stand-alone selling price and therefore the allocation of revenue to the different performance obligations, which impacts timing of the related revenue recognition, is complex and judgemental. In addition, auditing the revenue recorded by the Group is complex due to the multiple IT systems and tools utilised in the initiation, processing and recording of transactions, which includes a high volume of individually low monetary value transactions. Complex auditor judgement was involved, and IT professionals were utilised, in the design of the audit approach and testing of IT systems and automated processes, as well as manual adjustments made to the underlying data recorded by the IT systems, to recognise revenue in accordance with IFRS 15.
>
> Our response to the risk
>
> Our audit procedures included, among others, obtaining an understanding of, evaluating the design and testing the operating effectiveness of controls over the Group's revenue recognition process, which includes management's review of contracts, their identification of performance obligations, the estimation of the relative standalone selling price for each performance obligation, and the determination of the timing of revenue recorded. We also evaluated the design and tested the operating effectiveness of controls over the processing of billing data, assisted by our IT professionals.
>
> We evaluated management's accounting policies and the methodology used by management to determine the standalone selling price, where relevant.
>
> In addition, our audit procedures included, testing of reconciliations between the data records from the billing systems to the general ledger. Also, on a sample of basis:

- we tested the accuracy of the billing data used in the IFRS 15 accounting process;
- assessed the determination of performance obligations;
- compared the standalone selling price to observable pricing;
- recalculated the allocation of revenue between performance obligations and the revenue recognised during the period; and
- tested the associated manual and automated adjustments posted in the general ledger to record revenue.[3]

[3] Vodafone Group plc, 'Annual Report 2020', 2020 <https://www.vodafone.com/content/dam/vodcom/files/vdf_files_2020/pdfs/vodafone-annual-report-2020.pdf> (accessed 19 January 2024).

16.2 Purchases and expenses

Purchases are usually 'direct costs' of a business. For example, a retailer of goods has to purchase those goods from a wholesaler and the cost of those goods to the retailer form part of its purchases for the year. Purchases are usually referred to as 'cost of sales' in the financial statements. Table 16.1 shows hoe cost of sales is calculated.

Table 16.1

	£
Opening inventory	X
Plus purchases	X
	X
Less closing inventory	(X)—per the statement of financial position
Cost of sales	X

Cost of sales usually appears as a single line item in the 'trading account' which appears on the face of the statement of profit and loss and is deducted from revenue to determine gross profit.

16.2.1 Purchases—audit risks

The most common audit risk is that purchases are incomplete at the reporting date. Incomplete purchases will mean that cost of sales is understated and hence so are liabilities (i.e. trade payables or accruals). This is because of the double-entry when a company incurs costs on credit:

Dr Cost of sales/other expenses (statement of profit or loss)	X
Cr Trade payables/accruals (statement of financial position)	X

It could also be the case that cut-off is incorrect and so the company could have recognized purchases that belong in the next accounting period, hence cost of sales are overstated meaning liabilities in the statement of financial position are also overstated. Over or understated cost of sales and associated liabilities can present a very misleading picture in the financial statements and can distort the gross profit margin.

As we saw in Chapter 14, when an auditor is carrying out the audit of a company's inventory, work can also be performed on purchases at the same time, such as verifying whether purchase invoices have been authorized or have been included in the general (nominal) ledger at the correct value. This is because goods which have been purchased but not sold by the reporting date will be included in the company's closing inventory valuation.

As we know, when the auditor is planning the audit, they will carry out analytical procedures to identify where the risks of material misstatement may be in the financial statements. One tool which the auditor will use at the planning stage is ratio analysis to identify 'peaks and troughs' in certain areas of the financial statements which may be beyond the auditor's expectations, or which may be inconsistent with the auditor's knowledge and understanding of the entity. Where cost of sales is concerned, a key ratio the auditor uses is recalculation of the gross profit margin.

The gross profit margin represents the amount of profit made by the company simply by buying and selling goods. So, if a company makes 40 per cent gross profit margin, this means that for every £1 sold the company makes 40p gross profit. Deducted from this gross profit is the overhead expenditure (such as administration costs) which we will look at later in the chapter.

Ideally, a company wants its gross profit margin to be as high as possible because then the company will make more net profit (i.e. profit before tax). The lower the gross margin, the less profit before tax the company will make.

The gross profit margin for most entities remains relatively constant from one reporting period to another and so any significant variation in gross margin will usually indicate a risk of misstatement.

Auditing scenario 16.2 Calculation of gross profit margin for analytical purposes

Extracts from the draft financial statements of Whitaker Industries Ltd for the year ended 31 December 20X9 are as follows:

Table 16.2

	31.12.20X9	**31.12.20X8**
	£m	£m
Revenue	24.1	26.2
Cost of sales	(10.7)	(14.6)
Gross profit	13.4	11.6
Gross profit %	55.6%	44.2%

During the planning phase of the audit, the audit senior performed various analytical procedures. One of the points they noted is that the company's gross profit margin has increased from 44.2% in 20X8 (11.6/26.2) to 55.6% in 20X9 (13.4/24.1). The finance director was unable to provide any convincing reason as to why the gross profit margin should increase by some 11.4% when it has remained consistent over the last five years.

You are being assisted by an audit junior who has asked why this increase would matter and what audit procedures should be performed to address it.

Gross profit margins usually stay relatively constant from one reporting period to the next. The table below shows the potential reasons for the increased gross profit margin and the audit procedures which should be performed:

Table 16.3 Using gross profit margin analysis to plan audit procedures

Potential reason for the increase in gross margin	**Audit procedures**
Revenue has been overstated due to incorrect cut-off—i.e. sales in the next accounting period have been recognized in this year's financial statements.	Perform extended cut-off testing on the sales cycle ensuring that all goods sold immediately pre- and post-year end are recognized as sales in the correct accounting period.
Opening inventory has been brought forward into the current year's accounting records at an incorrect value.	Agree the opening inventory per the trial balance to the closing inventory in the prior year's audit working papers file and ensure that it has been brought forward correctly into the 20X9 general ledger.
Purchases have not been recorded completely due to incorrect cut-offs—i.e. purchase invoices relating to the 20X9 year have been recognized in the next accounting period.	As with revenue, perform extended cut-off testing to ensure that purchases have been recognized in the correct accounting period and that any goods or services received up to the year end but not yet invoiced have been recognized as accruals.

Potential reason for the increase in gross margin	Audit procedures
The year end inventory valuation is overstated.	Obtain the final inventory valuation and carry out substantive testing to ensure the **valuation** assertion is correct. Agree the final inventory valuation to the general ledger, trial balance and financial statements.
Direct costs have been included in overhead expenditure (administrative expenses).	Review the company's operating margin or carry out analytical review over the overhead expenditure items in the statement of profit or loss to identify any significant increase in the current year which may indicate that direct costs have been incorrectly classified as overhead costs.

16.2.2 **Audit procedures: purchases**

As we mentioned earlier, the auditor may carry out work that could be used in other areas of the audit. For example, whilst auditing the company's inventory, the auditor could carry out some procedures over purchases which could be used as audit evidence in the cost of sales audit as this may save time when carrying out substantive work.

Substantive procedures which the auditor should carry out over an entity's purchases include the following:

- Inspect goods received notes (GRNs) immediately pre- and post-year end and ensure they have been recorded in the correct accounting period (verifies *cut-off*).
- Select a sample of purchase orders and agree these to GRNs and purchase invoices and follow through to inclusion in the purchases day book (verifies *completeness*).
- Recalculate the values, including discounts, on a sample of purchase invoices (verifies *accuracy*).
- Recalculate value added tax (VAT) on a sample of purchase invoices (verifies *accuracy*).
- Enquire with management whether there have been any changes in key suppliers and compare this to the purchase ledger to assess *completeness* and *accuracy* of purchases.

Tests of control which the auditor may carry out over the purchases cycle of the business include the following:

- Inspect a sample of purchase orders to ensure they are generated by a central purchasing department (where one exists) rather than by individuals within the organization.
- Inspect a sample of purchase orders for evidence of authorization by a responsible individual (such as the purchasing manager or finance director) to ensure that only necessary goods and/or services are procured for the entity.
- For a sample of purchase orders, inspect the order and written confirmation from the supplier to ensure all (and only necessary) goods and services are received.
- Observe the ordering process in action to ensure that the ordering clerk checks inventory levels BEFORE ordering. This ensures that only necessary goods/services are ordered so company resources are not wasted.
- Inspect a sample of purchase orders for evidence that they have been authorized by a responsible official prior to the order being placed. In addition, observe a sample

of purchase orders being processed to ensure they have been authorized before the purchasing department places the order.

- Review the entity's procedures to ensure correct cut-offs over purchases and, for a sample of purchases immediately pre- and post-year end, carry out a review to ensure that the controls have operated effectively.
- For a sample of purchase orders, carry out sequence checks of order numbers for completeness.
- Review the entity's purchasing policy such as tendering processes and obtaining quotations to ensure the company is obtaining value for money.

The auditor should also carry out analytical procedures over the entity's cost of sales in the statement of profit or loss by calculating the gross profit margin for the current year and comparing it to the prior year, or reviewing actual costs against budgets. Any unusual fluctuations in cost of sales or the gross profit margin would need to be investigated as it could represent a material misstatement.

16.2.3 **Expenses**

So far we have concentrated on a company's direct costs—i.e. those costs which it incurs as a result of selling goods and/or services and which are referred to in the statement of profit or loss as cost of sales. A business will also incur overhead expenditure, the costs of which are necessary in order to continue running the business. Overhead expenditure appears underneath the gross profit line on the face of the statement of profit or loss and is classified accordingly.

Activity 16.3 Examples of overhead expenditure

List five examples of commonly incurred overhead expenditure.

The auditor must carry out procedures over a company's overhead expenditure to ascertain that it is correctly classified as overhead expenditure and not cost of sales and has been recorded in the financial statements at the correct amount. If a company's operating profit margin (operating profit/revenue x 100) has increased beyond expectations, this may indicate that overhead expenditure has been classified incorrectly as, say, cost of sales. This would also be reflected by a reduced gross profit margin and the auditor would then devise specific procedures to investigate the distortion.

16.2.4 **Expenses—audit risks**

As with cost of sales (purchases), the most common risk associated with expenditure is the completeness of expenses. A company must record all expenses incurred during the period in the right period.

At the year end, a company may not have received invoices for all goods received and services rendered up to the reporting date and up to the date on which it closes its purchase ledger. In this situation, the company must make accruals for goods and services received but not yet invoiced which relate to the accounting period. The auditor will need to be provided with a schedule of accrued expenditure so that audit procedures can be applied to ensure it is complete and valued appropriately.

Accruals may need to be estimated in some respects. Care must be taken with such estimates to ensure they are not too high or too low. Auditors will need to carefully check the client's estimates—for example, against prior years—to ensure they are reasonable, or by tracing the estimate to any invoices that have been received after the reporting date to compare the actual expense against the estimate.

A good tool the auditor can use to check whether there is a risk of misstatement in the accruals figure is to use analytical review. The auditor can compare the current year accruals total to the prior year's and devise procedures to investigate any significant differences—for example, an omission or an over/understatement.

Auditing scenario 16.3 Auditing accruals

You are carrying out the audit planning of an existing client, Osbourne Ltd, for the year ended 31 December 20X9. Preliminary analytical procedures that have been carried out over the overhead expenditure in the statement of profit or loss have revealed the following:

- Rent expense has reduced by 25% from the prior year
- Computer costs have increased by 45% from the prior year
- Repairs and renewals have increased by 60% from the prior year and include a large provision for work that is to be carried out next year

The audit engagement partner has asked you to devise initial responses to the above three issues which will go towards designing specific audit procedures to address the risk of material misstatement.

Rent expense

Rent would usually be regarded as a fixed overhead and hence would remain consistent (although there may be some increase in rent during the year due to, for example, annual rent increases per the lease agreement). However, in Osbourne's case, the rent expense has reduced by 25%. As 25% is equivalent to one-quarter, this may indicate that the year-end accrual has been missed meaning that rent expense and accruals are both understated in the draft financial statements. The auditor will need to review the rent account in detail, calculate any necessary accrual and agree this to the schedule of accruals.

Computer costs

Computer costs increasing by 45% may indicate that the company has written off items that are of a capital nature to the statement of profit or loss. This will overstate expenditure in the statement of profit or loss, reduce profit and understate non-current assets and depreciation charges. The auditor should obtain a schedule of computer expenses for the year and ensure that no items of a capital nature have been included.

Repairs and renewals provision

A provision has been included in repairs and renewals for future expenditure. A provision can only be recognized if the company has a legal or constructive obligation as a result of a past event and is likely to result in an outflow of economic benefits which can be measured reliably (IAS 37 *Provisions, Contingent Liabilities and Contingent Assets*). If the recognition criteria in IAS 37 is not met, the entity must not recognize a provision as this would overstate expenditure and liabilities and understate profit. If the provision does not meet the recognition criteria, the auditor must then consider whether the entity has a contingent liability that may need to be disclosed.

16.2.5 **Audit procedures: expenses**

Audit procedures that should be applied over the company's overhead expenditure should be a mix of substantive tests, tests of control, and analytical procedures. In some cases, there may be an opportunity for the auditor to use some of the work carried out in other areas (e.g. trade payables and accruals) as audit evidence over a company's expenditure.

Substantive procedures which the auditor should perform over an entity's overhead expenditure include the following:

- Obtain a schedule of accruals at the year end, inspect the date on the goods received note (GRN) to ensure they have been included within expenses in the correct accounting period and that goods received post-year end are not included (verifies *cut-off*).
- For a sample of expense accounts in the nominal (general) ledger, agree the entries to purchase invoices (verifies *accuracy* and *completeness*).
- Inspect unmatched GRNs not yet invoiced and if they relate to the current year agree to the schedule of accruals (verifies *completeness*).
- For GRNs immediately pre- and post-year end, ensure they have been recorded in the correct accounting period (verifies *cut-off*).
- Recalculate discounts for a sample of large purchases (verifies *accuracy*).

Tests of control the auditor may carry out over the entity's expenses include the following:

- For a sample of overhead expenses, review these to ensure they have been authorized by a responsible official and that official has signed within their limits (e.g. a purchasing manager may be able to authorize up to £5,000 and the purchasing director must authorize expenditure in excess of this amount).
- Observe the process for authorization of expenditure, particularly expenditure which is reimbursed to staff, to ensure it is authorized by a senior official before payment.

The auditor should carry out **analytical procedures** to identify possible sources of misstatement in overhead expenses as follows:

- Compare expenses for each category with the same category in the prior year and investigate any significant fluctuations (verifies *accuracy*, *completeness* and *occurrence*).
- Compare expenses against the company's budget and investigate any significant fluctuations (verifies *accuracy* and *completeness*).
- Calculate the operating profit margin and compare to the prior year and investigate any significant differences (verifies *accuracy*, *completeness* and *occurrence*).

- Calculate the gross profit margin and compare it to the prior year to identify any possible misstatement of purchases and overhead expenses (verifies *accuracy*, *completeness*, and *occurrence*).

16.3 Payroll and directors' remuneration

Payroll is a very sensitive area and it is important that the auditor observes confidentiality at all times where this is concerned.

Payroll is often a material area of the financial statements and there are various procedures which the auditor can use to verify:

- the total payroll charge in the statement of profit or loss; and
- associated payroll assets or liabilities which are owed to or by the entity at the reporting date.

16.3.1 Audit risks

Payroll is an area of the financial statements which gives rise to a fraud risk factor. Statistics indicate that payroll fraud costs the UK economy up to £12 billion per year[4] and auditors need to be on high alert for signs of fraud in this area. Red flags of payroll fraud include:

- Employees with no deductions for payroll taxes, pension contributions, or other deductions
- Several employees using the same bank account number or address
- Unusually high overtime pay
- Significant variances in pay for employees with the same job

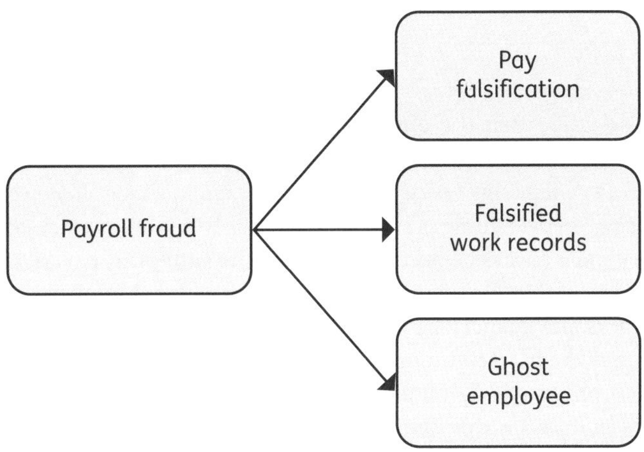

Figure 16.3 Common payroll fraud schemes

[4] The Chartered Institute of Payroll Professionals, 'Payroll fraud costs UK firms £12bn per year', 2016 <https://www.cipp.org.uk/resources/news/pf12bnpa.html> (accessed 19 January 2024).

- Pay falsification – this happens when an employee's payroll details are changed so that they receive extra pay. This is common if there is collusion between someone who has access to payroll and can change the amount that someone else is paid, the two then spilt the extra income between them. In companies with poor controls over access to the payroll system and limited authorization controls, this can easily be achieved.
- Falsified work records – here an employee simply claims more than they are entitled to, and their manager either innocently, or as part of a collusion, approves the payment. This can be achieved by falsifying time sheets, clocking in or out of work at the wrong time or claiming to have worked shifts when not actually being present at work.
- Ghost employee – this is when a fictitious employee is created in the payroll records, with the payment diverted into the fraudster's bank account. This can be quite an easy fraud to set up, especially if someone leaving the company is not removed from the payroll, so all the fraudster has to do is change the payment details to his or her own bank account.

Auditing in practice 16.3 Payroll fraud

In a famous case in 2014, Dennis Harold, a payroll worker who was found guilty of a £2.9 million payroll fraud, was sent to prison for four years. Harold had created more than 20 ghost employees, in this case temporary workers, diverting their pay into his possession. The fraud lasted for more than six years before being discovered by audit. At court, the judge summed up by saying:

> This was an appalling breach of trust. You, Mr Harold, were employed as a payroll administrator who was trained to use the computer system. You created false temporary staff to disguise payments to accounts controlled by you. In excess of 20 accounts were created and nearly £3m was taken from the fraud. It went on for six years and I have no doubt it would have continued but for an audit carried out and the fraud discovered. I accept you showed great remorse. It's hard to imagine a worse abuse of trust. You squandered your £1.2m in casinos and taxis and as I understand it you have nothing to show for it.[5]

Employee misclassification is a different type of fraud because it is perpetrated by the company rather than by employees. The company might classify employees as part time or casual workers, to avoid paying taxes. Management fraud in a payroll, however, would usually arise because of an overriding of internal controls. This is always viewed as a significant risk and this risk must always be borne in mind by the auditor. A payroll cycle could have sound controls in place, but this would not prevent management from overriding those controls to achieve personal financial gain.

Aside from fraud, the most common audit risks associated with payroll are misstated payroll expenses and misstated payroll liabilities. Payroll liabilities generally include employment tax payable at the reporting date that are paid in the next accounting period (e.g. 'Pay

[5] Press Association, 'Fraudster jailed for four years after stealing £3m and gambling it away', *The Guardian*, 2014 <https://www.theguardian.com/uk-news/2014/aug/29/city-worker-dennis-harold-3m-fraud-four-years-prison> (accessed 19 January 2024).

as You Earn', National Insurance Contributions and Student Loan deductions payable to HM Revenue and Customs). Payroll liabilities can also include other forms of liabilities such as mandatory deductions from an employee's wage/salary due to a court order that is then paid to a third party. The auditor will need to apply audit procedures to ensure that the total payroll expense in the statement of profit or loss is complete and accurate and that associated payroll liabilities owed by the entity at the reporting date are also complete.

Auditing scenario 16.4 Incomplete payroll expense

Ratchford Ltd pays all its staff monthly in arrears. Therefore, hours worked by staff in the month of January are paid in February.

Ratchford Ltd is preparing its financial statements for the year ended 31 December 20X9. Staff are paid for hours worked in the month of December 20X9 in January 20X0. Therefore, the company must make an accrual in the financial statements for hours worked by the employees upto and including 31 December 20X9 together with the associated payroll liabilities. If the company does not make this accrual, the payroll expense in the statement of profit or loss will be understated by one month and the liability presented in the statement of financial position will also be understated. The auditor must therefore devise procedures that provide sufficient and appropriate audit evidence that the payroll expense per the statement of profit or loss and the associated liabilities presented in the statement of financial position are complete.

The auditor should also carry out procedures to ensure that the opening accrual as at 1 January 20X9 is also correctly reversed in the current year.

This scenario also demonstrates the importance of the auditor gaining a sound understanding of an entity's payroll cycle. If the auditor does not understand the various cycles of the business, there is a risk that they will overlook a material issue. In this example, if the auditor does not fully understand the pay structure of the business (i.e. a month in arrears), they could miss the fact that the company should be making an accrual for employee hours worked in December that are paid in January. This would increase audit risk (the risk the auditor expresses an incorrect opinion on the financial statements) and illustrates how important it is to clearly understand all aspects of the client's business, especially where the audit client may be a new client.

Another audit risk which the auditor must be mindful of is in respect of directors' remuneration. Directors' remuneration can be contentious because some companies are reluctant to disclose such sensitive information. In many jurisdictions, including the UK, although with some exceptions for smaller companies, disclosure of directors' remuneration and other benefits is a legally required disclosure and must include:

- Wages and salaries paid
- Benefits provided (e.g. company cars, medical insurance, and such like)
- Bonuses
- Pension contributions from the employer

There is a risk that the directors have failed to adequately disclose directors' remuneration and other benefits in the financial statements and may, for example, try to include them within the wages and salaries expense so they are not immediately apparent. In the UK, for example, directors' remuneration does not have to be split into its component parts such as salary and bonus.

It must also be noted that any transaction with a director is regarded as material by nature. This means that, regardless of the amounts involved, the disclosure must be made due to its qualitative importance.

16.3.2 **Audit procedures: payroll**

As we mentioned earlier in this section, payroll is likely to be a material area of the financial statements—especially directors' remuneration. It is therefore important that the auditor devises specific audit procedures at the planning phase of the audit which reflects the risk of material misstatement and which addresses the relevant assertions properly.

Substantive procedures which the auditor should perform over the payroll expense in the statement of profit or loss and associated payroll liabilities include the following:

- Agree the total wages and salaries charge per the payroll system to the general ledger, trial balance and financial statements (verifies *completeness* and *presentation*).
- Obtain the monthly payroll reports and cast them to verify the accuracy of the payroll listings (verifies *accuracy*).
- For a sample of employees on the payroll during the year, recalculate the gross and net pay and agree to the payroll records (verifies *accuracy*).
- Select a sample of joiners and leavers and agree their start/leaving dates to the first/last payroll run (verifies *accuracy*).
- For a sample of employees, reperform the calculation of employment taxes (PAYE, NIC, and student loan deductions) and confirm that these have been included in the payroll expense for the year (verifies *accuracy*).
- For a sample of monthly payrolls, agree the total net pay per the payroll records to the bank transfer listing of payments and agree these to the cash book and an original bank statement (verifies *occurrence*).
- Agree the year end employment tax liability to the payroll records and agree the liability to a post-year-end payment.
- For a sample of employees, agree individual wages and salaries to human resources records and records of hours worked per time sheets or other time logging system (verifies *accuracy*).

Auditing scenario 16.5 Payroll fraud

You are the audit senior of Charnley Ltd and are in the process of preparing the draft audit programmes for the final audit of the financial statements for the year ended 31 December 20X9. The audit engagement partner has held a meeting with the finance director and has provided you with notes of that meeting. One issue that has been flagged as significantly important is a payroll fraud that was discovered during the year.

During the year a payroll clerk set up a fictitious employee on the payroll and diverted the funds into her own bank account. The prior year's working papers file confirms that the previous year's audit revealed a lack of segregation of duties as being a major weakness in the payroll processing function of the business and this had been notified to management and those charged with governance in accordance with ISA (UK) 265 *Communicating Deficiencies in Internal Control to Those Charged with Governance and Management.*

The payroll clerk was immediately dismissed and internal controls were strengthened to prevent such a fraud reoccurring. This includes having the payroll reviewed prior to finalizing by the HR department and a final check on the payments to be made to the employees by the finance director. The finance director told the audit engagement partner that they were satisfied the matter had now been resolved. However, the audit engagement partner is concerned that additional frauds may have taken place in the payroll department and has asked you to devise specific procedures to address his concerns.

Audit procedures which the auditor should carry out in respect of the payroll fraud include the following:

- Discuss with management and those charged with governance of the entity as to whether they are aware of any additional payroll frauds or potential frauds.
- Review board minutes for evidence of a discussion among management in terms of its materiality and to the existence of any additional frauds or suspected frauds.
- Discuss with the payroll supervisor the nature of the payroll fraud, in particular how it arose and the financial impact of amounts that were incorrectly paid into the former payroll clerk's own bank account.
- Review supporting documentation to confirm the total of the fraudulent payments made and ascertain the materiality of this misstatement.
- Review and test the internal controls in respect of setting up new employees and payments to them and assess whether this process gives rise to a fraud risk factor.
- Consider whether other information obtained by the audit team indicates risks of additional misstatements in respect of a payroll fraud.
- Obtain a written representation from management and, if applicable, those charged with governance, acknowledging that they have disclosed to the auditors all knowledge of actual and suspected payroll frauds.

The auditor should also carry out tests of control over the payroll cycle, including the following:

- Review of a sample of time sheets, particularly where overtime has been worked during a week/month, to ensure they have been authorized by a responsible official prior to being processed through the payroll system.
- Review the log of amendments to payroll master file information (standing data) to ensure that changes have been authorized by a responsible official.
- For bonuses paid to staff and directors, review board minutes for approval of the bonus.
- Observe the clocking-in/out process at the entity to ensure that it is adequately supervised (this ensures that staff are only paid for hours they have actually worked).
- Review the payroll processing to ensure there are adequate segregation of duties in place. For example, one person processing the payroll and another individual reviewing it prior to it being finalized. Note, the stronger the segregation of duties, the less likely a fraud will be committed.

- Review starter and leaver forms to ensure they have been completed correctly and have been authorized by a responsible official.
- Where the company has a HR department, inquire of the directors as to whether HR set up new employees on the payroll, including setting rates of pay (ideally HR should set up new joiners on the payroll system, including setting their rates of pay, and payroll should process their wages/salaries to enable segregation of duties).

Analytical procedures which the auditor should apply over the company's payroll expense include the following:

- Perform a proof-in-total test by taking last year's payroll charge, incorporate joiners and leavers and the annual pay increase or bonus. Compare this expectation to the actual payroll expense in the statement of profit or loss and investigate any significant fluctuations (verifies *completeness* and *accuracy*).
- Compare the current year's payroll charge to the prior year and identify any unusual fluctuations (verifies *completeness and accuracy*).
- Compare the monthly payroll expense against the monthly payroll charges in the prior year and investigate any significant differences (verifies *completeness* and *accuracy*).
- Compare monthly budgeted payroll expense against actual monthly payroll expense and compare any significant differences (verifies *completeness* and *accuracy*).

16.3.3 **Audit procedures: directors' remuneration**

We mentioned earlier that in many jurisdictions, including the UK, directors' remuneration must be disclosed separately from other payroll amounts and the auditor must carry out procedures to ensure that directors' remuneration has been adequately disclosed in accordance with accounting standards and legislation. If disclosure is inadequate or does not comply with accounting standards or legislation, it will have implications for the auditor's opinion which may be modified accordingly. Don't forget that all transactions with directors are material by nature regardless of the amounts involved.

The auditor should devise specific procedures to be applied over directors' remuneration given its sensitivity and its materiality. Audit procedures over directors' remuneration include the following:

- Obtain a schedule of directors' remuneration split between wages and salaries, bonuses, benefits, pension contributions, and other remuneration and agree to the financial statement disclosures (verifies *completeness*).
- Agree directors' wages/salaries to payroll records and human resources records (verifies *completeness*, *occurrence*, and *accuracy*).
- Recalculate the value of directors' remuneration from payroll records and agree the recalculated amounts to the trial balance and financial statements (verifies *completeness* and *accuracy*).
- Agree a sample of directors' wages/salaries to the cash book and original bank statements or bank transfer listings (verifies *occurrence*).

- Inspect board minutes for discussion and approval of directors' bonuses or other additional remuneration (verifies *accuracy* and *occurrence*).
- Obtain a written representation from management and, where applicable, those charged with governance that they have disclosed directors' remuneration to the auditor (verifies *completeness*).

Chapter round-up

- It is important to understand the difference between 'income' and 'gains' and 'expenses' and 'losses' as they are not the same thing and contribute to profit or loss in different ways.
- The auditor is primarily concerned with ensuring that revenue has been recognized at an appropriate amount at the correct time.
- Any deliberate acceleration or delaying of revenue recognition usually presents a misleading picture in the financial statements and would be regarded as earnings management or fraudulent financial reporting.
- Regarding revenue, the key assertions which the auditor is concerned with are cut-off, accuracy, completeness, and occurrence.
- Revenue can be difficult to account for example when there are multiple elements of a contract, and in some industries it is common to see revenue discussed as a Key Audit Matter in the auditor's report.
- Various audit procedures, including analytical review, are applied over purchases and expenses. Gross profit margins can be a useful tool in identifying any potential risk of material misstatement (e.g. misclassification of expenditure or incorrect cut-offs).
- Goods and services received up to the reporting date but not invoiced must be accrued in the financial statements to avoid understating expenses and liabilities and the auditor will be interested in ensuring the completeness assertion in these respects is covered.
- Payroll and directors' remuneration is a sensitive area of the financial statements and the auditor must focus on the completeness of payroll charges in the statement of profit or loss as well as the completeness of any associated payroll liabilities.

End of chapter case study

Introduction

The ability to design appropriate audit procedures is a key skill which auditors must possess. While some 'standard' audit procedures which can be applied to any audit client are useful, it is usually necessary to tailor audit procedures to fit the particular circumstances of the audit client. This is the best way to ensure that sufficient, appropriate evidence is obtained for all of the relevant assertions for a specific balance or transaction.

This activity will test your ability to design audit procedures for use in obtaining sufficient, appropriate evidence in relation to revenue and expenses.

This activity links to the following learning outcomes:

- Design and explain audit procedures to obtain sufficient and appropriate audit evidence over an entity's revenue and gains.
- Design and explain audit procedures to obtain sufficient and appropriate audit evidence over different expense cycles of the business including cost of sales administrative expenses; and other expenses.
- Design and explain audit procedures to obtain sufficient and appropriate audit evidence over directors' remuneration and payroll costs.

Scenario

You are auditing Nano Ltd, a software developer. The company develops software, e.g. accounting packages, inventory management systems and database software, which it sells to commercial customers. The company employs 25 software developers, five admin staff and a small team of business developers. The company has more than 25,000 customers and is has grown quickly in the last 12 months due to a significant increase in demand for software relating to support for e-commerce.

It is now 1 March 20X7. Nano Ltd's financial year ended on 31 December 20X6 and you are a member of the audit team, working on revenue and expenses. The company's finance director, John Dayton, has provided you with some information regarding contracts with customers, payroll, and directors' bonuses. Assume that each of these matters is material to the financial statements.

Contracts with customers

When the company sells a software package a licence is sold for a telephone technical support service which lasts for two years, after which time the customer can extend the service by purchasing additional years of technical support. The company's finance director has estimated the following relating to the support service obligation at 31 December 20X6:

Number of contracts including 2 year support service:	30,000
Estimated average obligation remaining per contract:	9 months
Standalone selling price of one year of support service:	£125

John Dayton, the finance director, has used this information to estimate that revenue of £1.4 million relates to the support service obligation and should be recognized as deferred revenue.

Overhead expenses

During the year, Nano Ltd incurred the following expenses which are recognized within operating expenses:

£120,000	Training costs for staff

Directors' bonuses

Nano Ltd has five directors, each of whom are entitled to a bonus based on the company's profit before tax. Each director has a different criteria for the calculation of their bonus, ranging from 2 per cent to 10 per cent of profit before tax.

The draft financial statements include a bonus accrual of £165,000, which represents 7 per cent of profit before tax. The previous year's total bonus payment was £150,000. The bonuses are due for payment on 30 April 20X7.

Required

For each of the matters described above, explain any relevant risks of material misstatement.

You should recommend the audit procedures to be performed including a brief explanation of the purpose of the procedure.

Answer

As a general observation, there is a risk that revenue has been overstated and expenses have been understated in order for the directors to maximize the company's profit before tax, as this will increase the bonus they will receive. The auditors must carry out detailed audit procedures on revenue and expenses to confirm that the figures are not misstated.

Contracts with customers

There is an inherent risk with revenue recognition where a contract relates to several distinct obligations. This is because IFRS 15 *Revenue from Contracts with Customers* requires revenue to be allocated between the two obligations and recognized accordingly. So, in the case of Nano Ltd, the finance director is correct to allocate part of the revenue arising on a contract to the provision of a telephone support service, which should be deferred and recognized over time. The part of revenue relating to recognition of the sale of the software should be recognized immediately. This can be a subjective allocation of revenue and is based on estimates made by the finance director, increasing the risk of management bias. It is in the interest of the finance director for as much revenue to be recognized as possible this year, to maximize profit and therefore bonus payments to the company's directors, including himself.

Audit procedures relating to the revenue will be based on the auditor developing their own estimation of the revenue relating to telephone service support. This can then be compared to the value estimated by the finance director, and discrepancies discussed.

To develop their own estimate, the auditor will need to:

- Using data extracted from the sales system and/or customer information records, confirm the number of contracts containing a two-year telephone support service, and using the date of sale, confirm how long remains on the contract at 31 December 20X5.
- For a sample of these contracts, review the terms and conditions to confirm that Nano Ltd has an obligation lasting two years from the date of sale.
- Confirm that the price of a support service as a standalone product is £125, from agreement to sales documentation, e.g. invoices or a published price list.
- Recalculate the allocation of total revenue for the year between the sale of software and the sale of the support service.
- Using the above, determine an expectation of the value of the deferred consideration and compare to that prepared by the finance director.

Training cost

For the training cost, as with any other type of expense, there is a risk that the expense is not complete and therefore understated. This is especially true given the incentive for management to manipulate expenses to boost profit before tax and maximize their bonus.

Audit procedures relating to the training expense could include:

- Review Nano Ltd's approved training budget to understand the overall level of planned spending on training. If this is significantly different from the £120,000 expense recognized as an operating expense, discuss with management.

- Recalculate the annual training spend per employee. Compare with the prior year and discuss any significant variation with management.
- Review supplier invoices received after the year-end for any training-related invoices and ensure that if the training was provided before the year end, the cost is accrued for.
- Obtain a breakdown of the £120,000 and:
  - Review for any items that may have been mis-classified as training costs e.g. should be classified as other expenses or as capital expenditure.
  - Agree a sample of items included in the £120,000 to supporting documentation such as contracts with training providers and to invoices received from those providers.
  - Agree a sample of items to cash book and/or bank statements.

Bonus

There is a risk that bonuses are overstated. It is in the interest of the directors to maximize their remuneration and the finance director could be under pressure from his fellow directors to inflate the bonus payment.

The bonus has increased by £15,000, which is a 10 per cent increase compared to the previous year. If profit before tax has increased by 10 per cent then the trend appears reasonable. However, even if there has been a 10 per cent increase in profit, the audit team need to apply a high level of professional scepticism in their audit of income and expenses, especially with regards to items where management bias could have been exercised. There is a high risk of manipulation of income and expenses to maximize the bonus payable to the directors.

Audit procedures could include:

- Obtain a list of the directors' bonuses to be paid on 30 April 20X7, and cast the schedule to ensure accuracy of the total.
- Using HR records, confirm the basis for each director's bonus payment, i.e. % of profit before tax, and recalculate their individual bonus.
- Read board minutes to confirm that the amounts of bonus per director has been approved.
- Confirm the amount of each bonus paid on 30 April 20X7 by agreeing to the company's cash book and bank statements.
- Confirm the bonus accrual is included as a year-end liability within current liabilities.
- Obtain a written representation from management confirming the completeness of directors' remuneration including the bonus.
- Review the disclosures made regarding the bonus paid to directors and assess whether these are in compliance with IFRS requirements (e.g. IAS 24 *Related Party Disclosures*) and legislation.

Activity solutions

Activity 16.1—Audit risks relating to revenue

Trinity Ltd sells garden furniture and the audit team is working on the audit of revenue for the current accounting period. The draft financial statements include revenue of £3.5 million.

Audit procedures have revealed that on the last day of the accounting period, sales invoices totalling £90,000 were posted, but the inventory to which these invoices relate was still in Trinity's warehouse until three days after the year end.

The audit team is aware that Trinity Ltd has in place a bonus scheme for management based on the company meeting certain targets, one of which is based on revenue growth.

What are the audit risks indicated in this scenario?

Suggested answer points:

IFRS 15 states that revenue in respect of the sale of goods is recognized when a performance obligation has been met, which in this case means the goods being delivered to, and accepted by the customer. The fact that the inventory relating to £90,000 sales on the last day of the accounting period is still physically held by Trinity Ltd indicates that this has not happened, and that these sales invoices should not be recognized within revenue.

This could be a cut-off error, perhaps due to deficiencies in the accounting system. However given that management receive a bonus based on revenue growth, the early recognition of revenue could be a deliberate misstatement.

It will be necessary to obtain further information regarding the sales, because there could be a reason why the sales have been recognized despite the inventory not being delivered to customers. For example, the customers may have requested that the goods remain at Trinity's warehouse for a few days after the sale of goods took place. The auditors need to obtain audit evidence in order to conclude as to whether IFRS 15 has been breached and whether there is a material misstatement of revenue due to its early recognition.

Activity 16.2—Audit procedures over revenue

Stour Ltd manufactures four types of engine which are used in large vehicles. Sales are made to commercial customers through the company's team of business development managers. Each business development manager can allow a discount of up to 5 per cent on list price, with all discounts needing approval of the company's sales director. Customer orders are taken by the business development managers, who then inform the warehouse. At the point at which an engine is despatched, a Goods Despatch Note is raised and a sales invoice generated, based on the customer order details.

Can you recommend four audit procedures relevant to the audit of Stour Ltd's revenue?

Suggested answer points:

- Compare the overall level of revenue against prior years and budgets and investigate any significant fluctuations by discussion with management.
- Obtain a schedule of sales for the year disaggregated (e.g. by month, by product line, by business development manager) and compare this to the same prior year breakdown investigate any significant fluctuations by discussion with management.
- Calculate the gross profit margin for the company as a whole and, if possible, by product line, and compare this to the prior year and investigate any significant fluctuations.
- Select a sample of customer orders and agree the sales price to company's standard prices and that discounts have been approved by the sales director.
- For the sample of customer orders, match the order with GDN and invoice and trace through to the sale included in revenue by confirming that the invoice is included in the general ledger.
- Select a sample of GDNs for pre and post year end and follow these through to sales invoices in the correct accounting period to ensure that cut-off has been correctly applied.

Activity 16.3—Examples of overhead expenditure

List five examples of commonly incurred overhead expenditure.

Suggested answer points:

Examples of overhead expenditure include:

- Heat and light
- Telephone
- Office costs, e.g. stationery
- Cleaning
- Payroll costs
- Rent and rates
- Postage
- Repairs and maintenance
- Legal and professional
- Bank and finance charges—these are categorized as finance costs in the statement of profit or loss but are commonly audited alongside other expenses

17

Auditing Related Parties, Subsequent Events, and Going Concern

Introduction

In the last three chapters, we looked at how assets, liabilities, equity, income, and expenses are audited. There are some other important aspects of the financial statements which the auditor must consider as part of the audit process. These are related parties, subsequent events (sometimes called 'post balance sheet events' or 'events after the end of the reporting period'), and going concern.

The biggest problem for the auditor where these three areas are concerned is that there is a lot of subjectivity attached to them. For example, in respect of related parties, the auditor is, to a certain extent, reliant on management to be open and honest with the auditor and tell them who all the related parties are. The auditor can, of course, carry out their own checks and procedures to identify all known related parties, but it will require some degree of input from management and, where applicable, those charged with governance.

The audit of subsequent events and going concern will usually be done towards the end of the audit. However, at the planning stage, the auditor will have to do some work on going concern to understand the financial, operating, and other risks facing the business. The auditor needs to understand whether the accounts have been prepared on a going concern basis and evaluate whether that basis appears to be appropriate. Other planning work might indicate that the going concern basis of accounting may not be appropriate—for example, if the company has made a loss in the year or if it has been adversely affected by external factors, such as high inflation or recession.

In this chapter, we will focus on the following ISAs (UK):

- ISA (UK) 550 Related Parties
- ISA (UK) 560 Subsequent Events
- ISA (UK) 570 Going Concern

Learning outcomes

- Explain and apply the process for identifying related parties and recommend the audit procedures to obtain sufficient and appropriate audit evidence over related parties and transactions with related parties.
- Discuss the responsibilities of auditors in respect of subsequent events and recommend the audit procedures to be carried out in performing a subsequent events review.
- Discuss the responsibilities of management and the auditor in respect of going concern, identify and explain events and circumstances which may impact going concern, and recommend relevant audit procedures.
- Discuss the auditor's reporting implications in respect of going concern.

By the end of this chapter, you will be able to:

- Discuss the difficulties in auditing related parties and going concern.
- Discuss the expectation gap in respect of going concern.

17.1 Related parties

17.1.1 Related parties and audit risk

We will look at the technical definition of related parties shortly. For now, let's assume that a related party is an individual or another entity with control or a close connection to the reporting entity. An example might be where one person controls two companies, so those two companies would be called related parties. Or, a related party can be a person, for example, the spouse of a company's managing director.

Financial reporting standards require disclosure of related parties and transactions between them. A key problem for the auditor is that unless management tell the auditor about the existence of related parties, they can be very hard to identify. Even where management are willing to inform the auditor about related parties, management may not understand the definition, leading to incomplete disclosure. This is particularly the case in smaller companies, which may lack informed management.

Internal controls are often not set up to specifically deal with related parties and transactions with them. So, for example, if two companies under common control trade with each other, these transactions might not be separately identified within the accounting system as related-party transactions, so again there is a risk of incomplete disclosure.

Finally, management may deliberately conceal related parties and transactions with them. This is because related parties are sometimes used as vehicles for fraud, and this type of fraud often involves senior management. An academic study[1] found that frauds involving related-party transactions were more likely to involve the chief executive officer (CEO) and/or chief finance officer (CFO) of an organization than other employees, but the transactions involved were not necessarily high value. The implication for the auditor is that senior management can override controls, making it easy for frauds involving related parties to be concealed.

[1] Henry, E., Gordon, E., Reed, B., & Louwers, T. (2012) 'The role of related party transactions in fraudulent financial reporting', *Journal of forensic & investigative accounting*, vol. 4, no. 1.

Activity 17.1 Related parties and fraud

Discuss the ways that related-party transactions could be used for fraudulent activity.

Auditing in practice 17.1 The Tyco scandal and related parties

One of the most famous frauds involving related parties involves the US company Tyco. This case dates back to 2002, but it serves to demonstrate how related-party transactions can be used to carry out significant frauds by senior management.

In the Tyco case, the company's CEO Dennis Kozlowski and CFO Mark Swartz were found to have given themselves loans amounting to $120 million, often disguised as bonuses, which were interest-free or had very low rates of interest. The company had a legitimate key employee loan programme, which was set up to help senior management to acquire loan stock in the company. However, Kozlowski and Swartz abused this policy, making loans without appropriate authorization leading to significant theft from the company as the loans were never intended to be repaid.

In addition to the unapproved loans, the company's funds were misused by Kozlowski for extravagant personal expenses, famously including a $6,000 shower curtain, works of art, and houses worth many millions of dollars, and a $2 million birthday party for his wife. Kozlowski clearly believed that the company's assets were 'his money'—a concept known as 'commingling'.

Both Kozlowski and Swartz were found guilty of grand larceny, falsifying business records, securities fraud, and conspiracy in 2005. They both received lengthy prison sentences and were ordered to pay fines totalling over $230 million.

In addition to the misappropriation of assets, on investigation, it was discovered that Tyco's financial statements were misstated by a $5.8 billion overstatement of profit.

The company's audit firm, PwC, was investigated by the Securities and Exchange Commission. The audit engagement partner was found guilty of recklessly violating the antifraud provisions of federal law, of engaging in improper conduct, and was barred from acting as an accountant. PwC ultimately paid $225 million in settlement of legal claims against the audit firm.

The disclosure requirements for related parties are contained in IAS 24 *Related Party Disclosures*. IAS 24 is a 'disclosure-only' standard and it's important to understand why related-party disclosures are necessary in the financial statements.

Irrespective of fraud risk, it is important that disclosures are made so that users of the financial statements can understand the impact of related parties and transactions with them.

The primary reason for disclosing related-party relationships and transactions is so that the user of the accounts understands that the financial position and performance of the business may have been affected by the presence of related-party transactions. These transactions may have been carried out on an arm's-length basis (i.e. at a 'normal market rate') but, in some cases, they may not have.

Let's imagine you are looking at buying one of two businesses, both of which rent their premises. In one business, the rent expense in the statement of profit or loss is significantly lower than in the other business. Without any further information, you invest in the business with the cheaper rent expense. However, if the building is owned by the director's father who is charging a much lower rent than market rate that may change your view. For that reason, IAS 24 requires all related parties, and transactions with them, to be disclosed.

ISA (UK) 550 *Related Parties* provides the guidance that auditors need to carry out their audit of related-party disclosures. ISA (UK) 550 recognizes that transactions with related parties may carry no more risk than other transactions with non-related parties. However, a fraud between related parties is something the auditor must consider because as we have seen, it is relatively easy for individuals, especially senior management, to collude with a related party of the entity in order to commit fraud.

17.1.2 **Related parties–definitions, requirements, and audit risk**

ISA (UK) 550 contains the following definition:

> A related party is a party that is either:
>
> (i) A related party as defined in the applicable financial reporting framework; or
>
> (ii) Where the applicable financial reporting framework establishes minimal or no related party requirements:
>
> a. A person or other entity that has control or significant influence, directly or indirectly through one or more intermediaries, over the reporting entity;
>
> b. Another entity over which the reporting entity has control or significant influence, directly or indirectly through one or more intermediaries; or
>
> c. Another entity that is under common control with the reporting entity through having:
>
> i. Common controlling ownership;
>
> ii. Owners who are close family members; or
>
> iii. Common key management.
>
> However, entities that are under common control by a state (that is, a national, regional or local government) are not considered related unless they engage in significant transactions or share resources to a significant extent with one another.[2]

For our purposes, because we are using IFRS as the applicable financial reporting framework, we apply the IAS 24 definition, which is similar to the definition per (ii) above, but it specifically includes members of key management personnel, and it also extends to close family members of key management personnel.

IAS 24 also contains examples of the kinds of transactions that would need to be disclosed if they are with a related party:

- purchases or sales of goods, property, and other assets;
- rendering or receiving services;
- leases;
- transfers of research and development;
- transfers under licence agreements;
- transfers under finance arrangements including loans and equity contributions;
- provision of guarantees or collateral;
- settlement of liabilities on behalf of the entity or by the entity on behalf of another party.

The list is quite long, and you can see that it includes a wide range of transactions and arrangements.

[2] FRC, 'ISA (UK) 550', 2022, para 10(b) <https://media.frc.org.uk/documents/ISA_UK_550_-_Updated_May_2022.pdf> (accessed 18 January 2024).

The principal audit risk is that of inadequate or incomplete disclosures. Auditors must keep in mind that some disclosures are material by nature. For example, a transaction with a director (regardless of value) is always considered to be material in nature. So, if a transaction with a director is not disclosed the financial statements will still contain a material misstatement, even if the value of the transaction is immaterial in monetary terms.

IAS 24 requires a number of disclosures about related parties and transactions with them (see also Figure 17.1):

- Related-party relationships—regardless of whether there have been transactions between a parent and a subsidiary, an entity must disclose the name of its parent and, if different, the ultimate controlling party.
- Where there have been transactions between related parties, disclose the nature of the related-party relationship as well as information about the transactions and outstanding balances necessary for an understanding of the potential effect of the relationship on the financial statements. The disclosure should include:
  - the amount of the transactions;
  - the number of outstanding balances, including terms and conditions and guarantees;
  - any allowances related to the number of outstanding balances;
  - expense recognized during the period in respect of bad or doubtful debts due from related parties.
- IAS 24 also requires disclosure of key management personnel compensation including salary, bonuses, pension contributions, and share-based payment benefits.

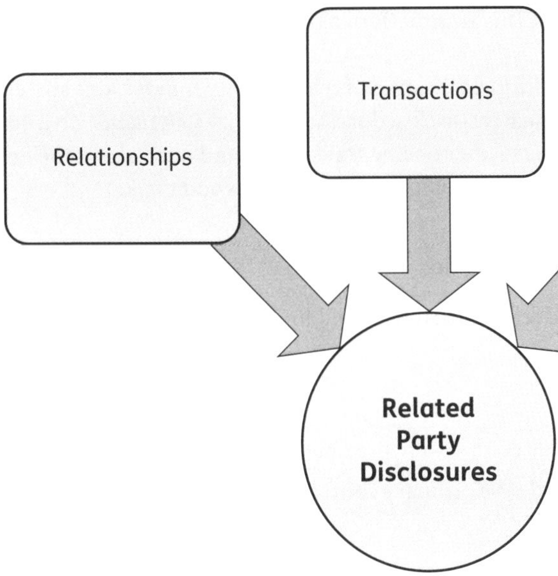

Figure 17.1 Related-party disclosure

Management may not want to make certain disclosures because they could be considered to be too sensitive, for example, details of salaries, bonuses, and pension contributions. Just because a transaction, or a series of transactions, may be considered sensitive, it does not preclude the directors from disclosing them as related-party transactions. If management insist on *not* disclosing those transactions, it is likely the auditor will have to modify their audit opinion.

The other audit risk is that the auditor has not been made fully aware of the entity's related parties. This could just be an oversight on the part of management or, where applicable, those charged with governance. On the flip side, it could also be a deliberate concealment. Where it is the latter, the auditor will have to be careful and consider that the lack of disclosure about related parties is a fraud risk factor.

ISA (UK) 550 recognizes that the nature of related-party relationships and transactions may, in some situations, give rise to a higher risk of material misstatement that transactions with unrelated parties. For example:

- Related parties may operate through an extensive and complex range of relationships and structures, with a corresponding increase in the complexity of related party transactions.
- Information systems may be ineffective at identifying or summarizing transactions and outstanding balances between an entity and its related parties.
- Related party transactions may not be conducted under normal market terms and conditions; for example, some related party transactions may be concluded with no exchange of consideration.[3]

Consider the last of these bullet points—a related-party transaction could have taken place with no exchange of cash involved. For example, a director could gift a car or other asset from the company to a related party for no consideration. It might therefore be difficult for the auditor to spot this transaction, as there would be no record of cash movement.

Management is responsible for the identification of related-party transactions and ensuring that such transactions are adequately disclosed in the financial statements. To a certain extent, the auditor is reliant on management being transparent and open about the entity's related-party transactions and balances, which, in turn, increases audit risk.

17.1.3 **Audit procedures–related parties**

The audit procedures in respect of related parties are put into 'stages' as follows:

- the risk assessment stage;
- the fieldwork stage;
- related parties which are discovered that were previously unknown to the auditor; and
- related-party transactions outside the ordinary course of business.

[3] Ibid., para 2.

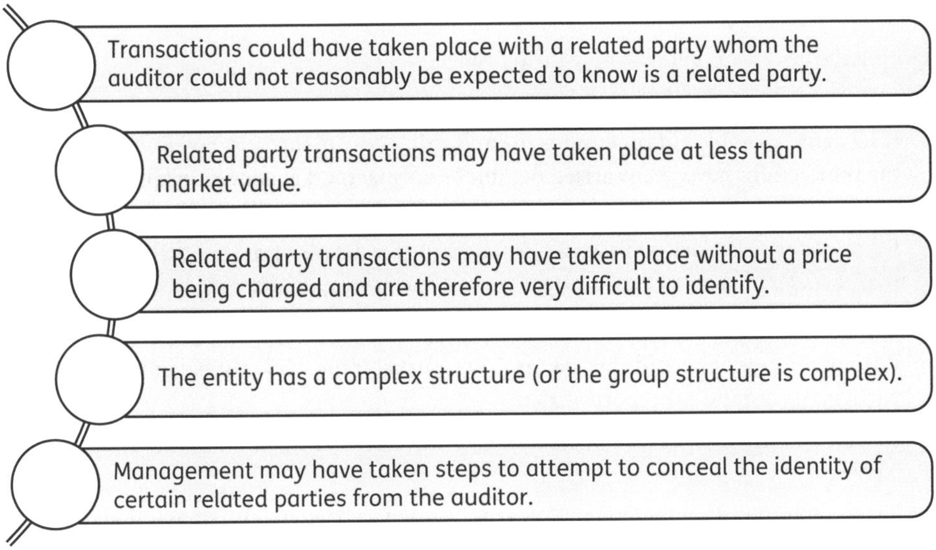

Figure 17.2 Summary of audit risks for related parties

17.1.3.1 **The risk assessment stage (which is usually at the planning stage)**

At the risk assessment stage, the auditor must:

- Discuss among the engagement team the susceptibility of the financial statements to material misstatement due to related parties or transactions with them.
- Inquire of management as to:
  - the identity of related parties, including any changes from the prior year;
  - the nature of the relationship between the entity and its related parties;
  - whether any transactions have taken place between the entity and its related parties during the reporting period;
  - the controls which are in place governing related parties and transactions with them (including the approval of related-party transactions); and
  - what controls are in place to approve significant transactions and arrangements outside the ordinary course of business.
- Apply professional scepticism (i.e. maintain a questioning mind) at all times throughout the course of the audit, recognizing the possibility that there may be related parties or related-party transactions which the auditor may not be aware of.
- When significant transactions, outside the ordinary course of business, are discovered, discuss with management the rationale behind them and whether related parties could be involved.
- Ensure there are procedures in place to enable the sharing of information obtained in connection with related parties with the rest of the audit team.

17.1.3.2 **The fieldwork stage**

During the fieldwork (evidence-gathering) stage:

- Inquire of management as to whether transactions with related parties have taken place. If so, agree a sample of transactions to supporting documentation, ascertaining whether the transactions have been carried out under normal market conditions (i.e. on an arm's-length basis).
- Review the prior year's audit working papers file for details of related parties.
- Review information held on public records (such as Companies House or an equivalent public registry) for evidence of directors' involvement in any other entities.
- Review accounting records for any large or unusual transactions or balances, particularly around the reporting date.
- Review confirmation of loan balances—in particular, if any guarantors are related parties.
- For the amounts disclosed in the notes to the financial statements (transactions and balances), agree to the accounting records and investigate any significant differences.
- Review investment transactions, such as a purchase or sale in a joint venture or an associate to identify if this indicates a related-party transaction.
- Review invoices and correspondence from lawyers or regulatory bodies for indications of the existence of related parties or related-party transactions.
- Inspect the bank confirmation letter (sometimes called the 'bank audit letter' or 'bank certificate') for evidence of any related-party transactions.

17.1.3.3 **Related parties are discovered which were previously unknown to the auditor**

There may be situations when the auditor identifies related parties that have not been disclosed to them. This can be an innocent oversight by management, but it can also be a fraud risk factor and ISA (UK) 550 requires the auditor to perform specific actions when they discover related parties of which they were previously unaware, as follows:

- Inform the rest of the audit team as quickly as possible.
- Request that management identify all transactions with those related parties.
- Inquire of management as to why the entity's internal control environment has not identified all related parties.
- Perform substantive procedures over the related parties by:
  - making inquiries of third parties, such as lawyers, who may have knowledge of the related-party relationships (management authorization will often be required before the auditor can make inquiries of third parties about matters concerning the entity);
  - analysing accounting records for transactions with the related parties; and
  - verifying the terms and conditions of transactions by looking at related contracts.

- Revisit the risk assessment over related parties and consider its appropriateness in light of the findings.
- If the non-disclosure of the related parties to the auditor appears to be intentional, therefore indicative of a fraud risk factor, consider the implications for the audit as additional procedures will be necessary.

Auditing scenario 17.1 Discovery of a previously unknown related party

The audit of Sunnie Ltd for the year ended 31 December 20X9 is being carried out. During the audit of receivables, it came to the attention of the audit senior that a loan had been provided to a third party amounting to £100,000.

Investigations concluded that this third party is the brother of the CEO of Sunnie Ltd who is a senior manager in the company. The loan has not been disclosed as a related-party transaction in the draft financial statements.

In this example, the auditor must notify the audit team immediately of the newly identified related party and request that management identify all transactions with the brother of the CEO. There must also be inquiries as to why the internal control environment of Sunnie Ltd failed to disclose this transaction as a related-party transaction.

The audit team must also perform substantive procedures over the loan and consider whether this is indicative of a 'one-off' isolated related party or whether there may be other unidentified related parties. This is in addition to considering whether any additional fraud risk factors need to be considered as well.

17.1.3.4 Related-party transactions outside the ordinary course of business

A transaction is said to be 'outside the ordinary course of business' when it is unusual in terms of its substance and/or value. For example, disposing of a company asset at a value that is substantially lower than market rate can be said to be 'outside the ordinary course of business'.

When the auditor identifies related-party transactions which they consider to be outside the ordinary course of business, they must:

- Inspect contracts and agreements to evaluate:
  - the business rationale (or lack thereof) and whether this gives rise to a fraud risk factor;
  - whether the terms of the transactions are consistent with management's explanations; and
  - whether the transactions have been accounted for and disclosed correctly.
- The auditor must also obtain evidence that the transactions have been appropriately authorized and approved.[4]

[4] Ibid., para 23.

Where management have made an assertion that all related-party transactions have been conducted on an arm's-length basis, the auditor must obtain sufficient and appropriate audit evidence that this assertion is correct by reviewing the terms of any contract, paying particular attention to:

- prices charged;
- terms of credit granted;
- specific charges; and
- any contingencies.

17.1.3.5 **Written representations for related-party transactions**

Remember that a written representation is a statement from the entity's management (and/or those charged with governance) about certain material issues that relate to the financial statements. Written representations are only one form of audit evidence and can only be used to complement other forms of audit evidence. It's important to remember that written representations, on their own, are a very weak form of audit evidence because they are internally generated by the entity itself.

ISA (UK) 550 requires management to obtain a written representation from management and, where appropriate, those charged with governance, that:

- they have disclosed to the auditor the identity of the entity's related parties and all the related party relationships and transactions of which they are aware; and
- they have appropriately accounted for and disclosed such relationships and transactions in accordance with IAS 24.[5]

17.2 Subsequent events

17.2.1 **What are subsequent events?**

ISA (UK) 560 *Subsequent Events* provides the auditor with the requirements in respect of events that take place after the client's financial year end.

The term 'subsequent events' is defined as follows:

> Events occurring between the date of the financial statements and the date of the auditor's report, and facts that become known to the auditor after the date of the auditor's report.[6]

Subsequent events are often referred to as 'post balance sheet events' or 'events after the end of the reporting period'. Subsequent events relate to events that arise between the entity's reporting date (i.e. balance sheet date or 'year end') and the date on which the financial statements are authorized for issue (i.e. approved).

[5] Ibid., para 25.

[6] FRC, 'ISA (UK) 560', 2016, para 5(e) <https://media.frc.org.uk/documents/ISA_UK_560_-_June_2016.pdf> (accessed 18 January 2024).

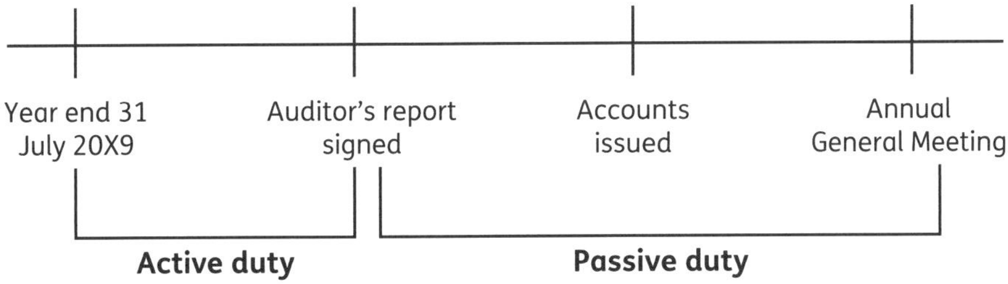

Figure 17.3 Active and passive duty regarding subsequent events

If you think about the timing of the audit, the bulk of the fieldwork takes place after the company's year end, and it can be many months after the year end when the auditor completes the audit and issues their report. Therefore, there is often a long period of time after the year end when significant events may take place. These events can impact the year-end financial statements, and this is why the auditor needs to be aware of them.

Two types of duty apply to the auditor where subsequent events are concerned (Figure 17.3):

- An active duty whereby the auditor must obtain sufficient appropriate audit evidence that all subsequent events that require adjustment or disclosure have been identified. This duty applies between the reporting date and the date on which the auditor's report is signed.
- A passive duty where there is no requirement for the auditor to perform audit procedures. This applies after the auditor's report has been signed. However, if a fact becomes known to the auditor after they have signed the auditor's report which may have caused a different opinion to be expressed if that fact had been known at the time, they must take appropriate action.

17.2.2 **Adjusting and non-adjusting events**

There is an accounting standard which deals with adjusting and non-adjusting events—IAS 10 *Events after the Reporting Period*. There is therefore close interaction between IAS 10 and ISA (UK) 560. IAS 10 categorizes events that occur after the year end as follows:

- adjusting events which provide evidence of conditions that existed at the reporting date; and
- non-adjusting events which are indicative of conditions that arose after the reporting date.

17.2.2.1 **Adjusting events**

Adjusting events are reflected in the financial statements even though they arise after the reporting date. This is because their conditions existed at the reporting date. For example, if a company which owes money to the client goes into liquidation shortly after the reporting date, this is evidence that the company had suffered a loss at the reporting date and therefore any trade receivable that is recognized in the financial statements needs to be written off. The circumstances leading to the bad debt were in existence at the reporting date.

17.2.2.2 **Non-adjusting events**

Non-adjusting events are not reflected in the financial statements. Instead, they are disclosed in the notes to the financial statements if they are considered to be material. This is because their conditions did not exist at the reporting date, but they have arisen between the reporting date and the date on which the auditor signs their report. For example, a company could suffer damage to assets due to a fire taking place after the year—this has nothing to do with a 'year-end condition' so it is a non-adjusting event.

Auditing scenario 17.2 Adjusting and non-adjusting events

Orbital Ltd has a reporting date of 31 August 20X9. Included within the year-end inventory valuation is a batch of products that cost £120,000. Orbital Ltd has experienced competition from a rival company for the last six months. The products were sold on 20 September 20X9 for £100,000. The finance director has not made any adjustment to the year end carrying amount of this inventory as he said he did not know on 31 August 20X9 that the inventory would be sold at a price lower than cost.

The inventory must be valued at the lower of cost and net realizable value, in accordance with IAS 2. Inventory which is sold after the reporting date for a price that is lower than cost is an adjusting event and so the finance director must make an adjustment to closing inventory in the financial statements for the year ended 31 August 20X9. If this adjustment is not made, inventory and profit before tax will both be overstated which could present a misleading picture in the financial statements.

If this adjustment is not made, and the £20,000 adjustment is considered to be material (either in isolation or in combination with other misstatements), the auditor's report must be modified.

On 6 October 20X9 an ex-employee commenced a legal claim against Orbital Ltd for unfair dismissal. The amount claimed by the employee is considered to be a material amount. The finance director is reluctant to make any disclosures in the financial statements about this issue in case users view the entity in an unfavourable light.

This is an example of a non-adjusting event. The claim was brought against the entity after the reporting date but before the auditor's report has been signed and the financial statements authorized for issue. As the amount claimed by the former employee is considered to be material to the financial statements the entity must disclose:

- the nature of the event; and
- an estimate of its financial effect, or a statement that such an estimate cannot be made,

in order to comply with the requirements of IAS 10.

If this non-adjusting event is not disclosed, the auditor will have to modify their audit opinion accordingly due to the lack of disclosure because the issue is material.

Activity 17.2 Adjusting and non-adjusting events

Can you think of further examples of both adjusting and non-adjusting events?

17.2.2.3 Impact of a non-adjusting event on going concern

There may be situations when a non-adjusting event may have an impact on the entity's ability to continue as a going concern. For example, if the non-adjusting event is a fire which destroys the company's premises and its inventory and the company is not adequately insured, the company may not be in a financial position to replace the premises and its inventory. As a consequence, the financial statements may need to be prepared on a basis other than the going concern basis.

Auditing in practice 17.2 Adjusting event and non-adjusting events in respect of Covid-19

Covid-19 was first detected in the UK in February 2020. The timing of company year ends had a significant impact on how the pandemic was treated in financial statements. All businesses were required to consider the impact that Covid-19 had on them. In some cases, the impact was minimal; whereas in others, the impact was devastating.

For businesses with a reporting date before or on 31 January 2020 it was more than likely that the effect of the pandemic would be a non-adjusting event. This is because at 31 January 2020, the pandemic had not reached the UK and was therefore not a 'year-end condition'. Hence, companies would explain the impact of the pandemic using a disclosure note in the accounts, as required by IAS 10 for non-adjusting events. The entity would not adjust the carrying amounts of assets and liabilities in the financial statements because even if in the period after the year end the pandemic had a significant impact on the business, it would not be considered to be related to a year-end condition.

In such cases, the auditor would review the adequacy of any non-adjusting event disclosure notes in respect of the virus and challenge any lack of disclosure or incomplete disclosures, especially where the impact of the pandemic is clearly material.

For companies that had 31 March 2020 year ends onwards, the impact of the virus may have given rise to an adjusting event. This is because, by 31 March 2020, the pandemic was a recognized event, the first of the UK's lockdown measures had come into law, creating a 'year-end condition'. For example, a client in the hospitality sector running a chain of restaurants would have had to write down the value of their inventory of food at the year end because the business had been forced to close. Other companies may have had to write down the value of other assets due to indicators of impairment. These are all adjusting events that would have needed to be reflected in the accounts as a result of the pandemic being a year-end condition by 31 March 2020.

In some more serious cases, the impact of the pandemic would have meant the directors had no alternative but to cease trading—even though the business had previously been profitable prior to the pandemic. This would have meant the financial statements would not have been prepared on a going concern basis hence additional disclosures would need to be made to describe the basis on which the financial statements have been prepared together with details of the reasons why the business is no longer a going concern.

Auditors carrying out audits of financial statements during the Covid-19 pandemic would have had to carefully plan additional procedures to ensure they address the risks of subsequent events and going concern issues. The extent of the auditor's work would depend on how significant the effect of the pandemic has been on the business.

Auditing scenario 17.3 Non-adjusting event disclosure

Polaris Ltd has prepared its financial statements for the year ended 31 January 2020. Management have concluded that the impact of Covid-19 on the business is a non-adjusting event because the restrictions and business interruption occurred after the year end. The directors are satisfied that the going concern basis of accounting remains appropriate. The company has made the following disclosure:

Note 29: Non-adjusting event

Since February 2020, the impact of Covid-19 has impacted many local economies around the world. Since 23 March 2020, non-essential businesses in the UK were forced to close by the government as a means of controlling the virus. Travel bans were also imposed as well as quarantines and social-distancing measures. This has resulted in a significant economic slowdown as businesses try to deal with the effects of the virus. The government has instigated financial measures as a means of assisting businesses throughout the period of disruption including loans at favourable rates and introduction of the Coronavirus Job Retention Scheme (CJRS).

Since the year end, the company has furloughed approximately 60 per cent of its workforce due to the pandemic. The costs of retaining these employees have largely been met by the government through the CJRS grant. Three of the company's subsidiaries are also showing indicators of impairment since the year end.

The directors have concluded that these events are non-adjusting events. Therefore, the financial position and results of operations for the year ended 31 January 2020 have not been adjusted to reflect their impact. At the date of approval of these financial statements, the duration and continuing effect of Covid-19 was uncertain and it is not possible to reliably estimate the duration and severity of these consequences, as well as their impact on the company's financial performance, financial position, and cash flows for future periods.

17.2.3 **Audit procedures–subsequent events**

17.2.3.1 **Audit procedures when the auditor has an active duty**

To recap, the auditor's active duty arises between the reporting date and the date on which the auditor's report is signed. ISA (UK) 560 requires that the auditor performs audit procedures designed to obtain evidence that all subsequent events which require adjustment or disclosure in the financial statements are identified.

Such procedures will include:

- Making inquiries of management if they are aware of any subsequent events that require adjustment in the financial statements.
- Reviewing accounting records such as budgets, forecasts, and interim accounts for evidence of any subsequent events.
- Inquiring of management's procedures for the identification of subsequent events.
- Reviewing minutes of directors and shareholders meetings.
- Reviewing correspondence with lawyers to identify any potential subsequent events.
- Inspecting post-year-end cash receipts from customers to identify any potential irrecoverable receivables which may need to be written off.

- Reviewing post-year-end sales invoices to identify any inventories that may have been sold after the reporting date for less than cost price.
- Reading the entity's latest subsequent interim financial statements, if any are available.
- Requesting a written representation from management that they have identified all subsequent events that need to be adjusted or disclosed in the financial statements.
- Reviewing the disclosure notes in the financial statements to confirm that they are in compliance with IAS 10.

Activity 17.3 Inquiry of management

Imagine you have been tasked by your audit supervisor with asking management some questions about subsequent events. Your objective is to find out whether any subsequent events have taken place which may need further investigation.

What inquiries might you make with management?

17.2.3.2 **Audit procedures when the auditor has a passive duty**

To recap: an auditor's passive duty arises between the date of the auditor's report and the date on which the financial statements are issued. In other words, the auditor has signed the auditor's report and the audit for that particular accounting period is now complete.

The auditor does not have any obligation to perform further audit procedures on the financial statements once they have issued their auditor's report. However, if facts become known to the auditor between the date of the auditor's report and the date on which the financial statements are authorized for issue, which, if known previously, would have caused the auditor to express a modified opinion on the financial statements, the auditor must take further action as follows:

- Discuss the issue with management and consider if the financial statements require amendment.
- Request that management amend the financial statements.
- If the financial statements are amended, perform audit procedures on those amendments to ensure they have been processed correctly.
- Issue a new auditor's report.
- If management do not intend to amend the financial statements and the auditor's report has not yet been issued to the entity, the auditor can still modify the opinion accordingly.
- If the auditor's report has been issued to the entity, the auditor must notify management and those charged with governance **not** to issue the financial statements before the amendments are made.
- If management issue the financial statements despite being requested not to do so by the auditor, the auditor must take action to prevent reliance being placed on the auditor's report. This will usually involve the auditor seeking legal advice in this respect.

The above procedures relate to the period between the date of the auditor's report and the date on which the financial statements are authorized for issue. The auditor is not under any obligation to perform audit procedures on the financial statements once the auditor's report has been issued. However, if they become aware of a fact which would have caused them to modify their audit opinion if they were aware of the issue, they must take action as follows:

- Discuss the matter with management to ascertain if the financial statements require amendment.
- Request management to make the amendments.
- Request management to take the steps necessary to ensure that anyone who is in receipt of the previously issued financial statements is informed of the matter.
- Perform audit procedures on the amendment to ensure they have been processed correctly.
- Issue a new auditor's report on the financial statements which includes an emphasis of matter paragraph (see Chapter 20) to draw attention to the fact that the financial statements and auditor's report have been reissued.
- If management refuse to recall and amend the financial statements, the auditor must take action to prevent reliance on the auditor's report. This will usually involve the auditor seeking legal advice.

17.3 Going concern–responsibilities and evaluation

17.3.1 What is 'going concern' in the context of audit?

The evaluation of going concern is a crucial aspect of the audit. This is where the auditor considers the future prospects of the company and whether enough information has been provided by management in the financial statements to allow users to understand whether the company has financial distress, operational problems, or other difficulties, which might impact its ability to survive.

The auditor's responsibilities in relation to going concern are clearly laid out in ISA (UK) 570 *Going Concern*. However, there is a significant expectation gap, with the general public thinking that auditors have a wider scope in their duties. This often leads to auditors being 'blamed' when an audit client goes bankrupt.

IAS 1 *Presentation of Financial Statements* requires that an entity prepares its financial statements on a going concern basis unless management either intends to liquidate the entity or to cease trading, or has no realistic alternative but to do so. In other words, management have concluded that the entity will continue in business for the foreseeable future.

The term 'foreseeable future' is not a defined term. Care needs to be taken where the foreseeable future is concerned because different jurisdictions may have different requirements. For example, in the UK the foreseeable future is twelve months from the date on which the financial statements are authorized for issue (i.e. approved). In practice, it is imperative that national requirements are also considered as they may differ from the requirements of IFRS.

17.3.2 Management's responsibilities in respect of going concern

Management is responsible for assessing the entity's ability to continue as a going concern. This should be part of their ongoing monitoring of business performance and risk management processes.

Of course, assessing going concern will involve judgement for both management and auditors because going concern is a forward-looking concept and the use of judgement increases uncertainty. The further into the future the evaluation of the company's prospects is made, the level of subjectivity and judgement increases.

Management can only carry out their assessment of going concern using information at their disposal at the time of the assessment. However, IAS 1 says that when management is carrying out their assessment of going concern, it must take into consideration all available information about the future, which is at least, but not limited to, twelve months from the end of the reporting period. Therefore, management will usually extend their assessment of going concern beyond twelve months.

If management are aware of any material uncertainties which may cast doubt upon the entity's ability to continue as a going concern for the foreseeable future, the entity must disclose those uncertainties in the financial statements. Factors which management should consider include:

- current and future levels of profitability;
- loan repayment schedules;
- up-to-date cash flow forecasts;
- renewal of borrowing facilities; and
- ability to continue to provide goods and/or services to customers.

Activity 17.4 Going concern problems

Think of as many different reasons as you can for a company to have going concern problems.

The impact of management's assessment of going concern on the financial statements is summarized in Figure 17.4.

It should be noted that it is very rare to see financial statements produced on a basis other than the going concern basis—it really only happens if a company is already in liquidation or is very close to being put into liquidation. When financial statements are prepared in this situation, they are sometimes known as 'break-up basis' financial statements, though this is not a technical term. Essentially it means that the financial statements are not prepared using IFRS or other usual accounting rules. Instead, the assets are valued at disposal value, liabilities recorded at their current value, and terms such as 'non-current' are not used, because there is no long-term future for the company. This basis usually cannot be used if the financial statements are being prepared under IFRS or other accounting standards as it is inconsistent with the recognition and measurement requirements.

It is more common to see financial statements prepared using the going concern basis but with a disclosure about material uncertainties. It is a matter of significant judgement for management to decide how much information to provide about the uncertainties, as

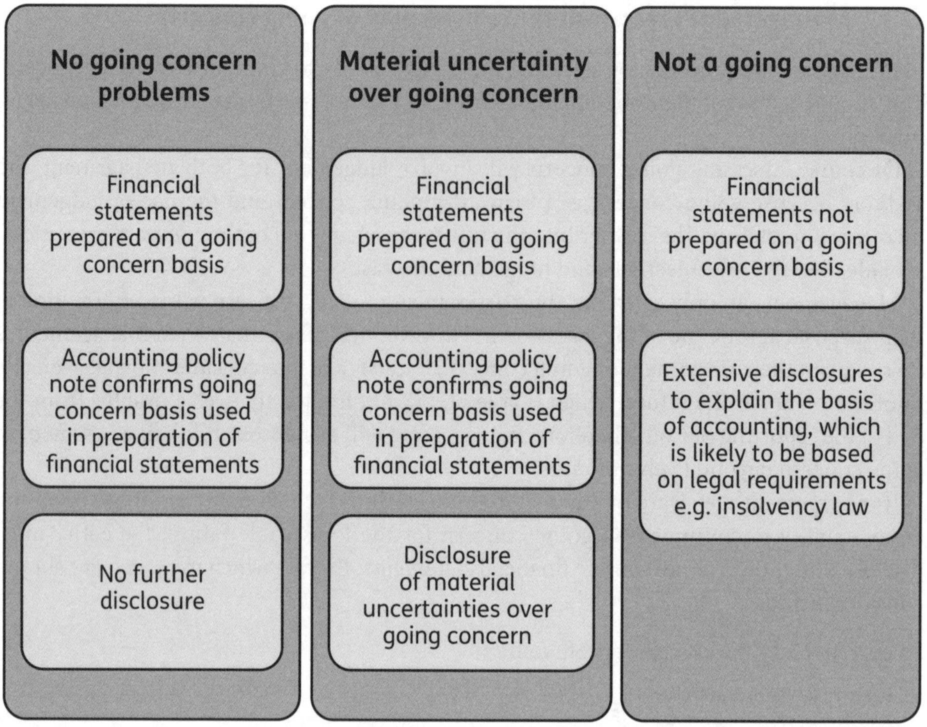

Figure 17.4 Impact of going concern assessment on financial statements

IAS 1 does not specify exactly what has to be disclosed. You can see why management may be reluctant to disclose very much information about the company's problems, as the information may itself trigger further difficulties (e.g. make it harder for the company to raise finance).

This is one of the reasons why ISA (UK) 570 contains specific requirements for the auditor to maintain professional scepticism throughout the audit and also to evaluate whether events or conditions that may cast significant doubt on the entity's ability to continue as a going concern give rise to a risk of management bias in the preparation of the financial statements.

Auditing in practice 17.3 Going concern and viability

In the UK, new requirements were introduced following the Sharman Inquiry, which took place after the financial crisis of 2008. The Sharman Inquiry identified that the going concern disclosures required by IAS 1 were not sufficient for investors' needs and that investors would benefit from more information about longer-term future prospects. As a result, listed companies are required to include a viability statement within the annual report. The viability statement provides information on longer-term prospects and viability.

The viability statement should link to principal risks facing the business, which are discussed in the Strategic Report. Management should provide details of how the board monitors factors which impact viability, include information on assumptions used by management in their evaluations, and discuss any relevant actions planned by management. Discussion of business model resilience and stress testing are also useful. The regulations do not specify a time horizon for the assessment of viability, and periods of three to five years from the reporting date are usually seen.

The inquiry also recommended that:

> in addition to addressing the basis of accounting and material uncertainty disclosures, the auditor also considers the directors' going concern assessment process and narrative disclosures about the going concern status of the entity and includes a statement in the auditor's report as to whether the auditor has anything to add to or emphasise in relation to the disclosures made by the directors about the robustness of the process and its outcome.[7]

17.3.3 **Auditor's evaluation of going concern**

The auditor's responsibilities are to obtain sufficient appropriate audit evidence regarding, and conclude on:

- whether a material uncertainty related to going concern exists; and
- the appropriateness of management's use of the going concern basis of accounting in the preparation of the financial statements.

These responsibilities exist even if the financial reporting framework used in the preparation of the financial statements does not include an explicit requirement for management to make a specific assessment of the entity's ability to continue as a going concern.[8]

To achieve these responsibilities, ISA (UK) 570 requires the auditor to consider going concern from the start of the audit process, when performing risk assessment procedures. This is an important point to note—going concern is often thought of as a 'completion issue' but ISA (UK) 570 requires auditors to consider it all the way through the audit, starting with the planning stage. As we saw when we looked at risk assessment in Chapter 9, the auditor must obtain information about the entity and its environment, including its risk assessment process and specifically risks which may impact the ability to continue as a going concern. Considering going concern at the planning stage means that appropriate audit effort can be planned, and relevant audit procedures designed.

ISA (UK) 570 specifically requires auditors to remain alert throughout the audit for audit evidence of events or conditions that may cast significant doubt on the entity's ability to continue as a going concern.[9] Obviously, events may arise after audit planning which impact going concern, and the audit plan may need to be adjusted accordingly.

[7] *Sharman Inquiry—Going concern and liquidity risks: Lessons for companies and auditors* (2012).

[8] FRC, 'ISA (UK) 570', 2022, para 6-1 <https://media.frc.org.uk/documents/Revised_Going_Concern_Updated_May_2022.pdf> (accessed 18 January 2024).

[9] Ibid., para 11.

17.3.4 **Audit procedures–going concern**

According to ISA (UK) 570, the auditor must evaluate management's assessment of the entity's ability to continue as a going concern. The auditor must also obtain sufficient appropriate audit evidence about:

(a) Whether events or conditions exist that may cast significant doubt on the entity's ability to continue as a going concern;

(b) Whether or not a material uncertainty related to going concern exists; and

(c) The appropriateness of management's use of the going concern basis of accounting in the preparation of the financial statements.[10]

Once this assessment has been carried out, the auditor must then perform audit procedures. These audit procedures include:

- Evaluating management's method to assess going concern. This must include determining if:
  - The method selected is appropriate in the context of the applicable financial reporting framework and the auditor's understanding of the entity;
  - Changes from the method used in prior periods are appropriate; and
  - Whether the calculations are applied in accordance with the method and are mathematically accurate.
- Evaluating the relevance and reliability of the underlying data used to make the assessment.
- Evaluating the assumptions on which management's assessment is based by determining whether there is adequate support for the assumptions underlying management's assessment. This shall include determining:
  - Whether the assumptions are appropriate in the context of the applicable financial reporting framework, and if applicable, changes from prior periods are appropriate; and
  - Whether the assumptions are consistent with each other and with related assumptions used in other areas of the entity's business activities, based on the auditor's knowledge obtained in the audit.
- Evaluating management's plans for future actions in relation to its going concern assessment, including determining whether the outcome of these plans is likely to improve the situation and whether management's plans are feasible in the circumstances.
- Considering whether any additional facts or information have become available since the date on which management made its assessment.
- Requesting written representations from management and, where appropriate, those charged with governance, regarding their plans for future actions and the feasibility of those plans.[11]

[10] Ibid., para 12-1. [11] Ibid., para 12-2.

By carrying out the procedures listed above, the auditor is forming their own view on the company's going concern status, and comparing it with the assessment performed by management. The auditor therefore can evaluate how well management is performing their assessment.

Where the auditor concludes that there are doubts over the going concern ability of the entity, the following procedures should be carried out, to obtain sufficient evidence to support the auditor's conclusion on going concern:

- Obtain the cash flow statement (see section 17.3.5) and other relevant budgets and forecasts and discuss these with management to understand the basis on which they have been prepared and consider the reliability of the data underpinning these cash flow statements/budgets/forecasts.
- Obtain the latest available interim accounts (e.g. management accounts) and assess whether these indicate going concern uncertainties.
- Review the terms of loan agreements and determine if any have been breached.
- Review/recalculate loan covenants and assess whether any breaches have arisen.
- Review correspondence from the bank for any indication that a loan or overdraft may be recalled.
- Read minutes of meetings of the shareholders and the directors and remain alert to any issues about the entity's financing.
- With the client's permission, discuss any litigation claims with the entity's lawyers and the impact the outcome of these claims will have on cash flow.
- If borrowing facilities are not being renewed, discuss how the company will source alternative working capital requirements.
- Review the work done on subsequent events (see section 17.2) to identify any issues which may mitigate any going concern uncertainties or events which may create uncertainties in respect of going concern.
- Review correspondence with customers for evidence of any disputes which may affect the recoverability of receivables.
- Obtain a written representation from management regarding its plans for the future and how management's plans address the going concern problems.

17.3.5 **Cash flow forecasts**

Companies maintain a cash flow forecast which aims to predict cash inflows and cash outflows to help companies manage their cash flow properly to avoid running out of available cash. These are often maintained on a month-by-month basis for a period of twelve months or longer but shorter periods such as week to week or day to day are sometimes maintained and can also be maintained for a longer period than twelve months; for example, two years or even five years.

A cash flow forecast can provide the auditor with some comfort over the going concern status of an entity. However, the auditor cannot just accept a cash flow forecast as sufficient and appropriate audit evidence; they have to carry out audit procedures over that cash flow forecast to make sure the underlying data within the forecast is reasonable. The auditor may also consider it necessary to test the controls over that data to ensure operating effectiveness. Typical procedures over an entity's cash flow forecast include the following:

- Agree the opening balance of the cash flow forecast to the closing balance of the cash book so as to ensure the starting position of the forecast is correct.
- Review prior years' audit procedures over the cash flow forecast to determine how accurate the entity's forecast has been in the past. If previous forecasts have been reasonable, the likelihood is that the current year's will also be reasonable.
- Determine the assumptions that have been used in the cash flow forecast. For example, if costs are increasing then there should be an increase in cash payments.
- Agree the timing of receipt of cash from receivables and payments of cash to payables are in line with the company's credit period for receivables and payables.
- Examine budgets and forecasts and assess whether the cash flow forecast is in line with these budgets and forecasts.
- Examine current-year management accounts and determine whether the cash flow forecast is consistent with those management accounts.
- Agree cash outflows for non-current assets to supplier quotations.
- Consider the adequacy of increased working capital requirements and whether this has been accurately reflected in the cash flow forecast.
- Recalculate the cash flow forecast to verify arithmetical accuracy.
- Inspect board minutes for any other relevant issues that should be reflected within the cash flow forecast.

17.4 Reporting on going concern and the expectation gap

17.4.1 Material uncertainties relating to going concern

As we saw earlier, where management conclude that the going concern basis is appropriate but there are material uncertainties present, then disclosures about the material uncertainty must be made in the financial statements to comply with the requirements of IAS 1.

The auditor must review the disclosures in respect of going concern that have been made in the financial statements. The auditor must conclude as to whether those going concern disclosure are adequate or not, by considering whether the financial statements:

> a) Appropriately disclose the principal events or conditions that may cast significant doubt on the entity's ability to continue as a going concern and management's plans to deal with these events or conditions; and
>
> b) Disclose clearly that there is a material uncertainty related to events or conditions that may cast significant doubt on the entity's ability to continue as a going concern and, therefore, that it may be unable to realize its assets and discharge its liabilities in the normal course of business.[12]

If the auditor concludes that the disclosures are adequate, then they must include a 'Material Uncertainty Related to Going Concern' paragraph in the auditor's report. This is

[12] Ibid., para 19.

a separate section of the auditor's report and is usually placed after the 'Basis for Opinion' paragraph.

The material uncertainty related to going concern paragraph will cross-refer to the relevant disclosure note in the financial statements which addresses the material uncertainty. In addition, the paragraph must also confirm that the auditor's opinion is not modified in respect of this uncertainty. Typical wording of the paragraph is shown by this example:

Material Uncertainty Related to Going Concern

We draw your attention to Note 20 which indicates that the effects of high inflation and challenging economic circumstances has had a detrimental impact on the company's operations and cash flows. In addition, the company's bank will not make any decisions concerning renewing the company's borrowing facilities until after the financial statements have been approved. As stated in Note 20, these events or conditions, along with other matters as set forth in Note 20, indicate that a material uncertainty exists that may cast significant doubt on the company's ability to continue as a going concern. Our opinion is not modified in respect of this matter.

A material uncertainty related to going concern paragraph can only be used when the entity has adequately disclosed material uncertainties related to going concern (i.e. the financial statements comply with the IAS 1 disclosure requirements).

When the auditor reports on key audit matters (KAMs) in accordance with ISA (UK) 701 *Communicating Key Audit Matters in the Independent Auditor's Report* a material uncertainty related to going concern is considered to be a KAM by its nature. In such cases, the auditor may discuss how the matter was addressed in the audit (although they are not specifically required to do this). We will consider KAMs in detail in Chapter 20.

If the auditor concludes that there is a material uncertainty over going concern and that the disclosures made by management are inadequate, the auditor will modify the opinion and express a qualified opinion or an adverse opinion instead (see Figure 17.5). We will look at modified audit opinion in more detail in Chapter 21.

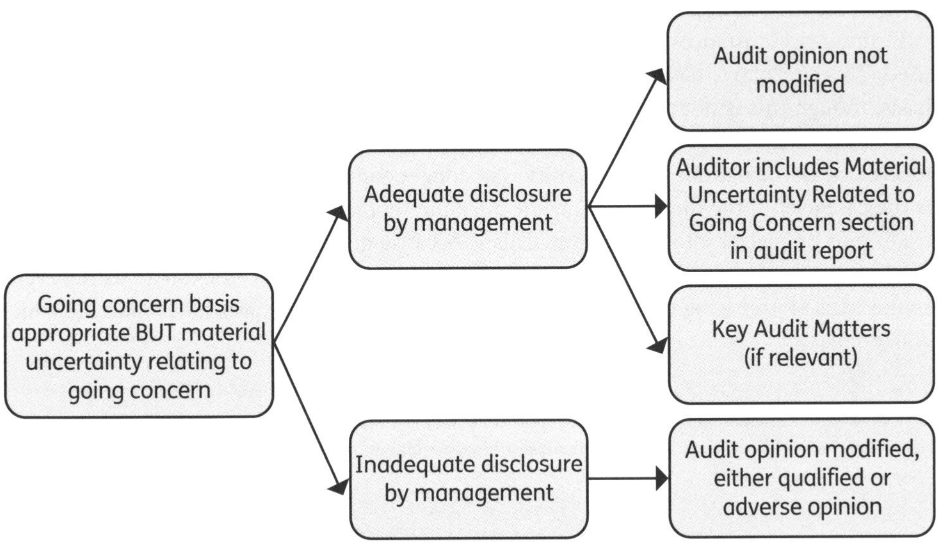

Figure 17.5 Impact on audit report of a material uncertainty relating to going concern

Auditing in practice 17.4 Material uncertainty related to going concern

The auditor's report for Cineworld plc, for the year ended 31 December 2019, included a material uncertainty related to going concern section:

Material uncertainty related to going concern

In forming our opinion on the financial statements, which is not modified, we have considered the adequacy of the disclosure made in Note 1 to the financial statements concerning the Group's and Company's ability to continue as a going concern. The Group's forecasts and projections assume that the Cineplex deal will complete which will result in increased borrowings of $2.3 billion, of which the $0.3 million bridge facility has an associated covenant, equivalent to that of the existing revolving credit facility. Unlike the revolving credit facility, the covenant applies at all times, irrespective of the bridge facility drawing levels. There are also cross default clauses in respect of the existing term loans and the additional term loan required to complete the Cineplex transaction. In the event that admissions were to be restricted or cinemas were to be closed, resulting in a loss of revenue equivalent to a period of between two and three months, as a result of COVID-19, then the Group would be in breach of its covenants and would need to negotiate a waiver with the majority of the lenders in order to avoid its borrowings becoming repayable immediately. These conditions, along with other matters explained in Note 1 to the financial statements, indicate the existence of a material uncertainty which may cast significant doubt about the Group's and Company's ability to continue as a going concern. The financial statements do not include the adjustments that would result if the Group and Company were unable to continue as a going concern.[13]

You can see that the auditors clearly state that the audit opinion is not modified, there is an explanation of the material uncertainties, and a reference to the note to the financial statements where management have provided a full description of the material uncertainties.

17.4.2 **Going concern basis is not appropriate**

Unfortunately, the impact of events or conditions such as economic recession could be disastrous for some companies and the directors may conclude that they have no alternative but to liquidate the business or cease trading.

In these circumstances, IAS 1 requires a basis other than the going concern basis to be used. This alternative basis for the financial statements is sometimes called the 'break-up basis', though this is not a 'technical term' derived from financial reporting requirements. The directors must disclose on which basis the financial statements have been drawn up together with the reasons why the entity is no longer considered to be a going concern. This is the case even if the directors conclude after the reporting date that the entity will cease trading or be placed into liquidation. This is because going concern is a forward-looking concept so what would normally be a non-adjusting event now becomes an adjusting event so the basis of preparing the financial statements is changed to a basis other than the going concern basis.

[13] Cineworld Cinemas Limited, 'Annual report and financial statements', 2019 <https://www.cineworldplc.com/sites/cineworld-plc/files/cineworld-cinemas-limited-annual-accounts-for-the-year-ending-31122019.pdf> (accessed 19 January 2024).

Auditing scenario 17.4 Going concern basis of accounting is inappropriate

Pastures Ltd has experienced a significant decline in profitability and cash flow over the last couple of years. The company has prepared its financial statements for the year ended 30 June 20X3 but on 16 July 20X3 the directors decided the company will cease trading as the bank has confirmed that it is unwilling to support the business any further.

The financial statements for the year ended 30 June 20X3 include the following note in respect of the basis of preparation of the financial statements:

Basis of preparation of the financial statements

As explained in Note 13 to the financial statements, the company will cease trading on 16 July 20X3 and the financial statements have been prepared on a basis other than the going concern basis. This basis includes, where applicable, writing the company's assets down to net realizable value. Provisions have also been made in respect of contracts that have become onerous at the reporting date. No provision has been made for the future costs of terminating the business unless such costs were committed to at the reporting date.

In this scenario, the directors have concluded the going concern basis of accounting is inappropriate because the company is to cease trading after the reporting date has passed.

Assuming that the disclosure note provided by management is appropriate, the audit opinion will be 'true and fair' and the auditor's report will include an emphasis of matter paragraph which will cross-reference to the relevant disclosure and confirm that their opinion is not modified in respect of this issue.

When both management and auditors agree that going concern is not appropriate and the financial statements have been prepared on an alternative basis, if the auditor is satisfied with the disclosures made in the financial statements, they will express an unmodified opinion with an emphasis of matter paragraph which will cross-reference to the relevant disclosure and confirm that their opinion is not modified in respect of this issue. A material uncertainty related to going concern paragraph is not used in such a circumstance because the financial statements have not been prepared on a going concern basis.

However, if the auditor concludes that the entity's use of the going concern basis of accounting is inappropriate but management refuse to change the basis, the auditor must express an adverse opinion accordingly. This could happen, rarely, if management conclude that the entity will continue in operational existence for the foreseeable future, and have prepared the financial statements on that basis, but the auditor disagrees, having evaluated the evidence and concluding that the entity will not continue in operational existence.

In this situation, ISA (UK) 570 requires the auditor to express an adverse opinion because the fact that the entity has used the going concern basis of accounting inappropriately is both material and pervasive. An adverse opinion will state that the financial statements do not give a true and fair view (or present fairly, in all material respects) and is a very serious modified opinion.

Investors would take this to mean that the financial statements cannot be relied upon. We will look at adverse opinions in Chapter 21.

17.4.3 **Expectation gap in relation to going concern**

We have looked at the expectation gap in a number of previous chapters, and in particular, we explored the expectation gap in relation to fraud in Chapter 13. We should therefore be familiar with the concept of the expectation gap—the issue being that there is a difference between what auditors do, and the public expectation of what auditors do.

Here, we turn our attention to the expectation gap in relation to going concern. One way to consider this issue is to think about the media attention which is focused on an audit firm when a high-profile audit client goes bankrupt. Often the audit firm is 'blamed' for not giving adequate warnings about the company's financial distress or operational problems, and sometimes worse, the audit firm can be perceived as contributing to the company's failure.

Auditing in practice 17.5 The collapse of Thomas Cook and the role of EY

The UK-based travel company Thomas Cook collapsed in September 2019. Shortly after the announcement of the company's bankruptcy, the UK government launched an inquiry. Rachel Reeves, Chair of the Business, Energy and Industrial Strategy Committee (BEIS), stated:

> On the question of the role of auditors, the Committee has noted with concern various press reports surrounding the collapse of Thomas Cook and the role of its auditors PwC and EY. *The Times* reported yesterday that the company's former Chief Executive revealed that the Group had a balance sheet deficit in excess of £3.1bn, including £1.9bn of debt and guarantees. Despite this, the *Daily Telegraph* reported that Thomas Cook executives had awarded themselves more than £20m in bonuses over the past five years. *The Times* further reported that the company had used 'aggressive accounting methods to flatter its financial performance'. The *Financial Times* has drawn particular attention to the use of 'separately disclosed items' and 'exceptional one-offs' in its balance sheets and its treatment of goodwill. EY in its 2018 audit of Thomas Cook's accounts noted that: 'Separately disclosed items are not defined by IFRS and therefore considerable judgement is required in determining the appropriateness of such classification'. The Committee is dismayed that similar issues that we identified in the collapse of Carillion and BHS may have occurred at Thomas Cook, including the role of auditors in identifying and addressing problems. This latest collapse reinforces the need for urgent and meaningful reform of the audit industry.[14]

The statement above indicates the government's concern that the auditors had failed to highlight the company's problems and that this is not an isolated incident.

As part of the inquiry, auditor partners from PwC, Thomas Cook's auditor until 2016, and audit partners from EY, who took over from PwC from 2017, were called to a BEIS committee meeting. After a long and heated discussion, in which the auditors were repeatedly asked to explain how they

[14] Letter from Rachel Reeves MP to Andrea Leadsom MP dated 26 September 2019 <https://www.parliament.uk/globalassets/documents/commons-committees/business-energy-and-industrial-strategy/correspondence/190926-chair-to-sec-of-state-thomas-cook.pdf> (accessed 30 June 2023).

had audited going concern, as well as other aspects of the financial statements including goodwill, Rachel Reeves MP said:

> I wonder how many more company failures, how many more egregious cases of accounting do we need? We've had BHS, we've had Carillion, we've had Patisserie Valerie and now we've had Thomas Cook. How many more do we need before your industry opens its ideas and recognises that you are complicit in all of this and that you need to reform? We can't rely on you to do the right thing and legislation is needed. We need tougher regulation because your industry is not willing to make the changes needed. Reform is long overdue and the evidence today makes it clear that that moment has got to come and got to come soon otherwise we'll have more business failures and you will be complicit in those.[15]

The final words in this quote are interesting—Rachel Reeves is saying that auditors could be complicit in company failure. This is a strong statement and goes beyond criticizing auditors for not highlighting going concern problems.

During the committee hearing, the auditors were also criticized for lack of challenge of management assumptions and for not obtaining sufficiently robust evidence regarding impairment.

The Thomas Cook example shows that the expectation gap clearly exists in relation to the audit of going concern. This, and other company collapses in which the role of the auditor has been questioned, including Carillion, Patisserie Valerie, and BHS, have led the UK government to undertake a review of the audit profession as a whole. Part of this review focuses on going concern. Sir Donald Brydon's review into the quality and effectiveness of audit commented that:

> Arguably, the information shareholders want most is reassurance about the resilience of a company.[16]

Resilience to principal risks should already be part of management's evaluation of going concern and the longer-term viability of the company but Brydon proposes that more information should be provided and that auditors should have specific responsibilities. The Brydon Report includes the following recommendations in respect of resilience:

- The board should make a Resilience Statement that incorporates, enhances, and builds on the current Going Concern and Viability Statements.
- Auditors should report to the Board of Directors if they have encountered any information in the course of their audit which leads to an anxiety about the resilience of the business not reflected in the Resilience Statement. If they consider the Board does not pay sufficient attention to their anxieties, they should have an obligation to report to the regulatory body.

[15] Business, Energy and Industrial Strategy Committee, Tuesday 22 October 2019 <https://parliamentlive.tv/Event/Index/25c0408b-4e19-4527-beb7-c707bc0375b7> (accessed 30 June 2023).

[16] *Assess, assure and inform—Improving audit quality and effectiveness*. Report of the Independent Review into the Quality and Effectiveness of Audit (2019) <https://assets.publishing.service.gov.uk/media/5df8edfced915d0938597e1f/brydon-review-final-report.pdf> (accessed 19 January 2024).

These proposals aim to ensure that high-quality, useful information is provided to investors about a company's resilience, and that auditors have a clear mechanism for reporting concerns to users of the auditor's report. Brydon considers that the reporting currently provided is often boilerplate in nature and not very useful. Additionally, there is currently no requirement for auditors to provide specific assurance on the viability statement. Brydon suggests that assurance should be provided but does not specify that the external auditor must provide this assurance.

It is yet to be seen whether Brydon's proposals will be fully implemented, and if they are, if it leads to a reduction in the expectation gap.

Chapter round-up

- Related parties can often be a subjective area of the financial statements because the auditor is, to a certain extent, reliant on the client's management being transparent and honest about the existence of related-party relationships.
- The principal audit risk for related parties is inadequate or missing disclosure.
- The stages for related parties which must be covered are: the risk assessment stage, the fieldwork stage and dealing with any related parties which the auditor was previously unaware of, or which have entered into transactions with the entity that are outside the ordinary course of business.
- Subsequent events include events which are 'adjusting' and 'non-adjusting' events. Adjusting events are reflected in the financial statements, whereas non-adjusting events are disclosed when material.
- The auditor has both an active duty and a passive duty where subsequent events are concerned.
- Going concern is a particularly important (and forward-looking) concept and the auditor will need to ensure that the going concern basis of accounting has been used appropriately when the entity has prepared its financial statements.
- Management is responsible for assessing the entity's ability to continue as a going concern. The auditor is responsible for obtaining sufficient and appropriate audit evidence that management's use of the going concern basis is appropriate and for evaluating the appropriateness of disclosures in relation to material uncertainties related to going concern.
- Cash flow forecasts and budgets are often provided to the auditor to support the going concern basis of accounting. These must be carefully audited to ensure the underlying data, and the controls over that data, are sound. Professional scepticism must be applied when evaluating the assumptions used by management in preparing a cash flow forecast.
- The auditor uses a material uncertainty related to going concern paragraph in the auditor's report when the client has made adequate disclosures in respect of going concern uncertainties.
- If the auditor concludes the going concern basis is inappropriate, but the client has prepared the financial statements using the going concern basis, the auditor expresses an adverse opinion.
- The expectation gap in relation to going concern is a significant issue, which current proposals for reform of the audit profession attempt to resolve.

End of chapter case study

Introduction

This chapter has examined the responsibilities of the auditor in relation to the audit of related parties, subsequent events, and going concern. In this case study we focus on the issue of going concern as this is a very significant part of the audit and one which is often difficult to audit due to the levels of judgement used by both management and auditors in their evaluations of going concern. The case study uses the Covid-19 pandemic as an example of a significant disruption to business activities which may impact going concern. Of course, the pandemic is now over, but the example is still relevant, as business operations can be severely disrupted by other events such as political unrest, which auditors may have to deal with.

This case study links to the following learning outcomes:

- Explain and apply the process for identifying related parties and recommend the audit procedures to obtain sufficient and appropriate audit evidence over related parties and transactions with related parties.
- Discuss the responsibilities of management and the auditor in respect of going concern, identify and explain events and circumstances which may impact going concern, and recommend relevant audit procedures.

Scenario

You are working on the audit of Raja's Retail Company (RRC) Ltd for the year ended 31 March 20X0. The company operates from a large number of retail outlets in the UK but has warehouses located in Spain and Italy. In addition to operating its own retail outlets, the company also supplies goods to online retailers.

The company is preparing its financial statements for the year ended 31 March 20X0 and the impact of Covid-19 has had an adverse effect on operations. All of the retail outlets were closed for a significant part of the year, and much of the revenue generated is through contracts with online retailers, which have struggled to recover. The company has also experienced significant problems in sourcing goods due to border closures and manufacturers in overseas countries that had to close down due to lockdown restrictions. In addition, on 27 April 20X0, a significant contract to supply goods to an online retailer was cancelled indefinitely. At the time of the audit, the government's lockdown legislation means that retail outlets must remain closed until July 20X0, and it is not certain how soon after that date the restrictions on retail activity will be eased.

RRC's overdraft is due for renewal three months after the year end. Currently the company has an overdraft of £155,000, and the limit agreed with the bank is £170,000.

The company's loan agreement is due to be reviewed by the bank in July 20X5 and contain covenants including that interest cover is maintained at 1.2. The bank loan is secured on the company's retail outlets, which are all owned by the company.

The financial statements disclose a contingent liability which relates to a letter of support dated 31 January 20X0, provided by RRC to a company called Yew Property Ltd. On further investigation, you discover that RRC owns 5 per cent of the equity share capital of Yew Property Ltd. In addition, RRC's finance director is also on the board of Yew Property Ltd.

The company's management has prepared cash and profit forecasts to support the negotiations with the bank for continued financial support. However, both management and the auditor consider that there are material uncertainties over RRC Ltd's ability to continue as a going concern.

Table 17.2

	20X1 £'000	20X0 £'000
Revenue	1,500	1,900
Operating expenses	(1,370)	(1,560)
Operating profit	130	340
Finance charge	(300)	(280)
(Loss)/Profit before tax	(170)	60
Total assets	8,760	9,500
Long-term liabilities—bank loan	2,000	2,000
Disclosed in notes to financial statements:		
Contingent liability (in relation to Yew Properties Ltd)	100	-

The notes to the financial statements contain a disclosure relating to the impact of Covid-19 on the business, but they do not specifically disclose information in relation to the company's financial position.

Extracts from the company's draft financial statements are shown in Table 17.2.

Required

1. Using the information provided, identify and discuss the matters which should be taken into account by the auditor when evaluating the company's going concern status.
2. Recommend the audit procedures to be performed in relation to going concern issues identified.
3. Discuss whether Yew Properties Ltd could be a related party of RRC and outline the audit implications should they be related parties.
4. Assuming that the note to the financial statements does *not*, in the auditor's judgement, adequately explain the material uncertainties related to going concern, discuss the potential impact on the auditor's reports.

Answer

1. Evaluation of the company's going concern status

Revenue and profitability

The financial statements show that revenue has fallen by 21 per cent, operating profit by almost 62 per cent. The operating margin is now only 8.6 per cent, compared to 18 per cent in the previous year. Overall the company is loss-making. The trends observed are highly significant and are likely to be due to the impact of the Covid-19 pandemic, which has led to the closure of retail stores and therefore a loss of a significant stream of income.

The loss-making position does not in itself mean that the company is not a going concern. However, the operational problems facing the company (discussed below), are extremely concerning and will have further negative impacts on the company's financial performance.

Financial position

The company's total assets have reduced by 7.8 per cent. This could indicate that there is no reinvestment being made in assets or that assets have been sold in order to raise cash.

The bank loan is significant, amounting to 22.8 per cent of total assets this year end. RRC has no cash and is reliant on an overdraft which is due for renewal shortly. If the bank does not agree to renew the overdraft, RRC will be left with very little in terms of liquidity, and it could struggle to make necessary payments such as payroll or to suppliers.

The bank loan includes a covenant that interest cover must be maintained at 1.2. In 20X0 this was just achieved, but in 20X1, the interest cover is only 0.4. The covenant has been breached which makes it unlikely that the bank will extend further borrowing, and the existing loan could be recalled.

The bank loan is secured on the company's retail outlets, so if the company defaults on payments of interest or capital, the bank has the right to seize the assets in order to recoup their funds. If this were to happen, which seems likely given the company's limited cash resources, RRC would lose its operational facilities and it is difficult to see how the company could continue to survive, unless all of its sales were moved online.

The letter of support provided to Yew Properties Ltd exposes RRC to a possible future cash outflow of £100,000. Given the company's current lack of cash and bleak prospects for the future, if the financial support is called upon, it is unlikely that RRC would have cash available to provide the financial support which the company has agreed to. Even if some finance were available, it is a cash outflow which the company can ill-afford to make.

Operational problems

The ongoing operational problems caused by the Covid-19 pandemic means that the company faces a range of significant business risks. Its retail outlets have been closed, and it is not clear at the time of the audit when they will be allowed to reopen. There is the risk that the government may impose further lockdown restrictions, leading to uncertainty over the sustainability of cash inflows and revenue generation. Closure of borders has disrupted the supply of RRC's goods into the UK, adding to the operational problems facing the company. Again, it is not clear when the borders will be fully open for trade.

2. Audit procedures to be performed in relation to going concern

- Obtain and review management accounts for the period after the reporting date and perform analytical review to ascertain the trends in profitability and cash flows since the year end.
- Discuss with management the strategy which is being developed to improve the company's financial performance (e.g. plans to maximize online sales).
- Discuss with management the cancellation of the contract to supply an online retailer to understand the circumstances and consider whether other contracts could be cancelled.
- Obtain cash flow and profit forecasts and review assumptions to ensure they are in line with auditor's expectations.
- Confirm that the data used to prepare the forecasts is reasonable and reliable.
- Perform sensitivity analysis on the forecasts to evaluate the impact of changes in key variables e.g. predictions of when retail outlets will be allowed to reopen.
- As part of a subsequent events review, as close as possible to the date of signing the auditor's report, evaluate the impact of the government's lockdown regulations and consider their impact on RRC (e.g. is there an update on when retail outlets can reopen and on when importation of goods will become easier?).
- Obtain and review the documentation relating to bank loan to confirm the following:
  - the amount of the loan;
  - the interest rate and repayment dates;

  - the details of the charge over the company's properties; and
  - the details of the covenant and the repercussions of the company breaching the covenant.
- Review correspondence with the bank in relation to the loan and overdraft to form a view on the bank's level of support for RRC.
- Obtain the letter of support in relation to Yew Properties to confirm the conditions under which RRC would become liable for payment of the £100,000.
- Discuss the letter of support with management to understand the rationale for providing the support.
- Review the minutes of management meetings where the letter of support was discussed and approved and for any other relevant details.
- Obtain a written representation from management regarding going concern.

3. Discuss whether Yew Properties Ltd could be a related party of RRC and outline the implications should they be related parties

According to IAS 24 two entities are not related to each other simply because they have a director or key manager in common. So, the fact that the finance director of RRC is also on the board of Yew Properties Ltd does not necessarily make the two companies related parties.

However, the facts that RRC owns 5 per cent of the share capital of Yew Properties Ltd, and that RRC has provided the letter of support to Yew Properties could provide evidence that there is a related-party relationship. In particular, the exact nature of the finance director's role in Yew Properties needs to be understood. If he or she exerts control over Yew Properties Ltd, for example, by being the sole director, then it is likely that the two companies should be treated as related parties.

The auditor should perform specific procedures to determine the nature of the relationship between the two companies, including:

- Discuss the situation with the finance director, to obtain understanding as to their level of involvement with Yew Properties Ltd, the extent of their control or influence over the company.
- Using a Companies House search, obtain the most recent financial statements of Yew Properties Ltd to confirm the names of the company's directors and shareholders.

Should the two companies be related parties, the financial support provided by RRC to Yew Properties Ltd should be disclosed as a related-party transaction. This is because according to IAS 24, provision of guarantees or collateral is an example of a transaction that should be disclosed if it is with a related party. In this case, the auditor would need to confirm that a note to the financial statements has been provided which provides the information as required by IAS 24.

4. Potential implication for the auditor's report in respect of material uncertainty related to going concern disclosure

If the details provided in the note to the financial statements are inadequate and do not fully explain the significant uncertainties affecting the going concern status of the company, the auditor should express a modified opinion, as the disclosure requirements of IAS 1 have not been followed, causing a material misstatement. The auditor would need to use judgement to decide whether a qualified or an adverse opinion should be given. A qualified opinion would be given if the misstatement is considered to be material, an adverse opinion would be given if the misstatement is considered to be both material and pervasive to the financial statements.

ISA 705 *Modifications to the Opinion in the Independent Auditor's Report* provides guidance on the presentation of the auditor's report in the case of a modification of the audit opinion. The auditor's report should include a paragraph entitled 'Basis for Qualified Opinion' or 'Basis for Adverse Opinion', which contains specific reference to the matter giving rise to material or pervasive misstatement. The paragraph should include a clear description of the uncertainties and should be presented immediately before the opinion paragraph.

ISA 705 states that when the auditor expects to modify the opinion in the auditor's report, the auditor shall communicate with those charged with governance the circumstances which led to the expected modification and the proposed wording of the modification. Therefore, the situation must be discussed with those charged with governance, who should be given opportunity to amend the financial statements by providing sufficient information in respect of the material uncertainties relating to going concern.

Activity solutions

Activity 17.1—Related parties and fraud

Discuss the ways that related-party transactions could be used for fraudulent activity.

Suggested answer points:

Sales of assets could be made to related parties at below market price, this has the effect of extracting assets from the company and transferring wealth to the related party. For example, a company could sell a car with a market value of £25,000 to a related party for £1,000. This type of fraud, a misappropriation of assets, is common in smaller businesses (e.g. where the owner-manager could arrange the transaction and sell the car to their spouse).

Another mechanism that could be used to transfer wealth to a related party is by fake purchases, or purchases from a related party where the price is above market value.

A company could create fictitious sales invoices with a related party. The invoices are recognized as revenue and a corresponding trade receivable is recognized. However, it is a fake transaction used to inflate profit and assets. This type of fraud is fraudulent financial reporting.

A loan could be made or received from a related party. The interest could be manipulated to be above or below market value, or interest-free, depending on the objective of the fraud. For example, if a company makes a loan to a related party, and charges interest above market rate, wealth is transferred from the related party to the company.

In groups of companies, it is easy to transfer assets and liabilities between companies using related-party transactions (e.g. one subsidiary can make an intercompany transfer of debt to another subsidiary). At group level, the intercompany transaction would be cancelled out as a consolidation adjustment, but the accounts of the individual subsidiaries would be misstated.

Activity 17.2—Adjusting and non-adjusting events

Can you think of further examples of both adjusting and non-adjusting events?

Suggested answer points:

Examples of adjusting events include:

- Sale of inventories after the year end which gives evidence of their year-end valuation.
- Evidence of impairment of non-current assets at the year end.

- Settlement of court cases or insurance claims which were in process at the year end.
- Discovery of fraud or errors that show the financial statements were incorrect.

Examples of non-adjusting events include:

- Destruction of assets or damages caused to assets by a catastrophe such as a fire or flooding.
- A decision to discontinue an operation or carry out major restructuring.
- Major purchases or disposals of assets.
- A decline in the value of assets since the year end (e.g. decline in the market value of investments).
- Entering into significant borrowing arrangements, significant commitments, or contingent liabilities.
- Commencing major litigation arising out of events that occurred solely after the reporting period.
- Sale of a major subsidiary.
- Dividends declared after the year end.

Activity 17.3—Inquiry of management

Imagine you have been tasked by your audit supervisor with asking management some questions about subsequent events. Your objective is to find out whether any subsequent events have taken place which may need further investigation.

What inquiries might you make with management?

Suggested answer points:

- Whether new commitments, borrowings, or guarantees have been entered into.[17]
- Whether sales or acquisitions of assets have occurred or are planned.
- Whether there have been increases in capital or issuance of debt instruments, such as the issue of new shares or debentures, or an agreement to merge or liquidate has been made or is planned.
- Whether any assets have been appropriated by government, or destroyed (e.g. by fire or flood).
- Whether there have been any developments regarding contingencies.
- Whether any unusual accounting adjustments have been made or are contemplated.
- Whether any events have occurred or are likely to occur that will bring into question the appropriateness of accounting policies used in the financial statements, as would be the case, for example, if such events call into question the validity of the going concern assumption.
- Whether any events have occurred that are relevant to the measurement of estimates or provisions made in the financial statements.
- Whether any events have occurred that are relevant to the recoverability of assets.

Activity 17.4—Going concern problems

Think of as many different reasons as you can for a company to have going concern problems.

Suggested answer points:

Table 17.3 illustrates situations which may indicate there are going concern problems.

[17] Answer points taken from ISA 560, para A9.

Table 17.3

Indicator of going concern	Why it is an issue
The statement of financial position shows a net current liabilities or net liabilities position	This indicates that the entity may be unable to meet its debts as they fall due
The bank does not renew borrowing facilities or does not approve a loan application	A lack of cash makes it difficult for a company to pay suppliers, employees, and other liabilities
The terms of a loan agreement or covenants have been breached	Breaches of a loan agreement or a loan covenants may trigger immediate repayment of the loan hence placing additional pressure on cash flow
Staff are not paid on time	This indicates a lack of working capital and potential loss of employee goodwill
Legal claims have been brought against the entity	If successful, these claims may result in significant cash outflows thus placing additional pressure on cash flow
Loss of key staff	This may make it difficult for the entity to trade
Changes in law and regulation	Such changes may make it costlier for the business to comply and the costs of compliance may be more than the company can realistically afford
Withdrawal of credit facilities by suppliers or a failure to obtain credit	This indicates a bad credit-rating which usually arises from a failure to pay liabilities
Missing payments to the tax authority	Payments to tax authorities must be prioritized and any missed payments may indicate the company has a lack of working capital
Negative cash flows	This indicates overtrading and/or lack of management of working capital
Significant bad debts	Significant bad debts will place pressure on the company's cash flow resulting in an inability to meet its liabilities
Successful competitors	Successful competitors will have a detrimental effect on revenue if customers decide to buy from the competitor
Uninsured catastrophes	A fire, flood or other disaster which is uninsured may mean the company cannot survive
Major technological change	An inability to keep up with major technological changes or an inability to afford to keep up with such changes may result in a loss of customers and inventory obsolescence

18 Completing the Audit

Introduction

The completion stage of the audit is of critical importance and is the culmination of the entire audit process. It is at this stage that the audit engagement partner will review the audit evidence obtained during the fieldwork stage and evaluate its sufficiency and appropriateness. The partner will review the audit documentation to establish how difficult and/or contentious issues have been resolved and if there are any outstanding issues to be discussed with the client. The financial statements are subject to final analytical review with the objective of forming the overall audit opinion that will be included in the auditor's report. The opinion in the auditor's report is the audit engagement partner's responsibility; they cannot delegate any aspect of this responsibility to another team member.

A key objective of the audit partner's review is to evaluate the misstatements that have been identified during the audit, and to consider appropriate actions. If adjustments to the financial statements are needed, the auditor will raise this with management of the audit client. Material misstatements will need to be corrected in order to avoid a modification to the auditor's opinion.

The review of audit work is not the sole review that takes place. On many audits, an engagement quality review (EQR) is carried out, by an independent senior auditor. This is typical for the audits of listed companies and other high-risk engagements and is part of a system of audit quality management within the audit firm. We looked at audit reviews and audit quality in Chapter 5, so we will recap the key points here as they are highly relevant to this stage of the audit.

There are final audit procedures to complete in relation to opening balances, comparative information, and the 'other information' which is to be published alongside the financial statements. These procedures are usually performed at the completion stage of the audit as this is when the final version of the financial statements and accompanying information is made available to the auditor.

In this chapter, we will examine the application of the following ISAs:

- ISA (UK) 520 Analytical Procedures
- ISA (UK) 450 Evaluation of Misstatements Identified during the Audit
- ISA(UK) 710 Comparative Information—Corresponding Figures and Comparative Financial Statements
- ISA (UK) 720 The Auditor's Responsibilities Relating to Other Information

Learning outcomes

- Describe and apply the use of analytical procedures when evaluating and reviewing the financial statements.
- Evaluate the effect of misstatements on the financial statements and recommend appropriate actions to be taken by the auditor.
- Explain the auditor's responsibility in respect of opening balances and comparative information.
- Explain the auditor's responsibility for other information contained in the annual report and recommend actions to be taken if there are inconsistencies.
- Describe the quality review which should take place by the audit engagement partner and discuss the main features of an EQR.

By the end of this chapter, you will be able to:

- Evaluate audit evidence to confirm if sufficient and appropriate evidence has been obtained.
- Discuss the importance of quality reviews and the different types of review that take place.

18.1 Final analytical review

As we saw in Chapter 10, analytical procedures are dealt with in ISA (UK) 520 *Analytical Procedures*. To recap: analytical procedures are generally used at three stages of the audit. Remember that analytical review is mandatory as part of risk assessment at the planning stage of the audit and it is also mandatory at the final stage of the audit, which is the focus of our attention in this chapter (Figure 18.1).

Towards the end of the audit process, the audit client will prepare the final draft of the financial statements which will include adjustments based on any misstatements identified by the auditor. The auditor will then review the final draft of the financial statements in line with ISA (UK) 520. The objective of this review is for the auditor to form an overall conclusion as to whether the financial statements are consistent with the auditor's understanding of the entity and whether the financial statements are free from material misstatement.

In Chapter 10, we identified various analytical review procedures including comparison of current figures with prior year figures, calculation of ratios (such as gross profit margin, receivables collection period, and gearing ratios) and comparison of the figures in the client's draft financial statements with the financial statements of other entities in the same industry.

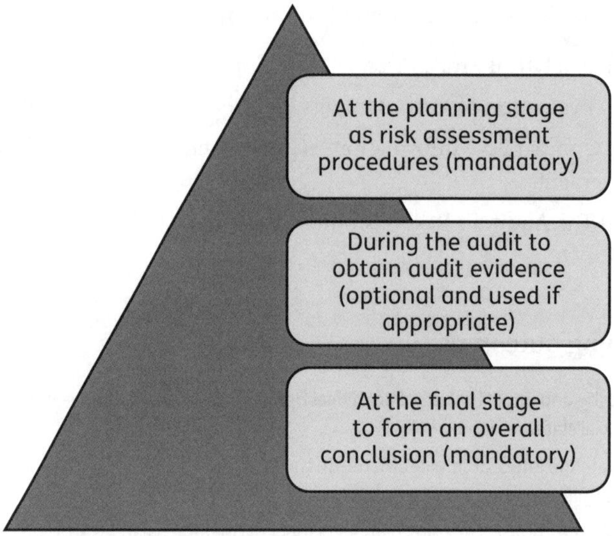

Figure 18.1 Analytical review during the audit process

The analytical review procedures that the auditor carries out at the final stage of the audit will not differ from those performed at the planning stage.

While the auditor will carry out the same analytical procedures at the final stage of the audit as they did at the planning stage, the difference is that at the completion phase the auditor should have sufficient audit evidence available to explain the issues that have been highlighted by the analytical procedures and hence should be able to conclude as the overall reasonableness of the financial statements. If, at this stage, the auditor finds any previously unidentified risks of material misstatement, further audit evidence will need to be obtained.

Auditing scenario 18.1 Final analytical procedures

Table 18.1 provides sample final draft financial statements.

Table 18.1 Final draft financial statements for Sunnie Ltd (year ended 31 December 20X9)

	31.12.20X9	31.12.20X8
	£'000	£'000
Revenue	15,200	13,150
Cost of sales	(9,641)	(7,136)
Gross profit	5,559	6,014

During the planning stage of the audit, the audit senior calculated the gross profit margins as set out in Table 18.2.

These ratios tell us that for every £1 that Sunnie Ltd sells, it made a gross profit of 36.6p in the £ in 20X9 before administrative expenses and a gross profit of 45.7p in the pound in 20X8 before administrative expenses. Something has happened in the current year which has meant that the gross profit margin has declined. In most businesses, gross profit margins will remain relatively stable, but,

Table 18.2 Gross profit margins for Sunnie Ltd (year ended 31 December 20X9)

20X9:	£5,559/£15,200 x 100	=	36.6%
20X8:	£6,014/£13,150 x 100	=	45.7%

in this case, they appear to have declined by nearly 20 per cent. The auditor will have devised audit procedures at the planning stage to ascertain the reasons for this decrease in gross margin.

When performing those audit procedures, the auditor has discovered that in 20X9, the company suffered price increases from four of its major suppliers which it could not pass on to its customers. Sufficient audit evidence should have been obtained by the auditor to corroborate this explanation and, assuming the evidence is sufficient, at the final review stage, the audit engagement partner can conclude that the decrease in the gross profit margin is reasonable and supported by appropriate audit evidence.

Now, consider if the gross profit margin had decreased because some purchase invoices for 20Y0 had been included in the 20X9 financial statements (i.e. they have been included in the incorrect accounting period) and the client refuses to correct the misposting. In this case, assuming that the error is material, it is likely that there may be a modified audit opinion issued because the financial statements contain a material misstatement.

Carrying out analytical procedures at the end of the audit will help the auditor to justify any trends or relationships within the figures which may be beyond expectations. Essentially, the auditor is obtaining corroboratory information so they, too, can explain why certain trends and relationships are as they are in the financial statements. This helps when the audit file is being reviewed for quality control purposes as the reviewer is also likely to inquire why certain fluctuations (e.g. in the gross profit margin above) have arisen.

Remember, it is not just about the auditor looking at the numerical information in the statement of comprehensive income, statement of financial position, statement of changes in equity, and statement of cash flows. The auditor must also review the notes to the financial statements as these contain crucial information which essentially breaks down the figures in the primary financial statements into more detail, as well as containing narrative information which the users will need to help make informed decisions about the entity. Auditors often use a 'disclosure checklist' to confirm that all of the necessary disclosures have been made in the notes to the financial statements.

The auditor must review the notes to the financial statements to check that:

- They are consistent with the financial statements themselves.
- They comply with the applicable financial reporting framework (e.g. IFRS).
- They deal with material information which may not be presented in the primary financial statements (e.g. non-adjusting subsequent events and related-party disclosures).
- They comply with the requirements of legislation, such as the Companies Act 2006.

If disclosures are inadequate, or have been completely omitted, the auditor will ask the client to correct the inadequacy or include the disclosures which are absent. If the client refuses, this could result in a modified audit opinion being expressed. Remember that the auditor is looking at material information which is qualitative as well—it is not just about the numerical information in the financial statements.

18.2 Evaluating the effect of misstatements

18.2.1 Types of misstatement

During the course of the audit, the auditor may come across various misstatements present in the draft financial statements. Misstatements can arise due to:

- mathematical mistakes;
- misapplication of an accounting standard;
- cut-off problems such as closing the ledgers down too late; or
- discrepancies within the accounting system.

ISA (UK) 450 *Evaluation of Misstatements Identified during the Audit* sets out the auditor's responsibilities where misstatements are concerned. Essentially, the auditor must consider the effect of misstatements on both the audit procedures performed and, if left uncorrected, on the financial statements as a whole (Figure 18.2).

ISA (UK) 450 contains a useful summary of the types of misstatements that can arise. The auditor is not required to classify misstatements using this terminology, but it provides a useful framework for identifying and evaluating misstatements and for discussion with management.

- Factual misstatements are misstatements about which there is no doubt (e.g. an arithmetic error in determining a value included in the financial statements).

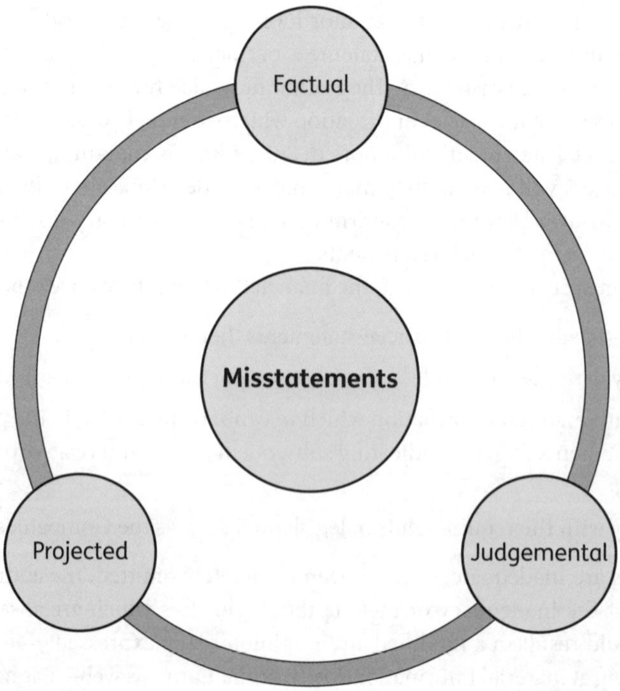

Figure 18.2 Types of misstatements

- Judgemental misstatements are differences arising from the judgements of management including those concerning recognition, measurement, presentation, and disclosure in the financial statements, including the selection or application of accounting policies, that the auditor considers unreasonable or inappropriate (e.g. use of an inappropriate assumption which forms the basis of an impairment calculation).
- Projected misstatements are the auditor's best estimate of misstatements in populations, involving the projection of misstatements identified in audit samples to the entire populations from which the samples were drawn.

Activity 18.1 Types of misstatements

Can you think of three examples of factual misstatements and three of judgemental misstatements which may be identified at the final stage of the audit?

During the course of the audit fieldwork, the auditor must:

- Record all identified misstatements on a 'Schedule of unadjusted error', unless the misstatement is clearly trivial. It is a matter of judgement as to whether an error is trivial—ISA (UK) 450 describes misstatements that are 'clearly trivial' as misstatements that are clearly inconsequential, whether taken individually or in aggregate and whether judged by any criteria of size, nature, or circumstances.[1] ISA (UK) 450 also states that clearly trivial does not mean the same as 'not material'. Both materiality and triviality will be determined at the planning stage of the audit as revised as necessary during the audit process.
- Consider whether the existence of a misstatement indicates that other misstatements may exist in the financial statements. For example, if the application of an inappropriate assumption regarding valuation has resulted in the material misstatement of one category of asset, then other assets could be similarly misstated in value. Such other misstatements may then be aggregated with the identified misstatements which then may become material.
- Consider whether the audit strategy and resulting audit plan need to be revised.
- Assess the materiality of the misstatement in both quantitative and qualitative terms.
- Report all identified misstatements during the course of the audit to an appropriate level of management at the entity on a timely basis. According to ISA (UK) 450, the appropriate level of management is usually the one that has the responsibility and authority to evaluate the misstatements and to take the necessary action, for example, the finance director.
- Request that all misstatements are corrected when preparing the final draft financial statements.
- When management refuses to correct all or some misstatements identified during the audit, the auditor must consider the reasons for this refusal and take these into consideration when establishing whether the financial statements are free from material misstatement.

[1] FRC, 'ISA (UK) 450', 2022, para A2 <https://media.frc.org.uk/documents/ISA_UK_450_Revised_June_2016_Updated_May_2022.pdf> (accessed 18 January 2024).

18.2.2 **Evaluating uncorrected misstatements**

In many cases, the audit client will be willing to correct identified misstatements as they will want the financial statements to present fairly, in all material respects (i.e. to give a true and fair view). In some cases, however, management may not wish to correct some or all identified misstatements. In this case, ISA (UK) 450 requires the auditor to:

- Revisit the assessment of materiality to identify whether materiality levels (financial statement and performance materiality levels) are still appropriate in the circumstances. See Chapter 10 for more on materiality.
- Determine whether the uncorrected misstatements, either individually or in the aggregate, are material to the financial statements as a whole. The auditor must consider both the size and nature of the misstatements.
- Report uncorrected misstatements to those charged with governance of the entity and explain the effect that these misstatements may have on the auditor's opinion. This is usually done with the audit engagement partner or another senior member of the team present.
- Request a written representation (see Chapter 12) from those charged with governance that they believe the effects of uncorrected misstatements are immaterial.

Auditing scenario 18.2 Evaluating the effect of identified misstatements

The draft financial statements of Shepherd Ltd for the year ended 31 March 20X9 show the following:

- Profit before tax £6m
- Total assets £31m

At the planning stage of the audit, the audit engagement partner agreed the following levels of materiality:

- Materiality to profit before tax: 5%
- Materiality to revenue and total assets: 1%

During the course of the audit, the following misstatements were identified:

- Lamb Ltd, who is a large customer of Shepherd Ltd, went into liquidation on 17 April 20X9 owing £217,000. The finance director has refused to write this off in the financial statements for the year ended 31 March 20X9, arguing that as the liquidation took place after the year end, it should be written off in next year's financial statements.
- On 6 April 20X9 a batch of inventory costing £360,000 was sold for £100,000.

Trade receivable

As the large customer has gone into liquidation shortly after the year end, IAS 10 *Events after the Reporting Period* would regard this as an adjusting event (see Chapter 17). The finance director's argument that the receivable should be written off in the following year's financial statements is invalid because Shepherd Ltd had already sustained a loss by the reporting date as Lamb Ltd was clearly in a position not to be able to pay their outstanding balance due to cash flow difficulties. If this adjustment is not made, receivables will be overstated and expenses understated.

The receivables balance of £217,000 equates to 3.6 per cent (£217k/£6m) of profit before tax and 0.7 per cent (£217k/£6m) of total assets and hence is immaterial to the financial statements.

Sale of inventory post-year end

IAS 2 *Inventories* states that inventory must be valued at the lower of cost and net realizable value. A batch of inventory costing £360,000 was sold immediately after the reporting date for £100,000. In this case, net realizable value is lower than cost and hence IAS 10 would require the inventory to be written down because the sale of inventory immediately after the reporting date at below cost is evidence that the inventory was impaired at the reporting date. If this adjustment is not made, inventory will be overstated by £260,000 (£360k – £100k) and cost of sales understated.

The overstated inventory equates to 4.3 per cent (£260k/£6m) of profit before tax and 0.8 per cent (£260k/£31m) of total assets. Again, this misstatement is immaterial in isolation.

Considering the impact of the two misstatements

Just because the two misstatements are immaterial individually, this does not mean that is the end of the issue. This is because ISA (UK) 450 also requires the auditor to consider the effect of the misstatements in the aggregate as well. Remember, that cumulatively misstatements may have a bigger effect on the financial statements.

The total misstatements are £477,000 (£217k + £260k). This aggregate amount represents 7.95 per cent (£477k/£6m) of profit before tax and 1.5 per cent (£477k/£31m) of total assets which means the misstatements now become material when aggregated. As a consequence, the two amounts will need to be adjusted in order to avoid a modified audit opinion.

18.3 Opening balances and comparative information

Opening balances are those balances in the closing statement of financial position of the previous period which become the opening balances in the current period. A set of financial statements will show the current year and, at least, the previous year as the 'comparative' period. Comparative financial information must be presented in an entity's annual financial statements so that comparisons can be made between the current year outcomes and the prior year outcomes.

18.3.1 Opening balances

We looked at opening balances in Chapter 12. To briefly recap, if you imagine that a company has closing inventory valuation as at 31 March 20X8 of £500,000, this amount will be shown in the closing statement of financial position as a current asset at that date. On 1 April 20X8, which is the start of the new accounting period, the £500,000 closing inventory valuation becomes the opening inventory valuation. In other words, it 'rolls over' into the next accounting period along with other items on the closing statement of financial position. The items making up profit or loss are cleared out and are included in accumulated retained earnings which is within equity on the statement of financial position.

ISA (UK) 510 *Initial Audit Engagements—Opening Balances* requires auditors to carry out audit procedures to confirm that opening balances have been brought forward from the prior period correctly. We can see how this requirement is applied using an example.

Auditing scenario 18.3 Opening balances of inventory

On 17 April 20X9, Dexter & Co were appointed as auditors to Morley Ltd to carry out the audit of the financial statements for the year ended 31 March 20X9. Morley Ltd manufactures computer equipment and has a material amount of finished goods and inventory at the reporting date. A full inventory count was undertaken on 31 March 20X9, although no audit firm attended the count as Dexter & Co were not appointed in time. The previous audit firm, Churchill & Co, resigned on 31 January 20X9 due to them having insufficient resources to carry out this year's audit.

ISA (UK) 501 *Audit Evidence—Specific Considerations for Selected Items* requires the auditor to attend the inventory count when inventory is material to the financial statements. As Dexter & Co did not attend the inventory count, there is an immediate problem in that they have not obtained sufficient appropriate audit evidence concerning the existence, completeness, and condition of the inventory at the reporting date. If the auditor cannot obtain sufficient appropriate audit evidence about the existence, completeness, and condition of the inventory at the reporting date through other means, the auditor will have to modify their opinion.

The fact that Dexter & Co were appointed too late to attend the inventory count as at 31 March 20X9 is only one side of the issue. This could cause a modified audit opinion on its own if the audit engagement partner is not satisfied there is sufficient appropriate audit evidence concerning the inventory valuation as at 31 March 20X9.

The other issue is the fact that the closing inventory valuation as at 31 March 20X9 becomes the opening inventory valuation on 1 April 20X9. Issues leading to a modified audit opinion due to the closing inventory valuation as at 31 March 20X9 are likely to lead to a further modified audit opinion for the year ended 31 March 20Y0 as the opening inventory will impact the statement of profit or loss.

While there should always be some audit evidence obtained in respect of opening balances, the amount of work performed will vary considerably. Where the audit firm has audited the client for some time, there is a low historic risk of material misstatement, and the client routinely adjusts the misstatements identified during the audit, the evidence required is much less than for a new client, or an existing client with a higher risk of material misstatement.

ISA (UK) 510 suggests that the nature and extent of audit procedures necessary to obtain sufficient appropriate audit evidence regarding opening balances depend on such matters as:

- The accounting policies followed by the entity.
- The nature of the account balances, classes of transactions and disclosures and the risks of material misstatement in the current period's financial statements.
- The significance of the opening balances relative to the current period's financial statements.
- Whether the prior period's financial statements were audited and, if so, whether the predecessor auditor's opinion was modified.[2]

[2] FRC, 'ISA (UK) 510', 2016, para A3 <https://media.frc.org.uk/documents/ISA_UK_510_Revised_June_2016.pdf> (accessed 18 January 2024).

18.3.2 **Comparative information**

'Comparative information' is the amounts and disclosures which are included in the financial statements in respect of one or more prior periods in accordance with the applicable financial reporting framework. 'Comparative financial statements' are the amounts and other disclosures for the prior period which are included for comparison with the financial statements of the current period and, if audited, are referred to in the auditor's opinion (see Figure 18.3).

When the auditor issues their report on the current year's financial statements, it does not provide any assurance relating to the prior period, except there is an implicit requirement that the financial statements presented to shareholders (and other interested parties) must not be misleading.

If an unresolved matter in the prior year gave rise to a modified opinion (as in the Morley example), it may affect the auditor's report for the current financial year. If the matter is resolved, then no further consideration is necessary.

If the comparative figures were audited by another audit firm, the current auditor must state in the 'Other Matters' paragraph that this was the case and include details of the type of opinion expressed, including details of any modification to the auditor's opinion and the date.

ISA (UK) 710 *Comparative Information—Corresponding Figures and Comparative Financial Statements* requires the auditor to obtain sufficient appropriate audit evidence that the comparative figures from the previous accounting period are fairly stated.

In most cases, the auditor of the current period will have been the auditor in the previous period (i.e. a 'continuing auditor'). If this is the case, and the auditor issued an unmodified opinion in the previous period, the auditor must:

- Consider whether the audit of the current period has revealed any issues which may cast doubt on the prior year's figures.

	31.12.20X9	31.12.20X8
	£'000	£'000
Revenue	X	X
Cost of sales	(X)	(X)
Gross profit	X	X
Distribution costs	(X)	(X)
Administrative expenses	(X)	(X)
	(X)	(X)
Finance income	X	X
Finance costs	(X)	(X)
	(X)	(X)
Profit before tax	**X**	**X**
Tax expense	(X)	(X)
Profit after tax	**X**	**X**

The shaded figures are referred to as the comparative year so the user can compare the current year outcomes to the prior year outcome. This will be the case for all the primary statements and the notes.

Figure 18.3 Comparative financial statements

- Confirm that the balances have been properly brought forward into the current period and have been correctly included in the accounting records.
- Obtain evidence that the preceding period's figures have been correctly and consistently classified and disclosed as comparative figures.
- Confirm that the client's accounting policies have been consistently applied.

Auditing scenario 18.4 Previous year's financial statements audited by another auditor

Alex's Attires Ltd sells clothing for adults and hires suits for formal events such as weddings. Ralph & Co have accepted appointment as auditor of the financial statements for the year ended 31 March 20X9. The previous firm, Elliott & Co (who audited the financial statements for the year ended 31 March 20X8) resigned due to the retirement of the firm's only audit partner.

The financial statements for the year ended 31 March 20X9 will be the first set of financial statements audited by Ralph & Co. When the preceding period's financial statements were audited by another firm, the current auditors will have to carry out further audit procedures to comply with the requirements of ISA (UK) 710 which may include the following:

- Inquire of client's management as to any issues that were faced during the course of the prior year's audit.
- Consult with the predecessor auditor and review their working papers and relevant reports to obtain sufficient appropriate audit evidence relating to opening balances.
- Review the client's accounting records, working papers and control systems (e.g. a 'procedures manual') as they will affect the current year's audit.
- Consider whether work carried out on the current year's audit may provide audit evidence concerning opening balances and comparative information.
- Carry out substantive testing, where appropriate, on comparative information and opening balances (e.g. opening receivables, payables, and inventory).

18.4 Other information

18.4.1 What are the auditor's responsibilities regarding 'other information'?

The term 'other information' is quite broad. It may include amounts or other items which are intended to be the same as, to summarize, or to provide greater detail, about amounts or other items contained in the financial statements. In many jurisdictions, for example in the UK, the content of the annual report is governed by regulations such as the Companies Act 2006 and stock exchange listing requirements. Management is responsible for preparing the other information which is required, or which they choose, to present in the annual report.

ISA (UK) 720 *The Auditor's Responsibilities Relating to Other Information* sets out the auditor's responsibilities relating to other information. ISA (UK) 720 defines 'other information' as follows:

> Financial or non-financial information (other than financial statements and the auditor's report thereon) included in an entity's annual report.[3]

[3] FRC, 'ISA (UK) 720', 2022, para 12(c) <https://media.frc.org.uk/documents/ISA_UK_720_Revised_2019_Updated_May_2022.pdf> (accessed 18 January 2024).

Activity 18.2 Other information

Prepare a list of examples of 'other information' which may form part of an annual report.

The auditor's opinion does not cover the other information. The auditor does not 'audit' the other information, but they have a responsibility to consider whether, or not, the other information is consistent with the financial statements that they do have a responsibility to audit.

ISA (UK) 720 outlines the auditor's responsibilities relating to other information, focusing on identifying and responding to inconsistencies in the other information:

(a) To consider whether there is a material inconsistency between the other information and the financial statements;

(b) To consider whether there is a material inconsistency between the other information and the auditor's knowledge obtained in the audit;

(c) To respond appropriately when the auditor identifies that such material inconsistencies appear to exist, or when the auditor otherwise becomes aware that other information appears to be materially misstated;

(d) Where required by law or regulation, to form an opinion on whether the information given in the other information is consistent with the financial statements and the auditor's knowledge obtained in the audit; and

(e) To report in accordance with ISA (UK) 720.[4]

To meet these objectives, the auditor first needs to determine exactly what 'other information' is going to be included in the annual report. This is done through a discussion and confirmation with management.

Management should provide the auditor with the other information prior to the date that the auditor is expecting to issue the auditor's report. Given the potential for the other information to run to more than one hundred pages in length, there needs to be enough time for the auditor to read and review it all, in order to identify any inconsistencies with the audited financial statements.

Auditing in practice 18.1 The nature of annual reports

Annual reports have changed in format and nature in the last few years. Until relatively recently, an annual report would be a PDF document, made available in hard copy to shareholders and to other individuals on request. These days, due to digital innovations, the content of an annual report is available on company websites, and they are often interactive in nature and in a variety of formats including spreadsheets as well as web pages. Auditors need to be very careful when determining the exact content of the annual report in such situations.

Also, in recent years, the volume of the typical annual report has increased significantly. A survey by Deloitte in 2020[5] found that the average number of pages in the annual report of FTSE

[4] Ibid., para 11.

[5] Deloitte, 'Annual company report insights 2020', 2020 <https://www2.deloitte.com/uk/en/pages/audit/articles/annual-report-insights-2020.html> (accessed 19 January 2024).

100 companies was 185 pages, of which on average 115 pages are 'other information' and 70 pages are the financial statements. The remuneration report alone averaged twenty-one pages in length.

All of this means that for auditors, dealing with other information can be very challenging. The work needs to be carefully planned because of the amount of information that needs to be reviewed and due to the deadlines involved—often the other information is not available until very late in the audit process. Management needs to be made aware of these issues so that they are prepared to have the other information ready in good time for the auditor's review.

ISA (UK) 720 requires the auditor to read the other information and consider whether there is a material inconsistency between:

- the other information and the financial statements; and
- the other information and the auditor's knowledge obtained in the audit.

It is important to remember that the other information is not being audited. There is no requirement for every fact, figure, or comment in the other information to be compared with the financial statements or the auditor's knowledge of the business.

ISA (UK) 720 acknowledges that it is a matter of judgement to select the elements of the other information to the financial statements. It is suggested that in deciding which elements should be compared, the following should be considered:

- The significance of the amount or other item in the context in which it is presented, which may affect the importance that users would attach to the amount or other item (for example, a key ratio or amount).
- If quantitative, the relative size of the amount compared with accounts or items in the financial statements or the other information to which they relate.
- The sensitivity of the particular amount or other item in the other information, for example, share-based payments for senior management.[6]

Auditing in practice 18.2 Reporting on other information

In the UK, the auditor's report will include a 'Reporting on other information' section, an example of which is shown below.

Reporting on other information

The other information comprises all of the information in the annual report other than the financial statements and our auditor's report thereon. The directors are responsible for the other information. Our opinion on the financial statements does not cover the other information and,

[6] FRC, 'ISA (UK) 720', 2022, para A27.

accordingly, we do not express an audit opinion or, except to the extent otherwise explicitly stated in this report, any form of assurance thereon.

In connection with our audit of the financial statements, our responsibility is to read the other information and, in doing so, consider whether the other information is materially inconsistent with the financial statements, or our knowledge obtained in the audit, or otherwise appears to be materially misstated. If we identify an apparent material inconsistency or material misstatement, we are required to perform procedures to conclude whether there is a material misstatement of the financial statements or a material misstatement of the other information. If, based on the work we have performed, we conclude that there is a material misstatement of this other information, we are required to report that fact. We have nothing to report based on these responsibilities.

With respect to the strategic report and the directors' report, we also considered whether the disclosures required by the UK Companies Act 2006 have been included.

Based on the responsibilities described above and our work undertaken in the course of the audit, ISAs (UK) require us also to report certain opinions and matters as described below:

Strategic report and directors' report

In our opinion, based on the work undertaken in the course of the audit, the information given in the strategic report and directors' report for the year ended 31 March 20X9 is consistent with the financial statements and has been prepared in accordance with applicable legal requirements.

In light of the knowledge and understanding of the company and its environment obtained in the course of the audit, we did not identify any material misstatements in the strategic report and directors' report.

18.4.2 **Information which is materially inconsistent**

If the auditor identifies a material inconsistency in the other information, ISA (UK) 720 requires the auditor to discuss the issue with management and, if necessary, perform other procedures to conclude whether:

(a) A material misstatement of the other information exists;

(b) A material misstatement of the financial statements exists; or

(c) The auditor's understanding of the entity and its environment needs to be updated.[7]

As part of the auditor's discussion with management about a material inconsistency in the other information, the auditor can request management to provide support for the basis of the facts, figures, and the comments made in the other information section. Based on management's further information or explanations, the auditor may be satisfied that the other information is not materially misstated.

In situations where the auditor concludes that a material misstatement of the other information exists, they must ask management to correct the other information. If management agree to the correction, the auditor must carry out procedures to ascertain that the correction has been made. If management refuse to make the correction, the auditor must communicate the matter with those charged with governance and request that the correction be made.

[7] Ibid., para 16.

Auditing scenario 18.5 Inconsistency with the other information

The financial statements of Casper Ltd show a profit before tax of £1.2m for the year ended 31 March 20X1. The comparative figure for the year ended 31 March 20X0 was £2.1m. The reduction has arisen due to the impact of high inflation on the company's results for the year ended 31 March 20X1. The auditor has obtained sufficient and appropriate evidence that this explains the trend in profit.

The report by the Chair of the board of directors, which is included in the Annual Report containing the financial statements, states that profit before tax has reduced by some 20 per cent on the prior year and that the company hopes profitability will be restored in the forthcoming financial year. The report also states that forecasts indicate that this will be the case.

The reduction in profit for the year ended 31 March 20X1 is actually 43 per cent (£1.2m/£2.1m) lower than the prior year, not 20 per cent as indicated in the report by the Chair of the board. This is a material inconsistency which must be corrected. If it is not corrected, the auditor must consider the implications of the inconsistency on the auditor's report and the auditor should also consider the implications for management integrity and continuance with the audit engagement.

18.4.3 **Reporting on other information in the auditor's report**

The auditor's report will contain an 'Other Information' section which must include:

- A statement that management is responsible for the other information;
- An identification of:
  - Other information, if any, obtained by the auditor prior to the date of the auditor's report; and
  - For an audit of financial statements of a listed entity, other information, if any, expected to be obtained after the date of the auditor's report;
- A statement that the auditor's opinion does not cover the other information and, accordingly, the auditor does not express (or will not express) an audit opinion or any form of assurance conclusion thereon, except to the extent otherwise explicitly stated in the auditor's report;
- A description of the auditor's responsibilities relating to reading, considering, and reporting on other information as required by this ISA (UK); and
- When other information has been obtained prior to the date of the auditor's report, either:
  - A statement that the auditor has nothing to report; or
  - If the auditor has concluded that there is an uncorrected material misstatement of the other information, a statement that describes the uncorrected material misstatement of the other information.[8]

Therefore, where the auditor discovers a material inconsistency between the other information and the financial statements which has not been corrected by management or those charged with governance, the auditor must describe the material inconsistency in their auditor's report so that the user is aware of the discrepancy.

[8] Ibid., para 22.

If the auditor does not discover any material inconsistencies between the other information and the financial statements, the auditor states in their auditor's report that they have nothing to report.

18.5 Audit engagement reviews

Reviewing the audit is a key part of the audit quality management process. Within the audit team, audit work is reviewed hierarchically, and it is crucial that these reviews take place in good time for any problems with the audit work to be resolved (see Figure 18.4). As well as review within the audit team, on some audits an independent review is required by regulations or considered necessary by the audit firm.

18.5.1 Audit engagement partner review

Throughout the course of the audit, the audit work carried out will be reviewed by senior members of the audit team. For example, an audit junior's work will be reviewed by an audit senior and an audit senior's work will be reviewed by an audit supervisor or audit manager (Figure 18.4).

The audit engagement partner will generally not review every working paper that is on file. They will usually concentrate on the material areas of the financial statements and those areas of the financial statements which are considered to be high or significant risk, for example, revenue recognition and complex financial instruments. The audit engagement partner will review the audit evidence to ascertain whether it is sufficient or whether it contradicts other forms of audit evidence. If the audit engagement partner concludes that audit work in a specific area is insufficient or contradicts other audit evidence, they may request that further audit procedures be carried out.

The audit work should be reviewed in accordance with ISA (UK) 220 *Quality Management for an Audit of Financial Statements*, which requires that:

> The engagement partner shall review audit documentation at appropriate points in time during the audit engagement, including audit documentation relating to:

- Significant matters
- Significant judgments, including those relating to difficult or contentious matters identified during the audit engagement, and the conclusions reached, and

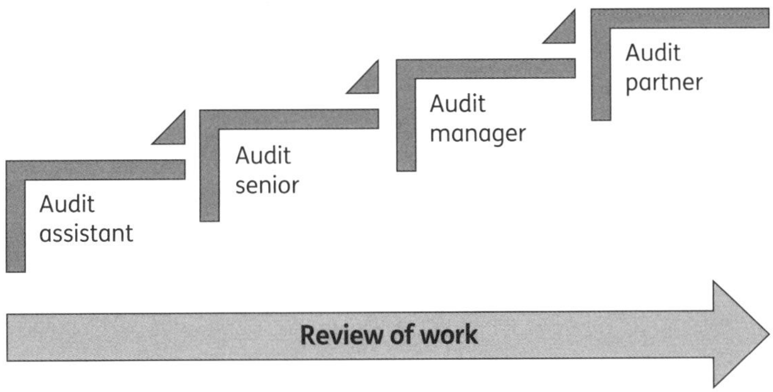

Figure 18.4 Hierarchical review within the audit team

- Other matters that, in the engagement partner's professional judgment, are relevant to the engagement partner's responsibilities.[9]

The engagement partner's review must be carried out as the audit progresses, so that problems can be resolved quickly. However, it is fair to say that in most audits, the bulk of the engagement partner review of working papers takes place during the completion stage of the audit.

The audit engagement partner may focus their attention on the difficult or contentious areas of the audit, or on the work performed by more junior members of the audit team, to ensure that any problems with the quality of the audit performed are identified and resolved.

Ultimately, as a result of this review, the audit engagement partner should be able to conclude that sufficient appropriate audit evidence has been obtained to support the conclusions reached and for the auditor's report to be issued.

The audit engagement partner is also required to review the financial statements and the auditor's report as well as any written communications with the management or those charged with governance of the audit client.

18.5.2 **EQRs**

In Chapter 5 we looked at the requirements in ISQM 2 *Engagement Quality Reviews*. In this chapter, we will recap the key issues. An EQR is defined as an objective evaluation of the significant judgements made by the engagement team and the conclusions reached thereon, performed by the engagement quality reviewer, and completed on or before the date of the engagement report.[10] Therefore, at the completion stage of the audit, an EQR must take place for certain audit clients.

As part of the audit firm's system of quality management, an EQR is required for:

- audits of listed entities;
- audits where an EQR is required by law or regulation; and
- audits where the audit firm determines that an EQR is an appropriate response to address one or more quality risk(s).

ISQM (UK) 2 deals with the appointment and eligibility of the engagement quality reviewer, and the engagement quality reviewer's responsibilities relating to the performance and documentation of an EQR. A key point is that the engagement quality reviewer is not a member of the audit engagement team, enabling an objective review to take place.

It is also required that the engagement quality reviewer has the competence and capabilities, including sufficient time, and the appropriate authority, to perform the EQR.[11] For an individual to be appointed as an engagement quality reviewer, they must possess good technical and regulatory knowledge as well as an understanding of circumstances specific to

[9] FRC, 'ISA (UK) 220', 2021, para 31 <https://media.frc.org.uk/documents/ISA_UK_220.pdf> (accessed 18 January 2024).

[10] International Auditing and Assurance Standards Board, 'ISQM (UK) 2', 2020, para 13.

[11] Ibid., para 18.

the audit they are reviewing, for example in respect of the industry sector in which the audit client operates. This would be particularly important where the audit involves a specialized or complex industry. An engagement quality reviewer who lacks industry knowledge and experience may not be able to adequately evaluate and, where appropriate, challenge significant judgements made by the audit team. For these reasons, engagement quality reviewers are usually senior individuals from the audit firm, often partners with considerable experience and authority, who will have the confidence as well as the knowledge necessary to perform an effective audit quality review.

ISQM (UK) 2 also recognizes that an audit firm's culture plays an important role in securing the success of EQRs. There should be a culture of respect for the engagement quality reviewer, so that they are less likely to be intimidated by members of the audit team (Figure 18.5).

To ensure than an objective EQR is carried out, the engagement quality reviewer should not have been involved with the audit engagement in the previous two years. This is to safeguard against any potential self-review threat which could be created if the engagement quality reviewer has been involved with significant judgements made by the engagement team, in particular, if they had previously acted as the audit engagement partner for the audit under review.

Activity 18.3 Ethical threats relating to the engagement quality reviewer

We have explained that there may be a self-review threat which threatens the objectivity of the engagement quality reviewer, and as a safeguard there is a two-year cooling-off period.

Can you think of any other specific threats to objectivity which may reduce the efficacy of the EQR?

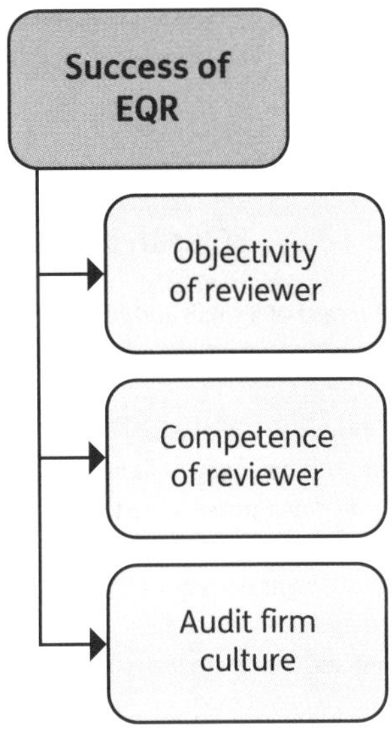

Figure 18.5 Factors impacting the success of an EQR

18.5.2.1 Performing the EQR

The EQR need not take place solely at the completion stage of the audit. It will often be relevant for elements of the review to take place earlier in the audit process, for example, the audit planning documentation could be reviewed at the completion of the planning phase of the audit and work performed at the interim stage of the audit may be subject to EQR before the final audit commences. However, there should not be too much interaction between the engagement quality reviewer and the audit team, as this may create a threat to the objectivity of the reviewer.

There is no 'right or wrong' way for the EQR to be performed. It is not the case that all audit working papers need to be reviewed as part of the EQR—the engagement quality reviewer must use their judgement to determine the extent of their review and in the selection of working papers to review. The nature and extent of the EQR procedures will vary depending on a range of factors, including the complexity of the audit engagement, the size, and structure of the audit client, and whether it is a listed entity.

ISQM (UK) 2 places particular emphasis on the review of significant judgements made by the audit team. The engagement quality reviewer must discuss with the engagement partner and other members of the engagement team the significant matters and significant judgements made in planning, performing, and reporting on the engagement.

Specifically, the engagement quality reviewer must evaluate:

- the basis for making those significant judgements, including, when applicable to the type of engagement, the exercise of professional scepticism by the engagement team;
- whether the engagement documentation supports the conclusions reached; and
- whether the conclusions reached are appropriate.

If the engagement quality reviewer has concerns over the significant judgements made by the audit team, the concerns must be discussed with the audit engagement partner. If there is not a satisfactory resolution to these concerns, the concerns should be escalated to a different individual in the audit firm, for example, a partner responsible for audit quality within the firm.

Auditing in practice 18.3 EQRs in smaller audit firms

In some situations, for example, in the case of a small audit firm or even a sole practitioner, there may not be an independent partner or other individual with the necessary experience and knowledge to perform an EQR.

In these circumstances, the audit firm may use external individuals to perform the EQR.

There are external consultants who can be engaged to carry out an EQR in a smaller audit firm. Such consultants will be suitably qualified and possess the technical competence and experience required to carry out the review. Appointments of external consultants are usually based on their expertise and reputation and some audit firms do request the consultant to provide a CV so they can ensure they are suitably qualified and experienced.

Client confidentiality is paramount and therefore the external consultant will usually be subject to a letter of engagement which will outline their responsibilities as well as the audit firm's responsibilities. Included within the letter of engagement will be a specific requirement for the consultant to maintain client confidentiality.

As well as freelance external consultants, an audit firm could also engage the services of a relevant training company to carry out reviews of their audit work. Quite often training companies which carry out continuous professional development courses to update accountants and auditors on matters relevant to them will often provide EQR services.

At the end of the review, a meeting is usually held between the EQR and the audit engagement partner to discuss the findings which are then followed up in a final report. Many consultants request that the audit firm respond formally to the findings in the form of an 'action plan' to address any deficiencies noted in the review. Some consultants also 'grade' files using a scoring system, such as 1 being very poor through to 5 which would be excellent.

Chapter round-up

- Final analytical procedures must be applied in accordance with ISA (UK) 520 to enable the auditor to form an overall conclusion as to whether the financial statements are consistent with their understanding of the entity.
- Misstatements that have been identified during the course of the audit must be evaluated to determine the effect they have on the financial statements. Misstatements must be assessed both individually and in the aggregate.
- The auditor must ensure that opening balances have been correctly brought forward from the prior year and that comparative information has also been presented correctly.
- Unresolved matters from the prior year may impact the current year's audit opinion if they are material.
- The auditor is required to read other information presented in the entity's annual report (such as the directors' report or the Chair's statement) to ensure it is consistent with the financial statements. The auditor does not express an opinion on the other information, but is required to ensure it is consistent.
- Any material inconsistencies identified between the other information and the financial statements must be appropriately described in the auditor's report.
- At the completion stage of the audit, the audit engagement partner must review the audit work carried out in accordance with ISA (UK) 220, as this provides a basis for their audit opinion.
- An EQR is required for certain audit engagements, and the focus of the review is on the evaluation of significant judgements made by the audit team.

End of chapter case study

Introduction

In this chapter, we have examined a number of matters which the auditor needs to consider at the completion stage of the audit. In this case study we focus on evaluating the sufficiency of audit evidence and evaluating misstatements identified during the audit. This is a very practical issue, and you will think from the point of view of the audit engagement partner, reviewing the audit working papers, to consider the type of evidence you would expect to see in the audit working papers, and the further actions which should be taken.

This case study links to the following learning outcomes:

- Evaluate audit evidence to confirm if sufficient and appropriate evidence has been obtained.
- Evaluate the effect of misstatements on the financial statements and recommend appropriate actions to be taken by the auditor.
- Describe the auditor's responsibility in respect of opening balances and comparative information.

Scenario

You are the audit engagement partner assigned to the audit of Cesar Ltd, a company that operates forty hotels across the country. The company's financial year ended on 31 December 20X1 and the audit is in the completion stage. Your audit firm is performing the audit for this first time this year, having been appointed as auditor in June 20X1.

The final version of the financial statements recognizes profit before tax of £30 million (20X0: £33 million) and total assets of £143 million (20X0: £150 million).

Materiality has been determined at £1.5 million, and this has been consistently applied during the audit.

You are performing a review of the audit working papers and you have noted the following issues which require further attention

1. Impairment of head office

After a flood damaged the company's head office building, the finance director calculated that an impairment loss of £1.8 million needs to be recognized. The only audit evidence obtained in respect of the impairment is as follows:

- Arithmetic check of the finance director's calculation.
- Notes of a discussion with the finance director and a comment that 'this accounting treatment appears reasonable'.
- Confirmation that total assets has been credited and expenses have been debited in the final version of the financial statements with a loss of £1.8 million.

2. Land

The statement of financial position at 31 December 20X1 includes a specific piece of land at a carrying amount of £3 million. The property was gifted to Cesar Ltd two years ago by one of the original founders of the company. The land is adjacent to one of the company's flagship hotels, in an area of natural beauty, and access is allowed to hotel guests during their stay. The company's finance director informed the audit team that the £3 million valuation is an estimate, but because the land is unique, it is impossible to obtain a fair value for it. No audit evidence has been obtained, except for a note of this comment made by the finance director, and confirming that the land was included in the previous year's financial statements at £3 million.

3. Exclusive use of hotel

For a weekend in August 20X1, the company provided one of its smaller hotels, free of charge, for the exclusive use of the finance director, whose daughter held her wedding at the hotel. The finance director has agreed to pay £10,000 towards the catering costs incurred for the wedding and paid for by the company.

The audit working papers note the following:

> We have confirmed that the hotel was used by the finance director for his daughter's wedding, by examining the booking register for the weekend. This is the only audit evidence obtained because the £10,000, which is recognised as a receivable, is immaterial to the financial statements.

4. Strategic report

The strategic report, which is to be published in the annual report along with the financial statements, contains the following statement:

> The management team at Cesar Ltd is very pleased with the company's performance this year. We have expanded our operations and managed to generate an increased return for shareholders this year as our profit has increased.

Required

Explain the implications of each of these matters for the completion of the audit. You should consider, where relevant:

- the adequacy of the audit evidence obtained and further audit evidence which should be obtained;
- whether the issues give rise to a material misstatement; and
- any further actions to be taken by the auditor.

Answer

Impairment of head office

The audit evidence obtained is not sufficient. The impairment loss of £1.8 million is above the materiality threshold and further evidence needs to be obtained to ensure that the value is not materially misstated.

A discussion with the finance director regarding the accounting treatment of the impairment is relevant, as it is important to understand how the impairment has been calculated, including any assumptions used. However, the accounting treatment should not be accepted at face value and the appropriateness of the calculations should be corroborated through further audit procedures.

Impairment is an area of high subjectivity and can be complex to account for, and the audit team should have applied a higher degree of professional scepticism when auditing this transaction. An arithmetic check confirms accuracy, but it does not provide any evidence regarding the rationale underpinning how the impairment loss was determined.

Agreeing that total assets has been credited by £1.8 million is not robust audit evidence. There should be specific confirmation as to the category of asset which has been adjusted. There could be an error whereby the impairment has been posted to the wrong account in the nominal ledge resulting in the wrong asset's value being reduced.

Further audit procedures should now be performed, for example:

- Obtain the finance director's impairment calculation and review the assumptions used to confirm if they appear reasonable and in line with the auditor's knowledge of the business.
- Obtain documentation relating to the damage to the head office, for example, insurance claims, damage reports, to confirm that there has been significant damage to the property.
- Review minutes of meetings where the damage has been discussed (e.g. board minutes).
- Trace the impairment adjustment to the nominal ledger and confirm that the head office has been reduced in value by £1.8 million.

Land

The land is recognized at £3 million, which exceeds the materiality threshold. Insufficient audit evidence has been obtained, as there is no documentation on the audit file relating to the land, just a note of a comment made by the finance director, which is not sufficient, appropriate evidence for this material amount.

The auditor should discuss the matter further with management and with those charged with governance, in order to obtain an understanding about the £3 million valuation, including:

- who provided it and when it was provided (presumably two years ago when the land was gifted to the company, but this needs to be confirmed);
- the assumptions used to determine the amount;
- whether any development of the land has taken place in the last two years which may impact its valuation;
- whether there are any restrictions on its use, given that it is an area of natural beauty; and
- details of insurance policies held in respect of the land, which should confirm ownership and possibly provide some evidence on valuation.

There may be some documentation or correspondence relating to the gifting of the land, which it is important to see because the auditor needs to confirm that the land is owned by the company, and that the company has the right to use it within the business (i.e. to allow hotel guests to access the land).

The audit team should also attempt to communicate with the previous auditor of Cesar Ltd, to discuss their views on the matter and to ask if they were able to obtain any evidence to support the valuation of the land.

Given the materiality of the land, the auditor may consider the appointment of an auditor's expert, to provide an up-to-date and independent valuation.

Exclusive use of hotel

The finance director is a member of key management personnel and is therefore a related party of Cesar Ltd. The use of the hotel by the finance director is a related-party transaction and is governed by IAS 24 *Related Party Disclosures*. IAS 24 states that a related-party transaction should be disclosed if it is material. Based on monetary value the amount of the transaction is not material. However, because the transaction is with a member of key management personnel, it is material by nature, regardless of monetary amount.

In relation to a material related-party transaction, IAS 24 requires disclosure of the nature of the related-party relationship along with information about the transaction itself, such as the amount of the transaction, any relevant terms and conditions, and any balances outstanding.

The auditor should consider the recoverability of the £10,000 owed to Cesar Ltd by the finance director. If the amount is not recoverable and needs to be written off, this will not be material in monetary terms for Cesar Ltd but an adjustment may be necessary overstatement of receivables and operating profit.

If the related-party transaction has not been disclosed, the auditor should consider the implications for the audit report, which may need to be modified on the grounds of material misstatement.

The audit evidence obtained is insufficient and further procedures should now be carried out, though there is likely to be limited evidence available in respect of this. The auditor can review the company's bank statement and cash books to confirm if the £10,000 has been received in the subsequent events period.

The auditor should also review the board minutes, or any other meetings held by management at which the exclusive use of the hotel was discussed and that this was appropriately authorized, including that the company would pay the costs relating to the wedding, other than the £10,000 to be received from the finance director.

A standard procedure in respect of related parties and transactions is to obtain a written representation from management stating that management has disclosed to the auditor the identity of the entity's related parties and all the related-party relationships and transactions of which they are aware, and that management has appropriately accounted for and disclosed such relationships and transactions in accordance with the requirements of IAS 24.

Strategic report

The strategic report falls under the definition of 'Other information' because it is going to be published in the annual report, along with the financial statements. The auditor needs to apply the requirements of ISA (UK) 720 *The Auditor's Responsibilities Relating to Other Information*, which requires the auditor to read the other information to identify any inconsistencies with the financial statements.

In this case, the strategic report states that the company's profit has increased. However, the financial statements indicate that profit before tax has reduced by £3 million, a decrease of 9 per cent compared to last year.

There appears to be an inconsistency between the comment in the strategic report and the financial statements. If this inconsistency remains, it could confuse readers of the annual report and undermine the credibility of the financial statements.

The auditor should discuss the issue with management, asking what information the comment is based on. It could be that profit after tax has increased, meaning that the comment is truthful and does not need to be changed. However, unless there are unusual movements in the tax expense recognized, it is likely that profit has reduced in which case management should be asked to amend the comment in the strategic report.

The auditor should include a section in the auditor's report in which the responsibilities of management and of the auditor in respect of the other information are outlined. Assuming that the inconsistency in the other information is removed, the auditor can comment that the other information is consistent with the financial statements.

Activity solutions

Activity 18.1—Types of misstatements

Can you think of three examples of factual misstatements and three of judgemental misstatements which may be identified at the final stage of the audit?

Answer points (more than the required number of answer points are given)

Factual misstatements:

- incorrect tax calculations (e.g. payroll taxes, company tax);
- errors in determining discounts offered to customers;
- inaccurate disclosure in notes to the financial statements (e.g. incorrect statement of depreciation policy);
- disclosures omitted in error (e.g. no note to the financial statements to provide information on contingent liabilities); and
- incorrect or incomplete disclosure of related-party transactions.

Judgemental misstatements:

- inappropriate assumptions (e.g. assumptions used as part of going concern evaluation);
- inconsistent application of judgement (e.g. assuming a different growth rate in two separate impairment reviews);

- unreasonable conclusions reached by management (e.g. in determining the probability of a payment being made and hence whether to recognize a provision or contingent liability); and
- changes to assumptions used from the prior period with no rationale (e.g. changing the method for estimating sales returns).

Activity 18.2—Other information

Prepare a list of examples of 'other information' which may form part of an annual report.

Suggested answer points:

Any content of the annual report that is distinct from the financial statements meets the definition of other information. Examples may include:

- directors' report
- strategic report
- chairman's statement
- remuneration committee report
- operating and financial review
- key performance indicators
- corporate governance statement
- report on sustainability and environmental matters

Activity 18.3—Ethical threats relating to the engagement quality reviewer

Can you think of any other specific threats to objectivity which may reduce the efficacy of the EQR?

Suggested answer points:

- The engagement quality reviewer could be intimidated by members of the audit team, in particular senior members such as the audit engagement partner.
- There could also be a familiarity threat, if the engagement quality reviewer has a close personal relationship with a member of the audit team.

19 The Auditor's Report

Introduction

In this chapter, we will start to look at the auditor's report. This is the document issued at the very end of the audit which contains the auditor's opinion on the financial statements. The auditor's report is the output of the audit which is addressed to the shareholders (also known as the 'members') and is included in the reporting entity's annual report containing the financial statements.

The concept of the auditor's report is fundamental to the audit process. It is the only really visible product of the audit and it therefore must contain all of the information which the auditor wishes to provide to the shareholders. We therefore need to consider the requirements for the content of the auditor's report which are given in the relevant International Standards on Auditing (ISAs) (UK). We also need to take a step back from the actual regulations and consider whether the amount and type of information contained in the auditor's report is as relevant and useful as it can be to the users of the financial statements.

In recent years there have been new regulations which extend the scope of the auditor's report of both public interest entities and private entities, and we will think about why these regulations were brought in and how successful the introduction of the new requirements has been. Auditors' reports have become a lot longer, and while the new content that is required is useful, some argue that the auditor's report has lost conciseness and perhaps is less user-friendly due to its wider scope. We have provided an illustrative unmodified auditor's opinion in Appendix 19.1 so that you can see how the report is worded and reflect on the usefulness of the disclosures within the report.

When the auditor's report contains a statement expressing the opinion that the financial statements are 'true and fair' or 'free from material misstatement', the opinion is known as an unmodified opinion. This is sometimes known as a 'clean' audit opinion and implies that the financial statements can be relied upon. Where the financial statements cannot be relied upon because they are not true and fair, or where the auditor cannot reach an opinion, the opinion must be modified. We will consider modified opinions in Chapter 20.

There are several ISAs which relate to the auditor's report:

- ISA (UK) 700 (Revised) Forming an Opinion and Reporting on Financial Statements
- ISA (UK) 701 Communicating Key Audit Matters in the Independent Auditor's Report
- ISA (UK) 705 (Revised) Modifications to the Opinion in the Independent Auditor's Report—we will cover this in Chapter 20
- ISA (UK) 706 (Revised) Emphasis of Matter Paragraphs and Other Matter Paragraphs in the Independent Auditor's Report

It is also worth remembering that we have already looked at some matters which impact the auditor's report including going concern (Chapter 17), comparative amounts and corresponding figures (Chapter 18), and other information published with the financial statements (Chapter 18). It is important to think holistically in respect of the topic of auditor's reports.

Learning outcomes

- Explain the purpose of the auditor's report and discuss current issues, including the expectation gap, in respect of the auditor's report.
- Describe the elements of an unmodified auditor's report.
- Discuss the meaning of the term 'true and fair' in the context of the auditor's opinion and explain the matters that auditors consider in reaching their opinion.
- Discuss the use of emphasis of matter paragraphs and other matter paragraphs and identify when their use may be appropriate.
- Identify and explain the matters which may be selected as key audit matters (KAMs) in the context of an audit of financial statements.

By the end of the chapter, you will be able to:

- Evaluate the matters which auditors consider in forming an audit opinion.
- Discuss developments in regulations seeking to extend the scope and usefulness of the auditor's report including KAMs.

19.1 The purpose of the auditor's report

19.1.1 The overall objective of the auditor's report

According to ISA (UK) 700, the objectives of the auditor are:

- To form an opinion on the financial statements based upon an evaluation of their conclusions drawn from the audit evidence gathered; and
- To express clearly that opinion through a written report.[1]

[1] FRC, 'ISA (UK) 700', 2022, para 6 <https://media.frc.org.uk/documents/ISA_UK_700_Updated_May_2022.pdf> (accessed 18 January 2024).

Note that ISA (UK) 700 uses the term 'express clearly'—remember that the auditor's report is the mechanism by which the auditor communicates their findings and it is imperative that users of the report understand what it is saying.

Over the years there has been a large amount of criticism of the auditor's report. Users have complained that the wording of the report is often ambiguous because it uses technical jargon and that some non-financially orientated users do not understand the message(s) which the auditor's report is conveying. Remember that the auditor's report is the only method by which the auditor can communicate with some user groups as they have no direct contact with any user group other than the shareholders. In the UK, the auditor has rights to communicate with shareholders, for example by speaking at the annual general meeting of shareholders, but the exact nature of these rights will depend on the legislation and regulations in the relevant jurisdiction. Therefore, the auditor's report should be seen as a communication tool. Communication is hindered where the auditor's report is not understandable or perhaps is not made available in an appropriate format to the various user groups.

Availability is governed by local rules. In most jurisdictions the auditor's report is 'attached' in a legal sense to the financial statements, so if the financial statements are held on public record, then so is the auditor's report. In many countries, such as the UK, listed companies are required to publish financial statements and the accompanying auditor's report on their website. This of course enhances the availability of the report. Perhaps one downside is that electronic publication and wide accessibility of the auditor's report may impact the perception of who the auditor's report is intended to address.

Auditing in practice 19.1 Perceptions of the auditor's report

In 2006 the International Auditing and Assurance Standards Board (IAASB), in conjunction with the American Institute of Certified Public Accountants (AICPA), and the American Accounting Association started a project[2] aimed at understanding more about how users perceive the auditor's report and how the auditor's report influences their decisions. Remember that usually (but not always), when the IAASB release an updated ISA (or a new ISA/ISQM), countries such as the UK will adopt that standard and make 'tweaks' to the ISA so that it is country specific, so this project had implications for the UK regulatory body.

Following on from the research projects, the IAASB issued a consultation paper which identified several issues arising from the academic research conducted and from the other outreach activities that have been performed which is summarized as follows:

- Users of financial statements and the auditor's report value the independent auditor's opinion.
- Other than the auditor's opinion, the content of the auditor's report was not viewed as very useful or informative.

[2] IAASB, 'AICPA, AAA and IAASB launch research project to better understand users' perceptions of the auditor's report on financial statements', 2006 <https://www.iaasb.org/news-events/2006–08/aicpa-aaa-and-iaasb-launch-research-project-better-understand-users-perceptions-auditors-report> (accessed 19 January 2024).

- Users wanted to understand more about the reporting and entity and the audit process and would value auditor's insight on a range of matters. The IAASB termed the issue the 'information gap'.
- Users thought that the structure of the auditor's report could be changed to better convey useful information.[3]

The Consultation Paper and a subsequent Invitation to Comment elicited a wide range of comments and suggestions and furthered the debate around how to improve the auditor's report as a means of communicating useful information to user groups.

The IAASB embarked on the final stage of the project in 2015 which led to significant changes in the way in which the auditor's report is structured. The revised reporting ISAs in the 700 series, including a brand-new ISA covering the new issue of KAMs became mandatory for audits of financial statements for periods ending on or after 15 December 2015. The UK adopted the new ISAs which became ISAs (UK).

On issuing the ISAs relating to the revised auditor's report, the IAASB said the following:

> The auditor's report is the key deliverable addressing the output of the audit process. While users of the financial statements have signalled that the auditor's opinion on the financial statements is valued, many have called for the auditor's report to be more informative and relevant.
>
> Enhanced auditor reporting is viewed as critical to the perceived value of the financial statement audit and thus to the continued relevance of the auditing profession. The new and revised Auditor Reporting standards lay the foundation for the future of global auditor reporting and improved auditor communications.[4]

The current format of the auditor's report is believed to provide the following benefits:

- Communication between the auditor and those charged with governance and users is enhanced.
- Increased attention is drawn by management and those charged with governance to KAMs which are now required to be disclosed in the auditor's report for listed entities.
- The auditor is required to apply increased professional scepticism over Key Audit Matters (KAMs).
- Users are expected to perceive that audit quality has been increased.

19.1.2 **The expectation gap and the auditor's report**

As we explored in Chapter 1, there is an expectation gap between what members of the public *think* the auditor does/should do versus what the auditor actually does and the form of their reporting. One of the examples of the expectation gap is the fact that many users of the financial statements and auditor's report think that the opinion expressed is in some way

[3] IAASB, 'Enhancing the value of auditor reporting: Exploring options for change', 2011 <https://www.iaasb.org/publications/enhancing-value-auditor-reporting-exploring-options-change-1#:~:text=Enhancing%20the%20Value%20of%20Auditor%20Reporting%3A%20Exploring%20Options%20for%20Change,-IAASB%20Consultation%20Paper&text=The%20consultation%20paper%20seeks%20to,the%20usefulness%20of%20auditor%20reporting.> (accessed 19 January 2024).

[4] IAASB, 'The new auditor's report: Greater transparency into the financial statement audit', 2015 <https://www.ifac.org/_flysystem/azure-private/publications/files/Auditor-Reporting-Fact-Sheet.pdf> (accessed 19 January 2024).

certifying the accounts as being completely accurate and containing no errors or omissions. Other misconceptions relating to the auditor's opinion are that a clean audit opinion is guaranteeing the financial stability and longevity of the reporting entity.

It is important for you to understand that the auditor does not express absolute assurance that the financial statements are 100 per cent accurate. Instead, the auditor provides reasonable assurance that the financial statements are prepared, in all material respects, in accordance with the applicable financial reporting framework and applicable legislation. When the auditor draws this conclusion through evaluating the audit evidence gathered during the course of the audit, they express an unmodified opinion.

As noted above, an auditor only ever provides reasonable assurance on the financial statements. While this is a high level of assurance, it is not absolute assurance because of the inherent limitations of an audit (Figure 19.1). Such limitations mean that it is not possible for the auditor to provide 100 per cent assurance and examples of the inherent limitations of an audit:

- Financial statements include estimates and judgements which are usually subjective.
- Auditors will place some reliance on the entity's internal controls.
- Representations from management will be required for certain areas of the financial statements, and these representations may be the only source of evidence available.
- The nature of audit evidence which is persuasive rather than conclusive.
- Auditors do not test all transactions and balances; instead, they test on a sample basis.

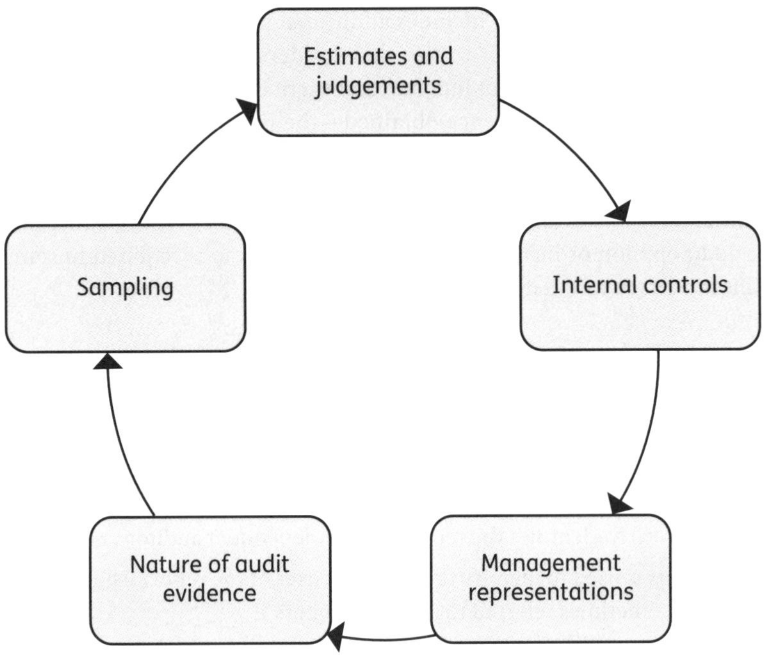

Figure 19.1 Inherent limitations of auditing

19.2 Content of the auditor's report

When the auditor concludes that the financial statements are prepared in all material respects in accordance with the applicable financial reporting framework and relevant legislation, they will express an unmodified auditor's opinion. The opinion is just one element of the auditor's report and it is important to be aware of the other required content of the report.

19.2.1 Modified and unmodified auditor's report

An unmodified auditor's report is one which contains an unmodified opinion (true and fair) and which also contains no additional paragraphs, in other words, it is the 'standard' (sometimes called the 'clean') audit report.

The terminology can be a little confusing because the auditor's report and the auditor's opinion can be 'modified'. This means that the standard report is not being issued. Let's think first about modifications to the opinion:

- An unmodified opinion is issued when the auditor is satisfied that the evidence obtained is sufficient and appropriate and supports the view presented in the financial statements (i.e. a 'true and fair view' is presented).
- A modified opinion is issued when the auditor is either not satisfied with the sufficiency or appropriateness of the evidence that has been obtained, compared with what could reasonably be expected, or concludes that there is a material misstatement of the financial statements. In Chapter 20 we will look at modified opinions.

In some situations, the auditor includes additional paragraphs in the auditor's report which provide extra information to the shareholders above that which is ordinarily required. These paragraphs do not indicate that there is anything wrong with the financial statements or the audit evidence obtained—the financial statements are still 'true and fair'. These paragraphs include required under ISA (UK) 706 which we will look at in section 19.4.

When the auditor makes amendments to a standard auditor's report, either due to modifying the audit opinion or including the additional paragraphs required in some circumstances, this is referred to as a modified auditor's report.

19.2.2 The required content elements of an unmodified auditor's report

The unmodified auditor's report must contain certain 'elements' (i.e. sections) in order to comply with ISA (UK) 700. Audit firms may use an innovative approach and they can restructure the report provided that it contains at least the following elements:

- Title—which clearly identifies the report as an independent auditor's report.
- Addressee—this is used to identify the intended user of the report which is generally the shareholders (sometimes referred to as the 'members').
- Opinion—this section provides the auditor's conclusion as to whether the financial statements give a true and fair view (or present fairly in all material respects).

As well as expressing the opinion, this section should also:

- state the name of the reporting entity whose financial statements have been audited;
- state that the financial statements have been audited;
- identify the title of each statement comprising the financial statements;
- refer to the notes, including the summary of significant accounting policies; and
- specify the date of/period covered by the financial statements.

- Basis for opinion—this paragraph provides a description of the standards which the auditor has applied (e.g. ISAs and the FRC Ethical Standard) when carrying out the audit and it aims to provide users with confidence that the report can be relied upon. This section should also state whether the auditor believes that the audit evidence the auditor has obtained is sufficient and appropriate to provide a basis for the auditor's opinion.
- Going concern—the auditor must report in accordance with ISA (UK) 570 *Going Concern* on aspects relating to the entity's application (or non-application) of the going concern basis of accounting. We looked at the auditor's responsibilities in respect of going concern, including reporting implications, in Chapter 17.
- Irregularities including fraud—the auditor's report must include a description as to what extent the audit was considered capable of detecting irregularities, including fraud (note, this is a UK-specific requirement in ISA (UK) 700).
- KAMs—this section is only compulsory for listed entities (although that does not mean auditor's reports of private entities are precluded from having a KAM section if they wish). This section of the report draws attention to significant matters which the users must be aware of in order to aid their decisions about the entity. We look at KAMs in more detail in section 19.6.
- Other information—this is used to clarify that management are responsible for the other information. ISA (UK) 720 (Revised) applies to other information. We looked at the auditor's responsibilities in respect of other information, including reporting responsibilities in Chapter 18, remember that the auditor's responsibility is usually limited to only reading the other information to ensure it is consistent with the audited financial statements.
- Responsibilities for the financial statements—this section clarifies that it is management who is responsible for preparing the financial statements and for the applicable internal controls. This section should also describe management's responsibility for assessing the entity's ability to continue as a going concern and whether the use of the going concern basis of accounting is appropriate. It should also identify those responsible for the oversight of the financial reporting process if they are different from management. This paragraph serves to reduce the expectations gap (i.e. the incorrect belief that the auditors are responsible for the preparation of the financial statements) and clarifies responsibilities relating to going concern.
- Auditor's responsibilities for the financial statements—this section clarifies that the auditor is responsible for providing reasonable assurance as to whether the financial statements give a true and fair view (or present fairly in all material respects). This section also describes the auditor's responsibilities in respect of risk assessment, internal controls, going concern, and the entity's significant accounting policies. As with the responsibilities of management section, this section aims to reduce the expectations gap.

- Other reporting responsibilities—this section highlights any additional reporting responsibilities where applicable, see section 19.2.3 for more detail on relevant requirements of the Companies Act 2006. There may also be reporting requirements stemming from Listing Rules relevant to listed companies, for example in the UK the auditor is required to review and report by exception on matters relating to the corporate governance statement and director's remuneration. In other jurisdictions, other reporting responsibilities may differ.
- Name of the engagement partner—this is required to identify the person responsible for the audit. In the UK the Senior Statutory Auditor (a concept we discussed in Chapter 2) is the signatory. In some rare circumstances, this information may be concealed if there could be a personal security threat to the auditor.
- Signature of the auditor—this shows the audit engagement partner or firm who is accountable for the auditor's opinion.
- Auditor's address—this is shown in the event that there are any queries.
- Date of the auditor's report—the auditor's report is dated up to the date on which audit work has been performed.

We should mention that the section which describes the auditor's responsibilities for the audit of financial statements can be very long due to the many matters which have to be included. The length of this section creates tension with the conciseness and understandability of the auditor's report and for this reason this section can be included as an appendix to the auditor's report rather than within the main body. Alternatively, the auditor's report may contain a reference to a description of auditor's responsibilities which is contained on the website of an appropriate authority. For example, in the UK, the Financial Reporting Council (FRC) maintains on its website a generic 'Description of the Auditor's Responsibilities for the Audit of the Financial Statements' of private sector entities, which can be cross-referenced from an auditor's report.

19.2.3 **Reporting by exception**

In the UK, the Companies Act 2006 and the Listing Rules require auditors to 'report by exception' on certain matters. This usually means that the audit report simply has to state that nothing has come to the attention of the auditor in respect of these matters. In the UK, the auditor is required to express an opinion as to whether the information in the directors' report is and the strategic report (when this is presented) are consistent with the financial statements.

Auditing in practice 19.2 Reporting by exception

Here is an example of the typical disclosure in a UK auditor's report in respect of reporting under the Companies Act requirements.

Opinions on other matters prescribed by the Companies Act 2006

In our opinion, based on the work undertaken in the course of the audit:

- the information given in the strategic report and the directors' report for the financial year for which the financial statements are prepared is consistent with the financial statements; and
- the strategic report and directors' report have been prepared in accordance with applicable legal requirements.

Matters on which we are required to report by exception

In light of the knowledge and understanding of the company and its environment obtained in the course of the audit, we have not identified material misstatements in the strategic report or directors' report.

We have nothing to report in respect of the following matters in relation to which the Companies Act 2006 requires us to report to you if, in our opinion:

- adequate accounting records have not been kept, or returns adequate for our audit have not been received from branches not visited by us; or
- the financial statements are not in agreement with the accounting records and returns; or
- certain disclosures of directors' remuneration specified by law are not made; or
- we have not received all the information and explanations we require for our audit.

19.2.4 **The date of the auditor's report**

According to ISA (UK) 700:

> The auditor's report shall be dated no earlier than the date on which the auditor has obtained sufficient appropriate audit evidence on which to base the auditor's opinion on the financial statements, including evidence that:
>
> - All the statements and disclosures that comprise the financial statements have been prepared; and
> - Those with the recognized authority have asserted that they have taken responsibility for those financial statements.[5]

It might seem obvious, but the auditor must not issue their report until they are satisfied that they have obtained all the evidence which they need to support their audit opinion. In the UK there is an additional requirement that the auditor must not issue the report earlier than the date on which all the other information contained in the annual report has been approved by those charged with governance and the auditor has considered all necessary available evidence.

These requirements are in place to ensure that the auditor's report is issued on the very final version of information which is to be released to shareholders and placed on public record. If there were to be any changes to this information after the auditor's report is issued, a new report would have to be issued after the auditor had received and reviewed the new information to consider if any change is needed to the auditor's report.

19.2.5 **Additional UK requirement—reporting in relation to going concern**

In some jurisdictions, including the UK, the auditor is also required to report on the entity's ability to continue as a going concern. This is usually worded as follows:

> We have nothing to report in respect of the following matters in relation to which the ISAs UK require us to report to you where:
>
> - the directors' use of the going concern basis of accounting in the preparation of the financial statements is not appropriate; or

[5] FRC, 'ISA (UK) 700', 2022, para 49.

- the directors have not disclosed in the financial statements any identified material uncertainties that may cast significant doubt on the company's ability to continue to adopt the going concern basis of accounting for a period of at least 12 months from the date when the financial statements are authorized for issue.

The UK regulators think it important for the auditor's report to make this disclosure as it highlights that the auditor has considered management's use of the going concern basis of accounting and whether disclosure of going concern matters is appropriate. Note that the wording is phrased as 'we have nothing to report . . .'—this signals that the auditor is satisfied with how management has prepared the financial statements in relation to going concern.

It should be emphasized that the management of companies in the UK are required to consider a going concern period of at least twelve months from the date of approval of the financial statements. ISA 570 *Going Concern* (as issued by the IAASB) and IAS 1 *Presentation of Financial Statements* only require such an assessment for a period of twelve months from the reporting date and hence some jurisdictions may have different requirements where reporting on going concern is concerned.

19.2.6 **Limiting liability using a disclaimer paragraph**

In Chapter 5 we looked at the issue of auditor's liability to third parties and at the mechanisms used by auditors to limit their liability. One of the ways that auditors can attempt to limit their liability is by including a liability disclaimer paragraph, known as a *Bannerman* paragraph in the auditor's report.

To recap: the *Bannerman* paragraph limits the audit firm's duty of care to third parties and is very common in auditors' reports as well as other reports issued by professional firms. The paragraph is typically worded as follows:

> This report is made solely to the company's members, as a body, in accordance with Sections 495 and 496 of the Companies Act 2006. Our audit work has been undertaken so that we might state to the company's members those matters we are required to state to them in an auditor's report and for no other purpose. To the fullest extent permitted by law, we do not accept or assume responsibility to anyone other than the company and the company's members as a body, for our audit work, for this report, or for the opinions we have formed.

It is common practice to include a *Bannerman* paragraph at the end of the auditor's report directly before the auditor's signature. Some commentators have argued that placing it at the end of the auditor's report is inappropriate and it should be given more prominence towards the beginning of the report.

It is recommended that when used, audit firms also need to be consistent in where they position the disclaimer paragraph in their audit reports, so that clients and other users of the audit report know where to expect to see it.

It should be kept in mind that *Bannerman* paragraphs are a risk management tool developed by audit firms and the advice is that audit firms should think carefully about reservations they put on who the audit is undertaken for.

19.3 The auditor's opinion

19.3.1 The wording of the auditor's opinion

ISA (UK) 700 requires that the auditor form an opinion as to whether the financial statements are prepared, in all material respects, in accordance with the applicable financial reporting framework. The auditor's opinion must be clearly stated in the auditor's report.

In some jurisdictions, for example in the UK, specific wording must be used. In the UK, when expressing an unmodified opinion on financial statements, the opinion paragraph shall clearly state that the financial statements give a true and fair view. Section 393 of the Companies Act 2006 states that the directors of a company must not approve the financial statements unless they are satisfied they give a true and fair view and therefore the concept of the true and fair view is fundamental to accounting in the UK. It is perhaps surprising to learn then, that there is no statutory definition of 'true and fair'. The concept of true and fair is critical as it enhances the credibility and reliability of financial information for stakeholders, including investors, creditors, regulators, and the general public. It helps to build trust in an organization's financial reporting and promotes transparency in the financial markets.

When thinking about the meaning of 'true and fair', a good starting point is to consider what it does *not* mean. It does not mean that the financial statements are 100 per cent accurate or that they contain no errors whatsoever. It does not mean that every figure has been 'proven' to be correct by the auditor.

Activity 19.1 True and fair

What do you understand by the term 'true and fair'? What does 'true' relate to? What does 'fair' imply?

- The idea of 'truth' in financial statements implies a high, but not absolute, degree of technical accuracy and conformity with relevant legal or financial reporting requirements. It means that fundamental accounting concepts such as those relating to going concern and accruals have been followed. True can also be interpreted as meaning that information is factual and conforms to reality and that the financial statements have been correctly extracted from the books and records.
- The 'fairness' aspect of the opinion is more about the judgements that have been used by management in preparing the financial statements. It implies that the financial statements are free from bias and have been as objectively prepared as they can be. The financial information is presented in a balanced and fair way and reflects the commercial substance (i.e. the commercial reality) of the company's underlying transactions.

Auditing in practice 19.3 Legal opinion on 'true and fair'

Over the years, regulators in the UK have sought legal counsel on the term 'true and fair' and its use, notably obtaining the legal opinion of Leonard Hoffman QC and Dame Mary Arden in 1983 and 1993. The issue became particularly important when UK listed entities had to start preparing financial statements using IFRS rather than UK accounting standards in 2005. At this time there was concern that the move to a different applicable financial reporting framework might impact whether 'true and fair view' remained a fundamental part of accounting practice and therefore an appropriate term for the auditor's opinion. In 2008, the UK's FRC commissioned a further legal opinion to consider this issue, which confirmed that while there had been some significant changes in accounting standards and company law, the true and fair requirement remained central to the preparation of financial statements in the UK. The legal opinion concluded that the use of 'true and fair' is still appropriate and that it means the same as the term 'fair presentation' which is a common wording for the auditor's opinion seen outside the UK.

We should at this point remind ourselves that the unmodified audit opinion relates to financial statements which are free from material misstatement. Remember that during the course of the audit, the auditor may have discovered misstatements within the financial statements, but for the audit opinion to be unmodified, these misstatements must be below financial statement materiality. When considering whether misstatements are material, the auditor considers them both in isolation and in the aggregate. If they are immaterial both individually and, in the aggregate, the auditor can still express an unmodified opinion.

Auditing in practice 19.4 The Brydon Review and 'true and fair'

Sir Donald Brydon's review of the auditing profession included some commentary on the term 'true and fair'. Brydon is not supportive of continued use of the term and his report suggests that the term contributes to the audit expectation gap, stating that 'since the introduction of IFRS, the financial statements contain many estimates and assumptions (generally required to be set out in the notes to the accounts) that are dependent on judgments about the future. It does not need a philosopher to question how an opinion about judgments relating to the future can be "true"'.[6]

Brydon recommends that 'true and fair' is replaced by 'present fairly, in all material respects', explaining that, in his view, this wording will strengthen the value of the audit opinion.

19.3.2 **Matters to consider in reaching audit opinion**

In determining whether the financial statements are fairly presented or show a true and fair view, ISA (UK) 700 requires the auditor to consider matters including whether:

(a) The financial statements appropriately disclose the significant accounting policies selected and applied. In making this evaluation, the auditor shall consider the relevance of the accounting policies to the entity, and whether they have been presented in an understandable manner;

(b) The accounting policies selected and applied are consistent with the applicable financial reporting framework and are appropriate;

(c) The accounting estimates made by management are reasonable;

[6] *Report of the independent review into the quality and effectiveness of audit*, 2019.

(d) The information presented in the financial statements is relevant, reliable, comparable, and understandable. In making this evaluation, the auditor shall consider whether:

i. The information that should have been included has been included, and whether such information is appropriately classified, aggregated or disaggregated, and characterized.

ii. The overall presentation of the financial statements has been undermined by including information that is not relevant or that obscures a proper understanding of the matters disclosed.

(e) The financial statements provide adequate disclosures to enable the intended users to understand the effect of material transactions and events on the information conveyed in the financial statements; and

(f) The terminology used in the financial statements, including the title of each financial statement, is appropriate.[7]

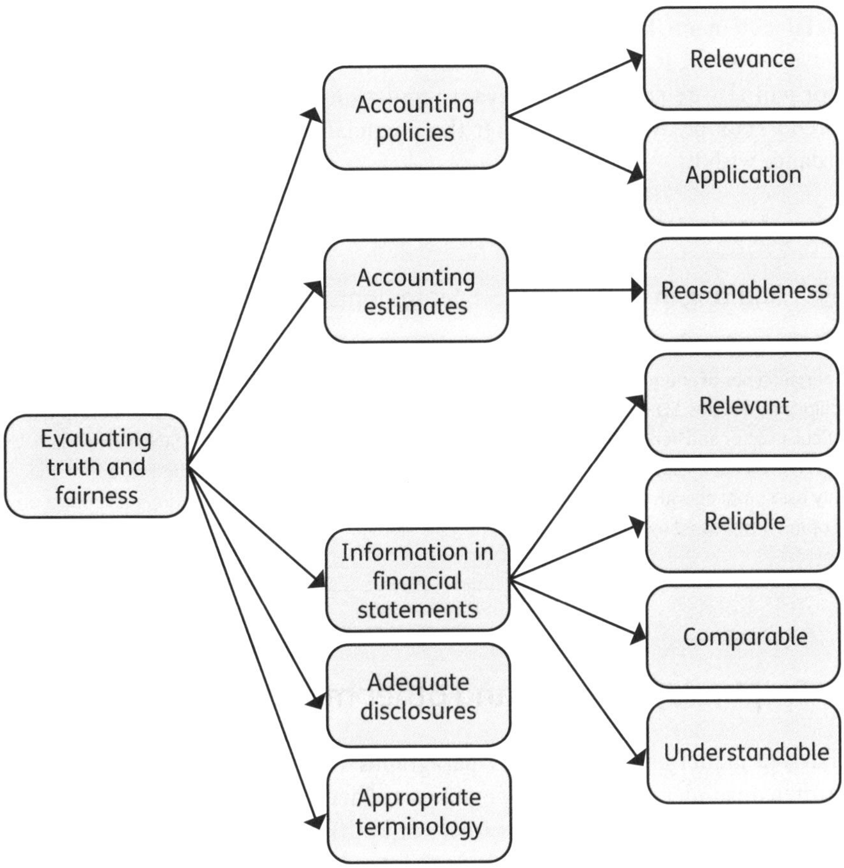

Figure 19.2 Matters to consider in evaluating truth and fairness of financial statements

[7] FRC, 'ISA (UK) 700', 2022, para 13.

Remember that in preparing the financial statements, management makes many judgements and estimates. Even in relatively simple financial statements, there will be judgements and estimates relating to matters such as the useful life of assets, the recoverability of receivables balances and the valuation of inventory. The auditor needs to consider whether the use of judgement has been appropriate and is free from management bias, so that there is no material misstatement of the financial statements. The accounting policies themselves need to be appropriate to the reporting entity, in conformance with the relevant financial reporting standards, and the accounting policies must be presented and adequately described clearly in the financial statements.

In assessing the understandability of the information in the financial statements, the auditor must consider whether it is concise and easy to follow, including evaluating whether important issues have been given appropriate prominence in the financial statements and if disclosures are cross-referenced, making the information easy to navigate.

When the auditor expresses an unmodified opinion, they must confirm that the financial statements have been properly prepared in accordance with the applicable financial reporting framework (e.g. IFRS) and relevant legislation or regulations. The auditor will also refer to other relevant regulations or legislation which the entity is required to comply with and whether the financial statements have been prepared in accordance with it.

Auditing in practice 19.5 Statements of recommended practice

In the UK, some entities are subject to *statements of recommended practice* (SORPs). A SORP is issued for certain types of entity, for example, for charities, pension funds, housing associations, and limited liability partnerships. SORPs interpret generally accepted accounting practice in the context of that particular sector and hence the entity is required to comply with any applicable SORPs or explain why they have not complied. The auditor will also confirm in their auditor's report whether, or not, the entity has complied with any relevant SORPs. Non-compliance could have a detrimental impact on the opinion expressed by the auditor which may be modified (see Chapter 20 for modified auditor's opinions).

19.4 Emphasis of matter and other matter paragraphs

Emphasis of matter and other matter paragraphs are dealt with in ISA (UK) 706. Students often misunderstand the use of emphasis of matter paragraphs in particular, so pay attention to this section! Including either (or both) paragraphs in the auditor's report means that the report is modified. This does not mean that the opinion is modified—the opinion is still 'true and fair'. There is nothing 'wrong' with the financial statements—all these paragraphs do is highlight information which is of relevance to the shareholders (see Figure 19.3).

A further matter which can lead to a modified report which does not impact the audit opinion is the inclusion of a 'Material Uncertainty Related to Going Concern' section in accordance with ISA (UK) 570 (see section 17.4).

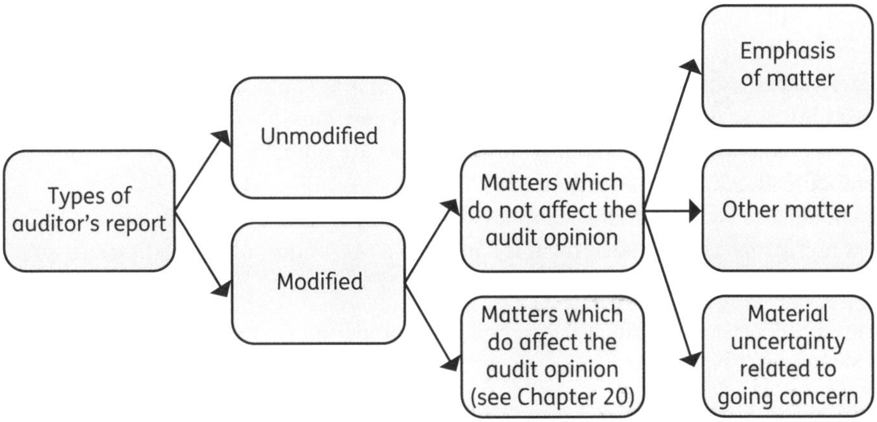

Figure 19.3 Unmodified and modified audit reports

19.4.1 **Emphasis of matter paragraphs**

ISA (UK) 706 defines 'Emphasis of Matter paragraph' as follows:

> A paragraph included in the auditor's report that refers to a matter appropriately presented or disclosed in the financial statements that, in the auditor's judgment, is of such importance that it is fundamental to users' understanding of the financial statements.[8]

The key thing to understand is that an emphasis of matter paragraph is *only* included in the auditor's report to refer to a fundamental matter which has already been adequately disclosed by management in the financial statements. The auditor uses an emphasis of matter paragraph to highlight an issue that has been appropriately accounted for and/or disclosed in the financial statements because, in the auditor's professional judgement, the issue is of fundamental importance to the users' understanding of the financial statements.

Emphasis of matter paragraphs are never used as a means of modifying the auditor's opinion in any way. Students often get confused as to the overall purpose of an emphasis of matter paragraph and sometimes mistakenly regard the emphasis of matter as a means of modifying the auditor's opinion. The paragraph must always confirm that the auditor's opinion is not modified in respect of the matter it is referring to. In addition, the emphasis of matter paragraph must always cross-refer to the relevant disclosure note in the financial statements.

ISA (UK) 706 requires that:

> When the auditor includes an Emphasis of Matter paragraph in the auditor's report, the auditor shall:
>
> (a) Include the paragraph within a separate section of the auditor's report with an appropriate heading that includes the term 'Emphasis of Matter';
>
> (b) Include in the paragraph a clear reference to the matter being emphasized and to where relevant disclosures that fully describe the matter can be found in the financial statements. The paragraph shall refer only to information presented or disclosed in the financial statements; and
>
> (c) Indicate that the auditor's opinion is not modified in respect of the matter emphasized.[9]

[8] FRC, 'ISA (UK) 706', 2016, para 7(a) <https://media.frc.org.uk/documents/ISA_UK_706_-_Revised_June_2016.pdf> (accessed 18 January 2024).

[9] Ibid., para 9.

If the matter which the auditor considers is of fundamental importance to the users' understanding of the financial statements and it has not been adequately disclosed in the financial statements, the auditor will modify their opinion accordingly.

In addition, an emphasis of matter paragraph is never used to draw attention to immaterial misstatements. The fact that the misstatements are immaterial means that they do not warrant the shareholders' attention.

It should also be noted that an emphasis of matter paragraph cannot be used to highlight an issue that has already been included in the KAMs section of the auditor's report. ISA (UK) 706 states that:

> the use of Emphasis of Matter paragraphs is not a substitute for a description of individual key audit matters.[10]

Activity 19.2 Examples of matters of fundamental importance

Can you list four examples of matters which may be of fundamental importance and included in an emphasis of matter paragraph?

Auditing scenario 19.1 Emphasis of matter paragraph

Browns Ltd is facing a legal claim, the outcome of which, at the time of issuing the auditor's report and financial statements, is uncertain. The company is defending its position and the company's legal advisers consider that the likelihood of the company paying damages is possible, but not remote. The auditor, having performed relevant procedures, agrees with management that the matter should not be provided for, and that a disclosure should be given in the notes to the financial statements. The auditor also considers this issue to be material.

On reviewing the note to the financial statements, the auditor agrees it to be in compliance with the requirements of IAS 37 *Provisions, Contingent Liabilities and Contingent Assets.*

In this case, the impact on the auditor's report is that an emphasis of matter paragraph should be included. The auditor's report is therefore modified. The emphasis of matter paragraph must describe the situation giving rise to the emphasis of matter and its possible effects on the financial statements.

The audit opinion is not modified—the financial statements are true and fair (i.e. they comply with the relevant requirements of IAS 37 and the auditor has obtained evidence to support their opinion on this matter).

The emphasis of matter paragraph may state wording such as this:

Emphasis of matter—legal claim

> In the forming of our opinion on the financial statements, which is not qualified, we have considered the adequacy of the disclosures made in note X to the financial statements concerning the possible outcome of a legal claim against the company, which is being defended. The outcome of the legal claim is uncertain, and no provision for any liability that may result has been made in the financial statements. Our opinion is not modified in respect of this matter.

[10] Ibid., para A1.

19.4.2 Other matter paragraphs

An 'other matter' paragraph is included in the auditor's report if the auditor considers it necessary to communicate on matters which are not presented or disclosed in the financial statements which, in the auditor's opinion, are relevant to an understanding of:

- the audit;
- the auditor's responsibilities; or
- the auditor's report.

An other matter paragraph should not be used to discuss matters which are also deemed to be KAMs and communicated as such in the auditor's report.

It is not very common to see other matter paragraphs, but they are used to highlight where the prior period financial statements were audited by another auditor or where the prior period financial statements were not audited at all.

An example of wording that may be used in an other matter paragraph is shown below. In this case, the other matter being referred to relates to the fact that the previous year's financial statements were audited by a different audit firm:

The financial statements of Smith Co Ltd for the year ended 31 December 20X8 were audited by a predecessor auditor whose opinion dated 31 March 20X9 was unmodified.

If the auditor expects to include an emphasis of matter or other matter paragraph in the auditor's report, the auditor will communicate with those charged with governance regarding this expectation and the proposed wording of the paragraph.

19.4.3 Placement of emphasis of matter and other matter paragraphs

There is no specific placement for the emphasis of matter or other matter paragraphs within the auditor's report. ISA (UK) 706 states:

> The placement of an Emphasis of Matter paragraph or Other Matter paragraph in the auditor's report depends on the nature of the information to be communicated, and the auditor's judgment as to the relative significance of such information to intended users compared to other elements required to be reported in accordance with ISA (UK) 700.
>
> (Revised June 2016)[11]

For example, if a matter disclosed in the emphasis of matter paragraph relates to the applicable financial reporting framework, it may be sensible to position the emphasis of matter paragraph immediately following the basis of opinion paragraph where the matter may be discussed further.

When a KAMs section is presented in the auditor's report (see next section), an emphasis of matter paragraph may be presented either directly before or after it depending on the auditor's judgement as to the relative significance of the information included in the emphasis of matter paragraph.

[11] Ibid., para A16.

19.5 Key Audit Matters (KAMs)

19.5.1 Enhanced auditor reporting

According to the IAASB's research and public consultation projects, enhanced auditor reporting is critical to influencing the perceived value of the financial statement audit. Investors and other financial statement users asked for a more informative auditor's report—in particular for auditors to provide more relevant information to users about key matters which arose during the audit.

As a result of its consultations, the IAASB suggested that the intended benefits of enhanced auditor reporting include the following:

- Enhanced communication between auditors and investors, as well as those charged with corporate governance.
- Increased user confidence in auditor's reports and financial statements.
- Increased transparency, audit quality, and enhanced information value.
- Increased attention by management and financial statement preparers to disclosures referencing the auditor's report.
- Renewed auditor focus on matters to be reported that could result in an increase in professional scepticism.
- Enhanced financial reporting in the public interest.[12]

The changes to auditor reporting, in particular, in relation to KAMs, which we will now explore, should be viewed not just as a development affecting individual financial statement audits, but as a move to enhance audit quality generally, which in turn will improve the credibility of financial reporting and the audit profession.

19.5.2 Determining KAMs

KAMs are dealt with in ISA (UK) 701 *Communicating Key Audit Matters in the Independent Auditor's Report*. A KAM section is compulsory for listed entities although auditors of private entities may include a KAM section if they wish.

The term 'key audit matters' is defined as:

> Those matters that, in the auditor's professional judgment, were of most significance in the audit of the financial statements of the current period. Key audit matters are selected from matters communicated with those charged with governance.

The purpose of communicating KAMs is:

> to enhance the communicative value of the auditor's report by providing greater transparency about the audit that was performed. Communicating key audit matters provides additional information to intended users of the financial statements ('intended users') to assist them in understanding those matters that, in the auditor's professional judgment, were of most significance

[12] IAASB, 'The new auditor's report: Greater transparency into the financial statement audit' (2015).

in the audit of the financial statements of the current period. Communicating key audit matters may also assist intended users in understanding the entity and areas of significant management judgment in the audited financial statements.[13]

The objectives of the auditor according to ISA 701 are to:

- determine key audit matters; and
- having formed an opinion on the financial statements, communicate those matters by describing them in the auditor's report.[14]

KAMs are usually matters which were a key focus during the audit, often the areas of high audit risk, and where significant audit work was performed. They often relate to accounting issues which involve a high degree of judgement or issues which are complex.

Activity 19.3 KAMs

What matters do you think are often disclosed as KAMs?

Given the multitude of matters that can arise during the audit process, the auditor may find that there are many matters that potentially could be included in the KAM paragraph. Determining the KAMs to be discussed in the auditor's report is a matter of judgement. A filtering process is applied, to ensure that the auditor applies appropriate judgement in determining the KAMs (Figure 19.4)

- KAMs are selected from those matters which the auditor has communicated with those charged with governance.
- Matters which are discussed with those charged with governance are then evaluated by the auditor who determines those matters which required significant auditor attention

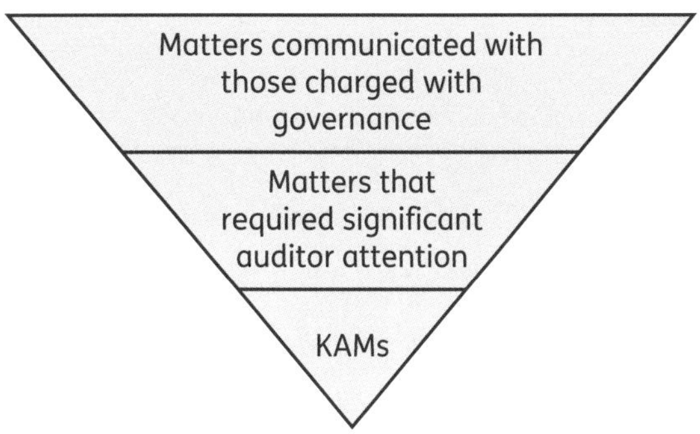

Figure 19.4 Determining KAMs

[13] FRC, 'ISA (UK) 701', 2022, para 2 <https://media.frc.org.uk/documents/ISA_UK_701_Updated_May_2022.pdf> (accessed 18 January 2024).

[14] Ibid., para 7.

during the course of the audit. ISA (UK) 701 states three matters which the auditor must take into account when making this determination:

(a) Areas of higher assessed risk of material misstatement, or significant risks identified in accordance with ISA (UK) 315 (Revised July 2020).

(b) Significant auditor judgments relating to areas in the financial statements that involved significant management judgment, including accounting estimates that are subject to a high degree of estimation uncertainty.

(c) The effect on the audit of significant events or transactions that occurred during the period.[15]

ISA (UK) 701 does not state a particular number of KAMs that should be communicated, discussing that the volume of disclosure will be affected by the size and complexity of the entity, the nature of its business and environment, and the facts and circumstances of the audit engagement.

In deciding how many KAMs should be included, the auditor should bear in mind that the volume of disclosure will be affected by the size and complexity of the entity and the nature of its business and environment. Auditors should try to avoid including lengthy descriptions of a large number of KAMs as this works against the idea of KAMs being those issues of most significance in the audit. Auditors need to be mindful in exercising professional judgement in prioritizing the audit matters to be included in the KAMs disclosure.

Auditing in practice 19.6 Disclosure of KAMs

A report produced by the ICAEW, including analysis based on analysis of listed company audit reports in the UK, found that the following matters were the most commonly reported as risks within KAMs, each being reported in more than 10 per cent of all audit reports:

- revenue
- carrying value of goodwill/intangibles
- taxation
- accounting for acquisitions
- pensions
- valuation of property
- inventory
- litigation and regulation

Of the matters listed above, revenue was by far the most reported KAM, being included in more than 60 per cent of audit reports.

The report also found that most reports included two to four KAMs but that a small number included as many as nine KAMs.[16]

[15] FRC, 'ISA (UK) 700', 2022, para 9.

[16] Institute of Chartered Accountants in England and Wales, 'The start of a conversation—The extended audit report', 2017 <https://www.icaew.com/-/media/corporate/files/technical/audit-and-assurance/audit-and-assurance-faculty/publications/extended-audit-report.ashx> (accessed 19 January 2024).

19.5.3 Communicating KAMs

Once the auditor has determined those matters which are to be included as KAMs, the auditor must then ensure that each matter is appropriately described in the KAM section of the auditor's report. This must include a description of:

a) Why the matter was determined to be one of most significance and therefore determined to be a key audit matter; and
b) How the matter was addressed in the audit, including significant judgments made by the engagement team with respect to the matter.[17]

Though there is not a specific requirement in terms of placement of the KAM paragraph within the auditor's report, ISA (UK) 701 does comment that placement of the KAM paragraph 'in close proximity to the auditor's opinion may give prominence to such information and acknowledge the perceived value of engagement-specific information to intended users'.[18] The auditor may need to use judgement in deciding on the best position of the KAM paragraph.

The ordering of items within the KAM paragraph itself is also a matter of professional judgement. ISA (UK) 701 suggests that the information may be organized in order of relative importance, based on the auditor's judgement, or may correspond to the manner in which matters are disclosed in the financial statements.

In deciding the amount and nature of description of each item within the KAM paragraph, the auditor is required to use their professional judgement, in order to ensure that each matter is adequately described in an understandable way.

The description of each KAM should be a succinct and balanced explanation to enable intended users to understand why the matter was one of most significance in the audit and how the matter was addressed in the audit. ISA (UK) 701 suggests that technical jargon should be avoided, stating that:

> limiting the use of highly technical auditing terms also helps to enable intended users who do not have a reasonable knowledge of auditing to understand the basis for the auditor's focus on particular matters during the audit.[19]

It is likely that many KAMs will have been discussed in the financial statements, in other words, there will be an overlap between information given in the financial statements and matters included as a KAM. For example, information in relation to a significant estimated value for a provision should have been disclosed in the notes to the financial statements in accordance with the relevant IFRS requirement. ISA (UK) 701 suggests that the description of a KAM should not be a duplicate of information that is already disclosed in the financial statements. However, a reference to any related disclosures should be included to enable intended users of the auditor's report to further understand how management has addressed the matter in preparing the financial statements.

[17] FRC, 'ISA (UK) 701', 2022, para 13. [18] Ibid., para A31. [19] Ibid., para A34.

The amount of detail to be provided in the auditor's report to describe how a KAM was addressed in the audit is also a matter of professional judgement. The auditor may choose to describe:

- aspects of the auditor's response or approach that were most relevant to the matter or specific to the assessed risk of material misstatement,
- a brief overview of procedures performed,
- an indication of the outcome of the auditor's procedures, or
- key observations with respect to the matter.

Where KAMs are concerned, the auditor must also keep in mind the importance of considering ethical issues. For an auditor to conclude that a KAM should be disclosed in the auditor's report will usually involve significant discussion with management and/or those charged with governance. These discussions can be intense and pressure may be put on the auditor not to disclose an issue (or a number of issues) as KAM.

Auditors are compelled to comply with the ethical principles of integrity, objectivity, professional competence and due care, and professional behaviour. Hence, the auditor must not be tempted to exclude KAMs which would otherwise be included for fear of being disengaged by the client or other such reasons.

Appendix 19.2 contains the KAM disclosure for AstraZeneca, extracted from the company's audit report for 2018. Note the length of the KAM disclosure and the nature of the items that are described. You should also consider the usefulness of the disclosure—do you think it is a helpful section to include in an audit report?

Chapter round-up

- An unmodified auditor's opinion confirms that the auditor has obtained reasonable assurance that the financial statements are free from material misstatement and have been prepared in compliance with the applicable financial reporting framework and applicable legislation.
- The auditor's report must contain a number of elements including a basis for opinion paragraph, description of the responsibilities of management and auditors, and the name and signature of the audit engagement partner.
- An emphasis of matter paragraph is used when the auditor wishes to highlight an issue which is fundamental to users' understanding and which has been appropriately reflected in the financial statements.
- Using an emphasis of matter paragraph does not modify the audit opinion.
- The audit reports of public interest companies must include a section dealing with KAMs.
- It is a matter of judgement for the auditor in determining the KAMs to disclose in the auditor's report.
- Auditors can choose to include a liability disclaimer paragraph within the auditor's report, but this is not mandated.

End of chapter case study

Introduction

The auditor's report is the key output of the audit and the means by which assurance is provided in the financial statements. The auditor's report is therefore a crucial piece of communication and to provide the most benefit to the users of the report, it must convey important messages in a user-friendly way.

ISA (UK) 700 requires the unmodified auditor's report to contain a set of elements, each of which is important in making the report as useful as possible. Requirements of other ISAs (UK) require the auditor to deal with a range of issues which should be highlighted with the report.

This activity will test your ability to explain the content of an auditor's report and to identify the matters which the auditor should address within the auditor's report.

This activity links to the following learning outcomes:

- Identify and explain the matters which may be selected as KAMs in the context of an audit of financial statements.
- Discuss the auditor's reporting implications in respect of going concern (Chapter 17).
- Explain the auditor's responsibility for other information contained in the annual report and recommend actions to be taken if there are inconsistencies (Chapter 18).

Scenario

You are working on the audit of Craig plc, a listed company with a diverse range of operations including retail, construction, and property development. It also has a small but growing logistics division, which currently contributes around 5 per cent to the company's overall revenue. The audit is drawing to a close, the audit fieldwork is complete, and the audit report is due to be issued next week.

Materiality for the audit of Craig plc is set at £1.2 million.

The audit engagement partner has asked for your help in preparing the auditor's report as she has been called away on urgent business with another audit client. She has left you with some information about several issues relating to the audit, which is shown below.

You should read the information provided and then attempt the tasks which are given at the end of the information.

1. Significant issues arising in the audit

Revenue recognition

Revenue recognition was identified as an area of high audit risk at the planning stage of the audit. There were several risks identified including those relating to the timing of revenue recognition on construction contracts. In addition, a risk was identified with the measurement of revenue arising on retail sales where a customer loyalty scheme means that an element of revenue generated on the sale of goods to a customer is deferred. Both of these elements of revenue are material to the financial statements. As a result of the audit procedures performed, the auditor's conclusion is that revenue is recognized in an appropriate way in the financial statements.

Financial instruments

Due to the international nature of Craig plc's operations, the company manages its exposure to exchange rate fluctuations using derivative financial instruments. These derivatives are measured at fair value through profit and loss and management has developed a model to determine the fair value of the financial instruments at the year end. The financial instruments are valued at £4.5 million in this year's financial statements, and the previous year were valued at £1.2 million. As a result of the audit procedures performed, the auditor's conclusion is that the derivatives are recognized in an appropriate way in the financial statements.

Loan covenants

The property development part of Craig plc's operations is suffering poor performance due to difficult economic conditions and new regulations brought in by the government. The financial statements for this year recognize a loss before tax of £3.4 million. In addition, due to problems in managing liquidity, the company is in breach of loan covenants in relation to loans provided by its bank. While management is optimistic about the company's ability to raise additional finance and to return to profitability, the audit evidence led to a conclusion that there is doubt on the Group's ability to continue as a going concern.

2. Operating and financial review

The Annual Report in which the financial statements and auditor's report will be issued contains an Operating and Financial Review including several Key Performance Indicators (KPIs) and related management commentary. The Operating and Financial Review states that while financial performance this year is not strong, the company is in a sound financial position and that the company's management team is confident of a return to profitability in the next financial year, largely due to the new logistics division now contributing a significant amount of revenue and profit to the company.

Required

You have been asked to help with drafting the auditor's report for Craig plc.

The tasks that you are required to perform are as follows:

1. Discuss whether the issues identified as 'Significant issues arising in the audit' should be disclosed and explained as KAMs within the auditor's report. If the matters are not KAMs, how should they be dealt with in the auditor's report?
2. Explain how the auditor should approach the problem with the management commentary included in the operating and financial review, including action to be taken by the auditor and the potential impact on the auditor's report.

Answer

1. Significant issues arising in the audit

KAMs are the matters which, in the auditor's judgement, were of most significance in the audit of the financial statements.

For both the revenue recognition and valuation of financial instruments, these appear to be areas of significant audit judgement with a high risk of material misstatement. Therefore, their inclusion as KAM is appropriate. Within the disclosure, there should be explanation of the factors which led the auditor to determine the matters are a KAM. For example, the explanation could describe the materiality of both of the issues, the reasons they were identified as having high risk of material misstatement and explained the impact of both matters on the nature and extent of the audit effort. The auditor should also describe how each KAM was addressed in the audit, and although this is a matter for auditor judgement, the auditor may describe aspects of the auditor's response or approach, provide a brief overview of the procedures performed and an indication of the outcome of the procedures.

The breach of loan covenants should be discussed in a 'Material Uncertainty Relating to Going Concern' section of the auditor's report, which should explain the financial distress faced by the company and refer to the note to the financial statements where the matters has been discussed. The 'Material Uncertainty Relating to Going Concern' section should state that the auditor's opinion is not modified in relation to this issue.

2. Operating and financial review

The Operating and Financial Review is not part of the financial statements and the auditor's opinion therefore does not extend to it. However, ISA (UK) 720 *The Auditor's Responsibilities Relating to Other Information* requires that the auditor must read the other information contained within the annual report in order to consider whether there is a material inconsistency between the other information and the financial statements.

A material inconsistency arises where the other information contradicts information in the audited financial statements. This undermines the auditor's opinion and the financial statements, impacting the credibility of both.

In the case of Craig plc there is an inconsistency because the management commentary states that the new logistics division provides significant revenue to the company, but the auditor's understanding of the business is that it contributes 5 per cent of the company's revenue. Although what classifies as a 'significant' amount of revenue is judgemental, 5 per cent is unlikely to be considered to be significant. A user of the annual report would therefore be confused about this inconsistency as the operating and financial review describes the logistics division as significant, but it would not be disclosed as such in the financial statements, for example, it would not be large enough to be a cash-generating unit or an operating segment to be separately disclosed in the notes to the accounts.

The auditor is likely to consider this inconsistency to be important as management is using the commentary relating to the new logistics division to discuss the company's going concern issues and to reassure readers of the report that going concern is not a problem. The management commentary is therefore misleading about the company's future.

Assuming that the auditor concludes that it is the other information which appears to be materially misstated (not the financial statements), the auditor should request management to correct the other information. If management agrees to make the correction, the auditor should determine that the correction has been made by requesting and reviewing a revised version of the management commentary.

If management refuses to make the correction, the auditor should communicate the matter with those charged with governance and request that the correction be made.

If the other information then remains uncorrected, the auditor should consider the implications for the auditor's report. As it is the other information which is incorrect, the auditor's opinion is not impacted. However, the auditor's report should include a statement which describes the uncorrected material misstatement. In the UK, the Companies Act 2006 requires auditors to report by exception if the information given in the strategic report and the directors' report for the financial year for which the financial statements are prepared is inconsistent with the financial statements.

Activity solutions

Activity 19.1—True and fair

What do you understand by the term 'true and fair'? What does 'true' relate to? What does 'fair' imply?

Suggested answer points:

True: the financial statements should be based on factual and accurate information. The financial statements presented should be free from intentional misrepresentation, errors, or omissions.

Fair: the financial statements should be impartial and balanced. They should not be biased towards any particular group or stakeholder, and they should reflect both positive and negative aspects of the organization's financial performance.

Activity 19.2—Examples of matters of fundamental importance

Can you list four examples of matters which may be of fundamental importance and included in an emphasis of matter paragraph?

Suggested answer points:

Examples of matter which the auditor may judge to be of fundamental importance include the following (note the list below is not conclusive):

- there is uncertainty relating to the future outcome of a legal case;
- a significant subsequent event takes place between the reporting date and the date of the auditor's report (sometimes referred to as an 'event after the reporting date' or a 'post balance sheet event');
- a major catastrophe has occurred after the reporting date but before the financial statement is authorized for issue;
- corresponding figures have been restated due to an accounting error.

Activity 19.3—KAMs

What matters do you think are often disclosed as KAMs?

Suggested answer points:

- judgemental areas of accounting including goodwill, impairment of assets, intangible assets, revenue recognition, provisions and contingencies, fair values;
- complex areas of accounting including financial instruments, complex group structures, taxation;
- deficiencies in internal controls; and
- fraud risks.

Appendix 19.1 Illustrative unmodified auditor's report

Independent auditor's report to the members of Cordley Co Ltd for the year ended 31 August 20X9

Opinion

We have audited the financial statements of Cordley Co Ltd ('the company') for the year ended 31 August 20X9 which comprise the statement of financial position, the statement of comprehensive income, the statement of changes in equity, the statement of cash flows and notes to the financial statements, including a summary of significant accounting policies.

In our opinion the financial statements:

- give a true and fair view of the state of the financial position of the company and its performance and cash flows for the year ended 31 August 20X9;
- have been properly prepared in accordance with International Financial Reporting Standards; and
- have been prepared in accordance with the requirements of the Companies Act 2006 [or other legislation].

Basis for opinion

We conducted our audit in accordance with International Standards on Auditing (UK) (ISAs (UK)). Our responsibilities under those standards are further described in the 'Auditor's Responsibilities for the Audit of the Financial Statements' section of our report. We are independent of the company in accordance with ethical requirements that are relevant to our audit of the financial statements in the United Kingdom, and we have fulfilled our other ethical responsibilities in accordance with these requirements. We believe that the audit evidence we have obtained is sufficient and appropriate to provide a basis for our opinion.

Key audit matters

Key audit matters are those matters which, in our professional judgement, were of most significance in our audit of the financial statements of the current period. These matters were addressed in the context of our audit of the financial statements as a whole and in forming our opinion thereof, and we do not provide a separate opinion on these matters.

[Provide a description of each key audit matter in accordance with ISA (UK) 701].

Conclusions relating to going concern

In auditing the financial statements, we have concluded that the directors' use of the going concern basis of accounting in the preparation of the financial statements is appropriate.

Based on the work we have performed, we have not identified any material uncertainties relating to events or conditions that, individually or collectively, may cast significant doubt on the company's ability to continue as a going concern for a period of at least twelve months from when the financial statements are authorized for issue.

Our responsibilities and the responsibilities of the directors with respect to going concern are described in the relevant sections of this report.

Other information

The directors are responsible for the other information. The other information comprises the Chairman's statement and the statement of directors' responsibilities but does not include the financial statements and the auditor's report thereon.

Our opinion on the financial statements does not cover the other information and we do not express any form of assurance conclusion thereon.

In connection with our audit of the financial statements, our responsibility is to read the other information and, in doing so, consider whether the other information is materially inconsistent with the financial statements or our knowledge obtained in the audit or otherwise appears to be materially misstated. If, based on the work we have performed, we conclude that there is a material misstatement of this information, we are required to report that fact. We have nothing to report in this regard.

Opinions on other matters prescribed by the Companies Act 2006

In our opinion, based on the work undertaken in the course of the audit:

the information given in the strategic report and the report of the directors for the financial year for which the financial statements are prepared is consistent with the financial statements; and

the strategic report and the report of the directors have been prepared in accordance with applicable legal requirements.

Matters on which we are required to report by exception

In the light of the knowledge and understanding of the company and its environment obtained in the course of the audit, we have not identified material misstatements in the strategic report or the report of the directors.

We have nothing to report in respect of the following matters where the Companies Act 2006 requires us to report to you if, in our opinion:

- adequate accounting records have not been kept, or returns adequate for our audit have not been received from branches not visited by us; or
- the financial statements are not in agreement with the accounting records and returns; or
- certain disclosures of directors' remuneration specified by law are not made; or
- we have not received all the information and explanations we require for our audit.

Responsibilities of directors and those charged with governance

As explained more fully in the statement of directors' responsibilities set out on page X, the directors are responsible for the preparation of the financial statements and for being satisfied that they give a true and fair view, and for such internal control as the directors determine necessary to enable the preparation of financial statements that are free from material misstatement, whether due to fraud or error.

In preparing the financial statements, the directors are responsible for assessing the company's ability to continue as a going concern, disclosing as applicable, matters related to going concern and using the going concern basis of accounting unless management either intends to liquidate the company or to cease operations, or has no realistic alternative but to do so.

Those charged with governance are responsible for overseeing the company's financial reporting process.

Auditor's responsibilities for the audit of the financial statements

Our objectives are to obtain reasonable assurance about whether the financial statements as a whole are free from material misstatement, whether due to fraud or error, and to issue an auditor's report that includes our opinion. Reasonable assurance is a high level of assurance but is not a guarantee that an audit conducted in accordance with ISAs (UK) will always detect a material misstatement when it exists. Misstatements can arise from fraud or error and are considered material if, individually or in the aggregate, they could reasonably be expected to influence the economic decisions of users taken on the basis of these financial statements.

The extent to which our procedures are capable of detecting irregularities, including fraud is detailed below:

[Describe the extent to which the audit was capable of detecting irregularities, including fraud. There is no standard text for this as the relevant audit procedures will be specific to the audit client.]

As part of an audit in accordance with ISAs (UK), we exercise professional scepticism and judgement throughout the audit. We also:

- Identify and assess the risks of material misstatement of the financial statements, whether due to fraud or error, design and perform audit procedures responsive to those risks and obtain audit evidence that is sufficient and appropriate to provide a basis for our opinion. The risk of not detecting a material misstatement from fraud is higher than for one resulting from error as fraud may involve collusion, forgery, intentional omissions, misrepresentations, or the override of internal control.
- Obtain an understanding of internal control relevant to the audit in order to design audit procedures that are appropriate in the circumstances, but not for the purpose of expressing an opinion on the effectiveness of the company's internal control.
- Evaluate the appropriateness of accounting policies used and the reasonableness of accounting estimates and related disclosures made by management.
- Conclude on the appropriateness of management's use of the going concern basis of accounting and, based on the audit evidence obtained, whether a material uncertainty exists related to events or conditions that may cast significant doubt on the company's ability to continue as a going concern. If we conclude that a material uncertainty exists, we are required to draw attention in our auditor's report to the related disclosures in the financial statements or, if such disclosures are inadequate, to modify our opinion. Our conclusions are based on the audit evidence obtained up to the date of our auditor's report. However, future events or conditions may cause the company to cease trading as a going concern.

- Evaluate the overall presentation, structure, and content of the financial statements, including the disclosures, and whether the financial statements represent the underlying transactions and events in a manner that achieves fair presentation.

We communicate with those charged with governance regarding, among other matters, the planned scope and timing of the audit and significant findings, including any significant deficiencies in internal control that we identify during our audit.

We also provide those charged with governance with a statement that we have complied with relevant ethical requirements regarding independence, and to communicate with them all relationships and other matters that may reasonably be thought to bear on our independence, and where applicable, related safeguards.

From the matters communicated with those charged with governance, we determine those matters that were of most significance in the audit of the financial statements of the current period and are therefore the key audit matters. We describe these matters in our auditor's report unless law or regulation precludes public disclosure about the matter or when, in extremely rare circumstances, we determine that a matter should not be communicated in our report because the adverse consequences of doing so would reasonably be expected to outweigh the public interest benefits of such communication.

Report on other legal and regulatory requirements

[Provide a report on other legal and regulatory requirements as required by local legislation or regulation].

Use of our report

This report is made solely to the company's members, as a body, in accordance with Chapter 3 of Part 16 of the Companies Act 2006. Our audit work has been undertaken so that we might state to the company's members those matters we are required to state to them in a report of the auditors and for no other purpose. To the fullest extent permitted by law, we do not accept or assume responsibility to anyone other than the company and the company's members as a body, for our audit work, for this report, or for the opinions we have formed.

John Smith
John Smith FCA FCCA
Senior Statutory Auditor
ABC & Co LLP
Chartered Accountants/Chartered Certified Accountants and
Statutory Auditors
123 Street Name
Town
County
AB1 2CD
31 October 20X9

Appendix 19.2 AstraZeneca KAMs

The financial statements of AstraZeneca for the year ended 31 December 2018 show the following KAMs in the independent auditor's report and how the auditor addressed them during the course of the audit.[20]

We determined that there were no key audit matters applicable to the Parent Company to communicate in our report.

Table 19.1

Key audit matter	How our audit addressed the key audit matter
Recognition and measurement of accruals for rebates and returns in the US Refer to page 115 (Audit Committee Report), page 154 (Accounting Policies) and Note 19 in the Group Financial Statements. In the US the Group sells to customers under various commercial and government mandated contracts and reimbursement arrangements that include rebates and provide a right of return for certain products, of which the most significant are Medicare Part D, Managed Care and Medicaid. These arrangements lead to material deductions to gross sales in arriving at revenue to recognise the obligations for the Group to provide customers with rebates, discounts, allowances and the right of return, for which unsettled amounts are accrued. The directors have determined an accrual of $4.043m to be necessary at 31 December 2018. Rebate, discount, allowance and return arrangements are complex and establishing an appropriate accrual requires significant estimation on the part of management. Changes in estimates can have a significant financial impact.	We evaluated the design and tested the operating effectiveness of controls over the recognition and measurement of rebates and returns. We determined that we could rely on these controls for the purposes of our audit. We obtained management's calculations for accruals under applicable schemes and assessed the assumptions used by reference to the Group's stated commercial policies, the terms of the applicable contracts, third party data related to patient enrolment in US government funded benefit schemes and historical levels of product returns. We compared the assumptions to contracted prices, historical rebates, discounts, allowances and returns levels (where relevant) and to current payment trends. We also considered the historical accuracy of the Group's estimates in previous years and the effect of any adjustment to prior year's accruals in the current year's results. We formed an independent expectation of the largest elements of the accrual at 31 December 2018 using third party data (where relevant) and compared this expectation to the actual accrual recognised by the Group. Based on the procedures performed, we did not identify any material misstatements in the accruals.
Assessment of the recoverability of the carrying value of intangible assets (product, marketing and distribution rights) Refer to page 115 (Audit Committee Report), page 155 (Accounting Policies) and Note 9 in the Group Financial Statements The Group has product, marketing and distribution rights and other intangible assets totalling $21,720m, out of a total intangible asset value of $21,959m at 31 December 2018	We evaluated the design and tested the operating effectiveness of controls in assessing the carrying value of intangible assets. We determined that we could rely on these controls for the purposes of our audit. For those assets tested we obtained the Group's impairment analyses and: • we tested the accuracy of the impairment models and agreed the cash flow forecasts used in the impairment models to the Board approved Long Range Plan;

Continued

[20] https://www.astrazeneca.com/content/dam/az/Investor_Relations/annual-report-2018/PDF/AstraZeneca_AR_2018.pdf

Table 19.1 (Continued)

Key audit matter	How our audit addressed the key audit matter
The carrying values of intangible assets are contingent on future cash flows and there is a risk that the assets will be impaired if cash flows are not in line with expectations. The projections in management's impairment models contain a number of significant estimates including peak year and erosion sales curves, probability of technical and regulatory success factors and discount rates. Changes in these assumptions could lead to an impairment to the carrying value of intangible assets. Our work on intangible assets focussed on assets that were in development (and not being amortised) and launched assets which were individually significant, had lower levels of headroom or where there have been concerns over the recoverability of the carrying value of specific assets in previous periods.	• we tested the reasonableness of key assumptions including revenue and profit growth or decline, the expected loss of drug exclusivity and the impact of the expiry of patents including comparing certain assumptions to industry and economic forecasts; • for higher risk assets we performed sensitivity analysis focusing on what we consider to be reasonably possible changes in key assumptions; and • we assessed the historical accuracy of forecasts to assess management's forecasting ability. We utilised our in-house valuation experts to assess the valuation techniques used, to independently corroborate the discount rate used by management by reference to market data and to assist with the evaluation of other key assumptions for higher risk assets (primarily probability of technical and regulatory success factors). As a result of our work, we determined that the net impairment charge of $683m recorded for intangible assets was appropriate. We reviewed the disclosure in Note 9 of the Group Financial Statements, including sensitivity analysis based on reasonably possible downsides. We are satisfied that these disclosures are appropriate.
Accounting for externalisation and collaboration arrangements—in-license and out-licensing arrangements and other types of complex development and collaboration agreements Refer to page 115 (Audit Committee Report), page 155 (Accounting Policies) and Note 1 in the Group Financial Statements. The Group routinely enters into development and commercialisation arrangements and collaborations with other pharmaceutical companies. These include in-license and out-licensing arrangements and other types of complex agreements. In 2018, the Group recognised externalisation revenue of $1,041m. The nature of these arrangements mean that the accounting for externalisation revenue is often inherently complex and judgemental, unusual by definition and presents a higher level of risk.	We evaluated the design and tested the operating effectiveness of controls in place over significant contracts and collaboration agreements. We determined that we could rely on these controls for the purposes of our audit. For each material externalisation revenue transaction we reviewed the underlying contract and management's accounting analysis to understand both the formal terms of the agreement and its commercial substance. We assessed whether components of the transaction were at fair value and whether the rights transferred under the agreement qualified for revenue recognition having regard to the remaining performance obligations under the arrangement. Where there were ongoing performance obligations we assessed whether an appropriate proportion of revenue had been deferred, including an appropriate margin for the work yet to be performed. Where there was a related intangible asset we assessed whether an appropriate amount of the intangible asset had been derecognised on transfer of the relevant rights. Based on the procedures performed, we consider management's judgements reasonable and did not identify any material misstatements.

Continued

Table 19.1 (Continued)

Key audit matter	How our audit addressed the key audit matter
Recognition and measurement of litigation and contingent liabilities Refer to page 116 (Audit Committee Report), page 158 (Accounting Policies) and Notes 20 and 29 in the Group Financial Statements The pharmaceuticals industry is heavily regulated which increases inherent litigation risk. The Group is engaged in a number of legal actions, including patent litigation, product liability, anti-trust and related litigation. At 31 December 2018, the Group held provisions of \$198m in respect of legal claims These provisions are based on judgements and reflect accounting estimates made by management in determining the likelihood and magnitude of an unfavourable outcome on the claims. Accordingly, unexpected adverse outcomes could significantly impact the Group's reported profit and balance sheet position.	We evaluated the design and tested the operating effectiveness of controls in respect of the recognition and measurement of litigation matters. We determined that we could rely on these controls for the purposes of our audit. We read the summary of litigation matters provided by management and held discussions with the Group's legal counsel. We requested and obtained legal letters from certain of the Group's external legal advisors with respect to the matters included in the summary. Where appropriate we examined correspondence connected with the cases. We considered management's judgements on the level of provisioning to be reasonable. We also evaluated the appropriateness of the disclosures in Note 20 and Note 29 which we considered appropriate.
Recognition and measurement of uncertain tax positions Refer to page 116 (Audit Committee Report), page 156 (Accounting Policies) and Note 29 in the Group Financial Statements. The Group operates in a complex multinational tax environment and is subject to a range of tax risks during the normal course of business including transaction related tax matters and transfer pricing arrangements Where the amount of tax payable is uncertain, the Group establishes provisions based on management's judgement and estimates of the probable amount of the future liability At 31 December 2018, the Group has recorded provisions of \$942m in respect of uncertain tax positions	We evaluated the design and tested the operating effectiveness of controls in respect of the recognition and measurement of uncertain tax provisions. We determined that we could rely on these controls for the purposes of our audit. With the assistance of our local and international tax specialists, we evaluated management's judgements and estimates of tax exposures and contingencies in order to assess the adequacy of the Group's tax provisions. In understanding and evaluating management's judgements, we considered the status of recent and current tax authority audits and enquiries, judgemental positions taken in tax returns and current year estimates and developments in the tax environment. Where appropriate, we also read documentation to understand the positions reached. We noted that the assumptions and judgements that are required to formulate the provisions mean that there is a range of possible outcomes. However, from the evidence obtained, we considered the level of provisioning to be acceptable in the context of the Group Financial Statements taken as a whole. We reviewed the disclosures in Note 29 of the Group Financial Statements. We are satisfied that these disclosures are appropriate.

20 The Modified Auditor's Opinion

Introduction

In Chapter 19 we examined the circumstances when an auditor will conclude, based on the audit evidence they have obtained, that the financial statements do not contain material misstatement and have been prepared in accordance with the applicable financial reporting framework (e.g. IFRS) and relevant legislation and regulation. As we saw, in such cases, the auditor will express an **unmodified opinion**, but may also include additional paragraphs within the report such as an emphasis of matter paragraph to highlight fundamental issues, or a section in respect of material uncertainty relating to going concern, to discuss matters relating to going concern problems facing the company. Including these additional paragraphs modifies the audit report, but neither of these affects the audit opinion which remains 'true and fair'.

There are, however, situations which may present themselves where the auditor must modify their opinion, which essentially means that the auditor cannot say that the financial statements are true and fair. There are two situations where this may happen:

- Where the auditor has obtained sufficient appropriate evidence to conclude that the financial statements are not true and fair (e.g. the financial statements do not comply with IFRS requirements).
- Where the auditor has not been able to obtain sufficient appropriate evidence to reach a conclusion about the true and fair view (e.g. when there is a restriction on the auditor being able to carry out necessary audit procedures).

In either one of these situations, the auditor will express a **modified opinion**, and the type of modified opinion expressed will all depend on the severity of the matter giving rise to the modified opinion as well as the reason for it.

In this chapter, we will look at the requirements of ISA (UK) 705 *Modifications to the Opinion in the Independent Auditor's Report* which provides plenty of guidance for auditors in situations where a modified opinion is needed.

In reality, modified audit opinions are quite rare. You can probably imagine the reasons why the management of a company will not want to end up in a situation where their financial statements attract a modified audit opinion. There could be negative implications for the company's share price, reputation, credit-rating, and status. In addition, a modified audit opinion would most likely trigger a lack of shareholder confidence in the governance of the company and possibly lead to calls for the directors to be removed from office. Banks and financiers will also not look favourably on a modified opinion, and this could (and, in reality, often does) affect lending decisions. So, management will certainly do their best to avoid a modified opinion being issued on the financial statements which they are responsible for, and this is why modified opinions are very uncommon.

It should be emphasized that, in practice, an auditor will only express a modified opinion as a last resort. The auditor will always give the client ample opportunity to resolve the issue(s) giving rise to the potential modification. If, however, the client refuses or the matter cannot be resolved, the auditor must express a modified opinion.

The topics covered in this chapter build heavily on the previous chapter, where we considered the content of an unmodified auditor's report, and also Chapter 17, where we looked at going concern. The issue of modified opinions cannot be considered in isolation because the opinion forms just part of the overall auditor's report, and reaching an opinion must include consideration of going concern.

Learning outcomes

- Describe and distinguish between qualified, adverse, and disclaimers of opinion.
- Discuss the use of qualified audit opinions, identifying and explaining the factors to be considered when forming a qualified audit opinion.
- Discuss the use of adverse audit opinions, identifying and explaining the factors to be considered when forming an adverse audit opinion.
- Discuss the situations when it is appropriate for the auditor to disclaim the auditor's opinion, identifying and explaining the factors to be considered when forming a disclaimer of opinion.
- Explain how an auditor should respond to management-imposed limitations.
- Identify and discuss situations when going concern matters could result in a modified audit opinion.

By the end of this chapter, you will be able to:

- Justify an audit opinion consistent with the results of audit procedures.
- Explain the actions to be taken by an auditor when issuing a modified audit opinion.
- Consider the reasons why, in practice, it is rare for a modified audit opinion to be issued.

20.1 Modified opinions—overall objectives and key definitions

20.1.1 Objective in relation to modified opinions

The overall objective of the auditor in relation to modified opinions is given in ISA (UK) 705 as follows:

> The objective of the auditor is to express clearly an appropriately modified opinion on the financial statements that is necessary when:
>
> (a) The auditor concludes, based on the audit evidence obtained, that the financial statements as a whole are not free from material misstatement; or
>
> (b) The auditor is unable to obtain sufficient appropriate audit evidence to conclude that the financial statements as a whole are free from material misstatement.[1]

This objective indicates to us that there are two very different reasons why an audit opinion can be modified—either due to the financial statements containing a material misstatement (i.e. not complying with the relevant law, financial reporting standards, or other regulations), or due to the auditor being unable to reach a conclusion because they are unable to obtain sufficient appropriate audit evidence.

Activity 20.1 Inability to obtain sufficient and appropriate audit evidence.

List four examples of circumstances which could lead to the auditor being unable to obtain sufficient and appropriate audit evidence.

Auditing scenario 20.1 Reasons for modified opinion

An audit partner in the firm Emery Associates is completing the audit of two unconnected manufacturing clients, Hall Ltd and Parkes Ltd. Problems have arisen in both audits in respect of inventory:

- Hall Ltd—the financial statements include an inventory balance of £75,000 which the auditor, based on evidence obtained, concludes should be written off in full. The level of materiality for the audit is determined to be £50,000 and management of Hall Ltd have refused to make the adjustment to write off the inventory.

  The audit partner determines that there is a material misstatement and will issue a modified opinion based on the evidence obtained.

- Parkes Ltd—this client is headquartered in London, but its entire manufacturing operation is based in a foreign country which the audit team has not been able to visit due to a war and restrictions on travel to the country. Due to this, the audit team has not been able to obtain sufficient audit evidence on inventory, which is material to the financial statements.

[1] FRC, 'ISA (UK) 705', 2016, para 4 <https://media.frc.org.uk/documents/ISA_UK_705_Revised_June_2016.pdf> (accessed 22 January 2024).

The audit partner determines that the evidence obtained is not sufficient and appropriate to conclude that the financial statements are free from material misstatement, so a modified opinion due to lack of evidence will be expressed. To put it simply, the audit partner does not know if the inventory is accounted for correctly and therefore cannot say that the financial statements show a true and fair view in respect of inventory.

20.1.2 **Qualified, adverse, and disclaimers of opinion**

According to ISA (UK) 705, there are three types of modified audit opinion:

> This ISA (UK) establishes three types of modified opinions, namely a qualified opinion, an adverse opinion, and a disclaimer of opinion.
>
> The decision regarding which type of modified opinion is appropriate depends upon:
>
> (a) The nature of the matter giving rise to the modification, that is, whether the financial statements are materially misstated or, in the case of an inability to obtain sufficient appropriate audit evidence, may be materially misstated; and
>
> (b) The auditor's judgment about the pervasiveness of the effects or possible effects of the matter on the financial statements.[2]

To put it simply, the ISA (UK) requires auditors to consider *why* a true and fair view cannot be expressed in the financial statements—this is the nature of the matter, and also to consider how *severe* the problem is—this is about the pervasiveness of the matter. The second matter is very judgemental, and it takes an experienced auditor to reach a decision about the severity of the matter and its impact on the audit opinion.

Let's now look at each of the types of modified opinion in a little more detail:

Qualified opinion—this is used when the auditor disagrees with an accounting treatment, adequacy of a disclosure, or other non-compliance in relation to a material item, or when the auditor has been unable to obtain sufficient appropriate audit evidence for a material item. This type of opinion is often called the 'except for' opinion, because the opinion contains the phrase 'except for', indicating that 'except for' the matter giving rise to the qualification, the rest of the financial statements show a true and fair view. A key issue is that a qualified opinion is issued in relation to an issue which is *material, but not pervasive*, to the financial statements.

Auditing scenario 20.2 Emery Associates revisited

If you look back to the example discussing Emery Associates in section 20.1.1, the auditor's opinion for both Hall Ltd and Parkes Ltd would be qualified opinions–for Hall Ltd the qualification of the opinion is due to material misstatement, for Parkes Ltd the qualification of the opinion is due to lack of evidence. In both cases, the matters leading to the qualified opinion are material, but not pervasive to the financial statements.

[2] Ibid., para 2.

Adverse opinion—an adverse opinion is very serious because an adverse opinion means the auditor is saying that the financial statements, as a whole, do not give a true and fair view. This indicates to the users that they cannot rely on the financial statements. This could happen when there are serious instances of non-compliance with the relevant financial reporting standards, of such significance that the accounts cannot be relied upon. The key issue here is that the misstatements are more than material. The wording of ISA (UK) 705 is that the misstatements are *both material and* ***pervasive*** to the financial statements.

Disclaimer of opinion—here the auditor is unable to express an opinion on the financial statements as a whole and makes this conclusion when they have been unable to obtain sufficient appropriate audit evidence on which to form a conclusion. This could have happened, for example, because the accounting records have been destroyed, or not kept, or management has refused to provide written representations (see Chapter 12 for more on written representations). Again, a key issue here is the severity—a disclaimer of opinion is issued when the auditor cannot reach a conclusion over matters which could be *both material and* ***pervasive***.

In Table 20.1 you can see that the left-hand column deals with the reason for the modification (i.e. the *reason why* a true and fair view cannot be expressed). As explained above, this is either due to material misstatement (i.e. the auditor has obtained sufficient appropriate evidence to conclude that there is a non-compliance which is at least material to the financial statements), or due to being unable to reach an audit opinion due to lack of evidence. It is usually clear-cut as to the reason for the modification.

Remember that a misstatement is a difference between the reported amount, classification, presentation, or disclosure of a financial statement item and the amount, classification, presentation, or disclosure that is required for the item to be in accordance with the applicable financial reporting framework.[3]

Table 20.1 Types of modified auditor's opinion

Overall conclusion	**Auditor's conclusion as to the effects on the financial statements**	
	Material but not pervasive	**Material and pervasive**
The financial statements contain material misstatements	Qualified opinion 'except for' Basis for Qualified Opinion paragraph	Adverse opinion Basis for Adverse Opinion paragraph
The auditor is unable to obtain sufficient appropriate audit evidence	Qualified opinion 'except for' Basis for Qualified Opinion paragraph	Disclaimer of opinion Basis for Disclaimer of Opinion paragraph

Activity 20.2 Material misstatements

Briefly describe three types of matters which could give rise to a material misstatement.

[3] FRC, 'ISA (UK) 450', 2022, para 4 <https://media.frc.org.uk/documents/ISA_UK_450_Revised_June_2016_Updated_May_2022.pdf> (accessed 18 January 2024).

20.1.3 Material, or material and pervasive?

The auditor needs to use judgement in deciding the level of severity of the problem, as shown in the second and third columns of Table 20.1. The decision as to severity includes considering whether the matter giving rise to the modified opinion is material or both material and **pervasive**. This is a very important issue, so we will explore this in more detail.

A matter is considered material, but not pervasive, when the issue is determined to be material to the financial statements but only affects a specified area in the financial statements. These types of misstatements will generally only affect specific elements, accounts, or items of the financial statements rather than multiple areas and hence will be regarded as material but not **pervasive**.

Examples include:

- recognizing research expenditure on the statement of financial position in contravention of IAS 38 *Intangible Assets*;
- failing to adequately disclose a material related-party transaction in accordance with IAS 24 *Related Party Disclosures*; and
- failing to disclose details of a material contingent liability in contravention of IAS 37 *Provisions, Contingent Assets and Contingent Liabilities*.

A material and pervasive misstatement is serious. Pervasive effects on the financial statements are those that in the auditor's judgement:

- are not confined to specific elements, accounts or items of the financial statements;
- if so confined, represent or could represent a substantial proportion of the financial statements; or
- in relation to disclosures, are fundamental to users' understanding of the financial statements.[4]

Hence, a pervasive matter must be fundamental to the financial statements therefore rendering them unreliable as a whole.

Examples of matters which would be considered material and pervasive include:

- using the going concern basis of accounting inappropriately;
- failing to consolidate a significant subsidiary in the group accounts.

Remember that a matter that is material and pervasive leads to either an adverse opinion (if the matter relates to a material misstatement), or a disclaimer of opinion (if the matter relates to inability to obtain sufficient appropriate evidence) (see Figure 20.1).

[4] FRC, 'ISA (UK) 705', 2016, para 5.

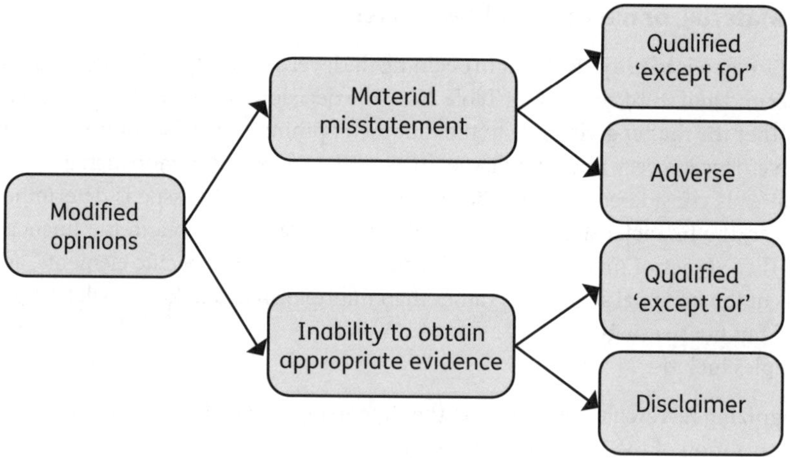

Figure 20.1 Types of modified opinion

Auditing in practice 20.1 How are potential modifications to the audit opinion dealt with?

When the auditor concludes that a modified auditor's opinion is necessary, it will invariably result in lengthy discussions with the client. This discussion can often be fraught and result in pressure being placed on the auditor not to express a modified opinion because such opinions can result in:

- the company's credit rating being impacted;
- suppliers withdrawing credit facilities;
- banks and financiers viewing the modified opinion unfavourably hence leading them to withdraw or refuse borrowing facilities; and
- customers deciding to source goods and/or services elsewhere as they may feel the company is acting unethically or the directors lack integrity.

A modified opinion can have significant detrimental impacts which is why the auditor will always give the client ample opportunity (where the issue is within the client's control) to remedy the issue giving rise to the potential modification. The auditor must not 'give in' to the client under any circumstances and issue an unmodified report where there is a material or a material and pervasive misstatement—even if the client threatens to disengage the auditor and change auditors after the current year's audit is complete.

The auditor is always required to comply with the ethical principles of integrity, objectivity, professional competence, and due care and professional behaviour. Hence, the auditor cannot issue an unmodified opinion in circumstances where a reasonable third party would conclude that a qualified opinion should be issued. Doing so is reckless and usually results in heavy sanctions being taken against the auditor by professional bodies and regulators which can, in more serious circumstances, lead to the auditor losing their auditing practising certificates and the individual being excluded from membership of a professional body, together with a hefty fine and publication of their details in the professional press.

20.1.4 **Basis for opinion paragraph**

In Chapter 19 we saw that an unmodified auditor's report must contain a Basis for Opinion paragraph. The same is true where the audit opinion is modified, but ISA (UK) 705 requires the paragraph to be titled according to the nature of the modification of the opinion, and to contain details which enable users of the auditor's report to understand the circumstances of the modification.

ISA 705 states:

> When the auditor modifies the opinion on the financial statements, the auditor shall, in addition to the specific elements required by ISA (UK) 700 (Revised June 2016):
>
> (a) Amend the heading 'Basis for Opinion' required by paragraph 28 of ISA (UK) 700 (Revised June 2016) to 'Basis for Qualified Opinion,' 'Basis for Adverse Opinion,' or 'Basis for Disclaimer of Opinion,' as appropriate; and
>
> (b) Within this section, include a description of the matter giving rise to the modification.[5]

When the reason for the modification is material misstatement relating to specific amounts in the financial statements, the basis for opinion paragraph should include a description and quantification of the financial effects of the misstatement, unless this is impracticable. For example, the basis for opinion section in the auditor's report could include the quantification of the effects of the material misstatement on income tax, income before taxes, net income, and equity if inventory is overstated.

Sometimes the material misstatement is more qualitative in nature (e.g. the adequacy of a disclosure note), in which case the basis for opinion paragraph should explain how the disclosures are misstated. Omitted disclosures should be described if necessary.

If the reason for the modification is from an inability to obtain audit evidence, the reasons for this should be explained in the basis for opinion paragraph.

20.1.5 **Communication with those charged with governance**

According to ISA (UK) 705:

> When the auditor expects to modify the opinion in the auditor's report, the auditor shall communicate with those charged with governance the circumstances that led to the expected modification and the wording of the modification.[6]

It is important that the auditor informs those charged with governance about any intention to modify the auditor's opinion. It is possible that those charged with governance are unaware of the matter(s) giving rise to the modification, or they may be able to provide further information and explanations regarding the matter(s).

In the UK there is a further requirement that the auditor must report to relevant regulatory bodies if a modified opinion is to be issued on the financial statements of certain public interest entities.

[5] Ibid., para 20. [6] Ibid., para 30.

Having looked at the different types of modified opinion and the requirements for the Basis of Opinion paragraph when the opinion is modified, we will now look at each type of modified opinion in more detail, using an example to illustrate each.

20.2 Qualified 'except for' opinion

A qualified 'except for' opinion is expressed by the auditor when the issue giving rise to the modification is material but not pervasive. The auditor's opinion states that 'except for' the matter, the financial statements give a true and fair view—in other words the matter is material to the area of the financial statements affected but does not affect the remainder of the financial statements.

The basis for qualified opinion paragraph will describe the effects of the issue, together with quantification where appropriate.

Remember that any form of modified opinion does not look good for the company and its management, and in almost all cases where there is a disagreement about accounting treatments which may give rise to a material misstatement, after some discussion, the financial statements are amended so that they do show a true and fair view, avoiding the modified opinion.

Auditing scenario 20.3 Request to a client to amend the financial statements prior to the auditor issuing their report

Harrison Ltd has prepared its financial statements for the year ended 31 May 20X9 showing revenue of £15m, profit before tax of £3.2m, and total assets of £9.4m. During the course of the audit fieldwork, the auditor discovered that revenue for the year had been overstated by £1m. This misstatement had arisen because the sales order processing system, which is linked to the accounting system, had not been closed at the correct time. This resulted in several invoices which related to sales made in June 20X9 being included in the 31 May 20X9 revenue figure (i.e. a 'cut-off' error) and recorded as trade receivable at that date.

The finance director of Harrison Ltd is reluctant to amend the financial statements as he has stated that the sales can simply be reversed in the next year's financial statements.

In this situation, the auditor has discovered that Harrison Ltd's revenue is overstated by £1m which is 6.7 per cent (1m/15m) of revenue, 31.2 per cent (1m/3.2m) of profit before tax, and 10.6 per cent (1m/9.4m) of assets, hence the misstatement is material.

The auditor cannot just accept the finance director's solution that the sales can be reversed next year because that will not resolve the material misstatement.

The auditor will give the finance director ample opportunity to correct the misstatement. The auditor must discuss the implications for the auditor's report if the finance director chooses not to amend the financial statements and how this may affect the company, such as an unfavourable view taken by the bank, creditors, and credit-rating agencies and the reputational damage the company will inevitably suffer as a result of the modified audit opinion.

The auditor is also required to communicate with those charged with governance which provides a further opportunity for the client to amend the financial statements, thus avoiding a modified audit opinion.

Auditing scenario 20.4 Qualified 'except for' opinion due to material misstatement relating to incorrect accounting treatment for intangible assets

Medidrug plc operates in the pharmaceutical industry and has a significant amount of development expenditure on its statement of financial position. The company reports under IFRS and is required to comply with the Companies Act 2006. It has a year end of 30 September 20X9 and draft profit before tax is £1.2 million.

During the year, the company capitalised an amount of £450,000 in relation to development expenditure on the statement of financial position which is considered material to the financial statements. No amortization has been charged on the additional development expenditure as the project was still nearing completion at the year end.

During the audit fieldwork, the auditor discovered that of the £450,000 development expenditure, £220,000 was, in fact, research expenditure which should have been written off to the statement of profit or loss account per IAS 38 *Intangible Assets*. Management have refused to correct this misstatement on the basis that they disagree with the auditor's conclusion and the auditor disagrees with management that it should be recognized on the statement of financial position. All other misstatements identified during the audit have been corrected.

In this example, the auditor disagrees with management's accounting treatment of the research expenditure. The research expenditure that has been incorrectly recognized on the statement of financial position amounts to 18.3 per cent (£220k/£1.2m) of profit before tax and hence, in the judgement of the auditor, is material. Intangible assets and profit are overstated but the misstatement, despite being material, is not pervasive. The auditor concludes that the requirements of IAS 38 have not been complied with and hence will express a qualified opinion as follows.

Qualified opinion

We have audited the financial statements of Medidrug plc [. . .]
In our opinion, except for the matter described in the Basis for Qualified Opinion section of our report, the accompanying financial statements:

- give a true and fair view of the state of the company's affairs as at 30 September 20X9 and of its profit for the year ended;
- have been properly prepared in accordance with International Financial Reporting Standards; and
- have been prepared in accordance with the requirements of the Companies Act 2006.

Basis for Qualified Opinion

The company has recognized an amount of £220,000 of research expenditure as capitalized development expenditure on the statement of financial position as at 30 September 2019 which, in our opinion, is not in accordance with the requirements of IAS 38 *Intangible Assets*. The company should have recognized the research expenditure in profit or loss for the year ended 30 September 2019 to comply with IAS 38. Accordingly, the company's intangible assets should be reduced by an amount of £220,000 with a corresponding reduction in profit.

We conducted our audit in accordance with International Standards on Auditing (UK) (ISAs (UK)) and applicable law. Our responsibilities under those standards are further described in the auditor's responsibilities for the audit of the financial statements section of our report. We are independent of the company in accordance with the ethical requirements that are relevant to our audit of the financial statements in the UK, including the FRC's Ethical Standard, and we have fulfilled our other ethical responsibilities in accordance with these requirements. We believe that the audit evidence we have obtained is sufficient and appropriate to provide a basis for our qualified opinion.

Keep in mind that it is not just monetary amounts which may give rise to a modified opinion in the auditor's report. Certain narrative disclosures may be required in the financial statements to comply with the applicable financial reporting framework (such as related-party disclosures to comply with IAS 24 *Related Party Disclosures*) and if management have failed to adequately disclose those issues, this will also give rise to a modified opinion being expressed by the auditor.

Auditing scenario 20.5 Qualified 'except for' opinion due to material misstatement relating to lack of related-party disclosures

Pastures Ltd has entered into a number of related-party transactions during the year ended 30 September 20X9 but has failed to disclose two related-party transactions that have been undertaken with a company owned and controlled by the wife of the chief executive officer. The monetary values stated in the financial statements (i.e. the statement of comprehensive income, statement of financial position, statement of cash flows and statement of changes in equity) are not affected. It is the fact that management have not disclosed a material related-party transaction that has given rise to the modified opinion. As examined in Chapter 10, materiality is not just confined to quantitative issues—the concept of materiality also has qualitative factors as well.

In such cases, the auditor is required to make the relevant disclosures in their auditor's report but will still express a qualified 'except for' opinion as follows.

Qualified opinion

We have audited the financial statements of Pastures Ltd [. . .]
In our opinion, except for the matter described in the Basis for Qualified Opinion section of our report, the accompanying financial statements:

- give a true and fair view of the state of the company's affairs as at 30 September 20X9 and of its financial performance and cash flows profit for the year the ended;
- have been properly prepared in accordance with International Financial Reporting Standards; and
- have been prepared in accordance with the requirements of the Companies Act 2006.

Basis for Qualified Opinion

The company has entered into a number of material related-party transactions during the year. The directors have failed to disclose the relationships or amounts of these transactions which is required by IAS 24 *Related Party Disclosures*. The company awarded a contract to an entity owned by the wife of the Chief Executive Officer for £120,000 and a consulting contract was also awarded to the same company amounting to £200,000.

We conducted our audit in accordance with International Standards on Auditing (UK) and applicable law. Our responsibilities under those standards are further described in the Auditor's responsibilities for the audit of the financial statements section of our report. We are independent of the company in accordance with the ethical requirements that are relevant to our audit of the financial statements in the UK, including the FRC's Ethical Standard, and we have fulfilled our other ethical responsibilities in accordance with these requirements. We believe that the audit evidence we have obtained is sufficient and appropriate to provide a basis for our qualified opinion.

In both of these examples, the reason for the qualified opinion is material misstatement. Remember that a qualified opinion can also be issued in relation to a lack of audit evidence to support an audit conclusion in relation to a matter which is material but not pervasive to the financial statements.

Auditing scenario 20.6 Qualified 'except for' opinion due to inability to obtain sufficient appropriate audit evidence

Browns & Co were appointed as auditor to Bills Ltd on 15 January 20X4.

When auditing the financial statements for the year ended 31 December 20X3, the audit evidence available to the auditor in respect of inventory valued at £500,000 was limited because the auditors did not attend the inventory count which took place on 31 December 20X3. The auditor was unable to obtain sufficient and appropriate audit evidence as to inventory quantities by other audit procedures due to poor record keeping by the client, meaning that inventory records are not adequately maintained.

In such cases, the auditor is required to express a qualified 'except for' opinion as follows.

Qualified opinion

We have audited the financial statements of Bills Ltd [. . .]
In our opinion, except for the matter described in the Basis for Qualified Opinion section of our report, the accompanying financial statements:

- give a true and fair view of the state of the company's affairs as at 31 December 20X3 and of its financial performance and cash flows profit for the year ended;
- have been properly prepared in accordance with International Financial Reporting Standards; and
- have been prepared in accordance with the requirements of the Companies Act 2006.

Basis for qualified opinion

With respect to inventory having a carrying amount of ££500,000 the audit evidence available to us was limited because we did not observe the counting of the physical inventory as at 31 December 20X3, since that date was prior to our appointment as auditor of the company. We were unable to obtain sufficient appropriate audit evidence regarding the inventory quantities by using other audit procedures.
We conducted our audit in accordance with International Standards on Auditing (UK) and applicable law. Our responsibilities under those standards are further described in the Auditor's responsibilities for the audit of the financial statements section of our report. We are independent of the company in accordance with the ethical requirements that are relevant to our audit of the financial statements in the UK, including the FRC's Ethical Standard, and we have fulfilled our other ethical responsibilities in accordance with these requirements. We believe that the audit evidence we have obtained is sufficient and appropriate to provide a basis for our qualified opinion.

Matters on which we are required to report by exception

In respect solely of the limitation on our work relating to inventory, described above:

- We have not obtained all the information and explanations that we considered necessary for the purpose of the audit.
- Adequate accounting records have not been kept.

Note that the points made in this final section of the auditor's report relate to matters which the auditor comments on by exception, as required by the Companies Act 2006. Due to the inadequacy of the company's accounting records, the audit firm is reporting to shareholders that they have not received all of the information and explanations that normally would be made available and adequate accounting records have not been maintained. If you want a reminder about matters reported by exception, we looked at this in section 19.2.3.

20.3 **Adverse opinion**

An adverse opinion is expressed when a misstatement is considered to be material *and* pervasive. This will mean that the financial statements do not give a true and fair view, and such an opinion can have serious repercussions for the entity.

As noted earlier in the chapter, an adverse opinion is very serious and signals to the users of the financial statements that the financial statements cannot be relied upon to make economic decisions. This can also send a message that management and those charged with governance are not acting ethically or appropriately.

Auditing scenario 20.7 Adverse opinion

Purley Enterprises Ltd has prepared its financial statements for the year ended 31 October 20X9 on a going concern basis. On 14 November 20X9, the bank confirmed that they would no longer be willing to support the company as it had defaulted on its loan terms, breached its overdraft facility on a number of occasions during the year, and had failed to supply the bank with management accounts as requested. In addition, the company had entered into an arrangement with the tax authority to pay a large sum of additional tax owing following an investigation into the company's affairs by the tax authority. The company was already in arrears with the tax authority who have now threatened to issue winding up proceedings.

The directors have approached a number of other banks who have refused to help the company, but they are confident that eventually the company will find a bank to support it.

The auditor has concluded that the going concern basis of accounting is inappropriate. The directors have refused to prepare the financial statements on a basis other than the going concern basis of accounting as they feel this may adversely influence the decision of any potential lender, which the directors still continue to actively seek.

ISA (UK) 570 *Going Concern* says that if the financial statements have been prepared using the going concern basis of accounting but, in the auditor's judgement, this basis is inappropriate, the auditor must express an adverse opinion. This is because the effects of the inappropriate use of the going concern basis of accounting are both material and pervasive. The adverse opinion will be expressed as set out below.

Adverse opinion

We have audited the financial statements of Purley Enterprises Ltd [. . .]

In our opinion, because of the significance of the matter discussed in the Basis for Adverse Opinion section of our report, the financial statements:

- do not give a true and fair view of the state of the company's affairs as at 31 October 20X9 and of its loss for the year then ended;
- have not been properly prepared in accordance with International Financial Reporting Standards; and
- have not been prepared in accordance with the requirements of the Companies Act 2006.

Basis for adverse opinion

As explained in note X of the financial statements, the financial statements have been prepared on the going concern basis. However, in our opinion, due to the number and significance of the material uncertainties, the company is not a going concern in accordance with IAS 1 *Presentation of Financial Statements* and therefore the financial statements should not be prepared on the going concern basis.

Following a breach of the company's loan terms and overdraft facility, the company's bank has expressed their unwillingness to support the company, and the directors have so far been unable to source financiers to continue to support the business. In addition, the terms of an arrangement to pay with the tax authority in respect of additional tax arising following a tax investigation have also not been complied with.

We conducted our audit in accordance with International Standards on Auditing (UK) and applicable law. Our responsibilities under those standards are further described in the Auditor's responsibilities for the audit of the financial statements section of our report. We are independent of the company in accordance with the ethical requirements that are relevant to our audit of the financial statements in the UK, including the FRC's Ethical Standard, and we have fulfilled our other ethical responsibilities in accordance with these requirements. We believe that the audit evidence we have obtained is sufficient and appropriate to provide a basis for our adverse opinion.

For audited entities falling under the scope of ISA (UK) 701 *Communicating Key Audit Matters in the Independent Auditor's Report*, the auditor is still required to include a key audit matters (KAMs) section in the auditor's report when the report includes an adverse opinion. The matter giving rise to the adverse opinion is by its nature a KAM. However, this is not described in detail as part of the KAMs section of the auditor's report, and the auditor should refer in the KAMs section of the report to the basis for adverse opinion paragraph of the report where the necessary details will be provided.

Auditing in practice 20.2 Adverse opinion on the financial statements of Ordnance Survey

It is very rare in practice to see an adverse opinion issued, as the potential damage to the reporting entity's reputation and the reaction of stakeholders is so severe. However, very occasionally they are seen in practice, often in situations where the impact on stakeholders is minimal.

A famous example in the UK is that of Ordnance Survey, the national mapping agency for the UK. The Ordnance Survey is now a limited company but at one time it was a government agency with no shareholders, giving a proportion of profit to the UK Treasury. The Ordnance Survey was, and still is, audited by the National Audit Office.

For several years from 1999, the National Audit Office issued an adverse opinion on the financial statements issued by the Ordnance Survey. The adverse opinion related to a misstatement, considered by the auditor to be both material and pervasive to the financial statements. The adverse opinion arose from a disagreement between the auditor and management over the accounting treatment for the

National Topographic Database—essentially the database and accompanying management system relating to the UK's mapping information—which is a major resource of the Ordnance Survey.

Without going into the minute detail of the disagreement, it revolved around application of the UK accounting standards which were the applicable financial reporting framework at that time. The key issue was whether the database should be recognized as a tangible fixed asset, which was the view of the auditor, or whether it should not be capitalized (i.e. written off as an expense in profit or loss) because it does not meet the relevant recognition criteria. The debate surrounding the accounting treatment went on for many years, with neither the auditor nor management willing to change their view, and so every year the auditor qualified their opinion on this issue. Each year the financial statements included a statement by the auditor justifying their opinion. An extract of the audit opinion from the 2001-2002 auditor's report is shown below.

Adverse Opinion

Ordnance Survey's turnover of £102.6 million derives principally from the exploitation of data contained on the National Topographic Database, the creation of which has been funded from public monies over many years. As disclosed in Note 1.7 to the accounts, the Agency has not capitalised the costs of setting up and maintaining the National Topographic Database in its Balance Sheet. In the Agency's view, the database is an intangible fixed asset that does not meet the conditions for capitalisation set by Financial Reporting Standard 10. In my opinion, the National Topographic Database is a tangible fixed asset that should be capitalised in accordance with Financial Reporting Standard 15. Having taken expert advice about the valuation of the database, in my view the value to the business is not less than £50 million. Had the National Topographic Database been capitalised at that value, the effect would have been to increase tangible fixed assets included in the Balance Sheet at 31 March 2002 from £39 million to £89 million.

In my opinion in view of the effect of the decision not to capitalise the National Topographic Database as a tangible fixed asset in accordance with Financial Reporting Standard 15, the financial statements do not give a true and fair view of the state of affairs of Ordnance Survey at 31 March 2002 or of its deficit, total recognised gains and losses and cash flows for the year then ended.[7]

The situation was eventually resolved in 2010 when, along with other government agencies, Ordnance Survey implemented IFRS. This meant that due to the application of IAS 38 *Intangible Assets*, the database was recognized for the first time in the financial statements and the auditor determined that the accounting treatment was in compliance with the applicable financial reporting framework and hence true and fair.

20.4 **Disclaimer of opinion**

A disclaimer of opinion is issued in circumstances where the auditor is unable to obtain sufficient appropriate audit evidence on which to base their opinion and concludes that the possible effects are likely to be material and pervasive to the financial statements.

Technically speaking a disclaimer of opinion is not an opinion—it confirms that the auditor chooses not to express an opinion. When a disclaimer is issued, the auditor's report should state that 'the auditor was engaged to audit the financial statements' instead of stating 'the financial statements have been audited'.

[7] Ordnance Survey, 'Annual Report and Accounts 2001–02', 2002 <https://www.geos.ed.ac.uk/~gisteac/proceedingsonline/Source%20Book%202004/SDI/National/UK/Ordnance%20Survey/OS_Annual%20Report_2001-02.pdf> (accessed 22 January 2024).

Examples of situations which may lead the auditor to issue a disclaimer of opinion include:

- a failure by the client to keep adequate (or any) accounting records; or
- a failure by the client to provide evidence over a single account balance which represents a substantial proportion of the assets or profits or over multiple balances in the financial statements.

The two situations above relate to cases where the auditor is unable to reach an opinion due to an inability to obtain the necessary audit evidence. As we have seen, this leads to a disclaimer of opinion if the auditor considers the issue to be material and pervasive.

ISA (UK) 705 also requires the auditor to disclaim their opinion when

> in extremely rare circumstances involving multiple uncertainties, the auditor concludes that, notwithstanding having obtained sufficient appropriate audit evidence regarding each of the individual uncertainties, it is not possible to form an opinion on the financial statements due to the potential interaction of the uncertainties and their possible cumulative effect on the financial statements.[8]

In practice, disclaimers of opinion are rare, but they do arise. When a disclaimer of opinion is issued, ISA (UK) 705 requires the auditor to:

(a) State that the auditor does not express an opinion on the accompanying financial statements;

(b) State that, because of the significance of the matter(s) described in the Basis for Disclaimer of Opinion section, the auditor has not been able to obtain sufficient appropriate audit evidence to provide a basis for an audit opinion on the financial statements; and

(c) Amend the statement required by paragraph 24(b) of ISA (UK) 700 (Revised June 2016), which indicates that the financial statements have been audited, to state that the auditor was engaged to audit the financial statements.[9]

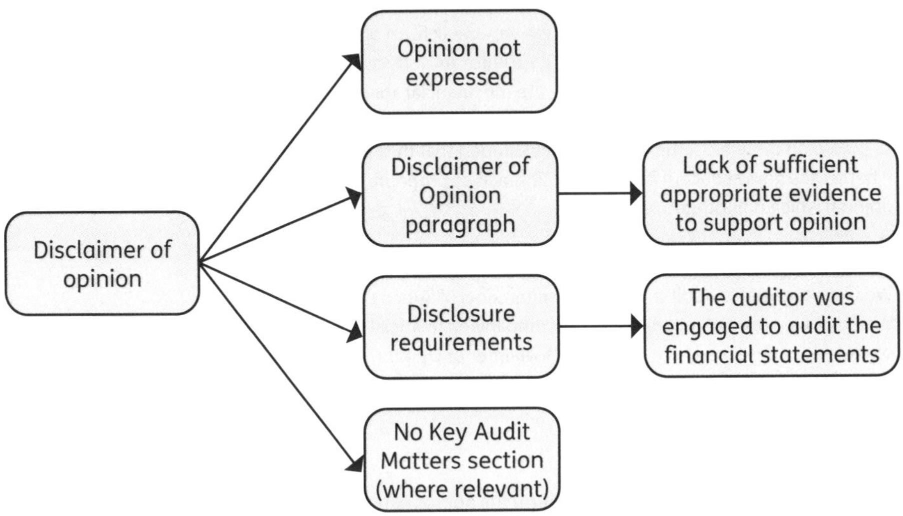

Figure 20.2 Reporting implications of disclaiming the audit opinion

[8] FRC, 'ISA (UK) 705', 2016, para 10.
[9] Ibid., para 19.

In addition, when the auditor is going to issue a disclaimer of opinion there are implications for the auditor's report other than the modified opinion:

- the statement that sufficient appropriate audit evidence to provide a basis for the auditor's opinion in the auditor's report is not included;
- the statements regarding the audit being conducted in accordance with ISAs (UK) and independence and other ethical responsibilities are positioned within the auditor's responsibilities section and not the basis for disclaimer of opinion paragraph; and
- the KAMs section and other information section (where applicable) is not included in the auditor's report as to do so would suggest the financial statements are more credible in respect of those matters which would be inconsistent with the disclaimer of opinion on the financial statements as a whole.

Auditing scenario 20.8 Disclaimer of opinion

Subco Ltd is a wholly owned subsidiary of Holdingco Group Ltd and has prepared its financial statements on a going concern basis for the year ended 31 July 20X9. Management of the subsidiary have prepared the financial statements on the going concern basis of accounting on the grounds that the parent of the group itself will support the business. The parent company has also expressed their willingness to provide a letter to the subsidiary's auditor confirming this support (often referred to as a 'comfort letter').

The auditor of the subsidiary has discussed the issue with the group auditor who has confirmed that the group has a significant level of overdue debt owed to it and, in the group auditor's opinion, the group, nor the parent, has been able to produce any detailed projections, in the form of budgets or forecasts, which demonstrate the group's ability to continue as a going concern. The subsidiary is reliant on additional finance/investment which has not yet been secured.

The auditor of the subsidiary cannot just rely on the comfort letter from the parent company because this is internally generated and is a very weak form of audit evidence to support the going concern basis for the subsidiary. The auditor must try to obtain sufficient appropriate audit evidence from other sources to corroborate the financial ability of the parent to provide the subsidiary with support. In this example, the auditor has been unable to obtain this evidence.

Based on these facts, the auditor has concluded that they are unable to form an opinion as to whether the going concern basis of accounting is appropriate and has expressed a disclaimer of opinion which is illustrated as follows.

Disclaimer of opinion

We were engaged to audit the financial statements of Subco Ltd [. . .]
We do not express an opinion on the accompanying financial statements. Because of the significance of the matter described in the Basis for Disclaimer of Opinion section of our report, we have not been able to obtain sufficient appropriate evidence to provide a basis for an audit opinion on these financial statements.

Basis for disclaimer of opinion

The audit evidence available to us to confirm the appropriateness of management's use of the going concern basis of accounting was limited because the company is reliant on support from the Group. The Group has not been able to provide any corroboratory evidence that it is able to continue to trade for the foreseeable future as a going concern.

The Group has significant levels of indebtedness and has not provided any financial projections which would indicate that it has the ability to continue to trade as a going concern for the foreseeable future. As a result, we were unable to determine whether the going concern basis of accounting is appropriate in the company's circumstances.

Auditor's responsibilities for the audit of the financial statements

We conducted our audit in accordance with International Standards on Auditing (UK) and applicable law. Our responsibilities under those standards are further described in the Auditor's responsibilities for the audit of the financial statements section of our report. We are independent of the company in accordance with the ethical requirements that are relevant to our audit of the financial statements in the UK, including the FRC's Ethical Standard, and we have fulfilled our other ethical responsibilities in accordance with these requirements.

Our objectives are to obtain reasonable assurance about whether the financial statements as a whole are free from material misstatement, whether due to fraud or error, and to issue an auditor's report that includes our opinion. However, because of the matter described in the Basis for disclaimer of opinion section of our report, we were not able to obtain sufficient appropriate evidence to provide a basis for an audit opinion on these financial statements.

20.5 Management-imposed limitations

In rare situations, the entity's management may impose a limitation which causes the auditor to be unable to obtain sufficient, appropriate audit evidence. For example, a refusal by the directors to provide the auditor with written representations as required by ISA (UK) 580 *Written Representations*.

If it is not possible to obtain evidence from alternative sources, then the opinion should be qualified if the issue relating to the management-imposed limitation is material but not pervasive. So far, what we have said in relation to a management-imposed limitation is the same as other situations where the auditor is unable to obtain sufficient appropriate audit evidence (i.e. where the inability to obtain evidence has not been imposed by management).

However, if the issue is both material and pervasive (i.e. where the opinion would normally simply be disclaimed) in a case where there is management-imposed limitation, the auditor should consider whether it is necessary to withdraw from the audit engagement. This is because management imposing a limitation on the ability of the auditor to obtain evidence is a very serious matter especially if it relates to a material and pervasive issue. ISA (UK) 705 states that where qualification of the opinion would be inadequate to communicate the gravity of the situation, the auditor shall:

(i) Withdraw from the audit, where practicable and possible under applicable law or regulation; or

(ii) If withdrawal from the audit before issuing the auditor's report is not practicable or possible, disclaim an opinion on the financial statements.[10]

Withdrawing from the audit allows the auditor to remove themselves from this difficult situation and, depending on local regulations, there may be a professional, legal, or regulatory

[10] Ibid., para 13.

requirement for the auditor to communicate the matters relating to the withdrawal to stakeholders such as shareholders. This enables the auditor to explain management's actions, and the implications which have resulted in the auditor leaving office.

20.6 Going concern and modified audit opinions

In Chapter 17 we looked at the issue of going concern and the requirements of ISA (UK) 570 *Going Concern*. In that chapter, we considered in overview the reporting implications of going concern, and at this point we need to come back to look specifically at situations where going concern matters in relation to an audit client could result in a modified opinion for that client's financial statements.

20.6.1 Use of going concern basis in inappropriate situations

In an extreme situation, the auditor, having completed their audit procedures on going concern, may reach the conclusion that the going concern basis should not have been used in the preparation of the financial statements. This essentially means that management has used the incorrect basis when preparing the financial statements and there is a fundamental disagreement between the management, who considers the going concern basis appropriate, and the auditor, who does not consider it appropriate.

In this situation, ISA (UK) 570 requires the auditor to issue an adverse opinion. It is not an option for the opinion to be qualified on the basis of material misstatement. This is because using the going concern basis to prepare the financial statements when it is not appropriate is automatically deemed as both material and pervasive. The adverse opinion must be issued regardless of whether the financial statements include disclosures relating to going concern. We saw an illustrative example of an auditor's report relating to this situation (see section 20.3), when we discussed the adverse audit opinion.

Auditing in practice 20.3 Alternative bases of preparation of financial statements

In some countries, depending on local regulations, where the going concern basis is not an appropriate basis of preparation for the financial statements, an alternative basis of preparation may be required or permitted. Note that alternative bases, sometimes known as the 'liquidation basis' or 'break-up basis', are not covered by IFRS requirements. Depending on local regulations, either of these bases might be used when an entity has ceased trading and its assets are being sold off as part of the process of liquidating the entity (although care needs to be taken with these bases if the entity wishes to adhere to state compliance with IFRS because there are inconsistencies between the liquidation/break-up basis and IFRS Accounting Standards).

The only relevant requirement is contained in IAS 1 *Presentation of Financial Statements*, which says:

> An entity shall prepare financial statements on a going concern basis unless management either intends to liquidate the entity or to cease trading, or has no realistic alternative but to do so. When

an entity does not prepare financial statements on a going concern basis, it shall disclose that fact, together with the basis on which it prepared the financial statements and the reason why the entity is not regarded as a going concern.[11]

All of this means that if an entity has ceased trading, or is close to doing so, management needs to very carefully consider how to prepare the financial statements and the disclosures which need to be made to explain the accounting policies applied, which will be a departure from 'normal' IFRS requirements.

Let's now think about this situation from an audit point of view. The fact that the financial statements are not prepared using the usual financial reporting framework does not necessarily mean that the audit opinion should be modified. The auditor may be able to issue an unmodified opinion on the financial statements which have been prepared on an alternative basis, provided that they can obtain sufficient appropriate audit evidence and that they conclude that there is appropriate disclosure within the financial statements about the basis of accounting on which they have been prepared. In such situations, the accounts may be prepared following insolvency legislation, and it might be that the auditor's report would need to contain a lot of additional information so that users can understand the report that has been issued.

Obviously, this is a very unusual situation and one that is rarely seen in practice, but it is a common misconception that the auditor would have to modify their opinion if their audit client has, or is about to, cease trading. We have seen that this is not the case. Of course, the auditor in this situation would almost certainly choose to highlight the situation in an emphasis of matter paragraph. In addition, the auditor would be well advised to seek legal counsel in this very unusual and high-risk situation.

20.6.2 **Lack of disclosure of material uncertainty relating to going concern**

In earlier chapters, we have seen that where there is a material uncertainty relating to going concern, management is required by IAS 1 to provide a description of the relevant uncertainties. We have also seen that the auditor is required to determine whether the disclosures are appropriate (see Chapter 17).

Looking at the implications for the auditor's report, we have also seen in Chapter 19 that if the disclosures made by management are considered by the auditor to be appropriate, the requirements of IAS 1 have been complied with, and there is no impact on the auditor's opinion—the financial statements are true and fair. However, the auditor is required to include a section in their report entitled material uncertainties relating to going concern which describes the relevant issues and cross-refers to the relevant disclosure note in the financial statements.

Now we think about what happens if the disclosures made by management in relation to going concern are *not* considered to be appropriate by the auditor. In this situation, ISA (UK) 570 requires the following:

[11] International Financial Reporting Standards Foundation, IAS 1 *Presentation of Financial Statements* (2023) para 1.25 <https://www.ifrs.org/issued-standards/list-of-standards/ias-1-presentation-of-financial-statements/#-standard> (accessed 22 January 2024).

If appropriate disclosure about the material uncertainty related to going concern is not made in the financial statements, the auditor shall:

- Express a Qualified Opinion or Adverse Opinion, as appropriate, and
- In the Basis for Qualified (Adverse) Opinion section of the auditor's report, state that a material uncertainty exists that may cast significant doubt on the entity's ability to continue as a going concern and that the financial statements do not appropriately disclose this matter.[12]

This means that the auditor needs to use judgement to decide whether the lack of disclosure made by management in relation to going concern is a misstatement which is material but not pervasive, in which case a qualified 'except for' opinion is issued, or both material and pervasive, in which case an adverse opinion is issued.

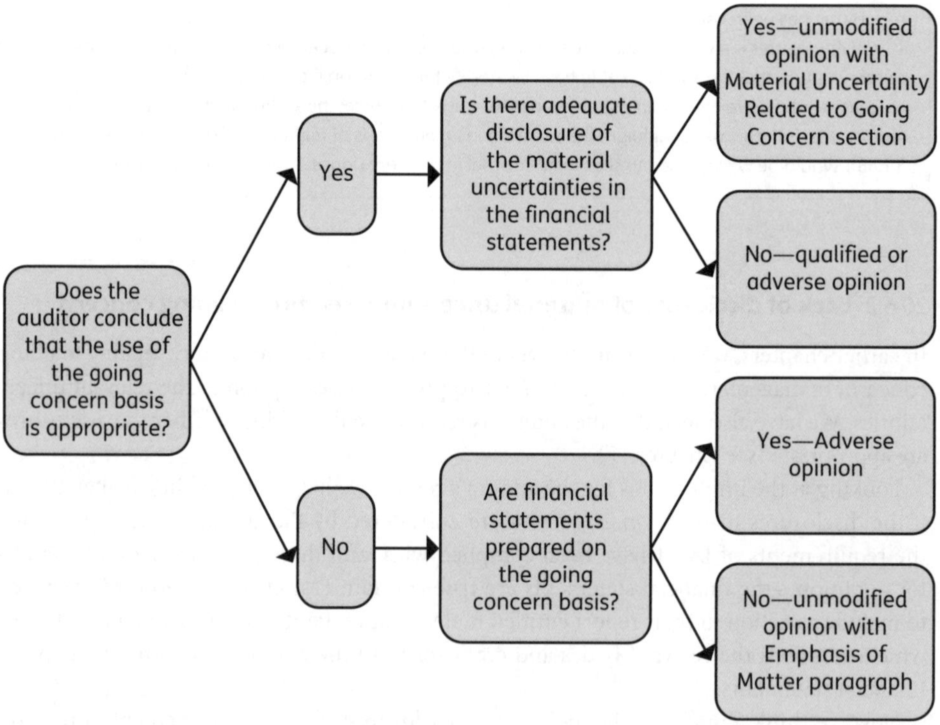

Figure 20.3 Impact of going concern on auditor's reports and opinions

[12] FRC, 'ISA (UK) 570', 2022, para 23 <https://media.frc.org.uk/documents/Revised_Going_Concern_Updated_May_2022.pdf> (accessed 18 January 2024).

[13] IAS 1 requires management to make an assessment of an entity's ability to continue as a going concern. If management has significant concerns about the entity's ability to continue as a going concern, the uncertainties must be disclosed.

Chapter round-up

- A modified auditor's opinion is a serious issue for companies and should always be avoided wherever possible to prevent reputational damage and other serious consequences.
- Auditors must also keep in mind their ethical responsibilities and not be forced into expressing an unmodified opinion when it would be inappropriate to do so.
- There are two main reasons for a modified opinion—misstatement and lack of evidence to support an opinion.
- There are two levels of severity for a modified opinion—material and material and pervasive.
- A qualified opinion (also known as the 'except for' opinion) relates to either a material misstatement or a material issue about which the auditor is unable to reach an opinion due to lack of evidence.
- An adverse opinion relates to a misstatement which is both material and pervasive—the financial statements as a whole are not true and fair.
- A disclaimer of opinion is where the auditor does not express an opinion on the financial statements due to lack of sufficient appropriate evidence.
- In all cases the auditor's report must include a basis for opinion paragraph, with the title of this paragraph aligned to the opinion, which explains the reason for the modified opinion and the details including financial impact.
- Going concern issues can lead to a modified audit opinion—an adverse opinion is given if the financial statements are prepared using an inappropriate basis, and either an adverse or qualified opinion is given if there is a lack of disclosure relating to going concern in the notes to the financial statements.

End of chapter case study

As we have seen over the last two chapters, there are many factors which the auditor must consider when preparing the auditor's report. The opinion is a crucial element of the auditor's report, and when the opinion is modified this has potentially very serious consequences for the audited company.

ISA (UK) 705 requires modified opinions to be issued in a range of circumstances, including material misstatement and an inability to reach an audit opinion. In all cases, the reasons for modification must be clearly communicated to the users of the auditor's report.

This activity will test your ability to evaluate a situation in which a modified opinion may be necessary. The scenario also recaps several issues seen in Chapter 19, when we covered unmodified audit opinions. It is important to be able to think holistically and apply the many ISAs (UK) which deal with the auditor's report, all of which the auditor must consider when dealing with the auditor's report to be issued in a specific situation.

This activity related to these learning outcomes:

- Discuss the use of qualified audit opinions, identifying and explaining the factors to be considered when forming a qualified audit opinion.
- Identify and discuss situations when going concern matters could result in a modified audit opinion.
- Justify an audit opinion consistent with the results of audit procedures.
- Explain the actions to be taken by an auditor when issuing a modified audit opinion.

- Identify and explain the matters which may be selected as KAMs in the context of an audit of financial statements (Chapter 19).

Scenario

You are preparing the auditor's report in respect of Ranger Ltd, a company which develops health and beauty products. The company's financial statements recognize profit before tax of £6.4m and total assets of £37.2m for the financial year ended 31 December 20X8.

Several matters are identified for your consideration in preparing the auditor's report:

During the audit, the audit team discovered that the inventories balance includes £880,000 related to a new range of shampoo which has been recently launched. According to the audit evidence obtained, there are quality issues with this new product as it has been found to cause skin irritation. As a result, the product has been withdrawn from sale. The finance director has suggested that no adjustment be made in the 20X8 financial statements as she is confident that any losses on this product will be more than compensated by profits on the sale of other product lines in 20X9.

In July 20X8, Ranger Ltd implemented a new payroll system due to a cyberattack which destroyed parts of the old system. During the audit of this new system, several errors were found affecting the wages and salaries expense recorded in the financial statements. The new accounting system was not run in parallel with the old system, and due to the cyberattack, the old data files have been corrupted and are not available for use by the audit team. No audit procedures can be performed to determine the significance of the errors that have arisen on the implementation of the new system. In previous years, wages and salaries have formed a material balance within the company's reported profit.

The finance director has informed the audit team that Ranger Ltd's bankers will not decide on the renewal of the overdraft facility until after the auditor's report is signed. The audit engagement partner is satisfied that the use of the going concern basis is appropriate, but that there is a material uncertainty over going concern because of this issue. The directors are reluctant to include detailed going concern disclosures in the draft financial statements, as they fear this will worsen the company's credit rating, making it more difficult to raise the finance necessary to fund further product development. However, they have agreed to include a brief note in the financial statements to state that the bank is considering the overdraft renewal at the time that the financial statements are issued.

Ranger Ltd is not a listed company, but it is aiming to become listed next year. The company's finance director has asked you to briefly explain how the auditor's report will be different once the company achieves a listed status.

Complete the following tasks in relation to the scenario above:

- Explain the impact that the three issues identified will have on the auditor's report.
- Discuss the use of judgement by the auditor in forming the audit opinion.
- Recommend any actions to be taken by the auditor.
- Respond to the finance director's question regarding KAMs.

Answer

Note—forming an audit opinion involves significant judgement, in particular, the decision as to whether a modified opinion should be qualified 'except for' or extended to the whole set of financial statements by using a pervasive opinion is difficult. The auditor should consider the view of the users of financial statements in forming their opinion. This means that there is not necessarily a 'right or wrong answer' for this case study. The important thing is to justify the opinion reached.

Inventories

The inventory of shampoo which has been withdrawn from sale represents 2.4 per cent of total assets and 13.75 per cent of profit before tax. Depending on the auditor's assessment of materiality, this is likely to be considered material to the financial statements. This is an area of judgement, as materiality thresholds are determined by the auditor dependent on a range of matters including the risk of the audit and the specific risk attached to the balance or transaction in question. In this case, the auditor may conclude that the inventory is marginally material to the statement of financial position, but much more material in terms of profit.

It seems that the inventory identified as being of poor quality should be written off to the statement of profit or loss. According to IAS 2 *Inventories*, items of inventory should be valued at the lower of cost and net realizable value. From the information provided, the inventory appears to have no value and therefore should be written off in full. If this adjustment for £880,000 is not made, the financial statements contain a material misstatement. Inventories are overstated and profit is overstated by a material amount.

This matter should be discussed with those charged with governance. They should be told that if the adjustment is not made, the auditor's opinion will be modified due to material misstatement. If management still refuses to amend this error, a qualified opinion would be necessary because the misstatement is material to the financial statements but not pervasive. The impact of the misstatement in the financial statements is relatively isolated and does not destroy the credibility of the financial statements as a whole. The opinion paragraph would be qualified 'except for'.

A basis for qualified opinion paragraph would be needed after the opinion paragraph and this would explain the material misstatement in relation to the incorrect treatment of inventories (i.e. the non-compliance with IAS 2), and the monetary value of the effect on the financial statements.

Payroll system

The audit firm is not able to carry out planned audit procedures as the data files relating to the old payroll system have been destroyed. This system was used for the first six months of the year and therefore relates to a significant proportion of the wages and salaries for the year. There are likely to be errors in how data was input to the new system, and errors have been found when testing the new system. Because the level of error cannot be determined, there is a limitation on scope, meaning that the auditor is unable to reach an opinion.

Historically, wages and salaries have been material to the financial statements. Therefore, the auditor should issue a modified opinion as they are unable to say whether the wages and salaries figure is true and fair within the financial statements.

Judgement will be needed to decide whether a qualified ('except for') opinion or a disclaimer of opinion should be given. The qualified opinion would apply to just the wages and salaries, whereas a disclaimer would state that the auditor is unable to reach an opinion with regard to the whole set of financial statements because the limitation on scope is pervasive. The former would seem to suffice in this situation unless there was some indication that the systems problems had extended to other areas of the financial statements and impacted other balances and transactions.

A basis for qualified opinion paragraph would be needed after the opinion paragraph and this would explain the limitation on scope in relation to the wages and salaries expense, and that it is not possible to quantify the monetary value of any error that may be contained within the wages and salaries expense recognized in the statement of profit and loss.

Overdraft

As the outcome regarding the negotiations for the overdraft facility renewal will not be known at the time of signing the auditor's report, there is a material uncertainty which may cast significant doubt on the company's ability to continue as a going concern. The impact on the auditor's report depends on whether this uncertainty is deemed to be adequately disclosed in the financial statements.

The auditor must carefully review the 'brief note' to the financial statements to consider whether it provides enough information about the situation, for example, does it describe how reliant the company is on the overdraft? Does it contain an indication of the amount of the overdraft and on management's contingency plans in case the overdraft is not secured? All of this might be necessary for users of the financial statements to understand the degree of uncertainty that exists over the company's funding and the implications of this for the use of the going concern assumption.

The auditor should discuss the disclosure with management and those charged with governance, encouraging full and detailed disclosure to ensure that the requirements of IAS 1 *Presentation of Financial Statements*[13] are satisfied.

Disclosure adequate: if the disclosures are adequate, there is no material misstatement as the financial statements comply with the requirements of IAS 1 and a true and fair opinion can be given on the financial statements. In accordance with ISA (UK) 570 *Going Concern*, due to the existence of a material uncertainty over going concern which has been appropriately discussed in the notes to the financial statements, the auditor's report will need to include a paragraph to highlight this material uncertainty to the users of the financial statements by the inclusion of a material uncertainty related to going concern paragraph. The paragraph will state that the audit opinion is not modified with respect to the going concern disclosures. The paragraph should indicate that there is a material uncertainty over going concern and will cross-reference to the disclosure note made by management. The paragraph itself would be included after the opinion and basis for opinion paragraphs.

Disclosure inadequate: if the disclosures made by management are not adequate, the audit opinion will need to be modified as there is a material misstatement relating to inadequate disclosure. The auditor will need to consider whether the failure to adequately disclose information on going concern is material or pervasive to the financial statements. This is a matter of significant judgement. Perhaps in this situation, if there are no other uncertainties over going concern, and due to the ongoing nature of the funding negotiations, the auditor may conclude that the lack of disclosure is material but not pervasive, and so a qualified opinion will be issued.

In this case, the opinion paragraph will state that 'except for' the failure to adequately disclose the uncertainty, the financial statements give a true and fair view. The report will contain a basis for opinion paragraph, subsequent to the opinion paragraph, explaining that a material uncertainty exists and that the financial statements do not adequately disclose this matter.

If the auditor felt that the lack of disclosure about the uncertainty over going concern was pervasive (i.e. meant that the whole set of accounts cannot be relied upon), then they should issue an adverse opinion.

Given that there are several issues which may lead to a modified opinion, the auditor will need to carefully consider the position in aggregate. ISAs (UK) do not provide specific guidance on how the auditor should report on multiple modifications to the opinion within the same auditor's report. The auditor may wish to consult with their professional body or with an independent engagement quality reviewer to help them reach a decision on how to communicate these issues in the most effective way.

KAMs

When Ranger Ltd becomes listed, the auditor will be required to follow ISA (UK) 701 *Communicating Key Audit Matters in the Independent Auditor's Report* and include a section dealing with KAMs within the auditor's report. KAMs are those matters which, in the auditor's professional judgement, were of most significance in the audit of the financial statements of the current period.

KAMs are selected from the matters communicated with those charged with governance (i.e. discussed with the client at the end of the audit).

The purpose of including KAMs in the auditor's report is to help users understand the key issues which impacted the audit process, and to provide a basis for the users to discuss with management and those charged with governance about matters relating to the entity and the financial statements.

An important part of the definition is that KAMs are the most significant matters to be highlighted to users of the auditor's report. Identifying the most significant matters involves using the auditor's professional judgement. ISA (UK) 701 suggests that in determining KAMs the auditor should take the following into account:

- Areas of higher assessed risk of material misstatement, or significant risks.
- Significant auditor judgements relating to areas in the financial statements which involved significant management judgement.
- The effect on the audit of significant events or transactions which occurred during the period.

Generally speaking, KAMs tend to be directly related to significant audit risks which were identified during the audit, and the discussion in the auditor's report will include a description of the audit risk, its materiality, why it was identified as a risk, and the auditor's response (i.e. how was audit evidence obtained to address the risk). The description of each KAM should include a reference to the related disclosures in the financial statements and cover why the matter was considered to be one of most significance in the audit. The discussion should also indicate whether the KAM was identified in previous years, and if its significance has increased or decreased.

KAMs can only be excluded if the disclosure would be prejudicial to the company, for example, if it involved the disclosure of commercially sensitive information, or could impact the outcome of litigation. It is extremely rare for KAMs to be excluded on this basis.

Activity solutions

Activity 20.1—Inability to obtain sufficient and appropriate audit evidence.

List four examples of circumstances which could lead to the auditor being unable to obtain sufficient and appropriate audit evidence.

Suggested answer points:

- Destruction of accounting records (e.g. due to cyberattack or other IT failure).
- Client not keeping appropriate accounting records (e.g. failing to record all transactions or maintain a nominal ledger).
- Limitations imposed by the management of the client (e.g. refusing to allow the auditor to review board minutes or contact legal advisers/providers of finance).
- The auditor is appointed too late to attend the inventory count.

Activity 20.2—Material misstatements

Briefly describe three types of matters which could give rise to a material misstatement.

Suggested answer points:

- The appropriateness of the selected accounting policies—for example, this could mean that the company's accounting policies are not compliant with the applicable financial reporting framework, or that the policies have not been properly described.
- The application of the selected accounting policies—this could relate to accounting policies not being consistently applied or perhaps an unintentional error in application.
- The appropriateness or adequacy of disclosures in the financial statements—examples here could include disclosures that have been omitted or not properly presented in the notes to the financial statements.

21 Communicating with Management and Those Charged with Governance

Introduction

When considering the reports made by the auditor, attention is usually focused on the report issued by the auditors to shareholders, which contains the audit opinion. However, there are other important reports produced as a result of the audit process: the auditor's communication to those charged with governance and the communication with management regarding internal controls.

Communication with senior members of the client's staff throughout the course of an audit is critical and helps in the performance of a good-quality audit. Indeed, at the end of each audit, the auditor must consider whether the two-way communication between the client and the auditor has been effective enough to yield an adequate audit.

Two-way communication is important because it assists both the auditor and those charged with governance in understanding matters that are related to the audit as well as serving to develop a constructive working relationship. To put it simply, the important issues relating to the audit need to be discussed between the auditor and appropriate individuals at the audit client. A good relationship between auditor and client means, among other things, that issues can be quickly resolved.

In addition, effective communication between the auditor and the client is important so that the auditor can obtain the information needed to perform the audit. This means that senior people within the organization may assist the auditor in understanding the entity and the environment in which it operates, assist in providing sufficient appropriate audit evidence, and provide information about specific transactions and events.

The auditor has specific reporting responsibilities to management and those charged with governance. Significant issues which arise during the audit and significant deficiencies in internal controls must be reported.

There are two ISAs (UK) that the auditor has to comply with where communication issues are concerned:

- ISA (UK) 260 Communication with Those Charged with Governance
- ISA (UK) 265 Communicating Deficiencies in Internal Control to Those Charged with Governance and Management

In this chapter, we will examine the requirements of these ISAs and outline the procedures necessary to ensure that communication issues are properly addressed during the course of the audit.

Learning outcomes

- Explain the terms 'management' and 'those charged with governance' in the context of auditor reporting.
- Explain the methods of communicating with management and those charged with governance.
- Describe the requirements for, and methods of, communicating significant deficiencies in internal control to management and those charged with governance.

By the end of this chapter, you will be able to:

- Recommend the content of reports to those charged with governance and management.
- In respect of deficiencies in internal control, provide recommendations to management and those charged with governance.

21.1 What do we mean by 'those charged with governance' and 'management'?

Before considering the type of reporting required by the auditor, and to whom within the client organization they should report, it is important to understand what we mean by 'management' and how this differs from 'those charged with governance'.

21.1.1 Terminology

ISA (UK) 260 *Communication with Those Charged with Governance* defines those charged with governance as:

> The person(s) or organization(s) (e.g., a corporate trustee) with responsibility for overseeing the strategic direction of the entity and obligations related to the accountability of the entity. This includes overseeing the financial reporting process. For some entities in some jurisdictions, those charged with governance may include management personnel, for example, executive members of a governance board of a private or public sector entity, or an owner-manager.[1]

[1] FRC, 'ISA (UK) 260', 2022, para 10(a) <https://media.frc.org.uk/documents/ISA_UK_260_Updated_May_2022.pdf> (accessed 22 January 2024).

Those charged with governance include the board of directors as a whole, including both executive and non-executive directors and the audit committee (if one exists). Those charged with governance are responsible for the strategic direction of the company and for overseeing management. In public sector organizations, those charged with governance could be a board of trustees or governors appointed by a regulatory body.

21.1.1.2 Management

ISA (UK) 260 defines management as:

> The person(s) with executive responsibility for the conduct of the entity's operations. For some entities in some jurisdictions, management includes some or all of those charged with governance, for example, executive members of a governance board, or an owner-manager.[2]

The individuals making up the management team of an organization are responsible for the day-to-day operations. Management includes the executive directors but would not normally include the non-executive directors.

The management team is responsible for the preparation of the financial statements, including designing, implementing, and maintaining effective internal control over financial reporting.

Those charged with governance and the management team are not always two separate groups of people. For example, in an owner-managed business, the managing director meets the definition of both those charged with governance and management, and it is likely that no one else is performing a governance role. The identity of the relevant person(s) to whom the communication will be addressed may be clarified in the engagement letter.

21.1.2 Board structures

In different countries and in different types of organization, governance and management structures differ. The auditor must determine the appropriate person(s) within the entity's governance structure with whom to communicate. Where the entity is a public interest entity, such as a listed company, it is likely the entity will have an audit committee with whom the auditor will primarily communicate. If the entity does not have an audit committee, the auditor will usually communicate with the body performing an equivalent function within the entity.

As we saw in Chapter 3, when we looked at corporate governance, audit committees are a subgroup of those charged with governance. There may be other subgroups of those charged with governance. Where the auditor communicates with a subgroup, they must determine whether they should also communicate with the governing body itself. For a reminder of board structures, look back to Chapter 3 (sections 3.2 and 3.3, in particular) and see Figure 21.1.

[2] Ibid., para 10(b).

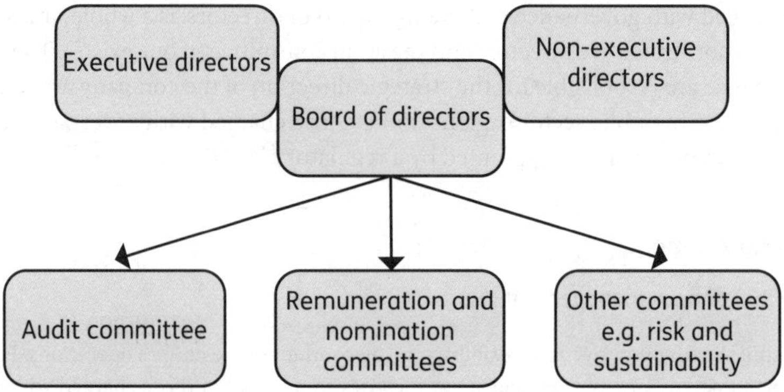

Figure 21.1 Typical board structure for a UK company

Auditing scenario 21.1 Management and governance structures

Dexter Ltd is a large mobile phone retailer with branches across the country and a head office in central London. It has eleven directors and approximately fifty shareholders. There is a small audit committee in place, comprised of non-executive directors.

For Dexter Ltd, there are separate management and governance responsibilities. The directors will clearly have management responsibilities to run the company in the best interests of the shareholders. Those charged with governance will include the audit committee.

Contrast the governance structure of Dexter Ltd with that of Sunnie Ltd, a smaller company which is a retailer of children's clothing. It operates from three stores in a vibrant city centre location. The company is owned by two shareholders, Neil and Amanda, who are a married couple, and both are 50% shareholders in the business. In addition, Neil and Amanda are the directors.

In this scenario, Neil and Amanda act as management and as those charged with governance. There is no other person involved in a governance role.

In this particular structure, any matters required to be communicated to management need not be communicated twice. However, the auditor needs to be satisfied that communicating with those individuals with management responsibilities adequately informs all of those with whom the auditor would also communicate in their governance capacity.

In all audits, there is a significant amount of communication between the audit team and the client. At the beginning of an audit, the auditor will start the communication process with management and, where applicable, those charged with governance. This involves issuing or reviewing the letter of engagement (see Chapter 6) which communicates the responsibilities of the auditor and the client and holding a pre-planning meeting with management where the scope and timing of the audit will be discussed.

At the end of the audit, the auditor will usually send another form of written communication in the form of a 'management letter' or 'letter of comment' (see section 21.3). Hence, the 'main' forms of formal communication between the auditor and the client are the engagement letter and the management letter.

Communication is clearly an important issue. However, there may be issues that are particularly sensitive and may need to be communicated in a particular way and in a timely manner—it may be the case that the issue can't wait until the end of the audit to be communicated in the management letter.

Consider a situation where an audit team member discovers a fraud. In some situations, for example, if the fraud involves a member of staff of the client, the fraud must be communicated with the appropriate level of management. However, where fraud involves management, it may be appropriate to discuss the issue with those charged with governance. In either case, the communication should take place quickly.

So, while communication with the client at all times during the audit is important, there are some important rules that have to be complied with where certain issues are concerned.

21.2 Communicating with those charged with governance

ISA (UK) 260 sets out the objectives of the auditor as follows:

> (a) To communicate clearly with those charged with governance the responsibilities of the auditor in relation to the financial statement audit, and an overview of the planned scope and timing of the audit;
>
> (b) To obtain from those charged with governance information relevant to the audit;
>
> (c) To provide those charged with governance with timely observations arising from the audit that are significant and relevant to their responsibility to oversee the financial reporting process; and
>
> (d) To promote effective two-way communication between the auditor and those charged with governance.[3]

Meeting these objectives means that the highest level of governance within the audit client is made aware of issues identified by the auditor which impact the financial reporting process, as well as providing a mechanism for those charged with governance to tell the auditor about important events, situations, or facts which may impact the audit.

21.2.1 What needs to be communicated with those charged with governance?

ISA (UK) 260 requires certain issues to be communicated with those charged with governance (Figure 21.2).

21.2.1.1 The auditor's responsibilities in relation to the audit

This will usually be included in the letter of engagement. The content of the letter of engagement was covered in Chapter 6. Remember that it contains the terms of the audit engagement, including the scope of the audit and any specific responsibilities that have been agreed (e.g. reporting to regulators in certain industries).

[3] Ibid., para 9.

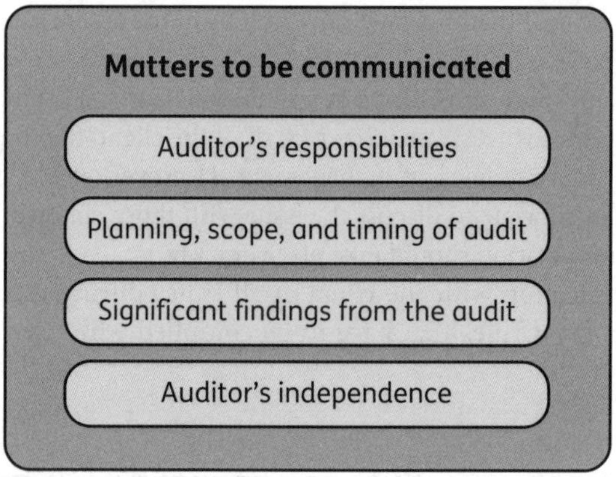

Figure 21.2 Matters to be communicated with those charged with governance

21.2.1.2 **Planning, scope, and timing of the audit**

Providing those charged with governance with information about how the audit is planned to take place will help them to understand practical issues such as timing of interim and final audit work. It also enables those charged with governance to ask questions about the planned audit approach. At the planning stage of the audit, the auditor will discuss significant risks and how the audit team plan to address those risks. However, care must be taken not to go into too much detail about the planned nature, timing, and extent of audit procedures to the extent that the procedures become too predictable.

Activity 21.1 Communication regarding the planned audit approach

What are the main issues that you think the auditor is likely to communicate with those charged with governance regarding the planned audit approach?

21.2.1.3 **Auditor's independence**

The matters communicated regarding independence should normally include a discussion of any threats to independence that arose during the audit and the safeguards which have been used to reduce the threats to an acceptable level. This communication is particularly important where the client has established an audit committee, as part of the remit of the audit committee is to have oversight on issues relating to auditor objectivity.

21.2.1.4 **Significant findings from the audit**

These are the issues communicated towards the end of the audit, after the bulk of the audit evidence has been obtained (Figure 21.2). However, even at this stage of the audit, the auditor may use this communication as a way to complete the audit evidence obtained (e.g. by asking those charged with governance to confirm their understanding of particular facts or situations, such as going concern, or a significant subsequent event).

ISA (UK) 260 provides a list of the significant findings from the audit which should be communicated:

(a) The auditor's views concerning qualitative aspects of the entity's accounting practices, including accounting policies, accounting estimates and financial statement disclosures. When applicable, the auditor shall explain to those charged with governance why the auditor considers a significant accounting practice, that is acceptable under the applicable financial reporting framework, not to be the most appropriate to the particular circumstances of the entity. [This is particularly relevant to the use of judgement in financial reporting, e.g. whether management has used reasonable assumptions to determine accounting estimates. The auditor may also communicate regarding indicators of possible management bias, or whether accounting estimates need to be revised.]

(b) Significant difficulties, if any, that have been encountered during the audit. [This could include matters such as uncooperative staff or difficulties in obtaining sufficient appropriate audit evidence.]

(c) Unless all of those charged with governance are involved in managing the entity:

  (i) Significant matters arising during the audit that were discussed, or subject to correspondence, with management; [this may include any material misstatements that have been identified]; and

  (ii) Written representations the auditor is requesting

(d) Circumstances that affect the form and content of the auditor's report, if any; [this may include any expected modifications to the auditor's opinion and Key Audit Matters to be communicated in accordance with ISA 701 Communicating Key Audit Matters in the Independent Auditor's Report] and

(e) Any other significant matters arising during the audit that, in the auditor's professional judgment, are relevant to the oversight of the financial reporting process.[4]

The point is that these matters need to be brought to the attention of the people responsible for the accounting and financial reporting function of the entity. Those responsible can then discuss the matters and decide any actions that need to be taken in respect of them. For example, if the management of the entity was totally unaware that a material misstatement exists within the financial statements, they can then resolve the problem by making the necessary adjustments. Those charged with governance must be given the opportunity to correct the financial statements in order to avoid a modified auditor's report.

Activity 21.2 Significant difficulties encountered during the audit

Can you think of some examples of difficulties which the auditor may have encountered during the audit? Why do you think these should be communicated with those charged with governance?

[4] Ibid., para 16.

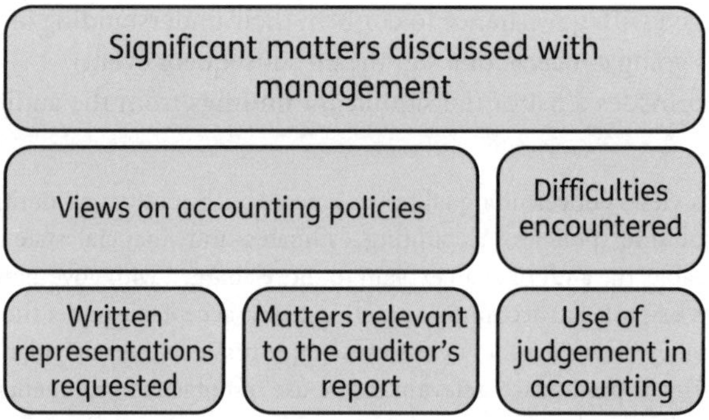

Figure 21.3 Significant findings from the audit to be communicated with those charged with governance

To summarize what we have seen so far: various communications will take place with those charged with governance depending on the stage of the audit. Table 21.1 shows some of the more notable communications that take place at each of the three stages of the audit.

21.2.2 **The communication process**

Given the importance of the issues that are discussed with those charged with governance, it is crucial that the auditor establishes a clear communication process. Remember that the communication must be a two-way process, so both the auditor and the client need to be aware of:

- the purpose of each communication;
- the form it will take;
- the specific individuals who will be responsible for the communication; and
- the process for reporting back and taking any necessary action.

Table 21.1 Timing of communication with those charged with governance

Stage of the audit	Communication
Pre-planning	• Engagement letter
Planning	• Significant risks identified by the auditor
	• How the auditor plans to address those significant risks
	• Materiality and how it will be applied during the course of the audit
	• How, and the extent to which, reliance will be placed on the entity's system of internal control
Audit fieldwork stage (evidence-gathering stage)	• Any situation that presents itself that warrants communication with management e.g.. difficulties obtaining audit evidence
Completion	• Major findings from the audit
	• Any uncooperation from management or others within the entity from whom the auditor has requested information
	• Problematic issues discovered

Regarding the form of the communication, written communication is most appropriate. ISA (UK) 260 does not require that all communications are in writing but does explain that for some issues, for example, significant findings from the audit, oral communication is not likely to be adequate. Usually, matters are discussed at a meeting between the auditor and representatives of those charged with governance, often the audit committee, so it is important that these meetings have accurate minutes to serve as a record of the discussion and action points agreed.

Effective communication could be made using a presentation by the auditor as well as less formal discussions. When communication is made orally it is important that the auditor has a written record within the audit working papers of the discussion of significant matters with management. Email serves as a written record of matters discussed.

In terms of the timing of communications, significant issues should be communicated without delay, for example, if a fraud or significant internal control deficiency is discovered or the auditor faces a limitation on the scope of their work which is imposed by management. Timely communication means that the problem can be quickly investigated and resolved by the client.

Finally, ISA (UK) 260 requires the auditor to evaluate whether the two-way communication between the auditor and those charged with governance has been adequate for the purpose of the audit. If it has not, the auditor must evaluate the effect, if any, on the auditor's assessment of the risks of material misstatement and ability to obtain sufficient appropriate audit evidence, and must take appropriate action.[5]

No specific procedures need to be performed as part of this evaluation. Instead, the effectiveness of the two-way communication can be assessed based on the auditor's observations, for example, of the ease by which matters have been resolved by those charged with governance, their willingness to meet with the auditor, and the openness of the discussions.

Auditing in practice 21.1 Ineffective two-way communication

In some situations, the auditor may determine that the two-way communication has not been effective. This may arise because audit issues have not been taken seriously by those charged with governance or because they have not appeared to understand the issues being raised.

In a case like this, the auditor is in a difficult position. They may consider that there is a lack of integrity among those charged with governance, or just a lack of understanding of their responsibilities in relation to the audit. Either of these could have serious consequences for the audit.

In more serious situations, where those charged with governance have been severely uncooperative, the auditor may consider modifying the auditor's opinion due to a limitation of scope. They could also consider communicating with the company's shareholders, for example, at the annual general meeting, about the difficulties faced. They could even consider withdrawing from the audit and taking legal advice. The key point is that the auditor is unlikely to want to perform the following year's audit under the same circumstances.

[5] Ibid., para 22.

21.3 Communicating significant deficiencies in internal control

21.3.1 Deficiencies and significant deficiencies

We looked at internal controls in detail in Chapter 8. The key point to remember is that as part of audit planning, the auditor must understand and document the elements of internal control that relate to financial reporting. The auditor also evaluates the strength of internal controls in order to devise an appropriate audit strategy and may choose to perform tests of control as a way to obtain audit evidence.

ISA (UK) 265 *Communicating Deficiencies in Internal Control to Those Charged with Governance and Management* deals with how the auditor should report on problems that they have identified with the client's internal controls to the client. This is not a communication to shareholders—the point of the reporting is to alert management to internal control deficiencies, explain why they are a problem, and provide a constructive recommendation. The report is known as the 'Management Letter' and gives the client useful advice which, if implemented, could improve the operations and financial reporting of the company.

ISA (UK) 265 requires the auditor to communicate deficiencies in internal control to management (see Figure 21.4).

According to ISA (UK) 265, a deficiency in internal control exists when:

(a) A control is designed, implemented or operated in such a way that it is unable to prevent, or detect and correct, misstatements in the financial statements on a timely basis; or

(b) A control necessary to prevent, or detect and correct, misstatements in the financial statements on a timely basis is missing.

The term 'A significant deficiency in internal control' is defined in ISA (UK) 265 as:

> A deficiency or combination of deficiencies in internal control that, in the auditor's professional judgment, is of sufficient importance to merit the attention of those charged with governance.[6]

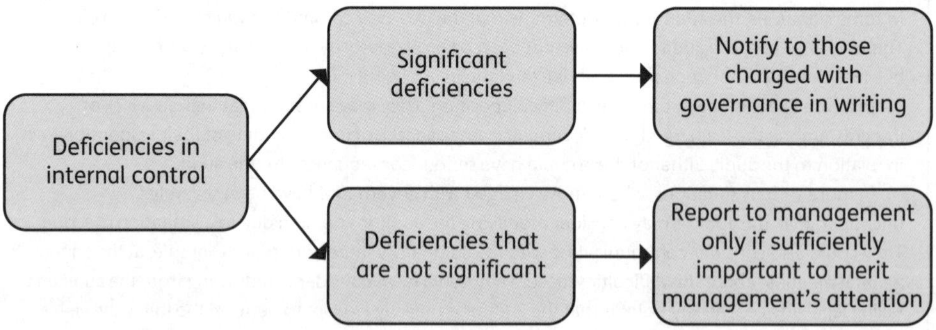

Figure 21.4 Communicating deficiencies in internal control

[6] FRC, 'ISA (UK) 265', 2022, para 6 <https://media.frc.org.uk/documents/ISA_UK_265_-_May_2022.pdf> (accessed 22 January 2024).

Significant deficiencies must be notified to those charged with governance in writing.[7] Communicating significant deficiencies in writing serves to emphasize the importance of these matters and assists those charged with governance in fulfilling their oversight responsibilities including putting measures in place to overcome the identified deficiencies.

Deficiencies that are not considered to be significant should be reported to management if, in the auditor's professional judgement, the deficiencies are of sufficient importance to merit management's attention.

It will be left to the auditor's professional judgement to determine whether a deficiency is a *significant* deficiency, warranting the attention of those charged with governance, warranting just the attention of management and not those charged with governance if the auditor considers this important.

Examples of matters which the auditor would usually consider when determining whether a deficiency in internal controls is significant include:

- The likelihood of the deficiencies leading to material misstatements in the financial statements in the future.
- The susceptibility to loss or fraud of the related asset or liability.
- The subjectivity and complexity of determining estimated amounts, such as fair value accounting estimates.
- The financial statement amounts exposed to the deficiencies.
- The volume of activity that has occurred or could occur in the account balance or class of transactions exposed to the deficiency or deficiencies.
- The importance of the controls used in the financial reporting process, for example:
  - General monitoring controls (such as oversight of management).
  - Controls over the prevention and detection of fraud.
  - Controls over the selection and application of significant accounting policies.
  - Controls over significant transactions with related parties.
  - Controls over significant transactions outside the entity's normal course of business.
  - Controls over the period-end financial reporting process (such as controls over non-recurring journal entries).
- The cause and frequency of exceptions detected as a result of the deficiencies in the controls.
- The interaction of the deficiency with other deficiencies in internal control.[8]

When an auditor identifies deficiencies in internal control, reporting to management and those charged with governance is just one response. Depending on the type of deficiency and its significance, the auditor may consider extending audit procedures and there could be implications for the auditor's report.

[7] Ibid., para 9. [8] Ibid., para A6.

Auditing scenario 21.2 Control deficiencies and auditor responses

During the audit of the financial statements of Merry Ltd for the year ended 31 December 20X9, the auditor noted several deficiencies in internal control and, in some cases, evidence of absent controls.

The audit manager and audit engagement partner have reviewed the audit evidence obtained and have concluded that the audit evidence is insufficient to support the audit opinion. The audit manager has asked the audit engagement partner if there is anything else that can be done to try to remedy the situation.

There are some options available to the audit team before concluding that the audit opinion may need to be modified.

Extend testing of controls

The audit team could extend the testing of controls in those areas where deficiencies have been noted. This could have the result that the controls are not as deficient as first thought, although absent controls will need to be communicated to management together with their implication.

Raise the issue with those charged with governance

If the auditor concludes that the deficiencies in internal control are significant deficiencies, then they should be communicated with those charged with governance, in accordance with ISA (UK) 265, so that they are aware of the issue.

Perform additional substantive testing

Remember, substantive testing aims to detect misstatements in the financial statements. The audit team could perform additional substantive testing on areas where controls are weak. This is usually the best approach the auditor will take in such circumstances because additional substantive procedures will help to quantify the extent of errors and compensate for a weak control system.

Issue a modified auditor's opinion

If the issue of a lack of audit evidence cannot be addressed by other means, the auditor will have no alternative but to express a modified audit opinion. Depending on the magnitude of the lack of audit evidence, a disclaimer of opinion may be appropriate.

21.3.2 Management letter points

Deficiencies in internal control will usually be addressed in the 'management letter' to the client at the end of the audit. Depending on the number of deficiencies noted, and the level of detail provided on each, it may be included within the main body of the letter itself or as an appendix to the letter.

ISA (UK) 265 requires particular issues to be communicated in writing with respect to significant deficiencies in internal control:

(a) A description of the deficiencies and an explanation of their potential effects; and

(b) Sufficient information to enable those charged with governance and management to understand the context of the communication. In particular, the auditor shall explain that:

   (i) The purpose of the audit was for the auditor to express an opinion on the financial statements;

(ii) The audit included consideration of internal control relevant to the preparation of the financial statements in order to design audit procedures that are appropriate in the circumstances, but not for the purpose of expressing an opinion on the financial statements; and

(iii) The matters being reported are limited to those deficiencies that the auditor has identified during the audit and that the auditor has concluded are of sufficient importance to merit being reported to those charged with governance.[9]

Generally, the auditor will set out the deficiencies or 'management letter points' in tabular format as in Table 21.2, using an internal control deficiency relating to purchase orders to illustrate:

Table 21.2

Deficiency	Implication	Recommendation
During the course of the audit, we noted that only purchase invoices over £5,000 are authorized by a senior official	The company is exposed to fraud risk as goods under £5,000 could be ordered which are not required hence creating a loss to the business	All invoices under £5,000 should be reviewed by a responsible official. Invoices over £5,000 should be reviewed by a more senior official, such as the finance director

The points raised in the management letter should be discussed with appropriate individuals before the letter is sent. This allows the client an opportunity to consider the issue and possibly to provide further information to the auditor. It also allows the auditor to check their understanding of the issue, to avoid any inaccuracies in their description of the deficiency and its implications for the business.

Auditing scenario 21.3 Reporting significant deficiencies in internal control

Superstores Ltd is a supermarket chain with 350 supermarkets across the country. It also has a significant online grocery division with over 450,000 regular customers.

The company has an internal audit department which monitors controls over operations and financial reporting. Due to significant capital expenditure being incurred during the current financial year, the internal audit team produced a report on the internal controls operating over capital expenditure relating to items including store fixtures and fittings, warehousing equipment, and delivery vans. An extract from the report is shown below:

> The internal audit investigations found that only capital expenditure over £35,000 in value is routinely approved by a senior manager. Capital expenditure in excess of £100,000 has to go through a tendering process which involves at least three potential suppliers. When the supplier sends the invoice for payment, the invoice is passed to the employee who requested the item to be purchased, who then approves the payment and passes the invoice to the accounts department for processing.

[9] Ibid., para 11.

The auditor would evaluate this information to determine whether there are significant deficiencies in internal controls in this system over capital expenditure, and a report to management will be prepared. The report will outline each deficiency, including its implication for the business, along with a recommendation, as illustrated in Table 21.3.

Table 21.3 Illustrative communication regarding deficiencies in internal control

Deficiency	Implication	Recommendation
Approval is not routinely sought for capital expenditure with a value under £35,000	The company is exposed to the risk that items under £35,000 could be ordered which are not required by the business, creating unnecessary cash outflows	All capital expenditure requisitions should be reviewed and approved by a responsible official A limit that is less than £35,000 may be more appropriate, to reduce the risks
Capital expenditure below £100,000 value does not go through a tendering process	Best prices may not be achieved, resulting in the company paying too much for their assets. Value for money will not be achieved.	Management should review the threshold for requiring a tendering process, and set a more appropriate, lower level
There is no segregation of duty in that the person who requested the item also approves payment	This creates a significant risk of fraud. There is nothing to stop employees ordering capital expenditure items for their personal use (e.g. new computer equipment and approving it for payment).	Segregation of duty should be introduced, so that different individuals are responsible for ordering the items, receiving the goods, and approving payment

Note that the issues do not need to be quantified, and the implications of the deficiency need not be financial—internal control deficiencies which cause operational or compliance problems should also be reported to management.

It is a matter of judgement as to how much detail the auditor should provide when communicating about significant deficiencies. Providing sufficient detail, especially regarding the implications of control deficiencies, should encourage management to act to address the deficiencies described. The implications do not have to be quantified, though this could serve to indicate the severity of the issue and encourage management to take action.

Activity 21.3 Communicating information about significant deficiencies

List as many factors as you can which may influence how much detail is provided to management and those charged with governance about significant deficiencies.

The auditor needs to consider the most appropriate individual(s) to receive the management letter, bearing in mind that it should be the person or group of people in the best position to understand the auditor's comments and to evaluate whether remedial action should be taken. In other words, should the auditor's recommendation be taken up? Often, the management letter is addressed to the audit committee, who then determine the best recipient, which may be a member of management or those charged with governance.

Auditing in practice 21.2 The report to management

The report to management on significant deficiencies in controls should include caveats, including that the report is for the sole use of the audit client, that the content should not be disclosed to third parties, and that the auditor accepts no responsibility for actions taken by management as a result of the recommendations made.

The report should also include that only significant deficiencies are being reported. There may be other, insignificant deficiencies which have been identified.

An example of the wording which can be used is shown below.

> Dear Sirs,
>
> Audit of Spiral Ltd for the year ended 30 November 20X3
>
> Please find enclosed the report to management on significant deficiencies in internal controls identified during the audit for the year ended 30 November 20X3.
>
> The appendix to this report identifies deficiencies in the payroll and capital expenditure systems, explains the implications of those deficiencies and provides recommendations to address those deficiencies.
>
> Please note that this report only addresses the deficiencies identified during the audit and if further testing had been performed, then more deficiencies may have been reported.
>
> This report is solely for the use of management and if you have any further questions, then please do not hesitate to contact us.
>
> Yours faithfully
>
> Helix & Co, Auditors

You may be wondering whether the client has any obligation to take action, that is, do they have to follow the auditor's recommendations? The simple answer is 'no'—it is up to management to decide whether to do so. There may be cost constraints which deter management from implementing the recommendations, or simply management believes that it is not a priority for the business.

Management should acknowledge receipt of the management letter, and if action has been taken or is planned to be taken in response to the issues raised, the auditor should be made aware. If matters are very significant, the auditor may request a meeting with management to discuss them.

The auditor can reiterate control deficiencies in subsequent periods, if they have not been corrected. Indeed, the auditor is likely to ask why the recommendation has not been followed. According to ISA (UK) 265, the failure of management or those charged with governance to follow the auditor's recommendations, in the absence of a rational explanation, may in itself represent a significant deficiency.[10]

[10] Ibid., para A17.

Chapter round-up

- Communication is critical throughout the audit so that both parties (the auditor and the client) understand their responsibilities properly. Communication will be in the form of verbal discussions, in the letter of engagement, and in the final management letter.
- Communication processes start at the very beginning of the audit and continue throughout the course of the audit (usually up to the point at which the auditor's report is signed).
- Those charged with governance, and in particular the audit committee, must be made aware of significant findings from the audit in order for them to fulfil their responsibilities regarding oversight of the audit process.
- Significant deficiencies in internal control must be communicated to those charged with governance.
- Deficiencies in an entity's system of internal control are usually notified in writing in the form of a management letter with an appendix to the letter providing a table showing:
  - the deficiency;
  - the implication of the deficiency; and
  - a recommendation to address the deficiency.
- The auditor must carry out an assessment as to whether the two-way communication process has been efficient in order to yield an adequate audit.

End of chapter case study

Introduction

In this chapter, we have considered the reports that the auditor is required to make to the client. These communications are very important as they provide management and those charged with governance with vital issues that have arisen during the course of the audit including significant audit findings and significant deficiencies in internal controls. The management letter provides the client with constructive recommendations and is often seen as a particularly useful outcome of the audit by management.

This case study links to the following learning outcomes:

- Explain the methods of communicating with management and those charged with governance.
- Describe the requirements for, and methods of, communicating significant deficiencies in internal control to management and those charged with governance.
- Recommend the content of reports to those charged with governance and management.
- In respect of deficiencies in internal control, provide recommendation to management and those charged with governance.

Scenario

You are working on the audit of Pixie plc, a listed company which operates gyms and leisure centres across the country. The company's financial statements for the year ended 31

December 20X4 recognize revenue of £215 million, profit before tax of £7 million, and total assets of £80 million.

The audit work is almost complete, and you have been tasked with drafting the reports to those charged with governance and management. Pixie plc has a board of directors including four non-executive directors, who also form the audit committee.

From your review of the audit working papers, you have identified the following issues.

Delays in receiving information

As part of the planned audit procedures on payroll, the audit team had requested access to the company's human resources records. In particular, information on starters and leavers was needed, but there was a four-week delay in this being provided to the audit team. This caused a delay in the completion of the audit procedures and incurred additional costs.

Inventory management software

Audit procedures performed on inventory revealed that the inventory management software used by Pixie plc is outdated. The software, called 'GoodStock', is no longer supported by the supplier. This could lead to loss of data and errors in recording inventory transactions which cannot be resolved. A discussion with management revealed that the financial controller refused to approve the cost of purchasing new inventory management software due to cash flow problems suffered by the company in the last financial year, resulting in other expenditure being prioritized. No material misstatement of inventory was discovered as a result of audit procedures performed.

Outstanding gym membership fees

During the audit of revenue, it was noted that the process for chasing outstanding gym membership fees from customers has changed due to a shortage of staff. This has led to an increase in trade receivables of £2.5 million in the year. No material errors in the financial statements were revealed by audit procedures performed on trade receivables or revenue.

Impairment of assets

Audit procedures have identified that due to an economic recession and the number of gym members reducing by 15 per cent in the year, management has not performed an impairment review on non-current assets. The audit team determined that an impairment of £3.5 million should be recognized. Despite having been informed of this, management decided not to amend the draft financial statements to recognize the impairment loss suggested by the audit team or to perform their own impairment test.

Offer to audit team members

The sales director of Pixie plc offered all of the audit team members free gym membership for a year, for themselves and their family members.

Review of management accounts

It has been noted that the board of directors does not routinely review the monthly management accounts prepared by the finance director at their board meetings.

Required

For each of the matters described, discuss the implications for the auditor to report to those charged with governance and management.

Answer

Delays in receiving information

The information on starters and leavers not being provided for four weeks caused a delay in the completion of the audit fieldwork. ISA (UK) 260 *Communication with Those Charged with Governance* requires that the auditor communicates significant difficulties encountered during the audit, and significant delays in management providing required information is an example of such an instance. The auditor should communicate the delay to those charged with governance and explain the impact on both the completion time of the audit and outline any additional costs incurred. They should explain that any additional costs have been added to the audit fee and that in future years if such delays are avoided the audit will be completed more efficiently.

Inventory management software

The auditor has identified a deficiency in internal controls in that the software being used appears to be obsolete. This could create problems if the software malfunctions, there is no support from the supplier, meaning that data could be lost or corrupted and the software is likely to become increasingly inefficient as it gets older. The auditor was right to raise this with management and an explanation has been received as to why the software has not been replaced. However, the auditor now needs to consider the significance of the issue. If it is deemed to be significant then it must be communicated in writing to those charged with governance. If it is not deemed to be significant, the auditor may choose to include the issue in the management letter, if in the auditor's professional judgement, the issue is of sufficient importance to merit management's attention. In making this judgement call regarding the significance of the internal control deficiency, the auditor may consider the following:

- The materiality of the issue—is inventory material to the financial statements? Possibly not, given that Pixie plc operates gyms, so inventory is not likely to be a significant asset.
- The reason for not upgrading the software—those charged with governance may not be aware that the financial controller has refused to approve the expenditure.
- The fact that no material misstatements have been found in respect of inventory.

Without further information, it is not possible to reach a firm conclusion, but on balance this issue is unlikely to be significant enough to warrant disclosure in writing to those charged with governance, but it could be included in the management letter, in which case the report should describe the deficiency, the implications and a recommendation.

Outstanding gym membership fees

The deterioration in controls over income from gym members has not led to any identified material misstatements but this could represent a significant deterioration in internal controls which should be reported to those charged with governance.

The increase in the trade receivables is material, representing 3 per cent of total assets and this increases the risk of irrecoverable receivables. This can lead to cash flow problems for the company and a deterioration in working capital management. This could have a significant impact on the business, including going concern, especially given the economic recession and decline in the number of gym members. For these reasons, the deterioration in controls should be reported in the management letter as described above in relation to the inventory management software. The auditor should also consider whether the issue is significant enough to warrant disclosure in writing to those charged with governance.

Impairment of assets

The failure to recognize the impairment of assets appropriately is a misstatement of the financial statements. The misstatement has overstated non-current assets and overstated profit by an estimated £3.5 million. This represents 50 per cent of profit before tax which is highly material to the financial statements. The auditor should communicate the uncorrected misstatement to those charged with governance in accordance with ISA (UK) 260. Those charged with governance should be asked to correct the misstatement and to discuss with management why they did not perform their own impairment test. The auditor should also report that if the misstatement remains uncorrected, a modified audit opinion will be issued.

Offer to audit team members

This is a potential threat to the auditor's objectivity. Offering free gym membership creates a self-interest threat because it creates a financial benefit to the audit team members, whose judgement may be impaired by the offer (e.g. they may choose to overlook problems identified during the audit). The offer could also be seen as a bribe. Matters relating to auditor independence should be communicated with those charged with governance in accordance with IAS (UK) 260. The auditor should report the circumstances of the offer made, for example, when was the offer made? Was there any reason for the offer? The auditor should also report how the situation was dealt with by the audit team—for example, was the offer declined by the audit team? Armed with this information, those charged with governance can discuss the issue with the sales director, explaining why it is inappropriate and to ensure that the offer is not made again.

Review of management accounts

This is an internal control deficiency, so the auditor will need to use judgement to decide whether it is a significant deficiency to be reported to those charged with governance. Regular review of the management accounts is an important element of the internal control process over financial reporting. If there is no regular review of the management accounts, errors are not likely to be detected, and inappropriate accounting policies may be applied. Given that Pixie plc is a listed company with an audit committee, this review is very important and should be a function of the audit committee. For these reasons, the auditor will probably conclude that this is a significant deficiency to be reported to those charged with governance.

Activity answer points

Activity 21.1—Communication regarding the planned audit approach

What are the main issues that you think the auditor is likely to communicate with those charged with governance regarding the planned audit approach?

Suggested answer points:

Matters will be discussed that will usually include:

- Any significant risks of material misstatement that have been identified and how the audit strategy and audit plan should address the significant risks of material misstatement.
- Business risks faced by the business, including new or emerging risks, such as new competitors entering the marketplace, which may impact the financial statements or on going concern.

- How materiality has been determined and how it will be applied during the audit.
- The auditor's approach obtaining audit evidence, whether the strategy is to use tests of controls or to rely on substantive testing.
- Accounting policies and any changes to accounting policies that have taken place during the year.
- Disagreements that could arise during the course of the audit between the auditor and the client (e.g. on a specific accounting treatment or a required disclosure note).
- Any areas that require special audit consideration (e.g. whether the auditor plans to use an auditor's expert for any part of the audit or how the auditor plans to communicate with component auditors in the case of a group audit).
- How audit quality will be addressed (e.g. the process for review within the audit team) and whether an engagement quality review will be performed.

Activity 21.2—Significant difficulties encountered during the audit

Can you think of some examples of difficulties which the auditor may have encountered during the audit? Why do you think these should be communicated with those charged with governance?

Suggested answer points:

- Significant delays caused by management or other client staff in providing information to the audit team.
- Individuals being unable or unwilling to answer questions or assist the auditor in other respects.
- Unreasonable deadlines to complete the audit.
- Extensive unexpected effort required to obtain sufficient appropriate audit evidence.
- Restrictions imposed on the auditor by management (e.g. not allowing access to information, or to external parties such as the client's bank or legal adviser).

It is important that these issues are discussed to avoid problems in the future. Some of the issues may also have implications for the audit fee (e.g. if significant additional work had to be carried out), so the client needs to understand the reason for this.

Activity 21.3—Communicating information about significant deficiencies

List as many factors as you can which may influence how much detail is provided to management and those charged with governance about significant deficiencies.

Suggested answer points:

- The type of significant deficiencies—the more complex they are, the more detail should be provided.
- Whether the significant deficiencies appear to be recurring (e.g. if they had previously been communicated to the client but no actions seem to have been taken), more detailed explanations may need to be provided.
- Whether the significant deficiency caused a material misstatement within the financial statements.
- If the deficiency is related to fraudulent activity or other breaches of laws and regulations, the explanation should be more detailed.
- The size, complexity, and structure of the client (e.g. the communication may need to be more detailed for a listed company or a company operating in a specialized industry).
- The level of knowledge and experience of the client (e.g. if management or those charged with governance are not familiar with the nature of the significant deficiency or the financial reporting area to which it relates).

22 Group Audit

Introduction

Almost all large audits, especially those of listed entities, are actually audits of groups of companies rather than an audit of a single company. Auditing a group of companies creates some unique challenges, including the potential need to liaise with other audit firms and risks of material misstatement that arise due to the complexities of group accounting.

When organizations grow and expand, this is often done through the acquisition of other companies to form a group which is under the common control of a parent company and its shareholders. When a group is created, each member of the group will prepare its own financial statements (which are called the 'individual' or 'separate' financial statements). In addition, the parent company must prepare consolidated financial statements (or 'group accounts') in addition to its own individual financial statements. The group accounts essentially consolidate the results of each individual member of the group into one set of financial statements. The objective of group accounts is to show the results of the group in line with its economic substance, which is that of a single reporting entity.

The audit of a group is twofold. First, each company within the group will have to have their individual financial statements audited if the company cannot claim any exemption from audit. Second, the group accounts also must be audited. The group audit report is in addition to the audit reports which are issued on the financial statements of the individual components of the group.

Providing the audit service to a group of companies can be a challenging process for a number of reasons. A particular difficulty arises when there is more than one audit firm performing the audit of companies within the group. For example, if there is a foreign group company which is audited by a local firm of auditors, but the rest of the group companies are audited by a different firm. In this situation, it is imperative that there is good communication between the two audit firms so that no duties go unperformed (or performed inadequately).

In addition, the financial reporting requirements for groups of companies can be complex to apply, and certain aspects, for example, accounting for goodwill, can require the use of significant judgement. The risk of material misstatement that arises from the consolidation process is often high, meaning that a group audit can require careful planning to ensure that all risks are identified and responded to in an appropriate manner through the audit strategy that is developed.

In this chapter we will look at the content of ISA (UK) 600 *Special Considerations—Audits of Group Financial Statements (Including the Work of Component Auditors)* and consider how the complex requirements are applied to a group audit.

Note: we are conscious that not all students will have studied group accounting at this point in their studies, and that many auditing modules will not include group audit within their content. For this reason, this chapter is more of an overview of group audit issues, and the chapter may not be relevant to all students.

Learning outcomes

- Explain the role and responsibilities of the group auditor and component auditors within a group of companies.
- Describe the factors that need to be considered before accepting appointment as group auditor and discuss the requirements for the group auditor to understand the component auditor.
- Describe the nature of communication between group and component auditors.
- Identify and explain the matters specific to planning the audit of a group including audit risks and responses to those risks.
- Explain the audit procedures relevant to a group audit including the consolidation process.
- Explain how the group auditor evaluates audit evidence specific to group situations, communicates with management, and discusses the matters to be considered when issuing a group audit report.
- Describe and explain the terms 'transnational audit' and 'joint audit' and consider when a joint audit would be appropriate.

22.1 Identifying a group of companies and the group and component auditors

22.1.1 How is a group of companies created?

A group is formed when one company (the parent) has a controlling ownership interest in another company (the subsidiary). For clarity, IFRS 10 *Consolidated Financial Statements* states that:

> An investor controls an investee when it is exposed, or has rights, to variable returns from its involvement with the investee and has the ability to affect those returns through its power over the investee.[1]

[1] International Financial Reporting Standards Foundation, 'IFRS 10 Consolidated Financial Statements', 2023, para 6 <https://www.ifrs.org/issued-standards/list-of-standards/ifrs-10-consolidated-financial-statements/> (accessed 22 January 2024).

In the broadest terms, an entity is said to have control over another entity when it has an ownership interest of more than 50 per cent in the net assets or voting rights of the entity. Numeric benchmarks are not the only indicator of control, but they are generally a reliable indicator because an equity shareholding of more than 50 per cent usually demonstrates control through voting rights.

Some subsidiaries may be wholly owned by the parent company (i.e. the parent owns 100 per cent of the subsidiary) and others may not be. When a subsidiary is not wholly owned by its parent there is 'non-controlling interest' (sometimes referred to as a 'minority interest' in the UK). Non-controlling interest is the external shareholders who are not connected to the group. So, for example, a parent company may own 80 per cent of a subsidiary so the non-controlling interest is 20 per cent.

In Figure 22.1, Topco Ltd is the parent company, which has a controlling interest in three subsidiaries. Topco Ltd and its three subsidiaries will prepare their own individual financial statements. Once these individual financial statements have been prepared, Topco will then consolidate the results of Subcos 1, 2, and 3 into its own financial statements, subject to consolidation adjustments, to arrive at the group financial statements.

Preparing group financial statements can be a complex exercise in practice as there is a lot of technical detail to comply with. For example, eliminating intra-group trading and balances, eliminating intra-group dividends and finance income/expenses, and bringing in additional transactions and balances, such as goodwill, fair value adjustments, and non-controlling interests. Detailed accounting and financial reporting requirements for group accounts are beyond the scope of this book but the key point to bear in mind where group accounts are concerned is that they report the results of the group as if the group were a single trading entity with the outside world.

For example, individual members of a group will often trade with each other during the year, but for group accounts purposes this intra-group trading is not recognized because it is within the group and not a transaction between the group and outside. It is for that reason that care must be taken in correctly eliminating all intra-group transactions and balances from the consolidated financial statements of the group. If this is not done, the group

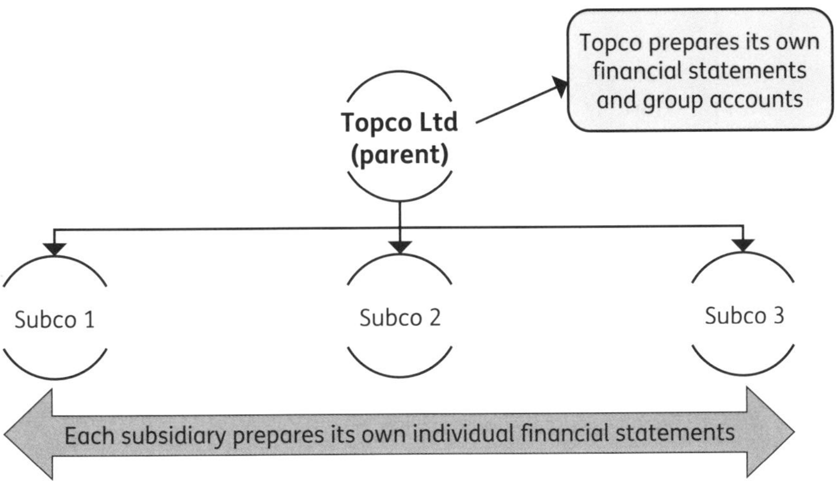

Figure 22.1 Example group structure

accounts will be materially incorrect and misleading. It is this type of issue which could give rise to audit risk at group level, but not at the level of the individual financial statements, and which the group auditor needs to carefully consider.

22.1.2 **Components**

ISA (UK) 600 (Revised September 2022) defines a 'component' as:

> An entity, business unit, function or business activity, or some combination thereof, determined by the group auditor for purposes of planning and performing audit procedures in a group audit.[2]

Therefore, in the context of a group, the term 'component' relates to the individual companies within the group, hence you will see phrases such as 'component management' and 'component materiality', all of which refer to the management and materiality levels set at individual company level rather than at group level.

Prior to the issuance of ISA (UK) 600 (Revised September 2022), the standard dealt with 'significant components'. These are no longer dealt with in ISA (UK) 600 now because emphasis is given instead to the consideration of risks of material misstatement at the assertion level of the group financial statements that are associated with components.

22.1.3 **Group and component auditors**

When a group audit is being carried out, there are two types of auditor involved: the group auditor and the component auditor (Figure 22.2). The group auditor is the auditor who will be responsible for expressing an opinion on the group accounts. The component auditor is the auditor who audits the subsidiary and issues an audit report on their individual financial statements, and, in addition, at the request of the group engagement team, performs work on the individual subsidiaries that is relevant to the group audit. In many cases, the group auditor and the component auditor will be the same audit firm, which makes the auditing process considerably more straightforward. However, there may be situations where several audit firms are involved in a group audit.

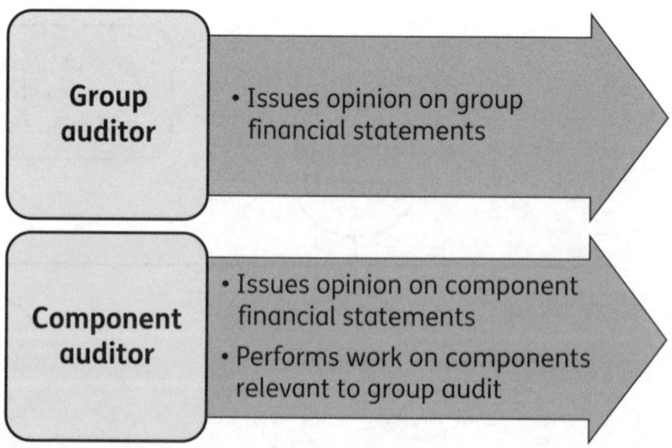

Figure 22.2 Group and component auditor responsibilities

[2] FRC, 'ISA (UK) 600', 2022, para 14(b) <https://media.frc.org.uk/documents/ISA_UK_600_Revised_November_2019_Updated_May_2022.pdf> (accessed 22 January 2024).

Activity 22.1 Component auditors

List as many situations you can think of in which a component of the group could be audited by a different audit firm than the firm appointed as group auditor.

The key point to appreciate is that the group auditor has the sole responsibility for the group audit opinion. They can use component auditors as a source of audit evidence, to support the opinion on the group financial statements, but this is only after the group auditor has considered how much reliance they can place on the work performed by the component auditor on the individual financial statements which feed into the group financial statements.

ISA (UK) 600 states that the objectives of the group auditor are to:

(a) With respect to the acceptance and continuance of the group audit engagement, determine whether sufficient appropriate audit evidence can reasonably be expected to be obtained to provide a basis for forming an opinion on the group financial statements;

(b) Identify and assess the risks of material misstatement of the group financial statements, whether due to fraud or error, and plan and perform further audit procedures to appropriately respond to those assessed risks;

(c) Be sufficiently and appropriately involved in the work of component auditors throughout the group audit, including communicating clearly about the scope and timing of their work, and evaluating the results of that work; and

(d) Evaluate whether sufficient appropriate audit evidence has been obtained from the audit procedures performed, including with respect to the work performed by component auditors, as a basis for forming an opinion on the group financial statements.[3]

You can see that one of the matters emphasized in the ISA (UK's) objectives is the need for clear communication between group auditor and component auditor. This is one of the practical challenges of conducting a group audit, especially if a component auditor is a firm located in a foreign country which may have different auditing regulations to those followed by the rest of the group. The structure and complexity of the group of companies and its auditors, including where they are located, is a key issue for group auditors to consider when deciding to take on a group audit. We will now go on to look at client acceptance for a group of companies in more detail.

22.2 Accepting a group audit, and understanding component auditors

22.2.1 Accepting a group audit engagement

The various factors which must be considered prior to accepting a group audit are not very different from when deciding to accept an individual entity audit. Prior to accepting a group audit, the engagement partner must:

(a) Consider ethical issues such as any reasons which may compromise their objectivity and independence. If such issues exist, the engagement partner is unlikely to accept the group audit unless they can be reduced to an acceptably low level.

[3] Ibid., para 13.

(b) Establish whether the firm has adequate resources available to carry out the group audit in accordance with the ISAs (UK) and other legal and regulatory requirements. This is a particularly important consideration if there are components of the group which are located abroad (international audits are briefly examined in section 22.7.1).

There is an interaction between ISA (UK) 600 and that of ISA (UK) 220 *Quality Management for an Audit of Financial Statements*. The group engagement partner must determine whether sufficient appropriate audit evidence can be obtained in respect of the consolidation process and the financial information of the components on which to base the group audit opinion. To that end, ISA (UK) 600 requires the group engagement team to obtain an understanding of the group, its components, and the environments in which they operate. This is important to enable the group auditor to evaluate whether they will be sufficiently involved with the group as a whole for the appointment as group auditor to be appropriate.

Auditing scenario 22.1 Frites Group

The Frites Group is a global distribution company, offering its services to business and residential customers in eighty countries. The Group is headquartered in London, where the majority of the senior executives are based. The Group has a parent company and twenty-five subsidiaries.

The Group has approached the audit firm Mac Associates to inquire whether the firm would be willing to tender for the Group audit. Mac Associates has been told that eighteen of the Group's subsidiaries are based in foreign countries and they are all audited by local firms of auditors who have specialist knowledge of tax and other regulations in their country of operation. The Group management team have also said that should Mac Associates be appointed as auditor to the Group, they would provide the audit opinion on the Group financial statements and also be appointed as auditor to the seven UK-based subsidiaries.

In this situation, Mac Associates should carefully consider the scope of work they have been asked to perform and the level of involvement they would have with the Group as a whole. It appears that while Mac Associates would be auditing seven of the Group's subsidiaries, the other eighteen subsidiaries would be audited by other firms. This means that Mac Associates would be relying heavily on the component auditors to perform high-quality audits, and Mac Associates should consider how appropriate this would be. Should Mac Associates take on the engagement, they would need to carefully evaluate the competence of the component auditors and their independence, to ensure that the individual financial statements of the subsidiaries have been robustly audited prior to them being consolidated into the Group accounts, for which Mac Associates has sole responsibility.

In addition to considering the extent of their involvement with the Group, Mac Associates would need to consider a range of other factors including:

- How easy it would be to communicate with the other audit firms and how likely the other firms are to cooperate, for example, with requests for information?
- Will the component auditors allow the Group audit team access to their audit working papers?
- Whether members of the Group audit team will need to travel to any of the foreign countries in order to obtain evidence relevant to the Group audit.
- What experience does Mac Associates have with the laws and regulations in the countries in which the Group operates?

You can see that it is not a straightforward decision for Mac Associates. The Group audit could be a lucrative audit engagement, but dealing with a number of different audit firms in so many countries could prove to be logistically challenging. In addition, the extent of reliance on other audit firms makes the audit engagement potentially a very high-risk audit, which is another reason why the engagement may be declined.

22.2.2 **Understanding component auditors**

The group auditor should obtain an understanding of component auditors, which is particularly important when the component auditor is responsible for material components of the group or where the group auditor requests the component auditor to perform some work on the individual financial statements of the component. In practice, the matters that would be considered in obtaining an understanding of component auditors would include:

- Whether the component auditor understands and will comply with the ethical requirements that are relevant to the group audit and, in particular, is independent.
- The component auditor's professional competence.
- Whether the group engagement team will be able to be involved in the work of the component auditor to the extent necessary to obtain sufficient appropriate audit evidence.
- Whether the component auditor operates in a regulatory environment that actively oversees auditors.

Activity 22.2 Understanding component auditors

Assuming that a group auditor is planning to request the component auditor to perform some work on the component's financial information, how do you think the group auditor can obtain the necessary understanding about the component auditor?

If the group auditor has concerns over any of these matters relating to the component auditor (e.g. that they are not sufficiently independent), then the group auditor should not request the component auditor to perform work relevant to the group audit, and should obtain evidence using alternative means (e.g. by using members of the group audit team).

22.2.3 **International audits**

A group may have a subsidiary, or multiple subsidiaries, which are located overseas, and this may cause the group auditor some logistical problems (Figure 22.3).

- The subsidiary may be in a jurisdiction which creates differences between the local audit and the requirements of the ISAs (UK). This may give rise to the need to request the component auditor to carry out additional procedures to comply with the requirements of the ISAs (UK), for example, local audit regulations may have a different way to determine materiality, different requirements for performing audit risk assessment, different forms of audit opinion.

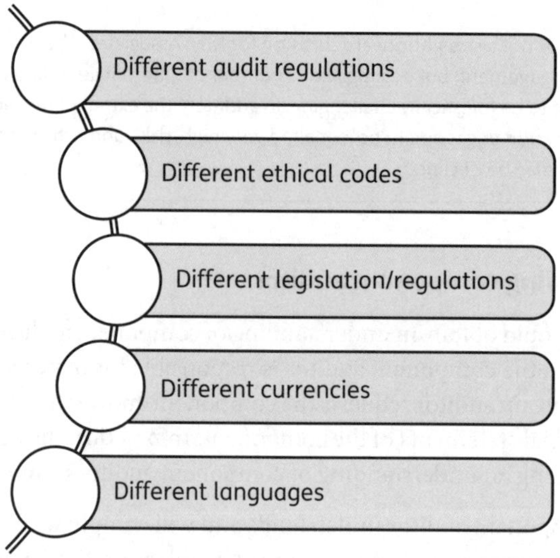

Figure 22.3 Complications in international audits

- There could be a different ethical code for auditors which may have different requirements to the UK Ethical Standard, for example, there may be different requirements on audit firm and key audit partner rotation, fee dependency, and the provision of non-audit services to audit clients.
- The financial statements may have been prepared to different regulations (e.g. companies legislation), and may have different formats or notes to the financial statements.
- If the financial statements of the subsidiary are prepared in a local currency, these will need to be translated to be included in the consolidated financial statements of the group. This creates additional work to be performed on the translation process to ensure the component's financial statements have been translated correctly.
- Language barriers may have a detrimental impact on the ability of the group auditor to obtain sufficient appropriate audit evidence.

In practice, where a parent has an overseas subsidiary which is material to the group, the group auditor will take account of these factors during the pre-acceptance process when determining whether to accept the audit engagement.

22.3 Communication

In a group audit, there must be effective communication between the group audit engagement team and the component auditors. ISA (UK) 600 requires the group audit team to communicate its requirements to the component auditor on a timely basis.[4] This will include the work to be performed by the component auditor and the form and content of the

[4] Ibid., para 31.

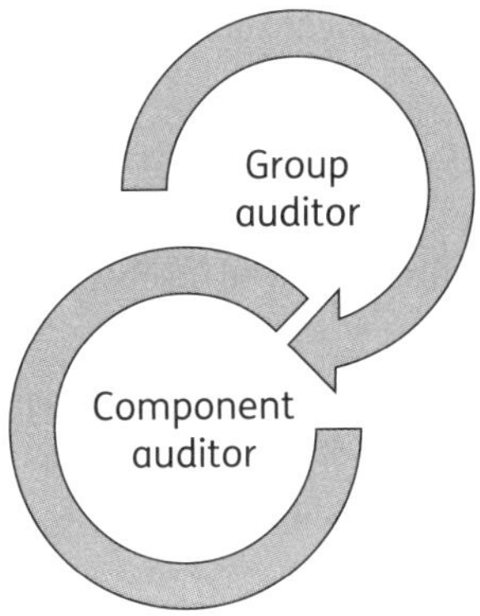

Figure 22.4 Two-way communication in a group audit

information to be provided by the component auditor to the group auditor. Effective communication is critical throughout the course of the audit—if communication is weak, there is a risk that key information is missed meaning that audit risk increases.

Remember, it is the group auditor who is responsible for the audit opinion on the consolidated financial statements and hence the group audit engagement team must determine the overall audit strategy and materiality levels and identify key risks of material misstatement. To do this properly, the group audit engagement team must communicate with the component auditors. However, the direction of communication is not one-way; it is a two-way process (Figure 22.4).

22.3.1 **From group auditor to component auditor**

Practical audit planning matters must be communicated to the component auditors in good time. Examples of such matters include:

- the timetable for the audit and deadlines by which the component auditor must provide information to the group auditor;
- dates of planned visits to review component audit work;
- key points of contact;
- specific procedures that are needed at individual component level following completion of the group audit strategy and group audit plan;
- details of subsequent events and going concern reviews to be carried out; and
- information for statutory reporting purposes.

Group auditors must communicate information on a timely basis—particularly where there are any specific deadlines that are imposed by regulatory authorities (such as compliance with Listing Rules). The following non-exhaustive list highlights some of the key issues that the group auditor must agree with the component auditor:

- The work that is to be performed and whether that work can be used by the group audit engagement team.

- The form and content of the component auditor's communication with the group engagement team.
- Confirmation that the component auditor will cooperate with the group audit engagement team.
- Confirmation that ethical requirements will be observed, especially in respect of independence requirements.
- Significant risks of material misstatement of the group financial statements due to fraud or error where these can be identified.
- Component materiality levels and the threshold at which a misstatement could not be regarded as 'clearly trivial'.
- A schedule of related parties that have been prepared by group management together with any other related parties of which the group audit team is aware. Component auditors must inform the group auditor of any related parties that have been discovered which were not previously notified to them by group management or the group audit engagement team.

22.3.2 **From component auditor to group auditor**

Practical matters which the component auditor will communicate to the group auditor include information that is required for the consolidation, such as intra-group transactions, balances, and information which may be relevant for the consolidated financial statements, but not necessarily the component's individual financial statements.

The component auditors should acknowledge receipt and understanding of group audit instructions which should be in writing. In addition, various other matters must be communicated to the group audit engagement team and group audit engagement partner including the following non-exhaustive list:

- Confirmation that the component auditor has complied with all ethical requirements, including independence and professional competence.
- Confirmation that the component auditor can comply with the group engagement team's instructions and carry out the required work.
- Information concerning instances of non-compliance with laws and regulations which could give rise to a material misstatement in the group accounts.
- A schedule of uncorrected misstatements at the component (generally this does not need to include misstatements which are below the threshold for clearly trivial misstatements).
- Significant deficiencies in the system of internal control at the component.
- Significant matters which the component auditor has, or will, communicate to those charged with governance which must include fraud, employees who have significant roles in internal control at the component or others where fraud has resulted in a material misstatement of the financial statements of the component.
- Indicators of potential management bias.
- Any other matters which may be relevant to the group audit.
- The component auditor's overall findings, conclusions, or opinion.

Communication may not be a straightforward issue within a group audit. A particular problem arises in an international audit scenario, when the group auditor should bear in mind that the component auditors may not be able to speak the language of the group auditor, making it difficult to communicate effectively. The component auditor may not fully understand the instructions given to them by the group auditor or to respond clearly to them.

Activity 22.3 Communication difficulties

What measures do you think can be put in place to resolve communication difficulties in a multinational group audit scenario?

22.4 Planning the group audit

22.4.1 Risk assessment

Once the group auditor has gone through the acceptance protocol, the next task is to plan the group audit. When formulating the audit strategy and plan, the group auditor needs to have a good understanding of the structure of the group, the significance of each component of the group, the mechanics of the consolidation process, and the risk of material misstatement presented by each of the company's financial statements.

Planning a group audit is inherently more complex than planning an audit of an individual entity because there are more factors to consider. At the outset, it is worth noting that it is the responsibility of the group auditor to develop the overall audit strategy and audit plan to audit the group accounts. The group auditor cannot rely on the work of component auditors for 'group level' issues (e.g. fair value adjustments required on consolidation), because the component auditor will not consider group-level issues as part of the audit of the individual component of the group.

ISA (UK) 600 requires the group auditor to identify and assess the risks of material misstatement by developing understanding of the group, its components, and their environments, including group-wide controls. In many ways, this is very similar to how an auditor would plan a single company audit—using business knowledge and understanding to evaluate inherent risks and control risks (Figure 22.5). One issue particular to group audit is that IAS (UK) 600 requires the group auditor to obtain an understanding of the consolidation process, including the instructions issued by group management to components.

Planning a group audit can be quite challenging, depending on the size and complexity of the group. In particular, the group auditor must consider:

- The size and geographical spread of each component within the group.
- The existence and effectiveness of group-wide controls, such as:
  - use of an internal audit function across the group;
  - regular meetings between management teams of the group and components where performance is discussed;

— reviews of financial information at group level;
— whether the group financial reporting system is centralized or not;
— consideration of the group's risk assessment processes;
— the results of previous tests of controls carried out at group level; and
— the group's fraud prevention strategy.

- Existence of processes for dealing with group-specific balances and transactions (e.g. identification and elimination of intra-group transactions and balances).
- Whether there have been any problems or history of errors in previous consolidation exercises (which can link into the work on group-wide controls).
- Whether the components of the group use the same accounting reference dates as the parent or whether further consolidation adjustments are needed where coterminous reporting dates are not used (e.g. some group companies have a financial year end 31 December, others use 31 March).
- Consistency of accounting policies (e.g. some group companies report using IFRS as the applicable financial reporting framework, while other group companies use US GAAP).

ISA (UK) 600 requires the group auditor to assess the risks of material misstatement of the group financial statements whether due to fraud or error.[5] As part of this assessment, the group auditor must carry out an evaluation as to how much work should be carried out by each component auditor or by the group engagement team. If a component has a sound system of internal control, then the group auditor may place reliance on those controls. The main advantage of doing this is that less substantive procedures will need to be carried out which can save time and reduce costs.

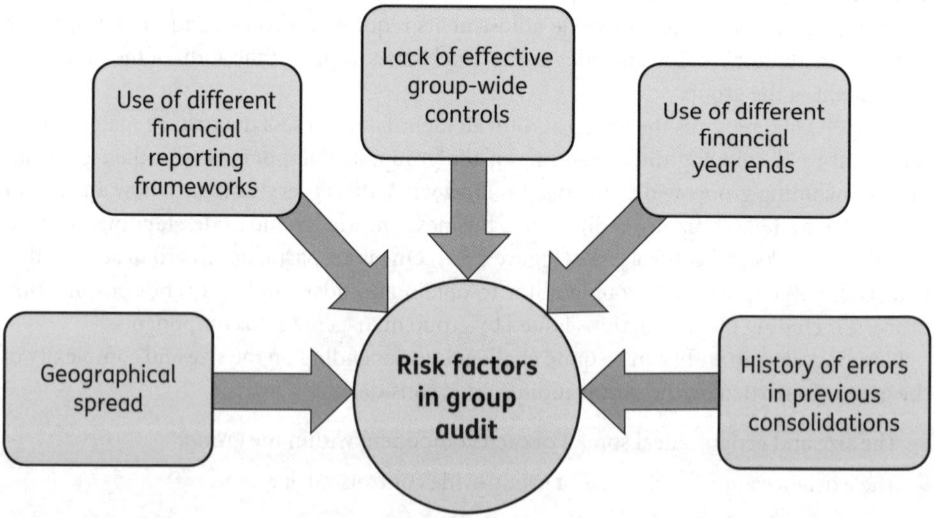

Figure 22.5 Examples of risks in a group audit

[5] Ibid., para 31(b).

Auditing scenario 22.2 Individual subsidiary with deficiencies in internal controls

The group auditor of the Holding Group is planning the audit for the year ended 31 December 20X9. Last year's group audit revealed significant deficiencies in the system of internal control of Subco Ltd, one of five material subsidiaries of the group.

Weaknesses in the system of internal control included:

- a lack of segregation of duties in the payroll department;
- control account write-offs without any investigation as to the imbalances;
- no restricted access to financial reporting systems (i.e. all staff within the subsidiary could access the accounting system);
- the company's finance director lacked knowledge of up-to-date accounting standards resulting in the financial statements needing material adjustments to avoid a modified opinion; and
- no authorization process for major items of expenditure (such as capital items).

Last year's auditor's opinion for Subco Ltd was unmodified but only because significant and material adjustments had to be put through to correct the financial statements as a result of the audit. The group auditor's opinion was also unmodified last year.

Although last year's auditor's opinion on both the component and the group financial statements was unmodified, there is a risk of material misstatement in the current year's audit due to the significant problems encountered last year.

The group auditor would therefore design additional substantive procedures to be carried out either by the group engagement team or by the component auditors on Subco Ltd's financial statements for the year ended 31 December 20X9. While the system of internal control would be tested to see if any improvements had been made since the prior year, reliance on the system of internal control could not be placed and a more substantive audit would be needed given last year's difficulties.

In this example, Subco Ltd was deemed a 'material component' hence further audit procedures would need to be performed to obtain sufficient appropriate audit evidence. However, if the component is not material to the group, the group auditor can perform a minimal amount of audit work which may just consist of analytical procedures at group level. The expectation would be that the results of the analytical procedures should corroborate the group auditor's conclusions that there are no significant risks of material misstatement of the financial information of components. Remember, analytical procedures do not reveal material misstatements on their own.

Sometimes, having performed analytical procedures and having assessed group-wide controls and the consolidation process, the group auditor may consider that more audit evidence is needed. This may happen, for example, if the results of the analytical procedures contradict other evidence that the group auditor has obtained. In this case, ISA (UK) 600 requires the group auditor to perform more audit work, which may include an audit of specific balances, transactions or disclosures, or a more detailed review of the component's financial information using a lower level of materiality. This additional work may be performed by the group audit team or by the component auditor.

In practical terms, the group auditor would usually meet with the component auditor of a material component of the group, to discuss the company being audited and its environment. The group auditor may also be involved in the work of the component auditor in other ways (e.g. review the audit strategy and audit plan, designing audit procedures, and taking part in meetings, e.g. the audit closing meeting between the component auditor and component management).

22.4.2 **Materiality of the group and components**

We looked at materiality in Chapter 10 in the context of a single company. ISA (UK) 600 contains specific requirements regarding materiality in a group audit. The group auditor is required to determine:

- Materiality for the group financial statements as a whole.
- Component performance materiality—this is the materiality for components where audit procedures are performed on financial information that is disaggregated. The component performance materiality amount may be different for each component. Also, the component performance materiality amount for an individual component need not be an arithmetical portion of the group performance materiality, and, consequently, the aggregate of component performance materiality amounts may exceed group performance materiality.[6]
- A threshold above which misstatements cannot be regarded as clearly trivial to the group financial statements.

Group materiality should be higher than the materiality levels set for each individual component of the group. The reason for this is to reduce the risk of material misstatement in the group accounts. It would not be appropriate to have group materiality lower than a significant component and this will effectively increase audit risk.

Auditing scenario 22.3 Group and component materiality

The auditor of the Garage Group, which has three subsidiaries, has determined that materiality for the Group financial statements is £12,000.

The auditor needs to determine component materiality, which does not have to be 'allocated' equally between the three subsidiary companies (i.e. £4,000 per subsidiary). If one of the subsidiaries has particular risk factors, such as deficient internal controls or a history of material misstatements, then that subsidiary could have a lower level of component performance materiality than the other subsidiaries.

Remember that materiality is a wholly judgemental issue and there is no prescribed method for calculating materiality (although as we examined in Chapter 10, benchmarks such as 1–2 per cent of revenue, 5–10 per cent of profit before tax, and 1–2 per cent of total assets are often used, but only as a guide). Remember, the higher the risk of material misstatement, the lower the level of materiality must be. If the group audit engagement team set materiality levels too high in a group audit which contains higher risks of material misstatement, this increases audit risk.

[6] Ibid., para A116.

22.5 Obtaining audit evidence

ISA (UK) 600 requires the group auditor to take responsibility for designing and performing further audit procedures to respond to the assessed risks of material misstatement of the group financial statements arising from the consolidation process (Figure 22.6), including:

(a) Evaluating whether all entities and business units have been included in the group financial statements as required by the applicable financial reporting framework and, if applicable, for designing and performing further audit procedures on sub-consolidations;

(b) Evaluating the appropriateness, completeness and accuracy of consolidation adjustments and reclassifications;

(c) Evaluating whether management's judgments made in the consolidation process give rise to indicators of possible management bias; and

(d) Responding to assessed risks of material misstatement due to fraud arising from the consolidation process.[7]

We will now consider the ways in which the group auditor can obtain evidence in response to risks identified.

22.5.1 Auditing the consolidation

As we mentioned earlier in the chapter, the group audit engagement team must obtain an understanding of the group-wide controls and the consolidation process and assess their effectiveness. This will involve the group audit engagement team carrying out tests of controls to assess if they are operating as expected. If they are operating as expected, the group audit engagement team may place reliance on them, which can help reduce the level of substantive testing. Tests of controls may also be necessary where substantive procedures alone are not capable of providing sufficient appropriate audit evidence at the assertion level.

Standardized audit programmes will often be used by the group audit engagement team; however, these must be tailored so that some procedures are client-specific and respond to the assessed levels of the risk of material misstatement arising from the consolidation

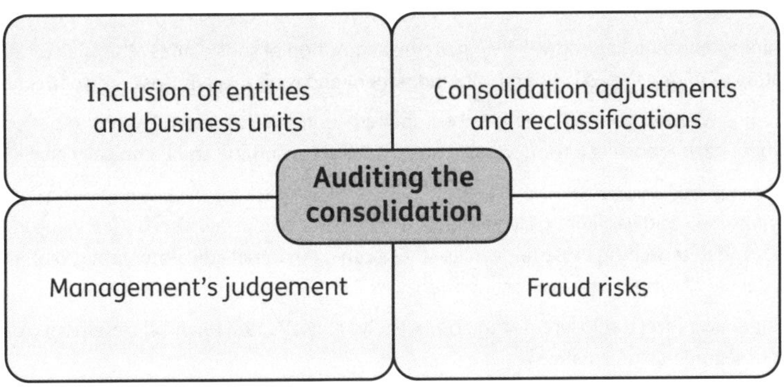

Figure 22.6 Responding to assessed risks of material misstatement

[7] Ibid., para 38.

process. For example, if the group-wide controls are assessed as poor by the auditor, this will create a higher risk of material misstatement than if they were operating effectively. To address this risk, the group engagement team would move away from reliance on the control environment and would carry out more substantive procedures on the consolidation process. Remember, substantive procedures test for misstatement, whereas tests of control focus on the operating effectiveness of the controls rather than a specific monetary amount in the group accounts.

During the audit of the consolidation, the group auditor may test the operating effectiveness of controls by reviewing exception reports, making inquiries of group management as to any problems that were encountered during the consolidation, or using test data to assess the effectiveness of the control process.

In practice, a detailed consolidation schedule will be maintained by the parent entity, and this should be reviewed in detail by the group auditor to identify any omissions or misstatements which may have arisen.

Auditing in practice 22.1 Consolidation

The consolidation of group companies will be performed by group management. In simple terms, this means obtaining the individual financial statements of all group companies and combining them together into the group accounts. As part of the consolidation process, a number of adjustments need to be made, and disclosures provided. Examples of areas that will need to be addressed in preparing the group financial statements include (but not limited to):

- Ensuring that the same accounting policies are applied across the group—this means that if individual companies have used different accounting policies (e.g. because they do not use the same financial reporting framework as the rest of the group), the figures need to be adjusted to bring them in line with group accounting policies.
- Eliminating all intra-group balances and transactions (e.g. receivables and payables balances owed between group companies). This applies to trading transactions, any transfers of assets between group companies, and management charges which are often paid from subsidiary companies to the parent company.
- Determining the value of goodwill arising on the acquisition of subsidiaries—this is a complex area of accounting requiring the use of significant judgement and is often a high-risk area of the audit.
- Determining whether goodwill needs to be impaired—under IFRS goodwill needs to be tested for impairment each reporting period, which can be a time-consuming and technically challenging process.
- Identifying assets and liabilities of subsidiaries which need to be recognized at fair value in the group accounts and determining those fair values—these can be material adjustments at group level and a certain degree of subjectivity may be involved.
- Preparing group-level disclosures for the notes to the consolidated financial statements (e.g. in respect of segmental information).

In practical terms, to perform the consolidation, group management will usually issue detailed instructions to the management teams at the group component companies. These instructions specify the financial information of the components that need to be included in the group financial statements and information relevant to the adjustments and further procedures (e.g. goodwill impairment testing) to be performed at group level. The instructions usually include a 'reporting package' which consists of standard formats for providing financial information for incorporation in the group financial statements.

From the group auditor's perspective, they need to obtain an understanding of the group instructions and evaluate whether they are complete and able to capture all of the relevant information that will enable the group management team to perform the consolidation.

If the group instructions are not sufficiently clear or are unlikely to provide the necessary information, the group auditor may consider this to create a risk of material misstatement.

Typical audit procedures which the group audit engagement team will perform over the consolidation include:

- Confirm that figures taken into the consolidation have been accurately extracted from the financial statements of the components and that all components are included.
- Evaluate the classifications of the components of the group—for example, whether the components have been correctly identified and treated as subsidiaries, associates, or joint ventures.
- Review the disclosures necessary in the group financial statements, such as related party transactions and non-controlling interests.
- Investigate the treatment of any components which have a different financial year end or accounting policies from those of the rest of the group.
- Reconcile group equity including retained earnings.
- Gather evidence appropriate to the specific consolidation adjustments made necessary by financial reporting standards, including, for example:
  - the calculation of goodwill and its impairment review;
  - cancellation of intra-group balances and transactions;
  - provision for unrealized profits as a result of intra-group transactions;
  - fair value adjustments needed for assets and liabilities held by the component; and
  - retranslation of financial statements of components denominated in a foreign currency.
- Obtain intra-group balances (e.g. trade and sundry receivables and/or trade and sundry payables) and agree these to the individual receivables and payables ledgers.
- If the group has intra-group loans among subsidiaries, agree these to any supporting documentation (e.g. loan terms) and agree a sample of transactions.
- Obtain direct confirmation from group members concerning any intra-group balances; whether these arise from direct trading or from loan transactions.
- If considered appropriate, contact the component auditors directly and ask for confirmation of balances from components and discuss their knowledge of related party transactions to identify any undisclosed related parties.

- Where intra-group loans have been entered into, ensure that amounts included in the calculation of the closing balance comply with the requirements of the financial reporting framework (e.g. use of an effective interest rate under IFRS 9 Financial Instruments).
- Ensure that no netting-off has taken place between intra-group receivables and payables.
- Where group balances have been outstanding for a long period of time, assess recoverability as this may indicate an impairment issue at parent or subsidiary level.
- Inquire of management of any security that has been pledged for intra-group loans and review any associated disclosures in the financial statements for adequacy.
- If management charges are incurred within the group, agree the terms of these and determine whether they are concluded under normal market conditions (i.e. on an arm's-length basis).
- Where there are any loss-making subsidiaries in the group, consider the carrying amount of the subsidiary in the parent's individual financial statements as the fact they are making losses may indicate the need for an impairment write-down.
- Where a subsidiary is loss-making, consider the need for a 'support letter' or 'letter of comfort' from the parent.
- For loss-making subsidiaries, ensure any support granted from a third party (e.g. the parent) is realistic and that the supporter can provide the necessary support to enable the loss-making subsidiary to be regarded as a going concern.
- Review fair value adjustments carried out at the date of acquisition (e.g. in respect of property, plant, and equipment) and ensure these have been correctly calculated and agree the fair values to supporting documentation.

In respect of intra-group balances and transactions, detailed work is required, including:

- Obtain or prepare reconciliations of intra-group transactions and balances and ensure these have been correctly eliminated in the consolidated financial statements. This will include:
  - intra-group sales, purchases, receivables, and payables;
  - intra-group transfers of property, plant, and equipment;
  - intra-group finance costs and finance income and associated loans receivable and payable;
  - management recharges; and
  - unrealized profits in inventory.

Auditing scenario 22.4 Classification of group investments

The Raindrop Group has a number of existing subsidiaries, and this year it has acquired a new investment, a 56 per cent equity shareholding in Storm Ltd. Based on its financial information, the Group auditor has determined that Storm Ltd is material to the Group.

Under the terms of the share purchase, the Group has the right to appoint two directors to the board of Storm Ltd. The other four directors are the original founders of the company, each of whom retains an 11 per cent equity shareholding.

The classification of the investment can create a risk of material misstatement. In this case, just looking at the shareholding, it would appear that Storm Ltd is a subsidiary, because the Group owns a controlling equity shareholding. IFRS 10 states that, 'an investee is a subsidiary where the investor is exposed, or has rights, to variable returns from its involvement with the investee and has the ability to affect those returns through its power over the investee'.

The key issue is whether the Group has power over Storm Ltd. The Group can only appoint two out of six board members, so power in terms of board decisions remains with the company's four original founders, who may work together to block proposals made by the Group. In addition, the original founders collectively hold 44 per cent of the company's equity shares, which may be enough to block certain shareholders' resolutions.

Due to these factors, it may be more appropriate to classify Storm Ltd as an associate of the Group, as it seems that the Group can exercise a significant influence rather than control. Should Storm Ltd be consolidated inappropriately as a subsidiary, the Group accounts would contain at least a material misstatement, and possibly the impact of the inappropriate consolidation could be pervasive to the Group accounts.

Auditing scenario 22.5 Intra-group transactions

The Link Group has a range of operations, including processing agricultural products to manufacture paper and textiles. The Group has a number of subsidiaries, many of which trade with each other, supplying products to be processed by a different subsidiary.

The Group auditor, Richards and Co, which audits all components of the Group, has identified that one subsidiary, Chain Ltd, has made sales to another subsidiary, Bolt Ltd, in the last week of the financial year. Chain Ltd has recognized revenue of £55 million in respect of these sales, on which it generates 15 per cent gross margin. However, Bolt Ltd did not receive the inventory until the first week of the next financial year, and has therefore not recorded the purchase or included the inventory within its financial statements.

In this situation, from the Group perspective, the intra-group transaction that has been recorded correctly in the individual financial statements of Chain Ltd needs to be eliminated as part of the consolidation process. As it stands, should no adjustments be made, Group revenue, gross profit and receivables are overstated because the transaction recorded by Chain Ltd needs to be eliminated—assuming that it is material to the Group financial statements.

A further issue is that Group inventory is understated because the goods are in transit at the year end and not recorded in the individual financial statements of any component company.

The Group auditor should obtain evidence around this issue, which should include:

- Confirm the details of the intra-group transaction to documentation including the sales invoice, goods despatch notes raised at Chain Ltd, dated before the year end.
- The 15 per cent gross margin should be confirmed to production records and management accounts at Chain Ltd.

Based on this evidence the Group auditor should discuss the necessary adjustments required to eliminate the intra-group transaction from the consolidated financial statements.

22.5.2 **Analytical procedures**

To quickly recap: analytical procedures look at the relationships and trends between certain figures. This is useful to the auditor because they can quickly identify whether any fluctuations between figures and/or ratios indicate a risk of misstatement. For example, if the gross profit margin in the current year is 40 per cent but last year it was 25 per cent, the auditor would need to corroborate the reasons for such an increase (especially as in most companies and groups, the gross profit margin is expected to remain relatively consistent from one reporting period to the next).

For components which are judged as being immaterial, analytical procedures may be performed by the group audit engagement team *as a minimum*. Even though the component may be deemed as being immaterial, this does not mean the group auditor can completely ignore it.

Analytical procedures which may be applied over intra-group balances and transactions include:

- Reviewing the number and size of intra-group balances and comparing these to the prior year and investigating any significant variations. The group auditor can also use their knowledge and understanding of the group to assess current-year expectations.
- If management charges have been levied across the group (for example because one group member performs administrative functions for another group member), the group auditor can compare the value of these in the current year against the prior year or against the auditor's knowledge and investigate any significant variations.

Analytical procedures which may be applied over the consolidation process include:

- Where unrealized profits exist (e.g. in inventory), assess the value of these against the prior year and/or the auditor's knowledge and expectations and investigate any significant variations.
- Perform a proof-in-total (i.e. a 'reasonableness test') on the depreciation or payroll expenses and identify any misstatement between the auditor's expected charge and the charge per the group accounts.
- Review the level of non-controlling against the auditor's expectations.

22.5.3 **Audit of goodwill**

The audit of goodwill can be one of the most challenging aspects of a group audit. The detail of the financial reporting requirements is outside the scope of our discussion, but put simply, when the cost of an investment in a subsidiary exceeds the fair value of the net assets acquired, positive goodwill is recognized as an intangible asset at group level. Conversely, but this is very rare in practice, when the fair value of net assets acquired exceeds the amount paid, this gives rise to a 'bargain' purchase and negative goodwill arises.

The determination of goodwill is difficult in many situations for the following reasons:

- The cost of the investment may not be as straightforward as cash being paid at the date of acquisition. If there is a deferred element to the consideration (this just means what is being paid) this needs to be recorded at present value. Any contingent consideration (i.e. an amount which may or may not be paid), depending on certain future events, should be recognized at fair value, based on the probability of payment. All this brings an element of subjectivity to the calculation, and the auditor may need to challenge the assumptions made by management.

- The net assets acquired need to be measured at fair value—this again introduces some subjectivity and it may be necessary for an expert to assist the auditor in obtaining evidence.
- In addition, the group may need to recognize assets and liabilities which are not recognized in the individual financial statements of the acquired company. This is because IFRS 3 *Business Combinations* requires the group to recognize identifiable assets and liabilities (e.g. contingent liabilities), even if they are not included in the individual financial statements.
- Where a non-controlling interest is present, there are different ways that this can be measured for the purpose of goodwill calculation—at fair value or using the proportion of net assets method.

Auditing scenario 22.6 Goodwill

The Tester Group acquired 75 per cent of the equity share capital of Nonstop Ltd on 1 December 20X4. The Group management team determined the goodwill arising on the acquisition to be £17 million, as follows:

	£ million
Cash paid on 1 December 20X4	60
Contingent consideration–to be paid on 1 December 20X7 if Nonstop Ltd reaches revenue growth of 5% per annum	25
Total consideration	85
Fair value of non-controlling interest	15
	100
Less: Fair value of identifiable net assets acquired–including a fair value adjustment of £5 million to recognize an internally generated brand name	(83)
Goodwill	**17**

The Group auditor should consider the following issues with respect to the goodwill.

The terms and conditions of the acquisition should be confirmed by reference to the legal documentation supporting the acquisition, including the percentage shareholding acquired, the details of the cash and contingent consideration–the date it is potentially payable, and the factors on which payment depends.

The cash paid is relatively low risk as it can be agreed to the acquiring company's cash book and bank statement.

For the contingent consideration, the auditor should consider the requirements of IFRS 3–contingent consideration is recognized at fair value at the time of the business combination, involving an evaluation of the probability of payment. The contingent consideration should also be discounted to present value as required by IFRS 3. The group auditor will need to carefully evaluate how management arrived at the £25 million value for contingent consideration, assessing the likelihood of payment and the other relevant assumptions used by management.

The non-controlling interest has been measured at fair value. The group auditor needs to establish how management has determined this fair value. If Nonstop Ltd were a listed company, then the market value of its shares at the date of acquisition can be used and this is a reliable measurement. However, Nonstop Ltd appears to be non-listed so management should have estimated the fair value in line with IFRS 13 *Fair Value Measurement*. This introduces subjectivity into the measurement and the method of determining fair value must be clearly understood by the auditor.

The net assets acquired should be all identifiable assets and liabilities at the date of acquisition. This is usually determined by an independent due diligence expert. There is a risk that not all acquired assets and liabilities have been identified, or that they have not been appropriately measured at fair value, which would lead to over or understatement of goodwill and incomplete recording of assets and liabilities in the group financial statements.

The fair value adjustment made in respect of Nonstop Ltd's brand name should be justified by group management. The group auditor should obtain documentation supporting the existence of the brand name, and how the £5 million valuation for it has been determined. This is another area of subjectivity and should be approached with professional scepticism.

We have seen that goodwill is a difficult balance to audit when it is initially determined and recognized in the first year that a new subsidiary is included in the group consolidation. In subsequent years, goodwill continues to be a challenging area of financial reporting and audit because according to IAS 36 *Impairment of Assets*, goodwill should be tested for impairment annually and not written off by way of amortization.

Goodwill impairment testing is another technically challenging aspect of group accounting, and it can also be very subjective, as impairment tests are usually based on cash flow forecasts. Management determines the inputs to the impairment testing model, and auditors need to approach this with a healthy degree of professional scepticism, as even small changes in the assumptions can change the decision as to whether goodwill needs to be impaired or not, and if impairment is necessary, how much should be recognized.

For these reasons, there is an inherent audit risk that goodwill could be overstated, and expenses understated, if any necessary impairment loss is not correctly determined and recognized.

Auditing in practice 22.2 Goodwill impairment and professional scepticism

Regulators frequently state that auditors fail to sufficiently challenge management, with implications for the quality of audit. In November 2020, the Financial Reporting Council (FRC) issued their annual Developments in Audit report, in which they outlined the results of their audit quality inspections for that year.

One of the key issues noted by the FRC in their audit inspections was that in many cases, auditors failed to sufficiently challenge management and that auditors often have an unconscious bias towards corroborating management's assumptions, such as the assumptions used to underpin impairment testing. The report contains an example illustrating how an audit team did not conduct a thorough audit of management's goodwill impairment assessment because the team:

- did not interrogate the data provided by management in support of their impairment assessment;
- over-relied on management representations as a source of audit evidence; and
- did not assess whether the forecasts produced by management were realistic and achievable.

In the investigations into the collapse of some companies, such as Carillion and Thomas Cook, and the role of the external auditors of these companies, goodwill impairment is highlighted. The investigators accuse the audit firms of not challenging why goodwill has not been impaired when there are indications that it should be, for example, due to loss-making business divisions to which the goodwill is attached.

In December 2021, the FRC announced that group audits and impairment of assets were both areas of focus in the next round of audit quality inspections. The FRC hoped to see improvements in the quality of audit of goodwill impairments and in particular, more robust challenges of management regarding the assumptions used in forecasts.

22.5.4 **Additional procedures**

Depending on the size and complexity of the group, the group engagement team can undertake additional procedures to obtain sufficient appropriate audit evidence as follows:

- Where the parent has disposed of subsidiaries during the year, recalculate the gain or loss on disposal and agree to the general ledger, trial balance, and financial statements. Agree disposal proceeds to supporting documentation, such as the cash book and bank statement and ensure any related goodwill is removed.
- For acquisitions of further ownership interest in a subsidiary during the reporting period, ensure that such transactions are accounted for correctly.
- Review questionnaires regarding internal controls and consider whether the responses give rise to a potential risk of material misstatement at group level.
- Select a sample of subsidiaries' individual financial statements and review these against budgeted information for that subsidiary. Inquire of management and investigate any significant variations.
- Obtain details of the group structure at the reporting date and consider whether all components have been included in the consolidation. For any subsidiaries not included in the consolidation, inquire of management as to the reasons why and confirm this is acceptable.
- Where individual components' financial statements are prepared on a different basis than the group (e.g. different year ends and different accounting policies), ensure adequate consolidation adjustments have been made and test these consolidation adjustments for accuracy.
- Obtain the working papers for all components and ensure that the work is done in accordance with the instructions from the group audit engagement partner and sufficient appropriate audit evidence has been obtained on which the auditor's opinion can be based.

- Ensure that all difficult and contentious matters at component level have been resolved properly and have been adequately documented on the file.
- Ensure that all components in the consolidation are being provided with an unmodified audit opinion. If this is not the case, assess the impact of any modification on the group auditor's opinion for the consolidated financial statements.
- Obtain the consolidation schedule and cast it to confirm accuracy.
- Agree all eliminating journals and reconciliations in respect of intra-group trading and balances to ensure all intra-group matters are eliminated from the consolidation. This will involve obtaining the consolidation schedule and agreeing the elimination process has been carried out correctly.
- Perform subsequent events procedures to identify events at those components which occur between the reporting date and the date of the auditor's report on the group accounts which may require adjustment or disclosure in the consolidated financial statements.
- Ensure documentation in the group audit working papers file includes an analysis of components, and the type of work performed on the financial information.
- Ensure the group audit file contains documentation outlining the communications between the group engagement team and the component auditors concerning the group engagement team's requirements.
- Obtain written representations from group management that the consolidation process is complete, and all applicable subsidiaries have been included in the consolidation.

22.6 Evaluating audit evidence, communicating with group management and the group audit opinion

22.6.1 Evaluating audit evidence

In all audits, the auditor is compelled to obtain sufficient appropriate audit evidence to reduce audit risk to an acceptably low level. Hence, the group engagement team must evaluate whether sufficient appropriate audit evidence has been obtained from the audit procedures performed on the consolidation process as well as the work performed by both the group engagement team and the component auditors.

ISA (UK) 600 requires the group engagement team to carry out a review of the work performed by the component auditor. In practice, this will often be done in conjunction with the group audit engagement partner because it is the engagement partner who is ultimately responsible for the auditor's report in the consolidated financial statements.

If the group engagement team conclude that the work of the component auditor is insufficient, the group engagement team must then determine the additional procedures that are necessary to remedy this situation. In addition, the group engagement team must decide who is to perform these additional procedures (i.e. whether it will be the component auditor or the group engagement team).

In situations where the audit evidence is insufficient and the group engagement team conclude that this is because the component auditor lacks technical ability or knowledge, it would normally be the case that the group engagement team will carry out the required procedures (although the group auditor could decide to outsource these procedures to another audit firm if they considered this appropriate). Doing this aims to minimize the risk of a potential modification to the group auditor's opinion.

In all audits it is more than likely that some misstatements will be found by the audit team and group audits are no different. Misstatements can remain uncorrected without any impact on the audit opinion, but only if those misstatements are immaterial both individually and when aggregated (this is a requirement of ISA (UK) 320 *Materiality in Planning and Performing an Audit*).

It is the responsibility of the group engagement partner to evaluate uncorrected misstatements which have been identified during the group audit and to assess the impact of these misstatements on the auditor's report. Where there have also been limitations of scope (i.e. the auditor has been unable to obtain sufficient appropriate audit evidence) placed on the audit team at either group level or component level, the group engagement partner must assess whether this inability to obtain sufficient appropriate audit evidence will give rise to a modified group auditor's opinion.

22.6.2 **Communicating with group management and those charged with governance**

ISA (UK) 600 requires the group auditor to determine which deficiencies in internal control are to be reported in accordance with ISA (UK) 265 *Communicating Deficiencies in Internal Control to Those Charged with Governance and Management*. The group auditor should consider reporting to group management identified deficiencies in group-wide internal controls and deficiencies in internal control at components that have been identified by either the group auditor or the component auditor. As usual, any frauds or suspicions of fraud should be communicated.

The group auditor should communicate to those charged with governance in accordance with ISA (UK) 260 *Communication with Those Charged with Governance* (see Figure 22.7), and in a group scenario the following matters should be addressed as part of this communication:

(a) An overview of the type of work to be performed at the components of the group and the nature of the group auditor's planned involvement in the work to be performed by component auditors.

(b) Instances when the group auditor's review of the work of a component auditor gave rise to a concern about the quality of that component auditor's work, and how the group auditor addressed that concern.

(c) Any limitations on the scope of the group audit, for example, significant matters related to restrictions on access to people or information.

(d) Fraud or suspected fraud involving group management, component management, employees who have significant roles in the group's system of internal control or others when the fraud resulted in a material misstatement of the group financial statements.[8]

[8] Ibid., para 57.

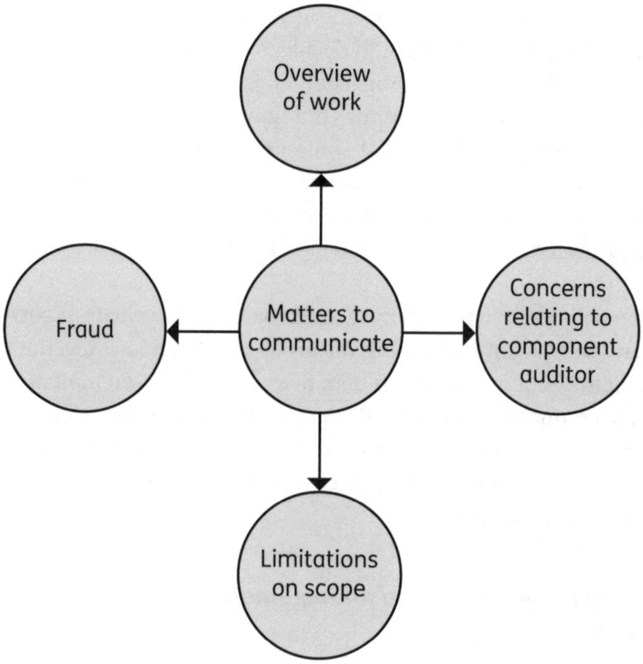

Figure 22.7 Matters to communicate to those charged with governance

22.6.3 **The group auditor's report**

ISA (UK) 600 does not specifically deal with the steps which should be taken by the group auditor in issuing the group audit opinion. Determining the opinion to be given on group financial statements follows the same process as we saw in Chapters 19 and 20, though there are a few particular issues to consider.

The group will normally publish the group financial statements in the same document as the financial statements of the parent company. The group auditor is therefore expressing two separate opinions: one on the entity financial statements of the parent itself and another on the consolidated financial statements of the group. The basis for opinion paragraph should also refer to both the parent company and the group financial statements.

ISA (UK) 700 *Forming an Opinion and Reporting on Financial Statements* contains the following requirements in relation to the description of the auditor's responsibilities in a group audit engagement:

> The group auditor's report shall state that:
>
> - The auditor's responsibilities are to obtain sufficient appropriate audit evidence regarding the financial information of the entities or business activities within the group to express an opinion on the group financial statements;
> - The auditor is responsible for the direction, supervision, and performance of the group audit; and
> - The auditor remains solely responsible for the auditor's opinion.[9]

[9] FRC, 'ISA (UK) 700', 2022, para 39(c).

You can see that ISA (UK) 700 prohibits the group auditor from making any reference to the work of any other experts or auditors, as doing so would diminish the credibility of the audit opinion and allow the group auditor to allow others to take responsibility for part of the audit.

A particular issue that may arise is when the component auditor issues a modified opinion on the financial statements of the component. Should this impact the group auditor's report? The answer simply depends on whether the issue giving rise to the modified opinion in the component is material at group level. For example, if a component has a material misstatement caused by, say, inappropriate inventory valuation, the group auditor would consider whether that misstatement is material to the group financial statements. If it is not, then the group audit opinion is unaffected, and the issue need not be referred to in the group auditor's report.

Activity 22.4 Group audit opinion

Here is a short example of group audit opinion.

Leek Associates is the group auditor of the Flintlock Group. The group auditor has determined group materiality to be £750,000.

The component auditor of one of the group subsidiaries, Tawny Ltd, has issued a modified auditor's report. The component auditor's opinion is qualified as a result of a material misstatement. The amount of the misstatement is £500,000.

What is the implication of this for the group audit opinion?

22.7 Transnational audits and joint audits

22.7.1 Transnational audits

A transnational audit is an audit which may be relied upon in more than one country for the purposes of significant lending, investment, or regulatory decisions. In other words, the audit may be relied upon outside the group's home jurisdiction. A transnational audit can relate to a group or to a single company, but it is more often seen in a group situation.

Auditing scenario 22.7 The Knight Group

The Knight Group is listed on the London stock exchange and the Group has recently obtained a listing on the New York stock exchange. The Group has further planned to become listed on more stock exchanges in Europe and Asia as a means of raising finance.

Because the Group is listed on the stock exchange of two countries, and is planning to raise more finance by obtaining further listings in different countries, the Group is subject to the regulations of all stock exchanges on which it is listed. The audit opinion on the Group financial statements will therefore be used by investors in different countries, making the audit of the Group a transnational audit.

A transnational audit may cause issues for local auditors because there may be some significant differences in legislation and regulation of the audit profession between countries. Issues primarily faced by auditors of transnational audits include:

- The regulation and oversight of auditors may take different forms, and the quality of the audit work may not necessarily be at the same standard as the local auditor, hence there may be inconsistency in audit practice.
- There may be variations in audit quality due to different audit firms using different audit methodologies.
- Corporate governance requirements will be different in other jurisdictions that, for example, in the UK. This will affect listed groups in certain countries (such as the UK) which have transnational audits. Where corporate governance is weak in a certain country, this may lend itself to the potential for poor oversight of directors and poor internal structures (such as a lack of an internal audit function) which will usually lead to a poor system of internal control.
- There may be differences in accounting requirements. However, with increased harmonization to IFRS over recent years, this has become less of a problem. However, if a company is reporting under, say, US GAAP, there are significant differences between that and IFRS.

Auditing in practice 22.3 Forum of Firms and the Transnational Auditors Committee

The Forum of Firms is a membership group established by the International Federation of Accountants (IFAC). Audit firms can join the Forum of Firms if they perform transnational audits or are interested in performing such audits. According to the Forum of Firms:

> The objective of the Forum of Firms (Forum) is to promote consistent and high quality standards of financial reporting and auditing practices worldwide. The Forum brings together firms that perform transnational audits and involves them more closely with the activities of the International Federation of Accountants (IFAC) in audit and other assurance-related areas.[10]

The Forum of Firms plays a role in encouraging audit firms to conduct high-quality international audits by requiring the commitment to comply with certain international standards as a condition of membership. In particular, members commit to maintain quality management issues for audits, use audit methodologies that are in line with ISA requirements and follow the principles of the IESBA International Code of Ethics for Professional Accountants.

The Transnational Audit Committee, which is an executive arm of the Forum of Firms, also supports audit quality by identifying audit practice issues relevant to transnational audits, taking these issues forward to the relevant standard-setting body for discussion, and providing a forum for firms involved with transnational audits to discuss best practices.

[10] 'Forum of Firms—An overview of the roles, responsibilities and activities of the Forum of Firms and TAC', 2019.

22.7.2 **Joint audits**

A joint audit is when two audit firms are appointed to jointly provide an audit opinion on a set of financial statements. This can sometimes happen in group audits, where a component may be audited by both the group auditor and the component auditor. When a joint audit is performed, the two audit firms will work together to plan the audit, gather evidence, review the work done, and to finally provide the opinion.

Auditing scenario 22.8 The Barber Group

The Barber Group is audited by Newhall Associates, which is appointed to audit the consolidated financial statements and to perform the audit of all Group components. The Group has a number of subsidiaries and has recently acquired a new subsidiary, Heather Inc, a foreign subsidiary located in South America. Heather Inc is currently audited by Morgan Philips, a local audit firm based in the same country.

The Group management team are considering appointing both Newhall Associates and Morgan Philips, to jointly audit Heather Inc.

The advantage of a joint audit being performed on Heather Inc is that it is beneficial to retain the involvement of subsidiary's existing audit firm, which will have the knowledge and experience of the company. However, Newhall Associates will benefit from involvement with the audit of Heather Inc so that they can develop knowledge of Heather Inc, and become familiar with the audit methods and procedures used by Morgan Philips. Working with the component auditor will make communication between the two audit firms easier as well as allowing the group auditor to form a view of the competence of Morgan Philips and the quality of their audit work.

Activity 22.5 Problems of joint audit

What do you think might be the problems or difficulties of performing a joint audit? In addition, what problems could there be for the client?

Chapter round-up

- A group is formed when the parent has control over a subsidiary which can usually be achieved with an ownership interest by the parent of more than 50 per cent in the net assets of the subsidiary.
- In a group, the individual subsidiaries' financial statements will be combined with those of the parent to create the consolidated financial statements of the group.
- ISA (UK) 600 requires the group auditor to engage the component auditors and to issue instructions to the component auditors. The component auditors are those who will be auditing the subsidiaries' financial statements for inclusion in the group accounts.
- The group auditor is ultimately responsible for the audit opinion contained in the consolidated financial statements.

- The same acceptance protocol as that for a single company must be followed for a group (e.g. technical competence, available resources) but additional factors will also need to be considered (e.g. location of components and group-wide controls).
- Additional planning considerations will be needed for a group audit as group-wide controls will need to be considered in addition to group members' accounting financial year ends and accounting policies that have been used.
- Group materiality levels should be higher than those of the components to ensure the risk of material misstatement is minimized to an acceptable level at group level.
- Various communications must take place between the group audit engagement team and the component auditors and vice versa.
- The group audit engagement team must carefully audit the consolidation. This will involve a mix of tests of controls and substantive procedures being performed on the consolidation.
- For components which are deemed to be immaterial to the group, the group audit engagement team must carry out analytical procedures as a minimum.
- The group audit engagement partner is responsible to evaluate uncorrected misstatements to determine whether these are immaterial to the group audit.
- International audits may pose specific logistical problems for the group audit engagement team (e.g. the geographic spread or when the individual financial statements of a component are denoted in a foreign currency).
- A transnational audit can also cause specific problems as these are audits which can be relied upon in more than one country.

End of chapter case study

Introduction

This chapter has introduced some of the complexities of auditing in a group environment. Planning a group audit can be particularly challenging, and the group auditors need to develop a very good understanding of the group structure, the activities of components of the group, and the work performed by component auditors. These matters are made more challenging when auditing a multinational group, when the risk of material misstatement is likely to be high and the logistics of managing the audit is made difficult by the presence of foreign companies within the group.

This case study links to the following learning outcomes:

- Identify and explain the matters specific to planning the audit of a group including audit risks and responses to those risks.
- Explain the audit procedures relevant to the consolidation.
- Explain how the group auditor should obtain and evaluate audit evidence specific to group situations.

Scenario

The group structure of the Mixed Nuts Group is presented in Figure 22.8.

Additional notes:

1. The revenue of each of the components is:

Mixed Nuts Ltd	£30 million
Cashewnut SA	£15 million (retranslated from local currency)
Brazilnut Inc	£10 million (retranslated from local currency)
Peanut Farmers	£8 million (retranslated from local currency)

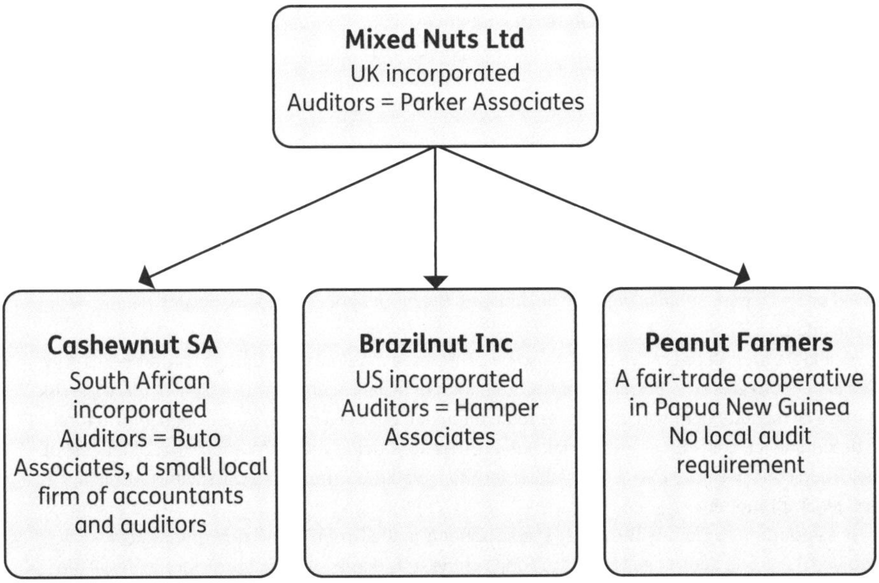

Figure 22.8 Group structure of the Mixed Nuts Group

2. Mixed Nuts Ltd is a company that provides nuts to manufacturers of processed foods, such as breakfast cereals, confectionery, and ready-made curry sauces. It buys nuts as a raw material and processes them into the format required by customers. Mixed Nuts Ltd has been trading successfully for twelve years with steady growth in revenue. The accounting year end is 31 March to coincide with the tax year end.
3. Cashewnut SA was acquired two years ago. Mixed Nuts holds 60 per cent of the share capital of Cashewnut SA. It has a 31 March year end. Cashewnut SA sells 75 per cent of its product to Mixed Nuts Ltd. It has recently received bad press due to contamination of a banned chemical pesticide in its cashew nuts. Cashewnut SA is incorporated in South Africa where IFRS is mandated as the applicable financial reporting framework.
4. Brazilnut Inc is based in the United States and has a 31 January year end. Mixed Nuts Ltd holds 65 per cent of the equity share capital of the company. Being a relatively small company, the regulations of the state in which Brazilnut Inc is located do not require a full audit of the financial statements to be conducted. Instead, the audit focuses on tax compliance.
5. Peanut Farmers is a new initiative started this year. Mixed Nuts Ltd helps to subsidize the farmers' incomes and puts money back into the local community to help general economic and social development. Peanut Farmers is a cooperative, and because it is not a company there is no local legal requirement for statutory accounts to be filed and audited.
6. In addition to the above, Mixed Nuts Ltd also acquired this year an 80 per cent shareholding in Moody Blues Ltd, a beachwear manufacturing company, an investment made to diversify the activities of the group. As its activities are dissimilar to the rest of the Group, the Finance Director feels that it should not be consolidated into the group accounts at the year end.

Required

Using the group structure and additional notes of information, identify the matters which will impact planning the group audit.

In particular, you should consider:

- Are the companies within the group material components?

- Are there any specific risks of material misstatement?
- What matters should be considered in relation to the component auditors?

Answer

Material components

Using total revenue as a benchmark, Cashewnut SA represents 23.8 per cent and Brazilnut Inc represents 15.9 per cent of group revenue (which is £63m before any intercompany transactions are eliminated—we do not know the value of intercompany transactions for all companies so it is not possible to determine an accurate consolidated revenue figure for the Group as a whole). Based on these percentages, both Cashewnut and Brazilnut appear to be financially material to the group audit.

Peanut farmers cooperative should also be considered material even though it contributes only 12.7 per cent to group revenue. This is because it has unusual circumstances which increase the risk of material misstatement (circumstances to be discussed below). There is not enough information to determine if Moody Blues is material, but its operations being very different to that of the rest of the Group could give risk to risk of misstatement so it would be prudent to classify this subsidiary as a material component.

It is important to identify the material components in the Group as this determines how involved the group auditor will be in the audits of the subsidiaries. In short, the more material the component, the more involvement the Group auditor will have.

Risks of material misstatement

Foreign exchange

For all of the foreign subsidiaries, a risk of material misstatement arises due to the fact that their individual financial statements need to be translated from local currency into the currency of the parent company. There is a risk that incorrect exchange rates have been used or that exchange gains and losses have not been recognized appropriately in the consolidation.

Goodwill

In a Group, goodwill is almost always classified as high risk of material misstatement. This is because the determination of goodwill can be complex and involved judgement calls, for example, in relation to fair value adjustments or contingent consideration. In addition, goodwill must be tested for impairment every year and this process is also very judgemental. Group management may have an incentive not to impair goodwill—to avoid the expense in the Group financial statements—therefore the auditor should always be sceptical when reviewing management's accounting treatment of goodwill.

The following looks at each subsidiary in turn.

Cashewnut SA

Risks of material misstatement arise in relation to the consolidation of intercompany transactions which need to be eliminated at Group level. The Group auditor will need to obtain evidence that the cancellation has taken place and may also instruct the component auditor to obtain evidence on how they have been accounted for in Cashewnut individual financial statements. If intercompany transactions are not cancelled out there is a risk that sales, purchases, receivables, and payables in the Group accounts are all overstated. In addition, if any provisions for unrealized profit are not recognized, inventory and profit will be overstated.

The bad press indicates that a provision or liability may be needed in Cashewnut's financial statements. The group auditor should ask the component auditor how they have audited the provision and can ask to look at the evidence which supports the accounting treatment. We are not provided with any figures, so we can't determine whether the provision would be material in the subsidiary's individual financial statements or at Group level. The Group auditor will need to obtain information to make this assessment.

The fact that Cashewnut uses IFRS reduces the risk of material misstatement at Group.

Brazilnut Inc

This company has a different year end to the rest of the Group. Under IFRS it is allowed to consolidate financial statements with different year ends as long as they are not more than three months different. However, it is not common to consolidate companies with different year ends because it becomes very difficult to cancel out intercompany balances. Usually, the year end of the subsidiary will be changed so that it coincides with the rest of the Group.

If the year end stays at 31 January for Brazilnut, the Group auditor will need to plan how to obtain assurance over the accounting in February and March, as these months have not been audited. The Group auditor can ask the component auditor to audit these months in addition to auditing the financial statements up to 31 January. Alternatively, the Group auditor could perform their own audit procedures.

An additional risk arises for Brazilnut because this subsidiary uses US GAAP as its financial reporting framework. The financial statements will need to be aligned from US GAAP to IFRS prior to consolidation and the Group auditor will need to perform audit procedures on the changes that have been made. This can be extremely complex and requires a skilled auditor who is technically competent in both IFRS and US GAAP to understand the adjustments that would be required.

In addition, the audit that has been performed on Brazilnut has a different purpose from an audit of financial statements, as it focused on tax compliance. The Group auditor needs to ask the component auditor about the scope of the audit that was conducted and the way that the audit was planned and performed. The audit is unlikely to comply with ISA requirements, and there is a risk that the figures being consolidated from the accounts of Brazilnut have not been sufficiently verified.

To cover all of these issues, the Group auditor should meet with the component auditor to discuss where additional work may be necessary, and may ask to review the audit files of the component auditor. The Group auditor should also confirm the nature of the opinion that was given on the financial statements, as it is unlikely to be a 'true and fair' opinion. In the worst-case scenario, the whole audit of Brazilnut may need to be reperformed by the Group auditor. or performed by an alternative audit firm.

Peanut Farmers

This is extremely high risk. There are no statutory accounts and no audit requirement. The Group auditor would have no assurance at all that the figures feeding into the consolidation are correct. The Group auditor needs to ask the Group's management team to ensure that proper accounts are prepared and that some kind of audit or limited assurance review takes place. The Group auditor could probably be appointed as the auditor of Peanut Farmers, this would not be a statutory audit, as this is not required, but an audit of financial information just for the purpose of reducing risk at Group audit level. Alternatively, a local firm could provide the necessary assurance, in which case the Group auditor would need to carefully evaluate the regulations under which the firm is operating, and the competence and independence of the firm. There may be language problems so the Group auditor may need to engage a translator to ensure they understand the content of the financial information provided by the cooperative.

Papua New Guinea, where this cooperative is located, may not use IFRS as the applicable financial reporting framework for non-listed companies or have a strong regulatory environment. The Group auditor will need to consider these matters as they contribute to risk. In addition, the fact that £8m revenue has been generated in the first year of existence seems suspicious and the Group auditor should investigate the sources of income and how the revenue figure has been determined.

Finally, it is not even clear whether this cooperative needs to be consolidated. There is no shareholding, it is not a company, and it is not clear how the Group exercises control over its operations. All we know is that the Group subsidizes its activities. Whether this conveys control is not clear. It might be that the Group exercises some influence, but not control, in which case the cooperative should be treated as an associate in the Group accounts. Perhaps the Group is keen to consolidate due to the £8 million increase in Group revenue which arises from consolidation (before any cancellation of intercompany trading).

Moody Blues

We have limited information on this company. However, it does not seem justified that it is not consolidated. IFRS 3 requires consolidation of all subsidiaries and dissimilar activities from the rest of the group is not a reason to exclude a subsidiary from consolidation. There is a risk that the Group accounts are incomplete if this company is wrongly excluded.

Therefore, the Group auditor will need to investigate this company fully, and find out who audits the company, as communication will need to be established with the component auditor with a view to assessing whether their work can be relied upon.

Dealing with component auditors

Where Group auditors use the work of other component auditors, the Group auditors must consider the professional competence of the other auditor in the context of the specific assignment. Specifically, the Group auditor will consider whether the component auditor has the necessary skills and technical competence in order to carry out the audit work effectively. Professional qualifications on their own may not necessarily mean that a component auditor has the necessary knowledge or experience required to perform any additional audit work required for the purpose of the Group audit, especially if the component auditor is not used to dealing with Group-related issues such as goodwill, fair values, or intercompany trading.

The Group auditor must perform procedures to conclude whether the work of the other auditor is adequate for the Group auditor's purposes. Factors which the principal auditor needs to address with the other auditor are:

- Independence issues.
- Whether the other auditor will comply with ethical guidelines.
- How the work of the other auditor will be used.
- The accounting and auditing requirements of the component entity—in particular, areas requiring special consideration (key risks, control environment).
- Timescales for performing and completing the work.
- Whether the other auditor has the resources available to enable an effective audit to be carried out.

Activity solutions

Activity 22.1—Component auditors

List as many situations you can think of in which a component of the group could be audited by a different audit firm than the firm appointed as group auditor.

Suggested answer points:

- A group has acquired a new subsidiary in the year and there has not been enough time to remove the incumbent auditor and replace with the group auditor.

- A group has a subsidiary located in a foreign country, and it makes sense for that subsidiary to be audited by a local firm of auditors (e.g. because the local firm is more knowledgeable about local regulations and the business environment).
- A subsidiary could have a very specialized activity, different from the rest of the group, and it makes sense for an audit firm with specialist knowledge to conduct the audit.

Activity 22.2–Understanding component auditors

Assuming that a group auditor is planning to request the component auditor to perform some work on the component's financial information, how do you think the group auditor can obtain the necessary understanding of the component auditor?

Suggested answer points:

- Visit the component auditor to discuss matters as required by ISA (UK) 600.
- Obtain a written confirmation from the component auditor (e.g. to confirm that the component auditor follows the same ethical standards as the rest of the group audit team), to confirm adequacy of resources and the appropriate skills to perform the required audit work.
- Ask the component auditor to complete questionnaires.
- Obtain references or other supporting documentation about the component auditor from their professional body.
- If the group auditor has previous experience with the component auditor, then prior year's working papers, communications with the component auditor can provide useful information

Activity 22.3–Communication difficulties

What measures do you think can be put in place to resolve communication difficulties in a multinational group audit scenario?

Suggested answer points:

In such a situation, the group auditor could consider the following measures to help communication between the two audit teams:

- using translators to assist in meetings;
- inquire whether there are staff at the component auditor who could translate documents when necessary;
- using translators to provide summaries of documents;
- allowing extra time for all of the above to take place.

Activity 22.4–Group audit opinion

Here is a short example of group audit opinion.

Leek Associates is the group auditor of the Flintlock Group. The group auditor has determined group materiality to be £750,000.

The component auditor of one of the group subsidiaries, Tawny Ltd, has issued a modified auditor's report. The component auditor's opinion is qualified as a result of a material misstatement. The amount of the misstatement is £500,000.

What is the implication of this for the group audit opinion?

Suggested answer points:

- If the opinion on a component is modified the group audit opinion is only affected if the matter is material to the group.

- Only a matter which is material in a group context will affect the group audit opinion, and because the issue leading to qualification of Tawny Ltd's audit opinion is not material to the group, the group opinion is not modified.

Activity 22.5–Problems of joint audit

What do you think might be the problems or difficulties of performing a joint audit? In addition, what problems could there be for the client?

Suggested answer points:

Difficulties in performing a joint audit could arise from:

- Coordinating efforts between two audit firms might be challenging, leading to misunderstandings and potentially duplication of effort or gaps in the work performed, especially if there is ambiguity about which firm is responsible for specific audit areas.
- In case of problems in how the audit is conducted, there may be a tendency for audit firms to shift blame onto each other.
- Ensuring a consistent audit approach and methodology across the audit firms may be difficult; audit firms may have different approaches (e.g. in determining materiality or using different audit data analytics tools).
- Joint audits can take longer because of the time involved in coordinating efforts and they can be inefficient.

For the client, there may be problems or disadvantages such as:

- Joint audits can be more expensive than single audits due to the coordination efforts, additional resources, and time required.
- A joint audit can be more expensive for the client, due to it taking longer, as outlined previously.
- Some clients may find it challenging to work with multiple audit firms simultaneously, and it may impact the client–auditor relationships.

23 Non-Audit Engagements

Introduction

In Chapter 1, we looked at what is meant by the terms 'audit' and 'assurance', and we saw that audit is just a specific type of assurance engagement. As a reminder, the International Auditing and Assurance Standards Board (IAASB) defines an 'assurance engagement' as:

> An engagement in which a practitioner expresses a conclusion designed to enhance the degree of confidence of the intended users other than the responsible party about the outcome of the evaluation or measurement of a subject matter against criteria.[1]

Remember that an audit engagement provides reasonable assurance on historical financial statements. A limited assurance engagement, on the other hand, does not go into as much detail as a reasonable assurance engagement and hence the practitioner does not express an 'opinion', but instead forms a conclusion, based on performing a limited range of procedures to obtain evidence. Assurance can be provided on financial and non-financial information. There is currently an increasing demand for firms to provide assurance on sustainability reports and similar information published by companies. Firms can also be engaged to report on business issues such as internal controls or risk management.

In addition to review or limited assurance engagements, firms of auditors can be asked to perform engagements which do not result in any opinion or conclusion being reached. These engagements could include compilations, where the firm is requested to prepare information for the client, and due diligence, which is basically a fact-finding exercise conducted on a target company which is being considered for acquisition by the client.

[1] International Federation of Accountants, 'International framework for assurance engagements', 2005, para 7 <https://www.ifac.org/_flysystem/azure-private/publications/files/B002%202013%20IAASB%20Handbook%20Framework.pdf> (accessed 22 January 2024).

Learning outcomes

- Explain the framework for assurance engagements and explain the level of assurance provided in non-audit engagements.
- Explain the nature and purpose of different types of limited assurance engagements that a firm may be asked to conduct.
- Explain the nature and purpose of different types of non-assurance engagements that a firm may be asked to conduct.

By the end of this chapter, you will be able to:

- Consider and evaluate the matters to be considered by an audit firm when accepting an assurance or non-assurance engagement.
- Plan an assurance or non-assurance engagement, including recommending appropriate procedures to obtain relevant information and evidence.

23.1 The framework for assurance engagements

23.1.1 Elements of an assurance engagement

The IAASB first published the International Framework for Assurance Engagements (the framework) in 2004. The framework sets out high-level principles which apply to all assurance engagements (including audit engagements). The key issue is that in an external assurance engagement, five elements must be present:

- A three-party relationship involving a practitioner, a responsible party, and intended users.
- An appropriate subject matter.
- Suitable criteria.
- Sufficient and appropriate evidence.
- A conclusion or opinion, expressed in a written report appropriate to a reasonable assurance engagement or a limited assurance engagement.[2]

Let's use an example to illustrate these five elements. A company may be looking to raise finance and approaches its bank to see if they are willing to advance a loan. The bank is likely to ask the company to provide cash flow and profit forecasts, which they will then evaluate as part of its lending decision. The bank may require assurance on the forecasts, to enhance the credibility of the financial information. To provide this assurance, the company engages an external firm of auditors to perform procedures on the forecast, obtain evidence, and report a conclusion (Figure 23.1).

In this situation, the elements are as follows:

- The three-party relationship is between the company (the responsible party), the bank (the intended user), and the audit firm (the practitioner).

[2] Ibid., para 20.

- The cash flow and profit forecasts are the subject matter.
- The suitable criteria are the benchmarks used by the practitioner to evaluate the forecasts (e.g. the use of appropriate assumptions and whether appropriate accounting treatments have been applied).
- The evidence obtained by the practitioner will be obtained in a similar way than in an audit, with the use of materiality, identifying risks of misstatement in the financial information, performing procedures, and reviewing the results to ensure that sufficient and appropriate evidence is obtained.
- The conclusion or opinion is reported by the practitioner, based on the results of the evidence obtained.

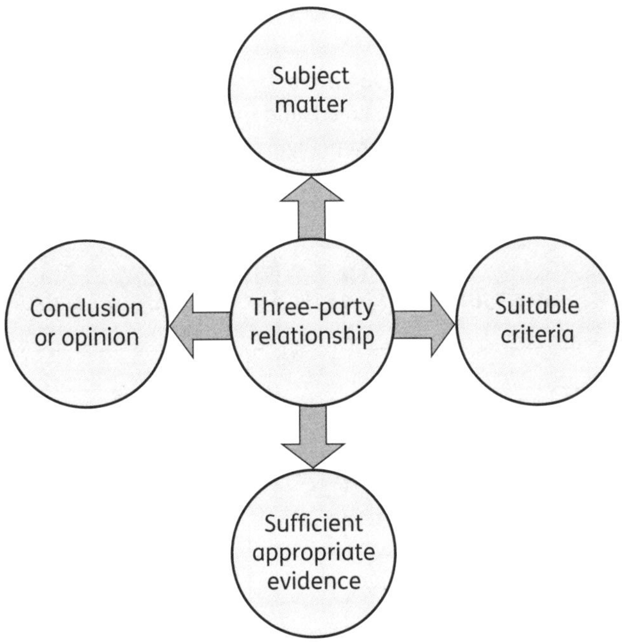

Figure 23.1 Elements of an assurance engagement

Activity 23.1 Subject matter

What do you think could be examples of the subject matter of an assurance engagement? Remember it can be anything over which an intended user requires assurance. Think of as many examples as you can.

There are many types of assurance engagements that are commonly performed. In the next part of this chapter, we will look at some examples but do bear in mind that these are just illustrations of the wide variety of assurance engagements that can take place.

It is also worth remembering that firms conducting assurance engagements must comply with ISQM (UK) 1 *Quality Management for Firms that Perform Audits or Reviews of Financial Statements, or Other Assurance or Related Services Engagements*, and the IESBA *Code of Ethics for Professional Accountants*, which must also be complied with as they apply to all assurance engagements.

23.1.2 **Levels of assurance**

In practice, there are two levels of assurance that can be provided:

- Reasonable assurance—the level of assurance given is high, and is a positive expression of opinion.
- Limited assurance engagements—the level of assurance is limited or moderate, and is often termed 'negative assurance'.

Clients might not understand the difference between the levels of assurance provided so it is important that this is discussed and agreed, and that the level of assurance for an engagement is confirmed in the engagement letter (Figure 23.2).

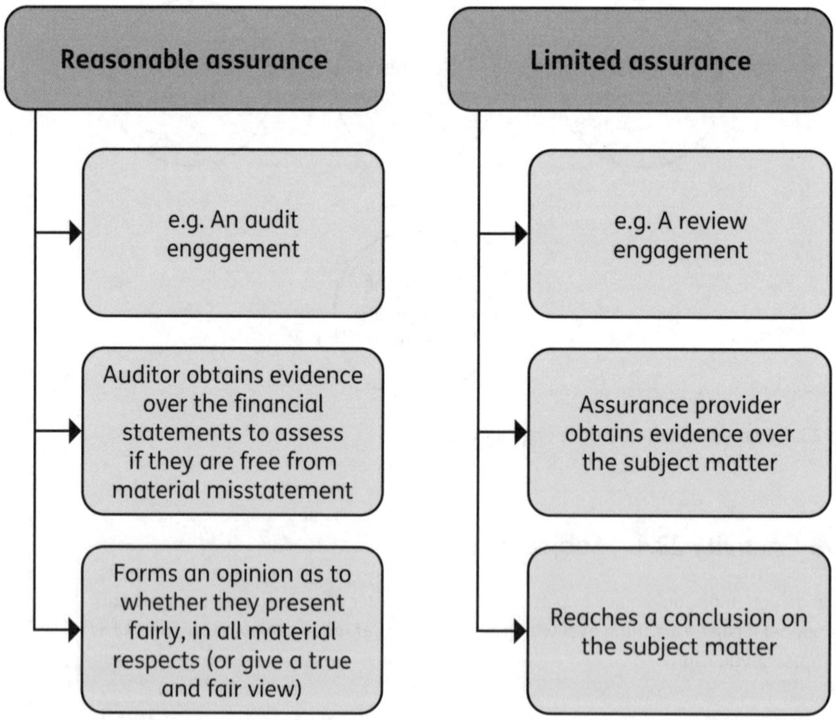

Figure 23.2 Different levels of assurance

To provide guidance on performing non-audit engagements, the IAASB has issued a number of standards:

- International Standards on Review Engagements
- International Standards on Assurance Engagements
- International Standards on Related Services.

While we will refer to some of these standards in our discussions, the detail of them is outside the scope of this book. In the UK, only one of these standards (ISAE 3000 International Standard on Assurance Engagements) has been adopted for use.

23.2 Limited assurance or review engagements

23.2.1 Characteristics of a limited assurance or review engagement

A review engagement is an example of a limited assurance engagement. A limited assurance engagement is not as in-depth as an audit and hence the practitioner does **not** express an opinion. Remember, an 'opinion' provides a reasonable level of assurance; in a limited assurance engagement, the same level of work as that required in an audit will not have been carried out and so the practitioner cannot express an opinion. Instead, they express a 'conclusion'.

When carrying out a limited assurance engagement, the practitioner will:

- Collate sufficient appropriate evidence to enable them to draw limited conclusions.
- Perform significantly fewer procedures which will mainly consist of inquiry and analytical procedures.
- Conclude that the subject matter is plausible in the circumstances, having regard to the identified criteria on which the conclusion is to be made.
- Provide a negatively worded assurance conclusion.

In Chapter 19 we explained how an unmodified auditor's report is worded. Such a report is *positively* worded:

> In our opinion, the financial statements present fairly, in all material respects.

In a limited assurance engagement, the practitioner's conclusion must be negatively worded:

> Nothing has come to our attention that causes us to believe that the financial statements of Byrne Ltd for the year ended 31 December 20X9 are not prepared, in all material respects, in accordance with the applicable financial reporting framework.

Table 23.1 distinguishes between a **reasonable assurance engagement** and a **limited assurance engagement**:

Table 23.1 Comparison of reasonable assurance and limited assurance engagements

Reasonable assurance engagement	Limited assurance engagement
Sufficient appropriate evidence is gathered to draw reasonable conclusions	Sufficient appropriate evidence is gathered to draw limited conclusions
A conclusion is drawn that the subject matter complies in all material respects with identified suitable criteria	A conclusion is drawn that the subject matter is plausible in the circumstances and complies to identified suitable criteria
Rigorous procedures are carried out to obtain sufficient appropriate evidence such as tests of controls and substantive procedures	Significantly fewer procedures are carried out which mainly consist of inquiry and analytical procedures
A positively worded assurance opinion is expressed	A negatively worded assurance conclusion is expressed
A reasonable (high) level of assurance is provided	A lower level of assurance is provided

Practitioners can provide limited assurance on a wide range of subject matters. We are going to illustrate the range of activities by considering four types of engagement which are common in practice (Figure 23.3).

23.2.2 **Limited assurance on historical financial information**

A limited assurance engagement on historical financial statements is increasingly being used by smaller companies as an alternative to the statutory audit. In the UK, it is quite common for a limited review of financial statements for companies below the audit exemption threshold—think of this like a 'mini' audit. These limited assurance engagements do not give the same level of assurance as a 'full' audit, but instead give a lower level of assurance based on more limited procedures than are required with a statutory audit.

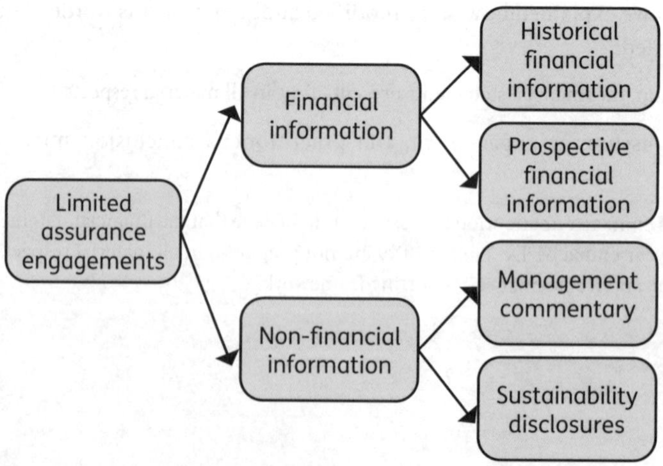

Figure 23.3 Examples of limited assurance engagements

The assurance that is provided is known as 'negative assurance' with the wording of the assurance provider's conclusion being typically as follows:

> Based on our review, nothing has come to our attention to indicate that the accompanying financial statements contain material misstatement.

Activity 23.2 Benefits of a limited assurance review

What do you think are the benefits to a small company which is exempt from statutory audit of having a limited assurance review of its financial statements?

The IAASB has issued ISRE 2400 *Engagements to Review Historical Financial Statements* which deals with this type of engagement. ISRE 2400 states that:

> In a review of financial statements, the practitioner expresses a conclusion that is designed to enhance the degree of confidence of intended users regarding the preparation of an entity's financial statements in accordance with an applicable financial reporting framework. The practitioner's conclusion is based on the practitioner obtaining limited assurance. The practitioner's report includes a description of the nature of a review engagement as context for the readers of the report to be able to understand the conclusion.[3]

To reach their conclusion on the financial statements, the assurance provider will mainly obtain evidence using analytical procedures and inquiry. If there is a potential material misstatement, additional procedures are performed to enable a conclusion to be reached. ISRE 2400 also requires the assurance provider to confirm that management is aware of its responsibilities for producing the accounts.

The report would usually be issued to the company directors, rather than the shareholders, because it is the directors who have appointed the firm to perform the limited review of the financial statements.

23.2.3 **Limited assurance on prospective financial information**

Specific guidance is given by the IAASB in ISAE 3400 *The Examination of Prospective Financial Information*. The standard defines prospective financial information (PFI) as 'financial information based on assumptions about events that may occur in the future and possible actions by an entity'.[4]

PFI is based on assumptions about future events and ISAE 3400 identifies two types of PFI:

- Forecast—this is based on best-estimate assumptions (i.e. events which management expects to take place).
- Projection—this is based on hypothetical assumptions (i.e. less certain than best estimations).

[3] International Federation of Accountants, 'International Standard on Review Engagements 2400 (Revised)', 2013, para 6 <https://www.ifac.org/_flysystem/azure-private/publications/files/B012%202013%20IAASB%20Handbook%20ISRE%202400%20(Revised).pdf> (accessed 22 January 2024).

[4] ISAE 3400, para 3.

Activity 23.3 Types of PFI

Companies produce different types of forecasts and projections. Note down as many as you can.

ISAE 3400 recognizes that, because PFI relates to events and actions that have not yet occurred and may not occur, PFI work is highly subjective in its nature, and its preparation requires the exercise of considerable judgement.

ISAE 3400 requires that before accepting a PFI engagement, the terms of the engagement must be agreed on and sufficient knowledge of the business should be obtained. The period of time covered by the PFI should be clarified, which could be a forecast (usually a period of up to 12 months) and/or a projection (usually up to five years).

ISAE 3400 also requires that written representations should be requested from management regarding the intended use of the PFI, the completeness of significant management assumptions, and management's acceptance of its responsibility for the PFI. The assurance report should make it clear that management is responsible for the PFI and also the assumptions on which it is based. Given the subjective and speculative nature of the PFI, an opinion cannot be given on whether the results shown in the report will be achieved, so only negative assurance can be given.

The assurance provider should plan their work to obtain sufficient and appropriate evidence to support their conclusion. ISAE 3400 specifies that the assurance provider should obtain evidence as to whether:

- Management's best-estimate assumptions on which the prospective financial information is based are not unreasonable and, in the case of hypothetical assumptions, such assumptions are consistent with the purpose of the information;
- The prospective financial information is properly prepared on the basis of the assumptions;
- The prospective financial information is properly presented, and all material assumptions are adequately disclosed, including a clear indication as to whether they are best-estimate assumptions or hypothetical assumptions; and
- The prospective financial information is prepared on a consistent basis with historical financial statements, using appropriate accounting principles.[5]

ISAE 3400 also requires that the assurance provider obtains a sufficient level of knowledge about the business to be able to evaluate the assumptions that underpin the PFI.

Auditing scenario 23.1 Review of PFI

Horton Ltd is a book and magazine publisher. The company is planning to invest £90,000 in developing a digital publishing division, and the finance director has prepared a profit forecast to be used to support an application to the bank for this finance (Table 23.2).

[5] International Federation of Accountants, 'International Standard on Assurance Engagements 3400', para 2 <https://www.ifac.org/_flysystem/azure-private/publications/files/B006%202013%20IAASB%20Handbook%20ISAE%203400.pdf> (accessed 22 January 2024).

The bank has requested that an external assurance report be provided on the profit forecast. Roe Associates has been engaged to perform this review. Roe Associates does not provide the external audit to Horton Ltd.

Table 23.2

	Forecast profit or loss				
	Six months ended 30.06.X2 £'000	Six months ended 31.12.X2 £'000	Six months ended 30.06.X3 £'000	Six months ended 31.12.X3 £'000	Six months ended 30.6.X4 £'000
Revenue	175	190	216	230	240
Operating expenses	(150)	(170)	(188)	(200)	(205)
Operating profit	25	20	28	30	35
Finance costs	(5)	(5)	(5)	(5)	(5)
Profit before tax	20	15	23	25	30

In this situation, Roe Associates needs to develop a good knowledge of Horton Ltd's business in order to be able to properly evaluate the assumptions on which the profit forecast has been based.

Roe Associates will perform some basic but important procedures, including agreement that the accounting policies used in preparing the forecast are consistent with those used in the company's financial statements and that the policies comply with IFRS. The forecast should be cast to confirm arithmetical accuracy.

Roe Associates should discuss how the forecast has been prepared and should obtain the assumptions that underpin the forecast and evaluate them to ensure that they appear reasonable and are consistent with their knowledge of the business.

Analytical review should be performed to establish the trends in the forecast which can be compared to historic financial information and discussed with management. For example, revenue is forecast to increase by 8.5 per cent in the second six-month period and to continue increasing over the whole period of the forecast. How can management justify this? Can they provide corroborating evidence, for example, marketing plans, customer orders, the results of market research? The operating margin is 14.2 per cent in the first six-month period, falls to 10.5 per cent, then increases to 13 per cent, and reaches 14.5 per cent by the end of the forecast. How can management explain this trend? What are the main categories of operating expenditure and why are they fluctuating over time?

Specific figures included in the forecast should be recalculated (e.g. any depreciation expenses), and some can be agreed to supporting documentation (e.g. the finance costs should be confirmed to loan documentation).

There should also be a review of capital expenditure budgets, cash flow forecasts, and any other information which accompanies the profit forecast, for consistency.

ISAE 3400 provides guidance on the content of an assurance report given when a professional accountant has examined forecasts or projections. The report should include:

1. Title and addressee—
2. Identification of the PFI; this should be by reference to a page number within a business plan, or to the titles of the statements which have been evaluated. There should also be a reference to the period that the PFI covers.

3. A reference to ISAE 3400 or other relevant regulations that are applicable to the examination of PFI; this adds credibility to the report because it has been prepared according to a recognized regulatory statement.
4. A statement that management is responsible for the PFI including the assumptions on which it is based.
5. Where applicable, a reference to the purpose and/or restricted distribution of the PFI. In this case, the report would reference the bank and limit distribution of the report to the bank for the objective of their lending decision.
6. A statement of negative assurance as to whether the assumptions provide a reasonable basis for the PFI. This would typically be stated as follows: 'nothing has come to our attention which causes us to believe that the assumptions do not provide a reasonable basis for the projection . . .'.
7. A statement as to whether the PFI is properly prepared on the basis of the assumptions and is presented in accordance with the relevant financial reporting framework.
8. Appropriate caveats concerning the achievability of the results indicated by the PFI.
9. The date, name of the audit firm, and a signature.

23.2.4 **Limited assurance on management commentary (non-financial information)**

Management commentary or non-financial reporting is an increasingly important topic. It can include information relating to a wide range of aspects of a business including:

- the organization's business model;
- an outline of strategy, key activities, risk profile, and management;
- operating and financial review often focusing on financial performance and position; and
- environmental, social, and governance information.

Non-financial information is often included in the 'front end' of the annual report of large companies, and it can include a broad range of information which is intended to help readers to understand how the organization is managed, its risk factors, and its performance, both financial and non-financial, during the reporting period. In the UK, there are requirements for companies to publish a strategic report and a governance report, which can be long and detailed, covering a wide range of information which is related to, but separate from, the audited financial statements. In Chapter 18, we looked at this in the context of ISA (UK) 720 The Auditor's Responsibilities Relating to Other Information, which requires auditors to read the other information published with the financial statements to consider whether any inconsistencies exist between the 'other information' and the financial statements and auditor's knowledge obtained during the audit.

In some countries, as well as adhering to International Financial Reporting Standards (or national Generally Accepted Accounting Practice) for their financial statements, some companies, particularly large and/or listed companies, are required or encouraged to produce information in line with:

- legislation of the home jurisdiction
- stock exchange listing rules
- Global Reporting Initiative

- Integrated Reporting Framework
- Sustainability Accounting Standards
- Climate Disclosures Standards Board
- Task Force on Climate-Related Disclosures (TCFD)
- indicators and goals based on the United Nations Commission on Sustainable Development

Mechanisms can be put in place to enhance the credibility of non-financial reporting. Stakeholders will benefit from knowing that this information is trustworthy so demonstrating that the information is accurate, complete, and reliable is important.

Auditing in practice 23.1 Assurance on non-financial information in an integrated report

One way in which companies can provide narrative information is by publishing an integrated report. Briefly, integrated reporting is a way for a business to present a holistic view of how its business model creates value over time. There is discussion of the various 'capitals' which flow into the business model, and how these capitals are increased or diminished as a result of business activities. One of the capitals is financial, but the other capitals include intellectual capital, human capital, social and relationship capital, and natural capital. This approach to narrative reporting is becoming 'the norm' in many countries and while obtaining assurance on the information is not mandatory, many companies do obtain independent assurance on at least part of the integrated report, often on the key performance indicators (KPIs) that are included.

The Value Reporting Foundation was consolidated with the IFRS Foundation in 2022 and supports the principle of obtaining independent assurance on integrated reporting. In their 2014 publication, they comment that, 'If providers of financial capital are to trust integrated reports as a key input to their decision making, then those reports need to contain "investment grade" information. Information provided by an organisation without independent assurance of any kind is not likely to achieve this level of credibility and trust.' [6]

Assurance can be provided in several ways. An organization's internal audit team are well placed to provide input into evaluating the appropriateness of existing systems and processes, and the design and implementation of performance measures.

External assurance is also a possibility. An independent assurance provider can be appointed to provide an unbiased conclusion, and the audit firms are used to planning and performing investigative procedures on a range of financial and non-financial information. The assurance provider will only be able to give limited assurance on many of the matters included in a narrative report, due to the subjective and sometimes hypothetical nature of the information.

Assurance could be obtained just on specific parts of the narrative report. Often the KPIs are subject to external scrutiny as these are quantified and therefore more robust evidence can be obtained as to their validity.

Rather than providing assurance on a whole non-financial report (e.g., an integrated report or a strategic review), it is common for assurance to be sought on certain aspects and specified content. Assurance is often given on KPIs that are included within a wide body of management commentary.

[6] IIRC, 'Assurance on <IR>: An introduction to the discussion', 2014 <https://integratedreporting.ifrs.org/wp-content/uploads/2014/07/Assurance-on-IR-an-introduction-to-the-discussion.pdf> (accessed 22 January 2024).

Auditing in practice 23.2 Independent assurance on KPIs

Here is an extract from the independent assurance practitioner's report on selected KPIs of Sappi, a South African company which operates in the wood and pulp industry.

Limited Assurance Conclusion

Based on the procedures we have performed and the evidence we have obtained and subject to the inherent limitations outlined elsewhere in this report, nothing has come to our attention that causes us to believe that the selected KPIs as set out in the Subject Matter paragraph above for the year ended September 2019 are not prepared, in all material respects, in accordance with Sappi's reporting criteria.

The conclusion does not provide a guarantee that the KPIs are complete or accurate—this is a low level of assurance based on obtaining a limited amount of evidence. This does not mean that the conclusion is without value—stakeholders can be assured that independent experts have conducted many relevant procedures. The report outlines the nature of the procedures carried out:

- Interviews of management to obtain an understanding of the internal control environment, risk assessment process, and information systems relevant to the sustainability reporting process.
- Inspection of documentation to corroborate the statements of management in our interviews.
- Inspection of supporting documentation on a sample basis and performed analytical procedures to evaluate the data generation and reporting processes against the reporting criteria.
- Evaluation of the reasonableness and appropriateness of significant estimates and judgements made by the directors in the preparation of the selected KPIs.
- Evaluation of whether the selected KPIs presented in the Report are consistent with our overall knowledge and experience of sustainability management and performance at Sappi.[7]

Stakeholders are able to see that management have been challenged on some important aspects of the KPIs and this should provide some credibility on the metrics disclosed.

23.2.5 **Limited assurance on sustainability disclosures**

Metrics relating to climate change and other matters relating to sustainability have been relevant to corporate reporting for many years, with many organizations having established reporting processes in relation to greenhouse gas emissions, carbon footprint, and other environmental matters. Users of annual reports have become very interested in environmental disclosures, and investors are increasingly calling for companies to report more specifically on climate change. As an example of a relevant reporting framework, the Task Force on Climate-Related Financial Disclosures (TCFD) was founded in 2015 to develop recommendations for voluntary climate-related financial disclosures that are consistent, comparable, reliable, clear, and efficient, and provide decision-useful information to lenders, insurers, and investors.

Governments and regulators are setting out proposals for enhanced sustainability disclosure requirements and it is fair to say that this is a rapidly changing area of corporate reporting. For example, in 2022, the Corporate Sustainability Reporting Directive was approved in

[7] Sappi reports, 'Independent assurance practitioner's report on selected key performance indicators', 2019 <https://sappi-reports.co.za/reports/sappi-gsr-2019/iaud.php> (accessed 22 January 2024).

Europe, and in June 2023, the International Sustainability Standards Board issued two IFRS sustainability disclosure standards:

- IFRS S1 General Requirements for Disclosure of Sustainability-related Financial Information
- IFRS S2 Climate-related Disclosures

The sustainability reporting frameworks, guidelines and regulations are extremely complex and the detail is outside the scope of our discussion. Companies in the oil, gas, and petrol industries generally provide much more comprehensive and extensive social and environmental reports than a company in, say, a service sector. Some environmental reports may describe events which have resulted in the company being fined (e.g. if water pollution has arisen). When such events are disclosed in the company's environmental report, stakeholders would want some assurance that the company has learnt from its mistake so that confidence can be restored. Hence, the report must be balanced—it cannot be biased on positive aspects; negative or potentially threatening aspects must also be included.

Environmental reporting does not necessarily have to take place within the company's annual report. Some companies have stand-alone reports purely dedicated to social and environmental reporting and others have a dedicated page on their websites. Stand-alone reports are becoming more common simply because of the cost involved in producing these sorts of reports because of the varying levels of detail and quality of information which they need to contain.

Auditing in practice 23.3 Climate-related KPIs

To illustrate, the metrics in Table 23.3 are disclosed by Land Securities Group plc in the 2019 annual report.[8]

Table 23.3

Climate-related financial metrics

	2018–19	2017–18	Change
	£m	£m	
Capital expenditure on low-carbon equipment and products	4	5	(1)
Avoided energy consumption costs measured against 2013/14 baseline	4	3	1
Forecast increase in energy costs resulting from climate change by 2100	1	1	0
Insured value of assets exposed to possible significant increase in river flood risk due to climate change by 2100	7	6	1
Insured value of assets exposed to possible significant increase in coastal flood risk due to climate change by 2100	257	281	(24)

Like many companies, Land Securities Group plc provides some climate-related information in its annual report, but publishes a separate sustainability report, which is where the majority of the TCFD are given.

[8] Land Securities Group plc, 'Annual Report 2019' (2019) <https://landsec.com/annual-report-2019> (accessed 22 January 2024).

As with any non-financial information, assurance can be obtained to enhance credibility. Most large audit firms now have specialist departments that can obtain the necessary evidence to reach a conclusion on environmental disclosures.

A particular risk in respect of sustainability disclosure, and a reason for obtaining assurance, is 'greenwashing'. Greenwashing refers to the deceptive or misleading practice of portraying a company's products, policies, or practices as environmentally friendly when, in reality, they are not. It is a strategy employed by businesses to create a false perception that they are committed to sustainability and environmental responsibility, often to appeal to environmentally conscious investors and consumers. Obtaining assurance on sustainability disclosures is a way to hold companies accountable for their environmental disclosures. In 2024, the IAASB issued International Standard on Sustainability Assurance 5000: General Requirements for Sustainability Assurance Engagements. ISSA 5000 is very detailed and is suitable for application in any sustainability assurance engagement. It contains requirements and provides guidance on engagement acceptance, planning, obtaining evidence and forming a conclusion.

Auditing in practice 23.4 Non-authoritative guidance on extended external reporting

In April 2021, the IAASB issued non-authoritative guidance on applying ISAE 3000 to extended external assurance engagements. The guidance was issued as part of a project relating to sustainability, supported by the World Business Council for Sustainable Development. Extended external reporting (EER) can include integrated reports, sustainability reports, and reports focusing on environmental, social, and governance matters.

The IAASB recognized, at the start of the project, that there are an increasing number of companies producing this type of report and obtaining assurance on at least some of the content. There are existing standards that can provide relevant guidance (e.g. ISAE 3000), but the IAASB wanted to look into how this guidance could be enhanced.

As part of their project, the IAASB considered a number of challenges which are often present when assurance providers are engaged to perform this type of work. Challenges can include how to apply materiality, how to identify suitable criteria for evaluating information and how to deal with the future orientation of much of the reported information.

The guidance published in 2021 provides a framework for approaching EER, which suggests that the assurance provider should obtain understanding of:

- the subject matter (e.g. environmental KPIs);
- the framework for reporting (e.g. TCFD); and
- the underpinning system of internal control including the process of preparing the subject matter information.

The guidance is extensive and provides detailed examples relevant to all stages of the EER. Guidance is given on a wide range of matters including evaluating the competence and capabilities required to perform the work, determining the scope of the engagement, considering the relevant internal controls and processes, obtaining evidence, using assertions, and applying materiality, and addressing qualitative and future-oriented information.

Performing this type of assurance engagement is definitely challenging, but by using this guidance, the quality of the work performed will be enhanced, leading to a higher level of credibility for both the assurance report and the subject matter itself.

23.3 Non-assurance engagements

23.3.1 Agreed-upon procedures engagement

In an agreed-upon procedures engagement, the party who engages the practitioner or the intended user will determine the procedures which are to be performed. The practitioner will then provide a report of factual findings following the performance of those procedures.

The key thing to remember where an agreed-upon procedures engagement is concerned is that this is not an assurance engagement, hence no opinion or conclusion is expressed.

In an agreed-upon procedures engagement, the procedures to be carried out are determined by the client or the end user of the report. This means that the accountant is merely acting on instructions from their client.

ISRS 4400 *Engagements to Perform Agreed-upon Procedures Regarding Financial Information* provides requirements and guidance to practitioners for this type of engagement.

In practice, an agreed-upon procedures engagement will follow a specific process (Figure 23.4).

When the work has been carried out, the report of factual findings will simply recite the agreed procedures. It does not provide any assurance at all. However, it could be the case that the accountant is additionally asked to provide some level of assurance. In such a situation, the assignment becomes an assurance engagement and additional work must be carried out by the accountant.

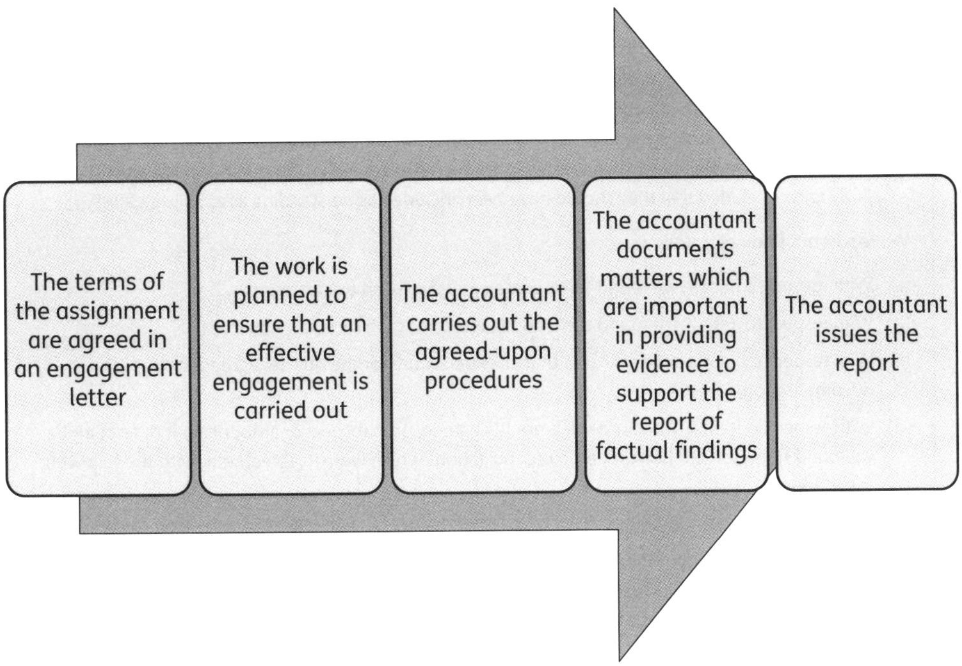

Figure 23.4 Stages of an agreed-upon procedures engagement

Auditing scenario 23.2 Agreed-upon procedures

Harper Arts has agreed to provide a grant to Tennyson Ltd on the basis that the income and expenditure for the quarter ended 30 June 20X9 is correct. Harper Arts has issued Tennyson with a list of procedures that must be carried out by a qualified accountant and then certified by them in a report of factual findings. The procedures are as follows:

1. Agree income for the quarter ended 30 June 20X9 to source documents.
2. Agree income for the quarter ended 30 June 20X9 to cash received.
3. Agree expenditure for the quarter ended 30 June 20X9 to receipts or purchase invoices.
4. Agree a sample of supplier balances as at 30 June 20X9 with supplier statements.

The accountant of Tennyson Ltd has carried out the above procedures and has concluded that everything is in order. The report of factual findings is issued as follows.

Report of factual findings

To Harper Arts

We have performed the procedures agreed with you and reviewed the income and expenditure of Tennyson Ltd for the quarter ended 30 June 20X9 which are set forth in the accompanying schedules. Our engagement was carried out in accordance with International Standard on Related Services 4400 applicable to agreed-upon procedures. The procedures were performed solely to assist you in evaluating the validity of the income and expenditure and are summarized as follows:

(a) We obtained and checked the income for the quarter ended 30 June 20X9 to source documents which comprised of sales invoices.

(b) We compared the income to cash received. This involved tracing the sales invoices paid to bank statements.

(c) We agreed the expenditure for the quarter to purchase invoices and petty cash receipts.

(d) We compared supplier statements to confirm balances owing as at 30 June 20X9. Some of these did not agree and we obtained reconciliations from Tennyson Ltd. In respect of the reconciliations, we identified outstanding invoices, credit notes, and outstanding payments. We obtained and examined such invoices and credit notes subsequently received and payments made after 30 June 20X9 and concluded that they should have been included as outstanding as at 30 June 20X9.

We report our findings as follows:

(a) With respect to item 1, we found the income agreed to source documents.

(b) With respect to item 2, we found the income agreed to cash received.

(c) With respect to item 3 we confirmed that all expenditure for the quarter agreed to supporting documentation.

(d) With respect to item 4, we found the amounts agreed, or in respect of amounts that did not agree, we found Tennyson Ltd had prepared reconciliations which were in agreement, with the following exceptions:

[List the exceptions]

As the above procedures do not constitute an audit or a review made in accordance with International Standards on Auditing, or International Standards on Review Engagement, we do not express any assurance on the income and expenditure of Tennyson Ltd for the quarter ended 30 June 20X9.

Had we performed additional procedures, or had we performed an audit or review of the income and expenditure in accordance with International Standards on Auditing or International Standards on Review Engagements, other matters may have come to our attention that would have been reported to you.

Our report is made solely for the purpose set forth in the first paragraph of this report and for your information and is not to be used for any other purpose or distributed to third parties without our express permission. This report relates only to the financial statements and items specified above and does not extend to any financial statements of Tennyson Ltd, taken as a whole.

ABC Accountancy Services Ltd
20 July 20X9

23.3.2 **Due diligence engagements**

In a due diligence engagement, the practitioner is asked to carry out inquiries into specific aspects of another entity's financial statements. This will usually be because the practitioner's client is looking to either buy the business or invest in it. Prior to purchasing or investing in the business, the client will want to know that the business is viable, and find out information relevant to the investment. Essentially, due diligence is a fact-finding exercise, the purpose of which is to ensure that the acquirer has all the necessary facts and that the perceived business opportunities are in fact real. This is important when determining purchase price. Similarly, due diligence can also be requested by sellers (vendor due diligence).

A letter of engagement is issued at the outset by the practitioner which outlines how the engagement will be performed and who the intended user of the report will be.

Auditing scenario 23.3 Due diligence assignment

King Ltd is looking to take over Queen Ltd. Negotiations are at an advanced stage and the professional accountants of King Ltd have been asked to carry out due diligence on Queen Ltd to ensure that all the assets of Queen Ltd do exist and that they have been valued appropriately.

The accountants will be specifically focused on the assets of Queen to ensure that they exist, that they belong to the company and that they are valued appropriately (usually in accordance with the requirements of accounting standards). Once the due diligence work has been completed, the professional accountant will issue a report of their findings, and the takeover will usually not be completed until this report has been issued.

Activity 23.4 Due diligence—fact-finding

Imagine that you are planning to invest a significant amount in a company. You already own a business, and you are hoping to merge the acquired business with your own, in order to expand your operations and customer base.

What information would you be interested in finding out about the target company?

There is no specific IAASB document that deals with due diligence. In fact, due diligence assignments are not always carried out by accountants. They can be carried out by actuaries, surveyors, lawyers, and other professionals who have expertise in the area of interest by the client. In some cases, a due diligence assignment can be carried out by the client themselves, if the management team has the time and expertise to perform the work.

The scope of the engagement will be determined by the client (Figure 23.5), and often includes that the due diligence team will obtain information about a number of issues.

Organizational due diligence—how is the business structured, who are the major shareholders, and what type of governance arrangements are in place? How is risk monitored and managed? Is there an effective internal control framework?

Financial due diligence—investigations into the financial performance and position of the target company, including both historic and PFI. There will be an evaluation of the quality of earnings, the asset base of the business, the level of debt, planned capital expenditure, etc. Often, due diligence can uncover assets and liabilities that are not included in the financial statements (e.g. brand names and contingent assets).

Operational due diligence—focuses on the commercial operations of the business including an evaluation of the business model, resources used, relations with customers and suppliers, and the company's strategy.

Legal due diligence—this part of the due diligence investigation examines contracts such as those relating to loans, leases or rentals of assets, employment, patents and copyrights, and any legal claims relating to the company.

People due diligence—the focus is on the employees and directors of the company, the skills, and talent of the workforce.

Figure 23.5 Scope of due diligence

This is not meant to be an exhaustive list of the areas that can be covered by a due diligence engagement. As mentioned before, the client may have specific interests and request that the due diligence engagement focuses on fact-finding in relation to those issues (e.g. some engagements might focus on the identification and valuation of intangible items such as intellectual property and customer relationships), others look into IT and systems in more detail, and others might emphasize regulatory compliance.

Due diligence will have a future orientation. The acquirers of the target company or business will want to consider the business plan, forecasts, and projections and consider how realistic they are, as well as evaluating how the two businesses can operate successfully under common ownership in the future.

Activity 23.5 Benefits of due diligence

Make brief notes on what you think the main benefits of having due diligence performed on a target company are for the potential acquirer.

International Standard on Related Services (ISRS) 4400 *Engagements to Perform Agreed upon Procedures Regarding Financial Information*, provides relevant, but not mandatory, guidance on reporting the results of agreed-upon procedures including due diligence.

The report of the factual findings of the due diligence engagement should normally contain the following:

- Title and addressee (ordinarily the client who engaged the auditor to perform the agreed-upon procedures).
- Identification of specific financial or non-financial information to which the agreed-upon procedures have been applied.
- A statement that the procedures performed were those agreed upon with the recipient.
- A statement that the engagement was performed in accordance with the International Standard on Related Services.
- Identification of the purpose for which the agreed-upon procedures were performed.
- A listing of the specific procedures performed.
- A description of the auditor's factual findings including sufficient details of errors and exceptions found.
- Statement that the procedures performed do not constitute either an audit or a review, and, as such, no assurance is expressed.
- A statement that the report is restricted to those parties that have agreed to the procedures to be performed.
- A statement (when applicable) that the report relates only to the elements, accounts, items, or financial and non-financial information specified and that it does not extend to the entity's financial statements taken as a whole.

Auditing scenario 23.4 Due diligence

Kilda Ltd is considering the acquisition of the entire share capital of Melbourne Ltd, and the directors of Kilda Ltd have engaged Geelong Associates to perform due diligence on the target company. As part of their work, Geelong Associates has discovered that Melbourne Ltd has five key customers, but one of them is facing going concern issues and is likely to go bankrupt. In addition, Melbourne Ltd has a widely recognized brand name, which is internally generated, and which generates approximately 70 per cent of the company's revenue.

In relation to the customer, Geelong Associates should make further inquiries to establish the potential impact on revenue, should the key customer go bankrupt. This is an important issue because the forecast revenue and cash flows of Melbourne Ltd will be critical in determining the business valuation and in negotiating the consideration to be paid. Losing one out of five key customers could even be a deal-breaker, and Geelong Associates should inquire as to whether this customer can be replaced, to make up the lost revenue. The going concern issues facing this customer should also be investigated, as, if the issues are not isolated, the other customers could also be impacted, which would be a significant problem for Melbourne Ltd.

Regarding the brand name, Geelong Associates should perform further investigations. A key point is that the brand name should be valued, either by Geelong Associates, if they have the necessary expertise, or by brand valuation experts. This could be an extremely valuable asset, which impacts the business valuation. From an accounting perspective, should the acquisition go ahead, and the two companies form a group, when the accounts are consolidated, the brand name should be recognized at fair value. The valuation of the brand is therefore important from a commercial and a technical accounting perspective. The management team at Kilda Ltd may have concerns that 70 per cent of the company's revenue is derived from the sales relating to this brand, as this shows some over-reliance on the brand, and they may wish to consider how this would fit in with the existing product lines of Kilda Ltd.

Geelong Associates will report their factual findings to Kilda Ltd. It is up to the management team at Kilda Ltd to evaluate the report, take the findings into account in deciding whether or not to go ahead with the acquisition and to negotiate the consideration to be paid.

23.3.3 Compilation engagements

This type of engagement is probably the most common type of engagement in practice. In a compilation engagement, the accountant will prepare financial statements (or other forms of financial information) from information and accounting records provided by the client. ISRS 4410 *Engagements to Compile Financial Statements* will apply to such engagements.

In practice, the process as set out in Figure 23.6 will apply.

In a compilation engagement, such as an accounts preparation assignment, the financial statements may contain some form of accountant's report. Unlike an auditor's report on audited financial statements, an accountant's report is not legally required because it is the client who is legally responsible for the financial statements, which will be based on the information and explanations provided to the practitioner from the client. An accountant's report may be required by the practitioner's professional body.

The engagement letter that is issued at the outset of an engagement will make it clear that the accountant is not carrying out any form of audit or assurance work and that

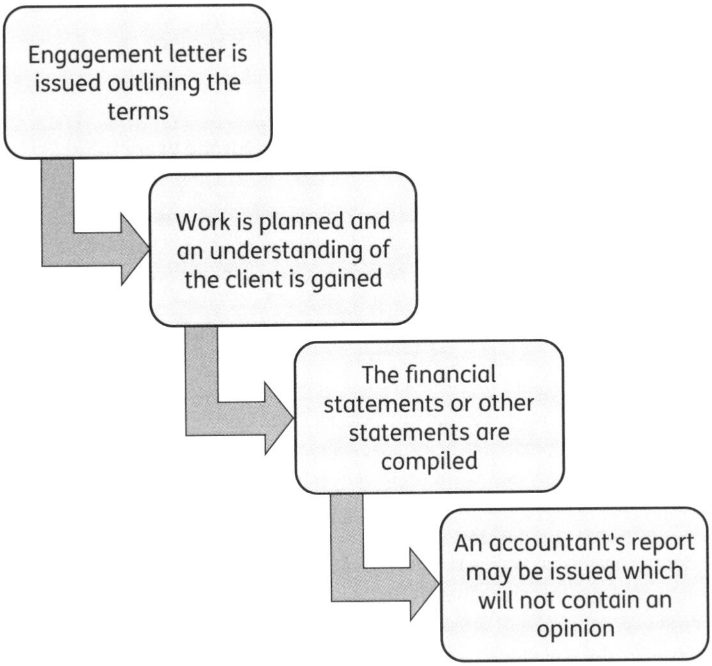

Figure 23.6 Stages of a compilation engagement

management will be responsible for the information produced. Where the work involves preparing financial statements, those financial statements must be prepared using Generally Accepted Accounting Practice (such as IFRS) and relevant legislation (e.g. Companies Act 2006).

In a compilation engagement, the accountant will typically use some form of analytical procedures. For example, when the draft financial statements are completed, the accountant may calculate gross profit margins to ascertain whether there have been any fluctuations in the margins beyond normal expectations. They may also review income and expenditure on a line-by-line basis to request confirmation of any unusual increases or decreases in income and expenditure from the prior year. The purpose of doing this is to make sure that income and expenditure do not contain any errors or mis-postings.

It's important to keep in mind that in a compilation engagement, while no opinion is being expressed by the practitioner and they will be relying on information and explanations provided to them by the client, they must carry out their work with diligence and in accordance with standards. Professional accountants cannot have their name associated with any information which is misleading and hence the professional accountant must question any dubious transactions or information rather than simply relying on it because it has been provided to them by the client.

Auditing scenario 23.5 An accountant's report

A typical accountant's report is as set out below.

Accountant's report to the Directors of Revere Limited for the year ended 31 December 20X9

In order to assist you to fulfil your duties under the Companies Act 2006, we have prepared for your approval the financial statements of Revere Limited for the year ended 31 December 20X9 as set out on pages 2 to 12 from the company's accounting records and from information and explanations you have provided to us.

As a member of [insert relevant professional body], we are subject to its ethical and other professional requirements which are detailed at www.

This report is made solely to the board of directors of Revere Limited, as a body, in accordance with the terms of our engagement letter dated 1 October 20X9. Our work has been undertaken solely to prepare, for your approval, the financial statements of Revere Limited and state those matters that we have agreed to state to the board of directors of Revere Limited, as a body. To the fullest extent permitted by law, we do not accept or assume responsibility to anyone other than Revere Limited and its board of directors as a body for our work or for this report.

It is your duty to ensure that Revere Limited has kept adequate accounting records and to prepare statutory accounts that give a true and fair view of the assets, liabilities, financial position and profit or loss of Revere Limited. You consider that Revere Limited is exempt from the statutory audit requirement for the year ended 31 December 20X9.

We have not been instructed to carry out an audit or a review of the financial statements of Revere Limited. For this reason, we have not verified the accuracy or completeness of the accounting records or information and explanations you have given to us, and we do not, therefore, express any opinion on the statutory accounts.

ABC Accountants Limited
Address
Date

The above report is purely for illustrative purposes and the wording is not specific. Different professional bodies will have different wording depending on their requirements. The key aspects to any sort of accountant's report are that it must:

- Refer to the fact that the information prepared is based on information and explanations provided by the client.
- Confirm that the client is responsible for the financial statements.
- Confirm that the client considers the entity is eligible to claim exemption from audit.
- Confirm that the firm has not been instructed to carry out an audit or review of the financial statements and hence no opinion is expressed.

Chapter round-up

- Firms of auditors and accountants are often engaged to perform non-audit engagements, which can be very wide-ranging in their scope.
- Limited assurance engagements are based on less rigorous procedures compared to an audit of historical financial statements, and provide a lower level of assurance.

- Limited assurance engagements can be performed on historical financial statements, forecast, or projected financial information, or on non-financial information such as KPIs.
- Limited assurance is increasingly provided on sustainability metrics, and this is an area that has recently been the focus of regulatory non-mandatory guidance.
- Agreed-upon procedures engagements, including due diligence engagements, are used to confirm or provide specific information or investigate specific facts, and do result in an opinion being provided.
- Compilation engagements are very common, and often performed for small businesses below the audit threshold, where a firm of accountants prepares financial information and may issue an accompanying report, which does not contain an opinion.

End of chapter case study

Introduction

We have examined a wide range of assurance and non-assurance engagements in this chapter. One type of engagement which is quite common is due diligence—we saw that this is when a company identifies a target company for potential acquisition, and the due diligence engagement provides information about the target company to the potential acquirer.

This case study links to the following learning outcomes:

- Explain the nature and purpose of different types of non-assurance engagements that a firm may be asked to conduct.
- Plan an assurance or non-assurance engagement, including recommending appropriate procedures to obtain relevant information and evidence.

Scenario

You work at Marie & Co, a firm of accountants and auditors, which offers a range of services to its clients. You are currently assigned to work on the Slate Group (the Group), which operates leisure centres across the country. The leisure centres include cinemas, restaurants, and activities including trampolining and indoor rock-climbing facilities.

The Group is looking to acquire a hotel business, and management has identified Lodge Ltd as a potential target for the acquisition. The Group has requested Marie & Co to perform a due diligence review of Lodge Ltd's operations, finances, and any other relevant issues for them to consider. This is the first time that management has considered an externally provided due diligence review.

Today's date is 9 September 20X5. This morning, you attended a meeting with representatives of the Group's management team, who provided you with the following information regarding Lodge Ltd.

- Lodge Ltd is a large, privately owned company. Four members of the company's management team are from the same family, which established the company twenty years ago.
- The company operates the 'Econolodge' chain of budget hotels, with sixty hotels across the country. The hotels are mainly located near airports, train stations, and motorway junctions. Recently, several hotels have been opened in city centres and near to business centres.
- Due to a general economic recession causing a reduction in travel, the company has been operating at its overdraft limit for the last twelve months.

- The company has £2 million debt, which is due for repayment in three years. The debt has associated covenants relating to interest cover and operating profit.
- Last month, Lodge Ltd received a legal claim against the company. The claim alleges that several hotel guests were injured when some light fittings that had not been properly installed fell from the ceiling. The company denies any liability, because the light fittings had been installed by a third party.
- The auditor's report on Lodge Ltd's financial statements for the last financial year to 31 December 20X4 contained an unmodified audit opinion.

You are also provided with the following financial information:

- Statement of profit or loss and statement of financial position—actual to 31 December 20X4 and projected to 31 December 20X5.

Required

- Explain the benefits to the Group management team of engaging Marie & Co to perform a due diligence review on Lodge Ltd.
- Outline the differences in scope between an audit of financial statements and a due diligence review.
- Based on the information that has been provided, suggest further information that should be made available for your due diligence review of Lodge Ltd, and explain the need for the information.

Table 23.5

Statement of financial position	Projected 31 December 20X5 £'000	Actual 31 December 20X4 £'000
Assets		
Non-current assets		
Property, plant, and equipment	47,400	36,090
Intangible assets—development costs	200	-
Total non-current assets	**47,600**	**36,090**
Current assets		
Inventories	5,000	2,000
Trade and other receivables	900	750
Total current assets	**5,900**	**2,750**
Total assets	53,500	38,840
Equity and liabilities		
Equity		
Equity share capital	15,000	13,000
Revaluation reserve	10,000	-
Retained earnings	19,470	15,040
Total equity	**44,470**	**28,040**
Non-current liabilities		
Loans	2,000	2,000

Statement of financial position	Projected 31 December 20X5 £'000	Actual 31 December 20X4 £'000
Current liabilities		
Trade payables	2,820	2,600
Tax payable	1,210	1,500
Overdraft	1,000	300
Provisions	2,000	4,400
Total current liabilities	**7,030**	**8,800**
Total equity and liabilities	**53,500**	**38,840**

Table 23.7

Statement of profit and loss for the year to 31 December	Projected 20X5	Actual 20X4
	£'000	£'000
Revenue	20,700	19,300
Operating expenses	(14,800)	(15,440)
Operating profit	5,900	3,860
Finance costs	(50)	(50)
Profit before tax	5,850	3,810
Tax expense	(210)	(800)
Profit for the year	**5,640**	**3,010**

Answer

Benefits of an externally provided due diligence to the Group management team

Due diligence is essentially a way to reduce the risk of a potential acquisition, by obtaining relevant facts and a target company. Due diligence ensures that the acquiring company has full knowledge of the target company's financial performance and position, strategy and operations, governance structure, legal and tax position, and plans for the future. Due diligence helps identify and assess potential risks associated with the target company. This includes financial risks, legal liabilities, operational issues, regulatory compliance, and any other factors that could impact the business's performance and future prospects.

Due diligence will help the management team of the acquiring company to assess the potential commercial benefits and drawbacks of the acquisition. For example, it could be used to determine potential synergies, and associated costs, of merging the businesses together. There will be a number of acquisition-related costs to consider, such as the costs of reorganization and the potential redundancy payments to staff.

By thoroughly examining the target company's financial statements, contracts, and assets, due diligence aids in determining the company's true value. It ensures that the purchase price reflects an accurate assessment of the business's worth. This means that the Group is in a stronger position to negotiate the terms and conditions of the acquisition.

Due diligence ensures that the acquirer is aware of any potential legal or compliance issues that the target company may be facing. Addressing these issues before completing the acquisition can prevent costly legal problems in the future. This is important for the Group, given the legal claim that has been made against Lodge Ltd.

Due diligence may reveal undisclosed information that the target company may not have willingly shared during initial negotiations. This can include hidden debts, other legal claims, or other factors that could significantly impact the deal.

An externally provided due diligence review, as opposed to a review conducted by management of the Group, will provide objective information. The due diligence team will be experienced in this type of work, which should ensure that high-quality work is performed. This adds credibility to the planned acquisition, which may help secure any finance which is needed to fund the acquisition.

Differences in scope

In a due diligence engagement, the scope of the review will be determined in the terms of the engagement, and it will have a much wider scope than an audit of financial statements. The company requesting the due diligence review will usually require the due diligence team to investigate a broad range of matters and to obtain facts that are relevant to the potential acquisition.

The type of issues that might typically fall under the scope of a due diligence engagement include:

- Identification of assets and liabilities—this is vital to the valuation of the business and for negotiating the consideration to be paid. In some cases, it is intangible or other assets that are not recognized in the company's financial statements which are particularly crucial and often this will be a specific matter outlined in the terms of the engagement.
- Financial issues—the due diligence team will investigate the company's financial position including its liquidity, longer-term solvency, how working capital is managed, past and future planned capital expenditure, how costs are controlled, the drivers of profit and cash generation.
- Operational matters—the acquiring company will need to understand the target company's current business model, including its inputs, processes and outputs and related issues such as research and development, quality control, staff recruitment and training, information systems, and use of technology. Key contracts with customers, suppliers and any other stakeholders should be evaluated.
- Legal and compliance issues—it is important to understand any significant problems the company may have with respect to compliance with relevant laws and regulations.

The type of work performed during a due diligence engagement is different to an audit engagement. Due diligence work relies on inquiry as means of gathering information and analytical procedures will be performed on financial information, past and forecast, to obtain information about financial performance and position. Tests of detail are not performed unless they are specifically requested by the acquiring company, in which case they are likely to focus on a specific issue. This is in contrast to an audit of historical information, where a wide range of tests of control and substantive tests are performed.

Another difference is that due diligence is much more forward-looking than an audit, with much of the financial investigation looking at forecasts of profit, cash flow, and capital expenditure.

Additional information

In relation to the financial information that has been provided:

- A list of the accounting policies that have been used to prepare this information, to confirm the applicable financial reporting framework (IFRS? UK and Ireland GAAP?) and to evaluate the appropriateness of these accounting policies.

- Information on the development costs valued at £200,000—what does this relate to? It is unusual for a hotel company to be capitalizing development costs, so there needs to be some supporting information to indicate the type of asset that is being created by Lodge Ltd. Will this asset be valuable to the Slate Group?
- The inventories are projected to more than double in value over the year, so questions should be asked to management about this trend. What inventory is held? Presumably food and drink—the increase seems very large and could indicate that the assets are overvalued.
- Details relating to the £2 million share issue during the year should be obtained. Who holds these new shares—the existing family members who are the company owners, or outside parties? How much were the shares issued for? What has the cash been spent on? The company has no cash surplus, which seems unusual if £2 million was raised during the year.
- A reconciliation of retained earnings b/d and c/d—the projected profit for the year does not explain the movement in retained earnings, so there could be an accounting error (or a number of errors) in the projections.
- Loan agreements should be obtained so that the terms of the loan can be understood in particular the debt covenants and confirmation of repayment dates and finance charges. How close is the Lodge Ltd to breaching any debt covenants and have they been breached in the past?
- Similar for the overdraft—the terms should be scrutinized, so that there is understanding of interest payments, the extent of the overdraft facility and whether there are penalties for breaching the terms.
- A breakdown of the provisions figure to understand the nature of these uncertain liabilities, what do they relate to? The provisions figure is projected to decrease significantly, the reason for this needs to be understood—has a significant amount been paid in the year to settle a provision?
- Segmental analysis of the revenue and profit made by each hotel, to see which are the most successful, and assess whether the new hotels opened in city centres and near to business parks are making a good return on investment.
- A breakdown of operating expenses to confirm the main categories of costs included and to perform analytical review—this is important as operating expenses is projected to reduce at the same time as revenue is increasing—this variance needs to be understood.
- Correspondence with tax authorities or other supporting documentation for the projected tax expense which looks low when compared with the prior year and with the higher level of projected profit this year.
- In addition to the financial information that has been provided, Marie & Co should request a full set of projected financial information including notes to the financial statements, to allow a more detailed analysis to take place.
- Profit and cash flow forecasts for the next two or three years should also be obtained for analysis and review of underlying assumptions.

Relating to the legal claim against the company:

- The legal correspondence should be obtained for a full understanding of the details (e.g. has a specific financial settlement been claimed?).
- Discuss the legal claim with the company's legal team to understand the likelihood of the claim against Lodge Ltd being successful.

Activity solutions

Activity 23.1—Subject matter

What do you think could be examples of the subject matter of an assurance engagement? Remember it can be anything over which an intended user requires assurance. Think of as many examples as you can.

Suggested answer points:

The subject matter of an assurance engagement can take many forms. The International Framework for Assurance Engagements provides the following categories and examples:

- Financial performance or conditions (e.g. historical or prospective financial position, financial performance, and cash flows) for which the subject matter information may be the recognition, measurement, presentation, and disclosure represented in financial statements.
- Non-financial performance or conditions (e.g. performance of an entity) for which the subject matter information may be key indicators of efficiency and effectiveness.
- Physical characteristics (e.g. capacity of a facility) for which the subject matter information may be a specifications document.
- Systems and processes (e.g. an entity's internal control or IT system) for which the subject matter information may be an assertion about effectiveness.
- Behaviour (e.g. corporate governance, compliance with regulation, human resource practices) for which the subject matter information may be a statement of compliance or a statement of effectiveness.[9]

Activity 23.2—Benefits of a limited assurance review

What do you think are the benefits to a small company which is exempt from statutory audit of having a limited assurance review of its financial statements?

Suggested answer points:

- Increased credibility: a limited assurance review enhances the credibility of the financial statements. While it does not provide the same level of assurance as an audit, it still involves a degree of examination and analytical procedures by a qualified professional.
- Identifying errors and inconsistencies: the review process involves analytical procedures and inquiries, which can help identify errors, inconsistencies, or unusual trends in the financial statements. This helps improve the accuracy and reliability of the information presented.
- Early detection of potential issues: the review process can help in early detection of potential financial problems or issues, allowing management to address them before they escalate into more significant challenges.
- Improved financial reporting: the review engagement often includes recommendations and suggestions for improving financial reporting practices, which can be valuable to the management in ensuring their financial statements are presented in accordance with applicable accounting standards.
- Cost-effectiveness: compared to a full audit, a limited assurance review is generally less time-consuming and expensive. It provides some level of assurance without the same extent of detailed testing required in an audit.

[9] International Federation of Accountants, 'International Framework for Assurance Engagements', 2005, para 31.

- Stakeholder confidence: external stakeholders, such as investors, creditors, suppliers, and customers, may gain confidence in the financial information presented by the entity after knowing that it has undergone a limited assurance review by an independent professional. In turn, the benefit to the company is that it can be easier to raise finance.

Activity 23.3—Types of PFI

Companies produce different types of forecasts and projections. Note down as many as you can.

Suggested answer points:

Companies produce forecasts or projections of:

- cash flow
- profit, and specific elements of profit (e.g. payroll costs)
- financial position
- capital expenditure
- debt or net debt
- non-GAAP performance measures (e.g. EBIT)
- customer numbers or orders

Activity 23.4—Due diligence—fact-finding

Imagine that you are planning to invest a significant amount in a company. You already own a business, and you are hoping to merge the acquired business with your own, in order to expand your operations and customer base.

What information would you be interested in finding out about the target company?

Suggested answer points:

- past levels of profit and cash generation
- forecasts of profit and cash flows
- level of debt and when existing debt is due for repayment
- range and type of products
- the company's business model and operations
- names of the directors and major shareholders
- details of key customers and suppliers
- the regulatory framework in which the company operates
- the geographical spread of the operations
- information on the property, plant, and equipment which is owned or leased
- details of any legal claims outstanding

Activity 23.5—Due diligence—benefits

Make brief notes on what you think the main benefits of having due diligence performed on a target company are, for the potential acquirer.

Suggested answer points:

- Enables the acquirer to evaluate the operational benefits of the acquisition (e.g. will economies of scale be achieved, allow access to new customer markets, bring new skills and talent into the business).
- The due diligence might reveal potential problems (e.g. high levels of debt, old assets that need replacing, legal claims against the company)—which may be 'deal-breakers' or may be issues that the acquirer can resolve.
- Obtaining past financial performance and future projections allows the financial health of the business to be evaluated and this information is often used as part of the business valuation which helps the acquisition price to be determined.
- Identify and value all of the assets and liabilities to be acquired—this is especially important if there are intangible assets that are not recognized in the financial statements and which represent 'hidden value' in the company.
- From a practical point of view, having due diligence is often an essential part of the corporate finance arrangements, should the acquirer need to obtain funding for the consideration to be paid.
- When due diligence is performed by independent experts, their report adds credibility to the due diligence report as well as freeing up management time.

Glossary of Terms

Acceptable level A level at which a professional accountant, using the reasonable and informed third-party test, would likely conclude that a professional accountant complies with the fundamental ethical principles.

Accounting records The records of initial accounting entries and supporting records, such as invoices, contracts, general and subsidiary ledgers, journals and other adjustments to the financial statements that are not reflected in journal entries; and records such as worksheets and spreadsheets supporting cost allocations, computations, reconciliations, and disclosures.

Accounts preparation A responsibility of management involving an accounting system to identify, record, and classify all the transactions and events relating to an entity that occur during a reporting period. To maintain accountability for assets, liabilities, revenues, and expenditures and to convert that data into information in the form of financial statements.

Agreed-upon procedures engagement A non-assurance engagement where the practitioner agrees with the client to undertake procedures agreed by both parties. The practitioner reports the factual findings arising from applying those procedures, but no conclusion is expressed, and no assurance is provided. The users draw their own conclusion and derive assurance from the information provided.

Analytical procedures Evaluations of financial information through analysis of plausible relationships among both financial and non-financial data. Analytical procedures also encompass such investigations as is necessary of identified fluctuations or relationships that are inconsistent with other relevant information or that differ from expected values by a significant amount.

Anomaly/Anomalous error A misstatement or deviation that is demonstrably not representative of misstatements or deviations in a population.

Appropriateness (of audit evidence) The measure of the quality of audit evidence; that is, its relevance and its reliability in providing support for the conclusions on which the auditor's opinion is based.

Assertions Representations by management, explicit or otherwise, that are embodied in the financial statements, and used by the auditor to consider the different types of potential misstatements that may occur.

Assurance An independent professional opinion, the objective of which is to reduce information risk (risk from incorrect information) to users of financial and other information to improve the reliability and credibility of information so that users can make more informed decisions.

Assurance engagement An engagement in which a practitioner aims to obtain sufficient appropriate evidence to express a conclusion designed to enhance the degree of confidence of the intended users other than the responsible party about the outcome of the measurement or evaluation of the underlying subject matter against criteria. The outcome of the measurement or evaluation of an underlying subject matter is the information that results from applying the criteria to the underlying subject matter.

Audit committee A standing committee of the Board of Directors, composed of a majority of independent directors, who oversees the financial reporting and external and internal audit functions within an entity.

Audit evidence Information used by the auditor in arriving at the conclusions on which the auditor's opinion is based. Audit evidence includes both information contained in the accounting records underlying the financial statements and other information. (*See also* **Sufficiency (of audit evidence)** and **Appropriateness (of audit evidence)**)

Audit objective An engagement where the auditor provides reasonable assurance by issuing a positive expression of opinion that enhances the credibility of assertions about a subject matter or directly on the subject matter.

Auditor's legal liability Auditor's legal liability to their clients and third parties arises when auditors fail to exercise professional care and skill in conducting an audit of financial statements. Auditors can be held liable to their clients and third parties under law.

Audit risk The risk that the auditor expresses an inappropriate audit opinion when the financial statements are materially misstated. Audit risk is a function of the risks of material misstatement and detection risk.

Audit sampling (sampling) The application of audit procedures to less than 100 per cent of items within a population of audit evidence such that all sampling units have a chance of selection in order to provide the auditor with a reasonable basis on which to draw conclusions about the entire population.

Business risk A risk resulting from significant conditions, events, circumstances, actions, or inactions that could adversely affect an entity's ability to achieve its objectives and execute its strategies, or from the setting of inappropriate objectives and strategies.

Clients Persons or organizations using the services of the audit firm.

Code of Ethics Professional standards which set out fundamental principles of ethics for professional accountants, reflecting the profession's recognition of its public responsibility. The principles establish the standards of behaviour expected of a professional accountant in business, in public practice, and for independence in audit and other assurance engagements.

Component An entity or business activity for which a group or component of management prepares financial information that should be included in the group financial statements.

Component auditor An auditor who, at the request of the group engagement team, performs work on financial information related to a component for the group audit.

Computer-assisted audit techniques (CAATs) Any automated audit tool or technique, such as generalized audit software, test data generators, computerized audit programmes, and specialized audit tools which help the auditor carry out audit procedures.

Conceptual framework for ethics The approach that auditors are to apply to identify, evaluate, and address threats to compliance with the fundamental ethical principles. It involves the auditor identifying any threats to the fundamental principles, evaluating their significance, and either applying safeguards to reduce it to an acceptable level based on a reasonable and informed third-party test or, if no safeguards are available, eliminating the circumstances or declining or discontinuing an engagement.

Control activities Those policies and procedures that help ensure that management directives are carried out. Control activities are a component of an entity's system of internal control.

Control environment This includes the governance and management functions and the attitudes, awareness, and actions of those charged with governance and management concerning the entity's system of internal control and its importance in the entity. The control environment is a component of the entity's system of internal control.

Control risk The risk that a misstatement which could be material, either individually or in aggregate with other misstatements, will not be prevented, or detected and corrected, on a timely basis by the entity's system of internal control.

Corporate governance A set of rules, measures, reforms, practices, and processes that dictate how a business is directed, managed, and controlled.

Criteria The benchmarks used to measure or evaluate the underlying subject matter. The 'applicable criteria' are the criteria used for the particular engagement.

Detection risk The risk that the procedures performed by the auditor to reduce audit risk to an acceptably low level will not detect a misstatement that exists and that could be material, either individually or when aggregated with other misstatements.

Direct assistance The use of internal auditors to perform audit procedures under the direction, supervision, and review of the external auditor.

Emphasis of matter paragraph A paragraph used in the auditor's report that cross-refers the user to a disclosure or item presented in the financial statements that, in the auditor's professional judgement, is of such importance that it is fundamental to users' understanding of the financial statements. An emphasis of matter paragraph does not modify the auditor's opinion in any way.

Entity's risk assessment process A component of a system of internal control that is the entity's process for identifying business risks relevant to financial reporting objectives and deciding about actions to address those risks, and the results thereof.

Error An unintentional misstatement in the financial statements, including the omission of an amount or a disclosure.

External auditor Independent professional contractors appointed by the shareholders to audit the company's financial statements. They perform an audit in accordance with the International Standards on Auditing (UK).

External confirmation Audit evidence obtained as a direct written response to the auditor from a third party (the confirming party), in paper or electronic form or other medium.

Financial statement audit An audit undertaken to provide reasonable assurance that financial statements prepared by management are in accordance with the applicable financial reporting framework, to enhance the degree of confidence of intended users in the financial statements.

Fraud An intentional act by one or more individuals among management, those charged with governance, employees or third parties, involving the use of deception to obtain an unjust or illegal advantage.

Fraud risk factors Events or conditions that indicate an incentive or pressure to commit fraud or provide an opportunity to commit fraud.

Governance Describes the role of person(s) in organizations with responsibility for the direction of the entity and obligations relating to the accountability of the entity.

Group engagement partner The partner or other person in the firm who is responsible for the group audit engagement and its performance, and for the auditor's report on the group financial statements that is issued on behalf of the firm. Where joint auditors conduct the group audit, the joint engagement partners and their engagement teams collectively constitute the group engagement partner and the group engagement team.

Historic financial information Information expressed in financial terms in relation to a particular entity, derived primarily from the entity's accounting system, about economic events occurring in the past, or about economic conditions at points in time in the past.

Independence Comprises:

(a) Independence of mind—the state of mind that permits the expression of an opinion without being affected by influences that compromise professional judgement, thereby allowing an individual to act with integrity, and exercise objectivity and professional scepticism.
(b) Independence in appearance—the avoidance of facts and circumstances that are so significant that a reasonable and informed third party would be likely to conclude that a firm's, or an audit or assurance team member's, integrity, objectivity, or professional scepticism has been compromised.

Information risk The risk of making incorrect decisions because of incorrect or unreliable information.

Inherent risk A function of the risk of material misstatement. It is the risk that a misstatement which could be material, either individually or in aggregate with other misstatements, is present in the financial statements *before* the consideration of the entity's system of internal control.

Intended users The individual(s) or organization(s) or group(s) that the practitioner expects will use the assurance report. In some cases, there may be intended users other than those to whom the assurance report is addressed.

Internal audit function A function of an entity that performs assurance and consulting activities designed to evaluate and improve the effectiveness of the entity's governance, risk management, and internal control processes.

Internal control The process designed, implemented, and maintained by those charged with governance, management, and other personnel to provide reasonable assurance about the achievement of an entity's objectives with regard to reliability of financial reporting, effectiveness and efficiency of operations, and compliance with applicable laws and regulations. The term 'controls' refers to any aspects of one or more of the components of a system of internal control.

International Standards on Auditing (UK) A set of standards that provide auditing guidelines for external auditors in conducting a statutory audit.

Limited assurance engagement *see* Assurance engagement.

Logical access controls The policies, procedures, organizational structure, and electronic access controls designed to restrict access to computer software and data files.

Management The person(s) with executive responsibility for the conduct of an entity's operations. For some entities in some jurisdictions, management includes some, or all, of those charged with governance.

Material uncertainty related to going concern paragraph A paragraph used in the auditor's report to cross-refer the user to a disclosure relating to the entity's ability to continue as a going concern for the foreseeable future. A material uncertainty related to going concern paragraph does not modify the auditor's opinion in any way.

Materiality Something is material if its omission or misstatement, individually or in the aggregate, would influence the decision-making process of the users taken on the basis of the financial statements as a whole.

Misstatement A difference between the reported amount, classification, presentation, or disclosure of a financial statement item and the amount, classification, presentation, or disclosure that is required for the item to be in accordance with the applicable financial reporting framework. Misstatements can arise from fraud or error.

Modified audit opinion An opinion expressed by the auditor where there is a material and/or pervasive misstatement contained in the financial statements that has not been resolved. There are three types of modified audit opinion:

(a) Qualified 'except for'.
(b) Adverse.
(c) Disclaimer of opinion.

Non-response A failure of the confirming party to respond, or fully respond, to a positive confirmation request, or a confirmation request that is returned undelivered.

Other board committees Are governance, compliance, IT, risk, security, and disclosure committees.

Overall audit strategy Sets the scope, timing, and direction of the audit, and guides the development of the detailed audit plan.

Performance audit An audit of the entity's activities or operations to assess economy, efficiency, or effectiveness.

Performance materiality The amount or amounts set by the auditor at less than materiality for the financial statements as a whole to reduce to an appropriately low level the probability that the aggregate of uncorrected and undetected misstatements exceeds materiality for the financial statements as a whole. If applicable, performance materiality also refers to the amounts set by the auditor at less than the materiality level(s) or particular classes of transactions, account balances, or disclosures.

Pervasive A term used, in the context of misstatements, to describe the effects on the financial statements of misstatements or the possible effects on the financial statements of misstatements, if any, that are undetected due to an inability to obtain sufficient appropriate audit evidence. Pervasive effects on the financial statements are those that, in the auditor's judgement:

(a) are not confined to specific elements, accounts, or items of the financial statements;

(b) if so confined, represent or could represent a substantial proportion of the financial statements; or

(c) in relation to disclosures, are fundamental to users' understanding of the financial statements.

Population The entire set of data from which a sample is selected and about which the auditor wishes to draw conclusions.

Positive confirmation request A request that the confirming party respond directly to the auditor indicating whether the confirming party agrees or disagrees with the information in the request or providing the requested information.

Preconditions (for an audit) The use by management of an acceptable financial reporting framework in the preparation of the financial statements and the agreement of management and, where applicable, those charged with governance with the premise on which the audit is conducted.

Professional scepticism An attitude that includes a questioning mind, being alert to conditions which may indicate possible misstatement due to error or fraud, and a critical assessment of evidence.

Professional standards International Standards on Auditing (UK) and relevant ethical requirements.

Reasonable assurance engagement *see* **Assurance engagement**.

Remuneration committee A standing committee of the board of directors responsible for evaluating directors and senior executives and design compensation schemes for directors and executives.

Responsible party The party(ies) responsible for the underlying subject matter.

Review engagement The objective of a review engagement is to enable an auditor to state whether, on the basis of procedures which do not provide all the evidence that would be required in an audit, anything that has come to the auditor's attention that causes the auditor to believe that the financial statements are not prepared, in all material respects, in accordance with the applicable financial reporting framework.

Risk of material misstatement The risk that the financial statements are materially misstated prior to audit. This consists of two components, described as follows at the assertion level:

(a) Inherent risk—The susceptibility of an assertion about a class of transaction, account balance, or disclosure to a misstatement that could be material, either individually or when aggregated with other misstatements, before consideration of any related controls.

(b) Control risk—The risk that a misstatement that could occur in an assertion about a class of transaction, account balance or disclosure and that could be material, either individually or when aggregated with other misstatements, will not be prevented, or detected and corrected, on a timely basis by the entity's internal control.

Safeguards Actions, individually or in combination, that the auditor undertakes to effectively reduce threats to compliance with the fundamental ethical principles to an acceptable level.

Sampling risk The risk that the auditor's conclusion based on a sample may be different from the conclusion if the entire population were subjected to the same audit procedure. Sampling risk can lead to two types of erroneous conclusions:

(a) In the case of a test of controls, that controls are more effective than they actually are, or in the case of a test of details, that a material misstatement does not exist when in fact it does. The auditor is primarily concerned with this type of erroneous conclusion because it affects audit effectiveness and is more likely to lead to an inappropriate audit opinion.

(b) In the case of a test of controls, that controls are less effective than they actually are, or in the case of a test of details, that a material misstatement exists when in fact it does not. This type of erroneous conclusion affects audit efficiency as it would usually lead to additional work to establish that initial conclusions were incorrect.

Sampling unit The individual items constituting a population.

Significant risk An identified and assessed risk of material misstatement that, in the auditor's judgement, requires special audit consideration.

Software Programs and systems that facilitate the use of a computer. Software controls the operation of the hardware.

Statutory audit An audit undertaken in compliance with the requirements of the law.

Stratification The process of dividing a population into sub-populations, each of which is a group of sampling units which have similar characteristics (often monetary value).

Subject matter information The outcome of the measurement or evaluation of the underlying subject matter against the criteria, that is, the information that results from applying the criteria to the underlying subject matter.

Substantive procedure An audit procedure designed to detect material misstatements at the assertion level. Substantive procedures comprise:

(a) Tests of details (classes of transactions, account balances and disclosures).
(b) Substantive analytical procedures.

Sufficiency (of audit evidence) The measure of the quantity of audit evidence. The quantity of the audit evidence needed is affected by the auditor's assessment of the risks of material misstatement and also by the quality of such evidence.

Sufficient appropriate audit evidence Audit evidence that in quality and quantity is adequate to support the auditor's conclusions and opinion.

Test data Data that is used to test the operation of a client's IT system. Test data may be used from the client's live files or from copy files provided to the auditor.

Test of controls An audit procedure designed to evaluate the operating effectiveness of controls in preventing, or detecting and correcting, material misstatements at the assertion level.

Tests of detail Audit procedures which are used to verify individual transactions and balances.

Third parties Persons or organizations not directly involved in an arrangement (such as the arrangement between the company being audited and the auditors), but instead those that would rely on the audited financial statements to make rational business decisions.

Tolerable misstatement A monetary amount set by the auditor in respect of which the auditor seeks to obtain an appropriate level of assurance that the monetary amount set by the auditor is not exceeded by the actual misstatement in the population.

Tolerable rate of deviation A rate of deviation from prescribed internal control procedures set by the auditor in respect of which the auditor seeks to obtain an appropriate level of assurance that the rate of deviation set by the auditor is not exceeded by the actual rate of deviation in the population.

Unmodified opinion The opinion expressed by the auditor when the auditor concludes that the financial statements are prepared, in all material respects, (or give a true and fair view), in accordance with the applicable financial reporting framework.

Using the work of an internal auditor Using work performed by internal audit during the course of their work within the entity to reduce the extent or nature of audit procedures undertaken by the external auditor. The work is to be assessed by the external auditor.

Verification Checks that data is entered correctly.

Viruses Malicious programs designed to spread and replicate from computer to computer through telecommunications links or through the sharing of files.

Written representation A written statement by management provided to the auditor to confirm certain matters or to support other audit evidence. Written representations in this context do not include financial statements, the assertions therein, or supporting books and records.

Index

D

E

F

N

O

U

V

W